Encyclopedia of
Catholicism

ENCYCLOPEDIA OF WORLD RELIGIONS

ENCYCLOPEDIA OF
Catholicism

Frank K. Flinn

J. Gordon Melton, Series Editor

Facts On File
An imprint of Infobase Publishing

Encyclopedia of Catholicism

Copyright © 2007 by Frank K. Flinn

Facts On File, Inc.
An imprint of Infobase Publishing
132 West 31st Street
New York NY 10001

ISBN-10: 0-8160-5455-X
ISBN-13: 978-0-8160-5455-8

Library of Congress Cataloging-in-Publication Data

Flinn, Frank K.
    Encyclopedia of Catholicism / Frank K. Flinn.
        p. cm.—(Encyclopedia of world religions)
    Includes bibliographical references and index.
    ISBN 0-8160-5455-X
    1. Catholic Church—Encyclopedias. I. Melton, J. Gordon. II. Title. III. Series.
    BX841.F55 2006
    282.03—dc22   2006009645

Text design by Erika Arroyo
Cover design by Cathy Rincon
Illustrations by Dale Williams

Printed in the United States of America

VB Hermitage 10 9 8 7 6 5 4 3 2 1

This book is printed on acid-free paper.

To my family:
Alice, My Beloved
Adam Pablo and Kristin
Mark Hosteen and Jenny
Lolita and Caleb

Aunt Rhoda and Uncle Leland
Lyle, Paula, and Michael
Serena and Barry

Edward, Allison, and Haley

CONTENTS

ABOUT THE EDITOR

Series editor J. Gordon Melton is the director of the Institute for the Study of American Religion in Santa Barbara, California. He holds an M.Div. from the Garrett Theological Seminary and a Ph.D. from Northwestern University. Melton is the author of *American Religions: An Illustrated History, The Encyclopedia of American Religions, Religious Leaders of America,* and several comprehensive works on Islamic culture, African-American religion, cults, and alternative religions. He has written or edited more than three dozen books and anthologies as well as numerous papers and articles for scholarly journals. He is the series editor for Religious Information Systems, which supplies data and information in religious studies and related fields. Melton is a member of the American Academy of Religion, the Society for the Scientific Study of Religion, the American Society of Church History, the Communal Studies Association, and the Society for the Study of Metaphysical Religion.

LIST OF ILLUSTRATIONS

PREFACE

The Encyclopedia of World Religions series has been designed to provide comprehensive coverage of six major global religious traditions—Buddhism, Hinduism, Islam, Judaism, Roman Catholicism, and Protestant Christianity. The volumes have been constructed in an A-to-Z format to provide a handy guide to the major terms, concepts, people, events, and organizations that have, in each case, transformed the religion from its usually modest beginnings to the global force that it has become.

Each of these religions began as the faith of a relatively small group of closely related ethnic peoples. Each has, in the modern world, become a global community, and, with one notable exception, each has transcended its beginning to become an international multiethnic community. Judaism, of course, largely defines itself by its common heritage and ancestry and has an alternative but equally fascinating story. Surviving long after most similar cultures from the ancient past have turned to dust, Judaism has, within the last century, regathered its scattered people into a homeland while simultaneously watching a new diaspora carry Jews into most of the contemporary world's countries.

Each of the major traditions has also, in the modern world, become amazingly diverse. Buddhism, for example, spread from its original home in India across southern Asia and then through Tibet and China to Korea and Japan. Each time it crossed a language barrier, something was lost, but something seemed equally to be gained, and an array of forms of Buddhism emerged. In Japan alone, Buddhism exists in hundreds of different sect groupings. Protestantism, the newest of the six traditions, began with at least four different and competing forms of the religious life and has since splintered into thousands of denominations.

At the beginning of the 19th century, the six religious traditions selected for coverage in this series were largely confined to a relatively small part of the world. Since that time, the world has changed dramatically, with each of the traditions moving from its geographical center to become a global tradition. While the traditional religions of many countries retain the allegiance of a majority of the population, they do so in the presence of the other traditions as growing minorities. Other countries—China being a prominent example—have no religious majority, only a number of minorities that must periodically interface with one another.

The religiously pluralistic world created by the global diffusion of the world's religions has made knowledge of religions, especially religions practiced by one's neighbors, a vital resource in the continuing task of building a good society, a world in which all may live freely and pursue visions of the highest values the cosmos provides.

In creating these encyclopedias, the attempt has been made to be comprehensive if not exhaustive. As space allows, in approximately 800 entries, each author has attempted to define and explain the basic terms used in talking about the religion, make note of definitive events, introduce the most prominent figures, and highlight the major organizations. The coverage is designed to result in both a handy reference tool for the religious scholar/specialist and an understandable work that can be used fruitfully by anyone—a student, an informed lay person, or a reader simply wanting to look up a particular person or idea.

Each volume includes several features. They begin with an essay that introduces the particular tradition and provides a quick overview of its historical development, the major events and trends that have pushed it toward its present state, and the megaproblems that have shaped it in the contemporary world.

A chronology lists the major events that have punctuated the religion's history from its origin to the present. The chronologies differ somewhat in emphasis, given that they treat two very ancient faiths that both originated in prehistoric time, several more recent faiths that emerged during the last few millennia, and the most recent, Protestantism, that has yet to celebrate its 500-year anniversary.

The main body of each encyclopedia is constituted of the approximately 800 entries, arranged alphabetically. These entries include some 200 biographical entries covering religious figures of note in the tradition, with a distinct bias to the 19th and 20th centuries and some emphasis on leaders from different parts of the world. Special attention has been given to highlighting female contributions to the tradition, a factor often overlooked, as religion in all traditions has until recently been largely a male-dominated affair.

Geographical entries cover the development of the movement in those countries and parts of the world where the tradition has come to dominate or form an important minority voice, where it has developed a particularly distinct style (often signaled by doctrinal differences), or where it has a unique cultural or social presence. While religious statistics are amazingly difficult to assemble and evaluate, some attempt has been made to estimate the effect of the tradition on the selected countries.

In some cases, particular events have had a determining effect on the development of the different religious traditions. Entries on events such as the St. Bartholomew's Day Massacre (for Protestantism) or the conversion of King Asoka (for Buddhism) place the spotlight on the factors precipitating the event and the consequences flowing from it.

The various traditions have taken form as communities of believers have organized structures to promote their particular way of belief and practice within the tradition. Each tradition has a different way of organizing and recognizing the distinct groups within it. Buddhism, for example, has organized around national subtraditions. The encyclopedias give coverage to the major groupings within each tradition.

Each tradition has developed a way of encountering and introducing individuals to spiritual reality as well as a vocabulary for it. It has also developed a set of concepts and a language to discuss the spiritual world and humanity's place within it. In each volume, the largest number of entries explore the concepts, the beliefs that flow from them, and the practices that they have engendered. The authors have attempted to explain these key religious concepts in a nontechnical language and to communicate their meaning and logic to a person otherwise unfamiliar with the religion as a whole.

Finally, each volume is thoroughly cross-indexed using small caps to guide the reader to related entries. A bibliography and comprehensive index round out each volume.

—J. Gordon Melton

ACKNOWLEDGMENTS

First and foremost I owe deep gratitude to my beloved wife, Alice, who saw me through the bright days and dark days of this project. Second, sincere thanks go to J. Gordon Melton, the general editor of this set of encyclopedias, who shared suggestions, information, and expertise, especially on issues touching on Protestantism. A third sincere thanks goes to Steven Scharre, my graduate assistant, who helped with much preliminary writing and contributed his expertise on Islam. Thanks also go to John Huston for his expert photography, to Frs. Vincent Heier and Martin Swanson for help in filming vestments and church furnishings, and to Patricia Woods of St. Louis Art Museum and Erin Davis of Washington University for assistance in obtaining images, which their institutions have kindly permitted to be reproduced.

CATHOLICISM
AN INTRODUCTION

Beginnings to c. 110 C.E.

The *Encyclopedia of Catholicism* seeks to cover the landmark people, movements, institutions, practices, and doctrines of Roman Catholicism from its earliest origins. It is most important for Christians and Catholics to realize that Christianity emerged from the matrix of late Judaism. Jesus of Nazareth was a Jew; he was born a Jew; he lived as a Jew; he taught and preached as a Jew within the religious concerns of Judaism; and he died as a Jew. In short, Jesus was not a Christian. The term did not even arise until late in the first century, c. 95 C.E. (Acts 11:26). The historical understanding of Jesus cannot be seen apart from the theo-political situation in ancient Judea, as the Holy Land was called. Jesus appeared in the midst of the conflicts and compromises of Pharisees, Sadducees, Essenes, Zealots, and others, who were all under the thumb of Roman power.

In the reconstructed "Gospel of Q" Jesus speaks very much as a "prophet like" Moses (Acts 7:37) or Elijah (Mark 6:15); he called for the renewal of the terms of the Covenant between God and the Jewish people and for bringing the gospel in word and deed to the disenfranchised population of Galilee. This aspect of Jesus' own self-understanding and mission became almost completely obscured by later emphasis on his miraculous birth and status as the only Son of God.

To those who see in the gospel only a spiritual (and not a political) message, the religious historian has to point out that the term *gospel* was commonly used in various pagan Roman altar inscriptions dedicated to the "savior" Augustus Caesar (who had brought peace to the empire). The title *the gospel of Jesus Christ,* with which the earliest canonical gospel, Mark, begins, must be seen as a "counter-gospel" to the gospel of Caesar.

Jesus's message and person evoked many different responses from the earliest times. The "Gospel of Q," which probably reflects the views of the earliest of Jesus' followers in Galilee, contains neither birth nor Resurrection stories. Matthew sees Jesus as a Moses-like lawgiver and reflects a very Jewish tradition that was taken into Syria; Mark sees Jesus through the lens of Hellenistic wonderworkers; and Luke—an *apologia christiana* to the Roman authorities of his time—presents Jesus as the founder of a new, legitimate religion. Scholars have uncovered multiple gospel traditions, some of them unorthodox from a later standpoint. Jesus was many things to many people: prophet, lawgiver, miracle-worker, messiah, Son of God, founder, savior, wisdom teacher, enlightener, and so on. A view common to an earlier age could wind up being heretical in later circumstances.

One thing is certain: the gospel spread rapidly from Galilee to Judea, Samaria, and Antioch, and, through the missionary activity of Paul, to Greece and Asia Minor. By the end of the first century, it had begun to spread far and wide into the known Roman world, which stretched north to York in England, west to Gibraltar, south to North Africa, and east to Syria. Perhaps Christianity spread under the broader mantle of the "mystery religions," all of which promised personal salvation, immortality, and intimacy with a deity beyond the public civic religion of the Roman Empire and the imperial cult. Soon various assemblies or churches arose in urban centers, welded together through the central rituals of baptism and the Eucharist. Differing traditions, customs, and even theologies were built up under the names of apostles: Paul in Asia Minor; Thomas and Matthew in Syria and farther east; Paul and Peter in Rome; and John in Asia Minor. Tradition has both Peter and Paul being martyred in Rome, two events that became central for later Catholicism.

Persecutions and Disputes (110–313)

As Christianity spread throughout the empire and more and more people came to espouse the gospel of Jesus Christ, Christians started coming to the attention of the Roman authorities. Emperor Nero (d. 68) pinned the great fire of Rome on the Christians in 64, bringing about the first of the great persecutions and expulsions. This pattern was repeated on a large scale under Domitian (d. 96), Trajan (d. 117), the philosopher-emperor Marcus Aurelius (r. 161–180), Decius (r. 249–251), and Diocletian (r. 284–305), until Constantine I and Licinius issued the Edict of Milan in 313, tolerating Christians.

Romans accused Christians of *flagitia* (incest, cannibalism, lechery), superstition, and atheism—the latter for not sacrificing to the Roman gods. Probably no more than 1,000 martyrs were killed in the entire era of persecution, but such Christian

"heroes" as Sts. Perpetua and Felicity (d. c. 203) inspired admiration among many Romans, and even some members of the imperial household converted. Memorials at martyrs' tombs gave rise to the later practice of veneration of the saints and pilgrimages to holy sites. The attacks also attracted the attention and the eventual conversion of members of the philosophical schools such as Justin Martyr (c. 100–c. 165), who began to write apologies in defense of Christianity. The apologies became the basis for framing the gospel in the language of Hellenistic philosophy, leading to the development of Christian theology in a more formal sense.

Internally, however, Christianity experienced intense disputes. One can witness an early example in 1 John, which insists that the Logos became flesh while criticizing "false prophets" who embraced what looks like the beginnings of Docetism, which taught that God is pure spirit and could not become incarnate (1 John 4:1–3). During the second century, ideas that what would later be deemed "heresy" bloomed everywhere: Marcionism, Montanism, and many varieties of Gnosticism. Many early Christian thinkers such as Clement of Alexandria (d. c. 215) embraced varying tendencies of Neoplatonism that bordered on Gnosticism.

The lines between heterodoxy and orthodoxy began to be drawn. The orthodox tradition fought heresy on two fronts. First, early in the second century the church began to assume a hierarchy of bishops, priests, and deacons who could boast an unbroken "apostolic succession" in teaching and practice from the first apostles. This served to curb the influence of the freewheeling Gnostic teachers, who in fact were following the wandering lifestyles of the original apostles. Second, the early theologians—Irenaeus of Lyon (d. c. 200), Hippolytus of Rome (d. c. 236), and Tertullian of Carthage (d. c. 225)—developed what came to be known as the rule of faith, the church's tradition of teaching on creation, redemption, and sanctification, which was used to undermine the arguments of the "heretics." The rule of faith served as the foundation of later creeds and provided the criteria for admitting biblical books into the canon of Scripture. Modern historians have been more generous to Gnosticism, the losing party in the struggle, following the discoveries of early Gnostic texts at Nag Hammadi, Egypt, in 1945–46. The orthodox side showed the first lineaments of what we now call early Catholicism: a hierarchical church, creedal beliefs, and an emphasis on sacramental life as opposed to the Gnostic reliance on free prophets, mythopoetic treatises, and spiritual enlightenment.

Christian art first showed itself in funerary inscriptions and catacomb depictions. The first churches were house churches, some of which were gradually modified to enclose baptisteries decorated with wall murals, such as at Dura Europos. Christian sculpture first appeared in a significant way on sarcophagi or stone burial caskets, which were carved in late Greco-Roman style. The first image of Jesus was as the Good Shepherd, painted on the earlier models of Orpheus and Apollo.

Imperial Christendom (313–600)

The next phase of Christianity produced what we now know as Christendom, a realm unified around a common religion and governed by Christian rulers. The three factors that brought this about were the toleration and eventual establishment of Christianity as the state religion beginning with Constantine I, the flourishing of monasticism, and the first seven ecumenical councils.

Church historian Eusebius of Caesarea (d. c. 340) offered up a flattering portrait in his *Life of Constantine,* but the emperor seems to have had his finger to the wind when he decided to tolerate Christians in 313. Similarly, when he called the first ecumenical council at Nicaea (325), he was not so much seeking orthodoxy as political unity in the empire. Subsequent emperors had a tendency to slide into Arianism when the occasion allowed.

Helena, Constantine's mother, began a massive building project in the Holy Land, beginning with the Church of the Holy Sepulcher; Constantine himself began building the Old St. Peter's Basilica and laid the foundations for major churches in Constantinople. This architectural explosion gave Christianity its first grand edifices, which were tinged with imperial splendor. The basilicas of Constantinople and Ravenna were further ornamented with jewel-like mosaics of Christ as Pantokrator (Ruler of All) and Mary as Theotokos (Begetter of God). The Christ image took on the regal posture of the churches' imperial donors.

The rise of monasticism in Egypt was a very important development in the history of Christendom. The pattern soon went from the solitary hermit (St. Anthony of Egypt) to the communal monastery (Pachomius), as monastic communities spread from Egypt to Palestine, Asia Minor, and the West. St. Athanasius' *Life of Anthony* inspired monastic foundations of men and women from Syria to France and Ireland. St. Basil established the model rule for the East and St. Benedict for the West. There is no evidence that Jesus led anything like a monastic life. There is not even evidence that he was not married, as most Jewish teachers of his time would have been. Monks could point to Jesus' time of temptation in the desert (Matthew 4:1–11), but the monastic impulse grew out of traditions of repentance, conversion, and philosophical discipline. Over the next millennium the monastery became the repository of both religious and secular learning, the laboratory for new inventions in agriculture, and the seedbed for the medieval universities. English and Irish monks would return to the Continent to missionize the German tribes of the North.

The first seven ecumenical councils, preceded by many local synods, achieved three major things: they fixed the canon of Scripture, they clarified the definition of the nature of Jesus as Christ and Son of God, and they clarified the theology of the Trinity. The Council of Nicaea (325) introduced the new term *homoousios,* or "of the same being," to establish the equality of the Father and Son against Arius of Alexandria (d. 336). (John Henry Newman was later to note that more than half the bishops were Arian, while the common faithful remained orthodox.) Theodosius I (381) issued the Nicene-Constantinopolitan Creed and upheld the divinity of the Holy Spirit. Ephesus (431) defended the title of Mary as Theotokos, or "Begetter of God," thereby establishing the doctrine of the Incarnation of God the Son in the flesh and the feast of Christmas. Chalcedon (451) defended the formula that Christ was one person but fully human and fully divine in nature; the Coptic Church then split off. The councils also came to a gradual understanding of the Trinity as three persons who share one divine substance. Ultimately, however, these formulas could not totally explain the deepest mysteries of salvation, which remained accessible primarily through faith. The last of the seven councils, Nicaea II (787), defended the veneration of images, or icons. The councils also established a tradition of ecclesiastical discipline that later came to be codified and known as canon law.

By the end of this period, the shape of Catholic tradition, in the broad sense of the term, was clearly delineated. The key theologians who determined the tradition were Sts. Athanasius, Jerome, and Augustine in the West and the Cappadocian Fathers Sts. Basil, Gregory Nazianzus, and Gregory Nyssa in the East. Later medieval theology is to a great extent a reflection on the theological milestones of these thinkers on creation, sin, and the Fall, the Incarnation and redemption, the role of Mary, the sacraments, and the life of the Trinity.

A difference in style between Eastern and Western Christianity was discernible by the fourth century. The East was much more prone to theological disputes (Arianism, Nestorianism, etc.), while the Achilles' heel of the West was a tendency to disciplinary disputes (although some of them had a strong theological component as well, such as Donatism and Pelagianism). The East looked to councils to work out differences; the West, though it had plenty of local synods, looked to the bishop who, in turn, looked to the bishop

of Rome to settle disputes. The spiritual orientations also differed. The East was deeply mystical, whereas the West took a more moral and legal direction. These differences, although not absolute, contributed to the eventual schism between Constantinople and Rome in 1054.

Papacy and Reform, Church and State, East and West (600–1150)

A central development in the second half of the fist millennium was the increasing importance of the papacy in western Christendom. Several factors contributed to papal primacy. First, by the end of the fourth century Eastern Christendom was divided ecclesiastically between the patriarchies of Jerusalem, Antioch, Alexandria, and Constantinople, with the last assuming second rank after Rome at the Council of Constantinople I (381). (Still today the Ecumenical Patriarch of Constantinople, or Istanbul, is deemed a *primus inter pares,* or "first among equals," with his fellow Eastern Orthodox bishops.) The region under each of the Eastern patriarchates was smaller, and eventually far less populous, than the immense territory administered by the bishop of Rome, the patriarch of the entire West.

Second, during the theological struggles of the first seven councils, Eastern bishops often appealed to the papacy as a court of last appeal. Third, the successive waves of invasions by the Visigoth Alaric in 410 and Attila the Hun in 453 left a weakened civilian rule in Italy; the pope, for good or ill, was called upon to fill the vacuum. Thus evolved the Papal States and the popes' secular role in the affairs of kingdoms and nation-states, which lasted until 1870.

All along the bishops of Rome claimed St. Peter as their first bishop (despite the lack of any hard evidence), and appealed to Jesus' statement that Peter, or Cephas, which means "rock" in Aramaic, is the "rock upon which I will build my church" (Matthew 16:18–19). Rome also benefited from the astute leadership of popes such as Damasus I (r. 366–384) and Leo I (r. 440–461).

In the East a unique relation between church and state developed. From the beginning of the Constantinian era emperors assumed quasi-ecclesiastical roles at ecumenical councils and saw themselves as legitimate heirs of the biblical King David, anointed by God the Father. This tradition, called caesaropapism, continued into the early 20th century, with the Ottoman sultans and the Russian czars (the Russian spelling of *caesar*) fulfilling the imperial role. (Some detect a reemergence of the tradition in post-Soviet Russia.)

In contrast, in the West a rivalry soon developed between emperors and bishops and between emperors and popes, which enabled the church to be more independent of civil rule. St. Ambrose of Milan (d. 397) excommunicated Emperors Valentinian II and Theodosius I. Soon popes began stressing the primacy of the papacy over both East and West. St. Gregory I the Great (d. 604) led a great papal reform, enhancing the prestige of monasteries, excluding laity from Vatican offices, standardizing the liturgy of the Mass and chant, promoting the veneration of saints, and challenging the use of the title "Ecumenical Patriarch" by the bishop of Constantinople. The struggle between church and state came to a head in the showdown between Gregory VII Hildebrand and the Holy Roman Emperor Henry IV at Canossa in 1076 over the claims by princes that they had a right to invest bishops and abbots under their jurisdictions. Although emperors and kings would often invade Italy and challenge papal power, the ecclesiastical extreme was reached by Innocent III (1198–1216), who likened himself to the greater light of the Sun, destined to rule over people's souls, while the kings, likened to the lesser light of the Moon, would rule over the body (papal bull *Sicut Universitatis Conditor,* 1098).

Not all relations between emperors and the church were hostile. On Christmas Day, 800, Pope Leo III crowned Charlemagne emperor of the West. Charlemagne and his chamberlain, Alcuin, proceeded to shore up the interests of the church. The Carolingian Renaissance brought the estab-lishment of the feudal system, which benefited abbot and prince alike. The new state established cathedral schools, out of which sprang the universities, and spread the Roman liturgy throughout the West.

The second half of the first millennium also saw the reform of monasticism, first at Cluny and then at Cîteaux; the development of the theology of the sacraments; and a flowering of both faith and reason in the first moves toward a systematic theology by scholars such as Peter Lombard (c. 1105–c. 64) and Peter Abelard (1079–1142). The renaissance of theology and philosophy was aided in no small part by the Spanish *convivencia,* during which Jewish, Muslim, and Christian cultures influenced one another. The works of Aristotle found their way into the Western curriculum via celebrated Muslim and Jewish philosophers such as Ibn Sina (Avicenna), Al Farabi, Ibn Rushd (Averroes), and Maimonides.

Middle Ages (1150–1450)

The Middle Ages may be said to begin with the Crusades, campaigns at once pious and cruel, to regain the holy sites of pilgrimage from the demonized "Saracens" (Muslims). On their way to the Holy Land, Christian knights not only waged a systematic persecution of Jews in cities such as Frankfurt am Main, but also succeeded in finally alienating the Eastern Church by sacking Constantinople.

In contrast, new impulses of reform were stirring. Some of the movements were deemed outside the pale of orthodoxy (Cathars, Beguines, and Waldensians), and others were within. Outstanding among the latter were the mendicant orders of Sts. Dominic and Francis at the beginning of the 13th century. The friars eschewed the luxurious lifestyles of the diocesan clergy and of many monasteries, preaching the gospel of the poor Christ. Their influence spread throughout Europe and even as far as China, where they went to preach with the word and not the sword. The pope appointed Dominicans and Franciscans as inquisitors to root out heresy, a tradition that would develop into the fateful institution of the Inquisition in Spain in 1492 and in the universal church in 1542.

The friars were central to that other medieval current, the rise of the universities in Bologna, Paris, Salamanca, Oxford, Cambridge, Cologne, Prague, and elsewhere. Theology flourished, with philosophy as a handmaid. While Bonaventure (d. 1274) stayed within the older Neoplatonic Augustinian tradition, Thomas Aquinas and Duns Scotus charted a new course, weaving Aristotle's metaphysical system with the interpretation of the Bible and the patristic tradition. The twins peaks of medieval philosophy remain Thomas's unfinished *Summa Theologiae* and its literary reflection in Dante's *Comedia Divina*. The realism of the high Middle Ages, which the church endorses to this day, came under attack by the nominalist William of Ockham (d. 1347).

Perhaps the crowning artistic achievement of the Middle Ages was the cathedral, which in stone and glass summed up Bible and legend, learning and lore, piety and pilgrimage for the ordinary Catholic. The cathedral was like a bejeweled New Jerusalem that Émile Mâle has compared to a "symbolic calculus" weaving together the threads of sacred history and nature.

But big cracks began to appear in Christendom toward the end of the Middle Ages. Pope and anti-pope played ruler against ruler. Bishops played council against the warring popes. The faithful were scandalized not only by schism but also by lavishly living prelates, absentee priests, and hair-splitting theological disputation. John Wycliffe (d. 1384) contrasted the true spiritual church with the sullied material one he saw around him. Jan Hus (d. 1415) introduced the Wycliffite message to the Continent. The innovative impulse in Catholicism seemed to go inward in the mysticism of Meister Eckhart (d. c. 1328) and Julian of Norwich (d. c. 1420), but the official church always distrusted mystics. The followers of the Brethren of the Common Life introduced the Devotio Moderna, a simple, direct piety centered on humble devotion to Jesus. The devotion appealed to cleric and layperson alike, but it was not strong enough to reform the church of its errant ways.

Reformation, Without and Within (1450–1650)

Many see the Reformation as a movement coming from outside Catholicism to reform the corruption within. Actually, the reformational impulse had periodically arisen *within* Catholicism, as for example in the Cluniac and mendicant reforms in the early and high Middle Ages, respectively. In the 15th century there was the unrelenting voice of Desiderius Erasmus (d. 1536), a follower of the Devotio Moderna, who heaped scorn on episcopal greed, pilgrimages, the veneration of saints and relics, and indulgences in his *Praise of Folly* (1509). There were also reformers within the Vatican such as the Oratorians Reginald Pole (d. 1558) and Gasparo Contarini (d. 1542). But these voices could not overcome the scandalous life of popes such as Alexander VI Borgia (d. 1503), who gained the papacy through bribery and fathered illegitimate children. Imitating the Medici Renaissance princes, Julius II (d. 1513) and Leo X (d. 1521) undertook elaborate restorations and decorations of St. Peter's and the Vatican palaces, employing the great artists of the day like Michelangelo and Raphael. To pay for this they sent the likes of the Dominican Johannes Tetzel (d. 1519) to sell indulgences in the north.

The question of indulgences was the trigger that sent Martin Luther (d. 1546) to the doors of Wittemburg cathedral in 1517, but the Reformation was about much more than doctrine. It was also about how the sacraments were to be administered and the authority of Scripture in the life of the church. The Reformation was also about the relationship between the Holy Roman Emperor and the other kings and princes in Christendom. In response, the papacy underwent a phase of inaction. Luther called for a council free of Vatican control, and popes were reluctant to return to the issue of who held supremacy, pope or council, that dominated the 15th century ecumenical councils. Finally, the popes relented and called for the Council of Trent (1545–63).

Trent was the key force, but not the only one in the Counter-Reformation. Nearly as central were the new or reformed religious orders, notably the Jesuits, Theatines, and Capuchins; the internal reform of the papacy along with a reorganization of the Vatican offices; the rise of new types of mysticism exemplified by Sts. Ignatius of Loyola (d. 1556) and Teresa of Ávila (d. 1582); the great missionary expansion to the New World and Asia; and the establishment of the Inquisition and the Index of Forbidden Books. Trent determined for the next 400 years the overall Catholic understanding of the doctrines of Scripture and tradition, original sin and justification, the sacraments and the Mass, liturgy and seminary training. A new style of religious architecture reflected the "baroque" spirituality of Teresa and Ignatius.

After Trent one hard reality Catholicism had to face was that there would now be intense competition not only from Orthodoxy to the East but from Protestantism inside western and central Europe and from nonreligious forces. Galileo (d. 1642) signalled the emergence of a new kind of empirical and experimental science that was a challenge to the medieval church, which had wedded biblical interpretation to the Ptolemaic system. Catholics shored up their losses by conducting internal devotional missions within the Catholic heartland, especially Italy, which they coupled with devotion to the Blessed Sacrament, Mary, and the saints, accompanied by processions and music. The other method was intense missionary work in the New World and Asia.

Christianity had experienced two great types of missionary expansions prior to the worldwide expansion in the 16th century. The first period witnessed the phenomenal growth of Christianity from a small Jewish sect to a population that numbered perhaps a third of the Roman Empire at the time Constantine tolerated it in 313. During and after this initial expansion important missionary undertakings focused on specific populations: Pantaenus to India (c. 190), Gregory of Ilium to Armenia (c. 312), the Arian Ulphilas to the Goths (c. 325), Patrick to Ireland (c. 450), Augustine of Canterbury to England (c. 600), the Nestorian Alopan to China (c. 635), and Boniface to Germany (c. 720). In the Middle Ages Raymond Lull (d. c. 1315) tried a mission to the Muslims in North Africa, and the Franciscan John of Monte Corvino founded the first bishopric of Beijing (c. 1290).

Nothing can match the organization, determination, and scope of the Catholic missionary effort following Columbus's discovery of the New World in 1492 and Ferdinand Magellan's circumnavigation of the globe in 1519–22. The Jesuit St. Francis Xavier (d. 1552) led the Jesuit mission to India and Japan, to be followed by Matteo Ricci (d. c. 1610) to China and many to Mexico and South America. The Jesuit Eusebio Kino (d. 1711) and the Franciscans Antonio Margil (d. 1726) and Junipero Serra (d. c. 1786) missionized Sonoran Mexico, Texas, and California, respectively. To this day the Philippines and Latin America are overwhelmingly Catholic by birth if not practice.

The division of Europe between Protestant and Catholic propelled the continent into a series of religious wars that did not come to an end until the Peace of Augsburg (1648). Thereafter, European Roman Catholicism, while maintaining the all-important link to Rome, started taking on national characteristics and is best understood by consulting the entries under France, Germany, Italy, Spain, and Latin America. Catholicism in England barely survived the rise of the Anglican Church, beginning with Henry VIII (d. 1547).

Enlightenment and After
(1650–1900)

The Catholic Counter-Reformation maintained the church throughout the difficulties presented by the rise of nation states and the critique of religion during the late Renaissance and throughout the Enlightenment. It is false to see the philosophical currents that span the time between Rene Descartes (d. 1650) and Immanuel Kant (d. 1804) as irreligious. Rather, the Enlightenment posited the religion of reason (Deism) against the religion of superstition that the philosophes believed Catholicism to be.

The Enlightenment was ambiguous for Catholicism. In the newly formed United States the Enlightenment principle of the separation of church and state proved a boon for the growth of Catholicism. By contrast, the Enlightenment's hostile side led to the suppression of Catholicism and the confiscation of churches and monasteries in France. That hostility was inflamed by the political roles that the Catholic cardinals Armand Richelieu (d. 1642) and André-Hercule de Fleury (d. 1743) had played in the French court.

The French Revolution shaped the reaction of the papacy to most of the currents of modernity well into the 20th century. Modernity meant different things to different people, but basically it included the embrace of Newtonian science, a historical view of doctrine and the Bible, the adoption of new sociological and philosophical methods, and the championing of democracy and labor movements. Pius IX opposed much of this agenda in his celebrated *Syllabus of Errors* (1864) and, facing the onslaught of a democratic movement in Italy, strove to shore up papal authority with the declaration of papal infallibility at Vatican Council I (1870). St. Pius X continued this antimodernism (and anti-Americanism) trend in his encyclical *Pascendi Domini Gregis* (1907).

But there were other currents astir. Beginning in the 19th century, Benedictines and others fostered liturgical renewal, centered on the Abbey of Solesmnes. Leo XIII gave a cautious approval of democracy and labor unions in *Rerum Novarum* (1891) and of new methods in biblical studies in *Providentissimus Dei* (1893), while simultaneously enshrining St. Thomas Aquinas as the official theologian for the universal church. John

Henry Newman (d. 1890) demonstrated that the historical study of doctrine was not only not inimical to Catholic faith but precisely the royal road that led him into the Catholic fold. These modernist trends were also accompanied by Catholic social action movements in most of the countries in Europe.

Pope Benedict XV (d. 1922) muted the voices of the antimodernist nay-sayers. This released new energies in the study of the fathers (and later, mothers) of the church and in the use of phenomenological and existential philosophical methods in the reinterpretation of the faith by members of the Nouvelle Theologie circle. Theologians like Ives Congar, Henri Chenu, Henri de Lubac, and Karl Rahner had a determining hand in Vatican Council II, but during the 1930s–50s their voices were often suppressed.

The role of the papacy under the rule of Italian fascism and German Nazism remains ambiguous to this day. The kindest way to see it is as an attempt to preserve the rights of Catholicism in a hostile situation, but there is no doubt that both the Catholic and Protestant stance helped toward the destruction of 6 million Jews and another 6 million, including countless Catholics themselves. During and after World War II, Pius XII, though liberal on issues like biblical studies, tried to preserve the old centralized view of the church, but the tide in the other direction was too great. John XXIII (d. 1963) called Vatican Council II and unleashed a swell that brought the Catholic Church fully into the 20th century.

In the 1980s John Paul II (d. 2005) had a not insignificant role in the demise of communism in Eastern Europe. Today his successor strives to work out an arrangement with the last major surviving communist government in China, which now tolerates the Catholic Patriotic Association, but apart from papal control. There has been a noticeable movement away from Vatican II, beginning under the papacy of Paul VI (d. 1978) and continuing under his successors, John Paul II and Benedict XVI.

Today Catholicism is struggling between two views of the church, one more hierarchical in the traditional sense, the other more collegial as it wends its way through issues of social justice among the nations and personal morality, the inculturation of the church in non-European societies, the status of women, and the struggles over sexual morality, abortion, euthanasia, and environmental degradation. Today there are more than a billion Catholics around the world. The future will prove very different for Catholicism as the preponderant number of Catholics has shifted from the Northern Hemisphere to Latin America, Africa, and Asia. There can be little doubt that the resilient Roman Catholic Church will be able to find its way through these challenges.

—Frank K. Flinn

CHRONOLOGY

B.C.E. c. 04–06

- Probable birth of Jesus of Nazareth during the reign of Caesar Augustus (r. 31 B.C.E.–14 C.E.).
- Priene Inscription proclaims "gospel" of Augustus as "savior" and "benefactor" bringing Pax Romana.

C.E. 29, 30, or 33

- In Galilee, Jesus preaches the renewal of the Covenant in the coming kingdom of God. Judea under the heel of Rome and divided between different factions: Pharisees, Sadducees, Essenes, and intermittent messianic rebels and Zealots.
- Crucifixion of Jesus in Jerusalem under Procurator Pontius Pilate during reign of Tiberias (14–37).

49

- Ministry of Paul to Greece and Asia Minor (49–64). Council in Jerusalem debates whether Gentile followers of Jesus need to follow Jewish ritual law. Paul goes to Gentiles, Peter and James to Jews.

60–100

- Gospels committed to writing after circulation of oral traditions of sayings and parables, dialogue stories, passion narratives, infancy and post-Resurrection stories. Mark is first written Gospel, c. 70; Matthew, Luke c. 90–95; John c. 110. Different followers of Jesus take different and sometimes conflicting trajectories.

64

- Christians blamed for great fire in Rome.
- Peter and Paul probably executed under Nero (54–68).

70

- Jewish Revolt (66) followed by destruction of Jerusalem by Titus during emperorship of Vespasian (69–79). Temple spoils depicted on Arch of Titus in Rome.

84

- Expulsion of Nazoreans (Jewish-Christians?) from the synagogue in Palestine. (Christians still attend synagogue till fifth century and even later.)

c. 112

- Letter of Pliny the Younger to Trajan (r. 98–117) that Christians are law-abiding and no threat.

140–200

 ◆ Marcion excommunicated (144) and sets up own church. Montanus prophesies (c. 160). Gnostic movements thrive, challenged by Irenaeus of Lyons, Tertullian of Carthage, and Hippolytus of Rome. Justin Martyr writes *Apologies*.

250

 ◆ Persecution of Christians under Decius (r. 249–251).

280

 ◆ Armenia converted by Gregory the Illuminator.

305

 ◆ Anthony of Egypt founds anchoritic monasticism, to be followed by cenobitic monasticism of Macariaus and Pachomius.

313

 ◆ Edict of Toleration for Christians at Milan by Emperors Constantine and Licinius.

324

 ◆ Constantine sole emperor (r. 306–337). His mother, Helena, makes a pilgrimage to Jerusalem in 326 and starts a program of construction at the holy sites. Holy Land becomes focus of Christian institution of pilgrimage. Athanasius of Alexandria persecuted by Arian-leaning emperors.

325

 ◆ Constantine presides over the Council of Nicaea, the first empirewide council, which attacks Arius and declares Christ "one in being with the Father."

361

 ◆ Julian the Apostate (361–63) attempts to reinstate the old Roman order.

365–400

 ◆ Major bishop-theologians in Christendom include Basis at Caesarea, Ambrose at Milan, and John Chrysostom at Constantinople. Jerome translates Bible into Latin Vulgate and settles in Jerusalem. As a signal for future church-state relations, Ambrose excommunicates Theodosius I (r. 378–395) for massacre at Thessalonica.

381

 ◆ Council of Constantinople I grants Constantinople episcopate second rank behind Rome but ahead of Jerusalem, Antioch, and Alexandria.

410

 ◆ Augustine of Hippo flourishes. Defends orthodoxy against Donatism, Manichaeism, and Pelagianism.

431

 ◆ Council of Ephesus condemns Nestorius, defends title Theotokos, or Mother of God, for Mary.

451

 ◆ Council of Chalcedon affirms Christ is one person with two natures. Copts and some Syrians, heirs to the language of Cyril of Alexandria, reject this formula and are called Monophysites (one-nature adherents) by their enemies.

430

 ◆ Patrick begins missionary work in Ireland.

455

 ◆ Vandals sack Rome. Pope Leo the Great (r. 440–461) negotiates in absence of civil leader.

496

 ◆ Clovis, Merovingian king of Franks, becomes a Christian, leading to conversion of France.

527–65

◆ Reign of Emperor Justinian. Reconquers North Africa from Vandals and Italy from Goths. Promulgates Justinian Code, basis of all future canon and civil law in the West, and rebuilds Hagia Sophia in Constantinople.

550

◆ Benedict of Nursia at Monte Cassino, which becomes the catalyst for the spread of monasticism in the West. Council of Constantinople II (553) counteracts Nestorians.

560–600

◆ Columba founds monastery on Iona, seedbed for spread of Irish monasticism. Gregory I the Great (r. 590–604) centralizes Vatican, fosters monasticism, spreads Roman liturgy, and sends Augustine, later of Canterbury, to missionize England.

◆ Isadore of Seville provides West with encyclopedia of knowledge.

622–38

◆ Hejira of Prophet Muhammad. Year 1 in Islamic calendar.

◆ Arabs conquer Jerusalem in 638.

681

◆ Constantinople Council III. Chalcedon affirmed; Christ said to have two wills.

726

◆ Iconoclast controversy breaks out in Eastern Church.

732

◆ Charles Martel stops advance of Muslims into Europe at Poitiers.

780–830

◆ Alcuin becomes adviser to Charlemagne, who is crowned first Holy Roman Emperor, Christmas Day, 800. Carolingian Renaissance. Cyril and Methodius missionize the Slavs. Greek philosophers translated into Arabic in Baghdad.

◆ Beginning of *convivencia* between Muslims, Jews, and Christians in southern Spain.

843–1000

◆ Triumph of Orthodoxy: icons restored to churches in East. Arabs sack Rome (846) and conquer Sicily (848). Emperor Basil expels Arabs from upper Italy (880). Prince Vladimir introduces Christianity to Russia (990). Holy Roman Emperor Otto I (962) makes bishops and abbots lords of the realm.

909

◆ Cluny monastery founded, center for reform throughout early Middle Ages.

961

◆ Mt. Athos founded; becomes focus of Eastern monasticism lasting till today.

1000–1200

◆ Anselm of Canterbury (fl. 1080) writes *Cur Deus Homo*. Pope Gregory VII Hildebrand excommunicates Emperor Henry IV in investiture controversy (1076). Urban II preaches First Crusade (1099). Cistercians founded (1098), led by Bernard of Clairvaux, who contends with Abelard over the use of reason in theology. Thomas à Becket murdered at English king Henry II's orders (1170). Beginnings of scholastic theology. Suger inspires building of first Gothic cathedrals.

1200–1300

◆ Founding of mendicant orders by Francis of Assisi (1209) and Dominic de Guzmán (1215). Innocent III (r. 1198–1216) is pope; Lateran Council IV defines change in Eucharist as transubstantiation, and requires yearly penance and Communion. Crusaders capture Constantinople and set up Latin kingdom (1204), alienating Eastern Church. Magna Carta signed (1215), establishing habeas corpus. Marco Polo to China (1271–95). Great medieval theologians Bonaventure and Thomas Aquinas flourish c. 1250, followed later by Duns Scotus. Inquisition founded to counteract Cathari (Albigensians). Meister Eckhart opens path to new mysticism, and Dante writes *Divine Comedy*.

1300–1500

- Boniface VIII issues *Unam Sanctam* (1302), claiming supremacy of pope over both spiritual and temporal affairs. Avignon papacy (1309–77) scandalizes church; St. Catherine of Siena urges pope to return to Rome. Hundred Years' War (1337–1453) tears fabric of Europe; Joan of Arc saves France. Pope fights antipope during Western Schism (1378–1417). Struggle between pope and councils for supremacy dominates Councils of Constance (1414–18) and of Basel-Ferrara-Florence-Rome (1431–45).

1453

- Constantinople falls to the Turks.

1491

- Ferdinand and Isabella defeat and expel the Moors in Spain; send Columbus to the New World. Christian missions expand in Asia. Spanish Inquisition established (1492) with papal approval.

1500

- Renaissance in Italy. Corruption pervasive, especially among princely popes like Alexander VI Borgia (r. 1492–1503). Massive building in Rome under Julius II and Leo X; Michelangelo and Raphael commissioned to decorate Vatican. Selling of indulgences to pay for this.

1517

- Martin Luther begins Protestant Reformation, followed soon by John Calvin, Huldrich Zwingli,

and later by Henry VIII (1534). Europe divides religiously.

1545–1600

- Catholic Counter-Reformation with new religious orders (Jesuits), spirituality (Teresa of Ávila, Ignatius of Loyola), architecture (baroque), and reformed theology at Council of Trent (1545–63). Inquisition and Index of Forbidden Books established by Vatican. Jesuit mission reaches China (1582).
- Spanish Armada defeated off coast of Spain (1588).

1600–1700

- Vincent de Paul establishes new kind of charity; baroque Catholicism flourishes throughout Europe. African slaves brought to North America (1619). Galileo condemned by papacy, and Copernicus put on Index (1632). Peace of Westphalia (1648) puts end to religious wars. French develop independent ecclesiastical powers (Gallicanism).

1700–1800

- Jesuits suppressed by pope (1773). Missions flourish in Asia (Philippines) and Latin America, reaching up into Texas and California. U.S. Declaration of Independence (1776) and Constitution (1788) and French Revolution (1789–93) unleash both democracy and terror. John Carroll consecrated first bishop in United States (1790).

1800–1900

- German Romantic movement, giving rise to organic conception of theology. Modernist tendencies in history, philosophy, and theology. Critical interpretation of biblical sources. Marx issues *Communist Manifesto* (1848); radical labor movements unsettle many. John Henry Newman studies development of doctrine, becomes Catholic. Reaction against modernism in *Syl-*

labus of Errors of Pius IX (1854), who declares as Catholic dogma the Immaculate Conception of Mary (1854) and papal infallibility at Vatican Council I. Old Catholics split from Rome. Garibaldi liberates Papal States (1870). *Kulturkampf* in Germany against Catholics, Jews, and others. Leo XIII becomes first "modern" pope, accepting democracy and historical biblical research, but condemns "Americanism."

1900–2000

♦ A century of World Wars (1914–18, 1939–45) and isms: fascism and communism. Benedict XV seeks peace 1914, issues *Code of Canon Law* in 1917, and quiets the modernism debate. Russian Revolution (1917) frightens many believers. Papacy enters into concordats with fascists (1929) and Nazis (1933), yet distrusts Axis intentions. Great Depression provokes Catholics into social thinking (Dorothy Day, Catholic Action, etc.). Pius XII remains ambiguous pontiff; declares dogma of the Assumption of Mary (1950). New theological voices are heard: Karl Rahner, Thomas Merton, and Ives Congar. New movements in liturgy, recovery of early theologians, and biblical studies prepare way for John XXIII's radical gesture in calling for Vatican Council II (1962–65).

2000

♦ Post–Vatican II church pulled between liberalizing and traditionalizing forces. Decline in vocations to priesthood and religious life, while Catholic population grows. Largest Catholic population has shifted to Latin America, Africa, Asia. John Paul II (r. 1978–2005), immensely popular yet ultratraditional. Birth control, abortion, and euthanasia in forefront of debate. Pedophilia scandal strikes hard at church credibility and finances. Benedict XVI (2005–   ) seeks to reconcile with the Eastern Orthodoxy and Catholics in China.

CHRONOLOGICAL LIST OF POPES AND ANTIPOPES

*Names of antipopes are in italic
**Names of popes with entries in the encyclopedia are in small capital letters

until c. 64	Peter[1]	257–258	Sixtus II
	Linus	259–268	Dionysius
	Anacletus	269–274	Felix I
c. 96	Clement I	275–283	Eutychianus
	Evaristus	283–296	Caius
	Alexander I	296–304	Marcellinus
c. 117–c. 127	Sixtus I	c. 307–308/9	Marcellus I
c. 127–c. 137	Telesphorus	310	Eusebius
c. 137–c. 140	Hyginus	310/11–314	Miltiades
c. 140–c. 154	Pius I	314–335	Sylvester I
c. 154–c. 166	Anicetus	336	Mark
c. 166–c. 175	Soter	337–352	Julius I
c. 175–c. 89	Eleutherius	352–366	Liberius
189–198	Victor I	355–365	*Felix II*
198–217	Zephyrinus	366–384	Damasus I
217–222	Callistus I	366–367	*Ursinus*
217–c. 235	*HIPPOLYTUS*	384–399	Siricius
222–230	Urban I	399–401	Anastasius I
230–235	Pontian	402–417	Innocent I
235–236	Anterus	417–418	Zosimus
236–250	Fabian	418–422	Boniface I
251–253	Cornelius	418–419	*Eulalius*
251–257/8	*Novatian*	422–432	Celestine I
253–254	Lucius I	432–440	Sixtus III
254–257	Stephen I	440–461	LEO I

461–468	Hilarus
468–483	Simplicius
483–492	Felix III (II)
492–496	Gelasius I
496–498	Anastasius II
498–514	Symmachus
498–499, 501–506	*Laurentius*
514–523	Hormisdas
523–526	John I
526–530	Felix IV (III)
530–532	Boniface II
530	*Dioscorus*
533–535	John II
535–536	Agapetus I
536–537	Silverius
537–555	Vigilius
556–561	Pelagius I
561–574	John III
575–579	Benedict I
579–590	Pelagius II
590–604	GREGORY I
604–606	Sabinianus
607	Boniface III
608–615	Boniface IV
615–618	Deusdedit or Adeodatus I
619–625	Boniface V
625–638	Honorius I
640	Severinus
640–642	John IV
642–649	Theodore I
649–655	Martin I
654–657	Eugenius I
657–672	Vitalian
672–676	Adeodatus II
676–678	Donus
678–681	Agatho
682–683	Leo II
684–685	Benedict II
685–686	John V
686–689	Cono
687	*Theodore*
687	*Paschal*
687–701	Sergius I
701–705	John VI
705–707	John VII
708	Sisinnius
708–715	Constantine
715–731	Gregory II
731–741	Gregory III
741–752	Zacharias
752	Stephen II
752–767	Stephen II (III)
757–767	Paul I
767–769	*Constantine*
768	*Philip*
768–772	Stephen III (IV)
772–795	Hadrian I
795–816	Leo III
816–817	Stephen V
817–824	Paschal I
824–827	Eugenius II
827	Valentine
827–844	Gregory IV
844–847	Sergius II
844	*John*
847–855	Leo IV
855–858	Benedict II
855	*Anastasius Bibliothecarius*
858–867	Nicholas I
867–872	Hadrian II
872–882	John VIII
882–884	Marinus I
884–885	Hadrian III
885–891	Stephen VI
891–896	Formosus
896	Boniface VI
896–897	Stephen VII
897	Romanus
897	Theodore II
898–900	John IX
900–903	Benedict IV
903	Leo V
903–904	*Christopher*
904–911	Sergius III
911–913	Anastasius III
913–914	Lando
914–928	John X
928	Leo VI
928–931	Stephen VIII
931–935	John XI

936–939	Leo VII	1105–11	*Sylvester IV*
939–942	Stephen IX	1118–19	Gelasius II
942–946	Marinus II	1118–21	*Gregory VIII*
946–955	Agapetus II	1119–24	Callistus II
955–964	John XII	1124–30	Honorius II
963–965	Leo VIII	1124	*Celestine II*
964	Benedict V	1130–43	Innocent II
965–972	John XIII	1130–38	*Anacletus II*
973–974	Benedict VI	1138	*Victor IV*
974, 984–985	*Boniface VII*	1143–44	Celestine II
974–983	Benedict VII	1144–45	Lucius II
983–984	John XIV	1145–53	Eugenius III
985–996	John XV	1153–54	Anastasius IV
996–999	Gregory V	1154–59	Hadrian IV
997–998	*John XVI*	1159–81	Alexander III
999–1003	Sylvester II	1159–64	*Victor IV*
1003	John XVII	1164–8	*Paschal III*
1003/4–9	John XVIII	1168–78	*Callistus III*
1009–12	Sergius IV	1179–80	*Innocent III*[2]
1012–24	Benedict VIII	1181–85	Lucius III
1012	*Gregory*	1185–87	Urban III
1024–32	John XIX	1187	Gregory VIII
1032–44	Benedict IX	1187–91	Clement III
1045	Sylvester III	1191–98	Celestine III
1045	Benedict IX (for the second time)	1198–1216	Innocent III
		1216–27	Honorius III
1045–46	Gregory VI	1227–41	Gregory IX
1046–47	Clement II	1241	Celestine IV
1047–48	Benedict IX (for the third time)	1243–54	Innocent IV
		1254–61	Alexander IV
1048	Damasus II	1261–64	Urban IV
1048–54	Leo IX	1265–68	Clement IV
1055–57	Victor II	1271–76	Gregory X
1057–58	Stephen X	1276	Innocent V
1058–59	*Benedict X*	1276	Hadrian V
1059–61	Nicholas II	1276–77	John XXI
1061–73	Alexander II	1277–80	Nicholas III
1061–72	*Honorius II*	1281–85	Martin IV
1073–85	Gregory VII	1285–87	Honorius IV
1080, 1084–1100	*Clement III*	1288–92	Nicholas IV
1086–87	Victor III	1294	Celestine V
1088–99	Urban II	1294–1303	Boniface VIII
1099–1118	Paschal II	1303–04	Benedict XI
1100–01	*Theodoric*	1305–14	Clement V
1101	*Albert*	1316–34	John XXII

1328–30	*Nicholas V*	1590	Urban VII
1334–42	Benedict XII	1590–91	Gregory XIV
1342–52	Clement VI	1591	Innocent IX
1352–62	Innocent VI	1592–1605	Clement VIII
1362–70	Urban V	1605	Leo XI
1370–78	Gregory XI	1605–21	Paul V
1378–89	Urban VI	1621–23	Gregory XV
1378–94	*Clement VII*	1623–44	Urban VIII
1389–1404	Boniface IX	1644–55	Innocent X
1394–1417	*Benedict XIII*	1655–67	Alexander VII
1404–6	Innocent VII	1667–69	Clement IX
1406–15	Gregory XII	1670–76	Clement X
1409–10	*Alexander V*	1676–89	Innocent XI
1410–15	*John XXIII*	1689–91	Alexander VIII
1417–31	Martin V	1691–1700	Innocent XII
1423–29	*Clement VIII*	1700–21	Clement XI
1425–30	*Benedict XIV*	1721–1724	Innocent XIII
1431–47	Eugenius IV	1724–230	Benedict XIII
1439–49	*Felix V*	1730–40	Clement XII
1447–55	Nicholas V	1740–58	Benedict XIV
1455–58	Callistus III	1758–69	Clement XIII
1458–64	Pius II	1769–74	Clement XIV
1464–71	Paul II	1775–99	Pius VI
1471–84	Sixtus IV	1800–23	Pius VII
1484–92	Innocent VIII	1823–29	Leo XII
1492–1503	Alexander VI	1829–30	Pius VIII
1503	Pius III	1831–46	Gregory XVI
1503–13	Julius II	1846–78	Pius IX
1513–21	Leo X	1878–1903	Leo XIII
1522–23	Hadrian VI	1903–14	Pius X
1523–34	Clement VII	1914–22	Benedict XV
1534–49	Paul III	1922–39	Pius XI
1550–55	Julius III	1939–58	Pius XII
1555	Marcellus II	1958–63	John XXIII
1555–59	Paul IV	1963–78	Paul VI
1559–65	Pius IV	1978	John Paul I
1566–72	Pius V	1978–2005	John Paul II
1572–85	Gregory XIII	2005–	Benedict XVI
1585–90	Sixtus V		

[1]There is ample historical evidence that Peter was an Apostle, some evidence that Peter died in Rome, some but slighter evidence that he is buried beneath the high altar at St. Peter's Basilica, and no evidence that he was "bishop" of Rome, although Catholics claim this status for him.

[2]Lotario di Segni (c. 1160–1216) chose the same name when he became pope in 1198.

ENTRIES A TO Z

A

abbess/abbot (Aram.: *abba,* "father")

An abbess (female) or abbot (male) is an experienced NUN or MONK who serves as a) the spiritual guide of beginners in the monastic life, whether eremitical or cenobitic; or b) who canonically serves as the religious superior of 12 or more nuns or monks.

The word *abba* was used by Jesus to refer to his Father in heaven (Mark 14:36). This word was first applied around 335 to eremitical monks—charismatic figures like St. ANTHONY OF EGYPT who acted as "vicars" of the Father to their followers. In the East a chief nun was originally called by the Aramaic title *amma* ("mother"). The West later developed the term *abbatissa,* from which the English word *abbess* is derived.

Abbesses and abbots have played significant roles in Christian history, contributing to reform movements and innovative forms of spirituality. Noted abbesses include Sts. JULIAN OF NORWICH, HILDEGAARD OF BINGEN, and Hilda of Whitby (614–80). Noted abbots were PACHOMIUS, Sts. BENEDICT OF NURSIA, BERNARD OF CLAIRVAUX, and Abbot SUGER.

See also MONASTICISM, MONASTERY.

Further reading: Venerable Bede, "Lives of the Abbots," in *Ecclesiastical History,* tr. J. E. King (London: Heinemann, 1971–1976); Benedict of Nursia, *The Rule of St. Benedict,* ed. T. Fry (Collegeville: St. John's Abbey, 1982); Dick Harrison, *The Age of Abbesses and Queens* (Lund: Nordic Academic, 1998).

Abelard, Peter (1079–1142) *medieval French philosopher*

A key, if controversial, philosopher, dialectician, and theologian, known in his lifetime as Doctor Peripateticus Pallatinus—Peripatetic (Aristotelian) doctor from La Pallet—Peter Abelard cofounded a school that would become the University of Paris and helped develop both the theoretical framework and the logical methods of high medieval philosophy. However, he is popularly remembered as much for the dramatic details of his private life as for his intellectual achievements.

Born of minor nobility at La Pallet, he studied first with the nominalist Roscelin of Compiegne (c. 1050–c. 1125) and the Neoplatonic hyperrealist William of Champeaux (1070–1121) at the Cathedral School of Notre Dame in Paris. He also studied under Anselm of Laon (d. 1117), the foremost theologian of his time. A brilliant student, Abelard soon gained his own following, teaching logic as a part of the liberal arts curriculum at Melun,

Corbeil, and Mont Ste. Genevieve in Paris. Abelard was a contentious thinker, often coming into public conflict with his teachers and opponents. He had many famous students and followers, including John of Salisbury (c. 1115–76), Arnold of Brescia (c. 1090–1155), and Peter Lombard (c. 1110–60).

While teaching at Notre Dame, Abelard took on as a student, HELOISE, the gifted and beautiful niece of Fulbert, canon of the cathedral. In *The Story of My Calamities*—nothing less than an ecclesiastical *Romeo and Juliet*—Abelard recounts how the two fell wildly in love. Heloise became pregnant and secretly bore a son, Astrolabius. Although Abelard had been ordained to the minor orders, the lovers married secretly to avoid scandal. The outraged Fulbert hired thugs who broke into Abelard's sleeping quarters and castrated him. Both Abelard and Heloise entered the cloistered life, he at the Abbey of St. Denis above Paris and she at Argenteuil nearby. Later she became abbess at the Oratory of the Paraclete in Troyes that Abelard helped to establish, while he retired to the abbey of Cluny, dying at the priory of St. Marcel-sur-Saone.

The lovers corresponded their entire lives and elevated their love to the spiritual plane. When she died, Heloise was placed in Abelard's tomb at the Paraclete. In 1817 their remains were transferred to Père Lachaise cemetery in Paris.

As a philosopher, Abelard stands at the turning point between the Neoplatonism, which prevailed after the CAROLINGIAN RENAISSANCE, and the new paradigm of learning that was ushered in with the incorporation of Aristotle's physics and metaphysics into Christian thought, culminating in the theology of ST. THOMAS AQUINAS in the high MIDDLE AGES.

Abelard helped invent the medieval dialectical method. In the preface to *Sic et Non* (Yes and no), he reveals his method by saying he is going to pit contradictory quotations from the TRADITION (BIBLE, Fathers of the Church, CANON LAW) against one another, inviting students to seek out the truth for themselves: "I venture to bring together various statements of the holy fathers and to formulate certain questions which were suggested by the seeming contradictions in the statements. These questions are meant to stir beginning students to a zealous pursuit of the truth so as to sharpen their wits." Referring to the questioning method Aristotle promotes in the *Categories*, Abelard concludes in a statement that fully anticipates René Descartes: "By doubting we come to examine, and by examining we reach the truth." This methodology, coupled with the format of Peter Lombard's *Sentences*, provided the template by which all future medieval theology would be written.

Abelard's predecessors wanted to repeat the tradition; he wanted to explain it. In his logic studies Abelard severely criticized his former mentor William of Chapeaux (c. 1070–1121). Chapeaux maintained that universals were real; for example, human nature was a universal that existed whole and complete in the persons of both Socrates and Plato. Abelard argued that, in that case, there was no difference between Socrates and Plato, that is, that Socrates existed in two places at the same time. By contrast, Abelard favored the nominalist position that universals are names and that only individuals exist in reality, although he did not go as far as Roscelin, who said that universals were nothing but the breath of the voice. While not real in and of themselves, universals have linguistic and logical reality in their reference to particular things.

Abelard sought to apply his dialectical method to the theology of the TRINITY in *On Unity and the Divine Trinity*, which underwent three revisions/expansions. Abelard was the first Western thinker to use the term *theology* in the sense it is still used today. Prior to that time the word was used for the study of the Greco-Roman gods and was interchangeable with *mythology*. Although Abelard accepted that language is limited by finitude and temporality and that we can speak of the divine nature only in a figurative or metaphorical way, we nevertheless can speak something that approximates truth (*verisimilis*).

Starting with the traditional formula of one substance and three divine persons, Abelard spoke of the Trinity as manifesting respectively the power, wisdom, and goodness of the Godhead. Abelard put strong emphasis on the Holy Spirit as the love that unites the power (Father) and wisdom (Son) of God. One could understand the Trinity not directly but indirectly through human similes. His favorite was the bronze bar from which is "begotten" the seal, from which "proceeds" the sealing.

Such "new thought" and rational daring was condemned at the Synod of Soissons (1121), where Abelard was required to recite the Athanasian creed while tossing his tome *On the Trinity* into the flames. This synod was clearly illegitimate by ecclesiastical standards, as Abelard was not given a chance to rebut the charges.

Abelard also wrote an ethical treatise, *Know Thyself,* in which he asserts, in anticipation of Kant, that intentions are paramount over deeds. In his *Exposition of the Epistle of Romans* he embraces a moral or exemplary theory of ATONEMENT, while not refuting the earlier satisfaction or penal theory formulated by St. ANSELM OF CANTERBURY. The Cross is meant to incite in us the love of God rather than fear of punishment for sin: "Our redemption through the suffering of Christ is that deeper love within us which not only frees us from slavery to sin, but also secures for us the true freedom of the children of God so that we may do all things out of love rather than fear—love for him who has shown us such grace that no greater can be found."

Late in his life, Abelard resumed public teaching and once again incurred the wrath of traditionalists, this time in the person of the formidable abbot of Citeaux, St. BERNARD OF CLAIRVAUX, whose approach to theology was based on a Neoplatonic mystical union with the divine and opposed to rational analysis. There is no doubt that Abelard was feisty and boasted of his skill in dialectics, but the unscrupulous Bernard did everything to stack the deck against him at the Synod of Sens (1140), maliciously accusing him of heresy, assaulting the majesty of God, and reducing everything to reason. Abelard appealed to Rome and was given refuge by Abbot Peter the Venerable (c. 1092–1156) at Cluny, but once again he was condemned before he could muster a defense. This time the condemnation was by Pope Innocent II (r. 1130–43), whom Bernard had helped to elect as pope. Abelard died soon after, reconciled with both church and adversary, but never once recanting his positions, which he believed in true accord with Christian teaching. On the relation of FAITH AND REASON, Bernard won the battle but lost the war. The great medieval theologians followed Abelard's path.

Further reading: Abelard and Heloise, *The Letters of Abelard and Heloise,* tr. by C. K. Scott Moncrieff (New York: Cooper Square, 1974); Peter Abelard, *Christian Theology,* tr. by J. Ramsey MaCallum (Oxford: Blackwell, 1948); Henry Adams, *Mont St. Michel and Chartres* (Harmondsworth: Penguin, 1986); G. R. Evans, ed., *The Medieval Theologians* (Oxford: Blackwell, 2001); Lieff Grane, *Peter Abelard* (Harcourt, Brace & World, 1964).

abortion (Lat.: *ab,* "away from" + *oriri,* "to arise," "emerge"; combined: "to perish")

The term refers both to the natural and the artificially induced termination of a pregnancy most often ending in the death of the fetus. Catholic moral teaching deals exclusively with artificially induced abortion ending in the death of the fetus.

The Catholic teaching on abortion has complex origins in Jewish teaching, Greek thought, and early Christian doctrine. Jewish teaching in general shows great reverence for life as a gift from God. Nevertheless, the law of compensation in Exodus 21:22 seems to make a distinction between the penalty for striking a pregnant woman that ends in the loss of a fetus (a monetary amount) or the mother (death). The Septuagint (LXX) version of this verse, showing the influence of Greek thought, distinguishes between an incompletely and a completely formed fetus and exacts a penalty of death in the case of the abortion of the latter. This likely refers to Aristotle's distinction between the nutritive, sensitive, and rational aspects of the soul (*On the Soul* 415a). Aristotle taught that the rational or specifically human faculty of the soul is infused not immediately at conception but only when the embryo takes on a human form. In his *Natural History* (8.3) Aristotle said human ensoulment took place 40 days after conception for males and 80 for females.

Early Christian teachings against abortion must be understood against the background of Greco-Roman custom. Both Plato and Aristotle held that the *polis,* or state, was supreme and could permit abortion for the good of the state. Greeks and Romans had no qualms about using abortificants, nor did they object to exposing defective infants or even healthy female children. Like the Jews, the early Christian communities rejected abortion, as witnessed in the *Didache* (2.2) and the *Epistle of Barnabas* (19.5). In *On the Soul* 37 TERTULLIAN OF CARTHAGE refers to Exodus 21:22 and Jeremiah 1:4–5 in condemning abortion of a fetus that is the "cause of a human being." Finally, against the false charge that Christians ate children during their AGAPE feasts, Athenagoras of Athens (c. 130–90) makes a defense that if Christians abhor both abortion and infant exposure, how could they tolerate killing a child to devour it (*Plea for the Christians* 37).

Several early local councils of bishops condemned abortion, in part due to its association with adultery: Council of Elvira in 306 (canon 63), Council of Ancyra in 314 (canon 21), and Council of Tullo/Quinsext in 692 (canon 91). Augustine, however, affirmed the Aristotelian teaching in *On Exodus* (21.80) and claimed in the *Enchiridion* (23.86) that he did not have an answer about the status of a fetus.

The abortion question entered into a new phase during the MIDDLE AGES. In *On Virginal Conception and Original Sin* 7 ANSELM OF CANTER-BURY gave the most forceful statement in favor of the delayed hominization thesis: "No human intellect accepts the view that an infant has the rational soul from the moment of conception." After Aquinas accepted Aristotle's hylomorphic theory of the soul as the form of the body (*Summa Theologiae* la.77.4), the theory of late ensoulment was in the ascendancy; he saw the abortion of the unensouled fetus as a sin against marriage but not murder. The jurist Gratian combined the theory of God's immediate creation of the soul with the Aristotelian theory of the delayed implantation of the soul until the human form was present: "He is not a murderer who brings about abortion before the soul is in the body" (*Decretals* 8.32.2).

The Council of Vienne (1312) under Clement V (r. 1305–14) affirmed the teaching on delayed hominization. The teaching suffered a setback in 1588 when Sixtus V (r. 1585–90) issued the bull *Effraenatum,* excommunicating anyone who used contraception or induced abortion at any time during pregnancy. However, three years later Gregory XIV (r. 1590–91) rescinded the severity of Sixtus's punishments and reinstated the doctrine of delayed hominization, or "quickening," of the fetus, approximately 16 weeks after conception. This rule remained in effect until Pius IX, whose *Apostolicae Sedis* (1869) reinstated excommunication for abortion at any stage of pregnancy. Implicitly, Pius's teaching embraced a theory of immediate ensoulment, or hominization at the moment of conception.

This position was affirmed in the VATICAN COUNCIL II declaration *Gaudium et Spes* 51. The Declaration on Procured Abortion (1974), issued by the Congregation for the Doctrine of Faith, stated that it "expressly leaves aside the question of the moment when the spiritual soul is infused" because there is so much disagreement in the tradition. In *Donum Vitae* (1984) the congregation argued that a fertilized egg will become nothing but a human being and that human life is to be absolutely respected from the moment of inception. This seems to place insurmountable restrictions on the delayed hominization theory.

However, moral theologians, arguing on the latest biological findings, note that the fertilized egg at the blastosphere stage is not a physical individual—it can split into twins, for example, or split and be reabsorbed by the original set of cells—until it is restricted by implantation in the wall of the uterus. This again argues for delayed ensoulment.

Practically speaking, Catholic moral theology forbids all direct abortions, that is, abortions that deliberately aim at the removal of a fetus plain and simple. In *Humanae Vitae* (1968) Paul VI condemned direct therapeutic abortion. Contrary to popular misconceptions even on the part of some priests, Catholicism does allow for indirect abortions, that is, abortions that aim not directly at the fetus but at the removal of a diseased or endangering condition, such as a cancerous uterus or an ektopic pregnancy in the fallopian tube. The moral reasoning is based on the principle of double effect: in seeking the good result a bad result may be indirectly and incidentally tolerated.

The Catholic Church has sought to influence civil society to move away from the option of direct abortion. The options are not monolithic. Catholic politicians are considered free to seek compromises, such as the restriction of some abortions, laws that discourage abortion, or legislation that addresses the conditions that give rise to the need for abortion. The Catholic politician is free to measure the whole worth of a piece of legislation even though an abortion plank may be part of it. For example, it can be statistically shown that an increase in employment decreases the number of unwanted pregnancies and abortions in the general population. In this case, a Catholic politician may support a political platform that supports abortion in theory yet also seeks to expand employment because the latter, in fact if not in theory, actually reduces the number of abortions. Conversely, a political platform can embrace an antiabortion plank in theory, yet follow employment policies that radically increase the number of abortions.

Recently in the United States, a small number of bishops have claimed that Catholic politicians who support abortion even indirectly, and Catholics who vote for them, are to be denied Holy Communion. Others oppose this as smacking of DONATISM or JANSENISM, stringent and purist positions that have generally been shunned in the orthodox Catholic tradition in favor of positions like the equiprobabilism of St. Alphonsus LIGUORI.

See also SEXUALITY; THEOLOGY.

Further reading: Norman M. Ford, *When Did I Begin? Conception of the Human Individual in History, Philosophy and Science* (Cambridge: Cambridge University, 1988); Patricia B. Jung and Thomas A. Shannon, eds., *Abortion and U.S. Catholicism* (New York: Crossroads, 1988); J. Gordon Melton, *The Churches Speak on Abortion* (Detroit: Gale Research, 1989); John T. Noonan, *The Morality of Abortion* (Cambridge Mass: Harvard University Press, 1970); Thomas A. Shannon and Lisa Sowie Cahill, *Religion and Artificial Reproduction* (New York: Crossroads, 1988); Allan B. Wolter and Thomas A. Shannon, "Reflections on the Moral Status of the Pre-embryo," *Theological Studies* (December, 1990) 51: 603–26.

accident   *See* SUBSTANCE; TRANSUBSTANTIATION.

acts, everyday religious   *See* DEVOTIONS.

Adam and Eve

The Book of Genesis 2–4 portrays Adam and Eve as the first humans, and thus the parents of all humankind. The name *Adam* is derived from the Hebrew *adamah*, red earth, and the name *Eve,* from *hayyah,* life. The Genesis story depicts the pair in the Garden of Eden, where the Serpent (later understood as Satan) tempts them to eat the forbidden fruit. They are expelled by the avenging

Adam and Eve in the Garden of Eden with serpent on tree. Engraving by Albrecht Dürer (1471–1528). The hare, cat, ox, and elk symbolize the four tempers (sanguine, choleric, phlegmatic, and melancholic), which were in perfect harmony before the Fall. *(St. Louis Art Museum, with permission)*

in the painting of the Renaissance. MICHELANGELO depicted them in one of the panels on the ceiling of the Sistine Chapel.

Adam and Eve figure heavily in the theology of CREATION, the FALL, anthropology, SPIRITUALITY, and CHRIST/CHRISTOLOGY. Sts. CYPRIAN OF CARTHAGE and AUGUSTINE OF HIPPO refer to Adam and Eve's sin in their development of the doctrine of original SIN.

Further reading: Jean Danielou, *From Shadows to Reality* (London: Burns & Oates, 1966); R. Scroggs, *The Last Adam: A Study in Pauline Anthropology* (Philadelphia: Fortress Press, 1966); Elaine Pagels, *Adam, Eve and the Serpent* (New York: Random House, 1988).

adoptionism

The heresy of adoptionism arose in the eighth century but had roots in even earlier teachings about the relation of Jesus to the Father. The adoptionist teachers Elipandus (717–812), archbishop of Toledo, and Felix (d. 818), bishop Urgel, taught that Jesus was not the true but the adopted Son of God. Adoptionism was condemned at the Council of Frankfurt (794), called by CHARLEMAGNE, by Pope Leo III, and ALCUIN OF YORK who wrote many treatises against the doctrine.

Later theologians tried to claim that PETER ABELARD, Gilbert of Porrée, DUNS SCOTUS, and FRANCESCO SUAREZ all had adoptionist Christologies, but the charges are now suspect. Protestant historian of doctrine Adolf Harnack (1851–1930) applied the term, somewhat anachronistically, to the earlier Christologies of the Ebionites, Theodore of Mospeutsia (c. 350–428), and others.

See also CHRIST/CHRISTOLOGY.

Further reading: John C. Cavadini, *The Last Christology in the West: Adoptionism in Spain and Gaul* (Philadelphia: University of Pennsylvania Press, 1993); Celia Martin Chazelle, *The Crucified God in the Carolingian Era: Theology and Art of Christ's Passion* (New York: Cambridge University Press, 2001).

angel of God and given specific curses: the serpent to crawl on its belly, Eve to suffer labor pains, and Adam to labor by the sweat of his brow.

Adam and Eve are important in Jewish, early Christian, Gnostic, Manichaean, and Islamic thought. Luke 3:38 depicts Adam as an ancestor of Jesus. Paul sees sin entering into the human race through Adam (Rom. 5:6), who is an antitype of Christ, through whom grace enters. In the MIDDLE AGES Mary came to be seen as the antitype of Eve (*Eva, Ave*). Adam, Eve, and the Serpent were among the first images painted in Christian catacombs. They are often depicted in the sculpture and stained glass of medieval cathedrals and

adoration (Lat.: *adorare,* "to worship")

Adoration is the highest attitude of devotion or prayer, reserved for God alone, in contrast to VENERATION, which is offered to SAINTS as models of holiness in imitation of Christ. *Adoration* translates the Greek term *latreia,* and *veneration* the term *dulia.* Mary, because she is the Mother of God (THEOTOKOS), is offered adulation, translated from *hyperdulia,* or "super-veneration."

Beginning in early medieval art, the Adoration of the Magi (Matt. 2:10–11), the Adoration of the Shepherds (Luke 2:15–16), and the Adoration of the Lamb (Rev. 5) became favorite themes for artists and sources of popular devotion. The Adoration of the CROSS is part of the Good Friday service.

In the late MIDDLE AGES devout Catholics developed a theology of Eucharistic adoration that they called "ocular Communion." In this religious, practice a large Host (consecrated at MASS as the Body of Christ) is put in a MONSTRANCE, which is placed in a prominent place in a church, chapel, or sanctuary. Some religious communities have developed the pious practice of the Perpetual Adoration of the Real Presence of Christ in the EUCHARIST. Many Protestant reformers objected strenuously to this practice, maintaining that Christ instituted the Eucharist as a sacred supper and not as worship. Today Catholics place the meal aspect above the adoration aspect, although the latter practice continues. In many cathedrals and churches a side chapel is reserved for the Adoration of the Host in a monstrance.

See also UTENSILS, SACRED.

Further reading: Jeremy Driscoll, "Adoration of the Blessed Sacrament," in Paul K. Hendersen, Emily A. Davis, and Margie Kilty, eds., *A Book of Readings on the Eucharist* (Washington, D.C.: National Conference of Catholic Bishops, 2000); Benedict J Groeschel, *In the Presence of the Lord: The History, Theology and Psychology of Eucharistic Devotion* (Huntington, Ind.: Our Sunday Visitor, 1997); Nathan Mitchell, *Cult and Controversy: The Worship of the Eucharist Outside Mass* (New York: Pueblo, 1982).

Advent   *See* LITURGICAL YEAR.

Africa

Christianity has been in Africa from its earliest times. The story of Simon of Cyrene, who was forced to carry Jesus' cross (Mark 15:21; Matt. 27:32), points to the many Greek-speaking Jews from Cyrene and Alexandria who visited Jerusalem for religious feasts. Simon, Lucius (Acts 13:1), and possibly Stephen (Acts 6:9) were part of this community through which Christianity was transmitted back to the Greek-speaking Jews of Africa. By the fourth century the temple of Apollo in Cyrene had been transformed into a Christian church.

The church expanded rapidly into all regions of coastal North Africa. The many acts of martyrs that occurred there, most notably those narrated in the *Passion of Perpetua and Felicity* (207), testify to the extensive inroads the church made into the African Roman populations. The early theologians ORIGEN and CLEMENT OF ALEXANDRIA conducted a catechetical school in Alexandria. By the third century TERTULLIAN OF CARTHAGE, CPYRIAN OF CARTHAGE, and CYRIL OF ALEXANDRIA provided the leadership that fostered church growth in the face of persecution on the one hand and the DONATISM schism on the other. African Christianity was noted for its stress

Wood door panel of Christ carrying cross, by Lamidi Olonade Fakeye (Our Lady Seat of Wisdom Catholic Chapel, University of Ibadan, Nigeria) *(Drawing by Frank K. Flinn)*

on morality against pagan practices, frequent episcopal councils, and rigorous legalism. By the time of AUGUSTINE OF HIPPO the African church had become one of the pillars of orthodox faith in the late Roman world.

Egypt witnessed the rise of hermits and the monastic life for both men and women. Notable are PACHOMIUS and ST. ANTHONY OF EGYPT. The monastic pattern spread from Egypt to Palestine and Syria and then to the rest of the empire. North African Christianity went into a severe decline after the sweep of Islam across the continent in the late seventh century, though it persisted as a strong minority in Egypt itself (*see* ETHIOPIAN CATHOLIC CHURCH).

The story of Christianity in Africa goes into abeyance until the arrival of Portuguese traders and missionaries on the west coast and in Angola and Mozambique in the 15th and 16th centuries. Regrettably, Pope Nicholas V (r. 1447–55) in his bull *Romanus Pontifex* (January 8, 1455) legitimized the taking of slaves among the Saracens (Muslims) and pagan peoples by the Portuguese. Although Franciscans converted the Congo king Nzinga Nkuwu in 1491 and Augustinians founded a monastery in Mombasa, the combination of imperial Portuguese brutality, slaveholding even by missionaries, and Islamic resistance thwarted real growth of the church.

A third wave of Catholic missions began after 1850. It received its initial impulse from Charles Lavigerie (1825–92), who founded the missionary orders of the White Fathers and White Nuns. Although the colonialist mission to North Africa was successful in terms of gaining converts, it soon lapsed when the North African Islamic nations gained independence. The missionaries, along with the Holy Ghost Fathers and other traditional religious orders, were far more successful south of the Sahara.

In the 20th century Christianity experienced an explosion in Africa. VATICAN COUNCIL II (1963–65) had a significant impact. The translation of the Bible and the liturgy into local languages increased participation of the laity. Vatican II's deemphasis of folk religious elements in Catholicism (holy water, blessings, healing shrines, candles, religious artifacts) was resisted in the African Church, but its stress on moving the local church to indigenous leadership under African bishops, priests, and especially lay catechists fostered the growth of home-grown liturgies. The celebrated *Missa Luba* includes complex choral singing, dancing, and the use of drums. However, there has been much debate about how far one can take the INCULTURATION or adaptation of the Gospel into indigenous contexts.

African Christianity tends to be traditional, orthodox in belief, yet tinged with Pentecostalism. Many indigenous African Christian movements, such as those formed by William Wade Harris (c. 1860–1929) and Simon Kimbangu (c. 1889–1951), both now members of the World Council of Churches, pose a problem and a challenge to mainline Christians. By the 1994 African synod in Rome 90 percent of the bishops in Africa were indigenous. Today there are 136,000,000 Catholics throughout the continent

African Catholicism has experienced several difficulties. Because of the complex nature of African ceremonial marriage and the shortage of priests, many marriages are not solemnized in a regular fashion. The lack of priests also means that church worship is not centered on the sacraments, especially the EUCHARIST, as it is in other parts of the world. The church's compromised position during the civil war in Rwanda created a scandal: both the Hutu and Tutsi are Catholics; many on both sides took refuge in churches but were killed nonetheless. Finally, the recent conflicts between Catholics and Muslims in the Sudan, Nigeria, and elsewhere have raised alarms. Despite such concerns, many scholars note that the future growth of Christianity and Catholicism lies in Africa, Latin America, and Asia.

Further reading: David B. Barrett, *World Christian Encyclopedia* (Nairobi: Oxford University Press, 2000);

Vincent J. Donovan, *Christianity Rediscovered* (Notre Dame: Fides/Claretian, 1978); Adrian Hastings, *African Catholicism* (London: SCM, 1989); Philip Jenkins, *The Next Christendom* (New York: Oxford University Press, 2002); Aylward Shorter, "The Roman Catholic Church in Africa Today," in *Christianity in Africa in the 1990s*, ed. by C. Fyfe (Edinburgh: University of Edinburgh, 1996) 22–38.

agape (Gk.: "love")

Agape is the common term used for love in the Greek New Testament, usually translated as *caritas* in Latin texts. It includes both the love and affection between human beings and between humans and GOD and is often contrasted with *eros* (love including sexual passion) and *philia* (affection between friends), although there are no hard and fast distinctions. The fact that *agape, philia,* and *eros* are all translated as *love* in English often leads to a confusion concerning Christian love. For example, the meaning of passages such as John 21: 15–17 swings on the distinction between *philia* and *agape.* The term has a secondary meaning as the *love feast* common among early Christians.

In the Greek translation of the Hebrew Bible, *agape* often represents the Hebrew *'ahabah*, which is used both for the steadfast love between a husband and wife and the covenantal relationship between God and Israel (Deut. 6:5). In the Christian Scriptures this love is the bond of humans to the Father and Christ and of Christ and the Father to humans. The verbal cognate *agapao* is used for the great commandment to love God and one's neighbor (Mark 12:28; Matt. 22:39–40). Paul sees love as the expression of God's saving will toward humankind (Rom. 5:5). It is also the abiding ethic of self-giving and mutual support in the believing community, and Paul gives it preeminence over faith and hope (1 Cor. 12–13). In John love means the boundless love of God for humankind: "For God so loved the world that he gave his only begotten son so that all who trust in him may not be destroyed but come to have eternal life" (John 3:16). In the Johannine tradition God is identified with love itself (John 4:16).

Agape theology continued into the second century (1 *Clement* 49–50) and became an enduring aspect of Christian theology in all its phases. The *Didache* begins with the command to love. IRENAEUS OF LYON finds a unity of God's saving history in the command to love given both by Moses and Jesus (*Heresies* 4.12.2). In CLEMENT OF ALEXANDRIA the true Gnostic is one who is in love with God (*Miscellanies* 7.11.67), and the martyr is one who loves God the best. BASIL THE GREAT mentions love frequently in his Rule and sees it as the force that binds the community together. Whereas Clement and Basil discussed love in the context of a spiritual elite, St. JOHN CHRYSOSTOM saw love as open to all and able to transform each person into the likeness of God. AUGUSTINE OF HIPPO taught that the FALL resides in the deviation from the rightly ordered love between God and creature. He saw the inner dynamic of the TRINITY itself as *amor amorans*, or "love loving," involving a lover, a beloved, and the love relation itself, a love that is shadowed even in human fleshly love (*On the Trinity* 8.14.10).

In the MIDDLE AGES the theology of love received a chivalric cast through commentaries on the Song of Songs, which was interpreted allegorically as the quest of the soul (the lover) for God (the beloved) or the bond between Christ and his church. Love theology entered into the mainstream of Christian mysticism. It also became a characteristic of the Franciscan school, which continued the thought of Augustine. St. BONAVENTURE centered his love theology on the overwhelming love God showed in offering up his own Son: "There is no other path but through the burning love of the crucified" (Preface, *Journey of the Soul into God*). The whole of DUN SCOTUS'S theology is dominated by the notion of love, which is marked by absolute freedom. The more free the love, the more it ennobles the relation between God and humans and among humans themselves. Creation itself is an act of loving will, and the end of human beings is not so much an intellectual BEATIFIC VISION but pure delight in the love of God. In his *Reportatio* Scotus wrote "God wills to love. God wills to be loved. God wills to have co-lovers of God's self."

St. THOMAS AQUINAS gives a formal treatment of love in relation to the three theological virtues in his *Summa Theologiae* 2–2.23–46. He correlates charity with Aristotle's notion of friendship in the *Nicomachean Ethics* 8. Charity or love is our friendship with God. The Holy Spirit is the motive force of love working in cooperation with human will. We are to love our neighbor because in so doing we love God's self, who is our greatest good and final end. However, love does not free us from the effects of sin and can even be lost.

The early Christian *agape*, or love feast, symbolized the fellowship of love between God and the community and pointed back to the meals Jesus shared with his disciples, especially the Last Supper (Mark 14). This feast was at first identified with the EUCHARIST itself (1 Cor. 11:17–34), which was also signified by "the breaking of bread" (Acts 2:42–47). Agape meals had a root in contemporaneous Jewish fellowship meals (*haburah*) and also echoed the cultic meals of fraternities or associations in Greco-Roman religion.

The agape meals, however, became subject to abuse: heavy drinking, class distinctions, and partisan strife, which was already noted by Paul in 1 Corinthians 11:17–22. Because of the abuses, by the early second century the agape meal and the Eucharist went their separate ways in most circumstances. TERTULLIAN OF CARTHAGE saw the agape meal as relief for the hungry and needy (*Apology* 39). At the end of the patristic period the practice fell into disuse. Some contemporary Catholic congregations have revived the agape meal as a part of the Holy Thursday liturgy.

Further reading: John Keating, *The Agape and the Eucharist in the Early Church* (London: Methuen, 1901); Anders Nygren, *Agape and Eros* (Philadelphia: Westminster, 1953); G. H. Oukta, *Agape: An Ethical Analysis* (New Haven, Conn.: Yale University Press, 1972).

agnosticism (Gk.: *a-gnosis*, "the state of not knowing")

Somewhere between atheism and faith lies agnosticism, the attitude that finite minds such as ours cannot know whether GOD or any ultimate reality exists. It is often identified with skepticism.

The term was coined by Thomas H. Huxley (1825–95), defender of Charles Darwin (1809–82) against Samuel Wilberforce (1805–73) at the 1859 Oxford Debate. His 1889 essay *Nineteenth Century* used the word to counter what he called "Gnostics," that is, believers who claim to know about God and ultimate reality, things of which Huxley claimed to be ignorant (*Science and Christian Tradition*, 239–40). Huxley grounded his arguments on the new sciences arising in the 19th century and the new critical methods of reading the BIBLE such as the documentary hypothesis and form criticism. The term *agnostic* gained immediate currency but has come to mean many different things to many different people.

Following Locke, the classic agnostic claims not to accept more propositions than are warranted by empirical evidence. In this sense an agnostic appeals to Immanuel Kant (1724–1804), who claims in his *Critique of Pure Reason* that since God, freedom, immortality, and the soul can be both proved and disproved by theoretical reason, we ought to suspend judgment about them. Kant, nevertheless, insisted that practical reason had to posit the existence of these realities in order for there to be a rational morality. In a more mundane sense, agnosticism is identified with a secular way of life that neither relies on God on the one hand, nor indulges in antireligious or anticlerical attitudes, atheism, free thought, or positivism on the other.

One kind of agnosticism can be associated with religious belief. Certain apophatic (Gk. "unsayable") mystical theologians such as GREGORY OF NYSSA claimed that God was ultimately unknown and unknowable, so that true believers should not engage in apologetics but simply submit to a union with the Godhead in a process of theosis. Apophatic theology is also known as negative theology: whatever finite quality one can discover, God is not that because God transcends it infinitely. In the beginning of *The Orthodox Faith* St. JOHN OF DAMASCUS notes that God is "ineffable and incomprehensible": what we do know of God comes through Scripture, the prophets, and the Son (Jesus Christ), but even then we never attain God's essence. This path of theology is much stronger in Eastern than Western Christianity. In the 19th century the existential theologian Søren Kierkegaard embraced a kind of religious agnosticism, confronting proud reason with a God, unreachable except through a "leap of faith."

See also ATHEISM; GOD; FAITH AND REASON; THEOLOGY.

Further reading: Thomas H. Huxley, *Science and Christian Religion* (New York: D. Appleton, 1896); James Ward, *Naturalism and Agnosticism,* The Gifford Lectures (New York: Macmillan, 1899).

Alacoque, St. Margaret Mary   *See*

MARGARET MARY ALACOQUE, ST.

Albertus Magnus, St. (1193–1280) *medieval scientist, philosopher, and theologian*

Known as the Doctor Universalis, Albertus Magnus was a towering figure in medieval science, philosophy, and theology in his own right as well as teacher of St. THOMAS AQUINAS. He was canonized in 1931 and made patron of natural scientists in 1941. His feast day is November 15.

Born near Ulm, Germany, Albertus studied at the University of Padua in Italy, where he joined the DOMINICAN ORDER while also developing his life-long interest in the natural sciences. He studied theology at Cologne and lectured at Paris, where Thomas was his most famous student. Back in Cologne, Albertus introduced the study of ARISTOTLE into the medieval curriculum. He

wrote the *Summa de Creaturis* (1246), wrote a commentary on the *Sentences* of PETER LOMBARD, and lectured on the Neoplatonic mystical writer DIONYSIUS the Pseudo-Areopagite. Albertus also wrote commentaries on the Bible and at the end of his life embarked on a *Summa Theologiae*. Albertus defended apophatic theology, the thesis that God is ultimately incomprehensible and that the theologian must at some point "stop speaking" (Gk. *apophasis*) about the Godhead.

Albertus was a skillful diplomat and mediated many conflicts, although he preached the Crusade in Germany. He defended Thomas Aquinas against charges of heresy and assisted at the second Council of Lyons (1274). He reluctantly accepted an appointment as bishop of Regensburg, Germany, but soon resigned., Because of his interest in nature, Albertus was long accused of practicing black magic, a charge that delayed his eventual canonization. He wrote on animals, the properties of minerals, the movement of the heavens, and many similar topics. There is a wonderful portrait of him by FRA ANGELICO in the Church of San Marco in Florence.

Further reading: Albertus Magnus, *Opera Omnia* (Aschendorf: Monasterii Westfalorum, 1951–   ); Ingrid Craemer-Ruegenberg, *Albertus Magnus* (Munich: Beck, 1980); James A. Weisapel, *Albertus Magnus and the Sciences* (Toronto: Pontifical Medieval Institute, 1980).

Albigensians   *See* CATHARI.

Alcuin of York (c. 730–804) *early medieval scholar and educator*

The English MONK Alcuin of York, a scholar and Neoplatonic philosopher, played a key role in reviving intellectual and scholarly life in Western Christendom and preserving the heritage of antiquity. He founded the imperial cathedral school for CHARLEMAGNE at Aix-la-Chapelle (Aachen), where he established the seven liberal arts as the core of the curriculum and stimulated the ferment that was later known as the CAROLINGIAN RENAISSANCE.

Alcuin was born in Northumbria and educated at the cathedral school of York. In 782 Charlemagne invited him to head the cathedral school of Aix-la-Chapelle, where his program laid the foundation for subsequent Christian ideas of learning and education. He codified the medieval division of learning into the seven "liberal arts," including the trivium (grammar, rhetoric, dialectic) and quadrivium (arithmetic, geometry, astronomy, music). This division is based on Plato's discussion of education in Book III of the *Republic*. As Plato subordinated sense experience to the true knowledge of ideas, Alcuin subordinated the liberal arts and philosophy to theology and contemplation of the divine. This hierarchy of learning prevailed until scholars of the high Middle Ages, most notably Sts. ALBERTUS MAGNUS and THOMAS OF AQUINAS, turned to ARISTOTLE, who gave much greater authority to sense experience and the sciences derived from them.

The cathedral school sent scholars and clergy throughout the empire to assume key positions in schools and monasteries. Alcuin became abbot of the Abbey of St. Martin in Tours in 796, where he devised the majuscule/minuscule system used in copying manuscripts. This became standard procedure for monk copyists throughout Christendom, as they embarked on the preservation of classical, biblical, and patristic texts for future generations. Alcuin also revised the Vulgate version of the Bible and reformed the LITURGY, joining with Charlemagne in promoting the Roman rite over the many variants of the Gallican rite. At the end of his life he partook in the debates with Spanish proponents of ADOPTIONISM, arguing the Carolingian viewpoint at the regional council of Frankfurt in 794.

Further reading: Alcuin, *The Rhetoric of Alcuin & Charlemagne,* tr. Wilbur Samuel Howell (New York: Russell & Russell, 1965); Luitpold Wallach, *Alcuin and Charlemagne* (Ithaca, N.Y.: Cornell University Press,

1959); Andrew Fleming West, *Alcuin and the Rise of the Christian Schools* (New York: Scribner's, 1903).

Alexander VI, Pope (1431–1503) *Renaissance pope (1493–1503), politician, and art patron*

Born in Valencia, Spain, Roderigo Borgia made a name for himself in his notorious family well before bribing his way to the PAPACY in 1493. He became perhaps the most corrupt pope, abusing both his spiritual and temporal powers, yet he acted as a generous patron of the arts during the Renaissance.

His family had great prominence by marrying into the powerful Italian Colonna and Orsini families. His uncle Pope Callixtus III (r. 1455–58) made him a cardinal in 1456 at the age of 25, whereupon he became one of the key agents of intrigue at the papal court. As Pope Alexander he lived a lavish life style and worked to further his family's interests in Italy and Spain. Of his numerous illegitimate children, he made his son Cesare Borgia (1475–1507) ARCHBISHOP of Valencia and a cardinal before he was 20 years of age and then released him from his clerical status to lead the armies that secured the PAPAL STATES in central Italy. Nicoló Machiavelli (1469–1527) was a great admirer of Cesare. Through his daughter Lucretia's multiple marriages, Alexander was able to forge alliances with the powerful Sforzas of Milan and the d'Estes of Ferrara and Modena. The Dominican reformer of Florence Girolamo SAVONAROLA preached against papal degeneracy and so riled Alexander that the he had him excommunicated and burned at the stake in 1498.

On the international plane Alexander's goal was to preserve the Papal States from the ambitions of France, the kingdom of Naples, and the feuding Italian principalities, which Machiavelli described with unvarnished truth. His most notable international act was to divide the non-European world between Spain and Portugal in 1493. He also sponsored a crusade against the Moors in 1499. As a RENAISSANCE prince, Alexander was a great patron of the arts. He oversaw the renovation of the papal apartments, Castel Sant'Angelo, and commissioned MICHELANGELO's *Pietà* for the Vatican. His great grandson St. Francis Borgia (1510–72) became general of the Jesuits in 1565.

Further reading: Johann Burchard, *At the Court of the Borgias* (London: Folio Society, 1963); Michael de la Bedoyere, *The Meddlesome Friar and the Wayward Pope: The Story of the Conflict between Savonarola and Alexander VI* (Garden City, N.Y.: Hanover House, 1958); Michael Mallett, *The Borgias* (London: Granada, 1981).

Alexandrine School

The early CHRISTIAN philosophers of Alexandria, who shared a certain theological bent, are often referred to as the Alexandrine School. Alexandria, located on the Mediterranean coast at the tip of the Nile delta, was the second most important city in the Roman Empire with the largest population of Jews outside of Palestine. In the first century it became a center of Jewish and Christian thought. PHILO OF ALEXANDRIA (c. 20 B.C.E.–50 C.E.) established the allegorical method of interpreting scripture that allowed him to reconcile it with Neoplatonic philosophy. St. CLEMENT OF ALEXANDRIA and especially ORIGEN espoused this allegorical method as a way to uncover the spiritual meaning of the text of the BIBLE, in contrast with the ANTIOCHENE SCHOOL, whose bias was toward the literal, historical sense of Scripture.

While Antioch stressed the human nature of Christ, Alexandria placed emphasis on his divine nature as well as the unity of his person. At the Council of EPHESUS (431) St. CYRIL OF ALEXANDRIA became the chief opponent of Nestorius, who denied that the human and divine natures of Christ were united into one person. But Cyril often confused the term *physis* (nature) with *hypostasis* (person), a confusion that opened the door to MONOPHYSITISM after the Council of CHALCEDON (451).

See also ALLEGORY; COPTIC CHURCH; EPHESUS, COUNCIL OF.

Further reading: Charles Biggs, *The Christian Platonists of Alexandria* (Oxford: Clarendon, 1884); Johannes Quasten, *Patrology* 2:1–118 (Utrecht: Spectrum, 1950–60).

allegory (Gr.: *allos,* "other" + *agoreuō,* "to speak openly")

Allegory has often been called an extended or narrative metaphor whereby symbols used on one level imply deeper, hidden, or spiritual meanings.

The BIBLE has a number of famous allegorical stories. Most notable are Jotham's political allegory of the trees, a comment on kingship in Israel (Judg. 9:7–15); Nathan's ethical allegory of the rich man and poor man in reproach of David (2 Sam. 12:1–6); and Isaiah's allegory of the vineyard, a prophetic indictment of Israel and Judah for their sins (Isa. 5:1–7). In the New Testament the PARABLES of Jesus are often seen as allegories. Paul in his epistle to the Galatians (4:24) explicitly used the word *allegory* in his theological comparison of Hagar (slavery, present Jerusalem) and Sarah (freedom, Jerusalem above).

In Greek literature the most celebrated allegory is Plato's myth of the cave (*Republic,* book 7, 514a–541b), where the philosopher ascends from images and objects to the realm of ideas in general and justice in particular. During the Hellenistic era the allegorical method was employed to save Homer from charges of impiety and ignorance. Gradually this method became adopted and adapted by Jews of the Diaspora in their attempt to reconcile the Bible with philosophy, especially Neoplatonic philosophy. The most noted exponents of this school were Aristobulus (second century B.C.E.) and PHILO OF ALEXANDRIA (c. 20 B.C.E.–50 C.E.).

This allegorical mode of biblical interpretation had significant impact on the ALEXANDRINE SCHOOL and was used by CLEMENT OF ROME, TERTULLIAN OF CARTHAGE, ORIGEN OF ALEXANDRIA, and Sts. AMBROSE OF MILAN and AUGUSTINE OF HIPPO. For the Alexandrines allegory was the vehicle of secret Christian gnosis, or knowledge, uncovering the hidden references to Christ in the vast texts of the Hebrew Bible. Its reach stretched from controlled typology (e.g., crossing the Red Sea // baptism), to wild psychology (Eve = senses; Adam = mind), and even speculative cosmology.

The penchant for allegory ran loose in the MIDDLE AGES, its chief exponent being BERNARD OF CLAIRVAUX, who vehemently opposed more rational and literal interpretation. Protestants often complained that Catholics used too much allegory in Bible interpretation; Martin Luther (1483–1546) sought to replace fanciful allegory with plain interpretation in which confusing passages were interpreted in light of other passages where the meaning is clear. Today, both Catholics and Protestants reject the allegorical and "metaphysical" interpretations that dominate the approach to the Bible in many contemporary spiritualist and New Thought churches.

VATICAN COUNCIL II studiously avoided overly allegorical interpretation in its Dogmatic Constitution on Divine Revelation. Instead it embraced a salvation history viewpoint with an emphasis on the literal and spiritual meaning of Scripture.

See also ANALOGY, TYPOLOGY.

Further reading: Raymond E. Brown, ed., *New Jerome Biblical Commentary* (Englewood Cliffs, N.J.: Prentice Hall, 1990); Walter Burghardt, "On Early Christian Exegesis," *Theological Studies* (1950) 11: 78–116; R.P.C Hanson, *Allegory and Event* (London: Westminster, 2002); Henri de Lubac, *Catholicism* (New York: Mentor-Omega, 1964); Samuel Sandmel, *Philo of Alexandria* (Oxford: Oxford University Press, 1979).

All Saints, feast of

A feast of the first rank (*see* FEAST DAYS). All Saints commemorates all the known and unknown deceased saints of the church. It is celebrated on November 1 in the West and on the first Sunday after Pentecost in the East. It is also a holy day of obligation. In England All Saints was formerly known as All Hallows or Hallowmas. The feast is still celebrated by non-Catholics in the Church of England (Anglican), some Lutherans, and the Church of Sweden.

In New Testament times believers in general were addressed as "saints" or holy persons who remained faithful to CHRIST throughout their lives (1 Cor. 1:1). Gradually, however, the term acquired a more restricted usage, referring to MARTYRS, those who witnessed to Christ by both their lives and their deaths. To Christians of the second century the martyrs were the spiritual equivalent of the Greek heroes and athletes. The middle second century *Martyrdom of Polycarp* tells how Christians regularly assembled to celebrate "the birthday of his martyrdom" at his tomb, most likely with a EUCHARIST.

The feast became firmly established on May 13, 609/10 when Boniface IV dedicated the Roman Pantheon, whose ecclesiastical name became St. Mary of the Martyrs. Gregory III (731–41) moved the feast to November 1, and Gregory IV (827–44) dedicated a chapel to All Saints in the Constantinian basilica of St. Peter's in Rome, no doubt a repository for relics of the saints. The feast teaches the connection between the living (the church militant) and those who have gone before (the church triumphant) and points to the ultimate destiny of the believing faithful in the communion of all the saints who enjoy the BEATIFIC VISION of GOD with God's heavenly hosts.

Further reading: John Chrysostom, *Laudatio sanctorum omnium* (Praise of All the Saints), *Patrologia Graeca* (1857–66), ed. J. P. Migne, 1:705–12; B. Luykx, "Allerheilgen," *Liturgisch Woordenboek* (1958–68) 1:99–102; Pius Parsch, *The Church's Year of Grace* (Collegeville, Minn.: Liturgical Press, 1953–1959).

All Souls, feast of

This feast commemorates all of the faithful departed so that they may "rest in peace." It is celebrated on November 2. As with ALL SAINTS, the feast of All Souls is meant to point to the ultimate destiny of the faithful in sharing life eternal with God, Christ and all the saints.

In contrast with All Saints, however, All Souls is a late feast day added to the liturgical calendar in the early Middle Ages. Odilo of Cluny (961–1049) helped spread the feast by ordering it observed in all Benedictine monasteries. It is associated with the theological ideas of dying in peace with Christ but still needing purification, and of PURGATORY as a place intermediate between heaven and hell where the soul grows to see God (Eastern Christianity) or suffers and is purified for lesser sins (Western Christianity).

Christians who want to honor their dead observe All Souls very intensely, often by paying to have a mass said in their memory. To meet the increasing demand, Benedict XV allowed three masses to be said by each priest on All Souls' Day, the same as on Christmas. The mass of the dead, formerly called a requiem mass, contains the famous hymn "Dies Irae" ("Day of Wrath") by Jacapone di Todi. The hymn is now optional.

The idea of purgatory has been deemphasized ever since the PROTESTANT REFORMATION, which was in part triggered by scandals associated with it. The feast is, however, widely commemorated in Latin America, especially Mexico where it is associated with the pre-Christian Aztec Days of the Dead (Días de Muertos) and other indigenous feasts.

Further reading: John Greenleigh and Rosalind Rosoff Beimler, *The Days of the Dead: Mexico's Festival of Communion with the Dead* (San Francisco: Collins, 1991); Pius Parsch, *The Church's Year of Grace* (Collegeville, Minn.: Liturgical Press, 1953–1959).

Alphonsus Liguori, St. (1696–1787) *moral theologian and founder of the Redemptorists*

Alphonsus Liguori was the founder of the Redemptorists and perhaps the most influential moral theologian in Catholic history. He was declared a Doctor of the Church in 1871.

Alphonsus was the son of a Neapolitan nobleman. He took a degree in law at the age of 16 and practiced for several years. Upon losing a suit against the grand duke of Tuscany involving a large sum, he became disenchanted, withdrew, and started living an abstemious religious life. With the help of Tommaso Falcoia (1663–1743) he founded the Congregation of the Holy Redeemer both for men and women; it was approved by Benedict XIV in 1749–50. Members of the order pursued pastoral ministry and missionary work, especially among the poor. Liguori was named bishop of St. Agatha of the Goths in 1762; in the famine of 1763 he emptied the bishop's pantry to feed the hungry. He retired to Nocera in 1775.

In contrast to the flamboyant preaching style of the time, Liguori sought to speak directly to the heart. He opposed equally the rigorist, puritanlike moral teaching of the Jansenists (*see* JANSENISM) and the casuistry of some Jesuits; in a famous dialogue with the Jesuit casuist Hermann Busembaum (1600–68), he laid out his own morality of the heart. He published his noted *Theologia Moralis* in two volumes in 1753 and 1755. His theory is called equiprobabilism, which sought a middle path between excessive moral rigorism and the laxity often falsely attributed to Jesuits. Alphonsus was a prolific spiritual writer, publishing many works of devotion that are still in use today, notably *Visits to the Blessed Sacrament and the Blessed Virgin* (1745), *Novena of the Heart of Jesus* (1758), *The Means of Prayer* (1759), and *The Way of Salvation* (1767). He stressed that God wants repentance not out of wrath but out of mercy.

See also THEOLOGY.

Further reading: *Selected Writings*, ed. Frederick M. Johns (New York: Paulist, 1999); Alphonsus Maria de Liguori, *The Way of Salvation and Perfection*, ed. Eugene Grimm (St. Louis: Redemptorist Fathers, 1926); Frederick M. Jones, *St. Alphonse de Liguori* (Westminster: Christian Classics, 1992); Théodule Rey-Mermet, *Moral Choices: The Moral Theology of Alphonsus Liguori* (Ligouri, Mo.: Ligouri, 1998).

altar (Lat.: *altare,* "altar" [or *altus,* "high"])
This Latin term refers to an elevated flat table, generally made of stones, upon which the sacrifice of animals (slaughter) and grains (burning) were made to the gods. Christians use the term to refer to the sacred table upon which is celebrated the sacramental EUCHARIST. The Wycliffe and King James English translations used this Latin word to translate the Hebrew term *mizbe'ah.* The Greek Septuagint (LXX) translation of the Hebrew Bible used two terms for this Hebrew term: *bômos* (Lat. *ara*) for pagan altars and *thusiasteron* (Lat. *altare*) for the altar of Israel's GOD.

In the Old Testament, Abraham is the first Israelite to erect an altar (Gen. 22:9). Moses was commanded by God to build two altars of acacia wood for burnt offerings (Ex. 27:1) and for incense (30:1). When the Israelites entered Canaan they were ordered to destroy all the altars dedicated to the Canaanite gods Baal and Asherah (Judg. 6:25). Early Israel had many shrines and altars for the worship of God. Worship became centralized under Solomon, who built an elaborate temple, ambiguously like the Canaanite temples of surrounding cultures, with a bronze altar for animal offerings (1 Kings 8:62). Psalm 26:6 refers to the Temple altar as the place of God's mercy.

The New Testament does not pay much attention to the altar of the Temple other than to say that sacrifice does not count until one is reconciled with one's brother (Matt. 5:23) and that Jesus performed a symbolic action against the commercialization taking place in the Temple (Matt. 21:12–17). In Christian times St. Ambrose of Milan fought for the removal of the Altar of Victory from the Roman Senate. Paul speaks of partaking of the "table of the Lord" (1 Cor. 10:21), so early Christians used the term *table* interchangeably with *altar.* Echoing the prophet Ezekiel,

Revelation speaks symbolically of the heavenly Temple and altar of incense from which ascend the prayers of the faithful and especially the offerings of the souls of martyrs (6:9–11; 8:3). The latter reference likely refers to the early Christian celebration of the Eucharist at the tombs of martyrs (*Martyrdom of Polycarp* 18), many of which later became sites for martyrion BASILICAS.

Early Christian altars were made of either wood or stone, on Old Testament models. Celebrating the Eucharist over tombs evolved into the practice of placing relics of saints under the table or altar and then incorporating relics into small altar stones or altar coverings, a practice that continues to this day (*Code of Canon Law* 1237.2). The belief is that the Eucharist establishes a communion with the saints who have gone before in the hope of the death and resurrection with Christ, "the first born from the dead" (Col. 1:18).

A circular row of seats with the throne of the bishop (Gk. *synthronon*) was placed around the altar in early churches. Eastern churches place a canopy over the altar and later sealed off the altar from public view by an iconostasis (*see* ICON). In the era of Constantine altars were incorporated into the form of the Roman BASILICA, many of which, like the original St. Peter's, were built over the tombs of apostles and martyrs. In the Middle Ages the altar was placed in the transept of cathedrals, and the celebrant still faced the people. Many reformers, rejecting the sacrificial interpretation of the Mass, tore down the altars and replaced them with wooden tables to commemorate the Lord's Supper. This caused an abreaction among Counter-Reformation Catholics, who started elevating the altar even higher, separating it from the common laity with an altar rail and ornamenting it with elaborate baroque baldachins. Bernini's altar in St. Peter's is an illustration of this magnificence. In Spain and Latin America many church altars are backed by *reredos,* high, elaborately carved pieces with niches for statues of many saints and decorations of flora and fauna. During the baroque period side chapels were added, sometimes the complete length of the nave, to accommodate private masses, especially for the nobility and the wealthy.

Since VATICAN COUNCIL II altars have been brought closer to the congregation and simplified in their ornaments. The celebrant now faces the congregation. The U.S. Catholic Bishops Conference issued a directive, *Environment and Art in Catholic Worship 72,* which instructs that the altar should be an "attractive, impressive, dignified, noble table . . . in pure and simple proportions." Because the altar is so important to Catholic worship, almost all parishes throughout the world traditionally had altar societies, often composed of women, who tended the altar and church, provided flowers for Eucharists, and sewed altar coverings. After Vatican II worship committees have replaced these altar societies. Many pious Catholics have installed altars, adorned with crucifixes, pictures, statues and candles, in their homes, not so much for the celebration of the Eucharist but for individual and family devotions.

Further reading: *Environment and Art in Catholic Worship* (Washington, D.C.: National Council of Catholic Bishops, 1978); Klaus Gambler, *The Reform of the Roman Liturgy* (San Juan Capistrano, Calif.: Una Voce, 1993); J. P. Kirsch and T. Klauser, "Altar," *Reallexikon für Antike und Christentum* (1950–) 1:334–354; Cyril E. Pocknee, *The Christian Altar in History and Today* (London: Mowbray, 1963).

Ambrose of Milan, St. (c. 339–97) *bishop of Milan and theologian*

An influential early bishop of Milan and the author of a treatise on the SACRAMENTS, many sermons, and hymns, Ambrose is considered one of the Doctors of the Church in the West along with Sts. JEROME, AUGUSTINE OF HIPPO, AND GREGORY THE GREAT. Unlike Augustine, he knew Greek, and he helped introduce Greek theology to the West. His feast day is December 7.

Ambrose was born the son of a praetorian prefect of Gaul at Trier, Germany. He studied law in Rome, practiced at Sirmium, and around 370 was appointed *consularis* (governor) of Aemilia-Liguria with his seat in Milan. Upon the death of the Arian bishop Auxentius a feud broke out between Catholics and the followers of ARIUS. Ambrose intervened to settle the dispute, and although the unbaptized son of Christians, he was elected bishop by acclaim. Tutored by St. Simplicianus (d. 400), who was to succeed him as bishop and who also instructed Augustine in the faith, Ambrose was baptized, ordained, and undertook a deep study of theology.

Ambrose accepted ORIGEN's threefold interpretation of Scripture (literal, moral, allegorical). His fondness for elaborating typologies between the Hebrew Bible and the New Testament heavily influenced medieval typology, especially the types depicted in the windows and sculptures of Gothic CATHEDRALS. He authored *De Sacramentis* ("On the Sacraments"), a celebrated treatise on BAPTISM, CONFIRMATION, and the EUCHARIST, which contains the earliest witness to the Roman CANON OF THE MASS. He saw the Eucharist as a *figura* ("figure") of the body and blood of Christ. He also wrote a treatise on the ethical conduct of the clergy, modeled on Cicero's *On Duties,* and fostered the ascetic life in the West. Ambrose once melted sacred vessels to make coins for the redemption of captives. With St. Hilary of Poitiers (c. 315–c. 367), Ambrose was among the first to compose dignified, metered, and rhymed hymns for the liturgy, some of which are still in use today, such as "Te lucis ante terminum" ("Now that the daylight dies away") sung at Compline, the evening prayers in the PRAYER OF THE HOURS, on Sundays. In the *Confessions* Augustine witnesses to weeping on hearing Ambrose's hymns.

Ambrose strongly defended the church from the challenges put to it by the emperors, many of whom, like CONSTANTINE, had strong Arian tendencies. He fought against Emperor Valentinian II (375–392) over the reintroduction of the Altar of Victory into the Roman senate and excommunicated Theodosius I (378–95) for the slaughter of civilians at Thessalonica in 390. More sadly he opposed Theodosius's attempt to rebuild the synagogue at Callinicum, burned down by Christians. Ambrose set the pattern for relations between CHURCH AND STATE later taken up by GREGORY VII HILDEBRAND and ST. THOMAS À BECKET. The church historian Theodoret of Cyrrhus (393–457) depicts Ambrose's humiliation of Theodosius, a scene that was later replayed between Hildebrand and Henry IV (*Ecclesiastical History* 5.17–18). Tradition ascribes to Ambrose the founding of the Ambrosian rite and Ambrosian chant, but all the manuscripts attesting to these traditions date from the 12th century.

See also CHANT; RITES.

Further reading: Many of Ambrose's writings are available online. Ambrose of Milan *De Sacramentis,* tr. by T. Thompson, ed. J. H. Stawley (London: S.P.C.K., 1950); John Moorhead, *Ambrose: Church and Society in the Late Roman World* (London: Longman, 1999); Angelo Paredi, *St. Ambrose: His Life and Times* (Notre Dame: University of Notre Dame, 1964).

Americanism

Americanism was a catch-all term used to describe a variety of attempts by 19th-century American church leaders, notably John IRELAND, James GIBBONS, and John J. Keane (1839–1918), to adapt Catholicism to American values. It often included support for separation of church and state, state schools, and labor unions. The tendency generated great controversy among American Catholics, and some considered it a heresy; LEO XIII condemned it in the apostolic letter *Testem Benevolentiae* (January 22, 1899), which had a stifling effect on the American church until VATICAN COUNCIL II.

In its first phase, the Americanist controversy remained relatively polite. Orestes Brownson (1803–76) and ISAAC THOMAS HECKER (1819–88) began advocating for an accommodation of Catholicism to the character of America, particularly the separation of church and state enshrined in the First Amendment, and many church leaders later supported their position. Archbishop John Ireland affirmed the civil state's right to educate the young and offered to lease his parochial schools to the local public school board. He also favored the prohibition of the use of European languages as the medium of education in ethnic immigrant schools. In this he was opposed by the German Catholic Association and Archbishop Michael A. Corrigan (1839–1900) of New York. The conflict was between the residual European nationalism of immigrant groups and the desire to present Catholics as true, patriotic Americans in the face of Protestant nativism. Within the church, ethnic nationalism threatened a balkanization of bishoprics throughout America according to language and culture. On another front Cardinal James Gibbons of Baltimore, an ally of Ireland, supported the Knights of Labor in their quest for better wages and labor conditions.

Along with John J. Keane, first rector of Catholic University of America, and Monsignor Denis J. O'Connell (1849–1927), rector of the American College in Rome, Ireland and Gibbons became apologists for the American separation of church and state as beneficial to the spread of Catholicism itself. They also saw the chance to cooperate with Protestant denominations. Keane, Ireland, and Gibbons went so far as to participate in the World Parliament of Religions, a sequel to the Chicago's World's Fair, in 1893 and one of the first interreligious gatherings of all the religions of the world. They even joined in prayers with those of other faiths. Ireland especially envisioned a leadership role for America in the renewal of the world and of the Catholic Church itself.

In an encyclical, *Longinqua Oceani* (January 6, 1895), Leo XIII recognized that Catholicism in the United States flourished in no small part because it was "unopposed by the Constitution and government . . . fettered by no hostile legislation, protected against violence by common laws and the impartiality of tribunals." Nevertheless, he firmly maintained that the American example was not a "type of the most desirable status of the Church, or that it would be universally lawful or expedient for State and Church to be, as in America, disseevered and divorced." Ireland and Gibbons escaped censure, but the pope demanded the resignations of Keane and O'Connell (as usual, the lower officials suffered the consequences) and appointed Francesco Satolli (1839–1910) as the first apostolic delegate to keep an eye on the American hierarchy.

There were two countervailing currents here. On one hand, American Catholicism was benefiting enormously from the separation of church and state. On the other, the papacy had suffered the loss of the PAPAL STATES in 1870, as a consequence of the unification of Italy, and the pope was fighting for his independence as a sovereign head of state who was at the same time an ecclesiastic. Also in the background was Pius IX's 1854 condemnation of the proposition "The Church ought to be separated from the State, and the State from the Church" in the *Syllabus of Errors* 55.

The second phase of the controversy was nastier, characterized by the charge of heresy. The issue was triggered in 1897 by a translation into French of a biography by Walter Eliot of Isaac T. Hecker, founder of the PAULISTS. Felix Klein (1862–1953) of the Institut Catholique in Paris wrote a long preface. The French version created a storm in Europe. Hecker promoted a vigorous, active spirituality based on the teaching of the indwelling of the Spirit in bishop, priest, and layperson alike. The Holy Spirit, he believed, was adapting itself to the age, and the age was that of America. Upholding the separation of church and state, he opposed the passive "mechanical piety" of devotionalism, so characteristic of many immigrants from Latin cultures. Denis O'Connell, John Keane, and John L. Spalding (1840–1916), bishop of Peoria, Illinois, espoused similar views. O'Connell in particular gave an address in 1897 on "political" versus

"ecclesiastical" Americanism at the International Catholic Congress, Fribourg, Switzerland, which stirred debate.

Archbishop Corrigan, bishop Bernard J. McQuaid of Rochester, some Jesuits, and a host of traditional Catholics opposed these progressive ideas. The dispute was temporarily muted at the Third Plenary Council of Baltimore in 1884. Conservatives found allies in Europe, especially in the voice of Fr. Charles Maigren, who attacked "Americanism" in a series of articles in the French Catholic journal *La Verité*. This brought the Vatican into the dispute, which terminated in the apostolic letter of Leo XIII *Testem Benevolentiae* (January 22, 1899), addressed to Gibbons in Baltimore. The papal letter speaks more to the preface by Klein than to the content of Hecker's program. The pope questioned American adaptionism, contrasting it with the "eternal" deposit of faith. While praising Hecker's emphasis on the indwelling, the letter challenged Hecker's distinction between active and passive piety and defended—out of context—traditional Catholic forms of religious life.

In France Felix Klein called Americanism a "phantom heresy." The American bishops promulgated the letter and, for the most part, ignored its prescriptions. The letter put the principle of separation of church and state under suspicion until VATICAN COUNCIL II. It also stifled the intellectual ferment then flourishing in American seminaries and laid the foundation for the implementation of neo-scholasticism as the officially sanctioned philosophy of Catholicism. As for ecumenism, Pope JOHN PAUL II's sponsorship of a Day of Prayer for World Peace together with leaders of other world religions at Assisi, January 22, 2002, signaled a vindication of Gibbons's cooperation with Protestants and others.

See also CHURCH AND STATE; NORTH AMERICA.

Further reading: Jay P. Dolan, *The American Catholic Experience* (Notre Dame: University of Notre Dame, 1992); Gerald P. Fogerty, *The Vatican and the American*

Hierarchy 1870 to 1965 (Collegeville, Minn.: Liturgical Press, 1985); Leo XIII, *The Great Encyclical Letters of Leo XIII* (New York: Benziger Bros., 1908).

Americas, Catholicism in *See* LATIN AMERICA; NORTH AMERICA.

Anabaptists *See* PROTESTANT REFORMATION.

anagogical sense *See* BIBLE.

analogy (Gk.: *ana,* "according to" + *logos,* "ratio" = proportion)

Analogy may be said to be proportional speech: A is to B as C is to D, or GOD is to his creation as the potter is to her or his pot. As in the latter example, analogy is based on the resemblance or similarity, but not absolute identity, between two objects of speech. Analogy falls between equivocation, or using the same term with two different semantic references (*bat* is used equivocally when referring both to the animal and a sport instrument for striking balls), and univocity, using a term with identical meaning (*dog* is used univocally when referring to Fido and Rover).

The Jewish philosopher/theologian Maimonides (1135–1204), arguing in favor of negative theology (we cannot say what God is, only what God is not), favored equivocation of "being" the term when used of God and creatures. Because human beings are limited to human terms when speaking of God, they must speak analogically. The Fourth Lateran Council (1274) stated on the relation between the Creator and the creature: "No similarity so great can be discovered that the dissimilarity is not even greater." While it makes perfect logical sense to say that Solomon is wise in a way that God is wise, the wisdom of God is greater by an infinite or eminent degree.

On this basis St. THOMAS AQUINAS argued for a theory of signification based on the analogy of being, truly and fully possessed by God and only secondarily possessed by creatures by way of privation or negation (*Summa Theologiae* 1a.13.5). Thomas's teaching was furthered by the Dominican philosopher and theologian Thomas de Vio Cajetan (1469–1534) and continued in our time by the Jesuit philosopher Erich Pryzywara (1899–1972). The Franciscans DUNS SCOTUS and WILLIAM OF OCKHAM argued that ultimately analogy leads to equivocation and that God and creatures must in some sense share a univocity of being and qualities. Protestant theologian Karl Barth (1886–1968), maintaining God's total otherness to creatures, argued against the analogy of being in favor of an analogy of faith.

Further reading: G. P. Klubertanz, *St. Thomas on Analogy* (Chicago: Jesuit Studies, 1960); Battista Mondin, *The Principle of Analogy in Protestant and Catholic Theology* (The Hague: Martinus Nijhoff, 1968).

Andrew, St.

In the New Testament he is an APOSTLE of Jesus and the brother of ST. PETER (Matthew 1:16–20). His feast day is November 30.

Andrew appears in a number of New Testament passages (John 1:35–42; Matt. 4:18–20, etc.). Eusebius says that he later went to Scythia in southern Russia (*Ecclesiastical History* 3.1.1). A later legend, associated with the apocryphal *Acts of St. Andrew* by the ascetical Encratite sect, tells how he was crucified on an X-shaped cross in Patras, Greece. According to another legend, his bones were translated to the town of St. Andrew's in Scotland by St. Regulus of Patras, known also as Riaghail of Scotland. Andrew is patron of Scotland, Greece, and Russia as well as of fishermen because he pointed out the boy with the loaves and fishes to Jesus (John 6:8). St. Andrew's cross, in the shape of a large X, is on the flag of Scotland and thus part of the Union Jack, the flag of the United Kingdom.

Further reading: F. Dvornik, *The Idea of Apostolicity in the Legend of Andrew the Apostle* (Cambridge Mass.: Harvard University Press, 1958); P. M. Peterson, *Andrew, Brother of Simon Peter* (Leiden: Brill, 1958).

angel (Gr.: *angelos,* "messenger," "herald")

Angels are spiritual beings who serve as members of GOD's heavenly council and sing his praises; they are classed in several orders, or choirs. Angels also bear God's commands to human beings, and they may also serve as guardians of nations and individuals. Fallen angels are identified with DEVILS.

All religious traditions of the world express a belief in angels or similar beings, and Christianity is no exception. The root of the idea goes back to the ancient Near East, with its conception of high gods surrounded by heavenly courts of celestial ministers who carry out the gods' commands; from there the idea passed into biblical literature. The Hebrew Bible sometimes refers to angels as the "sons of God" (Gen. 6:1–4, Job 38:7), "holy ones," or hosts of heaven. They are said to be an innumerable multitude (Gen. 32:1). Cherubim were depicted above the Ark of the Covenant (Exod. 25:18–20). The prophets, who bear the messages of the heavenly tribunal to earth, often give descriptions of the proceedings of the heavenly court and its angels (1 Kings 22–19–23; Isa. 6:1–13). Cherub angels keep Adam and Eve from reentering the garden (Gen. 3:24); angels guide the Israelites through the desert (Exod. 23:20–23); and Satan functions as a kind of prosecuting attorney before the heavenly council in the testing of Job (Job 1:6–12).

In the post-exilic period angelology became very developed in various traditions, including the writings of Philo Judaeus, the apocalyptic works of Qumran, and the books of Enoch. Angels serve as controlling spirits of natural phenomena, the ends of the earth, celestial bodies, wind currents, the four seasons, nations, peace, healing, death, and more. Angels became a key part of popular Judaism, with the exception of the Sadducees, who denied their existence (Acts 23:6), and they appear frequently in the New Testament as well. They serve as intermediaries between God and humans, and they promulgate the Torah (Gal. 3:19; Acts 7:53). Their numbers increased, especially in the Book of Revelation, where vast throngs worship God, and Michael leads the heavenly hosts in a cosmic battle against the dragon of the abyss (Rev. 12:07).

Some angels became known by name. Michael was archangel commander of the heavenly hosts (Dan. 10:13). Gabriel was the revealer of the Day of Judgment (Dan. 8:16) and angel of the Annunciation to Mary (Luke 1:27–38); he also appeared to Muhammad in Islamic tradition. Raphael was the angel of healing (Tob. 3:17).

Under the influence of Zoroastrian religion with its struggle between the forces of good (Ahura Mazda) and evil (Angra Mainyu, later Ahriman), a strain arose in Jewish tradition, especially in QUMRAN literature, which divided the angels into those who helped believers in their path to the Last Judgment and those who impeded them. Among the evil angels—variously called "satans," "angels of destruction," "angels of punishment"—are Satan, now as an evil spirit, Belial, Asmodeus, and Beelzebub. In apocalyptic literature there was an elaborate expansion of the passage in Genesis 6:1–2 about the "sons of god" cavorting with the "daughters of men." This gave rise to the idea of the fallen angels as recounted in the pseudepigraphic treatise Enoch 1.6–16 and rendered into riveting poetry by John Milton in *Paradise Lost.*

Jesus confirmed the importance of angels. In the gospels angels appear at every important juncture in his life: his birth (Luke 1), after his temptation (Matt. 4:11), during his agony in the garden (Luke 22:43), and at his resurrection (Matt. 28:2–7 John 20:12). Angels will be present in the heavenly court at the Last Judgment (Matt. 25:31–46). Some early Jewish-Christian theologians presented Jesus as a kind of angel.

Colossians 1:16 and Ephesians 1:21 give two lists of ranks, or orders, of angels. These lists gave rise to the nine choirs of angels meticulously arranged by DIONYSIUS the Pseudo-Areopagite in his *Celestial Hierarchy:* 1) seraphim, 2) cherubim, 3) thrones 4) dominations, 5) virtues, 6) powers, 7) principalities, 8) archangels, and 9) angels. Early church theologians debated whether angels had ethereal bodies (ORIGEN OF ALEXANDRIA, AUGUSTINE OF HIPPO) or were pure spirits.

In the Middle Ages PETER LOMBARD, ALBERTUS MAGNUS, THOMAS AQUINAS, BONAVENTURE, and DUNS SCOTUS conducted learned debates about whether angels had immediate intuitive knowledge (Aquinas) or could reason (Scotus). Angels were also associated with the geocentric motion of the heavens in medieval cosmology. Cherubim and seraphim were responsible for the *primum mobile* (the first moved), to which were attached the fixed stars, thrones for Saturn, dominations for Jupiter, principalities for Mars, powers for the Sun, virtues for Venus, archangels for Mercury, and angels for the Moon. Angels were also equated to Aristotle's "intelligences" as transmitted in Arabic philosophy.

Associated with the general notion of angel is the idea of particular, personal guardian angels. It seems that in the ancient Near East the messengers of the gods also functioned as guardian spirits of particular cities and nations. Plato says that each person is assigned a guardian angel to protect both body and soul at birth (*Phaedo* 108b). Jesus says angels protect children (Matt. 18:10), and angelic guardians for adults are implicit in Acts 18:10. The Book of *1 Enoch* (100:5) says that angels are assigned to the just. AMBROSE OF MILAN said that angels are withdrawn from the just to test them, but most church fathers take the opposite opinion. The current notion was given definitive shape by Honorius of Autun (d. c. 1151) in the early 12th century, who said that each soul was entrusted to an angel the moment it entered a body. Although the doctrine of guardian angels is not an official doctrine of the Catholic Church, Pope PAUL V extended the Feast of the Holy Guardian Angels to the whole church in 1608, and Clement X fixed it for October 2.

Angels are also a major theme in Christian art. Their winged nature survives from the cherubim of the ancient Near East, which were often depicted as winged sphinxlike creatures. In catacomb art angels were depicted in human form, often without wings in order to distinguish them from the pagan winged goddesses Victory, Glory, and Fortune. The last was patroness of the emperor. In Byzantine iconography angels assumed a fixed set of motifs. They are portrayed as young men with wings and haloes bearing heralds, staffs, palm branches, flags, censers (attending the throne of God as in Revelation), swords to ward off a return to paradise and fight the devil, lilies (purity), and trumpets (announcing the Last Judgment). In the Middle Ages and especially in the Renaissance angels assume androgynous features. Putti, or little baby cherubs, make their appearance, signifying innocence and incorporeality. Angels are often painted in Nativity scenes, ascending Jacob's ladder, as the three men who meet Abraham at the oak of Mamre, and as accompanying the cherublike souls of the deceased to heaven. In 19th and 20th centuries the image of the angel became very sentimentalized as the guardian of children.

Further reading: Hans Biedermann, *Dictionary of Symbolism* (London: Wordsworth, 1996); Gustav Davidson, *A Dictionary of Angels* (New York: Free Press, 1967); Jean Danielou, *The Angels and their Mission according to the Fathers of the Church,* tr. by David Heimann (Westminster: Christian Classics, 1993); J. Duhr, "Anges gardiens," *Dictionaire de Spiritualité* (1937) 1:586–598; James R. Lewis, Evelyn D. Oliver, and Kelle Sisung, *Angels A to Z* (Detroit: Gale Group, 1995); Morris B. Margolies, *A Gathering of Angels* (Northvale, N.J.: Jason Aronson, 2000).

Angelico, Bl. Fra (1387–1455) *Dominican friar and Renaissance painter*

Fra Angelico was one of the masters of Italian religious painting; departing from the late Gothic style of his early work, he eventually paved the way to the high Renaissance with his vivid use of color and realistic rendering of figures in space.

The artist was born Guido di Pietro, and he was also known as Giovanni di Fiesole. He entered the DOMINICAN ORDER when he was 20. Among his most noteworthy works are *Annunciation* (Cortona, c. 1434), the *Descent from the Cross* (San Marco, c. 1434), and the many frescoes in the cells of the friars at the Convento San Marco in Florence and in two chapels in the Vatican. The theology of "the garden of the soul," developed by his prior, St. Antonius of Florence, directly influenced the grace, sweetness, and delicacy of his many paintings of the Virgin. He was beatified by JOHN PAUL II in 1984.

Further reading: Giorgio Vasari, *Lives of the Painters* (Harmondsworth, U.K.: Penguin, 1965); Jacqueline and Maurice Guillard, *Fra Angelico: The Light of the Soul* (Paris: Guillard, 1986).

Angelus   *See* DEVOTIONS.

Anglican Ordination

After the Church of England broke away from the Roman Catholic communion during the reign of Henry VIII (1491–1547), a lively debate arose within the Roman church about the VALIDITY of the Anglican ordination of bishops, priests, and deacons. The question centers on the validity of the Ordinals (rules for ordinations) adopted under the Protestant monarch Edward VI in 1549. The successor, Catholic Queen Mary (r. 1553–58), appealed to Pope Julius III (r. 1550–55) to rule on the issue, but no firm policy was set, and the pope left Cardinal Reginald Pole (1500–58) much latitude to reordain or not. Objections against the validity of Anglican orders fall under three arguments: 1) the charge that the continuity of the rite of laying-on-the-hands was broken, an argument now generally admitted as not having a historical

basis; 2) a claim that the omission of the handing over of the instruments of the office (paten, bread, chalice) renders the rite invalid, a second argument now seen as spurious as no such rite existed in the early church; and 3) the argument that the general intention of the Anglican Church in saying the words of priestly ordination "Receive the Holy Spirit" did not include a specific mandate to offer the sacrifice of the Mass as defined by the Council of TRENT.

The last point is the heart of LEO XIII's seemingly definitive statement in the encyclical *Apostolicae Curae* (September 18, 1896) that Anglican orders are invalid. The key to the argument was that a defect of form and intention rendered invalid the ordination of Matthew Parker (1504–75) as archbishop of Canterbury in 1559; as a consequence, all subsequent ordinations of the Anglican Church were also invalid.

The Anglican archbishops of Canterbury and York replied in 1897 that present Anglicans trace their episcopal heritage to Archbishop William Laud, who was consecrated by bishops whose Irish and Italian apostolic succession is certain. In addition, they wrote, the Church of England explicitly teaches a doctrine of the Eucharistic sacrifice similar to that of the Roman church in the CANON OF THE MASS. Since Catholics believe that ordination is a sacrament that confers an indelible mark, it may not be conferred a second time. Today all Anglican bishops, priests, and deacons who convert to the Roman church are reordained conditionally, not absolutely, on the possibility that their original ordination was valid. The presumption is in favor of validity.

The joint Anglican-Roman Catholic International Commission (1969–) has come to several agreements on the EUCHARIST, ministry, ordination, and authority, but Anglican orders remain a bone in the throat. The situation is steadily shifting. In 1968 Pope PAUL VI simplified the rites of ordination, so that there is now not a great difference between the two churches. Many theologians no longer subscribe to the theory of intention that lay behind *Apostolicae Curae*. In 1982 JOHN PAUL II reopened the archive documents that lay behind Leo XIII's decision in order to further Anglican-Catholic dialogue, but then seemed to slam the door shut with the apostolic letter *Ad Tuendam Fidem* (May 18, 1998), which hints that Leo's original letter contains infallible teaching. The original makes no such claim for itself.

Further reading: Charles Wood Halifax, *Leo XIII and Anglican Orders* (London: Longmans, Green, 1912); R. William Franklin, ed., *Anglican Orders: Essays on the Centenary of Apostolicae Curae, 1896–1996* (London: Mowbray, 1996); J. J. Hughes, *Absolutely Null and Utterly Void: The Papal Condemnation of Anglican Orders, 1896* (London: Sheed & Ward, 1968); E. Yarnold, *Anglican Orders—a Way Forward?* (London: Catholic Truth Society, 1977).

annulment   *See* MARRIAGE.

Annunciation

The term *Annunciation* refers to both a feast day (March 25) and the event it celebrates—the proclamation to Mary of Nazareth, betrothed to Joseph of the house of David, that she would conceive a son, Jesus, called the Son of the Most High (Luke 1:26–35). In Daniel 8:16–17 Gabriel is the ANGEL, or messenger of God, who is to reveal the Day of Judgment. In the PSEUDEPIGRAPHA he attains greater importance; he is depicted along with Archangel Michael among God's glorious heavenly hosts. In Luke he brings tidings of reassurance and joy. His greeting "Hail, full of grace" has become a part of the second most popular Catholic prayer, the Hail Mary; the event itself is celebrated in the Angelus. The Annunciation in the gospel of Luke and the Book of Acts is part of an elaborate literary diptych in which the birth of John as the last of the old covenant is set against the birth of Jesus as the first of the new covenant.

The Archangel Gabriel announces to Mary the coming birth of the Messiah as the Holy Spirit hovers over her (Luke 1:26). Wood engraving by Albrecht Altdorfer (1480–1538) *(St. Louis Art Museum, with permission)*

In Luke the overshadowing of the Holy Spirit over Mary implies a virginal conception of Jesus by the "power of the Most High."

The feast of the Annunciation, also called Lady Day in English-speaking tradition, is celebrated March 25, nine months before Christmas. Early evidence for the feast in the East appears in a sermon by Abraham of Ephesus in c. 550 and in the West in the Gelasian Sacramentary (a list of feast days) in c. 750. The feast is now called in full the Annunciation of Our Lord to the Blessed Virgin Mary. The theme of the Annunciation has been a frequent subject in Christian art. A celebrated version is that by Fra angelico in the church of San Marco in Florence.

See also angel; incarnation; mary of nazareth; virgin birth.

Further reading: Raymond E. Brown, *The Birth of the Messiah: A Commentary on the Infancy Narratives in Matthew and Luke.* (Garden City, N.Y.: Doubleday, 1993); Carroll Stuhmueller, "The Gospel According to Luke," *The Jerome Bible Commentary,* ed. Raymond E. Brown (Englewood Cliffs, N.J.: Prentice Hall, 1968), 121–123; S. Vailhé, "Origines de la fête de l'Annonciation," *Échos d'Orient* (1906) 9:138–145; R. A. Fletcher, "Three Early Byzantine Hymns and Their Place in the Liturgy of Constantinople," *Byzantinische Zeitschrift* (1958) 51: 53–65.

anointing

Anointing is the ritual practice of pouring oil on the head or body of a person or of an object, transforming the recipient's status from secular to sacred. The anointing of persons and objects was a common practice in ancient Mesopotamia and egypt. Egyptians anointed officials, and Sumerians anointed wedding couples. The Hebrews had many words for anointing, which they performed on priests (Exod. 29:7), prophets (1 Kings 19:6), and kings (1 Sam. 10:1; 16:13). The Hebrew Bible also reports the anointing of the Tent of Meeting (Exod. 30:26).

The promise made by Nathan to David (2 Sam. 7:8–16) gave rise to hopes for an "anointed of the Lord" who would come and restore Israel to splendor. In Greek the word for *anointed* is *christos;* in Hebrew it is *mashiah* (which gives us the word *messiah*). The Qumranites referred to both a priestly and a royal messiah. In the New Testament Jesus is reluctant to accept the title of messiah, which might feed popular expectations for a mighty human king; he relates instead to the theme of the Suffering Servant in Second Isaiah (Mark 8:29–33; Isa. 53:10–12). Early Christian confessions directly proclaim Jesus the Anointed One (Rom. 1:1–4; Acts 2:36).

The New Testament also speaks of Jesus sending out disciples to heal the sick with anointing (Mark 9:6) and of elders anointing the sick and praying over them (James 5:14). From the earliest times anointing accompanied the Christian sacraments of baptism, confirmation, Ordination and the anointing of the sick. In later times anointing was used for the consecration of kings and churches, especially their altars and bells.

Many contemporary Pentecostals, including Catholic Charismatics, speak of being "anointed with the Holy Spirit." They are referring not to the anointing accompanying the sacrament of confirmation, but to a special spiritual infusion of power and grace that sets some leaders apart as the "Lord's anointed."

See also charismatic renewal; christ/christology; sacrament.

Further reading: Gerard Austin, *Anointing with the Spirit* (New York: Pueblo, 1985); Martin Dudley and Geoffrey Rowell, *The Oil of Gladness: Anointing in the Christian Tradition* (Collegeville, Minn.: Liturgical Press, 1993); Michael G. Lawler, *Symbol and Sacrament* (Omaha: Creighton University Press, 1995).

Anointing of the Sick

Beginning in the middle ages, the sacrament of the Anointing of the Sick was called Extreme Unction, meaning "last anointing." It was generally limited to the terminally ill and dying. At vatican council II, council participants sought to restore early Christian practice in regard to anointing in *Sacrosanctum Concilium* 73, the Constitution on the Sacred Liturgy. The new rite was promulgated by Pope paul VI in the apostolic constitution "The Sacrament of the Anointing of the Sick" (November 30, 1972).

The theology behind the sacrament affirms that Christ took on human pain and suffering (Phil. 2:6–11; Col. 1:22) not only to bring to believers the hope of resurrection but also the hope for healing in this life. The early church placed strong emphasis on Christ as physician who heals the lame and the sick (Mark 2:5–12; IGNATIUS OF ANTIOCH, *Ephesians* 7:2). Pope Paul VI also affirmed that the sick themselves also have a ministry to offer the church in their immediate identification with Christ's passion and death. The Council of TRENT (Session 13, Doctrine on Extreme Unction 1) based the institution of the sacrament on Christ's many healings and the reference to anointing for affliction in James 5:13–15.

The new rite encourages the presence and participation of family and friends in the rite. The rite is administered by a priest or deacon and, besides the anointing of the recipient on the extremities of the body, is generally accompanied by prayer and the reception of the EUCHARIST. The rite can also be administered during the Eucharist for those who suffer from emotional, spiritual, and physical afflictions. As a consequence, many more people than formerly receive the sacrament. The rite is now considered a central part of pastoral care of souls.

See also DEATH AND DYING.

Further reading: Michael Alhstrom, Peter Gilmour, and Robert Tozik, *A Companion to Pastoral Care of the Sick* (Chicago: Liturgy Training, 1990); Lizette Larzon-Miller, *The Sacrament of the Anointing of the Sick* (Collegeville, Minn.: Liturgical Press, 2005).

Anselm of Canterbury, St. (c. 1033–1109)
Medieval theologian

An Italian by birth, Anselm became abbot of the monastic school of Bec in Normandy and later ARCHBISHOP of Canterbury. He was a learned author of several important treatises. Clement XI (r. 1700–21) declared him a doctor of the church in 1720. Together with PETER LOMBARD, he may be considered one of the anchors of the medieval intellectual renaissance. After AUGUSTINE OF HIPPO he was the foremost western theologian until THOMAS AQUINAS. Never formally canonized, Anselm still enjoys a saint's feast day on April 21.

Anselm was born in Lombardy and spent a profligate youth before crossing the Alps to study at the monastery of Bec in France, where he was tutored by Lanfranc of Pavia (c. 1010–89). He took monastic vows in 1060 and became noted for both his devotion and his intellectual acumen. He succeeded Lanfranc both as prior and later as abbot and still later as archbishop of Canterbury. At Bec he wrote his famous *Monologium* and *Proslogion,* as well as treatises on truth, free will, and dialectic. After paying many visits to England, Anselm was nominated as archbishop of Canterbury in 1093 by King William II (r. 1087–1100). He immediately ran into conflicts with William and his successor, Henry I, (r. 1100–1135) over the question of INVESTITURE. In Italy he attended councils at Bari and the Vatican, meanwhile authoring his books *On the Incarnation of the Word* and *Cur Deus Homo?* ("Why God Became Human").

Anselm is known chiefly for two great ideas: the ontological argument for the existence of GOD and the penal or satisfaction theory of the ATONEMENT. Both versions of his ontological "proof" are found in *Proglogion,* but he qualifies them with a meditation, quoting Augustine: he believes first in order to understand (*credo ut inelligam*). The central argument is this: God is a being greater than which none can be conceived; since existence is greater than nonexistence, God must partake of it; therefore, God must necessarily exist. Anselm's argument was opposed by his fellow monk Gaunilo (1033–1109) and by philosopher Immanuel Kant (1724–1804). The argument was modified by Thomas Aquinas in his Five Proofs and variously defended by Leibnitz and especially Hegel in his *Lectures on the Philosophy of Religion.* Modern versions of the proof have been given by the mathematician Kurt Gödel and the philosopher Alvin Plantinga.

Anselm's second idea belongs to the theology of redemption, or the ATONEMENT. His argument fits into what is called the penal or satisfaction theory of the atonement. In *Cur Deus Homo?* (5:12) he argues that the infinite God was offended by the sin of humankind. A mere human can offer him only finite satisfaction. Therefore, only a God-man, the incarnate Christ, would have the ability (as infinite God) and the obligation (as a human) to render the proper amends to God. The weakness of the argument is: how can a finite being produce an infinite offense? This theory can be contrasted to the exemplary or moral theory of the atonement as proposed by ABELARD.

Further reading: Anselm of Canterbury, *Basic Writings,* 2nd. ed. Translated by S. N. Deane (LaSalle: Open Court, 1968); Jasper Hopkins, *A Companion to the Study of St. Anselm* (Minneapolis: University of Minnesota Press, 1972); Alvin Plantinga, *The Ontological Argument from St. Anselm to Contemporary Philosophers* (Garden City, N.Y.: Doubleday, 1965); Richard W. Southern, *St., Anselm: A Portrait in a Landscape* (Cambridge: Cambridge University Press, 1990).

Anthony of Egypt, St. (c. 251–356) *founder of Christian monasticism*

Anthony is considered by many to be one of the first true CHRISTIAN hermits and a father of MONASTICISM. His feast day is January 17.

As a young man Anthony gave away all his belongings and started living an eremitical life at home. Later he retired to the desert in Lower EGYPT. He pursued solitude for 20 years, but, being of cheerful disposition, he attracted many to his way of life, so he set up a rule for the community of monks who gathered occasionally for religious feasts. His sister became abbess of a community of women. About the year 316 he retired again to the desert at a place between the Nile and the Red Sea he called his "Inner Mountain"; it remains today as the monastery Dêr Mar Antonios, where Coptic monks still observe his rule.

Anthony supported St. ATHANASIUS OF ALEXANDRIA in the latter's struggle against the heresy of ARIANISM. In turn, Athanasius wrote his famous *Life of Anthony,* in which he recounts his life, miracles, and especially temptations by demons. The Temptations of St. Anthony became a favorite subject of Christian art, and many different versions have been rendered in art and literature, notably by Hieronymus Bosch, Pieter Brueghel, Matthias Grünewald (Isenheim Altar), Gustave Flaubert, and Salvador Dali. Athanasius's *Life* did much to elevate the monastic ideal and strongly influenced the rise of monasticism in both East and West. In the West the Carthusians best preserved the Antonian monastic model. Some of Anthony's authentic words are preserved in the *Life* (16–43) and in the *Sayings of the Fathers.*

St. Anthony in the desert holding a double cross with bell attached and pig, also with bell in ear. Etching by Martin Schongauer (1450–91). The double cross signifies Anthony's abbatial status; the swine, his overcoming of the desires of the flesh; and the bells, his power of exorcism. In the Middle Ages he was patron of swineherds. *(St. Louis Art Museum, with permission)*

Further reading: Athanasius of Alexandria, *The Life of Antony* in *The Nicene and Post-Nicene Fathers,* ed. Philip Schaff and Henry Wace, 2nd series 4: 194–221 (Grand Rapids, Mich.: Eerdmans, 1981); James Cowan, *Journey to the Inner Mountain: In the Desert with St. Antony* (London: Hodder & Stoughten, 2002); Samuel Rubenson, *The Letters of St. Antony* (Lund: Lund University Press, 1990).

Anthony of Padua, St. (c. 1191–1231) *friar and miracle worker*

Anthony of Padua was a Portuguese FRANCISCAN friar who became noted for his preaching in ITALY. Celebrated for working miracles, he was canonized only a year after his death. Pope PIUS XII declared him a DOCTOR OF THE CHURCH in 1946. He is known as the Evangelical Doctor. A patron to the poor, Anthony is one of the most popular saints in the world. His picture or statue is in almost every Catholic church, and people pray to him to find lost objects.

Anthony joined the Augustinian canons of Coimbra, Portugal, at the age of 15. He became very learned in Scripture and the fathers but was unhappy with his fellow friars' way of life. He switched to the Franciscans upon learning about the martyrdom of Franciscan missionaries in Morocco, but illness kept him from becoming a missionary. He attended the noted general chapter of the friars at Assisi in 1221. He preached at an ordination, and his eloquence astounded all. FRANCIS OF ASSISI assigned him to teach theology to the friars, first at Bologna, then at Toulouse and Montpelier in France.

Pope Gregory IX (r. 1227–41) assigned him to explain the rule to his fellow friars in the 1230 chapter. The rest of his life he spent in Padua, preaching against usury, avarice, enmity, and hatred. He was instrumental in getting the city of Padua to pass an ordinance in relief of debtors. The Bread of St. Anthony has become a tradition of collecting alms for the poor.

Many legends surround Anthony, some of which Donatello illustrated in bronze bas-reliefs for the Basilica di Sant' Antonio in Padua. In one he preached to the fishes of the Brenta River near Padua the way Francis preached to the larks. In another the Christ-child appeared to him, and he held the infant in his arms. This is often the subject of paintings and holy cards. In yet a third, a novice absconded with his Psalter, and Anthony appeared to him. Thus, he became the patron saint for lost objects. The popular Anthony has been adopted as the patron saint of the poor, sailors, various animals, and pregnant women.

Further reading: Anthony of Padua, *Sermons for the Easter Cycle,* tr. George Marcil (St. Bonaventure: Franciscan Institute, 1994); Sophronius Clasen, *St. Anthony, Doctor of the Church* (Chicago: Franciscan Herald Press, 1973).

anti-Catholicism

Anti-Catholicism includes discrimination, prejudice, and open hostility against Catholic persons and institutions on the basis of their FAITH. The reasons for anti-Catholicism can be many: political, philosophical, social, and moral.

In the earliest periods of the Catholic tradition one must speak of anti-Christianity rather than anti-Catholicism. It was present practically from the start. Jesus warns his disciples to expect persecution (Matt. 20:26–28), referring to the persecution of the prophets and especially to the Isaianic figure of the Suffering Servant. Christianity began as a sect within Judaism and partook of all Jewish rites, but by the end of the first century conflicts between the two became marked. The GOSPEL of John reflects this mutual hostility, which Raymond Brown attributes to the expulsion of CHRISTIANS from the synagogues in Asia Minor after the Jewish Council of Javneh (Jamnia) in c. 100. Acts recounts several acts of persecution by Jewish authorities against early followers of Jesus. This pattern was repeated throughout the empire wherever Jewish authorities had legal status.

In the second century Christians tried to answer the Jewish charges in a series of apologies called "Against the Jews," in which they referred to the Old Testament to demonstrate Christ's divinity and the extension of salvation to the Gentiles. JUSTIN MARTYR's *Dialogue with Trypho* is classic in this context. Justin, ORIGEN OF ALEXANDRIA, and St. JEROME all mention the "curse of the Christians" in the synagogue services, where the *nozerim* (Nazarenes, as Christians in general or Judean Christians were called) were included among the *minim* (heretics) who were cursed in the Twelfth Benediction. (Christians continued to attend synagogue services well into the fourth century throughout the empire and maybe even the seventh century in Palestine! Conversely, there was not a little belittling of Jewish and pagan faith and practices in these apologetic tracts.)

The Romans viewed Jesus as a political threat and hence condemned him to the political death of crucifixion. Thereafter, Christians, when they are mentioned in Roman literature, are accused of forming *hetaeriae,* seditious political clubs. The First Epistle of Peter, a late document, notes that "the pagans accuse [Christians] of doing wrong" (1 Peter 2:12). During the reign of Trajan (98–117), Pliny the Younger noted that merely bearing the name "Christian . . . is punishable, even if innocent of crime" (*Letter* 96). Romans accused Christians of many heinous acts such as incest, eating the flesh of children, and ritual intercourse. However, the crime Christians were most often accused of was *superstitio,* which did not have the modern connotation of "superstition," but rather referred to foreign cults that failed to honor sufficiently the civil gods of the Roman state and especially refused to worship the emperor. Thus when Tacitus (*Annals* 15.44) and Suetonius (*Lives of the Caesars, Nero* 16) accuse Christians of superstition, they are accusing them of lacking civil piety and, in effect, of being atheists. This political prejudice led to a number of systematic persecutions of Christians and others by imperial authorities, most notably by Nero

(54), Domition (95), Trajan (98–117), Hadrian (124–125), Marcus Aurelius (161–168), and others until the last great purge under Diocletian (302–305). However, not more than a thousand martyrs died in the 300-year Roman persecution, and the policy probably backfired, as many came to admire the bravery of Christians, even young women like Sts. PERPETUA AND FELICITY, and were inspired to follow the Christian way secretly.

The most sustained pagan critique of Christianity came from Celsus (c. 275), a middle Platonist philosopher whose treatise *True Doctrine* is quoted almost *in toto* in Origen's *Against Celsus;* the philosopher/physician Galen shared some of Celsus's views. Celsus had much knowledge of Christian as well as GNOSTIC and Marcionite texts (*see* MARCION) and uses wit, satire, and logic in his arguments. He also alludes to a Jewish critic of Christian claims. Celsus says that Jesus was the bastard offspring of Mary and a Roman soldier who went down to Egypt to learn the magic by which he performed miracles; that Christianity was derived from "barbarous" Judaism though it claims it is different; and that Christians place irrational, superstitious faith above reason, thus appealing to low-class women, children, and slaves. His critique anticipates that of Nietzsche: Christianity represented the resentment of the inferior masses against the noble Romans.

After the Edict of Milan (313) under CONSTANTINE THE GREAT, Christians experienced not only toleration but even favor. Although many subsequent emperors believed in ARIANISM, most of them favored the orthodox Catholic party for the sake of imperial unity. This policy, buttressed by the CHURCH AND STATE political theology of AUGUSTINE OF HIPPO, laid the foundation for the two-sword theory of medieval Catholicism. The pope and the church wield the spiritual sword, and the state wields the bloody sword in defense of the former.

In the GREAT SCHISM (1054) between Eastern Orthodoxy and Western Roman Catholicism it is fair to say that there was unfair bias and prejudice on both sides. And while the sectarian movements of the Middle Ages like the CATHARI held low opinions of the official clergy, the church itself wielded deadly power over them and persecuted them mercilessly with the INQUISITION. Thus, anti-Catholicism was matched by equal or stronger sentiments on the part of the Catholic world.

Modern anti-Catholicism arose as the natural result of the PROTESTANT REFORMATION. There is no doubt that by the time of the late RENAISSANCE the Roman papacy, the Catholic clergy, and religious life in general had become widely corrupted, but Martin Luther's response was excessive if not inflammatory. Wanting to reform the Roman church in the beginning, he wound up calling it Babylon and the pope its whore, using the rhetoric of the Book of Revelation. Thereafter, Protestants of various denominations continued to rail against Catholics for their devotion to Mary and the saints, for their use of novenas and pilgrimages, and for the ritualism of their services, which was dubbed "superstition" or "fetishism." In England Catholics like St. Edmund Campion (1540–81) were martyred for their faith even though they were willing to take an oath of loyalty to the Crown. It must be admitted that in the lands they dominated, Catholics typically returned the favors in kind.

In North America, Catholicism had a strong influence in the Hispanic Southwest, in Quebec, and in the states of Louisiana and Maryland, but Catholics were a clear minority and suffered systematic discrimination in most parts of the United States and Canada. Despite his authorship of the Virginia statute on religious liberty, Thomas Jefferson was particularly distrustful of Catholics, even though they contributed their full share in the Revolutionary War. To his credit George Washington suppressed the burning of the pope in effigy on Guy Fawke's Day by Protestant troops out of deference to his loyal Catholic troops and to Catholic France's support of the Revolution. In an attempt to retain the loyalty of the American colonies during the Revolutionary War, Anglican England granted them, especially the French-speaking ones (Quebec), religious rights it would only later grant to its own citizens.

In the 19th century U.S. anti-Catholicism found expression in the spheres of education and immigration. Catholics founded parochial school systems long before public education became universal (partly in reaction to Catholic schools). Although the Catholic schools were noticeably successful, they were often objects of derision and vandalism. One notorious instance occurred in 1834 when a Protestant mob, under the false information that a young woman was being held against her will at the convent school of the Ursulines in Charlestown, Massachusetts, ascended the hill and reduced the institution to ashes. Stories like this fed anti-Catholic screeds, most notably *The Awful Disclosures of Maria Monk,* a lurid tale written by Protestants in the late 19th century about sex and sadism in convent schools. It is still in print. Another notorious incident was the tarring and feathering in 1854 of the Jesuit Indian missionary John Bapst (1815–87) by Protestant nativists in Ellsworth, Maine. Bapst went on to become the first president of Boston College.

Toward the middle of the century the massive immigration of Catholics from Ireland, Germany, and Italy provoked a nativist reaction among the Protestant majority, inflamed by the Know-Nothing Party and later (sometimes literally) by the Ku Klux Klan (in 1920 the author's mother witnessed a cross burning on her parents' lawn in Topeka, Kansas, by the Klan). Much of anti-Catholic sentiment was nourished in fundamentalist circles under the influence of the premillennial dispensationalism of John Nelson Darby (1800–82), who did much to foster the image of the Roman Catholic Church as the "Whore of Babylon" on the American shore.

In the 20th century American anti-Catholicism manifested itself most notably in the political arena. Protestant forces mustered to defeat Al Smith (1873–1944), the Democratic candidate for president in 1928 and a Catholic. This scenario was almost repeated in 1960 by a coalition of conservative and fundamentalist preachers—among them Billy Graham, Bob Jones, Sr., and Carl McIntire—who sought to portray the John Kennedy candidacy as a threat to the separation of church and state. Some dispensationalists painted him as the "Beast" of the Book of Revelation. Kennedy's speech to a group of Protestant ministers in Houston, Texas, disarmed the fundamentalist opposition, although many of the latter still privately label the Catholic church as the Whore of Babylon.

Even in the nominally Catholic countries of Europe and Latin America, the rationalist approach of the 18th century Enlightenment gave rise to strong currents of liberal ANTICLERICALISM, which joined forces with traditional Protestant bias. Religious orders, especially the JESUITS, were expelled from several countries, including France, and even universally suppressed in 1773. Such anticlericalism became endemic in parts of Latin America, leading to a 1929 ban on wearing religious and clerical garb in public in Mexico, which was only recently repealed.

The openness of and public interest in VATICAN COUNCIL II, plus the active participation of Catholics in ecumenical dialogue and action, sharply reduced expressions of anti-Catholicism toward the end of the 20th century and gave Catholics a chance at full participation in public life on all levels in many parts of the world. Anti-Catholic sentiment, however, is still alive at certain flashpoints around the world: East Timor, Nigeria, the Sudan, and elsewhere. In some Muslim countries Catholics and followers of other religions are still prohibited from worshiping in public and from seeking converts, but in others, such as Indonesia, the largest Muslim country in the world, Catholics are relatively secure.

Further reading: Philip Jenkins, *The New Anti-Catholicism: The Last Acceptable Prejudice* (New York: Oxford University Press, 2003); Gustavus Myers, *History of Bigotry in the United States* (New York: Capricorn Books, 1960); William M. Shea, *The Lion and the Lamb: Evangelicals and Catholics in America* (Oxford: Oxford University Press, 2004); Robert Wilkins, *The Christians as the Romans Saw Them* (New Haven, Conn.: Yale University Press, 1984).

anticlericalism

Anticlericalism is a belief or attitude that opposes or condemns church hierarchies on principle and is hostile to anyone who holds clerical office. Historically, it has targeted Catholic CLERGY more than those of other faiths. It can come from within the church or from without.

Church reformers themselves have been the source of anticlericalism. In the early MIDDLE AGES St. BERNARD OF CLAIRVAUX railed against abuses by secular clergy who failed to serve their parishes or live holy lives. In the Middle Ages many friars from the DOMINICAN and FRANCISCAN ORDERS sent out preachers who spoke against absentee and high-living clerics. Later the humanist ERASMUS, though never joining the REFORMATION of his friend Martin Luther (1483–1546), satirized the lifestyles of errant clergy in his *Praise of Folly* and their sale of indulgences for money. Martin Luther himself can be seen as a type of anticlerical reformer. In modern times, during VATICAN COUNCIL II several bishops, most notably Bishop Emile-Josef De Smedt (1909–95) of Bruges, Belgium, felt that the new Dogmatic Constitution on the Church was too clerical and legalistic in its original form; they succeeded in gaining a rewrite. Several of the council's reforms may have helped take the steam out of anticlericalism.

Anticlericalism from without could often be found in literature; there is a strong anticlerical streak in Geoffrey Chaucer's *Canterbury Tales* and Boccaccio's *Decameron*. By the 18th century anticlericalism was associated with liberal political movements, most often associated with the philosophes of the French Enlightenment. A key figure was Voltaire (born François-Marie Arouet, 1694–1778), a deist who stridently and bitingly opposed the Roman Catholic Church as a dangerous, superstitious, and fanatical institution, which he contrasted to his vision of a kind and forgiving Jesus. Virulent anticlericalism led to the 1773 suppression of the JESUITS, whom many believed to be sinister political agents of the pope. In many cases the laxity of the clergy and their too-ready support of repressive regimes provided justification to the waves of anticlericalism that spread throughout Europe during the 19th century, especially in France and Portugal (1830s), Spain (1836), Italy (1870), Germany during Bismarck's KULTURKAMPF, Mexico during its revolution (1910), and Italy, Spain, and Germany during their fascist periods.

Pope PIUS IX, self-defeatingly, urged Catholics not to participate in the new Italian state founded by Garibaldi. Later, faced with the threat of the virulent anticlericalism of communist regimes, the papacy made compromises by signing concordats with Italian (1929), German (1933), and Spanish (1953) fascists in order to preserve the church's standing. In the German case, the concordat did little good in the long run. Anticlericalism appears to be on the wane throughout the world except in states that maintain proscriptions against Christianity in general.

See also FASCISM; NAZISM.

Further reading: S. J. Barnett, *Idol Temples and Crafty Priests: The Origins of Enlightenment Anticlericalism* (New York: St. Martin's, 1999); Christopher Clark and Wolfram Kaiser, *Culture Wars: Secular-Catholic Conflict in Nineteenth Century Europe* (Cambridge: Cambridge University Press, 2003); José Sanchez, *Anticlericalism* (Notre Dame: University of Notre Dame Press, 1972).

Antiochene School

The early CHRISTIAN philosophers of Antioch in Syria developed a style of theology focused on practical morality and a tradition of biblical interpretation that relied on a literal reading of the sources. The ANTIOCHENE SCHOOL thus stood in opposition to the more mystical and allegorical ALEXANDRINE SCHOOL.

Antioch in Syria was founded in 300 B.C.E. by Seleucus I (d. 280 B.C.E.); by the third century C.E. it was the third-largest city of the Roman Empire, with a large Jewish quarter. It was the site of early Christian missionary activity to both Jews and Gentiles and the jump-off for Paul's circuit of Asia Minor (Acts 11: 13). Antioch had many famous bishops, including IGNATIUS and JOHN CHRYSOSTOM, who was later drafted to become patriarch of Constantinople.

In the developing Christian world Antioch became locked in a struggle for pride of place first with Alexandria and then with Constantinople. As a crossroads between East and West and North and South, it became a hotbed of theological currents and controversy. Paul of Samosata, bishop from 260 to 268, seemed to have taught that Jesus was not the Son of God but rather a real man united with the Word at his baptism. An emphasis on the humanity of Christ became a hallmark of the Antiochene tradition, heretical or not.

Antiochene biblical exegesis was first developed by Lucian, martyred in 312 under Maximin Daza (r. 306–313). Lucian's version of the Septuagint, the Greek translation of the Hebrew Bible, is still in use today. His more literal interpretations of Scripture influenced Arius (c. 250–336) and his followers, who claimed Lucian as their teacher. Eustathius, bishop of Antioch from 324 to 327, opposed both the literalist humanism of Arius and the word-flesh allegorizing of ORIGEN OF ALEXANDRIA.

In the fourth century, the Antiochene tradition was shaped by the local Judaism, by Neoplatonist philosophers such as Iambilichus, and by a Christology that placed equal emphasis on Christ's humanity and divinity. Its key representatives were the rhetorician Diodore of Tarsus (d. c. 390) and his student Theodore of Mopsuestia (c. 350–428), an astute biblical commentator who applied critical, philological, and historical methods in his interpretation. He rejected Trinitarian formulas that had been read into into the Hebrew Bible and severely limited predictive prophecy. Theodore advocated a modest form of TYPOLOGY to relate the two testaments together. His interpretations do not ride above the text the way allegory does. He was a close friend of St. JOHN CHRYSOSTOM. Many of his works have been lost.

In his Christology Theodore apparently held that the divine Word in Christ is the subject of his divine actions, and the "assumed man" is the subject of his human actions. He had difficulty accounting for the unity of Christ, but his main purpose was to counter the Alexandrine Apollinarius of Laodicea (c. 315–92), who subscribed to the formula "one nature of the Logos made flesh," which was based on the soul-body allegory dear to the Alexandrine School. According to Theodore this formula denied the full humanity of Christ by denying him a human mind or soul. Nestorius was the final and most flamboyant member of the Antiochene tradition. He allowed Mary the title *Christotokos,* or Christ-bearer, but denied her the title *Theotokos,* or God-bearer, thus implying that Jesus was a mere man.

In accord with Antioch's stress on the human side of Christ, it also stressed human moral behavior, as manifest in Nestorius's sympathy to PELAGIUS. By contrast, the Alexandrines tended to devalue human action in favor of the mystical contemplation of and absorption into GOD.

Apollinarianism was condemned at the Council of CONSTANTINOPLE I (381). Nestorius was condemned at the Councils of EPHESUS (431) and CHALCEDON (451). Nestorius stated that he never denied the orthodox formula "two natures united in one person," and many modern scholars believe that CYRIL OF ALEXANDRIA was unfair in his attacks. Much of the problem revolved around a confusing mix of terminology (*see* COPTIC CHURCH). Theodore of Mopsuestia was condemned at the Council of CONSTANTINOPLE II (553). The Antiochene School eventually came under severe restrictions, and Theodore's far-

sighted methods fell into disuse until revived by modern biblical scholarship.

See also GNOSTIC/GNOSTICISM.

Further reading: Raymond Brown and John P. Meier, *Antioch and Rome: New Testament Cradles of Christianity* (New York: Paulist Press, 1985); J. Guillet, "Les exégèses d' Alexandrie et d'Antioche: conflit ou malentendu?" *Rescherches de Sciences Religieuses* (1947) 34:257–302; D. S. Wallace-Hadrill, *Christian Antioch: A Study of Early Christian Thought* (Cambridge: Cambridge University Press, 1982).

antipope

An antipope is a person who lays claim to the office of BISHOP of Rome and tries to act as head of the Roman Catholic Church, in opposition to the person duly holding that ecclesiastical office in the eyes of the church as a whole. There have been some 39 antipopes throughout Catholic history. The rules for validity have changed over time. Even a correct election is not an infallible indicator, as those rules, too, have changed. Today the pope is elected by all members of the College of Cardinals under the age of 75 in a duly convened consistory at the Vatican.

The first antipope was actually a saint: St. HIPPOLYTUS OF ROME (r. 217–35), a noted church writer and author of *Refutation of All Heresies* and *Apostolic Tradition,* who challenged Pope Callistus (r. 217–222). Hippolytus later died a martyr but remains an antipope. By way of contrast, a Roman synod excommunicated John XII (r. 955–964) for his gross immorality.

Because of political danger in Rome, Clement V (r. 1305–14) moved the seat of the papacy to AVIGNON, France in 1309, where it remained until 1377. This became known as the "Babylonian Captivity." During the Western Schism from 1377 to 1415, four antipopes reigned in Avignon, while valid popes reigned from Rome. The last antipope was Felix V (r. 1439–49), the former duke Amadeus of Savoy, who renounced his duchy after his wife's death, founded the Order of St. Maurice, and was inducted as pope by the schismatic Council of BASEL in 1439. He finally submitted to Nicholas V (r. 1447–55).

Further reading: Richard P. McBrien, *Lives of the Popes* (San Francisco: HarperSanFrancisco, 2000); Daniel MacCarron, *The Great Schism: Antipopes Who Split The Church* (Dublin: D.M.C. Universal, 1982).

anti-Semitism

Although Arab peoples can also be called "Semites," or descendants of Shem in the BIBLE (Gen. 10:21–32), the term *anti-Semitism* has come to mean antipathy toward Jews, discrimination against them, and persecution of them. The roots of anti-Semitism are complex and precede the emergence of Christianity. The Assyrians in 722 B.C.E. and the Babylonians in c. 589 B.C.E. conquered the Israelites of Palestine and dispersed them throughout Asia Minor and the Near East. Some rulers showed them favor, as did Cyrus the Great (580–29 B.C.E.); his release of the captive Jews from Babylon in c. 539 B.C.E. and arrangement for the rebuilding of the Temple earned him the title "Messiah" from Second Isaiah (Isa. 45:1). Most were like Antiochus Epiphanes (r. c. 175–64 B.C.E.), the Hellenistic tyrant who desecrated the Temple precinct with a statue of Zeus and forbade Jews to circumcise their male children. By this time many Jews had dispersed as minorities throughout the Mediterranean as far away as the Straits of Gibraltar.

Under Roman rule the status of Jews remained precarious until Julius Caesar (102?–44 B.C.E.) offered them protection. In 1 B.C.E. his grandnephew Augustus Caesar (Octavian) issued an edict protecting the Jews' religious observances but imposed the Temple tax to be paid to Rome. Thereafter Jews were freed from offering sacrifices to the Roman gods. Periodically Jews and later Christians experienced persecutions and expulsions from Rome. Writers like Suetonius and Tacitus, while recognizing Judaism as a religion, still believed it to be "barbarous." Romans were stringently opposed to any bodily mutilation and repulsed by the practice of circumcision. While some Greco-Romans, called *Theoseboi* (Gk.: "Those devout to God"), were attracted to the synagogue for its moral and spiritual teaching and for its celebration of the Sabbath day, most Romans found the rites and practices of the Jews to be abhorrent.

A discussion of Christian anti-Semitism requires an understanding of the complex relation between Judaism and its offspring religion, Christianity. Modern scholars point out the obvious fact that Jesus was born a Jew and that he lived and thought as a Jew. The "scripture" that Jesus refers to was the existing Hebrew Bible, which Christians now call the Old Testament. Jesus was not a "Christian," a word that did not come into common use until c. 95 C.E. (Acts 11:26). Paul, for example, never uses the word "Christian" but calls his fellow believers "saints" or "brothers and sisters in the Lord." All the first followers of Jesus thought of themselves as Jews. According to Josephus there were many "schools" or "philosophies" of Judaism around the time of Jesus—Sadducees, Pharisees, Zealots, and Essenes—all competing for the soul of Judaism. The followers of Jesus were just one among many.

Jesus first appears as an Elijahlike prophet, raising the dead, healing the sick, and calling for a renewal of the original covenant between God and his people (Lev. 19). There is no doubt that he had conflicts with the Jerusalem authorities, but so did most of the prophets who preceded him such as Jeremiah and Isaiah, who eventually were accepted into the Jewish canon despite those conflicts. These conflicts with Jewish authorities continued among the early followers of Jesus, as recorded in the early chapters of the Book of Acts. However, they should be seen as intra-Judaic rather than Jewish-Christian disputes. The conflict seems to have escalated after the Jewish War in 70 C.E., when the Temple was destroyed, the

Sadducees lost all their power, and the Pharisees regrouped at the Council of Javneh/Jamnia, c. 90 C.E., and formed the early Rabbinate.

Thus, looking at the New Testament (NT) from its own perspective and not from the viewpoint of much later and more fateful history, the conflicts between Jesus and the Sanhedrin, the Sadducees, and the Pharisees were intramural and did not involve anti-Jewish sentiments. Even the early Christian criticism of "Judaizers" was not anti-Jewish per se. When Paul argued against circumcision for Gentiles, he was not arguing against the practice among Jews, whom he still regarded as the chosen people of GOD, but against Gentiles who wanted to move backward in the timetable of salvation by adopting Jewish ways for themselves. God, Paul believed, was extending salvation to include the Gentiles, just as Second Isaiah had promised; he was not excluding the Jews. In the famous Romans 9–11 passage he states unequivocally that Israel, God's own name for the Jews, have their hearts hardened "for the time being" but in the end "all Israel will be saved" (11:26). By *Israel* he meant the Jews in the flesh, not some "true" Israel such as the Christian Church, as later generations believed.

Mark, the earliest surviving Gospel, was written c. 60–70 C.E., some 30 years after the events it retells. It describes Jesus as the victim of collusion between Jewish authorities and Pilate, but 15:15 makes it clear that it was Pilate who had Jesus crucified. In fact, Josephus and Roman sources both record that Pontius Pilate was a particularly cruel governor who brooked no opposition.

Matthew and Luke were written a generation later, c. 95, and reflect different interests and viewpoints. Matthew portrays Jesus as an exalted teacher, or rabbi, on the model of Moses, but since Matthew was a Jewish follower of Jesus, his Gospel also reflects the conflicts that had broken out between his community and the rabbinic Javneh Jews. Surviving rabbis at the Council of Javneh (c. 90) tried to drive the "Nazoreans" (followers of Jesus) from synagogues by including them among the *minim*, or heretics, who were denounced in the Twelfth Benediction of the early synagogue liturgy.

(The rabbis may not have been too successful. Recent archeological research indicates that later Jewish Christians partook in the synagogue until the seventh century in the Galilee. Throughout the Roman Empire the early Christian house-churches were built in close proximity to Jewish synagogues, as at Dura Europos, implying that Christians worshipped at both. This is not surprising: to this day, according to many Christian theologians, a Christian can go to any Jewish service and say *all* the prayers without violating his or her religious convictions.)

Matthew goes to some length to remove blame from the Roman authorities. He has Pilate's wife interceding for Jesus (in fact, later emperor's wives interceded for Christians in Rome) and has Pilate washing his hands as a sign of innocence. No doubt because of intra-Jewish rivalry, Matthew puts the ultimate blame for Jesus' death squarely on the shoulders of the Jewish authorities by adding the verse "His blood be upon us and our children" (Matt. 24:25).

In Luke, the responsibility of the Romans is diminished even further. The Gospel of Luke and the Book of Acts, which should be read as one work, were written for a Roman audience, probably nobles, and Luke goes beyond Matthew to establish Roman innocence. The work unfolds in ascending diptychs, proceeding from JOHN THE BAPTIST to Jesus, from Galilee to Jerusalem, from Peter to Paul, and from Jerusalem to Rome. Luke is trying to justify Christianity in the face of criticism by the Romans, who accused it of being "superstition" and thus a threat to Roman authority. Luke removes the crowning with thorns and mocking of Jesus by Roman soldiers. Luke finesses Pilate's responsibility: three times Pilate declares Jesus' innocence to the crowd, but in the end "Jesus [was] delivered up [by Pilate to the crowd's] will" (Luke 23:26).

Most scholars believe that the Gospel of John in its present form (c. 100–110 C.E.) stands by itself. One of the signs of its lateness is that John lays Jesus' death not so much on Pilate or on the Jewish authorities alone, but on "Jews" as a group (John 19:12). The break with Judaism is nigh complete. The stereotype is set for the later, fateful charge that "the Jews killed Jesus" although John does not say this. The irony is that the Johannine community began in Palestine as a thoroughly Jewish group of Jesus' followers.

While there are many statements against Jews in the NT, it would not be accurate to say that the NT and the Christian writings are "anti-Semitic" in the strict sense of the term. In the second century Gentiles replaced Jews as the largest group among the followers of Jesus. Christian apologists such as St. JUSTIN MARTYR portrayed the "Jews" as a "stiff-necked people" who refused the light of salvation. Biblical interpretation shifted accordingly. The Old Testament was now a dim, fleshly "type" of the true, spiritual reality revealed in the NT. Along with this, the theology of supercession took over (see TYPOLOGY). Whatever was promised to the Jews was turned over to the true worshippers of God, the Christians, and the Covenant with the Jews was cancelled.

Still, it was not until after CONSTANTINE brought about a full breach with Judaism at the Council of NICAEA that the phrase *Christ-killers* was put to use. Although some say that full-scale anti-Semitism did not emerge until the Middle Ages, the author of this work believes that Constantine's exclusion of contact with Jewish rabbis set the necessary condition for anti-Semitism by rendering the Jews a hated, pariah people to be shunned and despised.

The phrase *Christ-killers* has an interesting subtext. JOHN CHRYSOSTOM, bishop of CONSTANTINOPLE (c. 398–407), was the first to accuse Jews of being "Christ-killers" (*Homilies* 6.2.10) when he was bishop of Antioch, but his reason for doing so was that his Christian congregants were continuing to attend the local synagogue, no doubt because the rabbis were more learned than many priests and were better biblical preachers!

In the post-Constantinian world there were many who advocated the outright extermination of the Jews, but the view of AUGUSTINE came to prevail. He quotes Psalms 59:10–11 for his policy on the Jews: "Slay them not lest they forget thy law; disperse them in thy might" (Vulgate). Jews remain enemies of Christians, but they are to be preserved and dispersed, as an example of a rejectionist, homeless people. Their pariah status was guaranteed for the future. Some have argued that post-Constantinian stress on the Cross and the death of Jesus, culminating in the satisfaction theory of the ATONEMENT in the theology of St. ANSELM OF CANTERBURY, fixated Christians' attention on seeking retribution from those whom the tradition held to be the "cause" of Christ's death.

In the MIDDLE AGES the epithet *Christ-killers* became the verbal club justifying the ghettoization, persecution, and murder of Jews. Three important factors shaped Catholic anti-Semitism across the Middle Ages: 1) the CRUSADES, 2) the legal status of Jews, and 3) the growing power of the INQUISITION.

Although the Crusades were originally called to rescue the holy sites of Palestine from Saracens (Muslims), much of the fervor they excited was directed against Jews and against Eastern Orthodox Christians. Peter the Hermit preached the first Crusade at the behest of Pope Urban II (r. 1088–99). He collected a band of ragamuffin knights and sailed down the Rhine, stopping off in Frankfurt and Worms to slay Jews en route to the Holy Land. The knights repeated the act against Byzantine Christians in Constantinople.

The Frankfurt event signaled the subsequent pattern of pogroms against Jews and heretics throughout Europe and Russia. The overt violence against Jews was fed by the "blood libel"—the myth that Jews kidnapped and crucified young Christian males to use their blood in their ritual services. Another myth that gained wide currency was that Jews ritually desecrated the hosts used in the EUCHARIST. Apart from violence, discrimination against Jews blossomed. Following Augustine's recommendations, Jews were prevented from owning land, and they were periodically expelled from various countries in western Europe, notably England under King Edward I in 1290.

In the High Middle Ages the preachings of both DOMINICANS and FRANCISCANS focused on the poor life of Christ, including his death and crucifixion, ironically providing fuel for the later fires of prejudice when Jews were consigned to the "usurious" trade of banking. At the Council of Sens in 1205, Pope INNOCENT III, without doubt the most influential pope in the Middle Ages decreed "The Jews, by their own guilt, are consigned to perpetual servitude because they crucified the Lord . . . As slaves rejected by God, in whose death they wickedly conspired, they shall by the effect of this very action, recognize themselves as the slaves of those whom Christ's death set free." At the Lateran Council IV in 1215, Jews and Muslims were required to wear special garb, a practice that spread throughout Europe and fatefully anticipated the yellow star decreed by Hitler in 1938.

All these trends culminated in the Spanish Inquisition and the policy of FERDINAND OF ARAGON and ISABELLA OF CASTILE.: Jews were forcibly converted, expelled from Spain, or executed if they refused the first two options. Even those who converted, the *conversos,*—suffered discrimination. For example, they could not serve as superiors in religious orders. St. TERESA OF ÁVILA, the granddaughter of a *converso,* was a true exception, but even she was persecuted much of her life. Despite the waves of persecution, Jews continued to find pockets of protection both in the Old and New Worlds, especially in places like Amsterdam, Prague, Poland, and Recife, in Brazil.

The PROTESTANT REFORMATION was no better to the Jews than its Catholic predecessor. Aiming to convert the Jews, Martin Luther (1483–1546) wrote a pamphlet, "That Jesus Christ was Born a Jew" (1523). However, when Jews did not respond by converting, he wrote "On the Jews and Their Lies" (1543); as a cantankerous old man, he

even proposed that synagogues be burnt, Jewish literature banned, and vengeance be taken for the killing of Christ, a fateful foreshadowing of the Nazi's Kristallnacht in 1938. The great exception in the Protestant world was pluralistic Reformed Amsterdam and its colony New Amsterdam (New York), which became great Jewish havens. Some Protestant religious and civil leaders, such as Andreas Osiander of Nuremberg (1498–1552) and Landgrave Philip I of Hesse (1504–67) opposed Luther and anti-Semitic policies, but most held on to the age-old image of "stiff-necked" people who had spurned the Gospel.

The Enlightenment seemed to beckon the dawn of a new day. In 1791 the French National Assembly emancipated the Jews and granted them full rights as citizens. Full implementation occurred with Napoleon Bonaparte's 1806 proclamation granting Judaism equal status before the law. Many Catholics, including Napoléon's uncle Cardinal Fesh (1763–1839), opposed this move. Earlier in 1797 Napoléon had first proposed Palestine as a Jewish state, but the failure of his campaign in Egypt put an end to that plan. The legal emancipation of the Jews throughout Europe followed apace, including Germany in 1819.

Other forces were at work. In 1805 the Jesuit Abbé Barruel published a treatise stating that the French Revolution, which had devastating effects on Catholicism, had been plotted by the Freemasons. Later he blamed the Jews, setting into motion the idea of a Jewish conspiracy behind all major political activity. PIUS IX reimposed restrictions on Jews within the Papal States of central Italy. A short while later, during the KULTURKAMPF in Germany, Bismarck pitted Protestants against both Jews and Catholics. The negative forces came to a head with the Dreyfus Affair. Captain Alfred Dreyfus (1859–1935), a French military officer, was falsely convicted of treason and sentenced to prison on Devil's Island. His conviction was overturned, but not before waves of anti-Semitism, some of which were abetted by Catholics, swept over Europe. The publication of the scurrilous

Protocols of the Elders of Zion in Russia in 1905 fanned the allegations of a Jewish conspiracy to take over the world. Anti-Semitism went hand-in-hand with ANTI-CATHOLICISM in 19th-century America and was part and parcel of the Nativist Movement (*see* ANTI-CATHOLICISM). Beginning in the 1920s *The Protocols* had great influence on certain strands of Protestant fundamentalism in the United States and indirectly influenced Catholic attitudes, notably in the vehemently anti-FDR and anti-Jewish radio addresses of Father Charles E. Coughlin (1891–1979) during the 1930s.

The next phase of anti-Semitism is the most shameful one. Although the fascist movement, at least in its Italian and German forms, was bitterly hostile to Christianity, what Nazism perpetrated could not have been accomplished without the centuries of overt and covert anti-Semitism that preceded it. There is no doubt that many Catholics and Protestants gave safe harbor and exit to countless Jews during the Holocaust, but a far greater number succumbed to silence or complicity. Pope PIUS XI began an opening attack on the Nazis with *Mit brennender Sorge* ("With burning anxiety," March 14, 1937), a strongly worded letter to the German bishops condemning Nazism and read from all pulpits. He had another in the works but died before it was issued. Pope JOHN XXIII was noted for ferreting Jews through Turkey to Palestine, and, while PIUS XII helped many behind closed doors, he nonetheless assisted in legitimating the Nazi regime by signing the concordat with Hitler in 1933 as Vatican secretary of state. No doubt Pius XII felt his first responsibility was to protect Catholics, but some critics argue that his silence about the Holocaust must be judged as a monumental moral failure.

At VATICAN COUNCIL II the Catholic Church, recognizing Christianity's common heritage with Judaism, formally and decisively declared in *Nostra Aetate* 4, the Declaration on the Relation of the Church to Non-Christian Religions: "True, authorities of the Jews and those who followed their lead pressed for the death of Christ (cf. John 19:6), still what happened in His passion cannot be blamed on all the Jews then living, without distinction, nor upon the Jews of today.... The Church ... deplores the hatred, persecutions, and displays of anti-Semitism directed against the Jews at anytime and from any source." Following the council numerous dialogue groups and organizations formed between Christians and Jews, especially in the United States. Catholics are fully active in these efforts.

Aided by a Jewish boyhood friend, Pope JOHN PAUL II sought to bridge the gap that divided Christians and Jews. In 1986 he met with the chief rabbi of Rome, Elio Toaff (1915–), at the Great Synagogue of Rome, where the two sat in identical chairs at the same level. The pope asked forgiveness for the sins of commission and omission done by sons and daughters of the church during the Shoah (Holocaust). Later, in *Crossing the Threshold of Hope,* he referred to all Jews as "our elder brothers in faith" (99). The Vatican formally recognized the State of Israel in 1994, and the pope continued his mission of opening the church up to dialogue and prayer with Jews around the world until his death in 2005. Many conservative Tridentine Catholics bitterly opposed the pope's steps in this direction.

Anti-Semitism continues. Political anti-Semitism today is complicated by the Arab-Israel conflict. However, it can no longer find even lingering sanction in the official teachings of Catholicism.

Further reading: James Carroll, *Constantine's Sword: The Jews and the Church* (New York: Houghton Mifflin, 2001); Bishops' Committee for Ecumenical and Interreligious Affairs, *The Bible, the Jews and the Death of Jesus* (Washington, D.C.: United States Catholic Bishops Conference, 2003); John Dominic Crossan, *Who Killed Jesus?* (San Francisco: HarperSanFrancisco, 1994); John Paul II, *Crossing the Threshold of Hope* (New York: Knopf, 1994); Miri Rubin, *Gentile Tales: The Narrative Assault on Late Medieval Jews* (New Haven, Conn.: Yale University Press, 1999); Edward A. Synan, *The Popes and the Jews in the Middle Ages* (New York: Macmillan,

1965); John Weiss, *Ideology of Death: Why the Holocaust Happened in Germany* (Chicago: Dee, 1996).

apocalypse (Gr.: *apocalypsis,* "revelation," "unveiling")

In the Jewish and early Christian apocalyptic literature, an otherworldly being portends an imminent cosmic catastrophe, which will usher in the End Time and God's triumph over the forces of EVIL. Apocalypses are characterized by cryptic references to earthly and transcendant events and dense symbolic imagery. According to the apocalyptic worldview, the present age is falling away from God at an alarming rate, and salvation is possible only by divine intervention. A faithful remnant are told to await their deliverance and the ultimate judgment upon and destruction of the ungodly majority.

Only one full apocalypse is part of the Hebrew canon, the Book of Daniel. There are many apocalypses among the PSEUDEPIGRAPHA: *1, 2 Enoch, 2 Baruch, 4 Ezra, Jubilees, Testament of Abraham.* The visions in Daniel 7–12, which refer symbolically to the "four kingdoms" (Babylon, Media, Ptolemaic, and Seleucid Greece), are thought to refer to the time of the Macabbean revolt (c. 168–64 B.C.E.) as a manifestation of the End Time. Daniel 7 mentions the famous "Son of Man," probably a reference to Michael, God's warrior angel. The Book of Daniel seems to have been intended to give comfort and hope during a time of persecution.

In the New Testament several minor apocalypses were incorporated into the Gospels: Mark 13, Matthew 24, and Luke 21. These revelations, put into the mouth of Jesus, refer to the coming destruction of Jerusalem, the abomination of desolation, the great tribulation, and the final judgment of God.

The Book of Revelation is modeled on Daniel. The revealer is John of Patmos (not the author of the Gospel of John). Its guiding image is the number seven (seven churches, seals, and trumpets), a reference that the End Time will be like a new seven-day creation. The Son of Man figure is now clearly associated with Jesus. The "great beast" undoubtedly refers to Nero, who, according to Tacitus, was the first to persecute Christians. In the Hebrew and Aramaic number system the letters of the title *Neron Caesar* add up to 666, the mark of the beast. Revelation ends with the eschatological vision of the loosening of Satan, the battle of Armageddon (referring back to the destruction of Megiddo by the Assyrians), and the inauguration of a new heaven and a new earth.

Revelation became the foundation stone for the historical dispensationalism of JOACHIM OF FIORE (c. 1135–1202) and the Irish Protestant divine John Nelson Darby (1800–1882). Contrary to many who want to turn Revelation into an army manual for the End Time, its underlying theme is a call for patient and abiding faith (*hypomōnē*) in the midst of persecution (1:9).

Further reading: John Barclay and John Sweet, *Early Christian Thought in its Jewish Context* (Cambridge: Cambridge University Press, 1996); Norman Cohn, *Cosmos, Chaos, and the World to Come: The Ancient Roots of Apocalyptic Faith* (New Haven, Conn.: Yale University Press, 1995); John Joseph Collins, *Daniel: A Commentary on the Book of Daniel* (Minneapolis: Fortress, 1993); H. H. Rowley, *The Relevance of Apocalyptic* (London: Lutterworth, 1963); Timothy P. Webber, *Living in the Shadow of the Second Coming* (Chicago: University of Chicago Press, 1987).

Apollinaris of Laodicea (c. 315–392) *bishop and theologian*

Apollinaris was an extreme opponent of Arius; he stressed the divinity of Christ over his humanity. He and his father, the priest and rhetorician Apollinaris of Alexandria, were supporters of the Council of Nicaea and befriended ST. ATHANASIUS OF ALEXANDRIA on his return from exile. The father wrote biblical poems in Homeric style, and the son wrote Gospel dialogues.

Apollinaris is associated with the formula "One nature of the Logos made flesh." His opponents— Sts. BASIL THE GREAT, GREGORY OF NYSSA, and GREGORY OF NAZIANZUS—claimed that Apollinaris denied that there was a human subject or rational soul in Christ and that his divine nature took over. Apollinarianism was censured at the Council of EPHESUS (351), the Council of CONSTANTINOPLE I (381), and by a synod in Rome under Pope Damasus I (r. 366–384). For the orthodox the issue is fully resolved by the decree of the Council of CHALCEDON (451), which declared that the Lord Jesus Christ is "consubstantial with the Father as to his divinity and consubstantial with us as to his humanity" and that the two natures unite to form one person, the Christ. In brief, Christ is fully human and fully divine. Apollinaris's ideas live on in the "Monophysite" churches, like the Coptic Church.

Further reading: G. L. Prestige, *St. Basil the Great and Apollinaris of Laodicea* (London: S.P.C.K., 1956); Charles E. Raven, *Apollinarianism* (New York: AMS, 1978).

apostle (Gr.: *apostolos,* "one sent out")

The earliest Christian use of the word *apostle* occurs in the writings of St. PAUL (1 Cor. 12:28). Paul used the word broadly to refer to any missionary, man or woman, who bears the good news of the death and resurrection of the Lord. Paul also used the term in a polemic against those who denied he was a true apostle. He bases his apostolic authority on having seen the risen Christ as had James, Peter, and others in Jerusalem (Rom. 1:1; Gal. 1:1,19).

In the Gospel of Luke the term is used more specifically to refer to the group of the 12 original followers of Jesus (6:13–16). The election of Matthias to replace Judas Iscariot lists the criteria for being an apostle: a man who accompanied Jesus since his baptism in the Jordan by John and a witness to the RESURRECTION (Acts 1:21–22). The different use of the term affects the contemporary debate over the role of women as both apostles and disciples of Jesus from the earliest times.

In later New Testament writings and the early church the term continued to be restricted to one of the 12, or to someone who was selected by one of the 12 to carry on the work of the predecessor. This standard frames the arguments about APOSTOLIC SUCCESSION, which began in the second century and continues to this day. Likewise, a link to one of the 12 became a criterion for the inclusion of a book into the CANON of the New Testament. The *Didache,* or Teaching, of the Twelve Apostles however, retained the earlier, broad understanding of the word (11:3–6).

In later times outstanding missionaries, who established churches among formerly unevangelized peoples, came to be called apostles. Thus, Sts. CYRIL AND METHODIUS are called Apostles of the Slavs, and St. PATRICK is called the Apostle of Ireland. At VATICAN COUNCIL II, all Catholics, clerical and lay alike, were called to partake in the APOSTOLATE, the transmission of the saving message of the Gospel to the world, according to each person's vocation in life.

The Eastern Churches have a special, liturgical use of the word. It refers to a selection from one of the Epistles or the Book of Acts that is read in the first part of the LITURGY. Among contemporary Pentecostals, the term is applied to those who are responsible for establishing and offering leadership to multiple congregations on the theory that those who do the work of an apostle deserve the title and the acknowledgement that goes with it. Pointing to Ephesians 4: 11–13, Pentecostals teach that apostles are one part of the fivefold leadership that any biblical church must have.

Further reading: Bill Hamon, *Apostles and Prophets and the Coming Moves of God* (Santa Rosa Beach, Fla.: Christian International, 1997); Karen King, *The Gospel of Mary of Magdala: Jesus and the First Woman Apostle* (Santa Rosa, Calif.: Polebridge, 2001); John P. Meier, *A Marginal Jew: Companions and Competitors* (New

York: Doubleday, 2001); Walter Schmithals, *The Office of Apostle in the Early Church* (Nashville: Abingdon, 1969).

Apostles Creed   *See* CREEDS.

apostolate

Each segment of the Catholic family has its own special apostolate, or MISSION, in spreading or witnessing to the message of Christ to the world at large. BISHOPS, PRIESTS, and deacons are charged with administering the sacraments and preaching the Word, religious are charged with fulfilling the special missions of their orders, married lay persons with witnessing the sacrament of marriage and instructing engaged couples, and the laity in general with witnessing to the Gospel in their secular vocations and with participating in the ministries of the church, such as serving on pastoral councils, teaching the young and catechumens, and caring for the sick. In the civic sphere Catholics are urged to partake fully in political and social causes in order to promote the common good. In some cases, especially in LATIN AMERICA, AFRICA, and ASIA, nuns and lay catechists are the primary participants in the church's apostolate. They bring Communion to the people, conduct baptisms and worship, and even preach the word.

The word *apostolate,* with special reference to the laity, is widely used throughout the declarations of VATICAN COUNCIL II. The Decree on the Apostolate of the Laity (*Apostolicam Actuositatem*) was given prominent place at the council; it sparked increased participation of lay people in the liturgy and the life and mission of the church. Protestant reformers have sought to abolish the distinction between the laity and the clergy, largely by shrinking the latter's role. Catholicism, by contrast, has sought to expand the role of the laity through the apostolate by including them in the sacramental life of the church and in witness to

the word of salvation. In recent times, under the papacy of JOHN PAUL II, there were efforts to rein in the energies thereby released, but the impetus toward lay action in the ministry of Christ to the world remains at full throttle, especially in Latin America, Africa, and Asia, where there is a dire shortage of priests.

Further reading: Walter M. Abbott, *Documents of Vatican II* (New York: America Press, 1966); Bryan Froehle and Mary L. Gautier, *Global Catholicism: Portrait of a World Church* (Maryknoll, N.Y.: Orbis Books, 2003); Brian Garvey. *Bembaland Church* (Leiden: Brill, 1994).

apostolic letter   *See* ENCYCLICAL, PAPAL.

apostolic succession

When a church claims apostolic succession, it argues that its ecclesiastical officeholders derive their legitimacy from an unbroken line of clergy reaching back to the 12 apostles. The claim is especially important for the bishops, who have the power to ordain priests, who in turn confer all the sacraments to the faithful. Arguments over apostolic succession have figured in intra- and interchurch conflict for centuries.

Apostolic succession has three elements. First, the bishops' commission goes back to the Apostles. Second, bishops continue the functions of the apostles, most especially in conferring the sacraments to the faithful. Third, bishops succeed in the sees first established by the apostles from the earliest times. In the opening paragraph of *Christus Dominus,* the Decree on the Bishops' Pastoral Office in the Church, the bishops at VATICAN COUNCIL II affirmed the tradition of apostolic succession deriving from the apostles appointed by CHRIST.

At the end of the first century Clement I describes how the Apostles appointed their successors (called bishops), who in turn appointed their own successors (1 *Corinthians* 44:2). However, the institution of one bishop per diocese, key to the notion of succession, was not developed until well into the third century. Besides, the terms *bishop* (*episcopos*) and *priest* (*presbyteros*) were interchangeable in early Christian writing.

Hegisippus (c. 175) is the first to use the technical term *succession* in reference to the see of Corinth (Eusebius, *Ecclesiastical History* 4.22.2). In the same century St. IRENAEUS OF LYON, in his disputes with the free-wheeling and wide-ranging Gnostic apostles, appeals to apostolic succession of bishops in fixed sees, especially to the bishops of Rome as the successors of Sts. PETER and PAUL (*Against Heretics* 3.3.1). The weakness of this argument is that though there is some late evidence that Peter and Paul were buried in Rome, there is no hard historical evidence that either one was called bishop of Rome in his lifetime.

A claim that there had been a breach in the line of succession of Anglican bishops was the grounds for LEO XIII's denial of the VALIDITY of ANGLICAN ORDINATION in 1896, although there have been attempts to reopen the discussion on this issue. The papacy has refused to comment on the validity of Swedish Lutheran orders. Many Protestant denominations recently have taken up the theme of apostolic succession and mutual recognition, most notably with the Porvoo Declaration in 1993.

Currently, apostolic succession is claimed by the Eastern Orthodox churches, most of whom claim a succession from one of the 12 apostles other than Peter; the Old Catholic churches, which broke with Rome after Vatican Council I; the Anglicans; and various other Protestant bodies. Some of these claims are recognized by Rome, some recognized as valid but irregular (the Old Catholics), and some not recognized, such as those of the Anglicans. Many Protestant groups, such as the Methodists, have bishops but make no claim to apostolic succession.

See also APOSTLE.

Further reading: Arnold Ehrhardt, *The Apostolic Succession in the First Two Centuries* (London: Lutterworth, 1953); Thomas M. Kocik, *Apostolic Succession in an Ecumenical Context* (New York: Alba House, 1996); Hans Küng, *Apostolic Succession: Rethinking a Barrier to Unity* (New York: Paulist Press, 1968); Ola Tjørhom, ed., *Apostolicity and Unity: Essays on the Porvoo Common Statement* (Grand Rapids, Mich.: Eerdmans, 2002).

apparitions of Mary   *See* MARY OF NAZARETH.

archaeology (Gr.: *arche,* "beginning" + *logos,* "study of")

Archaeology is the science of recovering the material remains of the past in order to understand the everyday life, thought, and beliefs of the people who left them. Finds can include texts, buildings, mosaics, pottery shards, and multifarious artifacts.

The archaeological discoveries of the past century pertaining to ancient Israel and Judaism, early Christianity, and the Byzantine periods have been just short of overwhelming. Here, the focus is on those aspects that illuminate the rise of Christianity and its relationship to the surrounding culture.

The methods of archaeology have burgeoned and advanced, from finding and deciphering texts (e.g., the Rosetta Stone) and using geological surveys to explain findings, to dating sites via subtle changes in pottery shapes and scripts, to carbon 14 analysis, to aerial surveys, and to complex analysis of multiple factors such as pollen and other ecological elements. The methods advance so quickly that archaeologists no longer dig up an entire single site, but dig trenches or small sections so that future scholars can use newer and better methods on established sites.

FIRST CENTURY FINDINGS

Among the most illuminating finds on the earliest CHRISTIAN era have been texts of New Testament books and other related writings by various communities and groups, some of which apparently held traditions different from those preserved in the canonical Gospels. Prominent among these are the many papyri found in a rubbish heap at the ancient city of Oxyrhynchus, 10 miles west of the Nile near the modern city of Behnesa. The discoveries began in 1897 and continued many years. The texts date from the late first to the seventh century and include Christian as well as non-Christian classical Latin and Greek texts. They include the famous P(apyrus) 52, the earliest known New Testament manuscript (John 18:31–33, 37–38), dating from around 125. Stunning discoveries include PP 654 and 655, which have alternate sayings of Jesus and point to different Gospel traditions. Only after the discovery of the Gnostic Nag Hammadi codices (see below) was it recognized that P 655 contains the Greek version of sayings 36–41 of the Coptic Gospel of Thomas. Other papyri of note are a tightly written text for a Christian amulet (P 840), an ecclesiastical calendar from around 535 (P 1357), and a hymn with the earliest known Christian musical notation dating from the late third century (P 1786).

A second major discovery was the Dead Sea Scrolls, found in 1947 by two Bedouin boys in cliff caves above Wadi Qumran near the Dead Sea. More scrolls were later found nearby at Wadi Muraba'at, relating to the revolt by bar Cochba in 132–35. These discoveries shook the world of scholarship and faith alike, spawning many wild speculations. The scrolls were written on parchment, papyrus, and copper sheets. One quarter of the texts are from the Hebrew Bible, all 39 of whose books are represented with the exception of the Book of Esther, as are the books of the Apocrypha contained in the Septuagint. Other fragments are *pesher*-like commentaries on biblical texts. Another set of texts relate to the beliefs of the Qumran community, which fled Jerusalem during the time of the Maccabees, claiming to represent a purer priestly line. The community had priestly rulers, conducted purificatory baptisms, held communal end-time meals, and preached the coming of both priestly and royal messiahs.

The community was almost certainly related to the Essenes described by Josephus and Philo of Alexandria. The texts shed much light on the context of the emerging Christian community in Palestine.

A third set of texts, like the first, also comes from Egypt. In 1945 Egyptian boys found 12 codices in a jar near the city of Nag Hammadi on the west bank of the Nile. The texts, mostly Gnostic in their tone, were most likely buried by Coptic monks from the nearby ancient monastery of Chenoboskion after Gnostic scriptures came under severe attack from such early orthodox teachers as Irenaeus of Lyons. The texts both verify the writings of the antiheretical fathers and demonstrate that early Christianity had many trajectories branching off of Jesus' teaching. Most important for the New Testament is the Gospel of Thomas, a collection of the sayings of Jesus similar to the postulated Gospel of Q, deduced from Matthew and Luke at the end of the 19th century (see Bible). The Nag Hammadi discoveries did not become widely known until the publication of the Jung Codex in 1956.

There have been important excavations yielding information about the first century at the Temple Mount in Jerusalem; Masada, the fortress of Herod overlooking the Dead Sea; the Herodium near Bethlehem; Herod's winter palace at Jericho; Caesarea Maritima, the Roman capital of Judea; and the tomb of Caiaphas in Jerusalem, the high priest, including his ossuary. The Theodotus Inscription testifies to a possible Greek-speaking synagogue in Jerusalem prior to 70 and sheds light on Greek-speaking Jews such as Stephen (Acts 7). In 1968 building contractors in northeastern Jerusalem unearthed the only first century evidence of a crucifixion ever found: a tomb with an ossuary bearing the crucified bones of one Jehohanan ben HGQWL. His feet were attached on the sides of an upright beam and were nailed through the ankles. Presumably, his arms were securely wrapped around the crossbeam.

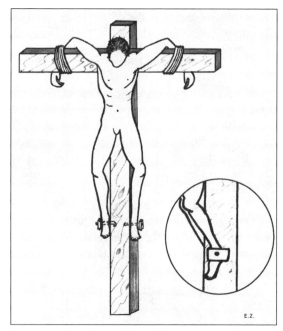

Reconstruction of crucifixion of ben HGQWL. The ankles were nailed to the main beam of the cross on the side, which is the most likely way Jesus was crucified. (Israel, first century) *(Drawing by Eitan Zias, with permission)*

There have been numerous discoveries in the Galilee of cities, synagogues, and house churches, as well as harbors, anchorages, and a boat along the Sea of Galilee. Of special note is the city of Sepphoris, some five miles from Nazareth, which Herod Antipas made his capital. The triclinum, or reception hall, synagogue, and Nile House contain outstanding mosaics. One figure in the triclinum has been designated the "Mona Lisa of the Mediterranean." The synagogue includes depictions of the Visitation of Angels to Sarah and Abraham and the Sacrifice of Isaac, which reoccur in early Christian art as the ANNUNCIATION and the Sacrifice of Jesus on the Cross. Parallels to Sepphoris were found in DURA EUROPOS in Syria, both in the use of images in a synagogue and the themes portrayed.

Of special importance is the discovery by Franciscan archaeologists of what many believe to be the original house of St. PETER in Capernaum, which was later converted into a house church and then reworked into an octagonal Byzantine chapel in the fifth century. Capernaum was Jesus' home after Nazareth (Matt. 4:13) and served as a center of Jesus' ministry in Galilee. Graffiti in Aramaic, Syriac, Greek, and Latin invoking the "Lord Jesus Christ" and Peter himself indicate that the house was a place of pilgrimage from the earliest times. The house, the first known to have been converted into a house church, or *domus ecclesiae,* around 90, was adjacent to the synagogue. There now seems little doubt that there was a lively interchange going on between Judaic instruction and worship and the early followers of Jesus. In her account of her travels in the Holy Land in 381–84, Egeria, an abbess from Spain or Gaul, recounts: "The house of the prince of the Apostles in Capharnaum was changed into a church; the walls, however, are still standing as they were" (*Pilgrimage of Egeria*).

LATER FINDINGS

The archaeology of the second century onward uncovers specifically Christian art and architectural themes emerging out of the Roman and Jewish matrices. At that time TERTULLIAN, still adhering to the Biblical Jewish prohibition of images (Exod. 24:4), roundly forbade images in *On Idolatry*. However, the evidence of the synagogues at Sepphoris and Dura Europos and of early Christian house churches, catacombs, burial art, sarcophagi, votive inscriptions, artifacts, and churches shows that the prohibitions of Exodus and the advice of Tertullian were given a liberal interpretation at best by Hellenistic Jews and Christians alike.

The art shows complete conformity to the late Hellenistic styles evident in Roman houses and mausolea such as those uncovered at Pompei. Very likely the same artists found clientele among Jews, devotees of Mithra and Isis, and Christians. The cemeteries and catacombs are notoriously pluralistic. Most Christian catacomb art begins with Jewish motifs, typically God's rescue of those in peril: Noah and the dove bearing an olive branch, Isaac rescued from sacrifice, Moses leading the Israelites through the Red Sea, Moses striking the rock for water, Jonah and the whale (often portrayed in the form of the mythical figure Endymion), Daniel in the lion's den, the three young men in the fiery furnace, and Susannah and the lecherous elders. These scenes may reflect typical prayers from early funeral liturgies: "Lord, receive the soul of . . . as you rescued Noah from the flood of destruction . . . Daniel from the lion's den, etc." The Jonah image is a very early instance of Christian TYPOLOGY sanctioned by Scripture itself: "For as Jonah was three days and three nights in the whale's belly; so shall the Son of Man be three days and three nights in the heart of the earth" (Matt. 12:40). Equivalent New Testament scenes matched these Old Testament tableaus: Jesus making wine at Cana, with the Samaritan woman, raising Lazarus, healing the paralytic, and so on. Of special note is the image of Jesus as the Good Shepherd, depicted either as the bucolic Apollo or as Orpheus with his lyre. Later in the third century, a mosaic shows Christ riding in a quadriga chariot as Sol Invictus (Unconquered Sun) in the Coemeterium Majus beneath St. Peter's.

Themes in third-century art include the *orans,* or figure praying with uplifted arms; Adam and Eve; the Adoration of the Magi; vine and branches (see John 15:5); loaves and fishes, sometimes shown at communal banquets and symbolizing the EUCHARIST; baptisms; and birds and flowers, perhaps signifying paradise. Recent analysts of the banquet scenes argue that some of the officiants offering the bread and cup are women. The inscriptions, most often accompanying burial sites, are simple and touching, such as, "Sabina, may you live in God" (Vatican Gallery). Class rank is almost never noted, although it is evident that rich and poor are buried at the same sites. Symbols also include palm branches,

fish in water (fish survived the Flood!), ships and anchors ("Heaven is my haven"), scales, and the ubiquitous Chi-Rho, or monogram of Christ.

Of special mention is the cemetery found underneath the high altar and nave of St. Peter's Basilica in Rome. In preparation for a burial site for PIUS IX in 1939, Vatican workmen discovered what turned out to be a complete cemetery including a *tropaion* or *martyrion*—martyr's altar—that archaeologists believe was built over the grave of ST. PETER around the year 90. These markers are typical of Greco-Roman heroes. Peter's, if the martyrion was his, was enclosed in the apse of Constantine's basilica over the site.

Some scholars claimed that they found Peter's actual bones near the martyrion. PAUL VI affirmed this belief in 1976. Other, perhaps more reliable, archaeologists have raised strong doubts, as the

Tomb trophaion of St. Peter beneath the high altar of St. Peter's Basilica. Tradition maintains that Peter was buried here. (Vatican City) *(Drawing by Frank K. Flinn)*

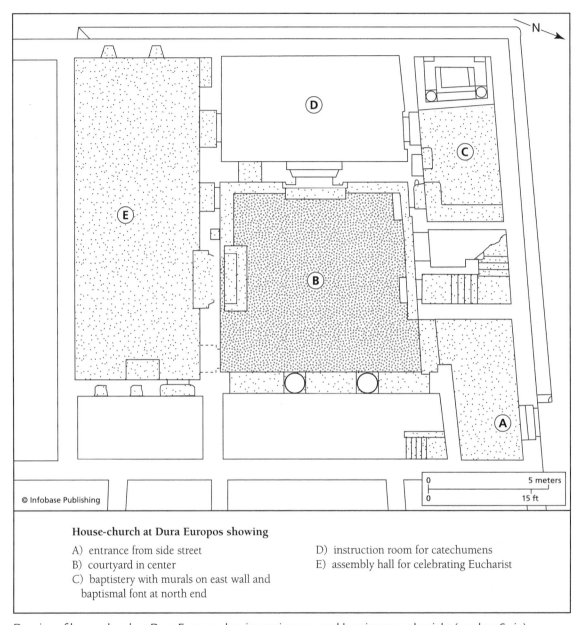

N

House-church at Dura Europos showing

A) entrance from side street
B) courtyard in center
C) baptistery with murals on east wall and
   baptismal font at north end
D) instruction room for catechumens
E) assembly hall for celebrating Eucharist

© Infobase Publishing

| 0 | 5 meters |
| 0 | 15 ft |

Drawing of house-church at Dura Europos showing main room and baptistery on the right (modern Syria)

bone collection included animals, a second man, and a woman (Peter's wife?). Others claim that a shrine at San Sebastiano on the Appian Way is Peter's tomb.

Another major find was a house church with a baptistery at Dura Europos on the Euphrates dating from around 250. It was located near the synagogue and shares similar biblical imagery.

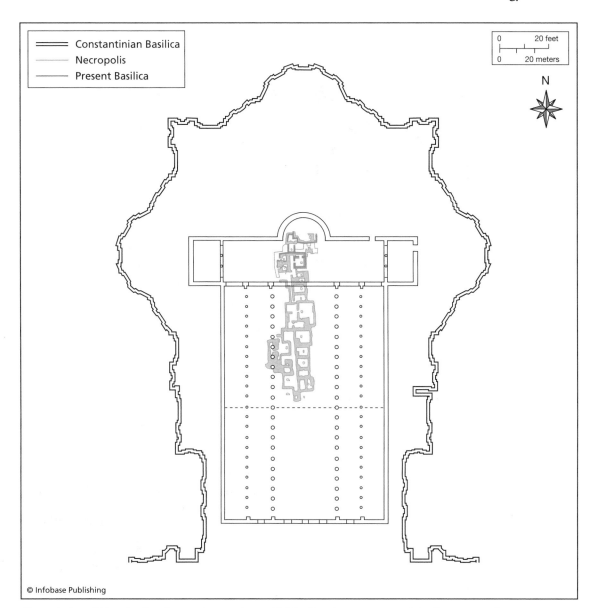

Ground plan of New St. Peter's superimposed over Old St. Peter's, grottoes, and the first-century Roman cemetery where tradition says St. Peter is buried (Vatican City)

Two rooms were modified into an assembly hall, and an adjacent room was converted into a baptistery with depictions of the Good Shepherd, Adam and Eve, Women at the Tomb, and Miracles of Jesus. There is a replica of the baptistery at Yale University.

Archaeology has also uncovered the earliest forms of church architecture after CONSTANTINE's

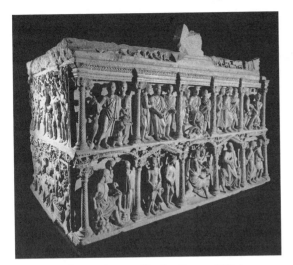

Side view of sarcophagus of Junius Bassus, 359. Lower register: Christ arriving in Jerusalem on Palm Sunday (center); flanked by Job and his wounds and Adam and Eve being evicted from the Garden of Eden (left); and Daniel in the lions' den and St. Paul led to his martyrdom (right). Upper register: Christ enthroned as a Roman emperor (center); flanked by the sacrifice of Isaac and the arrest of St. Paul (left); Christ before Pilate and before Herod (right). *(Erich Lessing/Art Resources, NY)*

Edict of Milan (313), which supported toleration for Christians. Through the influence of his mother, the emperor had earlier Roman basilicas converted to churches and undertook the construction of new ones in modified basilica form. Basilicas were long public halls used for imperial audiences, law courts, and even markets. Chief among these are the Old St. Peter's dismantled to make way for the new one, on Vatican Hill, St. John Lateran (a converted Roman structure), the Church of the Holy Sepulcher in Jerusalem, and the Church of the Nativity in Bethlehem. The nave of Old St. Peter's was modified with a cruciform transept between the apse and the rest of the church, with a narthex added at the front. This basic form became standard for most future Romanesque and Gothic churches. The following diagram shows the new St. Peter's superimposed on Constantine's basilica, in turn, superimposed over the circus of Nero.

Another type of early Christian archaeological find is the sarcophagus, a casket modeled on Roman prototypes. Christian sarcophagi have been found in Rome, Constantinople, Ravenna, and Arles dating from as early as 120. Most celebrated is the sarcophagus of Junius Bassus, prefect of Rome, who died around 359. The top tier shows Jesus handing on the law between two apostles (Peter and Paul), enthroned as emperor over the Roman mythological figure Coelus (Heaven). To the left are the capture of St. Paul and the sacrifice of Isaac; to the right Jesus is taken into custody and presented before Pilate. In the bottom tier Christ is riding into Jerusalem on Palm Sunday, probably a reference to the enthronement of Christ above. On the left are Adam and Eve and Job; on the right, Daniel in the lions' den and Paul being led to execution. The end reliefs show harvesting cupids (paradise?) and cupids as the seasons of the year. This and other sarcophagi show the influence of late Roman artistic styles and even mythological motifs.

Further reading: William H. C. Frend, *The Archaeology of Early Christianity* (Minneapolis: Fortress Press, 1998); Joachim Gaehde, "The Rise of Christian Art" in Geoffrey Barraclough, ed., *The Christian World* (New York: Abrams, 1981), 61–74; Margherita Guarducci, *The Tomb of St. Peter* (New York: Hawthorn Press, 1960); R. Krautheimer, *Early Christian and Byzantine Architecture* (Harmondsworth: Penguin, 1986); Eric M. Meyers, "Early Judaism and Christianity in Light of Archaeology," *Biblical Archaeology Review* (June, 1988), 69–79; E. Struthers, *The Iconography of the Sarcophagus of Junius Bassus* (Princeton, N.J.: Princeton University Press, 1990).

archbishop (Gk.: *arche,* "principal" + *episcopos,* "overseer")

Used since the fourth or fifth century, the term *archbishop* refers to a bishop or metropolitan from an archdiocese who presides over a province or region of the church, comprised of subordinate dioceses. Originally the title seems to have been reserved for PATRIARCHS or holders of prominent sees such as

Jerusalem, Antioch, Alexandria, CONSTANTINOPLE, or Rome. Later it was extended to any metropolitan or primate who presided over a province of suffragan (subordinate) bishops. Historically, archbishops exerted considerable power over church governance within their jurisdiction, including the selection of clergy for the church. By today many of these powers have been either transferred to the papacy or vested in regional or national conferences of bishops. In the *Code of Canon Law,* an archbishop or metropolitan has largely honorary or ceremonial rights unless duties are specifically prescribed by the Apostolic See, the pope (cnn. 435–38). These canons codify the policy of the papacy since PIUS IX to concentrate more and more power into the hands of the pope himself.

An archbishop receives the pallium, a wool stole, upon his installation as bishop of an archdiocese. The pope chooses archbishops as well as bishops, often after consulting with local leaders.

See also BISHOP; HIERARCHY.

Further reading: *Code of Canon Law* (Washington, D.C.: Canon Law Society of America, 1983); A. S. Popek, *The Rights and Obligations of Metropolitans* (Washington, D.C.: Canon Law Society of America, 1947).

architecture (Gr.: *archos-,* "chief" + *tektein,* "to construct")

In its primary meaning "architecture" is the science of making buildings or structures. This book focuses on the secondary meaning of the word: the method and style of making such structures. Catholic architecture concerns churches and cathedrals, shrines, sanctuaries, monasteries, grottoes, and other edifices that have been shaped by the beliefs first of Judaism (all the first "Christians" were Jews) and then of early Christianity in general and Catholicism in particular. Christian architecture evolved from house churches, to cemetery and martyrion churches, to monastic structures, and eventually to episcopal sees and cathedrals with their outlying parish churches.

BEFORE CONSTANTINE

The early followers of Jesus frequented ordinary Galilean and Judaean houses, public squares, and synagogues, and many may have visited the Temple in Jerusalem. The religious environment of the time was pluralistic, so they also must have experienced Greek and Roman temples, homes, and graveyards as well.

Jesus taught in synagogues (Matt. 4:23). The first synagogues were simple rooms for prayer, study of the Torah, and preaching. Perhaps they began as structures converted from one or more houses, as was the case with both the synagogue and the early house church at Dura Europos from around 250. After the destruction of the Temple in Jerusalem, synagogues became larger, with columns in the center, benches around the wall, and a niche in which to keep a scroll of the Torah. They probably took on many of the religious functions no longer possible in the Temple (apart from animal sacrifice), such as services for the new year and the Day of the Atonement. There is no evidence that the Judaean Christians, who thought of themselves as one with their religious environment, developed a separate architectural and iconic tradition. Peter's preaching began in the precincts of the Temple (Acts 2), and the first followers naturally partook of the Temple and synagogue.

Alongside their participation in Temple and synagogue, from the earliest times Jesus' followers began to use private houses for breaking bread, preaching, and teaching (1 Cor. 16:19; Phil. 1:2; Rom. 16:5; Col. 4:5; *see also* Acts 12:12, 16:40). Some of these houses came to be modified into what scholars call a *domus ecclesiae* (a house for use by the assembly of people).

There is strong evidence that Peter's house in Capharnaum had become a pilgrimage site by around 90 (Christian graffiti refer to "Lord, Jesus Christ" and "Peter" on plastered walls). In the fourth century the compound around the house was walled in, and the reception room was expanded and given an arched ceiling. The Spanish or Gaulish abbess Egeria visited this site in

381–84: "The house of the prince of the Apostles in Capharnaum was changed into a church; the walls, however, are still standing as they were" (*Pilgrimage of Egeria*). In the next century this structure was torn down and replaced with an octagonal Byzantine church, an architectural form typically used by the Byzantines for memorial sites (such as San Apollinare in Ravenna, Italy). The *domus ecclesiae* form achieved its pre-Constantinian peak at Dura Europos on the Euphrates, where several houses were modified into an assembly hall with a baptistery to the side (*see also* ARCHAEOLOGY).

Besides house churches, a number of warehouses, apartment houses, or other ordinary structures were converted into churches during the third century, when Christianity began to be tolerated, at least informally. Examples of this form are the churches of Sts. John and Paul and St. Clement in Rome. Churches were evolving larger, rectangular halls to accommodate the increasing number of Christians and the more elaborate liturgies (*see* LITURGY).

Baptistery at Dura Europos, which shows narrative scenes from the Gospels, including women at the tomb, Jesus' miracles, the Good Shepherd, plus other early Christian symbols *(reproduction at Yale University Art Gallery Dura-Europos Collection)*

UNDER CONSTANTINE

Following his Edict of Milan (313), which officially tolerated Christianity for the first time, CONSTANTINE set in motion a massive church building program throughout the empire. The architectural form his builders followed with remarkable consistency was that of the late Hellenistic BASILICA, examples of which have been found at Leptis Magna and Timgad in North Africa. Basilicas were originally imperial audience halls, halls for law courts, and even marketplaces. The form included an entrance hall (narthex), a nave sometimes colonnaded with one or two side aisles, a clerestory for windows above the nave, and an apse for a statue, throne, or meeting place for dignitaries. Often basilicas were entered through an atrium surrounded by a colonnade with its own entrance gate and steps leading up to it. Without doubt Constantine ordered his architects to use a version of his own audience hall that he had built in Trier, Germany, around 310. The first churches they constructed were St. John Lateran (314–16), which was built as and still is the episcopal seat of the bishop of Rome, and the Old Church of St. Peter on Vatican Hill (317–24), which was built as a martyrion basilica to honor the supposed remains of St. Peter (*see also* ARCHAEOLOGY). St. John Lateran had immense proportions for its day—98 feet high, 180 feet wide, and 246 feet long; it symbolized the audience hall for Christ the heavenly king and represents the first, fateful step in the imperialization of the image of the Christ figure.

In 326 St. Helena Augusta made a pilgrimage to the holy sites in Palestine, some say as penance for her part in the assassination of her daughter-in-law and grandson, although that story is almost certainly window dressing. She claimed to have found the true CROSS, pieces of which are still enshrined at St. John Lateran. Inspired by her trip, she pressured Constantine into a massive building program in the East. The results were the Church of the Holy Sepulcher, a martyrion basilica incorporating the tomb of Jesus, the Church of the Nativity in Bethlehem, plus the smaller basilicas at

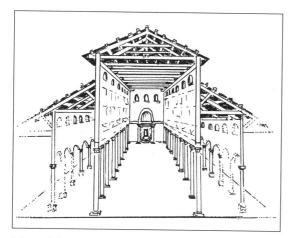

View of the nave of Old St. Peter's looking toward the grotto of the apse, which led to the tomb of St. Peter (Rome, Italy) *(drawing by Frank K. Flinn after 16th-century sketch)*

Mamre near Hebron and on the Mt. of Olives (the Eleona Church). Many of these structures have been radically modified over the years.

Constantine was also responsible for the mausolea churches in Rome for his mother (Sts. Peter the Deacon and Marcellinus) and for his daughter Constantina (Church of the Apostles/St. Sebastian). His crowning achievements were the two major churches in his new capital city of Constantinople: Hagia Eirene (Holy Peace) and the original HAGIA SOPHIA (Holy Wisdom). After Herod's Temple, the new Hagia Sophia built by Justinian (527–65) set the standard for all churches and mosques to come. The church was converted into a mosque by the Muslim conquerors and served as the standard by which the great Turkish architect Sinan (1489–1588) measured his own edifices.

Three variations were often incorporated into the basic basilica design: a centralized dome, based on Hadrian's Pantheon, an octagon, and the expansion of the apse. The centralized forms (rotunda, hexagon, octagon, or square) had often been used for mausolea in Rome, and the rotunda was employed for the anastasis of the Church of the Holy Sepulcher in Jerusalem. In the fourth to sixth centuries the octagon became very common in Greece and elsewhere, as in the redesigned House of St. Peter at Capharnaum and at San Vitale in Ravenna. The number 8 symbolized both the day of RESURRECTION after the seven days of creation and, symbolically, paradise and eternity itself. Apse expansion and the rotunda form encouraged the increased use of mosaics in church art. The San Vitale design survives in Charlemagne's chapel at Aachen (Aix-la-Chapelle) built around 800.

Scene of pilgrims entering the tomb of Christ, Church of the Holy Sepulchre, Jerusalem. Worshippers have to kneel down in order to enter the cave and touch the marble slab that covers the rock where Jesus' body was laid. *(Steven C. Scharre)*

Exterior view, Arian Baptistery, Ravenna, showing the classical octagonal design (Ravenna, Italy) *(drawing by Frank K. Flinn)*

Of special note are early baptisteries. The earliest preference was for baptism in running streams or in the sea (Mark 1: 9; Acts 8:36; *Didache* 7). Next in preference was total immersion in a fountain or bath-sized tank (Tertullian, *Baptism* 4). Total immersion recalled the abyss of the Flood or the Red Sea, and reemergence into the light of day reenacted the death and resurrection of Jesus (Rom. 6:1–5). Here the covered and ornamented baptistry at Dura Europos takes pride of place (*see* ARCHAEOLOGY). Some baptisteries were attached to their churches, and some were freestanding. The shapes were multifarious: rectangle, square, cross, octagon, circle, and cloverleaf. Special sites include the cruciform shape found at Mamshit in the Negev, the Donatist baptistery at Timgad, Algeria, and the two mosaic-covered baptisteries at Ravenna, one built by the orthodox and one by the Arian Ostrogoth Theodoric (c. 455–526).

CAROLINGIAN TO ROMANESQUE

The Byzantine style continued during the Carolingian dynasty, as can be seen clearly at the imperial chapel at Aachen. The basilica form originally had a flat wooden roof. In the late Carolingian and Ottonian periods, the basic form of the church changed into what we now know as the Romanesque. It was noted for 1) its high ceilings and barreled vault, which demanded thick walls and small windows; 2) the development of single and twin towers, often along with an ornamented façade; 3) the extension and amplification of the transept; and 4) the extension of the apse into an ambulatory with side chapels. The last change resulted from the increasing daily celebrations of the Eucharist by priests who received stipends from individuals to say Mass for the souls of their dead loved ones. The Romanesque eventually took two directions, one lean, the other ornamented.

With each new foundation, monks from Cluny spread the lean Romanesque style throughout Europe. When first built Cluny was the largest church in Christendom. The Cluniac and especially the later Cistercian monks insisted on sparseness and simplicity of form and ornament, as at the Abbey of Fontenay. Other abbey churches moved in the direction of more ornament, especially in the elaborate tympana on the façade and the capitals atop the pillars in the main nave. St. Madeleine, at Vézelay, in Burgundy, illustrates this tendency well.

Other noted Romanesque churches include the cathedral of Speyer, the pilgrimage church of San Juan Compestello in Spain, and the cathedral and baptistery of Pisa. In different regions the Romanesque merged with the Norman and even Moorish styles, as in the cathedral of Cefalù in Sicily.

GOTHIC

With the rise of Gothic, something new entered Christian architecture. Romanesque architects had already used arched and ribbed vaults, but the anonymous architects and craftspersons of the great Gothic CATHEDRALS (St. Denis, Chartres, Notre Dame in Paris, Rheims, Westminster, Milan, etc.) combined those two elements with the flying buttress, vast expanses of filtered light in stained glass, and the spire to create an architectural reality that was new in both a spiritual and material sense.

The key figure was Abbot SUGER, chief adviser to Kings Louis VI (1108–37) and VII (1137–80) of France, who began the Gothic revolution with the renovation of the chancel and apse of the royal

Abbey of St. Denis north of Paris. Suger employed symbolism that merged the Neoplatonic mystical light theology of Dionysius the Pseudo-Areopagite (c. 500) with the Old/New Testament TYPOLOGY of the epistle to the Hebrews. The typological schema—encompassing the mirrors of nature, history, learning, and morals—became central to the construction and experience of the medieval Gothic cathedral.

Suger's use of lavish ornament, gems, brocades, gold, and silver was meant, as he states in an inscription on the central West portal, "to bring light to minds, allowing them to journey from the [reflected] lights [of this world] to the True Light,

Flying buttresses, Abbey Church of St. Denis, north of Paris. The Abbot Suger began the Gothic renaissance at this abbey. *(Photo by Frank K. Flinn)*

where Christ is the True Door." Entering into the cathedral was entering into the womb of the heavenly Jerusalem, the church, the Bride of Christ, all of which symbols were summed up in the Blessed Virgin Mary. Hence, most medieval cathedrals, like Chartres, were dedicated to the Virgin.

The multiple flutes of the portals allowed for sculptures of Old Testament and New Testament prophets and saints and the personification of virtues and vices, the seven liberal arts, and the seasons of the year, that is, the sum of sacred and profane learning from the ancient world. Following the prototypes of Romanesque cathedrals, the central portal was always a scene of the Last Judgment, with Christ sitting in majesty. The flying buttress permitted the redistribution of the weight of the ceiling away from the inner walls, allowing them to become thinner. This in turn allowed for the ceiling to be higher, which, in turn, enabled the architects to add an upper clerestory of windows, which let in still more light. Upon entering, the viewers eye is taken both forward to the altar and upward to the vault, itself a material reflection of the spiritual vault of heaven.

Not everyone approved of Suger's lavishness. St. BERNARD OF CLAIRVAUX excoriated Suger for spending so extravagantly on a church while neglecting the condition of the poor and sick.

RENAISSANCE TO BAROQUE

If the Gothic reached heavenward and beyond time from the soaring cruciform shape of the church, the Renaissance took the measure of man. Whereas Suger took his symbolic numbers from theology (Trinity: trifold portals, trifolium window lights, etc.), the Renaissance architect took his numbers from nature (Pythagorean musical ratios, Fibonacci series, the Golden Ratio, etc.). Most of the architects of medieval cathedrals remain anonymous, but we know almost all the names of the architects from the Renaissance on. Great architects such as Filippo Brunelleschi (1337–1446), Leon Battista Alberti (1406–72), and Andrea Palladio (1508–80) revived the principles of perspective and geometrical proportion

Sky view showing Giovanni Lorenzo Bernini's baroque colonnade, St. Peter's Basilica *(Scala/Art Resource, NY)*

Baroque cathedral, Altersheim, Switzerland, showing ornate and curvilinear style of the period *(photo by Frank K. Flinn)*

of the Roman architect Vitruvius. The circle rather than the cross became their humanist architectural ideal, a model best seen in the celebrated drawing "Vitruvian Man" by LEONARDO DA VINCI.

Brunelleschi employed mathematical perspective in his construction of the church of San Lorenzo in Florence, and the dome for the Duomo Santa Maria del Fiore has the same diameter (43 m) as the Pantheon in Rome. The cupola became the paradigm of all future ecclesiastical domes, including MICHELANGELO's dome for ST. PETER'S BASILICA in Rome. Many Renaissance façades were added on to Romanesque and Gothic naves, but without the twin towers, and ground plans were designed according to the Golden Ratio or Section (a line cut such that the

smaller section is to the larger as the larger is to the whole), a ratio taken from the Pantheon, whose horizontal lines form a Golden Section. The façade of Alberti's Santa Maria Novella in Florence is a lesson in the proportions of harmonic progression.

Renaissance architecture passed rapidly into the baroque with an interlude in Mannerism. The baroque took the classical vocabulary of the Renaissance and transformed it into a new architectural medium. Long narrow naves were replaced with circular and broader structures with a dramatic use of light and darkness, called *chiaroscuro* in Italian. Ornament became opulent with the use of faux marbling, plaster and stucco, dramatic altars, and side chapels. Often trompe l'oeil ceiling paintings reach to the high heavens and flow down the walls terminating in stucco sculptures. Baroque art and architecture were shaped by the directives of the Council of TRENT on what is appropriate in Catholic art and devotion. The elevation of the altar, along with the status of the priesthood, to a prominent level was one of the effects.

The mediating prototype of the Renaissance to baroque style is St. Peter's in Rome, which began as a circular Greek cross in the designs of Danato Bramante (1444–1514) and Michelangelo, to which Giacomo della Porta added the nave and Giovanni Lorenzo Bernini (1598–1680) the fully baroque colonnade.

The once proportional and rectilinear façades of the classic Renaissance church succumbed to the curvilinear volutes of high baroque, as in San Carlo alla Quattro Fontane by Francesco Borromini (1599–1677) in Rome. The baroque style reached an apex with the ceiling trompe l'oeil fresco *The Triumph of the Name of Jesus* by Giovanni Battista Gaulli (1639–1709) in Il Gesu, Rome, and the audaciously ornamental rococo pilgrimage church of Vierzehnheiligen in Franconia, Germany, designed by Johann Balthasar Neumann (1687–1753).

The baroque and its late incarnation, rococo, established the style of the great colonial churches and missions in the Philippines and the Americas. The great Latin American cathedrals reformulated the Romanesque twin tower motif, which they wedded to the baroque dome while incorporating floral motifs from local indigenous cultures. The cathedral of Mexico City is a prime example of Latin American baroque. The same baroque elements were employed in the many Jesuit compound missions of South and Central America and the Franciscan missions of California and Texas.

Cathedral Church of Mexico City. All the architecture in the Americas was influenced by European baroque and rococo styles. *(www.shutterstock.com)*

Assumption Cathedral, built in a Federalist style, with spare baroque features and a Greek temple facade *(Baltimore, Maryland) (Z24.1619 Basilica of the Assumption—c. 1965 the Maryland Historical Society)*

Mission San Jose, in San Antonio, Texas, is a prime example of a simplified mission baroque style.

RECOMBINATION AND REVIVAL

It is somewhat difficult to describe the church architecture of the late 18th and the 19th centuries. In place of radical innovations there were new and inventive combinations of earlier periods (classical, Romanesque, Gothic, Renaissance, and baroque) into some surprisingly pleasing churches. The Basilica of the Assumption in Baltimore, designed by Benjamin Latrobe (1764–1820), was the first major church built after the U.S. Constitution went into effect in 1789. Latrobe was also the architect of the White House and the Capitol in Washington. Often described as Neoclassical, Assumption is really a satisfying combination of a spare baroque church with a Greek temple facade, whereas St. Patrick's Cathedral in New York is straightforward Gothic Revival (*see* CATHEDRAL). Of special note among Neo-Romanesque revivals is the Cathedral Basilica of St. Louis, Missouri, which contains more mosaic surface than any other church in the world.

TWENTIETH CENTURY

The 20th century brought many new innovations in Catholic architecture. New churches were shaped both by new religious forces like the LITURGICAL MOVEMENT but also by new materials, especially reinforced concrete. As if to signal a new artistic age, JOHN XXIII commissioned the Italian sculptor Giacomo Manzù (1908–91) to cast new doors, called the Doors of Death, for the far left entrance to St. Peter's in Rome. Following VATICAN COUNCIL II, Pope PAUL VI expressly embraced modern forms of art and architecture as appropriate for liturgical and ecclesiastical use.

One of the first churches to combine both liturgy and concrete was Notre-Dame du Raincy in Le Raincy, France, designed by August Perret (1874–1954). It transformed Gothic elevation and glass into something entirely new. In a similar vein, the renovated Church of Our Lady of Loretto at St. Mary's College, Notre Dame, Indiana, reflected liturgical space according to the new directions in the Constitution on the Liturgy at Vatican Council II. A circular colonnade highlights the key ritual actions of the preaching of the Word (the ambo), the Eucharistic table, and an open step-down baptismal font.

Perhaps the most revolutionary new architectural form was the chapel of Notre-Dame-du-Haut at Ronchamps, in the Franche-Comté, France, by Le Corbusier (Charles Edouard Jeanneret, 1887–1965). The small Expressionist chapel is both severely simple and surreal, delicate, and massive, with broken planes and irregular window shafts letting in varying light. Many people of faith and no faith find serenity there.

Le Corbusier's chapel had direct influence on two of the most important recent additions to Catholic ecclesiastical architecture, the cathedral of Los Angeles, California, and Dio Padre Misericordioso. Designed by the noted Spanish architect José Rafael Moneo, the Cathedral of Our Lady of the Angels was meant to reflect the many-faceted ethnic and cultural diversity of modern Los Angeles. The gull-winged church of Dio Padre Misercordioso by noted American architect Richard Meier was first commis-

Neoromanesque Cathedral Basilica of St. Louis, which has the most mosaic painting of any church in the New World (St. Louis) *(photo by John Huston)*

Interior view of the Church of Our Lady of Loreto, St. Mary's College, Notre Dame, Ind. Renovated in 1992 according to new liturgical directions of Vatican Council II. Note baptistery within the sanctuary on the right. *(architects: Woollen, Molzan and Partners; photo: Balthazar Korab)*

Nortre-Dame-du-Haut, 1950–54, by noted architect Le Corbusier. This church is an influential watershed in contemporary church architecture. *(© 2006 Artists Rights Society (ARS), New York ADASP, Paris/FLC/Anthony Scibilia/Art Resource, NY)*

Cathedral of Our Lady of the Angels, 2002. This modernist cathedral was designed by the Spanish architect José Raphael Moneo to reflect the many-faceted cultural diversity of Los Angeles. (Los Angeles) *(photo by George Machados, with permission)*

sioned by Pope JOHN PAUL II to celebrate the year 2000 church Jubilee. Both churches, unlike many of their predecessors, are completely open to outside light from multiple sources, including the ceiling, as if to let the modern world experience the Light of Christ in its present spiritual darkness.

Further reading: Richard Krautheimer and Slobodan Curcic, *Early Christian and Byzantine Architecture* (New York: Pelican, 1992); Jeannette Mirsky, *Houses of God* (Chicago: University of Chicago Press, 1965); Nicholas Pevsner, *An Outline of European Architecture* (Harmondsworth: Penguin, 1970); Bernhard Schütz, *Great Cathedrals of the Middle Ages* (New York: Abrams, 2002); L. Michael White, *The Social Origins of Christian Architecture: Building God's House in the Roman World* (Valley Forge, Pa.: Trinity, 1996); L. White, "House Churches," *Oxford Encyclopedia of the Archaeology of the Ancient Near East* (Oxford: Oxford University Press, 1997) 3:118–121.

Arianism

Arianism was an ancient Christian HERESY named after Arius of Libya (d. 336), a student of Lucian of Antioch (d. 312), who taught that the person of the Son was subordinate to the person of the Father who created him. Arius was ordained deacon by Peter of Alexandria (d. 311) and priest by Achillas (312). He was put in charge of the Baucalis, a chief church of Alexandria. He traveled to Syria and Palestine to seek supporters, among whom he found EUSEBIUS OF CAESAREA, the famous church historian, and Eusebius of Nicomedia (d. c. 342). In his letter to the latter Arius wrote: "We are persecuted because we say, 'the Son has a beginning, but God [the Father] is without beginning.'" (Letter to Eusebius of Nicomedia).

St. ATHANASIUS OF ALEXANDRA fought against Arius's teaching, which was condemned at the Council of Nicaea (325). The council declared the Son to be "begotten but not made" and equal to or "of the same being" (homoousios) with the Father. Arius was exiled to Illyria.

Arianism has a long life and split into several branches, some claiming that the Son is dissimilar to the Father, some similar but less than, and others both similar and dissimilar. ST. JEROME lamented that the whole world had become Arian. Cardinal JOHN HENRY NEWMAN noted that while many bishops became Arian, the laity retained the orthodox faith. The Christian emperors were often Arian, since the lower status of Christ implied the lower status of bishops in relation to the emperor, who traced his authority from the eternal Creator Father. The kings of the invading Vandals were mostly Arians and repressed orthodox Christianity until defeated by Justinian's general Belisarius in 534. Arianism spread as far as the Goths through the missionary Uphilas (311–81) but lost out when the Franks converted to Catholicism in 496. Arianism was revived in the thought of Isaac Newton and many of his successors at Cambridge. Most Deists and Unitarians may be said to be Arian in their views of Jesus.

Further reading: Arius, "Letter to Eusebius of Nicomedia," in Theodoret, Ecclesiastical History 1.4 (available online); Maurice F. Wiles, The Archetypal Heresy: Arianism through the Centuries (Oxford: Clarendon Press, 1996); Rowan Williams, Arius: Heresy and Tradition (Grand Rapids, Mich.: Eerdmans, 2002).

Aristotle (384–332 B.C.E.) Greek philosopher

Perhaps the greatest philosopher and systematizer of knowledge in the ancient Greek world, Aristotle also had enormous influence on medieval Catholic theologians, who referred to him as "the Philosopher." Aristotle was a Macedonian who studied under Plato (472–347 B.C.E.) in Athens, tutored Alexander the Great (356–323 B.C.E.), and founded his own school, the Lyceum, in Athens; his followers were known as peripatetics. Whereas PLATO was an "idea-ist," Aristotle was a realist. Plato's thoughts have come down to us in dialogues, Aristotle's in treatises, although he also wrote dialogues, now lost.

Aristotle's writings encompass the whole of ancient learning with the exception of mathematics. His main treatises cover the fields of ethics, politics, logic, physics, metaphysics, poetics (literature), interpretation, and rhetoric; several shorter treatises deal with the natural philosophy (science) of the heavens, parts of animals, generation and corruption, and the soul. Plato viewed the empirical world as a "copy," or imitation, of the Ideas to which the Demiurge referred in fashioning the universe. Aristotle said that ideas do not float "up there somewhere" but exist only in individual, concrete objects. Objects are the conjunction of form and matter. To explain the conjunction of form with matter he developed a theory of causation. What makes the world go is ultimately a Prime Mover, or First Cause, an impersonal being who is, in Aristotle's words, a circular "thinking of thinking." Aristotle calls the Prime Mover "God" and takes the natural world to be eternal, that is, uncreated. The natural world imitates this circularity as the oak tree generates the acorn which in turn generates the tree. Every object has a formal, efficient, final, and material cause. The carpenter (efficient) fashions wood (material) from a pattern (formal) so that people can sit on it (final).

Aristotle's logical studies established the categories that gave shape to all subsequent Western thought: substance and accident, subject and object, cause and effect, quantity and quality and so on. His logical system remained authoritative, although it was expanded by medieval logicians and given a new form by Gottlob Frege (1848–1925) and Bertrand Russell (1872–1970) at the end of the 19th century.

Early Christian thinkers, most of whom subscribed to a form of NEOPLATIONISM, suspected Aristotle of materialism. Nearly all traces of his writings disappeared in the Western Christian world by the fifth century with the exception of the logical treatises: the Roman Christian philosopher BOETHIUS (c. 480–524) uses the *Categories* and *On Interpretation*. But Aristotle's writings did not die. They were translated into Syriac by Christian writers, then into Arabic and Hebrew by Islamic and Jewish thinkers, and finally in the middle of the 12th century made their way into Latin in Spain. The encounter of ALBERTUS MAGNUS and THOMAS AQUINAS with Aristotle's thought led to the great renaissance of Christian theology in the high MIDDLE AGES. A renewed interest in Aristotle was sparked by LEO XIII's encyclical *Aeterni Patris* (August 4, 1879), which established Thomas Aquinas as the principal theologian of the Catholic Church.

Further reading: Aristotle, *The Complete Works of Aristotle,* 2 vols., ed. Jonathan Barnes (Princeton, N.J.: Princeton University Press, 1984); Jonathan Barnes, *Aristotle* (Oxford: Oxford University Press, 1982); Brian Davies, ed., *Thomas Aquinas: Contemporary Philosophical Perspectives* (Oxford: Oxford University Press, 2002); Richard Sorabji, ed., *Aristotle Transformed: The Ancient Commentators and Their Influence* (Ithaca, N.Y.: Cornell University Press, 1990).

Armageddon (Heb.: *har,* "mountain" + *megiddo,* "Meggido")

Armageddon is a prominent city mentioned in Revelation 16:16 as the scene of the final future battle between good and evil. Megiddo was a Canaanite and then Israelite stronghold overlooking the Plain of Jezreel. It figured heavily in the history of northern Israel and was destroyed and rebuilt many times. Eventually it came to sym-

bolize devastation and destruction (Judg. 5:19; 2 Kings 9:27; 23:29; Zech. 12:11). Revelation refers to Ezekiel 38–39, in which the invading nations will be defeated at Megiddo.

See also APOCALYPSE.

Further reading: Jean-Louis D'Aragon, "The Apocalypse," in *The Jerome Biblical Commentary,* ed. Raymond E. Brown (Englewood Cliffs, N.J.: Prentice-Hall, 1968), 467–493.

Armenian Catholic Church

The Armenian Catholic Church, one of the several Eastern-rite jurisdictions now in full communion with Rome, was formally organized in the 18th century as the outgrowth of several centuries of missionary activity by Roman Catholics among members of the Armenian Apostolic Church residing in Lebanon. Many important manuscripts of PHILO OF ALEXANDRIA, IRENAEUS OF LYONS (*Proof of Apostolic Preaching*), and St. Ephraim the Syrian (c. 306–73) are preserved only in Armenian.

The bishops in Armenia had separated from their colleagues in CONSTANTINOPLE when they found themselves unable to affirm the teachings promulgated by the Council of CHALCEDON (451) concerning the two natures of CHRIST. The Armenian position, traditionally termed Monophysitism, affirmed that Christ had only one nature, the divine. Chalcedon affirmed both the full human and full divine natures of Christ, united but not confused in one person. The Armenians argued that they were not against Chalcedon but simply not ready to embrace its wording. Many within other Christian communities considered the Armenians to be Monophysite heretics. Today Armenian Catholics often claim that the dispute was only about canon. 28 of Chalcedon, which granted primacy to the patriarch of Constantinople over the Armenian patriarch.

During the period of the Crusades, Armenians came into contact with Latin Christians who visited Lesser Armenia (Cilicia) on the southern coast of Turkey. In 1198, the church in Cilicia established an alliance with the bishop of Rome. That union proved unacceptable to most Armenians, but the issue became moot after the Mongol conquest of Cilicia in 1375.

Roman Catholics remained interested in union, and at the Council of FLORENCE (1415) the two churches published a union decree. Several Armenian congregations accepted papal authority. In 1742 the Armenian bishop Abraham Ardzivan (1679–1749) united with Rome. Seizing the moment, Pope Benedict XIV (r. 1740–58) established the Armenian Catholic Church as a formal body of believers and named Ardzivan their Catholicos patriarch. He took the name Abraham Pierre I, and his successors continue to add Pierre (or Bedros in Armenian) as part of their episcopal title. The church continued to use the old Armenian liturgy though making a few minor adjustments to resolve any theological questions.

The Armenian Catholic Church ran into immediate problems with the Ottoman authorities, who wanted all the Armenians in the empire to be under the Armenian Apostolic Church and its bishop in Constantinople. Only in 1829 did the government recognize the Catholic believers by permitting the naming of a second bishop who would reside near the sultan's court in Constantinople. In 1867, the two bishoprics were combined into a single patriarchal office in Constantinople.

The church was decimated when the Turks turned on the Armenian community at the end of World War I. Some 100,000 Armenian Catholics were murdered along with many of their Orthodox compatriots. After the fall of the empire, the patriarch relocated to Lebanon. During the next decades, many Armenians left the Middle East, settling in France, the United States, and Argentina. The present patriarch is Nerses Bedros XIX (1999–   ). Headquarters remain in Beirut, Lebanon, and the majority of the church's 150,000 members still reside in Lebanon and Syria. There are also dioceses in Turkey, Iran, Iraq, Egypt, Europe, and the United States. The church relates to the Roman church through the Congregation for the Oriental Churches.

Further reading: Donald Attwater, *The Catholic Eastern Churches* (Milwaukee: Bruce, 1937); Nikolaus Liesel, *The Eastern Catholic Liturgies: A Study in Words and Pictures* (Westminster, Md.: Newman Press, 1960); Ronald G. Roberson, *The Eastern Christian Churches—A Brief Survey*. 5th ed., (Rome: Pontifical Oriental Institute, 1995).

art   *See* ARCHAEOLOGY; ARCHITECTURE; PAINTING AND SCULPTURE; RELICS; UTENSILS, SACRED.

Ascension

The term refers to both the event described in the second article of the CREEDS, in which CHRIST "ascended into heaven to be seated at the right hand of the Father," and to the liturgical feast day held 40 days after Easter. The doctrine of the Ascension of Jesus as the Christ is based mainly on Acts 1:1–9, which recounts how the resurrected Jesus remained on earth for 40 days and then ascended into heaven from the Mt. of Olives. The Ascension affirms the belief in bodily RESURRECTION. Luke 24:50–53 seems to recount a different tradition. After appearing to the disciples at Emmaus, Jesus leads them out to Bethany, where he ascends into heaven.

Belief in the ascension, or apotheosis, of important religious and political figures was common in the ancient world. The BIBLE recounts many holy figures being taken up into heaven: Enoch (Gen. 5:24), Elijah (2 Kings 2:1–14), and, according to later Judaic tradition, Baruch, Ezra, and Moses. In the Greco-Roman world heroes such as Hercules and emperors such as Alexander the Great underwent an apotheosis, or elevation to the ranks of the gods, after their deaths.

In the New Testament Jesus' Ascension is seen as part of the cycle of his descent from a heavenly realm, incarnation, earthly ministry, death, harrowing of hell, resurrection in the flesh, reascent, and enthronement at the right hand of God as a vindication over his enemies (John 6:62; Heb. 1:3–4; Phil. 2:6–11). Similarly, the apocryphal wisdom literature also speaks of the descent and reascent of Wisdom, or Sophia (Sir. 24:8–12; 1 Enoch. 42:1–2).

By the fourth century the feast of the Ascension was celebrated on the sixth Thursday (40 days) after EASTER. Before the reform of the liturgy after VATICAN COUNCIL II, the Easter candle, lit at the Easter Vigil service, was extinguished on Ascension Thursday. The Ascension has figured prominently in Christian iconography as the affirmation of bodily life after death and the fulfillment of salvation. A noted painting of the Ascension by Tintoretto (1518–94) is in the Scuola di San Rocco in Venice.

Further reading: Peter Atkins, *Ascension Now* (Collegeville, Minn.: Liturgical Press, 2001); Brian K. Donne, *Christ Ascended* (Exeter: Paternoster, 1983); Douglas Farrow, *Ascension and Ecclesia* (Grand Rapids, Mich.: Eerdmans, 1999).

asceticism (Gk.: *askēsis,* "practice," "discipline")

The Greeks originally used the term *askēsis* to describe the practice and the associated discipline that athletes undertook in order to prepare for the Olympic and other games. The verb form also means "to strive." Greek philosophers, notably the Stoics, used the term to describe the moral discipline and purification of the soul from passions that one needs in order to engage in the philosophical life.

Christian asceticism has two aspects: a negative denial of self and the positive following of CHRIST in bearing the cross (Mark 8:34). Among ascetic disciplines advocated are 1) fasting (Matt. 6:16–18), 2) giving up one's possessions, and 3) chastity or celibacy (Matt. 19:12).

Early Christians applied the term *asceticism* to the bravery and self-denial a martyr demonstrated when faced with the threat of death (*Martyrdom of Polycarp* 18.3). Following the lead of the philosophers, the second-century Christian apologist Athenagoras of Athens extended the term to include the "discipline/practice of virtue" (*On the Resurrection of the Dead* 15).

In the second and third centuries, as martyrdom decreased, the ascetic ideal was taken up by desert monks and anchorites (*see* MONASTICISM). Some went to extreme lengths, but when monastic rules began to take shape, the great rule-givers (Sts. BENEDICT and BASIL) advised more moderate ascetic measures. The practices were often connected to the practice of repentance, or PENANCE for past sins.

Many theologians like AUGUSTINE OF HIPPO recommended ascetic practices to contain the concupiscence associated with the *calor genitalis* ("genital heat"). Though the Christian creed emphasizes that GOD created material and spiritual nature equally good, many modern commentators have argued that Augustine's line of thinking ended up alienating Christians from their bodies, healthy marriage, and simple sensual delight in physical living that necessarily accompanies life in the natural world.

Fasting and abstinence from certain foods became common among the desert monks of Egypt, Palestine, and Asia Minor and continued with the stricter monastic orders of the early medieval period such as the Carthusians, Cistercians, and Trappists. Ascetic practices also found a liturgical expression: beginning in the MIDDLE AGES all Christians were urged to fast and abstain from meat on Wednesdays and Fridays during the penitential seasons of Advent and Lent, on all Fridays throughout the year, and on rogation days and VIGILS.

The MENDICANT ORDERS in the Middle Ages developed an intense asceticism in their desire to imitate the suffering of the crucified Christ. St. FRANCIS OF ASSISI's mystical asceticism led to his receiving the STIGMATA. During the period of the DEVOTIO MODERNA, devout teachers like THOMAS À KEMPIS recommended ascetic practices for the laity as well as for clergy.

During the PROTESTANT REFORMATION, the reformers rejected stringent ascetical practices as not being in keeping with the spirit of the New Testament. Spiritual masters of the COUNTER-REFORMATION, like Sts. IGNATIUS OF LOYOLA and JOHN OF THE CROSS, geared asceticism into the direction of ministerial service, or of guiding the soul toward union with God.

VATICAN COUNCIL II turned Catholics' attention away from the external formalism that encroached on traditional ascetical practices toward the broader social practices of building community and developing a richer spiritual life. Penance is not an end in itself. The paschal fast looks to the joy of the RESURRECTION (*Sacrosanctum Concilium* 110, Constitution on the Sacred Liturgy). In the Apostolic Constitution on Penance *Paenitemini* (February 17, 1966) PAUL VI reduced the number of penitential days to Fridays, Ash Wednesday, and Good Friday. The Eastern Church generally continues to adhere to stricter norms of fasting and abstinence.

In contemporary life what once were called ascetical practices have now become emotional and spiritual disciplines to counteract the numerous addictions the modern world inflicts on believers. Questions of spiritual asceticism are also starting to emerge in the critique of consumerism and the devastation of the environment.

See also CELIBACY; PENANCE; MONASTICISM.

Further reading: *Asceticism Today* (Petersham: St. Bede's, 1991); John Behr, *Asceticism and Anthropology in Irenaeus and Clement* (Oxford: Oxford University Press, 2000); Everett Ferguson, *Early Christians Speak: Faith and Life in the First Three Centuries,* 2 vols. (Abilene: Abilene Christian University Press, 2002); Augustine Holmes, *A Life Pleasing to God: The Spirituality of the Rules of St. Basil* (London: Darton, Longman & Todd, 2000); Jerome Kroll and Bernard Bachrach, *The Mystic Mind: The Psychology of Medieval Mystics and Ascetics* (New York: Routledge, 2005).

Asia

Asia, or at least its western littoral, was the birthplace of Christianity, which began in first-century Palestine as a sect of Judaism, itself a western Asian religion. Asia Minor, Armenia, Syria, and other regions of the Asian continent hosted many of the most important early Christian communities and were a dynamic theater of theological development.

Because much of early Christian literature survived in Greek and then Latin texts, Western Christians are predetermined to think that the earliest trajectories of Christianity are Jerusalem, Antioch, Asia Minor, Greece, and Rome, in that order. This view neglects the other early trajectories that went from Jerusalem to Galilee, Syria, and Egypt and included other forms of Christianity, most especially Judaean Christianity, that later survived in such groups as the Ebionites and Elkasites. This entry recounts the spread of Christianity and Catholicism in various Asian countries in rough chronological order based on when Christianity and Catholicism arrived.

SYRIA AND CHALDEA (IRAQ)

We now know that early communities of followers of Jesus survived in the Galilee and Transjordan after the destruction of the temple in Jerusalem in 70. Most traces of these groups have disappeared owing to their heretical positions (from a later standpoint). Such were the Ebionites and Elkasites who left some mark in Transjordan and Mesopotamia. The later Syrian church centered itself in Edessa and developed a rich theological literature, including important biblical commentaries and the liturgical poetry of St. Ephraem the Syrian (c. 306–73) and Jacob of Sarug (c. 451–521). The Syrian church later split into western Nestorian and eastern Jacobite branches. The Jacobite tradition rejected the Council of CHALCEDON and remains

Monophysite in belief. Various forms of Syriac, derived from Aramaic, survive as the liturgical language of the West Syrian, Chaldean, Maronite, and Syro-Malabar rites.

The Syrian Catholic Church owes its origins to the time of the CRUSADES, when some Syrian Orthodox bishops developed warm relations with Catholics. There were various attempts at union ending at the Council of FLORENCE in 1439. In 1626 Jesuit and Capuchin missionaries began working in Aleppo. Many Syrians united with Rome; they elected a Catholic patriarch in 1662. The Catholic line ended in 1702, and Catholics were not favored under Ottoman Turkish rule. In the 1780s the Syrian Orthodox patriarch Michael Jarweh united with Rome and moved to Lebanon, where he established the important monastery of Sharfeh. The Turkish government recognized the Syrian Catholic Church in 1829. The seat of the patriarchate, first in Aleppo, was moved to Mardin, Turkey, in 1850. Today there are more than 100,000 Syrian Catholics in Syria, Lebanon, and Iraq. They follow the west Syrian rite and trace their eucharistic liturgy back to the Jerusalem liturgy of St. James.

Franciscan and Dominican missionaries began to operate in Baghdad in the 13th century. Temporary unions with Rome came and went. In 1552 a group of Assyrian bishops refused to recognize a Syro-Assyrian patriarch, elected the abbot Yuhanan Sulaka (d. 1555) instead, and sent him to Rome. Julius III (r. 1550–55) consecrated him bishop and appointed him Patriarch Simon VIII of the Chaldeans. The pasha of Amadya martyred Simon in 1555, but the church thrived nonetheless despite later persecution, especially during World War I.

Today there are more than 460,000 Chaldeans, mostly in Baghdad. They received protection from Saddam Hussein (1937–2006). After the Iraq War (2003–), they were once again being persecuted by the Sunni and Shiite Muslim population. The head of the church, called the Catholicos patriarch, is presently His Holiness Mar Rophael I

Bidawid. The Chaldeans use the ancient Syriac rite of Addai and Mari. There are two archdioceses in Iraq and Iran and members in Lebanon, Syria, and Turkey.

INDIA

The present-day Thomas Christians, also known as Syrian Malabar Christians, use the Syrian rite and trace their ancestry to St. Thomas the Apostle. This tradition (and according to legend, Thomas himself) passed through Edessa and Baghdad on its way to Southwest India. The early adherents were followers of NESTORIUS. The Alexandrine cosmographer Cosmas Indiopleutes attests to the presence of Christians in western India c. 550.

After the explorer Vasco da Gama (active c. 1496–1524) established Portuguese colonies at Goa and Cochin on the west coast of India, a majority of the Thomas Christians renounced Nestorianism at the regional Council of Diamper in 1559. Much of their liturgy was latinized, and later overzealous Jesuit missionaries further interfered with their rites and sparked a SCHISM. Carmelites later brought about a reconciliation with a majority of the community. The dissenters affiliated with the Jacobite Syrian Orthodox Church of Antioch and maintain close relations with the Church of England and the Church of South India.

St. FRANCIS XAVIER established the Jesuit mission in India in 1542. In 1603 the Jesuit missionary Roberto DeNobili adopted the ascetic lifestyle of a Brahman *sanyasi* in hopes of winning the approval of the Indian populace. This was the beginning of a missionary method that came to be known as indigenization, or INCULTURATION. Missionaries won entry into the Muslim court of the grand mogul in Lahore and even reached the heart of Tibet. Franciscans and other missionaries worked among the lower castes. The Jesuits ended up dividing their congregations according to the Indian caste system (Brahmans, Ksashtriyas, Vaisyas, and Sudras).

In 1637 a Brahman from Goa was appointed the first native Indian vicar apostolic, but there were few native bishops thereafter. A Dalit (Sanskrit "trampled upon"), or Untouchable, Marampudi Joji (1942–   ), made history in 2000 as the first archbishop of Hyderabad, appointed over the protest of some Brahman bishops.

The European-led Indian mission was always torn between competing interests and policies: between the Portuguese *padroada,* or patron, system and the missionary policies of the Sacred Congregation for the Propagation of the Faith; between converting high or lower castes; between Latin and Syrian rites; and later between competing Christian denominations (Syrian Orthodox, Roman Catholic, Church of England, Dutch Reformed, German Lutheran, and English Baptist).

After troubles with the Portuguese and the suppression of the Jesuits in the 18th century, the pope placed the Indian mission directly under the Congregation for the Propagation of the Faith. Tension between Italian and Portuguese hierarchies lasted until LEO XIII established a single hierarchy for the whole of India in 1886. Tensions between Latin and Syro-Malabar rite hierarchies remained, motivating JOHN PAUL II to erect the Syro-Malabar segment as a major archepiscopal church, roughly equivalent to a patriarchy, by the apostolic constitution *Quae Maiori* (December 16, 1992) with His Eminence Cardinal Antony Padiyara (1921–   ), the archbishop of Ernakulam, as the first major archbishop.

As a footnote, a third Catholic-affiliated church came to be in 1926 when two Syrian Orthodox bishops of the Malankara rite joined Rome. The Jacobite Episcopal Synod at Parumala had empowered Mar Ivanios (d. 1953), metropolitan of Bethany, to enter into negotiations with Rome to effect a reunion with the Catholic Church under the express condition that the ancient and venerable tradition of the Malankara Church should be kept intact. Pope PIUS XI graciously accepted the condition and welcomed the reunion.

Today there are more than 16 million Catholics in India with 150 dioceses. About 3.5 million belong to the Syro-Malabar rite, and about 300,000 belong to the Syro-Malankara rite. The remainder are Latin rite.

CHINA

There is evidence that Jewish traders may have reached China as early as the second century. Unverifiable legends say that St. Thomas the Apostle missionized China as well as India even earlier than that. More likely the legends reflect a mission carried from Syria with roots back to Thomas. A Christian stele discovered in Xian in 1625 and examined by MATEO RICCI narrates how A-lo-pen (Abraham?), most likely a Nestorian from Syria, arrived in western China in 655 and how the Christian Church grew until 781. Ricci found a synagogue still operating in Kaifeng (K'ai-feng). In 1294 the Franciscan missionary JOHN OF MONTE CORVINO established a diocese in Nanjing (Nanking), but the Christian efforts came to naught by the beginning of the Ming dynasty (1368–1644).

In 1582 Michele Ruggieri and Mateo Ricci began the important Jesuit mission at the court of Nanjing. Accompanied by Frs. Adam Schaal, a physicist, and Ferdinand Verbiest, an astronomer, the mission ingratiated itself to the Chinese emperor mostly by their learning. Even Chinese mandarin scholars recognized Ricci's phenomenal command of the complex Chinese language and its ideograms. Following the pattern of Roberto de Nobili, they introduced another stage of inculturation with what came to be known as the Chinese Rites: the use of the vernacular, wearing of mandarin garb, translation of catechism and Scripture into Chinese, allowing honor to be paid to ancestors, and use of Chinese terms *tian* (*tien,* heaven) and *Shangti* (Shang-ti, Lord of Heaven) for God. The coming of the DOMINICAN and FRANCISCAN ORDERS in the 17th century set the stage for the Chinese Rites Controversy and the intervention of the papacy into Chinese affairs, always an offense to the emperor and still an offense to the present-day

Communist leadership in Beijing (Peking). As a result the emperor banned Christianity.

The successes of the Jesuits came to an abrupt halt when their mission was suppressed in 1773. There was a missionary lull until the 19th century, when members of several Catholic orders, now joined by Protestant missionaries, renewed the mission to China. Great effort was put into founding educational, medical, and charitable institutions, but by the time of the victory of the Communists in 1949 there were only about 4 million Catholics and less than 1 million Protestants in the country.

Of note were the missionary efforts of John Nevius (1829–93), a Presbyterian missionary who adopted many of the principles of Mateo Ricci and founded the Three Self Movement, which aimed to make the mission in China self-administering, self-propagating, and self-financing as quickly as possible. In the middle of the century Hong Xiuquan (Hung Hsiu-ch'uan; 1813–64) led a nativist attempt to overthrow the Qing (Ching) dynasty in a movement known as Taiping (1850–64), a curious blend of Christianity, Taoism, and Chinese messianism. More than 30 million died during the Taiping Rebellion.

The 20th century was marked by several violent upheavals, often aimed against foreign interference, and in the 1900 Boxer Rebellion thousands of Chinese Christians lost their lives. The imperial regime was overthrown in 1911 by Sun Yat-sen (1866–1925). In the face of continued violence and turmoil, Rome ordained six native Chinese bishops in 1926. The Japanese incursion into Manchuria (1937–45) caused untold hardship both for the people and the churches and intensified the bitter rivalry between the Koumintang (Guomindang) of Chang Kai-shek (Jiang Jieshi 1887–1975) and the Communist Party of Mao Zedong (Mao Tse-t'ung 1893–1976).

The Communists won control in 1949 and began a policy of progressively excluding foreign Christian influence. The government embraced a nativist version of John Nevius's Three Self Move-ment for Protestants and enforced the Catholic Patriotic Association on Catholics, severing them from the authority of Rome. Both Catholic and Protestant underground churches nevertheless grew and are still growing at a phenomenal rate. Religions of all persuasions suffered a setback during the lawless and self-destructive Cultural Revolution (1966–76), an attempt by Mao, Madame Mao (also known as Jiang Qing [Chiang Ch'ing] 1914–91) and others to mask the devastating effects of earlier failures like the Great Leap Forward in 1957. Since 1979 Chinese policy has alternated between loosening up and again tightening restrictions against Christianity.

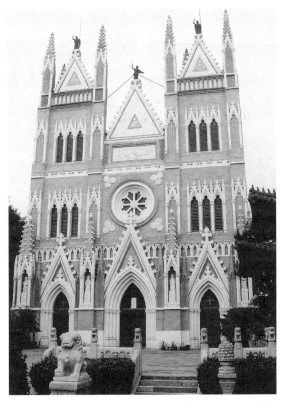

Xishiku Cathedral, Beijing, China, built by the French in 1890, now under Patriotic Catholic Church. This is the largest church building in China to this day. *(J. Gordon Melton)*

In the mid-1990s there were 113 officially sanctioned Catholic dioceses, more than 900 officially ordained priests, and 1000 nuns, in addition to many underground bishops, priests and laity. Growth for both Protestants and Catholics has been amazing, and Christianity has taken on a thoroughly Chinese character. Great throngs of pilgrims have returned to the Basilica of Mary at Sheshan near Shanghai. Due to the official isolation of Catholicism, the church in China has largely been untouched by the reforms of VATICAN COUNCIL II.

After the Tiananmen Square massacre in 1989 the government has become more wary of religion. It has severely repressed the Falun Gong movement, which is loosely based on Taoist beliefs, and has begun to apply some of the same methods to independent Christians. The Communist government, like the imperial dynasties of old, operates with a long memory and recalls vividly the violent power exerted by religion during the Taiping Rebellion.

Because of government control of information and the murky areas between the officially sanctioned and underground churches, it is very difficult to estimate the number of Catholic Church adherents in China. An educated guess gives a figure at 13 million, with the possibility of several million more underground. The VATICAN under Pope BENEDICT XVI is taking delicate steps to reach a reconciliation with the patriotic church in China.

JAPAN

The Jesuit missionary extraordinaire St. FRANCIS XAVIER first brought Christianity to southern Japan in 1549. The new religion was given protection by southern daimyos, or lords, but drew suspicion from the central government to the north. Many converts were made until the once-friendly shogun Toyotomi Hideyoshi (1536–98) proscribed the religion in 1596 and executed 27 converts and missionaries the following year (they were canonized as the NAGASAKI MARTYRS in

1862). Persecutions broke out again in 1613, and many more thousands died up to 1640. In 1616 the Tokugawa government banned all foreigners. True believers went underground and have survived to this day without any priests in the southern parts of Kyushu.

After Matthew Perry opened Japan in 1853, the Paris Missionary Society sent Fr. Bernard-Thadée Petitjean (1829–84), who located 20,000 surviving Christians. Persecution recommenced, but the Meiji government eventually issued an edict of toleration. Soon after, many religious congregations sent missionaries who helped found new dioceses, universities, and high schools. Outstanding among these institutions are the Nanzan Institute of Religion and Culture in Nagoya and the Jesuit Sophia University in Tokyo.

During the rise of Japanese nationalism in the 1930s Catholicism was put in a difficult place. Shinto, the native religion of early Japan, was revived and given a military caste. All citizens were required to bow at Shinto shrines. Catholics objected, and the government declared the bowing a civil act. In 1941 Japanese bishops replaced all foreign personnel. Since World War II Catholicism has held its own, but it has not grown with the population. A number of important writers are Catholic, among them Endo Shusaku and Sono Ayako (1913–97). Today there are only about 500,000 Catholics out of a population of 140 million.

VIETNAM

Modern-day Vietnam comprises the former Cochin China, Annam, and Tonkin. Spanish Franciscan and Portuguese Dominican missionaries arrived in the 1580s, if not earlier. The Jesuit mission was founded in 1615 by missionaries driven out of Japan. Among them was the Frenchman Alexander of Rhodes (1591–1660), who, like Mateo Ricci, was an outstanding linguist and who invented the Latin-based phonetic script for Vietnamese still in use today. Also like Ricci and Roberto DeNobili, Alexander attempted

Vietnamese houseboat church on Ton Le Sap Lake near Siem Reap, Cambodia. Though in Cambodia, it serves a Vietnamese community. *(Margaret Mooney)*

to indigenize the church by using lay catechists and founding an order of nuns. Expelled in 1645, Rhodes returned to Paris where he founded the Paris Missionary Society. The first native priests were ordained in 1668. Compared to other parts of Asia, the number of conversions was significant. By 1800 there were more than 300,000 Catholics.

The church suffered periods of persecutions, leading the French vicar apostolic to ask for French political intervention. In 1884 the Paris government made Cochin China a French colony. During the colonial war against the French in 1945–54, Catholics took sides against the nationalist movement that was controlled by the Communists. After the defeat of the French and the division of the country, Catholics fled to the south and supported the Republic of South Vietnam, which the United States propped up. With the collapse of the Nguyen Van Thieu (1923–2001) government in 1975, the Communist government adopted policies like those used by the Chinese and expelled all foreign missionaries. By 2000 Vietnam and the United States had reached an accord, and churches are once again thriving. Christians number about 4 million, some 7% of the population. More than 90% of these are Catholic.

KOREA

Early Christians in Korea had the unusual experience of having converted themselves. Jesuits made the first Korean converts in southern Japan at the end of the 16th century, but the Korean embassy in Beijing made its own contacts with the Jesuit missionaries at the Chinese court. Some diplomats were baptized; they brought back to Pyongyang a catechism with selections from the Bible made by Mateo Ricci. When a priest arrived in the 1790s he found 4,000 Catholics. The Congregation for the Propagation of the Faith established an apostolic vicariate in 1831, and the Paris Missionary Society sent missionaries in 1835. By the middle of the 19th century there were 15,000 Catholics, but many were made martyrs by the Confucian Korean emperors. In 1984 Pope John Paul II canonized the Korean martyrs.

In 1883 Korea, following the precedent of Japan, opened relations with the Western powers. This opened the doors not only to more Catholic missions but also to many Protestant denominations. Presbyterians adopted the Three Self Principles of John L. Nevius. Protestants founded many institutions of higher learning. After Japan annexed Korea in 1910, many Protestants supported the cause of Korean independence, while Catholics were more self-protective and neutral. The first Korean bishopric was created in 1942, and a hierarchy was established in 1962.

During the Korean War (1950–53) the Communist government in North Korea attempted to eradicate all forms of Christianity, and many Christians fled south. Korea has been a seedbed of many forms of "blended" Christianity that mix elements of native shamanism, Confucianism, and Buddhism together with Christian millennialism. Notable among these is the Holy Spirit Association of World Christianity (the Unification Church), founded by Rev. Sun Myung Moon (1920–), which has spread throughout the world. The largest Christian congregation in the world is the Yoido Full Gospel Christian Church in Seoul, with 800,000 members. The Catholic cathedral masses are full every Sunday. Today there are some 14 million Christians in South Korea, a quarter of them Catholic, organized in three archdioceses and 11 dioceses. Two other dioceses operate in North Korea. Together the Protestants and Catholics are 30 percent of the population, the highest proportion in the Far East outside the Philippines.

PHILIPPINES

The Philippines is Catholicism's greatest success story in the Far East. Priests accompanying Ferdinand Magellan (c. 1480–1521) made the first converts on Cebu Island in 1521. From 1565 until 1898 Spain ruled the Philippines as a colony; during that long period the Spanish Crown both supported and controlled ecclesiastical affairs. Manila, on Luzon Island, was made an episcopal see in 1579. Franciscan, Jesuit, Augustinian, Dominican, and Augustinian Recollect missionaries succeeded in converting a majority of the population and in founding many institutions of higher learning and charity.

Spain pursued a policy under which no native peoples were appointed to the hierarchy; native priests were reduced to a status inferior to the Spanish bishops and religious orders. The first native bishop was appointed only in 1905. This policy produced movements marked by nationalism and typical ANTICLERICALISM during the 19th century. In 1902 two priests, Gregorio Aglipay and Ignacio de los Reyes, founded the Philippine Independent Catholic Church, which claimed a fourth of the population before it declined and then entered into formal union with the Episcopal Church of America in 1961. Many forms of blended Catholicism have arisen throughout the islands, some especially shaped by faith healing. In the late 20th century Cardinal Jaime Sin (1928–2005) was the most important Filipino in bringing about the resignation of the dictator Ferdinand Marcos.

After the Spanish-American War the Philippines became an American protectorate, resulting in the separation of CHURCH AND STATE. This led to an influx of Protestant missionaries. The Philippines gained independence in 1946 after Japanese occupation.

From the start Filipinos nurtured their own brand of Catholicism. They have retained many pre-Christian beliefs including ancestor homage. Today they are much given to faith healing. They enjoy religious fiestas, processions, and devotion to the saints, especially the Santo Niño, or the Christ Child. Likewise they treasure sacramentals such as relics, the use of holy water, and the wearing of medals. Beginning in the 1970s some Filipino theologians developed their own form of LIBERATION THEOLOGY, in strong contrast to the conservative majority among the clergy. Today there are about 53 million Catholics, 83 percent of the population.

INDONESIA

Christianity came to Indonesia almost as a by-product of trade between East and West. There is some evidence that the Assyrian Church of the East founded a small community there in the seventh century. Franciscan missionaries on their way to China visited in the 14th century, and in 1534 Portuguese Franciscans established churches in the Moluccas, the prized center of the spice trade. Dominicans and Jesuits followed, including St. FRANCIS XAVIER, who stayed from 1546 to 1547. Throughout this time Catholicism was in strong competition with Islam, spread by Muslim traders throughout Sumatra beginning in the 13th century.

In the early 17th century the Dutch East India Company took control of the Sumatra islands. They favored Dutch Reformed and other Protestant missionaries at the expense of Catholics. In the 20th century Roman Catholic missionary activity resumed, especially in the Lesser Sunda Islands. The first native bishop was appointed in 1940, and a general Indonesian hierarchy was established in 1960.

Today the Indonesian government, while favoring Islam, officially recognizes Protestantism,

Catholicism, Confucianism, and Buddhism. Nonetheless, the rise of Islamic fundamentalism, particularly the version known as the Jemaah Islamiya, has led to bloody conflicts in East Timor and other islands. The peace-based Catholic resistance in East Timor was led by Bishop Carlos Filipe Ximenes Belo (1948–   ), who won the Nobel Peace Prize in 1996.

Indonesia has the single largest Muslim population in the world. About 10 percent of the population is Christian. Of the Christians, about 5 million are Catholic.

Further reading: Donald Attwater, *The Catholic Eastern Churches* (Milwaukee: Bruce, 1935); Miguel A. Bernard, *The Christianization of the Philippines* (Manila: Filipiniana, 1972); James Huntley Grayson, *Korea: A Religious History* (New York: RoutledgeCurzon, 2002); Paul Hsiang, *The Catholic Missions in China during the Middle Ages, 1294–1368* (Washington, D.C.: Catholic University Press, 1949); Jason Kindopp and Carol Lee Hamrin, eds., *God and Caesar in China* (Washington, D.C.: Brookings Institution, 2000); Liesbeth Labbeke "'There is so much involved . . .' The Sisters of Charity of Saint Charles Borromeo in the Period from the Second World War" in Pieter N. Holtrop and Hugh McLeod, eds., *Missions and Missionaries* (Rochester, N.Y.: Boydell, 2000) 186–199; Kenneth Scott Latourette, *A History of Christian Missions in China* (New York: Russell & Russell, 1967); Edward Maclagan, *The Jesuits and the Great Mogul* (New York: Octagon, 1972); Phát Huon Phan, *History of the Catholic Church in Viet Nam* (Long Beach, Calif.: Cuu The Tùng. 2000); Scott W. Sunquist, ed., *A Dictionary of Asian Christianity* (Grand Rapids, Mich.: Eerdmans, 2001); Edmond Tang and Jean-Paul Wiest, *The Catholic Church in Modern China* (Maryknoll, N.Y.: Orbis Books, 1993); Ines G. Zupanov, *Disputed Mission: Jesuit Experiments and Brahmanical Knowledge in 17th Century India* (New Delhi: Oxford University Press, 1999).

Assumptionists

The Assumptionists of Augustine (A.A.) is a religious congregation of PRIESTS who follow a form of the Rule of St. Augustine for the active life. It was founded in Nimes, France, by the Ultramontanist priest Ven. Emmanuel d'Alzon (1810–80) in 1845. The Ultramontanists defended the papacy as a bulwark against the disintegrating effects of 19th-century liberalism and science. Many congregations of religious women arose inspired by Assumptionist spirituality, which has strong Trinitarian and Christological roots.

Assumptionists are dedicated to education, missions, publications, and Christian unity. Their journal *Échos d'Orient* (founded 1897) fosters understanding and dialogue between Christianity of the East and West. Dispersed by a French state decree in 1900, the congregation spread throughout the world. Assumptionists founded Assumption College in Worcester, Massachusetts, in 1904. The congregation also sponsors the Institute of Augustinian Studies and the Institute of Byzantine Studies, both in Paris.

Further reading: Lucien Guissard, *Les assomptionnistes d'hier à aujourd'hui* (Paris: Bayard, 1999); Andrew Beck, *Assumptionist Spirituality* (London: Washbourne & Bogan, 1933).

Assumption of the Blessed Virgin Mary

See MARY OF NAZARETH.

Athanasius of Alexandria (c. 296–373)
theologian, patriarch, and early church father
A feisty patriarch of Alexandria, Athanasius was the chief opponent of Arianism. He wrote the noted Easter Festal Letters that defined the canon of Scripture and set the date for EASTER. His feast day is May 2.

Athanasius trained in the catechetical school founded by ORIGEN and was ordained deacon by his predecessor, Alexander (d. 328). After serving as secretary to the Council of Nicaea I in 325, Athanasius succeeded Alexander as patriarch, inheriting two major problems: 1) the so-called Militian schism, named after Militius of Lycopolis (fl. 310), who opposed lenient treatment of believers who had lapsed under persecution; and 2) the aftermath of Arius, who had been declared a heretic at Nicaea. The Militian bishops allied themselves with pro-Arian bishops in the East, and their schism with the orthodox endured for centuries.

CONSTANTINE THE GREAT, who always remained a crypto-Arian, exiled Athanasius to Trier in 335. Constantius II allowed him to return two years later in 337 but exiled him again to Rome under the influence of pro-Arian bishops. He returned again in 346, was threatened again, and fled to Upper Egypt, where monastics kept him hidden. He was exiled yet again for a short time under the influence of the Arian bishop Valens of Mursa. He returned in 366 and died in 373, having been bishop 45 years.

Athanasius formally refuted Arius in his seminal treatise *On the Incarnation,* which clarified the Incarnation of the eternal Logos in the human Jesus. The work set the parameters of orthodox doctrine concerning not only the Incarnation, but also creation, redemption, and the Trinity. Most of his voluminous writings, however, were against Arius and in defense of Nicaea. His *Life of Anthony* set the pattern for all future lives of the saints (*see* HAGIOGRAPHY); it also gave great impetus to the monastic movements in both East and West by inspiring numerous readers to follow Anthony's example.

Further reading: Most of Athanasius writings are available online. Khaled Anatolios, *Athanasius: The Coherence of His Thought* (New York: Routledge, 1998); Duane W.-H. Arnold, *The Early Episcopal Career of Athanasius of Alexandria* (Notre Dame: Notre Dame University Press, 1991); Timothy D. Barnes, *Athanasius & Constantius* (Cambridge, Mass.: Harvard University Press, 1993); David Brakke, *Athanasius and Asceticism* (Baltimore: Johns Hopkins University Press, 1998).

atheism (Gk.: *a,* "without" + *theos,* "god")

The term atheism originated in Greek philosophy, designating those who did not honor or questioned the gods of the state. Socrates was the prime example. The Romans continued to use the term, in particular against CHRISTIANS who would not offer sacrifices to the gods of the state and to the emperor. In the Christian world, the term came to be limited to those who either seriously doubted or denied the existence of GOD. Since the invention of the term AGNOSTICISM by Thomas H. Huxley, the term *atheist* is generally restricted to one who formally denies the existence of a deity in both the philosophical and theological senses.

Modern atheism was fed by several currents. First, modern scientific theories (Descartes, Newton, Boyle) seemed to say that the dynamism of the world could be explained solely by efficient and material causes (*see* ARISTOTLE), without recourse to formal or final causality (Francis Bacon). Second, Enlightenment thought encouraged a form of deism, the assertion that, though the deity created the universe, it was now essentially on its own and governed by the laws of nature (*see* CRITIQUE OF CHRISTIANITY/CATHOLICISM).

In the 19th century formal atheism came into its own in the school of "left-wing" Hegelians. Ludwig A. Feuerbach (1804–72) maintained that ideas of God are merely projections of human ideals onto a transcendent being. Karl Marx (1818–83) thought that belief in God was an opiate that distracted human beings from truly caring about their material and social well-being. Friederick Nietzsche (1844–1900) proclaimed the "death of God," because he felt that current understandings of deity inhibited humans from taking the next step into "trans-humanity" (*Übermenschlichkeit*). Nietzsche's thought was apotheosized in the "death of God" theology of Thomas J. J. Altizer (1927–   ), which did not, however, seem to find many followers. Sigmund Freud (1856–1939) followed all three of the 19th-century thinkers in saying that religious feelings are infantile wish-fulfillment projected onto reality in order to give a sense of security, to keep people from recognizing that the forces of nature are uncaring and unfeeling.

Philosophy in the 20th century (existentialism, pragmatism) seemed to say that human beings had come of age and were able to deal with existence without the "crutch" of a deity. Instead of theology, scientific inquiry was now supreme. Christians were slow to respond to modern atheism. Some, like the Lutheran Jürgen Moltmann (1926–), welcomed atheism when it protested against false gods, a theme embraced in *Gaudium et Spes* 19–21, the Pastoral Constitution on the Church in the Modern World at VATICAN COUNCIL II. Conversely, the Marxist philosopher Ernst Bloch (1885–1977) interpreted religious symbols and longings as anticipations of the classless society, which would not need a God.

Traditionally, Catholicism has taken a harsh view of atheism. VATICAN COUNCIL I condemned anyone who denied that God created visible and invisible creatures (On God Creator of All Things, Session 3, cn. 1). Karl RAHNER (1904–84) wrote that Christians are partially responsible for atheism in so far as they promote defective forms of theism both in theory and practice. His answer to the challenge of atheism is a self-critical life that is free of superstition and false security and open to the challenge of God's self-revelation to humanity.

The 21st century pope BENEDICT XVI, (2005–) was shaped in part by his 1968 encounters, as a theologian at Tübingen, with revolutionary students, in whom he saw "the unveiled and cruel face" of a "pious atheism." The pope sees his pontificate as a mission to save Europe from Godless atheism and relativism. This signals a return to the Vatican I approach toward atheism as an ideology to be combated.

Further reading: Ignace Lepp, *Atheism in Our Time* (New York: Macmillan, 1963); Henri de Lubac, *Drama of Atheistic Humanism* (San Francisco: Ignatius, 1995); Karl Rahner, *The Pastoral Approach to Atheism* (Mahweh, N.J.: Paulist Press, 1967).

atonement (Eng.: at-one-ment, of one accord)

The doctrine of the atonement teaches that GOD forgives humans through a merciful reconcilia-tion with them. For CHRISTIANS this reconciliation is centered on Christ's loving suffering, death, and RESURRECTION. The atonement has been a much debated doctrine in the history of Christian thought, yet it has never been formally defined in Christian confessions. The different aspects of atonement theory are discussed here under the themes of reconciliation, ransom, debt payment or expiation, and penal and moral atonement.

A primary aspect of atonement is reconciliation (Gk. *katallege*). As God is absolutely righteous, no one stained with sin or impurity dare approach; reconciliation must be initiated by the divine self. In the Old Testament the people were reconciled to God through the intercession of Moses and then of the high priest on the Day of Atonement (Heb. *Yom Kippur,* Lev. 16:30; Heb. 9:22). The idea of atonement was later expanded; God was seen to create a new covenant of the heart (Jer. 31:31 ff.), and to send a Suffering Servant who would mediate between the downtrodden people and God (Isa. 53:5,12). In late Judaism the death of a martyr could mitigate the wrath of God (2 Macc. 7:38).

Though the term *atonement* does not occur in the New Testament, the idea that God desires to be reconciled with fallen humanity continues there in full force. Some later theories of the atonement divide the Father, who almost vengefully demands a sacrifice for the sins of humanity, and the Son, who offers himself as the expiation (Gk. *hilasmos,* Lev. 25:9; 1 John 2:2), but the dominant theme in the New Testament is that God and Christ together effect the reconciliation: "God was in Christ reconciling the world to God's self" (2 Cor. 5:19). The New Testament never associates the divine "wrath" with the death and resurrection of Jesus. For Paul the consequences of the atonement are both anthropological ("peace" Rom. 5:1) and cosmic ("liberation of creation" 8:21).

The idea of atonement as a ransom comes from ORIGEN, who taught that the FALL placed humans under bondage to Satan and that Christ's death and resurrection release humanity to freedom under God. This idea found favor with many Western theologians, including AUGUSTINE and LEO I THE GREAT. ATHANASIUS OF ALEXANDRIA expressed the new sovereignty in terms of the INCARNATION: "He became human that we might be made divine" (*On the Incarnation* 54).

In the early MIDDLE AGES the idea of atonement began to take a significant turn, shifting to the debt/expiation/satisfaction theme. ANSELM OF CANTERBURY argued in *Why God Became Human* that Adam's sin was an offense against the infinite God, and only an infinite satisfaction could appease God's wrath. This theory was taken to the extreme by manipulating biblical evidence. By conflating the theory of the scapegoat in Leviticus 16, the figure of the Suffering Servant in Isaiah 52:13–53:12, and random verses from Paul (Rom. 8:3; Gal. 3:13), some theoreticians turned God into a bloodthirsty parent seeking vengeance upon the divine Son by making him pay the ultimate price of the Passion. This theory has two fatal shortcomings: Adam was finite and therefore could not commit an "infinite" sin, and the biblical tradition never sees the death of Jesus apart from the RESURRECTION and always interprets it as the gracious and merciful act of God acting in concert with the Son.

Other theologians followed a lead of Augustine in *On the Trinity* (13.11.15), when he questioned the sacrificial theory of atonement. This position sometimes goes by the label of the moral, as opposed to the penal, theory of the atonement. ABELARD taught that the Son became human not to appease the anger of God but to communicate God's love by reconciling humans to God and to one another. Christ is not an objective victim of divine wrath but the exemplary agent of God's love. Aquinas followed Anselm's theory but softened it even further by saying God has no need to exact full satisfaction. Luther rejected the satisfaction theory in favor of a substitution theory—Christ was reckoned a sinner in place of sinful humanity. Calvin radicalized this idea by saying that Christ took up the role of a "condemned and maimed man."

Christians, including Catholics, have never decided which side to favor in the atonement debate. Those who favor the penal theory favor the ideas of sacrifice, expiation, and satisfaction, with a cloud of divine wrath in the background. Those who favor the moral or exemplary theory say that the atonement is the model of love of God for humans and humans for one another.

Further reading: Stanilas Lyonnet and Léopold Sabourin, *Sin, Sacrifice, and Redemption: A Biblical and Patristic Study* (Rome: Pontifical Biblical Institute, 1970); John Milbank, *Being Reconciled: Ontology and Pardon* (London, Routeledge, 2003); Gerald S. Sloyan, *Why Jesus Died?* (Minneapolis: Fortress, 1995).

attributes of God   *See* GOD.

Augustine of Hippo (354–430) *foremost Western Christian theologian*

Bishop of Hippo from 395 till his death in 430, Augustine was a prolific author who became the most influential theologian of early Western Christianity one of the western FATHERS AND MOTHERS OF THE CHURCH. His feast day is Aug. 28.

It was Augustine who conceived and formulated the fundamental structure of Christian biblical theology as a grand schema reaching from CREATION, to the FALL, to REDEMPTION, and finally to RESURRECTION after the judgment of the dead. He uncovered psychological and philosophical interiority and subjectivity; His social theories and sacramental theology had lasting influence on the MIDDLE AGES. He was the principal source, after the Scriptures, for the Protestant reformers in their theologies of grace, justification, and predestination.

We know a great deal about Augustine's life from his own writings, especially the *Confessions, Letters,* and *Retractions.* In addition his disciple Possidius (c. 370–c. 440) left us a *Life of Augustine.* Augustine was born of a Christian mother,

St. Augustine with angel. Woodcut from Hartmann Schedel (1440–1514), *Liber chronicorum* (1493). Augustine wears the bishop's miter and opens a book, symbolizing he is a doctor of the church. *(Washington University Library, Special Collections, with permission)*

Monica, and a non-Christian father, Patricius, in Tagaste, Numidia, a province of North Africa now in Algeria. He had a brother and maybe more than one sister; his nephew, also named Patricius, was a member of the clergy of his church in Hippo. His parents sent him to school in Tagaste, and a wealthy patron, Romianus, furthered his education at Madaura and Carthage. At Carthage he took a Christian concubine (never named), by whom he had a son, Adeodatus, born c. 373. He read Cicero's *Hortensius*, which instilled in him a love of philosophy and wisdom and which he later saw as a first step in his process of conversion (*Confessions* 3.4.7).

At the same time he became a "hearer" of the Manichees (*see* MANICHAEISM), whose deter-

ministic dualism seemed to explain his own dual propensities toward sensuality and the spiritual life. Augustine sailed for Rome, the jumping off point for advancement, even though the emperors now resided in Milan. The Manichees helped get him an appointment as professor of rhetoric at the royal court of Valentinian II (r. 375–392) in Milan. Augustine's secular career was launched, though his Christian mother remained close behind. As law is today, rhetoric was the profession leading to positions of power in Roman society. Monica arranged for a society marriage, and the concubine was packed off to Africa, probably to become a Christian "widow" in a community in Tagaste. Meanwhile, Augustine took another concubine.

Something, however, was changing in him. He grew dissatisfied with the Manichees, especially their teacher Faustus, who struck Augustine as sincere but ignorant. He began associating with a group of Neoplatonist Christians, most notably Sts. AMBROSE OF MILAN, bishop of the city, and Simplicianus, mentor of Ambrose and later of Augustine. In the *Confessions* 8.12 he recounts a classic conversion scene. In a garden he heard the voice of a child in the distance saying "*Tolle! Lege!*" ("Take and read!") over and over again. Picking up his BIBLE, he read at random Romans 13:13, which speaks against reveling, drunkenness, debauchery, and lust. He gave up his past life, including his imperial position, and was baptized in 387. He returned to Africa with his son and companions, planning to found a monastic community under the inspiration of St. ANTHONY OF EGYPT. While visiting Hippo Regius on the way home to Tagaste, Augustine was chosen priest by popular acclaim; he remained at Hippo and was elected bishop in 395.

Three controversies mark Augustine's theological career: his relation to his own Manichaeism, and the two controversies he encountered as bishop of Hippo, namely DONATISM and Pelagianism (*see* PELAGIUS). Augustine's early involvement with Manichaeism helped define some of the most important Christian teachings on good and evil. The Manichees subscribed to the dualistic teaching that good and evil were real, enduring forces in the universe, and that good sided with the spirit and evil with the body. Like many Gnostics, they held that the material world was the work of evil powers and that the "elect" should shun even procreation. Following the Christian CREEDS, Augustine asserted in opposition that all CREATION, material and spiritual, was created good: "Whatever is, is good" (*Confessions* 7.12.18). Evil enters through the disordered will of both angels and humans and is a temporary phenomenon that will last only until the City of God is established at the RESURRECTION.

Adam and Eve at first delighted in God and had an ordered love for all other creatures. After the FALL their love could delight in creatures even to the exclusion of God. Augustine saw his own act of stealing pears when he was a boy to win favor with a gang of troublemakers as a manifestation of this disorder (*Confessions* 2.4). Following CYPRIAN OF CARTHAGE, Augustine taught that children should be baptized to counteract the "contagion of death" inherited from Adam, which Augustine was the first to call original sin; critics often condemned this approach as a physicalist, quasi-Manichaein notion. Under the anti-Manichaean rubric, Augustine contributed four themes that ever since have been held to be essential to Christian faith in the West: the priority of goodness in the creation; the emergence of evil after the fact not as a positive force but as the absence or defect of the good; the Fall as disorder of love in the will (concupiscence), which is passed on through the act of generation; and the temporary rule of evil over the City of Man until the Kingdom of God comes.

When he became bishop of Hippo, Augustine walked into a beehive of DONATISM. This schismatic movement was named after Donatus (d. 355), who was consecrated rival bishop to the orthodox bishop of Carthage during the Great Persecution of Diocletian (303–05), when *traditores* ("betrayers") reportedly handed over the Scriptures to be burned or offered sacrifices to the Roman gods.

The purist Donatists insisted that these betrayers needed to repent and that those who received BAPTISM from them needed to be rebaptized. The Donatists wanted to keep the church as the bride of Christ, pure and untainted by the state. Augustine's answer was both theological and biblical. First, he declared that the sacraments are administered by Christ, who is not dependent on the spiritual or moral condition of the priest. This laid down the principle later stated as EX OPERE OPERATO (Lat. "from the deed done"), whereby a SACRAMENT is valid even if the priest acts in an unworthy state and outside the pale of the law. Against the rigorist view of the Donatists, Augustine also appealed to the parable of the wheat and the tares (Matt. 13:24–29, 36–43), in which God lets good and evil coexist until the harvest (Last Judgment), lest the good be destroyed along with the bad.

In the beginning of the controversy Augustine declared in a letter to the Donatist bishop Eusebius that "no one should against his will be coerced into the Catholic communion" (*Letters* 34), yet in 405 he gave approval to the imperial Edict of Unity, which deprived the Donatists of legal standing. After the Council of Carthage in 411, Augustine agreed to the Roman tribune Marcellinus's use of force in suppressing the Donatists. Unlike his predecessors, he established the use of religious force in *theory*, citing (out of context) a line from the parable of the wedding banquet: "Compel them to come in" (Luke 11:23; Augustine, *Sermons* 112.2). While Augustine saw the church as a mixed bag of struggling believers ever tending toward great charity, his sinister policy on the Donatists helped pave the way for the INQUISITION and violated his earlier declaration of liberty of conscience in religious disputes and his own theology of God's unbounded love.

The controversy with the Pelagians was more complicated (*see* PELAGIUS). At first Augustine engaged and defeated the Celtic British lay ascetic Pelagius and his followers (many of whom misrepresented their leader). Later he contended with JULIAN OF ECLANUN over some of the same issues.

Today scholars are radically reevaluating Pelagius's writings; they view him as first and foremost an ascetic and moral theologian who grounded his views in a particular theology of creation. Pelagius, in Rome at the time, challenged Augustine's assertion "Give what you command and command what you will" (*Confessions* 10.24.40), which expressed Augustine's conviction in his later years that God's grace must precede all human merit, including faith itself. According to Augustine, all humans inherited Adam's sin after the Fall, which had vitiated human will itself. Pelagius had a much higher theology of creation: even after the Fall humans could still choose between good and evil. Adam's sin was a pattern but not an inheritance (*Commentary on Romans* 5:12–21). Pelagius points to all the righteous followers of God in the Book of Genesis who chose good over evil even after the Fall (*Letter to Demetrias*).

Accused of HERESY, Pelagius went before two episcopal councils in Palestine and was found sound in his teaching. (Eastern Christianity has never subscribed to the legalistic trends in Western theology in general and to its theology of sin in particular.) Conniving with JEROME, Augustine appealed to Pope Innocent I (r. 401–11), who charged Pelagius with HERESY. Innocent promptly died, and his successor, Zosimos (r. 417–18), reversed the decision. Jerome and Augustine appealed to the emperor, Honorius (r. 395–423), now residing in RAVENNA. Honorius's opposition to Pelagius forced Zosimos's hand, and he issued his own condemnation. These maneuvers again reflect on Augustine's willingness to go beyond dialogue in winning arguments.

Like Pelagius, Julian of Eclanum, bishop of Apulia in central Italy, took umbrage with the remnants of Manichaeism in the African bishop's theology, especially his physicalist and fatalist understanding of original sin and the assertion that every act of sexual intercourse involves sin. Augustine won the day with his treatise *Marriage and Concupiscence*. Julian was sent into exile around 418 and condemned at the Council of EPHESUS (431).

In between the Pelagian and Julian controversies, Augustine wrote *City of God*, his monumental apologia of Christianity. Dedicated to Marcellinus, the massive tome undertakes to defend Christianity against the charges that it was responsible for the decline and fall of the Roman Empire. Augustine refutes the charges and goes on to unfold the grand scheme of salvation as a struggle between the City of God (grace, the good, love, justice) and the City of Man (sin, evil, domination) stretching from creation and the Fall to redemption and sanctification in the resurrection. His most systematic theological work was *The Trinity*, in which the interrelations among the persons of the Godhead (*amor amorans*, or "love loving love") are related to the inner psychological realities of humans and to human love itself (the lover, the beloved, and the relation that is love itself).

Augustine's place in the West is paramount. He bequeathed to Christian theology the grand schema of creation to resurrection, the doctrine of original sin, and the fundamentals of sacramental theology. His portrayal of the hierarchy of the soul (reason, the supernatural, the ruler) over the body (passion, the natural, the ruled) laid the foundations for the theory of society in the Middle Ages (*City of God* 19.13–15). His teachings on grace, predestination, and justification as well as his principles of scriptural interpretation provided fuel for the fires of the Reformation. No other theologian has been as influential in the West.

See also THEOLOGY.

Further reading: Augustine's cited writings are readily available in the series *Nicene and Post-Nicene Fathers, Fathers of the Church* and *Library of Christian Classics* and on the Internet. Peter Brown, *Augustine of Hippo*, 2nd ed. (Berkeley: University of California Press, 2000).; J. Patout Burns, "Augustine on the Origin and Progress of Evil," in *The Ethics of St. Augustine*, ed. by William S. Babcock (Atlanta: Scholars Press, 1991); Frederik van der Meer, *Augustine the Bishop* (New York: Sheed & Ward, 1962); Eugene TeSelle, *Augustine the*

Theologian (New York: Herder & Herder, 1970); Gary Wills, *St. Augustine* (New York: Viking Penguin, 1999).

Augustinians

The term *Augustinians* has been used over the centuries by various monastic and mendicant movements and orders, who generally adopted the Rule of St. AUGUSTINE OF HIPPO. The rule is variously found in three of the latter's texts: *Order for a Monastery,* the *Precept,* and *Letter* 211. Unlike other monastic rules, the Augustinian is very flexible and adaptable to different ways of life. Versions of it were accepted by the DOMINICANS, Servites, ASSUMPTIONISTS, and the orders of nuns called the Ursulines and Visitation Sisters.

The Augustinian Canons had their origin in communities of clergy and CANONS in northern Italy and southern France who in the 11th century sought to live lives of poverty, chastity, and obedience. They received official approval in the Lateran synods of 1059 and 1063 and soon became known as Canons Regular. A number of Augustinian congregations, including the Victorines and Premonstratensians, adopted practices from the CISTERCIANS. Canons suffered from the disorders of the late Middle Ages. Many groups were absorbed into other orders.

The Augustinian Friars or Hermits is the name given to a number of congregations of MENDICANTS who also followed the rule of St. Augustine. They are known today by the initials OSA (Order of St. Augustine). During the Middle Ages the papacy both organized the central offices of the Vatican and loose orders of religious such as the Augustinians. Pope Innocent IV (r. 1243–54) united some groups in what is known as the "little union" by his decree *Incumbit Nobis* (December 16, 1243). Later, Alexander IV (r. 1254–61) brought about a "grand union" in 1256.

Augustinian Hermits began to join their counterpart friars in urban settings, and the movement, like other mendicant orders, spread throughout Europe and the Holy Land. Augustinians stressed

Augustine's primacy of grace. It is no accident that Martin Luther (1483–1546) was a member of the Augustinian friars. Despite Luther's break with Catholicism, most Augustinians were stout defenders of the papacy; they served as papal chaplains from 1352 to 1991. The famous geneticist Gregor Johann Mendel (1822–84) was an Augustinian in Brno, Czechoslovakia.

Augustinians founded Villanova University near Philadelphia in 1842. They are still active in Europe, North and South American, and the Philippines. There are now about 3,000 friars worldwide and 1,500 nuns in enclosed convents.

Further reading: John Gavigan, *The Augustinians from the French Revolution to Modern Times* (Villanova: Augustinian Press, 1989); David Gutierrez, *The Augustinians in the Middle Ages* (Villanova: Villanova University Press, 1984).

authority (Lat.: *auctoritas*, "authority"; *augere*, "to increase")

The Latin term translates the New Testament Greek *exousia*, meaning the hierarchical exertion of power from the top. Religious authority is the legitimate power or competence to shape and to guide the belief and practices of adherents without resorting to force or threat of force. Needless to say, many religions, Catholicism included, have not always kept to the ideal but often have resorted to physical violence, directly and indirectly, to enforce their credos and laws.

Catholic authority derives from the authority given by GOD as revealed in Jesus. In the Gospel of Matthew (28:18–20) Jesus says: "All authority in heaven and on earth has been given to me. Therefore, go and make disciples of all nations, baptizing them in the name of the Father and of the Son and of the Holy Spirit, and teaching them to obey everything I have commanded you. And surely I am with you always to the very end of the age." In this late gospel, the primary authority of St. PETER THE APOSTLE is already established as the "rock" to whom the keys of binding and loosening have been given (16:18–19), and the authoritative position of the 12 apostles (19:28) has also been fixed. Matthew's text is fortified with a passage in John, the latest of the four gospels, wherein Jesus promises the disciples that after he departs the "Spirit of truth" will be with them (16:12–15).

The earliest sources for church life are the letters of PAUL. Although Paul could appeal to his apostleship when challenged by opponents (Gal. 1:15–17), he was not interested in top-down authority, preferring the round-table model where the gifts of the Spirit can be manifested equally through APOSTLES, prophets, teachers, miracle workers, healers, speakers in tongues, and interpreters (1 Cor. 12), in order to build up the one body of the church. Authority implied first and foremost service (Gk. *diakonia*) to the whole of the church, not a claim to rank. Authority was the love of the Christ manifested in the mutuality of the believing members of the church (1 Cor. 13).

Toward the end of the first century and into the second this ethic of mutuality gave way to a hierarchy of power. As Christianity moved out into the Greco-Roman world, it started taking on more and more of the structures of patriarchal Roman society. This ethic shows up in the typically Roman *Haustafeln*, or Home Rules, of the deutero-Pauline and other letters (Col. 3:18–4:1; Eph. 5:22–6:9; 1 Peter 2:18–3:6), in which the subjection of women to men was the rule. Likewise, the struggle against the free-wheeling Gnostics in the second and third centuries resulted in the all-male structure of bishops, priests, and deacons with authority concentrated in bishops who could claim direct decent from one of the apostles (*see* APOSTOLIC SUCCESSION) and who could enforce ORTHODOXY on a more passive laity. Max Weber (1864–1920) called this a shift from charismatic to bureaucratic authority.

Another phase was inaugurated after CONSTANTINE; subsequent emperors established bishops as men of civil rank who exercised both administrative and juridical functions. While EASTERN ORTHODOXY tended in the direction of the theological and the mystical, the West tended in the direction of the ethical and the legal. In the interplay between church and state, as the state became officially CHRISTIAN, ecclesiastical authority became more legalistic and secular, while spiritual authority took refuge in monasticism. Almost all subsequent spiritual reforms of the church came out of the monasteries, such as the reforms of Hildebrand (GREGORY VII) and St. BERNARD OF CLAIRVAUX.

The accretion of power in the PAPACY was not solely the result of a power grab. In the bitter theological disputes between the third and eighth centuries even eastern bishops and councils appealed to the bishop of Rome for support. The consequence was that more and more power became concentrated in the papacy, as it can be called by this time, as at least *a,* if not *the,* final court of appeal. Popes LEO I, Gelasius I (492–96), and GREGORY I THE GREAT augmented papal authority after the fall of the Western Roman Empire.

In the MIDDLE AGES, imperial and royal authority began to expand and cross over into ecclesiastical territory, leading up to the INVESTITURE CONTROVERSY. Gregory VII fought to extricate the church spiritual from the temporal authority of kings and princes who had replaced the Roman emperor and who were, in effect, appointing bishops and bestowing benefices. He succeeded too well; thereafter, ecclesiastical authority crossed over into the temporal sphere. Gregory and all future popes claimed they held an autonomous power directly from God, independent of and superior to secular power. This trend terminated in INNOCENT III, who intervened ceaselessly in the moral affairs of sovereigns and boldly declared to the Holy Roman Emperor: "You are the moon; I am the sun."

The supremacy of papal authority attained during the Middle Ages has remained significant for Catholicism. It became perverted when Lateran Council IV (1215) demanded that the secular authority aid in exterminating heretics. In the face of this centralizing trend, theologians like St. THOMAS AQUINAS strongly defended the role of individual conscience. Lateran IV set the stage for the INQUISITION, where with the church directly exercised spiritual authority in condemning heretics and indirectly exercised temporal authority in turning the condemned over to the state to be killed.

The AVIGNON PAPACY and the subsequent Western Schism brought to the fore the question of the pope's ultimate authority vis-a-vis the ecumenical council. Papal supremacy generated opposition on many levels from the CATHARI, WALDENSIANS, Franciscan Spirituals, Lollards, Wycliffites, and Hussites. All of these movements, especially the last, converged in the PROTESTANT REFORMATION.

The Reformation was as much a dispute about ecclesiastical authority as it was about doctrine. The reformers placed Scripture above all else (*sola scriptura*) as the final authority and guide to salvation; everyone, bishop and serf alike, was asked to submit to it. After the Council of TRENT (1545–60), Catholic bishops and theologians of the COUNTER-REFORMATION reaffirmed and formalized the medieval theory of dual authority. Authority, including the authority to interpret Scripture, was traced both from Scripture and from unwritten traditions handed down through the apostles, recorded in the teachings of the fathers, and vested in the teaching office, or MAGISTERIUM, of the pope and the bishops. This came to be called the DEPOSIT OF FAITH—as it were, goods contained in a trunk; authority became lodged in the church as an instutition, with the pope holding the keys to the trunk.

This Counter-Reformation idea of authority climaxed in the Ultramontanist VATICAN COUNCIL I, which vested the papacy with the quality of INFALLIBILITY when speaking *ex cathedra* in matters of faith and morals. At the outset many bishops and theologians north of the Alps, including many American bishops, opposed this idea of authority. The council had intended to balance the papal decrees with further statements about

the teaching office of the bishops, but the Franco-Prussian War broke out in 1870, putting an end to the deliberations. In the interim some noted bishops, theologians, and laity left the Catholic Church entirely in protest, forming the Old Catholic Church.

Others attempted to bring balance into the discussion through learned studies. Outstanding was the work of JOHN HENRY NEWMAN on the role of the episcopate in the magisterium and on the interplay between reason, conscience, and authority. In *On Consulting the Faithful in Matters of Doctrine* he demonstrated that even the laity have a role in the magisterial office of the church. During the Arian controversy a majority of bishops in the East sided with Arius; it was the ordinary faithful who upheld the orthodox teaching on the nature and person of the Christ.

Newman, whose ideas on authority were dismissed in his own time, found vindication at VATICAN COUNCIL II, which in many ways is the counter-council to Vatican I. Vatican II established the principle of collegiality. *Lumen Gentium*, the Dogmatic Constitution on the Church, stated unequivocally that the bishops, individually and collectively, share with the pope in the teaching authority of the church (18) as "one apostolic college," and that the true meaning of authority is *diakonia*, service or ministry (24). Infallibility is coshared by bishops when assembled in ecumenical council with the successor of Peter. The council also promoted local synods and councils, and regional and national conferences of bishops.

Immediately after Vatican II authority became more widely distributed in the Catholic Church, especially in national conferences of bishops. Of note are the many declarations of the Conference of Latin American Bishops (CELAM) and the United States Conference of Catholic Bishops. In the latter part of JOHN PAUL II's papacy there was a great retrenchment in matters of collegiality through the appointment of "Vatican bishops," often unqualified for pastoral ministry, and through the one-sided intervention of the Congregation for the Doctrine of the Faith, under the presidency of Cardinal Joseph Ratzinger (now Pope BENEDICT XVI), in local affairs, especially on issues like politics and ABORTION.

The theological question of authority has always involved tension between individual conscience and the communal church, between the prophetic office and the administrative offices of the church, between Scripture and its interpretation in the life of the church, and between the guidance of the clergy and the concurrence of the laity. With the exception of Newman, the authority of the laity in witnessing the Gospel message to the church has been all but ignored in the various Catholic debates. Such authority is acknowledged only post mortem when lay people are beatified and canonized.

See also BIBLE; CHURCH; ECCLESIOLOGY.

Further reading: John Barton, *People of the Book? The Authority of the Bible in Christianity* (London: S.P.C.K., 1993); Hans von Campenhausen, *Ecclesiastical Authority and Spiritual Power in the Church of the First Three Centuries* (Peabody, Mass.: Hendrickson, 1997); Gerard Minion, *Readings in Church Authority* (Burlington, Vt.: Ashgate, 2003); V. Alan McClelland, *By Who's Authority? Newman, Manning and the Magisterium* (Bath: Downside Abbey, 1996); John Henry Newman, *On Consulting the Faithful in Matters of Doctrine* (New York: Sheed & Ward, 1962); Thomas F. O'Leary, *Pope and Bible: The Search for Authority,* William K. Warren Lecture, University of Tulsa (October, 1988); Noel Timms and Kenneth Wilson, *Governance and Authority in the Roman Catholic Church* (London, S.P.C.K., 2000).

Averroes (ibn Rushd)   *See* ISLAM.

Avignon Papacy

This phrase describes one of the most scandalous periods in the history of Catholicism, during which the seat of the PAPACY was transferred to the city of Avignon in southern FRANCE from 1309 to 1377. The Italian poet Petrarch metaphorically referred to the period as the "Babylonian Captivity" of the church or papacy, referring to the exile of the Judaeans to Babylon under the Assyrian Nebuchadnezzar from 604 to 562 B.C.E. (1 Kings 24:14–16). Martin Luther (1483–1546) popularized the phrase in his *Babylonian Captivity of the Church.*

Under threat from the Holy Roman Emperor Henry VII (r. 1312–13), the French pope Clement V (r. 1305–14) moved the seat of the papacy to Avignon, where he managed to patch up relations with Philip VI of France (r. 1328–50). The Avignon popes purchased property from Queen Joanna I of Naples (r. 1343–81) and built a sumptuous court that presaged the lavish building projects of the Renaissance popes. Under the spiritual pressure of St. CATHERINE OF SIENA, Gregory XI (r. 1370–78) transferred the papacy back to Rome in 1378. French bishops rejected the move and elected rival popes. This sparked the Western SCHISM, sometimes called the Great Schism (not to be confused with the GREAT SCHISM between the Eastern and Western Churches). The Avignon papacy undertook financial and judicial changes leading to a further bureaucratization of the Western Church.

Further reading: Robert Coogan, *Babylon on the Rhone: A Translation of Letters by Dante, Petrarch and Catherine of Siena on the Avignon Papacy* (Madrid: José Porrùa Turanzas, 1983); B. Guillemain, *Le Court Pontificale d'Avignon 1309–27* (Paris: Bibliothèque des écoles francaises, 1962); Yves Renouard, *The Avignon Papacy 1305–1403* (Hamden Conn.: Archon Books, 1970).

B

Baader, Franz von (1765–1841) *mystical Romantic theologian*

Franz von Baader, a rare lay theologian of the Romantic era, championed mysticism as opposed to pure reason in both philosophy and theology. His rich but complex ideas have found echoes in many modern philosophers.

Baader had careers in mining engineering and medicine before he turned to speculative philosophy, the philosophy of religion, and ecumenism while teaching at the University of Munich in southern Germany. His thought is difficult to penetrate, presented as it was in German with a dense, metaphoric style. He detected distortions both on the side of faith (Pietism against reason) and on the side of reason (Enlightenment autonomous reason opposed to faith).

Baader championed the mystical thought of Jakob Boehme (1574–1624) and MEISTER ECKHARDT and the social speculations of Claude Saint-Simon (1760–1825). He advocated uncovering the inner harmonies between the realms of nature and the spirit. A true Romantic, he embraced organic thinking in opposition to the mechanical ideal (Newton's laws) of the Enlightenment. GOD is not just abstract being or substance but dynamic action and interaction. This anticipates the process thought of Alfred North Whitehead (1861–1947). Against the individualistic autonomous reason of Descartes—*cogito, ergo sum* "I think, therefore I am"—he posited a social reason—*cogitor ab alio (a Deo), ergo sum* "I am thought by another (by God), therefore I am." Before Marx, he detected the alienation of the masses in a mechanical, hierarchical social system.

Like some earlier GNOSTICS, he posited an androgynous understanding of Adam as the *Urmensch,* or primal human being, and taught that one of the chief functions of marriage was for the wife to solicit the female aspect from the husband and vice versa. The first offspring of marriage, he believed, should not be a physical child but love itself.

Baader felt that Eastern Orthodoxy preserved the Christian mystical tradition much better than the West and sought to establish long-lasting relations with Russian Orthodox leaders, especially Prince Alexander von Gallizin (1773–1844). He had both friendly and argumentative relations with Friedrich Schelling (1775–1854) and Georg F. W. Hegel (1770–1881). His influence spread to Søren Kierkegaard (1813–55) and Nicholas Berdyaev (1874–1948) in the 19th century and to the neo-Calvinist philosophers Abraham

Kuyper (1837–1920) and Herman Dooyeweerd (1894–1977) in the 20th.

Further reading: Franz von Baader's works: "Concerning the Conflict of Religious Faith and Knowledge" (1833), "On the Concept of Time" (1818), and "Elementary Concepts of Time" (1831), available online. ———, *Sämtliche Werke* (Aalen: Scientia, 1963); David Baumgardt, *Franz von Baader und die Philosophische Romantik* (Halle: Max Niemeyer, 1927); Ramon J. Betanzos, *Franz von Baader's Philosophy of Love* (Vienna: Passagen, 1998).

Balthasar, Hans Urs von (1905–1988)
influential 20th-century theologian

Champion of aesthetic theology, member of the NOUVELLE THÉOLOGIE circle, and colleague of many non-Catholic philosophers, Balthasar's creative energies were very influential at VATICAN COUNCIL II, although he himself did not attend. Becoming more traditional in his later years, he cofounded the theological journal *Communio* with Cardinal Ratzinger (later BENEDICT XVI).

Hans Urs von Balthassar was born in Lucerne, Switzerland. He studied at Benedictine and Jesuit schools and finished a doctorate on the question of eschatology in German literature at Zurich in 1928. After a retreat he decided to join the Jesuits, with whom he studied neoscholastic philosophy and theology. He was ordained in 1936.

Soon dissatisfied with the dry and narrow neoscholastic system, von Balthasar found fresh winds in the thought of Erich Przywara (1889–1972) and HENRI DE LUBAC, a Jesuit philosopher and theologian who are little known in the English world but who had enormous influence on the outcome of VATICAN COUNCIL II and formed the nucleus of the Nouvelle Théologie circle. Przywara introduced von Balthasar to a wider theological and philosophical world, including the Swiss Reformed theologian Karl Barth (1886–1968), the Jewish theologian Martin Buber (1878–1965), and the philosophers Edmund Husserl (1859–1939) and Edith Stein.

Przywara provided Balthasar with the key concepts of the polarity and analogy of being. Henri de Lubac introduced him to the Church fathers, the springtime thinkers of the church. Both fonts of theology allowed him to drink deeper in the tradition and to open up to new experience beyond the strictures of scholastic philosophy and theology as it had been taught since the Council of TRENT. He did several seminal studies of early Christian theologians, including ORIGEN, Evagrius (c. 536–600), AUGUSTINE, and DIONYSIUS the Pseudo-Areopagite.

In 1940 von Balthasar formed the lay spiritual Community of St. John with Adrienne von Speyr (1902–67), a doctor who converted to Catholicism under his direction and became a mystic and possibly a stigmatic. Because of this association he eventually left the Jesuit order in 1950, but he always remained loyal to the spirituality of the *Spiritual Exercises* of St. IGNATIUS OF LOYOLA.

Von Balthasar's theology is expressed in what he called his "Trilogy," comprising many volumes. Using the medieval transcendental categories of *pulchrum, bonun et verum* ("the beautiful, the good, and the true") he formulated a loose theological system encompassing 1) theophany, or a theological aesthetics, 2) theo-drama, and 3) theo-logic. The first describes his fundamental theology, for which he draws on myth, drama, music, dance, art, and poetry as well as philosophy. His anchor is the incarnate Logos, or Word, that beckons both from REVELATION and from the beauty of CREATION. The second is the drama of salvation in which Christianity subsumes tragedy and elevates it to hope in God's glory. The third focuses on truth, language, and interpretation. He himself explained this threefold, overlapping theological enterprise in "A Resume of My Thought": "A being *appears*, it has an epiphany in that it is beautiful and makes us marvel. In appearing it *gives* of itself, it delivers itself to us: it is good. And in giving itself up, it speaks itself, it unveils itself: it is true in itself, but in the other to which it reveals itself."

Many view von Balthasar, along with KARL RAHNER, as one of the preeminent theologians of the mid-20th century. Both appeal to the *Spiritual Exercises* of St. Ignatius of Loyola. Rahner's basic theological orientation is ethical decision in light of the mystical experience of everyday life. For him centeredness on human subjectivity opens to centeredness on God. Von Balthasar appeals to our openness to hear and accept the Word spoken in Revelation. For him centeredness on God opens the human as intersubjectivity. The first begins with immanence, the second with transcendence.

Balthasar became theologically cautious after Vatican Council II. In his later life he sought reentry into the Jesuit society and was nominated as a cardinal by Pope JOHN PAUL II in 1988, but he died before either event could take place. Since the 1980s conservative Catholics, often anti-Vatican II, have appealed to von Balthasar's writings as support for their position, but the thought of his creative period will survive his later caution and its distorted use.

Further reading: Von Balthasar's writings are too voluminous to list here. Most useful is *Hans Urs von Balthasar: The Von Balthasar Reader,* ed. Medard Kehl and Werner Loser (New York: Crossroads, 1982); Hans von Balthasar, *The Glory of the Lord: A Theological Aesthetics,* tr. Joseph Fessio and John K. Riches (San Francisco: Ignatius; New York: Crossroads, 1983–1991); ———, *Theo-drama: Theological Dramatic Theory* (San Francisco: Ignatius, 1988–1998); Werner Loser, "Karl Rahner and Hans Urs von Balthasar," *America* (Oct. 16, 1999) 181:11–16; Louis Roberts, *The Theological Aesthetics of Hans Urs von Balthasar* (Washington, D.C.: Catholic University of America Press, 1987); David L. Schindler, *Hans Urs von Balthasar: His Life and Work* (San Francisco: Ignatius Press, 1991).

Baltimore Catechism

The "Baltimore Catechism" was the chief instrument for teaching Catholic doctrine to millions of lay people in the United States for more than 100 years. Published in 1885 under the title *A General Catechism of Christian Doctrine, Prepared and Enjoined by the Order of the Third Plenary Council of Baltimore,* the book defined Catholicism for generations of immigrants and American-born faithful.

The work was supervised by Cardinal JAMES GIBBONS. The Italian priest Januarius di Concilio of the diocese of Jersey City prepared a rough draft, with 421 questions in 37 chapters. Responding to criticism, di Concilio revised the work with the help of Bishop John L. Spalding (1840–1916) of Peoria. The final version, eventually known as *Baltimore Catechism No. 1,* with 208 questions in 33 chapters, received the imprimatur of Cardinal John McCloskey (1810–85) of New York. The CATECHISM followed the topical order of the Roman Catechism of St. Charles BORROMEO: creed, sacraments, and commandments. The text followed a rather infantile question and answer style: Q: Who made me? A: God made me.

The catechism came in for a lot of theological criticism. It dealt with the RESURRECTION in only one question, and the HOLY SPIRIT received short shrift. Answers were simplistic. Rival catechisms were put out. Finally, Archbishop Edwin V. O'Hara (1881–1956), founder of the National Catholic Rural Conference and promoter of the influential CONFRATERNITY OF CHRISTIAN DOCTRINE, supervised a revision that appeared in 1941 as *The Revised Baltimore Catechism.* Redemptorist theologian Francis J. Connell had input on the revision. In 1994, the more sophisticated *Catechism of the Catholic Church* finally replaced the Baltimore Catechism, although many conservative Catholics still use the Baltimore text on an unofficial basis.

Further reading: All earlier editions of the Baltimore Catechism are available online; *A Catechism of Christian Doctrine, Prepared and Enjoined by Order of the Third Plenary Council of Baltimore* (New York: Benziger, 1885; Rockford, Ill.: Tan, 1974); *Father Connell's Confraternity Edition, New Baltimore Catechism,* official revised edition 1949 (New York: Benzinger Brothers, 1955); John

K. Sharp, "How the Baltimore Catechism Originated," *Ecclesiastical Review* (1929) 81: 573–586.

banns of marriage (Middle Eng.: *ban,* "proclamation")

Banns are the formal, public proclamation of a couple announcing their intention to marry. The institution arose after CHARLEMAGNE decreed that there be an inquiry into all marriages to determine the possibility of consanguinity. The banns are discussed in cn. 1067 of the current *Code of Canon Law,* and the practice was confirmed at the Lateran Council IV in 1215 (*see* COUNCILS, ECUMENICAL). It is up to the local BISHOP or ordinary to determine the manner of publishing banns. Most often they are published in the local parish bulletin.

Further reading: James B. Roberts, *The Banns of Marriage* (Washington, D.C.: Catholic University of America Press, 1931).

baptism (Gr.: *baptizō,* "to plunge into," "wash in water")

Baptism, found in the New Testament, is the primary SACRAMENT of initiation for Christianity in general and Catholicism in particular. During baptism, a person is washed or ritually purified of her or his SINS, and through that purification is renewed to life and to a new spiritual relationship as a child of GOD. For Catholics baptism is also the rite of entry into the church, removing all stain of original sin and conferring a plentitude of GRACE.

There are not many references to baptism as a ritual in the Hebrew Bible. In 2 Kings (5:14), Naaman, commander of the army of Aram and a leper, washes seven times in the Jordan at the behest of the prophet Elisha and is cleansed. St. IRENAEUS OF LYONS, followed by other church fathers, took this event as a "sign" pointing toward baptism (*Fragment* 34). The laws of Leviticus prescribe ritual baths (*mikvaoth*), washings, sprinklings, and cleansings for a number of impurities (touching a corpse, shedding blood, bodily discharges, etc.) that impede participation in worship (Lev. 14–15). Early Christian writers saw circumcision, passing through the Flood, and the Red Sea as types of baptism (Col. 2:9–12; 1 Peter 3:20–21; Cor. 10:1–2).

The mystery religions that spread through the Hellenistic world in the time of Alexander the Great (356–23 B.C.E.) practiced various libations, lustrations or washings, baptisms, and other cleansings as part of their initiation ceremonies. In the cult of Isis, for example, the initiand went through various stages of purification before being revealed the secret teachings, clothed in a new garment and carrying a lighted torch (Apuleius, *Metamorphoses* 11:22–26). The initiation established an intimate relation between the devotee and the cult god. Attached to all initiations was the hope of immortality. Many claim the initiation rites of the mystery religions shaped the wording and practices of CHRISTIAN baptism, although others argue that the influence could have been the other way. At the least, there seems to have been an interchange between the two.

Among the immediate precedents to Christian baptism were the ritual purifications attested to in the Qumran writings, and JOHN THE BAPTIST's activity at the Jordan River just before Jesus' own ministry. The Qumran Community Code relates that new members are "cleansed for sprinkling with purifying waters," which unite them with the Spirit of the Counsel of Truth (1QS 3:7–10). The rite must be accompanied with the right intention. The Qumranites saw themselves as an advance community in preparation for the eschatological Age to Come; their baptisms thus had a messianic component. Many scholars have argued that John the Baptist may have had intimate connections with the Qumranites or other Essenes, and, in fact, he preached a baptism of repentance for the forgiveness of sins (Mark 1:1–5).

Jesus' own messianic mission is revealed at his baptism by John when the heavens open and the

Spirit descends (Mark 1:10). A problem arises: how is it that the sinless Son of God repents and seeks forgiveness for sins through baptism? Matthew 3:1–11 finesses the point by stressing Jesus' superiority to John, in that his baptism draws down the Spirit. Luke provides a similar rationale, while John drops the baptism scene altogether. The problem perplexed later writers who adopted the formula that Jesus became like humans "in all things save sin (*see* Heb. 2:17)." They stressed his closeness to the human condition in saving humanity from sin. Some of the earliest depictions of John "baptizing" Jesus, as in the orthodox and Arian baptisteries of Ravenna, do not show the pouring of water but only John placing his hand on Jesus' head to facilitate the descent of the Spirit in the form of a dove. On the other hand, many

Baptism of Jesus in the Jordan by St. John the Baptist (Mark 1:9–11). Rococo drawing and wash by François Boucher (1703–70). *(St. Louis Art Museum, with permission)*

early church theologians maintained that Christ's baptism instituted the church's sacrament of baptism (St. Ambrose of Milan, *On Luke* 2.83).

Paul bears witness to the earliest theology of baptism. Baptism unites the believer to the death and resurrection of Jesus (Rom. 6:4); it cleanses a person of sin (1 Cor. 6:11); through it the Spirit incorporates a person into the Body of Christ beyond social categories of being a Jew or a Greek, a slave or a free person (1 Cor. 12:13). Luke, in Acts, associates baptism with the reception of the Spirit (8:15; 10:47). The Great Commission at the end of Matthew enjoins the followers of Jesus to preach the Gospel to all nations, "baptizing them in the name of the Father, the Son and the Holy Spirit" (28:19–20). Although some passages in Acts (2:38; 10:48) speak of baptism "in the name of (the Lord) Jesus (Christ)," the standard formula and ritual soon became a triple immersion or sprinkling while reciting the names of the TRINITY. Anabaptists argue against infant baptism, but the New Testament attests to whole households being baptized (Acts 10:47; 16:15; 1 Cor. 1:16), and early Christian art in the CATACOMBS shows very young children receiving the rite.

In the second century the theology, rules, and rites of baptism began to assume canonical form. St. IGNATIUS OF ANTIOCH and the earliest theologians stated that baptism is the regeneration of the person to a new state. The *Didache,* or Teaching of the Twelve Apostles, lays down rules for baptism, such as using the name of the Father, Son, and Holy Spirit, a preference for flowing water, and fasting prior to the rite (8:1–4). Both TERTULLIAN in *On Baptism* and HIPPOLYTUS OF ROME in *Apostolic Tradition* fill out the details of the early rite. Those elements include 1) a catechumenate, or instruction period, lasting upwards of three years (*see* CATECHESIS/CATECUMENATE), 2) fasting and a vigil of prayer, 3) confession of sins, 4) renunciation of Satan followed by an anointing with the oil of exorcism, 5) at cockcrow a threefold profession of faith (the earliest form of the CREED) with a threefold baptism by triple immersion/sprinkling in the name of the Father, Son, and Holy Spirit, including children, 6) anointing with the holy oil of thanksgiving, 7) laying on of hands by a bishop or appointed minister, and 8) a symbolic meal of milk and honey with a EUCHARIST. Later some of the last elements of the baptism liturgy were separated off into the rite of CONFIRMATION. By the MIDDLE AGES Christianity became pervasive in the culture, and the catechumenate, or instruction period, was no longer needed and all but disappeared.

In the third century a controversy arose over the VALIDITY of baptisms (and other sacraments) administered by "heretics" or ungodly bishops or priests. Rebaptism was defended by TERTULLIAN, St. CYPRIAN OF CARTHAGE, and the Councils of Carthage in 255 and 256. Pope Stephen I (r. 254–57) refused to recognize rebaptism. The debate came to a head in the dispute between the Donatists and orthodox parties in North Africa. Following the decree of the Council of Arles (314) that all baptisms are valid if done in the name of the Trinity, St. AUGUSTINE OF HIPPO argued that sacraments performed by sinners and heretics are nonetheless valid because the true minister and agent of the sacrament is Christ himself bestowing his grace on the believer (*On the Gospel of John* 6.7). This became the basis for the doctrine of EX OPERE OPERATO, basing the validity of the rite on the "doing of the deed" rather than *ex opere operantis,* on the "doing of the doer." Later in his arguments with the Pelagians on infant baptism, Augustine maintains that even an infant inherits an original sinfulness from Adam (*Letters* 166.6).

One final element of baptism is that, like confirmation and HOLY ORDERS, it produces an indelible mark, seal, or character (*sphragis*) on the soul of the recipient. The term occurs in the New Testament (John 6:27; 2 Cor. 1:22), but it was CLEMENT OF ROME (*2 Clement* 7:6) and the author of the *Shepherd of Hermas* (8.6.3) that first used it as synonymous with the guarantee of the effect of baptism. Sts. Cyril of Jerusalem and Augustine of Hippo developed the idea further to mean a mark produced by the Spirit, whether or not grace is

bestowed, to mark the soul as a possession of God (Augustine, *Against Gaudentius* 1.12.13). Augustine compared it to the military mark (*nota militaris*), showing which commander a soldier belonged to.

The Reformation brought changes to the theology of baptism. For Martin Luther (1483–1546) the baptized person, while justified by imputation of Christ's grace, remains a sinner in nature (*simul justus et peccator*). For Huldrich Zwingli (1484–1531) all depended upon faith; baptism was only an external sign or figure admitting a person to the church. Calvin, following a hardline doctrine of predestination, believed that baptism was efficacious only for the elect. Quakers, appealing to Christ as the Inner Light, dispensed with the external rite altogether. Enlightenment theology was relatively indifferent toward the theology of baptism until the Tractarians of the OXFORD MOVEMENT revived the early Catholic teaching of baptism as regeneration.

Today the ordinary ministers of baptism are bishops, priests, and deacons. However, in an emergency any person, believer or not, who intends to fulfill the intentions of the baptisand can administer the rite both lawfully and validly. Catholics, like most Christians, consider baptism necessary to obtain the grace of salvation.

The early Christians recognized the baptism of blood, by which catechumens witnessed to their faith if they suffered martyrdom before undergoing the rite (*see* MARTYR). This demonstrates that intention springing from faith takes precedent over the actual rite. Likewise, an unbaptized person can attain salvation through the desire to do all things necessary to fulfill God's will even though the person has never heard the Gospel. The Council of TRENT called this the "baptism of desire" (*votum*) and VATICAN COUNCIL II identifies it with the pure conscience emanating from God's grace (*Lumen Gentium,* 16 Dogmatic Constitution on the Church).

Following the instruction of Vatican Council II, the Congregation for the Liturgy issued the Rite for the Initiation of Adults (1972) and reinstated the model of Hippolytus's *Apostolic Tradition*, as presented in the *Catechecism of the Catholic Church* (1213–84). The council also reinstated both the ancient form of baptism for the Easter Vigil service and the Rite of the Catechumenate, which ends with the Rite of Election, an intense period of study, prayer, and fasting corresponding to Lent, immediately prior to the public baptism conducted as part of the Easter Vigil Resurrection Mass. The Rite for Baptism of Children was also reformed in 1969, including a session questioning the parents' willingness to instruct their children in the faith.

Contemporary Pentecostal and charismatic groups stress the "baptism of the Spirit," which confers the gifts mentioned in 1 Corinthians 12. They argue that there are just as many texts in the New Testament illustrating Spirit baptism as water baptism, especially in the Book of Acts (2:4; 11:15, etc.). The Pentecostal movement, whose roots go back to the American holiness movements, themselves derived from John Wesley's doctrine of perfection, has strongly shaped the Catholic charismatic movement (*see* CHARISMATIC RENEWAL.)

Further reading: The body of early Christian writing on baptism is enormous. The following primary sources are available online: *Didache* 7; Tertullian of Carthage, *On Baptism*; Cyril of Jerusalem, *Catecheses* 19–21; Ambrose of Milan, *On the Mysteries*; Augustine, *On Baptism*; *Enchiridion* 13; Thomas Aquinas, *Summa Theologiae* 3.66–71; *Catechism of the Catholic Church* (Ligouri Mo.: Ligouri, 1994); James D. G. Dunn, *Baptism in the Spirit* (Philadelphia: Westminster, 1970); Maxwell E. Johnson, *The Rites of Christian Initiation: Their Evolution and Interpretation* (Collegeville, Minn.: Liturgical Press, 1999); Aidan Kavanagh, *The Shape of Baptism: The Rite of Christian Initiation.* (Collegeville, Minn.: The Liturgical Press/Pueblo, 1978); Kilian McDonnell and George T. Montague, *Christian Initiation and Baptism in the Holy Spirit* (Collegeville, Minn.: Liturgical Press, 1991); Rudolf Schnackenburg, *Baptism in the Thought of St. Paul* (Oxford: Blackwell, 1964).

baptistery (Gk.: *baptisērion*, "bathing [swimming] pool")

A structure, either free-standing or attached to a cathedral or church, where catechumens receive instruction in the CHRISTIAN faith and undergo BAPTISM, especially during the Easter Vigil service. The early evidence shows that the first followers of Jesus, following the model of Jesus' baptism by John in the Jordan (Mark 1:9), chose to be baptized in flowing water wherever possible (Acts 3:36; 16:13). The DIDACHE 7 gives various options. Jews built their synagogues near flowing water for their ritual baths (*mikvaoth*). In the second and third centuries Christians adapted the form of the Hellenistic bathing pool for ritual purposes as baptismal fonts. Various terms were used: *fons* or fountain; *piscina*, or fish pond; and *kolumbe thra*, or bird bath.

The earliest known baptistery is in the house church of Dura Europos; it is decorated with murals of CHRIST as Good Shepherd, Adam and Eve, the Samaritan Woman at the Well, Women at the Tomb, and the Miracles of Jesus (*see* ARCHAEOLOGY). Later baptistery pools took many shapes: rectangle, square, cross, circle, oval, clover trefoil, hexagon (Christ died on the sixth day of the Hebrew week), octagon (Christ rose on the eighth day), or a mixture of shapes. The baptistery of Santa Thecla in Milan, built by AMBROSE, and those in Ravenna set the octagon style. The baptisteries of North Africa are outstanding for their mosaics and rich symbolism.

The cruciform font from the church of the priest Felix in Kélibia, Tunisia, shows a dedication to Sts. CYPRIAN and Adelphos by the donors, Aquinius and his wife, Juliana. It is adorned with the Chi-Rho christogram underhung by the Alpha and Omega on the bottom and duplicated inside and outside the font in the four directions. This font illustrates amply all the imagery associated with baptism. Water symbols abound, including Noah's ark, fish, Leviathan (?), and dolphins; also depicted are doves, candles, and flora, all framed by four kraters, or urns, from which grow grape

Mosaic inlaid baptismal font, Church of the Priest Felix, Kélibia, Tunisia, dedicated to Sts. Cyprian and Adelphos, fifth to sixth centuries. This exceptional baptismal font demonstrates all the symbolism surrounding baptism: the Christ monogram surrounded by the Alpha and the Omega, the Paschal candle, flowering branches, birds, doves, fish, dolphins, the Tree of Life, and a large sea creature, perhaps symbolizing the Leviathan of the deep and the waters of creation. *(Bardo Museum, Tunis, Tunisia)* *(photo by J. Patout Burns, with permission)*

vines. At the base are the three words "Peace, Faith, and Love" (not visible) instead of the more standard Faith, Hope, and Love (1 Cor. 3:13); peace and unity were ardently sought by Cyprian and the church in North Africa in the face of the long-lasting Donatist controversy.

Generally, the baptisand entered from the west (symbolizing the darkness of sunset, renunciation of Satan, old life) to the east (brightness of sunrise, entrance into the grace of Christ, new life). There were usually three steps down, corresponding to the questions about the TRINITY in the baptismal ritual. The four lobes probably signified the four rivers of Paradise from which flow the living waters of CREATION and re-creation. Descending was also imaged as entering into the womb/tomb and ascending as rebirth/resurrection to new life.

The baptistery at St. John Lateran, begun around 315 but much modified over time, estab-

lished an octagonal standard that was later followed by the baptisteries at Ravenna (*see* ARCHITECTURE,) and lasted into later times. The famous baptistery at Florence, begun c. 1059, graced with the famous "Gate of Paradise" doors by Lorenzo Ghiberti (1378–1455), is in the Lateran pattern. Other celebrated baptisteries include those at Pisa, Poitiers, and Parma.

Further reading: John G. Davies, *The Architectural Setting of Baptism* (London: Barrie & Rockliff, 1962).

baroque *See* ARCHITECTURE; PAINTING AND SCULPTURE.

Bartholomew's Day Massacre, St.

On the feast of St. Bartholomew on August 23–24, 1572, between 5,000 and 10,000 French Calvinist Huguenots were massacred in Paris and throughout France, including their champion, Admiral Gaspard de Coligny (1519–72), at the instigation of Catherine de' Medici (1519–89), relative of Pope Clement VII [Guilio de' Medici] (r. 1523–34) and regent queen mother of the French king, Charles IX (1560–74). Together with Henri de Lorraine, third duc de Guise (1550–88), Catherine had begun by plotting the murder of de Coligny; when that failed she unleashed a tide of slaughter mostly carried out by the League, a Catholic alliance of anti-Protestants. The massacre marked the fourth of the Wars of Religion in France, which were ended only by the Edict of Nantes (1598) under Henry IV (r. 1589–1610).

Adding salt to the wound, Pope Gregory XIII (r. 1572–85) struck a medal commemorating the event in gory detail. He also commissioned Giorgio Vasari (1511–74) to paint a mural of it in the Vatican. It is an ugly blot in Catholic history and became a major obstacle to later attempts at rapprochement between Catholics and Protestants.

Further reading: Robert M. Kingdom, *Myths about the St. Bartholomew's Day Massacres, 1572–1576* (Cambridge Mass.: Harvard University Press, 1988); Nicola M. Sutherland, *The Massacre of St. Bartholomew and the European Conflict, 1559–1572* (New York: Barnes & Noble, 1973).

base communities

In LIBERATION THEOLOGY, base communities (from the Spanish *comunidades eclesiales de base*) are the praxis or community-formation aspect of liberation theology. The concept also has deep roots in the CATHOLIC ACTION movement among the working classes in Belgium, France, and other European communities early in the 20th century.

An early supporter of base communities was Joseph Cardijn (1882–1967), founder of the Young Christian Workers, who was an inspiration to the French worker priest movement and to DOROTHY DAY and the Catholic Workers movement in the United States. Cardijn's method, influenced by unionists in England and Europe, was to get working Christians to enact the threefold task: "observe-judge-act." The priest trained leaders of small cells of workers and then took a secondary role as an adviser. The action was to come "from the base." The YCW movement spun off into the Christian Family Movement, which spread to North and South America during the late 1940s and early 1950s where it took on a very middle-class character.

Another source for the base communities movement was the Cursillos de Christianidad, intense retreats that began in Spain and spread to the Americas. Brazilian Paolo Freire (1921–97) was an immediate source; his *Pedagogy of the Oppressed* (1968) promoted education based on life experience and honed through dialogue. The goal was to build on social capital toward liberation through critical *conscientização,* or consciousness-raising. Proponents of liberation theology argue that the early Christian house-churches were none other than base communities. Unlike parishes, which are defined by territory, base communities are defined by common needs and interests.

Base communities have had significant influence in the church life of Central and South America, altering the church's relations with the social world, the education of the faith, and the practice of the sacraments, especially the EUCHARIST, in the life of the oppressed. In *The Gospel in Solentiname* (1978) Ernesto Cardinal illustrates using the Gospel reading as an occasion for critical dialogue among the faithful. While base communities have had a strong influence in LATIN AMERICA and parts of the Third World, they have failed to catch on in the United States except among a portion of the Hispanic population, which, however, has now become the largest minority in the United States.

Base communities are not directly mentioned in the documents of Vatican II. In *Evangelii Nuntiandi* (December 8, 1975) Pope PAUL VI refers to them as a way to a renewed evangelization of the world but warns against the critical attitude of some against the "institutional" church (58). Their role was affirmed at the Medellin Conference of Latin American Bishops (1968), reaffirmed by JOHN PAUL II at Puebla (1979), and again affirmed by the Latin American bishops in Santo Domingo (1992).

There have been strong critiques of base communities and the liberation theology that undergirds them. Most criticisms focus on what opponents take to be Marxist elements in liberation thinking and its no-holds-barred attack on what it considers the deleterious effects of unrestrained capitalism. The lay theologian Michael Novak (1933–), for example, critiques the movement for its rejection of capitalism and the multinational corporation, which he legitimates as the chief moral force in the modern world. Most formidable has been the "Instruction on Certain Aspects of the 'Theology of Liberation'" (August 8, 1984) issued by the Vatican Congregation for the Doctrine of the Faith under the presidency of Cardinal Joseph Ratzinger. The document forcefully asserts the hierarchical authority of the magisterium and all but accuses liberation theology of being a Marxist front. The congregation, with the apparent approval of the pope, formally silenced the Franciscan LEONARDO BOFF, perhaps the foremost Catholic liberation theologian, in 1985. The punishment boomeranged and added to Boff's prestige on the world stage.

Despite papal praise for small Christian communities, the Vatican has appointed bishops who have sought to minimize the effect of base communities in their midst. Vatican support seems to be going to traditional Catholic institutions instead, such as OPUS DEI and the Legionnaires of Christ, from which the papacy apparently hopes to obtain more priests to ease a worldwide shortage. Base communities are primarily of the laity, by the laity, for the laity; they do not produce new priests, and are perceived to be beyond the control of the Vatican. Nonetheless, base communities are surviving and thriving in many parts of Central and South America.

Further reading: Leonardo Boff, *Church, Charism, & Power* (New York: Crossroads, 1988); John Burdick and W. E. Hewitt, *The Church at the Grassroots in Latin America* (Westport, Conn.: Praeger, 2000); Phillip Berryman, *Liberation Theology* (Philadelphia: Temple University Press, 1987); John Eagleson and Philip Scharper, *Puebla and Beyond* (Maryknoll, N.Y.: Orbis Books, 1980); Barabard Fraser and Paul Jeffrey, "Base Communities, Once Hope of Church, Now in Disarray," *National Catholic Reporter* (November 12, 2004).

Basel, Council of (1431–1449) *first stage of the 17th Ecumenical Council of Basel-Ferrara-Florence*

The Council of Basel was a follow-up to the Councils of Pisa and CONSTANCE; all three were attempts to deal with the consequences of the demoralizing AVIGNON PAPACY and WESTERN SCHISM. The Florence stage will be discussed separately under Council of FLORENCE. Basel was the most democratic of all church councils; it included papal legates and bishops, but also abbots, religious

superiors, clerks, and theologians in its deliberations. Nevertheless, it eventually failed in its attempts to reform the church or reign in the power of the papacy.

Following the procedures agreed upon at Pisa and Constance, Martin V (r. 1417–31) duly called the council, which was presided over by Cardinal Juliano Cesarini (1398–1444). The agenda included church reform, the problem of the Hussites, and a possible reunion with the EASTERN ORTHODOX churches. The Byzantine Emperor John VIII Paleologos and the Patriarch Demetrios Protonostiarius Palaeologos Metotides sent ambassadors to seek support from the papacy against the advancing Turks and possible reunification with the West.

Martin's successor, Pope Eugenius IV (r. 1431–47), tried to dissolve the council in 1431 against the judgment of Cesarini and the other bishops in attendance; the bishops, relying on the decrees at Constance, and upholding the principle of the superiority of the council over the PAPACY, did not disband. They had the support of the northern princes. In the face of increased attendance, including many abbots, religious, and doctors of the church (including NICHOLAS OF CUSA), Eugenius revoked his decree of dissolution in the bull *Dudum Sacrum* (December 15, 1433). Emboldened, the council proceeded to put more pressure on the papacy, seeking to regulate the selection of cardinals and to reorganize the VATICAN CURIA itself. In the Hussite controversy it conceded Communion in both kinds (bread and wine) to the Bohemian church, but it broke with the Eastern Orthodox over terms of reunion.

In 1437 Eugenius IV once more dissolved the Basel Council, transferring deliberations to Ferrara and then, in 1438, to Florence. This time he won the support of many bishops and of the previously neutral emperor Sigismund (r. 1433–37). A rump council at Basel excommunicated Eugenius and elected Duke Amadeus VIII of Savoy as pope. He reigned as antipope until 1449 under the name Felix V (r. 1439–49). Under pressure from bishops and princes the Basel party moved to Lausanne, where it dissolved itself in 1449.

The Eastern Orthodox representatives followed the pope to Florence. The new union proved short-lived, but more lasting unions were decreed with the Bosnians, the SYRIANS, the CHALDEANS, and the MARONITES of Cyprus (see ASIA).

The pope's victory in moving the council to Ferrara insured the monarchical conception of the Western Church. Basel's deliberations remain much disputed, but most theologians recognize as legitimate those decrees passed until the move to Ferrara.

See also COUNCIL/COUNCILIARISM.

Further reading: Joachim Stieber, *Pope Eugenius IV, the Council of Basel and the Secular and Ecclesiastical Authorities in the Empire* (Leiden: Brill, 1978); Ulrich Horst, *Autorität und Immunität des Paptes* (Paderborn: F. Schöningh, 1991); Antony Black, *Monarchy and Community: Political Ideas in the Later Conciliar Controversy* (Cambridge: Cambridge University Press, 1970).

basilica (Gr.: *basilikos*, "pertaining to the king [or emperor]")

A basilica was a certain type of Roman building that became the model for most major early CHRISTIAN churches. Canonically, the term refers to a church with a certain status and function.

Common in the third and fourth centuries, basilicas were large, high-ceilinged, rectangular buildings used as audience halls, courts, and marketplaces. Often the entrance looked toward a niche or apse at the far end, where thrones or daises for dignitaries were placed. Later the chair or cathedra of a bishop was placed in the apse, behind the altar. Prime examples include Constantine's Aula Palatina in Trier, now a Lutheran church, the Old St. Peter's (see ARCHITECTURE), and the Basilica of St. John Lateran. The last was a former imperial palace that Constantine donated to the bishop of Rome as his seat and residence.

The basic basilica form could take on additions: two or more aisles separated by rows of columns; an atrium or courtyard, sometimes with a fountain; a narthex or antechamber/porch with high doorways leading into the nave; and a transept in front of the apse and transverse to the nave giving the hall a cruciform shape. Some basilicas were built to enclose a martyrion, or martyr's shrine, in or beneath the apse. The Old St. Peter's is just such a martyrion basilica.

Canonically, Rome has four major basilicas, each traditionally dedicated to one of the four original patriarchies of the church East and West: St. John Lateran (Rome), St. Peter's (Constantinople), St. Paul outside the Walls (Alexandria) Santa Maria Maggiore (Antioch) and St. Lawrence outside the Walls (Jerusalem). All other basilicas are minor and so designated by the pope.

A basilica is a church that plays a significant role in the religious life of a region, enjoying certain privileges and INDULGENCES. They are often shrines of PILGRIMAGE. Noted examples are the Cathedral and Shrine of Our Lady of Guadalupe in Mexico City, Notre Dame Cathedral in Quebec City, the Cathedral of St. Louis, the Mission Dolores in San Francisco, and St. Patrick's Cathedral in New York City. Basilicas have three insignia, or signs, of recognition: an umbrella striped red and yellow, formerly accompanying Roman authorities and popes in procession, the papal coat-of-arms over the main door way, and a bell, formerly used to signal the approach of a papal procession.

Further reading: John G. Davies, *The Early Christian Church* (London: Wedienfeld & Nicolson, 1965); Richard Krautheimer, *Early Christian and Byzantine Architecture* (Harmondsworth: Penguin, 1981).

Basil the Great, St. (c. 330–379) *doctor of the church and monastic founder*

Basil was the son of aristocrats Basil the Elder and Emmelia, the brother of Sts. GREGORY OF NYSSA and Macrina, and the friend of GREGORY OF

NAZIANZUS. He was highly educated in both Greek and CHRISTIAN learning at Caesarea in Cappadocia, CONSTANTINOPLE, and Athens. He joined the monastic community set up by his mother and sister at Annesi, for which he cowrote the monastic rule still used in the East. He was called to the see of Caesarea, where he engaged in controversies with the Arians, the Pneumatomachoi (Gk.: "spirit-fighters"), and the patriarchs of Rome and Alexandria. His feast day is January 1 in the East and January 2 in the West.

Basil became noted for his charitable works, setting up dispensaries next to the monasteries he founded, a pattern for the future in both East and West. His treatise *On the Holy Spirit* countered the Pneumatomachoi ("spirit-fighters"), who denied the divinity of the Holy Spirit. His treatise *Against Eunomius* advanced the orthodoxy of the Council of Nicaea I against latter-day ARIANISM. He suggested the phrase "invariably like in being" to mediate the difference between the Arians and the orthodox (*Letter* 9).

He wrote two treatises on monks in the common life for those who make up one Body of Christ, called the *Small* and the *Great Asceticon*. These treatises, which favored communal existence over the life of a hermit, shaped both eastern and western MONASTICISM. His *Hexameron,* a commentary on the six days of creation, favored the literal interpretation of the ANTIOCHENE SCHOOL. His *Address to Young Men* became a favorite during the RENAISSANCE for its advocacy of classical learning.

St. Basil shaped the liturgy of the present EASTERN ORTHODOXY and the COPTIC CHURCH and was a source for the reformation of the LITURGY at VATICAN COUNCIL II. The Eastern Orthodox still use Basil's liturgy during Lent, on Maundy Thursday, on the eves of EASTER and Christmas, and on his feast day. Few churchman have had as deep and far-reaching influence as St. Basil.

Further reading: Many of Basil's writings are available online. Hans von Campenhausen, *The Fathers of the Church* (Peabody, Mass.: Hendrickson, 1998); Philip Rousseau, *St. Basil of Caesarea* (Berkeley: University of California Press, 1994); Joseph Tawil, *St. Basil the Great* (Newton: Sophia, 1981).

beatific vision

Beatific vision (literally, the vision that makes blessed) is the direct and immediate experience of GOD's being and love without the mediation of any creature; it can occur, according to Catholic teaching, after death. The teaching rests on two key texts. Exodus 33:11 speaks of Moses meeting God "face-to-face." Paul echoes this in his great Hymn on Love when he says "Now we see darkly as in a mirror, but then [in the age to come] we shall see face to face" (1 Cor. 13:12).

The nature of the beatific vision was much debated during the MIDDLE AGES. To refute the views of certain perfectionist Beghards and Beguines, the Council of Vienne (1311–12) decreed that the state of beatitude is beyond this life and hence is a supernatural gift of the "light of glory" (cn. 28.5). In the constitution *Benedictus Deus* (January 29, 1336) Benedict XII said that after death and even before reunion with the body, the soul would see "the divine essence intuitively and indeed face-to-face." THOMAS AQUINAS, referring to Moses (Exod. 34:28–35) and Paul (2 Cor. 12:2–4), maintained that the beatific vision can be granted to some blessed souls briefly in this life. Although humans have a natural desire for a vision of God, its bestowal is a supremely gratuitous and supernatural gift of God who freely and lovingly communicates the divine self (*Summa Theologiae* 2–1.5.5). In CATHEDRALS the rose windows illumined by the setting sun serve as a foretaste of the beatific vision. The doctrine of the beatific vision combines elements of ESCHATOLOGY, theological anthropology, and the theology of GRACE.

Further reading: Kenneth E. Kirk, *The Vision of God* (New York: Harper&Row, 1966); Christian Trottmann *La Vision Béatifique: des disputes scolastiques à sa définition par Benoît XII* (Rome: École française, 1995).

beatification   *See* SANCTIFICATION.

beatitudes

Beatitudes (literally "blessednesses") are statements of praise and comfort made to certain people for particular conditions or virtues. The primary background for the CHRISTIAN idea of beatitudes are the blessings and curses promised to the Israelites in recompense for keeping or violating the commandments of the Covenant (e.g., Deut. 28; Josh. 24:1–27). The prophets also declared curses or woes on Israel and the nations in what are known as prophetic lawsuits (Mic. 1–2), as well as promised blessings when Israel was at a low point. Other Hebrew texts declare blessedness on various states of life or virtue: for having a good wife (Sir. 25:8), for being chosen by GOD (Psalms 84:4), for fearing the Lord (Ps. 1:1), for doing justice and aiding the poor (Ps. 41:1; 106:5), and for keeping the Sabbath (Isa. 56:2).

The beatitudes appear in Luke's Sermon on the Plain (6:20–23) and Matthew's Sermon on the Mount (5:13–12). In *Q,* or *Quelle* (Ger.: "Source"), the document believed to be a common source for Luke and Matthew, the beatitudes appear as part of the Covenant renewal ceremonies that Jesus conducted in Galilee as a central feature of his mission. Luke's version refers to coming blessedness for those currently suffering from hunger, poverty, and desolation. The blessings are accompanied with four woes upon those who have breached God's Covenant with Israel by neglecting the widow, the orphan, the poor, and the hungry. Matthew's version is spiritualized ("blessed are the poor in spirit") and reflects a condition of great persecution, perhaps under Nero. There is much devotional and often sentimental writing about the beatitudes in both Catholic and Protestant literature.

Further reading: Richard Horsley and Jonathan Draper, *Whoever Hears You Hears Me: Prophets, Performance and* *Tradition in Q* (Harrisburg, Penn.: Trinity, 1999); H. B. Huffmon, "The Covenant Lawsuit in the Prophets," *Journal of Biblical Literature* 78 (1959): 285–295; Gerald Vann, *The Divine Pity: A Study in the Social Implications of the Beatitudes* (Glasgow: Collins & World, 1977).

Bec, Abbey of   *See* MONASTERY.

Becket, St. Thomas à (c. 1120–1170)
English churchman and martyr

A close friend and chancellor to Henry II Plantagenet of England (1133–89) who appointed him archbishop of Canterbury, Becket defied the king to defend the church's independence and paid with his life. His death stirred outrage across Europe; Alexander III (r. 1159–81) canonized him in 1173, and his burial site in Canterbury Cathedral became a place of pilgrimage. His feast day is December 29.

Thomas was born in London of Norman parents. He studied at Merton Priory in Surrey and in Paris. Archbishop Theobald of Canterbury (d. 1161) made him a member of his household and sent him to study law at Bologna and Auxerre. Upon his return in 1154 Theobald made him archdeacon of Canterbury. Henry, now married to Eleanor of Aquitaine (c. 1122–1204), made Thomas chancellor of state. Thomas frolicked, hunted, and even fought alongside Henry on an expedition to France, the last act being clearly in violation of canon law for clerics.

Upon Theobald's death, Henry engineered Thomas's election as archbishop of Canterbury the following year. Once in office, however, Thomas began to uphold the rights of the archbishopric and the church against the claims of the king. At the time, the king was trying to reduce the power of ecclesiastical courts as part of his codification of secular law. Though at first compliant, Thomas eventually rejected the Conventions of Clarendon (1164), especially the "customary" provisions that would prevent clerics from appealing to Rome without the consent of the king, and would give the royal courts jurisdiction over criminal clerics. Pope Alexander III condemned these and other provisions.

Thomas was tried and condemned at the royal court at Northampton. He fled to France under the protection of Louis VII (1120–80). Meanwhile, Henry had his son Henry the Young, a protégé of Becket, crowned coking by the archbishop of York, a clear violation of the privileges of Canterbury. Thomas suspended the bishops who partook in the coronation.

Henry and Thomas reconciled in July 1170, but Thomas refused to absolve the bishops unless they accepted penance. Crying out "Who will rid me of this turbulent priest?" Henry raged against Thomas in the presence of four knights who made their way to Canterbury and slew the archbishop in the cathedral on December 29, 1170.

Europe rose in horror at the king's deed. Henry was forced to do public penance and provide financial support for the Knights Hospitaller and the KNIGHTS TEMPLAR in the crusader states. Canterbury became one of Europe's chief destinations of PILGRIMAGE. King HENRY VIII of England put an end to the veneration of Becket by destroying the pilgrimage shrine. There is much argument about what happened to the relics of St. Thomas. Some Anglican canons at Canterbury today claim to know where they are.

The conflict between Henry and Becket is one of the central cases in the CHURCH AND STATE controversy of the Middle Ages. The story of Thomas à Becket has often been treated in celebrated pieces of literature, most notably Geoffrey Chaucer's 14th-century *Canterbury Tales* and *Murder in the Cathedral* (1935) by T. S. Eliot.

Further reading: Frank Barlow, *Thomas Becket* (Berkeley: University of California Press, 1986); Thomas M. Jones, ed., *The Becket Controversy* (New York: Wiley, 1970); Richard Winston, *Thomas Becket* (New York: Knopf, 1967).

Bellarmine, St. Robert (1542–1621) *Jesuit theologian of the Counter-Reformation*

Robert Bellarmine was a prominent and articulate defender of Catholicism in the era of the COUNTER-REFORMATION. Born Francisco Romolo Bellarmino in Montepulciano, Tuscany, Bellarmine was trained by the JESUITS and made a professor of controversialist theology at Louvain and then at the Collegium Romanum in Rome. He became a cardinal in 1599 and archbishop of Capua in 1602–05.

Bellarmine was known as a reasonable man who engaged his Protestant opponents (James I of England (1566–1625), William Laud (1573–1645)) with reason rather than dogmatism in his *Disputations on Controversies of the Christian Faith* (1586–95); some of his Protestant opponents were not always as moderate in tone. He also wrote one of the very first Catholic CATECHISMS.

Though a controversialist, Bellarmine was known for taking sensible positions. Against Sixtus V (r. 1585–90), he maintained that a pope can have only indirect power in temporal affairs, a position that likely delayed his canonization. On the other hand, he defended papal infallibility in spiritual matters. He mediated between GALILEO and the Vatican in the latter's heresy trial, suggesting that Galileo could maintain the Copernican theory hypothetically to explain astronomical phenomena. At the end of his life he wrote spiritual treatises. He was canonized by PIUS XI in 1930 and declared a doctor of the church in 1931.

Further reading: Robert Bellarmine, *The Louvain Lectures*, ed. by Ugo Baldini and George V. Coyne (Vatican: Specola Vaticana, 1984); James Brodick, *Robert Bellarmine: Saint and Scholar* (London: Burns & Oates, 1961); Maurice A. Finnochiaro, *The Galileo Affair: A Documentary History* (Berkeley: University of California Press, 1989).

Benedict XVI (1927–) *21st century pope*

As one of the most powerful figures in the church HIERARCHY during the PAPACY of JOHN PAUL II, Cardinal Joseph Ratzinger helped enforce the pope's conservative doctrines on many controversial issues. Ratzinger served as a theologian and professor, an expert at VATICAN COUNCIL II, an archbishop, and the prefect of the Congregation for the Doctrine of the Faith. He has been a prolific author throughout all phases of his career. He was a significant theologian in the late 20th century. His election as Pope Benedict XVI in 2005 signaled for many the end of the era of Vatican Council II.

Benedict was born Joseph Alois Ratzinger in Marktl am Inn, Bavaria, Germany. His father was a strong anti-Nazi on the grounds that NAZISM went against his faith, and he suffered professionally as a result. Joseph himself from a young age aspired to high office in the Catholic Church, telling relatives he wanted to be a cardinal. He was forced into the Hitler Youth at the age of 14 but was lackluster in attendance. In 1943 he was drafted into the antiaircraft artillery. He deserted in 1945, was a prisoner of war briefly near Ulm, and was then repatriated.

Joseph studied at St. Michael Seminary, Traunstein, and at the Ducal Gregorian University at Munich. It is said he was influenced by the authors Gertrud von le Fort (1876–1961), a Catholic convert; Fyodor Dostoyevsky (1821–81), who turned from liberalism to fervent EASTERN ORTHODOXY; Theodore Steinbüchel (1888–1949), a Catholic moral theologian who wrote on socialism; Martin Heidegger (1889–1976), the existentialist philosopher; and Karl Jaspers (1883–1969), also an existentialist but open to the transcendent. Joseph wrote his dissertation on AUGUSTINE OF HIPPO; his *Habilitationsschrift,* a qualification for a professorship, was on St. BONAVENTURE's ecclesiology and his dispute with the ESCHATOLOGY of the Franciscan Spirituals, a theme Benedict returned to in later life.

Ratzinger was ordained with his brother Georg in 1951. He served as professor of theology at Bonn (1959) and Münster (1963) before serving as an expert to Cardinal Joseph Frings (1887–1978) of Cologne at VATICAN COUNCIL II, where he earned a reputation as one of the liberal young Turks. In 1966 he went to Tübingen University with the Swiss theologian HANS KÜNG as his colleague; years later, as prefect of the Congregation for the Doctrine of the Faith, he would censure Küng.

In his *Introduction to Christianity* (1968), Ratzinger argued that the Catholic Church was too rule-bound and centralized, positions he would later abandon. Many people say that he was taken aback by the European student riots of 1968, which he believed resulted from abandonment of traditional Catholic values. Going to Regensburg University in 1969, he founded and contributed to the Catholic journal *Communio* along with HANS URS VON BALTHASAR, Walter Kasper (1933–   ), and many others.

Ratzinger's rapid rise in the church hierarchy began with his appointment as archbishop (1977) and then cardinal (1977) of the diocese of Munich and Fresing. In 1981 John Paul II made him prefect of the Congregation for the Doctrine of the Faith, the successor to the Inquisition and the Holy Office. After his appointment to this office, the controversies surrounding Ratzinger began to mount. He acquired a certain international notoriety in the eyes of many as the pope's right hand man and "enforcer."

Benedict XVI when he was elected pope in 2005 *(Max Rossi/Reuters)*

As prefect, Ratzinger took a number of strong stances against the use of birth control and homosexuality, and he placed curbs on interfaith dialogue. Critics said that he ignored the *aggiornamento* (updating) aspect of VATICAN COUNCIL II in favor of the aspect of *ressourcement* (going back to traditional sources). The early shot across the bow was his Instruction Concerning Certain Aspects of the "Theology of Liberation" (August 6, 1984), in which he criticized liberation theology for its use of Marxist themes and methods. His efforts have dampered liberationist action in LATIN AMERICA.

Many Catholic theologians argue that papal infallibility should be restricted to rare, solemn EX CATHEDRA statements that include an appeal to the SENSUS FIDELIUM, or sense of the faithful, as JOHN HENRY NEWMAN argued. Ratzinger instead has sided with those who favor a VATICAN COUNCIL I–style papacy and has championed an expansive theory of infallibility for the "ordinary and universal MAGISTERIUM" anchored naturally in the papacy. In the declaration *Dominus Jesus* (August 6, 2000), he upheld the superiority of Catholicism over all other religions, a position not quite in the spirit and definitely not in the language of Vatican II.

In his Doctrinal Note on Some Questions Regarding the Participation of Catholics in Political Life (November 24, 2002), Ratzinger insisted that Catholic politicians uphold church teaching on moral questions as public policy, especially the teaching on ABORTION. This became a noisy issue in the 2004 presidential elections in the United States, where abortion is a key issue; six American bishops said they would deny Holy Communion to the Democratic candidate John F. Kerry (1943–   ), a Catholic who said that while he opposed abortion as a matter of faith, he supported women's rights to abortion as a matter of public policy.

In one of his most controversial teachings (among theologians), Ratzinger sought to divorce Catholic ESCHATOLOGY from utopian social or political ideas, thus sundering the kingdom of God from time. In his performance as prefect, Ratzinger has been criticized for often seeming to reduce Catholic teaching to a series of politically controversial issues, most often centered on sexual morality (such as abortion, birth control, in vitro fertilization, pornography, masturbation, and homosexuality), while remaining relatively silent on other more broadly social questions such as capital punishment, just wages, environmental degradation, and world income distribution.

The most serious charge against Ratzinger as prefect of the Congregation for the Doctrine of the Faith concerns his response to allegations of sexual abuse and PEDOPHILIA on the part of the clergy. Some allege that he dragged his feet woefully and even tried to cover up the issue by sending a letter in Latin to bishops warning them to keep their information from the public.

One aspect of Ratzinger's staunch defense of his and the pope's views was his inquisition, silencing, reprimanding, and demotion of several important Catholic theologians over the years. They include (with the main issues for which they were reprimanded in parentheses:) Hans Küng (infallibility), CHARLES E. CURRAN (birth control, sexual ethics), LEONARDO BOFF (LIBERATION THEOLOGY, church power), Jacques Dupuis (1923–2004) (pluralism of revelation and salvation in other religions), Anthony di Mello (incorporating Eastern spirituality into the Western tradition), and Tissa Balasuriya (Mary and liberation theology in an Indian context). Several bishops and cardinals publicly rebuked Ratzinger, claiming that his methods made clear what the church was against but not what the Gospel was for. Outspoken in their criticism were Cardinals Franz Konig (1905–   ), now emeritus, and Christoph Schönborn (1945–   ), both of Vienna.

Ratzinger was chosen dean of the College of Cardinals in 2002. After the death of John Paul II, he preached the funeral sermon for the dead pope. According to many observers, he did a considerable amount of politicking among various contingents of cardinals at the conclave. Upon assuming the papacy on April 19, 2005, Joseph Ratzinger took the name Benedict, harkening back both to BENEDICT OF NURSIA, a patron saint of Europe, and BENEDICT XV, a moderate pope who quieted the intra-Vatican wars over MODERNISM.

Benedict disclosed two major objectives at the start of his reign: to bring Europe back to the church and to reconcile Rome with EASTERN ORTHODOXY. Concerning the first goal, some scholars point out that under John Paul II, the number of priests relative to the population dropped dramatically in Europe and that anywhere between 25 million and 50 million Catholics stopped attending church altogether. Most predict this trend will continue and even grow sharper under Benedict XVI. On the second point, they say, he will have to abandon the Vatican I–style of monarchic papacy he upheld under his predecessor in order to win over CONSTANTINOPLE and Moscow.

In the first year of his papacy he made attempts to reconcile with radically different wings of the Roman church, meeting with members of the Society of St. Pius X, TRADITIONALISTS organized under the schismatic Archbishop Marcel Lefebvre, and his own former colleague at the University of Tübingen and harsh critic of the Vatican, Hans Küng. Whereas the theme of John Paul II's papacy was solidarity, the theme of Benedict XVI seems to be heading in the direction of unity. He has also sought contact with Catholics in China.

Further reading: All of the instructions that Ratzinger issued as prefect of the Congregation for the Doctrine of the Faith can be found online. There is a huge volume of material by and about Benedict XVI online, both under the name Ratzinger and his new papal name. John Allen, *Cardinal Ratzinger: The Vatican's Enforcer of the Faith* (New York: Continuum, 2000); ———, *The Rise of Benedict XVI* (New York: Doubleday, 2005); Aidan Nichols, *The Theology of Joseph Ratzinger* (Edinburgh: T&T Clark, 1988); Joseph Alois Ratzinger, *Introduction to Christianity* (San Francisco: Ignatius, 2000); ———, *The Spirit of the Liturgy* (San Francisco: Ignatius, 2000); ———, *Truth and Tolerance: Christian Belief and World Religions* (San Francisco: Ignatius, 2004); ——— and

Vittorio Messori, *The Ratzinger Report* (San Francisco: Ignatius, 1985).

Benedictines

The Benedictines are members of monasteries throughout the world that follow the Rule of St. BENEDICT OF NURSIA. They take vows of poverty, chastity, obedience, and stability. They go by the official name of the Order of St. Benedict (OSB). They are known as the black monks in contrast to the later CISTERCIANS, who wore white robes.

Benedict did not found a religious order in the later sense. Rather, he established a group of MONASTERIES whose members, men and women, followed his rule. One of them, Monte Cassino, south of Naples, became the first center of MONASTICISM in the West, but each monastery remained autonomous. A variety of monastic rules competed in Europe until the reign of CHARLEMAGNE and his son Louis I the Pious (r. 813–840), who promoted the Benedictine rule throughout the Holy Roman Empire. Earlier, St. Wilfrid (634–709) spread the rule to England.

Benedictine monasteries fostered the common life, built around prayer and work (*ora et labora*), learning and invention. Many claim that the first technological revolution in medieval Europe occurred through the agricultural efforts of monasteries, including the construction of water mills and the development of new farm implements. Some monasteries focused on education, especially of the nobility, others on art and architecture, and still others on missionizing new territories. St. BONIFACE carried the Benedictine message to the Anglo-Saxons. Many monasteries became centers of manuscript making, thereby becoming repositories of the ancient Western traditions stemming from Jerusalem and Athens. As time went on liturgical celebrations became more and more elaborate.

In the early 10th century the abbey of Cluny in Burgundy, founded in 909, became the center of monastic reform throughout northern Europe. More than a thousand monasteries were founded in affiliation with Cluny, which acted as a kind of arch abbey under the leadership of St. Odo (927–42). Cluny exercised a powerful influence toward reform, especially with respect to the practice of Simony and the question of the celibacy of the clergy. At the Fourth Lateran Council in 1215, Pope INNOCENT III mandated general chapters, Europe-wide meetings, and monastic visitations or inspections by ecclesiastical authorities to keep order.

Abbot SUGER of St. Denis Monastery in Paris is credited with being the catalyst for the lavish Gothic style in art and architecture. St. BERNARD OF CLAIRVAUX, who fought for the spare art and spirituality of the CISTERCIANS, opposed him. Sts. HILDEGARD OF BINGEN and JULIAN OF NORWICH were two towers of medieval Benedictine life. The principal theologian of the order was St. ANSELM OF CANTERBURY, famous for his theory of the ATONEMENT and for his ontological argument for the existence of God.

Benedictine monasteries waned at the end of the 12th century and gave way to the new orders of MENDICANTS like the FRANCISCANS and the DOMINICANS. New reforms in the 15th century led to the formation of unions or confederations of monasteries. This tendency was reinforced by a decree of the Council of TRENT (session 25, chap. 8) in 1563. A notable result was the establishment of the Maurist Congregations in France in 1621. After these reforms some monasteries developed great libraries and fostered biblical and patristic scholarship.

The PROTESTANT REFORMATION in England led to the dissolution of the monasteries under HENRY VIII. Monasteries also suffered greatly during the Enlightenment, the French Revolution, and the ANTICLERICALISM of the 19th century (*see* FRANCE).

In the mid-19th century the Benedictines experienced a revival with the founding of monasteries at Solesmes in France (1833), St. Vincent in Pennsylvania (1846), and Beuron in Germany, each of which became a nursery to new congregations. All three were key to the LITURGICAL MOVEMENT. In 1887 LEO XIII, who fostered the revival of the religious

orders, founded the Collegio Sant' Anselmo in Rome as a center for Benedictine studies, LITURGY, philosophy, and THEOLOGY. In 1893 he established an abbot general for all the monasteries, which nonetheless remain autonomous in their government. Two prominent monasteries in the United States are St. Meinrad's Abbey in Indiana and St. John's Abbey in Minnesota. The famed Liturgical Press is located at St. John's.

Perhaps the best-known Benedictine of the 20th century was DOM BEDE GRIFFITHS (1906–93), who converted to Catholicism from the Anglican Communion and then went on to found the Christian ashram Shantivanam in South India in 1968. The St. Ottilien Congregation and other groups of Benedictine nuns work in the fields of evangelizing, teaching, and health care around the world. A lay group of Oblates of St. Benedict also works in harmony with the orders of monks and nuns and shares their Benedictine spiritual practices. There are also Anglican Benedictines who have warm relations with their Catholic counterparts.

The present abbot primate is Nokter Wolf (1940–   ), who was elected by abbots worldwide in 2000. Today there are about 8,000 Benedictine monks and 15,000 nuns around the world. While membership has decreased in Europe and North America, it has increased in East Africa and South Korea.

Further reading: E. Cuthbert Butler, *Benedictine Monasticism* (New York: Barnes & Noble, 1961); Owen Chadwick, *The Making of the Benedictine Ideal* (Washington, D.C.: St. Anselm's Abbey, 1981); Terrence Kardong, *The Benedictines* (Wilmington, Del.: Glazier, 1988); Lowrie J. Daly, *Benedictine Monasticism: Its Formation and Development Through the 12th Century* (New York: Sheed & Ward, 1965).

Benedict of Nursia, St. (c. 480–c. 550)
pioneer of Western monasticism

A monk and prolific founder of monasteries in Italy, Benedict wrote the famous rule that set

MONASTICISM on firm foundations in the West and thus helped preserve classical and CHRISTIAN civilization. He helped set the tone of spirituality that informed Christianity in the Middle Ages. His feast day is July 11.

Benedict was born in Nursia, a mountain village northeast of Rome. St. SCHOLASTICA was his twin sister. He received a classical education in Rome, but, scandalized by the lifestyle of the decaying empire, he withdrew as a hermit to Subiaco in the Apennines, where he attracted his first followers. He left this group as well, disappointed in their laxity, and eventually founded 12 monasteries south of Rome, the most famous of which is Monte Cassino where he wrote his rule (*see* MONASTERY). He is buried there in the same grave as Scholastica. Benedict is known as the patriarch of Western monasticism and is one of the patron saints of Europe. Along with Sts. CYRIL and METHODIUS, Edith Stein (Sr. Teresa Benedicta of the Cross), CATHERINE OF SIENA, and Bridget of Sweden. Benedict's *transitus,* or passing, is celebrated March 21.

Much of what we know about Benedict is contained in the *Second Book of Dialogues* by Pope GREGORY I THE GREAT (590–604), a HAGIOGRAPHY filled with legends and miracle stories modeled on the miracles of the prophets and Jesus. A famous tale relates that Benedict was offered a pitcher of poisoned wine by Subiaco monks who thought his rules were too hard; when he blessed the pitcher it shattered into many pieces.

Benedict's rule revolves around what have come to be known as the Benedictine ideals of *Ora et Labora* ("Pray and Work"). Taking due notice of the rule of St. Basil, it lays down the qualifications for becoming a monk or nun and sets the hours of rising and lying down, the times allotted to the Divine Office or PRAYER OF THE HOURS, manual labor and study, procedures for leaving the order, and so on.

The monks are enjoined to obedience, poverty, and celibacy. They must also abide by the principle of permanent stability or residence in one monastery, unless sent by an abbot to a new foundation. This provision was designed to combat the disordered existence of the many wandering, and often pandering, monks of the times.

In general, the rule is marked by temperance, prudence, and humility. Jacques-Bénigne Bossuet (1627–1704), the bishop of Meaux, described it as "an epitome of Christianity, a learned and mysterious abridgement of all the doctrines of the Gospel, all the institutions of the Fathers, and all the counsels of perfection." The rule ends with the humble statement that it provides only for the minimum of justice—of rendering what is due to God and humans. "Whoever you are, therefore, who are hastening to the heavenly homeland, fulfill with the help of Christ this minimum Rule which we have written for beginners; and then at length under God's protection you will attain to the loftier heights of doctrine and virtue which we have mentioned above." Benedict's ultimate goal was the BEATIFIC VISION of God.

Benedict was one of the chief shapers of the European world. His well-run monasteries became centers of religion, learning, technological invention and economic activity, and their manuscripts preserved the core of the wisdom of both Athens and Jerusalem for later generations. Through CLUNY, founded in 909/910, the monastic movement became the hub for the reform not only of monasteries in northern Europe, but of the PAPACY and Catholicism itself.

Further reading: Benedict of Nursia, *Rule of St. Benedict,* available online; Gregory the Great, *Dialogues,* available online; E. Rozanne Elder, ed., *Benedictus: Studies in Honor of St. Benedict of Nursia* (Kalamazoo: Cistercian Publications, 1981).

Bernardin, Joseph Louis (1928-1996) *US cardinal and church leader*

Joseph Louis Bernardin was the cardinal archbishop of Chicago and the leading spokesperson of the Catholic Church in America during the 1980s. As a college student, Bernardin decided to drop plans for a medical career in favor of the priesthood. He was ordained in 1952, the same year he finished his M.A. at Catholic University of America. He rose swiftly after being named vice chancellor of the Charleston (South Carolina) diocese in 1954 and chancellor in 1956. A decade later he became the auxiliary bishop of New Orleans.

In 1972 Benardin became the archbishop of Cincinnati. During his posting, he emerged as a capable administrator with strong ties to his advisers, both priests and lay people. In 1974, his fellow bishops elected him the president of the National Conference of Catholic bishops; during his three-year term he emerged onto the national scene.

In 1982 Bernardin was tapped to succeed the recently deceased John Cardinal Cody (1907–82) as archbishop of Chicago. He inherited a position embroiled in a financial scandal and responded by opening the church's records to public scrutiny. He settled into office just as the AIDS epidemic became public knowledge, and he worked for the rights of people with AIDS. In particular, he ordered the Catholic hospitals to serve AIDS patients without discrimination. He won popular support for his broadly liberal social stance, though remaining more conservative on the specific issues of women's ordination, homosexuality, and ABORTION. He proposed the famous "seamless garment" argument that God favors human life at the beginning (v. abortion), in-between (for social justice) and at the end (v. euthanasia).

In the mid-1990s, Bernardin was diagnosed with cancer. In 1996, he turned his last months of life into public pilgrimage and an example of living with death as an imminent fact. During this time, President William Jefferson Clinton (1946–) presented him with the Presidential Medal of Freedom.

Further reading: Joseph Cardinal Bernardin, *The Gift of Peace* (Chicago: Loyola University Press, 1997); ———, *Selected Works of Joseph Cardinal Bernardin: Church and Society* (Collegeville, Minn.: Liturgical Press, 2000); Eugene Kennedy, *Cardinal Bernardin: Easing Conflicts and Battling for the Soul of American Catholicism* (New York: Bonus, 1989); Tim Unsworth, *I Am Your Brother Joseph: Cardinal Bernardin of Chicago* (New York: Crossroads, 1997).

Bernard of Clairvaux, St. (1090–1153)

CISTERCIAN Abbot of Clairvaux, Bernard exercised enormous influence in the political, theological, and ecclesiastical affairs of his time. He championed the KNIGHTS TEMPLAR, intervened in papal elections, preached for the second CRUSADE, and fought with PETER ABELARD over the place of reason in theology. His sermons and treatises on the ascetic life are written in a beautiful Latin. He was known as Doctor Mellifluus or Honey-tongued Doctor. He is patron of beekeepers and candlestick makers. He was canonized in 1174 and made a doctor of the church in 1830. His feast day is August 20.

Bernard was born at Fointaines near Dijon of noble parents. In 1112, together with 30 other noblemen, he entered the new Abbey of Cîteaux, whose abbot, St. Stephen Harding (d. 1134), asked him to make a new foundation. He chose La Ferte in northeastern France, where the brothers built their famous Abbey of Clairvaux. The beautiful Abbey of Fontenay in Burgundy, presently being restored, was one of Clairvaux's many daughter foundations. Cistercian abbeys and churches to this day have simple, clean lines with a minimum of decoration.

At the Synod of Troyes in 1129 Bernard won approval for the rule of the Knights Templar. He also preached for the second Crusade and when it failed condemned the crusaders for their lack of faith. Bernard engineered the election of Innocent II (r. 1130–1143) over Anacletus II (r. 1131–1138). One of Bernard's pupils became Pope Eugenius III in 1145 and bestowed countless favors on the Cistercians.

Later, Bernard attacked as a heretic Henry of Lausanne (d. c. 1145), a preacher of absolute poverty, who claimed, like the earlier DONATISM and later WALDENSIANS, that the effectiveness of the sacrament depended on the disposition of the priest. He confronted Peter Abelard at the Synod of Sens (1140), charging him with putting reason over faith. While Abelard thought certain doctrines were not being stated with logical precision, Bernard felt the philosophers were attacking the doctrines of tradition. He put God's grace above reason, which led later Protestant reformers to revere him. Through devious means he got Innocent II (r. 1130–43) to condemn Abelard, but he was given refuge at CLUNY by Peter the Venerable (c. 1092–1156), who effected a reconciliation. Bernard also attacked the Cluniacs and especially Abbot SUGER of St. Denis for their luxuriant churches and liturgical decorations. He felt that the money should have been spent to help the poor. One shining aspect of his life was his forceful sermons against the persecution of Jews in the Rhineland at the beginning of the Crusade. To this day many Jews consider him a "righteous Gentile" and bear his name. His last act was to reconcile the warring provinces of Metz and Lorraine.

Bernard's most celebrated treatise is an extended ALLEGORY on the Song of Songs, in which he treats Christ as the bridegroom and the church or his own soul as the bride. His sermons ranged from the practical to the mystical, with love often the theme: "Love is sufficient of itself; it gives pleasure by itself and because of itself. It is its own merit, its own reward. Love looks for no cause outside itself, no effect beyond itself. Its profit lies in the practice. Of all the movements, sensations and feelings of the soul, love is the only one in which the creature can respond to the Creator and make some sort of similar return however unequal though it be." He saw Christians as being "pilgrims in this world" on the way to heaven (Sermon 1). He felt that heretics "should be taken, not by force of arms, but by force of argument" (Sermon 64). He was deeply devoted to the Blessed Virgin Mary and wrote some of the most enduring hymns in the history of the Christian tradition, still used today by both Protestants and Catholics: "O Sacred Head, sore wounded"

(*Salve caput cruentatum*), "Jesus, the very thought of Thee" (*Jesu dulcis memoria*) and "O Jesus, King most wonderful" (*Jesu rex admirabilis*).

Further reading: Bernard of Clairvaux, *Commentary on the Song of Songs,* available online; Jean Leclercq, *Bernard de Clairvaux* (Paris: Desclée, 1989); Dennis E. Tamburello, *Bernard of Clairvaux: Essential Writings* (New York: Crossroads, 2000); John R. Sommerfeldt, *Bernard of Clairvaux on the Life of the Mind* (Mahwah, N.J.: Newman, 2004).

Bible (Gk.: *biblia,* "writings")

The various books of the Bible ("Scripture," "Holy Scripture," or the "Word") are believed by Jews and CHRISTIANS to be of divine origin or inspiration. They are held sacred as the Word of GOD and as the authoritative guide to faith and practice.

CONTENT

The Jewish Bible, or Tanakh, is divided into the Torah ("Law"), Nebi'im ("Prophets"), and Ketubi'im ("Writings"). The Torah includes Genesis, Exodus, Leviticus, Numbers, and Deuteronomy. Jews do not use these customary names for the five books of the Torah but refer to the first important words of the text. Thus, Genesis is called *B'reshith* ("In the beginning"). In Jewish belief the Torah contains the core teachings mediated from God to Moses and is considered the basis of all subsequent Jewish law. Nevertheless, Jewish theologians do not hold the written word apart but integrate the interpretation of Scripture with their oral tradition.

In later Judaism the Prophets and Writings have lesser authority. The Prophets include the "former prophets" (Joshua, Judges, Samuel, Kings) and "later prophets" (the three major prophets—Isaiah, Jeremiah, Ezekiel—and the 12 minor prophets—Hosea, Joel, Amos, Obadiah, Jonah, Micah, Nahum, Habakkuk, Zephaniah, Haggai, Zechariah, Malachi). Jews do not distinguish between 1 and 2 Samuel or 1 and 2 Kings.

Canon of the Old Testament

Judaism*		Roman Catholicism and Eastern Orthodoxy	Protestantism
(1) Bereshith	· · ·	Genesis	Genesis
(2) Shemoth	· · ·	Exodus	Exodus
(3) Wayiqra	· · ·	Leviticus	Leviticus
(4) Bemidbar	· · ·	Numbers	Numbers
(5) Devarim	· · ·	Deuteronomy	Deuteronomy
(6) Yehoshua	· · ·	Joshua	Joshua
(7) Shofetim	· · ·	Judges	Judges
(17) Ruth	· · ·	Ruth	Ruth
(8) Shemuel	· · ·	{ 1 Samuel	1 Samuel
		2 Samuel	2 Samuel
(9) Melakhim	· · ·	{ 1 Kings	1 Kings
		2 Kings	2 Kings
(24) Divre Hayomim	· · ·	{ 1 Chronicles	1 Chronicles
		2 Chronicles	2 Chronicles
(23) Ezra-Nehemyah	· · ·	{ 1 Ezra	Ezra
		2 Ezra (Nehemiah)	Nehemiah
(Noncanonical)	· · ·	Tobit	(Apocrypha)
(Noncanonical)	· · ·	Judith	(Apocrypha)
(21) Ester	· · ·	Esther	Esther
(15) Iyob	· · ·	Job	Job
(14) Tehillim	· · ·	Psalms	Psalms
(16) Mishle	· · ·	Proverbs	Proverbs
(19) Qoheleth	· · ·	Ecclesiastes (Qoheleth)	Ecclesiastes
(18) Shir Hashirim	· · ·	Canticle of Canticles	Song of Solomon
(Noncanonical)	· · ·	Wisdom	(Apocrypha)
(Noncanonical)	· · ·	Ecclesiasticus (Sirach)	(Apocrypha)
(10) Yeshaya	· · ·	Isaiah	Isaiah
(11) Yirmeya	· · ·	Jeremiah	Jeremiah
(20) Ekha	· · ·	Lamentations	Lamentations
(Noncanonical)	· · ·	Baruch†	(Apocrypha)
(12) Yehezqel	· · ·	Ezekiel	Ezekiel
(22) Daniel	· · ·	Daniel	Daniel
		Hosea	Hosea
		Joel	Joel
		Amos	Amos
		Obadiah	Obadiah
		Jonah	Jonah

Canon of the Old Testament

Judaism*		Roman Catholicism and Eastern Orthodoxy	Protestantism
(13) Tere Asar	· · ·	Micah	Micah
		Nahum	Nahum
		Habakkuk	Habakkuk
		Zephaniah	Zephaniah
		Haggai	Haggai
		Zechariah	Zechariah
		Malachi	Malachi
(Noncanonical)	· · ·	1 Maccabees†	(Apocrypha)
(Noncanonical)	· · ·	2 Maccabees†	(Apocrypha)

* Numbers indicate order in Hebrew Bibles.
† Part of the Roman Catholic, but not of the Eastern Orthodox, canon.

The Writings include Psalms, Proverbs, Job, Song of Songs, Ruth, Lamentations, Ecclesiastes (or Qoholeth), Esther, Daniel, Ezra-Nehemiah, and 1-2 Chronicles. The Jewish order of the books of the Bible differs from that of the Septuagint, the Greek translation of the Hebrew Scriptures made in the third century B.C.E., which Catholics follow.

Roman Catholics, like Protestants, divide the Bible into an Old and a New Testament. The Roman Catholic Old Testament (OT) contains 46 books (most of them from the Hebrew Bible). Some are called canonical or authoritative; others deuterocanonical, secondary, but nonetheless authoritative. Protestants term the deuterocanonical books "The Apocrypha" and consider them to be outside the CANON OF SCRIPTURE or, as JOHN WYCLIFFE stated, "outen autorite of bileue" (without authority for belief). For its Old Testament, Catholics follow the list of books included in the Septuagint, a Greek version that was the source of the Latin Vulgate translation. The following chart lists the agreements and differences between the order and content of the books of the Hebrew Scripture among Jews, Catholics, and Protestants. Some Eastern Orthodox communities include 1 Esdras, the Prayer of Manasseh, Psalm 151, and 3 Maccabees as part of their Old Testament canon.

Catholics and Protestants are in virtual agreement on the 27 books of the New Testament. These are the four gospels of Matthew, Mark, Luke, and John; 13 epistles, or letters, attributed to Paul—Romans, 1–2 Corinthians, Galatians, Ephesians, Philippians, Colossians, 1–2 Thessalonians, 1–2 Timothy, Titus (the Timothy and Titus letters are also called the "pastorals," because they offer pastoral advice to their addressees), and Philomen—some also ascribe Hebrews to Paul; the "catholic" epistles—so-called because they address no particular churches—James, 1-2 Peter, 1-3 John, and Jude; and the last book, is Revelation, or the Apocalypse.

INTERPRETATION

The Bible has been interpreted in multiple ways depending on the historical, social, and cultural circumstances of those doing the interpretation. The current general term for the theory of interpretation is called HERMENEUTICS.

It is paramount for Christians to acknowledge that the Bible of the earliest followers of Jesus was the Hebrew Bible, that the followers saw themselves as Jews, and that they interpreted these biblical texts in first-century Jewish modalities. Of particular importance are the exegetic methods of *midrash,* which is divided between commentary on legal portions of the Torah (*halachah*) and on the narrative portions (*haggadah*). A prime example of *haggadah,* or homiletic interpretation, is the extended sermon on the meaning of the Exodus event in Wisdom 11:1–12:2. Paul's intricate commentary on the faith in Romans 4 can also be seen as a subtle form of *midrash* on the story of Abraham and Sarah in Genesis 12–24.

It is equally important for Christians to realize that there has been an ongoing Jewish and Islamic biblical interpretation effort parallel to that of Christians. Pious Jews do not interpret the books of the Bible as isolated texts but as a living tradition in dialogue with the interpretation of the rabbis codified in the Mishnah and Talmud. Muslim theologians often comment that Christians distorted the original *ingil,* or gospel, of Jesus.

By the end of the first century, however, two principles of interpretation begin to set in: 1) the Old Testament is viewed as prophecy referring to the life and teachings of Jesus as recorded in the early Christian communities, and 2) these Old Testament prophecies (shadow) find their "fulfillment" in New Testament events (light). This is the beginning of the doctrine of supercession, first clearly demarcated in the Epistle to the Hebrews, in which Jesus fulfills the roles of Moses, Aaron, Melchisedech, Joshua, and David as the lawgiver, high priest, teacher, leader, and king of the new covenant that supplants the old. Later AUGUSTINE OF HIPPO would formulate this principle: "The New Testament lies hidden in the Old; the Old is made manifest in the New" (*Questions on the Heptateuch* 2.17).

The second century witnessed the emergence of divergent Christian and semi-Christian movements that challenged the unity of the Bible. MARCION, a proto-Gnostic, taught that the God of the Old Testament was a God of wrath, not to be confused with the God of mercy of the New Testament. He accepted only some letters of Paul and a truncated version of Luke as authentic Scripture. Marcion thus espoused a kind of ontological dualism.

Many GNOSTICS embraced a kind of nominalist dualism. There is indeed one true God, but he is not to be confused with the God of creation, and especially of the body, who was a kind of bungling Demiurge. Salvation is based on a path of self-knowledge or self-discovery whereby the initiate escapes the material and the bodily limitations of existence and comes to recognize the identity of the true self with the true Father, who is Spirit. IRENAEUS and other early fathers answered this challenge with the principle of *unus auctor,* one author of both the Old and New Testaments, one creator (Father) of heaven and earth (spirit and matter), who is identical with the one redeemer (Son) and the one sanctifier (Holy Spirit) of the church. This formulation was also identified with the hierarchical church (bishop, priest, deacon, and layperson in obedience) as opposed to the loose, nonhierarchical associations of the Gnostics.

Self-reflective Christian interpretation begins with the ALEXANDRINE SCHOOL of the theologian ORIGEN, who applied Neoplatonic ideas, especially those of the Jewish scholar PHILO OF ALEXANDRIA, to the biblical text. Origen distinguished between three levels of meaning to a given verse or text: the literal and historical, the moral and ethical, and the allegorical and spiritual. The allegorical meaning also included the symbolic or figurative senses and extended to the eschatological, or future, implications of Christian faith and practice. The eschatological sense was also called the anagogical. The allegorical meaning had the potential of riding above the text and hanging on by a thin thread. Thus, Philo in his massive commentary on Genesis allegorically identifies Eve with the body and the senses and Adam with the soul and the mind, an interpretive schema that bypasses or floats above the dramatic urgency of the biblical story itself. Christian allegory could also take on supercessionist overtones. The second-century *Epistle of Barnabas* says that Moses intended the dietary laws to be interpreted spiritually but that Jews interpreted them carnally, that is, literally. The prohibition against pork means that one should avoid swinish people who turn to the Lord only when in need. This interpretation belittles the devout Jew's attempt to uphold the distinct order of creation, as ordained by God in Genesis 1 and sustained by the kosher rules in Leviticus and Deuteronomy.

In the fourth and fifth centuries biblical exegesis was subordinated to the theological tasks of explaining and defining the problems of the TRINITY and Christology (*see* CHRIST/CHRISTOLOGY), establishing the CANON OF SCRIPTURE, and determining the text of the Scripture itself. These issues came to a head at the Council of Nicaea (325) and its successor councils. It was these problems that shaped the growth of the two schools of biblical interpretation that emerged in the heyday of the patristic era. The Alexandrine School, which arose in the hometown of Philo, naturally favored allegorical interpretation. The ANTIOCHENE SCHOOL, taking its cue from bishop Theodore of Mopsuestia (c. 350–428), favored a literal or historical emphasis when interpreting the biblical text. Both sides had their weaknesses. The Antiochenes had trouble attributing full divinity to Christ; Alexandrines, full humanity.

Origen exerted great influence on JEROME, who undertook the monumental task of translating the whole Bible into Latin and of commenting on many of its books. His translation, known as the Vulgate, remained the authoritative version for the Latin West for 1,500 years. Jerome, ever a rigid ascetic and cantankerous man, later denounced Origen, somewhat disingenuously, when the latter's orthodoxy began to be challenged. Nevertheless, through Jerome, Origen had enormous influence on AUGUSTINE, who, though never mastering Hebrew or Greek, wrote commanding commentaries on Genesis and Romans and numerous exegetical homilies on books of the Bible and subsumed the sweep of the whole Scripture into his monumental treatises *On the Trinity* and *The City of God.* Augustine shaped in equal measure the biblical interpretation of the Middle Ages and the Reformation.

The interpretative principles formulated by Origen, Jerome, and Augustine set the stage for Christian biblical interpretation in the Middle Ages. Scholars refer to a popular ditty that encapsulates the modes of biblical interpretation in the Middle Ages:

Littera gesta docet	The *letter* teaches deeds done;
Quid credas allegoria	What you are to believe—*allegory;*
Moralis quid agas	The *moral* what you are to do;
Quo tendas anagogia	Whither you are headed—*anagogy*

Thus, any one verse can have four different meanings. In his commentary on Genesis 1:3 "Let There Be Light" THOMAS AQUINAS says literally the verse refers to the act of creation; allegorically it refers to Christ as love; morally it means the illumination of the mind by Christ; and anagogically it means the leading of the soul to the glory of Christ. Late medieval interpreters added symbolic, synecdochic, and hyperbolic senses to complete the "seven seals" referred to in the Book of Revelation.

In his reading of Gothic art and architecture, Émile Mâle showed that the medieval mind was woven with a kind of symbolic calculus that packed meaning on top of other meaning. This eventually led to a kind of symbolic overload, most visible in the wildly allegorical and tendentious interpretations of the Songs of Songs, a frankly erotic Hebrew epithalamion (wedding song) etherialized into the mystical union of the soul with God and of Christ with the church. This biblical book was the most commented on Book of the Bible during the Middle Ages, perhaps both for its juicy content and susceptibility to allegorizing.

When the symbolic circuits shorted out, a correction was in order. We now call the correction the PROTESTANT REFORMATION, whose leaders took their adherents back to the plain senses of the letter and the spirit. They had Jewish and Catholic forerunners. Rabbi Solomon ben Isaac of Troyes (1040–1105), better known as Rashi, upheld the "simple sense" of the text. Spanish rabbi Abraham ibn Ezra (c. 1084–1164) noted five senses of Scripture but preferred the plain sense based on the historical and grammatical meaning of the biblical writer. This paring down had great influence on the great Franciscan biblical commentator Nicholas of

Lyra (1264–1349), who taught at the University of Paris. He insisted that the literal or historical sense of the biblical text is the primary one. Lyra in turn influenced Luther, who shunned allegory and urged "the proper and simple sense of scripture" in his *Pagan Servitude of the Church* (1520).

No less important was the DEVOTIO MODERNA ("up-to-date piety") of the Brethren of the Common Life in the 15th century, who stressed a plain lifestyle in service to God and fellow human beings, a plainness that corresponded to the new stress on the plain meaning of the Scripture. In brief, Protestantism espoused the principle of *sola scriptura* ("scripture alone"), placing the Bible above both ecclesiastical hierarchy and patristic tradition. The Protestant principle gave impetus to the work of establishing critical editions of the books of the Bible and translating them into the vernacular languages of Europe. Desiderius ERASMUS, a member of the Brethren and a friend of Luther, produced the first critical edition of the Greek New Testament.

The next stage in biblical interpretation is best seen as the period of rational, analytic biblical criticism. Hugo Grotius (1583–1645), famed international jurist and ambassador, started reading the Bible with the same critical acumen scholars applied to the texts of Tacitus or Virgil. Thomas Hobbes (1588–1659) became obsessed with questions of authorship. In *Leviathan,* his book on the theory of the state, he determines from Genesis 12:6, a reference to "Canaanites in the land," and Deuteronomy 34:6–12, an account of Moses' burial, that Moses could not have written the Torah, and that it was thus written by a later hand. (Abraham ibn Ezra had earlier noted that Genesis 12:6 contained a secret, but warned those who understood to keep silent.) Hobbes did critical analysis on many other Old Testament books but stayed clear of the New Testament. Following ibn Ezra, Baruch/Benedict Spinoza (1632–77) furthers this Enlightenment enterprise in his *Tractatus Theologico-Politicus* (1670), in which he sets out a program to apply the method of interpreting nature to the method of interpreting Scripture by describing "the life, character,

and aims of each book's author, who he was, what occasioned his writing, when he wrote, to whom, and in what language" (chap. 7). These are the kinds of questions modern biblical scholars today set out to answer. Spinoza determined that all the books from Genesis to II Kings were composed or compiled by one hand, probably Ezra's. Like Hobbes, Spinoza refrained from applying his critical analysis to the New Testament.

At the end of the 17th century the Catholic Richard Simon (1638–1712) produced a critical history of the Old Testament. He noted the contradictions, repetitions, and variety of styles in the sources of the Pentateuch and concluded that the text had been composed over a long period of time. Son of a Jewish convert to Protestantism and then to Catholicism, Jean Astruc (1684–1766), professor of medicine at the University of Paris, noted the same repetitions and chronological confusion in the Old Testament text. He differentiated two sources in Genesis, one using the name Elohim and the other using the tetragrmmaton ("four-lettered" name) of YHWH. Astruc also listed lesser sources. His insights were taken up by Johnnes G. Eichhorn (1752–1827).

In a more critical vein, Hermann S. Reimarus's "Wolfenbuettel Fragments," published by literateur Gotthold Lessing (1729–81) in 1778, had an explosive effect on New Testament interpretation. Written from a strict Enlightenment viewpoint, the "Fragments" questioned the authenticity of much New Testament material but also had genuine insights about the differences between the Synoptics and the Gospel of John. The critical era of interpretation set the stage for the introduction of the documentary hypothesis and the theory of form criticism, the methods of analysis that arose in the 19th century, were honed in the 20th, and are still in force today.

FORMATION AND GROWTH OF THE JEWISH BIBLE

The documentary hypothesis is primarily associated with the name of Julius Wellhausen (1844–1918), professor of Semitics at Göttingen and

Marburg, although many German scholars contributed to its development. Picking up on Astruc and Eichhorn, Wellhausen set out to demonstrate that the Pentateuch (Torah, or the first five books of the Old Testament) was composed of four different strands, or layers, of textual material.

The documentary hypothesis has gone through several recastings. Roman Catholic scholars are in a broad consensus with scholars of other faiths in generally subscribing to this hypothesis. The most recent form can be briefly stated in a schematic developmental formula:

$$J + E + R_{JE} + D + P + R_{JEDP} =$$
$$\text{Pentateuch (Torah)}$$

First, it should be stated that there is an underlying unity to the great Israelite national epic that extends from Genesis to 2 Kings and that lies behind and beyond the unfolding of the literary traditions. The unified theme is God's engagement with humankind in history. The common elements include creation stories, flood stories, stories of the patriarchs and matriarchs, the call of Abraham, the Exodus event, the covenant at Sinai, the entrance into Canaan, kings and prophets, and the divided kingdom. Second, all the strands contain elements, especially poetry, that reach back into the earliest oral and written traditions of the Israelites, such as the Song of Miriam in Exodus 15.

The letter J stands for the literary strand that uses Jehovah (YHWH) for the name of God. This tradition gathered up much older materials such as the Song of Miriam (Exodus 15) and reshaped them into an apology for the southern kingdom of Judah centered on David and his successors and the centralized temple worship in Jerusalem that David and his son Solomon established. It is composed almost entirely of story material such as the story of the Garden of Eden (Gen. 2:4b–4:1), it alludes to multiple places of worship, dreams, visions, and angels, and has almost no interest in legal matters except the law of revenge. Because the Jehovist takes great interest in women's issues (for example, the story of Judah and Tamar, Genesis 38), some

have suggested that the author or compiler was a woman inside the royal court of Jerusalem.

The letter E stands for the literary strand that uses the name Elohim for God. It is much skimpier than J. The Elohist represents the interests of northern Israel, if not the northern kingdom itself: a defense of decentralized worship of God in old shrines like Shechem and Shiloh; an elevation of Moses above Aaron, whose descendants exclusively staffed the temple in Jerusalem; and an attack on the Judaean policy of *missim*, or forced labor. At first scholars attributed the Elohist to the prophetic tradition, but the strand also shows interest in legal and ritual matters. Hence, some suggest that the author, almost certainly a male, was associated with the Levite priests of Shiloh who were cut out when Jerusalem was made the center of worship.

Whoever redacted the Jehovist and Elohist into a common text (R_{JE}) felt the pressure to preserve competing stories and different takes on common traditions. This redaction probably took place soon after the destruction of northern Israel by the Assyrian Sennacharib (r. 705–601 B.C.E.) in 701 B.C.E. Many northerners fled south, and that event ensured that their version of the religious epic would get a fair if subordinate hearing.

The letter D stands for the Deuteronomist, the person(s) responsible not only for the Book of Deuteronomy but also for the grand historical vision that shapes all the books that follow, from Joshua to II Kings. Scholars almost unanimously associate D with the "Book of the Torah" found by the priest Hilkiah during renovations undertaken at the order of King Josiah in 621 B.C.E. as part of his religious reforms (2 Kings 22–23). This scroll is identified as Deuteronomy or perhaps the Code of the Covenant within Deuteronomy 12–26. The Deuteronomic historian advocates centralized worship, praises Moses and Josiah, and upholds the two Covenants, one to Moses, conditional on the people being faithful (Deut. 34), and one to the house of David and unconditional (1 Sam. 7). Some propose that Deuteronomic history was revised after the destruction of Jerusalem and the

Judaic kingship in 587 B.C.E., arguing that the Davidic Covenant, too, was conditional—dependent on the faithfulness of the kings of Judah. Recent scholars claim that the author of D came out of similar Shiloh Levite circles as the author of E a century and a half earlier and identify this person as the prophet Jeremiah (or Jeremiah plus Baruch, his scribe), who lived c. 628–586 B.C.E..

The last strand is attributed to P, or the Priestly author. The Priestly author(s) is responsible for much of the final shape of the Pentateuch as we have it. Wellhausen thought he was postexilic, but others argue he was aware of D and necessarily preexilic with some postexilic additions. He gave us the first story of creation in Genesis 1 and used the earlier Book of Generations to frame the narratives in Genesis and possibly a Book of Sojourns to frame Exodus to Numbers. He placed his own material in a position of priority, for example, the opening verses of Exodus. The Priestly strand is very interested in all material relating to the desert tabernacle, the Jerusalem Temple, the ritual law and favors the Aaronic priesthood over the Mushite (Moses). This strand is an alternative to JE and even anti-JE, which talked about many altars of worship to God all over Canaan and many intermediaries between God and humans (prophets, dreams, and visions). With P, only the high priest makes contact with the transcendent God of justice and on only one day a year, the Day of Atonement (Lev. 16: 23–32). Some suggest that P came out of the Aaronic priestly circles associated with the reform of Hezekiah (c. 686 B.C.E.).

Finally, all the strands were conjoined by a final redactor (R$_{JEPD}$), most likely in the midst of the crisis of the Babylonian Captivity or shortly thereafter. Spinoza thought this person was Ezra, the priest-lawgiver-scribe who is always associated with the Book of the Law of Moses (2 Kings 14:6). Some scholars support a variant of this hypothesis. Ezra led a group of Israelites back to Jerusalem with the sacred vessels of the Temple, absent the Ark of the Covenant. With a writ from Cyrus the Great, he supervised the building of the second Temple and the reinstauration of the Mosaic Law includ-

ing temple worship and sacrifice. He was seen as a second Moses. In any case, the final redactor was also a creator. He artfully juxtaposes sometimes conflicting accounts (the two stories of creation), interweaves others (the Flood stories) and puts P's aloof, inaccessible deity of justice in counterpoint with JE and D's more anthropomorphic God, who gets angry yet forgives and is always ready to show mercy. In many ways P created the framework of the discussion of God in the revealed religions of the West: a transcendent being who is yet the immanent person walking with Adam in the Garden of Eden and engaging humans one-to-one in give-and-take.

THE FORMATION
OF THE NEW TESTAMENT

Form criticism or, better, the history of literary forms was first applied by Hermann Gunkel (1862–1932) to Old Testament texts and extended by Johannes Weiss (1863–1914) to the study of the literary genres, oral and written, that lie behind the received text of the New Testament. Form criticism began with a concerted effort to uncover the oral tradition behind the variety of literary forms in the Bible and especially the New Testament, in order to uncover the life-setting (Ger. *Sitz-im-Leben*) of the early communities that produced different genres, such as, preaching, liturgy, teaching, legal rulings, and so on. The initial types of genre include 1) paradigms or apothegms, stories ending in a saying of Jesus, such as rendering unto Caesar vs. rendering unto God (Mark 12:13–17); 2) miracle stories such as the healing of the Syrophoenician woman (Mark 7–24–30); 3) sayings, or *logoi*, such as the beatitudes in Matthew 5; and 4) legends or narratives such as the story of Judah and Tamar (Genesis 38) or the Passion narrative (Matt. 26:1–27).

In the 19th century the major question facing scholars of the New Testament was what has become known as the Synoptic Problem. First, scholars noted that Mark, Matthew, and Luke shared a common view of Jesus' ministry in Galilee and his ascent to Jerusalem to die: their view was "synoptic." John has a very different view. For example, he has Jesus going to Jerusalem more than once. Second, scholars noticed that Matthew and Luke were dependent on Mark, and not vice versa. Third, they noted that Matthew and Luke share a number of *Logoi,* or sayings, of Jesus with one another but not with Mark. This collection of sayings has become known as Q, for *Quelle,* the German word for "source." Today it is known as the Sayings Source or, somewhat erroneously, as the "Gospel According to Q." Fourth, scholars noted that both Matthew and Luke have their own special sources unique to each. For example, Matthew has the genealogy of Jesus, and Luke has the infancy narrative. The Synoptic Problem—or its solution from one perspective—can be illustrated as follows:

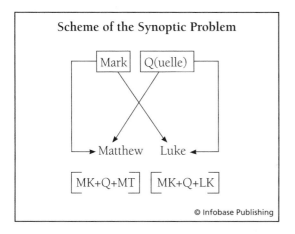

This solution, however partial, of the Synoptic Problem opened the door for further literary form criticism, tracing the oral origins of written traditions and marking out further literary characteristics. Scholars speculated that originally, at the oral stage, there were various collections of sayings separate from collections of miracle or healing stories, apocalypses, and Passion narratives. Earliest of all was the Passion narrative, derived from the preaching of the APOSTLES. Discoveries of ancient biblical texts and especially the library collection at NAG HAMMADI have augmented our understanding of the formation of the Gospels, both canonical and noncanonical. Most especially

the Gospel of Thomas, partially but not totally colored with later Gnostic elements, confirmed the existence of independent sayings sources.

Today there is a broad consensus that there was an original oral kerygma of the death, resurrection, and exaltation of Jesus in the earliest tradition. Good examples would be the sources behind the speeches of Peter in Acts 2:14–36 and 3:17–26. This kerygma became the basis for written Passion narratives. Independently there were separate collections of sayings, parables, miracle stories, and apocalypses, some dating back to Jesus' Galilean period and added to and/or modified in the varying life-settings of the early church. Recent studies have also uncovered the oral background of longer prophetic discourses in Q. Gradually, the oral traditions were committed to written form, and the three basic forms were melded into the Gospels as we now know them. The following simplified diagram illustrates this process with both canonical noncanonical gospels.

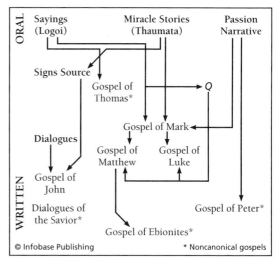

Scholars generally believe that Q dates from around 50 C.E., Mark from 60–70, and Matthew and Luke from 80–95. Many date the final form of John to 100, but some have shown that it, too, has undergone several stages of development.

Form-critical principles have been used also on other books of the New Testament and to uncover various additional genres, such as hymns (Phil. 2:6–11), baptismal confessions, and isolated sayings of Jesus (1 Cor. 11:23–25). Combined with textual criticism, these principles have also been used to differentiate Pauline (Rom., Gal., etc.) and deutero-Pauline letters (Eph., Col., etc.).

AUTHORITY OF THE BIBLE

The authority of the Bible rests on the belief that it contains revelation about God and God's plan for humankind. We can see elements of this belief within the Bible itself. The Book of Kings recounts how King Josiah's priest Hilkiah and secretary Shaphan found the "Book of the Torah" in the Temple and how the king was motivated to reform the institutions of Israel based on the prescriptions of this book (2 Kings 22:8–20). Scholars believe that the book was the Code of the Covenant in Deuteronomy 12–26. Similarly, a New Testament writer says "All scripture is inspired by God and is useful for teaching, for reproof, for correction and for training in righteousness that the man of God may be complete, equipped for every good work" (1 Tim. 3:16–17). Both Jews and Christians have looked to the Bible for guidance on what to believe (doctrine) and how to conduct life (morals), with Christians placing more emphasis on doctrine.

For Catholics, the authority of the Bible is a matter of dogma. The Council of TRENT, pointing to the list of 46 Old Testament books and 27 New Testament works compiled in the Decree of Damasus (382), decreed that "the entire books with all their parts, as they have been wont to be read in the Catholic Church and are contained in the old vulgate Latin edition, are to be held sacred and canonical" (4.1).

The authority of the Bible is associated with ideas of inspiration and inerrancy. Some Christians claim that God literally inspired every word a biblical writer put down and guaranteed that every jot and tittle was without error. However,

modern scientific discoveries about the origin of the universe and life, as well as historical criticism highlighting numerous factual errors in the transmission of the text of the Bible, militate against a too literal application of the teachings of inspiration and inerrancy, which modern popes have recognized.

While upholding inspiration and inerrancy, LEO XIII in his 1893 *Providentissimus Deus* (November 18, 1893) stated that the Bible is not meant to teach science, and uses the common language suitable to the times in which it originally appeared. In his 1907 *Pascendi Dominici Gregis* (August 9, 1907), which targeted the French biblical scholar Alfred Loisy, PIUS X invoked the doctrine of inspiration in his general condemnation of MODERNISM, but he did not explain it other than to say that it is not akin to poetic inspiration and that "God is the origin and inspiration of the Sacred Writings" (22). Benedict XV's 1920 encyclical *Spiritus Paraclitus* (September 15, 1920), an encomium to St. JEROME, the great biblical scholar of the fourth century and prime translator of the Latin Vulgate, praised the use of modern critical methods but warned against distinguishing too neatly between the divine or religious and human elements in inspiration. The encyclical maintained that "the effect of inspiration—namely, absolute truth and immunity from error—are to be restricted to that primary or religious element" (19).

The restrictive and cautious tone of these encyclicals was put to rest with PIUS XII's 1943 papal letter *Divino Afflante Spiritu* (September 30, 1943), the Magna Charta of Catholic biblical studies, written with considerable input from the noted biblical scholar Cardinal Augustine Bea (1881–1968). The letter emphasized the primary place of scriptural study in theological education, the primacy of the literal meaning, the return to the original languages of the Bible, and the employment of form critical methods of study developed in the previous hundred years. The pope embraced the recent linguistic, archaeological, and historical discoveries "which call for a fresh investigation, and which stimulate not a little the practical zest of the present-day interpreter" (n. 32).

All the key elements of *Divino Afflante Spiritu* were incorporated into *Dei Verbum,* the Dogmatic Constitution on Divine Revelation of VATICAN COUNCIL II. In reaction to the PROTESTANT REFORMATION Catholics had fallen into the habit of referring to the dual sources of faith in Scripture and tradition as if there were two fonts of revelation. Vatican II corrected this misinterpretation by asserting that Scripture holds the place of priority and that "sacred tradition and sacred scripture form one sacred deposit of the word of God" (n. 10). The function of tradition and the teaching office of the church is to serve the Word of God. Rejecting overly literalist readings of Scripture, the constitution says simply that "the books of scripture must be acknowledged as teaching firmly, faithfully, and without error that truth which God wanted to put into the sacred writings for the sake of our salvation" (n. 11). The facts of history and archaeology, world views, and textual transmission are not matters of salvation and therefore do not pertain to inerrancy. The official *Catechism of the Catholic Church* (1994) enumerates a number of crucial points Catholics are to hold about the Bible, namely, that it is a single work including both the Old and the New Testaments, that it teaches truth about salvation without error, that God inspired and assisted the authors, and that, as Catholics venerate the body of the Lord in the sacrament, they are to venerate the Word of God in the Bible as leading to salvation.

LANGUAGE, CODEX, TEXT, AND TRANSLATION

The Christian Bible is written in three languages. The vast majority of the text in the Old Testament is written in what is now known as classical Hebrew, except for Daniel 2:4b–7:28, Ezra 4:8–6:18 and 7:12–26, and Jeremiah 10:11; these are written in Aramaic, an East Semitic dialect that served as the chief Middle Eastern diplomatic and commercial language from around 1000 to 30 B.C.E. The vast majority of the New Testament is written in koine, or common Hellenistic Greek, except for a number of Aramaic phrases such as *talitha cumi* (Mark 5:41, "Young girl, arise"), *Marana tha* (1 Cor. 16:22, "Come, O! Lord"), and *Eloi, eloi, lama sabacthani* (Mark 15:34, "My God, my God, why have you forsaken me?"). Aramaic had gradually become the common language of Palestine and was the everyday language Jesus spoke.

The Palestinian recension of the Hebrew Scriptures was translated into Greek some time between 250 and 150 B.C.E. According to legend this was done by 72 scholars, hence this translation is called the Septuagint (LXX), the Greek term for the number 70. Theodotian (fl. c. 180) did a later Greek version, which influenced later LXX manuscripts, especially the Book of Daniel, as quoted in Revelation. Still later, Aquila (Second century) produced a literal Greek version in 128 C.E., following rabbinic rules of interpretation. The vast majority of quotations in the New Testament are from the LXX with the exception of Revelation's quotations from Daniel. After the return from the Babylonian Exile, the Hebrew Bible was also translated into Aramaic. These are called Targums, Aramaic for "translations."

Sometime late in the second century Latin translations began to appear. TERTULLIAN OF CARTHAGE and St. CYPRIAN OF CARTHAGE both cite a version known as the Old Latin. In the third century St. JEROME made a complete translation of the Bible known as the Vulgate (*vulgus,* "common, popular"). This version served as the official text of the Catholic Latin West until Vatican Council II. Three fourth- and fifth-century Greek codices of the Bible, now known as Codex Vaticanus, Codex Sinaiticus, and Codex Alexandrinus, have served as the anchors for critical editions of the Greek text (*see* CODEX). There were also early Syriac, Coptic, and Ethiopic translations.

The first complete English version of the Bible, translated by John Wycliffe (c. 1328–84), appeared in 1382. Wycliffe aimed for the general reader. He was excommunicated for his effort, and his version was condemned in 1415. With the same motive a hundred years later, William Tyndale (c. 1494–1536) believed that "it was impossible to stablysh layne people in any truth excepte the scripture were playnly layde before their very eyes in their mother tonge." He completed the New Testament from the Greek in 1525, and it was printed with the help of German printers. In 1530 he published the Pentateuch. He was attacked and killed in Antwerp. His translation was so eminent that more than 80 percent of the King James Version (KJV) is from Tyndale. Several more English versions followed until the great Anglican version under the sponsorship of King James I (1603–25) appeared in 1611. This version became the backbone for English worship and the Book of Common Prayer. Facing the music, Catholics produced a very faulty translation from the Vulgate of St. Jerome in 1610. It was done under the leadership of Gregory Martin (d. 1582) at the English college at Douay and Rheims, France, and is known as the Douay-Rheims version.

The next major English translation was the Authorized Version (AV) under Protestant auspices. New discoveries of manuscripts and papyri texts motivated a revision of earlier versions in the Revised Standard Version (1952). This version was and is used by Catholics and Protestants alike for study. The New Revised Standard Version (1989), done by Jewish, Protestant, and Orthodox and Catholic scholars, is considered to be the most ecumenical version of the Bible in the world. The New International Version (1978) is popular with Reformed and Evangelical churches. Many other versions attempt to put biblical language into colloquial and popular English, sometimes making the text and thought world of biblical times a little too up to date.

The most recent Roman Catholic translation into English from the original languages was the New American Bible (1970), which is still undergoing revisions. It is the translation officially approved by the United States Conference of Bishops for biblical study and liturgical worship. The now famous Jerusalem Bible, translated by members of the École Biblique in Jerusalem, appeared in full in French (1956) and then in English (1966), with scholarly footnotes. It became very popular as both a study and a liturgical Bible. A revised version appeared in English as the New Jerusalem Bible (1985).

Further reading: Walter M. Abbott, *Documents of Vatican II* (New York: America Press, 1966); Raymond E. Brown, ed., *New Jerome Biblical Commentary* (Englewood Cliffs, N.J.: Prentice Hall, 1990); Richard Elliott Friedman, *Who Wrote the Bible?* (New York: Harper & Row: 1987); Steven L. Harris, *The New Testament,* 4th ed. (St. Louis: McGraw-Hill, 2002); Louis G. Kelly, *The True Interpreter: A History of Translation Theory and Practice in the West* (Oxford: Blackwell, 1979); Helmut Koester, *History and Literature of Early Christianity,* 2nd ed. (New York: Walter de Gruyter, 1990).

bishop (Gr.: *episcopos,* "overseer")

The three ranks of HOLY ORDERS in Catholicism are bishop, PRIEST, and deacon. Of these, the bishop is the highest—he is a priest who possesses "the fullness of the sacrament of orders" (VATICAN COUNCIL II, *Christus Dominus* 15, Decree on the Bishops' Pastoral Office in the Church). Catholics see the college of bishops as successors to the college of APOSTLES in the New Testament.

In general, a bishop serves as the principal pastor of a DIOCESE, with many priests subordinate to him. Some bishops, however, serve as assistants to other bishops, sometimes as coadjutors (assistants with the right of succession); others are diplomats, and still others hold administrative positions in the Vatican. All of these are called titular bishops, and they bear the names of dioceses that are now defunct as a reminder of the original pastoral function of their rank. Some consider this practice a theological abuse, designed merely to give some administrators a higher ecclesiastical status. All bishops can bestow the full array of sacraments, including all the Holy Orders.

In the early Christian community, the term *bishop* did not yet have its later hierarchical connotation. In ancient Greek, an *episcopos* was a foreman or work boss, such as at a construction site or mine, or an overseer of slaves. The word first acquired a religious connotation as applied to the Greek gods in their roles as guardians of their devotees.

The word occurs only five times in the New Testament (e.g., Acts 20:28, Phil. 1:1, 1 Peter 2:25), where it is generally synonymous with *presbyteros* ("elder"), pastor, or steward. A bishop was apparently the overseer of the spiritual unity of a church and the chief celebrant of the EUCHA-RIST. The office was one of many mentioned by PAUL, who spoke of apostles, prophets, teachers, servants, bishops, preachers, helpers, healers, speakers-in-tongues, and interpreters (*see esp.,* 1 Cor. 12). Paul does not indicate any hierarchy among these figures, but rather considers them a circle of "gifts" mutually supporting one another in building up the assembly or church.

In the early church, bishops and other leaders were for the most part elected by the community of believers (*Didache* 15). IGNATIUS OF ANTIOCH (c. 115) is the first to attest the presence of one bishop per local assembly who, as first among equals, would preside over the presbytery (*Magnesians* 6.1). The pattern gradually spread to the West. By the middle of the second century, the Christian community, with its bishops, priests, and deacons, had become more conformed to the hierarchical structures of the Roman Empire, adopting the typical household rules of order and eliminating the active roles of women in ministering to and the governance of the assembly.

In the MIDDLE AGES the bishop's role developed in parallel to that of secular princes. Bishops came to be called "Lord" and held court like secular potentates, often in the same lavish style, leading to resentment and attacks by reformers. During the COUNTER-REFORMATION the Council of TRENT (1545–60) instituted a process of eliminating abuse by bishops.

As a result of VATICAN COUNCIL I (1870), the role of the diocesan bishop became overshadowed by the authority given to the supreme pontiff as the infallible Vicar of Christ. VATICAN COUNCIL II saw a strong movement in the opposite direction, with bishops seen as collegial partners of the pope in the ministry and governance of the church as a whole (*Lumen Gentium,* 3.22 Dogmatic Constitution on the Church). This role, however, was progressively hemmed in, first by PAUL VI and, more markedly, by JOHN PAUL II.

Today, a diocesan bishop is president of the eucharistic community under his jurisdiction. He is the chief administrator of the diocese, in charge of pastoral appointments, priestly formation, instruction of the faithful, and all temporal property and goods. Every five years he is obliged to make an official visit *ad limina* ("to the threshold") to the pope (*Code of Canon Law,* cnn. 399–400).

Bishops of larger dioceses, usually ARCHBISH-OPS, have auxiliary bishops to help them in their duties. A coadjutor bishop is an assistant bishop appointed by the Holy See with the right of succession, usually in cases of failing health of the bishop or scandal. A coadjutor bishop also serves as the vicar general of the diocese and prime consultant and collaborator of the diocesan bishop.

See also HIERARCHY.

Further reading: Henry Chadwick, ed., *The Role of the Christian Bishop in Ancient Society* (Berkeley, Calif.: Center for Ecumenical Studies, 1979); Jean Colson, *L'épiscopat catholique* (Paris: Cerf, 1963); Hermann J. Pottmeyer, "The Episcopacy" in Peter Phan, ed., *The Gift of the Church* (Collegeville, Minn.: Liturgical Press) 337–354.

bleeding statues

In the last half of the 20th century and into the 21st, cases of miraculously bleeding or weeping states or paintings seemed to have become more common in the Roman Catholic world. Images of Jesus Christ, the Virgin Mary, and various saints appeared to be shedding blood in a religiously significant manner. Most commonly, statues of the Virgin Mary were seen to bleed from the hands or forehead, places associated with the crucifixion wounds of Jesus. Such events have also been reported in Eastern Orthodoxy.

One of the most spectacular incidents occurred in a Catholic convent in Akita, Japan. In 1973, Sister Agnes Katsuko Sasagawa began to receive apparitions of the Blessed Virgin while experiencing the stigmata on the palms of her own hands. Sister Agnes was deaf, but she heard Mary speak to her; the words seemed to be coming from a wooden statue of the Virgin that resided in the convent's chapel. In subsequent years Sister Agnes experienced the visitations of an angelic being.

These apparitions and messages set the stage for the next remarkable occurrence. A tearlike liquid began to flow from the statue, which a laboratory found identical in composition to human tears. At one point the statue began to cry while a Japanese television crew was filming in the chapel. Simultaneously with the tears, a reddish fluid that laboratory analysis determined to be types O, B, and AB human blood oozed from the palm of the statue's right hand. Healing miracles began to occur, and Sister Agnes regained her hearing.

The phenomenon of bleeding and crying statues has evoked dramatically varied reactions among Catholics. Many believers have stressed the supernatural quality of the events and have tried to integrate them into a Catholic theological perspective. Skeptics have offered purely mundane explanations. They have suggested hallucinations, unusual natural phenomena (such as were discovered by scientists in India in the 1990s, when statues of the Hindu god Ganesh appeared to be drinking milk), or even deliberate fraud (which was uncovered in a few incidents). However, such purely natural explanations do not seem adequate to explain some of the cases, such

as Akita, where, following several investigations, the church authorized veneration of Our Lady of Akita. The devotion to bleeding statues of Mary stresses that Mary shared in Jesus' Passion both spiritually and physically.

Few cases of bleeding statues or crying pictures undergo the same scrutiny as those of Akita. Nevertheless, they can serve to increase piety among believers. Except when they contradict church teachings, they may be integrated into church life, at least at the local level. No doubt the increase in the number of such incidents is in part a factor of the media's increasingly global reach; a century ago most cases would have remained purely local stories.

Further reading: Joe Nickell, *Looking for a Miracle* (Amherst, N.Y.: Prometheus, 1998); Teigi Yashuda, *Akita: The Tears and Message of Mary* (Asbury, N.J.: 101 Foundation, 1991).

Boehner, Philotheus (1901–1955) *Historian and writer on medieval philosophy*

Boehner was the foremost Franciscan scholar of the mid-20th century, leaving his mark as a writer, editor, translator, and teacher. Boehner entered the Franciscan Order in 1920. He took a doctorate in biology at Münster in 1933 and continued to work as a bryologist (a specialist in mosses) all his life. However, during a bout with tuberculosis, he translated several of Étienne Gilson's works on medieval philosophy, which sparked a lifelong interest in the Franciscan philosophical tradition. He pursued those studies at Quaracchi, Rome, and Paris, and he coauthored a history of medieval philosophy with Gilson. In 1939 Gilson invited him to teach at the Pontifical Institute in Toronto.

When World War II broke out, Boehner could not return to Germany and Thomas Plassmann (1879–1959), president of St. Bonaventure's College in upstate New York invited him to teach Franciscan philosophy. There he reshaped the

Franciscan Institute and its learned journal *Franciscan Studies* to international acclaim. He taught and remained a close friend of THOMAS MERTON. Boehner was an expert in the philosophies of ST. AUGUSTINE, ST. BONAVENTURE, and especially WILLIAM OF OCKHAM. He oversaw the critical edition of several classic Franciscan philosophers including Ockham and Bonaventure. His popular translation and selection of Ockham's philosophical writings remains in print.

Further reading: "In Memoriam: Philotheus Boehner, OFM, 1901–55," *Franciscan Studies* (1955) 15:101–105; Philotheus Boehner, ed., *St. Bonaventure: Itinerarium Mentis in Deum* (St. Bonaventure: Franciscan Institute, 2002); ——— *Medieval Logic: An Outline of its Development 1250–1400* (Manchester: Manchester University Press, 1966); ——— ed., *William Ockham: Philosophical Writings, a Selection* (Indianapolis: Hackett, 1990).

Boethius (c. 480–c. 524) *Christian philosopher and transmitter of ancient knowledge*

Scion of a senatorial family, Anicius Manlius Torquatus Severinus Boethius served as master of offices at the Arian Ostrogoth court at Ravenna. A defender of orthodoxy, he was charged with treason and put to death. He was canonized as St. Severinus. His tomb is in Pavia, and his feast day is October 23.

Boethius was a transmitter of philosophical tradition. He condensed Greek works on the quadrivium, including Euclid's geometry, but his real love was logic. He translated and commented on Aristotle's *On Interpretation, Topics,* and *Hypothetical Syllogisms.* These were the key texts by which ARISTOTLE was known in the West in the early MIDDLE AGES until his rediscovery through Arabic texts. He also translated Porphyry's *Isagoge.*

Boethius contributed to the medieval discussion of universals. He was undecided whether they exist apart from particulars. He was noted for his definition of a person ("an individual substance with a rational soul"), which played a part in the debates about the Trinity and the person of CHRIST. Boethius's own philosophical position was close to that of the Neoplatonists Proclus Diadochus (410/412–485) and Ammonius Saccas (third century). His *Consolation of Philosophy,* written while in prison, is a Platonic meditation on attaining knowledge of God while facing impending death.

See also NEOPLATONISM.

Further reading: Boethius, *Consolation of Philosophy,* tr. Joel C. Relihan (Indianapolis: Hackett, 2001); John Marenbon, *Boethius* (Oxford: Oxford University Press, 2003).

Boff, Leonardo (1938–) *Liberation theologian*

Leonardo Boff, a Franciscan, is one of the foremost exponents of LIBERATION THEOLOGY in Latin America and indeed the world. He was born to Italian immigrant parents in Concórdia, Santa Catarina, Brazil; his brother, Clodovis, a Servite priest, is also a liberation theologian who studies its epistemological and ontological foundations. Leonardo was educated at the Franciscan seminary in Petropolis, Brazil, where he entered the order in 1959. He took his doctorate at Munich in 1970, and returned to Petropolis, where he taught at the seminary for 22 years, while also ministering in the *favelas,* or slums. Author of many books, he became famous for *Church, Charism and Power* (1985), a theology of the church that championed the community of the faithful poor against the institutional feudalism of much traditional Roman Catholicism.

With Pope JOHN PAUL II's approval, the Congregation for the Doctrine of the Faith under Joseph Ratzinger, now Pope BENEDICT XVI, censored the book, and Boff was put under silence. Ironically, this censorship ensured his fame. He served his penance until 1986, when he resumed his public writing and teaching. When Ratzinger challenged him again in 1992, he refused to remain silent and asked permission to leave the order and the priesthood. Unlike countless similar requests, the Vatican has yet to release Boff from his vows. He still considers himself a Franciscan Catholic.

Boff has written widely in theology, spirituality, philosophy, anthropology, and mysticism. In *Church, Charism and Power* he summed up his views on liberation theology, emphasizing "Christ from below"—Jesus as the radical liberation of the human being. That liberation he believes could best take place in BASE COMMUNITIES through which the church served the poor and dispossessed and shared its power with them. Like many other liberation theologians, Boff uses Marxist analysis to find structures of alienation and oppression in both ecclesiastical and social institutions. But he does not stop there. In *The Lord's Prayer* he reveals what he calls the "transparency" between the human and the divine, the prophetic and the priestly, and the active and the contemplative. In *St. Francis of Assisi* he presents both a protest against a society that expels its poor from its midst and the act of love in identification with them. In his later years he has developed a theological ecology that engages businessmen to think through economic policy in light of the future of the planet.

Further reading: Leonardo Boff, *Jesus Christ Liberator* (Maryknoll, N.Y.: Orbis, 1978); ———, *Saint Francis: Model of Human Liberation* (New York: Crossroad, 1882); ———, *The Lord's Prayer: The Prayer of Integral Liberation* (Maryknoll, N.Y.: Orbis, 1983); ———, *Church, Charism and Power* (New York: Crossroad, 1985); Harvey Cox, *The Silencing of Leonardo Boff* (Oak Park, Ill.: Meyer-Stone, 1988).

Bonaventure of Bagnoregio, St. (c. 1217–1274) *Theologian and churchman*

Born Giovanni di Fidenze in Bagnoregio, Bonaventure probably assumed his name upon entering the FRANCISCAN ORDER. Noted for his mystical theology, he was called the Seraphic Doctor. He served as minister general of the Franciscan Order, where he tried to find a path between the radical Spirituals and the Relaxti, who were fighting over how stringently the vow of poverty should be observed. Bl. Gregory X (r. 1271–76) made him cardinal bishop of Albano in 1273, and he played a key role at the Second Council of Lyons the following year. Bonaventure was canonized in 1482 and made a doctor of the church in 1588. His feast day is July 15.

He first studied at Paris under Alexander of Hales (c. 1186–1245), who first started doing theology by commenting on the *Sentences* of PETER LOMBARD. Bonaventure carried on the Christian Neoplatonic tradition established by AUGUSTINE and transmitted through ALCUIN and ANSELM. While accepting some aspects of Aristotle's concept of science, he shared Plato's critique of human insight based on a trust of the senses. Also unlike Aristotle and Aquinas, he thought that the creation of the world in time could be apprehended by human reason. In his *Reduction of the Arts to Theology* he argues that all human knowledge, summed up in the trivium and quadrivium of the seven liberal arts, is subsumed and superseded by theology.

Bonaventure's metaphysical theology is grounded in the TRINITY: from the Father emanates the wealth of being in the Word, the perfect exemplar of the divine art, which in turn returns to the Father through the personal love of the Spirit. This pattern is the hidden signature of all creation: "Every creature, because it bespeaks God, is a divine word" and thus reflects God as a shadow, a trace, or an image (*Sentences* 1.3.1.1–3). Following Augustine's *On the Trinity*, Bonaventure finds the image of the Trinity most reflected in the memory, intellect, and will of the human being.

Through sin humans have become "curved in" on themselves and fail to see the divine pattern in themselves or in creatures. Christ becomes incarnate to restore humanity to its true destiny; by his grace he refurbishes the image of the Trinity in the soul through faith, hope, and love. The mystical journey in *The Triple Way* takes place through the triple path of purgation of the senses, illumination of the mind by truth, and perfection of the soul through love. *Journey of the Mind into God* presents six stages of contemplation; eventually the soul, enraptured like St. Francis in the wings of the seraph, leaves even the intellectual plane and finds its "affection . . . transferred and transformed into God" (7.4). Bonaventure thought holistically. Theology cannot be separated from spirituality or nature from grace. In this he had a significant impact on KARL RAHNER in the 20th century. His thinking on ESCHATOLOGY has deeply influenced Pope BENEDICT XVI.

See also MYSTICISM; NEOPLATONISM.

Further reading: Almost all of Bonventure's writings are available online. Ewart Cousins, *Bonaventure and the Coincidence of Opposites* (Chicago: Franciscan Herald, 1978); Zachary Hayes, *The Hidden Center* (New York: Paulist Press, 1981).

Boniface VIII (c. 1234–1303) *medieval pope who expanded the papacy's power*

Born Benedict Caetani in Anagni, Boniface was educated at Todi and Spoleto. He entered the Roman curia in 1276, becoming a cardinal deacon and cardinal priest. He finessed the resignation of the weak Celestine V (r. 1294) and was elected pope at Naples in 1294. Among medieval popes he and INNOCENT III did the most to shore up the power of the papacy.

As pope he renewed the CRUSADES against the Turks to liberate the Holy Land. He condemned the Franciscan Spirituals known as the Fratecelli, and suppressed their supporters, the noble Roman Colonna family.

Boniface tried to mediate political disputes. His assertion of papal power grew out of his struggle against Philip IV the Fair (r. 1285–1314) of France, who wanted to tax church income. Against Philip, Boniface issued the bull *Ausculta fili* (December 5, 1301) claiming papal supremacy over princes and kings. This doctrine was radically expanded in the controversial bull *Unam Sanctam* (November 18, 1302), in which Boniface claims jurisdiction for the Roman pontiff over all living creatures and the prerogative of the spiritual power over the temporal.

The bull also contains the famous assertion that "the church is one, holy catholic and apostolic . . . and outside of her there is no salvation or remission of sins" (*extra ecclesiam nulla salus*). In his *Social Contract* Jean Jacques Rousseau (1712–78) states that anyone who makes such a claim should be excluded from civil society. In the 19th century Protestants and Catholics who opposed papal infallibility often referred to the seeming arrogance of Boniface's phrasing in their attacks on the papacy. In the 20th century the Jesuit Leonard Feeney of Boston was excommunicated for supporting a strict interpretation of the *extra ecclesiam* doctrine.

Boniface promulgated the *Sext* (*Liber sextus decretalium*), a sixth Book of CANON LAW to follow Gregory IX's five. It confirmed the centralization of church authority in the Vatican. In so doing, it overlooked the growing trend toward nationalism in Europe. Boniface established the tradition of the Jubilee Holy Year, a source of enormous income to the papacy. In the first Holy Year of 1300 more than 200,000 pilgrims made their way to Rome with the promise of a plenary indulgence for all their sins. The tradition continues to this day. Boniface also founded the Vatican Library and did much to embellish Roman churches. He ordered so many images and statues of himself that his opponents accused him of self-idolatry; in fact, Dante's *Inferno,* written while Boniface was still alive, prepares a ready-made place in hell for the pope on account of his vanity. There is a famous fresco of him by Giotto in the Lateran Basilica showing Boniface between two Holy Year pilgrims. After Boniface's death Philip the Fair sought redress against him from Avignon pope Clement V (r. 1305–14) in a process that accused him of many heretical opinions.

Further reading: Agostino Paravicini Bagliani, *Boniface VIII: un pape hérétique?* (Paris: Payot, 2003); Charles T. Wood, ed., *Philip the Fair and Boniface VIII* (Huntington N.Y.: Krieger, 1976); Herbert L. Kessler, *Rome 1300: On the Path of the Pilgrim* (New Haven, Conn.: Yale University Press, 2000).

Boniface of Germany, St. (c. 675–754)
missionary to Germany, monastic founder

Boniface, born Wynfrith in Wessex, England, became a Benedictine monk at Nursling. With St. Willibrord (658–739) he missionized the Norse tribes in Holland, GERMANY, and Denmark. Known for cutting down the Oak of Thor/Odin, he received the title Apostle of Germany. He is patron saint of Germany, woodcutters, brewers, and tanners. In art he is portrayed holding an axe. His feast day is June 5.

After failing in 716 in his mission to Frisia, Wynfrith went to Rome, where St. Gregory II (r. 715–31) commissioned him to missionize the German tribes along the upper Rhine. Probably at this time he received the name Boniface ("Doer of Good"). Accompanied by St. Willibrord, he returned to Germany, where legend says he single-handedly felled the sacred Oak of Thor/Odin with an axe near Greismar in Hesse, mounting the stump and proclaiming: "Where is your god? My God is stronger." Some claim that he felled whole copses of oaks throughout northern Europe to wean the Norse and Celts away from their nature gods. Many today challenge theologically his destructive policy of felling forests in order to win converts.

Boniface founded many monasteries throughout Germany, most notably the Abbey of Fulda, still in existence. After the death of Charles Martel (r. 714/719–41) in 741, Boniface, now a bishop, called a series of synods to reform the Frankish church. Pope Zacharias the Greek (r. 741–52) made him archbishop of Mainz in 746, but he soon returned to the missionary path. He was martyred in 754 and is buried at the Abbey of Fulda. Earlier in his monastic life Boniface wrote a Latin grammar and a book on metrics.

Further reading: St. Boniface of Germany, *Letters* (New York: Records of Civilization, 1940); T. Schieffer, *Winfrid-Bonafatius und die christliche Grundlegung Europas* (Darmstadt: Wissenschaftliche Buchgesellschaft, 1972); James M. Williamson, *The Life and Times of St. Boniface* (Ventor: W.J. Knight, 1904).

Book of Kells   See KELLS, BOOK OF.

Borromeo, Charles (1539–1584) *Counter-Reformation churchman*

Charles was born into the influential Medici family. He received his first benefice at the age of 12, in typically corrupt Renaissance fashion and went on to study humanities at Milan and Pavia. At 21 he was appointed cardinal and archbishop of Milan by his uncle Pope Pius IV. Contrary to all expectations, he became a leader at the third session of the Council of TRENT, reformed the lax lifestyle of the clergy in his diocese, and founded seminaries and orphanages for homeless children. He founded the Confraternity of Christian Doctrine to educate lay people in the faith. In the plague of 1576 he used much of his vast wealth to aid the poor and the sick. His model of a churchman had wide influence throughout Europe in his day and in later times. He was canonized in 1610 by PIUS V. His feast day is November 4.

Further reading: Giuseppe Alberigo, *Karl Borromäus: geschichtliche Sensibilität und pastorales Engagement* (Münster: Aschendorff, 1995); Margaret Yeo, *A Prince of Pastors: St. Charles Borromeo* (London: Longmans, Green, 1938).

Brazilian National Catholic Apostolic Church

The Brazilian National Catholic Apostolic Church is a schismatic body founded in 1945 in Brazil following the excommunication of the Most Rev. Don Carlos Duarte da Costa (1888–1961), Catholic Bishop of Maura in Sao Paulo State. Duarte da Costa had been ordained a priest in 1911 and consecrated in 1924 as bishop of Botucatu. He retired in 1937 and was given the title of titular bishop of Maura. He emerged as a liberal voice in the Brazilian hierarchy; he was an early opponent of celibacy for the priesthood and a supporter of liberalization of the Brazilian divorce law. The immediate cause of his excommunication in 1945 was not these controversial views, however, but his public complaints that the Vatican had aligned itself with FASCISM. Following his excommunication, he began to call for the formation of an independent church that would accept marriage for priests and permit divorce.

The new church, while never a real threat to the Catholic Church in Brazil, did spread, and by the time of his death in 1961 had established a dozen dioceses, though many of the parishes had to operate in a semiclandestine fashion. By 1973 it reported some 20,000 members under the guidance of some 34 bishops. Duarte da Costa was succeeded by Luis Fernando Castillo-Mendéz (b. 1922). He oversaw the canonization of Duarte da Costa by the church in 1970. By the 21st century, the church had emerged as a significant body with between 2 million and 3 million adherents.

Castillo-Mendéz attempted to extend the church in North America. In 1949 he consecrated Stephen Meyer Corradi-Scarella (1912–79), who subsequently founded the Holy Catholic Apostolic Church in North America with headquarters in Albuquerque. Though the North American church still exists, it has never grown beyond a handful of members.

Further reading: David Barrett, *The Encyclopedia of World Christianity*, 2nd ed. (New York: Oxford University Press, 2001); Gary L. Ward, ed., *Independent Bishops: An International Directory* (Detroit: Apogee Books, 1990).

Bulgarian Catholic Church

The Catholic Church maintained a presence in predominantly Eastern Orthodox Bulgaria for many centuries. It the mid-19th century it received a number of former members of the Bulgarian Orthodox Church into communion with Rome. These new members were allowed to retain their separate identity and retain a version of their Old Slavonic LITURGY. In 1859 the Bulgarian Catholic Church was formally constituted. Archimandrate Joseph Sokolsky (d. 1879?) was consecrated the first Bulgarian Catholic prelate in 1861.

The church got off to a shaky start. Soon after Sokolsky assumed his duties he was kidnapped by the Russians and imprisoned for 18 years. He died in Kiev. When in 1870 the Turkish sultan allowed the Bulgarian Orthodox Church to establish a jurisdiction independent of the Ecumenical Patriarchate in Istanbul, some three-quarters of the 80,000 members of the Bulgarian Catholic Church returned to Orthodoxy.

Membership in the Bulgarian Catholic Church reached its lowest point during the communist era. Only 7,000 members were reported in the 1970s. It has revived since the fall of the Soviet Union and as the new millennium begins has approximately 15,000 members. The church is headed by an apostolic exarch, who resides in Sofia and relates to the Roman Curia through the Congregation for the Oriental Churches.

See also EASTERN CATHOLICISM.

Further reading: Donald Attwater, *The Catholic Eastern Churches* (Milwaukee: Bruce, 1937); Ronald G. Roberson, *The Eastern Christian Churches—A Brief Survey*, 5th ed. (Rome: Pontifical Oriental Institute, 1995).

Byzantine Catholicism   *See* EASTERN CATHOLICISM.

C

Cabrini, St. Mother Frances Xavier

(1850–1917) *first U.S. saint, founder of charitable institutions*

Mother Cabrini was born in Lombardy, ITALY. Denied at first entrance into a religious order for her frail health, she worked in an orphanage for six years. She took vows in 1877. When the orphanage closed, her local bishop asked her to found the Missionary Sisters of the Sacred Heart of Jesus to work with poor children in schools and orphanages. At the urging of LEO XIII, she accepted Archbishop Michael Corrigan's (1839–1900) invitation in 1899 to work in New York. She arrived with six sisters. Corrigan regretted his invitation, but she stayed anyway, becoming a U.S. citizen and founding schools, hospitals, and orphanages in the United States, Europe, and South America. In 1946 PIUS XII made her the first U.S. citizen to be canonized. She is patron of immigrants, orphans, and hospital workers. Her feast day is November 13.

Further reading: A Daughter of St. Paul, *Mother Cabrini* (Boston: St. Paul, 1977); Segundo Galilea, *The Life and Missionary Activity of Saint Frances Xavier Cabrini.* Quezon City: Claretian Communications, 1996); Kathleen Jones, *Women Saints* (Maryknoll, N.Y.: Orbis Books, 1999); Theodore Maynard, *Too Small a World: The Life of Mother Cabrini* (New York: Censor Librorum, 1945).

caesaropapism (Lat. & It.: *caesar,* "emperor" + *papa* "pope")

Caesaropapism is an arrangement under which an emperor or king seeks to exercise supreme spiritual as well as temporal authority in his domain. In Europe the system has its roots in the Roman imperial tradition. From the time of Augustus (r. 31 B.C.E.–14 C.E.), the emperor acted as both the supreme ruler of the state and high priest, or *pontifex maximus* ("Supreme Pontiff" a term adopted by the popes by the 15th century) in Roman civic rites.

Once Christianity gradually became the state religion after CONSTANTINE THE GREAT, CHRISTIAN Byzantine emperors sought to have a say over the church's spiritual matters. Many emperors were the primary conveners of church councils. Emperors were consecrated in their offices and believed to be the legitimate successors of David, Solomon, and Jesus Christ himself. Sometimes the term *caesaropapism* is narrowly applied to the authority exercised by the Byzantine emperors over the Eastern patriarchate after the GREAT SCHISM between Roman Catholicism and EASTERN ORTHODOXY in 1054.

Russian czars, especially Peter I the Great (1672–1725), sought to control the patriarchate of Moscow through the newly created Holy Synod, through which he modernized the Russian liturgy. Somewhat ironically, the Soviet and Eastern European communist governments continued the caesaropapist system in their attempts to control the Russian Orthodox and other churches under their sphere of influence. Some people see the system reemerging in modern-day Russia.

See also CHURCH AND STATE.

Further reading: Gilbert Dagron, *Emperor and Priest: The Imperial Office in Byzantium* (Cambridge: Cambridge University Press, 2003).

calendar, liturgical *See* LITURGICAL YEAR.

Calvin, John *See* PROTESTANT REFORMATION.

Câmara, Dom Helder (1909–1999)
Brazilian archbishop and cofounder of CELAM
Câmara was born in Forteleza in northeast Brazil, became a seminarian under French Lazarists, and was ordained at 22. His pastoral abilities and work with Young Christian Workers brought him to Rio de Janeiro, where he was made auxiliary bishop. He became cofounder of the Latin American Bishops Conference (CELAM) and founded the Church of the Poor in Recife, where he served as archbishop.

Câmara was called to work with workers, youths, and the poor from his earliest days as a priest. At first he was attracted to the integralist ideas of the Portuguese dictator Antonio de Oliveira Salazar (1889–1970), but soon learned to work directly with workers, youths, and the poor. In Rio he worked with the Special CATHOLIC ACTION group and gained the attention of Vatican Secretary of State Giovanni Montini, later Pope PAUL VI, whom he convinced to set up the conference of bishops in Brazil in 1952 and the Latin American conference in 1955. These were the first truly decentralized conferences of bishops in the world.

Câmara became a central player in VATICAN COUNCIL II, where he worked closely with Cardinal LÉON JOSEF SUENENS in freeing the church throughout the world from the tight control of the Vatican curia. He also championed the needs and concerns of Third World bishops and facilitated dialogues with their First World counterparts. Back in Recife he founded the first BASE COMMUNITY, established a bank for the poor, and abandoned the espiscopal palace to live in the barrio, gaining worldwide attention. He once said, "If I feed the poor, I am called a saint; but if I ask why the poor have no food, I am called a communist." He became fully ecumenical in his proclamations, addressing all and hearing all as a servant of CHRIST.

Critical of the military coup in 1964, he became a nonperson but he wrote widely and traveled the world championing the cause of the poor and the principle of nonviolence. His most celebrated book was *Spiral of Violence* (1971). Though vigorous, he was forced to retire in 1985 at the age of 75. In his place, Pope JOHN PAUL II appointed the Carmelite José Cardoso Sobrinho (1933–), a canon lawyer and Vatican bureaucrat, who dismantled the Church of the Poor and reestablished a traditionalist church. Meanwhile Cardinal Ratzinger, later BENEDICT XVI, had launched his frontal attack from the Vatican on all aspects of the liberation movement and LIBERATION THEOLOGY, of which Dom Helder had been the episcopal champion. Dom Helder died almost an ecclesiastical nonperson, forgotten by the church that he had served with a full heart, but his memory, like that of the ignored Archbishop ÓSCAR ROMERO, burns brightly in the hearts and minds of many of the faithful beyond the borders of his homeland.

Further reading: Helder Câmara, *Through the Gospel with Dom Helder Câmara*, tr. Alan Neame (Maryknoll, N.Y.: Orbis, 1986); David Regan, *Why are They Poor?: Helder Câmara in Pastoral Perspective* (London: Lit, 2003).

canon (Gk.: *kanon,* "straight rod," "measure," "standard," "guide," "norm," "rule")
The term *canon* has several meanings in CHRISTIAN and Catholic ecclesiastical usage. The seven

most important are: 1) a RULE OF FAITH (later CREED) to instruct believers in basic theological principles; 2) the CANON OF SCRIPTURE, the list of books believed to be inspired by the Holy Spirit, which make up the BIBLE, or Holy Scriptures; 3) the order of prayers and procedures for conducting a liturgical rite, such as, the CANON OF THE MASS; 4) an official decree of a church council or synods; 5) one of the internal rules of the church that regulate and discipline the lives of its members and that comprise CANON LAW, as it was known in the MIDDLE AGES); 6) a cleric attached to a cathedral or living under a semimonastic rule such as that of the AUGUSTINIANS; a woman who lived according to similar rules received the title canoness; and 7) one of the nine odes, or canticles, used in the Orthros in the Eastern rite (*see* EASTERN CATHOLICISM), the equivalent of Matins and Lauds.

Further reading: Roger T. Beckwith, *The Old Testament Canon of the New Testament Church and Its Background in Early Judaism* (Grand Rapids, Mich.: Eerdmans, 1985); *Code of Canon Law,* cnn. 503–10 (Washington, D.C.: Canon Law Society of America, 1983); Bruce Metzger, *The Canon of the New Testament: Its Origin, Development, and Significance* (Oxford: Clarendon Press, 1987); H. Oppel, "KANΩN: Zur Bedeutungsgeschichte des Wortes und seiner lateinischen Entsprechungen," *Philologus* (Suppl. 1930) 30:1–108.

canonization

Canonization (or sanctification) is the definitive proclamation by which the pope, in the name of the church, declares a beatified deceased person to be a saint. A saint is one who has entered into eternal glory with GOD and the other saints and who may receive a public cult throughout the entire church.

There are three significant steps in the process of canonization. The first step generally begins at the local level through a bishop's curia. The bishop assigns a postulator, or *Promotor Justitiae,* to plead the cause of the candidate. The case then moves to the Congregation of the Causes of Saints in the Vatican, which weighs all the testimony and documentation, called the Acts of the Cause. Generally there is an advocate (called *Promotor Fidei,* or Promotor of the Faith) who argues the candidate's cause, and another who argues against it. The contrary party used to be referred to popularly as the *advocatus Diaboli,* or "Devil's Advocate." If the person is judged to be worthy of honor, he or she is first declared "venerable," and the case proceeds to the next step.

A rigorous investigation is then pursued to find out whether the candidate had attained heroic love and virtue and whether at least one uncontested miracle was wrought through her or his intercession. Both theological and scientific criteria are applied. If there is a positive answer at this stage, the person is declared "blessed" (beatified) by the pope at a ceremony in St. Peter's. The blessed are generally venerated on a local level. As a rule, more miracles must be demonstrated in further pleading before a person receives the title *saint,* issued through a papal bull at a formal ceremony in St. Peter's. A comparable investigative procedure is employed in the canonization of figures from the distant past.

A saint has seven honors: 1) her or his name is inscribed in the catalog of saints, 2) the saint can be invoked in public prayers of the church, 3) churches may be dedicated to the saint, 4) a EUCHARIST and Divine Office are composed in the saint's honor, 5) the saint receives a feast day in the LITURGICAL YEAR, 6) statues and paintings may be made showing the saint with a halo or nimbus signifying heavenly glory, and 7) the saint's relics may be enclosed in reliquaries and venerated by the faithful.

In the early church anyone who was a martyr for the faith in the waves of persecution by the Romans was treated as a saint through popular devotion. The honor was later extended to noted missionaries, virgins, doctors of the church, and other persons who attained heroic virtue. Because of abuses, local bishops and synods of bishops began to assume authority over the process. In the Eastern Church this procedure is still followed. In the West, by the 10th century the PAPACY started taking a direct role. The first officially canonized saint seems to have been St. Ulrich of Augsburg (c. 890–973), designated by Pope John XV (r. 985–96) in 993. In 1170 Alexander III (r. 1159–81) decreed in a letter to King Canute I of Sweden (r. 1167–95) that no one could be declared a saint without papal approval. This decree was incorporated into the Decretals of Gregory IX in 1264, thereby becoming part of CANON LAW. After the Council of TRENT the procedures for canonization were tightened; in 1588 Sixtus V entrusted the process to the Sacred Congregation of the Rites. The rules remained in effect until JOHN PAUL II radically simplified the process with the apostolic constitution *Divinus Perfectionis Magister* (January 25, 1983). Since then, less time and fewer miracles have been needed to clinch the case.

During his reign John Paul II beatified more than 1,300 venerables and canonized more than 500 blessed, more than any pope in history. His most notable mass canonizations all derived from ASIA—the 103 Korean martyrs (1984), the 116 Vietnamese martyrs (1988), and the 120 Chinese martyrs (2000), the last over the protest of the Chinese government. Notable individuals include the Franciscan MAXIMILIAN KOLBE and the Carmelite Edith Stein (1891–1942), both of whom died at Auschwitz. John Paul II canonized many Africans and Latin Americans, including Juan Diego, who received the vision of the Virgin of Guadalupe (*see* MARY OF NAZARETH). Also included were JUNIPERO SERRA, KATHERINE DREXEL, Padre Pio (1887–1968), and Josemaria Escrivá (1902–75), the controversial founder of OPUS DEI. In 2000 he beatified Pope JOHN XXIII, the most beloved pope in modern history, and PIUS IX. He beatified MOTHER TERESA OF CALCUTTA, perhaps the most popular religious figure in the world after the Dalai Lama, in 2003.

Further reading: Eric Waldram Kemp, *Canonization and Authority in the Western Church* (Oxford: Oxford University Press, 1948); Richard P. McBrien, *Lives of the Saints* (San Francisco: HarperSanFrancisco, 2001); T. J. Zubek, "New Legislation about the Canonization of the Servants of God," *Jurist* 43 (1983): 361–375; Kenneth L. Woodward, *Making Saints* (New York: Simon & Schuster, 1990).

canon law

The body of church laws imposed either by a council or a primate and dealing with matters of faith, morals, and discipline. The concept of canon law, and much of the content, is common to the Roman Catholic, Eastern Orthodox, and Anglican communions.

The body of canon law grew very slowly over time. The beginnings can be seen in early church rules governing CIRCUMCISION and foods offered to idols (Acts 15), head coverings during worship and appropriate conduct during the EUCHARIST (1 Cor. 11), and normative behaviors of CHRISTIAN life in general (*Didache*; Hippolytus, *Apostolic Tradition*). This stage was followed by legislation enacted at church councils called in the early 4th century to resolve disputes concerning both doctrine and discipline. Among these were the Councils of Ancyra (314), which laid down penalties for believers who lapsed under persecution, and Laodicea (date unknown), whose 59 canons dealt with the treatment of heretics, LITURGY, penance, church order, and Lent.

The canons derived from the decrees of the first ecumenical councils—Nicaea I (325), CONSTANTINOPLE I (381), and CHALCEDON (451)—enjoyed extraordinary universal authority. The canons dealt with topics such as church organization, the conduct of priests, and penance. The Roman church has often referred to Nicaea I's canon 6, which ranked Constantinople second to Rome, to justify the primacy of the PAPACY at Rome.

The African and Spanish provinces held many plenary councils that also produced a large body of canon law. Many councils gave canonical status to rulings of the church fathers by incorporating them into their decrees and canons. Of special importance were the letters on church problems, known as decretals, issued by popes beginning with Pope Siricius (r. 384–99) in 385; some eventually acquired status as canon law. The Code of Justinian (529), a civil code, recognized canon law as the parallel ecclesiastical body of law. When the Roman Empire fell in the West around 476, canon law took independent turns in different regions of Europe.

With the exception of a few organized subsections (e.g., on penance), the collections of law remained largely in ad hoc disarray. Around 550 John Scholastikos (d. 577) patriarch of Constantinople, sought to bring order out of this mess by organizing Greek canons according to topic in his *Synagōgē Kanōnōn,* which he later amplified from the Justinian law collection called the *Novellae.* In the West Dionysius Exiguus (fifth to sixth centuries), who fixed the date of the birth of Christ, translated Greek canons into Latin. He appended 39 papal decretals, in effect equating papal decrees with those of full councils. There were further redactions under CHARLEMAGNE around 800 and GREGORY VII around 1050.

A collection now known as the False Decretals gained currency in that era. Attributed to one Isidore of Mercator (in an attempt to use the legitimacy of St. Isidore of Seville, c. 560–636, the False Decretals defend direct relations between the papacy and diocesan bishops, to the detriment of the authority of metropolitan archbishops. They also contain the fake DONATION OF CONSTANTINE. Elements of the False Decretals made it into the collections of GREGORY VII and Gratian (d. c. 1160).

In the same period Ivo of Chartres (c. 1040–1115) laid down rules for interpreting and harmonizing conflicting canons in the Prologus to his *Decretum.* The peak in the systematization of canon law came with the *Decretum* of the great medieval canonist Gratian (fl. 1130). His treatise

divides the "old" from the "new law." Gratian, widely called the father of modern canon law, collected, codified, and harmonized more than 4,000 patristic, conciliar, and papal texts up to and including the decisions of the Lateran Council II (1139) in all the areas of church discipline.

Gratian's *Decretum* never received official sanction. Nonetheless, it was continuously cited as an official authority by all canonists until its formal incorporation into the *Code of Canon Law* (*Corpus juris canonici*) issued under the *motu proprio* of PIUS X in 1904 and promulgated in 1917. When JOHN XXIII declared his intention to call an ecumenical council, he also called for a revision of canon law. The Synod of Bishops in 1967 gave directions that the new code should reflect not just legal technicalities but pastoral concerns as well, that it should respect the principle of subsidiarity (i.e., higher organization structures should not overwhelm lower ones), and that it should protect the rights of the faithful. In recent times the last principle has been severely tested by the PEDOPHILIA cases involving the clergy.

The new revision appeared in 1983 for the Western Church and in 1990 for the Eastern Churches (*see* EASTERN CATHOLICISM)—the first time that Catholic Eastern canons have been codified. The 1983 edition is meant to reflect the decrees and spirit of VATICAN COUNCIL II (1962–65), but its canons on the authority of the pope seem to reflect more the spirit of VATICAN COUNCIL I.

The interpretation of canon law follows rather strict rules that have been incorporated into the new code itself. First, the lawmaker or his designate gives the official and authoritative interpretation of the law (cn. 16). There is no principle of *stare decisis* ("Let the decision stand") as in civil law, and judicial and administrative decisions do not necessarily set precedents. Second, there are guidelines, whether explicitly stated in the code or part of tradition, for determining the meaning of rules contained in the canons and their application. Third, the laws are to be interpreted according to "text and context" (cn. 17). In other words, the interpretation may depend on the type of law involved: a doctrinal declaration, a recommendation or exhortation, or an explicit command. Fourth, the purpose of the law shapes its meaning and application. Fifth, the mind of the lawgiver must also be taken into account. All interpretations are subject to the principle of equitable justice (Gr. *epikeia,* Lat. *aequitas*), derived from Aristotle and applied by THOMAS AQUINAS and FRANCISCO SUAREZ. It has pride of place: a law need not be obeyed if it is detrimental to the genuine common good or the good of individuals.

Laws imposing penalties or restricting rights are to be interpreted strictly and narrowly. Custom has a role, too: "Custom is the best interpreter of the law" (cn. 17). The practice of the community of faithful confirms and clarifies the meaning of the law. If the community refuses a law over time, then it is without effect. Although the official church is loathe to admit it, the restrictions and conditions the Vatican has imposed on the use of artificial birth control probably would fall under this rule, as married lay Catholics have almost universally rejected them de facto and follow their own consciences.

The goal of canon law is clearly stated in the final canon 1752: ". . . the salvation of souls, which is the supreme law of the Church." Canon law has had a civilizing effect in all the lands to which it has been imported. Along with the Justinian Code, it is one of the two legal anchors of European civilization.

Further reading: *Code of Canon Law* (Washington, D.C.: Canon Law Society of America, 1983); *Code of Canons of the Eastern Churches* (Washington, D.C.: Canon Law Society of America, 1991); James Coriden, Thomas Green, and Donald Heintschel, eds., *The Code of Canon Law: A Text and Commentary* (Washington, D.C.: Canon Law Society of America, 1985); James Muldoon, *Canon Law, the Expansion of Europe, and World Order* (Aldershot: Ashgate, 1998); Brian Tierney, *Church Law and Constitutional Thought in the Middle Ages* (London: Vari-

orum Reprints, 1979); Constant van de Wiel, *History of Canon Law* (Louvain: Peeters, 1991).

Canon of Scripture

The Canon of Scripture is the list of books of the Old Testament (Tanakh) and the New Testament that are officially sanctioned as having been inspired by GOD under the heading of Scripture or BIBLE. The Catholic canon includes 46 Old Testament and 27 New Testament books.

OLD TESTAMENT

The Torah, or the Five Books of Moses (Pentateuch), had canonical status by the time the Jews started returning c. 539 B.C.E. from the Babylonian Exile. Ezra (fl. 538 ft. B.C.E.) may well have been the final editor/redactor of the Torah. Within the next few centuries the rest of the books of today's Hebrew Bible had their canonical status confirmed, probably in their present division and order: Torah, Nebi'im (Prophets), and Ketubi'im (Writings). With the exception of the Book of Esther, all the books of the Hebrew Bible were represented at least in part among the scrolls discovered at Qumran; Esther, too, may yet be found among the countless undeciphered fragments.

The entire text of the Bible was long considered sacred and authoritative, but the first explicit mention of such a status within the Bible itself was in 1 Kings (22–23), when the "Book of the Law" was found by the priest Hilkiah during the reign of Josiah and proclaimed to be authoritative. The title most likely refers to Moses' Covenant discourse in Deuteronomy 5–12, which was later expanded into the present Book of Deuteronomy and used to frame the historical narration of the Israelites given in Joshua, Judges, 1 and 2 Samuel, and 1 and 2 Kings. After the destruction of the Temple in Jerusalem in 70 C.E., religious authority passed from the priests (Sadducees) to the rabbis (Pharisees), who continued to debate the authenticity or acceptability of Qohelet (Ecclesiastes) and the Song of Songs. In his discussion of Jewish sacred texts, Josephus enumerates the Five Books of Moses, 13 prophetic books, and four books of hymns (psalms) and precepts (proverbs). The first complete list of the 24 books of the Jewish Bible is in the Babylonian Talmud (b. B. Bat. 14b–15a), dating from the end of the fifth century but reflecting much earlier traditions.

SEPTUAGINT (LXX)

The Septuagint is the Greek translation of the Hebrew Bible known to the Greek-speaking Jews of Alexandria in the Hellenistic era. According to the legend recounted in the *Letter of Aristeas* (200 B.C.E.–33 C.E.?), Ptolemy II Philadelphus (285–46 B.C.E.) engaged 72 scholars (hence the name "Septuagint," or 70 in Greek) to translate the Hebrew Scripture for his famous library at Alexandria; they all independently came up with exactly the same translation. We now know that the text was produced by many authors working over a period of time; it was not completed until about 132 B.C.E.

The LXX was apparently translated from a Palestinian Hebrew recension of a still older manuscript tradition. It differs from the known Hebrew Bible in the order and number of books and in many cases in the text. Many scholars credit later Christian influence with the present arrangement of the books in the Hebrew Bible according to historical, poetic/didactic, and prophetic types.

Almost all the biblical quotes or references in the New Testament are to the LXX. Early Christian writers knew that the LXX contained books not found in the Hebrew version; they recognized these books as "deuterocanonical" but canonical nonetheless. In the LXX's favor, fragments of both Tobit and Sirach have been found at Qumran. Furthermore, in many instances the Hebrew text of the Bible at Qumran agrees with the Septuagint over the masoretic text, the standard Hebrew version of today.

Sts. Jerome, Gregory of Nazianzus, and Epiphanius favored the list in the Hebrew Bible and would not accept the Apocrypha as canonical, but Ambrose and Augustine disagreed. Protestants called the extra books or sections of books the Apocrypha and rejected them. The Council of Trent (Session 4, 1546), followed by Vatican Councils I and II, affirmed the Apocrypha as canonical.

(For a comparative list of canonical books of the Old Testament accepted by Roman Catholics and, for the most part, by the Eastern Orthodox, see under Bible. The Jewish and Protestant canons are listed for comparison.)

NEW TESTAMENT

It may seem odd to contemporary Christians, but the authoritative Bible familiar to the New Testament writers was what Christians today call the Old Testament; most New Testament books did not have the same authority until the end of the second century or later. No doubt the process of canonization of the New Testament was accelerated in reaction to Marcion, the second-century Christian radical who rejected the creator God of the Old Testament as an evil Demiurge and accepted only the letters of Paul and a truncated version of Luke as scripture. The use of Scripture in the Liturgy and in pastoral writing was another incentive to establish the canon.

The four familiar gospels and the 13 epistles of Paul were the first to receive informal canonical status. There was much debate about other books including Hebrews, Jude, 2 Peter, 2 and 3 John, and Revelation. Some churches accepted the Epistle of Barnabas and the Shepherd of Hermas as Scripture.

The oldest extant lists of New Testament books are 1) canon 60 of the fourth-century Council of Laodicea, and 2) the Muratorian Canon, which may have been composed at the end of the second century, although the earliest manuscript dates to the eighth. The earliest witness to the present New Testament canon is in the *Festal Letter* of 367 by Athanasius of Alexandria. At Rome Pope St. Damasius (r. 366–85) approved a canonical list of both the Old Testament and New Testament in

382. This list is identical with the list endorsed at the Council of Trent, which remains authoritative for Catholics to this day. Trent gave equal status to "canonical" and "deuterocanonical" texts, in part because 2 Maccabees 12:46 implies a doctrine of PURGATORY, that the reformers had rejected.

Further reading: Joseph Blenkinsopp, *Prophecy and Canon* (Notre Dame: Notre Dame University Press, 1977); Frederick F. Bruce, *The Canon of Scripture* (Downers Grove, Ill.: InterVarsity, 1988); Bruce Metzger, *The Canon of the New Testament* (Oxford: Clarendon Press, 1987).

Canon of the Mass

The Canon of the Mass is the order of prayers and procedures used in the Roman rite for the central part of the EUCHARIST (formerly called the Mass)—the consecration of the sacred elements of bread and wine. It is called the CANON because its basic form has never changed. The basic form is found in all ancient Eucharistic liturgies, Greek and Latin, and with the possible exception of the liturgies of Addai and of Mari, it always contains Jesus' words of institution: "This is my body . . . This is my blood." (Luke 22:19–20).

The text of the Roman canon is found in almost complete form in *On the Sacraments* by St. AMBROSE OF MILAN (d. 397). It was modified slightly by St. GREGORY I THE GREAT (d. 604). Other early versions are found in the Gelasian Sacramentary (c. 750), the Bobbio Missal (eighth century) and the Frankish Missal (seventh century).

The canon is preceded by the Liturgy of the Word, which includes the opening, scripture readings gloria and creed. The canon begins with the preface prayer "The Lord be with you" which ends in the "Holy, Holy, Holy, Lord God of Hosts;" it proceeds to the eucharistic prayer including the words of institution; continues with the memorial acclamation "Christ has died"; and ends with the doxology, or word of praise, and the Great

Amen. Communion, the distribution of consecrated bread and wine, follows the canon.

From about 800 to 1967 most of the canon was recited silently in the Western Church, and only in Latin, to reflect the exclusive status of priests. Following the directives of VATICAN COUNCIL II, a commission on the LITURGY in 1967 revised the form of the canon, allowed the prayers to be recited aloud, and allowed the use of local languages. Today there are four different Eucharistic prayers that may be used in the liturgy; what remains constant are the preface, the words of institution, and the great doxology.

Prior to Vatican II there was great emphasis on the Canon of the Mass and especially the words of institution, but today Catholic liturgical theologians, following the precedents of the earliest CHRISTIAN theologians, see the Eucharist in a holistic context and do not place one part of the service above another. The entire rite contributes to the spiritual life of the community of the faithful.

Further reading: Jerome Gassner, *The Canon of the Mass: Its History, Theology and Art* (St. Louis: Herder, 1950); Josef Jungman, *The Eucharistic Prayer* (Notre Dame: Fides, 1964).

capital punishment

Capital punishment is the infliction of death on a person by the authorities after conviction for certain serious crimes. Capital punishment appears in the world's earliest law codes. The Sumerian Laws of Eshunna and the Babylonian Code of Hammurabi recognize the death penalty for certain offenses. These laws find specific counterparts in the laws of Exodus, Leviticus, and Deuteronomy. For example, capital punishment for a false accusation of murder, cited in the Code of Hammurabi 1, is reflected in modified form in Exodus 23:1–3 and Deuteronomy 5:20. While the BIBLE prescribes certain capital sentences (Exod. 21:12–17), scholars have noted that it manifests a clear tendency to limit and restrict the number of instances to which such sentences may apply, as in the example cited above. Jewish rabbinic law further restricted the death penalty by putting up ever greater hurdles to its application.

Prior to the era of CONSTANTINE, the church was essentially pacifist in political terms and opposed to violence even under judicial decree, in part because CHRISTIANS themselves suffered unjustly from the imposition of the death penalty under the Romans. In *On Idolatry* 19 TERTULLIAN OF CARTHAGE noted the impediments to Christians serving in the army: not only were soldiers required to take part in pagan sacrifices as ordered by the emperors, but they had to enforce capital punishments as decreed by judges. Tertullian constantly highlighted the "sword that the Lord has taken away" from those who would follow him (Matt. 26:52; 2 Cor. 10:4). Many later Christians have taken this and other texts as support for Christian pacifism and a totally nonviolent civil order.

After Constantine Christians became more tolerant of capital punishment without actually approving it. Major thinkers did not undermine the legitimacy of capital punishment on the part of the state, but they made sure to display an underlying disapproval, such as by forbidding clerics to take part in the administration of a death sentence. Even though popes have condemned heretics and rebels to death, there has never been an official Catholic teaching mandating the death penalty for any crime.

Sts. AUGUSTINE and THOMAS AQUINAS both provided arguments for the death penalty. Aquinas argued that the body social could amputate a diseased member for the good of the whole (*Summa Theologiae* 2-2.64). The reformers followed this line of reasoning. However, if the common good can be obtained without inflicting death, then this argument loses some of its force for both Aquinas and the reformers. Ever since the Enlightenment opposition to capital punishment has grown. In all countries of the European Union it has been removed from the instruments of law.

In more recent times capital punishment has come under criticism from religious quarters as well. In 1980 the U.S. Catholic Bishops' Conference issued a *Statement on Capital Punishment*. It acknowledged the state's right to inflict capital punishment but challenged the exercise of that right on the basis that "the abolition of the death penalty would promote values that are important to us as citizens and as Christians." Today, many bishops are actually challenging the state's right to inflict capital punishment. They have been fortified in their argument by Pope JOHN PAUL II's *Evangelium Vitae* (March 25, 1995), which comes close to a ban on capital punishment: ". . . there is a growing tendency, both in the Church and in civil society, to demand that it be applied in a very limited way or even that it be abolished completely. The problem must be viewed in the context of a system of penal justice ever more in line with human dignity and thus, in the end, with God's plan for man and society" (56). The death penalty goes against the dignity of the human person, cutting off definitively the possibility of repentance and conversion of the criminal guilty of capital crime. The instances of its just application are "vary rare if practically non-existent." The pope's position was supported in a U.S. Catholic Bishops' statement *Confronting a Culture of Violence* (1995) and in the newly modified 1997 edition of *Catechism of the Catholic Church* (2265–67).

Cardinal JOSEPH BERNARDIN of Chicago proposed a "seamless garment" argument: the Christian is called to defend life both at the beginning (by opposing abortion), in-between (by supporting social justice), and at the end (by opposing euthanasia and capital punishment). If society can be made secure without the death penalty, he argued, then it should be done away with.

The new tendency in Catholicism is really a return to the stance of the early church. It takes due notice of the number of people, especially the minorities and the poor, who have been sentenced to death and later found innocent. It seeks to break the cycle of violence prevalent in modern life. It affirms the unique worth and dignity of each human being, including the possibility of his or her repentance and conversion to GOD. It submits that God alone is the Lord of life and that Jesus preached forgiveness even of injustice.

Further reading: Joseph Bernardin, "The Death Penalty in Our Time," Address to Criminal Law Committee Criminal Court of Cook County (May 14, 1985), available online. *Catechism of the Catholic Church* (Washington, D.C.: United States Catholic Conference, 1997); Avery Dulles, "To Kill or not to Kill: The Catholic Church and the Problem of the Death Penalty," in Charles Curran, ed., *Change In Official Catholic Moral Teaching* (New York: Paulist Press, 2003); John Paul II, *Evangelium Vitae* (March 25, 1995), available on the Vatican Web site; J. Gordon Melton, *The Churches Speak on Capital Punishment* (Detroit: Gale Research, 1989); U.S. Catholic Bishops, *Statement on Capital Punishment* (Washington, D.C.: U.S. Catholic Bishops Conference, 1980); U.S. Catholic Bishops, *Confronting a Culture of Violence* (Washington, D.C.: U.S. Catholic Bishops Conference, 1995).

Carmelites

The Carmelites are an order of hermits that began as a group of contemplatives gathered around the traditional cave of Elijah on Mt. Carmel in the 12th century. Their abbreviation is OCarm. They took their inspiration from Elijah's way of life and their devotion to the Blessed Virgin Mary. They were given a rule, modeled on the rules of the ancient Palestinian *lavrae,* or MONASTERIES by St. Albert (1149–1214), Latin patriarch of Jerusalem. Protected by the crusader Frankish kingdom, their life was dedicated to prayer and contemplation in individual caves, the common celebration of the EUCHARIST, and the recitation of the PSALTER.

When the last crusaders were expelled from the Holy Land in 1291, the Carmelites established foundations in Cyprus, Sicily, France, and England with the help of returning crusaders. Innocent IV (1243–54) granted the hermits permission to establish foundations in cities and modified their rule in conformity to the rules of the other MENDICANT ORDERS. In 1432 Eugenius IV (1383–1447) (r. 1431–1447) approved a mitigation of the rule with regard to abstinence from meat and silence, allowing the order to take a preaching function in society. Many women began to follow the Carmelite way; their communities were incorporated in 1452.

About 1370 Philip Ribot of Catalonia composed the *Institute of the First Monks,* which describes the mystical path of the Carmelite as withdrawal from the world, purification of the heart, and union with God. The book helped to spark a flowering of mysticism in the 16th century, centered on Sts. TERESA OF ÁVILA and JOHN OF THE CROSS, who founded the Carmelite tradition known as Teresan or Discalced ("without sandals").

Carmelites suffered greatly from the suppression of the monasteries under HENRY VIII (1491–1547) (r. 1509–1547) and again during the French Revolution (1789). François Poulenc (1899–1963) made the persecution of the Carmelite nuns in France the theme of his famous opera *Dialogue of the Carmelites* (1957). Beginning in the 19th century the Carmelite family of friars and nuns reconstituted themselves in various branches, including the friars of the Ancient Observance, the Discalced, the third order Regulars, lay associates, and the Carmelites of Mary Immaculate, founded in India in 1831. Sts. Thérèse of Lisieux and Theresa Benedicta of the Cross (Edith Stein, 1891–1942) were two noted modern Carmelite saints. The Carmelite ROLAND T. MURPHY is one of the great biblical scholars of the 20th century.

Further reading: Joachim Smet, *The Carmelites: A History of the Brothers of Our Lady of Mt. Carmel,* 4 vols. (Darien Ill.: Carmelite Spiritual Center, 1978–88); ———, *Cloistered Carmel: A Brief History of the Carmelite Nuns* (Rome: Carmelite Institute, 1986); Mary Jo Weaver, *Cloister and*

Community: Life within a Carmelite Monastery (Bloomington: Indiana University Press, 2002).

Carneiro, Melchior   *See* Nunes Carneiro Leitao, Melchior

Carolingian Renaissance

The cultural and religious flowering in the West under Charlemagne and his successors is known as the Carolingian Renaissance. It signaled the recovery from the destructive effects of the fall of Rome and helped lay the basis for medieval European culture.

Charlemagne reunited most of Christian Europe under centralized rule, which he enforced through legates (*missi dominici* "lord's emissaries") who had royal authority to correct abuses. Internal and external trade revived, aided by the emperor's silver standard for monetary exchange.

The social structures that would prevail in the Middle Ages took shape. Wealth and land tenure were concentrated in a noble class created by a web of intermarriage between various families based on military service to the emperor and other princes. Nobles tended to monopolize high church appointments as well, serving as bishops and abbots. Together this group ruled over peasants and serfs attached to landed estates. In parallel to government centralization, Charlemagne firmed up the archiepiscopal governance system. Liturgically he promoted the Roman rite and chant of Gregory I the Great, shunting aside the native Gallican rite. He induced bishops and abbots to found chapter schools on the model of the palace school that Alcuin founded at Aachen. The chapter schools served as the model for the teaching of the liberal arts in later university curricula. Charlemagne also promoted monastic scriptoria for the preservation and dissemination of ancient learning. They in turn gave rise to the traditions of luxuriant illuminated manuscripts.

One of the most prominent abbatial schools was at the abbey of Fulda, whose abbot was Rabanus Maurus, later archbishop of Mainz. Education was open to both clerics and, for the first time, lay students, especially children of the nobility and those appointed to imperial administration. The era also witnessed a revival of ecclesiastical history; one of the most famous practitioners was Venerable Bede (c. 672–715).

The era saw great advances in architecture and ecclesiastical decoration, including mosaics and ivory carving. Most celebrated are the octagonal Palatine chapel at Aachen and the astounding abbey of Sankt Gallen in Switzerland, plans of which have survived. Carolingian mosaics and decoration can be seen in the Oratory of Theodulf of Orleans at Germigny-des-Pres in the Loire Valley and in the chapel of St. Zeno in the church of St. Praxedes in Rome. The mosaics are Byzantine in heritage but begin to break out of the frozen mold characteristic of earlier Christian mosaics. A noted ivory is the cover of the Lorsch Gospels in the Vatican museum. Nothing can compare to the delicacy of drawing and painting of the many surviving Carolingian illuminated manuscripts, among which stand out the Gospel of Archbishop Ebbo of Reims and the Lothair Gospel.

Further reading: With patience, all the churches, architecture, mosaics, ivories, and manuscripts mentioned above can be found online on the Web. Rosamond McKittrick, ed., *Carolingian Culture* (Cambridge: Cambridge University Press, 1994).

Carroll, Charles (1737–1832) *signer of U.S. Declaration of Independence*

Charles Carroll was the only Catholic to sign the U.S. Declaration of Independence. He was born in Annapolis, Maryland, into one of the most prominent families of the colony, his grandfather having migrated to the New World in 1688. He was sent to Europe for his education and remained there from 1748 to 1765. In 1773 he debated the Tory Daniel Dulany (1722–97), arguing for the cause of independence. Outspoken on the issue of taxation without representation, Carroll represented Maryland as senator at the first Continental Congress in 1789. He became one of the wealthiest colonists in America and was an original director of the Baltimore & Ohio Railroad. His cousin, John CARROLL, became the first Roman Catholic bishop in America.

Further reading: Charles Carroll, *Journal of Charles Carroll, 1776.* New York: New York Times, 1969); Thomas O'Brien Hanley, *Charles Carroll of Carrollton: The Making of a Revolutionary Gentleman* (Washington, D.C.: Catholic University of America, 1970); Scott McDermott, *Charles Carroll of Carrollton* (New York: Scepter, 2002).

Carroll, John (1735–1815) *first American bishop and archbishop*

John Carroll was the first Catholic BISHOP of the United States. Born in Maryland (a colony founded as a refuge for English Catholics), he was educated under Jesuit auspices at St.-Omer, Flanders. Ordained a priest in 1761, he returned to the colonies in 1773 as a secular missionary after the suppression of the JESUITS by the pope. A strong supporter of independence, he accompanied Benjamin Franklin (1706–90) on a mission to gain Canada's neutrality in 1776. He organized Catholics to support the Constitution of the United States.

Following petitions from priests, Pope PIUS VI (1775–99) appointed Carroll the first bishop in the new nation in 1789. He became archbishop of Baltimore in 1808. His diocese was enormous, stretching from New York to Virginia but was later divided into four suffragan sees. He established the nation's first Catholic university at Georgetown and its first seminary, St. Mary's, in 1791, the same year he led the first Catholic synod in Baltimore. In 1793 he ordained Stephen Badin (1768–1853) the first priest created in the new nation. He enrolled the assistance of Carmelite and Visitation nuns and the Sisters of Charity in his church building projects. He adopted the trustee system by which lay people governed the secular aspects of their parishes. In spite of frequent troubles, he never abandoned faith in that system. He oversaw the building of the famous Cathedral of the Assumption in Baltimore, a treasure of federal ARCHITECTURE.

Carroll published widely in an attempt to make Catholicism understandable to the Protestant majority and vice versa, most notably *An Address to Roman Catholics of the United States* (1784). He wholeheartedly embraced the American principles of religious freedom and the separation of church and state, yet maintained warm relations with a papacy that had other ideas. No other cleric gave such sound bearing for the future of Catholicism in the United States.

Further reading: Joseph Agonito, *The Building of an American Catholic Church: The Episcopacy of John Carroll* (New York: Garland, 1988); Peter Guilday, *The Life and Times of John Carroll, Archbishop of Baltimore* (Westminster, Md.: Newman Press, 1954); T. O. Hanley, ed., *The John Carroll Papers,* 3 vols. (Notre Dame: University of Notre Dame Press, 1976).

catacombs (prob. Gr.: *kata,* "down" + *kumbas,* "at the hollows")

The catacombs are vast underground burial chambers and complexes used to bury CHRISTIANS and others in the vicinity of ancient Rome. The term *catacomb* probably referred originally to the natural cavity alongside the Via Appia in Rome, now occupied by the basilica of St. Sebastian, in which were buried the remains of Christians who refused to be cremated in the typical Roman manner. The 10th Roman bronze law tablet decreed that no corpse could be buried or cremated within the city. Hence, all the catacombs were outside the walls. Not all catacombs were dedicated to Christian burial. Some were devoted to adherents of Judaism, the mystery religions, especially Mithraism, and even Roman religion.

The entrance to St. Sebastian catacomb was known throughout history, but the sites and

Arcosolium (right), or an arched tomb, with a mensa, or table, at which the Eucharist was likely celebrated. (Via Latina Catacomb, Rome) *(Scala/Art Resource)*

entrances of most other catacombs were lost in time; they are still being discovered in modern times. The Via Latina catacomb was discovered only in the 1950s. More than 50 catacombs in Rome are now known, most of them built in the second to early fourth centuries. The most noted are the ones open to the public: Sts. Agnes, Callistus, Domitilla, Priscilla, and Sebastian.

Catacombs were laid out in the four cardinal directions, much like cities of the living, until crowding became uncontrollable. Airshafts were dug for ventilation. Most tombs started off as family plots with *loculi* ("little niches") placed in the wall and covered with marble, brick, or tile. These were frequently placed as close as possible to the remains of early Christian martyrs. Some sites were larger *cubicula* ("little rooms"), which might also have an *acrosolium*, or arched tomb, with a *mensa,* or slab, placed over it for funeral offerings. Often the ceilings, the walls, the front of the *mensa* and the niche above it had murals depicting scenes from the Old and New Testaments. The catacombs are a chief source for understanding the earliest Christian art forms and symbols, many of which were based on Roman and Jewish precursors (*see* PAINTING AND SCULPTURE).

During and shortly after the era of persecution, Christians would celebrate memorial rites and the EUCHARIST at the graves of the better-known martyrs. Contrary to novel and movie lore, they were not used as hiding places for Christians. After CONSTANTINE's Edict of Milan, tolerating Christians, the catacombs went into disuse, although Pope Damasus (r. 366–84) encouraged visits to the tombs of the martyrs and their decoration.

In the seventh century, the popes ordered the transfer of the relics of early Christian martyrs to basilicas above ground. Pillaged and overgrown with vegetation, the catacombs passed from memory until their rediscovery in 1578 and their archaeological exploration by Antonio Bosio (1575–1629) and Giovanni Battista de Rossi (1822–1894). One artistic effect of the rediscovery was that painters like MICHELANGELO and Carravagio (1571–1610) started to paint Jesus without a beard, as in the catacomb depictions.

Further reading: Pasquale Testini, *Le Catacombe e gli Antichi Cimiteri Cristiani in Roma* (Bologna: Capelli, 1966); Antonio Ferrua, *The Unknown Catacomb* (New Lanark: Geddes & Grosset, 1991); Fabrizio Mancinelli, *Catacombs and Basilicas. Early Christians in Rome* (Florence: SCALA, Instituto Fotografico Editoriale, 1981); James Stevenson, *The Catacombs. Rediscovered Monuments of Early Christianity* (London: Thames & Hudson, 1978).

catechesis/catechumenate (Gk.: *katechein,* "to echo," "to make to hear," "to teach")

Catechesis is the instruction or ministry of the Word given by teachers and catechists to new converts or neophytes to the CHRISTIAN faith. The term is used in Acts 18:25; Romans 2:18, and Galatians 6:6. The catechumenate refers to the period and institution of instruction covering scriptural, doctrinal, and moral aspects of belonging to the faith.

Evidence shows that Jews of the first century would instruct newcomers in the Ten Commandments and the basic teachings of Judaism. At the community of Qumran the *Rule of the Community* provides instructional materials not unlike those contained in the early Christian instruction of the "Two Ways" presented in the DIDACHE and the Epistle of Barnabas. Some claim that there are bits and pieces of catechetical material in 1 Thessalonians 4:1–5.1, Colossians 3:5–15, and 1 Peter. Many early Christian conversions appear to have been rather sudden, unprepared events (Acts 8:36–38; 16:33); it is not until the early second century that there is firm evidence of a period of instruction (*Didache* 1–6; JUSTIN MARTYR, *1 Apology* 61). A discipline of silence (*doctrina arcana*) was imposed on neophytes not only about the EUCHARIST, reserved for Christians, but also about the holiest of the teachings.

IRENAEUS OF LYON's *Proof of Apostolic Teaching* seems to be an instruction manual for catechists. HIPPOLYTUS OF ROME's *Apostolic Tradition* 16–20 speaks of a three-year catechumenate. ORIGEN founded a famous catechetical school at Alexandria in the second century. By the fourth century common instructional materials included 1) a preliminary instruction for inquirers, 2) a catechumenate proper, 3) immediate preparation for BAPTISM during Lent prior to the Pasch, or EASTER, and 4) a postbaptismal instruction in the sacraments and Christian living during which the neophytes wore a white garment. St. Cyril of Jerusalem (d. 386) is celebrated for his five *Mystagogical Catecheses,* an introduction to the mysteries of the Christian faith for catechumens.

The catechumenate was restored by the decree of VATICAN COUNCIL II in the Constitution on the Sacred Liturgy 64. The rite is presented in the *Rite of Christian Initiation of Adults* (1972).

The theological discipline of catechetics is dedicated to formulating the theory and praxis of the faith for the sake of teaching neophytes and baptized Christians the meaning of their faith and the ways to practice it in the world. Today catechectics has been much influenced by the revival of the liturgy and the models of faith development uncovered by Jean Piaget (1896–1980), Lawrence Kohlberg (1927–87), and James Fowler (1943–). Programs for catechetical instruction are fostered in Catholic universities, colleges, institutes, and dioceses throughout the world.

See also CATECHISM.

Further reading: All the classic Christian sources mentioned above can be found online; Michel Dujarier, *A History of the Catechumenate* (New York: Sadlier, 1979); *Sharing the Light of Faith: National Catechetical Directory for Catholics of the United States* (Washington, D.C.: United States Catholic Conference, 1981); Michael Warren, ed. *Sourcebook for Modern Catechetics,* 2 vols. (Winona, Minn.: St. Mary's Press, 1997).

catechism

A catechism is a manual of religious teaching written in simple, direct language and communicating the basic truths of the Catholic faith. Catechisms became very popular after the invention of the printing press and in response to the Protestant Reformation. Martin Luther (1483–1546) produced the first catechisms in the modern sense, known as the Large and Small Catechisms. The Catholic catechisms were intended to contain truths derived from both revelation (Scripture) and tradition. Generally, catechisms followed the topics format, sequentially covering creed, commandments, and SACRAMENTS.

The most noted catechisms are the *Catechism of the Council of Trent* (1566), also known as The Roman Catechism, prepared by St. Charles BOR- ROMEO at the request of St. PIUS V for instructing priests; the *Catechism of General Doctrine* (1885), popularly known as the BALTIMORE CATECHISM, issued by Cardinal JAMES GIBBONS after the third plenary session of the American Council of Baltimore and revised in 1941; and *Catechism of the Catholic Church* (1994), promulgated under JOHN PAUL II.

The Baltimore Catechism had a simple question-and-answer style: Q. "Who made me?" A. "God made me." The *Catechism of the Catholic Church,* which will probably come to be known as the "Vatican II Catechism," had its beginnings in the "General Catechetical Directory" (1971), issued in response to VATICAN COUNCIL II by the Congregation for the Clergy under the presidency of the American cardinal John Wright (1909–79). In 1985 an Extraordinary Synod of Bishops called for a new catechism. There was much struggle over the wording; objections by U.S. conservatives to the use of "feminist language" delayed publication for a year. It was published along with the earlier apostolic constitution *Fidei Depositum* (October 11, 1992) of John Paul II.

Going beyond the creed-commandments-sacraments formula of earlier catechisms, the new universal catechism gives a complete account of Roman Catholic teaching under four headings: 1) the profession of faith with an exposition of the Apostles CREED, 2) the SACRAMENTS, 3) the life of CHRIST with a discussion of the commandments, and 4) prayer, with an exposition of the Lord's Prayer. It includes teachings on contemporary ethical issues. Cardinal Joseph Ratzinger, now BENEDICT XVI, was chiefly responsible for the formulation of the text.

The 1994 Cathechism is not without its critics. Some have pointed out that it cites John Paul II an inordinate amount of times, putting it in danger of being out of date. There are no entries for "liberation" or "liberation theology" even though, the critics say, the theme of liberation is key to Jesus' proclamation (Luke 4:18–21). Sexual SIN and sexual deviation are dealt with extensively, but very little is said about the poor, social justice, or even the common good.

Further reading: *Catechism of the Catholic Church* (Ligouri Mo.: Ligouri, 1994, revised 1997); Alfred McBride, *Essentials of the Faith: A Guide to the Catechism of the Catholic Church* (Huntington, Ind.: Our Sunday Visitor, 2002); Ronald Lawler, Donald W. Wuerl, and

Thomas C. Lawler, eds., *The Teaching of Christ: A Catholic Catechism for Adults* (Huntington, Ind.: Our Sunday Visitor, 1976).

Cathari (Gr.: *katharos*, "pure"; possibly Ger.: *Ketter*, "heretic")

The Cathari were a group of sects with ideas similar to GNOSTICISM and MANICHAENISM that flourished during the 12th and 13th centuries, especially in the Languedoc region of France. They espoused dualistic teachings about good and evil and endorsed severe asceticism. The French followers were relentlessly pursued and slaughtered by the INQUISITION and its agents.

Cathari is the general term for a number of dualistic or quasi-dualistic medieval sects, including the Albigensians, the Bogomils, the Paulicans, the Patarenes, and others. The history of the Albigensians is the best documented because of the famous crusade launched against them. Although all the groups showed doctrinal, liturgical, and organizational kinships with earlier Gnostic and Manichaean groups, there is no clear evidence of a direct link between the latter second-to-fourth century groups and their medieval look-alikes. Some opponents linked them to Jewish and Muslim "heresies," but, again, the evidence is weak. Much of what we know about these groups comes from their opponents, so the sources should be interpreted with extreme caution.

In general, the Cathari viewed existence as a struggle between good and evil or light and darkness, as portrayed in the Gospel of John. As with MARCION and many early Gnostics, good is identified with soul and spirit, and EVIL with matter and body. Evil, personified in Satan, imprisons the soul in the body; the goal of Cathari asceticism is to detach the soul from matter and reattach it to spirit, culminating in BAPTISM. Jesus came to liberate the soul from is material imprisonment. As spirit, Jesus entered Mary through the ear (the Word) and only gave the appearance of having a body. He was not equal to God but

operated only as a redeeming creature of God. The crucifixion was not a real event but only an instructive demonstration.

The Cathari rejected the Catholic sacraments as tainted with material and moral corruption designed to justify a lax and vile priestly caste. Their rite of baptism consisted in the renunciation of their own ineffective infant baptism with water. Instead of communion they received a *consolamentun* ("consolation") that functioned as a spiritual baptism and was conferred by the imposition of hands. It was open only to full-fledged members.

Like Manichaeans, Cathari divided their membership between ordinary believers and the *perfecti,* who could receive the *consolamentum* and who renounced meat, excepting fish. Cathari rejected marriage because they rejected the material as not conducive to salvation. Opponents claimed that they advocated suicide through a rite they called *endura,* but the word meant simply fasting. Others accused them of holding concubinage in greater esteem than marriage, since it was a temporary arrangement, but this is most likely pure vilification.

Because the soul may remain attached to material pleasure even at the end of life, they embraced a doctrine of *metempsychosis,* or transmigration of the soul, from one body to the next or from one biological order to a lower one. When the soul attains sufficient purification it can enter the realm of the spirit. Although the concept is similar to *samsara* and *moksa* in Buddhism, there is no known connection between the two faiths. Adherents dressed in black, made no distinction between men and women, traveled about in pairs according to Jesus' command (Luke 10.1), and lived by their own labors.

The Albigensians constituted a problem in the social, ecclesiastical, and political spheres. Socially, the movement can be seen as a protest against the lax lifestyle of the clergy. Ecclesiastically, the Cathari were a threat to the orthodoxy of the day and especially the hierarchizing efforts of the papacy. Politically, they were pawns in the struggles between king and vassals and between nobles and the papacy. Many Albigensians served in the courts of southern France and were loyal subjects of their lords, although, like the later Anabaptists, they refused to swear oaths or bear arms. Rival lords, especially the kings of France, seized on the opportunity to aggrandize their own fiefdoms by attacking them as heretics.

In 1209 Pope INNOCENT III elicited the help of the Cistercian Abbots Arnaud Amaury (d. 1225) and Pierre de Castelnau (d. 1208), and of the Spanish cleric DOMINIC DE GUZMÁN, who later founded the DOMINICAN ORDER, to mediate between the Albigensians and the church. When these efforts failed, the pope declared a CRUSADE against the heretics and called on Simon de Montfort (1160–1218), a freebooting nobleman originally from England, to lead the struggle. In a gruesome application of the precedent established by St. AUGUSTINE in his struggle against the Donatists, the pope used both torture, deployed by the Inquisition, and all-out war. The Cathari strongholds, most notably at Albi, were put under siege and destroyed. Cathari were burned at the stake, their bodies disinterred and burned, their children scattered, and their goods looted. The crusade lasted until the scorching of their last strongholds at Montsegur (1243) and Queribus (1255). All scholars now recognize the episode as a black mark in the history of Catholicism.

See also GNOSTICISM; HERESY.

Further reading: John Arnold, *Inquisition and Power* (Philadelphia: University of Pennsylvania Press, 2001); Wouter J. Hanegraaff, Antoine Faivre, Roelof van der Broek, and Jean-Pierre Brach, eds., *Dictionary of Gnosis & Western Esotericism*, 2 vols. (Leiden: Brill, 2005); Mark G. Pegg, *The Corruption of Angels: The Great Inquisition of 1245–1246* (Princeton, N.J.: Princeton University Press, 2001); Michel Roquebert, *Histoire des Cathares* (Paris: Perrin, 2002).

cathedral (Gk.: *kata,* "down" + *hedra,* "seat")

The term *cathedral* has two basic meanings that overlap: 1) the seat of a BISHOP, placed within the sanctuary of the main church of a DIOCESE, and 2) the central diocesan church building itself. Traditionally, a CLERGY person attached to a cathedral church was called a CANON. A cathedral is often compared to and contrasted with a BASILICA and an ordinary parish church. As a church building, the cathedral evolved from the ancient Roman basilica, or imperial palace hall, first into a Romanesque form and then into the great Gothic structures of the high MIDDLE AGES.

Apart from its practical functions, the medieval cathedral served as a condensed symbolic structure that gave pilgrims a foretaste of the heavenly Jerusalem so lavishly portrayed in the Book of Revelation. In stone and glass, it was a mirror of nature (CREATION), sacred learning, and sacred history (BIBLE, church history). It also depicted scenes and themes of the secular world, such as the seven liberal arts, the seasons of the year, the zodiac, and the ancient philosophers.

Cathedrals were generally laid out on an east-west axis. The portals, windows, and statues of the north side depicted scenes of the Old Testament, which were interpreted as typological figures of scenes of the New Testament on the south side. The west portal facing the sun generally depicted the Last Judgment.

Almost all cathedrals became places of PILGRIMAGE, attracting pilgrims with relics of Mary and other saints. Pilgrims visited St. Madeleine of Vézalay to see the legendary relics of St. Mary of Magdala. Chartres Cathedral claimed the Veil of the Blessed Virgin Mary; Canterbury had the bones of St. Thomas à Becket; Santiago de Compostela in Spain had the legendary sarcophagus of St. JAMES THE GREATER.

The first Gothic style cathedral was built by Abbot SUGER at the French royal church of St. Denis north of Paris. It was quickly imitated throughout Europe. It introduced two fundamental architectural innovations. Tall Romanesque cathedrals and abbey churches like Cluny and Cîteaux had required massive walls that allowed for only narrow window slits. Gothic architects in effect sliced the thick walls and distributed the weight of the roof to flying buttresses. This allowed for even taller structures and for a great expansion of window space, making room for an explosion in stained glass images.

The "ideal" plan of a Gothic cathedral followed an east-west axis, with the facade facing west and the apse facing east. Generally, there were three portals each on the north, south, and west sides. The semicircular tympanum above the central portal on the west often depicted CHRIST sitting in judgment over the world at the end of time. Most cathedrals were originally planned to have at least nine spires, although as a rule only two or three were built at most. The central portion leading from the west facade is called the nave, and the section in the apse with stalls is called the choir.

The north and south windows were generally designed according to a typological plan, which

Cutaways of Romanesque nave with thick walls (a) and Gothic nave with thin walls supported by flying buttresses (b) *(drawing by Frank K. Flinn)*

often got obscured over the many years required for completion. In TYPOLOGY an Old Testament event is taken as a figure or prototype of a New Testament event. Thus, the crossing of Red Sea by the Israelites (Exod. 14) was interpreted as a prefiguration of the baptism of Jesus in the Jordan by John the Baptist (Mark 1:9–11). Many have described the Gothic cathedral as the Bible and the history of salvation carved in stone and painted in glass.

A handful of the greatest cathedrals of the world are described below. Others are treated under ARCHITECTURE and ST. PETER'S BASILICA.

CHARTRES

Without doubt, the cathedral at Chartres is the most famous in the world. Sculptor Auguste Rodin (1840–1917) called it "the acropolis of France." A Druid sanctuary seems to have occupied the site in pre-Christian times—it was common in Europe to build Christian churches over pagan shrines. Bishops Fulbert (d. 1028) and Ivo (d. 1116) oversaw the building of a Romanesque cathedral, where they also established a celebrated cathedral school.

The Gothic structure was completed in about 50 years. It has more than 4,000 carved statues and more than 5,000 figures depicted in stained glass. More than 175 of the images portray Notre Dame or Our Lady, to whom the cathedral is dedicated. Legend says that Frankish king Charles the Bald (r. 840–77) donated a chemise, or veil, of the Virgin to the original sanctuary in 876. This relic became the focus of pilgrimages to the shrine throughout the ages. In 1912 the French poet Charles Péguy (1873–1914) revived modern pilgrimages to the shrine by young people.

FLORENCE

The cathedral, called simply the Duomo, is a monument to the spirit of Florentine Gothic style and demonstrates the transition to the Renaissance. The BAPTISTERY, parts of which date to the fourth century, has 13th-century mosaics in Byz-

Chartres Cathedral, spires and western facade with rose window seen from the town *(photo by Frank K. Flinn)*

antine style. DANTE ALIGHIERI was baptized there. The south bronze doors of the baptistery are by Andrea Pisano (1270–1348) and the north and east ("Gates of Paradise") are by Lorenzo Ghiberti (1378–1455). The 276-foot-high campanile is by Giotto di Bondone (1267–1377), who also painted scenes of St. FRANCIS OF ASSISI's life in Santa Croce, Florence. The cathedral is noted for its marble inlay throughout. The dome, a miracle of engineering by architect Filippo Brunelleschi (1377–1446), was the tallest in Europe until the dome of St. Peter's in Rome by MICHELANGELO. The neo-Gothic facade was added only in 1877–87.

MEXICO CITY

This cathedral introduced the baroque style to the New World. It replaced an earlier sanctuary built over the Aztec Templo Major, a pyramidal structure dedicated to the Aztec gods Tlaloc (water) and Huitzlipochtli (war). All Latin American cathedrals can be seen as variations of Mexico City. The first stone was laid by Archbishop Pedro Moya de Contreras (c. 1520–91) in 1572, and the completed structure was inaugurated by the viceroy-duke of Albuquerque. The ornate exterior and elaborately carved benches contrast with the lean interior with its fluted columns reaching to the heavens. This combination of the sensual and the spiritual reflects the baroque mystical theology of Sts. TERESA OF ÁVILA, JOHN OF THE CROSS, and IGNATIUS OF LOYOLA. In 1813 the Spanish sculptor and architect Manuel Tolsa (1757–1816) added neoclassical elements like the square-topped bell towers and the statues of Faith, Hope, and Charity above the central portal.

ST. PATRICK'S CATHEDRAL

The present cathedral in New York City replaced the original at a different site, which is still used as a parish church. It was begun in 1858 under Archbishop JOHN JOSEPH HUGHES, who wanted a church worthy of the growing and sophisticated Catholic population of New York, and opened under Cardinal John McCloskey (1810–85) in 1879. The church was designed in Gothic Revival style by architect James Renwick (1818–95), who also designed the Smithsonian Institution in Washington, D.C.

The west towers were added in 1888 and the Lady Chapel, designed by Charles Mathews, in 1901. Tiffany and Co. designed the St. MICHAEL THE ARCHANGEL and St. Louis altars, and Paolo Medici of Rome did the St. Elizabeth altar. In more recent times the main ALTAR and baptistery were reconfigured to conform to the new liturgical requirements of VATICAN COUNCIL II. The cathedral seats about 2,200 and has 3 million visitors a year.

Further reading: Alain Erlande-Brandenburg, *Notre-Dame de Paris* (New York: Abrams, 1997); Jean Favier,

The World of Chartres (New York, Abrams, 1998); Emile Mâle, *The Gothic Image: Religious Art in France of the Thirteenth Century* (New York: Harper & Row, 1972); Bernhard Schütz, *Great Cathedrals of the Middle Ages* (New York: Abrams, 2002).

Catherine of Siena, St. (1347–1380)
mystical theologian

Catherine of Siena was a theologian whose tendencies toward mysticism did not prevent a deep involvement in the political matters of the day, both secular and religious. She authored *Dialogues on Divine Providence*, letters, and prayers, and she mediated disputes, especially during the SCHISM following the AVIGNON PAPACY. PAUL VI made her a doctor of the church in 1970. Her feast day is April 29.

Catherine was born in Siena, the 23rd child of Jacopo and Lapa Benincasa. Despite early opposition from her family, she dedicated herself to the mystical life. She joined the Dominican Mantellates, laywomen who remained at home but took the garb of the Dominican order. Her model was DOMINIC DE GUZMÁN, founder of the DOMINICANS, who preached far and wide. In a vision she received a confirmation of her calling to walk on two feet, serving both GOD and humans. She supported the CRUSADE against the Turks and preached against corruption among the clergy.

With the Dominican Bl. Raymond Capua (1330–99) as her spiritual guide, she preached throughout central Italy, gaining many followers among both men and women. She attended prisoners and mediated feuds. Soon she was asked to mediate disputes between Pisa and Florence, and between the popes in Avignon and Florence. In Avignon she convinced Pope Gregory XI (r. 1370–78) to return to Rome, his true bishopric; she later urged his successor, Urban VI (r. 1378–89), to institute reforms. This caused a schism, and Catherine died trying to mediate this intrachurch discord.

In her mystical theology, Catherine saw God as united with the soul from the moment of creation:

> You, eternal God, saw me and knew me in yourself
> And because you saw me in your light
> you fell in love with your creature
> and drew her out of yourself
> and created her in your image and likeness.

In her *Dialogue* she portrayed Christ as the Bridge of Mercy between God and fallen humanity. In 1375 she received the STIGMATA while passing through Pisa.

Further reading: Igino Giordani, *Saint Catherine of Siena, Doctor of the Church* (Boston: St. Paul Editions, 1975); Conleth Kearns, "The Wisdom of St. Catherine," *Angelicum* (1980) 57: 324–343 (1980); Mary O'Driscoll, *Catherine of Siena: Selected Spiritual Writings* (New Rochelle, N.Y.: New City, 1993); Raymond of Capua, *Life of St. Catherine of Siena*, tr. G. Lamb (London: Harvill, 1960).

Catholic Action

A variety of social or political movements in which Catholic laypersons have taken an active and leading part are collectively referred to as Catholic Action. The term often overlaps with the "lay apostolate."

PIUS X in *Il Fermo Proposito* (June 5, 1905) and PIUS XI in *Quadragesimo Anno* (May 15, 1931) gave their encouragement to these types of movements, which first sprang up in Europe. The movements dedicated themselves to the reconstruction of family and society through legislation and social action.

The first significant example was the Young Christian Workers movement, founded in Belgium in 1925 by Joseph Cardijn (1882–1967). Basing himself on the "observe-judge-act" organizing methods of English unionists, Cardijn set out to found a movement in which the laity and not the clergy had the primary say. This movement soon developed into the Christian Family Movement, in which cells of six couples each were to observe their environment, judge where Gospel principles might be relevant, and take action to apply them. Cardijn's model influenced not only DOROTHY DAY and Peter Maurin's Catholic Worker movement in the United States but also the BASE COMMUNITIES movement in LATIN AMERICA.

In the United States Catholic Action took many forms, but unlike in Europe, the groups were largely subordinate to the hierarchy. The leading organizations were the National Council of Catholic Men (1920), which sponsored the radio program *The Catholic Hour,* and of Catholic Women (1920), which now engages issues relating to housing, racism, and international peace; the Confraternity of Christian Doctrine (CCD), which was centered on religious instruction for children, especially those attending public schools and has now been replaced by parish catechetical and religious education programs; the Legion of Decency (1934), which imposed an indirect censorship on the moral content of most films and other media; the Grail (1921), an international women's movement that became headquartered in Loveland, Ohio; the Young Christian Student (1925); the Catholic Worker (1933); the Christian Family Movement (CFM), led by Pat (1911–74) and Patty (1913–2005) Crowley in the United States; and Friendship House (1930).

Although CFM declined in the 1960s, it still had considerable influence on marriage-centered Catholic action via the Cana Conferences and Marriage Encounter. The latter group spread from Catholic to Protestant circles.

VATICAN COUNCIL II placed great stress on the renewal of Catholic Action and the lay apostolate. In Europe Catholic Action often contributed to the formation of political parties. In Latin America and the Third World, Catholic Action has often taken the form of liberation movements centered on base communities and dedicated to social reform.

See also Apostolate; Charles Borromeo; Christian Democratic Parties.

Further reading: Yves Congar, *Lay People in the Church* (Westminster Md.: Newman, 1963); *Decree on the Apostolate of the Laity,* in Walter M. Abbott, *The Documents of Vatican II* (New York: America Press, 1966), 489–521; Gianfranco Poggi, *Catholic Action in Italy: The Sociology of a Sponsored Organization* (Stanford, Calif.: Stanford University Press, 1967); Roland Potvin, *L'Action catholique: son organization dans l'Église* (Quebec: Laval University Press, 1957).

catholic church (Gr.: *kata,* "down" + *holos,* "according to the whole," "universal")

The term *catholic church* can have any of several related meanings. In one sense, it means the universal church of all believers spread throughout the world. That is its meaning in Ignatius of Antioch's *Letter to the Smyrnaeans* 8.2 and in the Nicene-Constantinopolitan CREED: ". . . one, holy, catholic and apostolic church." Or it can mean the united, universal church to the exclusion of sectarians or separatists. Augustine of Hippo used the term *catholic* in this way during his struggle against the Donatists. Catholics may have this sense in mind when they use the distinctions Orthodox/Catholic and Protestant/Catholic. This usage can carry a pejorative connotation for the non-Catholic element, although it may also be used as a simple religious and sociological description.

In his *Catechetical Lectures* 18 Cyril of Jerusalem expanded the meaning of *catholic* to include membership, teaching, nonclass differentiation, and the universal spiritual gifts and healing from sin. At Vatican Council II the notion of catholicity was expanded to include not only the "visible" Catholic Church but other Christian churches and denominations not in full communion with Rome in whom "elements of sanctification and of truth can be found" (*Lumen Gentium* 8 Dogmatic Constitution on the Church).

Further reading: Ola Tjørhom, *Visible Church, Visible Unity* (Collegeville, Minn.: Liturgical Press, 2004).

CELAM (abbreviation for Sp.: Conferencia Episcopal Latinoamericano, "Latin American Episcopal Conference")

CELAM is the popular designation for the conference of bishops in Latin America. It has met in two major continentwide meetings at Medellín, Columbia, (1968) and Puebla, Mexico, (1979).

See also Dom Helder Câmara; Latin America; liberation theology.

Further reading: Louis Michael Colonese, ed., *The Church in the Present-Day Transformation of the Council* (Bogotá: General Secretariat of CELAM, 1970–73); John Eagleson and Philip Sharper, eds., *Puebla and Beyond* (Maryknoll, N.Y.: Orbis Books, 1980).

celibacy (Lat.: *caelebs,* "unmarried")

The Catholic tradition of unmarried, celebate clergy has a long but not always continuous history. The evidence from the New Testament is not clear. On one hand, Jesus implied that marriage is the normal state in society when he sharpened the Torah law and prohibited easy divorce (Mark 10:11). Further, many of the Apostles, from whom clerical status is derived, seem to have been married and even took their wives on their journeys (Matt. 8:14; 1 Cor. 9.5).

On the other hand, the Gospel of Matthew speaks of "eunuchs for the sake of the kingdom of heaven" (19:12), and Paul, expecting the imminent return of Christ, advised those married and those unmarried to abide in their present states, thus favoring neither state over the other. Later Latin church Fathers, possibly infected with misogyny during their struggle against Pelagius, claimed that virginity and celibacy were the highest forms of religious life.

The Eastern and Western Churches went their separate ways on this issue. Eastern Orthodoxy has continued to follow canon 13 of the Council of Trullo (692): "Although the Romans wish that everyone ordained deacon or presbyter should put away his wife, we wish the marriages of deacons and presbyters to continue valid and firm." To this day, the Eastern Churches, including those in union with Rome, allow priests and deacons to be married before ordination, although BISHOPS must be celibate.

The Western Church followed the precedent set by cn. 33 of the Spanish Council of Elvira (306): "Bishops, presbyters, deacons, and others with a position in the ministry are to abstain completely from sexual intercourse with their wives and from the procreation of children. If anyone disobeys, he shall be removed from the clerical office." LEO I THE GREAT had to forbid clergy from simply casting out their wives, enjoining them instead to live together—as brother and sister. The Gallican church required the wives to retire to nunneries or to join orders of widows or deaconesses. Beginning in the 11th century subdeacons were required to submit to a vow of perpetual chastity. Lateran Council IV decreed that clerical marriage was not just illegal but also invalid (see COUNCILS, ECUMENICAL). This rule was confirmed by the Council of TRENT (Session 24, cn. 9).

Throughout the MIDDLE AGES the rule of celibacy was difficult to enforce. Allowing marriage would have put the church at risk of losing church property through inheritance, yet the prohibition led to widespread clerical concubinage. With the decline in the number of priests worldwide in the 20th and 21st centuries, the problem of concubinage has returned to haunt the church, especially in AFRICA and LATIN AMERICA.

The debate over celibacy was reopened at VATICAN COUNCIL II, until PAUL VI removed the topic (along with the question of artificial birth control) from open discussion; he issued an encyclical *Sacerdotalis Caelibatus* (June 24, 1967), reaffirming the traditional Western position but continuing the exception for the uniate churches within EASTERN CATHOLICISM.

In the Vatican II decree on the priesthood *Presbyterorum Ordinis*, however, the council fathers noted that, given the overwhelming evidence and experience of the early church, celibacy is not by nature demanded of the priesthood (2.16). Meanwhile, the Roman church reinstituted the permanent diaconate for married persons in the 1983 edition of the Code of Canon Law without requiring celebacy. Likewise, in exceptional circumstances it has allowed married Episcopal, Lutheran, Methodist, and Presbyterian clergy who have converted to enter the priesthood without requiring them to give up the privileges of marriage. The decline in the number of priests, continuing sexual scandals (see PEDOPHILIA), the expanding number of exceptions to the rule, and the shift in cultural norms will continue to make celibacy a much-debated issue in the Catholic Church in the short and long term.

See also SEXUALITY.

Further reading: All the councils referred to above are available online; William Bassett and Peter Huizinga, *Celibacy in the Church* (New York: Herder & Herder, 1972); Stefan Heid, *Celibacy in the Early Church* (San Francisco: Ignatius, 2000); Richard A. W. Sipe, *Celibacy in Crisis* (New York: Brunner-Rutledge, 2003).

Chalcedon, Council of (451 C.E.)

The Council of Chalcedon (in Asia Minor, a short distance from CONSTANTINOPLE) completed the task of defining the nature of CHRIST for the early church. The first three ecumenical councils (see COUNCILS, ECUMENICAL), which had the task of finding the right balance and emphasis between the divine and the human in Christ, had left a number of problems unresolved. Chalcedon's formulations shaped and directed all future Christological definitions, East and West. Pope LEO I THE GREAT at first rejected its decisions but finally accepted them with the exception of canon 28, which gave Constantinople "equal but second place" with Rome.

Emperor Marcian (r. 450–57) summoned the council two years after the "Robber" Council of Antioch, at which Dioscorus of Alexandria (d. 454) defended the formulation of Eutyches (fl. 450), archimandrate of Constantinople, against the Antiochene position of Theodoret of Cyrus (c. 393–457) and Ibas of Edessa (d. 457). Following CYRIL OF ALEXANDRIA's formula at the Council of EPHESUS (431)—"one incarnate nature of God the Word"— Eutyches asserted that after the hypostatic union of God and humanity in the INCARNATION there was only one nature of Christ. Leo I quoted Eutyches as saying, "I confess that our Lord was of two natures before the union, but I confess one nature after the union." This theological position was later called monophysitism. Throughout the years-long debate the key terms, *physis* (nature), *hypostasis* (person, subject, substance), and *prosōpon* (person), were never clearly defined.

Chalcedon's "confession" of faith is more like a "formulation" of Christology (*see* CHRIST/CHRISTOLOGY): "So, following the saintly fathers, we all with one voice teach the confession of one and the same Son, our Lord Jesus Christ: the same perfect in divinity and perfect in humanity, the same truly God and truly man, of a rational soul and a body; consubstantial with the Father as regards his divinity, and the same consubstantial with us as regards his humanity; like us in all respects except for SIN; begotten before the ages from the Father as regards his divinity, and in the last days the same for us and for our salvation from Mary, the virgin God-bearer as regards his humanity; one and the same Christ, Son, Lord, only-begotten, acknowledged in two natures which undergo no confusion, no change, no division, no separation; at no point was the difference between the natures taken away through the union, but rather the property of both natures is preserved and comes together into a single person and a single subsistent being; he is not parted or divided into two persons, but is one and the same only-begotten Son, God, Word, Lord Jesus Christ, just as the prophets taught from the beginning about him, and as the Lord Jesus

Christ himself instructed us, and as the creed of the fathers handed it down to us."

The short form of Chalcedon is "one person, two natures." This formula remained definitive for future theologians, East and West: Catholic, Eastern Orthodox, and Protestant. The COPTIC CHURCH of Egypt has maintained the singularity (divine) of the nature of the Christ to this day. Other canons at Chalcedon dealt with practical problems: money, transfer of BISHOPS, bishops' authority, and others.

Further reading: Paulos Gregorios, ed., *Does Chalcedon Divide or Unite?* (Geneva: World Council of Churches, 1981).; J. N. D. Kelly, *Early Christian Doctrine* (San Francisco: Harper & Row, 1978); Johannes Quasten, *Patrology,* vol. 4 (Westminster Md.: Christian Classics, 1988); R. V. Sellers, *Council of Chalcedon: A Historical and Doctrinal Survey* (London: S.P.C.K. 1953).

Chaldean Catholic Church

The Chaldean Catholic Church serves Eastern-Rite Catholics residing in Iraq. Its origins can be traced to the 1550s.

The CHRISTIAN community in Iraq separated from the larger Christian community when it refused to accept the promulgations of the Council of CHALCEDON (451) concerning the two natures of CHRIST. Like the Armenians and Copts, the Iraqi (or Assyrian) church emphasized Christ's divine nature over his human one. The Iraqi Christian community has survived in a dominant Islamic milieu; the majority belong to the Apostolic Catholic Assyrian Church,

In the 13th century, Roman Catholic missionaries launched work in the Iraqi Christian community. They had little success until the 1550s, when they were able to take advantage of a peculiar situation. The Iraqi Church had a tradition of passing the patriarchal office from uncle to nephew within a single family. Occasionally this practice resulted in an untrained youth suddenly becoming the new patriarch. When such a youth was selected in 1552, some bishops refused to accept him and took the opportunity to unite with Rome. They selected a new patriarch to head what in 1553 was designated the Chaldean Catholic Church. The new church retained its former rite, the ancient East Syrian liturgy of Addai and Mari.

The Chaldeans experienced a difficult start, after local Muslim authorities arrested and executed the new patriarch, but it eventually survived and flourished. It is today headquartered in Baghdad, Iraq. The present patriarch is Mar Emmanuel III Delly (1927–). The patriarch's authority includes an American diocese along with 10 dioceses in Iraq, four in Iran, and seven additional dioceses in the Middle East. There are some 500,000 members worldwide. The church is active in the Middle East Council of Churches.

See also ASIA.

Sources: Nikolaus Liesel, *The Eastern Catholic Liturgies: A Study in Words and Pictures.* (Westminster, Md.: Newman Press, 1960); Ronald G. Roberson, *The Eastern Christian Churches—A Brief Survey,* 5th ed. (Rome: Pontifical Oriental Institute, 1995).

chalice   *See* EUCHARIST; UTENSILS, SACRED.

chant (Lat.: *cantus,* "song").
The term *cantus planus,* or plainsong, describes a type of monophonic, or single-voiced, sacred music performed a cappela, without instruments. It often accompanies the LITURGY, especially the EUCHARIST, and the Divine Office, or PRAYER OF THE HOURS, in the Byzantine and Latin rites, that became very widespread from the very beginnings of Christianity. Chant goes back to Jewish prototypes, but the trace lines are faint and the history obscure.

Almost all plainsong is fitted to a text, most often texts from the BIBLE such as psalms and selected verses but later also including hymns and sequences composed for special feasts. Chants are composed of neums, various groupings of notes that accompany and illustrate the meaning of the text. Neums of different shape have specific names: punctum, virga, podatus, clivis, scandicus, and so on. Most scholars believe that early chant was sung in an unmetered free rhythm (one stroke, or *ictus,* for every two to three notes), but others have recently challenged this theory.

Chants were composed for the Ordinary sections of the Mass (Kyrie, Gloria, Creed, Sanctus, Agnus) as well as the Propers (Introit, Alleluia, Gradual, Communion). Besides these, types of chants include antiphons, sequences, tracts, canticles, hymns, responsories, and psalm tones. There were various CHRISTIAN chant traditions in the ancient West until Gregorian chant was imposed as the dominant style during the Carolingian dynasty.

BYZANTINE CHANT
Like its Western counterpart, Byzantine chant is monophonic and unaccompanied by instruments. It received its impetus from the establishment of the Byzantine Empire by CONSTANTINE THE GREAT. Byzantine chant underwent various transformations with the translation of the Byzantine liturgy into the Syriac, Coptic, Armenian, Georgian, and Slavic languages. The Frankish developers of Gregorian chant most likely adopted the eightfold mode system of chants from Byzantium. Contemporary Byzantine chant is much altered from the original.

OLD ROMAN CHANT
Along with the Ambrosian chant of Milan and the Beneventan chant, Old Roman chant represents a musical tradition preceding the ascendancy of Gregorian. The melodic style of Old Roman is more florid, intricate, and steplike within a tight pitch range than the angular, gaplike Gregorian style. Old Roman chant was suppressed in the 13th century.

AMBROSIAN CHANT
Ambrosian chant has been preserved as a living tradition, no doubt because of the importance of

Milan as the capital of the Roman Empire from 354 to 404 and as one of the oldest Christian foundations on the Italian Peninsula. Church father AMBROSE OF MILAN, who, along with Hilary of Poitiers (d. 368), introduced the tradition of Christian hymnody to the Latin West, also provided authority to the Ambrosian chant tradition.

Like Gregorian, Ambrosian chant has been transmitted in pitch-accurate notation. Ambrosian chant is extreme in style. Some chants are lean and simple; others, like the *cantus* (Gregorian Tract) and the Gospel Alleluia are ornamental and melismatic, or florid, with many notes under a single syllable.

BENEVENTAN CHANT

This chant tradition owes its survival to the research of scholars. It is named after Benevento, the southern Italian city of the Lombards, where manuscripts of this liturgical tradition were discovered. Like one strain of Ambrosian, Beneventan chant is ornate, uses repetitive tropes, and proceeds stepwise. It does not have the accurate pitch system of Gregorian, so it is difficult to reconstruct.

GALLICAN CHANT

Gallican refers to the liturgical tradition and accompanying music that thrived in France prior to the imposition of Gregorian by the Carolingians in the late eighth century. The surviving chant repertoire of the Gallican rite is meager and dubious.

Like Old Roman and Beneventan, Gallican can be decorative and melismatic, often on the second- or third-to-last syllable. Gallican chants have made it into the Gregorian repertoire where the latter had gaps, such as the antiphon *O crux benedicta* for vespers of the feast of the Seven Dolors of the Blessed Virgin. Some claim that the famous *Exultet* in the Easter Vigil services is Gallican.

CELTIC CHANT

There is evidence that a Celtic form of the liturgy and chant preceded the imposition of Roman usages by Augustine of Canterbury (d. 604). No notation has survived. The Antiphonary of Bangor and the Irish *Liber hymnorum* contain early hymns that call for antiphonal singing but have no indications of what the early music would be. A few antiphons, unlike Roman types from Caen, are reconstructible from 13th-century manuscripts, including the chant *Ibunt sancti*, which the Irish monk Theobald of Bobbio was said to recite on his deathbed.

MOZARABIC CHANT

Mozarabic chant has an interrupted tradition but is still sung in one of the chapels of Toledo Cathedral

Parchment showing the Offertory prayer and Communion chant antiphone for the pre–Vatican II Feast of St. Joseph Calasanctius (August 27) from an ornamented medieval sacramentary *(possession of Kenneth R. Palmer, with permission; photo by John Huston)*

on a daily basis. Much has been recovered, but the pitches are lost for most manuscripts. Cardinal Francisco Jiménez de Cisneros (1436–1514) led a revival in 1500, and Cardinal Antonio Lorenzana y Butron (1722–1804) led another in the 18th century. As with the Gallican rite, there were at least four variants of the Spanish rite. Reconstructed Mozarabic chant is preserved in the *Liber ordinum mozarabicus*. Some detect Jewish and Moorish influences in the Mozarabic tradition.

GREGORIAN CHANT

Despite its name, Gregorian chant as we know it does not date from the period of GREGORY I THE GREAT (540–604) or Gregory II (669–731) but represents the reworking of Roman chant by Frankish cantors during the Carolingian period. In 754 Pope Stephen II (r. 752–57) visited Pepin III (r. 751–68) with his *schola cantorum*. In an effort to unify church and empire, Pepin and his son CHARLEMAGNE decreed that the Roman form of chant should supplant the Gallican. The imposition was complete about 900, by which time various systems of musical notation had been developed.

Unlike the notation for most other chant forms, Gregorian was accurately pitched by 900 with the use of Boethius's system. Attaching clef markers to stave lines was the invention of the famous Guido d'Arezzo (c. 990–1050). Today chant books are marked with either a Do or Fa clef at the beginning of a four-line stave. Like Byzantine but unlike the other forms of western chant, Gregorian has eight modes, or tones (*echoi* in Greek). The modes are grouped into a fourfold scheme divided between an "authentic," or principal, mode and a "plagal," or derivative, mode. These modes anticipate the major and minor chords of modern music. Modes are defined by the beginning notes, range of notes, dominant tone, and final notes. The modes start from D, E, F, and G rather than C or A as in modern music.

With the rise of organum, the doubling of each Gregorian note with a lower fourth or fifth, and

later polyphony, chant gradually fell into decline, which became almost complete with the publication of the Medicean edition of chants for the Mass and Divine Office, or PRAYER OF THE HOURS. This edition altered neums, truncated chants, and eliminated whole types entirely. Western chant experienced a second life with the rise of the LITURGICAL MOVEMENT and the Abbey of SOLESMES in France in the 19th century. Under the direction of Doms Joseph Pothier (1835–1923) and André Mocquereau (1849–1930) the Solesmes monks undertook critical studies and assembled editions of chant. These were the source of the many editions of the *Liber usualis*, the most widely used handbook of chant.

The translation of the liturgy into local languages after Vatican II served to truncate much of the chant tradition. It survives in cathedral liturgies, monasteries, and traditional Latin masses celebrated for those who do not like the musical results of the council. New forms of worship such as the Missa Luba in Africa, mariachi masses, and African-American liturgies that use spirituals are crowding out traditional chant, but many parishes preserve chant melodies for special feasts such as Christmas and Easter as well as popular chant hymns like Tantum Ergo and Salve Regina.

Further reading: Willi Apel, *Gregorian Chant* (Bloomington: Indiana University Press, 1990); Thomas F. Kelly, *The Beneventan Chant* (Cambridge: Cambridge University Press, 1989); David Hiley, *Western Plainchant* (Oxford: Clarendon, 1993); *Liber Usualis,* ed. Benedictines of Solesmes (Tournai: Desclée, 1956).

charismatic renewal

The charismatic renewal is a movement within mainline Protestantism and the Catholic Church beginning in the 1960s in which practices developed in older Pentecostal churches became widespread. Such movements emerged as far back as the second century, and they have continued to appear ever since. One can point to the MONTA-

NUS, the Joachimites, and the Franciscan Spirituals in the MIDDLE AGES (*see* FRANCISCAN ORDER) and the Doukhaboors in 18th/19th-century Russia.

Pentecostalism places great emphasis on what it calls the "baptism of the Holy Spirit," which bestows the nine gifts of the Spirit (*charismata*) mentioned in 1 Corinthians 11 and 12. The possession of the BAPTISM is evidenced by the individual's speaking in tongues (GLOSSALALIA). The nine gifts are wisdom, prophecy, knowledge, discernment of spirits, faith, speaking in diverse tongues, healing, interpretation of tongues, and working of miracles.

American Pentecostalism has deep roots in evangelical Protestantism, with its call for repentance and a personal relationship with Jesus. More specifically, it is tied to the Methodist-inspired Holiness movement inspired by Methodist founder John Wesley's call for personal sanctification, or a perfection in love. It is also anchored in the British pietist movement centered at Keswick, which stressed "living victoriously in the Spirit."

The key founders of the Pentecostal movement were Charles F. Parham (1873–1929) of Topeka, Kansas, who proposed the relationship between the baptism of the Spirit and speaking in tongues, and the African-American Methodist preacher William J. Seymour (1870–1922), who led the now-famous Azuza Mission in Los Angeles, which sparked the spread of Pentecostalism around the world. It now exists as a global movement, encompassing large international groups such as the Assemblies of God, the several Churches of God, the International Church of the Foursquare Gospel, and the United Pentecostal Church as well as hundreds of smaller bodies. The movement includes as many as 300 million adherents.

With the spread of the Pentecostal experience into mainline Protestant and Catholic churches in the 1960s, a new phase of charismatic renewal was launched. At VATICAN COUNCIL II some council members, notably Cardinal Ernesto Rufini of Palermo (1888–1967), claimed that the charisms, or gifts of the Holy Spirit, noted by St. Paul belonged only to the bride-time of the church while the APOSTLES were still alive (an argument that many mainline Protestants had used in the early 20th century). However, Cardinal LÉON-JOSEF SUENENS (1904–96) of Belgium challenged this limitation of the charisms; his position became the official position of the council in *Lumen Gentium,* 12, the Dogmatic Constitution on the Church.

Cardinal Suenens went on to become a champion of the charismatic renewal movement in the 1970s and 1980s. His six "Maline Documents" cover all aspects of the renewal. Pope PAUL VI gave papal approval to the movement in the Holy Year 1975 on the feast of Pentecost. In the *Hidden Hand of God* (1994) Suenens wrote: "As I look to the future, I cannot avoid stressing the role of the Holy Spirit in the church of tomorrow. He is always 'the life-giving Spirit,' in the fullest meaning of the words."

The charismatic movement was seen by many adherents as an action of the Holy Spirit in the wake of Vatican II signaling closer ties between Catholic and Protestant believers. Indeed, close ecumenical ties emerged among charismatics of both faiths. On the other hand, some Catholics were not comfortable with the phrase *baptism of the Holy Spirit;* they believed the Spirit is received in the SACRAMENTS of baptism and CONFIRMATION. Instead, Catholic charismatics began to speak of the "release of the Spirit" as descriptive of the experiences they shared as they began to speak in tongues and manifest the other charisms.

The charismatic movement began to manifest itself in the mid 1960s among Catholics at the Universities of Notre Dame, Duquesne, Pittsburgh, and Michigan. Among the early leaders were Benedictine theologian Killian McDonnell (b. 1923), Notre Dame theologian Josephine Massynbaerde Ford (b. 1928), layman Stephen J. Clark (b. 1940), layman Ralph Martin (b. 1942), and biblical scholar R. Francis Martin (b. 1930). In 1970 a national service committee was formed to coordinate the fast-spreading movement, which was also served by *New Covenant Magazine.*

Dominican priest Francis MacNutt (b. 1925) became engaged in Pentecostal healing. MacNutt was introduced to healing prayer through the Episcopal Church's Order of St. Luke, through which he also met such healing ministry pioneers as Agnes Sanford (1897–1982). The general charismatic phenomenon spread throughout the nation. Charismatic cells started appearing in a variety of parishes, and many priests joined in. In 1990 a variety of Catholic charismatic movements united under the canonically recognized Catholic Fraternity of Charismatic Covenant Communities and Fellowships.

Under pressure by the hierarchy, MacNutt and many other Catholic priests and lay people have left the official church, some for a limited time, to continue their Pentecostal ministry elsewhere. In 1994 MacNutt, officially laicized by the church, resumed his healing ministry among Catholics. Charismatic associations claim that there are as many as 100 million Catholic charismatics throughout the world, especially in AFRICA and LATIN AMERICA.

Although Pope JOHN PAUL II addressed the International Catholic Charismatic Renewal Office in 1992, official support for the movement has become very muted in most American dioceses. Charismatic cells still exist, and bishops still lend their support, but in a quieter manner. One explanation is that American Catholicism during the pontificate of John Paul II has become more hierarchized and bureaucratized. Many cells are sustaining themselves online through Web sites.

Further reading: Stanley M. Burgess and Eduard M. Van der Maas, eds., *International Dictionary of Pentecostal Charismatic Movements,* rev. ed.: (Grand Rapids, Mich.: Zondervan, 2002); Donald L. Gelpi, *Pentecostalism: A Theological Viewpoint* (New York: Paulist, 1971); John Paul II, *Address of Pope John Paul II to the ICCRO Council* (March 14, 1992); Francis MacNutt, *Healing* (Notre Dame: Ave Maria, 1974); J. Gordon Melton, *The Catholic Pentecostal Movement* (Evanston, Ill.: Garrett Theological Seminary Library, 1971), a bibliography; Vinson

Synan, *The Century of the Holy Spirit: 100 Years of Pentecostal and Charismatic Renewal, 1901–2001* (Nashville: Thomas Nelson, 2001); Léon Josef Suenens, *Charismatic Renewal and Social Action: A Dialogue with Dom Helder Câmarra* (Ann Arbor, Mich.: Servant, 1979).

charity (Lat.: *caritas,* "charity," "love")

See AGAPE.

Charlemagne (c. 742–814) (Lat.: *Carolus,* "Charles" + *magnus,* "the great") *emperor of the West*

Charlemagne was the founder and first emperor of what later came to be called the HOLY ROMAN EMPIRE. He united much of western Europe under his rule and presided over an economic, cultural, and ecclesiastical revival that laid the groundwork for much of subsequent European civilization.

Son of Pepin III (r. 751–768), king of the Franks, and Bertrada of Laon (720–83), he was anointed coruler with his brother Carloman by Pope Stephen III in 754. Carloman died in 771, leaving Charlemagne sole ruler. He fought and subdued the Lombards, Saxons, Danes, and Slavs and extended his kingdom into Bavaria. In 778 his liege Count Roland of Breton March (d. 788) led an expedition across the Pyrenees to fight both Muslims and Spaniards. Roland was later immortalized in *La Chanson de Roland*. Charlemagne was crowned emperor on Christmas Day, 800, in Rome, an event that did not please the Byzantine emperors. By the middle of the ninth century the western empire extended as far north as Denmark, as far west as the Atlantic Ocean, as far south as Barcelona in Spain and Monte Cassino in Italy, and beyond Salzburg to the east.

Together with ALCUIN and other leaders, Charlemagne was overseer of the CAROLINGIAN RENAISSANCE, centered in his famous palace school at Aachen (Fr. Aix-la-Chapelle). Similar schools were founded in archbishoprics and monasteries throughout the empire that became the seeds of later universities. Charlemagne fostered the renewal of learning, especially the liberal arts, and the reform of imperial legislation, and he promoted monastic, ecclesiastical, and liturgical reforms in the Frankish church as the virtual ruler over the dioceses of his realm. He promoted the Roman rite of the Mass to aid political unification. He presided over the Council of Frankfort in 794, which condemned ADOPTIONISM, the belief that the Father adopted Jesus as his son, and he participated in the controversy over iconoclasm.

Charlemagne had many wives and concubines. His heirs, Charles, Pepin and Louis I the Pious, were the children of Hildegard of Swabia (758–783). The court chronicler Einhard eulogized his life after his death.

Further reading: Einhard, *The Life of Charlemagne* (Ann Arbor: University of Michigan Press, 1960); Matthias Becher, *Charlemagne,* tr. David S. Bachrach (New Haven, Conn.: Yale University Press, 2003); Rosamond McKittrick, ed., *Carolingian Culture* (Cambridge: Cambridge University Press, 1994).

Charles V (1500–1558) *Holy Roman Emperor, king of Spain (as Charles I), most powerful European ruler of his era*

As heir to the vast Habsburg dominions all across Europe, Charles was the most powerful ruler of his era. However, he was unable to prevent the breakup of Christianity during the PROTESTANT REFORMATION.

Son of Philip I of Burgundy (1478–1506) and grandson of FERDINAND I (1452–1516) and ISABELLA (1451–1504) of SPAIN, Charles married the Portugese infanta Isabella and ruled over Burgundy, the Netherlands, Spain, and the Spanish Empire in the New World and had a claim on the duchy of Milan. Charles held firm power in the Netherlands and Spain, but was beset by enemies on all sides in his wider empire: the pope, the Turks, and the Protestant princes. Although he was present at the Diet of Worms (1521), at which Luther was banned, he pursued a policy of alternately repressing and tolerating his Protestant subjects. At the Diet of Augsburg (1555) Charles was forced to concede the principle *cuius regio, eius religio* (where a person lives determines his or her religion). Dismayed at persecuting his Protestant subjects in one region and protecting them in another, Charles retired to the monastery of Yuste at Estremadura, Spain.

Further reading: Martin C. Rady, *Emperor Charles V* (London: Longman, 1988); William S. Maltby, *The Reign of Charles V* (New York: Palgrave, 2002).

chastity (Lat.: *castus,* "chaste," "pure")

Chastity is the virtue by which human beings direct their SEXUALITY toward its proper end. A basic CHRISTIAN tenet is that sexuality may never be separated from the commandment of love. In earlier Christian times chastity was often incorrectly identified as, or limited to, continence, virginity, or abstinence from all sexual life. This was no doubt due to the premium placed on monastic and religious life in which members took vows of obedience, poverty, and "chastity," where the latter term meant abstinence from all sexual life. Beginning with the monastic ideal in the second century, chastity in the sense of abstinence was considered an evangelical counsel, recommended but not commanded.

Theologians like St. AUGUSTINE OF HIPPO taught that even Christians can hardly hope to escape from the "disease of concupiscence" within marriage, but they are commanded to desire intercourse solely for the purpose of generating children (*On Marriage and Concupiscence* 1.9). Augustine felt there could be no act of human love without some taint of concupiscence. This limited view of chastity was modified by PIUS XI, who distinguished between the primary (procreation) and secondary (mutual support) ends of marriage in his celebrated encyclical on "chaste marriage" (*Casti Connubii,* January 31, 1930). Pius invoked the great New Testament image of marriage as reflecting the relation between CHRIST and his spouse, the church (Eph. 5:28–32).

After VATICAN COUNCIL II a new understanding of chastity promoted a reverence for human sexuality, for the human body, and for the partner in marriage. Whether celibate, single, or married, CHRISTIANS are all called to a chaste life that reverences the sacred dimensions of sexuality and avoids selfish self-love and objectification of the partner in marriage.

Further reading: John S. Grabowski, *Sex and Virtue* (Washington, D.C.: Catholic University of America Press, 2003); Hanne Sigismund Nielson, "Men, Women and Marital Chastity: Public Preaching and Popular Piety at Rome," in John T. Fitzgerald, ed., *Early Christianity and Classical Culture* (Leiden: Brill, 2003), 525–554.

chasuble   *See* VESTMENTS.

Chaucer, Geoffrey (1343/4–1400) *pioneer English writer*

The son of a Thames merchant, Chaucer became a page to Elizabeth de Burgh (1337–63), wife of Prince Lionel (1338–68), second son of King Edward III (1312–77). He fought in France alongside the king, who ransomed him when he was captured; Chaucer entered imperial service as a diplomat and clerk of works at Windsor. He authored the *Canterbury Tales* and *Troilus and Cresyde*. The *Tales* are yarns told by pilgrims on their way to Canterbury Cathedral to honor St. THOMAS À BECKET. While fondly sympathetic to the foibles of human nature, Chaucer was nonetheless sharply critical of the lax life of the clergy (Prologue) and of the abuse of INDULGENCES (Pardoner's Tale).

Further reading: Peter Ackroyd, *Chaucer* (New York: Doubleday, 2005); Steve Ellis, *Chaucer: An Oxford Guide* (Oxford: Oxford University Press, 2005).

Chávez, César (Cesar Chavez) (1927–1993) *U.S. social activist*

César Chávez was a migrant worker and union organizer in California. In 1958 he formed the National Farm Workers Association and led a boycott from 1968 to 1970 that ended with growers agreeing to collective bargaining. Chávez was a devout Catholic who received much support from Catholics who identified with La Causa ("The Cause") and supported him on religious principles of social justice. Lay people, nuns, priests, brothers, and even bishops often accompanied him in the boycott.

Further reading: Frederick John Dalton, *The Moral Vision of César Chávez* (Maryknoll, N.Y.: Orbis Books, 2003).; Richard Grisworld de Castillo and Richard A. Garcia, *César Chávez: A Triumph of Spirit* (Norman: University of Oklahoma Press, 1995).

Chenu, Marie-Dominique (1895–1990) *Vatican II theologian*

Chenu was a French Dominican and a key participant in the NOUVELLE THÉOLOGIE movement, an authority on the theology of THOMAS AQUINAS, and an influential expert at VATICAN COUNCIL II. After getting his doctorate from the Angelicum, the Dominican school of theology in Rome, in 1920, Chenu taught at Le Saulchoir in Belgium, which moved to Étoilles south of Paris. He served as its rector from 1932. In the face of charges of MODERNISM, Chenu applied the historical method to the study of St. Thomas Aquinas, attempting to study him in the context of his own times. He founded the influential journal *Revue des sciences philosophiques et théologiques* and wrote several books on Aquinas, including the widely cited *Introduction à l'étude de s. Thomas d' Aquin* (Introduction to the study of St. Thomas Aquinas, 1950). Early on Chenu became interested in linking theology, sociology, spirituality, and mission to his historical studies. Like GEORGES-YVES CONGAR and HENRI DE LUBAC, he was banned from teaching for a period of time. He had significant influence on MATTHEW FOX and creation spirituality.

At Vatican II Chenu served as an expert at the direct invitation of Pope JOHN XXIII and had considerable input into *Gaudium et Spes,* the Dogmatic Constitution on the Church, which embraced an opening to CREATION and the modern world. After the council he strongly defended its confident openness against those who would backtrack.

Further reading: Marie-Dominique Chenu, *Aquinas and Theology* (Collegeville, Minn.: Liturgical Press, 2001); ———, *Faith and Theology* (New York: Macmillan, 1968); ———, *Theology and Work* (Chicago: Regnery, 1966); Christophe Potworowski, *Contemplation and Incarnation: The Theology of Marie-Dominique Chenu* (Ottawa: McGill-Queen's University, 2001).

Chesterton, G(ilbert) K(eith) (1874–1936)
English writer

G. K. Chesterton was a brilliant and eccentric English novelist, poet, journalist, essayist, dramatist, and apologist. He wrote the immensely popular Father Brown mystery series, later adapted for television, as well as best-selling biographies of Sts. FRANCIS OF ASSISI and THOMAS AQUINAS. He opposed the Boer War (1899–1902) and proposals for eugenics. He believed in "distributism," which he colorfully explained as every person being able to own "three acres and a cow." He became a Catholic in 1922. He received many honors, including Fellow of the Royal Society of Literature, Knight Commander with Star, and Knight of the Order of St. Gregory the Great. There are G. K. fan clubs all over the world.

Further reading: Gilbert Keith Chesterton, *The Catholic Church and Conversion* (New York: Macmillan, 1926); ———, *St. Francis of Assisi* (London: Hodder & Staughton, 1923); ———, *St. Thomas Aquinas* (New York: Sheed & Ward, 1933); Gary Wills, *Chesterton* (New York: Doubleday, 2001).

China, Catholicism   *See* ASIA.

Chinese Catholic Patriotic Association

The Chinese Catholic Patriotic Association is the Catholic Church officially recognized by the Peoples Republic of China but not in communion with Rome. Having supported the Nationalist (Koumintang) cause during the Chinese revolution, the Catholic Church fell from favor when Mao Zedong [Mao Tse-tung] (1893–1976) came to power. Repression followed. Because of the church's unwillingness to accommodate to the new political situation, in 1957 the government moved to establish the Chinese Catholic Patriotic Association with the goal of transferring the church from Vatican to Communist Party control. While giving lip service to the pope's spiritual authority, the association denied the Vatican any administrative powers within China and asserted its right to select and consecrate bishops in its own right. Speaking directly to the Chinese situation, Pope PIUS XII declared that the church is "supranational" in *Ad Sinarum Gentium* (October 7, 1954). In 1957 he declared the Catholic Patriotic Association schismatic and excommunicated its leaders. Meanwhile, a secret underground church remained loyal to Rome.

The Cultural Revolution that began in 1966 was devastating to both culture and religion, not just Catholic. All Christian churches were closed; Catholic priests were killed or arrested; those who survived were forced to marry. When the madness was over, the association was revived in 1979, and Catholic services were again held with government permission. Simultaneously, two additional organizations, the National Administrative Council of the Catholic Church in China and the Chinese Bishops College, were created. These three organizations currently represent and provide oversight to the Catholic community in China and provide its interface with the government. Average Catholics experience divided loyalties to the association and the underground church.

The revived church faced several problems, the most important being the lack of sufficient priests. At first the association used the Latin Mass, but in the 1990s it gradually accepted the liturgical reforms of VATICAN COUNCIL II. As the church became visible again in China, Pope JOHN PAUL II lent his support to those bishops who remained loyal to Rome; he also canonized 120 Chinese martyrs on October 1, 2000. Both the Chinese government and the association denounced the pope for this act. Nevertheless, the loyal bishops continue to operate sub rosa and under the continual threat of arrest.

The Chinese Catholic Patriotic Association is headquartered in Beijing. It is currently led by Bishop FU TIESHAN. There are an estimated 15 million Catholics in China, the majority of whom appear to favor the Patriotic Association, though precise numbers for either group remain elusive. Pope BENEDICT XVI is taking halting steps to reconcile with the dominant church in China.

Further reading: Alan Hunter and Kim-Kwong Chan, *Protestantism in Contemporary China* (Cambridge: Cambridge University Press, 1993); Richard Madsen, *China's Catholics. Tragedy and Hope in an Emerging Civil Society* (Berkeley: University of California Press, 1998): Charles E. Ronan and Bonnie B. C. Oh, eds., *East Meets West: The Jesuits in China, 1582–1773,* (Chicago: Loyola University Press, 1988); Luo Zhufeng, ed., *Religion under Socialism in China* (Armonk, N.Y.: M. E. Sharpe, 1991).

chrism   *See* ANOINTING.

Christ/Christology (Gr.: *christos*, "anointed one" + *logos*, "word about," "account of")

Christology is the critical and formal theological study of the person of Jesus as the Christ, especially of the union of the human and divine natures in him and of the importance of the Christ for CHRISTIAN faith. The New Testament is more concerned

Icon of Christos Pantokrator (Christ Ruler of All), seated in majesty and surrounded with medallions of symbols of the four Gospellers (Luke=angelic man; Mark=lion; Matthew=ox; John=eagle). Icon by contemporary icon painter Charlene Wetwood *(permission of the artist).*

about the acts and words of Jesus of Nazareth than his nature. The primary question it asks is was he the Messiah (the Anointed One) or not, and if so, at what point did he become Messiah? In what may be the earliest Christology of all, Peter's sermon in Acts 3:20 implies that Jesus is the Messiah *designatus,* the Christ appointed to return in the future. By contrast, the sermon in Acts 2:30–33 seems to say that Jesus was "made" Lord and Messiah at his RESURRECTION. Deeper reflection on the Christ event pushes Jesus' messianic status or its clear manifestation back ever earlier: at his baptism in the Jordan

(Mark 1:10–11), at his birth (Luke 1:31–33; Matt. 1:20–23), or, as the Gospel of John has it, before CREATION, when the incarnate Christ was identified with the Logos (John 1:1–14).

In addition to the messianic designation, a number of other titles were progressively applied to the historical figure of Jesus in New Testament writings. The Covenant renewal discourse from the Q source (Luke 6:20–49) points to Jesus as a prophet like Elijah bringing the renewal of GOD's rule to the people of Galilee. Mark focuses on the titles the Son of Man (Dan. 1:13–14), a being in the sky associated with the Godhead that many think first referred to the Archangel Michael, and Son of God, fully recognized only by the centurion (Mark 15:39). In his sermon in Acts, the first martyr, Stephen, refers to Jesus as a prophet like Moses and the Righteous One (7:37, 52). Matthew portrays Jesus as a rabbi, or teacher, like Moses preaching a heightened sense of the Torah, or Law (Matt. 19). The prologue to the Gospel of John identifies Jesus as the Logos from before Creation, and the Gospel itself points to him as the Way, the Truth, and the Life. Other passages identify Jesus with God's creative Wisdom, with whom he created all things (1 Cor. 1:24; Heb. 1:2), and the descent and reascent of personified Wisdom served as a pattern for the descent and reascent of the redeemer (Sir. 24: 8–10; 1 Enoch 42:1–2; Phil. 2:6–11).

Many other titles are applied to Jesus in the New Testament: Suffering Servant, Son of David, Lamb of God, Redeemer, Savior, Judge of the Living and the Dead, and so on. Most important is the title Lord (Gk. *kyrios*), which hearkens both to the holy name of God YHWH and to the title of address to Greco-Roman emperors and leaders. This title, often in the combination "the Lord Jesus," plus the title "the Christ" are the terms most favored by Paul (1 Thess. 1.6; 1 Cor. 5:4, etc.). Revelation 1:8 addresses Jesus as "the Alpha and the Omega, who is and who was and who is to come, the Ruler of All (Pantokrator)." This image of Jesus was to return as dominant in Byzantine iconography.

In following centuries the central question began to shift from "Who was Jesus?" to "What was the nature of the Christ?" The teaching about Jesus as divine faced external critiques (e.g., from the pagan writer Celsus) and internal disputes. Several problems emerge when one sees Jesus as divine. First and foremost, the earliest Christians were Jews who had a primary commitment to the singleness of God; any divinity of Christ could not be construed in a way that would challenge that singleness. (The Jewish Christian group of Ebionites seems to have accepted Jesus as master and teacher but not as God.) Second, all subsequent Christology is determined by two parameters: his humanity cannot be so maintained as to exclude his divinity and his divinity cannot overwhelm his humanity. (The Docetists and later Gnostics denied earthly humanity as beneath the Redeemer who descended to liberate humans from fleshly existence.) The descent of divine power of the one God on the person of Jesus as Son and Christ had the aim of bringing about the salvation of a fallen humanity. Christology cannot be separated from soteriology, the doctrine of REDEMPTION.

In the second century apologists like JUSTIN MARTYR applied the idea of Logos (reason and order) from Middle Platonism to Jesus. This approach started with eternity and looked at the historical Jesus in that light. This Logos, however, was an intermediary between God and the world and not quite equal to God's self. In the fourth century Arius (d. 336) concluded that the Son is less than the Father: "The Son has a beginning but God is without a beginning" (*see* ARIANISM). Under the goad of ATHANASIUS OF ALEXANDRIA, the fathers who produced the creed of the Council of Nicaea in 325 stated that the Lord Jesus Christ is "consubstantial (of the same being) with the Father" (Gk.: *homoousios tō patri*). The matter was finally formulated only by the addition of "begotten not made" to the Nicene Creed at the Council of CONSTANTINOPLE in 381.

This formula did not solve the problem. APOLLINARIS OF LAODICEA affirmed the Athanasian formula of Nicaea but maintained that the Logos took the place of the human soul in Christ. Apollinaris preserved the unity of Christ, but St. GREGORY OF NAZIANZUS argued that "what is not assumed is not healed and what is not united with God is not saved." The reasoning is: if the human mind and will of Christ was not assumed by God, then humanity itself is not saved. Athanasius and the Cappodocian fathers Sts. BASIL THE GREAT, Gregory of Nazianzus, and GREGORY OF NYSSA rose in opposition to Apollinaris. Apollinarianism was censured at the Synod of Antioch (379) and at Constantinople in 381 (cn. 1). No sooner was this Christological difficulty settled than another rose: Nestorius of Constantinople gave support to a subordinate, Anastasius, who was preaching against the use of the term *Theotokos* ("Begetter of God") when applied to Mary, the mother of Jesus. St. CYRIL OF ALEXANDRIA undertook to oppose the Nestorian position, and Nestorius and his supporters were condemned at the Council of EPHESUS in 431. Many claim that Cyril distorted Nestorius's true position, and that the conflict represents a typical dispute between Antiochene and Alexandrine theology. The Alexandrines fought to preserve the unity of the person of Christ; they believed that to say that Mary was not the Mother of God divided that unity.

The classic Christological debate was fully stated only at the Council of CHALCEDON in 451. Chalcedon was called to counteract the teaching of Eutyches of Constantinople (c. 380–c. 456), who maintained that after the union of God and man in Christ there remained only one divine nature. This was the beginning of monophysitism, which is attributed to Coptic Christianity to this day but not accepted by them as a fair designation. The "confession" of Chalcedon, which reads more like a dogmatic treatise than a confession of faith, states in brief that Christ is one and that he is fully human and fully divine.

Chalcedon did not solve all the problems of Christology, but it did set the parameters for all future debate. Later heretical tendencies emerged, most notably monenergism (there is only one energy active in Christ) and monothelitism (there is only one will in Christ), but the formulas of Chalcedon prevailed. The Christological discussions of the MIDDLE AGES were more refinements and elucidations of Chalcedon than new developments. They divided Christology between the "person" of Christ and the "work" of salvation and gave the latter the title "soteriology," or "the account of salvation." Of special importance is the difference in the understanding of Christ's ATONEMENT between ANSELM OF CANTERBURY, who saw it as a satisfaction against the infinite wrath of God, and PETER ABELARD, who saw it as the exemplary outpouring of God's infinite love.

The operative medieval formula was that Christ was one person who united in himself the divine and human natures (THOMAS AQUINAS,

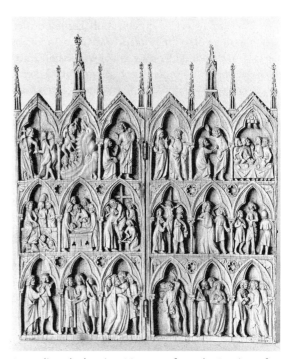

Ivory diptych showing 18 scenes from the Passion of Christ to the Ascension into heaven. Mid-13th century. *(St. Louis Art Museum, with permission)*

Summa Theologiae 3.2.2). Corollary to this was the patristic teaching of *communcatio idiomatum,* or the "interchange of properties," between the human and divine in Christ so that one could say that what God did the human did and what the human did God did (Bonaventure, *Sentences* 3.6.1.1). The one new innovation was DUNS SCOTUS's stress that Christ was the supreme manifestation of divine love, the fulfillment of creation itself and that the INCARNATION, would have taken place irrespective of the FALL.

The PROTESTANT REFORMATION did not depart from the Christological formulas of earlier ages but shifted the discussion more in the direction of what Jesus Christ did for humankind by gaining justification of all through his emptying of himself on the CROSS and his vindication by God in the Resurrection. The old Scholastic distinction between the person of Jesus and his work fell away.

With the Enlightenment and Romanticism the terms of discussion shifted radically. The emphasis was now on a historical understanding of Christ. Rationalist Protestant scholars like Hermann S. Reimarus (1694–1768) of Hamburg began to distinguish between the Jesus of history and the Christ of faith. Deists like Thomas Jefferson (1743–1826) rejected the view that Jesus was divine, choosing instead to see him as a moral exemplar. Georg F. W. Hegel (1770–1831) saw Jesus as the culmination and concrete reconciliation of the universal and the particular, the infinite and the finite, and the divine and the human in time. Scholars like David Friedrich Strauss (1804–74) and later Albert Schweitzer became very interested in the historical Jesus from psychological, historical, and social perspectives: his life, what he experienced, what he thought, how he felt, and how he saw himself in his historical situation.

The quest for the historical Jesus has passed through many phases and still goes on. In the theology of Friedrich Schleiermacher (1768–1834), religious experience became the key to interpreting Jesus, whom he saw as the paradigmatic example of the feeling for the Infinite in human life. In the late 19th century this Christology of feeling, strong in Jonathan Edwards (1703–58) and Schleiermacher, degenerated into a sentimental view of Jesus. Today some call this the "bourgeois Christ," whose image is promulgated through countless saccharine portraits of the "blond Jesus" and holy cards of the SACRED HEART. The noted New Testament scholar Rudolph Bultmann (1884–1976) gave up the historical quest completely and looked to the Christ of faith who calls for an existential decision toward authentic existence.

With the coming of VATICAN COUNCIL II, the context of Christological thinking among Catholic theologians changed in a fundamental way. Without challenging the tradition, the council no longer spoke of the doctrine of the Christ in isolation but in relation to theological anthropology, ECCLESIOLOGY, ECUMENISM, and other pressing pastoral concerns. While ontological Christology still speaks of Jesus' person and nature, this is seen in relation to the functional meaning of Jesus Christ, his message, and the import of his life, death, and resurrection in the life of the church. The Christ of Vatican II is the pastoral Christ, the Shepherd of his flock.

There are now many avenues to open the Christological question, following the lead of the Jesuit KARL RAHNER, the Dominican Edward Schillebeeckx, Johannes Metz (1928–), GUSTAVO GUTIÉRREZ, and LEONARDO BOFF. A "low" route begins with Jesus' humanity and seeks to show the opening of the human to the supernatural. The "high" route begins with the relation of the Son to the TRINITY and proceeds to God's self-disclosure in creation and history and the entrance of the divine into time and space in the INCARNATION. Christological reflection is also open to the meaning of the Christ as liberator of the poor and oppressed and of those discriminated against on the basis of their race, gender, or even belief. In the belief that the image of Jesus has been slanted by modern individualism, many theologians are reinterpreting the Christ in differing cultural contexts. Christology is now even open to the relation of Jesus to holy figures of other religious traditions, such as the Buddha, as christic instantiations or manifestations.

Further reading: Richard Cross, *The Metaphysics of Incarnation: Thomas Aquinas to Duns Scotus* (New York: Oxford University Press, 2002); Uchenna A. Ezeh, *Jesus Christ the Ancestor: An African Contextual Christology* (New York: P. Lang, 2003); Leonardo Boff, *Jesus Christ Liberator* (Maryknoll, N.Y.: Orbis, 1978); Karl Rahner, *The Foundations of Christian Faith* (New York: Crossroad, 1984); Thomas P. Rausch, *Who is Jesus?: An Introduction to Christology* (Collegeville, Minn.: Liturgical Press, 2003); Edward Schillebeeckx, *Jesus: An Experiment in Christology* (New York: Crossroad, 1979).

Christian

It is difficult for many Christians to understand that all the earliest adherents of what is now called Christianity thought of themselves as Jews and not "Christians." Paul made a distinction between Jews and Greeks or Gentiles in his letters to the Galatians and Romans, but he never used the term *Christian*. In the New Testament the term first appears in Acts 11:26: ". . . and in Antioch the disciples were called Christians for the first time." The term is formed on the model of "Herodian," that is, someone belonging to the party of Herod. It was almost certainly a pejorative term, meaning something like "Christers." All late first- and early second-century Roman authors saw the Christ-party as obstinate, "superstitious," and even "atheisitic" citizens who refused to honor the emperor and the Roman gods (Tacitus, *Annals* 15.44; Suetonius, *Nero* 16; Pliny the Younger, *Letters* 10.96). The term took on a more positive, if defensive, meaning when the apologists of the second century, such as Justin Martyr, defended the moral and spiritual integrity of the Christians

against the Roman charges of idolatry and vice. Today some who do not walk humbly in their faith often use the term arrogantly to distinguish themselves from others who are not followers of Jesus.

Further reading: Χριστιανός in Frederick W. Danker, *Greek-English Lexicon of the New Testament* (Chicago: University of Chicago Press, 2000); Justin Martyr, *First and Second Apologies,* in A. Cleveland Coxe, *Ante-Nicene Fathers* (Grand Rapids, Mich.: Eerdmanns, 1967) 1:163–193.

Christian Brothers

The Christian Brothers, an institute of lay brothers, was founded by St. Jean-Baptiste de La Salle in 1680 to educate poor and middle-class boys in Rheims, France. Its official title is Brothers of the Christian Schools, or Fratres Scolarum Christianarum, with the abbreviation FSC. The brothers brought about a revolution in educational methods, including teaching in the local language. The brothers do not aspire to become priests, but are trained in theological orthodoxy, pedagogical competence, and catechetical skills. Pope Benedict XIII (r. 1724–30) gave the institute formal approbation in the bull *In Apostolicae Dignitatis Solio* (January 26, 1725).

The brothers soon spread throughout France. They also took on special missions, such as educating the Irish children of followers of exiled king James II (1633–1701). The French Revolution led to their suppression, but they recovered and started spreading overseas, at first to Martinique, the Louisiana Territory, and French Canada. The institute suffered another difficult time under the secularization laws in France from 1904 to 1912.

The brothers responded actively to Vatican Council II by formulating a new educational mission statement, "The Brother of the Christian School in the World" (1967), and revising their original rule over a period of time ending in 1987. The brothers have embraced principles of INCULTURATION of the Gospel in local cultures. A number of institutes of sisters and catechists have become associated with the brothers in what is now called the Lasallian Family, including the Hermanas Guadalupanas de La Salle in Mexico and the Union of Catechists of Jesus Crucified and Mary Immaculate in Thailand.

Today there are brothers in 85 countries who, with associate lay teachers, educate more than 700,000 students. Brother Álvaro Rodríguez Echeverría of Costa Rica is the current superior general. The Christian Brothers have been very active in the United States, starting high schools in most major cities and founding several institutions of higher learning, including Christian Brothers University in Memphis, La Salle University in Philadelphia, Manhattanville College in New York City, and the College of Santa Fe in New Mexico.

Further reading: Bruno Alpago, *The Institute in the Educational Service of the Poor* (Rome: Brothers of the Christian Schools, 2000); Carl Koch, ed., *John Baptist de la Salle: The Spirituality of Christian Education* (New York: Paulist Press, 2004).

Christian democratic parties

Arising out of the political turmoil of late 19th-century Europe, Christian democratic parties were at first closely associated with the Catholic Church. They were given broad support by the papal encyclicals *Rerum Novarum* (May 15, 1891) by LEO XIII and *Quadragesimo Anno* (May 15, 1931) by PIUS XI.

Most Christian parties have tried to address economic suffering and social injustice in different ways than socialists and existing trade unions. In general, they opposed secular liberalism. Not challenging capitalism per se, they nonetheless have stressed that the economy should serve the common good. They favored the formation of unions and in some cases worked with socialist parties. On the other hand, some Christian parties have been very conservative. Somewhat tragically,

the Vatican's CONCORDATS with Mussolini in 1929 and with Hitler in 1933 led to the suppression of budding Christian democratic movements in Italy and Germany.

Perhaps the most successful of these parties was the Christian Democratic Union (CDU) of Germany, founded by Konrad Adenauer (1876–1967), which facilitated Germany's return to democracy after World War II. The conservative affiliate of the CDU in Bavaria, the Christian Social Union, has ruled that state since World War II. The Democrazia Cristiana, an offshoot of Don Luigi Sturzo's People's Party, was outlawed by the Fascists in 1925, only later to play a similar democratizing role in Italy after World War II. Widespread corruption led to its demise in 1994.

Most of these parties no longer have formal ties with the Catholic Church. In the Netherlands the Christen Democratisch Appèl is a coalition of Reformed, Protestant, and Catholic parties. There have been many Christian democratic parties in LATIN AMERICA. The newer parties in AFRICA and ASIA have a more Protestant flavor.

See also CHURCH AND STATE; FASCISM; NAZISM.

Further reading: Thomas Kselman and Joseph A. Buttigieg, eds., *European Christian Democracy* (Notre Dame: University of Notre Dame Press, 2003); Roberto Papini, *The Christian Democratic International* (Lanham Md.: Rowman & Littlefield, 1997); Scott Mainwring and Timothy R. Scully, eds., *Christian Democracy in Latin America* (Stanford, Calif.: Stanford University Press, 2003).

Christmas   *See* LITURGICAL YEAR.

church and state

The relationship between civil and ecclesiastical authority and power, whether amicable or not, has gone through many phases in CHRISTIAN history. A few are discussed in this entry.

BIBLICAL TIMES

Israelite history lays the framework for understanding the relation between church and state. The Israelites went through a phase as a confederation of tribes, through a period of "judges," or temporary leaders, and finally into a typical ancient Middle Eastern kingship. When the people asked Samuel to appoint a king to succeed him (1 Samuel 8), GOD tells him that they are rejecting not Samuel but their true king, God. A king was appointed nonetheless, but there remained an ongoing tension between the monarchy and the prophets. These prophets, who had access to the proceedings of the heavenly council of God (Isaiah 1), were the makers and breakers of kings. Like Nathan, they called the kings to justice and mercy when they violated the terms of the Covenant between God and the people (2 Samuel 12). This established the fundamental principle underlying the relation between church and state.

Many biblical scholars, past and present, have portrayed Jesus' mission as apolitical or even countercultural. They point to such sayings as "My kingdom is not of this world" (John 18:36) and "Render unto Caesar what is Caesar's" (Matt. 22.21). A careful reading and reconstruction of the Sermon on the Plain in Q (Luke 6:20–49) shows that it is a Covenant renewal ceremony deriving from Jesus' role as a prophet like Elijah, rallying Galilee against the corrupt and corrupting powers in Jerusalem, both Roman and Jewish, who were violating the terms of the Covenant by foreclosing on lands that originally belonged to the tribes. Thus, Jesus carries on the old king-prophet quarrel.

In the latter half of the first century, this theme became muted under the weight of persecution. Paul's seeming acquiescence to the powers that be (Romans 13) probably reflects an attempt to protect Jews and followers of Jesus from unnecessary persecution and should not be understood as enunciating a universal principle. The Book of Revelation, often taken as a militant tract against the violent power of Rome, actually recommends *hypomone*, an abiding, pacifist endurance in faith (1:9), in the face of persecution. And persecution from the Roman state is what Christians received during the era of martyrs.

The persecution backfired, as even the Roman nobility came to admire the bravery of young women like Sts. PERPETUA AND FELICITY as they stood up to the wild beasts like gladiators of the spirit. By the time of CONSTANTINE, between 30 percent and 40 percent of the empire had become Christian. The Edict of Milan (313), which did not establish Christianity but brought it toleration, was a political move on the part of Constantine to gain the support of a significant segment of the population.

POST-CONSTANTINE ERA

At the first Council of Nicaea (325), called by Constantine together with a number of BISHOPS, the emperor ceded to the bishops a role in civil affairs. Conversely, the emperor took an active role in ecclesiastical affairs. The stage was set for a struggle for supremacy. Emperors, often claiming legitimacy from God the Father, tended to place bishops, whose legitimacy was derived from the Son, in a secondary position. Many emperors secretly entertained ARIANISM, which placed the Son in a subordinate role and thus bolstered their political position. This imperial attitude later became known as CAESAROPAPISM. Western bishops like AMBROSE and various popes opposed this tendency, which was, however, more accepted in the East.

Pope St. Gelasius (r. 492–96) formulated a theory that was to prevail into the MIDDLE AGES in the West. Appealing to Roman law on the one hand and Ambrose and Augustine on the other, Gelasius drew a distinction between spiritual ecclesiastical *auctoritas*, the power to legislate, and temporal civil *potestas*, the power to execute, a principle that in a different version became inscribed in the American Constitution. Each power had its proper sphere, but it is obvious that the former is the greater in the mind of Gelasius.

In the words of Ambrose, the priest's authority is weightier because he must render an account before the divine tribunal for both king and priest. This became known as the two-sword theory of the state. The principle came under severe test in the time of St. GREGORY VII HILDEBRAND, who excommunicated the Holy Roman Emperor Henry IV (r. 1084–1105) over the right of investiture of bishops and made him do penance on his knees in the snow at Canossa in 1077.

By gaining full control of a territorial base, the Papal States, INNOCENT III ensured that future kings and princes could hold only limited sway over the PAPACY. He almost tipped the balance the other way in the PAPAL BULL *Sicut Universitatis Conditor* (October 30, 1198), in which he compared the power of the pope over the soul to the sun and the power of the prince over the body to the moon. The medieval political theologian John of Paris (d. 1306) tried to contain this papal claim by siding with Philip IV the Fair (1268–1314) against BONIFACE VIII, whose bull *Unam Sanctam* (November 18, 1302) borders on spiritual arrogance. WILLIAM OF OCKHAM boldly opposed the papacy's totalistic claims.

REFORMATION ERA AND AFTER

The Reformation and the contemporaneous rise of the nation-state meant the collapse of the unitary, papal-centered society of the Middle Ages. The Peace of Augsburg (1555) established the principle *cuius regio, eius religio,* under which the religion of the local prince become the locality's religion. This, coupled with the PEACE OF WESTPHALIA (1648), which ended the wars of religion, set a trend under which a state would establish a particular public religion, either Protestant or Catholic, and tolerate the private practice of the other.

Protestant polities, meanwhile, took a variety of shapes. Some became absolute theocracies (Geneva); others partially subjected church authority to the state (Luther's Germany). In still other varieties of Protestantism (England, Sweden, Denmark) national churches were established by

state sanction. In many countries Catholicism was established as the religion of the state (SPAIN, ITALY, LATIN AMERICA). In the United States, a new beginning was made based on freedom of conscience, freedom of worship, and a sense that duty was owed directly toward the Creator, not via a state religion. The duties toward God precede entry into the civil compact and remain free of the state's supervision (James Madison, *Memorial and Remonstrance,* 1785).

Even after the American breakthrough many Catholics and non-Catholics in Europe adhered to a principle that "error hath no rights." Until VATICAN COUNCIL II, Catholic political theory functioned under the medieval/theory that the true church should be established and the false ones suppressed. PIUS IX said in his *Syllabus of Errors* 77 that only the Catholic Church had the right to the status of a religion in the state, to the exclusion of all others. False religions could be tolerated only if their suppression would be impossible or would lead to disorder in society at large. At the time, Pius IX was still in the process of losing the Papal States. Bit by bit the defense of the medieval premise was given up, first by LEO XIII and then by PIUS XII, who started down the path of recognizing religious rights free from state interference.

In several addresses Leo XIII, especially in *Sapientiae Christianae* the duties of a christian citizen on (January 10, 1890), called for cooperation between church and state lest the citizen's right to conscience be violated. In *Ci Riesce* (December 6, 1953), an address to Italian jurists, Pius XII, recognizing the radical encroachment of 20th-century totalitarians on human freedom, stated: "The right to existence, the right to respect from others and to one's good name, the right to one's own culture and national character, the right to develop oneself, the right to demand observance of international treaties, and other like rights, are exigencies of the law of nations, dictated by nature itself." This comes close but fails to enunciate clearly a declaration of religious freedom.

PACEM IN TERRIS AND VATICAN II

Vatican II became a strong wind in the history of religious freedom, but its advance breeze was JOHN XXII's *Pacem in Terris* (April 11, 1963), a papal encyclical like no other because it was addressed not only or even primarily to Catholics but to the whole world. Grounding his argument on the dignity of the human person, John caused an uproar when he declared unequivocally, without any apologies to past papal pronouncements: "Also among man's rights is that of being able to worship God in accordance with the right dictates of his own conscience, and to profess his religion both in private and in public" (16).

The Vatican II document *Dignitatis Humanae* (1965), the Declaration on Religious Freedom, served to lay out in detail what John XXII announced in general. Some have claimed that this was the most fought-over declaration of the entire council. The American Jesuit JOHN COURTNEY MURRAY played a key role in the writing of the document. Together with *Lumen Genitium*, the Dogmatic Constitution on the Church in the Modern World, (1964), certain church-state principles emerged into the clear at Vatican II: 1) a key role for the church is to uphold human dignity; 2) even though Catholics believe their faith is the true faith, every person in the world has a right to religious freedom, and there can be no coercion to faith whatsoever; 3) the church is not identified with any political community, or party and its freedom vis-à-vis the state is a fundamental principle; 4) the state has a duty to the whole of society, and all are to serve the common good; and 5) the church favors limited, constitutional democratic government.

JOHN PAUL II built upon Vatican II, declaring in *Centesimus Annus* 47 (May 1, 1991) that, though there are many rights important to human dignity, "the source and synthesis of these rights is religious freedom, understood as the right to live in the truth of one's faith and in conformity with one's transcendent dignity as a person." This passage explicitly refers to *Dignitatis Humanae*.

Having lived under an oppressive totalitarian regime, John Paul II, unlike his 19th- and early 20th-century predecessors, was unequivocal and unwavering in his support of democracy.

Further reading: Herminio Rico, *John Paul II and the Legacy of Dignitatis Humanae* (Washington, D.C.: Georgetown University Press, 2002); John T. S. Madeley and Zsolt Enyedi, *Church and State in Contemporary Europe: The Chimera of Neutrality* (London: Frank Cass, 2003); John Courtney Murray, *We Hold These Truths: Catholic Reflections on the American Proposition* (New York: Sheed & Ward, 1960); Brian Tierney, *Church Law and Constitutional Thought in the Middle Ages* (London: Variorum Reprints, 1979).

church orders

In the early Christian church, "orders" were manuals of instruction for governing the church. They prescribed the functions of ministers and the proper rites for the administration of the SACRAMENTS. Early CHRISTIAN church orders contain a variety of other items including instructions on prayer, rules on training catechumens, and canons of Scripture.

PAUL's directions on immoral behavior, lawsuits, marriage, food offered to idols, the Lord's Supper, and spiritual gifts may be considered an early form of church order. The *Haustafeln* (tables for house governance) in Colossians 3:18–4:1, Ephesians 5:22–6:9, and 1 Peter 2:18–3:6, which have prototypes in Stoic ethical writings, are in the category of church orders. The *Rule of the Community* at Qumran has many affinities with later Christian manuals of order.

The first known systematic church order is the *DIDACHE,* or Teaching of the Twelve Apostles, variously dated from 60 to 110, of either Syrian or Egyptian provenance. Chapters 1 to 6 describe the Two Ways between life and death. They are based on Jewish models of instruction and show close affinities with the Qumran rule. This section may well have been originally a Jewish manual, as the

Latin version in *Doctrina Apostolorum* lacks the Christian interpolation (1.3–2.1), a collection of sayings very similar to Matthew and Luke's commandments to love one's neighbor. This moral preamble introduces the catechetical instruction on BAPTISM, fasting, prayer, and the EUCHARIST in chapters 7 to 10. Chapters 11 to 15 provide instructions for how to treat traveling apostles, prophets, and teachers, the necessity of reconciliation before the Eucharist, and the election of BISHOPS and deacons. Chapter 16 contains a short APOCALYPSE concerning the signs of the end time on the pattern of Matthew 24. There are many parallels to the *Didache* in the *Shepherd of Hermas* and the *Epistle of Barnabas*, two early second century writings.

The *Didache* marks Christianity between its birth in a Jewish matrix and its emergence as a separate religious stream. Much of it is reincorporated into the *Apostolic Constitutions,* a late fourth-century semi-Arian or Apollinarian treatise, which covers church ordinances in 16 chapters on the Two Ways (1–6), including variants on the Sermon on the Mount/Plain in Matthew's and Luke's GOSPEL; liturgical instructions on baptism, prayer, fasting, and the Eucharist; instructions on traveling apostles, prophets and teachers, bishops and deacons (11–15); and an apocalypse (16). Besides the *Didache,* the *Apostolic Constitutions* apparently relies on the *Didascalia Apostolorum,* an early third-century combination of church order and pastoral admonition directed to bishops, and on the *Apostolic Tradition* of HIPPOLYTUS OF ROME (d. c. 236). The last is a compilation dealing with ordination ceremonies and the Antiochene/Clementine liturgy (3–27) and prescriptions for Christian life (28–46).

Today most of the elements contained in older church orders can be found interspersed in the *Code of Canon Law* (1983), the *Roman Ritual* (1990), and the *Catechism of the Catholic Church* (1994). Some Protestant denominations, notably the Presbyterians, still publish "books of church order."

Further reading: J. V. Bartlet, *Church-Life and Church-Order During the First Four Centuries* (Oxford: Black-well, 1943); C. N. Jefford, ed., *The Didache in Context: Essays on Its Text, History and Transmission* (Leiden: Brill, 1994).

circumcision (Lat.: *circum,* "around" + *cidere,* "to cut")

This is the ritual of cutting off the foreskin of the penis as a sign of tribal membership and of a relationship with GOD. Egyptian priests and many Semitic peoples practiced circumcision from time immemorial.

In Israelite religion circumcision was a sign of the Covenant between God and the descendants of Abraham (Gen. 17:10–14). It was obligatory that every male child be circumcised on the eighth day after birth (Lev. 12:3) as a sign of the Covenant and as a mark of separation from other nations (Judg. 14:3). Both the Torah and the prophets use the metaphor of circumcision of other parts of the body as a sign of consecration to God and separation from SIN: the heart (Deut. 10:16; Jer. 4:4), the lips (Exod. 6:30), and the ears (Jer. 6:10). The New Testament continues this metaphoric usage (Rom. 2:29). PAUL, however, says that imposing physical circumcision on Gentiles is turning back God's plan of salvation (Gal. 5:2–12; Rom. 2:25–29). Nonetheless, Paul circumcised Timothy, who was a Jew by virtue of birth from a Jewish mother (Acts 16:3).

Jewish CHRISTIAN groups like the Ebionites continued physical circumcision (Irenaeus *Heresies* 1.26.2). Gentile Christians amplified the metaphoric use to signify spiritual purity before God, the Passion of Christ (*Epistle to Barnabas* 9), cutting off EVIL, and moral reform (Chrysostom, *Homily on Romans* 6.2; Ambrose, *Letters* 72). The HOLY SPIRIT was believed to be the agent of spiritual circumcision that was associated with BAPTISM (Col. 2:11–12; Cyril of Jerusalem, *Catecheses* 5.6; Augustine, *Letters* 187.11.34).

Further reading: Jean Daniélou, "Circoncision et baptême," in Johannes Auer, ed., *Theologie in Geschichte und Gegenwart* (Munich: Zink, 1957) 755–776; Everett

Ferguson, "Spiritual Circumcision in Early Christianity" *Scottish Journal of Theology* (1988) 41:485–497; Leonard B. Glick, *Marked in Your Flesh: Circumcision from Ancient Judea to Modern America* (Oxford: Oxford University Press, 2005).

Cistercians (Lat.: Cistercium, Latin name of Cîteaux)

The strict Cistercian Order of MONKS and NUNS was founded as a reformed Benedictine group by Sts. Robert of Molesme, Alberic, and Stephen Harding. They were originally known as "white monks" because they wore white robes with a black SCAPULAR. The motherhouse was in Cîteaux, France, from whence monasteries were established throughout France and Europe.

The Cistercian rule, based on the rule of BENEDICT OF NURSIA, is called Carta Caritatis ("Charter of Love") and was approved by Pope Calixtus II (c. 1119–24) in 1119. The order of nuns, called the Bernadines, began at the end of the 12th century in Flanders to perform works of charity.

The most celebrated early Cistercian was St. BERNARD OF CLAIRVAUX; the most famous in modern times was THOMAS MERTON. By 1400 the order had 740 monasteries in Europe. Tinturn Abbey, celebrated by William Wordsworth, was a Cistercian foundation before being dissolved by HENRY VIII in 1536. The Cistercian Abbey of Fontenay in France has been restored. The famous convent of Port-Royal, associated with JANSENISM, was a Cistercian nunnery.

The Cistercians embraced an austere and simple communal discipline, long hours in reciting the Divine Office, or PRAYER OF THE HOURS sustained periods of fasting or vegetarianism, silence (though, contrary to popular belief, they do not take a vow of silence), intense work, and study of sacred writings. Their churches were very plain in style, in contrast to the ornateness of the Gothic cathedrals then arising in Europe. Bernard criticized Abbot SUGER over the decoration of the CATHEDRAL St. Denis above Paris. Cistercian monasteries were often founded in remote places; the monks often turned uninhabitable land into productive farms. Monasteries were often places of technological and agricultural innovation. The wool industry in England received its jump-start from Cistercian husbandry methods.

Through its long history, the order has oscillated between strict observance and common observance rules. In 1666 the former French court cleric Armand-Jean Le Bouthillier de Rancé (1626–1700) led a reform based at the monastery of La Trappe in France. This monastery lent the name "Trappist" to the reformed strict observance group. Today there are 180 Trappistine monasteries for monks and nuns throughout the world. The French Revolution decimated all branches of the order.

The common observance group is now called simply the Order of Cistercians (OCist), and the strict group is called the Order of Cistercians, Strict Observance (OCSO). The former do both educational and parochial work. The OSCO today counts about 170 abbeys with about 2,500 monks and 1,800 nuns, while the OCist has about 30 abbeys with 800 monks and about 100 convents with some 3,000 nuns. There is also a small group of middle observance. The families of Cistercians today are in close cooperation.

Further reading: Many Cistercian texts are available online; Constance H. Berman, *The Cistercian Evolution: The Invention of a Religious Order in Twelfth-Century Europe* (Philadelphia: University of Pennsylvania Press, 2000); Chrysogonus Waddell, *Narrative and Legislative Tests from Early Cîteaux* (Nuit St. Georges: Abbaye de Cîteaux, 1999); Esther de Wahl, *The Way of Simplicity: The Cistercian Tradition* (Maryknoll, N.Y.: Orbis Books, 1999).

Clare of Assisi, St. (1192–1253) *founder of order of Poor Clare Franciscan nuns*

Clare was the cofounder with St. FRANCIS OF ASSISI of the Franciscan Second Order, the Poor Clares. She was canonized in 1255 and has most recently been designated the patroness of television. Her feast day is August 11.

Clare was the daughter of Count Favorino Scifi of Sasso-Rosso and Ortolana of Fiumi. After she heard Francis of Assisi preaching about Lady Poverty in the chapel of San Giorgio, she abandoned all thoughts of a noble marriage. After mass on Palm Sunday she fled to the Portiuncula chapel where, under the light of candles held by the brothers, she dedicated her life to Jesus the poor one and the way of Francis. Her father pursued, but Francis hid her in a Benedictine monastery on the slopes of Mt. Subiaco until he found a permanent home for her at the church of San Damiano outside the walls of Assisi. Soon her sisters Agnes and Beatrice, her aunt Bianca, and then her mother followed her.

Wherever the friars went, the Poor Clares were soon to follow. Houses spread throughout Europe. While Francis was in Egypt and the Holy Land, Cardinal Ugolino di Segni, protector of the Franciscans, got Honorius III (1216–27) to impose a rule on the Second Order in the bull *Sacrosancta* (December 9, 1219) that, in effect, turned it into a Benedictine order. While some friars under the influence of Brother Elias (c. 1180–1253), were seeking to modify the rule on absolute poverty, Clare held fast. Later Ugolino, now Pope Gregory IX (r. 1227–41), relented in his *Privilegium Paupertatis* (September 17, 1228), and to this day the Poor Clares follow the original ideal of Francis and Clare.

The Poor Clares still live a cloistered life of almost complete silence. The question of the nature of the poverty of Jesus and of the Franciscans has continued to be much debated and fought over by the Poor Clares (and other Franciscans) throughout history, causing divisions. St. Collete of Picardy in France (1381–1447) led a reform back to the original ideal of absolute poverty, bare feet, perpetual fasting, and abstinence except for the feast of Christmas.

Two notable miracles are attributed to St Clare. When hostile soldiers of FREDERICK II were about to attack Assisi, she held the sacred host in a monstrance at the window of the convent, and the soldiers were repelled. In art she is most often depicted holding a monstrance with the host. When she was old and infirm and could no longer attend the EUCHARIST, a moving image of the service would appear on the wall of her cell. In commemoration, PIUS XII named her patroness of television in 1958.

In 1801 there was an attempt to found a monastery in the United States by Poor Clares fleeing the French Revolution, but they eventually returned to Europe. Srs. Maria Maddelena and Maria Costanza Bentivoglio, from the celebrated monastery of San Lorenzo-in-Panisperma in Rome, came to America in 1875 and established monasteries in Omaha, New Orleans, and Evansville. Today there are some 20,000 Poor Clares living in monasteries in 76 countries.

Further reading: Marco Bartoli, *Chiara d'Assisi* (Rome: Istituto Storico Cappucini, 1989); René-Charles Dhont, *Clare Among Her Sisters* (St. Bonaventure: Franciscan Institute, 1987); Marianus Feige, *The Princess of Poverty: Saint Claire of Assisi and the Order of Poor Ladies* (Evansville, Ind.: Poor Clares, 1900).

Clement of Alexandria (c. 160–215)
theologian

Clement sought to reconcile Christianity and philosophy and even saw CHRISTIAN doctrine and practice as a kind of philosophy. He was noted for his Logos Christology and for teaching what he took to be true Christian gnosis in opposition to the GNOSTICS.

He was born Titus Flavius Clemens Alexandrinus. Describing himself as a seeker of truth, Clement traveled to Italy and Palestine in search of instruction before settling in Alexandria, where legends tells he founded a catechetical school that ORIGEN later took over. Just as Sirach (late second century B.C.E.) and Philo (20 B.C.E.–40 C.E.) taught Jewish wisdom as true philosophy, so Clement wanted to present Christianity.

Clement wrote what many take to be a kind of trilogy: 1) *Exhortation* (*Protreptikos*), an appeal to students, modeled on Greek prototypes, to convert to the true philosophy of the Logos incarnate in CHRIST; 2) *Tutor* (*Paidogogos*), the education of the children of GOD by the Logos through love; and 3) *Carpets* (*Stromata*), a miscellaneous collection of clues for one seeking a deeper gnosis, grounded in moral perfection and love of God. There are also a number of fragmentary and lost works. A very popular short work is *Who Is the Rich Man Who Shall Be Saved?* His answer is each of us.

According to Clement, God acts lovingly toward humans through the Logos. The Father became female to generate the Logos, who acts as the breasts of God, nourishing humans with the milk of true education (*paideia*). Unlike the teachers of GNOSTICISM, Clement saw no ranks among believers. The Logos, somewhat like the Platonic Demiurge, shaped the cosmos and brought it into harmony with God. True Gnostics are those who are initiated into the secret teachings of the Logos, Christ, transmitted through the APOSTLES.

Clement may have educated ORIGEN and DIONYSIUS, the Pseudo-Areopagite thereby having a direct influence on medieval mysticism. Michael Servetus (c. 1511–31), physician and anti-Trinitarian Calvinist heretic, claimed that Clement's Logos was the supreme angel and not coequal with God. Methodist founder John Wesley (1703–91) derived much of his theology of Christian perfection from Clement's theory of the moral perfection of the true Gnostic.

Further reading: G. W. Butterworth, *Clement of Alexandria* (London: William Heinemann, 1953); Henry Chadwick, *Early Christian Thought and the Christian Tradition* (Oxford: Clarendon, 1966); E. F. Osborn, *The Philosophy of Clement of Alexandria* (Cambridge: Cambridge University Press, 1957); Johannes Quasten, *Patrology. I. The Beginning of the Patristic Age* (Utrecht: Spectrum, 1949).

Clement of Rome, St. (d. c. 97) *early bishop of Rome*

According to IRENAEUS, Clement was bishop of Rome (c. 88–c. 97), succeeding Linus and Anacletus. He wrote an important first-century letter to the church in Corinth. A second letter in his name is really a sermon and probably not by Clement. Some believe that his home became the titular church of San Clemente, one of the most adorned in Rome. His feast day is November 23, and his name was included in the Roman canon of the Mass.

The letter, called *1 Clement,* is addressed from the pilgrim church in Rome to the pilgrim church in Corinth and takes up the problem of SCHISM. The council fathers at VATICAN COUNCIL II revived its metaphor of the church as a pilgrim. Some scholars, pointing to the "dire straits" mentioned in 1.1., date the letter to the persecution under Domitian (r. 81–96). The writer is familiar with the LXX version of the Old Testament and with many (but not all) New Testament books, thus perhaps indicating what first-century CHRISTIANS believed to be Scripture. It quotes the synoptics Gospels, and perhaps John, Acts, 1 Corinthians, Romans, Galatians, Ephesians, Philippians, 1 Timothy, Titus, Hebrews, and 1 Peter, as well as three wisdom-type citations from unknown scripture(s).

Among other interesting features, the epistle testifies to a hierarchizing distinction between laity and clergy, called variously BISHOPS, priests, and deacons but not ranked among themselves; an appeal to APOSTOLIC SUCCESSION for legitimacy (44.1–3); and an exhortation to the Christian virtues of penance, hospitality, piety, and humbleness in order to overcome the factionalism at Corinth. In an interesting blend of biblical theology and Stoic philosophy, Clement refers to the Creator of the universe as the one who instilled harmony into the motions of nature and who wants his creatures to live accordingly. Clement makes the famous analogy between the death and RESURRECTION OF CHRIST and the mythical phoenix bird that rises from its own dead flesh (25).

The second letter under Clement's name is really a sermon addressed to the Gentile church that Jesus Christ called into being and that he asked to live virtuously and with mercy. It likely dates from the early second century, with a Roman provenance.

Further reading: Harold Bertram Bumpus, *The Christological Awareness of Clement of Rome and Its Sources* (Cambridge: Cambridge University Press, 1972); Johannes Quasten, *Patrology. I. The Beginning of the Patristic Age* (Utrecht: Spectrum, 1949); Robert M. Grant and H. H. Graham, *First and Second Clement* (New York: Nelson, 1965); Donald Alfred Hagner, *The Use of the Old and New Testaments in Clement of Rome* (Leiden: Brill, 1997).

clergy (Old Fr.: *clerc*, "member of the clergy," "clerk" from Gr.: *klēros*, "lot," "allotment")

The clergy, as distinguished from the laity, are those who hold office and exercise a permanent ministry in the church. The LXX, the pre-CHRISTIAN Greek translation of the Hebrew Bible, uses *klēros* to mean both the lots cast by a victor over spoils and the allotment granted by GOD as a sign of favor. The apostolic writers of the second century use the term to signify the blessed lot bestowed by God at the end of time (Ignatius, *Ephesians* 11.2; Polycarp, *Epistle* 12.2).

The first person to use the term in the present technical sense was Clement of Alexandria (*Who is the Rich Man?* 42); Clement of Rome was the first to use "laic" (*1 Clement* 40). TERTULLIAN, ORIGEN, and Cyprian all applied the cleric-lay distinction. JEROME compared the clergy to the Levites, who owned no land because the Lord was their "lot" (*Letters* 52.5). AUGUSTINE suggests that the term refers to the election of Matthias to the college of APOSTLES in Acts 1:26 (*Psalms* 67.19).

By the middle of the second century the category of clergy included BISHOPS, presbyters (PRIESTS), and deacons. Presbyter-bishops were always distinct from deacons and deaconesses, but only in time were they clearly distinguished from one another. PAUL refers to Phoebe as *diakonos* in Romans 16:1, but in New Testament times the term probably meant something more like an intermediary, agent, or courier, whether of God or humans, in a wider sense than a cultic minister. A council of presbyters often advised a bishop and could act in his place. In time the ranks of clergy became called orders, in imitation of Roman social ranks. Tertullian gives evidence of a "clerical order" (*Idolatry* 7; *Prescription* 41). In the Eastern Church an order of deaconesses emerged in the early third century. They were drawn from among widows and virgins and had many of the functions of deacons.

Toward the end of the second century some of the duties of the deacon began to be relegated to "lower clergy," who received what were called minor orders in the MIDDLE AGES but not HOLY ORDERS in the technical sense. These came to include the functions of porter, acolyte, lector or reader, exorcist, and subdeacon. Isadore of Seville adds the office of psalmist to this list (*Etymologies* 7.12.3).

In early Christianity clergy attained their rank by various means. Augustine was elected bishop of Hippo by acclamation as he was passing through the city. Other clerics were appointed by a council of presbyters or directly by a bishop. Today only a local ordinary bishop can determine who will become a deacon or priest, and only the pope can appoint a bishop. In some instances a consultative body is appointed to recommend candidates for an episcopal post.

Over time a body of canon law developed to regulate the clerical orders. One of the first was to deny ordination to a twice-married man (1 Timothy 3:2). Slaves and serfs were excluded from orders. Self-made eunuchs and neophytes were excluded at the Council of Nicaea (cnn. 1–2), which also barred unrelated women from living with a cleric (cn 3). Clerics were also prohibited from moving from diocese to diocese without official sanction. The Council of CHALCEDON barred clerics from certain professions such as moneylenders, civil officers, and executioners; similar laws were passed in the Middle Ages. In that era, many of the disputes between popes and princes concerned who would control clerics. The most noted examples were the disputes between GREGORY VII and Emperor Henry IV (c. 1084–1105), and between BONIFACE VIII and Philip IV (r. 1285–1314) the Fair of France, against whom Boniface issued the notorious PAPAL BULL *Clericos Laicos* (February 25, 1296). Abuses by both civil authorities and clergy themselves contributed to waves of ANTICLERICALISM in Christian history.

Today clergy are subject to canonical requirements, including praying the PRAYER OF THE HOURS, obedience to their bishops, an annual retreat, and CELIBACY (except in the case of married deacons or deacons and priests in the Eastern Rites), and married Protestant ministers received into the priesthood. Permanent deacons do not have to follow most of the rules of celibate clergy but are prohibited from holding civil offices along with all clerics.

Since VATICAN COUNCIL II Catholics have returned to the simple major orders of the early church (bishop, priest, deacon), and the functions formerly performed by those in "minor orders" have been taken over by the laity. Rules governing the clerical rank are contained in the *Code of Canon Law* cnn. 232–93.

See also HIERARCHY.

Further reading: Hans von Campenhausen, *Ecclesiastical Authority and Spiritual Power in the Church of the First Three Centuries* (Stanford, Calif.: Stanford University Press, 1969); *Christus Dominus:* Decree on the Bishops' Pastoral Office in the Church, in Walter Abbott, ed., *The Documents of Vatican II* (New York: America Press, 1966) 396–423. *Presbyterium Ordinis:* Decree on the Ministry and Life of Priest in Walter Abbott, ed., *The Documents of Vatican II* (New York: America Press, 1966) 532–576.

cloister (Lat.: *claustrum,* "enclosed space")
The term means both the enclosed space reserved to members of a religious order and the canon

law pertaining to cloistered life. Religious orders of men and women are obliged to have cloistered areas in their monasteries and convents, generally their living and eating quarters, forbidden to members of the opposite sex. In exceptional circumstances the local ordinary or BISHOP and male medical personnel are allowed to enter a female cloister. Religious orders dedicated to the contemplative life, such as the Trappists and Poor Clares, fall under a special papally mandated form of cloister. The laws pertaining to cloister are in canon 667 of the *Code of Canon Law* (1983). Cloister became much less stringent after VATICAN COUNCIL II.

Further reading: Scholastica Crilly, "The Cloistered Model of Monastic Life," *Cistercian Studies Quarterly* (1997) 32: 345–361; Robert W. Crooker, *The Discipline of Enclosure in Clerical Congregations and Societies* (Toronto: Basilian, 1963); Mary Jo Weaver, *Cloister and Community: Life within a Carmelite Monastery* (Bloomington: Indiana University Press, 2002).

coadjutor bishop   *See* BISHOP.

Code of Canon Law   *See* CANON LAW.

codex (Lat.: *caudex,* "tree trunk; writing board, tablet")
This term has two basic meanings, a physical book and a collection of laws. In the first sense, a codex is a book composed of individual sheets, originally parchment, bound at the spine, in contrast to a continuous roll or scroll divided into running columns. The Latin word *caudex* originally referred to sheaves of waxed wooden tablets used for business transactions, household information, and literary drafts. The term was transferred to bound manuscripts. The New Testament epistle 2 Timothy 4:13 refers to *membrana,* a Latin loan word related to our word *membrane,*

to refer to a parchment notebook. Such a codex appears in a third-century catacomb fresco. In the Orthodox BAPTISTERY at Ravenna, dating from the fourth century, there is a mosaic depiction of four codices, standing for the four GOSPELS.

CHRISTIANS took the lead in spreading the parchment codex. Greeks, Romans, and Egyptians commonly used a papyrus roll. Jews produced mostly parchment scrolls composed of continuous columns of text. The Torah scrolls in Jewish synagogues today continue this practice. The earliest Christian codices contained one or two books. By the third century we find codices of PAUL's epistles.

There are three famous codices relevant to the BIBLE. *Codex Vaticanus* is an early fourth-century uncial (Greco-Roman capital script) codex originally containing the entire Bible with the exception of the Prayer of Manasseh and the books of the Maccabees. It has been much mutilated over time and now lacks about 60 of its original approximately 820 pages. It was listed in a catalogue of the Vatican Library in 1475; it is not known when it was acquired.

Codex Sinaiticus is a fourth-century copy of parts of the LXX (Greek Old Testament) and all 27 books of the New Testament, plus the Epistle of Barnabas and parts of the Shepherd of Hermas, which the compilers obviously considered scriptural. Everything before Ezra 9.9 is absent. The distinguished 19th-century biblical textual critic Constantin von Tischendorf (1815–74) discovered the codex at St. Catherine's Monastery at the foot of the traditional Mt. Sinai. He "borrowed" the manuscript from a monk in 1859, took it to Leipzig, and eventually presented it to the Czar. It remained in St. Petersburg until the British Museum purchased it from the Soviet Communists in 1933 for £100,000. There may be additional ancient codices in the monastery unknown to outside scholars, but the monks for years distrusted researchers. The library catalogue is now being put online.

Codex Alexandrinus is an early fifth-century codex presented by the British ambassador to Tur-

key by the patriarch Cyril I Lucaris (1572–1637) of CONSTANTINOPLE in 1624 as a gift to James I (1566–1625). It went into the Royal Library and thence to the British Museum in 1757. The original contained the entire Greek Bible plus 1 and 2 Clement and the Psalms of Solomon.

See also BIBLE.

Further reading: H. Y. Gamble, *Books and Readers in the Early Church: A History of Early Christian Texts* (New Haven, Conn.: Yale University Press, 1995); Scot McKenrick and Oralaith A. O'Sullivan, eds., *The Bible as a Book: The Transmission of the Greek Text* (New Castle Del.: Oak Knoll, 2003).

colors in liturgy

Since the 12th century certain colors have been associated with the seasons of the LITURGICAL YEAR. The Augustinian Canons in Jerusalem seem to be the first to have used these colors, which INNOCENT III mentions in his *Sacred Mystery of the Altar* (1204). The colors currently approved in the Roman Ritual are 1) white, 2) red, 3) green, 4) purple, and 5) black. Rose and gold can be used in special circumstances.

White is used from EASTER to the Feast of the ASCENSION. It is also used for the feasts of virgins and confessors. Since 1970 the funeral EUCHARIST is celebrated in white to signify hope for the RESURRECTION, replacing black, a sign of mourning. White also symbolizes creation, light, joy, resurrection, innocence, and perfection.

Purple or violet is used during Advent and Lent, symbolizing penitence, fasting, humility, suffering, and sympathy. On Gaudete Sunday in Advent and Laetare Sunday in Lent, rose, a sign of anticipatory joy, may be used in place of purple. (Both *gaudere* and *laetare* mean "to rejoice" in Latin; the words begin the opening song, or introit, on the respective feast days.) Purple is associated with Jesus' 40 days in the desert (Matt. 4:1–11) and with the purple garments Jesus wore when mocked (Mark 15:17).

Red is used on Pentecost, the feasts of the APOSTLES, excepting St. John the Evangelist, and, since 1970, for Good Friday (which used to be black) and Palm Sunday (which used to be purple). Green, the most common color, is used between EPIPHANY and Lent, and between Trinity Sunday and Advent. Green symbolizes hope and the growth of nature and the church. For major feast days gold or the most ornamented vestments may be used.

The colors are used for the chasuable, stole, chalice cover, veil, burse, and altar hangings (*see* UTENSILS, SACRED; VESTMENTS). The Eastern Churches have no fixed rules or traditions relating to liturgical colors, though there is a tendency to use restrained colors in penitential seasons. Protestants tended to keep the liturgical colors as developed in the Roman tradition, though many abandoned the practice as alien to the BIBLE. In the 20th century, with the development of the ecumenical movement, the use of liturgical colors (and the liturgical calendar) have experienced a marked revival among Anglicans, Methodist, and others (*see* ECUMENISM).

Further reading: Joseph Braun, *Die Liturgische Gewandung im Occident und Orient nach Ursprung und Entwicklung, Verwendung und Symbolik* (Darmstadt: Wissenschaftliche Gesellschaft, 1964); Clapton C. Rolfe, *The Ancient Use of Liturgical Colours* (Oxford: Parker, 1879); *The Rites of the Catholic Church* (New York: Pueblo, 1990).

Columba, St. (c. 521–597) *Irish missionary and monastic founder*

Columba founded the celebrated MONASTERY on the Scottish island of Iona, from where Christianity returned to Britain. His feast day is June 9.

St. Columba was born in Ireland of royal descent. Ordained at the age of 25, he spent the next 15 years building churches and monasteries all around Ireland. At the age of 42 he led 12 companions to Iona, where he lived the rest of his life, founding monasteries on neighboring islands and on the mainland. He succeeded in converting the king of the Picts. Celtic MONASTICISM was notably different in that monasteries often included both sexes and lay people living in close contact.

Further reading: Maire Herbert, *Iona, Kells, and Derry: The History and Hagiography of the Monastic Familia of Columba* (Dublin: Four Courts, 1996); Lucy Menzies, *Saint Columba of Iona; A Study of His Life, His Times, & His Influence* (New York: E. P. Dutton, 1920); William Douglas Simpson, *The Historical Saint Columba* (Edinburgh: Oliver & Boyd, 1963).

Columbus, Christopher (1451–1506) *explorer credited as discoverer of the New World*

Columbus is celebrated for discovering the New World on his first voyage across the Atlantic in 1492 under the sponsorhip of FERDINAND OF ARAGON AND ISABELLA OF CASTILE of Spain. Although his goal was to open a new trade route to the Far East, he never made it to South Asia; instead he spent the remainder of his career exploring the islands of the Caribbean. It is generally accepted that he was Genovese, although his nationality is still debated today. Some think he had Jewish ancestors; other claim he was a former Catalan pirate.

The purpose of his voyages was twofold: to open new trade routes to the Far East and to spread the Word of Jesus Christ. His signature read "Christ Bearer." On his first voyage in 1492 he did not conquer or kill any of the natives he encountered, believing he could convert them to Christianity through love. During his later voyages he captured hundreds of natives. He tried to convince Spanish royalty to use slavery for economic gain, but Isabella refused to condone slavery.

Columbus became more religious in his later years, frequently donning the Franciscan habit. He claimed to hear divine voices and pushed for another CRUSADE to capture Jerusalem. He became convinced that his explorations were part of God's eschatological plan that would soon bring the Last Judgment and the end of the world. To this day, most tend to view Columbus as either a hero or a villain: either he brought Christianity and the GOSPEL to the New World, or he destroyed the indigenous peoples and opened up the New World for European domination.

Further reading: Kay Bringam, *Christopher Columbus: His Life and Discovery in the Light of His Prophecies* (Barcelona: Editorial Clie, 1990); Christopher Columbus, *Christopher Columbus's Book of Prophecies* (Barcelona: Editorial Clie, 1991); George Grant, *The Last Crusade: The Untold Story of Christopher Columbus* (Wheaton, Ill.: Crossway, 1992).

commandments of the church

The ecclesiastical and moral precepts enjoined on all Catholics by church decree are together called the commandments of the church. One fulfills these commandments through external performance, whatever one's intention.

The only commands mentioned in the New Testament are the TEN COMMANDMENTS and the two great commandments: to love God and to love one's neighbor (Mark 12:29–31). Other commands began to be appear in the post-CONSTANTINE era; they became formalized during the MIDDLE AGES. In the late 16th century, Sts. Peter Canisius (1521–97) and ROBERT BELLARMINE were among the first to provide lists of commandments.

The number of commandments has never been formally fixed, but they usually include attendance at mass on Sunday and holy days, periodic reception of PENANCE and the EUCHARIST, fasting during certain periods and on certain days, and not contracting marriage during penitential times (Advent, Lent, and rogation days; *see* LITURGICAL YEAR).

The Council of TRENT did not issue a commandment list. The third plenary session of the Council of Baltimore (*see* BALTIMORE CATECHISM)

in 1886 included six: 1) keeping holy Sunday and holy days; 2) keeping appointed fast days; 3) penance at least once a year; 4) Communion at least once a year; 5) support of the pastor; and 6) no marriage of kindred to the third degree or during forbidden times. The only commandment among the biblical 10 that corresponds to the church commandments is the third, on "keeping holy the Sabbath."

In the post–VATICAN COUNCIL II period the commandments have been called "precepts of the Church." The *Catechism of the Catholic Church* (1994) gives them a theological foundation, puts them into a positive, pastoral light, and limits them to five: 1) Mass on Sundays and holy days commemorating the RESURRECTION; 2) confession of sins once a year to continue the work of BAPTISM unto conversion and forgiveness; 3) Holy Communion once during EASTER, the origin and center of Christian liturgy; 4) keeping of holy days, which complete the Sunday observance; and 5) fasting and abstinence that prepare the faithful for liturgical feasts and help them gain mastery over their instincts and freedom of heart (2041–43). Support of the church is listed as a duty but not a commandment.

Further reading: Antoine Villien, *A History of the Commandments of the Church* (St. Louis: Herder, 1915); *Catechism of the Catholic Church* (Liguori: Liguori, 1994).

communicatio idiomatum (Lat.: "interchange of properties"; Gk.: *antidosis tōn idiōmatōn*)

According to the principle of *communicatio idiomatum*, the properties, attributes, and actions of the divine in CHRIST can be attributed to the human, and vice versa, because both natures are united in one person, Jesus Christ, called the hypostatic union. The principle represents perhaps the last phase in the historical development of the classical theology of the INCARNATION, and thus of REDEMPTION. The interchange of properties is an attempt to explain how GOD can be born of Mary (Theotokos) and how God could die on the cross.

The teaching finds its origin in the Johannine assertion "the Word (Logos) became flesh" (John 1:14). The unfolding of this seemingly simple statement into an elaborate CHRISTOLOGY (*see* CHRIST/CHRISTOLOGY) is both dramatic and intricate. In the second century the teaching appears in the Old Roman Creed: the "Son was born / begotten of the holy Spirit and Mary the virgin." During the next two centuries theologians—now tending toward the ALEXANDRINE SCHOOL, now tending toward the ANTIOCHENE SCHOOL—fought over Jesus' divinity, and then over his humanity: The Council of Nicaea debated the question, "Was he equal to God (Father)?" while the Councils of EPHESUS and CHALCEDON asked, "Was he human?" and "Was he fully human?"

Chalcedon followed the imprecise formula of CYRIL OF ALEXANDRIA's *Second Letter to Nestorius:* there is a concurrence (*syndromē*) and union (*'enosis*) of the two natures in one nature. In his *Tome* LEO I stated that the Christ was born "true God, in the entire and perfect nature of true man, complete in his own properties and complete in ours," and that each nature "does the acts which belong to it, in communion with the other." The Chalcedon formula is expressed in a chain of negatives: "one and the same Christ, Lord, Only-begotten, recognized in two natures not confused, not changed, not divided, not separated." None of these formulas explain how the two natures actually interact except in the vaguest terms. In subsequent centuries theologians balanced these negatives with the positive idea of the *communicatio idiomatum,* or interchange of properties.

The medieval theologians advanced this discussion by stating that the communication is between concrete entities, divine and human, such that one can say that in *this* person, Jesus Christ, "God is human, and the human is God" (Bonaventure, *Sentences* 3.6.1.1; THOMAS AQUINAS, *Summa Theologiae* 3.16.5). The medievals, however, framed the doctrine in terms of the distinc-

tion between the absolute and ordained power of God. They began to ask from the viewpoint of God's absolute power: can God become incarnate in a stone (Aquinas, DUNS SCOTUS) or an ass? (Ockham). Thus, the discussion ended tangled up in a nominalistic propositional calculus.

The PROTESTANT REFORMATION took even further steps and applied the *communicatio idiomatum* to the theory of the EUCHARIST. When asked how the body of Christ can be in the Eucharist after the ASCENSION, Luther answered with the theory of ubiquitism, that is, the body of Christ is everywhere because God is omnipresent (*Confession on the Lord's Supper,* 1528). Lutheran theologians then developed a very complicated but biblically annotated theology of the *communcatio idiomatum.* Zwingli, however, stuck to the literal meaning of the Ascension texts (Acts 1:9–1) and stated that Christ is really at the right hand of the Father and could only be figuratively present in the sacrament and that there could only be a rhetorical exchange (*allaiosis*) of properties grounded in faith.

In 1699 Innocent XII condemned the proposition, found in FRANÇOIS FÉNELON's *Maxims of the Saints on the Interior Life* (1697), that "the lower part (nature) of Christ did not communicate to the higher its involuntary perturbences" (*Cum Aliis,* March 12, 1699). That is, in Innocent's view, God can indeed get "all shook up." In brief, the communication or exchange between the divine and human in Christ is complete in all aspects.

The *communicatio idiomatum* principle has at times become so tangled in theological niceties that its larger purpose became lost. The interchange is meant to express the full completion of humanity and the full communication of God's grace for the redemption of all humankind.

Further reading: Heiko Obermann, *Harvest of Medieval Theology* (Cambridge, Mass.: Harvard University Press, 1958); Reinhold Seeberg, *History of Doctrines,* 2 vols. (Grand Rapids, Mich.: Baker, 1964).

communion/communion of saints
(Lat.: *cum* + *unio,* "state of being united together"; Gr.: *koinonia*)

The word *communion* has two related senses: 1) the united community of the faithful, or of the saints, or of the church as a body of believers, and 2) the reception of the body and blood of CHRIST in Holy Communion during a Eucharistic rite or outside the rite. This entry is devoted to the first sense of the word (*see* EUCHARIST for the second meaning).

The early church saw itself as a *koinonia,* that is, communion or fellowship with the Son of GOD (1 Cor. 1:9), the HOLY SPIRIT, (2 Cor. 13:13), and one another (Acts 2:42), especially in help to the poor (Rom. 15:26). This powerful Greek word was translated by a host of Latin terms with English cognates: *communio, participatio,* or *communicatio.* Communion united the individual both vertically with God and horizontally with his or her neighbor in a fellowship with Christ. When people were on the outs with fellowship, they suffered *ex-communicatio,* disfellowshiping (1 Cor. 5).

A number of other terms and phrases used by early CHRISTIANS, many in the writings of St. AUGUSTINE, conveyed similar concepts: congregation, compact, society of believers, Christian society, society of the good, and united community of the body of Christ. The communion of the faithful (the church) is the primal SACRAMENT of Christ.

Communion was expressed in multiple ways: collecting money for the poor (1 Cor. 16:1–4); sharing means of income in dire straits (Acts 2:42–47; *Didache* 1:5); sharing letters from city to city (2 Cor. 16:1–4); celebrating BAPTISM and the Eucharist (*Didache* 7; 9); and breaking off a piece of the holy Bread at the Eucharistic rite (Luke 24:30–31, *fractio panis*) to share with fellow churches in mutual recognition of fellowship. The *fractio panis* could stand for the eucharistic rite itself and is depicted countless times in catacomb frescoes.

The phrase *communio sanctorum* (communion of holy things/saints) appears in the first canon of the Council of Nîmes in Gaul and in the creed of the Gallican Sacramentary. It seems that originally the phrase (Gr. *koinonia tōn 'agiōn*) meant the holy things that Christians shared in common (baptism, the Eucharist, the Scriptures, etc.) and that united them into a community of faith. This meaning is retained by Nicetas of Remesiana in his *Exposition of the Creed* and in AUGUSTINE's phrase *communio sacramentorum,* or communion of sacred things (*Sermons* 214.11). It also survives in Alexander of Hales (*Sentences* 3.69.1) and St. THOMAS AQUINAS (*Exposition of the Creed* 10) in the sense of "participation in holy things." However, the most common understanding of the phrase *communio sanctorum* in the western CREEDS is the fellowship of the faithful in Christ. The reality of *communio* is the church as the primal sacrament of Christ through which and in which the grace of God flows. In the East the phrase was not a part of early creeds.

The communion embraces all who have received the one baptism whereby they become united to the one body of Christ (1 Cor. 12:12–13). In modern times this unity has been expressed in the theology of the mystical body of Christ (Pius XII, *Mystici Corporis,* June 19, 1943). It includes the living and the dead (1 Thess. 4:16). From this developed the notion of the unity of the church triumphant (saints in heaven), the church suffering (souls undergoing purgation to enter heaven), and the church militant (those struggling on earth). This universal communion is manifest in prayers for the dead by the living and by saints in heaven (2 Macc. 12:43–46; Tertullian, *Resurrection* 43; Abercius Epitaph). The inclusion of the dead is the ultimate motive behind the development of the notion of PURGATORY. The communion is also manifest in the intercession of the saints in heaven by the living (Cyril of Jerusalem, *Catechetical Lectures* 29:3). Thomas Aquinas added the angels to the communion not because they are fallen and redeemed by Christ but because they receive their grace through the Son (*Summa Theologiae* 3.8.4).

Among the living the idea of communion expresses itself in the sharing of the sacraments, especially in the Eucharist, the sacrament of the unity of the church with Christ and God, in common prayer, in common acts of charity, and in other undertakings to build up the body of the church. It is also expressed in the union of the faithful with their bishops, who are united together in a collegiality of love and authority with the BISHOP of Rome. Communion is the theological component underlying the Catholic teaching on the common good, which extends beyond the confines of ecclesiastical unity.

At VATICAN COUNCIL II there was a decided shift away from corporate and centralized ECCLESIOLOGY toward a communion ecclesiology that is locally based and reaches out even to those not in full communion with the Catholic Church. This raised the question of intercommunion between Catholics and other Christians.

Over time the relations among the various Christian denominations have gone from open warfare, to open hostility, to concealed antipathy, to reluctant tolerance, and finally to dialogue and other forms of heartfelt exchange, at least among a good many churches. This process had its first beginnings at the faltering steps toward reconciliation between Rome and EASTERN ORTHODOXY at the fourth Lateran Council (1215) and the Council of FLORENCE (1438–45) and at unofficial meetings. The impulse in this direction was further enhanced in the age of ECUMENISM that dawned at the World Parliament of Religion in Chicago in 1892, where representatives of most of the religions of the world, including Catholic bishops, attended. Among Protestant Christians a milestone of dialogue and cooperation was reached at the World Missionary Conference at Edinburgh in 1910. These efforts were crowned with the founding of the World Council of Churches (WCC) at Amsterdam in 1948.

Although Catholics were not officially a part of the latter conferences, the Vatican gave formal approval to the ecumenical movement with the founding of the Secretariat for Promoting Christian Unity in 1960, under the deft direction of Cardinal Augustin Bea (1881–1968). This was eventually followed by the formal approval of a communion-oriented ecclesiogy in various declarations including *Lumen Gentium,* the Dogmatic Constitution on the Church; *Unitatis Redintegratio,* the Decree on Ecumenism; and *Nostra Aetate,* the Declaration on the Relation of Church to Non-Christian Religions. JOHN PAUL II affirmed this direction of the church in *Ut Unum Sint* (May 5, 1995), but some of his other actions cast this commitment into doubt especially his approval of some statements by Cardinal Ratzinger, now BENEDICT XVI.

Catholics are now official members of various World Council of Churches committees, and have participated in countless dialogues with a variety of Protestant denominations. They have entered into covenants of agreement on baptism, the Eucharist, and the doctrine of JUSTIFICATION. The 1983 Code of Canon Law allows Catholics to receive baptism, the Eucharist, and penance from priests not in union with Rome but who otherwise have valid orders (Eastern Orthodox, Coptic, the Syro-Malankara Rite, etc.), under special circumstances of either "necessity or a spiritual advantage" (cn. 844). Under similar conditions members of Eastern Churches may come to Catholic priests to receive these sacraments. However, most Eastern Churches have failed to reciprocate. The Roman Catholic Directory on Ecumenism (1993) also lists instances under which a Protestant may receive Communion at the Eucharist. One example: a Protestant who believes in the true presence of Christ in the Eucharist may receive Communion at his or her wedding to a Catholic.

At the broadest level intercommunion across religions has taken place on the level of prayer, as when John Paul II hosted the World Day of Prayer (October 17, 1986) at Assisi, the city of St. FRANCIS, who is Catholicism's most universal saint. Intercommunion on the level of the reciprocal reception of the Eucharist is taking place more and more on an unofficial basis.

While communion ecclesiology has moved forward on some fronts, the Vatican under John Paul II and at the instigation of Cardinal Joseph Ratzinger drew back from Vatican II's bold openness into a bulwark model of the church as a fortress of truth. John Paul II sometimes seemed conflicted on this issue. Sacramental intercommunion, which is becoming very common in Europe, has deeply disconcerted the PAPACY.

Further reading: Robert S. Bilheimer, *Breakthrough: The Emergence of the Ecumenical Tradition* (Grand Rapids, Mich.: Eerdmans, 1989); Avery Dulles, *Models of the Church* (New York: Doubleday, 2002); Miguel María Garijo-Guembe, *Communion of the Saints* (Collegeville, Minn.: Liturgical Press, 1994); Joseph Ratzinger, "Letter to the Bishops of the Catholic Church on Some Aspects of the Church Understood as Communion," May 28, 1992 (Vatican: Congregation for the Holy Faith), online.

communism, Christian

There was an aspect of early Christianity that can be called communist in a religioeconomic sense. It was grounded in the biblical injunction to love one's neighbors and succor them in all things, which places one close to the kingdom of GOD (Lev. 19:18; Mark 12:32).

In the Pauline churches an ethic of *koinonia,* or COMMUNION, seems to have prevailed, with mutual support and especially support of the poor in Jerusalem (Gal. 2:10; 1 Cor. 16:1–4). The Essene communities seem to have been communistic in some of their social arrangements and strongly opposed the private amassing of wealth.

The Book of Acts 2:44–47 states: "And all who believed were together and had all things in common. And they were selling their possessions and belongings and distributing the proceeds to all, as any had need. And day by day, attending the temple together and breaking bread in their homes,

they received their food with glad and generous hearts, praising God and having favor with all the people." Subsequent passages note that the Jerusalem church was penniless (3:6) and that "no one claimed that any of his possessions was his own but they shared everything in common" (4:32). Acts is probably describing Jerusalem after the destruction (66–70), when its community of Jesus' followers, as most of its other Jewish inhabitants, had fallen into dire straits; sharing all things in common was a practical matter necessary for group survival.

The Pauline churches, while not wealthy, probably had some resources. In the expectation of an imminent return of CHRIST, some members gave up their occupations to wait for the return (2 Thess. 3:6–10), but PAUL opposed this practice. Instead, he stressed using resources for mutual support in building up the assembly of the saints. Many second-century theologians depicted Eden as a communist order in which Adam and Eve shared all things in common.

In subsequent centuries CHRISTIANS accommodated themselves to the economic system of the empire. However, the ideal original communism or communalism was retained in the new cenobitic monasteries, which began to arise in Egypt and Asia Minor at the end of the second and into the third centuries. PACHOMIUS of Egypt called his original MONASTERY the Koinonia; this meant not only that material goods were held in common, but that all the members, men and women, humbly served one another. All his legends depict Pachomius assuming all the tasks of the monastery, even the lowliest, in imitation of Christ, the servant of all humankind. The earliest monasteries stressed an extremely abstemious and poor life in disdain of material luxury.

The communal ideal was pursued in the monasteries in the West as well. St. BENEDICT moderated the severity of the monastic life; he allowed monasteries to own property collectively, and discipline was not as severe. However, the "distribution to each according to need" (Acts 4:35) was maintained (*Rule of Benedict* 34). Monastic communism established the model for all future religious orders that are communist in their ways of life both in terms of property ownership and of service to the community and the church at large.

Ironically, monastic communism became an important supporting factor in the rise of the feudal system in the early MIDDLE AGES. The great abbey estates became entities parallel to the feudal estates of the lords and held serfs. This system lasted until the rise of the absolute monarchies, many of which sought to limit the monasteries if not to abolish them entirely in their own favor, as in the case of HENRY VIII. They did not fair better under the later nation states, and they suffered even more under the revolutionary democracies. St. THOMAS MORE, perhaps tongue-in-cheek, portrayed his *Utopia* as a communist society.

The Christian communist ideal reasserted itself in the 19th century both in the revival of monasteries throughout Europe (SOLESMES, Beuron) and more broadly in the rise of religiously tinctured movements that sought to revive an egalitarian early Christianity, such as the Saint-Simonians, the Rappites, and the Oneida community. Many of these groups were accused of an affinity for atheistic communism or MARXISM. In defense, they have often preferred the euphemistic term *communalism* to describe the Christian form of communism.

Although the modern papacy has often harbored nostalgic feelings toward monarchism, at the end of the 19th century the principle of "each according to his or her need" reemerged. Catholic leaders became deeply involved with labor causes such as unions, living conditions for the urban poor, and the principle of just distribution of wealth. The theme first surfaced in LEO XIII's *Rerum Novarum* (May 15, 1891) and was reaffirmed in PIUS XI's *Quadragesimo Anno* (May 1, 1931) and JOHN PAUL II's *Centesimus Annus* (January 1, 1991).

The social ideal of a shared life was sustained in CATHOLIC ACTION movements in Europe and America, such as the Catholic Workers of DORO-THY DAY and Peter Marin. The early Christian principle of the common life and mutual support also reasserted itself in the BASE COMMUNITIES that have contributed to the revitalization of Catholicism in LATIN AMERICA.

Further reading: Andrew Collier, *Christianity and Marxism* (London: Routledge, 2001); C. H. Lawrence, *Medieval Monasticism: Forms of Religious Life in Western Europe in the Middle Ages,* 3rd ed. (New York: Longman, 2000); Edward A. Lynch, *Religion and Politics in Latin America: Liberation Theology and Christian Democracy* (New York: Praeger, 1991); Kenneth J. Heineman, *A Catholic New Deal: Religion and Reform in Depression Pittsburgh* (University Park: Pennsylvania State University Press, 1999).

communism, secular   *See* MARXISM.

concordat (Lat.: *cum,* "together" + *cor,* "heart")

Corcordat is the ecclesiastical term for a treaty or agreement between the Vatican, as a sovereign power, and another sovereign or political entity. Only the Roman pontiff, who possesses "full and supreme power in the church" (*Code of Canon Law,* cn. 332.1), acting through his secretary of state, usually a cardinal, can conclude concordats.

Sometime during the fourth century popes began claiming not only spiritual power over the church but also temporal power over certain territories in Italy. As temporal sovereigns over what became known as the PAPAL STATES, situated in central Italy (and later including Avignon and Venaissin in France), they would from time to time conclude concordats. The PAPACY lost its claim to the French territories in the Revolution (1791); the rest of its territories were taken by the Kingdom of Italy in 1861 (the outlying provinces) and in 1870 (the city of Rome).

The most celebrated concordat of the MIDDLE AGES was the Concordat of Worms (1172), in which the word was used for the first time. It was an agreement between Pope Callixtus II (r. 1119–1124) and Emperor Henry V (r. 1111–25) over the question of lay investiture. The agreement stated that only the church could invest with sacred authority, but that the emperor could invest BISHOPS with the regalia of secular offices. In effect, princes continued to wield unwelcome authority over the appointment of bishops and other CLERGY.

In modern times the papacy has negotiated seven major concordats: with Napoleon (1801), Franz Joseph of Austria (1855), Poland (1925), Italy (1929), Germany (1933), Portugal (1940), and Spain (1953). On July 15, 1801, Napoléon (1769–1821) signed a concordat with Pope Pius VII (r. 1800–23), reestablishing the Catholic Church in France, but not to the exclusion of others. The emperor wisely believed the pact would help consolidate his rule, reconcile contending factions of the clergy, and mollify the peasants. The deal was less advantageous for the church, which was forced to consent to a form of lay investiture it had rejected at Canossa in 1077. The French state would nominate archbishops and bishops; the papacy would merely confer the office. The church was not compensated for property lost in the French Revolution, but clergy were compensated.

Unilaterally, Napoléon issued the Organic Articles (April 16, 1802), never agreed to by the papacy, which reinstated the traditional Gallican freedoms of the French church (*see* FRANCE). The state claimed a say in appointing *curés* to important parishes, processions were forbidden in towns with significant Protestant populations, and the state would regulate seminaries and control both the number of priests and their dress. As a result of the profound ANTICLERICALISM that swept France in reaction to the Catholic role in the Dreyfus Affair (1894), the French government abrogated both the concordat and the Organic Articles in 1905, thereby separating CHURCH AND STATE.

Following the loss of the Papal States in 1870, church-state relations in ITALY festered until PIUS XI

signed the Lateran Treaty/Concordat with Benito Mussolini, the Fascist head of the Italian state, on February 11, 1929. The Vatican gained sovereignty over Vatican City, including the outlying summer residence, Castel Gondolfo, and some of the major churches in Rome, including St. John's Lateran, the pope's cathedral seat. The Vatican was compensated for the loss of its territories. The two parties agreed that instruction in the Catholic faith would be provided in all public schools and that the clergy would be paid as if they were employees of the state. The last two terms were removed on June 3, 1985, when Pope JOHN PAUL II renegotiated the treaty with the Italian government. The Lateran Treaty had the unfortunate side effect of granting legitimacy to the fascist regime of Mussolini. One of the sadder effects was the suppression, with tacit agreement of the Vatican, of the antifascist, leftist Catholic Partito Populare, founded in 1919 by Dom Luigi Sturzo (1871–1959), who fled to the United States.

A much more fateful concordat was concluded between Adolf Hitler's vice chancellor Franz von Papen (1879–1969) and the Vatican on July 8, 1933. Cardinal Eugenio Pacelli, later PIUS XII, served as Vatican secretary of state at the time. From the Vatican perspective, the treaty, which came to be known as the Reichskonkordat, was a legitimate attempt to defend church interests: the church could continue to collect taxes from believers (art. 13); any state services provided to the church could be removed only by mutual agreement (art. 18); religion would be taught in public schools (art. 21) with church-approved teachers (art. 22); and Catholic organizations would be protected, as would freedom of worship (art. 31).

More ominous articles included those requiring bishops and clergy to swear an oath of fealty to the state (art. 16) and barring clergy from political parties (art. 32). Pacelli negotiated the treaty in the "universal" interests of the church and over the heads and against the interests of local clergy and laity. As with the Lateran Treaty, one of the immediate side effects was the suppression of the antifascist Center Party led by Heinrich Brüning (1885–1970), who had to flee to Holland and then the United States. Konrad Adenauer (1876–1957), leader of the Christian Democratic Union, which succeeded the Center Party, was imprisoned by the Nazis in 1933.

Prior to the concordat the German bishops had banned membership in the Nazi Party and stipulated that anyone wearing a swastika was to be refused COMMUNION. Two weeks after Pacelli offered the terms of the concordat these restrictions were lifted. As was the case with the Lateran Treaty, only after the Nazi regime began violating the freedom of Catholic organizations and religious practice did the Vatican criticize the regime, in PIUS XI's piercing encyclical to the German bishops *Mit brennender Sorge* ("With Burning Anxiety") (March 14, 1937). By then it was too late.

In 1953, Pius XII negotiated a concordat with Francisco Franco (1892–1975). It was renegotiated in 1979.

Further reading: Frank J. Coppa, ed., *Controversial Concordats: The Vatican's Relations with Napoleon, Mussolini and Hitler* (Washington, D.C.: Catholic University of America Press, 1999); James Carroll, *Constantine's Sword: The Church and the Jews* (Boston: Houghton Mifflin, 2000); Peter C. Kent, *The Pope and the Duce: The International Impact of the Lateran Agreements* (London: Macmillan, 1981).

confession   *See* RECONCILIATION, SACRAMENT OF.

Confirmation, Sacrament of (Lat.: *cum,* "together, with" + *firmare,* "to strengthen")

The rite of confirmation is understood by Catholics to be the completion or concluding part of the SACRAMENTS of initiation (which also include BAPTISM and the EUCHARIST, or First Communion). It consists of three actions: a laying on of hands as a sign of conferral of the HOLY SPIRIT in a new or fuller way, an anointing with holy chrism, or oil, via a sign of the CROSS on the forehead, and a light symbolic blow to the cheek by a BISHOP or his surrogate. Catholics believe that confirmation confers on the recipient an indelible character, or mark, as do the sacraments of baptism and HOLY ORDERS, and thus can be conferred only once. Unlike in the West, the Eastern Churches, reflecting early practice, confer the sacrament on neophytes and infants immediately following baptism and before first communion.

There is no clear evidence that confirmation was a separate sacrament in early Christianity. Some point to incidents of "laying on of hands" (Acts 8:17; 19:6) and "sealing with the Spirit" (2 Cor. 1:20; Eph. 1:13), but these are probably references to baptismal liturgies. HIPPOLYTUS OF ROME's *Apostolic Tradition* 21:1–24 describes a single continuous rite beginning with baptism and ending with what is now called confirmation.

By the fourth century CLERGY in the West began administering confirmation as a rite separate from Baptism, as evidenced by the Council of Elvira of 306 (?) (cn. 38). At first both rites were restricted to bishops, but with the dramatic increase in the number of believers, priests and deacons performed more and more baptisms, reserving confirmations to bishops or their appointed surrogates. Whoever performed the confirmation had to use oil consecrated by the bishop on Holy Thursday.

There has been no coherent or consistent theology behind confirmation as a separate sacrament. Some think it became a separate rite in order to receive heretics and schismatics back into the unity of the church. In a sermon in 460 the semi-Pelagian bishop Faustus of Riez (fl. 450) in Provence gave this justification: "In baptism we are born to new life; after baptism we are confirmed for combat. In baptism we are washed; after baptism we are strengthened." This military view was fortified both by BONAVENTURE, who saw it as "the sacrament of warriors," and by THOMAS AQUINAS, who also argued that confirmation imprints a character (*Summa Theologiae* 3.72).

Nor was there agreement about its origin. Aquinas said it was instituted by CHRIST, and Bonaventure attributed it to the successors of the APOSTLES. This confusion gave Luther a lot of ammunition. He called the arguments for its sacramental status "monkey business" (*Affenspiel*) and "mumbo-jumbo" (*Gaukelwerk*). Lutherans nonetheless kept the practice of confirmation as part of the church's educational ministry.

The Council of TRENT theologians could not even agree on the "matter" of the sacrament: was it laying on of hands or anointing with oil? Trent eventually stated that the rite consisted in the collective imposition of hands by the officiants and a prayer for the seven Gifts of the HOLY SPIRIT, an anointing on the forehead with the prayer "I sign you with the sign of the cross and anoint you with the chrism of salvation," a tap on the cheek, and a prayer for the indwelling of the Spirit.

VATICAN COUNCIL II called for the revision of the rite of confirmation in *Sacrosanctum Concilium* 71, the Constitution on the Sacred Liturgy. These revisions were effected in PAUL VI's apostolic constitution *Divinae consortium naturae* (August 15, 1971) and incorporated in the 1994 *Catechism of the Catholic Church*. The latter sees the sacrament as one of the rites of conferring a "fullness of the Spirit" that makes the recipients part of "the whole Messianic people." Confirmation "perpetuates the grace of Pentecost in the church" (Acts 2:38). The rite includes anointing with the chrism of Holy Thursday oil with the words "Receive the sign of the gift of the Spirit," the laying on of hands, and an episcopal prayer over the confirmands. A bishop can appoint a priest to confirm in special circumstances.

Further reading: Aidan Kavanaugh, *Confirmation: Origin and Reform* (New York: Pueblo, 1988); Paul Turner, *The Meaning and Practice of Confirmation: Perspectives from a 16th Century Controversy* (New York: Peter Lang, 1987); *Rediscovering Confirmation* (Vatican City: Pontifical Council for the Laity, 2000).

Confraternity of Christian Doctrine (CCD)

The Confraternity of Christian Doctrine was the principal official organ for instructing the laity in Catholic teaching in the modern era. Given official sanction in 1562 by PIUS IV and strongly supported by Sts. ROBERT BELLARMINE, FRANCIS DE SALES, and CHARLES BORROMEO, the group was reestablished by PIUS X in his apostolic letter *Acerbo Nimis* (May 15, 1905). It got further backing from PIUS XI in *Provido Sane Concilio* (January 12, 1935).

The confraternity got its kick-start in the United States under the supervision of the National Conference of U.S. Bishops on October 30, 1935, which declared a national catechetical day. It was used mostly to impart Catholic instruction to youth who attended public schools and adult converts, although the papal decrees called for instruction across the board. The confraternity had a publishing arm that promoted catechetical materials and sponsored a noted retranslation of the New Testament by biblical scholars as part of what was then intended to be the New American Bible. After VATICAN COUNCIL II local directors of religious education at the parochial level subsumed many of the functions of the Confraternity.

See also CATECHESIS; CATECHISM.

Further reading: *The Confraternity Comes of Age* (Paterson: Confraternity, 1956); Bernard Marthaler, "The Rise and Decline of the CCD," in Michael Warren, ed., *Sourcebook for Modern Catechectics*, vol. 2 (Winona: St. Mary's, 1997), 220–231; John S. Middleton, *A Handbook of the Confraternity of Christian Doctrine* (New York: Benziger, 1937).

Congar, Georges-Yves (1904–1995) *French theologian*

Georges-Yves Congar was a French Dominican theologian who specialized in the field of ECCLESIOLOGY. One of the founders of modern Catholic ECUMENISM, he had an enormous impact on VATICAN COUNCIL II, especially on its first officially published document, *Lumen Gentium,* the Dogmatic Constitution on the Church in the Modern World. In 1994, shortly before he passed away, Pope JOHN PAUL II named him a cardinal. He published under the names Marie-Joseph or simply Yves Congar.

Congar was born in Sedan, FRANCE, and studied at Le Saulchoir, the Belgian (and later French) Dominican school that became the seedbed of NOUVELLE THÉOLOGIE. Early in his career Congar established life-long contacts with Protestant and Orthodox theologians and became interested in ecumenism, a field first sponsored under Protestant and Orthodox auspices. He attended the ecumenical conferences at Oxford and Edinburgh in 1937 and wrote *Divided Christendom* (1937, Eng. 1939). The book laid down principles of ecumenical participation that took into account "feelings, ideas, actions or institutions, meetings or conferences, ceremonies, manifestations and publications directed to prepare the reunion in a new unity" of the CHRISTIAN churches. In 1941 he published his authoritative *Mystery of the Church.* After imprisonment by the Vichy government during World War II he wrote an appeal for the reform of the church and a defense of the Worker-Priest movement in France (*see* CATHOLIC ACTION). This last act merited him a prohibition from teaching in 1954 by the Vatican, but he had the quiet support of Cardinal Angelo Roncalli, then papal nuncio to France and later Pope JOHN XXIII.

In semi-exile at the École Biblique in Jerusalem Congar pursued his studies of the church in early Christianity, the role of the laity, and numerous historical studies. He returned to teach at Strasbourg, where he continued his ecumenical contacts. Pope John XXIII personally appointed him as consultor to Vatican Council II. He wrote much of the pope's opening "Message to the World" and contributed to several of its major documents on the church. His influence as a theologian at the council was matched only by that of KARL RAHNER.

Toward the end of his career Congar turned his attention to the doctrine of the HOLY SPIRIT in a three-volume work, *I Believe in the Holy Spirit* (1970–80). He also lent his support to the burgeoning CHARISMATIC RENEWAL movement in the Catholic Church. Congar's writings are voluminous.

Further reading: Congar, Yves, *Divided Christendom: A Catholic Study of the Problem of Reunion* (London: Bles, 1939); ———, *Mystery of the Church* (Baltimore: Helicon, 1960); ———, *Priest and Layman* (London: Darton, Longman & Todd, 1967); Timothy I. MacDonald, *The Ecclesiology of Yves Congar* (Lanham Md.: University Press of America, 1984); Aidan Nichols, *Yves Congar* (London: Chapman, 1989).

Congregations, Roman   *See* CURIA; VATICAN CURIA.

conscience (Lat.: *cum,* "with" + *scire,* "to know" = "to know within oneself")
In Catholic THEOLOGY, the conscience is the center of the human person that gives one the ability to know the moral rightness or wrongness of actions, whether past or presently to be performed. The Greek equivalent is *syneidēsis.* Geoffrey Chaucer and James Joyce referred to it as the "inwit" of a person. Though clearly manifest on the moral plane, conscience is deeper than moral judgment itself. CHRISTIANS believe that conscience was innate to human beings before the FALL and that it is increased through experience with the aid of divine GRACE.

The biblical foundation for the theology of conscience rests on the concept of living one's life in the sight of GOD. The Old Testament (OT) word *yad'a* ("to know") can include self-awareness, but in general the OT employs images like "heart" or "reins" to convey the nuances of conscience. That conscience was fully present is clearly demonstrated in Nathan's parable of the Poor Man's One Little Ewe (2 Sam. 12:1–13), by which he indicts

David for sexual greed. The later Wisdom of Solomon 17:10 in the LXX (Greek translation of the BIBLE) speaks of cowardly wickedness that is "convicted by its own testimony and distressed by its own conscience." In late Jewish thought there was much discussion about the inner conflict between *yezer hatov* and the *yezer hara* (the good and bad inclinations of the spirit) that in some ways corresponds to the "spirit" and the "flesh" in the New Testament. In the Hellenistic period conscience as the inner moral awareness of right and wrong emerged sharply in Stoic philosophy, which shaped much of the moral discourse of the New Testament writers.

PAUL uses the word *conscience* when he stresses that all parts of the assembly need to support and build up one another and that the "strong" conscience types should not scandalize the "weak" by eating food offered to idols (1 Cor. 8). In Romans 2:14 he refers to the law written on the heart, to which the conscience bears witness. In other New Testament passages *syneidēsis* means simply consciousness (1 Peter 2:19) or loyalty to the faith (1 Tim, 1:5).

The first theologians, and later the FATHERS and MOTHERS OF THE CHURCH, developed the religious meaning of conscience as the way to walk with God and to repent of any deed that takes one off that path. In the MIDDLE AGES theologians discussed the question of conscience in relation to their theology of virtue. They distinguished between *synderesis* and *conscientia*. The term *synderesis* harkens back to JEROME's commentary on Ezekiel 6: "This is that spark of conscience which was not quenched even in the heart of Cain . . . that makes us, too, feel our sinfulness when we are overcome by evil." *Synderesis* was the natural nucleus of conscience that was left intact after the Fall. It is the basis in mind and will of all acts of conscience. THOMAS AQUINAS and JOHN DUNS SCOTUS called *synderesis* the primary moral principles and called conscience the actual judgments based on them (Aquinas, *Summa Theologiae* 1–2.1; Duns Scotus, *Opus Oxoniense* 2.39). *Synderesis* points to

the general end of the rational being; conscience directs one in choosing the proximate means to that end. Because of the duty of conscience, individuals also have the obligation to inform themselves when doubts of conscience arise. In the end, however, one is obliged to follow one's conscience even though it may be in error.

In modern thought Immanuel Kant (1724–1804) spoke of conscience as a transcendental faculty of the mind. Kant's notion seems to correspond to the medieval notion of *synderesis* but not *conscientia*. Nietzsche spoke of the "bad conscience," by which he meant decadent, thwarted instincts that have turned in on themselves. Sigmund Freud spoke of conscience as the by-product in the superego of the repression of socially taboo instincts from the id that helps form the ego. Modern existentialists like Martin Heidegger (1889–1976) and Jean-Paul Sartre (1905–80) viewed conscience as the existential call to authenticity in the realization of the self. None of these views concern the end of human existence as it relates to practical moral action; they are rather concerned with the nexus of interiority that constitutes the self.

Without denying the nuances of the modern contributions to the notion of conscience, VATICAN COUNCIL II reaffirmed the centrality of conscience in the religious life: "Conscience is the most secret core and sanctuary of a person. There he or she is alone with God whose voice echoes in the person's depths" (*Gaudium et Spes* 16, Pastoral Constitution on the Church in the Modern World). The very sanctity of conscience guarantees the complete liberty of conscience in fulfilling one's religious calling (*Dignitatis Humanae* 3, Declaration on Religious Freedom).

The recent *Catechism of the Catholic Church* makes extended use of the treatment of moral conscience in Cardinal JOHN HENRY NEWMAN. In the section on conscience (5) in his celebrated "Letter to the Duke of Norfolk" (December 27, 1874) Newman quotes an earlier commentator: "He who acts against his own conscience, loses his soul." The conscience, Newman went on to say, is the "aboriginal Vicar of Christ" in the soul, adding the near humorous ending "I shall drink—to the Pope if you please—still, to the Conscience first, and to the Pope afterwards."

In their spiritual practices Catholics are urged both to form and to examine their consciences on a regular if not daily basis, especially when preparing to receive the SACRAMENT OF RECONCILIATION.

Further reading: Philip Bosman, *Conscience in Philo and Paul: A Conceptual History of the Synoida Word Group* (Tübingen: Mohr Siebeck, 2003); Joseph V. Dolan, "Conscience in the Catholic Theological Tradition" in William C. Bier, ed., *Conscience: Its Freedom and Limitations* (New York: Fordham University Press, 1971); John Henry Newman, "A Letter Addressed to the Duke of Norfolk on the Occasion of Mr. Gladstone's Expostulation" (Dec. 27, 1874), available online; Barbara M. Stilwell, Matthew R. Galvin, and Stephen Kopta, *Right Versus Wrong: Raising a Child with a Conscience* (Bloomington: Indiana University Press, 2000).

conscientious objection

Many states around the world exempt individuals from compulsory military service on the grounds of their conscientious objection to war, based on moral or religious teaching. There are generally two forms: total conscientious objection, which claims that any form of war is wrong, and selective conscientious objection, which opposes only those wars that fail to meet the criteria of a JUST WAR.

Christianity and Catholicism have a long and complex history of attitudes toward war that are relevant to issues of conscientious objection. Objectors can point to significant deeds and sayings of Jesus prohibiting the use of violence even in self-defense. When Peter drew a sword to defend Jesus, cutting off the ear of the High Priest's servant, Jesus rebuked: "Put your sword back in its place for all who draw the sword will die by the sword" (Matt. 26:52). In the Sermon on the Mount Jesus said: "Blessed are the peacemak-

ers for they shall be called the children of God" (Matt. 5:9). These, plus many admonitions to love one's enemy, point to a nonviolent strain in Jesus' teaching that shaped the practice of early Christianity.

There can be little doubt that the early church took a nonviolent if not actively pacifist stance toward the world. Most of the pre-Constantinian theologians found membership in the church to be incompatible with military service (TERTULLIAN, *On Idolatry* 19; *The Crown* 11). Many were fond of citing the famous prophecy in Isaiah 2:4 of a future time when "swords will be beaten into ploughshares" (JUSTIN MARTYR, *Dialogue with Trypho* 90) to demonstrate that the new Covenant is an era of peace and not war. There are some late second-century epitaphs memorializing CHRISTIAN soldiers, but they do not tell about the military status of the deceased at the time of burial.

By the time of CONSTANTINE THE GREAT many Christians were among his soldiers, and after the Edict of Milan in 313 tolerating Christians, theologians started changing their traditional positions on military service. Both ATHANASIUS OF ALEXANDRIA and AUGUSTINE OF HIPPO argued in favor of just wars, which legitimized participation in the military. Augustine fatefully called in the military commander Marcellinus to put down the Donatist schism.

Augustine's stance prevailed through the MIDDLE AGES. The old proscription against participating in war or violence survived only in medieval canon laws that prohibited clerics from personally engaging in war or participating directly in executions. Only heretical sectarians like the CATHARI, WALDENSIANS, Beghards, and Beguines upheld the primitive Christian proscription against military service. Renaissance popes could hardly tolerate the concept of conscientious objection; as temporal sovereigns of the PAPAL STATES they themselves mustered armies and sometimes even led them into battle, in violation of long-standing canon laws.

Luther and the other leading reformers adopted a version of Augustine's two-kingdoms theory that allowed a Christian state to resort to warfare. However, many Anabaptists reaffirmed the ancient Christian principle of pacifism and enshrined it in the Schleitheim Confession. Huldrich Zwingli (1484–1531) was the first to take a pacifist stance, although he later abandoned it, but it was the Hussite Brethren and the Anabaptists (Amish, Mennonites, Hutterites, and Schwenkfeldians) who carried principled pacifism into the modern world. They were joined later by the Quakers, Seventh Day Adventists, and Jehovah's Witnesses.

The Catholic Church's stand on conscientious objection radically shifted in the second half of the 20th century in a return to the values of the early church that paralleled the return to the early form of sacraments such as BAPTISM. Small circles like the Catholic Worker Movement of DOROTHY DAY and Peter Maurin kept the spark of pacifism glowing in the face of seemingly heavy odds. By contrast, Pope PIUS XII in his 1956 Christmas Message to the World proclaimed the old teaching that a Catholic citizen "cannot invoke his or her own conscience in order to refuse to render the services and perform the duties established by law." But only seven years later JOHN XXIII issued his groundbreaking encyclical *Pacem in Terris,* or Peace on Earth (April 11, 1963), which called into question the use of nuclear bombs in warfare and placed the highest value on the pursuit of peace.

VATICAN COUNCIL II in *Gaudium et Spes* 79–82, the Pastoral Constitution on the Church in the Modern World, recognized the right to lawful self-defense on the part of nations, but urged all nations to take measures outlawing war wherever possible. It also called for laws that make "humane provisions for the case of those who for reasons of conscience refuse to bear arms, provided however, that they accept some other form of service to the human community" (79). This established a principle of conscientious objection that could include citizens who objected to a particular war they deemed unjust.

The issue came alive during the Vietnam War, when many young Catholics, following the guidelines of numerous moral theologians, judged that war to fail the just war criteria. This principle of selective conscientious objection was upheld by the United States Catholic Bishops Conference in their pastoral directives *Human Life in Our Day* (1968) and *The Challenge to Peace* (1983).

Many nations now include provisions for conscientious objectors in their laws. The United States Selective Service Code provided alternative service options. However, the Supreme Court of the United States ruled in *Gillete v. United States* (1971) that the objector must be against war "in any form" and not just "a particular war." Many constitutional scholars believe *Gillete* was wrongly decided, in part because it may tend to discriminate against those Catholics who follow the principle of selective conscientious objection.

President Nixon ended the U.S. military draft in 1972. In 1980 President Jimmy Carter reinstituted draft registration in case of a threat of war. Many conscientious objectors and selective conscientious objectors register their objection to war on their registration forms.

Further reading: Patout Burns, ed., *War and its Discontents: Pacificism and Quietism in the Abrahamic Traditions* (Washington, D.C.: Georgetown University Press, 1996); *Declaration on Conscientious Objection and Selective Conscientious Objection* (Washington, D.C.: United States Catholic Conference, 1971); Michael F. Noone, Jr., ed., *Selective Conscientious Objection: Accommodating Conscience and Security* (Boulder, Colo.: Westview Press, 1989); Lillian Schlissel, *Conscience in America: A Documentary History of Conscientious Objection in America, 1757–1967* (New York: E. P. Dutton, 1968); Thomas A. Shannon and Thomas A. Massaro, eds., *Catholic Perspectives on Peace and War* (New York: Sheed & Ward, 2004).

consecration (Lat.: *cum,* "with" *sacrare* "to make sacred")

Consecration involves dedicating something, such as a person, a building, or a holy object, to the service of GOD. More narrowly, it refers to the pronunciation of Jesus' words over the bread and wine during the EUCHARIST: "Take this all of you, this is my body which shall be given up for you," and "Take this, all of you, and drink from it: this is the cup of my blood, the blood of the new and everlasting covenant" (Matt. 26:26–29; 1 Cor. 11:23). Catholics and Orthodox Christians believe that the elements of bread and wine are then changed into the body and blood of CHRIST.

Further reading: Enrico M. Mazza, *The Celebration of the Eucharist: The Origin of the Rite and the Development of its Interpretation* (Collegeville, Minn.: Liturgical Press, 1999). A. J. Schulte, *Consecranda: Rites and Ceremonies Observed at the Consecration of Churches, Altars, Altar-stones, Chalices & Patens* (New York: Benziger, 1907).

Constance, Council of (1414–1418)

The Council of Constance is considered the 16th valid council of the Catholic Church. It was the second (between the Councils of Pisa and BASEL) of the three councils provoked by the western SCHISM.

The Holy Roman Emperor Sigismund (1368–1437) urged the council on the ANTIPOPE John XXIII (Baldasarre Cossa, d. 1419), who was being challenged by two other claimants to the PAPACY, Pope Gregory XII (r. 1406–15) and the Avignon antipope Benedict XIII (r. 1394–1417). It soon became clear that the members of the council wanted all three popes to resign to allow the smooth election of a fourth. John XXIII fled but was forced to return only to be deposed for scandalous conduct. Gregory XII abdicated. Benedict XIII fled to the protection of the King of Aragon, Fernando I (1412–16). He was deposed in 1417.

In its fifth session in 1415 the council, under pressure from Sigismund, enacted the controversial decree *Sacrosancta*, which stated that "this same council, legitimately assembled in the Holy Ghost, forming a general council and representing the Catholic Church militant, has its power immediately from CHRIST, and every one, whatever his state or position, even if it be the Papal dignity itself, is bound to obey it in all those things which pertain to the faith and the healing of the said schism, and to the general reformation of the Church of God, in head and members." A second decree, *Frequens*, called for additional councils to be held after five, seven, and 10 years and every 10 years thereafter. This advice was shunned by later popes, thereby contributing to the explosion of the PROTESTANT REFORMATION.

On November 11, 1417, the cardinal deacon Oddo Colonna was elected pope and took the name Martin V (r. 1417–31). The remaining sessions dealt with additional ecclesiastical issues, and CONCORDATS with various nations were enacted to handle issues of exemption and taxation.

The council also dealt with the heretics JOHN WYCLIFFE, who inspired both the translation of the BIBLE into English and the Lollard movement, and his Hungarian disciple Jan Hus (c. 1371–1415), who advocated administering both species of the EUCHARIST to lay people. The council condemned more than 200 propositions of Wycliffe, including his elevation of the eternal spiritual church over the "material," or temporal, church, his denial of the scriptural origin of the papacy, and his assertion that Scripture was the sole criterion of doctrine. Not satisfied with verbal denunciation, the council ordered Wycliffe's remains removed from consecrated ground. Shamelessly, it ignored the safe-conduct pledge that Sigismund had issued to Hus. Instead, it convicted him of heresy and handed him over to be burned at the stake. The council failed to decide the cases of the Franciscan John Parvus (c. 1360–1411) and the Dominican John of Falkenberg (d. 1418), who taught that tyrannocide was legally justifiable.

See also COUNCILS/CONCILIARISM.

Further reading: Walter Brandmüller, *Konzil von Konstanz* (Paderborn: Schöningh, 1999); Christopher M.D. Crowder, *Unity, Heresy, Reform, 1378–1460: The Con-*

ciliar Response to the Great Schism (Kingston Ont.: Limestone, 1986); Norman P. Tanner, ed., *Decrees of the Ecumenical Councils* (London: Sheed & Ward, 1990).

Constantine the Great (c. 285–337) *Roman emperor*

Constantine, coemperor of Rome from 306 to 334 and sole emperor until 337, was the first Roman ruler to tolerate Christianity. He presided at the Synod of Arles (314) and the crucial Council of Nicaea in 325 (*see* COUNCILS, ECUMENICAL) and became the model for CAESAROPAPISM. Although he murdered his first wife and son, he is revered as a saint in the East (regrettably, according to some Catholics), and as the 13th apostle by Eastern Orthodoxy. His feast day is May 21.

Constantine was a momentous yet extremely problematic figure in the history of Christianity. He was born in Naissus, in today's Turkey, the son of emperor Constantius I Chlorus and Helena, a barmaid who exerted a strong influence on her son in later life. After a series of successful military campaigns, Constantine in 306 won his dying father's blessing to assume power and married Fausta (d. 326), daughter of the pagan coemperor Maximian (r. 306–12); she bore him a son, Crispus. Like his father, he ruled the western empire from Trier in present-day Germany.

Constantine took sole control of Rome in 312 by defeating Fausta's brother Maxentius at the battle of the Milvian Bridge over the Tiber River near Rome. In his *Life of Constantine* the church historian Eusebius of Caesarea, who paints a rosy picture of the emperor and glosses over his murders and pagan worship, says that Constantine dreamed of the sign of the cross in the form of the Chi-Rho before the battle (1.18–31). Constantine then had the Chi-Rho inscribed on the standards of the legions in place of the former pagan talismans. The new standard came to be called the *labarum*. Later legend says that in the dream Christ uttered the Latin words *In hoc signo vincis* ("With this sign you will conquer").

Drawing of labarum, used by Constantine I as his military standard. Drawing after fourth-century sarcophagus. (Pio Christian Museum, Vatican City) *(drawing by Frank K. Flinn)*

Scholars today challenge Eusebius's version of the event; they say that the cross was adopted by Constantine as a battle standard only in later years. Lactantius, in *The Death of the Persecutors* 44.5, says simply that Constantine saw a "celestial sign of God"; historians believe he may have been referring to a conjunction of Mars, Saturn, and Jupiter in the constellations of Capricorn and Sagittarius, that can look like a Chi-Rho This fortuitous sign was later merged with the symbolism of the cross in the *labarum*, Constantine's military standard.

The victory allowed Constantine and his coemperor, Licinius, to issue the Edict of Milan (313), imposing toleration of Christians and returning their churches and other property, confiscated earlier by order of the emperors, to them (*Death of Persecutors* 48; Eusebius, *Ecclesiastical History* 10.5). Though this act won him great praise from later Christian authors, Constantine may have been acting from mere political expediency—by this time the empire was already about 30 percent Christian. Constantine continued to partake in pagan sacrifices, build pagan temples, and consult the oracle of Delphi. However, he did abolish crucifixion as the preferred method of execution for rebels out of deference to his own victory standard.

In his later reign Constantine undertook major steps to solidify his hold on the Roman Empire. In 326 he had his wife, Fausta, and their son, Crispus, murdered. His mother, Helena, upon whom he bestowed the semidivine imperial title Augusta, had now become a devout Christian, at least outwardly, and had accused Fausta of adultery. Fond of his pagan ways, Constantine, like many nominal Christians, did not receive baptism until he was on his death bed, and that from Eusebius of Nicomedia, a follower of ARIANISM. He was buried in the Church of the 12 Apostles in Constantinople, among the legendary tombs of twelve Apostles, whence his posthumous title of "Thirteenth" Apostle. On the other hand, posthumous images on coins show the deceased Constantine receiving an apotheosis, or deification, as Apollo/Helios, in the manner of his pagan predecessors.

Constantine initiated the policy of caesaropapism, in which Christian emperors assumed direct roles in ecclesiastical matters. Such emperors were depicted in sacred art in quasi-ecclesiastical robes alongside saints and bishops. For example, Constantine tried to mediate the Donatist controversy (see DONATISM) at the Council of Arles in 314; when the schismatics did not buckle to his decisions he had them persecuted. He sent his own imperial theologian Hosius of Cordova (c. 256–358) to the East to mediate the Arian controversy, and he called and presided over the first major assembly of Christians from the whole Roman world, the Council of Nicaea of 325.

Constantine superficially abided by the decisions of the bishops, but he personally pardoned Arius and his ally Eusebius. In 336 he actually exiled the principal voice of orthodoxy at Nicaea, St. ATHANASIUS OF ALEXANDRIA, to Trier. His foremost goal was the unity of his empire, and unity in the church served that end. There are indica-

tions that he and many of his successors secretly favored the Arian party in the belief that Arians, who believed Jesus was a lesser being than the Father, would be more willing to subordinate the church to the emperor, who derived his dominion directly from the Father Creator (Genesis 1: 28).

Constantine initiated many great construction projects. At Trier in 306 he established the form of the BASILICA, which became the model for the first major churches of Christianity. To commemorate his victories he built the Arch of Constantine in Rome, parts of which were plundered from earlier pagan imperial monuments. He commissioned a colossal statue of himself for his Roman basilica next to the Forum, possibly as Kosmokrator, or Judge of the World; some segments are preserved in the Palazzo dei Conservatori in Rome. At the outskirts of the city he built the LATERAN BASILICA, the Church of St. JOHN, as the episcopal church of the bishop of Rome.

Following his mother's pilgrimage to Jerusalem to find the true CROSS, he approved the building of the Church of the Holy Sepulcher and many basilicas throughout the eastern empire (see ARCHAEOLOGY). In 330 he undertook the foundation of Constantinople, a "second Rome," built over the ancient Greek city of Byzantium. Many take this event to be the foundation of the Byzantine Empire. Out of his plans came the famous HAGIA SOPHIA and Hagia Eirene ("Holy Peace"), churches still standing in present day Istanbul.

Constantine stands at a turning point in Christian history. In an important sense he was the founder of Christendom, the civilization shaped by the combination of Roman law and institutions with the beliefs, practices, and hierarchical structures of the Christian church. His reign also fatefully marks the final separation of Christianity from its Jewish matrix: he ordered that Sunday become the Christian "Sabbath" and that Christians no longer consult the "detestable Jews" for the date of EASTER, and he imposed the death penalty on Jews who tried to prevent other Jews from converting to Christianity.

Some historians applaud what Constantine did for the church, and there is no doubt that he benefited the Christian cause enormously. Others, however, claim that his direct involvment in church matters skewed relations between CHURCH AND STATE for centuries, welded the cross to the sword, and paved the way for later problems such as the INVESTITURE CONTROVERSY, the entrapment of the papacy in secular rule (see PAPAL STATES; INNOCENT III), the horrors of the CRUSADES and the INQUISITION, and the systemic persecution of Jews by force of law (see ANTI-SEMITISM). In short, he signals the imperialization of the Gospel of Jesus of Nazareth.

Ironically, one of the most famous documents associating Constantine with imperial Christianity was a forgery, the infamous "Donation of Constantine." In this ninth-century Frankish forgery, Constantine allegedly confers episcopal primacy on the pope and crowns him a temporal ruler as well. The forgers got their facts wrong but their attribution symbolically right. Anabaptists, among others, see Constantinian Christianity as a falling away from the nonviolent Gospel of Jesus.

See also HOLY ROMAN EMPEROR.

Further reading: Lactantius's and Eusebius's writings are readily available on the Internet; Michael Grant, *Constantine the Great* (New York: Scribner's, 1994); T. D. Barnes, *Constantine and Eusebius* (Cambridge, Mass.: Harvard University Press, 1991); Johannes Burckhardt, *The Age of Constantine the Great* (New York: Pantheon, 1949); James Carroll, *Constantine's Sword: the Church and the Jews* (Boston: Houghton Mifflin, 2000); George H. Williams, "Christology and Church-State Relations in the Fourth Century," *Church History* (1951) 20: 3–33.

Constantinople

CONSTANTINE THE GREAT founded Constantinople, the new capital of the Eastern Roman Empire, in 330, over the remnants of the ancient Greek city of Byzantium. Except for the period from 1204 to 1261, when it was a Crusader kingdom, the city remained the Eastern capital until it was conquered by the Ottoman Turks in 1453. It was the Turkish capital until 1923, when Mustafa Kemal Ataturk (1881–1938) moved the government to Ankara. The Ecumenical Patriarch of the East still resides in the city, now named Istanbul.

Constantinople was home to the famous HAGIA SOPHIA and Hagia Eirene BASILICAS, the most noted in Byzantine Christendom. Seeking to be a "new Rome," the city emerged as a rival not only to its counterpart in the West but also to the patriarchate of Alexandria. The Council of Constantinople I gave the city's BISHOP preeminence after the bishop of Rome and conferred on him patriarchal powers (cn. 3). Beginning in the sixth century the bishop of Constantinople began to be recognized as the Ecumenical Patriarch. The growing tensions between the East and West led to the GREAT SCHISM in 1054, after which Constantinople ceased to yield pride of place to Rome.

After 1453 most of the city's Christian churches were turned into mosques under Turkish control. Their famous mosaics were either whitewashed or destroyed. Today Hagia Sophia is a museum; its remaining mosaics have been uncovered to the admiration of the world.

Further reading: Thomas F. Mathews, *The Early Churches of Constantinople: Architecture and Liturgy* (University Park: Pennsylvania State University Press, 1971); Jonathan P. Philips, *The Fourth Crusade and the Sack of Constantinople* (London: Jonathan Cape, 2004); David Talbot Rice, *Constantinople from Byzantium to Istanbul* (New York: Stein & Day, 1965); Philip Sherrand, *Constantinople: Iconography of a Sacred City* (London: Oxford University Press, 1963).

Constantinople I, Council of (381)
See COUNCILS, ECUMENICAL.

Constantinople II, Council of (553)
See COUNCILS, ECUMENICAL.

Constantinople III, Council of (680–681)

See COUNCILS, ECUMENICAL.

convent (Lat.: *cum,* "together" + *venire,* "to come" = *conventus,* "assembly")

The Latin term *conventus* originally referred to a provincial assembly of Roman citizens gathered to administer law and other civil matters. The more familiar ecclesiastical term refers to the association together of members of a religious group and the building in which they reside.

Convents have typically been cloistered, or off limits, to anyone not a member of a religious order. The Council of TRENT distinguished between major (12 or more members) and lesser convents. The 1983 Code of Canon Law (573–709) dropped the term entirely in favor of "institute," "house," or "MONASTERY." The houses of mendicant orders and nuns are still frequently referred to as convents.

Further reading: Linda Eckenstein, *Woman Under Monasticism* (New York: Russell & Russell, 1964); Helen Hils, *Invisible City: The Architecture of Devotion in Seventeenth-Century Neapolitan Convents* (Oxford: Oxford University Press, 2003).

conversion (Lat.: *cum,* "with" + *vertere,* "to turn")

The word *conversion* derives from a root meaning to revolve, turn around, or head in a different direction. This basic meaning is parallel to the biblical Hebrew *shuv* (to turn, return, in both a physical and religious sense) and the Greek terms *strepho* and *epistrepho.* Two other Greek words in the New Testament associated with the phenomenon of conversion convey overtones of repentance and regret. The first, *metamelomai* (to be anxious, regretful), describes the state of the subject undergoing a conversion experience. The second, *metanoia* (change of mind), describes the positive state or attitude of one who has undergone a conversion.

Closely related to but distinguishable from the phenomenon of conversion is the experience of vocation, or calling. Although people commonly refer to the conversion of Saul (Acts 9:1–30), PAUL himself never refers to himself as one converted but as one called—in Greek, *kletos* (Rom. 1:1; 1 Cor. 1:1)—to be an APOSTLE of the GOSPEL. Paul models his calling on the classic pattern of the calling of the prophets in the Old Testament (Isa. 49:1; Jer. 1:5). In contrast with conversion, which stresses the introspective aspects of consciousness, *calling* puts the emphasis on divine appointment and election to a mission to the community at large.

Conversion in contemporary thought is almost exclusively restricted to religious phenomena. However, Plato recounts a story of the conversion (Gr. *periagoge*) of the philosopher from the shadows of earthly existence to the light of eternal truth in Book VII of his *Republic* (515a–516b). While it is common to separate the cognitive aspect from the religious and emotional aspects of conversion, such rigid divisions appear false to experience. Plato's account of the philosopher's turn is colored with language adapted from the initiation of neophytes into the Greek mystery religions, such as the mysteries at Eleusis. In every conversion there seems to be a cognitive aspect, a religious aspect, a moral aspect, and an emotional aspect.

Popular accounts of conversion experiences such as the one recounted in *Seven Story Mountain* (1948) by THOMAS MERTON leave the impression that modern conversions are distinctly private and solitary affairs. The common experience, however, is that conversion is undergone in the context of wider communities. The most celebrated modern discussion of conversion is by William James in *The Varieties of Religious Experience* (1902), in which he describes it as an intensely personal and private event. Josiah Royce argued that conversion to faith is a spiritual reality that takes place within communities of interpretation. Indeed, conversion, following upon atonement, is conversion *into* community. Saul's reception into the Christian community in Acts 9 amply illustrates this communal aspect.

There have been two models of conversion. One sees it as a sudden event and escape from time (Plato). The other sees it as a stage of growth in the ongoing life cycle of a person (ARISTOTLE, THOMAS AQUINAS).

The case of St. AUGUSTINE OF HIPPO is instructive. In Book 8 of his *Confessions,* he recounts the immediate circumstances surrounding his decision to become a CHRISTIAN. He found himself in inner turmoil with his divided will struggling against himself until, sitting in a garden, he heard a child chanting over and over *"Tolle, lege"* ("Take up and read"). Thereupon he took up Paul's Epistle to the Romans and read verse 13:13. "Instantly," Augustine continues, "there was infused in my heart something like the light of full certainty and all the gloom of doubt vanished away" (*Confessions* 8.12). To someone who has read only book 8, Augustine's conversion would appear as sudden, rapid, and radical.

However, if we behold the full amplitude of Augustine's rich narrative, the event in the garden is but one of three garden scenes that can be understood as episodes of a long process. When Augustine was 16 he once stole some fruit from a garden. This experience made him conscious of his sinfulness: "And I become a wasteland unto myself" (2.10, whence the title of Thomas Stearns Eliot's famous poem). He likens his sin with Adam and Eve's sin and expulsion from the Garden of Eden (2.2). The other garden scene takes place long after the conversion event. Here he is with Monica, his mother, shortly before her departure and death. They are overlooking a garden in Ostia, conversing about celestial things and the Garden of Paradise (9.10). The recurring theme of the garden scene in the *Confessions* provides the dense background and context of the stages in Augustine's spiritual journey: remorse over SIN, surrender to GOD's will: and foretaste of celestial bliss. Augustine's dramatic conversion experience

in Book 8 is both a momentous event and a stage on life's way.

Contemporary theory of life development lends support to the reconciliation of the Plato-Augustine and Aristotle-Aquinas models of conversion. In his celebrated essay "Eight Ages of Man" and more recently in *The Life Cycle Completed* (1982), Erik Erikson notes that the human life cycle unfolds in ages or stages, beginning with the child's basic trust versus mistrust and ending with the older person's ego-identity versus despair. However, the transition to young adulthood (identity versus role confusion) is particularly marked by a call to "ideological" commitments and conversion-related orientations. The conversion experience required for the transition into young adulthood was the subject of Erikson's *Young Man Luther.* Conversion can be both maturational, or a stage in the unfolding of life's dialectic, and/or critical, a crucial event like Paul's road to Damascus experience that shapes the fundamental orientation of a person toward life. James Fowler united Erikson's psychosexual stages with Lawrence Kohlberg's stages of moral development in his seminal *Stages of Faith* (1981).

Conversion is an extremely complex phenomenon. It is both event and process. It is a state and a dialectical movement. That dialectic can be broken down into three moments: a turning away, or separation; a state of suspension; and a turning toward.

Turning Away Those who experience a conversion seem to undergo something akin to "spiritual dissonance." The horizon that the person is living within is now perceived, for one reason or another, as limited and unfulfilling. This turning has religious, emotional, psychological, intellectual, and even political components. William James summarized this by noting that the convert experiences a fundamental change in "the habitual center of his energy." It is imperative to note that all of the above factors—psychological, intellectual, religious, moral, sociological, and political—are latent in any conversion experience. The change is not unlike the paradigm shift in scientific revolutions.

Suspension The middle phase in the conversion process is very difficult to describe, and not much attention has been given to it. This phase also can be described as a state of indecision, of a divided mind (James), of dwelling in what Plato called the "in-between" (Greek, *metaxu*), or of standing on the threshold (Lat., *limen*), where the convert is not all the way out of one room ("the old man") and not all the way into the next ("the new man"). This last notion refers to the "liminal phase" in rites of passage, during which initiates are statusless, anonymous, and secluded from ordinary society. Although we are tempted to restrict rites of passage to primal societies, liminal transitions still occur in modern industrial society, but they are diffuse and fragmented (the "teen years") rather than compact and intense, as they are in tribal societies. During this phase the convert experiences what Jean Piaget calls "cognitive disequilibrium," Kohlberg calls "cognitive conflict," and James calls the "divided self."

Turning Toward Many theories of conversion stop with the *terminus a quo* of the conversion experience. The experiences accompanying the "turning away" phase are often colorful, dramatic, and even traumatic. That conversions have long-term effects is without question. Moses turned away from the luxury of the Egyptian court and founded a people of faith. St. FRANCIS OF ASSISI turned away from a quest for knighthood and founded instead one of the greatest religious orders of the MIDDLE AGES. James characterized the third phase of the conversion experience with terms like commitment, revitalization, renewal, regeneration, and a sense of sanctification, holiness, or blessedness. If the first two phases of the process can be said to be inner-directed, the third is other-directed in the sense that the convert dedicates himself or herself to new ideals; new codes of behavior; new spiritual disciplines such as prayer, fasting, and meditation; and works of charity or evangelization. The social impact of conversion is felt through the public expression of new modes of life. The third phase is also the seedbed of religious innovation.

Further reading: Darrol Bryant and Christopher Lamb, eds. *Religious Conversion: Contemporary Practices and Controversies* (London: Cassell, 1999); Robert Duggan, ed. *Conversion and the Catechumenate* (New York: Paulist Press, 1984); Erik Erikson, *The Life Cycle Completed* (New York: Norton, 1982); James Fowler, *Stages of Faith* (San Francisco: Harper & Row, 1981); R. Lewis Rambo, *Understanding Religious Conversion*. (New Haven, Conn.: Yale University Press, 1993).

Copernicus, Nicolaus (1473–1543) *astronomer*

Nicolaus Koppernigk was born in Torun, Poland. He studied at the cathedral school of Wloclawek, which prepared him to enter the University of Kraków in 1491. His uncle, a CANON in Frauenburg (Frombork), hoped that Nicolaus would choose a career in the church. He received a broad education in Latin, mathematics, astronomy (and astrology), geography, and philosophy. While at Kraków he began to use the Latinized version of his name by which he is better known.

After Kraków Nicolaus studied CANON LAW at Bologna, which had a large contingent of German-speaking students. He was appointed a canon at Frauenburg cathedral while at Bologna, but in the meantime he had become the enthusiastic assistant to Domenico Maria de Novara (1454–1504) of Ferrara, Bologna's astronomy professor. Nicolaus secretly pursued his astronomical studies while taking degrees in medicine at Padua and canon law at Ferrara.

After studying the heavens at Frauenburg, Nicolaus came to believe that the Earth moved around the Sun rather than the opposite, a view now known as heliocentrism. He first recorded this idea in a privately circulated text called the Little Commentary. Among his unique hypotheses was that the apparent backward movement of the other planets was caused by the Earth's movement around the Sun in relation to the planets. The mathematical calculations to confirm his theories had to wait until later. Only in 1543, as his life neared its end, did he finally publish *De revolutionibus orbium coelestium* (1543). It appears that he was finally motivated to finish his work by the 1539 publication of a preview and summary by a young colleague, Georg Rheticus (1514–74).

The Lutheran theologian and mathematician Andreas Osiander (1498–1552) oversaw the printing of the book in Nuremberg. Osiander stated in a preface that Copernicus intended his hypothesis not as an objective fact but as a simpler method to calculate the motions of the planets. Later GALILEO GALILEI would defend the Copernican hypothesis not simply as a theoretical model of explanation but as a description of objective reality. Following Galileo's condemnation, Copernicus's book was then placed on the Index of Forbidden Books along with Galileo's.

The heliocentric theory was not fully fleshed out until Johannes Kepler (1531–1630) and Isaac Newton (1643–1727). Kepler explained the motions in terms of three laws: the planets move in elliptical orbits with the Sun at one of the foci, the orbits move over equal areas in equal times, and the average distance to the sun of each planet is related to the square of its period of revolution. Newton explained the reasons for these laws with his own laws of motion and theory of gravity, which states that the gravitational force between two bodies is directly proportional to the product of two masses and inversely proportional to the square of the distance between them ($Fg = m \cdot m/d^2$), or the closer the bodies, the greater the gravitational force.

Further reading: Angus Armitage, *Copernicus: The Founder of Modern Astronomy* (New York: Thomas Yoreloff, 1957); Nicholas Copernicus, *Complete Works* (Baltimore: Johns Hopkins University Press, 1992); Pierre Gassendi and Olivier Thill, *The Life of Copernicus* (Fairfax, Va.: Xulon, 2002); Thomas Kuhn, *The Copernican Revolution: Planetary Astronomy and the Development of Western Thought* (Cambridge, Mass.: Harvard University Press, 1957); Edward Rosen and Erna Hilfstein, *Copernicus and His Successors* (London: Hambledon, 1995).

Coptic Catholic Church

After the Council of CHALCEDON in 451, the Coptic Orthodox Church and the Armenian Apostolic Church separated from both Rome and CONSTANTINOPLE by refusing to affirm the council's formulas concerning the nature of CHRIST. Chalcedon asserted that the divine and human natures were present in the one person of Christ. Egyptian CHRISTIANS tended to follow a position labeled monophysitism, which emphasized Christ's divine nature as the center of his personality. Both the Catholics and the Orthodox considered those rejecting Chalcedon to be heretics.

In 1442, several Coptic leaders tried to effect a reconciliation with Rome. They attended the Council of FLORENCE, where they signed the document *Cantate Domino* (February 4, 1442). However, upon their return to Egypt both the local leaders and the laity were unwilling to support their action.

Franciscan missionaries arrived in Egypt beginning in 1630. In 1741 Coptic bishop Amba Athanasius of Jerusalem became a Catholic, and Pope Benedict XIV (r. 1740–58) appointed him vicar apostolic of the small community of Egyptian Coptic Catholics, which at that time numbered no more than 2,000. Although Athanasius eventually returned to the Coptic Orthodox Church, a line of Catholic vicars apostolic continued after him.

With some minor changes the Catholic Copts continued to use the Coptic liturgy. Misreading the intentions of the Ottoman rulers, Pope Leo XII (r. 1823–29) created the Egyptian patriarchate in 1824, but the office was not filled until 1899 with the naming of Cyril Makarios as Cyril II, Patriarch of Alexandria of the Copts (r. 1899–1908). In office less than a decade, he resigned in 1908, partly because he tried to impose Latin features on the Coptic rite and met stiff resistance. A new patriarch was not named until 1947.

The Coptic Catholic Church has nine dioceses. The church supports a theological seminary and six religious orders. It is active in the Middle East Council of Churches. It relates to Rome through the Congregation for the Oriental Churches. The present patriarch of Alexandria of the Copts is Stephanos II Gatta (b. 1920, elected 1986). Today there are 243,000 members in Egypt, with 10,000 more abroad in Paris, Montreal, Brooklyn, Sydney, and Melbourne.

See also COPTIC CHURCH.

Further reading: Donald Attwater, *The Catholic Eastern Churches* (Milwaukee: Bruce, 1937); Nikolaus Liesel, *The Eastern Catholic Liturgies: A Study in Words and Pictures* (Westminster Md.: Newman, 1960); Ronald G. Roberson, *The Eastern Christian Churches: A Brief Survey,* 5th ed. (Rome: Pontifical Oriental Institute, 1995).

Coptic Church (Ar.: *Qibt,* from Gk.: *Aegyptos,* from Eg.: *Hikaptah,* one of the names of Memphis, the first capital of ancient Egypt)

The Christian Coptic Orthodox Church of Egypt is an autonomous, self-governing church encompassing most of the CHRISTIANS of EGYPT, Ethiopia, and Eritrea. It traces its religious ancestry to St. Mark the Evangelist, and lays claim to the origin of Christian MONASTICISM in the Egyptian desert in the late third century. Coptic is the last stage of the ancient Egyptian language; its writings have a Greek admixture, especially in the LITURGY. Coptics address the patriarch of Alexandria as "pope," a position currently held by Pope Shenouda III (1971–).

The Copts accept the first three ecumenical COUNCILS (Nicaea, Constantinople I, EPHESUS), but they separated from both Rome and CONSTANTINOPLE over the Christological formulation of the Council of CHALCEDON (451). Chalcedon speaks of CHRIST as "one person with two natures, divine and human." After the council Bishop Diocorus of Alexandria (444–51) was deposed by the Orthodox party, but in 460 the Copts chose to adopt his ECCLESIOLOGY along with the Christological wording of St. CYRIL OF ALEXANDRIA, who spoke of "one incarnate nature of God the Word."

In the Alexandrine tradition, *hypostasis* and *physis* were identical terms, whereas in the Chalcedon formula *hypostasis* meant "person" and *physis* meant "nature." Those who accept Chalcedon have long accused the Copts of monophysitism, which asserts that Christ has only one nature, the divine, which unites the human and divine aspects. Today Coptic theologians firmly state that they have never believed this; instead, they believe that Christ is perfect in his divinity, and he is perfect in his humanity, but his divinity and his humanity are united in one nature called "the nature of the incarnate word." Thus, the Copts believe in two natures, "human" and "divine," that are united in one being "without mingling, without confusion, and without alteration," as stated in the confession of faith at the end of the Coptic liturgy.

Coptic Christianity developed its own religious style centered on biblical spirituality, monasticism, and holy monks. Many of the MONASTERIES founded in the third century still flourish. The tradition is noted for its distinctive art, which blends Egyptian, Greek, and Byzantine styles. The Coptic cross is very distinctive.

After the Arabic conquest in 641, the Copts were given the status of a "protected people" according to the Qu'ran: socially restricted and subject to a poll tax. In recent times Coptic leaders have charged zealous Muslims with kidnapping young Coptic girls and trying to force them into Islam via marriage. The Coptic Church is a charter member of the World Council of Churches (1948). Today there are more than 9 million Copts in northeast Africa and about 1.5 million living in Europe, Australia, and the United States.

Further reading: Massimo Capuani, *Christian Egypt: Coptic Art and Monuments Through Two Millennia* (Collegeville, Minn.: Liturgical Press, 1999); Otto F. A. Meinardus, *2000 Years of Coptic Christianity* (Cairo: American University Press, 1999); M. Roncaglia, *Histoire de l'église copte* (Beirut: St. Paul, 1985); Birger Pearson and J. Goehring, eds., *The Roots of Egyptian Christianity* (Philadelphia: Fortress Press, 1986); *St. Mark and the Coptic Church* (Cairo: Coptic Orthodox Patriarchate, 1968).

cosmology/cosmological argument (Gr.: *cosmos,* "universe" + *logos,* "study, account of")

Cosmology is the study of the sum total of phenomena in space and time that make up the universe; it can also be defined as the study of the large-scale properties of the universe as a whole. The cosmological argument is an attempt to prove the existence of GOD via the evidence of cosmology.

Until the Enlightenment cosmology was considered a part of METAPHYSICS, the study of reality or being as being; later it became subsumed under the empirico-analytic sciences. The current cosmology, or model of the universe, is the Big Bang theory, which states that the universe began with a sudden explosion about 13.7 billion years before the present, followed by an expansion and the formation of the building blocks of matter and, eventually, the galactic structures we now see in the starry heavens.

During the early MIDDLE AGES what is known as the Kalām Cosmological Argument emerged among thinkers like Maimonides (1135–1204) and Al-Ghazali (1058–1111) and was adopted by the great CHRISTIAN thinkers ANSELM, THOMAS AQUINAS, DUNS SCOTUS, René Descartes, John Locke (1632–1704), and Gottfried Wilhelm Leibniz (1646–1716). The Jewish and Muslim thinkers based their arguments on Plato and ARISTOTLE. The term *kalām* means "speech" in Arabic and stood for natural theology and the arguments derived from it.

The argument begins with the statement "The universe had either a beginning or no beginning" and through a series of logical steps concludes with "A series of events in time without a beginning cannot exist." The ultimate conclusion is that God, an infinite being, created the universe. St. Thomas's version is contained in his famous five proofs (*Summa Theologiae* 1.2.3). Scotus's argument is in his *On the First Principle*. Descartes gives a version in his *Meditations* and Leibniz in his *Monadology*.

During the Enlightenment the cosmological argument came under severe criticism by David Hume (1711–76) and Immanuel Kant (1724–1804), although Georg F. W. Hegel (1770–1831) argued for its validity. The cosmological argument remains the most popular of the arguments for the existence of God and has lately been merged with the argument from intelligent design.

See also CRITIQUE OF CHRISTIANITY.

Further reading: William Lane Craig. *The Kalam Cosmological Argument* (New York: Barnes & Noble, 1979); John Duns Scotus, *A Treatise on God as First Principle* (Chicago: Franciscan Herald, 1966); Michael Rowan-Robinson, *Cosmology* (Oxford: Clarendon, 2004).

Coughlin, Charles E.   *See* ELECTRONIC CHURCH.

council/conciliarism (Lat.: *concilium,* "assembly")

A council is a formal meeting of BISHOPS, abbots, and other religious leaders called for the purpose of defining doctrine and/or regulating church discipline. Assemblies representing the whole church worldwide, where the collegial authority of the bishops is fully manifest, are called ecumenical councils (*see* COUNCILS, ECUMENICAL). Conciliarism is the view that recognizes the preeminence of councils over the hierarchy, including the pope.

Councils can be held on a national (plenary) or a regional (provincial) level. Such nonecumenical gatherings are often called synods, but the terminology is not fixed. The Council of Arles (314), which engaged the problem of DONATISM, was an example of a regional council. The Councils of Baltimore (1852, 1866, 1884) were examples of national plenary councils.

Some call the Council of Jerusalem (Acts 15) the first council, but its scope dealt almost exclusively with the question of Jewish law. The first formal ecumenical council was the Council of Nicaea (325); the most recent was VATICAN COUNCIL II (1962–65). In Eastern Orthodoxy and for many theologians the first seven ecumenical councils have extra authority since they defined the fundamental doctrines concerning the CREED, CHRISTOLOGY (*see* CHRIST/CHRISTOLOGY), and the TRINITY.

Beginning in the MIDDLE AGES, conciliarism became a burning issue: was council or pope preeminent in authority, indefectibility, inerrancy, and infallibility? The noted canonist Hugh of Pisa (d. 1210), also known as Huguccio, taught that a pope could become a heretic and thus distinguished between the local Roman Church and the Universal Church. The debate came to a head during the struggle between BONIFACE VIII and Philip IV the Fair of France (1268–1314). John of Paris (d. 1306) taught that the pope was God's steward in temporal and spiritual matters and could be deposed for injustice. In his *Defensor Pacis* Marsiglio of Padua (1276–1342) made the state supreme: the emperor could "correct, install or uninstall or punish" the pope. Pope John XXII condemned that thesis in the bull *Licet Juxta Doctrinam* (October 23, 1327). WILLIAM OF OCKHAM thought that both pope and general council could fall into error but that the church would remain indefectible in some part. Both Marsiglio and

Ockham were excommunicated and sought refuge from the antipapal Holy Roman Emperor Ludwig IV (1282–1347) of Bavaria.

The Western SCHISM (1378–1417), during which there were as many as three papal claimants at the same time, brought conciliar theory into acute focus. Like Marsiglio and Ockham, the preeminent canonist, Conrad of Gelnhausen (c. 1320–90), professor at Bologna and later first rector of Heidelberg University, made a distinction between the pope and his curia on the one hand, and the universal church on the other. The schism warranted a general council to resolve the impasse.

The Council of CONSTANCE did just that; its fourth and fifth sessions stated that all CHRISTIANS, including the pope, were bound by the God-authorized decrees of a council. Unfortunately for conciliarism, subsequent popes Martin V (1417–31) and Pius II (1458–64) declared invalid any appeal from the pope to a council. In the bull *Exsecrabilis* (January 18, 1460) Pius II (r. 1458–64), who, as Aeneas Silvio de Picollomini had defended Constance and even the radical reform at the Council of BASEL, condemned the conciliar theory.

From that point on the inviolability of papal claims seemed impregnable. NICHOLAS OF CUSA argued for a more balanced approach in his *De Concordantia Catholica* (1433). Many church historians claim that the failure of the Renaissance popes to undertake reforming councils paved the road to the PROTESTANT REFORMATION. The addition of the doctrine of papal INFALLIBILITY at VATICAN COUNCIL I kept the balance strongly in favor of the PAPACY. The 1917 edition of Code of Canon Law (cn. 2332) stated that anyone appealing from the papacy to a general council is suspect of "HERESY" (not just "SCHISM," which would have been the logical charge) and is automatically excommunicated. VATICAN COUNCIL II tried to redress the balance by affirming the collegiality of all the bishops in union with the pope. It said nothing about SENSUS FIDELIUM, or "sense of the faithful," and its role in shaping and maintaining doctrine.

Further reading: Luis M. Bermejo, *Church, Conciliarity and Communion* (Anand: Gujarat Shitya Prakash, 1990); Christopher M. D. Crowder, *Unity, Heresy and Reform, 1378–1460* (New York: St. Martin's, 1977); Brian Tierney, *Foundations of Conciliar Theory* (Cambridge: Cambridge University Press, 1955).

councils, ecumenical

An ecumenical council is an official gathering of BISHOPS, abbots, church officials, other clergy, and theologians from around the world, convened to provide guidance for the church on matters of doctrine, discipline, church organization, and pastoral care. Roman Catholics recognize 21 valid historical councils. The first seven of these councils are held to be authoritative by the EASTERN ORTHODOX and Anglican Churches and by many other members of the CHRISTIAN family. This entry will list all 21 councils, and briefly describe some. The Councils of BASEL, FLORENCE, CONSTANCE, CHALCEDON, EPHESUS, TRENT, VATICAN COUNCIL I, and VATICAN COUNCIL II have separate entries.

The first several councils, called by emperors, patriarchs, and/or popes, helped define the orthodox Christian faith in an era of doctrinal contention. The ecumenical councils of the MIDDLE AGES all took place under the direction and in the interest of strong popes. When the PAPACY underwent severe weakening during the AVIGNON PAPACY and the western SCHISM, the councils themselves stepped up to fill in the gaps. This gave rise to counciliarism, which tried to elevate the collective power of the bishops as a whole above even the papacy.

Nicaea I (325) The first ecumenical council, Nicaea I, was convened by Emperor CONSTANTINE THE GREAT in concurrence with the pope and bishops to deal with both organizational and doctrinal matters. It began the process of fixing the CREED for all Christians and setting the church apart from HERESY, in this case the "impiety and lawlessness of Arius" (*see* ARIANISM). The key doctrinal matter was the inclusion of the term *homoousios* ("of the same being/ substance") into the creed, thus affirming the equality of the Father and Son against the views of the Arians. Some 20 canons dealt with church discipline, for example, the exclusion of eunuchs from the priesthood (1), the qualifications, education, and conduct of CLERGY (2,3,9), the recognition of the patriarchates of Antioch, Alexandria, and Rome (6), proscription against military service (12), and praying standing up (20). Nicaea I also sundered Christians from Jews on the matter of fixing the date for EASTER.

Constantinople I (381) This council was convened by Emperor Theodosius I (r. 378–395). Pope Damasus I (r. 366–384) was represented by his famous *Tome*, a treatise on doctrine. GREGORY OF NAZIANZUS was one of the presiders.

The council affirmed the creed of Nicaea and addressed the heresies of Arianism; Sabellelianism, which taught that the three persons of the TRINITY were three modes, or aspects, of the one God—a related heresy was PATRIPASSIONISM, the belief that when Jesus suffered, the Father suffered, too; Anomoeanism, a radical Arianism that taught that the Son was not only less than the Father, but even unlike him (Gk.: *anomios*); the Apollonarians, who said there was only one active divine center in Christ, the Logos, thereby downplaying Christ's humanity (that issue was not resolved until Chalcedon); and the Pneumatomachi, or "Spirit-Fighters," who maintained that the HOLY SPIRIT was not divine. To refute the latter group, the creedal *Exposition of the 150 Fathers* affirmed belief "in the Spirit, the holy, the lordly, the life-giving one, proceeding from the Father, coworshipped, co-glorified with Father and Son."

The council issued several important canons (matters of church organization and discipline), one (cn. 2) limiting a bishop's power to his own diocese, and another (cn. 3) recognizing Constantinople as a patriarchal "second Rome," next in rank to the first, a canon that has never been fully accepted by the Roman church.

Ephesus (431) *See* Council of Ephesus.

Chalcedon (451) *See* Council of Chalcedon.

Constantinople II (553) The council was called by Emperor Justinian I (r, 527–65) and Pope Vigilius (r. 537–55). The focus was to condemn the popular teachings of Theodore of Mopseustia (c. 350–428), who was called the Interpreter for his many commentaries on the Bible in the tradition of the Antiochene School. Theodore was accused of Nestorianism, which taught that there were two separate persons in Christ—the orthodox formula established at Chalcedon was "one person, two natures."

Theodore used the analogy "grace-nature" to describe the relation of the divine and human in Christ. The council anathematized any teaching that limited the unity between the Word of God and the man in Christ to a relation "in respect of grace, or principle of action, or of dignty, or in respect to equality of honor, or of authority, or of some relation of affection or power." It attributed such teachings to Theodore.

Constantinople III (680–681) Called by Emperor Constantine IV (r. 668–685) and Pope Donus (r. 676–678), the council was later ratified by Pope Agatho (r. 678–681). It dealt with the issues of Monothelitism, the teaching that there was only one will (Gk. *thelema*) in Christ, and Monenergism, the teaching that there was only one mode of activity (Gk. *energeia*) in Christ. Pope Honorius (r. 625–638) had embraced the one-will formula, a historical fact that seriously challenges claims of papal infallibility. The council stated that it is "heresy" to maintain "a single will and a single principle of action in the two natures of the one member of the holy Trinity, Christ our true God," leading to "the blasphemous conclusion that [Christ's] rationally animate flesh is without a will and a principle of action."

Nicaea II (787) The council was convoked by Empress Irene (r. 797–802), acting as regent for Constantine VI (r. 780–97). Pope Hadrian I (r. 772–95) later concurred with the proceedings. The focus was on the inconoclasm controversy (*see* Icon). Influenced by the Jewish and Islamic proscription of idols and images in sacred spaces, Emperors Leo III (r. 717–741) and Constantine V Copronymus (r. 741–775) issued laws calling for the effacement of images throughout the empire. In opposition, as far back as 730 St. John of Damascus and other iconodules, or venerators of icons, had argued in favor of images on the basis of church tradition and the principles of the Creation and the Incarnation; he wrote that "the invisible things of God since the creation of the world are made visible through images," Christ being the visible image of God "in flesh and blood" (*Apology Against Those Who Decry the Use of Images* 1). In 843 Empress Theodora (d. 848), wife of iconoclast Emperor Theophilus (829–42), set about restoring images during the regency of her son Michael III (r. 842–867).

Constantinople IV (869–870) This council's aim was to resolve the first formal East-West schism. Pope Nicholas I (r. 858–867) had excommunicated Patriarch Photius I the Great (r. 858–67, 877–86), ostensibly over irregularities in Photius's election, but really and more shamefully over his claim to jurisdiction over Dalmatia and southern Italy. Photius countered by accusing the West of unilaterally inserting the FILIOQUE clause into its creed and promulgating a doctrine of PURGATORY not supported by the tradition. Canon 21 of the council established the priority of the patriarchates: Rome, Constantinople, Alexandria, Antioch, and Jerusalem. Photius was reinstated after the council: Nevertheless, Eastern Orthodoxy does not recognize the 869–70 council as ecumenical; instead it recognizes as ecumenical a later synod, held in 879–80.

Lateran I (1123) The council was held at the papal palace and LATERAN BASILICA of St. John in Rome, on the initiative of Pope Calixtus (r. 1119–24). It recognized the CONCORDAT of Worms (1122), which had settled the INVESTITURE CONTROVERSY. There are no officially recorded acts remaining. The council's canons dealt with simony, the "truce of God" (a peace period during times of war), indulgences for crusaders, and the administration of the SACRAMENTS.

Lateran II (1139) Pope Innocent II (r. 1130–43) called this "plenary synod" in order to remedy the effects of the schism caused by the rival pope Anacletus II (d. 1138). St BERNARD OF CLAIRVAUX played a key role in swinging support Innocent's way. The canons extended the reforms of GREGORY VII regarding usury and regarding the participation of monks and clerics in tournaments and in the study of law and medicine. Canon 7 enjoined CELIBACY on clerics and monks from the level of the subdiaconate and invalidated any subsequent marriages. Canon 28 established cathedral chapters, the association of priests and deacons assisting a cathedral bishop, and their right to elect the local bishop. Chapters become very important during the Middle Ages.

Lateran III (1179) Convened by Pope Alexander III (r. 1159–81), this council settled the political, territorial, and ecclesiastical dispute between the papacy and the Holy Roman Emperor FREDERICK I BARBAROSSA, who had put up rival candidates for the papacy. There are lists of the bishops and envoys from kings who attended.

The council issued several canons, which it called "chapters," setting qualifications for bishops (they had to be of legitimate birth and at least 30 years of age), forbidding multiple benefices to one person, barring Jews and Saracens (Muslims) from owning Christian slaves, and excommunicating the CATHARI. On the other hand, the council refrained from condemning the Poor Men of Lyons, later known as WALDENSIANS, who had sought approval for their Bible translation and their way of life. The attitude toward heretics was gradually changing. The early church sought to persuade heretics and, failing that, to isolate or exile them. The medieval church eventually tried to exterminate those it ruled to be heretics and appealed to the precedent Augustine established against the Donatists. This bloodthirsty attitude was soon reenforced by the INQUISITION.

Lateran IV (1215) Convened by INNOCENT III, this was the most important council in the Latin West during the Middle Ages. Emperor FREDERICK II and all the kings of the West sent representatives, and participants came from eastern Europe as well. The "chapters" include a profession of faith aimed at the Cathari, orders to the Inquisition to combat Cathari, Waldensians, Beghards, Beguines, and others; a declaration that CREATION was ex nihilo; and the use of the term TRANSUBSTANTIATION (change of substance of the bread and wine into the body and blood of the Lord) for the EUCHARIST. Chapter

21 required every Christian above the age of reason to receive penance (RECONCILIATION) and the Eucharist at least once a year. Several canons dealt with extending the pastoral ministry of bishops. Several dealt with the education of the clergy. Fatefully, Muslims and Jews were prohibited from appearing in public during Holy Week and commanded to wear distinctive garb. The council intervened directly in political affairs, putting Simon de Montfort (1160–1218) in power at Toulouse, where the Cathari lived, rejecting the Magna Carta, and recognizing Frederick II as emperor. Innocent III had told the emperor, "You are the moon; I am the sun."

Lyon [Lyons] I (1245) Called by Innocent IV (r. 1243–45), the council's principal purpose was to depose Emperor Frederick II in an attempt to settle the territorial dispute between the empire and the pope, the "prince" of the PAPAL STATES. This was a fateful and woeful invasion of the church into the affairs of the state. The emperor was deposed on grounds of perjury, disturbing the peace, and heresy. Some of the chapters dealt with CANON LAW and became part of the revised code in 1253. (As Sinibaldo Fieschi, Innocent IV had been a canon lawyer at Bologna, the preeminent medieval school of canon law in all of Europe.)

Lyon [Lyons] II (1274) After a long *sede vacante* (Lat. "the chair [of St. Peter] being empty"), the new pope Gregory X (r. 1271–76), convened the council to reform the procedures of papal conclaves, seek reunion with the Eastern Church, and start a new CRUSADE. Western kings, the eastern emperor Michael VIII Paleologus (1225–82), and even the Mongolian Kublai Khan (r. 1260–94) were invited, the latter on the rumor that he was thinking of converting. St. BONAVENTURE preached the opening sermon and played a key role at the start of the proceedings, but he died soon after; St. THOMAS AQUINAS had died on the way to the council.

At the fourth session the Greek representatives seemed willing to compromise: they accepted papal primacy, a version of the doctrine of PURGATORY, and seven as the number of sacraments (the East was never as concerned about numbers as the West), and they participated in a Latin mass at which the FILIOQUE phrase was sung in the CREED, with the understanding they would keep their own, differing creed. Back home, however, the general Greek hierarchy and laity failed to approve the agreement. The council added a nuance to the filioque doctrine by condemning anyone who dared "rashly to assert that the holy Spirit proceeds from the Father and the Son as from two principles and not as from one."

The fifth session issued the decree *Ubi Periculum* (July 16, 1274), which laid down strict rules for the election of popes that are still in force, although many intervening popes have tried to suspend them or bend them to their own advantage. Most important is the requirement that a successor be elected 10 days after the death of a pope, in a conclave of cardinals sealed off from contact with the outside world. Canon 23 approved the pastoral mission of the MENDICANT orders against opposition from many secular clergy. The pope decided the kingship of Germany in favor of Rudolph I of Habsburg (r. 1723–91). Throughout the proceedings, the pope exerted extraordinary power.

Vienne (1308–1312) The long shadow of BONIFACE VIII, the most powerful of the medieval popes, extended over the proceedings of Vienne, although it was convened by his second successor, Clement V (r. 1305–14). The council opened with a liturgical ceremony that became standard at later councils, including the reading of Luke 10:1–16 (Jesus sending out the disciples) and the singing of the *Te Deum*. Using stern language worthy of an Old Testament prophet, the pope condemned and suppressed the military order of the KNIGHTS TEMPLAR, accusing them of idolatry, apostasy, fornication, and sodomy. Although the knights were by no means innocents, the attack was instigated by Philip IV the Fair of France (r. 1285–1314) as a way to seize the Templar properties; he used torture to extract "confessions" of magic and heresy.

The council also gave dogmatic force to a philosophical position: it ruled that anyone who denied that "the rational or intellectual soul is . . . the form of the human body of itself and essentially" was to be considered a heretic. The council also pronounced against the strict observance of poverty by the Spirituals of the FRANCISCAN ORDER. It also laid down directives to protect the church from secular interference, especially from taxation. The council tried to rouse yet another Crusade, but Raymond Lull (1232–1315) convinced it instead to set up language schools to train missionaries, who could use persuasion rather than pillage to spread the faith.

Constance (1414–1418) *See* COUNCIL OF CONSTANCE.

Basel-Ferrara-Florence (1431–1442) *See* COUNCIL OF FLORENCE.

Lateran V (1512–1517) Convened by Julius II (r. 1503–13), Lateran V was concluded under LEO X (r. 1513–21). This council deliberately modeled itself on the strong papal councils of the Middle Ages and tried to avoid the style of the last two Councils of Constance and Florence. Its decrees took the form of PAPAL BULLS. The chief aim was to counteract the Council of Pisa, which had been convoked by cardinals in 1409 to end the western schism and which had proclaimed that the council was above the pope, thus leading to the independence of the two intervening councils. There is much debate about whether Pisa was a valid council.

Lateran V also declared that the individual human soul is immortal, in opposition to the Aristotelian philosopher Pietro Pamponazzi (1462–1525), who, while affirming revelation, asserted that natural reason could demonstrate that the soul is mortal. Several of the Camadolese monks proposed stringent reforms to counteract a growing tide of abuses, including multiple benefices, absentee clergy, and corrupt morals. However, Julius II (r. 1503–13) and Leo X (r. 1513–21), son of Lorenzo de Medici the Magnificent (1449–92) of Florence, were not up to reform, being themselves the epitome of lax Renaissance clergy. Unable to reform from within, the Roman church was forced from without to change. Lateran V ended March 16; on July 17 Martin Luther (1483–1546) tacked 95 theses to the door of Wittenburg cathedral, launching the PROTESTANT REFORMATION.

Trent (1545–1563) *See* COUNCIL OF TRENT.

Vatican I (1869–1870) *See* VATICAN COUNCIL I.

Vatican II (1962–1965) *See* VATICAN COUNCIL II.

Further reading: Philip Hughes, *The Church in Crisis: A History of the General Councils, 325–1870* (New York: Image, 1964); Hubert Jedin, *Ecumenical Councils of the Church* (Glen Rock, N.J.: Paulist Press, 1961); Edward Schwartz et al., *Acta Conciliorum Oecumenicorum* (Berlin: W. de Gruyter, 1914–); Norman P. Tanner, *Decrees of the Ecumenical Councils* (Washington, D.C.: Georgetown University Press, 1960).

Counter-Reformation

Most people define the Counter-Reformation as the Catholic reaction to the PROTESTANT REFORMATION, sparked in 1517 by Martin Luther's Ninety-five Theses. The reality was much more complex.

The Counter-Reformation was first and foremost a continuation of the reform movement within Catholicism itself, which had appeared well before the end of the 15th century. Second, it was an effort to preserve the unity of the church by containing the spread of Protestantism. Third, it was a creative movement that went beyond the Reformation with new forms of religious orders (e.g., the Jesuits), new types of spirituality (e.g., TERESA OF ÁVILA), a new aesthetic (baroque), and a new engagement with the world beyond Europe (missionary expansion).

The idea of reform was already built into the Catholic tradition. The most notable example was the Cluniac monastic reforms in the ninth to 11th centuries. Pope GREGORY VII THE GREAT used monks from Cluny and its daughter monasteries to carry out his own reform program. The Cistercian reform of the 11th century was exemplified in the life of St. BERNARD OF CLAIRVAUX, a medieval monk often later cited as a model by the great Protestant reformers. The rise of the MENDICANT ORDERS was another call to reform. Many of the heretical offshoots of the Middle Ages (CATHARI, WALDENSIANS, Beguines, Lollards, etc.) were not just heresies but also attempts by faithful Catholics to reform corrupt clerical practices. Two "heretics" in particular, JOHN WYCLIFFE (d. 1384), often called the "morning star" of the Reformation, and his Czech follower JAN HUS (1374–1415), anticipated the Reformation in many details, especially on the authority of the BIBLE and in preaching and living the Gospel life. Closer to the mainstream Catholic tradition were the Brethren of the Common Life founded by Geert Groote (1340–84), who promoted the DEVOTIO MODERNA, promised a personal relation with Jesus, and the simple, direct piety found in Thomas à Kempis's *Imitation of Christ* and painted in the celebrated Isenheim altar of Matthias Grünewald (1475–1528).

Closer in time to the Wittenberg cataclysm were the voices of the pre-Reformation reformers. At the two extremes were the radical firebrand Dominican GIROLAMO SAVONAROLA and the humanist scholar DESIDERIUS ERASMUS. No less than a prophet, Savonarola preached the "bonfire of vanities," into which even Botticelli (c. 1444–1510) tossed his artwork, and railed against the flagrantly corrupt Borgia pope ALEXANDER VI. His preaching sent him to the fiery stake. Erasmus, on the other hand, trained by the Brethren of the Common Life, was scholarly and cosmopolitan. His *Praise of Folly* (1509) mocked the sale of indulgences, the outlandish miracle stories about the saints, and corruption in clerical life. He preached a simple, direct piety like that of the Brethren. He accused bishops of being "overseers (*episcopi*) of their own gain and income." His critical edition of the New Testament, along with a completely new Latin translation, provided the reformers with ample justifications for interpreting the Bible outside the box of the medieval four-fold senses. Erasmus championed a new form of CHRISTIAN humanism and spirituality beyond the aridities, as they now appeared, of medieval disputations.

The Catholic side of the pre-Reformation reform was sustained by figures like Juan de Valdés (c. 1490–1541), who fled the Spanish INQUISITION and joined forces with the reforming noble families of the Gonzagas and the Colonnas in Naples. Giulia Gonzaga (1513–66) and Vittoria Colonna (1492–1547) also sponsored the Observant Franciscan and later Capuchin Bernadino Ochino (1487–1541) and the Dominican Peter Martyr Vermigli (1499–1562). This coterie of humanist theologians was given protection by the Oratorian cardinals Reginald Pole (1500–58) and Gasparo Contarini (1483–1542). All supported a return to inward spiritual sincerity, giving them the name Spirituali, and they all embraced a doctrine of JUSTIFICATION approaching that of Luther. In the end, many of their efforts came to naught, at least in the near term. With the Inquisition on their tails, Peter Martyr fled to Protestant Strasbourg and England, and Ochino soon followed via Geneva.

Both Contarini and Pole died under clouds of suspicion by Pope Paul IV (r. 1555–59).

The papacy had one last chance to reform at Lateran Council V under Julius II (r. 1503–13) and Leo X (r. 1513–21). Sadly, these two Renaissance princes spent so much time adding art to the Vatican, albeit the great art of MICHELANGELO and RAPHAEL that turned Rome into a baroque showplace, shoring up the PAPAL STATES through warfare, and preserving papal prerogatives that any chance for reform had to come from outside. Come it did. There can be no doubt that papal arrogance—and blindness—had reached new heights. Significantly, all the decrees of Lateran V were issued not as conciliar decrees but as papal bulls, as if they were the exclusive production of the pope alone, to which was appended the afterthought ". . . with the approval of the sacred council." Leo X had not only done little to ameliorate the spiritual condition of the church, it was he who sent forth the incendiary device that would spark a revolution in the form of the Dominican Johann Tetzel, who in 1517 came to Wittenberg itself preaching indulgences with maudlin effect: "Do you not hear the voice of your parents and loved ones crying out loudly and saying 'Have mercy on me, have mercy?'"

Luther shot back with his 95 theses decrying this clinking of coins and promise to pop parents from purgatory. He could not believe that the pope actually approved such outward buying and selling unconnected with any inward repentance and contrition, but he soon found himself on the outs with the pope and the emperor, too. Leo X excommunicated him in 1521. Though it was sparked by indulgences, the Reformation was much more. It was about the preaching of the GOSPEL, the proper delivery of the SACRAMENTS and their biblical foundation, and, finally, the organization and administration of the church itself.

One of the amazing aspects of the Counter-Reformation is how long it took for it to get underway after the Lutheran, then the Reformed, and finally the Anglican breakaways occurred.

There was a doomed attempt for reconciliation between Protestant and Catholic parties at the Colloquy of Regensburg (1541), but by this time the spiritual differences, shored up by secular political divisions, literally militated against any peaceful change.

Once the wheels of Catholic reform were oiled, however, the Counter-Reformation became remarkably successful in its own terms, if not for Christianity at large. Several factors undergirded the reforms: 1) the rise of new and reformed religious orders; 2) structural reform of the papacy, the Vatican bureaucracy, and the hierarchy; 3) the monumental Council of TRENT (1545–60), which redefined and refocused all aspects of Catholic doctrine, worship, and moral practice for the next 400 years; 4) the missions to new lands; and 5) the flourishing of a new spirituality, often called baroque.

1. The new religious orders and some of the newly reformed traditional orders provided the intellectual strength and lifeblood of the Counter-Reformation. Outstanding among these were the JESUITS, founded by St. IGNATIUS OF LOYOLA. The Jesuits contributed not only highly trained clergy to stem the Protestant tide in Europe but also fearless missionaries who spread the Catholic version of the Gospel to Asia and the New World. Not far behind were the Capuchins—a reformed order of Franciscans founded by Mateo of Urbino (d. 1552),—the society of the Theatines, and the Barnabites. The Oratory of Divine Love in Rome, which grew out of the Theatines, deserves special mention. Among its members who played a significant role in the Counter-Reformation were Jacopo Sadoleto (1477–1547), who later debated with Melanchthon and Calvin; Reginald Pole, who tried to turn England back to Rome under Mary Tudor (r. 1553–58); and Gian Pietro Caraffa (1476–1559), who became Pope PAUL IV.

Pope PAUL III called on these Oratorians to prepare for the Council of Trent.

2. The papacy was reformed under Clement VII, Paul III (r. 1534–49), and PAUL V. The College of Cardinals was reorganized into the congregations we have today, and their composition became more international. Gasparo Contarini led the internal Vatican reform that stressed a renewal of moral life. Much inspiration was drawn from the infamous *Concilium de emendanda ecclesia* ("Advice for Reforming the Church," 1537), a collective effort of Sadoleto and others noted for its ruthless critiques. It fell into the hands of the Vatican's Lutheran critics. Perhaps as a sign of the internal contradictions within Vatican Catholicism, Paul IV placed the *Concilium* as the first book on the Index of Prohibited Books in 1559!

As part of the reorganization the Spanish Inquisition was transferred to Rome and placed under the Congregation of the Holy Office (*see* VATICAN CURIA). The Inquisition was henceforth effective only in the Papal States, though attempts were made to extend it to the Netherlands and the other Habsburg territories. Its most notable victim was Giordano Bruno in 1600. The final Vatican organizational change was the creation of the Index of Prohibited Books, established in 1557 by the former reformer Giovanni Pietro Carafa (1476–1559), now the repressive Paul IV. The most noted book to be placed on the Index was GALILEO GALILEI's *Dialogues on the Two Chief World Systems* in 1633, much to the church's later regret.

3. The Council of Trent was held over four sessions between 1545 and 1560. Trent effected a monumental reform of morals, particularly among the clergy, and a reformulation of Catholic doctrine and practice, covering topics from the creed, Scripture, TRADITION, the SACRAMENTS, the veneration of saints, and daily Christian practice. In relation to doctrine, reformulation won out over change, to the disappointment of many Catholics as well as Protestants. Nevertheless, the reformulation provided both clarity and guidance to a church rocked by schism.

Trent did not outlaw indulgences per se but justified them on the basis of the plenipotentiary power granted to Peter (Matt. 16:18; 18:18) and claimed by the papacy. It outlawed their sale for "evil gains" (session 25, December 4, 1563). Free-will offerings were still welcome. Both Pius IV (r. 1559–65) and St. Pius V (1566–72) forbade indulgences involving fees or financial transactions and abolished the quasi-ecclesiastical office of pardoner, whose mercenary activities were so broadly derided in Chaucer's *Pardoner's Tale.*

4. Catholic missionary activity bourgeoned, both in the New World and in ASIA. One of the most interesting aspects of the post-Reformation world was the failure of mainline Protestants to take up the mission field. Some ascribe this to the prevailing doctrine of predestination, which consigned "heathen" nations to their foreordained fate. The one exception was the Moravians, who followed Jesus' command to send out missionaries two-by-two (Luke 10:1).

The most remarkable missionary was St. FRANCIS XAVIER, who worked in India, Indochina, China, and Japan. Missionary successes demanded better Vatican administration, which culminated in the establishment of the Congregation for the Propagation of the Faith by Gregory XV (r. 1621–23) in the bull *Inscrutabili Divinae Providentiae* (June 22, 1622).

Within Europe many religious orders, especially the Jesuits and Capuchins, treated the newly lost Catholic lands like mission fields. With the support of Catholic princes, large segments of France, southern

Germany, Austria, Bohemia, Czechoslova-kia, and Poland were won back from Prot-estantism or Protestant tendencies.

5. New forms of intense spirituality emerged, called baroque by some, documented in the *Spiritual Exercises* of St. Ignatius of Loyola and *The Interior Castle* of St. TERESA OF ÁVILA. To these can be added the robust if practical spiritualities of ST. FRANCIS DE SALES and CHARLES BORROMEO. Together these new forms of spirituality, including the practice of reciting the Rosary and the adoration of the Blessed Sacrament, bolstered the piety of clergy and laity alike (*see* DEVOTIONS; MARY OF NAZARETH). These spiritual mea-sures were augmented by new canons for religious art approved at Trent (session 25, December 3–4, 1563). The most celebrated painters who followed the Tridentine canons were El Greco (1541–1614) and Michelan-gelo Merisi da Caravaggio (1573–1610).

Further reading: Robert Cireley, *The Counter-Reforma-tion Prince* (Chapel Hill: University of North Carolina Press, 1990); A. G. Dickens, *The Counter Reformation* (New York: Harcourt Brace & World, 1969); Nicholas S. Davidson, *The Counter-Reformation* (Oxford: Blackwell, 1987); Diarmaid MacCulloch, *The Reformation* (New York: Viking, 2004).

creation (Lat.: *creare*, "to make, produce, fashion")

In theology creation is the teaching that the uni-verse ("the heavens and the earth") came into being through the free act of GOD at the beginning of time (Genesis 1:1). This teaching, understood in different ways, is shared by Jews, CHRISTIANS, Mus-lims, and, contrary to popular belief, many other primal religions. The teaching is expressed in the first article of the Christian CREED: "We believe in God, the Father, the maker of heaven and earth."

Creation can be contrasted with pantheism, which holds that all reality is imbued with the divine; emanationism, which teaches that God is the primordial source of being from which all oth-ers flow as in a continuum; and dualism, which maintains that there are two primordial forces, one good and another evil that are locked in eter-nal conflict.

The Christian teaching on creation, that it is different from God but still good, was implicit in all the New Testament writings but became explicit only in the second century, when Chris-tian orthodoxy went through the process of rejecting DOCETISM and the early forms of GNOSTI-CISM. The Docetists held that Jesus' humanity and suffering in the flesh (1 John 4:1–4) was only apparent (Gk.: *dokeō*, "to seem") and not real. The implication was that matter was in some way unworthy of the divine and perhaps evil. MARCION, who maintained that the true God is a God of Love as found in some books of the New Testament, and not the God of Law as found in the Old Testament, identified the Creator God of the Old Testament as a malevolent Demiurge, full of caprice, despotic and cruel. Later GNOSTICS found the material world itself to be an imprisoning web of ignorance; salvation required an escape into the true realm of the spirit. The orthodox tradi-tion answered this tendency to malify the mate-rial realm with the first article of the CREED: God created both heaven and earth, the visible and the invisible, spirit and matter, all of which are equally good (Genesis 1:31).

Some early Christian thinkers thought that God, like Plato's Demiurge in the *Timaeus*, fash-ioned the world out of preexistent matter (Clem-ent of Alexandria, *Stromata* 5.14). Later teachers, beginning with Theophilus of Antioch (c. 175), rejected this position in favor of creation ex nihilo (*Autolycus* 2.4). The doctrine of creation ex nihilo had to wait until Lateran Council IV (1215) for its first dogmatic formulation in the decree against the Albigensians and CATHARI. It was reaffirmed at VATICAN COUNCIL I (cn. 1).

The New Testament links creation with Jesus Christ as the Logos, through whom all things were made (John 1:3), and as the First Born of creation by whom all things were created (Col. 1:15–20). As a corollary, redemption is not a flight from creation but the renewal and "recapitulation of the original handiwork of the Father," interrupted by the sin of Adam, through the INCARNATION and obedience of the Savior (IRENAEUS OF LYON, *Against Heresies* 3.18.1; 5.14.2).

Most medieval theology of creation was hampered by a dependence on the theories of ARISTOTLE, who taught that the universe was composed of a hierarchy of motions. The highest beings, the fixed stars, moved circularly and eternally in imitation of the Unmoved Mover (*Physics* 8.6 206a; *Metaphysics* 12.7 1072b8–9). Aristotle's God neither created nor acted outwardly but was a pure inner "knowing of knowing" whose circle of thinking the rest of the universe sought to imitate. According to reason, THOMAS AQUINAS would argue, the world could be sempiternal, created but always so. Creation pertains to the principle of origin, not necessarily to the principle of duration in time. The creation of the world in time is "believable but not demonstrable or knowable [by reason alone]" (*Summa Contra Gentiles* 2.38). Creation in time can be known only through revelation.

In the first of his antinomies of transcendental reason in the *Critique of Pure Reason*, Immanuel Kant (1724–1804) argued that reason could both prove and disprove that the world had a beginning in time. This was an illustration of the principle that reason was limited and had to make room for faith.

The contemporary empirical-analytical sciences, biology, geology, and quantum and relativity physics, have presented an enormous challenge to any naive, literalist reading of the story of creation in Genesis and other passages in the BIBLE. The issue is whether the present universe and all that is in it came to be in a once-for-all act or through an evolving process (*see* EVOLUTION). Fully aware of the long, drawn-out GALILEO GALILEI fiasco, the participants at VATICAN COUNCIL II argued both for the autonomy of the things of creation "endowed with their own stability, truth, goodness, proper laws

and order" and for the autonomy of the sciences that study those complex phenomena (*Gaudium et Spes* 36, Pastoral Constitution of the Church in the Modern World). The challenge, however, is not about the fact of creation but about the manner.

There has been a tendency in modern theology to turn away from the primacy of creation theology (as in Irenaeus) toward the centrality of REDEMPTION in CHRIST. This tendency is most notable in the Reformed theologian Karl Barth (1886–1968), who derived the first article of the creed (creation by the Father) and the third (sanctification through the Spirit) from the second (redemption by the Son). The argument hangs on just how much damage one believes was rendered to creation through the FALL of humankind. Some more recent theologians have become once again attentive to the primacy of creation in the earliest formal theologies from which the creeds were derived. Key to a renewal of creation theology is the MEISTER ECKHARDT–inspired creation spirituality espoused by MATTHEW FOX; theologies of stewardship for the creation; the theology of the environment, or ecotheology, now promoted by the liberation theologian LEONARDO BOFF; and the incorporation of indigenous tribal perspectives into theologies of the Earth and the land.

See also COSMOLOGY: THEOLOGY.

Further reading: Richard A. Clifford and John J. Collins, eds., *Creation in Biblical Traditions* (Washington, D.C.: Catholic Biblical Association, 1992); Zachary Hayes, *The Gift of Being: A Theology of Creation* (Collegeville, Minn.: Liturgical Press, 2001); A. Wati Longchar and Larry E. Davis, eds., *Doing Theology with Tribal Resources* (Assam: Tribal Study Center, 1999); Gustav Wingren, *Creation and Gospel* (Lewiston, N.Y.: Edwin Mellen, 1979).

creeds (Lat.: *credo,* "to believe," "to have faith in," "to trust")

A creed is a short statement that summarizes the foundational principles of one's faith. The term in Greek for "creed" is *symbolon*. The standard Christian creed, after stating "I/We believe in God," is divided into three articles pertaining to the work of the Father, the work of the Son, and the work of the HOLY SPIRIT. The presupposition of the CHRISTIAN creed is the oneness of GOD as contained in the Jewish Shema: "Hear, O Israel, the Lord our God, the Lord is one." (Deut. 6:4).

It is almost certain that the Christian creedal formula grew out of the ritual of BAPTISM, which included the renunciation of Satan and darkness, the anointing with the oil of exorcism, and the threefold immersion in the baptismal font accompanied by the threefold profession of faith in the Father, the Son, and the Holy Spirit. A shortened form of the rite is alluded to in early Christian writings as baptism "in the name of the Father, the Son, and the Holy Spirit" (Matt. 28:19; *Didache* 7.1). A somewhat expanded version of the rite is contained in HIPPOLYTUS OF ROME's *Apostolic Tradition* (21:12–20). Some claim that baptism "in the name of Jesus" (Acts 2:38; 8:16, etc.) was the earliest form of the baptismal rite, but these texts in Acts do not refer to the ritual but to the authority by which one is to be baptized. All the texts referring to the rite itself also refer to the Father, Son, and Holy Spirit (JUSTIN MARTYR 1.61).

After a period of time the creedal formulas took on a life of their own beyond baptism, and various of the articles of the creed became expanded in response to doctrinal disputes. These additions and alterations became embodied in the various forms of the creed.

OLD ROMAN CREED

This creed, like the Apostles' Creed, was used only in the West. It refers to the Father Almighty, Jesus Christ his only Son—including his birth, suffering, death, RESURRECTION to sit at the Father's right hand, and coming again to judge the living and the dead—and the Holy Spirit, who was understood to have descended on the holy church for the remission of SINs, the resurrection of the flesh,

and life everlasting. This form probably dates from the end of the second century; it is contained in interrogatory form in Hippolytus's *Apostolic Tradition* and in declaratory form in Marcellus of Ancyra (Epihanius of Salamis, *Panarion* 72.3). The purpose of the expansion of the second article is to combat teachings like those of Cerinthus (late 1st, early 2nd century) and DOCETISM in general, who denied the INCARNATION of God in the flesh and, consequently, the resurrection of the flesh. The stress on the remission of sin was in contrast to the GNOSTIC idea of "salvation" as enlightenment by Jesus with true knowledge (gnosis) of our real predicament in the material world. On the other hand, the simplicity of the Roman Creed left it open to Montanist or Monarchist (modalist) interpretations (*see* GOD).

APOSTLES' CREED

This creed clearly developed out of the old Roman Creed. Although there is no basis in fact, legend traced each of its 12 "statements" back to one of the 12 apostles. The sixth-century Gallican version adds the phrase "descended into the lower regions" (Lat. *inferna* = Hades? Hell? Sheol? *See* HEAVEN AND HELL) to the second article, and "catholic" to the holy church, which it also called "a COMMUNION of saints." The descent was meant perhaps to affirm that Jesus truly died and not another in his place (as some Gnostics said), or perhaps to refer to the "harrowing of hell," by which Jesus reclaims the faithful dead of the first Covenant, such as Abraham, Moses, David, and Elijah, thereby uniting both testaments of the BIBLE together under one God and one line of redemption.

The Apostles' Creed as recited today also adds "creator of heaven and earth" to the first article. The phrase is contained in many western and eastern creeds, most likely to counter MARCION, who identified the creator with a malevolent Demiurge, and Gnostics and proto-Manicheans, who thought that the physical world was evil or a place of estrangement (*see* MANICHAEISM).

NICENE CREED

Two creeds go by this name. The first was issued at the Council of Nicaea I (325) (*see* COUNCILS, ECUMENICAL) to counter ARIUS. The latter taught that Jesus was not fully divine the way God the Father was, but only *homoios,* or "like" the Father. Likewise, Arius claimed that "begotten" when applied to the Son implies that there was a time when he was not. This Nicene Creed is without doubt derived from the Jerusalem baptismal liturgy creed, which can be reconstructed from St. Cyril of Jerusalem's *Catechetical Lectures.* The first article has a variant western version, that states that the "Father is maker of all things, visible and invisible." The Christological argument of the second article is greatly expanded to state belief in "one Lord Jesus Christ, the only-begotten Son of God, begotten of the Father before all ages, God of God, Light of Light, true God of true God, begotten, not made, being of one substance with the Father by whom all things were made; who for us men, and for our salvation, came down from heaven, and was incarnate." The key word is *homoousios,* or "of the same being" with the Father. The Latin translation says "of one substance." This statement places the second person of the Trinity on an equal footing with the first. To make it perfectly clear the Nicene statement adds that the same eternal Son who is united in being with the Father and through whom all things were created also became incarnate in time. Likewise the creed adds the coming of Jesus "in glory," again to emphasize his regal equality with the Father. The creedal part ends simply with "and in the Holy Spirit." Four anathematas were attached to the conciliar decree, thereby turning what was a positive confession of faith into a negative test of orthodoxy.

The second creed is often called the Nicene-Constantinopolitan Creed and is the version commonly recited in the EUCHARIST liturgies of Catholics, Eastern Orthodox, Anglicans, and Lutherans after the sermon and before the CANON OF THE MASS. The Council of Constantinople I (381) did not actually issue a creed. Rather, the creed, which is close to the Jerusalem baptismal creed of Cyril and is perhaps based on the Constantinopolitan baptismal creed, is contained in the *Exposition of the 150 Fathers,* which is associated with that council.

This version shows minor changes in the first two articles. Under the first article, the phrase "heaven and earth" was coordinated with "all that is seen and unseen." In the second, the phrases "crucified for our sake" and "according to the scriptures" were added. The big additions were under the third article. The Holy Spirit is also called "Lord, the giver of life, who proceeds from the Father; with the Father and Son he is worshipped and glorified." The Greek has "coworshipped" and "coglorified." (Later the Latin West unilaterally added "and the Son," or FILIOQUE, to the clause "who proceeds from the Father," thereby angering the Greek East and sticking one more thorn into the festering wound that became the GREAT SCHISM.) The church is now called "one" and "apostolic" besides "holy, catholic." The remission of sins is tied to baptism. Two notes of eschatological hope were appended, one to the second article, "and his kingdom will have no end," another to the third, "we look for . . . the life of the world to come. Amen."

The creeds were closely associated with the idea of the RULE OF FAITH (Lat.: *regula fidei*) or measure of truth (Gr. *kanōn tēs alethēias*). Unlike the baptismal confessions and the creedal formulations derived from them, the rule of faith was an instructional affair and never took on a fixed form. It was a flexible catechetical tool for instructing new converts into the essential scriptural truths of the Christian faith: the belief in one God who created all, the experience of salvation in Christ, and the reception of the Spirit who renews creation to God. In the New Testament the rule of faith as a guide to theological authenticity was measured by reference to the sermons preached by the Apostles (Acts 2; 3; 10; 13) or to the same Gospel preached by all the Apostles (1 Cor. 15:1–11). In postcanonical times, the rule of faith took on a Trinitarian modality in conformity to the baptismal confessions.

None of the creeds following the Nicene-Constantinopolitan version found a liturgical use. The reason is clear. The Definition of Chalcedon (451), which defines Christ as one person in two natures, reads like a theological disquisition. The same holds for the so-called Athanasian Creed, which begins with the Latin words *Quicunque vult,* which is an exposition on the TRINITY, CHRISTOLOGY (*see* CHRIST/CHRISTOLOGY), and the Apostles' Creed. At the Council of Toledo (589), which marked the conversion of the Arian Visigoths, the term *filioque,* derived from Augustine's *On the Trinity* (14.25.47), was added to read "proceeding from the Father and from the Son" to counter any doubts about the Son's divine status. It thus passed into the creedal expressions of the West, but not the East.

The Reformation saw a flurry of creedal statements, usually termed "confessions" of faith, by various branches of Protestantism: the Lutheran Augsburg Confession (1530) and Formula of Concord (1577); the Reformed First (1536) and Second (1577) Helvetic Confessions and the Dutch Reform Canons of the Synod of Dort (1618–19); the Puritan Reform Westminster Confession (1646) and Cambridge Platform; and finally the Anabaptist Schlecitheim (1527) and Dordtrecht (1632) Confessions. The Anglican Reformation produced many creedal statements, the most important of which were the Thirty-Nine Articles (1536), which were included in all subsequent editions of the *Book of Common Prayer.* The Catholics responded to the Protestant creeds with the dogmatic statements and summary Creed of the Council of TRENT, promulgated by Pius IV (r. 1559–65) in 1564. The Trent creed reads more like a dogmatic test of doctrine than a confession of faith. To Trent have been added the creedal statements on the Immaculate Conception and the Assumption of Mary. Metropolitan Peter Mohila of Kiev (r. 1633–47) produced an Orthodox Confession (1633) in the form of a catechetical interrogatory. The Orthodox Creed of Patriarch Dosethius

of Jerusalem (1641–1707) in 1672 was meant to counteract Protestant tendencies among some Orthodox believers.

Almost all of the many Protestant denominations have produced one or more creedal statements. Examples include the Theses Theologicae (1675) by Robert Barclay for the Quakers, the Methodist Articles of Religion (1784), and the Baptist New Hampshire Confession (1833). In the 20th century the most important creedal statement was the Barmen Declaration (1934), issued by the German Evangelical Union to counter the theological claims of the Nazis. It became the model for the Kairos Document (1985) and the Belhar Confession (1986) issued in South Africa as acts of protest against apartheid.

Through the 20th century, a variety of ecumenical creedal affirmations have been issued in NORTH AMERICA. Among the first was the "Social Creed" adopted by the Federal Council of Churches in 1908. A more recent example was the Hartford Appeal (1975), a call to return to earlier Christian doctrines written by Peter L. Berger, Richard John Neuhaus, and others. Harvey Cox, Max Stackhouse, and others thought that the appeal failed to measure up to the Social Gospel and answered with the Boston Affirmations (1976).

The tendency of modern theology has been to place greater and greater emphasis on the second article of the creed and the theology of redemption in Christ. This tendency has grown from Friederick Schleiermacher (1768–1834) to Karl Barth (1868–1968). A closer look at the formation of the early creeds, however, shows that a subtler process was going on. Whenever one article was "slighted" to the advantage of another, the tendency of the subsequent council or formulation was to bring the other articles of the creed up to theological richness and into reciprocal harmony with one another. We see this, for example, in the phrase "through whom all things were made," added to the second article of the Nicene Creed, which links the second to the first, thereby showing that salvation is not "away from the creation" but in it, of it, and for it. This closes off the avenue of escape from the material. The fullest possible Christian creedal theology will have a full theology of creation, a full theology of redemption, and a full theology of sanctification (or *theosis* in the Eastern tradition) and relate each of these elements to the other, for the Christian God is one in three.

Further reading: Peter L. Berger and Richard John Neuhaus *Against the World For the Word: The Hartford Appeal* (New York: Seabury, 1976); J. N. D. Kelly, *Early Christian Creeds* (London: Longsmans, Green, 1973); John H. Leith, *Creeds of the Churches* (New York: Anchor, 1963); Hans Lietzmann, *Symbole der Alten Kirche* (Berlin: Gruyter, 1961); J. Gordon Melton, *The Encyclopedia of American Religions: Religious Creeds,* 2 vols. (Detroit: Gale Research, 1988, 1994).

critique of Christianity/Catholicism

The critique of religion in general and of Christianity and Catholicism in particular can take two basic forms: a questioning or rejection of all religion, as in ATHEISM and skepticism, or a questioning, rejection, or modification of its rational foundations, as in critical theology. Not all critique is hostile to religion pure and simple.

When Christianity first became known to the Romans, they labeled it a *superstitio,* a term with deeper connotations than the modern term *superstition* (Tacitus, *Annals* 15.44; Pliny, *Letters* 10.97–7). The Romans used it to characterize the beliefs and practices of "barbarian" religions and their *collegia,* or associations. The charges included not only fear of demons and malevolent spirits and the concomitant use of charms, talismans, amulets, and exorcisms, but also the refusal to give due deference to the civil gods of Rome or to worship the emperors. Such beliefs and practices to the Romans amounted to political atheism.

In the second century CHRISTIAN apologists came to the defense of Christianity. The many charges placed at its doorstep included not only

political sedition, orgiastic sexual practices (naked baptism could give rise to this misperception), and cannibalism (partaking of the "body and blood of the Lord" could give rise to this). They also had to defend against charges of being heretics (*minim*) on the part of rabbinic Judaism and refute its claims of Jesus' illegitimate birth. Drawing upon the Logos philosophy of Stoicism, apologists like JUSTIN MARTYR and Athenagoras (fl. 170) tried to show that Christianity was politically harmless and morally superior to paganism. One astute critic, the philosopher Celsus, most of whose treatise *True Doctrine* can be retrieved from ORIGEN's *Against Celsus,* praised the Logos teaching and high morality but scoffed at the belief in miracles, allegorical interpretation of the Old Testament within the New Testament, Christian exclusiveness, the doctrine of the INCARNATION, and the ignominy of crucifixion (*see* CROSS).

After CONSTANTINE Christianity became legally equivalent to the old Roman religion and faced relatively little external critiques. The two exceptions were the muted critique of Jewish thinkers and Julian the Apostate (332–63). Julian became initiated into the Eleusian mysteries and tried to reinstate the noble religion of the Romans. He fomented dissension among the bishops to weaken their authority and wrote anti-Christian tractates.

Islam incorporates religious traditions from Judaism, Christianity, and GNOSTICISM. Muhammad (c. 570–632) wanted to lead everyone back to what he believed was the original religion of Abraham. He held both Moses and Isa (Jesus) to have been prophets of God. Jesus was created and born of a virgin but not eternally begotten, and his crucifixion was only apparent (influence of DOCETISM). St. JOHN OF DAMASCUS saw Islam as a Christian heresy (akin to ARIANISM) in his *Fount of Wisdom.*

In the early MIDDLE AGES the critique of Catholicism was mostly internal, revolving around the perennial problems of lax morality on the part of the clergy and the practice of lay investure. The critique originated in the successive reforms of monasteries like Cluny. By the Middle Ages the tension between reason and revelation fed the critique of religion. While most medieval theologians found harmony between theology and its "handmaid," philosophy, some found conflict. Ibn Rushd (1126–98), known in the West as Averroes the Commentator on the works of Aristotle, applied philosophy to Islamic belief and thought. In the places where he found the Qu'ran to contradict Aristotelian reasoning, he interpreted it metaphorically (allegorically) and maintained the supremacy of reason over revelation. Literal interpretation was fine for the common folk. This led to the medieval controversy of double truth, that is, something can be true in theology but false in philosophy, and vice versa.

Pope Alexander IV (r. 1254–61) ordered St. ALBERTUS MAGNUS to refute Averroes. He did so in *The Unity of the Intellect* and was followed in the same endeavor by Sts. BONAVENTURE AND THOMAS AQUINAS, who refuted the Latin Averroist Siger of Brabant (1240–84).

Many of the reforming yet heretical movements of the era (CATHARI, WALDENSIANS, Beguines, etc.) can be seen as critiques not of Christianity itself but of its perceived corruption. Much of the critique concerned the luxurious lifestyles of clerics and monks, but some was grounded in theological argument. In particular, JOHN WYCLIFFE (c. 1330–84) and others felt that theologians had subordinated the Scripture to folk customs, now given the status of theological tradition. Many argued for a return to the simplicity of the GOSPEL preaching. On the orthodox side of the critical camp were St. FRANCIS OF ASSISI and other MENDICANTS; on the heretical side were the Waldensians, Lollards, and Hussites.

In the later Middle Ages the critique combined the direct, Christ-centered piety of the DEVOTIO MODERNA with the critical, historical impulse of Renaissance humanism. The two streams are fully alive in DESIDERIUS ERASMUS. On the one hand, he excoriated corrupt clericalism (wealth, indulgences, pilgrimages, etc.) in *The Praise of Folly*. On the other, his learning produced the first critical edition of the Greek New Testament with a new Latin translation that was to provide ammunition to the reformers. The two currents in Erasmus combined in the more trenchant critique of the PROTESTANT REFORMATION.

From this point on, it is legitimate to talk about a critique of Catholicism. Much of the modern critique is grounded in the Renaissance sense of the exalted dignity of human nature despite the FALL (Giovanni Pico della Mirandola, 1463–94) and in the modern faith in limitless scientific progress (Francis Bacon, 1561–1626). The trial of GALILEO GALILEI did much to discredit Catholicism, especially as the heliocentric version of the solar system was progressively vindicated. The Catholic Church did not remove his *Dialogue on the Two Chief World Systems* (1632) from the Index of Prohibited Books until 1822, long after even Catholic scientists had embraced the new view. In 1979 Pope JOHN PAUL II conceded that Vatican inquisistors had erred in the Galileo affair.

The Protestant impulse planted the seeds that were later to emerge as the thoroughgoing Enlightenment critique of religion in general and Catholicism in particular. Some of the seeds came from within Catholicism, some from Protestantism and beyond. All involved applying rationalist criteria to religion.

Appealing to reason, Jakob Armenius (1560–1609) undermined the Calvinist doctrine of predestination. The Socinians, followers of Lelio Sozzini (1525–62), called into question both the divinity of Christ and the doctrine of the Triune Godhead. Thomas Hobbes (1588–1679), Benedict de Spinoza (1632–79), and others subjected the Scriptures to historical criticism, discovering multiple authors in the books of the Old Testament and putting the doctrine of their divine inspiration under a cloud of uncertainty (*see* BIBLE). Spinoza in particular asserted the Averroist principle that when a scriptural passage goes against reason and the laws of nature, it should be interpreted metaphorically.

These tendencies culminated in the many-sided Enlightenment, which embraced the humanitarian ideals of scientific progress, tolerance, universal justice, the moral and material betterment of humanity, and, in some instances, social revolution. Many Enlightenment thinkers, such as François-Marie Arouet (1694–1778), who published under the pseudonym Voltaire, embraced a Newtonian-inspired deism and attacked Catholicism for its remnants of superstition, fanaticism, and intolerance. Others like David Hume (1711–76) and Immanuel Kant (1724–1804) challenged the old metaphysical proofs for God's existence. Social thinkers like Jean-Jacques Rousseau (1712–78) posited a social contract that protected only the physical person and the material well-being of its members; this became an implicit challenge to the more organic Catholic conception of society, which embraces both spiritual and material aspects of humanity. In the 19th century, Enlightenment convictions often joined forces with intolerant prejudice to yield ANTICLERICALISM, ANTI-CATHOLICISM, and even persecution.

Although the Catholic Church did not repeat the Galileo error in the case of Charles Darwin (1809–82) and his theory of evolution, it seemed in the 19th and early 20th century to be engaged in a rear guard action, trying to hold back the inevitable forces of modernity. This tendency was most evident in Pius IX's *Syllabus of Errors* (December 8, 1864), which condemned pantheistic naturalism, opposed the idea that faith is a process of reason, and criticized political liberalism in so far as it affected the civil status of the church. Pius X issued two encyclicals, *Lamentabili* (July 3, 1907) and *Pascendi Domini Gregis* (September 8, 1907), that condemned what he considered the heresy of MODERNISM, including the biblical criticism and historical evolutionism of Alfred Loisy (1857–1940); the theological modernism based on religious experience of Lucien Laberthonniére (1860–1932) and George Tyrrell (1861–1909); and the social modernism that championed democracy and self-determination.

In the 19th and 20th centuries Christianity in general and Catholicism in particular came under three severe but influential critiques. The first was from Karl Marx (1818–88), who charged that religion, while it begins with the cry of the oppressed, benumbs that cry by deflecting religious yearning from earth to heaven, where all wrongs will be righted; it thus becomes "the opium of the masses." Friedrich Nietzsche (1844–1900) sought to unmask Christianity as a resentful "Platonism for the masses" (the quest for eternity) against the becomingness of time and history. Finally, Sigmund Freud (1856–1939) claimed that religion is a systematic infantile wish fulfillment by which humans abandon themselves to an "oceanic feeling" of protection by the divine in the face of the harsh cruelties nature deals humankind. Many Catholics reject these critiques outright, but others maintain that modern faith must pass through the fiery furnace of criticism in order to attain the "second naiveté."

Gradually, if reluctantly, Catholicism has come to absorb those aspects of the modern critique of religion that did not directly undermine supernatural faith. Pope BENEDICT XV curbed the more strident antimodernist voices within the Vatican. PIUS XII sanctioned the use of historical critical methods for the study of the Bible in his *Divino Afflante Spiritu* (September 30, 1943). The theologians associated with the NOUVELLE THÉOLOGIE movement quietly but insistently embraced many of the theological tendencies formerly condemned by the church. Finally, the great *aggiornamento,* or updating, of VATICAN COUNCIL II opened the doors to new ways of thinking that could help the church absorb, cope with, or critique the forces of modernity.

Under JOHN PAUL II, however, there was a partial retrenchment away from modern ideas, enforced by a more monarchical conception of the PAPACY. The church is now facing a 21st-century equivalent of the confrontation with Galileo over the question of stem cell research (*see* ETHICS).

Further reading: Anthony J. Cernera and Oliver J. Morgan, eds., *Examining the Catholic Intellectual Tradition*

(Fairfield, Conn.: Sacred Heart University Press, 2000); J. Heft, *Faith in Intellectual Life* (Notre Dame: University of Notre Dame Press, 1996); Paul Ricoeur, "The Critique of Religion," in Charles E. Reagan and David Stewart, eds., *The Philosophy of Paul Ricoeur* (Boston: Beacon, 1978), 213–222.

cross/crucifixion (Lat.: *crux,* "cross" + *fixere,* "to impale")

The New Testament reports that the Roman authorities sentenced Jesus to die on the cross (Mark 15:22–26). Roman sources indicate that crucifixion was indeed an accepted form of execution, generally used against political rebels; it dated from Persian times. The Romans were prone to use crucifixion as a deterrent against political resistance. Prior to the crucifixion of Jesus, the most notorious instance was the mass crucifixion of the rebel slave Spartacus and 6,000 of his followers along the Via Appia in 71 B.C.E. after their defeat by Pompey (106–48 B.C.E.) and Crassus (d. 91 B.C.E.).

We do not know the form of the cross for sure. It may have been in the form of the *crux commissa,* the Tau cross similar to an upper-case **T** (*Epistle of Barnabas* 9.8), or the *crux immissa,* the standard crossed beam **†**. Archaeologists in Israel have so far uncovered only one example of a first-century crucifixion. The victim was a man named Jehohannan ben HGQWL; his feet were fixed to the sides of the vertical beam and his arms were most likely strapped to a horizontal cross beam atop the vertical (*see* ARCHAEOLOGY). Legend has it that PETER was crucified on an inverted cross, and ANDREW on an X cross.

Surprisingly, the cross was not a widely popular symbol during the first three centuries of Christianity, just as the crucifixion and death of Jesus by itself were not the main focus of CHRISTIAN belief. When PAUL refers to the cross, it is often a rhetorical point directed against those who are scandalized by such a "disreputable" death (Gal. 5:11; *see* Deut. 21:22), or who claim

a superior wisdom apart from or above the "message of the cross" (I Cor. 1:18), or who are even hostile to the idea of the cross (Phil. 3:18). These intense passages can give the impression that the cross itself was central for Paul. Luther seems to enshrine this view in his Thesis 28 of the Heidelberg Disputation: "The 'theologian of glory' calls the good bad and the bad good. The 'theologian of the cross' says what a thing is." Paul's theology, however, is never fixated on the cross alone. The most fundamental rite of Christianity, BAPTISM, is baptism into the death *and* resurrection of CHRIST (Rom. 6:1–8).

Crosses appear at catacomb burial sites and on some early Christian sarcophagi, but there is no firm connection between the common form equilateral cross (+) and Christian beliefs. Various forms of the Chi-Rho symbol (chi-rho symbol) were common, but that was a monogram of the name "Christos" and not per se a symbol of the cross. Early Christian Fathers saw the cross prefigured in the Tree of Life (Gen. 2:9), the staff of Moses (Exod. 14:16), the Tree of Jesse (Isa. 11:1), as well as Odysseus tied to the mast of his ship (*Odyssey* 12). Some early theologians note that outsiders accused Christians of worshipping the cross as only GOD should be worshipped (TERTULLIAN, *Nations* 1.12).

Christian emphasis on the cross increased significantly after it was incorporated into the military standard of CONSTANTINE, as the *labarum,* by 325. In his *Life of Constantine* (1.28), the church historian Eusebius explains the emperor's choice of this symbol by relating the legend that God sent Constantine a vision of the cross before the battle at the Milvian Bridge (312). The story is most likely an embellishment promulgated by Constantine's propaganda agents. The *labarum* did not appear on the Arch of Constantine, which was built just three years after the Milvian Bridge battle, when memories would have been fresh. A noted fourth-century example appears on Lateran sarcophagus 171, now in the Museo Pio Cristiano.

The importance of the cross increased further after Constantine's mother, Helena Augusta, excavated the site of the Church of the Holy Sepulcher in Jerusalem, which now encompasses what is believed to be the empty tomb of Christ as well as the rock of Golgotha, or place of the crucifixion. According to some legends, the excavators found the "true" cross as well as the other instruments of the Passion (scourge, pillar of flagellation, crown of thorns, nails, spear, sponge). The early fifth-century *Pilgrimage of Egeria* (37.1–4) shows that the remnants of the cross plus the superscription ("Jesus Christ, King of the Jews") were kept in a silver casket and venerated on Good Friday.

Woodcut from the *Speculum passionis* (1519) showing Mary the Mother of Jesus and the apostle John beneath Christ on the cross (*Washington University Library, Special Collections, with permission*)

According to later legend, the cross of Christ was identified by the healing of a young man.

Whether or not this cross was authentic, the discovery led to three important feasts: 1) the Invention (or Finding) of the Cross, a feast originating in Gaul and then moving to Rome (originally May 3, but suppressed in 1961 in favor of the September 14 date celebrated in the East); 2) the Exaltation of the Cross, the Eastern equivalent of the Invention, celebrated on September 14; it was merged with the commemoration of the recovery of the cross from the Persians by Emperor Heraclus in 629; and 3) the Veneration of the Cross, part of the Good Friday service.

AUGUSTINE attests to the common practice of making the sign of the cross in his time. The earliest extant depictions of the crucifixion date from after the Constantinian period. The first is a carnelian intaglio known as the Constanza gem, now in the British Museum. The second is a wood carving on the cedarwood doors of Santa Sabina in Rome, showing Jesus crucified with the two thieves and dating from around 430. Pieces of the cross became premium relics throughout the Christian world. The BASILICA of Santo Toribio de Liébana in Spain holds the largest piece. The church of Santa Croce in Gerusalemme in Rome claims a larger piece of the cross of the good thief crucified with Christ, to whom legend has given the name Dismas. Medieval legend claimed that the Tree or Branch of Jesse, a frequent theme in Gothic stained glass windows and illuminated manuscripts, provided the wood for the cross of Christ. Piero della Francesco, drawing upon Jacopo de Voragine's *Golden Legend,* made all the events surrounding the finding and recovery of the True Cross the theme of a series of splendid frescoes in the cappela maggiore of the Basilica of San Francesco in Assisi in 1492. Although DESIDERIUS ERASMUS and Jean Calvin (1509–64) were fond of scoffing that there were enough pieces of the cross to build a boat, Rohault de Fleury calculated in 1870 that the then known relics

Pilgrims touching the top of the Hill of Golgotha, beneath the altar at the site of Christ's crucifixion, Church of the Holy Sepulchre, Jerusalem *(photo by Steven C. Scharre)*

would constitute only about a third of a Roman crucifixion cross.

The rise of the cross as an object of veneration, if not adoration, had important consequences for future Christian thought. First, the theology of Christ's death became more and more separated from the theology of his RESURRECTION and shaped the theory of the ATONEMENT in the MIDDLE AGES. This led to a devotional preoccupation with suffering and death rather than hope and resurrection, as in the Stations of the Cross and the Sorrowful Mysteries of the Rosary. While suffering and death underscore the humanity of Christ, extreme depictions of the crucifixion increasingly came to the fore, especially in western Christianity, most notably in many Spanish crucifixes and in the Isenheim Altar by Matthias Grünewald. Second, the EUCHARIST, which was once the sacred rite of breaking of bread and uniting the body of Christ (the believers) in common fellowship, came to focus on the supreme sacrifice of God as mediated through a priest who stood as the vicar of Christ on earth.

After the Reformation, Catholics continued to fashion crosses with the body of Christ on them. These are known as crucifixes. Evangelical and Reformed Protestants began to remove the body in order to stress a biblical point that Christ is risen and sits in heaven at the right hand of the Father (Acts 2:32–33). Eastern Orthodox ICONS of the crucified Christ never depict the extreme of suffering, so common in Spanish and Latin American art, but show a composed Christ as victor over death. In the East the cross is not death dealing but life giving.

Many forms of the cross have developed in various religious traditions. Below are images of various crosses and their associations.

Drawing after panel from cypress door showing one of the first depictions of the Crucifixion (Church of Santa Sabina, Rome) *(drawing by Frank K. Flinn)*

+ *crux quadrata,* equilateral or Greek cross, commonly used in Eastern Orthodoxy

X *crux decussata,* oblique cross associated with the legend of St. Andrew the Apostle's crucifixion

T *crux comissa,* or Tau cross, the likely form of the cross used in Jesus' crucifixion and associated with St. Francis of Assisi

† *crux immissa,* or Latin cross commonly used in the Roman rite

☦ Coptic cross

☥ *cruz ansata,* based on the Egyptian ankh, a sign of life and immortality

Further reading: George Willard Benson, *The Cross, its History & Symbolism,* (New York: Hacker Art Books, 1983); Erich Dinkler, "Comments on the History of the Symbol of the Cross," in James M. Robinson, ed., *The Bultmann School of Biblical Interpretation* (New York: Harper & Row, 1965); Martin Hengel, *Crucifixion* (Philadelphia: Fortress, 1977); Norman Laliberté and Edward N. West, *The History of the Cross* (New York: Macmillan, 1960).

Crucifixion   *See* CROSS/CRUCIFIXION.

Crusades (Lat.: *crux,* "cross")

The Crusades were a sequence of religiously motivated military expeditions from western Europe, sanctioned by the PAPACY, to retrieve the Holy Land from Muslim control and later to impede the further expansion of Islam under Ottoman rule. Two background factors enter into the motivation for the Crusades. The first was the conquest of former Christian territories by Muslim forces in the seventh and eighth centuries in the Holy Land and other territories in the Middle East and in North Africa, Sicily, and Spain. After the Battle of Manzikert (1071) the Seljuk Turks even threatened the patriarchy of CONSTANTINOPLE, "the second Rome." The second factor was the desire of pilgrims to visit the holy sites and churches in the Holy Land,

in the footsteps of CONSTANTINE's mother Helena, who built many of the first Christian BASILICAS in Jerusalem, Bethlehem, and elsewhere in the Holy Land. These sites had become the destinations of pilgrimages from the West, which was threatened by turmoil in the Muslim world.

Theologically, the Crusades vitiated the early Christian opposition to war and even challenged AUGUSTINE's theory of JUST WAR by suppressing the criteria that make a war just. Popes offered indulgences, remission from temporal punishment due to SIN, and the title "martyr" to those wearing the crusader cross and who died in combat. The ranks of crusaders attracted not only noble minded knights but also brigands and hangers-on out for profiteering. The campaigns witnessed not only warfare among combatants but also pillaging, rape, massacre, and wanton destruction. Innocent civilians were attacked, including both Jews along the Rhine and Eastern Orthodox in the Byzantine Empire.

Urban II (1088–99) called the First Crusade in response to an appeal from the Byzantine emperor. Peter the Hermit (d. 1115) preached the crusade after the Council of Clermont (1095). His advance force was defeated by the Turks in Anatolia before he could join the main army, which had reached Jerusalem in 1099. The conquerors divided the territories into Christian kingdoms. The Knights Templar, under the leadership of Hugh de Payens (c. 1070–1136), undertook to protect pilgrims, while the Knights Hospitaller provided lodging and medical care. Their practice of treating the sick as "ladies" and "lords" influenced later medical care throughout Europe. Godfrey de Bouillon (d. 1115) was appointed the first ruler of the Holy Land, and his brother Baldwin was crowned king of Jerusalem in 1100. Disputes among the Christian rulers arose immediately.

The Second Crusade was called by Eugenius III (1145–53) in 1147, preached by BERNARD OF CLAIRVAUX, and led by Louis VII of France (1120–80) and Conrad III of Germany (1093–1152). Its aim was to recapture the eastern kingdom of

Edessa. Crusaders on their way down the Rhine decided to stop off and waylay Jews residing in Frankfurt am Main and Mainz. To his great credit, Bernard preached against this persecution of the Jews. The Muslim commander Saladin (1137/38–93) overwhelmed this force and recaptured Jerusalem. Humanely, he gave the retreating crusaders safe passage out of Palestine.

Clement III (1187–91) called the Third Crusade in 1189, which was led by FREDERICK I BARBAROSSA of the Holy Roman Empire, Richard I of England, and Philip II of France. The aim was to retake Jerusalem, but the forces only managed to recover coastal cities like Acre.

Pope INNOCENT III called the Fourth Crusade in 1202, which headed for Egypt but was deflected by the Venetians to Constantinople, where Boniface de Montferrat (c. 1150–1207) set up a Latin kingdom and forced his Eastern Orthodox subjects to reconcile with Rome. This bullying engendered resentment among the Eastern Orthodox against the Latin Church, which remains unresolved to this day.

Still another international attempt to recover the Holy Land was staged in 1217–21; St. FRANCIS OF ASSISI accompanied the crusade in 1219, attempting to do by preaching before the Egyptian sultan Al-Kamil (d. 1238) what the knights were doing with the sword. FREDERICK II was able to negotiate Latin rule over Jerusalem from 1229 to 1244. However, the final major Crusade, launched by LOUIS IX of France in 1248–54, was less successful. By 1291 all attempts had failed, although the Spanish and Portuguese oceanic conquests in the 16th century encouraged hopes for eventual recovery of the Holy Land. Muslims keep the memory of the Crusades and their brutalities alive in their consciousness to this day; many view the foundation of the Jewish state of Israel in 1948, with some Western support, as a latter-day crusade.

Further reading: Aziz Surval Atiya, *The Crusade in the Later Middle Ages* (New York: Kraus Reprint, 1970); James A. Brundage, *The Crusades, Holy War, and Canon Law* (Brookfield, Mass.: Gower, 1991); Jonathan Harris, *Byzantium and the Crusades* (New York: Hambledon & London, 2003); Carole Hillenbrand, *The Crusades: Islamic Perspectives* (New York: Routledge, 2000); Steven Runciman, *A History of the Crusades* (New York: Harper & Row, 1964).

Curé d'Ars (1786–1859) *French parish priest and confessor*

Jean-Baptiste Marie Vianney became known to history as the *curé*, or parish priest, of Ars in France. In his lifetime he was celebrated as a confessor with remarkable sensitivity. He was canonized by PIUS XI in 1925 and named patron of parish priests in 1929. His feast day is August 4.

Growing up during the era of the French Revolution and Napoleonic wars, he received his first COMMUNION in secret. Drafted into Napoléon's army, he deserted to continue his studies at seminary. He was dismissed for his inability to learn Latin but finally was ordained in 1815. He succeeded as pastor at Ars and soon became famous as a confessor and spiritual director not only to the people of Ars but also to as many as 20,000 people per year who flocked to him from all over France. He was said to have spent as many as 18 hours a day in the confessional.

Further reading: George W. Rutler, *Saint John Vianney: The Curé d'Ars Today* (San Francisco: Ignatius, 1988); Michel de Saint Pierre, *The Remarkable Curé of Ars: The Life and Achievements of St. John Mary Vianney* (Garden City, N.Y.: Doubleday, 1963); Francis Trochu, *The Curé d'Ars, St. Jean-Marie-Baptiste Vianney (1786–1859): According to the Acts of the Process of Canonization and Numerous Hitherto Unpublished Documents* (Rockford, Ill.: Tan, 1977).

curia (Lat.: *cura,* "care")

The offices and agencies that constitute the staff of a BISHOP and do the work of a DIOCESE are collectively known as the curia. Most often the term refers to the curia of the Pope, the bishop of Rome. The term originally referred to the offices used by the Senate in the days of the Roman Republic.

The Roman curia is also generally known as the VATICAN CURIA or simply Vatican. Modeled on secular Roman prototypes, the curia took its definitive shape during the reigns of the great medieval popes such as INNOCENT III. It was reorganized by Pope JOHN XXIII during VATICAN COUNCIL II. Pope PAUL VI introduced further reforms in 1967, making the curia more pastoral. JOHN PAUL II continued this reform in his apostolic constitution *Pastor Bonus* (June 28, 1988), approving regulations on February 4, 1992 that are still in effect. The canon law pertaining to both the Roman and diocesan curia are in the *Code of Canon Law,* cnn. 360–61 and 469–94.

Further reading: John L. Allen, *All the Pope's Men: The Inside Story of How the Vatican Works* (New York: Doubleday, 2004); Thomas J. Reese, *Inside the Vatican: The Politics and Organization of the Catholic Church* (Cambridge, Mass.: Harvard University Press, 1996)

Curran, Charles E. (1934–) *priest and moral theologian*

Curran is a PRIEST in the DIOCESE of Rochester, where he was ordained in 1958. He studied moral THEOLOGY at the Academia Alfonsiana in Rome under Bernard HÄRING and received doctorates from there and the Pontifical Gregorian University in 1961.

Curran quickly became the foremost moral theologian in the United States, teaching the subject at Catholic University of America from 1965 to 1988. In 1968 he, along with many other moral theologians, disagreed with PAUL VI's rejection of artificial birth control, as stated in the ENCYCLICAL *Humanae Vitae* (July 25, 1968). As a result of his stance, his license to teach Catholic theology was removed on July 25, 1985 (the anniversary of *Humanae Vitae*), by the Vatican. He left Catholic

University in 1988 after a contentious legal battle. Catholic University is a pontifical university directly under the pope, and the courts sided with the university. However, the case raised serious questions about academic freedom in Catholic institutions. Curran subsequently was appointed the Elizabeth Scurlock University Professor of Human Values at Southern Methodist University in Dallas, Texas, in 1991.

Curran has been a prolific author of major works on social and moral theology, notably the authoritative *Catholic Social Teaching 1891–Present: A Historical, Theological and Ethical Analysis* (2002) and *The Catholic Moral Tradition Today: A Synthesis* (1999). He strongly upholds the Catholic tradition of the social common good against the individualism that prevails in modern society. He thinks that Catholic teaching on SEXUALITY has not kept up with its evolving social teaching. Curran has been president of many theological societies and received the John Courtney Murray Award from the Catholic Theological Society of America.

Further reading: Charles E. Curran, *Catholic Social Teaching 1891–Present: A Historical, Theological and Ethical Analysis* (Washington, D.C.: Georgetown University Press, 2002); ———, *Faithful Dissent* (Kansas City: Sheed & Ward, 1986); Larry Witham, *Curran vs. Catholic University: A Study of Authority and Freedom* (Riverside: Edington-Rand, 1991).

Cyprian of Carthage, St. (d. 258) *African bishop and theologian*

A pagan rhetorician who converted to Christianity around 246, Cyprian within two years acquired such a remarkable knowledge of the Scriptures that he was elected BISHOP of Carthage. With TERTULLIAN before him and AUGUSTINE after, he was one of the founding theologians of African and Latin theology. His feast day is September 16.

During the Decian persecution of 249–51, when the emperor demanded that CHRISTIANS sacrifice to the Roman gods, Cyprian fled to the hinterland but continued to govern his diocese by mail. Some Christians submitted during the persecution and offered sacrifices (*sacrifacati*), while others simply purchased letters saying they did so (*libellatici*). When many of these backsliders later sought reentry to the church, Cyprian, while opposing utterly lax conditions for reentry, came also to oppose the rigorist high-penance position of the schismatic followers of the Roman Novatian (d. 257/258) on the principle of preserving the unity of the church. However, he led a series of African councils that required schismatics to be rebaptized on the grounds that SACRAMENTS given outside the church were invalid. The Roman church argued to the contrary that sacraments administered by heretics and schismatics could still be valid. The controversy was not settled until Augustine argued against the DONATISTS that it was CHRIST and not the heretical or schismatic minister who conferred the grace of the sacrament (EX OPERE OPERATO).

Cyprian also contributed to the theology of original SIN, arguing for the BAPTISM of infants on the grounds that the entire human race was united with Adam in sin (*Letters* 151). This teaching, too, was given definitive form by Augustine. Cyprian's *On the Unity of the Church* has come down in two versions, one defending the unity of the church on the basis of the primacy of the see of PETER in Rome, and another that is silent on the subject, perhaps reflecting Cyprian's strong public disagreements with St. Stephen I, bishop of Rome. Today there is almost no instance of a bishop engaging in public debate with the papacy the way Cyprian did.

Further reading: Cyprian's major writings are available online; Edward White Benson, *Cyprian: His Life, His Times, His Work* (London: Macmillan, 1897); G. W. Clarke, trans., *The Letters of St. Cyprian of Carthage* (New York, Newman, 1984); Peter Bingham Hinchliff, *Cyprian of Carthage and the Unity of the Christian Church* (London: Chapman, 1974).

Cyril (826–869) and Methodius (c. 815–885), Sts. *apostles to the Slavs*

These two brothers from Thessalonica, known as the Apostles of the Slavs, were public servants before becoming monks; Cyril was known as Constantine before becoming a monk in 868. The brother went on imperial missions to the Khazars on the Dnieper River; Emperor Michael III sent them to Moravia, where they preached in the local language. Cyril invented the Glagolitic alphabet (commonly called Cyrillic) to fit the sounds of Slavic languages. The brothers created a LITURGY in Slavonic and translated Scripture into that tongue. Cyril is buried in San Clemente in Rome. Their feast day in the East is May 11 and in the West February 14. Pope JOHN PAUL II named them copatrons of Europe in 1980.

Further reading: Anthony-Emil N. Tachiaos, *Cyril and Methodius of Thessalonica: The Acculturation of the Slavs* (Crestwood, N.Y.: St. Vladimir's Seminary, 2001); Evangelos Konstantinou, *Leben und Werk der byzantischen Sklavenapostel Methodios und Kyrillos* (Münsterschwarzach: Vier-Türme, 1991).

Cyril of Alexandria, St. (c. 375–444) *bishop and theologian*

Cyril was born in Theodosiou, east of Alexandria. He succeeded his uncle Theolophilus as BISHOP of Alexandria. Often pugnacious in his arguments, he became the chief opponent of NESTORIUS and, ironically, the source of the later HERESY of Monophysitism. His feast day is February 9.

Cyril inherited a contentious situation in Alexandria from his uncle, with whom he attended the Synod of the Oak (403) that condemned JOHN CHRYSOSTOM. Some attributed the death of Hypathia, the famous mathematician and philosopher of Alexandria, to Cyril's machinations; indeed, his followers did appear to be responsible. He also inflamed his flock against the Jews.

In his letters to Nestorius of CONSTANTINOPLE (c. 386–c. 451), Cyril can be charged with distorting

Nestorius's views on the relation of Christ's humanity and his divinity to the extreme. Like his teacher Theodore of Mopseutia (c. 350–428), Nestorius was inclined to see Jesus as a fully human person with whom the Spirit was fully united. No other human could match this "fully" to the same degree as Jesus. Nestorius was reluctant to apply the term "Mother of God" (*Theotokos*) to MARY OF NAZARETH in other than a metaphoric sense, for which he was censured at the Council of EPHESUS in 431. In the *Second Letter* Cyril argued for the hypostatic union of the two natures in one being: there is a concurrence (*syndromē*) and union (*'enosis*) of the two natures in one nature. Cyril's imprecise language was taken up and given greater precision at the Council of Chalcedon, which used the terminology "one person (*hypostasis*), two natures (*physeis*)." Cyril often confused the terms "nature" and "person," thus giving rise to the Monophysitism problem in the post-Chalcedonian world. Besides many letters, Cyril wrote commentaries on the Pentateuch, the Gospel of John and other New Testament writings, the Nicene faith, and the TRINITY.

See also CHRIST/CHRISTOLOGY.

Further reading: Cyril of Alexandria, *Letters*, tr. John I. McEnearney (Washington, D.C.: Catholic University Press, 1987); Susan Wessel, *Cyril of Alexandria and the Nestorian Controversy* (Oxford: Oxford University Press, 2004).

Częstochowa, Our Lady of   *See* MARY OF NAZARETH.

D

Damien, Father (1840–1889) *minister to lepers*
Father Damien is the name by which the world
came to know Joseph de Veuster years before
his beatification by JOHN PAUL II in 1995. The
son of Belgian farmers, Joseph joined the Picpus
Society, a religious association dedicated to the
adoration of the Blessed Sacrament, in 1859. In
1863 he was sent to Honolulu, where he was
ordained. At his own request he was sent to the
island of Molokai, where for the rest of his life
he ministered to the spiritual, legal, and physical
needs of 600 lepers. He contracted the disease
(now known as Hansen's disease) in 1884. Along
the way, he was charged and later cleared of
illicit sexual contacts. In 1936 his remains were
removed to Louvain, Belgium, and placed in a
small church erected in his honor, a move he
almost certainly would have objected to. His life
was the subject of the 1999 movie *Molokai: The
Story of Father Damien.*

Further reading: Gavan Daws, *Holy Man: Father Damien
of Molokai* (Honolulu: University of Hawai'i Press,
1994); Hilde Eynikel, *Molokai: The Story of Father
Damien,* (New York: Alba House: 1999); Richard Stewart: *Leper Priest of Moloka'i: The Father Damien Story*
(Honolulu: University of Hawai'i Press, 2000).

**damnation (Lat.: *damnare,* "to condemn,"
"deprive of")**
Damnation is the state of those who fail to attain
salvation through CHRIST. It is an eternal banish-
ment from the presence of GOD (BEATIFIC VISION)
and absence of divine grace.

The New Testament speaks graphically about
the punishments accompanying the eternal loss of
God's grace (Matt. 3:12; Mark 9:43; 2 Thess. 1:9).
In his pronouncement on the damned who failed
to show mercy to the hungry and homeless, Jesus
puts the following words into the mouth of the
Lord of the Judgment: "Depart from me, ye cursed,
into everlasting fire prepared for the devil and his
angels" (Matt. 25:41). For some theologians (ORI-
GEN, GREGORY OF NYSSA) the punishments of hell are
symbolic and consist in the conscious awareness of
the loss of the joy of heaven, and for others (AUGUS-
TINE, THOMAS AQUINAS) the state is accompanied by
everlasting punishments such as physical torments.
Dante in his *Inferno* depicts these states in graphic
detail. The subject is also shown in the lower reliefs
of the central door tympana on medieval cathedrals
and in numerous medieval and Renaissance paintings, the most noted of which is MICHELANGELO'S
Last Judgment in the Sistine Chapel of the Vatican.

See also HEAVEN AND HELL.

217

Further reading: Alan E. Bernstein, *The Formation of Hell: Death and Retribution in the Ancient and Early Christian Worlds* (Ithaca: Cornell University, 1993); Alice K. Turner, *The History of Hell* (Orlando: Harcourt Brace, 1993).

Daniélou, Jean (1905–1974) *Jesuit theologian and scholar of early Christianity*

Daniélou was a Jesuit theologian, a noted patristic scholar, and an expert at VATICAN COUNCIL II. He was made a cardinal by Pope PAUL VI in 1969.

After studying at Jersey, Lyons (under HENRI DE LUBAC) and Mongré, he received his doctorate from the Sorbonne for a thesis on Platonism in patristic mystical theology. He was one of the innovators who contributed to the NOUVELLE THÉOLOGIE movement, urging theologians to go back to the earliest sources of CHRISTIAN history.

Daniélou became a principal investigator of the Jewish dimension of early Christianity. With de Lubac, he inaugurated the authoritative series of critical editions of patristic writings in 1942 under the title *Sources chrétiennes.* He is widely known for his book *Theology of Jewish Christianity.* He contributed significantly to *Gaudium et Spes,* the Pastoral Constitution on the Church, at Vatican II. After the council he became critical of what he took to be increasing secularism in the church. He died on the stairs of a Paris brothel.

Further reading: Jean Daniélou, *The Theology of Jewish Christianity* (London: Darton, Longman & Todd, 1964); Jean Daniélou and Henri Marrou: *The First Six Hundred Years* (New York: McGraw-Hill, 1964); Paul Lebeau, *Jean Daniélou* (Paris: Éditions Fleuris, 1967); Marie-Joséphe Rondeau, *Jean Daniélou, 1905–1974* (Paris: Éditions du Cerf/Axes, 1975).

Dante Alighieri (1265–1321) *philosophical Italian poet*

Author of *La Divina Comedia,* Dante was a founding giant of Italian literature who gave lasting expression to the moral and religious beliefs of his day. Born in Florence, Dante first encountered his muse, Beatrice, in 1273, probably Bice Portinari, the wife of Simone dei Bardi. She died in 1290; in *Vita Nuova* (1292) he promised her a poem like no other. That poem was the *Comedia,* later called *Comedia Divina,* or *Divine Comedy.*

The poem interprets human life as a sacred journey symbolized by the poet's passage through the realms of the afterlife in the *Inferno* (hell), *Purgatorio* (purgatory), and *Paradiso* (heaven). In 1300 the poet enters a forest and thence into the lower regions, where the Roman poet Virgil serves as his guide. At the earthly paradise of Adam and Eve Beatrice becomes his guide until they reach the empyrean, where St. BERNARD OF CLAIRVAUX takes over. Bernard, according to tradition, received a glimpse of the BEATIFIC VISION on Earth and is the theologian of divine love. The poem has been interpreted in many ways.

For all his orthodoxy, Dante, who was exiled by BONIFACE VIII in 1301, pictured many a pope in hell, showed compassion toward the doomed lovers Paolo and Francesca, and placed the "indifferent" in the lowest part of hell. Although Dante painted a harsh portrait of Muhammad and Ali, his nephew and son-in-law, in the *Inferno* (Canto 28:22-36), he had many positive things to say about the medieval Islamic philosophers Avicenna (Ibn Sina) and Averroes (Ibn Rushd). He places both in limbo instead of hell (Canto 4:143-44) and often cites them to agree with them in his other writings. He himself was probably a secret Averroist. Yet the poem affirms belief in the church. The poem ranks among the greatest pieces of literature of any time or any place. It has inspired many artistic interpretations, notably the engravings of Gustav Doré (1832–83) and William Blake (1757–1827).

Dante took an interest in both political thought and philosophy. His *Canzoni* are philosophical poems, later commented on in *On Vernacular Eloquence* and the *Convivio* (Banquet). In *On Monarchy* he argued that the PAPACY should abandon all temporal power. He placed hope in a universal monarchy, which he thought Emperor Henry VII of Italy (c. 1275–1313) would inaugurate.

Dante and Virgil gaze upon the tragic lovers Paolo and Francesca swirling in hell, *Inferno,* Canto 5.82–142, etching by Gustave Doré, 1867. *(possession of the author)*

Further reading: Morgan Alison, *Dante and the Medieval Other World* (Cambridge: Cambridge University Press, 1990); Michele Barbi, *Life of Dante, trans. by Paul Ruggiers (Berkeley: University of California Press, 1960); Rachel Jacoff, ed., The Cambridge Companion to Dante* (Cambridge: Cambridge University Press, 1993).

Day, Dorothy (1897–1980) *Catholic social activist*

Dorothy Day began life as a bohemian in New York City's Greenwich Village, where she bore a daughter, Tamara. In 1927 she converted to Catholicism and met the French personalist philosopher and peasant Peter Maurin (1877–1949). Together they founded the Catholic Worker movement in America. Their newspaper is still published as the *Catholic Worker.*

Day's commitment to PERSONALISM led her to uphold the dignity of each person and solidarity with the poor and oppressed. Her movement embraced CHRISTIAN socialism and was also one of the first 20th-century Catholic groups to embrace PACIFISM. She and Maurin opened a house of hospitality on Mott Street in New York City and a farming commune in upstate New York. The hospitality house served as a meeting place of the poor, activists, and intellectuals.

Under the influence of Robert Ludlow, and Ammon Hennacy (1893–1970), the movement took an activist role in peace and social justice causes, often serving to prick the conscience of civic authorities to do more for the down-and-out. Catholic Workers joined the civil rights marches led by the Rev. Dr. Martin Luther King, Jr., (1929–68) and led the Catholic opposition to both World War II and the Vietnam War. Catholic Workers played a key role in setting up numerous CATHOLIC ACTION groups in the United States, including the American Pax Association, the Catholic Peace Fellowship, and Pax Christi USA. The movement always has seen itself as a lump of leaven toward a new social order in the world. The group has been a frequent object of secret spying by the Federal Bureau of Investigation and, most recently, the National Security Agency.

Further reading: Robert Coles, *Dorothy Day: A Radical Devotion.* (Reading, Mass.: Addison-Wesley, 1987); Dorothy Day, *From Union Square to Rome.* (New York: Arno, 1978); ———, *House of Hospitality* (New York: Sheed & Ward, 1939); ———, *The Long Loneliness: The Autobiography of Dorothy Day,* 1952; reprint (San Francisco: Harper & Row, 1997); Jim Forest, *Love Is the Measure: A Biography of Dorothy Day* (New York: Paulist, 1986); Anne Klejment, *Dorothy Day and the Catholic Worker: A Bibliography and Index* (New York: Garland, 1986); William D. Miller, *A Harsh and Dreadful Love: Dorothy Day and the Catholic Worker Movement* (New York: Liveright, 1973).

deacon *See* CLERGY; HIERARCHY.

death and dying

All people go through the process of the disintegration and termination of biological life. The under-standing of death in the Western world has been shaped by both Jerusalem and Athens, religion and philosophy. In the Old Testament, adherence to the stipulations of the Covenant was life-giving. When a person died, he or she was believed to go to a place called *sheol,* a state of dark and cheerless suspended animation where there is no joy nor praise of GOD (Ps. 6.5; Isa. 38:18).

Later biblical books, influenced by Hellenistic philosophy, saw death as the separation of SOUL (*psychē*) from the body (*sōma*) as in Wisdom 3:1–5. The Greeks saw the soul as immortal, but not the body. Late biblical teaching, however, places emphasis on the RESURRECTION of the body at the Last Judgment (Dan. 12:2). In the New Testament, death is seen as the consequence of Adam's primal SIN (Rom. 5:1–12). CHRIST's resurrection, in which believers already participate even before death, is a victory over sin and its grip through death (Heb. 2:14; 2 Tim. 1:10).

Following St. PAUL THE APOSTLE, as interpreted by AUGUSTINE, Catholic theology views death as a consequence of original sin passed on to the human race through the act of sexual generation. Modern theology, influenced by the existential thought of Martin Heidegger (1889–1976), who viewed man as a "being unto death," sees death as a definitive moment in life, which manifests a person's disposition—humble or rebellious—toward the ultimate mystery of God.

Further reading: Glennys Howarth and Oliver Leaman, eds., *Encyclopedia of Death and Dying* (New York: Routledge, 2002); Henri J. M. Nouwen, *Our Greatest Gift: A Meditation on Dying and Caring* (New York: HarperSanFrancisco, 1994); Karl Rahner, *Theology of Death* (New York: Herder & Herder, l96l); Ron Wooten-Green, *When the Dying Speak: How to Listen to and Learn from Those Facing Death* (Chicago: Loyola, 2001).

decalogue *See* TEN COMMANDMENTS.

De Costa Nunes, José (1880–1979) *first cardinal of Macau*

José De Costa Nunes, archbishop of Macao (Macau) and cardinal, was born in the Azores on March 15, 1880. He accompanied Bishop de Azevedo e Castro (1852–80) to Macao in 1903. Late that year he was ordained a priest and placed in charge of the local Catholic orphanage. He also served as the diocesan administrator whenever the BISHOP's duties took him from the colony and succeeded Castro when he died.

The two decades of De Costa Nunes's leadership in Macau were times of expansion for the church. He oversaw the rebuilding of several churches and the expansion of educational work, which he turned over to the JESUITS. Among his duties as bishop of Macao was oversight of the mission in the Portuguese colony of Timor. He built up the work, so that on his completion of service in Macao, East Timor was set apart as a suffragan diocese under Goa. During the next 13 years (1940–53), De Costa Nunes served as the patriarch of the East Indies.

He retired to Rome and in 1962 was named a cardinal. He died November 29, 1976, in Rome.

See also ASIA.

Further reading: Sergio Ticozzi, "José De Costa Nunes," in Scott W. Sunquist, ed., *A Dictionary of Asian Christianity* (Grand Rapids, Mich.: Eerdmans, 2001).

de fide   *See* DOCTRINE.

Deism (Lat.: *deus*, "god")

Deism is a belief in the existence of one Supreme Being, but not necessarily in the theology and scriptures of any of the major monotheistic religions. It was commonly held during the Enlightenment era in Europe and the Americas.

The classic expression of Deism was *Christianity not Mysterious* (1696) by John Toland (1670–1722). The celebrated Samuel Clarke (1675–1729), student and disciple of Isaac Newton (1642–1727), differentiated four types of Deism in *Demonstrating the Being and Attributes of God* (1704): 1) God is Creator but takes no further interest in the universe; 2) GOD is Creator and exerts divine providence over the material world through the laws of nature but not over the spiritual and moral worlds; 3) God is Creator and has moral attributes, but there is no afterlife for humans; and 4) God is Creator, exerts divine providence on all levels, and is knowable through natural theology, but there is no supernatural REVELATION.

Newton himself was not a Deist, as he maintained that God could directly intervene in CREATION at any moment. However, he was a Unitarian who secretly denied the TRINITY and an Arian in his CHRISTOLOGY (*see* ARIANISM). Voltaire (François-Marie Arouet, 1694–1778) was the sharpest-witted Deist critic of Catholicism during the Enlightenment. Most of the founding fathers of the United States were Deists to varying degrees. Most deistic were Benjamin Franklin (1706–90), who wrote "A Deist's Creed," and Thomas Jefferson (1743–1826), who expunged all references to miracles from his cut-and-paste New Testament. In reaction to Deism, Pope PIUS IX condemned anyone who asserts "All action of God on humans and the world is to be denied" in his *Syllabus of Errors 2* (December 8, 1864).

See also CRITIQUE OF CHRISTIANITY; FAITH AND REASON; GOD.

Further reading: Edward G. Waring, ed., *Deism and Natural Religion: A Sourcebook* (New York: F. Ungar, 1967).

democracy (Gk.: *demos*, "people" + *kratein*, "to rule")

A spirit of democracy can be found in early Christianity and in many later movements and institutions within the church. It has become far more prominent in the past two centuries.

In political theory and practice, democracy is rule by all the people in contrast with aristocracy, rule by the nobility; plutocracy, rule by the rich; or monarchy, rule by one. Today democracy is closely allied with a commitment to inalienable rights and a separation of powers between the executive, the legislative, and the judicial branches of government. These rights include freedom of the vote, religion, assembly, and the press as well as habeas corpus.

In the New Testament PAUL paints a picture of a democracy of spiritual gifts (1 Cor. 12–15) in which each and all are called to contribute equally to the building up of the assembly (Gr. *ekklēsia*), or church of believers. Paul claimed a special status of equality with Peter and the other APOSTLES, but that status depended on having seen the Lord in a REVELATION, and not on any social or ecclesiastical superiority. Later Christianity, bowing to Roman institutional reality, developed a hierarchical system of ranks built around BISHOPS, priests, and deacons; began excluding women from governance roles; and placed special powers into the hands of leading BISHOPS (metropolitans, patriarchs, popes) in a quasi-monarchical manner. After the toleration of Christianity by CONSTANTINE and its establishment as the religion of the empire by his successors, Christianity became wedded to monarchism in society and a parallel hierarchical system internally. This principle was reinforced by AUGUSTINE'S subordination of the temporal to the spiritual and the peasant class to the rulers in his *City of God*.

This structure was continued in the feudal system of the MIDDLE AGES, which nonetheless maintained some protection for the lower classes. Under the Holy Roman Emperors, bishops became feudal "lords" of the land, equal in rank, privileges, and wealth to secular princes. Some religious orders during the Middle Ages, most notably the DOMINICANS, adopted democratic forms of self-government. When democratic movements and states began to arise in Western societies, the Catholic hierarchy, entrenched in its monarchist self-conception, was very distrustful. On the other hand, democratic movements and thinkers such as Thomas Jefferson (1743–1826) were often virulently anti-Catholic and anticlerical, driving many in the church into a defensive posture. This was

particularly true of PIUS IX, whose temporal rulership of the PAPAL STATES was ended by the democratic liberator Giuseppe Garibaldi (1807–82). But the tide was changing. Many democracies granted full rights to their citizens, including the right to vote, and own property, along with the right to make mistakes in life.

Sensing the changing times, Pope LEO XIII implicitly affirmed democratic rights and institutions when he recognized the rights of workers in his celebrated encyclical *Rerum Novarum* (May 15, 1891). The anniversary of this papal letter has been marked by a series of other encyclicals increasingly accepting of democratic government: *Quadragesimo Anno* by PIUS XI, *Octagesima Adveniens* by PAUL VI, and *Centesimus Annus* by JOHN PAUL II. VATICAN COUNCIL II in *Humanae Dignitatis* 6, the Declaration on Religious Freedom, upheld the protection of "inviolable rights" as a central function of government. Likewise, *Gaudium et Spes* 74, the Pastoral Constitution on the Church in the Modern World at Vatican II, declared that the form of government is left "to the free will of citizens." In *Centessimus Annus* 46 (May 1, 1991) John Paul II, echoing his support for the Solidarity movement in Poland during the 1980s, showed a preference for democracy because it allows for maximum participation, accountability, and replacement of rulers through peaceful means by the people.

Although the Catholic Church is not a democracy, neither is it a monarchy, even though it took on many of the trappings of monarchy throughout history, such as temporal power, tiara crowns, thrones, and royal-like garb. Vatican II, chiefly at the urging of JOHN COURTNEY MURRAY, sought to move beyond this confining heritage by stressing that the church is first and foremost a COMMUNION of the One Body of Christ, that BAPTISM confers a fundamental equality to all members (*Lumen Gentium* 30, Dogmatic Constitution on the Church), and that all within the church have fundamental rights as expressed in the revised *Code of Canon Law* (cnn. 208–31). Although those rights are still administered hierarchically, parishes and some dioceses are now functioning with consultative councils and bodies in their day-to-day affairs. The recent PEDOPHILIA scandal forced the American church to seek guidance from an outside consultative body composed of lay experts, clergy, and others.

Further reading: Eugene C. Blanchi and Rosemary Radford, Reuther, eds. *A Democratic Catholic Church: The Reconstruction of Roman Catholicism* (New York: Crossroad, 1992); Jay P. Corrin, *Catholic Intellectuals and the Challenge of Democracy* (Notre Dame: University of Notre Dame, 2002); William V. D'Antonio, "Autonomy and Democracy in an Autocratic Organization: The Case of the Catholic Church," *Sociology of Religion* (1995) 55:1004.

demythologization

Demythologization, or doing away with myth, is a method of interpreting the BIBLE and other CHRISTIAN religious texts by suspending their "mythic" elements (such as miracles, a tiered universe of heaven, Earth, and hell, ascensions, and resurrections) and seeking the existentially "authentic" proclamation (*kerygma*) of the GOSPEL ("the word of the Cross"). Demythologization is part of the larger conflict between modernity and antiquity and between a premodern and postmodern scientific understanding of the world and its events.

Demythologization is most often associated with the noted 20th-century New Testament scholar Rudolph Bultmann (1884–1976), who adapted his mode of existential analysis from the philosopher Martin Heidegger (1889–1976). It is thus a critique of religion arising from within the sacred sciences. It was preceded and accompanied by demystification, the critique of religion arising from outside. Both belong to the HERMENEUTICS of suspicion, manifested in the critical consciousness of modernity.

The medieval hermeneutic of the Bible, with its fourfold literal-historical, allegorical, moral, and anagogical senses, provided a template for the interpretation of nature and history, but it also bypassed the plain sense of Scripture in a symbolic web of TYPOLOGY and ALLEGORY. The hermeneutic of the PROTESTANT REFORMATION reduced the fourfold sense to the literal and the spiritual. Martin Luther (1483–1546) deallegorized the Scripture by a return to the letter and the principle that *scriptura suae ipsius interpres* ("Scripture interprets itself"). In offering the Bible to Christians in the vernacular, he asserted that it could be read and understood by the average person.

There is a hidden connection between Luther's project and that of Francis Bacon (1561–1626). As the reformers reduced the biblical texts to a set of evidences for FAITH, so Bacon sought to de-idolize the presumptions of human understanding in order to return to "things themselves" in a direct reading of the "Book of Nature." He reduced natural knowledge to an array of instances that humans could control and master through the judicious use of force. Bacon's project set the stage for the great hermeneutical reversal of Thomas Hobbes (1588–1679) and Benedict de Spinoza (1632–77), who resorted to the rational interpretation of nature in order to interpret the "Book of Scripture." This reversal enabled the historical-critical enterprise known as "higher criticism," which looks at the literary genres of the Bible not as divine inspiration or REVELATION but as human productions in given historical contexts. Later thinkers have argued that biblical religion's insistence on an absolutely transcendent God led to a "dedivinization of nature" (Friedrich Schiller) and a "demagification of the world" (Max Weber).

In the 19th and early 20th centuries the process of demystification reached unparalleled intensity. Georg W. F. Hegel (1770–1831) saw religious ideas as external, figurative husks from which the thinker must extract (Ger. *Enthüllen,* "dehusk" "shuck") the rational kernel. Karl Marx (1818–81) radicalized Hegel's critique, claiming that religious belief is a "holy illusion" that deflects the proletariat from their true material interests and transfigures them to an imaginary heaven.

Friedrich Nietzsche (1844–1900) and Sigmund Freud (1856–1939) brought the hermeneutics of suspicion to its pinnacle. As dedivinization and disenchantment were to the world as object, so Nietzsche's disillusionment (*Enttäuschung*) and Freud's decipherment (*Entzifferung*) were to the world as subject. Nietzsche unmasked Christianity as the resentment of the Christian masses against the becomingness of the world. Freud dethroned the modern ego, once so certain in its faith (Luther) and even in its doubt (Descartes), into an economy of drives (unconscious, preconscious, conscious) or a topography of conflict domains (id, ego, superego).

Postmodern faith could no longer find a footing on premodern religious representation. The search for critical faith was to appear in Karl Barth (1886–1968). Barth's dialectical theology made a radical distinction between faith and its cultural embodiment in cultural forms. Bultmann extracted the nucleus of faith—the kerygmatic event of the Word as judgment (*krisis*) addressed to existential depth—apart from the mythic forms in which it is embedded.

Bultmann's existentialist presuppositions and ahistorical relation to the Word of the Cross were superseded by the hermeneutics of deconstruction, which challenged the rational foundations of philosophical and theological discourse itself with a thoroughgoing historicity based on other aspects of Heidegger's thought. The herald of deconstruction was Jacques Derrida (1930–2004). In *Fides et Ratio* 82 (September 15, 1998) JOHN PAUL II averred that "a radically phenomenalist or relativist philosophy would be ill-adapted to help in the deeper exploration of the riches found in the word of God." Some Catholic theologians, however, say that deconstructive readings of the Kingdom in the Gospels can keep the believer open to the unexpected and incalculable in God's providence. Others show that deconstruction has an affinity with the *via negativa* in theology and the visions of the mystics like DIONYSIUS the Areopagite, JULIAN OF NORWICH, and TERESA OF ÁVILA.

Further reading: Rudolph Bultmann, *Jesus Christ and Mythology* (New York: Scribners, 1958); Frank K. Flinn, "The Phenomenology of Symbol: Genesis I and II," in William S. Hamrick, ed., *Phenomenology in Practice and Theology* (Dordrecht: Martinus Nijhoff, 1985), 223–249; Kevin Hart, *The Trespass of the Sign: Deconstruction, Theology and Philosophy* (New York: Fordham University Press, 2000); Paul Ricoeur, *The Philosophy of Paul Ricoeur*, ed. Charles E. Reagan and David Stewart (Boston: Beacon, 1978).

Denis, St. (third century) *martyred bishop of Paris*

Little is known of the early life of the semilegendary St. Denis (Dionysius). He emerges out of obscurity during the reign of Pope Fabian (r. 236–50), who sent him to Gaul to assist the recovery of the CHRISTIAN church following the persecution under the emperor Decius. Denis and his companions settled on the island in the Seine near what would become Paris. Their preaching was eventually rewarded with both a number of converts and torture and martyrdom at the hands of the pagan authorities. A shrine was erected over their graves.

One legend tells that St. Denis was beheaded near the Seine, picked up his head, and carried it north to where he fell, on the spot now known as the royal Abbey of St. Denis. Eventually a church was built over the site, and a BENEDICTINE monastery attached to the church. The Merovingian king Dagobert (622–38), whom another legend credits with moving the saint's remains to the site, saw to the adorning of the church.

Through succeeding centuries a cult of veneration of Denis spread through the emerging nation of France. The cult seems to have been fed by a serious historical error: Denis was identified with both DIONYSIUS the Areopagite, the first-century Athenian converted by PAUL's preaching on

Mars Hill (Acts 17:34), and the Pseudo-Dionysius, the sixth-century mystical writer who composed a book ascribed to Dionysius the Areopagite. The confusion between these three figures only intensified in the ninth century thanks to the *Areopagitica,* a volume attributed to Hilduin, the abbot of Saint-Denis's church in Paris, written at the request of Louis I the Pious (r. 814–40). In the 12 century, SUGER completely rebuilt the church of St. Denis, now renowned as the first of the great Gothic churches of France.

Further reading: Robert Cole, *A Traveler's History of Paris* (London: Weidenfeld & Nicholson, 2002); S. M. Crosby and P. Z. Blum, *The Royal Abbey of Saint-Denis from its Beginnings to the Death of Suger, 475–1151* (New Haven, Conn.: Yale University Press, 1987).

de' Nobili, Roberto (1577–1656) *missionary to India*

Roberto de' Nobili, a pioneer Jesuit missionary in India, was born in Rome in September 1577. Little is known of his life prior to his arrival in 1605 to assume control of the church in Madurai, in southern India. His congregation consisted entirely of expatriates, as his predecessor had been unable to make any converts among the native people.

De' Nobili pondered the problem of spreading the GOSPEL in India and decided that it was systemic. He needed to develop a new form of ministry that honored the culture and religion of the Indians. His rejection of the Portuguese, among whom he was sent to work, was made all the easier as he was an Italian.

After only a few months in India, de' Nobili adopted Indian dress as a *sannyasi* (a person who has taken the vows of a renunciant) and a vegetarian diet, began learning Sanskrit, and separated himself from the Portuguese community. In presenting the Christian message, he encouraged his hearers to remain Hindu in every way possible for a CHRISTIAN. He assembled about 100 converts over the first four years.

De' Nobili's work raised serious questions about missionary methodologies and the theological legitimacy of his approach. In 1612 he was ordered to stop baptizing people until a ruling on his unique methods came from Rome. That took 11 years, but in 1623, Rome ruled in his favor. He resumed his work. He was soon joined by other missionaries who shared his ideas, and the Madurai Mission prospered, claiming converts from all levels of society.

De' Nobili died at Mylapur on January 16, 1656, having made more than 20,000 converts. Both Catholics and Protestants continue to discuss the feasibility of attempting to contextualize the Gospel as de' Nobili did.

See also INCULTURATION; MATEO RICCI; MISSIONS.

Further reading: Vincent Cronin, *A Pearl to India: The Life of Roberto de Nobili* (New York: Dutton, 1959); S. Rajamanickam, *The First Oriental Scholar* (Madras: Diocesan Press, 1972); Augustine Souliere, *His Star in the East* (Anand: Gujarat Sahitya Prakash, 1995).

descent into hell   *See* CREED.

De Smet, Pierre Jean (1801–1873) *missionary to Amerindians*

De Smet was born in Termoncle, Belgium. He came to America in 1821 and was ordained a Jesuit in 1827. He carried the GOSPEL message to Amerindians of the Midwest and Pacific Northwest regions of the United States. In 1840 he headed for the Rocky Mountains to minister to the Flathead and others. In Montana, he worked among the Salish at Pierre's Hole and baptized about 600. A year later at Bitterroot Valley, he began St. Mary's Mission. In 1844, with fellow-priest Adrian Hoecken (1815–97), de Smet built the St. Ignatius Mission near Albeni Falls, Idaho. Under his ministrations, Standing Grizzly, a Kalispel chief, converted to Catholicism, but the mission lost support after his death. In 1850 it was abandoned. At times, de

Smet served as an agent of the U.S. government. He operated out of St. Louis, Missouri, where he is buried.

Further reading: Hiram Martin Chittenden and Alfred Talbot Richardson, eds., *Life, Letters and Travels of Father Pierre-Jean de Smet, S.J. 1801–1873.* 4 vols. (New York: Francis P. Harper, 1905; reprint, New York: Kraus, 1969).

devils and demons (Gk.: *diabolos*, "accuser" = Heb.: *satan*; Gk.: *daimon*, "possessing spirit")

In theological terminology the devil is the personification of EVIL and the chief of the fallen angels, often named Lucifer (Lat.: "light-bearer"). The fallen angels freely rebelled against the dominion of GOD and are eternally damned.

The Hebrew BIBLE shows little interest in devils and demons until the period after the exile. Not even the serpent in the Garden of Eden is a devil or demon, until so interpreted in postexilic literature (Wis. 2:24). Nor is Satan a devil in the Book of Job, where he functions like a prosecuting attorney in the heavenly council of God (1:9–12). Chronicles has Satan lead David to seek a census of the people (1 Chron. 21:1; *but see* 2 Sam. 24:1). Zechariah depicts Satan as an accuser of the high priest Joshua, very much like the picture in Job (Zech. 3:1–2).

Devils and demons grow exponentially in the postexilic Jewish and early CHRISTIAN literature. There are two reasons. First, during the exile in Babylon (c. 589–39 B.C.E.) Jews came into close contact with the ethical dualism of the ruling Zoroastrians, which saw time and history as a struggle between Good Mind (Ahura Mazda) and Evil Mind (Angra Mainyu) culminating in a final battle and judgment. This religious system shaped both the late Jewish and the early Christian apocalyptic understanding of good and evil, good angels vs. evil angels, and the final judgment. Second, the Hellenistic world saw a general increase of belief in demons and demon

possession. Archaeologists have uncovered countless prophylactics against demons: amulets, incantation texts inscribed in bowls, and so on. There is also evidence for widespread use of exorcism rituals against demons (*see* Mark 3).

The intertestamental literature performed a "demonization" of ambiguous texts. Thus, 1 Enoch 6:16 turned the "sons of God" (Gen. 6:1–4) into fallen angels. Similar transformations take place in Jubilees and the Testament of Twelve Patriarchs. The New Testament picks up on all the above themes and shapes them into a developed demonology. The devil tempts Jesus at the beginning of his ministry (Mark 1:13; Matt. 4:1–11). Jesus frees those rendered powerless by demons. Jesus sees the power of Satan who has "fallen from heaven like lightning" (Luke 22:31–32) as already broken, although the wheat cannot be sifted from the tares until the last judgment (Matt. 13:24–30), when Satan and his minions will be consigned to eternal fire (Matt. 25:41). Other texts amplify on the theme of the fall of the angels (1 Peter 1:6; Rev. 12:7–9).

There is no consistent systematic treatment of demons among the early Christian theologians. Some, like JUSTIN MARTYR, TERTULLIAN, and CYPRIAN, thought that the fall of the angels was due to their envy of humans, as in 1 Enoch. Others, like ORIGEN, rejected the tales of 1 Enoch and attributed the fall to pride. AUGUSTINE, who thought angels had bodies, combined the two theories. He also rejected Origen's Zoroasterlike theory that the fallen angels would ultimately become reconciled to God (*apokatatasis*).

In the MIDDLE AGES theologians like Sts. ALBERTUS MAGNUS and THOMAS AQUINAS distinguished between the angelic state and human grace and beatitude. The evil angels fell in the first instant of their creation through their pride in thinking they could reach divine beatitude by their own powers. The Franciscan DUNS SCOTUS located Lucifer's sin in an inordinate love of his own excellence. FRANCISCO SUÁREZ sought to reconcile the Dominican and Franciscan viewpoints.

Many modern theologians attribute manifestations of demon possession and similar phenomena to psychiatric disorders. There is no formal dogmatic statement about demons and devils in the Christian tradition other than that issued by the Council of Braga (561), which stated, against the alleged teachings of the Priscillianists, that the devil was created good and that he himself could not create. Lateran Council IV (*see* COUNCILS, ECUMENICAL) said that Satan became evil by his own will and not through some outside cosmic force.

Further reading: Peter Kreeft, *Angels and Demons: What Do We Really Know about Them?* (San Francisco: Ignatius Press, 1995); Jeffrey Burton Russell, *Lucifer: The Devil in the Middle Ages.* (Ithaca, N.Y.: Cornell University Press, 1984); ———. *Mephistopheles: The Devil in the Modern World* (Ithaca, N.Y.: Cornell University Press, 1986); ———. *Satan: The Early Christian Tradition* (Ithaca, N.Y.: Cornell University Press, 1981).

Devotio Moderna (Lat.: "Modern Devotion")

Devotio Moderna was a spiritual renewal movement that originated in the Netherlands at the end of the 14th century and spread to GERMANY. It stressed the inner life, meditation, and a simple, direct devotion to Jesus, and it quietly opposed the theological complexities of Scholastic theology. The *devotio* was associated with the Brethren of the Common Life. It was sustained by Geert de Groote of Deventer (1340–84), a member of the Brethren, and it came to fruition in the *Imitation of Christ* by THOMAS À KEMPIS, a Christocentric meditation on the interior life and on the life and Passion of Jesus. The movement drew its spiritual guidance from the mystical and devotional writings of Sts. AUGUSTINE, BERNARD OF CLAIRVAUX, and BONAVENTURE. The Brethren, composed of lay women and men, priests, and in some cases CANONS regular, lived in small communities. DESIDERIUS ERASMUS was a canon regular member of the Brethren. In many ways, the Devotio Moderna

anticipated the spiritual side of the PROTESTANT REFORMATION. Many find Matthias Grünewald's depiction of Christ in the Isenheim Altar to be the pictorial equal of the *Imitation of Christ.*

Further reading: Gerard Groote, *Gérard Grote, Fondateur de la dévotion moderne: lettres et traités* (Turnhout: Brepols, 1998); Diarmaid MacCulloch, *The Reformation* (New York: Viking, 2004); Regnerus R. Post, *The Modern Devotion: Confrontation with Reformation and Humanism* (Leiden: Brill, 1968).

devotions

Devotions are the various motions, gestures, and words, both liturgical and nonliturgical, that Catholics use to express their piety and the affective aspect of their reverence for GOD. Because Roman Catholicism is highly sacramental and ritual in nature, Catholics have many outlets to express their devotion to God and their veneration of saints and holy objects. Some acts are ritually prescribed in the Roman Ritual, the official Catholic book of prayers and ceremonies. They include making the sign of the cross, bowing, sprinkling with holy water, and bestowing blessings.

Devotions can be divided into two classes: isolated acts and sustained ceremonies. The most common Catholic religious act is the sign of the CROSS, often accompanied by the phrase "In the name of the Father, the Son, and the Holy Spirit." It consists of a movement of the thumb from forehead to breast and of the fingers from the left shoulder to the right. The sign is made upon entering churches, with worshippers first dipping their fingers in a Font containing holy water (*see* FURNISHINGS, CHURCH). It is also frequently made before commencing prayer or upon receiving a blessing from a priest or bishop. TERTULLIAN attests to this practice in the early third century. Catholics frequently kiss a crucifix and venerate the cross as a formal part of Good Friday services.

Catholics also regularly genuflect on one knee upon entering a church and before entering a pew to sit down, especially if a lit candle in a red-reflecting glass indicates that the Blessed Sacrament is present in the sanctuary (see EUCHARIST). They also kneel when praying, doing acts of contrition, and during the consecration portion of the Eucharist. Devout believers often crawl on their knees up the aisles of churches in a display of devotion and humility. Some Latin Americans are known to make kilometers-long pilgrimages on their knees, for example to the church of Guadalupe in Mexico and the Santuario de Chimayo in New Mexico.

Catholics often hang a crucifix above their beds and have various statues, pictures, and images of the Blessed Virgin Mary and other saints prominently displayed in their homes. Many have collections of holy cards depicting CHRIST, Mary, and other saints with prayers on the back. St. Christopher is still the most popular holy card although he has officially been removed from the list of saints. On Palm Sunday they bring home palm branches, which they weave into elaborate shapes. They keep these until the following Ash Wednesday when the dried leaves are burnt and used to mark the forehead as a sign of penance.

Some sprinkle their beds with holy water before sleeping and keep small wall fonts in their homes. Others frequently use what are known as ejaculations, or short prayers (such as "Jesus, Mary, Joseph," or "Lord, hear my prayer") before retiring or in times of stress.

Many Catholics say the rosary on a daily or weekly basis (see MARY OF NAZARETH). Other say grace before meals. Others say the Our Father or Hail Mary prayers before undertaking a task or journey or in a distressful situation.

The second class of devotions are continuous acts. They may be dedicated to the SACRED HEARTS OF JESUS or Mary, the Miraculous Medal, or Our Lady of Sorrows, the Blessed Sacrament, or objects of devotion. The Miraculous Medal is associated with the apparition of Mary of Nazareth to St. Catherine Labouré in 1830. They include the ritual circuit of the Stations of the Cross, done each Good Friday at the sacred sites in Jerusalem and often on every Friday in parishes around the world. There are also devotions to a particular saint who has a special function or is a patron. Popular saints and their specialties are St. Anthony of Padua (lost items), St. Jude (hopeless causes), and St. Maria Correti (purity). A novena, or cycle of prayer for nine days, is a very common form of devotion before a major feast or as an individual act. Some Catholics keeps shrines or altars in their homes on which they place statues of Christ, Mary, and other saints, holy cards, blessed candles, and holy water for use in blessings.

The wearing of Medals around the neck is very popular. Common images on medals include Jesus, the Blessed Virgin Mary, Our Lady of Fatima, or a favorite or patron saint, especially the saint after whom a person is named. Many wear what is known as the Miraculous Medal. Members of third orders, lay persons associated with an order like the FRANCISCANS, wear scapular cloth medals as a sign of their membership.

There has been much discussion in favor and in critique of the various types of devotions. Devotions became very popular in the early MIDDLE AGES when Eucharistic participation declined sharply. This led to long-lasting anomalies, such as a person coming to a Eucharist and saying the rosary throughout the entire service including while receiving the consecrated bread and wine. With the renewal of liturgical practice at VATICAN COUNCIL II, many theologians thought that privatistic devotions should be deemphasized in favor of communal liturgical worship. In *Sacrosamtum Concilium* 13, the Constitution on the Sacred Liturgy, Vatican II gave its blessing to devotions, especially those approved by the Apostolic See, with the proviso that "they harmonize with the liturgical seasons, are in accord with the sacred liturgy, are in some fashion derived from it, and lead people to it, since the liturgy by its nature far surpasses any of them." In the post–Vatican II period starting under JOHN PAUL II there has been a notable return to traditional devotionalism.

See also PRAYERS, COMMON.

Further reading: John G. Deedy, *Retrospect: The Origins of Catholic Beliefs and Practices* (Chicago: Thomas More, 2001); James Martin, *Awake My Soul: Contemporary Catholics on Traditional Devotions* (Chicago: Loyola, 2004); Michael Walsh, *A Dictionary of Catholic Devotions* (San Francisco: HarperSanFrancisco, 1993).

dialogue   *See* ECUMENISM.

Didache (Gk.: *didachē*, "teaching")

The full title of the early CHRISTIAN church order manual commonly known as the *Didache* is *The Teaching of the Lord through the Twelve Apostles*. Its date is unknown, but it contains material dating back to the early church, perhaps to the turn of the first century. The only known full manuscript, was discovered by Metropolitan Philotheos Bryennios (1833–1914?) in the library of the Hospice of the Jerusalem Church of the Holy Sepulcher in CONSTANTINOPLE in 1873, along with the Epistle of Barnabas and the two epistles of Clement to the Corinthians, and published by him in 1883.

The first section (chaps. 1–6) of the manual describes the Two Ways, the Way of Life and the Way of Death. It has quotations from the Sermon on the Mount (Matt. 5:1–7:27) and shows close affinities with the Manual of Discipline at Qumran. Chapters 7–15 contain church guidance on the celebration of BAPTISM and the EUCHARIST and on the treatment of church functionaries. It seems to make a distinction between itinerant APOSTLES and prophets on the one hand and sedentary BISHOPS and deacons on the other. Chapter 6 is an APOCALYPSE dealing with the Antichrist and the imminent Second Coming.

Further reading: Johannes Quasten, *Patrology*, vol. 1 (Utrecht: Spectrum, 1950–60); Aaron Milavec, *The Didache:*

Faith, Hope, & Life of the Earliest Christian Communities (New York: Newman, 2003).

diocese (Gk.: *dia*, "through," "throughout" + *oikesis*, "housekeeping," "administrative territory")

A diocese is the fundamental ecclesiastical unit in Roman Catholicism; in ecclesiastical law it constitutes a juridical person. Each Catholic diocese has a BISHOP or ARCHBISHOP at its head, who is directly answerable to the pope in Rome. Following the pastoral directives of VATICAN COUNCIL II, the *Code of Canon Law* (1983) now defines a diocese as "a portion of the people of God entrusted for pastoral care to a bishop" (cn. 369), which portion is understood to be the Eucharistic community of the faithful united in CHRIST.

A bishop is supreme in his diocese, over which he exercises ordinary jurisdiction. (*Ordinary* is a technical term for ecclesiastical governance.) The pope's most important ecclesiastical title is "bishop of Rome." A diocese is usually divided into parishes, with priests as their pastors. Larger archdioceses sometimes have auxiliary bishops to assist in ministering to the faithful. Sometimes groups of parishes are associated together in deaneries.

The New Testament does not use the term *diocese*. Its first occurrence is in Clement, 1 *Corinthians* 20.1, where it means administration, as it did in general Roman usage. In first-century Christianity the basic ecclesiastical unit was the *ekklesia*, or "church," a term that now applies to the Catholic or other CHRISTIAN communion worldwide. The Council of Nicaea (325) used the term *paroikia*—today "parish"—for what we now call diocese (cn. 16). By the MIDDLE AGES the term *diocese* was in common use. In the first millennium archdioceses exerted some control over lower dioceses. Today an archdiocese is simply an important diocese.

The Eastern Catholic and Orthodox Churches use the terms *eparchy* and *exarchy*, roughly corresponding to diocese and archdiocese in the West (Council of CHALCEDON, cn. 17). An exarch is often called a metropolitan, roughly equivalent to archbishop in the West.

Further reading: Charles Du Cange, "Dioikesis," *Glossarium ad Scriptores Mediae et Infimae Graecitatis* (Bratislava: Koebner, 1891); Henry Chadwick, ed., *The Role of the Christian Bishop in Ancient Society* (Berkeley, Calif.: Center for Ecumenical Studies, 1979).

Dionysius

Several important early saints and scholars were named Dionysius, and later tradition often confused them. This entry deals with the historically most important of them.

1. **Dionysius the Areopagite** (fl. 50) was converted by St. Paul (Acts 17:34) and was often referred to as the first bishop of Corinth.
2. **Dionysius of Paris**, also called St. Denis (c. 250) was, according to St. Gregory of Tours, sent to convert the Gauls in Paris. He is patron of France, along with St. Joan of Arc.
3. **Dionysius the (Pseudo-)Areopagite** (fl. 500), often identified with the previous two, was the prolific author who combined Neoplatonism and Christianity in a number of elaborate mystical treatises. The *Celestial Hierarchy* treats the sacraments and the hierarchical orders of the faithful. The *Divine Names* discusses the being and attributes of God. The *Mystical Theology* deals with the journey of the soul into God through purification, illumination, and perfection. Dionysius sees all creation as being taken up into the Godhead in a mystical union. Dionysius's writings had enormous influence on all the major Christian medieval philosophers and theologians and on the course of Mystical theology.
4. **Dionysius Exiguus** (fifth to sixth century) was a Scythian monk who contributed to church chronology and canon law. He calculated the new Easter cycle from the (supposed) day of the Incarnation, giving us the date we now call 1 A(nno) D(omini), or, in scholarly terms, 1 C(ommon) E(ra). By modern calculations Jesus was most likely born in 4–6 B.C.E.

Further reading: Gregory of Tours, *History of the Franks*, available online; H. Mordeck, "Dionysius Exiguus," *Lexikon des Mittelalsters* (1986) 3:1088 to 1092; René Roques *L'univers dionysien: structure hiérarchique du monde selon le Pseudo-Denys* (Paris: Aubier, 1954).

Docetism (Gk.: *dokein*, "to seem")

Docetism, a doctrine eventually ruled heretical, taught that the Christ only appeared to take up a human body for his ministry and then left the body of Jesus before it underwent suffering and death. Docetists seem to have overvalued Christ's divine origin at the expense of his humanity and therefore were led to deny a true Incarnation of the Word in the flesh. Docetists are the target of several passages in the New Testament: 1 John 4:1–3; 2 John 7; Colossians 2:9.

Cerinthus (fl. c. 100), the teacher of Marcion, seems to have been the first person to be called a Docetist. He may have come out of Ebionite circles. He taught that Jesus began as a mere man and that a divine power overtook him at his baptism in the Jordan but then departed from him before he underwent the Passion of the cross. Some Docetists taught that Judas Iscariot or Simon of Cyrene took Christ's place on the cross. Most subsequent forms of Gnosticism have Docetic tendencies. Ignatius of Antioch inscribed the first clear Christology while criticizing those who taught that Christ "suffered in mere appearance" (*To the Trallians* 9.10).

Further reading: Charles E. Hill, "Cerinthus, Gnostic or Chiliast? A New Solution to an Old Problem," *Journal of Early Christian Studies* (2000) 8.2: 135–172; Kurt

Rudolph, *Gnosis: The Nature and History of Gnosticism* (San Francisco: Harper & Row, 1983).

doctors of the church

The appellation *doctor of the church* is an honorific title granted to certain teachers of the universal church whose work has through the centuries been especially useful and authoritative both theologically and practically. All of the "doctors" are canonized saints. By the early MIDDLE AGES the title *doctor* was already being applied to Sts. GREGORY THE GREAT, AMBROSE OF MILAN, AUGUSTINE OF HIPPO, and JEROME. In the Eastern Church, three men had attained an equally honorable status: JOHN CHRYSOSTOM, BASIL THE GREAT, and GREGORY OF NAZIANZUS, with ATHANASIUS OF ALEXANDRIA soon added.

In more recent centuries, the granting of the title has become more formal. It is now issued, with the pope's approval, by the Vatican's Congregation of Sacred Rites, since it implies some changes to the LITURGY. The candidate's writings are reviewed before the title is granted. However, granting the title is not viewed as an ex cathedra (hence, infallible) ruling, nor does being named a doctor of the church mean that the person's writings are completely without error. Within these boundaries, however, the honor lifts the work of those so named above the writings of their peers.

In 1567 THOMAS AQUINAS became the ninth name added to the list. Since then, more than 20 additional people have been designated doctors of the church. Pope PAUL VI made history in September 1970 when he named TERESA OF ÁVILA the first woman to the very exclusive list. He followed a month later by naming CATHERINE OF SIENA. Pope JOHN PAUL II added THÉRÈSE OF LISIEUX to the list. As of 2006, a mere 33 people have been named a doctor of the church.

Further reading: Cecilia Bush, *A Walk Through History with the Doctors of the Church* (Wichita, Kans.: Spiritual Life Center, 2003); Ernest Simmons, *The Fathers and Doctors of the Church* (Milwaukee: Bruce, 1959).

doctrine/dogma (Lat.: *docēre,* "to teach")

Doctrine is the official teaching of the Catholic Church as a whole. A doctrine that has been formally defined as infallible or unerring is now called a dogma. The official teaching body of the church is called the MAGISTERIUM, which includes ecumenical councils, popes, and regional and national conferences of BISHOPS, all of which are informed by theologians.

The sum total of doctrine handed on from Jesus CHRIST in the apostolic tradition was called at the Council of TRENT the deposit of FAITH, now understood to be a treasure house of REVELATION and salvation entrusted to the church. A formal and conscious rejection of a dogma of the church is considered HERESY.

In past church history the voice of the laity was counted as part of the magisterium. JOHN HENRY NEWMAN wrote in *On Consulting the Faithful in Matters of Doctrine* that during the ARIANISM controversy all but a handful of bishops were on the Arian side. Thus, "the governing body of the church came up short, and the governed were preeminent in faith, zeal, courage, and constancy." For the most part the lay voice had long been radically muted until VATICAN COUNCIL II. Today there are many Roman Catholic lay theologians throughout the world.

In reaction to the implicit historicism of the Enlightenment, some Roman Catholics in the 19th century viewed church doctrine and the deposit of faith as a frozen body of truth always and everywhere infallibly presented by the church. By contrast, Newman, in *An Inquiry on the Development of Christian Doctrine,* and the theologians of the NOUVELLE THÉOLOGIE, attacked this rigid notion and presented doctrine as a living response of the community of believers at various times and circumstances to the revelation received from God in Christ and handed on through the apostolic tradition. In *Mysterium Ecclesiae* 5 (June 24, 1973) the Congregation for the Doctrine of Faith, while rejecting "dogmatic relativism," still stated that a dogma might reflect "the changeable conceptions of a given epoch." Old formulas sometimes merit updated explanations or may even be replaced by new expressions. The theory of the development of doctrine was enhanced by the studies of Newman, Johann S. von Drey (1777–1853), and Johann A. Moehler (1796–1838) at the University of Tübingen and Maurice Blondel (1861–1949), all of whom embraced an organic view of doctrine as a living phenomenon evolving and reshaping itself in time.

Today almost all theologians and scholars of historical theology admit that there has been a progressive development of doctrine. Although there are clear teachings and doctrines in the biblical record, the BIBLE itself is a collection of narratives, law codes, histories, psalms, prophetic oracles, GOSPELS, epistles, and APOCALYPSES and not a systematic treatise of THEOLOGY. The New Testament is much concerned about *who* Jesus is (Is he the Messiah or not?), not *what* Jesus is (Is he God or human, and how so?). Catholics believe that public revelation came to a close with the death of the last APOSTLE, but the HOLY SPIRIT continues with the church, deepening its understanding of the content of that revelation.

Formal doctrinal thought comes into focus only in the second century, when CHRISTIANS were faced with the challenges of DOCETISM, the doctrines of MARCION and MONTANUS, and the many varieties of GNOSTICISM. In response to these challenges, the structure of doctrine emerged in the three articles of the Christian CREED, as developed in the writings of IRENAEUS OF LYONS, TERTULLIAN OF CARTHAGE, and HIPPOLYTUS OF ROME. The doctrine of the CREATION of heaven and earth, and thus of both the material and the spiritual, refuted the denigration of matter and the body. The emphasis on the INCARNATION of the Word in the flesh in the article on REDEMPTION similarly refuted the attempt to downplay the human reality of the savior. Irenaeus's doctrine of the recapitulation and restoration of creation in Christ was meant to answer the wild-eyed eschatologies of the Montanists and others, who saw the end of all things as a flight from creation.

In the Nicene and post-Nicene era Christian doctrine concerned itself with four themes: 1) the relation of Christ to the Godhead; 2) the relation of the divine and human natures to the person of the Christ; 3) the status of Mary as the mother of Christ and/or mother of God (*Theotokos*); and 4) the relation of the Holy Spirit to the Father and Son and the three persons of the TRINITY to the one substance of the Godhead. In the debates with the Arians, Nestorians, Monophysites, and monothelites, a new vocabulary of terms not in the New Testament but derived from Hellenistic philosophy came into play: *homoousios* (of the same being/substance), *physis* (nature), and *hypostasis* (at first substance, later person). Necessary though they were, these disputes and their resolution became both intricate and intellectualistic, a significant departure from the style of the proclamation (*kerygma*) of the Gospel in the New Testament.

In the period after the first seven councils, doctrine in the West took on new directions and emphases, including sacramental theology, church-state relations, and papal authority. In the Scholasticism of the MIDDLE AGES the language of faith became wedded to the language of ARISTOTLE's categories: substance and accident, quality and quantity, cause and effect, and so on. Thus, THOMAS AQUINAS and other medieval theologians employed Aristotelian categories to explain the transformation of the elements of bread and wine into the body and blood of Christ as a TRANSUBSTANTIATION whereby the substance, or underlying element of the bread and wine, is changed, yet the outward accidents are preserved (whiteness of bread, redness of wine, taste, etc.).

One of the key doctrinal developments of the MIDDLE AGES was its ample theology of the INCARNATION and the correlate teaching on the Immaculate Conception of Mary, opposed by the Dominicans but championed by the Franciscans, especially DUNS SCOTUS. The nominalism of WILLIAM OF OCKHAM shaped doctrinal discussion in the late Middle Ages, especially the debates on Scripture, tradition, and mysticism, topics equally important both for the PROTESTANT REFORMATION and the COUNTER-REFORMATION. Nominalists like Gabriel Biel severely limited the scope of natural reason, thus paving the way for the mysticism of MEISTER ECKHARDT and Johannes Tauler (c. 1300–61).

During and after the Protestant Reformation Catholic doctrine went into a defensive and preservative mode. The doctrinal decrees of the Council of TRENT were formulated in precise, Scholastic terms and presented as a grand final summation of Catholic doctrine for all time. As far as the laity were concerned, this was the truth. All subsequent editions of the CATECHISM were grounded on the decrees of Trent until the new catechism in 1994.

While theology continued to develop with such thinkers as ROBERT BELLARMINE and FRANCISCO SUAREZ, doctrine, for the most part, was restricted to refinement and summation of already defined formulas. There was significant progress, however, in moral doctrine and spirituality by such luminaries as Sts. FRANCIS DE SALES and ALPHONSUS DE LIGUORI. Furthermore, the popular Marian devotions of modern times resulted in two important doctrinal additions. The first was the dogmatic definition of the doctrine of the Immaculate Conception of Mary by PIUS IX in 1854; the second was the doctrine of the bodily assumption of Mary into heaven, proclaimed by PIUS XII in 1950. But even these two doctrines had their theological foundations in much earlier times. The form of doctrine seemed frozen in a post-Tridentine grid, especially after LEO XIII made the Scholastic theology of Thomas Aquinas authoritative for seminary instruction.

This doctrinal freeze, however, began to break up in the most recent era as new theological undercurrents gained force. More and more theologians now shared a sense of doctrinal history as an organic, living process progressively unfolding in time. Catholic scholars began plumbing the riches of the early church theologians, not just for doctrine but also for their liturgical, pastoral, and spiritual treasures. Then, in the early 20th century, the doors were officially opened to the study of the Scriptures themselves using historical and literary critical methods. These trends unfolded and were summed up in the NOUVELLE THÉOLOGIE movement, which in turn had a far-reaching impact on VATICAN COUNCIL II.

Vatican II was primarily a pastoral council, a visionary updating of Catholic doctrine with a view to the church's pastoral mission in the world. Though many decrees were labeled "dogmatic" to demonstrate their doctrinal importance, none of them came with anathemas attached.

Nowhere can the results be better seen than in the new *Catechism of the Catholic Church* (1994). Unlike its predecessors—simplistic, propositional summaries of the decrees of Trent—this new instruction manual presented Catholic teaching in clear (though learned) terms, drawing on Scripture, early Christian writings like the DIDACHE, FATHERS AND MOTHERS OF THE CHURCH, medieval and modern theologians, and spiritual writers, namely, all the resources of the rich Catholic tradition, and applied these resources to the living questions of the day. From this perspective, faith is assent not simply to propositions but to the present mystery of God as revealed in Scripture and interpreted in the tradition.

Further reading: Jaroslav J. Pelikan, *The Christian Tradition: A History of the Development of Doctrine,* 5 vols. (Chicago: University of Chicago Press, 1971–1991); John Henry Newman, *An Essay on the Development of Christian Doctrine* (Notre Dame: University of Notre Dame Press, 1989); Bradford Hinze, *Narrating History, Developing Doctrine: Friedrich Schleirmacher and John Sebastian Drey* (Atlanta: Scholars, 1993).

documentary hypothesis   *See* BIBLE.

dogma   *See* DOCTRINE.

Doi, Peter Tatsuo Cardinal (1892–1970)
first Japanese cardinal

Peter Tatsuo Doi, the first Japanese to be named cardinal, was born December 22, 1892, in Sendai, Japan. As a youth of 10 he was baptized a Roman Catholic. He attended the seminary in his hometown and then went to Rome to study at the Pontifical Urbanian Athenaeum De Propaganda Fide. He was ordained in 1921.

Doi began his pastoral work in Sendai, where he worked for 13 years. In 1934 he was named the secretary to the apostolic delegate in Japan, from which position he was elected ARCHBISHOP of Tokyo in 1937 and consecrated the following year. He assumed additional duties as head of Catholic Relief during the years of World War II.

In 1956 he was named an assistant at the Pontifical Throne (a position in the Catholic hierarchy just below that of cardinal). In 1959 POPE JOHN XXIII signaled a new interest in Japan by making the Vatican's first radio broadcast to the country. The next year, as part of his reaching out to several neglected areas of the church, the pope named Doi a cardinal, the first ever from Japan. He was active through the years of VATICAN COUNCIL II (1962–65). Doi died in Tokyo and is buried there in the metropolitan cathedral.

Further reading: Johann Laures, *The Catholic Church in Japan: A Short History* (Rutland, Vt.: Charles E. Tuttle, 1954).

Döllinger, Johann J. Ignatz von (1799–1890) *theologian and Vatican critic*

Ordained in 1822, Döllinger became a professor of church history first at Aschaffenburg and then at Munich. He developed a warm lifelong friendship with JOHN HENRY NEWMAN and his student Lord John Acton (1834–1902). He published a number of important studies on early Church fathers, the PROTESTANT REFORMATION, and Luther.

At first Döllinger supported the position of Ultramontanism, which stressed strong ties with the Roman curia, but over time he became distrustful of the influence of Rome due to its opposition to liberalism both in politics and theology. In the *Letters of Janus* (1869) and the *Letters of Quirinus* (1869–70), to which Lord Acton contributed reports from the Vatican, he differed strongly with PIUS IX's *Syllabus of Errors* (December 8, 1864), with the upcoming VATICAN COUNCIL I, with the pope's insistence on retaining the PAPAL STATES, and especially with the declaration on papal INFALLIBILITY.

Döllinger was excommunicated in 1871 by the ARCHBISHOP of Munich and lost his Catholic professorship. Acton's lay status kept him from canonical censure. Thereafter Döllinger worked with the OLD CATHOLICS and enjoyed the support of the Bavarian government. His influence on the disciplines of church historiography and the development of DOCTRINE was lasting and far-reaching.

Further reading: Georg Denzler and Ernst L. Grasmück, *Geschichtlichkeit und Glaube: zum 100. Todestag John Joseph Ignaz von Döllingers* (Munich: Wewel, 1990); Johann J. Ignaz von Döllinger, *Declarations and Letters on the Vatican Decress, 1869–1887* (Edinburgh: T & T Clark, 1891); C. B. Moss, *The Old Catholic Movement* (Eureka Springs, Ark.: Episcopal Book Club, 1977).

Dominican Orders

The name *Dominicans* applies to a family of religious orders and institutes founded by or associated with St. DOMINIC DE GUZMÁN. It includes the Order of Preachers (OP), many congregations of Dominican NUNS, and lay institutes that follow the spiritual path of St. Dominic. Like FRANCIS OF ASSISI, Dominic insisted on the return to the apostolic form of life depicted in the New Testament: itinerant preaching, poverty, and service to both the physical and spiritual needs of the people. Early Dominicans stressed the worship of God in the LITURGY and private prayer and the study of the Word of God.

Dominicans espoused a form of government unique among Roman Catholic religious orders. The basic unit is a priory, headed by a chapter of the brethren who elect the prior. Priors in turn elect provincials who then elect a master of the order who governs with a bicameral system of chapters and whose tenure is limited. Many claim that this constitutional form of governance influenced the Parliament of England and the United States Constitution. It also helps explain why outstanding Dominican friars like Francisco de Vitoria (c. 1486–1546) and BARTOLOMÉ DE LAS CASAS (1474–1566) championed the cause of basic human rights for Amerindians against the claims of the colonists in the New World.

The early Dominicans keenly fostered the intellectual life of the new universities of Europe. Sts. ALBERTUS MAGNUS and THOMAS AQUINAS sought to replace the old paradigm of learning embodied in the Neoplatonic Augustinianism of the CAROLINGIAN RENAISSANCE with the new paradigm that reconciled ARISTOTLE with CHRISTIAN thought. Along with biblical scholar Hugh of St. Cher (1200–63) and Peter of Tarentaise (later Pope Innocent V, r. 1276), they believed that Aristotelian science and philosophy provided a sure foundation for the systematic presentation of the Gospel and THEOLOGY. Their accomplishments in the field of art found expression in the delicately nuanced work of FRA ANGELICO, the Dominican friar who painted the famous murals in the Dominican priory of San Marco in Florence.

Like many other religious orders, the Dominicans suffered during the 14th century. Confusion and laxity set in, but a spiritual revival was sparked by St. CATHERINE OF SIENA, who, along with the firebrand GIROLAMO SAVONAROLA, fostered a social spirituality to balance the earlier inward mystical spirituality of MEISTER ECKHART, Johannes Tauler (c. 1300–61), and Henry Suso (c. 1295–1366). A regrettable aspect of Dominican history was the active participation of friars both

in the INQUISITION and the sale of INDULGENCES. Two names came to the fore: Bernardo of Gui (c. 1261–1331), who composed a handbook for inquisitors, and JOHANN TETZEL (c. 1464–1519), who trafficked indulgences in Germany, sparking the wrath of Martin Luther (1483–1546). On the other hand, Dominicans played a key role in the reforms of the Council of TRENT. An especially unhappy Dominican story is that of hermetic philosopher Giordano Bruno (1548–1600), driven from the order and burned at the stake in Venice by the INQUISITION. Today Dominican scholars are taking a hard look at the order's entanglement in the Inquisition.

The order entered another decline after the French Revolution (1789–91) but experienced a renewal in the middle of the 19th century under the guidance of Henry Lacordaire (1802–61). LEO XIII's blessing of Thomism as the guiding philosophy and theology of the Roman church added to the revival, which produced such luminaries as Reginald Garagou-Lagrange (1877–1964), who taught at the Angelicum in Rome; Garagou-Lagrange defended the intellectual life of the church and the mystical path as open to all believers, not just elites. Two Dominicans were outstanding contributors to the success of VATICAN COUNCIL II. MARIE-DOMINIQUE CHENU sought to understand Thomas Aquinas in his historical context and was open to the ideas of the NOUVELLE THÉOLOGIE. As an expert at Vatican II, he contributed heavily to *Gaudium et Spes,* the Pastoral Constitution on the Church in the Modern World, later defending the council from its detractors inside the Vatican and out. YVES CONGAR blazed new trails in ECCLESIOLOGY and ECUMENISM in preparation for the council and later illuminated the workings of the council in numerous diaries.

Today there are more than 5,500 members of the First Order, 28,600 nuns of the Second Order in apostolic life, and 4,000 in contemplative life, many tertiaries or lay third order members. There is close cooperation among the various branches of the Dominican family.

Further reading: William A. Hinnebusch, *The History of the Dominican Order,* 2 vols. (Staten Island: Alba House, 1966–73); M. Hoyer, *The Dominicans and the Medieval Inquisition* (Rome: Institutum Historicum Fratrum Prædicatorum, 2004); Richard Woods, *Mysticism and Prophecy: The Dominican Tradition* (London: Darton, Longman & Todd, 1998).

Dominic de Guzmán, St. (c. 1170–1221)
founder of the Dominican Order

Dominic was born of a noble family in Calruega, Spain, and was educated at Palencia. He joined the canons of St. AUGUSTINE (*see* AUGUSTINIANS) under the guidance of Bishop Osma Martin Barzán. Early in life he became dedicated to poverty, like St. FRANCIS OF ASSISI. He accompanied the new BISHOP, Diego of Acebes, on a mission to northern Europe and on the way back became interested in counteracting the Albigensians or CATHARI in southern FRANCE by preaching the GOSPEL. At Diego's urging, Dominic adopted a lifestyle of itinerant preaching, like the APOSTLES in the New Testament (Matt. 10). Following the advice of INNOCENT III, he adapted the rule of St. Augustine for a new order, the mendicant Order of Preachers, known as the DOMINICAN ORDER. The rule was formally approved by Honorius III (r. 1216–27) in 1218. The order functioned in a very democratic manner. Dominic founded communities in France, SPAIN, and ITALY and established houses of study at the new Universities of Paris and Oxford.

Like Francis, he also established a Second Order of NUNS, founding houses in Prouilhe, Madrid, and Rome. He was both fearless and fraternal. Given his devotion to Mary, legend attributes to him the discovery of the Rosary. He stressed devotion through study and contemplation, a mark that shaped his learned followers Sts. ALBERTUS MAGNUS and THOMAS AQUINAS. He died in Bologna in 1221.

Further reading: Mary Jean Dorcy, *St. Dominic* (St. Louis: Herder, 1959); Vladimir J. Koudelka, ed., *Domi-nic* (London: Darton, Longman & Todd, 1997); Marie-Humbert Vicaire, *St. Dominic and His Times* (London: Darton, Longman & Todd, 1964).

Donation of Constantine

The "Donation" is a document purportedly issued by Roman emperor CONSTANTINE recording his conversion to Christianity and conferring vast powers and properties on the pope in Rome. Although a forgery, it was used in later centuries to justify papal supremacy. The Donation grants Pope Sylvester I (314–335) all the major church buildings in Rome; "primacy" over the historic church centers in Jerusalem, Antioch, Alexandria, and CONSTANTINOPLE and over all the provinces and cities of ITALY; and judicial authority over all CHRISTIAN clergy in the empire.

The terms of the Donation were incorporated into the *False Decretals,* said to be the work of Isadore Mercator (fl. ?850), and the *Decretals* of Gratian (d.c. 1160) (*see* CANON LAW). The document was often cited by popes to assert their rights over the PAPAL STATES and, beginning with Leo IX (1048–54), their claim to primacy over the Eastern Orthodox Church. In the 15th century NICHOLAS OF CUSA, Bishop Reginald Peacock (c. 1395–1460) of Chichester, and Lorenzo Valla (c. 1406–57) demonstrated that the document was a late ninth-century forgery.

Further reading: Lorenzo Valla, *De falso credita et emen-tita Constantini donatione declamatio,* English and Latin, ed. by Christopher B. Coleman (Toronto: University of Toronto Press, 1993); Horst Fuhrmann, *Das Constitu-tum Constantini* (Hannover: Hahn, 1968).

Donatism

The Donatists were a North African schismatic church who separated from the Catholics over the validity of SACRAMENTS administered by *traditores* ("betrayers"), those who had offered sacrifices to the emperor and pagan gods during the Diocletian persecution (303–05) or who had obtained *libelli* ("certificates") to that effect. The SCHISM started when sacramental purists refused to accept Caecilian (d. c. 345) as BISHOP of Carthage after he was consecrated around 311 by Felix of Aptunga (d. c. 318), a *traditor.* Numidian objectors to Caecilian consecrated the rival bishop, Majorinus (d. c. 314), who was succeeded by Donatus (d. 355), who gave his name to the movement. The schism lasted until the Muslim conquest of North AFRICA in the seventh and eighth centuries.

The Donatists appealed for support to local African feeling, but the emperor CONSTANTINE assigned Mitiades, bishop of Rome (r. 310–14), to rule on the matter. Mitiades decided against the Donatists, ruling that the sacraments bestowed by lapsed CLERGY were valid provided they were administered in the proper form. The ruling was backed up by canon 9 of the Synod of Arles (314).

The decision at Arles should have put an end to the matter, but the Donatist schism persisted, especially in the hinterland of Numidia. Donatists gradually became the largest CHRISTIAN party in North Africa. At one point, both Donatists and Catholics appealed to the prestigious CYPRIAN OF CARTHAGE for support. Cyprian was very strict on the readmission of lapsed members, but he was equally insistent on preserving the unity of the church. The Donatists were represented by Parmenian (362–92), bishop of Carthage, and by the layman Tyconius (fl. 380), while two able theologians, Optatus of Melevis (fl. 360) and AUGUSTINE OF HIPPO defended the Catholic cause.

A rebellion of Donatists against the emperor Honorius (r. 395–406) gave the Catholics the upper hand. Imperial edicts declared them heretics and deprived them of their offices and property. Finally, in 412 the imperial tribune Marcellinus enforced the edicts in favor of the Catholics at Carthage; Augustine backed his use of force in the subsequent repression of the Donatists, whose numbers rapidly decreased but never ceased.

The Donatists, appealing to Cyprian's image of the church as a "sealed fountain" and "closed garden," continued to insist on Christian purity, holiness, and integrity against the contamination of the heathen world. Thus, they held invalid any sacraments administered by *traditores* and those ordained by them. They embraced a martyr's attitude toward the state; the Circumcellian faction took on a program of radical apostolic poverty, attacking landowners and changing places with slaves. Apostolic poverty later became central to the Franciscan movement. Donatist EUCHARISTS were marked by enthusiastic displays and ecstatic singing. Their cry became *Deo Laudes!* ("Praises to God!"). The key to Augustine's response to their claim of invalid sacraments was that it is Christ, not the priest, who is the true minister of the sacrament and the conferrer of God's grace. Augustine starkly stated in his *Commentary on the Gospel of John* 5.18 "Those whom John [the Baptist] baptized, John baptized; those whom Judas baptized, Christ baptized."

Further reading: Marcus Dods, tr., *Anti-Donatist Works of St. Augustine,* Ante-Nicene and Post-Nicene Fathers, series 1 (1872) vol. 4 (repr. Peabody: Hendrickson, 1994); W.H.C. Frend, *The Donatist Church: A Movement of Protest in Roman North Africa,* 3rd ed. (Oxford: Clarendon, 1985); O.R. Vassal-Phillips, tr., *The Work of St. Optatus Against the Donatists* (London: Longmans, Green, 1917).

Douay-Rheims   *See* BIBLE.

doubt (Lat.: *dubitare,* "to be uncertain about")

Doubt is the mental state of being uncertain about a fact, a state of affairs, or the meaning of ultimate things. In Catholicism there are three forms of doubt: canonical, moral, and religious or philosophical.

Canonical doubt arises when there is uncertainty about either the existence of a law or the applicability of a law as discussed in *Code of Canon Law,* cn. 14. For example, there was canonical doubt about whether women may function as attendants at liturgical rites, especially the EUCHARIST.

Traditionally women were excluded from these kinds of liturgical roles, although abbesses had more privileges than ordinary religious and lay women. VATICAN COUNCIL II strongly advocated the involvement of all laity in the LITURGY. After the promulgation of the new *Code* in 1983, there was doubt whether the traditional prohibition had the force of law. Canon 230.1 seemed to restrict the function of acolytes or altar servers to the male gender, but canon 230.2 mentioned just "lay persons." Nonetheless, many ordinaries and BISHOPS, following the liturgical spirit of *Sacrosanctum Concilium,* the Constitution on the Sacred Liturgy, decided in favor of engaging women as altar assistants and dispensers of the Eucharist at Mass. The Holy See responded in the affirmative in 1994. Subsequently, the Congregation for the Liturgy and Discipline of the Sacraments put dampers on movement in this direction, insisting on clerical privilege and stating "non-ordained faithful do not have a right to service at the altar" (*Letter,* July 27, 2001; *Redemptionis Sacramentum,* March 25, 2004). When there is a doubt of fact, for example, as to whether the parties to a marriage meet the minimum canonical age (16 for men, 14 for women), the local ordinary may dispense from these restrictions.

Moral doubt arises when there is uncertainty about the morality of doing or not doing an action. A person can have moral certainty about a law but uncertainty about its application. There is much debate and disagreement about the degree of certainty needed to justify a course of action.

Religious and philosophical doubt arises when a person questions the foundations of his or her faith and the ultimate meaning of existence. A permanent state of doubt is called skepticism. This may also be called existential anxiety. Contrary to many simplistic presentations of FAITH, the biblical record shows a strong tradition not only of questioning GOD but also of doubt about the meaning of one's personal faith. In Genesis 18:16–33, Abraham questions God's righteousness in the threat to destroy both the righteous and the wicked in Sodom and Gomorrah. Genesis 32:24–30 shows Jacob "wrestling" with the angel of God. Because he challenged the angel, God changed his name to Israel ("He who struggles with God") and granted him the vision of the ladder reaching into the heavens. The Book of Job portrays the hero challenging the thoughtless, conventional faith of his interlocutors, Eliphaz, Bildad, Zophar, and Elihu, who believed naively that if you were materially successful, you were righteous and were blessed by God, and if not, you had sinned and were cursed. It is Job, who both challenges and doubts God's way, who receives the vision of the mystery of God's governance of the universe.

Christian mystical theologians like St. JOHN OF THE CROSS frequently talked about a purgative stage of the spiritual ascent of the soul to God. In this stage, the contemplator experiences an "obscure and dark and terrible purgation" of all external support, including the assurances of faith itself. The purgation prepares the soul for higher union with God.

Faith and doubt are not opposites. Faith and indifference are opposites. True faith takes the negation of doubt and personal anxiety into itself in its openness to the unconditional mystery of God.

Further reading: Angel Marzoa, Jorge Miras, and Raphael Rodriguez-Ocaña, *Exegetical Commentary on the Code of Canon Law* (Chicago: Midwest Theological Forum, 2004); Charles E. Curran, *The Catholic Moral Tradition Today: A Synthesis* (Washington, D.C.: Georgetown University Press, 1999); John of the Cross, *Ascent of Mt. Carmel,* ed. Henry L. Carrigan, Jr. (Brewster, Mass.: Paraclete, 2002); Paul Tillich, *Biblical Religion and the Search for Ultimate Reality* (Chicago: Chicago University Press, 1964).

dove

The dove is a frequent symbol in early CHRISTIAN art, found on sarcophagi and in the catacombs.

It recalled GOD'S Covenant of peace with Noah (Genesis 8:11), and by extension the soul resting in peace with the Lord, as well as the descent of the HOLY SPIRIT in BAPTISM (Mark 1:10). (Greco-Romans often associated the dove with Aphrodite as the goddess of love.)

In the Old Testament the dove symbolized peace and ritual purity. Doves were sacrificed for the purification of women after giving birth (Lev. 12:6; Luke 2:24). In later Christian thought (TERTULLIAN, AMBROSE, AUGUSTINE) the dove often symbolized the church as loyal Bride of Christ, with reference to the allegorical meaning of the Song of Songs 2:14. In medieval art the dove came to signify the wisdom of the Spirit bestowed on DOCTORS OF THE CHURCH such as Sts. GREGORY THE GREAT and THOMAS AQUINAS. In scenes portraying the Annunciation, the baptism of Jesus in the Jordan, and the TRINITY, the dove stood for the Holy Spirit. Seven doves signified the seven gifts of the Spirit (Hosea 11:11); 12 meant either the 12 fruits of the Holy Spirit (Gal. 5:22–23) or the 12 APOSTLES.

In the MIDDLE AGES artisans made Eucharistic Doves, hollow containers made of precious metals, for carrying the consecrated host from one location to another. They are still used in churches of the Byzantine rite.

Further reading: Friedrich Sühling, *Die Taube as Religiöses Symbol im Christlichen Altertum* (Freiburg im Breisgau: Herder, 1930); Diane Apostolos-Cappadona, *Dictionary of Christian Art* (New York: Continuum, 1995).

Drexel, St. Katherine Mary (1858–1955)
missionary founder and educator
Mary Drexel was the founder of the Sisters of the Blessed Sacrament, a missionary to Native Americans and African Americans in America, and founder of Xavier University in New Orleans. She was canonized by JOHN PAUL II in 2000. Her feast day is March 3.

Katherine was the second daughter of the wealthy Philadelphia banker Francis A. Drexel and Hannah Jane Drexel. After her mother's death in 1860 her stepmother, Emma Bouvier, lovingly raised her stepdaughters together with her own daughter. The children were taught that their vast wealth was only a loan by God to be shared with others.

Katherine was educated at home and traveled widely in Europe. Soon she became dedicated to the plight of Native Americans and African Americans in her country and committed her inheritance to this cause, establishing a school for Native Americans in Santa Fe, New Mexico. At the direct suggestion of LEO XIII, she herself became a missionary and studied with the Sisters of Mercy in Pittsburgh. In 1891 she founded the Sisters of the Blessed Sacrament for Indians and Colored People. Within her lifetime, more than 60 institutions were founded by her society, including Xavier University in New Orleans, opened in 1915 as the first Catholic institution of higher learning for blacks in America. After a stroke in 1937, she devoted herself to the adoration of the Blessed Sacrament, dying in 1955 at Cornwell Heights, Pennsylvania.

Further reading: Katherine Burton, *The Golden Door: The Life of Katherine Drexel* (New York: Kenedy, 1957); Consuela Marie Duffy, *Katharine Drexel, A Biography* (Cornwell Heights, Penn.: Mother Katharine Drexel Guild, 1972); Ellen Tarry, *Katherine Drexel: Friend of the Neglected* (New York: Farrar, Straus & Cudahy, 1958).

Duchesne, St. Rose Philippine (1769–1852)
missionary founder of religious order
Rose Duchesne cofounded the Society of the Religious of Sacred Heart of Jesus, or Societé du Sacre Coeur de Jesus (abbreviation RSCJ), founded the society in America, and served as missionary to the Potowatomi Indians of the Rocky Mountains. She was canonized by Pope JOHN PAUL II in 1988.

Rose was born into a wealthy, influential family in Grenoble, FRANCE. At an early age she heard a Jesuit missionary speak about his work among Native Americans and gained a desire to do the same. Trained at home, she entered the convent of the Visitation Sisters in Grenoble. During the Reign of Terror in 1792, her convent was closed. She lived a pious life as a laywoman, opening schools, orphanages, and refuges for fleeing priests.

After Napoléon's CONCORDAT with the church, she reclaimed her convent, but most of the sisters were long gone. Regrouping with a few sisters, her community restarted as the Society of the Sacred Heart ("Sacred Heart Sisters") under St. Madeline Sophie Barat (1779–1863). Rose took her final vows in 1805.

In 1815 she established a convent in Paris and left as a missionary to the Louisiana Territory in 1818. Her first mission was at St. Charles, Missouri, where she founded the first school west of the Mississippi. Her French methods of teaching caused some opposition, but her schools and orphanages were successful, although she never learned to speak English well.

At the ripe age of 71 she sought to fulfill her earliest calling, serving as a missionary to the Potowatomi in the West. The Potowatomi called her "She-Who-Always-Prays," but as she was unable to master the language, she returned to St. Charles, where she spent her remaining years praying and contemplating in a log cabin chapel.

Further reading: Catherine M. Mooney, *Philippine Duchesne: A Woman of the Poor* (New York: Paulist, 1990).

Duns Scotus, Bl. John (c. 1265–1308)
medieval theologian and philosopher

Duns Scotus was the foremost Franciscan metaphysician, philosopher, and theologian of the MIDDLE AGES. He lectured at Oxford, Paris, and Cologne, where his remains are venerated. His commentaries on the *Sentences* of PETER LOMBARD came to be known as the *Opus Oxionense* and the *Reportatio Parisensis*. His celebrated argument for the existence of GOD is called *On God as the First Principle*. Known as the Subtle Doctor or the Marian Doctor, he had many followers and influenced theologians of the PROTESTANT REFORMATION centuries later. Somewhat ironically, his name became the source for the epithet "dunce." He was beatified by JOHN PAUL II in 1994.

Scotus adapted Avicenna's conception of metaphysics as the science of being qua being. He sought to show that God is the first being and creator of all other beings. Reducing THOMAS AQUINAS's analogy of being to equivocation (using the same term to mean two different things), Scotus demonstrated that both God and creatures share being univocally in some same sense of the term. Otherwise, God would be completely unknowable by natural reason (*Reportatio* 1.2.12.2.11).

In his famous proof Scotus showed that if God can exist, God must exist (with ANSELM) but that the possibility of God's existence must be shown from creatures (with Aquinas). The demonstration grounds the contingency of all creatures on a necessary first being who is first in efficient and final causality and preeminence.

Alluding to 1 John 4:16 ("God is love"), Scotus argues that God's creative will holds primacy, and all other beings are radically dependent, or contingent, on this will to create out of love. This love bestows on each creature a common nature that is "contracted" in a particular being by a principle of individuation (*haecceitas* "thisness"), a concept that strongly shaped the poetry of GERARD MANLEY HOPKINS. Aquinas thought that matter provided individuation only when united with a form.

The common nature and thisness, Scotus argued, are not really nor logically but formally distinct in each creature. (He applied the formal distinction also to the faculties of the soul and the persons of the TRINITY). Scotus' position—often called moderate realism but more accurately critical realism—was halfway between the realist Aquinas and the nominalist WILLIAM OF OCKHAM.

God's motive for creation was love. God fore-willed (foreloved) CHRIST as the highest work, final end, and exemplary cause of all creation. Even had there been no original SIN in Adam, Christ would have become incarnate (*Oxoniense* 1.3.7.3.3). The good precedes and remains always greater than EVIL. God, out of love, desired that a lower nature share the glory of the highest being and both foresaw and foreordained the INCARNA-TION, the union of the lower human with the highest divine nature in the person of Christ, before Adam fell. Christ's love is most exhibited in the CROSS and the EUCHARIST. Because of the superabundant merit of Christ, God also willed that MARY OF NAZARETH, as mother of Christ and mother of God, be conceived without sin in the Immaculate Conception (ibid. 1.3.18.1.13).

Scotus also shows that in the rational soul it is the will, not the intellect, that is truly rational. The intellect is necessarily dependent on the input it receives from the senses, but the will, acting with reason, can choose to will or not to will this or that. The will possesses supersufficient potentiality for self-determination and can have an inclination (*affectio*) either to choose for its own advantage out of a desire for happiness or choose contrary to self-advantage out of an inclination toward justice. The affection for justice is the same as love of God above all as the ultimate good and source of beatitude. For Scotus beatitude is not so much an intellectual vision but a universal community of the beloved (*see* BEATIFIC VISION).

Scotus's ethical teaching, based as it is on radical freedom, is receiving new attention. We do not have as many writings on social theory from Scotus as we have from Aquinas and Ockham, but he did teach that society arises from the will of the people in a social contract, and he denied that private property was a right by natural law. That would follow from his ethic of love as justice seeking the greater, common good.

Scotus's thought gave birth to a Scotist school in the late Middle Ages and early Renaissance. Some followers were wont to pit the Angelic (Aquinas) against the Subtle Doctor, but Scotus's real discussants and opponents were Henry of Ghent (d. 1293), Gottfried von Fontaines (c. 1250–1306), and Giles of Rome (c. 1245–1316). The Jesuit FRANCISCO SUÁREZ sought to mediate between Aquinas and Scotus. The American founder of pragmatism, Charles Sanders Peirce (1839–1914), saw himself as a critical realist in the manner of Scotus.

Further reading: Olivier Boulnois, *Duns Scot: la riguer de la charité* (Paris: Cerf, 1998); Richard Cross, *Duns Scotus* (New York: Oxford University Press, 1999); John Duns Scotus, *Philosophical Writings*, tr. Allan B. Wolter (Indianapolis: Bobbs-Merrill, 1962); ———, *Questions on the Metaphysics of Aristotle*, tr. Girard J. Eztkorn and Allan B. Wolter (St. Bonaventure: Franciscan Institute); ———, *A Treatise on God as First Principle,* tr. Allan B. Wolter (Chicago: Franciscan Herald, 1982); Thomas A. Shannon, *The Ethical Theory of John Duns Scotus* (Quincy, Ill.: Franciscan, 1995).

E

Eastern Catholicism

The Eastern Catholic Churches all have spiritual, liturgical, and canonical traditions distinct from and independent of the dominant Latin tradition of the Roman Catholic Church. Although each of these churches has united with the Roman Catholic Church at one historical time or other, they all continue to maintain their separate traditions. The Western Church tends to use the term *uniate* when referring to the Eastern Churches, as if the union were unidirectional toward Rome. Easterners often find that term offensive. They see the union as a reciprocal recognition between autonomous communions.

Early on the Eastern and Western branches of Christianity developed distinctive ecclesiastical styles. The East was far more taken with theology and thus was prone to theological heresies such as ARIANISM and Nestorianism (*see* NESTORIUS). The West was more organizational and authority-driven, and thus its schismatic rebellions involved questions of practice like DONATISM. The West specialized in moral THEOLOGY, the East in mystical and liturgical theology. These tendencies evolved into many other differences as well; the Eastern Catholic Churches have preserved all these Eastern tendencies that also characterize the larger world of EASTERN ORTHODOXY.

The Eastern Catholic Churches for the most part are organized under the ecclesiastical form known as a patriarchate (*see* PATRIARCH). This system harkens back to the third- and fourth-century organization of various regions into the patriarchies of Jerusalem, Antioch, Alexandria, Rome, and CONSTANTINOPLE. The principle of patriarchy raises questions of autonomy and authority. There are presently patriarchs for the Chaldean, Coptic, Maronite, and Melkite Catholic Churches, while there are none for the Syro-Malabar and Ukrainian Churches, the two largest. Both of those churches have petitioned the PAPACY for patriarchal status.

In 1992 the papacy granted the Syro-Malabar and Syro-Malandara rites the status of a major archiepiscopy, a rank just beneath that of patriarchy. Many of the Syro-Malabar dioceses, however, remain under the direct administration of the pope. The Ukrainian synod requested patriarchal status in 2002. JOHN PAUL II said to the Ukrainian Church in 2004, "I share your aspiration, well-founded in the canonical and conciliar discipline, to have full juridical and ecclesiastical configuration." But, noting the objections of the Orthodox Ecumenical Patriarch Bartholomew I (1940–) of Constantinople and not wanting to irritate the patriarch of Moscow, the papacy has been reluctant to act on the matter.

The question of the Eastern Churches also raises the issues of variety in the forms and languages of rites. The five main rites are Byzantine, Antiochene, Alexandrine, Chaldean, and Armenian. Many of the rites predate the Roman rite and have been jealously preserved in the face of intrusions by the latter. Rome has often been insensitive on this question and has frequently tried to "Romanize" Eastern Churches in union with it in respect both to jurisdiction and to rites. The Romanizing policies of Portuguese missionaries in the 17th century provoked many Syro-Malankara Catholics to pull away and link up with the Syrian Orthodox (Jacobite) patriarchate of Antioch.

The Eastern liturgies were sung and spoken in local languages long before the Latin rite. For Eastern Churches the LITURGY, which most often means the EUCHARIST, is of prime importance in defining the relation of believers with the Godhead. The languages used include Greek, Coptic, Ge'ez (Ethiopia), Syriac, Arabic, Old Slavonic (Russia), Grabar (Old Armenian), Romanian, Hungarian, and Albanian. In the 20th century most rites, with the exception of those in ancient Christian Greek and Old Slavonic, adopted modern vernaculars.

The Eastern Catholic veneration of saints is markedly different than the Roman sanctoral cycle. Chaldeans favor Fridays for the commemoration of saints, whereas the Armenians can have saints' feasts on Sundays. Maronites have included many western saints. Some Eastern Catholic Churches do not venerate any Orthodox saints made after the GREAT SCHISM in 1054. Still others accept celebrated saints such as Orthodox St. Sergius of Rodonezh (c. 1314–92) and others who date after the schism but before the Orthodox rejection of the decree of union at the Council of FLORENCE. The lines remain fluid.

In the modern era Roman attitudes toward Eastern Catholics have shifted. In the bull *Etsi Pastoralis* (May 26, 1742) Pope Benedict XIV forbade the Latinization of the eastern rites, although Vatican administrators often ignored the instruction. In *Orientalium Dignitas* (November 30, 1894)

LEO XIII reaffirmed Benedict's principle and restricted Latin missions in the East. VATICAN COUNCIL II marked a watershed in the relation between Roman Catholicism and EASTERN ORTHODOXY and between the Roman Church and the Eastern churches in communion with it. In *Orientalium Ecclesiarum,* the Decree on the Eastern Catholic Churches, the council insisted on the autonomous patriarchal structure of those churches, their independent juridical traditions, and the integrity of their liturgical worship. The Melkite patriarch Maximus IV Sayegh of Antioch (1878–1967, r. 1947–67) spoke up strongly for the Eastern Churches, never using Latin and insisting that patriarchs rank above cardinals. He benefited the Latin rite by championing the use of the vernacular, arguing that every language in the world is liturgical.

The patriarchate for the Coptic Catholic Church is located in Alexandria, though the patriarch resides in Cairo. The Melkite patriarch of Alexandria-Antioch-Jerusalem resides in Damascus; the present patriarch is Gregorios III (1933– elected 2000). The Maronite patriarch of Antioch resides in Bherke, Lebanon; the present patriarch is His Beatitude Mar Nasrallah Boutros Sfeir, elected in 1986.

See also ARMENIAN CATHOLIC CHURCH; BULGARIAN CATHOLIC CHURCH; COPTIC CATHOLIC CHURCH; MELKITE CATHOLIC CHURCH; RUTHENIAN CATHOLIC CHURCH; SYRIAN CATHOLIC CHURCH; SYRO-MALANKAR CATHOLIC CHURCH; UKRAINIAN CATHOLIC CHURCH.

Further reading: Donald Attwater, *The Christian Churches of the East* (Milwaukee: Bruce, 1961); Victor J. Pospishil, *Eastern Catholic Church Law* (Staten Island, N.Y.: Saint Maron, 1996); Ronald G. Roberson, *The Eastern Christian Churches—A Brief Survey,* 5th ed. (Rome: Edizioni Orientalia Christiana, 1995).

Eastern Orthodoxy

The term *Eastern Orthodoxy* applies to all those branches of Eastern Christianity that see themselves as autonomous and autocephalous ("self-headed") and that are not in communion with the church of Rome. The Eastern Orthodox churches are in communion with one another and recognize the Ecumenical Patriarch of Constantinople as the sign of their unity and "first among equals."

The Eastern communions include 1) the four ancient patriarchies of Constantinople, Jerusalem, Antioch, and Alexandria; 2) the five later patriarchies of Russia, Serbia, Romania, Bulgaria, and Georgia; and 3) the autocephalous metropolitans of Cyprus, Greece, Czechoslovakia, Slovenia, Poland, and Albania. Among the semiautonomous churches are those of Finland, China, Japan, and the United States. Most Orthodox in the United States are of Greek origin, but Russia, which established a church at Kodiak, Alaska, in 1795, claims primacy over the American church.

A major break in the Orthodox communion occurred following the 451 Council of CHALCEDON, which in attempting further definition of the nature of CHRIST condemned a position termed monophysitism (Gk *monos* "only one" + *physis* "nature"). Monophysitists claimed that Christ was one person with one nature and adhered to the formula "one incarnate nature of the Word" from St. CYRIL OF ALEXANDRIA. Chalcedon said that Christ was "one person in two natures": of one substance with the Father in regard to his divinity and of one substance with humanity as regards his humanity. The Armenian and Coptic churches did not accept the Chalcedonian formulations and have continued as separate bodies not in communion with the other Orthodox bodies nor with Rome. They have claimed that they do not hold the position condemned at Chalcedon and have continued to uphold the pre-Chalcedon Nicaean CHRISTOLOGY common to the churches prior to 451. Today, Coptic and Armenian church leaders have suggested that they may have a less developed Christology, but not a heretical one.

Early on the Eastern and Western branches of Christianity developed distinctive ecclesiastical styles. The East was far more taken with theology and thus was prone to theological heresies such

as ARIANISM and Nestorianism (*see* NESTORIUS). The West was more organizational and authority-driven, and thus its schismatic rebellions involved questions of practice like DONATISM. The West specialized in moral theology, the East in mystical and liturgical theology. These tendencies eventually helped bring about a rupture between the two traditions.

The Eastern Orthodox tradition recognizes the first seven ecumenical COUNCILS between 325 and 787 as authoritative in terms of belief. Those councils defined the nature of Christ as equal with the Father, the Incarnation of the Christ as fully human and fully divine, Mary as the Theotokos, and the nature of the TRINITY as one substance in three divine persons. After the iconoclasm controversy (*see* ICON), the veneration of images of Christ, the Virgin Mary, and the saints became central in the Eastern Churches as the visible witness that GOD took on human flesh. Unlike the Western Church, the East does not venerate statues but only the two-dimensional ICON. More intensely than the West, the Eastern Churches see the spiritual life as a process of *theosis*, or "being taken up into the Godhead," by which they mean the full transformation of the human being, body and spirit, into the likeness of God. The LITURGY, by which the East means preeminently the celebration of the EUCHARIST, is central to this spiritual process.

In concert with the all-encompassing THEOLOGY of *theosis*, the Eastern Orthodox churches fully recognize not only bishops and priests but also the laity as guides to the holy life. Lay people have often served as influential theologians, as was Vladimir Soloviev (1853–1900), or religious guides, as was the *staretz* (Rus. "elder") of Russian tradition. The Eastern Churches, including those in union with Rome, allow seminarians to be married before diaconal ordination. Bishops are celibate and are selected from among MONKS or widowed priests.

While they recognize the seven SACRAMENTS defined by the Western Church at the Council of

TRENT, the Eastern Orthodox see other aspects of liturgical life as equally sacramental, such as the blessing of water and the anointing of monarchs. MONASTICISM has been central to Eastern Orthodoxy throughout its history. The monasteries follow the Rule of St. BASIL THE GREAT. Beginning in the 10th century, monks from all Eastern Orthodox traditions have founded monasteries on Mt. Athos, from which women are excluded. In contrast with the Western Church, where conflicts between CHURCH AND STATE have often arisen, the Eastern Orthodox embraced what is known as CAESAROPAPISM.

Eastern Orthodoxy does not recognize some doctrines defined in the Western Church after the GREAT SCHISM. The East has always accepted the teaching about the Assumption of Mary but has never formally defined it. For the most part the Eastern Churches do not subscribe to the doctrine of the Immaculate Conception. While sensing some intermediate state between HEAVEN AND HELL, Orthodox theologians have never defined it, as the West has in the idea of PURGATORY, for fear of blurring the primacy of the initial distinction.

The breach between Roman Catholicism and Eastern Orthodoxy was the result of a long process, played out against the difference in theological styles and in the methods for reckoning the date of EASTER. In the ninth century Pope Nicholas I (858–67) refused to recognize the election of Patriarch Photius (c. 810–c. 895) of Constantinople. Photius in turn challenged the pope's authority and the Western Church's unilateral insertion of the FILIOQUE phrase into its CREED. The East also differed with the West over the use of leavened as opposed to unleavened bread at the Eucharist. Finally, the differences terminated in the Great Schism of 1054, with Pope Leo IX (r. 1049–54) and Patriarch Michael Cerularius (d. 1058) mutually excommunicating each other. The sacking of Constantinople by Latin Christians during the Fourth CRUSADE in 1204 added to the bitterness.

There were forced attempts at reconciliation at the Councils of Lyon (1215) and FLORENCE (1438–39), but delegates from the East could not get their congregations back home to concur. The Eastern Orthodox Churches were among the early members of the Protestant-initiated World Council of Churches. During VATICAN COUNCIL II Eastern Orthodox delegates were invited to act as observers, and many had an indirect but active voice in the proceedings. In *Unitatis Redintegratio* 14–18, the Decree on Ecumenism, Vatican II went a long way toward accepting the autonomy and spiritual integrity of the Eastern Churches, including those in union and not in union with Rome. In 1966 Pope PAUL VI and Ecumenical Patriarch Athenagoras (1886–1972) lifted the mutual excommunication between the churches.

The current *Code of Canon Law* cn. 844.2 allows Catholics to receive Communion in separated churches under the following conditions: 1) when there is necessity or genuine spiritual advantage (e.g., intermarriage between a Catholic and a Syrian Orthodox); 2) when the danger of error or indifferentism is avoided; 3) when it is physically or morally impossible to approach a Catholic minister (e.g., when traveling); and 4) at a church that has valid sacraments. The Eastern Orthodox churches have not reciprocated this ecumenical gesture, but many quietly allow Catholics to partake.

See also ASIA, AFRICA.

Further reading: Thomas E. Fitzgerald, *The Orthodox Church* (Westport, Conn.: Greenwood Press, 1995); Vladimir Lossky and Leonid Ouspensky, *The Meaning of Icons* (Boston: Boston Book & Art, 1952); John Meyendoff, *Byzantine Theology: Historical Trends and Doctrinal Themes* (New York: Fordham University Press, 1983); Kallistos Ware, *The Orthodox Church* (Baltimore: Penguin, 1963).

East European Catholicism *See* EASTERN CATHOLICISM.

Easter/Pascha (Easter: ?Ang. Sax.: *Eoastre,* goddess of springtime; Aram.: *Pascha,* "Passover")

Easter is the oldest and foremost feast in the Christian LITURGICAL YEAR. It celebrates the death and RESURRECTION of Jesus the Christ, which is the central theme of the earliest *kerygma,* or proclamation of the Gospel, as in Acts 3:22–36. There is a probable indirect reference to the celebration in the liturgical hymn cited in 1 Corinthians 5:7–8: "For Christ, our paschal lamb, has been sacrificed. Let us then celebrate the festival, not with the old leaven, the leaven of malice and evil, but with the unleavened bread of sincerity and truth."

This reference shows that the Christian feast was intimately connected with its Jewish predecessor, Pesach, or Passover. Passover seems to have its origin in a combination of a Near Eastern nomadic tribal sacrifice of a lamb in springtime, a Canaanite-type festival of unleavened bread, and commemoration of the great event of the liberation of the Israelites from bondage in Egypt (Exod. 1–15; Deut. 6:20). It is the Jerusalem celebration of this feast that sets the background for the Last Supper, trial, death, and Resurrection of Jesus in the New Testament.

Today the feast is celebrated on the first Sunday after the spring equinox, sometime between March 22 and April 25. The feast is preceded by Lent, Passion Sunday, and Holy Week. It is followed by the paschal season during which the singing of the Alleluia at the EUCHARIST and the Divine Office, or PRAYER OF THE HOURS, occurs frequently, as a sign of joy in the Resurrection.

In the ancient church the Easter Vigil (held on the night before the holiday) was already a rich and crucial event, which St. AUGUSTINE called the "mother of all vigils" (*Sermon* 219). Candidates for BAPTISM went through a catechumenate (*see* CATECHESIS/CATECHUMENATE) prior to the festival. They were excluded from the holiest part of the Eucharist until they were baptized during the vigil and received into the church as neophytes. During the paschal season the new members received further instruction in the Christian mysteries, called the *mystagogia.*

During the vigil a new fire was lit in front of the church, from which the Paschal Candle was lit and borne through the nave to the chant *Lumen Christi,* or Light of Christ. The holy oils, or chrism, were consecrated in cathedrals, along with special chants and readings from Scripture, followed by the baptism of catechumens and the celebration of the Eucharist.

Over time elements of the Easter Vigil came to be dispersed across the entire day. Pope PIUS XII restored the Sacred Triduum ("Three Days") and Easter Vigil service to their early Christian form through the decrees of the Sacred Congregation for Rites *Dominiae Resurrectionis* (February 9, 1951) and *Maxima Redemptionis* (November 16, 1955). After VATICAN COUNCIL II the Congregation for Divine Worship issued an instruction covering the entire Lenten and Paschal season entitled *Paschales Solemnitatis* (January 16, 1988).

In the second century a dispute arose over the method for reckoning the date of Easter. This is called the Paschal or Quartodeciman Controversy. The church in Asia Minor followed the Jewish rabbis in reckoning the date for Pascha on the 14th of the lunar month of Nisan. St. Polycarp of Smyrna (d. c. 155) argued for this method. Pope Ancetus (c. 155–c. 166) disagreed but allowed the East to follow it. However, Pope Victor (189–98) took a hard line, thereby provoking a SCHISM. IRENAEUS OF LYON, noting the great antiquity of many varying customs, took Victor to task (Eusebius, *Ecclesiastical History* 5:23–25). A later dispute arose between the Alexandrine and Antiochene churches, with the Alexandrines adopting the present method of using the first Sunday after the vernal equinox. The emperor CONSTANTINE and the Council of Nicaea (*see* COUNCILS, ECUMENICAL) in 325 ruled that Christians should not go to the rabbis for the date of Easter. In the fourth and fifth centuries further disagreements arose between Rome and Alexandria, with Alexandria prevailing. The Celtic churches had their own various dates for Easter. The introduction of the GREGORIAN CALENDAR in 1582 resulted in a further difference between Rome and the Eastern churches, which continued to follow the Julian Calendar.

Easter is more than a single feast day but a symbol of the transformation of the Christian believer from sin and death to grace and life. The Easter feast is the template and exemplar of all other Christian feasts. It is appropriate to call all Christians "Easter people."

See also LITURGY.

Further reading: Rainero Canatalemessa, *Easter in the Early Church* (Collegeville Minn.: Liturgical Press, 1993); Anscar J. Chupungco, *The Cosmic Elements of Christian Passover* (Rome: Anselmiana, 1977); Anthony G. Koolamparampil, *From Symbol to Truth: A Syriac Understanding of the Paschal Mystery* (Rome: C.L.V. Edizioni Liturgiche, 2000); Stephen McCluskey, *Astronomies and Cultures in Early Medieval Europe* (Cambridge: Cambridge University Press, 1998).

ecclesiology (Gr.: *ekklesia,* "assembly" + *logos,* "account of")

This is the theological discipline that studies the nature and constitution of the church and its distinctive place in the economy of salvation through CHRIST. There are several threads of teaching about the church in the New Testament, although a formal ecclesiology does not start to emerge until the late second and early third centuries. Ecclesiology has its roots in earlier Jewish teaching about the *qahal,* the community GOD has gathered for worship, and in the proclamation of salvation to the nations. The New Testament uses several metaphors to convey the meaning of the church. PAUL saw the church as a local community of varied spiritual gifts that equally served to build the church (1 Cor. 12). It was also the single loaf or body, of which Christ was the head and the believers the members (1 Cor. 10:16–18; 12:12–30). The deutero-Pauline authors of Ephesians and Colossians see this body on a universal cosmic level.

Paul also used the image of Christ as bridegroom and the church as bride to show the covenantal intimacy between God and the people. This image is also related to the one of the church as the people of God with whom God makes an everlasting covenant (Ezek. 37:26; Rom. 9:25; Heb. 8:10). This image came to have dominant influence on the proceedings of VATICAN COUNCIL II. Luke-Acts sees the church as the community of the HOLY SPIRIT, which will spread to the ends of the Roman Empire, whereas John saw the church as the community of the beloved disciple (*see* GOSPEL).

The image of the church most favored by Catholicism throughout its history was the figure of Peter the "Rock" (Aram. *Cephas*) upon whom Jesus said he would build his church (Matt. 16:18). The authority and centrality placed on Peter became the chief justification for the later hierarchical church, anchored to the authority of the BISHOP of Rome. This idea of a hierarchical church, which came to the fore in the second century, led to a radical deemphasis of the laity in Western Christianity; they came to be seen as the recipients of the gifts of the church rather than its embodiment. The Eastern Churches stayed closer to the idea of the church as the mystical body and, despite having a HIERARCHY, have preserved the tradition of a closer unity between CLERGY and laity.

In the age of the CREEDS, ecclesiology stressed four marks of the church: "one, holy, catholic, and apostolic." St. CYPRIAN OF CARTHAGE argued for the unity of the church beyond SCHISM at the beginning of the DONATISM controversy. The church was holy because it was united with Christ as his bride and sanctified by the Holy Spirit as the locus through which God distributed grace to the world. AUGUSTINE argued against the sectarians of his day that the church was "catholic" because it was universal and orthodox in its belief. "Apostolic" means that the church can trace its foundations—authority, teaching, mission, and validity—back to the time of the APOSTLES. This last mark became crucial in the fight against heretics in the second and third centuries. In the second century the idea of APOSTOLIC SUCCESSION coalesced around bishops who could claim a direct line of descent from an apostle, for example, James for Jerusalem, Peter and Paul for Rome, Mark for Alexandria, John for Ephesus, and so on. Thus, the diocese became the basic organizational unit for the church and remains so for Catholics today.

In the MIDDLE AGES the focus of ecclesiology alternated between the sacramental and the institutional perspective. Western institutionalization, with its stress on power and authority, set the stage for the breach with EASTERN ORTHODOXY in 1054. In the high Middle Ages the PAPACY became both more centralized in the Vatican bureaucracy and more "monarchized," as popes like INNOCENT III and BONIFACE VIII exercized, and sometimes confused, both temporal and spiritual powers.

Protestants have placed great stress on the organization (or polity) of the church. Anglicans (in England) retained the greatest part of Catholic ecclesiology. Like Anglicans, Lutherans (in Germany and Scandinavia) retained bishops and a central emphasis on the sacraments of BAPTISM and EUCHARIST but placed the proclamation of the Gospel (Word) on an equal footing with them. The followers of John Calvin (the Reformed Church in Switzerland, France, and the Netherlands) rejected the episcopal polity in favor of a rule by presbyters, or elders. In Great Britain, Reformed Protestants became known as Presbyterians. The Anabaptists rejected not only the Catholic-style office of bishop but the church's ties to the state and adopted a polity that emphasized the leadership of independent congregations. Arguments over ecclesiology would be a major driving force within the larger Protestant movement.

Tridentine Catholicism (see Council of TRENT), while reforming the most notorious abuses attacked by the reformers, upheld the essential organizational aspects of the medieval church: a hierarchy focused on the papacy with a sharp division between clergy and laity, a strong sacramental emphasis, and a defensive posture based on juridi-

cal authority. These characteristics held sway until a more active model of the church emerged with the LITURGICAL MOVEMENT, CATHOLIC ACTION, and NOUVELLE THÉOLOGIE in the 20th century. In *Mystici Corporis* (June 29, 1943) Pius XII upheld traditional ecclesiology but also opened new reflections on the church as the mystical body that also has charismatic aspects through the presence of the Holy Spirit.

At VATICAN COUNCIL II the idea of the church was given a renovative biblical interpretation. In *Lumen Gentium,* or the Pastoral Constitution of the Church in the Modern World, the church is the people of God, a servant community, a pilgrim community, an ecumenical community facing other Christians and religions, a collegial community of sharing, and an eschatological community dedicated to bringing about the reign of God on Earth with justice and peace. While this church still retains key institutional, sacramental, and mystical functions, it also has a prophetic and leavening role in time and space.

In recent times there has been a pulling back of Vatican II's expansive and decentralized view of the church, most notably in the thinking of the long-time prefect of the Congregation of the Faith, Cardinal Ratzinger, now BENEDICT XVI. He has been challenged by Cardinal Walter Kasper (1933–), president of the Council for Promoting Christian Unity.

Further reading: Avery Dulles, *Models of the Church* (Garden City, N.Y.: Doubleday, 1987); Walter Kasper, "On the Church," *America* (April 23, 2001); Hans Küng, *The Church* (New York: Sheed & Ward, 1967); Joseph Ratzinger, "The Local Church and the Universal Church," *America* (November 19, 2001).

Eck, Johann (1486–1543) *theologian, opponent of Protestant Reformation*

Eck, an Augustinian canon of Eichstadt and professor of THEOLOGY at Ingolstadt, was the foremost Catholic theologian in Europe and opponent

of Luther and Melancthon during the PROTES-
TANT REFORMATION. Johann was born in Eck and
educated in humanist traditions at Heidelberg,
Tübingen, Cologne, and Freiburg im Breisgau. He
soon became known for his oratorical skills and
use of invective in debate. In 1510 he accepted the
chair in theology at Ingolstadt, where he turned
the town into a bastion of orthodox Catholicism.
In his *Chrysopassus* (1514) he adopted a Semi-
Pelagian understanding of predestination and
commented on ARISTOTLE and the logician Peter of
Spain, later Pope John XXI (r. 1276–77).

At first friendly with Luther, Eck later attacked
him in his *Obelisci* for promoting the HERESY of the
Bohemian Brethren. Luther counterattacked and
was defended by Andreas Karstadt (1480–1541).
By agreement, Eck and Karstadt were selected to
debate first at Leipzig in 1519. From a staunch free-
will position Eck was forced to concede that GOD's
grace and FREE WILL work in harmony to produce
good works. Karstadt maintained the Lutheran
position that all the good in good works is by
the grace of God. Eck fared less well with Luther,
but the university declared him winner. Whereas
Eck centered his attack on Luther's refusal to
submit to the authority of the pope, Luther and
Karstadt centered theirs on the doctrine of JUSTI-
FICATION by FAITH alone. Eck brought heresy suits
against Luther at Louvain and Cologne. In the
bull *Exsurge Domine* (June 15, 1520) Pope LEO
X condemned 41 propositions of Luther. Upon
receiving it Luther promptly burned it.

Eck sought by every means to have Luther's
writings condemned by Elector Friederich of Saxony (1503–54), who instead wound up becoming a Lutheran himself. The debate raged on,
with Philip of Melanchthon (1497–1560) joining
the fray. Eck produced a handbook listing 404
Lutheran theses worthy of condemnation. In
1539 he came forth with a German translation
of the Old Testament, published alongside the
New Testament version of Hieronymus Emser
(1477–1527). Despite the invective, Eck was willing to meet Melancthon halfway on the doctrine

of original SIN at the Imperial Diet of Regensburg
(1541), but by that time the reformers thoroughly
distrusted him.

Further reading: Johann Eck, *Enchiridion of Common-
places Against Luther and Other Enemies of the Church*
(Grand Rapids, Mich.: Baker, 1979); Max Ziegelbauer,
*Johannes Eck: Mann der Kirche im Zeitalter der Glaubens-
spaltung* (St. Ottilien: EOS, 1987).

Eckhart, Meister (c. 1260–1328) *mystical theologian*

Born in Hockheim, Thuringia, Eckhart was a
Dominican theologian who probably studied
under ALBERTUS MAGNUS at Paris. He himself
taught at Strasbourg, Cologne, and Erfurt and
wrote in a style of simple, mystical piety in both
German and Latin. Condemned in his time, Eckhart is now recognized as orthodox.

Eckhart proposed to encompass his THEOL-
OGY in a monumental but uncompleted *Opus
Tripartum*. He made a distinction between formal
and virtual being. Formally there is an absolute
distinction between the Creator and the creature.
Virtually, however, the creature has its being from
GOD and is destined toward ultimate union with
God, which calls for withdrawal from earthly
things: "To the extent that you withdraw from
creaturely things God enters you with all that
is his." Eckhart believed that we should break
through finite particulars to discover the "ground
of being," where God and SOUL are one.

Eckhart's enemies accused him of PANTHEISM.
He was tried and condemned by the archbishop
of Cologne in 1326. He appealed to Pope John
XXII (r. 1316–34) in Avignon but died before the
case could be adjudicated. The pope condemned
28 propositions attributed to Eckhart in *In Agro
Dominico* (March 27, 1329), but there was no way
to get at his true teaching. His works underwent
heavy editing yet had great influence on later mystics like Henry Suso (1295–1366) and NICHOLAS OF
CUSA. He also influenced the idealist philosophers

of the 19th century and the existentialist Martin Heidegger. There has been a revival of Eckhart's mystical thought in the creation spirituality of MATTHEW FOX.

Further reading: Oliver Davies, *Meister Eckhart: Mystical Theologian* (London: S.P.C.K., 1991); Meister Eckhart, *The Essential Sermons, Commentaries, Treatises, and Defense,* Classics of Western Spirituality 28, ed. Edmund Colledge and Bernard McGinn (New York: Paulist Press, 1981); C. F. Kelly, *Meister Eckhart on Divine Knowledge* (New Haven, Conn.: Yale University Press, 1977); Barry McGinn, "Meister Eckhart," in P. Szarmach, ed., *Introduction to the Medieval Mystics of Europe* (Albany, N.Y.: State University of New York Press, 1984), 237–257; Reiner Schurmann, *Meister Eckhart: Mystic and Philosopher* (Bloomington: Indiana University Press, 1978).

ecotheology (Gk.: *oikos*, "house," "dwelling" + *theologia*, "study of God")

Ecotheology is the relatively new study of humankind's relation to the environment in terms of its relation to GOD and its responsibility as steward of CREATION (Genesis 1:28). The study has both theological and ethical dimensions.

Theologically, ecotheology can be summarized in God's command to have "dominion" over the birds, fish, and land animals in the first chapter of Genesis. This dominion needs to be contrasted with the structures of "domination" among humans, animals, and the soil that arise as the result of SIN (Gen. 3:14–19). The Jewish *kashruth*, or kosher laws, can be seen as a hedge around human beings' exploitation of the natural world and a call to keep God's order of dominion in creation.

Ecotheology asks the key questions: What is our proper relation to the beauty of the creation given us by a providential God? How are the goods of the earth to be distributed with justice between the rich and the poor? What do we do about technologies that spoil the environment both for humans and other life forms, equally created by God? What are the limits to our experimental manipulation of the forces of nature and the keys to life such as DNA?

Ecotheology has deep roots in the BIBLE, which unfailingly, especially in the Psalms, exalts the handiwork of God in creation and beckons humanity to reverence and praise. It also has roots in AUGUSTINE OF HIPPO's reflections on the wonders of creation (*Confessions*, Book 13), BENEDICT OF NURSIA's nurturing attitude toward nature, HILDEGARD OF BINGEN's mystical herbalism, and FRANCIS OF ASSISI's hymn to Brother Sun and Sister Moon, in which he proclaims his kinship with all creation. Francis especially is seen as a paradigm of conservation in his successful effort to rescue the wolf of Gubbio from the wrath of the townspeople. The Jesuit poet GERARD MANLEY HOPKINS foresaw many of the 20th century's deforestation problems in his protest poem "Binsey Poplars" that both celebrated and lamented trees felled in Oxford in 1879 and in his poem "God's Grandeur," which marvels at God's creation yet underscores how much nature is "seared with trade; bleered, smeared with toil; and wears man's smudge."

Despite the THEOLOGY of the FALL, Catholic theology in the MIDDLE AGES continued to take a sacramental view of creation. God is known in shining light, flowing streams, fresh air, fertile soils, and the elements of the SACRAMENT of all sacraments, the EUCHARIST, which are wheat and grape juice worked by human hands. Against the loss of species through reckless development, the ecotheologian can point to THOMAS AQUINAS's assertion that the infinite God can only be manifested in the multiplicity of creatures (*Summa Theologiae* 1.49.2), which implicitly calls for the preservation of all species and environments on the living planet.

The Catholic HIERARCHY has become more aware of the threats to the environment in recent times. In 1988 the Philippine Conference of Bishops issued a pastoral letter, *What is Happening to Our Beautiful Land?* Taking his theme from "And God saw that it was good" (Gen. 1:3, 10,12, 18), Pope JOHN PAUL II issued a letter, *The Ecological Crisis A Common Responsibility: Peace with God the Creator, Peace with All Creation* (January 1, 1990) at the World Day of Peace. In 1992 the UNITED STATES CONFERENCE OF CATHOLIC BISHOPS issued a pastoral letter, *Renewing the Earth,* on the ecological crisis.

In more recent times, the theology of creation has received creative impulses from creation spirituality, which rejects the false distinction between mind and body and teaches the presence of the divine in both the material and spiritual dimensions of life. Thomas Berry, MATTHEW FOX, and ROSEMARY RADFORD RUETHER have contributed significantly to this development. There is now a convergence between feminist, environmentalist, ecotheological, and liberationist streams in theology. The ultimate aim of ecotheology is to show the interdependence and kinship of life, nature, and the worship of God.

Further reading: Thomas Berry, *The Dream of the Earth* (San Francisco: Sierra Club, 1988); Leonardo Boff, *Ecology and Liberation: A New Paradigm* (Maryknoll, N.Y.: Orbis, 1995); Sean McDonagh, *The Greening of the Church* (Maryknoll, N.Y.: Orbis, 1990); Rosemary Radford Ruether, *Gaia & God: An Ecofeminist Theology of Earth Healing* (San Francisco: HarperSanFrancisco, 1992).

ecumenism/ecumenical movement
(Gk.: *oikoumenē, "the whole inhabited world")*
Ecumenism is the effort to achieve unity among all CHRISTIAN churches both through and beyond CREED, cult, ethnic diversity, cultural tradition, and church polity. It is related to inter-religious relations, which promotes dialogue and exchange between religions. The term derives from the New Testament (Luke 2:1) and looks to the mission of the church to unite all humanity in this age and the age to come (Heb. 2:5).

Traces of ecumenism can be detected in the New Testament. In the Corinthian correspondence PAUL reveals his earnest efforts to overcome local church factionalism and preserve the unity of the believers as the one body of CHRIST (1 Cor. 10:16). The early COUNCILS of the church were efforts to preserve the "one, holy, catholic church" (Nicene Creed). This unity was not uniformity, for even then different branches of Christendom celebrated different rites, had different dates for EASTER, developed different theological styles, and functioned under different forms of authority. Ecumenism became a Christian necessity after the split between the orthodox and Monphysites (Copts, etc.) in 451 and between the Eastern and Western Churches in the GREAT SCHISM in 1054 and the multiple splits in Western Christian churches following the PROTESTANT REFORMATION. Though brief and partial reconciliations between East and West occurred at the Councils of Lyons II (1272) and BASEL (1431–45), and half-hearted attempts at dialogue between Catholics and Protestants were held at the Imperial Diet of Regensburg (1541) and at the Council of TRENT (1545–62), ecumenism faltered in a climate of enmity, fear, and suspicion.

There were, however, rare thinkers who continued to plea for ecumenism in the following centuries, notably the lay Catholic theologian FRANZ VON BAADER. The impulse received new life with the rise of the modern ecumenical movement, which began largely as a Protestant undertaking. In the 19th century various missionary Protestant denominations (Anglican, Presbyterian, Baptist) formed cooperative associations such as BIBLE and tract societies and united education and health agencies; they often divided mission fields to avoid competition. These trends culminated in the World Missionary Conference in Edinburgh, Scotland, in 1910, with 122 denominations attending from 43 countries. The conference declared that "a unity in Christ and the fellowship of the Spirit is deeper than our divisions."

The Edinburgh conference led to the Universal Christian Conference on Life and Work (1925) and the World Conference on Faith and Order (1927). In 1920, acting Ecumenical Patriarch of

Constantinople, Dorotheos of Prousa (r. 1918–21), called for "closer intercourse and mutual cooperation," and national councils of Christian churches appeared in many countries. These efforts culminated in the founding of the World Council of Churches in 1948, which included Eastern and Oriental Orthodox Churches from the beginning, and the Russian Orthodox Church from 1961.

Although Catholics were not officially part of this movement, important Catholic theologians like YVES CONGAR developed strong ecumenical contacts beginning in the 1930s. These contacts bore great fruit, notably in the visit to Pope PAUL VI of the Archbishop of Canterbury, Geoffrey Francis Fisher, in 1960. Catholics were now allowed to become official observers at the World Council of Churches.

VATICAN COUNCIL II ushered in a totally new era of ecumenism for Catholics and for the world. In *Unitatis Redintegratio,* the Decree on Ecumenism, and *Nostra Aetate,* the Decree on Non-Christian Religions, the council opened avenues of ecumenical interreligious dialogue, cooperation, and worship unimagined a mere decade before. Present-day ecumenical cooperation has moved far beyond the old dictum "Doctrine divides, action unites." Various Protestant denominations have united throughout the world, notably in India and the United States. Catholics, Protestants, and non-Christians join in the World Day of Prayer. Catholics have come to informal and formal agreements with many Protestant denominations on important theological issues, including BAPTISM, the EUCHARIST, and CONFIRMATION. Most significant was the Joint Declaration on the Doctrine of Justification of the Roman Catholic Church and the World Lutheran Federation (October 31, 1999). In 2004 the Anglican, Evangelical Lutheran, and Roman Catholic Churches of Papua New Guinea came forth with An Agreed Statement on Baptism.

Even prior to Vatican II, John XXIII had formed the Pontifical Council for the Promotion of Christian Unity (1960). It received the rank of conciliar commission in 1962, a status confirmed by PAUL VI in 1966. Beginning with the formation of the Joint Working Group of the Roman Catholic Church and the World Council of Churches in 1966, this commission then became the birthing place for a set of structures aimed at establishing formal dialogue between the Vatican and various world Protestant and Orthodox communions.

More recently, various Vatican offices under Pope JOHN PAUL II, notably the Congregation for the Doctrine of the Faith headed by Cardinal Joseph Ratzinger, now Pope BENEDICT XVI, have put up various theological hurdles in the path toward greater ecumenical cooperation. Specifically, Ratzinger issued a "Note on the Expression 'Sister Churches'" (June 20, 2000) and similar statements on the validity of ANGLICAN ORDINATION that seemed to place very cautionary hurdles in the path of ecumenical exchange. On the other hand, he was credited with saving the Catholic and Lutheran "Joint Declaration on the Doctrine of Justification."

See also COMMUNION/COMMUNION OF SAINTS; ECCLESIOLOGY.

Further reading: Carl E. Braaten and Robert W. Jenson, *The Ecumenical Future* (Grand Rapids, Mich.: Eerdmans, 2004); Yves Congar, *Divided Christendom: A Catholic Study of the Problem of Reunion* (London: Bles, 1939); Mariasusai Dhavamony, *Ecumenical Theology of World Religions* (Rome: Gregoriana, 2003); Joseph Ratzinger, "Note on the Expression 'Sister Churches,'" *Origins* (September 14, 2000), also available online; William G. Rusch, ed., *Justification and the Future of the Ecumenical Movement: The Joint Declaration on the Doctrine of Justification* (Collegeville, Minn.: Liturgical Press, 2003); Thomas E. Fitzgerald, *The Ecumenical Movement* (Westport, Conn.: Praeger, 2004).

Egeria, Pilgrimage of

This is an early fifth-century account of a pilgrimage by the NUN Egeria from her MONASTERY in

Galicia, SPAIN, to EGYPT, Judea, and Galilee. The extant text is not complete. Her descriptions are significant for both the study of the LITURGY and early Palestinian Christian ARCHITECTURE.

In Egeria's travels, various ascetics show her famous Old Testament sites, including Mt. Nebo, the tomb of Thomas the Apostle in Edessa, and the alleged tomb of Abraham in Carrhae. She also describes the tomb of St. Thekla near Seleucis.

The second part of the book describes the LITURGICAL YEAR in the Jerusalem liturgy and mentions the noted churches of the Holy Sepulcher, the Church of Zion, the Imbolon and Eleona on the Mount of Olives, the Basilica of the Nativity in Bethlehem, and the Church of Lazarus in Bethany. She also describes the house of Peter, converted into a church, in Capharnaum.

See also ARCHAEOLOGY.

Further reading: The text of *Egeria* is widely available on the internet; John Wilkinson, *Egeria's Travels*, rev. ed. (Warminster, Penn.: Aris & Phillips, 2002).

Egypt

Christianity in Egypt was shaped by the complex civilizations established by the ancient Egyptians, the successors of Alexander the Great (356–323 B.C.E.), and the Romans. In the first century the Neoplatonic philosopher PHILO OF ALEXANDRIA (20 B.C.E.–40) describes a vibrant intellectual community shared by Egyptians, Greeks, Romans, and Jews, including two sectarian groups, the Essenes and the monklike Therapeutae, who later may have converted to Christianity.

The arrival of Christianity is shrouded in mystery. Acts 18:24 mentions that Apollos, PAUL's opponent at Corinth (1 Cor. 1:12), came from Alexandria. He may have been a Therapeut. Later tradition says that Mark founded the church in Egypt (Eusebius, *Church History* 2.16), but there is no hard evidence. All mention of the first- and early second-century Egyptian Church seems to have been snuffed out of the historical record.

One explanation is that the early community was most likely Jewish Christian and was nearly wiped out by Trajan (98–117) along with the Jews.

Many famous GNOSTICS claimed Egypt as their homeland, including VALENTINUS, Basilides, and the Marcionite Apelles. Egyptian THEOLOGY took an orthodox direction in the subsequent spiritual interpretations of the ALEXANDRINE SCHOOL, founded by Pantaeus (late second century), CLEMENT OF ALEXANDRIA (c. 150–215), and ORIGEN (c. 185–c. 254). In the next century the church became divided between the intense intellectualism of Origen's successor, Dionysius of Alexandria (d. 264/5), and the rural faith of the native Egyptians, now known as Copts. Dionysius communicated with the BISHOPS of the world, fought against Sabellianism, and differed with CYPRIAN OF CARTHAGE on the readmission of *lapsi* into the church after the Decian persecution (249–50).

It was among the Copts that MONASTICISM first made its defining impact on Christianity. St. ANTHONY OF EGYPT inspired the spread of anchoritism, or hermetic asceticism, as PACHOMIUS set the pattern for the great cenobitic, or communal, monasteries which spread to Palestine, ASIA Minor, and Europe. The MONK Shenoute (d. 452) founded the famous White Monastery near Sohag. It came to house 4,000 monks and despite some gaps survives to this day.

By the fourth century Alexandria became elevated to the rank of a patriarchate, and its bishops wielded widespread influence. Theolophilus, patriarch of Alexandria (385–412), unscrupulously destroyed the famous pagan temple of Sarapis and engineered St. JOHN CHRYSOSTOM's condemnation at the Synod of the Oak (403). His sucessor, CYRIL OF ALEXANDRIA, did not play fair either in his attacks on Nestorius. Nevertheless, his *Second Letter to Nestorius* was incorporated into the acts of the Council of CHALCEDON in 451. Cyril's own CHRISTOLOGY was confusing.

Adhering to Cyril's Christological formulations, the Coptic Church could not come to agreement with the leading party at the Council of Chalcedon, which insisted on the formula of "one person, two natures, human and divine." In the following centuries the Chalcedonian Greeks persecuted the Copts until the conquest of Egypt by Islamic conquerors in 642. Thereafter Coptic Christianity remained relatively isolated until modern times (see COPTIC CHURCH). Contemporary Copts draw inspiration not only from the tradition of Mark's initially spreading the Gospel in their land, but Egypt's role in protecting the baby Jesus from Herod's slaughter of the innocents. (Matt. 2:13–18)

Egypt has been vital for the study of early Christianity. The dry sands along the Nile have preserved the earliest papyri texts of the New Testament. In 1945 young men discovered 13 Gnostic codices from the library at the monastery of Chenoboskion near Nag Hammadi, including the noted Gospel of Thomas.

See also COPTIC CATHOLIC CHURCH.

Further reading: Birger Pearson and J. Goehring, eds., *The Roots of Egyptian Christianity* (Philadelphia: Fortress Press, 1986); Otto F. A. Meinardus, *2000 Years of Coptic Christianity* (Cairo: American University Press, 1999); *St Mark and the Coptic Church* (Cairo: Coptic Orthodox Patriarchate, 1968).

electronic church

This term refers indiscriminately to those who produce or use electronic means (radio, television, Internet) to propagate or learn about their religion. Protestant preachers were among the first to make heavy use of both radio and television. Noted among these have been Southern Baptist Billy Graham (1918–) and his Crusade, Pentecostal healer Oral Roberts (1918–), whose broadcasts have been televised around the world since the 1950s, and more recent personalities such as Benny Hinn (1953–) and Pat Robertson (1930–), who have dominated the Sunday morning airwaves.

There were two notable Catholic exceptions. Fr. Charles E. Coughlin (1891–1979), founder of the Shrine of the Little Flower in Royal Oaks,

Michigan, in 1926, convinced Detroit radio station WRJ to give him airtime to counteract religious prejudice after a Klu Klux Klan cross burning in front of his church. Soon his message shifted from religious themes to economics and politics. At first approving of President Franklin Delano Roosevelt (1882–1945), he turned against him, charging the administration of being the stooge of communists. He soon gained a following of more than 50 million listeners. At the beginning of World War II he took a pro-Nazi stance and was silenced by his bishop.

The second notable Catholic broadcaster was FULTON J. SHEEN, who attracted a nationwide audience as a Catholic apologist, first with *The Catholic Hour* (1930–52) on the radio and then with the *Life is Worth Living* (1951–57) television series. The latter, which was aired weekly in primetime, had an audience of 30 million, by no means limited to Catholics.

Cable television and the Internet have greatly expanded the resources available to spread knowledge of the Catholic Church and Christianity in general. The Vatican has developed its own World Wide Web site (http://www.vatican.va), on which all important ecclesiastical documents, including many from the past, are available to the public. The UNITED STATES CONFERENCE OF CATHOLIC BISHOPS maintains a Web site (http://www.usccb.org/), on which it posts general documents and information. In 1981 Mother M. Angelica, a cloistered Poor Clare nun, founded the Eternal Word Television Network (EWTN) at Our Lady of Angels Monastery in Irondale, Alabama, which also provides a Web site with multiple links to Catholic themes. EWTN promotes a very traditional form of Catholicism. There are now multiple formal and informal Catholic Web sites throughout the world, including sites for almost all the Eastern Catholic rites.

Further reading: Ronald H. Carpenter, *Father Charles E. Coughlin: Surrogate Spokesman for the Disaffected* (Westport, Conn.: Greenwood, 1998); Jeffrey K. Hadden and Anson Shupe, *Televangelism: Power and Politics on God's Frontier* (New York: Henry Holt, 1988); Stewart M. Hoover, *Mass Media Religion: The Social Sources of the Electronic Church* (Newbury Park, Calif.: Sage, 1988); J. Gordon Melton, Phillip Charles Lucas, and Jon R. Stone, *Prime-Time Religion* (Phoenix: Oryx, 1997).

Elizabeth I   *See* PROTESTANT REFORMATION.

Elizabeth of Hungary, St. (1207–1231)

Elizabeth (also known as Elizabeth of Thuringia) was the daughter of King Andrew II of Hungary (1175–1235). A member of the Franciscan Third Order, she was canonized in 1235. Her feast day is November 17.

Early in her marriage to Landgrave Ludwig IV of Thuringia (d. 1227), she made an association with the newly arrived FRANCISCANS and became a member of the Third Order. She had a happy marriage and several children. After Ludwig died on a Crusade, she was driven out of court by Henry Raspe (d. 1247), Ludwig's brother, on charges of depleting state coffers through her charity. She ended her days doing works of charity for the sick and poor near Marburg under the spiritual direction of Conrad of Marburg (d. 1230), a masochistic papal inquisitor who was later murdered.

Further reading: Elizabeth R. Obbard, *Poverty, My Riches: A Study of St. Elizabeth of Hungary 1207–31* (Southhampton: Saint Austin, 1997).

emperor   *See* CHARLEMAGNE; CONSTANTINE; FREDERICK I BARBAROSSA; FREDERICK II; HOLY ROMAN EMPIRE; JUSTINIAN I.

encyclical, papal (Gk.: *enkyklikos*, "circular")

An encyclical is a formal pastoral epistle addressed by the pope to the universal church. Originally it referred to any letter sent out by a BISHOP to all those under his jurisdiction. Normally, encyclicals have been addressed to those in communion with the church of Rome, but in 1963 John XXIII proclaimed *Pacem in Terris* both to the church and "to all people of good will."

There is an informal hierarchy among ecclesiastical pronouncements. Most solemn are pronouncements EX CATHEDRA either by the pope speaking for the universal church or by the pope in concert with the bishops of the world. These are called statements by the extraordinary and infallible MAGISTERIUM. Of lesser import are statements of the ordinary magisterium, which include encyclicals, followed by doctrinal notes or clarifications. The principle of infallibility can operate on all levels, but formal belief is generally restricted to the extraordinary pronouncements.

The subject of encyclicals can include doctrinal, moral, or ethical matters important to the church. Encyclicals have become the common way for the pope to exercise his ordinary teaching authority. It is important to note that although encyclicals contain authoritative teachings, they are not definitive, infallible statements, and that some forms of respectful dissent can be tolerated. An encyclical has not usually been understood to close discussion of an issue once and for all.

However, current pope BENEDICT XVI may disagree; as Cardinal Ratzinger he publicly stated, for example, that JOHN PAUL II's teaching on the ordination of women in the Anglican Church in the encyclical *Ordinatio Sacerdotalis* (May 22, 1994), "requires definitive assent, since, founded on the written Word of God, and from the beginning constantly preserved and applied in the Tradition of the Church, it has been set forth infallibly by the ordinary and universal Magisterium" ("Concerning the Teaching Contained in *Ordinatio Sacerdotalis: Responsum ad Dubium*," October 28, 1995). Since the papal encyclical in question had not itself claimed infallibility, critics asked whether the cardinal was claiming infallibility for himself as prefect of a Vatican congregation.

Beginning with *Rerum Novarum* in 1891, 11 encyclicals were issued that became collectively known as the "social encyclicals" for their teaching about society, economics, labor rights, war, and other pressing social concerns. Because of their deep and wide impact, most will be discussed at length under the popes who issued them, with the exception of *Pacem in Terris*, which has a separate entry.

> *Rerum Novarum* (1891), *see* LEO XIII.
> *Quadragesimo Anno* (1931), *see* PIUS XI.
> *Mater et Magistra* (1961), *see* JOHN XXIII.
> PACEM IN TERRIS (1963), and *see* JOHN XXIII.
> *Populorum Progressio* (1963), *see* PAUL VI.
> *Laborem Exercens* (1981), *see* JOHN PAUL II.
> *Sollicitudo Rei Socialis* (1987), *see* JOHN PAUL II.
> *Centesimus Annus* (1991), *see* JOHN PAUL II.

Further reading: Thomas J. Massaro and Thomas A. Shannon, eds., *American Catholic Social Teaching* (Collegeville, Minn.: Liturgical Press, 2002); Francis A. Sullivan, *Magisterium: Teaching Authority in the Catholic Church* (Eugene: Wipf & Stock, 2002).

Endo Shusaku   *See* SHUSAKU ENDO.

England, John (1786–1842) *U.S. bishop*

England was the first Catholic BISHOP of Charleston, South Carolina, and the chief initiator of the First Provincial Council of Baltimore in 1829. England was born in Cork, Ireland, and trained for the priesthood there. An active priest, he taught catechectics to all his parishioners and advocated the emancipation of Catholics in Ireland long before it was granted. He came to Charleston as bishop in 1820 and soon became fully American in his outlook. His diocese included South Carolina and Georgia, and he later administered eastern Florida as well.

England was tireless in organizing parishes in his diocese and included laypeople in his many diocesan conventions. He was a frequent preacher and lecturer, often speaking before non-Catholic audiences. He was the first Roman Catholic bishop to speak before the U.S. Congress, in 1826. He founded a seminary and an order of the Sisters of Mercy and was an active participant in the Charleston Philosophical Society, where he promoted classical learning. He fought against dueling and against the Nullificationists, states-rights advocates who claimed that individual states had a right to nullify any federal law they deemed unconstitutional.

England was also very solicitous of his African-American congregants, gladly preaching to them and visiting them everywhere in his diocese. It was chiefly at his insistence that the First Council of Baltimore, which began the process of giving Catholicism an American character, took place in 1829. When he died, Catholic and non-Catholic alike mourned him. His style of free and open Catholicism in a free and open society would later be branded with the nebulous epithet AMERICANISM.

Further reading: Patrick W. Carey, *An Immigrant Bishop: John England's Adaptation of Irish Catholicism to American Republicanism;* (New York: U.S. Catholic Historical Society, 1982); Peter Clarke, *A Free Church in a Free Society: The Ecclesiology of John England* (Greenwood, S.C.: Attic, 1982); John England, *The Works of the Right Reverend John England,* ed. Sebastian Messmer, 7 vols. (Cleveland: Arthur H. Clark, 1908).

Ephesus, Council of (431)

The emperors Theodosius II (r. 401–450) in the East and Valentinian III (r. 425–455) in the West called the third ecumenical council at Ephesus to settle the controversy over the doctrines of NESTORIUS concerning the relation of the divine and the human in CHRIST. The council can also be seen as a struggle between the ALEXANDRINE and ANTIOCHENE SCHOOLS of theology.

Nestorius (d. 451), the patriarch of CONSTANTINOPLE who studied under Theodore of Mopsuestia

(c. 350–428), was alleged to have taught that there were two separate persons in Christ, one divine and one human. He rejected the title "Begetter of God" (*Theotokos*) for Mary, though he was willing to accept "Begetter of Christ" (*Christotokos*).

The council opened with the BISHOPS Memnon of Ephesus and CYRIL OF ALEXANDRIA present, but without the attendance of John of Antioch (d. 441), the bishop most suited to argue the cause of the Nestorians, and without the legates from Pope Celestine. The council passed eight canons, excommunicating and deposing Nestorius and condemning the Pelagianism of Celestius (*see* PELAGIUS). The council reaffirmed the CREED of Nicaea, asserting that the human and divine natures were united in the one Christ, which logically justifies the title *Theotokos* for Mary. The image of Mary as *Theotokos* has become a central ICON in Eastern Christianity (*see* MARY OF NAZARETH).

In response to the condemnations of Ephesus, the Antiochenes in turn excommunicated the Alexandrine party, although Cyril later reconciled with John of Antioch. Modern scholars note that Cyril often presented the case of his opponents unfairly. Recently discovered original manuscripts of Theodore show that, despite his formulations, his intentions were within the bounds of orthodoxy. Contemporary analysis of the Christological controversies is uncovering the political element that often trumped any genuine differences that may have existed.

Further reading: Leo Donald Davis, *The First Seven Ecumenical Councils (325–787): Their History and Theology* (Collegeville, Minn.: Liturgical Press, 1983); John L. Murphy, *The General Councils of the Church* (Milwaukee: Bruce Publishing, 1960).

Epiphany (Gr.: *epi-*, "upon," "forth" + *phanein*, "to appear")

This feast of Epiphany, much older than Christmas, originated in the middle of the second century in the Eastern Church. It celebrates the BAPTISM of Jesus in the Jordan by JOHN THE BAPTIST, when the status of Jesus as Son of GOD first became manifest (Mark 1:11). Some think that the feast arose to counteract the Roman feast day of Sol Invictus, or Unconquered Sun, which marked the end of the winter solstice. The eve of Epiphany is known as Twelfth Night.

In the West the feast, called Theophania, or Manifestation of God, was transferred to the earlier manifestation of the infant Jesus to the Magi (Matt. 2:1–12) and attached to Christmas, although Jesus' baptism and the wedding at Cana (John 2:1–11) were also considered epiphanies. In the East the blessing of holy water occurs on this feast. It ranks with the feasts of EASTER and PENTECOST as a solemnity.

See also FEAST DAYS; LITURGICAL YEAR.

Further reading: Theresa Cotter, *Christ Is Coming: Celebrating Advent, Christmas & Epiphany* (Cincinnati: St. Anthony Messenger Press, 1992); Thomas J. Talley, *The Origins of the Liturgical Year* (Collegeville, Minn.: Liturgical Press, 1986).

Erasmus, Desiderius (c. 1466–1536)
humanist scholar and philosopher

Erasmus was a celebrated Renaissance humanist scholar and philosopher, author of *Praise of Folly*, and editor of the first critical edition of the Greek New Testament. He was a forerunner of but not a participant in the PROTESTANT REFORMATION, with many friends on both sides. He liked a good wine and a good table.

Erasmus may well have been the first European celebrity in the contemporary sense of the term. Every prince, pope, and BISHOP wanted him at his court. He might also have been the first cosmopolitan European, even though his name is associated with Rotterdam. He lived first in the Netherlands, then at Cambrai, Paris, London, Oxford, Basel, Rome, Venice, and Freiburg, to name only the main places. Like other moderns, he invented himself, giving himself the name Desiderius because he thought it echoed his Dutch name Geert, which could be derived from the German word *begehrt,* or "beloved."

He was born the illegitimate son of a priest and a physician's daughter in Gouda. He was sent to study with the Brethren of the Common Life in Deventer, who imbued him with their inward, simple devotion to Jesus, which he called *philosophia Christi,* although he later rejected their mysticism (*see* DEVOTIO MODERNA). He became, to his everlasting regret, an Augustinian canon at Steyn, where he fell in love with a fellow MONK but was rejected. Seeking a way out, he became secretary to the bishop of Cambrai and soon went to Paris to study and later teach. Later the pope relieved him of his vow to live in a MONASTERY. Meanwhile, he had rejected the intricacies of Scholastic disputation, opting for the classics, the church fathers, and the new humanist learning.

At Paris he fell in love again, with Thomas Grey, marquis of Dorset, but it was William Blount, fourth baron of Mountjoy, who became a lifelong patron and induced him to come to England many times. There he befriended Sts. THOMAS MORE, JOHN FISHER, and John Colet (1467–1519), professor of Bible at Oxford and, like Erasmus, a severe critic of laxness and luxury among the CLERGY. Colet induced him to undertake the study of classical Greek, and this advice shaped his whole life. Later he was to develop off-and-on friendships with reformers Martin Luther (1483–1546) and Huldrich Zwingli (1484–1531).

While in England, Erasmus published his *Adages* (1500), snippets and proverbs from the classical world. Quoting it made everyone seem a learned humanist. It became a pan-European best seller and went through many editions, making its author world famous. A confirmed pacifist, he liked especially the saying *bellum dulce est inexpertis,* "War is sweet to those who have not suffered it." The book was followed by *Moriae Encomium,* or *Praise of Folly* (1509), by which he is most known today. It took a corrupt church

to task for traffic in relics, mindless devotions to saints, indulgence peddling, miscreant and absentee clergy, and countless other abuses. In *Colloquia Familiaria,* or *Friendly Conversations* (1518), he made fun of the pilgrimages, and all the trappings associated with them, that he himself had made to Walsingham and Canterbury in England. (Pope PAUL IV put the book on the very first Index of Prohibited Books in 1557.)

In 1516 Erasmus published the first critical edition of the Greek New Testament along with a new Latin version that challenged St. JEROME's time-honored Vulgate. Instead of *poenitentiam agite,* "do penance," he suggested *respi-*

Erasmus in his study with his books. Engraving (1520) by Albrecht Dürer (1471–1528) from a charcoal drawing taken from life. The Greek reads: "My writings will the better [image]." Erasmus did not like the portrait. *(St. Louis Art Museum, with permission)*

scite, "reconsider, look back," which is much closer to the *metanoeite* of Matthew 3:2. That one change could undermine the whole theology of indulgences. Similarly, he replaced *gratia plena,* "full of grace," with *gratiosa,* "gracious," in Luke 2:51, thereby threatening the elevated status of MARY OF NAZARETH in medieval piety. He attacked the wild use of ALLEGORY in medieval exegesis, whereby commentators stretched meanings to make all sorts of texts refer to the Virgin Mary. He doubted the validity of the translation in the LXX and the Vulgate of the Hebrew word *almah,* "young maiden, concubine" (Isa. 7:14) with *parthenos/virgo,* "virgin"; the passage was usually interpreted by Christians as a reference to Mary. Both William Tyndale (c. 1494–1536) and Luther used his New Testament for their translations.

Many orthodox Catholics felt that Erasmus was a secret traitor, but then in 1523 he wrote *De Libro Arbitrio,* or *On the Free Will,* in which he defended the concept against Luther's tractate. Toward the end of his life he had to flee Basel, dominated by the reformer Johannes Oecolampadius (1482–1531), to Freiburg im Breisgau, only later to return and die among his erstwhile Protestant friends. Always on the edge, he never left the Church of Rome. He produced critical editions of many of the church fathers, including Jerome and ORIGEN, his favorite.

Further reading: Cornelius Augustijn, *Erasmus: His Life, Works, and Influence* (Toronto: University of Toronto Press, 1991); Desiderius Erasmus, *Collected Works,* ed. Charles Trinkaus (Toronto: University of Toronto Press, 1991); L. E. Halkin, *Erasmus: A Critical Biography* (Oxford: Oxford University Press, 1993); John C. Olin, ed., *Christian Humanism and the Reformation: Selected Writings of Erasmus* (New York: Fordham University Press, 1975).

eschatology (Gk.: *eschata,* "last things" + *logos,* "study of")

Eschatology is the study of the final destiny of the created world in GOD's plan of salvation. It is inti-

mately bound up with Jesus' proclamation of the kingdom of God (Mark 4:30–32). The teaching is grounded in the FAITH and hope of CHRISTIANS that, despite the darkness of history, a communal and individual deliverance from SIN and DEATH has already begun through the death and RESURRECTION of Jesus CHRIST.

Eschatology touches on other important themes in Catholic theology: death, Last Judgment, PURGATORY, resurrection, eternal life, and HEAVEN AND HELL—the themes traditionally treated in Advent sermons. It is closely related to Jewish and Christian apocalyptics (*see* APOCALYPSE), which portray time and history as a struggle between the forces of good and EVIL, culminating in a final judgment and the millennial reign of the Messiah.

For some theologians, the kingdom will arrive after God breaks into human history from the future. Others believe, on the contrary, that the present world is already tending toward the kingdom, and that the creation is "groaning" for the full redemption (Rom. 8:18). MONTANUS and FRANCISCAN Spirituals tended to forsake the past and the present to concentrate on their hopes of the future. AUGUSTINE OF HIPPO, by contrast, abandoned his early hope in a millennial kingdom and turned his attention to the present: the church with its SACRAMENTS.

Pope BENEDICT XVI, as Cardinal Joseph Ratzinger, followed this Augustinian line of reasoning in claiming that orthodox belief "tears eschatology from time." What he is left with is the church, particularly the hierarchical church. Ratzinger incorporated this opinion into the 1994 *Catechism of the Catholic Church* (676). KARL RAHNER and HANS KÜNG argued in opposition that the church, which is the work of humans in response to God and through which the kingdom begins, does not exist for itself but serves as the herald and harbinger of the coming kingdom of God, when God will complete the divine work and Jesus' promises will be fulfilled. The church is both "already" and "not yet." The EUCHARIST is a present meal that is also the foretaste of the messianic banquet that God has prepared for God's children. The first view sees the church as a permanent holding pen until God unilaterally inaugurates the kingdom from beyond time and history. The second view sees the church as a catalyst toward the kingdom that will culminate history.

The conflict can be overcome by returning to the eschatological teaching of IRENAEUS OF LYONS. Irenaeus viewed the millennium through the prism of all of Scripture (*tota scriptura*), including the typological idea (*see* TYPOLOGY) that the Last Things (*ta eschata*) will be like the First Things (*ta prota*). His millennium doctrine embraced the three articles of the CREED, CREATION, REDEMPTION, and restoration. Thus, for Irenaeus the millennium is a restoration, recapitulation, and renovation of the structures of creation itself, including time and space. The millennium has already begun through the redemptive action of Jesus; it continues through the church but remains unfulfilled. Believers are called to partake in the restoration, not simply as passive witnesses but as the community of Christ spreading justice and mercy in concrete ways, including harvests justly distributed (*Against Heretics* 5.35.1–2).

Early Christians awaited the imminent return of Jesus (1 Thess. 4:15–18). The delay of the parousia, or Second Coming, caused severe theological problems. Some held on to the millennial belief in an imminent future (Rev. 20:4–6); the Montanists tied their millennial beliefs to ecstatic prophecy. In his *Dialogue with Trypho* 80 JUSTIN MARTYR stated that many other Christians abandoned the belief in the resurrection and the millennium outright. Others opted for a "realized eschatology" of the present (Gospel of John). The ALEXANDRINES allegorized the Second Coming into a spiritual dimension. GNOSTICS did much the same, interiorizing Jesus as the inner life of the enlightened. To a greater or lesser degree, all these groups saw the millennium as a flight from creation, a tendency to which Irenaeus offered a sound, realistic theological alternative but which

much subsequent theology has failed to articulate clearly.

Further reading: Frank K. Flinn, "Millennial Hermeneutics," in M. Darrol Bryant and Donald Dayton, eds., *The Coming Kingdom: Essays in American Millennialism and Eschatology* (New York: Paragon, 1983); Bernard McGinn, ed., *Visions of the End: Apocalyptic Traditions in the Middle Ages* (New York: Columbia University Press, 1998); Karl Rahner, "The Church and the Parousia of Christ," in *Theological Investigations* 6 (Baltimore: Helicon, 1969); Joseph Ratzinger, *Eschatology: Death and Eternal Life* (Washington, D.C.: Catholic University Press, 1989).

Ethiopian Catholic Church

The Book of Acts (8:26–40) tells how the disciple Philip baptized the first Ethiopian. In ancient times, the Ethiopian Orthodox Church existed as a branch of the Orthodox COPTIC CHURCH based in EGYPT; as such, it joined the Coptic Church in rejecting the formulations proposed by the Council of CHALCEDON (451) that CHRIST existed as one person with two natures. The Monophysites (from the Greek for "one nature"), who predominated in the Egyptian and Ethiopian churches, tended to emphasize the single divine nature of Christ.

Two centuries later Ethiopia was cut off from the rest of Christianity by the establishment of Islam in Egypt and North Africa. Westerners did not reestablish communication until the 13th and 15th centuries. Catholic missionaries attempted to bring the Ethiopian church under the papal banner. The effort found initial success, and events moved rapidly following the 1622 declaration by the Ethiopian king that his nation was a Catholic state. In 1623, the pope selected Alfonso Mendez, a Portuguese Jesuit, as the first patriarch of the new Ethiopian Catholic Church, and Mendez was installed in 1626. However, initial acceptance came to a standstill shortly thereafter when Mendez tried to institute the Latin LITURGY. He held on until the king died, but the new king banished

Mendez and brought a quick end to any union between the Ethiopian Church and Rome.

At the end of the 19th century Catholic missionaries again showed up, but they made little headway until Italy invaded the region in 1935. In 1940 Haile Selassie (r. 1930–74) invited Jesuits to open what is now Addis Ababa University. Their work expanded significantly during the first six years of Italian rule. Rather than build a Latin-rite church, the missionaries developed a church with a modified Ethiopian liturgy. Progress slowed with the spread of World War II (1939–45) and until the fall of Benito Mussolini (1883–1945).

The first BISHOP was appointed in 1961. The church had a stable life for a generation, but in 1993, Eritrea, where some half its members resided, became an independent nation. There are 10 diocese. Today, almost all of the church's 520,000 members reside in Ethiopia and Eritrea. The present metropolitan, ARCHBISHOP Berhaneyesus D. Souvaphiel, resides in Addis Ababa. He relates to the Roman Curia through the Congregation for Oriental Churches.

See also COPTIC CATHOLIC CHURCH; COPTIC CHURCH.

Further reading: Nikolaus Liesel, *The Eastern Catholic Liturgies: A Study in Words and Pictures* (Westminster, Md.: Newman Press, 1960); Ronald G. Roberson, *The Eastern Christian Churches—A Brief Survey*, 5th ed. (Rome: Pontifical Oriental Institute, 1995).

Eucharist (Gr.: *eu* "well," "good" + *charis* "graciousness"; together = "to give thanks")

Together with BAPTISM, the Eucharist ranks as a primary SACRAMENT of the Catholic Church. In it, the community assembles for the consecration of bread and wine into the body and blood of the Lord and the reception of the sacrament. Baptism and CONFIRMATION are sacraments of initiation into the communion of believers; the Eucharist is the full participation in that communion.

Christ at the Last Supper with four disciples (Mark 12:22). Woodcut from Marcus Vigerius (1446–1516), *Decachordum christianum* (1507). *(Washington University Library, Special Collections, with permission)*

The earliest mention of the Eucharist is in 1 Corinthians 11:23–26, where PAUL chastises factionalists who are dividing the community while hypocritically partaking of the Eucharist, the symbol of unity of the church as the body of CHRIST. Other primary references include Mark 14:22–25 and parallels in Matthew and Luke.

Early CHRISTIANS used a variety of terms to designate the Eucharist. "Giving thanks" is the primary term (DIDACHE 9) but other phrases and terms were also used: breaking bread (Acts 27:35); Lord's Supper (1 Cor. 11:20); AGAPE, or love feast (Jude 12); *anamnesis*, or commemoration (1 Cor. 11:24); *koinonia*, or communion fellowship (1 Cor. 10:16); and *mysterion*, or secret/sacred rite, which was translated by *sacramentum* in the West (Cyprian *Letters* 63.16).

In the Eastern rite the Eucharist is often referred to as the *Divine Liturgy*, while the West uses the general term *Mass*, a term derived from the final words of the Latin Eucharist: *Ite, missa est* ("Go! It is sent forth/ended"). Today the term *Eucharist* is coming back into greater use. The term *the sacrament* is commonly used for Eucharistic bread and wine.

In the early centuries the Eucharist was understood and interpreted in various ways. The theological meaning was generally associated with the EASTER, or Paschal, Mystery, the saving event of Christ's suffering, DEATH, and RESURRECTION, in which all of humanity and history is gathered to Christ, and he returns to the Father. Within this master model, the Eucharist was seen in varying lights as a pure thank offering (JUSTIN MARTYR, *Dialogue with Trypho* 41), a figure, sign, or symbol pointing to a spiritual reality (TERTULLIAN, *Against Marcion* 4.40), or a memorial of Christ's death and resurrection (JOHN CHRYSOSTOM, *Homilies on Matthew* 25.3).

In the MIDDLE AGES the emphasis shifted from the overarching model of the Paschal Mystery, although its influence continued, to the model of the Real Presence (of the body and blood of Christ in the sacrament). This shift can be traced back to both AMBROSE OF MILAN, who maintained a virtual identity between the sign and the reality in the sacrament (*Sacraments* 4.4.14–5.23) and AUGUSTINE, who tended to have some distance between the outward, visible sign and the inward, invisible supernatural grace (*Sermons* 227). All agreed that the reality of God's grace was present in the sacrament.

This focus on the physical objects of the consecration of bread and wine, apart from their context in church life in the celebration of communion, seduced people into terminological thickets and ended up in Eucharistic heresies. The first systematic theology of the Eucharist was by the Carolingian theologian St. Paschasius Radabertus (c. 790–c. 860), who proposed a hyperrealistic understanding of the body and blood as the physical flesh of the son of Mary. Ratramnus of Corbie (ninth century) and Rabanus Maurus (c. 780–c. 856) argued that this physicalist understanding slighted the spiritual meaning of the Eucharist.

The issue came to a head in the teaching of Berengar of Tours (c. 1010–88), who affirmed the Real Presence but argued that the material elements undergo no physical change. At the Synod of Rome in 1079 he was forced to admit that the bread and wine undergo a substantial change into the body and blood of Christ. The terminology remained confusing. Lateran Council IV (*see* COUNCILS, ECUMENICAL) introduced the term TRANSUBSTANTIATION in its struggle against the CATHARI, who rejected any connection between the spiritual and material worlds. St. THOMAS AQUINAS gave a brilliant interpretation of this term by combining Augustine's understanding of a sacrament with Aristotle's metaphysical terminology. In the Eucharist the underlying substance of the elements of bread and wine are supernaturally converted, that is, transubstantiated, into the real Body and Blood of Christ at the moment of the consecration, but the accidents of bread and wine remain (*Summa Theologiae* 3a.75). That is, the consecrated body and blood still taste like bread and wine.

Concurrent with the stress on the Real Presence was the development of nonsacramental devotions such as the adoration of the Blessed Sacrament. This led to a lessening of the Eucharist in the spiritual life of the church and a substitute for the reception of the sacrament. Coupled with outright abuses like "buying masses" for one's private intentions, these deflections of the original meaning of the Eucharist played a significant part in sparking the PROTESTANT REFORMATION.

The Eucharist became the most significant issue dividing Protestants, as they struggled to rid their THEOLOGY of what they considered magical and superstitious elements, retain a sacramental element in their life, and be biblically grounded. Martin Luther (1483–1546) remained the most traditional, wishing to retain a strong emphasis on the Real Presence. He used the term *consubstantiation*, an obscure term at best, to signify his acceptance of the fullness of Christ's presence in the Eucharist without accepting the effect of the ritual itself in transforming the material elements of bread and wine into the body and blood of Jesus. Calvinists retained the idea of Christ's presence in the sacrament but understood it to be a spiritual presence perceived by the eye of FAITH. Huldrich Zwingli, priest of the church at Zurich, first formulated the idea that Christ was not really present in the Eucharist but only figuratively present through the faith of believers, and its performance was purely a memorial of the original Last Supper celebrated by Christ and his disciples; this idea was adopted by the Anabaptists. Thus, while those in the Lutheran and Reformed camp retained a sacrament, Anabaptists (and later Baptists) said that the Eucharist was merely an ordinance to be followed because of biblical admonition. They commonly refer to it as the Lord's Supper and see its primary purpose as an affirmation of the communion of believers.

In reaction to the Reformation, the Council of TRENT corrected many corrupt simonistic abuses associated with the Eucharist, but it also held fast to the transubstantiation doctrine itself without, however, adopting the commonly held Thomistic language of substance and accidents (session 13.4). In the following centuries both Protestant and Catholic theologians continued to refine Real Presence teaching.

The next important phase in understanding the Eucharist came with the LITURGICAL MOVEMENT in the early 20th century, which sought to place the celebration back into its original Paschal Mystery context. The change took shape first in the revitalized liturgies of abbeys like SOLESMES, Beuron, and MARIA LAACH. PIUS XII gave cautious approval to the new liturgical understanding of the Eucharist, but a full embrace had to wait until VATICAN COUNCIL II. Its decree *Sacrosanctum Councilium,* The Constitution on the Sacred Liturgy, allowed celebrations in the vernacular and restored elements of the earliest forms of the Eucharist, including a variety of prayers and the reception of the sacrament by the laity under both species, wine as well as bread. The pre-Reforma-

tion Utraquists, who insisted on reception under both kinds, were at last vindicated, though not, of course, acknowledged. Vatican II repeatedly affirmed that the Eucharist lies at the very center of Christian life as both its source and its summit (*Lumen Gentium* 11, Dogmatic Constitution on the Church).

Further reading: Classic texts: *Didachē* 9–10, 14; Justin Martyr *1 Apology* 65; Hippolytus of Rome, *Apostolic Tradition* 4; Cyprian of Carthage, *Letter* 63; Cyril of Jerusalem, *Catechetical Lectures* 23; all of these are available online. Mark G. Boyer, *The Liturgical Movement* (Collegeville, Minn.: Liturgical Press, 2004); Joseph A. Jungman, *The Mass of the Roman Rite* (New York: Benziger, 1951); David Power, *The Eucharistic Mystery* (New York: Crossroads, 1992).

Eusebius of Caesarea (c. 260–c. 339) *early historian of the church*

Eusebius was the first major church historian of Christianity. He engaged both sides of the controversy over ARIANISM and became an apologist for CONSTANTINE I THE GREAT.

Eusebius studied under Pamphilus, a CHRISTIAN teacher at Caesarea Maretima in Palestine and a follower of ORIGEN. Eusebius was not an original thinker, but his *Church History* became authoritative for the history of early Christianity thanks to his many quotes from the original sources he found in Pamphilus's library. The author's aim was to show how major events in sacred and secular history found their fulfillment in Christianity. He also wrote the *Onomastikon,* a study of biblical geography and place names. Later, in *The Preparation of the Gospel,* he sought to demonstrate the superiority of Jewish and Christian teaching over Greek mythology and philosophy.

Eusebius at first sided with Arius on the question of the superiority of the Father over the Son in the TRINITY. After 325, however, he accepted the CREED of the Council of Nicaea (*see* COUNCILS, ECUMENICAL) and its homoousios formula but was wary of Sabellianism, which taught that the Son was not a separate hypostasis, or person, but simply a different mode of the Father. His commitment to Nicaea remained suspect as he supported the exile of ATHANASIUS OF ALEXANDRIA by Constantine.

Later in his life Eusebius elaborated the arguments for what came to be known as CAESAROPAPISM, the union of spiritual and temporal power in the person of the Christian emperor. His flattery of Constantine, who remained a pagan until his deathbed, reached its apex in his *Life of Constantine*.

Further reading: Many of Eusebius's works are available online; T. D. Barnes, *Constantine and Eusebius* (Oxford: Oxford University Press, 1981); Eusebius, *Ecclesiastical History* (London, William Heinemann/Cambridge, Mass.: Harvard University Press, 1975); Robert M. Grant, *Eusebius as Church Historian* (Oxford: Oxford University Press, 1980).

evangelization (Gk.: *euangelion,* "gospel," "good news")

Evangelization is the proclamation or preaching of GOD's message of favor upon the poor, the hungry, and the ill, the message rooted in the announcements of the Hebrew prophets and continued in the ministry of Jesus: "I must preach the good news of the kingdom of God to the other cities also, for this is why I was sent" (Luke 4:43). Early on the disciples and APOSTLES felt called to the same mission as Jesus (Mark 16:15; Matt. 28:18–20; 1 Cor. 9:16), but their proclamation included the hope for the restoration of the world through the death and RESURRECTION of Jesus.

The evangelical impulse within Christianity gives it a built-in directive in favor of missionizing. Within the first generation the Gospel had already reached beyond Jerusalem to Syria, ASIA Minor, EGYPT, North Africa, and ITALY.

Catholic evangelizing was given added impetus at VATICAN COUNCIL II, especially in *Lumen Gentium* 17, Dogmatic Constitution on the Church,

and *Ad Gentes,* Decree on the Church's Missionary Activity. These conciliar evangelization themes were gathered together in PAUL VI's *Evangelii Nuntiandi* (December 8, 1975). At Vatican II evangelization was seen as a duty incumbent on all members of the church including the laity as the people of God (*Apostolicam Actuositatem* 2–4, Decree on the Apostolate of the Laity). Indeed, the chief Catholic evangelizers in the Third World today are NUNS and lay catechists. Proclaiming the Gospel must begin first with the "witness of an authentic Christian life" (*Evangelii Enuntidandi* 41). Then comes preaching and CATECHESIS. This initial evangelical stage is then sustained and deepened by the LITURGY and the SACRAMENTS.

The kingdom or reign of God is one of justice and peace. Therefore, evangelization addresses all aspects of human existence that stand in need of liberation from SIN, DEATH, and destruction.

Further reading: Gerald H. Anderson, ed., *Evangelization* (New York: Paulist Press, 1975); Robert Bireley, *The Refashioning of Catholicism, 1450–1700: A Reassessment of the Counter Reformation* (Washington, D.C.: Catholic University Press, 1999); Johannes Hofinger, *Evangelization and Catechesis* (New York: Paulist Press, 1976); Robert S. Rivers, *From Maintenance to Mission: Evangelization and the Revitalization of the Parish* (New York: Paulist Press, n.d.).

Eve   *See* ADAM AND EVE.

evil (Old Eng.: *ypel:* "evil," "bad fortune")

The existence of evil presents a special problem for monotheistic religions. They assert that GOD created everything. If evil exists, then God created it, too. The problem is further compounded by certain biblical verses that seem to say that God indeed created evil: "I made the good and I created the evil" (Isa. 5:6–7). Such verses are often finessed in translations. Such problems belong to the field of philosophical THEOLOGY traditionally called theodicy, the JUSTIFICATION of God in the face of evil.

Catholicism usually treats the problem first from the ontological and then from the ethical point of view. Ontologically speaking, most Catholic thinkers follow AUGUSTINE OF HIPPO and THOMAS AQUINAS in defining evil as an absence, privation, or defect of being; for example, an inadequate degree of virtue in a creature that is properly virtuous, such as a lack of wisdom and foresight in a parent. Augustine reasoned 1) God created everything, 2) everything created is good, 3) evil is not good, and 4) therefore evil does not exist as a separate thing, or *res*. From this he concludes, "Evil has no positive nature; but the loss of some good has the name 'evil'" (*Confession* 7.5.7; *City of God* 11.9). In this argument Augustine was seeking to counteract the doctrine of MANICHAEISM, which posited a principle of evil that was coeternal and coactive with the principle of the good.

Aquinas gave the same argument a firmer metaphysical foundation using the terminology of ARISTOTLE (*Summa Theologiae* 1a.48–49. Although evil has no positive being, or substance, it nevertheless has real effects in bringing about the loss of good. Evil arises not directly from beings, who are good in themselves, but only accidentally through the imperfections of finite creatures and their wills.

Thus, the figure of the serpent in the Garden of Eden story remains undemythologized, as one can talk about evil only indirectly through the language of symbols. Humans are responsible for the evil they commit, yet the initiation to evil did not come solely from within but also through the external trickery of the serpent (Gen. 3:13; see Rom. 7:11).

Philosophically, however, the origin of evil remains a mystery, what Immanuel Kant (1724–1804) called the "mystery of iniquity." He viewed human beings as destined for the good but inclined toward evil. Placing too much emphasis on either side of this existential "contradiction" would propel one either to a rigid predestinationism or to a radical and rootless freedom.

In the Catholic view, ethical or moral evil (SIN) presupposes the ontological condition of the loss or deprivation of the good. Though not founded in being, sin is nonetheless rooted in a deformation of the human will such that it chooses the finite good over and above the infinite good, thereby distorting its relation to the finite good itself. Ethical evil manifests itself on all levels: the personal—the individual and God—(Adam and Eve), the social (Cain and Abel), and the political (Lamech and the nations). Human responsibility for evil necessarily implies a notion of freedom of the will, which, although damaged and distorted by the FALL, retains the core of its freedom.

CHRISTIANS generally hold that ethical evil leads to suffering and death both on the spiritual and physical levels (Rom. 5:12–14). Christ's death and RESURRECTION is the beginning and foretaste of evil losing its grip on CREATION. Christians retain the hope of overcoming the evil with the good even in face of the monumental evils of the 20th century: the Holocaust and two world wars. In the Book of Genesis evil irrupts into the good creation God had made and seems to take over time and space. But following the call of Abraham, the good begins to make its way back. In the story of Joseph, the prophetic word on evil first becomes clear: even though evil is now present in the world, God has the power to take the evil that Joseph's brothers perpetrated against him and turn it to the good (50:19–21).

Further reading: Gregory C. Higgins, *Twelve Theological Dilemmas* (New York: Paulist, 1991); Gottfied S. Leibniz, *Theodicy: Essays on the Goodness of God, the Freedom of Man, and the Origin of Evil* (London: Routledge & Paul, 1952); Michael L. Peterson, ed., *The Problem of Evil: Selected Readings* (Notre Dame: University of Notre Dame Press, 1992); Bruce R. Reichenbach, *Evil and a Good God* (New York: Fordham University Press, 1982).

evolution (Lat.: *ex,* "out of" + *volvere,* "to turn," "unfold")

Evolution is the scientific hypothesis that all present life forms evolved from a single celled organism far back in geological time. The mechanism that propels such evolution was long the subject of scientific research. Jean Lamarck (1744–1829) thought that species were modified over time through the passing on of acquired characteristics. The geologist Clarence King (1842–1941) thought it was natural catastrophes such as earthquakes and volcanic explosions that provoked evolutionary change.

The dominant theory today was the one proposed jointly in 1858 by Alfred Russel Wallace (1823–1913) and Charles Robert Darwin (1809–82), generally called modification through natural selection and most thoroughly treated in Darwin's *On the Origin of Species* (1859). The modification of organisms happens through chance variations in the environment that "selects" the types of species most suited to survive (natural selection). At the beginning of the 20th century Darwin's theory was combined with the theory of genetic inheritance discovered by the Augustinian friar Gregor Mendel (1822–84). There has been much corroborating evidence for the theory of natural selection coming from the fields of paleontology, comparative anatomy, geology, biochemistry, and genetics. Today scholars date the origin of life forms on earth to a time at least 4 billion years ago.

Nearly all biologists fully accept the theory of the evolution of species; indeed, nearly all scientists believe the universe itself evolved from the moment of the Big Bang. Many evangelical or fundamentalist CHRISTIANS, who interpret the CREATION story in Genesis literally, reject Darwinian evolution and accept instead a scientific hypothesis known as creationism or creation by intelligent design. Most Catholics, however, accept the Darwinian theories to varying degrees.

After the Inquisition's disaster in the GALILEO GALILEI affair, the Catholic Church has been very slow and very reluctant to embrace or reject any given scientific hypothesis. Provided that a scientific hypothesis does not entail "godless materialism" or relativism, the Catholic Church has taken a cautiously affirmative attitude toward modern scientific discoveries. In *Humani Generis* 36 (August 12, 1950) Pope PIUS XII asserted that while God immediately creates the soul, the "origin of the human body from pre-existent and living matter" is not contrary to Catholic FAITH. In his "Message to the Pontifical Academy of Science" 4 (October 22, 1996) JOHN PAUL II stated that the theory of evolution had become "something more than a hypothesis."

Recently, however, this seeming acceptance of Darwin is being qualified. With the approval of BENEDICT XVI, when he was still Cardinal Ratzinger, Cardinal Christoph Schönborn (1945–   ) published an essay claiming that there is ample evidence for design in nature and that neo-Darwinians are wrong to limit everything to "chance and necessity." Fearing falling into a neo-Galilean fiasco, the Vatican quickly withdrew and affirmed the stance of world-renowned Vatican astronomer, Jesuit George V. Coyne, who wrote of "God's chance creation."

Scientists, however, continue to assert that the wonderful structures and processes found in nature can evolve based on the operation of the known laws of nature and chance variation. Project Avida, jointly sponsored by Michigan State University and the California Institute of Technology, simulates evolution by generating "digital organisms" that experience natural selection through random mutations and competition for limited resources. These views contradict a literalist interpretation of Scripture but do not touch on belief or nonbelief in God.

Further reading: Barbara E. Bowe, ed., *Earth, Wind, and Fire: Biblical and Theological Perspectives on Creation* (Collegeville: Liturgical Press, 2004); George V. Coyne, "God's Chance Creation," *THE TABLET* (August 6, 2005); William Kramer, *Evolution & Creation: A Catholic Understanding* (Huntington: Our Sunday Visitor, 1986); Ernan McMullin, ed., *Evolution and Creation* (Notre Dame: Notre Dame University Press, 1985); Christoph Schönborn, "Finding Design in Nature," *New York Times* (July 7, 2005).

ex cathedra (Lat.: "from the chair")

Any doctrine "of faith or morals" issued by the pope in his capacity as successor to St. Peter, speaking as pastor and teacher of the universal church, from the seat of his episcopal authority in Rome, and meant to be believed "by the universal church," has the special status of an *ex cathedra* statement. VATICAN COUNCIL I in 1870 declared that any such *ex cathedra* doctrines have the character of INFALLIBILITY (session 4, Constitution on the Church 4).

Vatican I appeared to limit this infallible teaching authority to the PAPACY, but the council was interrupted by the Franco-Prussian War of 1870 and did not complete its work. VATICAN COUNCIL II discussed the teaching authority of the church (the MAGISTERIUM) in the context of collegiality. Such authority is derived through "the successors of Peter and the other apostles" (i.e., the pope *and* the bishops). Since Vatican II, however, popes and Vatican officials have sought to constrict the council's views on collegiality and to limit the teaching authority of the church more and more to the papacy and its offices.

In the 19th century, JOHN HENRY NEWMAN advanced a concept of the magisterium that included not only pope and BISHOPS but the laity as well. He showed that during the great Christological and Trinitarian debates of the third and fourth centuries it was the laity who most often remained closest to orthodox belief, while significant numbers of deacons, theologians, and bishops, including the bishops of Rome, strayed into heretical territory.

Since the 1870 declaration on infallibility, only one such *ex cathedra* pronouncement has been made: PIUS XII's definition of the dogma of the Assumption of the Virgin Mary in the encyclical *Munificentissimus Deus* (1950). (It is generally accepted that the 1854 doctrine of the Immaculate Conception, in *Ineffabilis Deus* [1854], was also an *ex cathedra* statement.) However, BENEDICT XVI, when he was prefect for the Congregation for the Doctrine of the Faith, sought to extend the reach of the "ordinary and infallible" teaching authority of the magisterium by stating that pronouncements of JOHN PAUL II on the ordination of women where infallible although the pope made no such claim (*see* HOLY ORDERS).

See also AUTHORITY; ENCYCLICAL.

Further reading: Hans Kung, *Infallible? An Unresolved Enquiry* (New York: Continuum, 1994); John R. Page, *What Will Dr. Newman Do?: John Henry Newman and Papal Infallibility, 1865–1875* (Collegeville, Minn.: Liturgical Press, 1994); Klaus Schatz, *Papal Primacy: From its Origins to the Present,* tr. John A. Otto and Linda M. Maloney (Collegeville, Minn.: Liturgical Press, 1996); Brian Tierney, *Origins of Papal Infallibility, 1150–1350: A Study on the Concepts of Infallibility, Sovereignty and Tradition in the Middle Ages* (Leiden: Brill, 1988).

excommunication (Lat.: *ex,* "out of" + *communio,* "communion, fellowship")

Excommunication is a formal penalty in CANON LAW by which a member of the church is excluded from its full fellowship and is prohibited from receiving any of its SACRAMENTS or partaking in other privileges. The penalty is more severe than and differs from INTERDICT, which bars one from participating in public worship but is not a full exclusion from the church itself. However, even an excommunicated person may remain in sanctifying grace.

Canon law is presently very wary about imposing excommunication, and the offenses must be genuinely serious. Certain excommunications are considered automatic (*late sententiae*) on the performance of a particularly notorious or offensive act. Acts that incur automatic excommunication include consecration of a bishop by an excommunicated bishop, the use of the confessional to absolve an accomplice in murder, a breach of the confessional, an abortion, the profanation of the EUCHARIST, and an assault of a pope. In June 2003 seven Catholic women in Austria, known as the Danube seven were ordained to the priesthood, an act that caused both the women and the others who actively participated in the event to be automatically excommunicated by the church. Other excommunications occur only as a result of an ecclesiastical trial or process (*ferendae sententiae*).

Excommunication can be lifted after the offender performs a suitable penance. Certain offenses, such as the desecration of the EUCHARIST, require Rome's permission in order to rectify an excommunicant's status.

In recent times certain conservative or traditionalist Catholics have incurred excommunication. Most notable have been the Jesuit Leonard Feeney (d. 1978), who taught that no one could be saved outside the Catholic Church. Archbishop Marcel Lefebre (d. 1991) was excommunicated for rejecting VATICAN COUNCIL II (*see* TRADITIONALISTS). In more recent times many theologians, notably LEONARDO BOFF, CHARLES CURRAN, Balasuriya Tissa, and many others, have been implicitly threatened with excommunication for their theological positions by the Congregation for the Doctrine of the Faith under the direction of Joseph Ratzinger, now BENEDICT XVI. In 2006 Archbishop Raymond Burke (1948–   ) of St. Louis excommunicated the trustees of St. Stanislaus Parish for refusing to turn over the financial assets to diocesan control.

Further reading: Francis Edward Hyland, *Excommunication, Its Nature, Historical Development and Effects* (Washington, D.C.: Catholic University of America Press, 1928); Elisabeth Vodola, *Excommunication in the Middle Ages* (Berkeley: University of California Press, 1986).

exegesis   *See* BIBLE.

ex opere operato (Lat. "from the work done")

This technical phrase originated in the 13th century to describe the objectivity of the GRACE of GOD conferred in the performance of a SACRAMENT, even when administered illegally by priest. The doctrine was formally defined at the Council of TRENT (session 7, On the Sacraments in General, cn. 8).

The reasoning behind this formula reaches back to AUGUSTINE OF HIPPO. His DONATIST opponents argued that a sacrament was invalid if it was conferred by a priest or other minister who had previously fallen away from the FAITH through SCHISM, HERESY, or corruption. Augustine argued that it is God and CHRIST who confer the sacrament, and the grace contained does not depend on either the minister's or the recipient's subjective state. To be effective the grace conferred does depend on the faith of the recipient.

Further reading: Alberto Dal Maso, *L'efficacia dei Sacramenti e la "Performance" Rituale: Ripensare l'"ex opere operato" a Partire Dall'antropologia Culturale* (Padua: Abbazia di Santa Giustina, 1999); Constantin von Schaezler, *Die lehre von der Wirksamkeit der Sakramente ex opere operato in ihrer Entwicklung innerhalb der Scholastik und ihrer Bedeutung fur die Christliche Heilslehre* (Munich: J.J. Lentner'schen Buchhandlung, 1860); Josep Lligadas Vendrell, *La Eficacia de los Sacramentos: "ex opere operato" en la Doctrina del Concilio de Trento* (Barcelona: Pontificia Universidad Gregoriana, 1983).

exorcism (Gk.: *ek*, "out of" + *horkizein*, "to cause to swear")

Exorcism is a religious (and not magical) rite that relieves people of demonic and other spiritually obsessive possessions. In early Christianity, exorcism became both an incidental ritual and a part of the standard baptismal rite.

There are few mentions of exorcism in the Old Testament. In the intertestimental apocryphal Book of Tobit (6:7–18 and 8:1–3) Raphael uses the gall, heart and liver of a fish to free a victim of possession. Exorcism was very common throughout the Greco-Roman world. Exorcists and magicians claimed the ability to cure people of demon possession by the use of ritual formulas and acts that included purifications, sacrifices, and the use of material elements like clay and herbs. (Plutarch, *Moralia* 706E). The Hellenistic wonderworker Apollonius of Tyana was renowned as an exorcist much like Jesus.

The GOSPEL of Mark places great emphasis on the many exorcisms of Jesus, who casts out EVIL spirits (5:1–10). The expulsion of demons was a sign of the coming kingdom of GOD (Luke 11:14–22). Acts mentions two exorcisms of pagan persons by PAUL (16:16–18; 19:12). In the Diaspora Jews were often seen as exorcists and sorcerers (Acts 13:6). Celsus accused CHRISTIANS of using magic in their exorcisms, but ORIGEN defended the moral aspect of exorcism (Origen, *Against Celsus* 1.6, 68).

Exorcism of evil spirits became a preliminary rite to BAPTISM among early Christians (Hippolytus, *Apostolic Constitution* 20–21). Fourth-century Christian texts include exorcists among the types of CLERGY. In the MIDDLE AGES exorcists ranked among the minor orders.

In modern times, the Catholic Church has shied away from exorcism, due in part to discoveries in psychiatry and in part as a reaction to sensationalized novels and movies like *The Exorcist* (1973). Exorcism has been judiciously reintroduced into the Rite of Adult Baptism (1972). Pope JOHN PAUL II reportedly performed at least three exorcisms, one each in 1982, 2000, and 2001.

Further reading: Roger Baker, *Binding the Devil: Exorcism Past and Present* (New York: Hawthorn, 1975); J. Forget, "Exorcisme," *Dictionaire de Théologie Catholique* (1913) 5:1762–80; S. Vernon McCasland, *By the Finger of God: Demon Possession and Exorcism in Early Christianity in the Light of Modern Views of Mental Illness* (New York: Macmillan, 1951); John Richards, *But Deliver Us from Evil: An Introduction to the Demonic Dimension in Pastoral Care* (New York: Seabury Press, 1974).

F

faith (Lat.: *fides,* "faith, trust")

The word *faith* has its ultimate origin in the Indo-European root *beidh,* meaning to trust or to set one's heart on. It is cognate with the Latin *foedus,* "covenant," from which the term *federal* is derived. The Hebrew word *'emunah,* the Greek *pisteuein,* and the Latin parallel term *credere* share many of the same meanings.

Sometimes scholars make a distinction between faith and belief in the religious context. In this context faith means the whole orientation and attitude of one's life before GOD, while belief means the assent to or affirmation of certain propositions implied by faith or held by the faith community. In practice, however, the term embraces a range of meanings from a truth to be believed (Eph. 4:5), to a confidence issuing in action (Heb. 11), or implicit trust.

Theologically, faith is defined as the open acceptance of God's self-communication, which places the believer into a free personal and communal relation with God. The paradigm and paragon of faith was Abraham, who along with Sarah and his family, left his secure home in Haran (Gen. 12:1–9). For many years Abraham wandered with only the promise of progeny, home, and livelihood. Because he had faith in God's blessing, God credited him with righteousness (15:6). PAUL sees Abraham and Sarah as the pattern of all who have faith, and, indeed, they are the true pattern for CHRIST (Rom. 4). They experienced the first RESURRECTION, since their "dead" loins and womb were regenerated to produce the new life of Isaac.

Faith is central to all of the Abrahamic religions (Judaism, Christianity, and Islam). Most often the term refers to the faithfulness of God who keeps God's covenant and word (Deut. 7:9; Ps. 145:13). But it also means Abraham's trust that God will keep the divine promises. This also means that Abrahamic faith has a historical dimension: God wills the salvation of all people (1 Tim. 2:3–7) and accomplishes the divine purposes in time and space, redeeming Israel from bondage and bringing the believer out of death to new life.

In the Book of Genesis faith is also a trust that CREATION and time are good from the beginning (1:31), a recognition that this original goodness was deflected and distorted by the entrance of SIN and EVIL in the world (3:17–19), and a deeper faith that God can take evil and turn it to the good the way he took the evil deed of Joseph's brothers and transformed it into good for the people of Israel (50:21) and indeed for EGYPT.

In the New Testament faith is centered on Jesus CHRIST, his special relationship to the Father, his mission as the fulfillment of the promise of a Messiah who will inaugurate the messianic kingdom of God, his power over natural forces and the demonic, and his atoning work of salvation and redemption from DEATH and evil (1 Cor. 15:12–28).

In the early Church faith entailed trust in the saving work of God as well as an ethical commitment to live one's life in accord with that faith. The supreme act of faith was the celebration of the EUCHARIST. Thus, there was no separation of "faith" and "works," no placing one against, above, or prior to the other (James 2:17). Paul's famous distinction between faith and "works of the law" was meant to be understood narrowly: new Gentile believers did not have to follow the rites of CIRCUMCISION or the kosher food laws in order to be followers of Christ. Paul was not formulating a general opposition between faith and works or ethical conduct. A broader distinction between faith and works is relevant to the issues of the PROTESTANT REFORMATION but does not accord with first-century Christian experience.

Beginning in the second century orthodox theologians began to develop a "rule of faith" (regula fidei) to counter what they took to be the "false" knowledge of the GNOSTICS. The rule pointed to three articles, or benchmarks, that later evolved into the three fundamental articles of the CREED covering 1) creation, 2) redemption, and 3) sanctification. All subsequent theologians agreed with CLEMENT OF ALEXANDRIA that faith is "a grace (charis) of God" (Stromata 1.7.38.4), yet they began articulating that faith using the language and concepts of Hellenistic philosophy (logos, or "word/reason," homoousios, or "same being," ousia, or "being/essence," etc.). Thus, reason came into relation with faith. Reason could fortify one's faith, which in turn could lead to the true gnosis, which leads to salvation.

Other theologians like CYPRIAN OF CARTHAGE began to understand faith in ecclesial terms as the assent or affirmation to the teachings defined, shaped, and guided by church authorities. This led to the later propositional understanding of faith. Following AUGUSTINE, St. THOMAS AQUINAS defined faith as "assent with cognition" and said that assent was the act of affirming or denying true or false judgments (On Truth 14.1). In this way the notion of faith became coordinate with the notion of reason (see FAITH AND REASON). In medieval theology faith was elevated to one of the theological virtues along with hope and love (1 Cor. 13:12–13). Most importantly, faith was necessary for salvation (Thomas Aquinas, Summa Theologiae 2a–2ae.2.3; DUNS SCOTUS, Oxoniense 1.3.23).

Medieval theologians distinguished between fides qua, the act of faith, and fides quae, the content of faith. As faith is a supernaturally infused virtue, the distinction is not exactly the same as between the purely subjective and purely objective aspects of faith. In general the medievalists thought that natural reason could deduce that God exists but not what God is in the divine inner nature nor the deeper truths of revelation in the Gospel (creation from nothing, INCARNATION, TRINITY, etc.). However, they often differed about the ultimate powers of unaided reason.

The Council of TRENT sought to counter what it believed to be Martin Luther's overemphasis on faith as subjective trust. Instead, it stressed that faith is a free response on the part of a believer, even though God infuses the initial grace. VATICAN COUNCIL I, following the lead of Pope Gregory XVI (r. 1831–46) in his Theses Argentoratenses (September 8, 1840) fought against two distortions in the understanding of faith: an overweening rationalism that denies all need for faith, and an overweening fideism that disparages the use of reason in matters pertaining to faith.

Without obscuring any of the above dogmatic content, VATICAN COUNCIL II revitalized the earlier CHRISTIAN understanding that faith is the response of the whole person to the saving revelation of God. It also recognized that the faith of Christians not in communion with Rome both nourishes and bears fruit (*Unitatis Redintegratio* 23, Decree on Ecumenism). The council declared that since faith is the absolutely free response to God's absolutely free self-communication to humanity, there can be absolutely no coercion when inviting someone to faith (*Dignitatis Humanae* 12, Declaration on Religious Freedom); this contradicted the practices of many earlier Catholics, including many in the HIERARCHY.

Further reading: Romanus Cessario, *Christian Faith and the Theological Life* (Washington, D.C.: Catholic University of America Press, 1996); William V. Dych, *The Mystery of Faith: A Christian Creed for Today* (Collegeville, Minn.: Liturgical Press, 1995); Heinrich Fries, *Fundamental Theology* (Washington, D.C.: Catholic University of America Press, 1996); Gilbert Meilaender, *Faith and Faithfulness: Basic Themes in Christian Ethics* (Notre Dame: University of Notre Dame Press, 1991).

faith and reason

Catholic teaching strives to avoid two pitfalls in the relation between faith and reason: an excessive rationalism that dismisses faith as superstition, and an excessive fideism that denies all power to natural reason to know GOD and God's attributes without the help of divine REVELATION. The faith-reason relation can be stated also as the relation between philosophy and THEOLOGY, or faith and knowledge, or reason and revelation.

In the New Testament, especially the Gospel of John, there was no conflict between faith and knowledge. Many early CHRISTIAN theologians like JUSTIN MARTYR were converts who had studied secular philosophy; their apologetic treatises were aimed not to contrast faith and knowledge but, on the contrary, to demonstrate that the Christian faith was the true philosophy (*Dialogue with Trypho* 2).

TERTULLIAN is often quoted as saying *credo quia impossibile/absurdum est*—"I believe because (the Gospel, and the miracle of the INCARNATION) is impossible/absurd." However, that quote is a mistranslation and taken out of context. Tertullian actually said *credibile est, quia ineptum est*—"It is believable because it is unlikely"—and was basing his argument on ARISTOTLE's *Rhetoric* (2.23.22), which argues that some stories are believable precisely because they are improbable—who would make them up?

Theologians and church councils did not hesitate to use Greek philosophical concepts in the explication of the faith—the *logos* (word, reason, cause) of Stoicism and Neoplatonism, the general notion of being (*ousia*) or of person (*hypostatis*). AUGUSTINE does not even distinguish philosophy from theology in his Christian Neoplatonic explication of the great themes of the Christian faith.

The MIDDLE AGES was interested in the overall role of natural reason in philosophy and its relation to theology and biblical revelation. The medievalists all followed the lead of Augustine and ANSELM, pursuing understanding out of faith (*credo ut intelligam,* "I believe that I may understand"). They thus needed to understand what they believed. When Aristotle (the "Philosopher") was brought into the medieval system of thought, the question was more sharply put: what can natural reason, unaided by revelation, know on its own? The usual answer was that natural reason could demonstrate the CREATION of the world, the existence of God, and many of God's attributes, such as infinity, goodness, omniscience, and omnipotence, but not those truths specifically dependent on revelation—providence, creation in time, the INCARNATION, and the nature of the TRINITY (THOMAS AQUINAS, *Summa Theologiae* 1.2.1–3; DUNS SCOTUS, *Ordinatio* 1.2.1.39–190; *On the First Principle*).

The medieval understanding of the relation was a continuum. There were truths that reason could know on its own, there were truths that faith and reason share, and there were deeper truths that could be known only through revelation. The medievalists also talked about the "preambles of faith," including the power of reason to deduce a God, the intellectual powers of humans to know the truth and to receive revelation, human freedom, and the ability to discern natural and moral law.

With WILLIAM OF OCKHAM the relationship began to tilt toward the side of faith. Ockham upheld both the BIBLE and church authority as the true foundations of faith, but not of reason. Luther dispensed with church authority and opted for "Scripture alone" and "faith alone." He believed that Aristotelian reason was the "devil's bride" and a "pretty whore" that cooked up laws and works to take the place of the word of God ("Last Sermon at Wittenberg"). Luther in effect created a dichotomy between faith and reason, a divide that even the rationalists of the 18th century failed to bridge.

The Enlightenment philosopher Immanuel Kant (1724–1804) took the divide for granted when he claimed to "deny *knowledge* in order to make room for *faith*" (*Critique of Pure Reason* Bxxx). The Enlightenment philosopher Voltaire showed the breadth of the split when he wrote in his *Dictionaire philosophique* "Faith consists in believing when it is beyond the power of reason to believe." G. F. W. Hegel (1770–1831), according to some, tried to "subsume" faith into absolute knowing, but in the *Lectures on Religion* (1832) he retained the dialectic of faith and reason to the end and spoke of the "piety of knowing." After Hegel, the idea of faith in European thought became increasingly downgraded and associated with superstition, fetishism, and self-projection (Ludwig Feuerbach), an opiate leading to self-delusion (Karl Marx), a resentment of the Christian masses against the pagan nobility (Friedrich Nietzsche), and infantile wish-fulfillment (Sigmund Freud).

VATICAN COUNCIL I in its Declaration on Faith (session 3.3) tried to counteract this divide by upholding the powers of natural reason to know God and to find the path to true religion, while sharply criticizing excessive fideism. Noting the human propensity to err, PIUS XII reaffirmed natural knowledge of God in *Humani Generis*

(August 12, 1950). Without abrogating Vatican I's traditional propositional understanding of the relation of faith and reason, VATICAN COUNCIL II saw revelation as the fundamental sacramental self-revelation of God in creation. Reason, though fully empowered, never operates outside the realm of grace in coming to know and love God. Culture and the human reason that shapes it is constantly renewed, purified, strengthened, and made fruitful by "the good news of Christ" (*Gaudium et Spes* 58–59, Pastoral Constitution on the Church in the Modern World).

Further reading: Curtis L. Hancock and Brendan Sweetman, eds., *Faith & the Life of the Intellect* (Washington, D.C.: Catholic University of America Press, 2003); Laurence Paul Hemming and Susan Frank Parsons, eds., *Restoring Faith in Reason: With a new Translation of the Encyclical Letter Faith and Reason of Pope John Paul II* (Notre Dame: University of Notre Dame Press, 2003); Alvin Plantinga and Nicholas Wolterstorff, eds., *Faith and Rationality: Reason and Belief in God* (Notre Dame: University of Notre Dame Press, 1983); Robert Sokolowski, *The God of Faith and Reason: Foundations of Christian Theology* (Notre Dame: University of Notre Dame Press, 1982).

Fall, the

Early CHRISTIANS referred to the first SIN of humanity in Genesis 3 as the Fall. In the traditional understanding, Genesis 1:1–2:4a shows that GOD created the world good. However, while God blesses the first humans and gives them dominion over the earth, they are not called good, perhaps in anticipation of their capacity to do EVIL. When Eve and Adam (*see* ADAM AND EVE) defy the Lord and eat of the tree of the knowledge of good and evil, the text of the BIBLE does not call this a "fall" or "lapse" on the part of humanity. Instead, it shows Eve and Adam tricked by the serpent. The deed results in enmity and discord between God and humans, Eve and the serpent, Adam and the earth, and Adam and Eve. The two first people are expelled from the settled ease of the garden to a life of nomadic wandering.

PAUL did not speak of original sin in AUGUSTINE's sense but of the primal sin of Adam that brings death with it and spreads further and deeper among the children of Adam and Eve (Gen. 4:1–6:8; Rom. 5:12). The life-giving righteousness of CHRIST, anticipated in the life-yielding faith of Abraham and Sarah (Rom. 4), begins the reversal of the sway of sin and DEATH over Jew and Gentile alike (5:15–18).

The early Greek theologians interpreted the events in Genesis as a "fall" from an original innocence and purity through an abuse of FREE WILL on the part of both Eve and Adam (JUSTIN MARTYR, 2 *Apology* 5; ORIGEN, *Principles* 3.2.2). The punishment—mortality and subjection to the passions—was contrasted with the original state (CLEMENT OF ALEXANDRIA, *Stromata* 3.12.88), variously described as an angelic state, immortality, or at least the potential for immortality. In any case, they lost it.

These theologians were hard put to explain how Adam, who enjoyed the direct vision of God in the divine goodness, fell into evil. Some speculated that though created good, the original pair had a defective nature and an inclination toward evil. The slip into carnality and sensuality after the Fall became the model of how not to behave, which helps explain later practices such as ASCETICISM.

AUGUSTINE OF HIPPO gave the West a most fateful interpretation of the Fall. He interpreted Genesis 3 both literally and figuratively. Adam and Eve had natural bodies but were able to hold off lust (*concupiscentia*) by partaking of the sacrament of the Tree of Life. When they rebelled out of pride and became the playthings of their senses, their sin was transmitted hereditarily (as original sin) through sexual intercourse. In consequence, he believed, intercourse was always attached to lust, even in sacramental marriage (*Marriage and Lust* 2.8.20). Augustine opposed PELAGIUS, who, in his judgment, underestimated the effects of the

Fall on subsequent humanity. Augustine's view prevailed; if anything, it became more influential during the PROTESTANT REFORMATION, whose leaders cited Augustine in their insistence on the total depravity of fallen humanity.

Many theologians, following Augustine, believed desire could not be reconciled to divine grace on earth. Others, like IRENAEUS OF LYONS, thought that Adam and Eve had merely been immature; the Fall motivated them to spiritual growth (*Heresies* 4.38.1–4). Augustine looked at the impossibility of perfection in time, Irenaeus at the possibility of progress. The Latin EASTER Vigil LITURGY expressed the ultimately redemptive and pedagogical effect of the Fall in a wonderful expression: "O happy fault (*felix culpa*) that merited as its reward so great and so good a redeemer."

Further reading: Frans Jozef van Beeck, *God Encountered: A Contemporary Catholic Systematic Theology,* vol. 2 (San Francisco: Harper & Row, 1989); Dietrich Bonhoeffer, *Creation and Fall: A Theological Interpretation of Genesis 1–3,* trans John C. Fletcher (New York: Macmillan, 1959); Ernest A. Dawson, *The Atonement: A Catholic Restatement* (London: Mowbray, 1993).

family (Lat.: *familia,* "a group of close kin")

In the BIBLE a family is a community of persons related by ties of marriage and descent. In the Old Testament people traced their descent through the male line; the governing structure of the kinship system was patriarchal, as the stories in Genesis make abundantly clear. (Today Jews trace descent through the maternal line.) The word *house* (Heb. *bet,* Gk. *oikos*) was the most common biblical term for the household family (Gen. 14:14; Matt. 12:15). The terms for clan and household were also used, as was the Greco-Roman patriarchal designation *patria* in the New Testament (Luke 2:4).

Honor to one's parents was one of the Commandments (Exod. 20:12), a longstanding pious tradition in ancient Israel (Eccles. 7:27–28) and a tradition upheld in the New Testament (Matt. 15:4;

Eph. 6:2). The New Testament also adopted and adapted the traditional Greco-Roman household codes for church life (Col. 3:18–4:1); the relation between a BISHOP and the church was expressed as a "household of God" (1 Tim. 3:1–16). The Romans stressed the family as the seedbed of the state (Cicero *On Duties* 1.54). AUGUSTINE saw the family as the first natural bond, or covenant, of society (*On the Good of Marriage* 1.1).

With the exception of Paul, it seems that all the early APOSTLES were married and had extended families, though this fact is in the background in the New Testament as it now stands. Marriage and family was the normal state for bishops, priests, and deacons until the rise of ascetic MONASTICISM in the third and fourth centuries. The wondrous stories of ascetic MONKs and NUNs began to overshadow the everyday reality of married CLERGY. This left a legacy of tension between the family and the ascetic and monastic life in Christianity. In the MIDDLE AGES the religious life was often valued over family life.

Despite this hierarchical tendency, many theologians saw the family as the true model of the church (JOHN CHRYSOSTOM, *Homilies on Genesis*). Pope LEO XIII reaffirmed this when he called the family the "first form of the church" in his encyclical on marriage, *Arcanum Divinae Spientiae* (February 10, 1880). In *Lumen Gentium* 11, The Dogmatic Constitution on the Church, VATICAN COUNCIL II declared that the family is "the domestic church." In fact, Vatican II gave great emphasis to the Catholic family, which it saw as a "community of love" (*Gaudium et Spes* 49, Pastoral Constitution on the Church in the Modern World) and the "apprenticeship for the apostolate" (*Apostolicam Actuositatem* 30, Decree on the Apostolate of the Laity).

These themes were repeated again and again in the subsequent encyclicals of PAUL VI, JOHN PAUL I, and JOHN PAUL II. In his visit to the United States in 1987, John Paul II said that the parish is a "family of families." At the direction of the Synod of Bishops in 1980, the Vatican issued a "Charter of the Rights of the Family" (November 24, 1983). In 1988 the United States Conference of Catholic Bishops issued "A Family Perspective in Church and Society," which summed up Catholic teaching since Vatican II and pledged to find pastoral ways for the family to move "from crisis to growth, from stress to strength." As many have said, as the Catholic family goes, so goes the church.

Today Catholic families are afflicted with a high incidence of divorce, family abuse of varying kinds, and a failure on the part of the church to support families as families and not just adjunct institutions attached to the local parish. On the other hand, many dioceses provide resources and programs to aid the Catholic family.

Further reading: Mitch and Kathy Finley, *Christian Families in a Real World: Reflections on a Spirituality for the Domestic Church* (Chicago: Thomas More, 1984); *Handbook for Today's Catholic Family: Foundations, Prayers, Resources* (Ligouri: Ligouri Press, 1979); Paulinus Ikechukwu Odozor, ed., *Sexuality, Marriage, and Family: Readings in the Catholic Tradition* (Notre Dame: University of Notre Dame Press, 2001); Julie Hanlon Rubio, *A Christian Theology of Marriage and Family* (New York: Paulist, 2003); John L. Thomas, *The American Catholic Family* (Westport, Conn.: Greenwood, 1980).

Farley, Margaret A. (1935–   ) *professor and moral theologian*

A contemporary moral theologian, Farley holds the Gilbert L. Stark Chair in CHRISTIAN Ethics at Yale University Divinity School and has been teaching since 1971. She specializes in medical, sexual, and social ethics. She is also involved with various organizations that promote a positive Roman Catholic Church response to HIV/AIDS in AFRICA. She has also emerged as one of the prominent voices for feminist concerns in the North American church, and in 1996 she coedited *Feminist Ethics and the Catholic Moral Tradition* with fellow moral theologian CHARLES CURRAN.

Further reading: Charles Curran, Margaret A. Farley, and Richard A. McCormick, eds., *Feminist Ethics and the Catholic Moral Tradition* (New York: Paulist Press, 1996); Margaret A. Farley, *Personal Commitments: Beginning, Keeping, Changing* (New York: Harper & Row, 1986).

fascism (Lat.: *fasces,* "bundle of rods")

A fasces, a bundle of rods tied around an axe, was a symbol of authority for higher magistrates in ancient Rome. It lent its name to a nationalistic, militarist political movement that managed to set up dictatorial governments in several European countries in the first half of the 20th century.

As an ideology, fascism was a mixed bag of Marxist, corporatist, nationalist, and socialist ideas with a dash of Nietzsche. Its ideologue in Italy, the first fascist country, was Giovanni Gentile (1875–1944). The early *fascisti* were left-wing socialists, or adherents of syndicalism, a political ideology that advocated giving control of industry and labor to labor federations. Benito Mussolini (1883–1945) was the first to use the name to describe his movement and the government system he established, which was supposedly based on a Romantic corporate notion of the nation and was opposed to both capitalism and socialism. He had wide support in the lower and middle classes for his stated policies: populism, separation of church and state, and progressive taxation. These policies were abandoned one by one as circumstances dictated.

Mussolini formed an army of thugs ("Black Shirts") to enforce his policies in every corner of civic, legal, religious, and economic life. Fascists were vehemently opposed to democracy, socialism, and communism. He ended parliamentary government in 1928 and ruled as a dictator ("Il Duce") thereafter. Adolf Hitler (1889–1945) adopted many of Mussolini's tactics of intimidation. After the latter's alliance with Hitler, fascism took on more and more of National Socialism's racist agenda.

Some scholars claim that Mussolini had church support for his philosophy by citing LEO XIII's *Rerum Novarum* (May 15, 1891), which spoke against the ill effects of unbridled free enterprise and used the language of class struggle as advocated by many socialists. However, in 1919, Dom Luigi Sturzo (1871–1959) founded the Popular Party as a Catholic party to counteract Mussolini. The party might have won support, but PIUS XI suppressed it in favor of the nonpolitical Catholic Action movement. When Mussolini tried to suppress even that group, the pope struck back with *Non Abbiamo Bisogno* (June 29, 1931), accusing the fascist of pagan "Statolatry." This tense situation did not prevent the Vatican from signing the Lateran Treaty/CONCORDAT with Mussolini in 1929, which created the modern VATICAN CITY.

In the World War II era, the Catholic Church found itself compromised in its relations with the fascist Austrian chancellor Kurt von Schussnigg (1897–1977) in the mid-1930s; with Monsignor Jozef Tiso (1887–1947), a priest who governed Slovakia under the Nazis and did their bidding; and with the Catholic-linked Ustashe party, led by Ante Pavelić (1889–1959), which governed Croatia under the Nazis. The Vichy government, which ruled much of FRANCE under Nazi hegemony, had links with the Catholic Action Française movement, which also fell under this heading. The closest link between Catholicism and a fascistlike government was with the Falange of Francisco Franco (1892–1975), who ruled SPAIN as a dictator from 1939 until his death in 1975. The link between fascism and Catholicism is not a flattering one for the latter.

Further reading: Carl Amery, *Katholizismus und Fascismus* (Dusseldorf: Patmos, 1970); Frank J. Coppa, *Controversial Concordats: The Vatican's Relations with Napoleon, Mussolini, and Hitler* (Washington, D.C.: Catholic University of America Press, 1999); Peter Godman, *Hitler and the Vatican: Inside the Secret Archives that Reveal the New Story of the Nazis and the Church* (New York: Free Press, 2004); John F. Pollard, *The Vatican* *and Italian Fascism, 1929–32: A Study in Conflict* (Cambridge: Cambridge University Press, 1985); Richard J. Wolff and Jorg K. Hoensch, eds., *Catholics, the State, and the European Radical Right, 1919–1945* (Highland Lakes, N.J.: Atlantic Research, 1987).

fate (Lat.: *fatum,* "something spoken and therefore determined")

Both the Greeks and Romans believed in fate, a force that determined the destinies of human beings. Fate was beyond the control of humans and even of the Olympian gods. The force was personified as the three Fates (Gk.: *moirai;* Lat.: *parcae*), known as Clotho, the one who spins fate; Lachesis, the one who assigns fate; and Atropos, the one who determines that fate is unavoidable (Hesiod, *Theogony* 219). They were represented respectively by a spindle, a pointing scepter, and scales. They also carried staffs or scepters as signs of authority equal to the gods.

The tension between the gods and fate and between freedom and fatalism is a theme in Greek thought (Plato, *Republic* 617c). The Old Testament contains some wisdom sayings that can be understood as semifatalistic, such as the famous "time for all things" passage in Ecclesiastes 3:1–8, but there is no concept of a fateful force governing human fortunes. Similarly, the New Testament does not use the word fate nor talk about it. Some texts seem to strongly oppose astrology as a means of determining one's fate (Rom. 8:38–39), and other early CHRISTIAN writings prohibited astrology altogether (*Didachē* 3.4). The Synod of Braga (561) in Portugal condemned the idea that the celestial bodies control the body or mind, which it attributed to the Priscillians.

Later Christian thinkers felt they had to deal with the question of fate, as it was such an important topic in Greek thought. Minucius Felix (fl. late 2nd century) insisted that the mind remains free but that fate may be understood as divine foreknowledge. ORIGEN argued strongly that what happens to us is determined not by outside forces but by our FREE WILL (*On First Principles* 3.11–2). GREGORY OF NYSSA wrote a whole treatise *Against Fate* along the same lines.

Notwithstanding long-term Christian prohibitions against the ideas of fate and astrology, the practice of getting one's astrological charts read became very popular in the Renaissance among princes and commoners, both Catholic and Protestant. The celebrated astronomer Johannes Kepler (1571–1630) earned much of his income preparing such charts.

Today nearly every newspaper in the world has a horoscope page. The recurrence of astrology, crystal magic, belief in reincarnation, palmistry, Tarot cards, and other "New Age" practices, all implying some belief in the idea of fate, has elicited a strong reaction on the part of the Vatican in a recent report, *Sects and New Religion Movements: A Pastoral Challenge* (May 3, 1986), issued jointly by the Vatican Secretariat for Promoting Christian Unity, the Secretariat for Non-Christians, the Secretariat for Non-Believers, and the Pontifical Council for Culture. The document is a mixture of scholarship, apologia, and, in some aspects, vitriol. The members of New Age movements, in turn, took the document to task for distortions, falsifications, and outright hostility. Following the arguments of the Vatican document, Archbishop Noberto Rivera Carrera (1942–   ) of Mexico City issued a pastoral letter "A Call to Vigilance: A Pastoral Instruction on New Age" (January 7, 1996).

Further reading: W. C. Greene, *Moira: Fate, Good and Evil in Greek Thought* (Cambridge, Mass.: Harvard University Press, 1943, 1963); Justin Martyr, *1 Apology* 43–44, available online; Joseph Owens, *Human Destiny: Some Problems for Catholic Philosophy* (Washington: Catholic University of America Press, 1985).

fathers and mothers of the church

The term *father* was at first applied to all BISHOPS, who carried on the tradition of the APOSTLES.

By the end of the fourth century the term had become restricted to certain theological writers in the church whose teachings carried special weight. Today priests are addressed as "father."

In the Christology (see CHRIST/CHRISTOLOGY) debates that marked the early church certain theologians were frequently cited as authorities for one or another party, and their status consequently increased. For example, the sixth-century Gelasian decree lists authoritative scriptures, teachings, and "Holy Fathers," which included bishops, theologians like St. JEROME, and the layperson Prosper of Aquitane (c. 390–c. 455). St. Vincent of Lérins (d. before 450) referred to authoritative teachings as *quod ubique semper, quod ab omnibus* ("what has everywhere [been believed], always and by all" (*Commonitorium* 2). In the East the following theologicans came to be seen as the most authoritative fathers: Sts. ATHANASIUS OF ALEXANDRIA, GREGORY OF NYSSA, BASIL THE GREAT, GREGORY OF NAZIANZUS, and JOHN CHRYSOSTOM. The West had Sts. Jerome, AMBROSE OF MILAN, AUGUSTINE OF HIPPO, and GREGORY THE GREAT.

In the past 10 years, as a result of the astonishing recovery and reconstruction of many early Christian texts written by Ammas (Aram. "mothers") in the desert, the expression fathers is being expanded to include mothers. The sayings of Sts. Sarah, Theodora, and Synelethia appear in the collection *Sayings of the Desert Fathers*, even though that collection has come down to us under an exclusively male title.

Further reading: Hans von Campenhausen, *The Fathers of the Church* (Peabody, Mass.: Hendrickson, 1998); Frederick J. Cwiekowski, *The Beginnings of the Church* (New York: Paulist, 1988); Mary Forman, *Praying with the Desert Mothers* (Collegeville, Minn.: Liturgical Press, 2005); Saint Jerome, *On Illustrious Men* (Washington, D.C.: Catholic University of America Press, 1999); John Henry Newman, *The Church of the Fathers* (New York: Lane, 1900); Laura Swan, *The Forgotten Desert Mothers: Sayings, Lives, and Stories of Early Christian Women* (New York: Paulist, 2001).

feast days

Feasts are special days in the LITURGICAL YEAR for the celebration of important events in the life of CHRIST, Mary, the saints, or the CHRISTIAN people as a community. The first and foremost Christian feast was EASTER, the day of RESURRECTION; all other feasts can be seen as derivatives from it. After CONSTANTINE's Edict of Milan (313) Sunday (Easter Day) became a universal day of rest, replacing the Jewish Sabbath. Early on Christians distinguished between movable and immovable feasts. Movable feasts can be celebrated on varying days; immovable are on the same fixed day each year. Easter is the prime movable feast: the Council of Nicaea (325) fixed its celebration to the first Sunday after the first full moon after the spring equinox, which could occur anywhere between March 23 and April 25 in today's calendar. This date in turn determines the date of the Feasts of the Ascension (40 days later), Pentecost (50 days later), as well as Ash Wednesday (forty days before). The most important immovable feasts are Christmas (December 25), and the various saints' birthdays and martyrs' days. Feast days have individual propers—special antiphons, hymns, and readings—for the EUCHARIST and PRAYER OF THE HOURS.

Since Vatican II the greatest feasts are called solemnities, and lesser feasts are called simply feasts or memorials. Some feasts are feasts of obligation, on which the faithful are required to hear mass on the day itself or on its vigil the day before. They are Sundays, Easter, Christmas, the Epiphany (January 6), the ASCENSION, Corpus Christi, the Solemnities of the Blessed Virgin MARY OF NAZARETH (January 1), the Assumption (August 15), the Immaculate Conception (December 8), and the feasts of St. JOSEPH (May 1), Sts. PETER and PAUL (June 29), and ALL SAINTS (November 1). They are listed in the *Code of Canon Law*, cn. 1246.

Further reading: Daniel Donovan, *Preparing for Worship: Sundays and Feast Days* (New York: Paulist, 1993); Meredith Gould, *The Catholic Home: Celebrations and Traditions for Holidays, Feast Days, and Every Day* (New York:

Doubleday, 2004); George Poulos, *Lives of the Saints and Major Feast Days* (Brookline, Mass.: Greek Orthodox Archdiocese of North and South America, 1974); *The Rites of the Catholic Church* (New York: Pueblo, 1983).

fees, ecclesiastical

In times past, BISHOPS, priests, and deacons received fees for the performance of liturgical functions. This practice led to much abuse, first in the purchasing of ecclesiastical offices as a source of income and second in the sale of spiritual matters (simony). Today the sale or purchase of a SACRA-MENT incurs the penalty of interdict or suspension for both parties (*Code of Canon Law,* cn. 1380). In many places, however, it is still very much the custom for parishioners make FREE-WILL offerings or donations either to an officiant or to the church on the occasions of BAPTISM, CONFIRMATION, MARRIAGE, and first Holy Communion.

Further reading: William Anthony Ferry, *Stole Fees* (Washington, D.C.: The Catholic University of America Press, 1930); Charles Frederick Keller, *Mass Stipends* (St. Louis: Herder, 1926).

feminism/feminist theology

Feminism is the belief that women and men deserve equality of opportunity in economics, politics, and social relations, as well as equal dignity and rights. Theological feminism argues for equal treatment of women in the church.

The classic expressions in English of the struggle for equality for women were Mary Wollstonecraft's *A Vindication of the Rights of Women* (1792) and John Stuart Mill's essay "The Subjection of Women" (1869). Some feminists like Margaret Fuller (1810–50) argued for equality on the basis of complimentarity, a balancing of male and female characteristics.

The modern feminist struggle arose in the midst of the liberationist movements of the 19th century and reached a point of clarity in the Decla-ration of Statements & Resolutions at the Women's Rights Convention in Seneca Falls, N.Y. (1848), with its assertion that "all men and women are created equal." The key text was Genesis 1:28, a biblical verse whose full meaning has taken a long time to be understood. The Seneca conference was followed by the publication of *The Women's Bible* (1895) by Elizabeth Cady Stanton (1815–1902). The women's religious emancipation movement of the 19th century paved the way in the United States for the political victory of the suffrage movement in 1919 with the passage of the Nineteenth Amendment giving women the right to vote.

In the 20th century feminist THEOLOGY has employed both critical philosophy (Frankfurt School) and liberation theology to analyze women's experiences. Feminist theologians have insisted that the solution to the question of women's status before GOD and humans requires a change not only in THEORY but also in PRAXIS. The structures that need to be critiqued and changed are andocentrism, patriarchalism, and hierarchalism. In Catholicism the central problem standing in the way of structural change is that despite PAUL's theology of mutuality in all relations centered on CHRIST (Corinthian letters), the tradition quickly was distorted into typical imperial Roman patriarchalism. Within this context, women's ecclesiastical and liturgical roles, once nearly on par with men, were pushed to the periphery. By the time the hierarchical system of BISHOP-priest-deacon was in place at the middle of the second century, women were being denied even the role of deacon, which they once enjoyed (Rom. 16:1).

Catholic feminist theology exploded on the American scene with the publication of *Beyond God the Father* (1972) by Mary Daly, professor of theology at Boston College. Daly traveled eventually beyond the Catholic tradition, but she paved the way for other important women theologians like Elizabeth Schussler Fiorenza (1938–) and Rosemary Radford Ruether.

Women theologians set out to liberate the biblical text and the theological tradition from sexist interpretation and to critique the structures of the church that thwart women's full participation. The question of the ordination of women to the priesthood became a central issue. JOHN PAUL II's *Ordinatio Sacerdotalis* (May 24, 1994), explicitly reserving ordination to men alone, came as a great setback to Catholic feminists.

Feminist theology has taken several paths. Some are revolutionary and aim at the overthrow of the CHRISTIAN tradition itself. Others think the tradition can be reconstructed and reformed. Others have taken a separatist path yet still have influence on the others. Feminist theology has frequently joined forces with other forms of social critique, including criticism of racism, classism, and environmentalism. In recent times, there has been a great retrenchment in many Christian churches, including among Catholics, on the issue of the status of women, though most liberal Protestant churches (Anglican, Methodist, Lutheran, and Presbyterian) have pushed ahead with ordaining women and admitting them to all levels of church lay leadership.

Further reading: Sally Barr Ebest and Ron Ebest, eds., *Reconciling Catholicism and Feminism?: Personal Reflections on Tradition and Change* (Notre Dame: University of Notre Dame Press, 2003); Nicholas King, *Whispers of Liberation: Feminist Perspectives on the New Testament* (New York: Paulist, 1998); Rosemary Radford Ruether, *Women and Roman Catholic Christianity* (Washington, D.C.: Catholics for a Free Choice, 2000); ———, *Sexism and God-Talk: Toward a Feminist Theology* (Boston: Beacon, 1993); Sandra Marie Schneiders, *Beyond Patching: Faith and Feminism in the Catholic Church* (New York: Paulist, 1991).

Fénelon, François de Pons de Salignac de la Mothe (1651–1715) *theologian and mystical churchman*

François Fénelon was born into a noble family in Périgord, FRANCE. He studied at the University of Cahors and transferred to the Collège du Plessis in Paris. Around 1672 he entered the Séminaire

de Saint-Sulpice to prepare for the priesthood. He was ordained in 1675 and joined the community of Saint-Sulpice.

The ARCHBISHOP of Paris, noting Fénelon's oratorical and theological skills, placed him in charge of a ministry for new Catholics, many of them recent converts from Protestantism. In 1685 the "Sun King," Louis XIV (1638–1715) of France, revoked the Edict of Nantes (1598), under which "Good King" Henry IV (1553–1610) had granted the Huguenots (French Protestants) considerable rights. Fénelon was assigned to a mission at Santonge, a former Protestant stronghold, to assist in the reconversion process. He advocated the use of persuasion rather than coercion. About this time, his first major book, *Refutation of Malebranche's System on Nature and Grace,* was completed, though it was not published until 1820.

In 1689 Fénelon became tutor to the dauphin, heir to the throne. To assist him in this difficult task, he authored several textbooks for the prince. The king rewarded him with an estate and saw to his appointment as the archbishop of Cambrai in 1696.

Fénelon's brilliant career was deeply affected by his collaboration with Madame Guyon (1599–1621), an independent itinerant mystic whose teachings appeared to many to agree with the Quietism of Miguel de Molinos (c. 1640–97), which Innocent XI (r. 1689–91) had condemned. At first Fénelon signed on to the findings of a commission that examined and mildly condemned some of Guyon's ideas, but the controversy led him to write *Explication of the Maxims of the Saints on the Interior Life* (1697), in which he lays out the progress of the spiritual life, the end of which is the CHRISTIAN's pure love of GOD. This book, too, became a matter of immediate controversy, calling into question his position with the king. Jacques-Bénigne Bossuet (1627–1704), also tutor to the Dauphin and bishop of Meaux, attacked the book in his *Relation sur le quietisme* (1698).

Fénelon submitted the book to Rome for review. In the bull *Cum Alias ad Apostolatus* (March 12,

1699) Innocent XII (r. 1691–1700) found many "errors" in the work, the chief of which was Fénelon's apparent belief that the "involutary perturbences" of Christ's lower, human nature were not communicated to his divine when he was on the CROSS (*see COMMUNICATIO IDIOMATUM*). Fénelon immediately accepted Rome's opinion, and he withdrew his work from circulation. He turned his attention to the administration of his archdiocese. This censure foreclosed his rise in the French hierarchy.

Fénelon maintained an extensive correspondence, especially with those who turned to him for spiritual guidance. While staying away from overt expression of the ideas that had led to his condemnation, he continued to point people to the pure love of God as a goal in life and secretly stayed in contact with Madame Guyon.

Fénelon's fame increased following his death. Many Protestants and Quakers were attracted to his ideas. An edition of his works appeared in French in the 1820s and was later translated into English. They were favorites of John Wesley (1703–91), the founder of Methodism. Though largely forgotten in his native land, his writings have remained in print in English as a source of spiritual reading to this day.

Further reading: Jean Robert Armogathe, *Le Quietisme* (Paris: Presses universitaires, 1973); Michael De La Bedoyere, *Archbishop and the Lady: The Story of Fénelon and Madame Guyon* (London: Collins, 1956); François Fénelon, *Best of Fénelon* (Plainfield: Bridge-Logos, 2002); ———, *Fénelon Meditations on the Heart of God* (Brewster, Mass.: Paraclete, 1997).

Ferdinand of Aragon (1452–1516) and Isabella I of Castile (1451–1504)
Spanish monarchs

Ferdinand and Isabella were married in 1474, and by that act they united nearly all of SPAIN. They conquered the remaining territory, Granada, in 1492. They immediately expelled all Jews who refused to convert; most took refuge in the Ottoman Empire, Portugal, the Netherlands, and the New World. They also imposed forcible conversion on the Moors, the Muslim citizens left in Spain. They made heavy use of the INQUISITION to guarantee that conversions of Muslims and Jews were "authentic," and to consolidate their power in Madrid. In 1492 they also sent CHRISTOPHER COLUMBUS on his fateful voyage to find a transatlantic sea route to India.

The Inquisition condemned many to be burned at the stake in what became known as autos de fe, the deliverance of a sentence in a matter of faith. The ritual involved a procession, a mass, a sermon, and the capital punishment. The last auto-da-fé took place in Seville in 1781. Many converts (*conversos*) and even their descendants continued to be under suspicion and were prohibited from serving as superiors even if they entered the religious life. The one bright spot in Isabella's record is that unlike the Portuguese, she officially refused to allow her subjects to engage in slavery; in practice, slavery nonetheless became widespread in the new Spanish colonial dominions.

In response to the discoveries on behalf of Portugal and of the new Spanish monarchy, in 1493 Pope ALEXANDER VI divided the known New World between Spain and Portugal by drawing a line 100 leagues west of the Cape Verde Islands extending to the poles. In the Treaty of Tordesillas (1494) the Spaniards and Portuguese renegotiated the line at 370 leagues. Though unknown at the time, this new line ended up giving Brazil and its mission fields to the Portuguese.

See also ANTI-SEMITISM.

Further reading: Felipe Fernández-Armesto, *Ferdinand and Isabella* (New York: Dorset, 1975, 1993); John Edwards, *Ferdinand and Isabella* (New York: Pearson/Longman, 2004).

filioque (Lat.: "and the Son")

The western, Latin-speaking countries of the CHRISTIAN world came to add the word *filioque* to the Nicene-Constantinopolitan CREED, which had been finalized in 381. The relevant clause now read: "The Holy Spirit proceeds from the Father *and the Son (filioque)*." By the late sixth century, this phrase became official doctrine, helping to drive a sharp wedge with the eastern Christian world, which did not accept this change.

There had been a common understanding at the Councils of EPHESUS (431) and CHALCEDON (451) that the Nicene-Constantinopolitan Creed, the product of two centuries of debate and struggle, was final and definitive. Any change that did not have the backing of a new ecumenical council would be resisted. Besides, many eastern theologians believed that the HOLY SPIRIT proceeded from the Father in a different way than the Son from the Father. They were content to affirm the biblical assertion in John 15:26: "The Spirit of truth who proceeds from the Son," and leave it at that. The western insertion of *filioque* caused untold ecumenical friction between Rome and CONSTANTINOPLE and continues to be a sore point to the present.

The East came to think of the Father as the cause (*aitia*) and origin (*arche*) that gives unity to the TRINITY. When they thought of the Son and the Spirit they did not think in terms of the inner Trinity ("substance trinitarianism") but in terms of its outward working in the plan of salvation ("economic trinitarianism"). Likewise, they thought of the procession of the Spirit as "*from* the Father" but "*through* the Son" as the mediation (Maximus the Confessor, *Questions to Thalassius* 63). The West extrapolated from the external processions of the Son and Spirit backward into the immanent life of the Trinity.

The first clear enunciation of an immanent, or interior, double procession of the Holy Spirit from both the Father and the Son is by AUGUSTINE OF HIPPO (*On the Trinity* 15.26). He was careful to note that the Spirit proceeds "originally" from the Father, even though "also through" the Son. He thus kept the primary relation to the Father, which was not incompatible with the teaching of the Eastern Church.

Augustine's supposed authority lies behind the western creed known as Quicumque vult, which states that "the Holy Spirit is from the Father and the Son, not made or created or begotten, but proceeding." This formula could possibly be acceptable to the East as it distinguished the procession of the Spirit from the Son. The Quicumque vult formula in turn shaped the creed of the Third Synod of Toledo (589), which anathematizes those who do not say that the Spirit proceeds "from (*ex*) the Father and the Son." This formula fails to distinguish *from* and *through,* and so would be totally unacceptable in the East. By the Third Synod of Braga (675) in SPAIN, the phrase "who proceeds from the Father and the Son" was included in the sung CREED at the EUCHARIST.

In 649 Pope Martin I (r. 649–53) used the *filioque* addition in a letter to Constantinople, much to the dismay of the eastern patriarch. Later, CHARLEMAGNE mandated the addition of *filioque* to the imperial LITURGY. The phrase made its way via MONKS to Jerusalem and via missionaries to the Balkans, stirring up more dismay. Charlemagne's theologians tried to get Leo III (795–816) to add the formula officially and condemn the Greeks. He refused, although he held the formula to be orthodox. By 1016 the formula had become part of the Roman liturgy.

In 967 the Constantinopolitan patriarch Photius (858–69, 877–86), countering Latin missionaries to Bulgaria, sharpened the split by stating that the orthodox formula is "the Holy Spirit proceeds from the Father only." The filioque controversy became central in the GREAT SCHISM. There were brief accords on the formula at the Councils of Lyons II (1274) and FLORENCE (1439), but they were only paper agreements without back-up in the East. Today EASTERN ORTHODOX theologians say that this is the only true doctrinal controversy they have with the Roman church.

See also COUNCILS, ECUMENICAL.

Further reading: Vladimir Lossky, "The Procession of the Holy Spirit in Orthodox Trinitarian Theology," in

Daniel B. Clendenin, ed., *Eastern Orthodox Theology* (Grand Rapids, Mich.: Baker, 2003), 163–182); Saint Photios, *On the Mystagogy of the Holy Spirit,* (Oxford: Studion, 1983); Henry Barclay Swete, *On the History of the Doctrine of the Procession of the Holy Spirit: From the Apostolic Age to the Death of Charlemagne* (Cambridge: G. Bell, 1876); Lukas Vischer, ed., *Spirit of God, Spirit of Christ: Ecumenical Reflections on the Filioque Controversy* (Geneva: World Council of Churches, 1981).

Florence, Council of (1438–1445)

Roman Catholics consider the Council of Florence to be a continuation of the Council of BASEL, which Pope Eugenius IV (r. 1431–47) moved to Ferrara (1438) and then Florence (1439) to facilitate the attendance of EASTERN ORTHODOX delegates. The goal of the council was reconciliation between the Eastern and Western branches of the church, to counteract the threat posed by the expanding Ottoman Empire. The council established the lasting principle of "unity of faith with diversity of rites"—a principle reaffirmed at VATICAN COUNCIL II in its declarations on Eastern rites and Eastern Orthodox churches.

The issues debated included the double procession of the HOLY SPIRIT (*see* FILIOQUE), the use of unleavened (West) and leavened (East) bread in the EUCHARIST, the doctrine of PURGATORY, and the primacy of the pope. The Greek emperor John VIII Paleologus (1423–48) and Patriarch Joseph II of CONSTANTINOPLE (1416–39) attended, along with a contingent of noted theologians. Metropolitan and later Cardinal Bessarion of Nicaea (1403–72) argued strongly for union, while Metropolitan Mark Eugenikos of Ephesus (d. 1444) argued strongly against.

On the filioque issue, the Latins asserted that the Council of EPHESUS's prohibition of changing the CREED had referred not to words but to meanings. This was a rather specious argument. Agreement was hard to come by until theologians from both sides argued that saints cannot err in matters of faith and that the saints who had formulated the theologies both East and West had to be in agreement. A shaky agreement was celebrated with the Decree of Union *Laetentur Coeli* (July 5, 1439). Once they returned home, however, the Greek participants could not persuade their fellow BISHOPS and flocks to follow them.

However, lasting agreements were reached with certain Armenian, Syrian, and Coptic churches and with the Maronites of Cyprus. The conquest of Constantinople by the Turks in 1453 put an end to further attempts at reconciliation on a grand scale. After the council ended, Eugenius IV (1431–47) issued a papal bull, *Etsi Non Dubitemus* (April 20, 1441), asserting the supremacy of popes over councils. It is clear that the council itself, having just dealt with the after-effects of the Western SCHISM, would not have agreed to this statement.

See also ARMENIAN CATHOLIC CHURCH; CHALDEAN CATHOLIC CHURCH; COPTIC CATHOLIC CHURCH; EASTERN ORTHODOXY; MARONITE CATHOLIC CHURCH; PAPACY; SYRIAN CATHOLIC CHURCH; UKRANIAN CATHOLIC CHURCH.

Further reading: Giuseppe Alberigo, ed., *Christian Unity: The Council of Ferrara-Florence 1438/39* (Leuven: University, 1991); Joseph Gill, *The Council of Florence* (Cambridge: Cambridge University Press, 1959); Oskar Halecki, *From Florence to Brest (1439–1596)* (Hamden, Conn.: Archon, 1968); J. M. Neal, ed., *The History of the Council of Florence,* (London: Joseph Masters, 1861); Constantine Tsirpanlis, *Mark Eugenicus and the Council of Florence* (New York: s.n., 1979).

font, baptismal   *See* FURNISHINGS, CHURCH.

Fools, Feast of

The medieval Feast of Fools, celebrated between Christmas and Epiphany in FRANCE and to a lesser extent in England and other countries, was an occasion for the ritual inversion of social status, with much buffoonery sometimes bordering on blasphemy. The festival was held in or on the front steps of cathedrals and churches and was often sponsored by the lower CLERGY, In some areas, an ass was dressed as a BISHOP and given mock obeisance.

The origins of the feast seem to be in early Celtic fertility cults and Roman celebrations like the Saturnalia. In some cases church authorities tried to divert the ribald aspects of the festivals by encouraging the performance of miracle or mystery plays. In other cases bishops like Robert Grosseteste of Lincoln (c. 1170–1253) forbade the feast entirely. The Council of BASEL in 1435 imposed penalties for observing the feast.

Aspects of the Feast of Fools have been transferred to the carnival festival that precedes Lent in many countries. In 1969 Harvard theologian Harvey Cox published *The Feast of Fools,* an influential book in which he promoted a theology of celebration and culture for our times.

Further reading: Harvey Gallagher Cox, *The Feast of Fools: A Theological Essay on Festivity and Fantasy* (Cambridge, Mass.: Harvard University Press, 1969); Jacques Heers, *Fetes des Fous et Carnavals* (Paris: Fayard, 1983).

forgiveness

Forgiveness is both the act and the condition of being restored to a right relationship with GOD, self, and others after a period of offense and alienation. In Christianity forgiveness involves the sinner's acceptance of the unconditional love and mercy of God through Jesus CHRIST and the extension of that mercy to others. Mercy and forgiveness are founded on God forgiving the sinner through Jesus (Mark 2:8–12). Forgiveness is perhaps the central aspect of the Lord's Prayer (Luke 11:1–4; Matt. 6:9–15).

In the CHRISTIAN tradition, forgiveness is extended to the sinner as he or she offers repentance of SIN. While forgiveness is absolute, it does not put aside the need of the sinner to make resti-

tution for the sin. Thus, it has been customary for the sinner to undergo a period of penance, almsgiving, and even seclusion before reconciliation with the community. Forgiveness plays a central role in the Sacraments of BAPTISM and RECONCILIATION. Reconciliation is accompanied by contrition, a confession of sin, and absolution by a confessor with the imposition of a penance. Since VATICAN COUNCIL II the church has stressed not only the individual but also the social and structural aspects of sin and forgiveness.

Further reading: David Michael Coffey, *The Sacrament of Reconciliation* (Collegeville, Minn.: Liturgical Press, 2001); Vincent Taylor, *Forgiveness and Reconciliation: A Study in New Testament Theology* (London: St. Martin's, 1956).

Foucauld, Charles-Eugène de (1858–1916) *French explorer and soldier*

Known as the "Hermit of the Sahara," Foucauld was a French explorer and army officer in Algeria. In 1887 he returned to the Catholic FAITH and was ordained a PRIEST in 1901. He was murdered in 1916 for rather obscure reasons. Although he had no followers during his lifetime, his writings and humble lifestyle inspired others to adopt a monastic lifestyle and found "Little Brothers" and "Little Sisters" of Jesus around the world.

As a lieutenant in the French army Foucault developed a passion for AFRICA and wrote his famous work *Reconnaissance au Maroc* (1888) after an expedition through Morocco. Upon returning to Catholicism, he made a pilgrimage to the Holy Land in 1888–89 and entered a TRAPPIST MONASTERY in 1890. Desiring a life of greater solitude with a stronger emphasis on humility, he left the order in 1897 and went to Algeria to lead a hermit's life, settling at Tamanrasset. As a desert monk, he studied the local language, wrote dictionaries, and focused on prayer and acts of charity. French soldiers and the local desert tribes admired his lifestyle, but he was killed in 1916 because apparently his good acts were resented for creating friendly feelings toward the French.

Foucault himself served as a solitary monk, but his instructions inspired René Voillaume (1905–2003) and four other priests to create a monastic community on the edge of the Sahara in 1933. Since then, Little Brothers and Little Sisters communities have sprung up around the world. Members live among the locals, earn a living, wear ordinary clothes, and exercise their influence by the example of their humble lifestyles. There is no explicit attempt to convert; the emphasis is witnessing by way of life.

Further reading: Jean Jacques Antier, *Charles de Foucauld* (San Francisco: Ignatius, 1999); Charles de Foucauld, *Meditations of a Hermit* (London: Orbis, 1981); Philip Hillyer, *Charles de Foucauld* (Collegeville, Minn.: Liturgical Press, 1990); Ali Merad, *Christian Hermit in an Islamic World: A Muslim's View of Charles de Foucauld* (New York: Paulist, 1999).

Fox, Matthew (1940–) *New Age Christian theologian and ecumenical activist*

As a young man Fox entered the DOMINICAN ORDER and was ordained to the priesthood in 1967. He received his doctorate in theology in 1970 from the Institut Catholique in Paris, where he studied MEISTER ECKHART, who inspired his creation spirituality. He joined the faculty of Mundelein College, a Catholic women's college in suburban Chicago. After difficulties with Catholic authorities, he became an Episcopal priest in 1994.

Fox gained attention with a book on prayer, *On Becoming a Musical, Mystical Bear,* which led to the establishment of the Institute for Culture and Creation Spirituality (ICCS) in 1977. In 1983 the institute moved to Holy Name College in Oakland, California.

Fox's creation spirituality focuses CHRISTIAN life and thought as an affirmation of GOD's work of creativity and emphasizes the good CREATION over and against the traditional Catholic emphasis on SIN and REDEMPTION. Fox became open to other-than-Christian approaches to the spiritual life. Creation spirituality thus seeks an integration of the wisdom of the West (traditional Christianity) with indigenous cultures from around the world and contemporary scientific understanding of the universe. Creation spirituality reverences artistic creativity and the interrelated nature of all life (the Gaia hypothesis of James Lovelock, 1919–).

Fox invited teachers from across the contemporary religious spectrum to join the staff of the ICCS, including the Wiccan priestess Starhawk (Miriam Simos, 1951–). This openness provoked a reaction from Catholic Church officials. The Vatican silenced him for a year in 1988. In 1991, his Dominican superiors ordered Fox to leave the ICCS or face dismissal. He refused and subsequently left the order and the Catholic Church. In 1994 Bishop William Swing accepted him into the Episcopal Diocese of California.

Since 1999, Fox has continued his work through the University of Creation Spirituality (UCS) in Oakland, California, a campus of Naropa University, the school founded by the Tibetan Buddhist group headed by Chogyam Trungpa (1939–87) and based in Boulder, Colorado. Fox has authored more than 20 books including *Original Blessing* (1983); *A Spirituality Named Compassion* (1979); *One River, Many Wells* (2000); and *Creativity: Where the Divine and the Human Meet* (2002). He also translated the works of the medieval mystic HILDEGARD OF BINGEN.

Further reading: Matthew Fox, *The Coming of the Cosmic Christ* (San Francisco: Harper & Row, 1988); ———, *Original Blessing* (Santa Fe: Bear, 1983); ———, *A Spirituality Named Compassion and the Healing of the Global Village, Humpty Dumpty and Us* (San Francisco: Harper & Row, 1979); Lawrence Wright, *Saints & Sinners: Walker Railey, Jimmy Swaggart, Madalyn Murray O'Hair, Anton LaVey, Will Campbell, Matthew Fox* (New York: Knopf, 1993).

France

Traditionally, France has been called the "eldest daughter of the church." It is more than likely that CHRISTIANS from Asia Minor missionized southern France at the beginning of the second century. By 150 there was a flourishing community in Lyons, whose BISHOP was IRENAEUS, the first true Christian theologian. The important Synod of Arles in 314, summoned by CONSTANTINE, dealt with the DONATIST controversy outside AFRICA.

France gave to the church St. Hilary of Poitiers (c. 315–67), who fought against the Arians in his *On the Trinity*, and St. Martin of Tours (d. 397), who established MONASTICISM in western Europe. France developed its own Gallican RITE and CHANT before being overrun by the Franks.

After an initial period of chaos, the conversion of the Frankish king Clovis (481–511) in 496 ensured the survival of Christianity. The Franks stabilized the country under the Merovingian Dynasty (fifth century–751), named after the founder, Merovich, and unified it under the Carolingian Dynasty (751–987), begun under Pepin III the Short (751–68) but named after CHARLEMAGNE. Charlemagne fostered a theological and educational renaissance under ALCUIN and imposed the Roman rite in place of the Gallican (*see* CAROLINGAN RENAISSANCE). Louis I the Pious (814–40) encouraged the spread of monasticism following the BENEDICTINE Rule. Romanesque ARCHITECTURE spread through the founding of many monasteries, notably at Vézelay, Autun, and Moissac. The Franks absorbed the Latin language, and from this original appropriation the French language eventually evolved.

Cooperation between CHURCH AND STATE continued under the early Capetian dynasty (987–1328), although French kings bestowed the ring and the crozier on new bishops at their installation, a practice that was challenged by the PAPACY during the INVESTITURE CONTROVERSY. France provided several popes during this period and was the starting point for the CRUSADES. The reforms of the Cluniac and CISTERCIAN monasteries had effects throughout Europe. At St. Denis north of Paris Abbot SUGER, chancellor to the kings, began what became known as Gothic style in CATHEDRALS; it flourished at Notre Dame, Chartres, Rheims, and elsewhere, affecting modes of piety and worship all across Christendom. St. BERNARD OF CLAIRVAUX opposed Suger's extravagance.

Chapter or cathedral schools, begun under Alcuin, developed into full houses of learning. With the founding of the scholarship-oriented MENDICANTS, full university systems began to take shape all across Europe. Among the masters France and Paris hosted were PETER ABELARD, PETER LOMBARD, THOMAS AQUINAS, and DUNS SCOTUS. The Dominicans took part in the Albigensian Crusade (1209–29) against the CATHARI, thereby contributing to the expansion of royal control. Under St. LOUIS IX's long reign (1226–70) France experienced extraordinary peace and prosperity. Capetian power reached its peak with Philip IV the Fair (r. 1285–1314), but feudal monarchs, who by now were becoming full sovereigns in their lands, started falling afoul of equally powerful popes like INNOCENT III and BONIFACE VIII over many issues, including lay investiture, legal jurisdiction over benefices, and taxation of church property.

Upon his election the French pope Clement V (1305–14) moved the papal seat to Avignon. The AVIGNON PAPACY caused untold damage to the reputation of the papacy and contributed to the rise of a flurry of ANTIPOPES. In this era the French church went through periods of Gallicanism, as clerics and laity asserted ecclesiastical autonomy vis-à-vis Rome, as in the Pragmatic Sanction of Bourge (1438), alternating with submission, as in the concordat of 1472.

In the concordat of 1516 between Francis I (1515–47) and Leo X (1513–21), the papacy conceded the right of the crown to nominate candidates for major benefices, including dioceses; in effect, French kings were given the right of lay investitute. The concordat made it possible later for many high-ranking French churchmen such as Richelieu (1585–1642) and Talleyrand (1754–1838) to play important roles in civil affairs. While compromising the status of the church, it also staved off the Protestant tide in France. It also explains why Henry IV's Edict of Nantes (1598), tolerating the Huguenots, could be ignored during the St. Bartholomew's Day Massacre (1672) and eventually revoked by Louis XIV in 1685.

The 16th and 17th centuries were periods of deep piety in France, but the piety was tinged with superstitious or near-superstitious devotions to the Blessed Virgin Mary of Nazareth and the saints, the purchase of private masses and indulgences, the building of chapels, and the fear of the consequences of this life in the afterlife. France, like the rest of the Catholic world, experienced a revival during the Counter-Reformation under the guiding lights of Jacques-Bénigne Bossuet (1627–1704), François Fénelon, and Sts. Vincent de Paul and Francis de Sales. King Louis XIV defended traditional Gallicanism (which championed the power of the state over that of pope or church) and struck out at the Jansenists (see Jansenism). His grandson Louis XVI (r. 1744–92) expelled the Jesuits in 1784.

The church's stringent measures against dissidents led to a wave of Enlightenment-led anticlericalism. The Enlightenment philosophers Jean-Jacques Rousseau (1712–78) and Voltaire (1694–1778) ratcheted up the critique of Christianity. With the explosion of the French Revolution (1789) the interests of the Catholic Church were put into grave peril. Church property was auctioned to pay public debt, monastic vows were abrogated, and tithing to the church ended. The situation did not improve until Napoléon Bonaparte (1769–1821) entered into a concordat with Rome in 1801. Ironically, the concordat weakened nationalist Gallicanism in favor of the Ultramontanist cause, culminating in Vatican Council I.

The church's close affiliation with Napoléon III (1852–70) sparked a second anticlerical wave in the Third Republic (1870–1940). Schools were secularized and religious orders expelled, and the church was totally separated from the state. At the same time Alfred Loisy (1857–1940), Maurice Blondel (1861–1945), and Lucien Laberthonnière (1860–1932) led an intellectual Catholic revival later tagged, pejoratively, as modernism. Meanwhile, reconstituted Benedictine abbeys like Solesmes were preparing the way for the liturgical movement of the 20th century.

During the first half of the 20th century, Jacques Maritain and Étienne Gilson led a revival in modern Catholic philosophy and in the study of its medieval predecessors, while Dominicans Reginald Garrigou-Lagrange (1877–1944) and Roland de Vaux (1903–71) pioneered a revival in Catholic biblical studies, culminating in the publication of the authoritative Jerusalem Bible (1944; English, 1966). The flight of the lower classes from the church led to the worker priest movement of the 1940s and 1950s and the renewal of Catholic Action. France contributed many noted theologians to the success of Vatican Council II, notably Jean Daniélou, Yves Congar, and Marie-Dominique Chenu.

While numerous Catholics compromised themselves with the Nazi-controlled Vichy regime (1940–45), others resisted at the risk of their lives. Clergy and religious fought side by side with laity against the Nazi occupation during World War II, thus lessening the anticlerical feeling so prevalent in France. France also welcomed the changes of Vatican II. Some also embraced the protests of 1968.

The status of the church suffered dramatically in 1905 by the laws on separation of church and state. A variety of subsequent laws have attempted to actualize the oft-stated policy of France being a secular country. For example, all public education must be secular, and clergy may not teach in primary or secondary schools. Today, France seems to have lost the fervor once roused at Vatican II. Though 70 percent of the population of about 60 million is nominally Catholic, less than 10 percent attend church on any regular basis.

Further reading: M. A. Fitzsimons, *The Catholic Church Today: Western Europe* (Notre Dame.: University of Notre Dame Press, 1969); James MacCaffrey, *History of the Catholic Church from the Renaissance to the French Revolution* (St. Louis: Herder 1915); John L. McNulty, and Julius S. Lombardi, *La France Catholique: A History of Catholic France* (New York: W. H. Sadlier, 1939); Steven Ozment, *The Age of Reform, 1250–1550. An Intellectual and Religious History of Late Medieval and Reformation Europe* (London: Yale University Press, 1980); Yves Renouard, *The Avignon Papacy 1305–1403,* trans. Denis Bethell (Hamden, Conn.: Archon, 1970).

Franciscan Orders

The term *Franciscans* applies to a family of orders that include regular communities and lay followers of St. FRANCIS OF ASSISI. It includes the First Order of Friars Minor and the various movements derived from them, including the Conventuals and Capuchins; the Second Order of Poor Clares and the many orders of Franciscan NUNS; and the Third Order, which includes regular communities and lay followers of St. Francis of Assisi. (A regular is a lay community that adopts a rule.)

The Friars Minor, or Lesser Brethren, was officially founded by Francis in 1209 when he gave his followers a rule approved by INNOCENT III, which is now lost. It was almost certainly composed simply of passages from the New Testament illustrating the life of Jesus. A second rule, known as the Regula Prima, or Bullata, was drawn up in 1221 and approved by Honorius III (r. 1216–27) in 1223.

Besides the imitation of the life pattern of Jesus, the rule is noted for its insistence on absolute poverty not only for individual friars but also for the community as a whole. In this aspect the mendicant, or begging, orders differ from previous orders of MONKS, who collectively owned their monasteries and estates. Friars were prohibited from owning any property or accepting money. They were to work with their hands for their daily needs or, if necessary, to beg. Beginning with

Innocent III the popes of the MIDDLE AGES saw in the Franciscans and other mendicant orders the means for the pastoral renewal of Christianity.

Although Francis wanted to promulgate the poor Gospel life of Jesus and at first attracted humble lay brothers, the order soon attracted the mighty and the educated. The character of the movement changed from lay to clerical, and Franciscan scholars established houses at Oxford, Paris, Cologne, Bonn, and other centers of learning throughout Europe. Soon great theologians dotted the Franciscan landscape: Alexander of Hales (1185–1245), the first to produce a commentary on the *Sentences* of PETER LOMBARD and whose students gathered his teachings into the first *Summa Theologica;* BONAVENTURE OF BAGNOREGIO, the great mystical theologian; JOHN DUNS SCOTUS, the great luminary of Oxford and Paris; and WILLIAM OF OCKHAM, the great logician and opponent of secular papal power.

Franciscan missionaries, following Francis's example, soon spread two-by-two throughout all of Europe and into the Near East, where they often served as ambassadors between the PAPACY and local peoples, even those of other faiths. Most notable was JOHN OF MONTE CORVINO (1247–1330), who carried the Gospel message all the way to the court of the great khan in Khambaligh (Beijing) and translated the Psalter and the New Testament into Tartar. He was to be followed in later centuries by Bernadino de Sahagun (1500–90), Spanish missionary to the Aztecs who composed the monumental study of Aztec culture *Historia general de las cosas in Neuva España* ("General History of Events in New Spain"); JUNIPERO SERRA, who founded the many missions of California; and ANTONIO MARGIL DE JESÚS, who founded the missions of Texas, including the famous Alamo.

The Franciscan movement spread with remarkable speed. The friars preached the Gospel in word and deed, but the increase in numbers brought the need for places to house the friars, an event that triggered a relentless conflict. The Spirituals, influenced by the radically dispensationalist view of history in the abbot Joachim of Fiore's *Eternal Gospel,* wanted to keep strictly to the provisions of the rule, but others argued for the ownership of convents and other mitigations of the rule. After Francis's death in 1224, the disagreements reached the point of violence. St. Bonaventure of Bagnoregio, minister general of the order from 1257 to 1274, attempted to mediate the conflict. The question whether Jesus and the Apostles owned property, implied in the key texts "The Son of Man has nowhere to lay his head" (Matt. 8:20) and the commission of the disciples in Mark 6:7–13, Matthew 10, and Luke 9, was debated before many popes. In 1317–18 John XXII (r. 1316–34) decided against the Spirituals, many of whom became schismatics under the pejorative name of Fraticelli. Some fled for cover into Benedictine monasteries, and others formed a separate church, including women preachers, under the leadership of Michael of Cesina (d. 1342). Such disputes, combined with the effects of the western schism and the Black Death (1348–52) led to a decline among the Franciscans.

The order experienced a reform and revival under the leadership of the Observants, especially Sts. Bernadino of Siena (1380–1444) and John Capistrano (1386–1446). By 1517 the Observants won the title as the true Order of Friars Minor (OFM) against the more lax Conventuals (OFM Conv). Another reform movement now known as the Capuchins (OFM Cap) won separate recognition in 1528. The 20th-century mystic and stigmatic St. Padre Pio of Pietrelcina (1887–2002) was a Capuchin (*see* stigmata).

The French Revolution sorely weakened all religious orders in Europe, and the numbers of Franciscans dropped steeply. The Observants included separate groups under a general umbrella—Reformed, Recollects, and Discalced—until Leo XIII formally united them with the bull *Felicitate Quadam* (October 4, 1897). In the 20th century Franciscans were key missionaries to China until the Communists expelled them. Because of the engagement of early Franciscans in the Holy Land, Franciscans are the guardians of the holy sites under the supervision of the Vatican. In 1979 John Vaughn of the province of Santa Barbara was elected the first American minister general of the order. Since Vatican Council II Franciscans have returned to their classic mission as ministers of the Gospel to the poor and the dispossessed. One of the foremost liberation theologians of the world, Leonardo Boff, began as a Franciscan. Today there are more than 16,000 members of the Franciscans proper, 11,000 Capuchins, and Conventuals.

Beginning with St. Clare of Assisi and the Poor Clares, the Second Order grew alongside the first. From the earliest times lay people were attracted to the way of St. Francis. These people became tertiaries, or members of the Third Order, married and not, who committed themselves to a Franciscan way of life. Sts. Louis IX (1214–70), king of France, and Elizabeth of Hungary (1207–31) were a members of the Third Order. Some groups of the Third Order assembled into formal associations, taking vows and living a communal life. These groups, male and female alike, are called Third Order Regulars. The 19th century saw the foundation of many orders of Franciscan sisters who follow the rule of Third Order Regular and the spirit of St. Francis. Religious orders of Franciscan sisters number in the hundreds. Many serve as missionaries and work in difficult situations.

Of all the religious movements in the Roman Catholic Church from the Middle Ages on, the Franciscans have been the largest and farthest reaching. Franciscan groups have sprung up especially in the Anglican Church. Fr. Paul Wattson and Sister Lurana White founded Graymoor on the banks of the Hudson above New York City in 1898. They were accepted into the Roman Catholic communion in 1909 as the Friars and Sisters of the Atonement and today work in the field of ecumenism, but not all Anglican Franciscans have converted. There are now several communities within the Church of England, whose members share a fond devotion to St. Francis along with their Catholic counterparts. Francis remains the most universal saint to the world at large.

Further reading: Lester Bach, *Called to Rebuild the Church* (Quincy, Ill.: Franciscan Press, 1997); John R. H. Moorman, *A History of the Franciscan Order* (Chicago: Franciscan Herald, 1988); William Short, *The Franciscans* (Wilmington, Del.: Glazier, 1989).

Francis de Sales, St. (1567–1622) *spiritual writer of the Counter-Reformation*

Francis de Sales, bishop of Geneva, was a leader in the Counter-Reformation, a cofounder of the Visitation Sisters, and a noted spiritual writer. He was canonized in 1665, declared a doctor of the church by Pius IX in 1877, and made patron of journalists by Benedict XV in 1923. His feast day is January 24.

Francis was born to a noble family in Savoy and educated at Annecy, Paris (Clermont and Sorbonne), and Padua. Rejecting an offer in civil service from the duke of Savoy, he was ordained in 1593 and became provost of Geneva. He engaged Calvinists in charitable and amicable debate, winning many back to Catholicism. He met St. Vincent de Paul in Paris in 1599 and, together with St. Jane Frances de Chantal (1572–1641), founded the Visitation Sisters, who became noted for their devotion to the Sacred Heart of Jesus. He became bishop of Geneva in 1602.

Francis was a model pastor, confessor, and spiritual director. His two major spiritual works, *Introduction to the Devout Life* (1609) and *Treatise on the Love of God* (1616), remain among the most widely read in the Catholic world.

Further reading: Eunan McDonnell, *God Desires You: St. Francis de Sales on the Living Gospel* (Blackrock: Columba, 2001); Christopher Harold Palmer, *The Prince Bishop: A Life of St. de Sales* (Ilfracembe: Stockwell, 1974).

Francis of Assisi, St. (1181/82–1226) *mystic and mendicant founder*

Without doubt Francis is the most beloved saint in all of Christian history. Known as Il Poverello ("the Poor One"), he founded the Franciscan Order and became author of the most famous early Italian poem, the "Canticle of the Sun." Tradition calls him the "seraphic saint" and the patron of animals and nature. Pope Gregory IX (r. 1227–41) canonized him in 1229. His feast day is October 4.

Francis was the son of Pietro and Pica di Bernadone. His father was a very wealthy cloth merchant who traded in France, owned estates around Assisi, and engaged in banking. His mother was probably French. Francis had two brothers, one of whom was named Angelo. As a youth Francis worked with his father, traveling to France and serving as master of revels to his companions. He aspired to become a knight, and the chivalrous ethic continued to shape his life thereafter. He was taken prisoner in a skirmish of the perennial war with neighboring Perugia. The overall politics of the time were determined by the disputes between the German Holy Roman Emperors and the pope in Rome.

Ransomed, Francis's life started taking an unusual turn. Long noted for dreams and visions, he began to engage in periods of prayer, fasting, and extreme almsgiving. Recaparisoned and on the way to another battle, he encountered a destitute knight and suddenly gave the man all his possessions. Meeting a leper on the road, he was first repulsed but then returned and gave the sufferer the kiss of peace. Before the Byzantine crucifix in the decayed chapel of San Damiano in Assisi, he heard Christ tell him "Rebuild my church." Taking this literally, he gathered some of his father's most precious bolts of cloth, sold them in a nearby town, and gave the money to the priest of San Damiano. Francis's father took him to court. As the property was then in the custody of the church, the trial was held before Bishop Guido. Francis stripped himself stark naked and returned his clothes and the money to his father, renouncing his patrimony. The BISHOP covered his nakedness and became his protector. Francis donned a simple dun-colored, T-shaped tunic with a hood and rope for a belt. This remains the habit of the Franciscan Order to this day. Throughout his life Francis engaged in sometimes extravagant symbolic actions to instruct others, like stripping naked on his death pallet or rubbing the walls of the friars' dwelling with meat on Christmas day to show that all should celebrate Jesus' birth.

Francis began rebuilding chapels in early Gothic style in and around Assisi. His favorite

St. Francis of Assisi. Carving by José Mondragon, 1973. (Chimayo, New Mexico) *(possession of the author; photo by John Huston)*

was Santa Maria degli Angeli. Known as the Portiuncula ("Little Portion"), it was owned by the Benedictine abbey of San Benedetto but later bequeathed by the abbot to Francis as the friars' mother church. (The city of Los Angeles is named after this chapel.) Hearing the word of Jesus "Preach as you go, saying 'The kingdom of heaven is at hand'" (Matt. 10:17) at mass, he began to preach in public. Throughout his life he was torn between preaching in public squares and retiring to hermitages to pray and meditate. Soon he attracted followers, including young noblemen from Assisi. Two by two the brothers spread the Gospel news around central ITALY, across the Alps, and into SPAIN. Soon there were 12 followers.

No doubt aware that the official church was on a campaign to suppress, with violence if necessary, rebellious lay movements such as the CATHARI in France, the WALDENSIANS (Poor Men of Lyons), and the Humiliati in northern Italy, Francis and some of the early companions went to Rome in 1209 to seek approval for his new fraternity of Fratres Minores, or Lesser Brethren, from the powerful Pope INNOCENT III. Curia officials suggested he follow the rules of established religious orders like the BENEDICTINES and AUGUSTINIANS. But Francis was proposing something radical: he wanted to follow the prescriptions of the Gospels simply and directly. The Benedictines took vows of personal poverty, chastity, and obedience, but also of stability, and they collectively owned their monasteries and princely estates. Likewise, the Augustinians were attached to cathedrals. Francis wanted his brethren to wander like Jesus with no place to lay their heads and, like him, to own absolutely nothing. He wanted poverty, obedience to God, prayer, work, harmony with the people, and preaching. The first rule of the order contained little besides quotations from the Gospels and a few exhortations. His goal was the apostolic life portrayed in the New Testament (to love God and one's neighbor), and his mission was to preach to the poor and oppressed and to alleviate the suffering of the sick and homeless. Innocent gave tentative approval. The early Franciscan movement, like the Dominican, was an urban youth revitalization project.

Returning to Assisi, Francis witnessed a phenomenal growth in the order. Soon Clare di Favarone (*see* St. CLARE OF ASSISI), daughter of a noble family of Assisi, sought to follow his lifestyle. If Heloise and Abelard are the carnal romance of the MIDDLE AGES, Clare and Francis are the spiritual romance. She became founder of the second Franciscan order, called the Poor Clares, although the order was later required to follow a rule more appropriate for cloistered Benedictines, under orders from Cardinal Ugolino dei Conti di Segni (later Pope Gregory IX r. 1227–41). San Damiano was assigned to her and her sisters. Lay people were also attracted and formed a loose spiritual association called the Brothers and Sisters of Penance. Later this was called the Third Order, and from it emerged several religious orders of men and women. Lucchesio da Siena, a grain broker, and his wife were among the first Third Order members, distributing their wealth to war victims and working to secure medicine for the poor. Another member, Olando da Chiusi, provided Francis with a *retiro*, or retreat, at Monte La Verna in Tuscany.

Francis followed a spontaneous leadership style, although he called chapter meetings on Pentecost and Michaelmas every year. By 1219 scholars estimate that 3,000 friars showed up for the Pentecost chapter. In 1213 Francis had no qualms to leave the friars in the care of Pietro of Catanio while he headed off to Spain to preach among the Saracens. He was firmly against the use of force to gain converts. In 1219 he traveled to Egypt on the coattails of King John of Brienne (c. 1148–1237) on the fifth CRUSADE, slipped through the military lines, and found a way to engage Sultan al-Malik al-Kamil (d. 1238) in what may have been one of the first ecumenical dialogues. Francis failed to convert the sultan or mediate the peace, yet FREDERICK II and Sultan al-Kamil eventually accepted his mediation proposals. The

next year he was in Acre but soon returned to Italy because of dissension among the brothers. Francis's vicars had amended the rule on the matter of absolute poverty. Recognizing his limits, he resigned as minister general of the order, turning over authority to Peter of Catanio. In the next year he struggled, sometimes contradictorily, to amend the rule that was finally approved by the pope in 1223.

Two events crowned the end of Francis's life. First, at his retreat in the hills of Greccio Francis reenacted the birth of Christ in a cave with live animals and began a tradition of distributing food and animals to the poor. This set the pattern for Christmas creches and plays in later history. Second, at Michaelmas in 1224 Francis received the STIGMATA (five wounds) of the crucified Christ from a seraph. He was in seclusion at his *retiro* at Monte La Verna, with only Brother Leo in attendance. Leo recorded the incident in red letters overwriting a blessing written in Francis's own hand and signed with his characteristic Tau (T-cross). This is the first recorded stigmata in Christian history. Francis died two years later, naked and lying on the earth at his request. He suffered from tuberculosis, trachoma, which he contracted in Egypt, and, some speculate, leprosy from caring for lepers.

Francis's life gave birth to many tales and legends. He preached to birds, and they alighted to listen; he reconciled the voracious wolf of Gubbio with the townsfolk; he bought live animals in the market to free them, a practice emulated by Leonardo da Vinci (1452–1519); he fasted fiercely, except when a brother needed nourishment, when he feasted to spare the sickly one embarrassment; he tossed his poor body into the rose bushes to check temptations of the flesh, but at the end of his life asked "Brother Ass" (his body) forgiveness for treating it too harshly. His favorite bird was the lark, dun-colored like a humble friar, yet able to rise in song in the clear blue sky, just as Francis himself sang in praise of God's creation in his Canticle to the Sun:

Be praised, my Lord, with all your creatures,
Especially my master Brother Sun,
Through whom he gives us the day
and through whom light shines.
He is beautiful and radiant with great splendor;
Of you, most High, he is the symbol.

There are Catholic, Anglican, and Lutheran religious orders that follow Francis's path. At the Anglican cathedral of St. John the Divine in New York City people of all faiths bring their pets of all species to be blessed on his feast day. He is the most universal of western saints. Francis's life and miracles became the subject of countless works of art, most notably by Giotto in the Basilica of St. Francis in Assisi and in the church of Santa Croce in Florence. Later the stigmatization of Francis and Francis contemplating a skull became favorite subjects for Renaissance and Mannerist painters, although the saint himself was not preoccupied with suffering or death, which he welcomed as a sister when it came.

See also FRANCISCAN ORDERS; MENDICANT ORDERS; POVERTY.

Further reading: Adrian House, *Francis of Assisi* (London: Chatto & Windus, 2000); J. R. H. Moorman, *Sources for the Life of St. Francis of Assisi* (Manchester: Manchester University Press, 1940); Paul Sabatier, *Life of St. Francis of Assisi* (London: Hodder & Stoughton, 1922).

Francis Xavier, St. (1506–1552) *Jesuit missionary to Asia*

Francis Xavier was a pioneering JESUIT missionary who introduced Christianity to India and Japan in the 16th century. Pope PAUL V beatified Xavier in 1619, and Pope Gregory XV (r. 1621–23) canonized both Francis and St. IGNATIUS OF LOYOLA in 1622. His body is enshrined in the Good Jesus Church at Goa, India. He is the patron of all missionaries, and his feast day is December 3.

Francis was born in Navarre, Spain, to a Basque family. He attended the University of Paris, where he met IGNATIUS OF LOYOLA and participated in the small group that served as the core of the Society of Jesus, or Jesuits. Xavier was one of the original members who made their vows with Ignatius on August 15, 1534.

Xavier continued his studies at Paris, earning a doctorate and an appointment as professor; he was ordained in 1537. Following a request by King John III of Portugal (1502–57) for priests to serve the new missions in India, Xavier was appointed as apostolic nuncio to Asia and sailed in 1541. Briefly landing in Goa in 1542, he proceeded to Cape Comorin in southern India, where he worked among the pearl fishers, or Paravas, on the Fishery Coast. He worked with great success throughout the region. In 1544 he was named the first provincial of the Society of Jesus in Goa, where he also headed the Jesuit college.

In 1545, Xavier sailed eastward to Malacca and the Moluccas. Again he worked with great success. Then in 1547, he met a fugitive from Japan named Yajiro who convinced him that he should go to his native land. With Yajiro as interpreter Francis sailed for Japan in 1549. Hopeful of securing the attention of Portuguese traders, the daimyo, or lord, of Kagoshima welcomed Xavier and allowed him to preach but under his control.

With Yajiro's assistance, Xavier published a translation of the CATECHISM. Yajiro proposed translating the biblical "God" as Dainichi, the name of the highest god in Shingon Buddhism, but after his Japanese audience, including *bonzes*, or Buddhist priests, took him as the representative of yet another Buddhist sect, Xavier then published a new edition with the primary religious terms transliterated from the Latin. After some success in Japan, Francis moved on to China. He died on Shangchuan, an island near Canton, on December 3, 1552, having failed to gain entrance into the Chinese kingdom.

He is now considered the patron of all the church's missions. Xavier's work continues in Catholic churches in India and Malaysia. In Japan, Christianity was banned by the shogun in 1614.

The faith survived through the approximately 300,000 converts that Xavier and his colleagues had made. These CHRISTIANS went underground; only in the 19th century were pockets of "hidden Christians" rediscovered. However, Christianity has never regained a firm footing in Japan. Today the Jesuits run Sophia University, a major institution of higher learning in Tokyo.

Further reading: James Brodrick, *A Biography of St. Francis Xavier* (New York: Wicklow, 1952); Francis Xavier, *The Letters and Instructions of Francis Xavier* (St. Louis: Institute of Jesuit Sources, 1992); Georg Schurhammer, *Francis Xavier: His Life, His Times* (Rome: Jesuit Historical Institute, 1973).

Frederick I Barbarossa (c. 1122–1190) *Holy Roman Emperor*

The reign of Frederick I ("Barbarossa," or Red Beard) was characterized by a struggle for preeminence by the German states in Europe, especially vis-à-vis the power of the PAPACY. Originally duke of Swabia, Frederick was elected Holy Roman Emperor in 1155. At once he began his efforts to expand his power through aligning the empire's interests with those of the constituent German principalities. He waged innumerable campaigns in northern Italy. His power vis-à-vis the papacy diminished with the Treaty of Constance in 1153, and in 1159 he sided with the ANTIPOPE against Alexander III, resulting in an ongoing conflict about the empire's role in papal affairs. Frederick had a heart attack and drowned in the Saleph River while on the Third CRUSADE.

See also HOLY ROMAN EMPIRE.

Further reading: Paul J. Knapke, *Frederick Barbarossa's Conflict with the Papacy: A Problem of Church and State* (Washington, D.C.: Catholic University of America Press, 1939); Ferdinand Opll, *Friedrich Barbarossa* (Darmstadt: Wissenschaftliche Buchgesellschaft, 1990); Otto I, Bishop of Freising, *The Deeds of Frederick Barbarossa,* tr. Charles Christopher Mierow (New York: Norton, 1966).

Frederick II (1194–1250) *Holy Roman Emperor, king of Sicily, crusader*

As a child of four, the future Holy Roman Emperor Frederick II became king of Sicily, the island where he grew up and lived most of his life. As ruler of a land just south of the PAPAL STATES, he found himself almost continually at war with his northern neighbor and on two occasions was excommunicated. In an apparently more pious role, he set out on a CRUSADE in 1228 and conquered Jerusalem, where he crowned himself king of Jerusalem in the Church of the Holy Sepulchre. He is often called one of the first modern rulers and Stupor mundi (Wonder of the World), being learned in science and economics. He was also fluent in Arabic and fascinated by the oriental world.

During his conflicts with Rome, Pope Gregory IX (r. 1227–41) called him the anti-Christ. This label stuck, and after his death many began to believe that he would return and rule over a 1,000-year *Reich* (Ger. "empire").

See also HOLY ROMAN EMPIRE.

Further reading: David Abulafia, *Frederick II: A Medieval Emperor* (New York: Oxford University Press, 1992); Ernst Hartwig Kantorowicz, *Frederick the Second, 1194–1250* (New York: F. Ungar, 1957); Paul Wiegler, *The Infidel Emperor and His Struggles Against the Pope: A Chronicle of the Thirteenth Century* (London: G. Routledge, 1930).

Freemasonry

Freemasonry is an international movement with roots in medieval European laborers' guilds that in the modern era often took on a coloration of anti-clericalism or anti-Catholicism. The movement was started in the 12th century by English masons as a religious fraternity under the protection of St. JOHN THE BAPTIST, in part to protect the secrets of their craft. The movement soon traveled to the Continent, where it took root in FRANCE, GERMANY, SPAIN, and ITALY. Edward VI (r. 1547–53) of England tried to abolish it for conspiracy.

In the 18th century, many men with no connection to the building crafts joined the group; they organized groups of "accepted" Masons whose purpose was to discuss esoteric and political ideas. Many occult and magical notions were pursued. Some Masons helped develop DEISM, believing that GOD had created the world like a craftsman but then set it loose to be governed by Newton's three laws. Politically, Masons often developed ideas of revolution and helped spark the American and French Revolutions. Such 18th-century notables as George Washington (1732–99) and Benjamin Franklin (1706–90) were Masons.

In Catholic countries (especially Italy and France) Freemasonry assumed both an antimonarchical and an anticlerical cast, attracting the condemnation of several popes (speaking as both rulers of the Papal States and leaders of the church), from Clement XII (r. 1730–40) in 1738 to LEO XIII in 1884. The papal attitude was influenced by the role of freemasons like Giuseppe Garibaldi (1807–82), who led the unification of Italy and the consequent destruction of the PAPACY's temporal powers. In the United States there is clear evidence of hostility between Freemasonry and Catholicism during the 19th century. The 1917 *Code of Canon Law* proscribed membership for Catholics (cn. 2335). Over the years, however, masonry has taken on more of a fraternal and less of an ideological demeanor.

In the past, their secret nature and occasional revolutionary activity created many enemies for the Masons, including the totalitarian regimes of the 20th century. A popular literature grew up portraying the movement as a sinister secret society planning to take over the world.

Masonry is not mentioned in the 1983 revision of the *Code*. However, Cardinal Ratzinger, now BENEDICT XVI, issued a Declaration on Masonic Associations (November 13, 1983), stating, "The faithful who enroll in Masonic associations are in a state of grave sin and may not receive Holy Communion." To the dismay of critics, the declaration did not distinguish between the different types of Freemason associations, such as the Afri-can-American type, which differs widely in theory and practice.

Further reading: Paul A. Fisher, *Behind the Closed Door: Church, State and Freemasonry in America* (Bowie, Md.: Shield, 1989); Arturo de Hoyos and S. Brent Morris, *Freemasonry in Context: History, Ritual, Controversy* (Lanham, Md.: Lexington, 2004); *A Study of Freemasonry* (Atlanta: Home Mission Board, Southern Baptist Convention, 1993).

free will

Free will is the human faculty of being able to decide between two or more courses of action without external force or internal compulsion. Catholic moral teaching, like common civil law, presumes that mature human agents are capable of freedom of action unless there are serious mitigating factors.

Many theologians of the PROTESTANT REFORMATION, relying primarily on St. PAUL (Rom. 7:15–24), argued that humans had entirely lost the capacity of free will, relative to issues of faith and salvation, due to the original SIN of ADAM AND EVE. Catholics argued that freedom was not destroyed in the FALL but only wounded.

Traditionally, Christianity has condemned notions of rigid determinism and predestination as found in the early heresies of GNOSTICISM and MANICHAEISM (Council of Arles, 473, On Grace and Predestination). The Council of TRENT stated that though GOD's preeminent grace is absolutely necessary to salvation, free human assent and cooperation is also necessary (session V, Decree on Justification 5). The council added that failure to believe in free will is grounds for expulsion from the Catholic Church.

Today theologians, philosophers, psychologists, and sociologists all ponder the conditions of and limitations to freedom. All recognize that free will does not occur in a vacuum but is to some extent conditioned by social and other factors, such as oppression, fear, ignorance, emotional instability, drug use, and entrenched habits. Some fatalist philosophers speak of being "condemned to freedom." Notwithstanding the limiting conditions, KARL RAHNER argued that the proper human response to the gift of freedom is thankfulness, a theological attitude that will steer the believer between scrupulosity and self-righteousness.

Further reading: Duns Scotus, *Duns Scotus on Divine Love* (Hant: Aldershot, 2003); F. Michael McLain, ed., *Human and Divine Agency: Anglican, Catholic, and Lutheran Perspectives* (Lanham, Md.: University Press of America, 2003); Karl Rahner, "Theological Freedom," in *Encyclopedia of Theology: The Concise Sacramentum Mundi* (New York: Seabury, 1975) 544–545.

fresco   *See* PAINTING AND SCULPTURE.

Freud, Sigmund   *See* CRITIQUE OF RELIGION.

fundamentalism   *See* TRADITIONALISM.

fundamental theology

In the past, the term *fundamental theology*, or foundational THEOLOGY, referred to the field of apologetics, the literature that presents rational and historical reasons in favor of FAITH. Today it also refers to the study of how theology is grounded in the self-revelation of GOD to humanity (Exod. 3:14–15) and in the faith by which humans receive that revelation (Gen. 15:6; Rom. 4).

Fundamental theology also includes questions that touch on the philosophy of religion (the existence of God and God's relation to the world), apologetics proper, the foundations of systematic theology, and the nature and methods of theology itself. It uses methods taken not only from theology but also from biblical studies, anthropology, history, philosophy, and linguistics.

The apologetic side of fundamental theology finds a biblical root in 1 Peter 3:15, which calls on the believer to make a "defense" (*apologia*) of the hope that comes from the Gospel in gentleness and reverence. Thus, there is also a kerygmatic, or preaching and missionary, aspect to making the case for the reasonableness of the Gospel to the world.

Modern fundamental theology has followed two methodologies. The first is a more epistemological approach, begun in the Tübingen School as a response to the modern understanding of Scripture and tradition and to other currents in philosophy. Key to this was the work of Johann Sebastian von Drey (1777–1853), who argued that REVELATION is not one dogma among others but the condition and presupposition of all others. This tradition is continued in the theology of KARL RAHNER, Heinrich Fries (1911–   ), and HANS KÜNG.

The second approach was found in the more metaphysical *philosophia perennis* of Neoscholasticism. It argued more apologetically, defensively, and polemically in favor of the Catholic faith. This approach was largely superseded by VATICAN COUNCIL II, which, while praising traditional Catholic philosophy, opened the doors to other methodologies.

ECCLESIOLOGY, or the doctrine of the church, plays a key role in fundamental theology, as the church is the transcendental condition for theology and the mediator of both the revelation received from God and the faith of the believer in that revelation. Fundamental theology has also been reshaped by the aesthetic theology of HANS URS VON BALTHASAR, the political theology of Johannes Baptist Metz (1928–   ), LIBERATION THEOLOGY, the cultural theology of David Tracey (1939–   ), and the FEMINIST THEOLOGY OF ELIZABETH SCHÜSSLER FIORENZA. Pope JOHN PAUL II addressed many questions of fundamental theology in his encyclical letter *Fides et Ratio* (September 15, 1998).

Further reading: Elizabeth Schüssler Fiorenza, *But She Said: Feminist Practices of Biblical Interpretation* (New York: Crossroad, 1984); Heinrich Fries, *Fundamental Theology* (Washington, D.C.: Catholic University Press, 1996); Hans Küng and David Tracy, *Paradigm Change in Theology* (New York: Doubleday, 1989); Karl Rahner,

Foundations of Christian Faith (New York: Seabury, 1978); David Tracy, *The Analogical Imagination: Christian Theology and the Culture of Pluralism* (New York: Crossroad, 1981).

funeral, Christian (Lat.: *funus,* "funeral," "burial")

Catholics have three rites for the final "passover" of the CHRISTIAN to his or her life with GOD in CHRIST. There are prayers at the time of a person's death and in conjunction with the vigil (wake) of the burial. These are followed by the EUCHARIST of Christian burial and then the rite of commital of the body or ashes at the burial site with further prayers of commending the soul to God and expression of hope in the RESURRECTION.

Before the reform of the Roman Ritual at VATICAN COUNCIL II, Catholics commemorated DEATH with the rather lugubrious Requiem Mass with its famous dirge *Dies Irae* ("Wrathful Day"), which stressed judgment and the sadness accompanying the departure of the deceased. The mass was celebrated in black vestments.

At Vatican II *Sacrosanctum Concilium* 81, the Constitution on the Sacred Liturgy, mandated that the rite of burial be reformed to reflect "the paschal character of Christian death" while taking into account local traditions. This reform reflects early Christian practice. The new Rite of Funerals was issued in 1969.

The new form of the burial Eucharist stresses the COMMUNION of the deceased with Christ in BAPTISM, the communion of saints to which the person is going, and the Second Coming, or *parousia,* of Christ, at which all the faithful will be reunited at the end of time. In effect, the new funeral service is a resurrection Eucharist and is celebrated with white garments, the same as are used at EASTER.

The church formerly prohibited cremation to contrast Christian hope in bodily resurrection with Roman funeral practices. It is now allowed for health, space, or financial reasons.

Further reading: *The Liturgy Documents: A Parish Resource* (Chicago: Liturgy Training, 2004); *Order of Christian Funerals: General Introduction with Pastoral Notes* (Washington, D.C.: United States Catholic Conference, 1989).

furnishings, church

When one approaches a Catholic church, the first thing one generally sees is a rather ornate facade with decorated entrance doors. Often there are one or more towers, either attached to or alongside the church, which house the church

Church door, Cathedral of Saint-André, Bordeaux, France. The central typanum depicts Christ in glory (top) with 12 apostles (center) and the Last Supper (bottom). *(J. Gordon Melton)*

bells. These facades have undergone considerable alteration in the history of Christian ARCHITECTURE. The doors, especially cathedral doors, often have sculpted or mosaic scenes from the BIBLE and the life of CHRIST, MARY OF NAZARETH, and other saints. Often there are niches in the facades with statues, also of Christ, Mary, and the saints. Many churches have images of the patron after whom the church is named.

When one enters the church, there is often an antechamber with church decorations and a set of inner doors to the sanctuary itself. Upon entering the sanctuary, called the nave, one sees rows of pews and kneelers divided by a central aisle. Sometimes there are side aisles separated from the main aisle by rows of columns. In European churches, especially Romanesque churches, the tops of the columns were carved with biblical scenes, gargoyle-like creatures, and folk motifs. A prime example is the Church of the Madeleine at Vézelay, in Burgundy, FRANCE. The far end of the church is called the apse, where one sees the main ALTAR for the celebration of the EUCHARIST. Often this area is called the sanctuary, a term that can also apply to the whole church itself.

Off to the side or as a separate chamber at the front of a church one will find the BAPTISTERY. In earlier churches BAPTISTERIES were often com-

High altar, All Saints Church, showing the figure of the lamb (Rev. 14:1–5) surrounded by the early Christian symbols of the fishes and loaves (Luke 9:12–17). (University City, Mo.) *(John Huston)*

pletely separate buildings, as at St. John Lateran in Rome and at Ravenna. After the reform of the LITURGY at VATICAN COUNCIL II, baptisteries were given a greater emphasis in church architecture, often being incorporated into the center of the church closer to the altar.

The side aisle(s) is often surmounted with stained glass windows depicting biblical scenes, the BEATITUDES (Matt. 5:3–11), works of charity, saints, theological virtues, and other edifying scenes. In earlier times, cathedral windows were arranged according to a rule of theological TYPOLOGY, with scenes of the Old Testament (north side, shadow) foreshadowing scenes from the New (south side, light).

Around the outer rim of the church in nooks and crannies one also sees statues of particular forms of Christ and Mary and special patron saints that have become central to popular Catholic devotion. EASTERN CATHOLICISM, like EASTERN ORTHODOXY, places emphasis on devotion toward ICONS rather than statues, although many Eastern rite churches in the West have succumbed to Roman practice. Among the most frequent statues are images of the SACRED HEARTS OF JESUS and Mary, the Infant of Prague, Sts. JOSEPH OF NAZARETH (the husband of Mary), ANTHONY OF PADUA, ROSE OF LIMA, Anne, the mother of Mary (see JOACHIM AND ANNE), and THÉRÈSE OF LISIEUX. Many ethnic immigrants in Europe and the United States have introduced images special to their native lands, such as the icons of Our Lady of Czestochowa from Poland and Our Lady of Guadalupe from Mexico. There are usually banks of vigil candles in front of these statues and images, which devotees light after making an offering and a prayer of special intention. Also around the church or along the walls of a side chapel one finds bas-reliefs of the Stations of the Cross, showing scenes of Christ's last hours. There are devotions which are held in front of these images, especially on Fridays, the traditional day of Jesus' death.

Also along the side of the church or in special alcoves are confessionals, boothlike structures used to administer the SACRAMENT OF RECONCILIATION. Today this sacrament often takes place with the penitent and the priest sitting face to face. Many churches have side chapels or side altars, harking back to the days when Mass was celebrated more as the individual act of the priest and not as the central celebration of the community. In many churches these side altars have been removed in response to the reforms of Vatican II. Today a side altar or chapel is set aside for the reservation of the Blessed Sacrament (the consecrated Host), the presence of which is signified by a lamp burning in front of a tabernacle. In the churches of Europe deceased nobles and famous people are interred either in the floor of the nave or in side altars. The church of St. Denis above Paris is the site of the tombs of French royalty. Bishops are often interred in their cathedrals, either in the nave or in a crypt below ground.

The altar in the apse is the focal point of the church. It is where the communal EUCHARIST is celebrated every Sunday and on special feast days. In baroque times the altar was placed right up to the far wall, and the priest faced the altar away from the congregation for the main parts of the Eucharist. In response to Vatican II altars were moved forward so that the priest could now face the people at the Eucharist. There is often a crucifix on or immediately behind the altar and large candlesticks either on or near the altar for lighting candles during the Eucharist. Off to the side are one or more lecterns (Lat. *ambo*) for reading the lessons from the Bible. In former times, there was an altar rail marking off the area for priests and the area for laity. These became very common after the Council of TRENT to emphasize the status of the ordained priest and to counteract Martin Luther's emphasis on the priesthood of all believers.

In many European and Latin American churches there is frequently a reredos, or elaborately carved altar backing, with statues of Mary, Joseph, and the APOSTLES. The altar of the Sistine

Chapel in Rome is adorned with MICHELANGELO's celebrated *Last Judgment*. Altars are often inlayed with mosaics, carvings, and other decorations, frequently of the lamb from the Book of Revelation 5:6, symbolizing the Eucharist as the sacrifice of the Lamb of God. The altar top is also inlaid with an altar stone containing RELICS of Martyrs. The priest consecrates the bread and wine over this stone. During the Eucharist the altar is covered with altar linens and is frequently adorned with pendants with liturgical COLORS appropriate to the season or the feast day.

In sum, a Catholic church is the chief site where the central sacraments of the Catholic faith—baptism and the Eucharist—normally take place, and where the word of God is preached to the faithful. Following Vatican II various conferences of BISHOPS throughout the world have issued guidelines on art and architecture for Catholic worship.

Further reading: *Built of Living Stones: Art, Architecture, and Worship* (Washington, D.C.: National Conference of Catholic Bishops, 2000); Pierre Grimal, *Churches of Rome* (New York: Vendome, 1997); Richard Krautheimer, *Early Christian and Byzantine Architecture* (Harmondsworth: Penguin, 1986); Peter Mazar, *To Crown the Year: Decorating the Church Through the Seasons* (Chicago: Liturgy Training, 1995); Mattheus C. Nieubarn, *Church Symbolism* (St. Louis: Herder, 1912).

Fu Tieshan (1931–) *government-backed Catholic prelate of China*

Fu Tieshan, chairman of the Chinese Patriotic Catholic Association, is the leading Catholic cleric recognized by the Peoples Republic of China. Fu was born in Hubei Province and graduated from Beijing Wensheng College. In 1956 he was ordained a PRIEST at the Xishiku Cathedral in Beijing. In 1957 he accepted membership in the Chinese Catholic Patriotic Association, created at the insistence of the Communist government. The association acknowledged the spiritual authority of the pope but rejected any direct administrative role for him in China.

Fu sat out the years of the Cultural Revolution when the Catholic churches in China were closed. He emerged as one of a small number of priests still left when the churches were allowed to reopen in the late 1970s. In 1979, the Chinese Catholic Patriotic Association was revived, and Fu was named the new BISHOP of the revived diocese of Beijing. He was consecrated in the Church of the Immaculate Conception, which had been the first Catholic Church allowed to reopen in Beijing. The church remains the center of the diocese of Beijing.

As the Catholic Church grew significantly through the 1980s, Fu accepted greater leadership roles and became a vocal advocate for the officially sanctioned church and an opponent of the continued efforts of bishops and priests who remained loyal to papal authority. Fu was elected vice chairman of the Chinese Patriotic Catholic Association in 1993 and succeeded Bishop Zong Huai-De as chairman in 1998. He has also participated in the Chinese People's Political Consultative Conference (CPPCC), an advisory body that includes non-Communists and usually meets in parallel to plenary sessions of the National People's Congress. In 2003, he was named vice chairman of the Standing Committee the National Peoples Congress, the highest political office ever held by a churchman under the Communist regime.

Over the years, Fu has openly supported the policies of government as he tried to rebuild and extend Catholicism in China in the post–Cultural Revolution era. His efforts have won him continued criticism internationally from papal loyalists and leaders of other religious bodies.

JOHN PAUL II's canonization of the Chinese martyrs on October 1, 2000, was seen in China as a political rather than religious act. On several occasions Fu has accused the Vatican of meddling in China's internal affairs, especially in regard to Taiwan. In 2000, he became the vice chair of the

Chinese Anti-Cult Association, the goal of which is to suppress the Buddhist group Falun Gong and other groups like it. In the same year Fu led the Chinese delegation to the millennium summit of religious leaders held in New York City, where he spoke against both Falun Gong and the Dalai Lama. Most recently, in 2003, he criticized the Roman Catholic bishop of Hong Kong, Joseph Zen Ze-kiun (1932–   ) for his effort to organize opposition to proposed changes in Hong Kong's civil rights laws.

Under BENEDICT XVI, the Catholic Church is making a new effort to reach an accommodation with the Chinese government. Fu was invited to the synod of bishops in the Vatican in October of 2005, but he did not attend.

Further reading: *Catholic Church in Beijing* (Beijing: Diocese of Beijing, 1990); Foster Stockwell, *Religion in China Today* (Beijing: New World, 1993); Scott W. Sunquist, ed., *A Dictionary of Asian Christianity* (Grand Rapids, Mich.: Eerdmans, 2001).

G

Galileo Galilei (1564–1642) *mathematician and scientist*

Galileo was an Italian mathematician and polymath scientist. As an astronomer he is known for inventing one of the first telescopes and for defending the heliocentric theory of planetary motion of NICOLAUS COPERNICUS (1473–1543). For the latter "offense" he was brought before the Holy Office of the INQUISITION, first in 1615 and then in 1633, where he was made to renounce his views.

Born in Pisa, Galileo at first wanted to enter the religious life but was prevented by his father, Vincenzio, a music theorist. He studied medicine at Pisa but switched to mathematics and became professor there in 1589. The field of mathematics at that time included what we now separate into physics and astronomy. Thereafter, he taught at Padua before becoming chief philosopher and mathematician to Cosimo II de' Medici, grand duke of Tuscany (1590–1621) in 1610.

In *Dialogues Concerning Two New Sciences* (1638) Galileo demonstrated empirically that unimpeded horizontal motion would continue indefinitely and that unimpeded vertical motion downward accelerates uniformly, two laws that anticipate the three laws of motion of Isaac Newton (1642–1727). He learned about the new instrument called the telescope and had prototypes made, after which he began studying the heavens empirically. He learned that Jupiter has four "planets" that move about it, perhaps giving him the clue that the planets move about the Sun in the same way. His results were published in *The Starry Messenger* (1610). He concluded, in defense of Copernicus's system, that it made more sense to say that the Earth moved around the Sun than the reverse, a view that he endorsed more openly in his private *Sunspot Letters* (1613).

The dowager grand duchess Christina (1565–1637) expressed dismay concerning this theory to the Benedictine Benedetto Castelli (1668–1743), a follower of Galileo, noting that the BIBLE, especially the passage about the Sun stopping in Joshua 10:12–13, seems to assert that the Earth does not move. In his letter to Castelli (December 21, 1613) and a subsequent letter to the grand duchess (1615), Galileo argued that one must consult both the Book of Scripture and the Book of Nature to find the truth, that the Bible frequently speaks figuratively (God's "hands"), and that the Aristotelian and Ptolemaic systems were even more in discord with the account in Joshua, as the sun would have set even sooner in that case. The sun's "motion of the other" would not have deterred the "motion of the same" of the empyream. This daring essay was widely circulated and elicited denunciations for heresy from Dominican preachers in Florence, leading to Galileo's first examination by the Inquisition in Rome. Though the JESUIT scientists confirmed his observations, Galileo was forced into delicate negotiations. Cardinal ROBERT BELLARMINE, taking an instrumentalist approach to scientific theory, suggested that Galileo could use Copernicus's hypothesis to explain the phenomena as observed by humans, but not as a description of the way the heavens really move. Copernicus's *On the Revolution of the Heavenly Spheres* (1543) and the books supporting him were placed on the Index of Prohibited Books until corrected (March 16, 1616), but Galileo escaped censure in 1615.

In 1623 Cardinal Maffeo Barberini, a friend of Galileo, was elected Pope Urban VIII (r. 1623–44). He held views similar to Bellarmine's about the nature of scientific hypotheses. In the same year Galileo published the *Assayer,* which argued for an atomistic theory of matter. Enemies claimed that it violated the doctrine of TRANSUBSTANTIATION, but Galileo was exonerated.

All this time Galileo privately upheld the reality of the Copernican system. Thinking he had the permission of the Inquistional authorities in Rome and Florence, he published *Dialogue on the Two Chief World Systems, Ptolemaic and Copernican* (1632), in which, though he argued for the Copernican view "hypothetically," he showed that he truly thought that the Earth's motion was factual, unconditional, and real. He also discussed Scripture. On top of that, he put Urban VIII's theory of hypothetical instrumentalism in the mouth of Simplicio, the simpleton of the *Dialogue.* Offended and pressed by the Thirty Years War (1618–48), the pope called Galileo before the Inquisition, where he was once more made to retract his position and this time placed under house arrest, where he remained for the rest of his life. Legend has Galileo saying in Italian under his breath on exiting from the trial *"Eppur si muove"* ("Nonetheless, [the Earth] still moves").

The Catholic Church lived to rue the Galileo condemnation. Against the overwhelming evidence provided by Isaac Newton in his *Philosophiae Naturalis Principia Mathematica* (1687), which gathered and transformed all the evidence in favor of the heliocentric system, the official church remained silent, even though by then Catholic scholars were teaching heliocentrism all over the world. It did not remove Copernicus's *Revolutions* from the Index of Prohibited Books until 1822. In 1979, JOHN PAUL II set up a commission to study the Galileo affair. Speaking for the Commission on Culture, Cardinal Joseph Jean Poupard (b. 1930) issued a report (October 31, 1992) during a papal audience that admitted "subjective error" on the part of "Galileo's judges," who confused matters of fact with matters of faith. Noticeably absent from the report is any explicit admission that the papacy itself committed any errors even in matters of fact.

Further reading: Stillman Drake, *Discoveries and Opinions of Galileo* (New York: Doubleday Anchor, 1957); Maurice A. Finnochiaro, *The Galileo Affair: A Documentary History* (Berkeley: University of California Press, 1989); Galileo Galilei, *Galileo on the World Systems,* abridged by Maurice A. Finnochiaro (Berkeley: University of California Press, 1997); David C. Linberg "Galileo, the Church, and the Cosmos," in David C. Lindberg and Ronald L. Numbers, eds., *When Science and Christianity Meet,* (Chicago: University of Chicago Press, 2003) 33–60.

Gaudium et Spes   *See* VATICAN COUNCIL II.

genuflexion (Lat.: *genu,* "knee" + *flectere,* "to bend")

Genuflexion is a momentary bending on the right knee with the torso erect as a sign of reverence. The act probably had its origins in the deference shown to nobility. In the early church and today in the Eastern Rite churches worshippers commonly stand during religious services, with bows at appropriate moments.

Before the revision of the Roman Rite in 1967 Catholics used to genuflect at the word *incarnatus,* or "became flesh," during the recitation of the Nicene-Constantinopolitan CREED. Today it is done only on Christmas Day (December 25) and the Feast of the Annunciation (March 25). Double genuflection on both knees is part of the Good Friday service during the Exposition of the CROSS.

It was also common to genuflect on one knee when entering the pew of a church, and when crossing past the tabernacle where the Blessed Sacrament is kept. Double genuflexion was used in case the Blessed Sacrament was exposed. In the rite of the MARONITE CATHOLIC CHURCH congregants have a special ceremony on the Feast of Pentecost of kneeling on the left knee to signify God the Father, on the right, the Son, and on both knees, the HOLY SPIRIT. The number and places at which genuflexions were made during the celebration of the EUCHARIST were reduced in the new ritual mandated by VATICAN COUNCIL II.

Further reading: E. Bertaud, "Génuflexions et Métanies," *Dictionaire de Spiritualité* (1967) 6:213–226; Rama P. Coomaraswamy, *What's Wrong with the New Mass* (London, Ont.: CCCP London, 1989).

Germany

In Roman times Germania included the lands roughly north of the Alps and east of the Rhine, although Teutonic tribes were never respecters of borders. Tacitus described the Germans as beer-swilling, milk-drinking, and meat-eating pastoralists who refused to settle in cities. Like the Celts, the Germans revered oaks and felt their gods dwelled in forests. The eastern Teutons included Goths, Vandals, Burgundians, and Lombards, who invaded lands to the west and south that now bear their names.

There is evidence of CHRISTIANS in Germany as early as 200. Maternus of Cologne-Trier (d. c. 325) attended the local councils of Rome (313) and Arles (314), which dealt with the DONATISM controversy. Uliphas (c. 311–c. 383), a disciple of Eusebius of Caesarea (c. 260–c. 341) and an Arian missionary from Cappadocia (*see* ARIANISM), converted the eastern Goths north of the Danube. He translated the BIBLE into Gothic but omitted the books of Kings, as their war-laden themes might overencourage the Germans in their natural propensity toward violence.

During the Merovingian dynasty (500–751) the Salian Frank Clovis I (466–511) converted to Christianity, bringing his subjects and conquered tribes into relation with Rome. He also defeated the Arian Visigoth Alaric II in 507, thereby stemming the Arian influence north of the Danube. In the early eighth century BONIFACE, the Apostle of Germany, came from England to convert the local tribes. The Carolingian dynasty (752–911) under CHARLEMAGNE brought the German tribes into close relations with Rome and all things Roman, including the LITURGY and CHANT, during the CAROLINGIAN RENAISSANCE. The Carolingian kings, however, never could consolidate their rule over the many duchies of Franconia, Saxony, Bavaria, Swabia, and Lorraine.

German history proper began, according to many historians, with the Saxon Dynasty (919–1024) and the election of Conrad I (r. 911–18). His grandson Otto I the Great (r. 936–73) was crowned Roman emperor in 962 by Pope John XII (r. 955–64), whom he delivered from the slough of Italian politics. Otto was the first of what later came to be called Holy Roman Emperors (*see* HOLY ROMAN EMPIRE). Under his rule, BISHOPS were elevated to the rank of princes and given generous land grants, which helped the king to expand into Bohemia and Poland. By inviting the sly Saxon into Rome, the pope paved the way for nearly a millennium of interference by German emperors and princes in the internal affairs of the church and the secular politics of Italy itself.

A CONCORDAT was reached at Worms (1022) under which the pope could appoint but the emperor could veto a bishop or abbot. The interference came to a head during the Salian Frank Dynasty (1024–1125) when Emperor HENRY IV went toe to toe with Pope GREGORY VII HILDEBRAND at Canossa in 1077 over the INVESTITURE CONTROVERSY. The crisis weakened the power of the emperor to the benefit of local princes. German intellectual vitality also declined, as France and Italy became the sponsors of the great new universities where theological learning flourished.

The rivalry within Germany between the rival dynasties of Saxon Welfs and Swabian Hohenstaufens spilled over into Italy in the form of the wars of the Guelfs and Ghibellines. FREDERICK I BARBAROSSA spent most of his time in Italy, where Pope Alexander III (r. 1159–81) thwarted his path. FREDERICK II reigned chiefly from Sicily and left the German princes and bishops to rule their own territories. Cities gained power, too. The East was colonized by the Knights of the Teutonic Order, a fierce fighting band of MONKS spreading the Gospel by violence, not preaching.

After an interregnum the Habsburgs of Austria took over the Holy Roman Empire. Typically, German factionalism continued to prevail, with power now divided between emperors, princes, bishops, and the mercantile cities of the Hanseatic League. But intellectual ferment began to rise with the founding of new universities: Prague (1348), Vienna (1365), Heidelberg (1386), and Cologne (1388). The invention of movable type by Johann Gutenberg (c. 1397–1468) facilitated the spread of independent religious thought first signaled by JAN HUS (1369?–1414), who had the support of Emperor Wenceslaus (1361–1419).

No one was prepared for the explosion that Martin Luther (1483–1546) unleashed on the German empire and Christendom itself with his calls for reform, resulting in the PROTESTANT REFORMATION. CHARLES V, triangulated between the French, the Turks, and the German princes, was weak from the moment he took the throne in 1519, while Germany's proverbial provincial factionalism aided Luther in pitting one elector against another. Luther released a tide of new religious currents, most not to his own liking, including in Germany the Peasant's War (1524), the Anabaptist movement, and varieties of millennialism. Subsequent wars of religion terminated in the Peace of Augsburg (1555), which laid down the informal rule *cuius regio, eius religio,* "whoever owns the region, his religion prevails," as long as it was either Catholicism or Lutheranism. Religious disputes were to be adjudicated in the courts and not on the battlefield.

Nevertheless, religious tension remained high. The Protestants refused to recognize the reformed GREGORIAN CALENDAR of Pope Gregory XIII (r. 1572–85), which corrected the errors of the old Julian Calendar, even though the brilliant Lutheran astronomer Johannes Kepler (1571–1630) urged them to do so. Everyone tried to jockey for territory, Catholic against Protestant, Catholic against Catholic, and Protestant against Protestant. Catholic princes formed the Catholic League for the purpose of thwarting Protestant rights and aspirations. France entered the fray to advance Bourbon interests versus the Habsburgs. Gustavus Adophus of Sweden (1594–1632) brought down an army to protect the Lutheran cause only to die in battle.

When everyone had had enough, some on both sides signed the Treaty of Prague (1634), to be followed by the more solemn PEACE OF WESTPHALIA (1648), which included Calvinism as an acceptable state religion and recognized the independence of Switzerland and the Netherlands. There followed a period of enlightened absolutism (1648–1789), which was shaken by the wars following the French Revolution (1789). Catholicism experienced a revival during the Romantic age with the founding of the Catholic faculty at the University of Tübingen School, and Catholic thought flourished. The blossom, however, was thwarted by the KULTURKAMPF, launched by Otto von Bismarck (1815–90) in an attempt to consolidate the German Lutheran states in the north and to isolate Catholic Austria. Meanwhile, many German Catholics became alienated from the PAPACY and its declaration of papal INFALLIBILITY at VATICAN COUNCIL I.

Germany was one of the seedbeds of the LITUR-GICAL MOVEMENT, centered at the Abbeys of Beuron and MARIA LAACH. All of Germany was devastated in the aftermath of World War I, but the Center Party led a Catholic revival during the Weimar Republic (1918–29). Unfortunately, the Vatican abandoned the party in its fateful CONCORDAT with Adolf Hitler (1889–1945) in 1933. Although there were a few bishops and church leaders like Cardinal Bl. Clemens August Graf von Galen (1878–1946) who stood up to Hitler on the issues of euthanasia and the persecution of the Jews, much of Hitler's staunchest support came from Catholic Bavaria and Austria (see NAZISM).

After World War II Catholicism experienced a remarkable revival on the liturgical, pastoral, and theological fronts. The country gave the world the outstanding theologians KARL RAHNER, Heinrich Fries (1911–), and Johannes Baptist Metz. Many believe that Rahner was the foremost theologian of the 20th century. He played the key theological role at VATICAN COUNCIL II. Among the group of outstanding theologians was also Joseph Ratzinger, now BENEDICT XVI. During the revolutionary fervor of 1968, some Catholics vented their belief that church authorities had not completed the promises of Vatican II, while others like Ratzinger were shocked into a desire to retrench. In effect, the church split between progressives and conservatives. Benedict XVI in effect leads the conservative wing, with Swiss theologian HANS KÜNG of the University of Tübingen remaining a voice of protest. But recently the pope invited Küng for a meeting in the papal residence.

There are about 29 million Catholics in Germany today in 18 dioceses, but church attendance and vocations to the priesthood have declined dramatically in recent decades. Catholic church attendance declined from 37 percent in 1970 to 23 percent in 1990. Many German Catholics favor allowing married priests and the ordination of women. Most German Catholic women practice birth control as a matter of conscience.

Further reading: John Cornwell, *Hitler's Pope: The Secret History of Pius XII* (New York: Penguin, 2000); Michael Gross, *The War Against Catholicism: Liberalism and the Anti-Catholic Imagination in Nineteenth-Century Germany* (Ann Arbor: University of Michigan Press, 2004); Robert A. Krieg, *Catholic Theologians in Nazi Germany* (London: Continuum, 2004); John McManners, *The Oxford Illustrated History of Christianity* (Oxford: Oxford University Press, 1990); Thomas O'Meara, *Church and Culture: German Catholic Theology 1860–1914* (Notre Dame: University of Notre Dame Press, 1991).

Gibbons, James (1834–1921) *pioneering U.S. Catholic archbishop and cardinal*

James Gibbons was the leading Catholic prelate in the United States in the era when the church came into its own as a major component in American life. Gibbons was born in Baltimore, Maryland, but spent much of his childhood in Ireland. After returning, he attended St. Mary's Seminary in Baltimore and was ordained a PRIEST in 1861. In 1868 he was consecrated BISHOP of North Carolina, a diocese with fewer than 1,000 Roman Catholics. He managed to open schools, build churches, and increase the number of priests from five to 15. He became the ARCHBISHOP of Baltimore in 1877 upon the death of Archbishop James Bayley (1814–77) and was made the second Roman Catholic cardinal in North America in 1886 by Pope LEO XIII.

Gibbons led American Catholics during turbulent times and helped the church deal with three major issues. He managed to keep the church together in the 19th century during the massive waves of immigration, which made Catholics the largest single religious denomination in the country, by mediating ethnic tensions among the immigrant groups. Second, he advised many presidents, showing that Roman Catholicism was compatible with American life at a time when many Protestants believed that loyalty to Rome was a threat to democracy. Third, Gibbons is justly famous as a staunch defender of the Catholic labor movement in its fight for better wages and working conditions, influencing the pope to support the labor cause. Gibbons wrote "It is the right of the laboring class to protect themselves, and the duty of the whole people to find a remedy against avarice, oppression and corruption."

For almost 40 years Gibbons was the public face of Roman Catholicism in America, and he was widely mourned at his death. He published *The Faith of Our Fathers,* a clear and simple exposition of Catholic FAITH that was widely distributed in the nation.

Further reading: John Tracy Ellis, *The Life of James Cardinal Gibbons* (Milwaukee: Bruce, 1963); James Gibbons, *The Faith of Our Fathers: Being a Plain Exposition and Vindication of the Church Founded by Our Lord Jesus Christ* (Baltimore: Murphy, 1904); Arline Boucher Tehan, *Prince of Democracy: James Cardinal Gibbons* (Garden City, N.Y.: Hanover House, 1962).

Gilson, Étienne (1884–1978) *Neothomist philosopher*

Étienne Gilson was one of the most important Catholic thinkers of the 20th century. Gilson made numerous contributions to the study of philosophy and its changing modalities in history. At the same time he brought about a greater appreciation for THOMAS AQUINAS, the subject of the bulk of his attention and writing.

Gilson was born June 13, 1884, in Paris and raised in a Catholic family. In 1904 he entered the Sorbonne, where he studied philosophy, and upon completion of his work in 1907 he taught in several secondary schools. In 1913 he completed his doctoral thesis and was appointed to a chair at the University at Lille. He subsequently taught at Strasbourg (1919–21) and the Sorbornne (1931–32); beginning in 1932, he held the chair of medieval philosophy at the Collège de France.

In 1926 Gilson traveled to North America, the first of many trips, one fruit of which was the establishment of a research institute centered on medieval studies in Toronto, which matured into the Pontifical Institute of Mediaeval Studies. Gilson considered Thomas Aquinas the epitome of Western thinking and did much to woo Catholic intellectuals back to him and away from other philosophical options that had been attracting them in the modern world. He saw Aquinas as the best means to wed the Christian faith to rational thinking. Besides his many travels and lectures, Gilson extended his influence with his many books, monographs, and scholarly articles. He died September 19, 1978, in Auxerre, France.

Further reading: Étienne Gilson, *The Christian Philosophy of St. Thomas Aquinas* (New York: Random House, 1956); ———, *The Spirit of Mediaeval Philosophy* (New York: Scribner's Sons, 1940); ———, *God and Philosophy* (New Haven Conn.: Yale University Press, 1959); ———, *Being and Some Philosophers* (1949); ———, *The Philosopher and Theology* (1960, tr. 1962); Margaret McGrath: *Étienne Gilson. A Bibliography/Une bibliographie* (Toronto: Pontifical Institute of Mediaeval Studies, 1982); A. C. Pegis, ed., *Gilson Reader* (Garden City, N.Y.: Image, 1962).

glory of God

Glory is a symbolic but real expression for the wondrous majesty and splendor of GOD's reality. It is also an expression of the adoration, praise, and worship due to the Godhead. The Hebrew word is *kabod* and the Greek *doxa*.

In the Old Testament, God is depicted with metaphors of majesty and power: the angels who visit Abraham at the oak of Mamre (Gen. 18:1–3), the burning bush of Moses (Exod. 3:2), the storm tossing Pharaoh's soldiers into the sea (Exod. 15:1–2), and the pillar of cloud before the Tent of the Meeting (Exod. 33:9). This sense of God's glory is continued in the New Testament, where it appears to the shepherds at the birth of Jesus

(Luke 2:9) and at the Transfiguration (Mark 9:2) Jesus' apparition with Moses and Elijah before Peter, James and John.

The theme of giving glory to God appears very early in CHRISTIAN writings (Rom. 16:27) in what were likely snippets from hymns and antiphons. These hymns of praise were no doubt derived from first-century Jewish *berakoth,* or blessings. The angels' anthem "Glory to God in the Highest" (Luke 2:14) became the opening words of the early Christian psalm known as the Greater Doxology and still sung or recited at the EUCHARIST. The *Gloria Patri,* known as the Lesser Doxology, was patterned on the baptismal formula at the end of the gospel of Matthew 28:19. It became widespread in the struggle against ARIANISM toward the end of the fourth century as the glory given to the three persons of the TRINITY implies equality of status. Today it is recited at the end of hymns and psalms in the Divine Office, or PRAYER OF THE HOURS or in conjunction with the PRAYERS of Our Father and Hail Mary.

Perhaps no other modern Christian has expressed the wonder of God's glory in greater depth than the Jesuit poet GERARD MANLEY HOPKINS in his sonnet "God's Grandeur":

The world is charged with the grandeur of God.
It will flame out, like shining from shook foil.

Further reading: Louis Bouyer, *Cosmos: The World and the Glory of God* (Petersham: St. Bede's, 1988); Herbert Thurston, *Familiar Prayers: Their Origin and History* (Westminster, Md.: Newman, 1953); Bernard Capelle, *Travaux liturgiques* (Louvain: Centre Liturgique, Abbaye de Mont César, 1955–67).

glossolalia (Gk.: *glossa,* "tongue" + *lalia,* "speaking")

Glossolalia is the ecstatic speaking in tongues. This 19th century term was invented to describe the phenomenon described by the Apostle PAUL in 1 Corinthians 14:1–25. Early CHRISTIANS took this *charisma,* or gift, as a sign of the HOLY SPIRIT's working (Acts 2:4–6; 10:46; 19:6). The aim of the speakers seemed to be praising and giving GLORY to God.

What precisely the "speaking" or "babbling" was remains obscure. Psychologists have described glossolalia as a loosening of conscious control over speech so that the unconscious expresses itself in both coherent words taken from the LITURGY (*Abba! Alleluia! Maranatha!* "Father! Alleluia! Come O Lord!") or babbled phrases. Some have compared it to the oracular style of the ecstatic prophets in the Old Testament (1 Sam. 10:5–11), others to the enthusiastic shouting that accompanied pagan Dionysiac rites.

A verse in Acts 2:13 seems to indicate that speaking in tongues was a sign of elevated excitation and exaltation, potentially placing the ecstatic individual above the community. One thing seems very clear: Paul insisted that the gifts were not for personal aggrandizement but came from the single Spirit and were meant to build up the body of the church. If there were to be speaking in tongues, there also had to be an interpreter for the benefit of others (1 Cor. 14:6–11).

Speaking in tongues experienced a revival with the rise of modern evangelistic Pentecostalism, which has had a significant impact on the CHARISMATIC RENEWAL movement among Catholics. There is much disagreement about the value of glossolalia in modern Christianity. For some it is the Spirit speaking to the church; for others it is religious showmanship.

Further reading: Raniero Cantalamessa, *The Mystery of Pentecost* (Collegeville, Minn.: Liturgical Press, 2001); Eddie Ensley, *Sounds of Wonder: Speaking in Tongues in the Catholic Tradition* (New York: Paulist, 1977); Christopher Forbes, *Prophecy and Inspired Speech in Early Christianity and its Hellenistic Environment* (Peabody, Mass.: Hendrickson, 1997); Frank Stagg, *Glossolalia: Tongue Speaking in Biblical, Historical, and Psychological Perspective* (Nashville: Abingdon, 1967).

Gnostic/Gnosticism (Gk.: *gnosis,* "knowledge," "insight")

The word *gnosticism* has the same Indo-European root as the English verb *to know.* In the context of the early CHRISTIAN era, *gnosis* meant revealed sacred knowledge accessible only to those who had been initiated into secret teachings. Christian Gnostics believed that only the secret teachings of Jesus, the Heavenly Revealer, could bring salvation and aid one to escape from the bonds of material existence.

The label *Gnostic* was coined by the orthodox opponents of the movement; those Gnostics who arose in the Christian stream believed themselves to be simply Christians. In modern times the term, with its connotation of HERESY, has often been used indiscriminately by devout Christians to criticize any political system, philosophical thought, or religion (such as Hinduism, Buddhism, or New Age) they happen to disagree with or dislike.

In the past, all we knew about the ancient Gnostics derived from refutations of their beliefs by orthodox church writers like TERTULLIAN OF CARTHAGE, HIPPOLYTUS OF ROME, and IRENAEUS OF LYONS, especially from the latter's *Against Heresies.* Some Gnostic texts like the Acts of Thomas, Pistis Sophia, and the Gospel of Mary were well known by the 19th century. Then in 1945 a number of Coptic manuscripts found near the ancient site of Chenoboskian, today Nag Hammadi, EGYPT, came to light that greatly expanded the available material. The texts were originally composed in Greek and translated into Coptic. They contain Gnostic, Neoplatonic, Hermetic (Greek metaphysical mysticism), and general ascetic and mystical writings, probably used in nearby Pachomian MONASTERIES (*see* PACHOMIUS) and buried perhaps to avoid detection by orthodox authorities in Alexandria. Among the writings was the celebrated Gospel of Thomas (*see* GOSPEL). As the monasteries associated with Pachomius were known to be orthodox, it is possible that the manuscripts were kept in monastic libraries for the purpose of refutations of the type noted above.

There seems to have been a fundamental Gnostic myth with many variants: the SOUL once enjoyed bliss in union with the dual Mother-Father of the All (in some variants, the primordial Monad), located above the planetary spheres of the heavens. A series of divine pairs, called syzygies, emanate from this Origin; they are called the Pleroma (Gk. "Fullness"). The soul experienced desire and, in the personification of *Pistis* (Gk. "Faith") or *Sophia* (Gk. "Wisdom"), fell toward the material world through the spheres of the heavenly bodies (*Hypostasis of the Archons*). The lower, material world was created by a Demiurge, sometimes called Yaldabaoth, in a bungled attempt to imitate the first divine being. MARCION identified this creator with the God of the Old Testament. While not exactly EVIL, the lower world abides in obscurity and at great distance from the Light of Truth. In its captive state in the body the soul exists in darkness and ignorance.

In order to return to the primordial Pleroma the soul first has to discover its true identity as a "spirit." Many Gnostics believed that Jesus descended from above, on the model of Wisdom in the late Judaic APOCALYPSE 1 Enoch 42:1–2, to provide this secret knowledge plus the passwords allowing the freed spirit to pass through the planetary spheres and return to the Godhead. In some versions Jesus becomes the syzygy, or partner, of Sophia. Gnostics believed that they were the true "pneumatics" (those aware of their inner *pneuma,* or spirit), while ordinary Christians were "psychics" (aware of their *psyche,* or soul), and all others were "hylics" (ignorantly stuck in *hyle,* or matter). The return of the spirit to the Pleroma was celebrated ritually as a marriage of the soul with its heavenly counterpart. Some taught that the true RESURRECTION is not of the body but has already occurred, when Jesus revealed the truth to the enlightened one, a point stressed by the Gnostic writer VALENTINUS in the *Treatise on the Soul.*

The Gnostic teachers were known as itinerant preachers, like the first APOSTLES; the movement accepted women teachers and prophets, who seem to have derived their authority from Mary of Magdala, presented as a rival to PETER in the *Gospel of Mary*. In general, Gnostics traced their roots back to the secret, post-RESURRECTION teachings Jesus committed to certain of his apostles, whereas the orthodox Gospels that are in the present CANON OF SCRIPTURE give preeminence to the public teachings of Jesus.

Gnostics had a very ambivalent attitude toward the body and marriage. The material cosmos was controlled by a bumbling and ignorant Demiurge, patterned after Plato's *Timaeus*. Since the passions of the flesh could hinder returning to the Pleroma, some Gnostics embraced solitary CELIBACY and extreme ASCETICISM. Later ORTHODOX writers accused Gnostics of engaging in libertinism to demonstrate that the body has nothing to do with salvation. Either way, matter and the body were hostile or indifferent obstacles in the way of finding one's true home. The Gnostics seem to have had magical and spiritualist interpretations of the SACRAMENTs like BAPTISM and the EUCHARIST. The late Gnostic rite of "redemption," or "restoration," seems to have been a form of second baptism for pneumatics that releases them from the world to the first Aeon (Gr. "Eternity"). Another rite called the "bridal chamber" seems to have been a ritual of spiritual marriage between the spirit and its syzygy, or heavenly partner.

Many Gnostics favored mythopoetic interpretations of the first six chapters of Genesis and the Jewish books of wisdom. Some speculate that Gnosticism originated in Jewish circles in cities like Alexandria in the second century, but there seem to have also been types influenced independently by Neoplatonic and Hermetic philosophical schools, as well as by the stringent Christian ASCETICISM that was widespread in Syria and Egypt. Neoplatonic philosopher Plotinus (c. 205–70) attacked libertine Gnostics, who claimed to be his followers, for their immoral behavior (*Enneads*, 2.9).

Christian Gnosticism saw Jesus as the Revealer of Wisdom, who did not really die a bodily death but left post-resurrectional secret teachings to

guide the soul to its true home (APOCRYPHON OF JAMES). This is similar to the teaching of Cerinthus, an early 2nd century Docetist. Several different schools or tendencies developed over the course of the second century, and there were a number of outstanding teachers, including Valentinus and Basilides of Alexandria. The latter identified Christ with the Neoplatonic *Nous*, or Mind, and thought that Simon of Cyrene died in Jesus' place. The epistle of 2 Timothy 2:18 speaks of the false teachers Hymenaeus and Philetus, who teach that the resurrection (of the spirit) has already taken place through BAPTISM, a teaching that recurs in Valentinus.

The most influential teacher was Valentinus of Alexandria (fl. 120–60), who taught in Rome and could almost be called the Gnostic pope. He was both profound and brilliant. His *Gospel of Truth* speaks to the deep human desire to escape ignorance and come to the mystical, saving knowledge of and union with GOD. Many of the later Nag Hammadi texts come from the Valentinian school.

Other Gnostic teachers saw themselves as heirs of Seth, the third son of ADAM AND EVE (Gen. 4:25), who retained the true image of the heavenly Adam; his heirs would soon return to their true home. Among the Sethian treatises at Nag Hammadi are the *Apocryphon of John* and *Hypostasis of the Archons*. The Ophites, or Naasenes (Gk. *ophis*, Heb. *nahash* "serpent'), taught that the FALL was not a fall at all but the beginning of enlightenment by the Serpent, who was counteracting the inferior creator of the material world, Yaldabaoth.

It is useful to contrast the basic tenets and practices of the Gnostics with orthodoxy, although at certain points there is some overlap. Whereas the Gnostics felt that the true self was a spark fallen from the divine and lost in matter, the orthodox insisted on a radical distinction between Creator and creature. The Gnostics believed humans were afflicted with illusion and that enlightenment was their salvation, whereas the orthodox taught that what separates the creature and God is SIN, and the way back is repentance. To the Gnostics Jesus was Revealer; to the orthodox he was Savior. The Gnostics were interested in the "Living Jesus" who was awakened when the enlightened person heard his Word within the self. The orthodox favored the elevated notion of Christ as Lord and Son of God who is far above the fallen self. The Gnostics tended to see the material world as an impediment or a hurdle to salvation, whereas the orthodox, in the first article of the CREED, proclaimed that the Father made matter and spirit equally good, although they have had trouble living up to this belief. Gnostics had a decided penchant for abstruse mythopoetic treatises, laden with symbolism and "secret" meanings, whereas the orthodox responded with clear creedal statements. While the Gnostics without doubt preserved the earlier apostolic pattern of wandering preachers, teachers, and prophets, including women, orthodoxy answered them with a male-dominated hierarchical system of resident BISHOPS, priests, and deacons who could claim APOSTOLIC SUCCESSION. This system guaranteed that orthodoxy would win the day. However, some orthodox thinkers such as CLEMENT OF ALEXANDRIA argued for a type of Christian gnosis that would be compatible with orthodox belief and was affirmed by Paul (1 Cor. 13:2; Rom. 15:14). Various forms and aspects of Gnosticism survived beyond the fourth century into the MIDDLE AGES, turning up in different forms among the MANICHEANS, CATHARI (Albigensians), Bogomils, Beguines, and Paulicians.

There have been several attempts to reconstitute the Gnostic Church in modern times, notably in FRANCE by Jules Doinel (1842–1903), who took the name Valintinus II. The Swiss psychiatrist Carl Jung (1875–1961) took a deep interest in Gnostic symbolism, as did Helena Petrovna Blavatsky (1831–91), the founder of Theosophy. In the United States there are many Gnostic societies, the most important of which is the Ecclesia Gnostica directed by the non-Catholic Rt. Rev. Stephan A. Hoeller (1931–).

Several significant studies have related Gnosticism to forms of modern thought. In *Science, Politics and Gnosticism* (1968), the political philosopher Eric Voegelin saw the survival of Gnostic thinking in the modern sense of alienation and in the attempt by modern totalitarianism to "immanentize the eschaton"—to bring the end time into the present. The *Catechism of the Catholic Church* 676 states that the attempt to immanentize the kingdom via secular messianism is the work of the Antichrist (*see* ESCHATOLOGY). Hans Jonas related the Gnostic themes of alien existence in matter to the themes of alienation and "throwness" into existence in the existentialist philosophy of Martin Heidegger in *The Gnostic Religion: The Message of the Alien God and the Beginnings of Christianity* (1958). Elaine Pagels gave Gnosticism an open and sympathetic reading in *The Gnostic Gospels* (1979).

See also DOCETISM.

Further reading: Robert McQueen Grant, *Gnosticism and Early Christianity* (New York: Columbia University Press, 1966); Birger Albert Pearson, *Early Christianity and Gnosticism in the History of Religion* (Claremont, Calif.: Institute for Antiquity and Christianity, 2001); James M. Robinson, ed., *The Nag Hammadi Library in English* (San Francisco: Harper & Row, 1988); Kurt Rudoph, *Gnosis: The Nature and History of Gnosticism* (San Francisco: Harper & Row, 1983).

God (Anglo Sax.: *gott;* Gk.: *theos,* "divine," "immortal being")

Christianity has its roots in the Jewish FAITH, whose belief that there is only one God is stated very clearly in its central prayer: "Hear O Israel, the Lord our God, the Lord is one" (Deut. 6:4). This Jewish faith shaped the monotheism of Christianity and Islam. In contrast with Judaism and Islam, however, CHRISTIANS came to affirm that their one God was a "Tri-unity," or threefold unity of Father, Son, and HOLY SPIRIT. This belief first manifested itself in the liturgical formula used in the BAPTISM ritual (Matt. 28:19).

BIBLICAL SOURCES

The early patriarchal and matriarchal notion of the "God of the fathers" began most likely as a "henotheistic" notion, such as "We have our God who protects us, but the other tribes/nations have their protective deities too." After Israel formed as a nation with a complex religious component this tribal deity was elevated into an exalted God who created heaven and earth (Gen. 1:1). He also became a Lord of history who enters into and renews covenants with those who have faith and demands obedience to the stipulation of those covenants (Gen. 17; Exod. 19–20; Josh. 24).

God reveals this divine self to Moses by a name (Exod. 3:2–15) that is usually translated as "I am who am" but that is most likely a causative, "I cause to be what is." When the voices of the prophets became clear, they declared that this God requires righteousness over ritual (Amos) yet shows mercy and lovingkindness (Hosea). The prophets Isaiah and Ezekiel speak of God's elevated holiness and transcendence. Many prophets spoke of the coming judgment of God on Israel and the nations if they did not convert from their sinful ways (Isa. 2:4). While many held on to a nationalistic concept of God, later prophets came to stress that God was the God of all nations, the savior of Gentiles as well as Jews (Isa. 49:6; Jon.). In the various writings of the Old Testament, God is personified as King (*melek*), Judge (*shophet*), Word (*dabar*), Spirit (*ruah*), Wisdom (*hokmah*), and Presence (*shekinah*). These terms are not so much internal attributes of the Godhead but terms of how God relates to the people.

The New Testament reaffirms all the fundamental Jewish ideas of God as creator, sustainer, providential ruler, and future judge of the universe. It gives particular emphasis to the idea of God as the loving Father (Aram. *Abba*), to whom we can appeal as children in the Spirit through righteousness won for us by CHRIST, his Son (Rom. 8:1–17; Gal. 4:1–7). However, the Spirit and the Son are also now part of God. There are many passages in the New Testament, such as the baptismal formula in Matthew 28:19, that relate the Father, Son, and Holy Spirit (2 Cor. 13:14) to one another, but there is no formal exposition of any doctrine of the TRINITY. The great focus of the New Testament was the proclamation of the GOSPEL of salvation won for all in Christ; any "doctrines" about God were subordinate to that primary message.

THEOLOGICAL DEVELOPMENT

In the second and subsequent centuries the THEOLOGY of God underwent a significant development, becoming both more complex and more precisely defined. Theologians, in debates over the nature of God, Christ, and the Holy Spirit, began to look for "proof texts" in the BIBLE. Simultaneously, Christians began to acquire the technical vocabulary of the various schools of Hellenistic philosophy, especially Neoplatonism and Stoicism, and apply it to their doctrine of God. As a result, formal doctrines about God began to emerge in the debates among Christians themselves and with their Jewish and Greco-Roman peers.

Some, like Tatian the Syrian (second century), rejected Greek philosophy outright, but the widespread use of Greek terminology was only to be expected, as many early apologists and theologians received their training in the philosophical schools. The new vocabulary included terms such as perfection, self-sufficiency, incomprehensibility, ineffability, invisibility (JUSTIN MARTYR), First Cause (TERTULLIAN), invisibility, impassibility (IGNATIUS OF ANTIOCH), and immutability (Aristides of Athens). By the time of the Council of Nicaea (325), the key ontological attributes of God were firmly and officially in place: eternity, omniscience, omnipotence, and immutability.

By the late third and early fourth centuries the speculative theologians of the ALEXANDRINE SCHOOL—especially Sts. CYRIL and ATHANASIUS—had formulated the key concepts to fight ARIANISM, the greatest HERESY of the first millennium. The Arians doubted that the Son was equal to Father, saying instead that he was only *homoios*, or "like unto," the Father. Athanasius argued in opposition that Christ had to have been divine for salvation to have taken place. At the Council of Nicaea, bishops and theologians agreed on a compromise wording: the Son was *homoousios,* or "of the same being/substance," as the Father. This became the major benchmark in what came to be called orthodoxy and a part of the Nicene-Constantinopolitan CREED.

Nicaea clarified Christological teachings, but questions remained about the status of the HOLY SPIRIT and the Trinity. Already in the second century the apologist Athenagoras of Athens had argued that the Holy Spirit is an "outflow" (Gk. *aporrsia*) of God and that the Father, Son, and Spirit relate to one another by a "power in union and distinction in order" (*Apology* 10). At the end of the fourth century the Neoplatonist Cappadocians Sts. Basil of Caesarea, GREGORY OF NAZIANZUS, and GREGORY OF NYSSA provided the terminological framework for the orthodox definition of the Trinity: the Father, Son, and Spirit share one common nature, being, or substance (Gk. *ousia,* Lat. *substantia*) and yet are distinct as three persons (Gk. *hypostases,* Lat. *personae*). This made it possible for the participants at the Council of Constantinope I (381) to affirm the equal divinity of the Holy Spirit (*see* COUNCILS, ECUMENICAL). The creedal formula in the *Exposition of the 150 Fathers* states: "We believe . . . in the Spirit, the holy, the lordly and life-giving one, proceeding from the Father, co-worshipped, and co-glorified with Father and Son."

The Cappadocians refined the theology of the second article (on the Son) by saying that the Son is begotten (*gennesia*) but not created (*genesia*). The divine essence, Gregory of Nazianzus argued, is not identifiable with unbegottenness and is ultimately unknowable (*Theological Orations* 2.4). This allowed them to counter Eunomius of Cyzicus (c. 325–c. 395), the radical Arian who equated deity and unbegottenness and argued that the Son was even "unlike" or "dissimilar" (*anomios*) to the Father on the grounds of his begottenness. The Cappadocians also maintained the biblical notion that the Father is the originating principle in creation, but everything is brought into being through the Son and perfected and sustained by the Spirit. The key to the Cappadocian understanding of divinity is that God is essentially "relation-to-another-who-is-equal." Eastern theologians have always emphasized the distinct roles of the divine persons in the "economy," or unfolding, of salvation in time. This theory is often called "economic, or external, trinitarianism."

In his brilliant and celebrated treatise *On the Trinity* AUGUSTINE OF HIPPO, also a Neoplatonist, began his exposition not with the distinct divine persons, but with the union of the divine substance common to all three. The Trinity is both psychological and anthropological in form. Augustine argues from the images of the Trinity in the operations of SOUL (mind, knowledge, love; memory, understanding, will) and in human perception (object, perception, attention). The soul has these distinct operations, but we do not say that there are three separate souls. This stress on the internal relations of the Trinity is often called "substance, or immanent, trinitarianism." The Eastern form of theology had a tendency toward subordinationism of the Son and Spirit to the Father; the Western form had a tendency toward tritheism. The modern theologian KARL RAHNER sought to resolve the dilemma by stating, "the economic Trinity is the immanent Trinity, and vice versa." Beyond the formal nature of the Trinity, Augustine also sought to tell the story of God's relation to humanity in the grand themes of creation, FALL, REDEMPTION, and Last Judgment in his *City of God.*

In the fifth century Christological theology shifted from soteriological concerns—how Christ saves us—to ontological concerns—how Christ is related to the Father, and what is the nature of the human and divine in Christ. The Council of EPHESUS in 431 tried to resolve one of these ontological conundrums by stating, against Nestorius, that the divine and human natures of Christ are united hypostatically in one person, thereby justifying calling Jesus' mother MARY OF NAZARETH *Theotokos,* or "Mother of God." The Council of CHALCEDON in 451 countered the alleged monophysitism (single, divine nature in Christ) of Eutyches of Constantinople (fl. 450) and Dioscorus of Alexandria (d. 451) by stating that Jesus Christ is "perfect in divinity and perfect in humanity, the same truly God and truly man, of a rational soul and a body; consubstantial with the Father as regards his divinity, and the same consubstantial with us as regards his humanity." In sum, Jesus Christ, the Incarnate Son of the Father, is fully human and fully divine.

This fifth-century formulation of the doctrine of God served as the pattern for the future, and very little was added to it. The fundamental doctrine states that there is one God who subsists in three persons (Father, Son, Holy Spirit), from whom there are two processions (the generation of the Son, and the spiration of the Spirit), and among whom there are four relations (fatherhood and sonhood between Father and Son, and active spiration of the Spirit from the Father and Son and passive on the part of the Spirit). The Greek theologians took great interest in the reality of *perichoresis* (Gk.)/*circumcessio* (Lat.), the "presencing" of the persons of the Trinity to one another in mutuality and reciprocity without confusion. *Perichoresis* means, literally, a "dancing around" one another in the manner of the three Graces. In their fundamental approach to the understanding of God, some theologians gave primacy to the intellect (THOMAS AQUINAS), while others gave primacy to the will (DUNS SCOTUS). Scotus defined the divine essence as love. This theme is important in mystical THEOLOGY.

BOETHIUS added to the theology of God by refining the idea of person as "an individual substance of a rational nature." The Western Church added the FILIOQUE phrase to the creed, much to the dismay of the Eastern Church. The MIDDLE AGES added subtler discussions of the COMMUNICATIO IDIOMATUM, or communication of properties, between the divine and human natures of Christ. Aquinas, employing the metaphysics of ARISTOTLE, defined a divine person as a "subsistent relation" (*Summa Theologica* 1.29.4) such that the divine essence is relational at its root. Aquinas also set the pattern for discussions about God by dividing the topic between "the One God" and "the Triune God."

Despite this division, Aquinas's own advance in trinitarian theology in the discussion of divine personhood as subsistent relation argues against hard-and-fast separation between the One and the Triune. Unfortunately, the Neothomist manuals that appeared after the Neoscholastic revival at the turn of the 20th century solidified the distinction and reduced discussions about God to a sequence of dry propositions.

With the partial exception of John Calvin (1509–64), the reformers rejected the abstract and formal creedalism and Aristotelianism of medieval Scholasticism. Concerned about their salvation, they turned directly to the message of the Bible and to the kind of Jesus piety foreshadowed in THOMAS À KEMPIS's *Imitation of Christ.* Jesus became the focus of evangelical theology.

Since the 19th century the theology of God has swung between the "liberal" theology of the Lutheran Friederich Schleiermacher (1768–1834), who shifted the understanding of God away from pure reason to a "sum feeling for the Absolute or Infinite," and the "orthodoxy" of the Reformed theologian Karl Barth (1886–1968), who returned to the centrality of faith against deformed modern reason. In his monumental *Church Dogmatics* (1932–68) Barth gave primacy to the second article of the creed (Jesus as "God for us") over the first (Father as "God above us") and third (Spirit as "God with us"). Barth paved the way to the Christocentrism—some would say Christomonism—of much 20th-century theology. In response to this Rahner and others have tried to bring a full Trinitarian theology back into the mainstream of Catholic thought and practice.

MYSTICAL THEOLOGY

As the reference to Gregory of Nazianzus above makes clear, there can be no absolute distinction between the formally theological and mystical aspects in discussions about God. Mysticism goes beyond trying to understand God and focuses on the experience of the soul's union with the divine. DIONYSIUS the Pseudo-Areopagite (c. 500) incorporated Neoplatonic speculation into his threefold schema of the approach to God through purification, illumination, and finally union, or perfection. This pattern shaped all subsequent forms of Christian and Catholic mystical theology, notably the *Threefold Way* of St. BONAVENTURE.

John Scotus Eriugina (c. 810–c. 817) maintained that reason might know that God is, but only contemplation could experience what God is. Neoplatonic Augustinianism informed the many kinds of Trinitarian love theology in the Middle Ages. Extending Augustine's psychological analogies to the realm of the social, Richard of St. Victor (d. 1173) argued that the true nature of charity requires a relation between not two but three persons, the third being the mutuality of the love between two (*On the Trinity* 3.19). The mystical understanding of God continued in the thought of MEISTER ECKHART, NICHOLAS OF CUSA, and St. TERESA OF ÁVILA.

PHILOSOPHICAL PROOFS

Attempts to demonstrate the existence of God arose very early in the Christian tradition. Some of the arguments are based on reason alone and some on reason informed by faith.

Already Athenagoras of Athens (fl. 170) provided an argument for the existence and oneness of God in his defense of Christians against pagan charges of atheism (*Apology* 8). In his many writings St. Augustine gave many arguments for the existence of God, from the contingency of the world, from the beauty and order of the universe, from the principles of reason, and from conscience. In his *Proslogion* 3 and *Monologion* 1–2 St. ANSELM OF CANTERBURY gave two versions of his famous "ontological argument," which he sees as beginning in faith. René Descartes (1596–1650)

and Gottfried Leibniz offered versions of this proof. The ontological proof has come up for intense discussion in contemporary philosophical thought. In *Fides et Ratio* 14 (September 14, 1998) Pope JOHN PAUL II cited Anselm's ontological argument approvingly.

St. Thomas distrusted the ontological argument. Instead, he presented five arguments for the existence of God from potentiality, efficiency, possibility, gradation, and the governance of the universe (*Summa Theologiae* 1.2.3). The last has come to be known as the "cosmological argument" and is behind much of the contemporary discussion of "intelligent design" in the universe. Many scholars say the tightest proof for the existence of God in the Middle Ages was provided by Duns Scotus in *On the First Principle,* which argues in many steps that "If something can exist . . . God necessarily exists."

The philosopher Immanuel Kant (1724–1804) argued that one could both prove and disprove the arguments for the existence of God, creating amphiboly (Gk. "tossed two ways") in pure reason and thereby undermining the arguments themselves (*Critique of Pure Reason* B612–658). Georg F. W. Hegel (1770–1832) argued in favor of the proofs in his *Lectures on the Philosophy of Religion* (1827). The logician Gottlob Frege (1848–1925), arguing that the ontological proof posits God by definition, claimed that existence can never be predicated on anything by definition alone, but the mathematician and logician Kurt Gödel defended the ontological argument with a proof based in modal logic.

Contemporary discussions about God have dealt with a variety of themes: the "death of God" movement in the 1960s; process theology based on Alfred North Whitehead (1861–1947) and Charles Hartshorne (1897–2000); LIBERATION THEOLOGY; ECUMENISM and interreligious dialogue; and FEMINIST THEOLOGY. Two recent Catholic theologies of God have had worldwide impact: HANS KÜNG's *Does God Exist?* (1978) and Karl Rahner's *Foundations of Christian Faith* (1978).

Further reading: Alfred J. Freddoso, ed., *The Existence and Nature of God* (Notre Dame: University of Notre Dame Press, 1983); Robert McQueen Grant, *The Early Christian Doctrine of God* (Charlottesville: University Press of Virginia, 1966); J. N. D. Kelly, *Early Christian Doctrines* (London: A. & C. Black, 1977); Catherine Mowry LaCugna, *God for Us: The Trinity and Christian Life* (San Francisco: HarperCollins, 1991); Thomas V. Morris, *Our Idea of God: An Introduction to Philosophical Theology* (Notre Dame: University of Notre Dame Press, 1991); Gerald O'Collins, *The Tripersonal God: Understanding and Interpreting the Trinity* (New York: Paulist, 1999); Gilbert L. Prestige, *God in Patristic Thought* (London: S.P.C.K., 1959).

Golgotha (Aram.: "skull")

Golgotha is the site of the crucifixion of Jesus and two others under the Roman procurator Pontius Pilate. The Greek equivalent is *kranion* (Luke 23:33), translated as *calvaria* in the Latin Vulgate version, the origin of the English term *calvary.*

Golgotha seems to have been a place of execution or ignominious burial (Judg. 9:53; 2 Kings 9:35). There is an early CHRISTIAN tradition (ORIGEN, *On Matthew* 27:33) that Adam was buried at Golgotha. In medieval paintings his skull is frequently depicted at the foot of the CROSS with a drop of Jesus' blood falling on it, signifying that Jesus' blood paid the price for Adam's sin, thus completing the circle. However, there is much dispute about where Adam was historically buried.

Legend has it that St. Helena, mother of CONSTANTINE THE GREAT, received visions as to the location of the holy sites in Jerusalem. Eusebius in his *Life of Constantine* 25–40 reports how Constantine removed a temple of Aphrodite at the place of Jesus' RESURRECTION (Gk. *Anastasis*) and began the Church of the Holy Sepulcher (c. 325–35). The reputed site of Golgotha, a rocky prominence, is included in the southeast corner of the original church. Others have proposed a site near Jerusalem's Damascus Gate as the site of Golgotha.

Further reading: Jack Finegan, *Archaeology of the New Testament* (Princeton, N.J.: Princeton University Press, 1992); Rivka Gonen, *Biblical Holy Places: An Illustrated Guide* (New York: Macmillan, 1987); Joan Taylor with Shimon Gibson, *Beneath the Church of the Holy Sepulchre, Jerusalem: The Archaeology and Early History of Traditional Golgotha* (London: Palestine Exploration Fund, 1994).

good

For the philosopher Plato (427–347 B.C.E.) the good (*agathon*) was the supreme form or idea of all ideas, in which all other beings participated according to their degrees of perfection. He often identified the good with justice. In the *Republic* he argued that the good of the soul is the well-ordered or harmonious relations between the mind, the will, and the passions. The city is the "soul writ large," and in the ideal city he posited in his *Republic,* its good consists in the harmonious relations between the philosopher kings, the guardian fighters, and the workers.

ARISTOTLE, following and adapting Plato, identified the good with "happiness" (*eudaimonia*), a term he identified more with doing right rather than getting pleasure. The good encompasses all the actions, the habits informed by VIRTUES—that orient a being toward its proper fulfillment and end. The virtues can be both intellectual (wisdom, knowledge of first principles) and moral (justice, prudence, fortitude, temperance). Moral virtue makes people good; intellectual virtue enables them to find the good.

Theses notions have come to influence CHRISTIAN thought. In the MIDDLE AGES, philosophical theologians discussed the good using the transcendentals: the one, the true, and the good (*unum, verum, bonum*). Some included more transcendentals, including the beautiful (*pulchrum*). These terms or concepts were deemed to apply to all beings regardless of their ontological status.

The great medieval theologians, especially St. THOMAS AQUINAS, wrote at length about the common good: the ultimate end and good of all human life is common and shared. This principle is based on the mutuality between love of God and love of neighbor (*Summa contra Gentiles* 3.117). Thus, if one truly loves one's neighbors, one will help them to attain tranquility and peace, including the material conditions of life, so that they, too, can come to the love of GOD. In addition, the person who seeks the good of the many seeks his or her own personal good (*Summa Theologica* 2–2.47.19. ad2). This message is barely audible in many modern Western societies that ground their idea of the good on private possessions and personal happiness.

In modern discussions the term *value* tends to replace the term *good*. This can have fateful consequences, as the new term carries with it the weight of subjectivity, if not an individually grounded understanding of the good. In the Catholic tradition, by contrast, the good is an objective and commonly-shared standard against which one measures all else, even if one cannot attain it. Ontologically speaking, many Christian thinkers, beginning with St. AUGUSTINE OF HIPPO, argued that EVIL is the absence or defect of good.

Further reading: Aristotle, *Nichomachian Ethics,* available online; Jonathan Jacobs, *Aristotle's Virtues: Nature, Knowledge & Human Good* (New York: P. Lang, 2004); James Keating. ed., *Moral Theology: New Directions and Fundamental Issues* (New York: Paulist, 2004); Dennis McCann and Patrick Miller, eds., *In Search of the Common Good* (New York: T & T Clark, 2005); Plato, *Republic,* available online.

Good Friday   *See* ASCETICISM; CROSS/
CRUCIFIXION; LITURGICAL YEAR.

Good Shepherd

In the ancient Near East gods, kings, and other leaders were often described metaphorically as shepherds. This imagery carried over into the Hebrew BIBLE, where GOD is frequently called the shepherd and Israel the flock (Isa. 40:10). In the New Testament the metaphor is widely applied to Jesus as the CHRIST (John 10:11–14; Heb. 13:10). In Luke 15:3–7 Jesus tells the Parable of the Lost Sheep, which the shepherd finds and brings home to great rejoicing.

The parable in Luke sets the pattern for the later depictions of Jesus as the Good Shepherd in poetry, painting, and sculpture. CLEMENT OF ALEXANDRIA names him the holy shepherd in his Hymn to Christ the Savior (*Paidogogos* 3.101.3). TERTULLIAN refers to images of the Good Shepherd painted on Communion cups (*On Modesty* 7:1–4). The image occurs in the lunette above the baptismal font at the Dura Europos house church (*see* BAPTISTERY). Frescoes and statues of the Good Shepherd are frequently found in third- and fourth-century CATACOMBS depicting him in the Greco-Roman style of Hermes the Rambearer or of Orpheus, who could soothe animals with his lyre. Christ is youthful and beardless.

After the legalization of Christianity by CONSTANTINE, the image of the Good Shepherd almost disappears in CHRISTIAN art, giving way to the imperial image of Christos Pantokrator, or Christ the Ruler of All. In the 19th century the Good Shepherd image returned in a very sentimental form; it is now one of the more popular images of Jesus in Christian art.

Further reading: Paul Corby Finney, *Art, Archaeology and Architecture of Early Christianity* (New York: Garland, 1993).

Goretti, St. Maria (1890–1902) *martyr, youngest Roman Catholic saint*
On July 5, 1902, 11-year-old Maria was attacked, stabbed 14 times, and mortally wounded by her neighbor, Alessandro Serenelli (1882–1970), who tried to assault her sexually. She died the next day after praying for and forgiving Alessandro, was beatified by the Roman Catholic Church in 1947,

and was declared the youngest saint in 1950 by Pope Pius XII. She is the patroness of modern youth. Her feast day is July 6.

Goretti was born in 1890 in Corinaldo, Italy, to poor sharecroppers and quickly was seen to grow in grace and humility. She showed strength and maturity after her father died from malaria. She did her chores with cheer. The highlight of her young life was her first Holy Communion in 1901.

Maria caught the eye of her next door neighbor, Serenelli, a pedophile, who frequently propositioned her and made sexual advances. She continued to deny him, claiming it was a SIN and against God's will, until he fatally attacked her. After his release from prison in 1932, Serenelli lived as a gardener in the Capuchin monastery of Macerata and wrote of the love he received from his "Guardian Angel."

Further reading: Marie Cecilia Buehrle, *Saint Maria Goretti* (Milwaukee: Bruce, 1950); Alfred Macconastair, *Lily of the Marshes: The Story of Maria Goretti* (New York: Macmillan, 1951).

Görres, Johannes Joseph von (1776–1848)
German Catholic reformist writer

Görres was born and educated at Coblenz, where he imbibed the rationalistic approach that prevailed during the late 18th century. In his early years he was an ardent supporter of the French Revolution (1789–91), but his enthusiasm disappeared after he visited Paris as a delegate in the fall of 1799. From 1800 to 1806 he taught physics at Coblenz. He lectured at the University of Heidelburg from 1806 to 1807 and became acquainted with the leaders of German Romanticism. During the Napoleonic wars he condemned Napoleon (1769–1821) and called for the independence of GERMANY.

Görres's relentless demand for political and religious liberty put him at odds with the German princes, and the Prussian government reacted

by ordering his arrest in 1819. However, he escaped to Strassburg, where he remained until he returned to Munich in 1827, when King Ludwig I of Bavaria (1786–1868) offered him a professorship at the university. There he became the leader of a group of Catholic intellectuals who strove to renovate the spiritual life of the church and fought for its freedom vis-à-vis the government. In 1837 he protested the arrest of the ARCHBISHOP of Cologne.

A gifted writer, Görres produced many political and religious treatises defending Catholic liberty. He founded the first German Catholic newspaper and many other periodicals in order to give Catholics a voice. From 1836 to 1842 he published his greatest work, *Christliche Mystik* (4 vols), a brilliant study of Christian mysticism. His writings helped spread Catholic ideas throughout Germany.

Further reading: Mary Gonzaga, *The Mysticism of Johann Joseph von Görres as a Reaction Against Rationalism: A Dissertation* (Washington, D.C.: Catholic University of America Press, 2001); Joseph von Görres, *Athanasius* (Regensburg: G. J. Manz, 1838); Jon Vanden Heuvel, *A German Life in the Age of Revolution: Joseph Görres, 1776–1848* (Washington, D.C.: Catholic University of America Press, 2001); Esther-Beate Korber, *Görres und die Revolution: Wandlungen ihres Begriffs und ihrer Wertung in seinem politischen Weltbild, 1793 bis 1819* (Husum: Matthiesen, 1986).

gospel (Old Eng.: "good spell/news"; trans. Gk.: *eu*, "good" + *angelion*, "news," "announcement")

The word *gospel* refers both to a theopolitical concept and a literary genre. Theologically, the term can be traced to the Septuagint Greek translation of Isaiah 52:7, where the prophet of the Exile proclaims to a broken Israel the promise of a covenant renewal: "How beautiful upon the mountains / are the feet of *the messenger who announces* (*euangelizomenou*) peace / [*the mes-*

senger] *who brings good news (euangelizomenos) / who announces salvation / who says to Zion, 'Your God reigns.'"* Jesus' own proclamation of the reign of God (Mark 1:14) and the Gospels' echo of that news in their own proclamation of salvation through Jesus harkens back to the theme of the Israelite prophets. GOD yet governs the actions of nations despite Israel's despair. This gospel theme is continued in Isaiah 61.1–2, where the prophet promises that one will come "to preach the good news to the poor . . . to bind up the brokenhearted / to proclaim freedom for the captives / and release from darkness for the prisoners / to proclaim the year of the Lord's favor." Jesus takes this Gospel as his own in Luke 4:18–19.

The term had political implications in the time of Jesus. Throughout Asia Minor during the reign of Caesar Augustus, (31 B.C.E.–14 C.E.), many client cities erected dedicatory calendar monuments in honor of the emperor. The most famous was the Calendar Inscription of Priene, a Greek city on the Ionian coast, modern-day Güllübahçe, Turkey, which dates from about 9 B.C.E.. It recounts how Providence sent Augustus Caesar as a savior (*soter*) and doer of good deeds (*euerges*) to bring peace to the world, winning Augustus the rights of a divine one (*theios*), including the naming of the month of August after him, as the "beginning of the gospel" (*euangelion*). Of course, the Pax Romana memorialized in Priene brought destruction and devastation in the Galilee and alienation of tribal lands that had originally been allotted by God (Num. 13:1–2). The term was also used in imperial proclamations to announce the coming of age and/or ascension of a new emperor to the throne. Given this imperial context, the Gospel proclaimed by and about Jesus was an "anti-gospel," proclaiming another kind of salvation and another kind of peace in the face of the overwhelming and self-deifying power of Rome.

THE GOSPEL GENRE

The gospel was a rich literary genre, going well beyond the familiar four books called by that name. PAUL'S "gospel" is his oral proclamation of the good news about Jesus' death and RESURRECTION (Rom. 1:1–3). The news includes an ethic of mutuality among CHRIST'S followers in building up his church, so different from the hierarchical patron-client relations prevailing in imperial Roman society (Phil. 4:15; 1 Cor. 12). Scholars do not know when the term became applied to the literary form we now call a "gospel." Sometime in the first century the superscript was added to the Gospel of Mark, "The beginning of the gospel of Jesus Christ, Son of God" (Mark 1:1). The use of the word is probably a direct challenge to the imperial "gospel" of Augustus. None of the other canonical Gospels are introduced like this, and their current titles were added later in the tradition: by the second century, JUSTIN MARTYR says that the "memoirs" of the APOSTLES are called "gospels" (*Apology* 1.67).

The Gospels as we now have them shared certain qualities with other Greco-Roman literary forms. The Greek *bios,* or life narrative (whence, biography), recounted the sayings, deeds, and marvelous workings of famous people. The story of the wonder-worker Apollonius of Tyana recounted in Philostratus's *Life of Apollonius* shares many qualities with the narrative of Jesus in Mark. Some compare the Gospels to the tales of virtuous heroes known as aretologies (from Gk. *arete* "virtue"). These tales recount the hero's wise sayings, miracle working, and martyrdom at the hands of tyrants.

Some have compared the Gospels to certain apocalyptic myths about wisdom revealers who descend from heaven and reascend after being rejected on Earth (*1 Enoch* 42.1–2), a theme very common in the GNOSTIC sects of early Christianity. Similar elements are indeed present in certain New Testament passages, as in the hymn used by Paul in Philippians 2:6–11 and the descent of the Logos in 1 John 1:1–18, but the Gospels are neither APOCALYPSES nor myths, even though colorings from both literary types entered into their composition.

Contemporary researchers agree that the four received Gospels were built up from smaller elements of varied genres: passion narratives, collections of sayings and parables (*logoi*), miracle stories, post-resurrection stories, and infancy narratives (Matt. and Luke) and then fashioned into the unique form we now read (*see* Bible). It is likely that the primitive apostolic preaching (*kerygma*) provided the principal framework for the Gospel narratives. Some think the form of that preaching can be reconstructed from the speeches in Acts and Paul's letters. Its basic elements state 1) that the Christ appeared to begin the New Age in fulfillment of prophecy; 2) that he was born of the seed of David; 3) that he preached and did wonders in Galilee; 4) that he went up to Jerusalem, died under Pontius Pilate, and was buried; 5) that he was raised from the dead on the third day, in accord with scriptural prophesy, and appeared to many; and 6) that he sits at the right hand of God as Lord and Christ, whence he will come again to judge the quick and the dead and restore the creation. Whatever the case, the Gospels remain the principal form of our understanding of Jesus, his message, and the faith his followers placed in him.

Scholars still refer to the "authors" of the Gospels as if they were specific individuals. The Gospels, however, represent a decades-long development from oral to written and rewritten stages. The celebrated New Testament scholar Raymond Brown (1928–98) proposes six stages of development in the Johannine material. Each of the four names probably refers to a school or tradition rather than an individual. Although all the names are masculine, there is no reason to doubt that women may have written or helped write any of these narratives. Women played a prominent role in the life of Jesus, were the first witnesses of the Resurrection, and were very influential in the early church, more so than in later centuries.

All the traditional identifications of the Gospel authors with figures mentioned in the New Testament have been rejected by historians: Mark with John Mark, the companion of Paul (Acts 12.12); Matthew with the tax collector of that name (Matt. 9:9); Luke with the physician companion of Paul (Col. 4:14); John with the apostle of that name (Mark 1:19), with the "beloved disciple" (John 21:20–23), and/or with the John of the Apocalypse (Rev. 1:1).

There seem to have been many gospels and gospel traditions, both "orthodox" and "unorthodox." Those other than the canonical four can be partially reconstructed from papyri fragments, especially those found at Oxyrhinchus in Egypt, from quotations gleaned from early church writers, and from the findings at Nag Hammadi, Egypt, in 1946.

CANONICAL GOSPELS

The formation of the Canon of Scripture took place against the backdrop of the struggle between orthodoxy and heresy, especially in the form of the many varieties of Gnosticism. The canonical Gospels are those now referred to as Mark, Matthew, Luke, and John. The noncanonical gospels belong to a class of secret writings, or apocrypha, generally dating from the second and third centuries, that identify themselves as gospels, acts, letters, and apocalypses in imitation of the books in the canon.

GOSPEL OF MARK

Mark is the earliest gospel by historical reckoning. Some date it to around 70 C.E., right after the destruction of the Temple by Titus (39–81 C.E.). It may well have been written for a Gentile audience, as the author(s) translates all Aramaic terms into Greek, and only the Gentile Roman centurion at the cross (15:39) fully acknowledges Jesus.

The story begins with Jesus' baptism in the Jordan by John and ends at the empty tomb, showing no post-resurrection appearances by Jesus (16:8). The most authoritative codices of the New Testament lack the more "satisfying" ending (16:9–20), added later to make Mark conform to Matthew and Luke (*see* codex). Various Canon(s) of Scripture placed Mark after Matthew, because teachers of DOCETISM and early Gnostics could have used it to back their claim that Jesus was not originally incarnated as the Son of God but only selected for his mission at his BAPTISM.

After Jesus' baptism and temptation by Satan in the desert, Mark is divided into two sections: what Jesus does in Galilee and outlying districts (1:14–10:52) and what happens to him in Jerusalem (11:1–16:8). Outside of Jerusalem he demonstrates power and authority in both word and deed, yet his own people reject him, and his disciples flat out misunderstand him. The demons know who he is, but his disciples do not! They think that his power will rub off on them and lead to positions of authority in the messianic kingdom Jesus is going to set up. In response, Jesus starts predicting that the Son of Man must suffer (8:31; 9:31; 10:33), as must the Suffering Servant foretold by 2nd Isaiah (Isaiah 42:1–9, etc.). He warns demons and disciples alike to keep his identity a secret (3:12; 8:30; 9:9).

In the second section, Jesus goes up to Jerusalem riding not a powerful charger like Alexander the Great on Bucephalus but a humble ass with her colt alongside. This is a prophetic mock theater performance worthy of Jeremiah about how the Son of David will really be received (11:2; Zechariah 9:9). Although Jesus seems to demonstrate authority when he tosses from the temple the coins bearing Caesar's idolatrous image, or when he debates his opponents with cunning and foretells a dire end to the Temple and Jerusalem (13), everything conspires to bring him low to a point of powerlessness, betrayal by his disciples (14:66–72), humiliation by the Romans (15:16–20), and seeming utter abandonment by God (15:34). When he gives up his last breath, once again the heavens open up, not with the Spirit descending (1:11), but with the God hidden behind the veil of the Holy of Holies revealing the true presence of divinity, not in power and wonders, but in this broken, defeated, dead body hanging on a gibbet (15:38–39), an abomination to Jew and Gentile alike. This is Mark's famous Messianic Secret shockingly revealed with expectations of messianic power displays turned upside-down. For decades scholars have been bemused over its "clumsy" style, yet Mark may prove to be the most profound gospel of all.

GOSPEL OF MATTHEW

Both Matthew and Luke adopt the Galilee/Jerusalem armature of Mark, but they add infancy narratives and post-resurrection appearances. Matthew is decidedly a Jewish gospel. The word "Christian" had not been invented in Matthew's circle, so it would be false to call it "Jewish-Christian." Today scholars generally date Matthew to a period between 90–95 when conflicts began to arise between early Rabbinic Judaism and the Jewish followers of Jesus. Matthew triggers all the incidents of Jesus life with formula quotations from the Hebrew Bible, especially the Book of Isaiah, e.g. the Virgin Birth (1:22 with Isaiah 7:17), and the birth in Bethlehem (2:5–6 with Micah 5:1 and 2 Samuel 5:12).

Matthew traces Jesus' ancestry through Joseph back to King David and to Abraham in a triple set of 14 generations. In the last set Jesus is the 13th, and the Christ is the 14th generation (1:16). Matthew then reports the Virgin Birth of Jesus from the HOLY SPIRIT (despite having just reported the genealogy of Jesus passing through Joseph). He narrates the visit to the newborn of the unnamed Magi (they received the names Melchior, Gaspar, and Balthasar only much later, in the Middle Ages). The Magi follow the star to honor the child instead of Herod the Great, who, enraged, slaughters the innocents and drives the Holy Family to Egypt, a favorite subject in late Gothic and Renaissance art. The half-Idumean Herodians had messianic pretensions of their own, so killing off potential rivals would make sense in their world, dominated by Roman imperial machinations.

Matthew then picks up the Markan account (3:1), adding new material to the narrative and teaching sections (M), including a series of sayings from a source he shares with Luke that is commonly called Q for *Quelle,* the German word for "source." All this he rearranges in a structure that has been called chiastic (from the Greek letter chi) or even ringlike, composed of a prologue (infancy, chapters 1–2) and epilogue (resurrection, 28) making up the bookends for six narratives (3–4, 8–9, 11–12, 14–17, 19–23, 26–27) and five discourses sandwiched in between (5–7, 10–13, 18, 24–25). The celebrated Sermon on the Mount is the first discourse (5–7) and the Passion is the final narrative (26–27).

The Torah, or Law, of course, is composed of the "five discourses of Moses," the teacher (rabbi) of all teachers for a pious Jew. In Matthew Jesus is addressed as "Rabbi" by another rabbi (8:19); he is the New Moses, and the church he founds is the New Israel. Jesus comes not to loosen the Law but to make it sharper (5:17–20; 18:17). Matthew has become the favorite Gospel of Catholic authorities because it places strong emphasis on church order and gives a central role to Peter (16:17–19), a passage often quoted by popes to shore up their authority as Peter's successor.

In Matthew one can discern the first signs of a phenomenon called supercessionism (*see* TYPOLOGY). The Gospel, once promised to the Jews (10:16) but rejected by them, now finds fulfillment among the Gentiles (28:19).

GOSPEL OF LUKE

Like Matthew, Luke employs the basic Markan armature, uses Q, and shapes the Jesus story with his own special material (L). The final shaper of Luke, using numerous sources and traditions, also composed the Book of Acts.

Luke's Gospel can be analyzed on its own, as some scholars do, but the two books seem to constitute a unit, following a sustained dyptichal pattern: John the Baptist / Jesus; Galilean ministry / Jerusalem ministry; Peter's mission / Paul's mission; Jerusalem / Rome. In sum, Luke in this wider scope unfolds a panorama of salvation history, beginning with the founding of a tiny Jewish religious movement in Galilee and marching all the way to imperial Rome, where the movement takes its place among the great religions of the ancient world.

Whereas Mark's Jesus can look like a Hellenistic wonder-worker and Matthew's like the rabbi of the new age, Luke's Jesus looks like the cosmopolitan founder of a universal religion. This universalism is a mark of Luke. He traces Jesus' genealogy back not to Abraham, the first Jew, but to Adam, the father of all the nations. Jesus assembles 70 disciples to go to all the nations (Luke 10:1–20; Acts 1:8). He associates and has banquets with all sorts of people (Luke 11:37–41; 14:7–24). He talks with Pharisees, with Samaritans, and with Gentiles. His is the only Gospel that has the Parable of the Good Samaritan (Luke 10:19–37).

Luke is very much in favor of the poor, sinners, women—and Roman authorities. When he says "Blessed are you who are poor" (Luke 6:20) he means the literal poor and not the "poor in spirit" (Matt. 5:3), and he praises the Roman centurion Cornelius for his almsgiving (Acts 10:2). Sinners, prodigals, and sinful women who were lost (dead) are once again found (resurrected) in Jesus' presence, as in the Parable of the Prodigal Son (15:24). Luke tells the stories of Elizabeth and Mary (Luke 1–2) and Mary and Martha (10:38 ff), places women at the foot of the cross (23:27), and talks about Priscilla, a missionary like Paul (Acts 18:1–3). Luke's real identity may have been "Lucia."

Luke portrays all Roman officials with sympathy, perhaps too much sympathy. He is trying to justify Christianity as a legitimate religion in the face of criticism by the Romans, who accused it of being a seditious "superstition." Luke goes beyond Matthew to establish Roman innocence in the death of Jesus. He removes the crowning with thorns and mocking of Jesus by the Roman soldiers. Then he has Pilate declare Jesus' innocence to the crowd three times. Luke finesses Pilate's responsibility: "But Jesus [Pilate] delivered up to [the crowd's] will" (Luke 23:26). A Roman, Cornelius, is the first convert to the Jesus movement. All the Roman officials treat Paul well (Acts 13:12; 18:14–15).

There are hints of institutionalization of the Christian message in Luke, inferred from the system of 12 apostles with Peter as their leader (Luke 2–5), the seven deacons who distribute food to the poor (Acts 6:1–6), the council of the Apostles in Jerusalem (15), the appointment of elders (20:28–35), and the rite of "laying on of hands" as a sign of transmitting spiritual authority (9:17). Luke also shows Jesus praying before every major event in his life, especially in the Garden of Gethsemane (Luke 22:4). Luke's Greek is the most sophisticated in the New Testament.

GOSPEL OF JOHN

Among the canonical Gospels the Gospel of John is the odd man out in more ways than one. John is the most theological of the Gospels and independent of the Synoptic tradition (which produced the other three), though there are affinities with the Gospel of Mark. There are many difficulties with the text. Catholic scholar Raymond Brown (1928–98) argued that the Johannine Gospel and letters emerged from a long-enduring community that went through six stages of development. It began with an in-group of Jesus people in Palestine with a very simple CHRISTOLOGY (see CHRIST/CHRISTOLOGY) (John 1:35–45) and ended with a split community that shared an evolved Christology but differed in their view of Jesus' physicality. The majority denied that the Man from Heaven had become flesh (the beginning of GNOSTICISM proper), while the minority insisted that Jesus the Savior could be seen and touched in the flesh (1 John 1:1–3; 4:1–3).

The Greek is simple and beautiful but shows many linguistic peculiarities. Many words are symbolically laden with double and even triple meanings and allusions. Nicodemus asks how he is to be born "again" (anothen), a term that can also mean "from above." The term to lift up (hypsoein) is used for Moses lifting up the serpent that heals (Num.

21:9), Jesus being lifted up on the cross (3:14), and the Son of Man being lifted up in glory (8:28). John also mixes up tenses: "Before Abraham was born, I am" (8:58). The entire Gospel is laden with a series of reduplicating dualisms: life and death, light and darkness, freedom and slavery, we and the world. Some have argued that the Gospel or part of it is frankly Gnostic, especially in its use of the Wisdom myth of a descending (8:42) and reascending (16:28) revealer. The Johannine community seems to have been insular, like the Qumran community, even in relation to the other movements that considered themselves followers of Jesus. John's Jesus says "Love one another" (13:34) but not "Love your enemies," as do the other Gospels (Matt. 5:44; Luke 6:27). John's enemies are the "world" and include not only the Jews who expelled the community from the synagogue (9:22; 12:42) but also inadequate believers like Peter who "fell behind" the true disciples (20:1–9).

Even in his Jesus narrative, John differs in significant ways from the other Gospels. The Synoptics have Jesus going up to Jerusalem once; John has him in and out of the city at least three times. Their last meal is a Passover Seder; John's is not (13:2 ff.). They show Jesus teaching in short sayings, discourses, and parables; John has Jesus engage in long involved monologues and dialogues. They show Jesus doing deeds and healings that cause wonder; in John Jesus works "signs" (semeia) pointing to his true identity (2:11; 3:2, etc.). They depict Jesus' opponents as separate groups (such as Pharisees, Sadducees, Herodians, leaders of the Sanhedrin); John has only one enemy, "the Jews," who now resemble the fateful stereotype that would haunt Christianity into the 20th century. In the Synoptics Jesus speaks of the kingdom of God or of Heaven; in John Jesus points to himself: "I am the way, the truth and the life." (14:6). Finally, in John the death of Jesus is not a tragedy but a fulfillment that Jesus consciously proclaims at the moment of his death, not as he passively "dies" but as he actively "gives up his spirit" to the Father (19:30).

Two Synoptic genres were transformed in the Johannine tradition. The miraculous deeds were transformed into "signs," and the sayings/anecdotes/parables were reshaped into monologues/dialogues, often appended to signs. John follows a pattern of action (sign or deed/discourse) → dialogue → monologue → coda or appendix with variations on the monologue/dialogue sections (e.g., 5:1–47; 9:1–10: 39). In the last sequence, the overall pattern is reversed (discourse/deed): washing of the feet, dialogue on Jesus' departure, farewell monologue on Christ and his church, final dialogue, prayer for the church, and Passion narrative (13:1–20:31).

The overall structure of the Gospel is divided into 1) the interpolated Logos hymn (1:1–51); 2) the Book of Signs (2:1–12:50); 3) final discourses and prayer for the church (13:17–26); and 4) the Passion narrative (18:1–20:31), with an epilogue appended later on (21–1–23).

The Logos hymn, which has its own peculiar language (e.g., "grace and truth"), probably came from Jewish Wisdom circles. The author adds touches to the hymn (1:6–9, 13, 15, 17–18) to fit it in with the Gospel and substitutes Logos (Gk. "word") for Wisdom, which is feminine in Hebrew (*hochma*) and Greek (*sophia*). The descent and "tenting" of Wisdom is found in Sirach 24:8–12 and *1 Enoch* 42:1–2. Philo of Alexandria identified Wisdom with the Word and the Son. Although the numbering got lost in the many cycles of editing, there seems to have been a Book of Seven Signs, beginning at verses 2:1, 4:46, 5:1, 6:1, 6.16, 9.1, and 11.1.

The overall purpose of the Gospel was to bring the hearer to belief in Jesus and the new life that belief makes real in the present (20:21). John has what scholars have called "realized ESCHATOLOGY." All things needed for salvation are already present in believing in Jesus now: the way, the truth, and the life. In this, John resembles and shares many features with the noncanonical Gospel of Thomas (*see below*). Because of its gnosticizing and dualizing tendencies, this Gospel had difficulties making it into the Canon of Scripture. Most date its composition to around 100. The earliest known text of a Gospel, Oxyrhinchus Papyrus 52 (John 18:31–33,37–38), dates from c. 125.

NONCANONICAL GOSPELS

Many of the noncanonical gospels made definite marks on the early Christian church before they sank from view. The following account of a few of the more important ones shows the range of material covered by the term *gospel*.

GOSPEL OF THOMAS

Today the most celebrated noncanonical gospel is the Gospel of Thomas. It is a sayings gospel, like Q(uelle), the collection of sayings of Jesus shared by Matthew and Luke. Much of the Thomas material goes back to the earliest Christian times. It was found together with the Nag Hammadi collection in 1945–46 as a Coptic translation of a Greek prototype.

Thomas includes variants of sayings found in both canonical and noncanonical gospels, but it attributes them to "Thomas the Twin," who is assumed to be the twin brother of "the living Jesus," the revealer of the secret teaching. Whoever reaches the right interpretation of the sayings "will not experience death." The gospel is intended to give the initiate the knowledge (gnosis) of the living Jesus within him or herself. Though Gnostic in color, the gospel belongs to no recognized school of Gnosticism. Its famous saying that Mary of Magdala will have to become a male probably refers to the restoration of the original Adam before he was split in two. The book's Christology sees Jesus as a bringer of light and wisdom into a world obscured by darkness and ignorance. Many of its sayings or *logoi* of Jesus are as old as anything in the canonical Gospels or Q; some are even the earliest.

EGERTON GOSPEL

This fragmentary gospel, also known as Papyrus Egerton 2, dates from around 125–50. It was discovered in Egypt in 1935; the later discovered Papyrus

Köln 255 is part of this gospel. Egerton contains a dialogue between Jesus and the Pharisees, precursor to the dialogues in the Gospel of John. It also includes the attempt to arrest Jesus, the miracle of the healing of the leper, and the dialogue/debate on paying taxes to kings (and not to Caesar, as in Mark 12:14).

GOSPEL OF EBIONITES

The Ebionites were Greek-speaking Jewish followers of Jesus who lived east of the Jordan. *Ebion* is Aramaic for "the poor." The gospel dates from around 100 to 150 and exists only in fragmentary quotes. Though the church historian Epiphanius said that the sect used only the Gospel of Matthew, the extant quotes indicate that their gospel was a compendium of the Synoptic three. The Ebionite gospel begins with the baptism of Jesus in the Jordan. The Ebionites held an adoptionist Christology (*see* ADOPTIONISM): Jesus was fully human but chosen as the Son of God at his baptism. Epiphanius writes that the Ebionites believed Jesus had been "created like one of the archangels" (*Panarion* 30). The gospel also implies that Jesus and John were vegetarians, modifying Luke 22:15, and changing the Baptist's diet from locusts (Gk. *akris*) to cake (*egkris*).

GOSPEL OF THE EGYPTIANS

There are two tractates by this name. The first, cited by early Christian writers, was used by the Encratites to justify their extreme asceticism. The Encratites were a 2nd century sect that rejected the use of wine, thought matter was created by a lesser Aeon, and prohibited marriage, to allow believers to return to the soul's primal androgynous state (Gen. 1:27) before the division into sexes and the Fall into sin. The Naasenes also used this text to support their notion of the soul's descent through the seven planetary spheres into matter. The Sabellians used it to argue for their modal theory of the TRINITY.

The second tractate is a Sethian Gnostic treatise found at Nag Hammadi. It describes the emanation of the Father, Mother Barbelo, and Son from the Great Invisible Spirit and the coming of Seth, the perfect third son of ADAM AND EVE; Seth takes on Jesus as a garment in order to save his race from the thralldom of the Archon Saklas ("Fool") and his cohorts.

GOSPEL OF PETER

The gospel of Peter as it stands is only a Passion narrative of 58 verses (Brown). It may be very early in its original form, from around 50. There are two statements that seem to have Docetic and/or Gnostic tendencies: 1) Jesus is said to experience no pain (v. 9) and 2) Jesus addresses God as "My Power, My Power (Gk. *dynamis*), why have you forsaken me?" when he expires. Otherwise, the narrative looks orthodox, though it blames Jesus' death solely on Herod and the Jews. It is probably of Syrian origin though it was found in Upper Egypt as part the Akhmîm Codex in 1886. Serapion, bishop of Antioch (190–211), refers to the gospel in a letter quoted by Eusebius of Caesarea (*Ecclesiastical History* 6.12.2–6).

GOSPEL OF MARY OF MAGDALA

The gospel of Mary of Magdala is really a dialogue that employs some of the sayings from the gospel tradition. It probably dates from the end of the second century or the beginning of the third. The first part is a dialogue between the Savior and his disciples, which implies that sin is not a moral but a cosmological category (*see* Rom. 7). The second section contains a description of an esoteric vision given to Mary by the Savior.

Mary's vision reveals that this world of illusion, chaos, ignorance, suffering, death, and domination is passing away. The Savior comes to reveal to each soul its "root" in the Good (a Platonic idea) and to guide it back to its place of silence in the eternal Sabbath rest, after Genesis 2:2–3. Mary's vision is a variant of the fundamental Gnostic myth of the descent and reascent of the spirit to its true home/state from before the Fall.

The vision is followed by a dialogue/contention between Mary and Peter and Andrew. Levi defends Mary as the one whom the Savior "loved more." This passage was famously (or infamously) used by Dan Brown in his bestselling novel *The Da Vinci Code* (2003).

GOSPEL OF TRUTH

See VALENTINUS.

Further reading: John Dominic Crossan, *Four Other Gospels* (Minneapolis: Winston, 1985); Helmut Koester, *Ancient Christian Gospels* (Philadelphia: Trinity, 1990); William L. Petersen, ed., *Gospel Traditions in the Second Century: Origins, Recensions, Text, and Transmission* (Notre Dame: University of Notre Dame Press, 1989); Donald Senior, *Invitation to the Gospels,* (New York: Paulist, 2002); Burnett Hillman Streeter, *The Four Gospels: A Study of Origins* (New York: Macmillan, 1925).

Gothic   *See* ARCHITECTURE; PAINTING AND SCULPTURE.

grace (Lat.: *gratia,* "free favor")

Grace is the free favor of GOD toward those who believe, through which they can share in the life of the divine essence, which is love. A more recent description of grace by KARL RAHNER says that it is God's absolutely free self-communication to creatures that allows them to share in the life of the divine. CHRISTIANS believe that the grace of God, won for all by Jesus Christ, is absolutely necessary for salvation.

In classic Greco-Roman culture the word *grace* (Gk. *charis*) had connotations of graciousness and benevolence. There were three words in Hebrew for the idea of grace, all with different connotations: 1) *hen,* the favor a master shows a slave; 2) *hesed,* steadfast mercy toward someone in a covenantal relation; and 3) RAHAMIN, a mother's love "from the womb." Several prophets of the Exilic period speak of God extending divine mercy to stricken people of Israel so that God's law will be written in their hearts (JER. 31:31–34; EZEK. 36:26–27).

In the New Testament the term *charis* occurs frequently in liturgical and other contexts, but it is PAUL who gives it theological weight. Grace is the favor God extends to humanity in the death and resurrection of Jesus, which justifies the sinner—makes him or her right before God. This grace extends into *charismata,* a term coined by Paul, by which God empowers individuals with spiritual gifts to aid them in the building up of the community (1 Cor. 12–13). All of these meanings come together in Paul's favorite greeting, "the grace of our Lord Jesus Christ" (Rom. 16:20; 1 Cor. 16:23, etc.).; The term has various meanings for other New Testament writers. For example, it could mean FORGIVENESS of sin (Mark 1:4) or the indwelling of God (John 14:23). In the next century MARCION radically sundered the God of creation (Law) from the God of grace (Gospel). He and the GNOSTICS were countered by theologians like CLEMENT OF ALEXANDRIA, who taught that God's gracious activity goes back to creation and that *charis* is the gentle, forgiving work, while *nomos* (law) is the corrective work of God. Others saw grace as medicinal, healing the wounds of the human soul.

The apostolic writers of the second century began to look at the moral consequences of grace and to reflect on the possibility of losing and regaining grace. Soon the eastern theologians added the theme *theosis,* God's bestowal of grace through the incarnate Son: "He became the son of man so that man might become the son of God" (IRENAEUS, *Against Heresies* 3.10.2). ATHANASIUS OF ALEXANDRIA reformulated this theme in his famous statement, the Word of God "was made human that we may be made divine" (*On the Incarnation* 54). St. BASIL THE GREAT (330–79) argued in favor of the divinity of the Holy Spirit since it is the Spirit who communicates the divine life to humans. Eastern theologies of grace stress that participation in the divine life comes through the sacraments, especially BAPTISM and the EUCHARIST.

This liturgical understanding of grace tended in the direction of the theological and the mystical.

Western concepts of grace, by contrast, were governed by more moral and forensic, or legal, concerns. The idea of grace came into sharp focus in the conflict between AUGUSTINE OF HIPPO and PELAGIUS. Relying on CYPRIAN's teaching about Original SIN, Augustine asserted that there is no way a fallen human can avoid sin. Pelagius did not argue, as his enemies charged, that we do not need grace for salvation, but only that it is possible to live, with God's help, without sinning. Augustine's view on the absolute gratuitousness of God's grace, the predestination of those chosen by God, and his psychology of grace and sin came to prevail in the West, notably at the Councils of Carthage (411) and Orange (529). From his own experience Augustine argued that his will had been deformed and could act freely only after an infusion of grace.

Medieval theologians adapted and applied ARISTOTLE's terminology in refining the theology of grace (habitual/actual grace, disposition, accidents, virtues, etc.). They framed the philosophicotheological discussion of grace in terms of nature-supernature. Through enabling grace humanity can once again attain its original natural end lost in the FALL: the BEATIFIC VISION. Supernatural grace does no violence to human nature but rather perfects it. Grace is "a glow of the soul, a real quality like the beauty of the body" (THOMAS AQUINAS, *Summa Theologiae* 1a–2a.110.2).

Following the PROTESTANT REFORMATION Catholics found themselves defending various aspects of the theology of grace: the restoration of human freedom under grace and the new creation of humanity through indwelling grace against the Reformers' idea of irresistible grace and Luther's formula "at once sinner and justified" (Council of TRENT, sessions 5 and 6.4–5); the totally supernatural character of grace versus the semi-Pelagian view of Michael de Bay (1513–89), the Louvain theologian known in Latin as Baius (PIUS V, *Ex omnibus afflictionibus,* May 1, 1572); and

God's universal will to save all humankind against the predestination of the elect according to Calvin and JANSENISM. The debate between the Jesuit Luis de Molina (1535–1600) and the Dominican Domingo Báñez (1508–1604) on the relation between divine efficacious grace and human freedom was left undecided (Paul V, *De Auxiliis,* January 28, 1621).

The theology of grace became a lively topic in the 20th century. HENRI DE LUBAC appealed to the richness of the early theologians to stress the "natural desire" for grace even on the part of fallen humans and God's completely free gift. KARL RAHNER, who restored the Trinitarian aspect of grace to theology, called grace the "supernatural existential," a transcendental horizon that touches humanity in its depth yet is totally dependent on the utterly free and gracious self-communication of God. He maintained that one comes closest to the full realization of the meaning of grace and freedom in the moment of prayer. He also argued that those who live faithful lives outside the Christian tradition can also receive God's free grace as "anonymous Christians." GUSTAVO GUTIÉRREZ held that grace transcends individual experience and liberates whole communities from shackles of oppression. Feminists have applied and extended these insights to questions of gender in the believing community. ECOTHEOLOGY is now returning to the early church thinkers who always taught that grace has a cosmic dimension and touches all levels of nature and all dimensions of life (Rom. 8:19–22).

Further reading: Leonardo Boff, *Liberating Grace* (Maryknoll, N.Y.: Orbis, 1979); Stephen Duffy, *The Dynamics of Grace: Perspectives in Theological Anthropology* (Collegeville, Minn.: Liturgical Press, 1993); Piet Franzen, *The New Life of Grace* (New York: Seabury, 1969); Karl Rahner, *Grace in Freedom* (New York: Herder, 1969); Basil Studer, *The Grace of Christ and the Grace of God in Augustine of Hippo: Christocentrism or Theocentrism?* tr. Matthew J. O'Connell (Collegeville, Minn.: Liturgical Press, 1997).

Grail, Holy (Middle Lat.: *gradalis*, "dish," "platter")

In medieval legend and romance, the Holy Grail is the sought-after cup that Jesus used at the Last Supper (Matt. 26:27). The cup made its first appearance in Chrétien of Troyes's *Perceval* (1180) and, in a more Christianized form, Robert de Boron's *Estoire de Graal* or *Joseph de Arimathie* (c. 1190). The Grail came to symbolize the eternal quest for an unattainable spiritual ideal.

The story of the Grail was integrated into the legends of Arthur and the Knights of the Round Table in *La Queste del Saint Graal* (bet. 1225–37) which may have been influenced by CISTERCIAN piety, and Wolfram von Eschenbach's *Parzival* (1205–15). In the latter the Grail is a sacred stone that preserves a beholder from death for a week. In *Le Morte d' Arthur* by Sir Thomas Malory (1405–71), Galahad and Bors, rather than Perceval, are assigned the task of finding the grail; Malory has the latter two succeed.

Medieval legend tells that Joseph of Arimathea, who arranged for Jesus's burial (Mark 15:43), brought the Grail to Glastonbury in England, where it became a focus of pilgrimage. In modern times the legend was refurbished by poets Alfred Tennyson (1809–1902) in his *Idylls of the King* (1859–82) and James Russel Lowell (1819–91) in *The Vision of Sir Launfal* (1848). Jessie Weston related the legend of the Grail to fertility cults in *From Ritual to Romance* (1920), a book that had enormous influence on T. S. Eliot (1888–1965) and his celebrated poem *The Wasteland* (1928).

More recently, the theme reappeared in Dan Brown's bestseller *The Da Vinci Code* (2003), which claims the Holy Grail is Mary Magdalene's womb, through which Jesus supposedly perpetuated his bloodline. The book, like its precursor *Holy Blood, Holy Grail* (1982) by Michael Baigent, Richard Leigh, and Henry Lincoln, is a pseudo-historical book based on French monarchist fantasies of divine descent from Jesus and Mary Magdalene, and continuing through the Merovingian line. Brown's novel, misconstrued as fact by many readers, accuses the Catholic Church and OPUS DEI of a massive cover-up of the truth. The Holy Grail legend has attracted a considerable following in a manner similar to the romantic (and largely baseless) theories concerning the pyramids of EGYPT and the Standing Stone of England.

Further reading: Mike Ashley, ed., *The Chronicles of the Holy Grail* (New York: Carroll & Graf, 1995); John Matthews, *The Elements of the Grail Tradition* (Rockport, Mass.: Element, 1996); D. D. R. Owen, *The Evolution of the Grail Legend* (Edinburgh: St. Andrew's, 1968); Richard Rohr, *Quest for the Grail* (New York: Crossroad, 1994); Andrew Sinclair, *The Discovery of the Holy Grail* (London: Arrow, 1999).

Great Britain

Legend has it that Christianity came to England via Joseph of Arimathea, who brought the Holy GRAIL to the site of the later Abbey of Glastonbury. Second- and third-century writers such as ORIGEN, JEROME, and ATHANASIUS attest to the presence of BISHOPS in Great Britain. Gallic writer Constantius of Lyons (fl. 480) mentions three English martyrs, Alban, Aaron, and Julius. Many churches in England are called St. Alban's, and Albion became the country's poetic name. The Roman Christian mosaics at Hinton St. Mary's in Dorset imply that early fifth century Britons mixed CHRISTIAN motifs with Greek and Roman mythological images. They show the earliest depiction of CHRIST in England.

After the last Romans abandoned Great Britain around 410, various Teutonic tribes from northern Europe invaded and settled, including the Angles and Saxons. The early medieval historian venerable Bede mentions St. Ninian (d. c. 432), missionary to the Picts in Scotland, in his *Ecclesiastical History* (3.4.1). Other sources speak of St. PATRICK, a Briton who missionized Ireland. At the end of the sixth century Pope GREGORY I sent Augustine (d. c. 610), prior of a Roman monastery, to missionize the Anglo-Saxons. He became the first ARCHBISHOP of Canterbury, established contact with Celtic BISHOPS, and missionized the whole land. The last Anglo-Saxon king, St. Edward the Confessor (d. 1066), who restored Westminster Abbey, was canonized by Pope Alexander III (r. 1159–81) in 1161.

The conquest of England by William I (r. 1066–87) after the Battle of Hastings in 1066 linked England's destiny more closely to that of the Continent. For example, the conflict between CHURCH AND STATE that riled Europe found expression locally in the struggle between St. Thomas à Becket (c. 1115–7), Archbishop of Canterbury, and Henry II (1183–89), who had him murdered. Thomas's relics at Canterbury became the focus of a pilgrimage, celebrated in GEOFFREY CHAUCER's *Canterbury Tales*. Christianity flourished in England during the MIDDLE AGES with the foundation and renewal of celebrated abbeys such as the CISTERCIAN Tintern Abbey, founded in 1131 and immortalized in the poem of that name by William Wordsworth (1770–1850). In the 14th century the English reformer JOHN WYCLIFFE anticipated many of the changes later brought by the PROTESTANT REFORMATION.

The peculiarly British and quasi-Catholic Church of England emerged during the Reformation under Tudor King HENRY VIII. Until the 19th century the Catholic Church underwent alternating periods of persecution and suppression in the country, beginning with the martyrdoms of Sts. JOHN FISHER, THOMAS MORE, and, later in the century, the Jesuit Edmund Campion (1540–81), who professed his loyalty to Queen Elizabeth and his allegiance to the church till death. Robert Catesby's and Guy Fawkes's 1606 Gunpowder Plot, which aimed to kill King James I (r. 1603–25) by blowing up Parliament, stoked popular fear of Rome and suspicion of English Catholics, as commemorated every year in the anti-Catholic Guy Fawkes Day on November 5.

During the years of persecution English Catholics trained priests at seminaries in Rheims and Douay in France for reinsertion to England—thus the famous "Douay-Rheims BIBLE," the English Catholic translation of the Vulgate. In the 17th century crypto-Catholics were caught in the middle of the violent struggle between the Church of England and the Puritans, who wanted to purge the church of vestiges of "papism." The fear that James II (r. 1685–88) might reintroduce Catholicism led to the Glorious Revolution and the introduction of Protestant Hannover royalty into the monarchy of England.

Some estimate that the number of English Catholics fell to a low of some 100,000 by the end of the 18th century. Immigration from Ireland increased that number, helping bring about Catholic Emancipation in 1829. The revival was greatly aided by the intellectual OXFORD MOVEMENT under the leadership of JOHN HENRY NEWMAN and Henry Edward Manning (1808–92), both of whom were made cardinals. In 1850 PIUS IX restored the Catholic hierarchy of England and Wales, soon to be headed by the able Cardinal Nicholas Wiseman (1802–67). Since that time Roman Catholicism has recorded steady growth and epics of renewal. The authors Lord (John) Acton (1834–1902), G. K. CHESTERTON, and Hillaire Belloc (1870–1953) gave credibility and exposure to the Catholic position. Today there are more than 5 million Catholics in England; they attend church in much greater numbers than their Anglican counterparts.

Further reading: John McManners, ed., *The Illustrated History of Christianity* (Oxford: Oxford University Press, 1990); V. Alan McCllelland and Michael Hodgetts, *From Without the Flaminian Gate: 150 Years of Roman Catholicism in England and Wales 1850–2000* (London: Darton, Longman & Todd, 1999); Edward R. Norman, *Roman Catholicism in England from the Elizabethan Settlement to the Second Vatican Council* (Oxford: Oxford University Press, 1986).

Great Schism

The ecclesiastical split between the two major streams of Christianity—the Eastern, Greek Orthodox, centered in CONSTANTINOPLE, and the

Western, Latin Catholic, centered in Rome—is known as the Great or East-West Schism. The separation of the two churches over the course of the early MIDDLE AGES was marked by centuries of theological and political discord. Some date the formal split to 1054, but it probably did not become irrevocable until 1204. (The term *Great Schism* is also often used to describe the 15th-century split surrounding the AVIGNON PAPACY; that event is called the Western SCHISM in this volume.)

The unraveling of the relationship had theological, political, social, and cultural aspects. From the third century onward the two major regions within the great early church began to develop different styles. Eastern Christianity revolved around multiple centers, primarily the ancient patriarchates of Jerusalem, Antioch, Alexandria, and Constantinople. Western Christianity revolved around the bishopric of Rome as the final court of appeal. The East had a tendency toward intense theological speculation leading to a heretical impulse, as in ARIANISM and Nestorianism (*see* NESTORIUS). Many of these conflicts were resolved in the great early ecumenical councils (*see* COUNCILS, ECUMENICAL), resulting in cooperation between the patriarchates. In the West, factions such as DONATISM tended to be practical and schismatic, rather than heretical, and were repressed by centralized authorities using firm discipline. Finally, Eastern spirituality tended in the direction of the mystical, whereas the West tended in the direction of the moral and the legal. These divergent inclinations provide the deep background for the eventual split.

The break in CHRISTIAN unity really began in the Christological controversies of the fifth century. After the condemnation of Nestorianism at the Council of EPHESUS (431) the Assyrian Christian Church went its own way. Following the condemnation of Monophysitism at the Council of CHALCEDON (451), the Armenian, Coptic, Ethiopian, and Syrian Orthodox Churches also departed from the united fold. The controversy over the unilateral insertion of the word FILIOQUE

(" and the son") into the CREED in the West in the sixth century, while it did not at first cause a formal split, inflamed feelings in the East.

Tensions between East and West were aggravated by misunderstandings, ecclesiastical rivalry, territorial infringement, and church-state conflict. Two notorious cases were the so-called Photian Schism in the mid-ninth century and the schism of Patriarch MICHAEL I CERULARIUS in 1054, both involving a pope's attempts to control the appointment of a patriarch.

Photius (c. 810–c. 895), a brilliant theologian noted for his writings on the iconoclasm and filioque controversies, was appointed patriarch of Constantinople by eastern emperor Michael III in 858. He was deposed through the intervention of Pope Nicholas I (r. 858–67) and then apparently reinstated. Two centuries later, Leo IX (r. 1049–54) tried to deny Michael I Cerularius (d. 1058) the title of Ecumenical Patriarch unless he recognized Rome as the *caput et mater ecclesiarum* ("head and mother of the churches"). In response, Michael excommunicated Leo, and the pope reciprocated in 1054, the date most often given as signaling the Great Schism.

The break, however, was not complete until the CRUSADES. Although the Crusades were ostensibly aimed at regaining land from Muslims, they also saw acts of Western Christian expansionism: the pope established competing Latin patriarchates in the East, especially in Antioch and Jerusalem, Latin missionaries intruded into territories like Bulgaria traditionally reserved to the Eastern Church, and Latin knights sacked Constantinople in 1204.

There were two major attempts to repair the breach. The first was the Council of Lyons II in 1275, attended by St. BONAVENTURE (St. THOMAS AQUINAS died on route to the meeting). Political necessity dictated an agreement: in order to block Charles of Anjou (1227–85), king of Sicily and brother of St. LOUIS IX, from becoming Latin Emperor of Constantinople, the representatives of Greek emperor Michael VIII Paleologus submitted to the authority of the Roman church and accepted the filioque formula and the council's definition of the double procession of the Holy Spirit. The union lasted barely a decade and was terminated in 1289. A final attempt at reconciliation was the Council of FLORENCE (1438–45), held under the gun of the Ottoman Turkish threat. Several prominent theologians attended on both sides, including Patriarch Joseph of Constantinople (r. 1464–65) and Metropolitan Bessarion of Nicaea (d. 1403–72). Many sessions were held on the filioque formula, the doctrine of double procession, purgatory, the primacy of the pope, and the EUCHARIST with unleavened bread.

Union was effected on all major points. The council proceeded to form unions with Armenians (1439), Copts (1442), Syrians (1444), some Chaldeans, and the Maronites. Most of the local Orthodox populations did not favor the reunion, and many older bishops refused it. The conquest of Constantinople by the Turks in 1453 put an end to the matter, and the Eastern Synod of Constantinople formalized the break in 1484. Only the Maronites remained steadfastly united with Rome, although a few other national churches later reconciled with it.

However, not all was lost. The Council of Florence did establish the principle of unity of FAITH with diversity in rite, and its sessions have never formally ended. The principle took on new vigor at VATICAN COUNCIL II, which radically altered relations with EASTERN ORTHODOXY. In *Unitatis Redintegratio,* Decree on Ecumenism, the council noted the special position of the Eastern Churches, including their right to govern themselves "according to their own disciplines" (3.16). Though the division remains, PAUL VI and the Ecumenical Patriarch Athenagoras (1886–1972) nullified in 1964 the anethemas of 1054. JOHN PAUL II frequently expressed a desire for unity with the Eastern Orthodox, as in the apostolic letter *Ut Unum Sint* (May 25, 1995). However, his return to a pre–Vatican II style of church governance probably militated against further

moves toward raproachment. Pope BENEDICT XVI, on a 2005 trip to Bari, Italy, a city on the border between East and West, pledged that one of the central goals of his papacy will be to end the rift with the Eastern Orthodox Churches.

See also ARMENIAN CATHOLIC CHURCH; CHALDEAN CATHOLIC CHURCH; COPTIC CATHOLIC CHURCH; EASTERN CATHOLICISM; EASTERN ORTHODOXY; MARONITE CATHOLIC CHURCH; ORTHODOX-CATHOLIC DIALOGUE; PAPACY; SYRIAN CATHOLIC CHURCH; UKRANIAN CATHOLIC CHURCH.

Further reading: Joan M. Hussey, *The Orthodox Church in the Byzantine Empire* (Oxford: Clarendon, 1990); Aidan Nichols, *Rome and the Eastern Churches: A Study in Schism* (Collegeville, Minn.: Liturgical Press, 1992); Steven Runciman, *The Eastern Schism* (Oxford: Oxford University Press, 1997).

Greek Catholic Church

Prior to 1829, a small number of Greeks residing in Greece and Turkey acknowledged the authority of Rome, but as Greece was then within the Ottoman Empire they were unable to organize into a separate church, as the sultan insisted that all CHRISTIAN worship be subject to the Ecumenical Patriarch who resided in CONSTANTINOPLE. Then, in 1829, the sultan ruled that Catholics could organize a separate diocese. The tiny Catholic community grew steadily over the next decades with the assistance of some Catholic missionary priests.

In 1895, the ASSUMPTIONIST Fathers settled in Constantinople and took charge of a seminary to train Greek priests. By 1911, the work had grown to the point that an exarchate was deemed appropriate, and Pope PIUS X named Isaias Papadopoulos (1855–1932) the first bishop. With the fall of the Ottoman Empire after World War I, most Greek Catholics moved to Athens as part of a larger agreement between Greece and Turkey calling for expatriates to return to the homeland.

After the Greek Orthodox Church was established as an autonomous body separate from the

Ecumenical Patriarchate in 1850, the position of Greek Catholics affiliated with Rome became more tenuous. The Greek Orthodox Church actively opposes the presence of Catholic and Protestant churches in the country. Its bishops view the Greek Catholic Church, with its traditional Eastern LITURGY, as a particular threat, since it might easily be confused with the Orthodox church. The government has imposed a special set of regulations on the Catholic community designed to prevent conversion of Orthodox Christians to Catholicism.

The Greek Catholic Church has remained relatively small, with a total of less than 2,500 members. The church is headquartered in Athens. The total number of Catholics in Greece—including Polish, Filipinos, Iraqi, Albanians, and Ukrainians—numbers above 200,000. The church is led by Archbishop Nikolos Foscolos (1936–) of Athens.

Further reading: Nikolaus Liese, *The Eastern Catholic Liturgies: A Study in Words and Pictures.* (Westminster, Md.: Newman, 1960); Ronald G. Roberson, *The Eastern Christian Churches—A Brief Survey,* 5th ed. (Rome: Pontifical Oriental Institute, 1995).

Greeley, Andrew (1928–) *popular U.S. priest, sociologist, and author*

Andrew Greeley studied at St. Mary of the Lake Seminary in Chicago, where he received an S.T.L. degree in 1954, and at the University of Chicago, where he received a Ph.D. in the sociology of religion in 1962. He has been an influential and popular Catholic thinker who has worked as a priest, sociologist, and author for more than 50 years, serving also as professor of sociology at the University of Chicago and the University of Arizona and research associate with the National Opinion Research Center (NORC) at the University of Chicago.

Greeley is a prolific writer, with more than 100 works of nonfiction and several dozen bestselling novels to his credit. He has published two autobiographies, *Confessions of a Parish Priest* and *Furthermore!* He writes a weekly column on political, church, and social issues for the *Chicago Sun-Times* and frequently contributes to the *New York Times,* the *National Catholic Reporter,* and other national newspapers. The themes of his witty commentary range from sex to politics to society to the environment.

In 1986 he established a $1 million Catholic Inner-City School Fund, which provides scholarships and financial assistance to schools within the archdiocese of Chicago that have a minority population of more than 50 percent. In 1984 he contributed a $1 million endowment to establish a chair in Roman Catholic studies at the University of Chicago. He also funds an annual lecture series, "The Church in Society," at St. Mary of the Lake Seminary.

Further reading: Andrew M. Greeley, *Confessions of a Parish Priest; An Autobiography* (New York: Simon & Schuster, 1986); ———, *Furthermore! Memoirs of a Parish Priest* (New York: Tom Doherty Associates, 1999); ———, *Crisis in the Church: A Study of Religion in America* (Chicago: Thomas More, 1979); ———, *How to Save the Catholic Church* (New York: Viking Penguin, 1984); John Kotre, *The Best of Times, the Worst of Times: Andrew Greeley and American Catholicism, 1950–75* (Chicago: Nelson-Hall, 1978).

Greene, Graham (1904–1991) *novelist*

A convert to Roman Catholicism, Graham Greene treated contemporary Catholic life and issues in many of his popular novels. Greene studied at the Berkhamstead School and Oxford Union, where he graduated with a B.A. in 1925. Early in his career he worked as a journalist, editor, and film critic. After his first novel, *The Man Within,* he left his job with the *London Times* to become a full-time novelist. He met his wife, Vivienne Dayrell-Browning, when she wrote to point out errors regarding Catholicism in his work; it was her urging that brought him to Catholicism. He was baptized in February 1926, and the couple were married a year later.

In 1934 Greene began traveling extensively, in part to explore the world and also to seek out colorful characters and story lines for his novels. In 1938 he made a trip to Mexico to investigate charges of persecution of Catholics, which became the story line for *The Power and the Glory*, possibly the best novel of his career. It received the Hawthornden Award for literary achievement but was condemned by the Vatican for its portrayal of a fallen priest through whom GOD works mercy.

By his own description, Green wrote two types of novels, "entertainments," such as spy and crime thrillers, and "Catholic novels," including *The Power and the Glory, The Heart of the Matter,* and *The End of the Affair.* Nevertheless, he rejected the label "Catholic novelist" because of all the limitations and theological expectations it implied.

Further reading: Mark Bosco, *Graham Greene's Catholic Imagination* (Oxford: Oxford University Press, 2005); Maria Couto, *Graham Greene: On the Frontier: Politics and Religion in the Novels* (New York: St. Martin's, 1988); Roger Sharrock, *Saints, Sinners, and Comedians: The Novels of Graham Greene* (Notre Dame: University of Notre Dame Press, 1984); William Thomas Hill, ed., *Perceptions of Religious Faith in the Work of Graham Greene* (New York: Peter Lang, 2002).

Gregorian Calendar

In 1582 Pope Gregory XIII (r. 1572–85) promulgated a new calendar via his bull *Inter Gravissimas* (February 24). Its purpose was to correct the accumulated errors of the Julian Calendar, which had been introduced by Julius Caesar (100–46 B.C.E.) in 46 B.C.E. Due to a slight imprecision in its estimate of the length of a solar year (which takes just under 365.25 days), by the 16th century the Julian Calendar was off by 10 days.

The new calendar went into effect on October 15, one day after October 4 on the previous calendar. To prevent any future time lags, century

years (which had all been leap years) were to be considered leap years only when divisible by 400 (e.g., 2000).

Despite the recommendation of the Lutheran astronomer Johannes Kepler (1571–1630), Protestants were reluctant to accept the new calendar. The English accepted it only in 1752. Many churches of the eastern rites, including those in union with Rome, stick to the Julian Calendar, a fact noted in the media twice a year when mention is made of the Orthodox celebration of Christmas and Easter (which now occur 13 days after the western celebrations). Much of EASTERN ORTHODOXY accepted the Gregorian Calendar under pressure from the communists in 1924, but many of the Orthodox churches that were never under communist rule continue to use the Julian Calendar.

Further reading: Peter Archer, *The Christian Calendar and the Gregorian Reform* (New York: Fordham University Press, 1941); George V. Coyne, ed., *Gregorian Reform of the Calendar* (Rome: Vatican, 1983); Aidan A. Kelly, Peter Dresser, and Linda M. Ross, *Religious Holidays and Calendars: An Encyclopedic Handbook* (Detroit: Omnigraphics, 1993).

Gregory I the Great, St. (540–604) *pope and church reformer*

As architect of the "Gregorian Reform," Gregory I, pope and DOCTOR OF THE CHURCH, became one of the most significant figures in the development of the Roman Catholic Church. As pope he referred to himself as *servus servorum Dei,* or "servant of the servants of God." His feast day is September 3 in the West, March 3 in the East.

Gregory was born around 540 into a wealthy Roman family. Little is known of his early life, though two of his aunts would later be canonized as saints by the church. He emerged out of obscurity in 573 when he was appointed prefect of the city of Rome. He left this important position in 574 to become a MONK. Concurrently, he gave his land in Sicily and Rome for the building of a set of MONASTERIES.

After several years in seclusion, he was called back into public life by the pope, who in 578 named him one of the seven deacons of Rome and later sent him as a permanent ambassador to Byzantium. He stayed in the East for some six years, during which he wrote a commentary on the Book of Job and engaged in an ongoing controversy with the patriarch of CONSTANTINOPLE, Eutychius (r. 552–65; 577–82), over the state of the dead and the doctrine of PURGATORY. Around 585 he returned to Rome to become the abbot of St. Andrew's Monastery and devoted much of his time in the following years to lecturing on the BIBLE. After he met some English slaves in Rome's market, he developed a desire to evangelize the British. He visited the island briefly but soon returned to Rome, where he had become one of the chief advisers to the pope.

In 590, very much against his will, he was elected pope, just before completing a treatise on the office of BISHOP, *Liber Pastoralis Curae*. Though a reluctant bishop, he set about his job with vigor and became a popular preacher. He oversaw the passage of a set of decrees reforming church organization and revising the LITURGY of the Mass, thereby stabilizing the Roman Rite. He dismissed the lay people working in the Vatican and replaced them with priests. He collected and published the melodies of Roman CHANT, now known as Gregorian Chant, which CHARLEMAGNE later did much to spread throughout the West. He also supported MONASTICISM. Gregory's actions collectively became known as the Gregorian Reform.

Gregory solidified and expanded papal authority, believing that as the successor of St. Peter he held a certain primacy over all other churches. This belief colored his relations with the eastern patriarchs. He opposed the use of the title "Ecumenical Patriarch" by the archbishop of Constantinople. His goals were aided by an accumulation of temporal authority at Rome, resulting from the weakness of the secular powers at the time.

Gregory came to his office with a desire to evangelize the northern lands, especially England and Gaul, and northern Africa. He sent St. Augustine of Canterbury (d. 605) to England; his traditional arrival date of 596 is considered the founding date of the Church of England. He was named first Archbishop of Canterbury in 597.

Gregory's health was already impaired when he became pope, and he suffered considerably from a variety of bodily ailments during the years in office. He eventually succumbed to his failing body and died on March 12, 604. He was canonized soon after his death. While not a creative theologian, he would become known as one of the four great doctors (teachers) of the Latin church (along with AMBROSE, JEROME, and AUGUSTINE OF HIPPO).

Further reading: John C. Cavadini, ed., *Gregory the Great: A Symposium* (Notre Dame: University of Notre Dame Press, 1996); G. R. Evans, *The Thought of Gregory the Great* (Cambridge: Cambridge University Press, 1986); Robert A. Markus, *From Augustine to Gregory the Great* (London: Variorum Reprints, 1983); Jeffrey Richards, *Consul of God: The Life and Times of Gregory the Great* (London: Routledge & Kegan Paul, 1980).

Gregory VII Hildebrand, St. (c. 1021–1085)
pope and church reformer

Hildebrand is recognized as one of the great reform popes of all time. He is most famous for his role in denouncing Simony and lay investiture and for his clash of wills with Emperor HENRY IV (r. 1084–1105) in the INVESTITURE CONTROVERSY. He was canonized in 1606 by Pope PAUL V; his feast day is May 25.

The future pope, saint, and DOCTOR OF THE CHURCH was born at Soana in Tuscany, ITALY, about 1023 and named Hildebrand by his rather impoverished parents. He received his education at a MONASTERY in Rome and at the Lateran school, and as a young man he became a BENEDICTINE monk. Recognized for his skills, a succession of popes used him as their assistant. During the brief reign of Gregory VI (1046–47) he was exiled from Rome but returned during the ascendancy of Leo IX (r. 1049–54). Pope Leo initiated the reforms that would culminate under Hildebrand.

In 1073, after the death of Alexander II (r. 1061–73), Hildebrand was elected pope and took the name Gregory VII. Within a year he issued a decree against simony, the buying or selling of church offices, and banned lay investiture. Under the latter practice, the secular ruler of a region would formally convey both the lands attached to a bishopric and the symbols of the bishops office to the newly appointed bishop. The pope's decrees were opposed in GERMANY, FRANCE, and England, where kings and princes had become used to installing bishops with the insignia of their office (ring, mitre, crozier).

In 1076 Holy Roman Emperor Henry IV reacted by declaring the pope deposed. Hildebrand responded in kind by deposing and excommunicating the emperor. A year later the emperor was forced to submit to the pope and was absolved for his actions, but the conflict soon resumed. In 1080 Hildebrand once again excommunicated Henry IV. While the public accepted the first excommunication, most felt that the second was an injustice. Henry IV took advantage of Hildebrand's diminishing power and marched on Rome, seizing it two years later. Hildebrand fled to Salerno, where he died.

During his PAPACY, Hildebrand recognized the existence of the state as part of GOD's plan but never considered the church and the state to be equal. The church remained superior even in political decisions. Ever trying to maximize power in Rome, he ran into conflict even with bishops who tried to maintain their independence. He also tried to restore the church's relationship with the Eastern Church, which he wanted to join him in a CRUSADE to recapture the Church of the Holy Sepulchre in Jerusalem.

Further reading: Uta-Renate Blumenthal, *Papal Reform and Canon Law in the 11th and 12th Centuries* (Brookfield, Vt.: Ashgate, 1998); H. E. J. Cowdrey, *Pope Gregory VII, 1073–1085* (Oxford: Oxford University Press, 1998); Kathleen Cushing, *Papacy and Law in the Gregorian Revolution,* (New York: Oxford University Press, 1998); Allan John Macdonald, *Hildebrand: A Life of Gregory VII* (London: Methuen, 1932); Marvin Richardson Vincent, *The Age of Hildebrand* (Edinburgh: T & T Clark, 1897).

Gregory of Nazianzus (c. 329–390)

Known in the Eastern Church as "The Theologian," Gregory of Nazianzus was one of the pillars of what came to be called orthodoxy. He is famous for defending the Nicene faith with his five sermons, which strongly influenced the Council of CONSTANTINOPLE I in 381. He also served as the BISHOP of Constantinople. His feast day in the East is January 25, and in the West, January 2.

The son of a bishop, Gregory of Nazianzus grew up in Cappadocia (central Turkey) in the generation immediately after the Council of Nicaea (325) (*see* COUNCILS, ECUMENICAL), which had settled the debate between Arius (*see* ARIANISM) and ATHANASIUS concerning the nature of CHRIST. Gregory is closely associated with BASIL THE GREAT (c. 329–79) and Basil's brother GREGORY OF NYSSA (c. 330–c. 394). The three are often referred to as the Cappadocian Fathers.

The decision at Nicaea, while setting the main body of the church in the Athanasian camp, did not end the conflict. Support for Arius remained strong in different regions, and many communities were home to both an orthodox and an Arian congregation. A few of the Roman emperors through the next century also favored Arius.

As Gregory of Nazianzus emerged as a CHRISTIAN teacher, among his first accomplishments (in concert with Basil) was to compile an anthology of the writings of the third-century theologian ORIGEN (c. 185–254). Basil went on to become the bishop of Caesarea in Cappadocia and used his position to have Gregory named bishop of Sasima. The appointment caused considerable friction between the two friends, as Sasima was a most undesirable place to reside, and Gregory refused to live there.

In the meantime, Constantinople had become a stronghold of Arianism during the reign of the Emperor Valens (r. 364–378). With the new emperor THEODOSIUS I (r. 378–95) in place, Gregory was invited to take up residence in Constantinople. His home became his first preaching center and the site where he delivered his most famous work, a series of five sermons on the TRINITY and the deity of Christ. His oratorical abilities soon won the majority of the city to the orthodox camp. Gregory became the new bishop of Constantinople and in 381 served as the presiding officer at the Council of Constantinople, which reaffirmed the Athanasian position and issued a more definitive statement on the two natures of Christ.

Following the council, feeling that his job was done, Gregory resigned his bishopric and retired to his hometown, where he quietly lived the remainder of his years. His Five Theological Orations became one of the valued statements of Christian thinking and earned him the title doctor of the church.

Further reading: Gregory Nazianzen, *The Theological Orations,* tr. C. G. Browne and J. E. Swallow, The Library of Christian Classics (London: SCM, 1954); John Anthony McGuckin, *St. Gregory of Nazianzus: An Intellectual Biography* (Crestwood, N.Y.: St. Vladimir's Seminary, 2001); Anthony Meredith, *The Cappadocians* (Crestwood, N.Y.: St. Vladimir's Seminary 1996); Rosemary Radford Reuther, *Gregory of Nazianzus, Rhetor and Philosopher* (Oxford: Oxford University Press, 1969); Donald F. Winslow, *The Dynamics of Salvation: A Study in Gregory of Nazianzus,* Patristic Monograph Series (Cambridge, Mass.: Philadelphia Patristic Foundation, 1979).

Gregory of Nyssa (c. 330–395)

Gregory of Nyssa was one of three Cappadocian fathers who lived and worked in the middle of the fourth century in what is now central Turkey. The three, including BASIL THE GREAT of Caesarea and GREGORY OF NAZIANZUS, provided significant support in the defense and reaffirmation of the orthodox CHRISTIAN position on the two natures of CHRIST (fully human and fully divine) as promulgated by the Council of Nicaea in 325 during the struggle against ARIANISM. Unlike the other two, Gregory was married.

Not formally educated in any of the prominent schools of the time, Gregory, younger brother of Basil the Great, was nevertheless widely read in both Greek philosophical thought and Christian THEOLOGY. Early in his life he was attracted to Greek pagan thought, as revived under the emperor JULIAN THE APOSTATE (c. 331–63), and became a teacher of rhetoric. Though attracted to monasticism, he married and never adopted a monastic lifestyle.

His brother Basil was able to have Gregory appointed BISHOP of Nyssa, but in the midst of the continuing struggle with the Arian Christians, who were strong throughout Cappadocia, he was deposed by the Arians in 376 and driven into exile two years later. However, with the ascendancy of THEODOSIUS I (378–95) to the emperor's throne, the orthodox party was favored once again in CONSTANTINOPLE, and Gregory was appointed to succeed his recently deceased brother as bishop of Caesarea.

As a bishop again, he assumed important duties at the Council of Constantinople I (381), which reaffirmed the Council of CHALCEDON's position on the two natures of CHRIST. He later wrote against Eunomius (d. c. 395), a theologian who favored the Arian position. While Gregory is respected for his defense of Christian orthodoxy, as a theologian he is most remembered for his discussion of the human SOUL and its movement toward perfection. He saw the attainment of perfection as part of a constant process. There is in his view no end to the gaining of perfection or virtue. The soul, having attained a level of perfection, is presented with a new level. It is constantly moving forward into the inner life of GOD but never becoming God.

Further reading: Jean Daniélou and Herbert Musurillo, *From Glory to Glory: Texts from Gregory of Nyssa's Mystical Writings* (Crestwood, N.Y.: St. Vladimir's Seminary, 1979); Henry Wace and Philip Schaff, eds. *Gregory of Nyssa: Dogmatic Treatises, Etc.* A Select Library of Nicene and Post-Nicene Fathers (Oxford: Parker and Co., 1911); Anthony Meredith, *Gregory of Nyssa* (London: Routledge, 1999).

Griffiths, Dom Bede (1906–1993)
Benedictine monk, mystic, and priest
Dom Bede Griffiths, also known as Swami Dayananda, was born Alan Richard Griffiths at Walton-on-Thames, England, in 1906. His father's bankruptcy and the family's subsequent poverty greatly affected the young Griffiths, but a scholarship allowed him to study at Oxford, where he graduated in 1929. The Anglican writer C. S. Lewis (1898–1963), a tutor during his college years, became a lifelong friend.

After a one-year experiment in communal living and natural lifestyle with two friends, Griffiths applied for ministry in the Church of England. This catalyzed a period of inner turmoil and spiritual searching, during which he was drawn to JOHN HENRY NEWMAN's book *The Development of Christian Doctrine* (1845). In 1931, he formally converted to Roman Catholicism. He entered Prinknash Abbey and on December 20, 1932, became a BENEDICTINE novice with the name of Bede. He took his final vows in 1937. In 1947 he was placed in charge of a MONASTERY at Farnborough (1947–51) and then at Pluscadin, Scotland (1951–55). While at Pluscadin, he penned an autobiography, *The Golden String* (1954).

In 1955, Griffiths accompanied Fr. Benedict Alapott to India, where they established a monastic residence at Kengeri, Bangalore. Finding the location too western, Griffiths moved in 1958 to Kurisumala, where he and Fr. Francis Acharya

developed a monastic LITURGY using the Syriac rite. They also dressed in orange robes, in identification with the Indian *sanyassin* community of ascetic Hindu monks. At this time Griffiths adopted the spiritual name Dayananda (meaning the bliss of prayer). His next book, *Christ in India* (1967), reflected his study of Indian culture and religion.

In 1968, Griffiths moved to Shantivanam, an ashram in Tamil Nadu founded by Fathers Jules Monchanin (d. 1957) and Henry LeSaux (Abhishiktananda) (d. 1973), two French missionaries who pursued a life of poverty in common with the Indians among whom they worked. The two had developed a liturgy in their daily prayer meetings using English, Sanskrit, and Tamil. Griffiths developed Shantivanam into a center focused on the contemplative life, the contextualization, or INCULTURATION, of Christianity into non-European cultures, and interreligious dialogue. His own books advanced this program, such as *Vedanta and the Christian Faith* and *Return to the Center* (1977). His commentary on the Bhagavad Gita, *Rivers of Compassion*, appeared in 1987.

In 1990, Griffiths suffered a stroke. He recovered and was able to resume his active life that now included travel worldwide. He died May 13, 1993, honored by CHRISTIAN and non-Christian alike. His life had embodied a compassionate mysticism that sought to embed Christianity within Indian culture and offer new opportunities for prayerful devotion for Christians. He is seen as a leading force in the development of contemporary Asian Christian theology, a major theme of which has been de-Westernization.

Further reading: L. Anandam, *Western Lover of the East: A Theological Enquiry into Bede Griffiths' Contribution to Christology* (Kodaikanal: La Salette, 1998); Beatrice Bruteau, ed. *The Other Half of My Soul: Bede Griffiths and the Hindu-Christian Dialogue* (Wheaton, Ill.: Theosophical Publication House, 1996); Shirley Du Boulay, *Beyond the Darkness: A Biography of Bede Griffiths* (New York: Doubleday, 1998); Bede Griffiths, *A Human Search: Reflection on My Life*, ed. John Swindells and Wayne

Teasdale (Ligouri, Mo.: Triumph, 1997); ———, *River of Compassion: A Christian Commentary on the Bhagavad Gita* (New York: Continuum, 1995).

Grotius, Hugo (1583–1645) *Dutch jurist and theologian*

Grotius is known as the "Father of International Law." His principal political and theological works have become standard references for CHRISTIANS of all denominations and jurists in general. In them, he developed influential notions of natural THEOLOGY and natural law, itself based on divine law as understood through REVELATION.

Huig de Groot was born into an influential Dutch family. A child prodigy, at the age of 12 he went to Leiden University and became a lawyer at 15. Siding with the FREE-WILL Arminians in their political-religious conflict with the predestinationist Calvinists, Grotius was in 1618 sentenced by Prince Maurice of Nassau (1567–1625) to life imprisonment for supporting the former. He escaped to Paris in 1621, where he continued to produce treatises about natural theology, international law, and social justice. "God," he wrote, "has given conscience a judicial power to guide human actions." FRANCISCO SUAREZ had a deep influence on him. Besides natural law, Grotius taught that nations are also governed by voluntary laws based on the consent of the people, thereby anticipating modern democratic theory.

Shocked by the Wars of Religion of the early 17th century, he proposed in *On the Law of War and Peace* (1625) a JUST WAR doctrine. War, he argued, must be limited to certain contained circumstances and may be waged only to protect and defend human rights. He also analyzed ways to negotiate peace. He defended the principle of the "freedom of the seas" in the face of international piracy, a principle soon adopted by the leading maritime nations. His influence on subsequent theories of government has been enormous.

Further reading: Christian Gellinek, *Hugo Grotius* (Boston: Twayne, 1983); Charles S. Edwards, *Hugo Grotius, the Miracle of Holland: A Study in Political and Legal Thought* (Chicago: Nelson-Hall, 1981); William S.M. Knight, *The Life and Works of Hugo Grotius* (London: Sweet & Maxwell, 1925); Hamilton Vreeland, *Hugo Grotius: The Father of the Modern Science of International Law* (Little, Colo.: F. B. Rothman, 1986).

Guadalupe, Our Lady of *See* MARY OF NAZARETH.

Guardini, Romano (1885–1968) *theologian and spiritual teacher*

Guardini was born in Verona, Italy, but raised and educated in GERMANY, first in chemistry and economics and then in theology at the Universities of Freiburg im Breisgau, Tübingen, and Bonn. He served as mentor to the youth group Quickborn, taught at Tübingen and Munich, opposed the Nazis, and wrote many books, including *The Lord* (1937), a popular meditative biography of CHRIST. At the end of his life, he declined the cardinalate offered to him by PAUL VI.

Guardini was a CHRISTIAN existentialist thinker and wildly prolific writer whose range extended from a THEOLOGY of the LITURGY to meditations on theologians, philosophers, and poets. Liturgy, he wrote in *The Spirit of the Liturgy* (1918), is comparable to the play of children, in which there is "the sublime mingling of profound earnestness and divine joyfulness." In a treatise on the beatitudes he wrote, "Blessed are . . . those who ask for no miracles, demand nothing out of the ordinary, but who find GOD's message in everyday life." His meditative biography of Christ, *The Lord,* is still popular among both theologians and lay people of all faiths. Many of the themes he discussed in more than 60 volumes read like anticipatory statements to VATICAN COUNCIL II.

The spiritual guidance center Burg Rothenfalls on the Main River, which he founded in 1927 for

Catholic youth was confiscated by the Nazis in 1939. Unlike other Catholic theologians under the Nazi regime, Guardini remained openly and publicly critical of the Nazi agenda. During the war years he wrote noted studies of the poets Friederich Hölderlin (1770–1843) and Rainer Maria Rilke (1875–1926), besides teaching philosophy of religion. After World War II Guardini taught the *Geisteswissenschaften* (sciences of the spirit) at Tübingen and Munich. He received many national and international awards, including the Peace Prize of the German Book Dealers (1952) and the Erasmus Prize of Brussels (1962).

Further reading: Romano Guardini, *The Lord* (Chicago: Henry Regnery, 1954); ———, *Selected Spiritual Writings,* ed. Robert A. Krieg (Maryknoll, N.Y.: Orbis, 2005); Robert A. Krieg, *Romano Guardini: A Precursor of Vatican II* (Notre Dame: University of Notre Dame Press, 1997).

guilt (Old Eng.: *gylt,* "responsibility for offense")

In theological terms, guilt does not refer to the psychoemotional state of "feeling guilty" for real or imagined offenses or wrongdoings. Rather, it is the state of being at fault with the attendant consciousness of that fault and liability for the punishment attached to it. In CHRISTIAN thought, the reality of guilt is addressed by the FORGIVENESS of GOD.

See also SIN; THEOLOGY.

Further reading: Jeffrey G. Sobosan, *Guilt and the Christian: A New Perspective* (Chicago: Thomas More, 1982); Merold Westphal, *God, Guilt, and Death: An Existential Phenomenology of Religion* (Bloomington: Indiana University, 1984).

Gutiérrez, Gustavo (1928–) *father of liberation theology*

Gutiérrez is a mestizo, part Hispanic and part Indian, born in Peru. As a child he had polio, an experience that led him to study medicine. He soon changed his mind and became a Roman Catholic priest, joining the DOMINICANS. In 1985 he received his doctorate from the Université Catholique de Lyon and has since received many honorary degrees. He is currently the John Cardinal O'Hara Professor of Theology at the UNIVERSITY OF NOTRE DAME.

Gutiérrez is most famous for his book *A Theology of Liberation: History, Politics, Salvation* (1971), which has earned him the title "Father of LIBERATION THEOLOGY." Liberation THEOLOGY calls on the church to educate its members in critical social consciousness, to identify with the poor, and to actively challenge political and economic systems that foster social injustice. His work has primarily focused on LATIN AMERICA but was influential in the development of liberation theologies around the world.

See also LEONARDO BOFF; FEMINISM; INCULTURATION.

Further reading: Curt Cadorette, *From the Heart of the People: The Theology of Gustavo Gutierrez* (Oak Park, Ill.: Meyer Stone, 1988); Margaret M. Campbell, *Critical Theory and Liberation Theology: A Comparison of the Initial Work of Jürgen Habermas and Gustavo Gutierrez* (New York: Peter Lang, 1999); Marc H. Ellis and Otto Maduro, eds., *Expanding the View: Gustavo Gutierrez and the Future of Liberation Theology* (Maryknoll, N.Y.: Orbis, 1990); Robert McAfee Brown, *Gustavo Gutierrez: An Introduction to Liberation Theology* (Maryknoll, N.Y.: Orbis, 1990).

H

Hagia Sophia (Gk.: *hagia,* "holy" + *sophia,* "wisdom")

Among second-century CHRISTIANS, Sophia, the personification of wisdom, referred to CHRIST as the "Wisdom of God" (Luke 12:49). The first and second cathedrals of CONSTANTINOPLE were both named Holy Wisdom. The first structure was built by CONSTANTINE over a temple dedicated to Artemis in 360. The second church was built on the same spot by Emperor JUSTINIAN I (482–565) and finished in 537.

Justinian's architects were Anthemius of Tralles (c. 474–c. 534) and Isadore of Miletus (fl. 537), whose goal was to surpass Solomon's Temple in Jerusalem. They developed the rounded dome set on a square and supported by buttresslike squinches, pendentives, and soffits. An earthquake damaged the first dome, which collapsed in 557. Isadore's nephew erected one even higher. The church had a golden star and 40,000 lbs of silver ornament. The first mosaics were decorative, based on a large Greek CROSS. The present mosaics date from the ninth century, after the iconoclasm controversy was resolved (*see* ICON).

Hagia Sophia was the jewel of all Christian churches and a model for all future architects of holy shrines, including the great Ottoman architect Sinan (1489–1588). The Turks turned the church into a mosque after they conquered Constantinople in 1453. Some mosaics survived, and in 1935 Mustafa Kemal Ataturk (1881–1938) turned the Hagia Sophia into a museum. Many mosaics have been restored.

Further reading: W. R. Lethaby and Harold Swainson, *The Church of Sancta Sophia, Constantinople: A Study of Byzantine Building* (London: Macmillan, 1894); R. J. Mainstone, *Hagia Sophia: Architecture, Structure, and Liturgy of Justinian's Great Church* (New York: Thames & Hudson, 1988); Robert S. Nelson, *Hagia Sophia, 1850–1950: Holy Wisdom Modern Monument* (Chicago: University of Chicago Press, 2004); Kalliopi Theoharidou, *The Architecture of Hagia Sophia, Thessaloniki: From its Erection up to the Turkish Conquest* (Oxford: B.A.R., 1988).

hagiography (Gk.: *hagios,* "holy," "saint" + *graphe,* "writing")

Hagiography, or "writing about the saints," is a CHRISTIAN literary genre that aims to inspire remembrance of the saints and imitation of their virtues. The genre had roots in judicial *acta,* or records, as in the *Martyrdom of Perpetua and Felicity,* passions, or martyrdom stories, and later leg-

Hagia Sophia (Holy Wisdom) was the first monumental church of Christendom built in Constantinople, now Istanbul, Turkey, under Emperor Constantine, 360. A second church, seen here, was built on the same spot by Emperor Justinian in 537. *(Photo: Jack Renard)*

endary miracle stories. Parallel to the development of hagiography was the proliferation of accounts about legendary acts of CHRIST, the APOSTLES, and other disciples, which abounded especially in the second century.

The *acta* were read at memorial feasts and EUCHARISTS celebrated at the tombs of martyrs on their "heavenly birthdays"—the anniversaries of their martyrdom. These *acta* and stories functioned as Christian hero-heroine tales to compete with those of Hercules and the other heroes of Greco-Roman culture. Martyrdom was the ultimate imitation of Christ, a baptism of blood. When persecution of Christians ceased, MONKS and NUNS in the Egyptian desert developed the notion of the BAPTISM of tears or repentance in imitation of

the martyrs that went before them. Their stories in turn became the hero stories for future Christians. ATHANASIUS OF ALEXANDRIA's *The Life of Antony* almost single-handedly served as the catalyst for the growth of MONASTICISM in the East and the West. The martyrs' memorials led to the honoring, preservation, and later transportation of RELICS, which today are part of every ALTAR stone.

Further reading: Gail Ashton, *The Generation of Identity in Late Medieval Hagiography: Speaking the Saint* (London: Routledge, 2000); Donald Attwater, *A Dictionary of Saints* (New York: Penguin, 1965); Thomas Head, ed., *Medieval Hagiography: An Anthology* (New York: Garland, 2000); Thomas F. X. Noble and Thomas Head, eds., *Soldiers of Christ: Saints and Saints Lives from Late*

Antiquity and the Early Middle Ages (University Park: Pennsylvania State University Press, 1995).

Häring, Bernard (1912–1998) *Vatican II moral theologian*

Bernard Häring was born on November 10, 1912, in Böttingen, Germany, one of 12 children in a devout Catholic family. His treatise on moral THEOLOGY, *The Law of Christ* (1954), had worldwide impact, and he was one of the most influential *periti*, or experts, at VATICAN COUNCIL II.

Häring studied at the Redemportist seminary at Gars-am-Inn and in 1933 entered the order, a missionary society founded by St. ALPHONSUS LIGUORI. He was ordained a priest in 1933. His order asked him to study moral theology, and he completed a degree in theology at Tübingen in 1947. After teaching for two years at Gars-am-Inn, he moved to the Alphonsian Academy, which the Redemptorists had just opened in Rome. He remained there throughout his career.

In 1954 Häring published *The Law of Christ*, which offered a new direction for moral theology within the church. Moral theology had often been bogged down in the practical problems of priests trying to sort out the distinctions between mortal and venial SIN in parishioners' confessions. He suggested a new approach based on GOD's Covenant of GRACE with the people and invited readers into a life in which moral issues were considered in the context of one's relationship to God, other people, and the world. He self-consciously moved away from legalistic approaches to a focus on overall moral conduct. *The Law of Christ* was immediately hailed as an important work and translated into more than a dozen languages.

Pope JOHN XXIII named Häring to the preparatory commission for the Vatican Council II and gave commendatory remarks to Häring's new approach to moral theology. He served as secretary to the committee that worked on *Gaudium et Spes* the Pastoral Constitution on the Church in the Modern World. His high regard by the papal office continued during the reign of PAUL VI, who invited Häring to lead the Curia's annual retreat.

In 1968 Häring publicly disagreed with *Humanae Vitae* (July 25, 1968), Paul VI's encyclical proscribing artificial contraception, and his statement was published by the *New York Times*. During the 1970s, he fell under the scrutiny of the Congregation for the Doctrine of the Faith, which contemplated a doctrinal trial concerning his writings. The issue was never pushed to a final resolution, but some of Häring's students who expressed similar views were forced to recant or, as in the case of American theologian CHARLES E. CURRAN at the Catholic University of America, to withdraw from their role as a teacher recognized by the church.

Häring continued to write and publish. His work culminated in his three-volume 1979 opus *Free and Faithful in Christ*. Then in 1979, he was discovered to have throat cancer. Despite several operations he lost the ability to lecture and preach, and he formally retired from his academic post in 1987.

Further reading: William Jerry Boney and Lawrence E. Molumby, eds., *The New Day; Catholic Theologians of the Renewal* (Richmond, Va.: John Knox, 1968); Daniel Callahan, ed., *The Catholic Case for Contraception* (New York: Macmillan, 1969); Bernard Häring, *Free and Faithful in Christ* (New York: Seabury, 1978–79); ———, *The Law of Christ: Moral Theology for Priests and Laity* (Westminster, Md.: Mercier, 1967).

heaven and hell (O. Eng.: *heofen*, "sky" and Gmc.: *haljo*, "covered place," "netherworld;" Heb.: *shamayim* and *sheol;* Gk.: *ouranos* and *hades*)

In Catholic doctrine, heaven is the dwelling place of GOD, the angels, and the saved dead who attain the BEATIFIC VISION. In the Old Testament the heavens (*shamayim*) means both sky and God's abode, where God sits in council with the heavenly hosts (angels) whose proceedings the prophets may glimpse. The netherword, or *sheol*, was not so much a place of punishment as a murky region of suspended animation apart from God's presence (Ps. 88:8).

There is little doubt that Zoroastrianism had significant influence on the next stage of late Jewish and early CHRISTIAN conceptions of heaven and hell. This influence likely took place during the Jewish exile in Bablyon (c. 589–540 B.C.E.), after the Persian Zoroastrian emperor Cyrus the Great (d. 529) freed them and helped them rebuild the Temple in Jerusalem; for that deed Second Isaiah named Cyrus "Messiah of the Lord" (Isa. 45:1). Exilic Judaism may have influenced Zoroastrianism, too.

Jews and later Christians brought to the interchange their concepts of CREATION, REDEMPTION (exodus from EGYPT, DEATH and RESURRECTION of Jesus), and consummation of history in a reign of God. Zorastrianism, a revealed monotheistic religion, added the conception that after creation history there will be a struggle between good forces, led by Ahura Mazda, and evil forces, led by Ainya Mainyu, culminating in a Last Judgment and a relegation of souls to heaven or hell. The combination of these concepts helped determine the Western worldview, at first through APOCALYPSE in the books Ezekiel and Daniel, the QUMRAN literature, and the Book of Revelation in the New Testament. The APOSTLE PAUL spoke of tiers of heavens (2 Cor. 12:2); the GNOSTICS were fond of multiple heavens corresponding to the planetary spheres.

At its root the Catholic concept of heaven entails dwelling in and enjoying the presence of God in a BEATIFIC VISION. Benedict XII (r. 1334–42) determined in *Benedictus Deus* (January 25, 1336) that the SOULS of the just could attain beatific vision immediately after death and did not need to await the general judgment and resurrection, and that the souls of those who die in mortal sin go immediately to hell.

The Christian concept of hell means the opposite of heaven: the total absence of God. More graphic Christian notions of heaven and hell

borrowed Greco-Roman religious motifs from the bliss of the Elysian Fields and the torture and torment of Hades. The Italian poet DANTE ALIGHIERI shaped all later Western images of heaven and hell in his *Comedia Divina.*

Neither heaven nor hell is a specific physical "location" but a condition of existence after death. The Council of Lyons (1274) said that souls are received into heaven after death (*see* COUNCILS, ECUMENICAL). The Council of FLORENCE (1439) says that heavenly souls see God as God truly is (*see* 1 Cor. 13:12).

Nevertheless, as the notion of heaven includes the teaching on the bodily resurrection of CHRIST, there is always a bodily component to the rewards of heaven and the punishments of hell (2 Cor. 5:10). Catholics and Christians in general have never clearly sorted out the relation between heaven and hell, the coming reign of God of which Jesus preached, or the New Jerusalem and the creation of a new heaven and new earth (Rev. 21.1–4). Theologian KARL RAHNER wrote that Christ entering into heaven is not a person entering an existing place but rather the very creation of heaven, as the fulfillment of the "supernatural existential," the capacity of humankind to enter into union with God.

Further reading: Bernhard Lang and Collen McDannell, *Heaven: A History* (New Haven, Conn.: Yale University Press, 1988); Christopher Rowland, *The Open Heaven: A Study of Apocalyptic in Judaism and Early Christianity* (New York: Crossroad, 1982).

Hecker, Isaac Thomas (1819–1888) *founder of the Paulists*

Hecker was born in New York to immigrant parents and at a young age became interested in the social conditions of the working class. His mother was a pious Methodist, but he rejected Protestantism. For a brief time he stayed at Brook Farm and befriended Henry David Thoreau (1817–62) and the Catholic Orestes Bownson (1803–76), but he ultimately found both Protestantism and Transcendentalism to be unsatisfactory and was drawn instead to Roman Catholicism, which he adopted in 1844. Attracted to the Redemptorist community, he joined their novitiate in Belgium in 1845 and was ordained in 1849. In 1851 he returned to work with the Catholic immigrant community in the United States.

Hecker's problems with his Redemptorist superiors led Pope Pius IX to release him from his vows in 1857. He soon founded a new congregation known as the Paulists devoted to missionary work, and he remained its superior until his death. In 1865 he founded the *Catholic World* magazine, geared toward the American Catholic experience. From the start the Paulists have been heavily involved in Catholic information, news, and book publishing; they have also sent missionaries to foreign lands throughout their history.

Hecker was passionate and zealous in adapting Catholicism to the American experience. He was a proud American and a staunch Catholic at a time when it was believed these two could not coexist. Were it not for his association with the alleged HERESY of AMERICANISM, he might well have been canonized long ago.

Further reading: John Farina, *An American Experience of God: The Spirituality of Isaac Hecker* (New York: Paulist, 1981); John Farina, ed., *Hecker Studies: Essays on the Thought of Isaac Hecker* (New York: Paulist, 1983); Isaac Thomas Hecker, *Questions of the Soul* (New York: Catholic Publication House, 1855); David J. O'Brien, *Isaac Hecker: An American Catholic* (New York: Paulist, 1992).

Henry IV (1050–1106) *Holy Roman Emperor*

The conflict between Henry IV and GREGORY VII, HILDEBRAND was a high point of the INVESTITURE CONTROVERSY. As part of a balance between CHURCH AND STATE, secular rulers traditionally had the authority to appoint church officials, known as lay investiture, or to sell church offices, known as simony, to those loyal to the state. As BISHOPS had temporal as well as spiritual powers in the Roman Empire from the time of CONSTANTINE and in the Holy Roman Empire from the time of Otto I (936–73), emperors and other princes thought it their right to invest new bishops with the insignia of office, including the crozier, the ring, and the miter, or bishop's hat. Indeed, even the appointment of bishops often required secular assent.

In 1073 Hildebrand was elected to the PAPACY and began a campaign to reform the church by banning simony and lay investiture. He hoped to strengthen the power of the church and curb the power of the Holy Roman Emperor to elect the next pope, but his reforms were strongly opposed in FRANCE, England, and GERMANY. In 1076 the emperor of Germany, Henry IV, reacted by declaring the pope deposed. Hildebrand responded by both deposing and excommunicating Henry IV.

Due to unrest in Germany, Henry IV was in a more precarious situation and was forced to submit to the pope a year later at Canossa by climbing the mountain on his knees in the snow. He was absolved for his actions, but the dispute revived. In 1080 Hildebrand once again excommunicated Henry IV for not fulfilling the promises he gave at Canossa. While the public accepted the first excommunication, most felt that the second was an injustice. Henry IV took advantage of Hildebrand's diminishing power and marched on Rome, seizing it after two years. Hildebrand fled to Salerno, where he died in 1085. Urban II succeeded him, and the Investiture Controversy ended in a compromise at the CONCORDAT of Worms in 1122. The ongoing conflict between church and state in the MIDDLE AGES has not been totally resolved, especially in those European countries where the Catholic Church (and some Protestant churches) are still tied to and supported by the state through various concordats.

See also BONIFACE VIII.

Further reading: Karl Leyser, *The Crisis of Medieval Germany* (London: British Academy, 1984); I. S. Robinson, *Henry IV of Germany, 1056–1106* (Cambridge:

Cambridge University Press, 1999); W. R. W. Stephens, *Hildebrand and His Times* (London: Longmans, Green, 1888); Marvin Richardson Vincent, *The Age of Hildebrand* (Edinburgh: T & T Clark, 1897); Gerold Meyer von Knonau, *Jahrbücher des Deutschen Reiches unter Heinrich IV* (Berlin: Duncker & Humblot, 1964).

Henry VIII (1491–1547) *king of England and founder of Church of England*

Henry VIII succeeded to the throne of England in 1509 upon the death of his elder brother, Henry VII (r. 1485–1509). He is most famous for breaking with the Catholic Church and laying the foundation for the Church of England, or Anglican Church, a defining moment in Western Christendom.

Born in Greenwich, Henry was an energetic and intelligent youth. As an engaged young monarch he wrote a book attacking Martin Luther's ideas and defending the Catholic Church, for which the pope gave him the title "defender of the faith" in 1521. Under the guidance of the powerful lord chancellor Thomas Wolsey, foreign policy dominated the first half of Henry's reign. He shifted his alliance from the kings of Spain and France to the Holy Roman Emperor with unfortunate results. His various campaigns against FRANCE and Scottish forces cost him huge sums of money.

Henry was obsessed with continuing the Tudor dynasty through a male heir. In 1509 he married Catherine of Aragon, his brother's widow, after receiving a papal license. After giving birth to Mary Tudor (1516–58), Catherine, however, was unable to produce a male, so Henry sought an annulment of the marriage, claiming it had never been legal. Besides, Henry had fallen in love with Anne Boleyn (c. 1501/1507–36) and wanted to marry her.

Pope Clement VII would not grant a divorce, so Wolsey's successor, Thomas Cromwell (c. 1485–1540) turned to the English Parliament for a decision. Parliament issued a series of acts to curb papal authority in England. In 1532 Thomas Cranmer (1489–1556) became Archbishop of Canterbury and a year later declared Henry's marriage invalid. The pope responded by excommunicating Henry, to which the Parliament reacted by issuing legislation that began England's break with Rome. Among other things, it dissolved Catholic MONASTERIES and declared the king the only head of the Church of England. The Act of Submission of the Clergy required all CLERGY to take an oath to the king.

Anne Boleyn also failed to produce a male heir, to which Henry responded by beheading her in 1536. Henry's third wife, Jane Seymour, finally produced a son, Edward VI. Henry made three more marriages in the few years he had left, executing only one of his later wives. Elizabeth I (1533–1603) was the daughter of Henry and Anne Boleyn (c. 1501/1507–1536).

Further reading: J. S. Brewer, *The Reign of Henry VIII: From His Accession to the Death of Wolsey* (New York: AMS, 1968); Great Britain Public Record Office, *Letters and Papers, Foreign and Domestic, of the Reign of Henry VIII* (London: H.M. Stationery Office, 1862); Reginald Pole, *Defense of the Unity of the Church* (Westminster: Newman, 1965); H. Maynard Smith, *Henry VIII and the Reformation* (London: Macmillan, 1962).

heresy and schism (Gk.: *hairesis,* "party," "sect," "faction"; *schizmos,* "split")

Heresy and schism are often confused in popular understanding, although to be sure, in the early stages of Christianity, the terms were not radically distinct. Today heresy is a division between those holding false beliefs and those having orthodox beliefs, while schism is a division between two parts of the church not on the basis of belief but on the basis of authority. ARIANISM and DONATISM are classic heresies; the split between Roman Catholicism and EASTERN ORTHODOXY, which does not recognize the primacy of the pope, is a classic schism.

In ancient Rome, if one did not honor the civil gods of the state and partake in the emperor cult, one was guilty of "superstition," meaning impiety or atheism, but not heresy, as the state was not interested in citizens' theological beliefs. In New Testament times the term *hairesis* had less theological weight than in the second century; it merely designated a religious group with distinctive tenets of its own. For example, the first century Jewish historian Josephus refers to the Sadducees, Pharisees, and Essenes as "heresies" in the sense of philosophical sects or schools. CHRISTIANS are called a "heresy" in this sense in Acts 24:5. PAUL writes about factions (*schismata*) in the church of Corinth not so much in terms of false doctrine, although that is involved, but as tearing apart the unity of the church. On the other hand, Paul, Jude, John, and the Book of Revelation all speak of false teachers and APOSTLES, who may have been DOCETISTS or proto-GNOSTICS, showing that the concept of false doctrine was not unknown.

With the rise of multiple Gnostic and other movements in the second century, such as the followers of MARCION and MONTANUS and the Encratites, theologian/BISHOPS like IRENAEUS OF LYONS gave heresy a formal definition. It was false doctrine in opposition to orthodox belief as measured by the RULE OF FAITH and established TRADITION. This understanding prevailed during the Christological and Trinitarian controversies of the first seven ecumenical councils.

Until the fourth century, heretics were generally fought with exile, silencing, or both. Some like Nestorius (c. 386–c. 451) went on to found rival churches. After AUGUSTINE OF HIPPO justified the use of force by civil authorities in the suppression of the Donatists, heretics began to be imprisoned and killed. The ascetic Priscillian of Ávila (d. 385), who was most likely not even a heretic, was beheaded by the emperor Magnus Maximus (r. 383–88) in Trier. This opened the door to the wholesale slaughter of heretic CATHARI in the Albigensian Crusade and the violent abuses of the INQUISITION in SPAIN and elsewhere. Famous victims of heresy in later history include the Dominican firebrand GIROLAMO SAVONAROLA (1452–98), executed after preaching against the corruption of ALEXANDER VI

and fomenting violent revolution, and Giordano Bruno (1548–1600), a brilliant Dominican philosopher burned at the stake by the Inquisition.

Further reading: John Henry Blunt, ed., *Dictionary of Sects, Heresies, Ecclesiastical Parties, and Schools of Religious Thought* (London: Longmans, Green, 1892); Harold O. J. Brown, *Heresies: Heresy and Orthodoxy in the History of the Church* (Peabody, Mass.: Hendrickson, 1998); Lester R. Kurtz, *The Politics of Heresy: The Modernist Crisis in Roman Catholicism* (Berkeley: University of California Press, 1986); Robert E. Lerner, *The Heresy of the Free Spirit in the Later Middle Ages* (Notre Dame: University of Notre Dame Press, 1972).

hermeneutics (Gk.: *hermeneuein,* "to interpret," possibly from Hermes + *neuein,* "to ferry")

Hermeneutics is the art of determining the context, meaning, and purport of original sacred texts and interpreting those texts in a contemporary setting. The need for hermeneutics arises from the ambiguity of sacred texts, which are typically couched in symbols and metaphors and embedded in cultures with ancient or radically different worldviews. The term probably derived from its association with the god Hermes, who "ferried" the intentions of the gods to humans and the prayers of humans to the gods.

The ANTIOCHENE and ALEXANDRINE SCHOOLS of biblical interpretation set fundamental parameters for later CHRISTIAN hermeneutics. St. AUGUSTINE OF HIPPO's *De Doctrina Christiana* and his *Literal Interpretation of Genesis* were other foundational works in the field. Medieval exegesis followed these third- to fifth-century models. Modern hermeneutics begins with the work of Protestant theologian Friederich D. E. Schleiermacher (1768–1834), who subsumed the interpretation of sacred texts within a general theory of interpretation, whereby he sought to comprehend the meaning of the original authors better than they could themselves. He, in turn, had a direct influence on Wilhem Dilthey (1833–1911), who distinguished between understanding (*verstehen*), which is proper to the humanistic sciences, including sacred literature, and explanation (*erkären*), which is proper to the natural sciences. These two shaped the existential hermeneutic of Martin Heidegger (1889–1976) in *Being and Time* (1927; Eng. 1962). From Heidegger's hermeneutic Rudolph Bultmann (1884–1976) developed his project of DEMYTHOLOGIZATION.

Contemporary hermeneutics is shaped by the tension between the hermeneutics of suspicion in the CRITIQUE OF RELIGION by Marx, Nietzsche, and Freud from outside THEOLOGY and the critique from within theology by Karl Barth (1886–1968) and Bultmann. Having passed through the fiery furnace of criticism, the French Huguenot philosopher Paul Ricoeur (1913–2005) charted a path toward a hermeneutics of restoration and the recovery of meaning in the face of the deconstruction of discourse in postmodernity. His writing has greatly influenced Catholic thinking. Today hermeneutics has received new impulses from the hermeneutics of PRAXIS championed in LIBERATION THEOLOGY, gender-aware interpretation in FEMINISM, and the theology of INCULTURATION in non-Western and non-Christian countries.

Further reading: Frank K. Flinn, "The Phenomenology of Symbol: Genesis I and II," in William S. Hamrick, ed., *Phenomenology in Practice and Theory* (Dordrecht: Martinus Nijhoff, 1985), 223–249; Robert Hollinger, ed., *Hermeneutics and Praxis* (Notre Dame: University of Notre Dame Press, 1985); James McConkey Robinson and John B. Cobb, Jr, eds., *The New Hermeneutic* (New York: Harper & Row, 1964); Sean E. McEvenue and Ben F. Meyer, eds., *Lonergan's Hermeneutics: Its Development and Application* (Washington, D.C.: Catholic University of America Press, 1989); Paul Ricoeur, *The Philosophy of Paul Ricoeur,* ed. Charles E. Reagan and David Stewart (Boston: Beacon, 1978); Elizabeth J. Smith, *Bearing Fruit in Due Season: Feminist Hermeneutics and the Bible in Worship* (Collegeville, Minn.: Liturgical Press, 1999).

Hesburgh, Theodore (1917–) *U.S. Catholic higher education leader*

Hesburgh was born in 1917 in Syracuse, New York, attended NOTRE DAME UNIVERSITY and the Gregorian University in Rome, and received his bachelor of philosophy degree in 1939. In 1943 he was ordained a PRIEST, and in 1945 he received his doctorate in theology from the Catholic University of America. At the age of 35 he was named the 15th president of Notre Dame, a position he filled for 35 years, the longest tenure in the university's history.

Hesburgh has served on numerous national and international commissions over the years, including the U.S. Civil Rights Commission from 1957 to 1972. In 1964 he received the Medal of Freedom, and in 2000 he was awarded the Congressional Gold Medal, becoming the first person from higher education to receive the award. He has received the most honorary degrees of any one person, more than 150. Under his leadership the University of Notre Dame opened its doors to women in 1972. Like JOHN IRELAND, he envisioned Catholicism making a broad contribution to American society and being a vital part of its religious and cultural mainstream.

Further reading: Joel R. Connelly, *Hesburgh's Notre Dame: Triumph in Transition* (New York: Hawthorn Books, 1972).; Theodore Martin Hesburgh, *God, Country, Notre Dame: The Autobiography of Theodore M. Hesburgh* (New York: Doubleday, 1990); John C. Lungren, *Hesburgh of Notre Dame: Priest, Educator, Public Servant* (Kansas City, Mo.: Sheed & Ward, 1987); Michael O'Brien, *Hesburgh: A Biography* (Washington, D.C.: Catholic University of America Press, 1998).

hierarchy (Gk.: *hieros,* "sacred" + *archos,* "ruler")

Religious institutions in the West have generally been classified as either hierarchical or congregational. In a hierarchy spiritual AUTHORITY is exercised from the top down. In a congregational body spiritual authority is exercised from the bottom up.

There is much debate about how authority was exercised in the early church. Each APOSTLE or group of apostles gathered a following after the DEATH of Jesus around 30 C.E. There was no unanimity of views among them, as the conflict over the status of Gentiles demonstrates (Acts 15; Gal. 2). With time, different GOSPEL traditions developed under the authority or purported authority of an apostle or disciple (Paul, Peter, Mark, Matthew, Luke, John, Thomas, etc.). Later church teachers were to ascribe special authority to certain but not all apostles (e.g., Thomas in the *Gospel of Thomas*).

In the second and following centuries a hierarchical system of BISHOPS-priests-deacons emerged in order to face the challenge of GNOSTICISM and other heresies. An even denser hierarchy took shape for the first time under the system of the patriarch in which certain episcopal sees were given primacy of place and authority (Jerusalem, Rome, CONSTANTINOPLE, Alexandria, and Antioch). When disputes arose even among the patriarchs and bishops under them, supreme authority was expressed in ecumenical councils (*see* COUNCILS, ECUMENICAL), convened with the blessing of both emperors and bishops, including the bishops of Rome and Constantinople.

Meanwhile, the bishop of Rome, the patriarch of the West, gradually became a theological judge of last appeal even from the East. This led Roman bishops to start insisting on the primacy of the See of Peter, whom they saw as the "prince" of the apostles (*see* St. PETER THE APOSTLE), and to claim authority over the entire church, East and West. This position led to the GREAT SCHISM with EASTERN ORTHODOXY in 1054.

In the late MIDDLE AGES, the rival supremacy claims of popes and councils, in part a reaction to the AVIGNON PAPACY and the western SCHISM, was the subject of debate at the Councils of BASEL and CONSTANCE. Over time, papal primacy was bolstered by the development of the elabo-

rate hierarchical structures of the Vatican CURIA. The declaration of papal INFALLIBILITY at VATICAN COUNCIL I seemed to place the supreme teaching authority of Catholicism solely in the office of the PAPACY, but that declaration was qualified and contextualized by the principle of episcopal collegiality at VATICAN COUNCIL II, which affirmed that bishops share with the pope in responsibility and care for the whole church in *Lumen Gentium* 22–23, the Dogmatic Constitution on the Church. In this view, bishops and pope share in the MAGISTERIUM, or teaching office of the church.

Of special note is the role of cardinals in the hierarchical system of the Catholic Church. The term is derived from the Latin *cardo,* "hinge," and was first applied to a priest attached to a specific church. By the eighth century the term applied to the seven suburbicarian, suburban, or bishops surrounding the diocese of Rome, priests of the major churches of Rome, and the seven (later 14) district deacons. This group served as counselors to the pope. When there was a *sede vacante,* or a vacant papal see, the cardinals served collectively as leaders of the church. Their rank paralleled that of princes of the royal blood in the secular hierarchy. The cardinals came to serve as electors of a new pope. Cardinals in the collective are called the College of Cardinals, and the meeting to choose a new pope is called a consistory.

Starting in the Middle Ages cardinals began to be appointed from metropolitan sees throughout Europe and the world. In 1586 Pope Sixtus V (r. 1585–86) fixed the number of cardinals at 70, but JOHN XXIII went beyond that number in 1958, and today there is no fixed number. Today all cardinals are priests or bishops, even though they may bear the title cardinal-deacon. Most cardinals are cardinal-priests.

All the major congregations, tribunals, councils, offices, and commissions of the curia are led by cardinals. The cardinal-bishop of Ostia is the dean of the College of Cardinals. The dean and subdean, who rank first among equals, are in effect the second-highest ranking clerics in the church.

The secretary of state of the Vatican ranks next. Cardinals, like bishops, are expected to retire at the age 75, although the pope may ask them to stay longer. The rules governing the cardinalate are in the 1983 *Code of Canon Law* (cnn. 349–59).

Believers and others routinely use the term *Catholic Church* to refer to the hierarchical institutions that hold the church together. At Vatican II, the term came to be used in a more fundamental sense to refer to the sacramental communion of the people of God (*Lumen Gentium* 12), that is, the ordained clergy together with all Catholic lay people. Since Vatican II many observers see a trend, led by the papacy, to return to a pre–Vatican II emphasis on hierarchy. Cardinals wear scarlet robes at liturgical functions.

Further reading: John V. Allen, *All the Pope's Men: The Inside Story of How the Vatican Really Works* (New York: Doubleday, 2004); Avery Dulles, *Models of the Church* (New York: Doubleday, 2002); W.H.C. Frend, *The Early Church* (Philadelphia: Fortress, 1982); William J. La Due, *The Chair of St. Peter: A History of the Papacy* (Maryknoll, N.Y.: Orbis, 1999); Harris M. Lentz, *Popes and Cardinals of the 20th Century: A Biographical Dictionary* (Jefferson, N.C.: McFarland, 2002).

Hildegaard of Bingen (1098–1179) *abbess and mystic*

Hildegaard was a remarkably influential woman for the MIDDLE AGES. She is best known as a mystic, but she also wrote, led a monastic community, and composed music. Her feast day is September 17.

Hildegaard was born to a noble family. As a weak and sickly child of eight, she was placed under the care of Jutta, the leader of a small nunnery near Disibodenberg MONASTERY in GERMANY. In 1136 she became superior of the community upon Jutta's death and moved the community to a larger convent on the Rupertsberg at Bingen on the Rhine.

Her ill health caused her to lead an interior life, and she began receiving visions at a very young age. In 1147, with the influence of St. BERNARD OF CLAIRVAUX, Pope Eugenius III (r. 1145–53) created a commission to investigate Hildegaard, and it determined she was indeed a true mystic. Her first visionary work, *Scivias,* is her most famous. It recounts 26 visions related to the CHRISTIAN doctrine of salvation. She also wrote plays, a medical encyclopedia and handbook, and several well-known hymns. She traveled frequently and gave public speeches at monasteries and cathedrals.

Hildegaard was a powerful and influential woman, corresponding with and advising popes, statesmen, emperors, and heads of monasteries. Although all four formal attempts at canonization failed, since the 15th century she has been granted the title of saint in Roman martyrology, the official list of saints.

Further reading: Hildegard von Bingen, *Hildegard von Bingen's Mystical Visions: Translated from Hildegard's Scivias,* tr. Bruce Hozeski (Santa Fe: Bear & Company, 1995); Sabina Flanagan, *Hildegard of Bingen, 1098–1179: A Visionary Life* (London: Routledge, 1990); Anne H. King-Lenzmeier, *Hildegard of Bingen: An Integrated Vision* (Collegeville, Minn.: Liturgical Press, 2001); Mary Palmquist, ed., *The Life of the Holy Hildegard* (Collegeville, Minn.: Liturgical Press, 1995).

Hippolytus of Rome (c. 170–c. 236) *saint and doctor of the church*

Hippolytus was one of the most important CHRISTIAN theologians of the third century, although little is actually known of his life and writings. The 1851 publication of *Philosophumena,* which many believe to be his work, has provided at least some evidence. A presbyter in Rome, he was elected as the first ANTIPOPE in 217 but later was reconciled with the church and died a martyr. He was largely forgotten in the West, possibly due to his schismatic activities and the fact that he wrote in Greek. He is not to be confused with a martyr of the same name, who was a BISHOP of the city of Portus. Hippolytus of Rome's feast day is August 13th in the West and January 30th in the East.

It is unclear whether Hippolytus was a disciple of St. IRENAEUS, but he was certainly an important figure, as ORIGEN (c. 185–c. 254) attended one of his sermons when he visited Rome. In the early decades of the third century Hippolytus began attacking the doctrines of Sabellius (c. third century). He also rejected the theological teachings of Pope Zephyrinus (198–217) and Pope Callistus (217–22). During the latter's reign he became the first antipope; from that post, as bishop of a schismatic church, he continued to criticize the teachings of Popes Urban (222–30) and Pontianus (230–35). Under the persecution of Emperor Maximin (235–38) he was exiled to Sardinia with Pontianus, and before he died he most likely was reconciled with the church, because in 236 Pope Fabian (236–50) brought his body back to Rome together with that of Pontianus. He is celebrated as a saint and martyr of the church.

The central element of Hippolytus's teaching is the Logos (Word) doctrine. He distinguished between two states of the Word; one is immanent and eternal while the other is exterior and temporal. He disagreed with Sabellius, who emphasized the unity of God too one-sidedly, locating almost the whole of the TRINITY within the CHRIST. Hippolytus, on the other hand, distinguished the persons of the Trinity, emphasizing a distinct difference between the Son and the Father.

His writings are numerous but fragmentary. His best-known work is the *Refutation of All Heresies,* but he also wrote commentaries on the Book of Daniel and the Song of Songs. He wrote on a wide range of subjects, including apologetics, polemics, and ecclesiastical law. His *Apostolic Tradition* was much consulted in the liturgical renewal following VATICAN COUNCIL II.

Further reading: Brent Allen, *Hippolytus and the Roman Church in the Third Century: Communities in Tension*

before the Emergence of a Monarch-Bishop (New York: E. J. Brill, 1995); Christian Bunsen, *Hippolytus and His Age* (London: Longmans, Brown, & Longmans, 1852); Johann Döllinger, *Hippolytus and Callistus* (Edinburgh: T & T Clark, 1876); Hippolytus, *The Refutation of All Heresies,* tr. J. H. MacMahon (Edinburgh: T & T Clark, 1868); Catherine Osborne, *Rethinking Early Greek Philosophy: Hippolytus of Rome and the Presocratics* (Ithaca, N.Y.: Cornell University Press, 1987).

Holy Ghost Fathers *religious order of priests*

This congregation of priests was founded in 1703 in Paris by Claude Poullart des Places (1679–1709), a young lawyer. It is formally known as the Congregation of the HOLY SPIRIT and the Immaculate Heart of Mary but is known as the Spiritans in continental Europe and the Holy Ghost Fathers in English-speaking countries.

After becoming a priest, Poullart chose to found the religious order specifically for men who felt called to the priesthood but were too poor to join. The order is dedicated to the Holy Spirit and ministers to the poor by placing chaplains in hospitals, prisons, and schools. The Holy Ghost Fathers are also involved in missionary work, specifically in AFRICA. The French Revolution almost forced the congregation into extinction, but in 1848 the Holy See combined it with the Society of the Immaculate Heart of Mary, founded by Fr. Francis Libermann (1802–52). The Holy Ghost Fathers run two schools in the United States, Duquesne University in Pittsburgh, Pa., and the Holy Ghost Preparatory School in Bensalem, Pa.

Further reading: Paul Coulon, et al. *Libermann: (1802–1852): Une Pensée et Une Mystique Missionnaires* (Paris: Editions du Cerf, 1988); Henry J. Koren, *Knaves or Knights? A History of the Spiritan Missionaries in Acadia and North America, 1732–1839* (Pittsburgh: Duquesne University Press, 1962); ———, *The Spiritans: A History of the Congregation of the Holy Ghost* (Pittsburgh: Duquesne University Press, 1958).

Holy Orders (Lat.: *ordo,* "arrangement," "rank") *sacrament of deacons, priests, and bishops*

Holy Orders is the sacrament consecrating men to the special ministry of GOD with the laying on of hands symbolizing the gift of the HOLY SPIRIT. The CHRISTIAN ministry traces its origins to Jesus' commission of the 12 (Matt. 10:1–5), or the 70 (Luke 10:1) to do the work of the kingdom of God.

That ministry took shape in the earliest church communities as described in the New Testament. The Apostle PAUL speaks of church leadership not in terms of titled positions within a HIERARCHY. Instead, different members of the community offered a variety of charismatic gifts that helped build up the one church in love: APOSTLES, prophets, teachers, healers, speakers-in-tongues, interpreters, and helpers (1 Cor. 12:27–31). Paul does mention a female *diakonos,* or "deacon"—Phoebe of Cenchrea (Rom. 16:1)—but scholars disagree about what that term meant at that stage. By the end of the first century, however, we read about elected and appointed *episcopoi,* "overseers" or bishops, and *presbyteroi,* "elders" (Acts 20:28). The two terms were relatively equal at first.

New BISHOPS and elders received their AUTHORITY through ordination—the laying on of hands by church leaders; by that act, the Spirit was conferred (Acts 6:1–6; 2 Tim. 1:6). This tradition reaches back to the Old Testament (Num. 27:15; Deut. 34:9). Ordination took place during the EUCHARIST and is first described in the *Apostolic Tradition* (2.1–4.13) of HIPPOLYTUS OF ROME. Pope PAUL VI reinstituted this rite in the ritual manual called the *Roman Pontifical* (1978).

Beginning in the second century the early spiritual democracy yielded to a monarchical episcopate, with a subordinate priesthood and deaconate. In part, the change was a response to the freewheeling behavior and writings of prophets and teachers, who spawned and developed a huge variety of movements, later seen as heretical and schismatic, such as DOCETISM, Marcionism (*see* MARCION), Montanism (*see* MONTANUS), and Gnosticism (*see* GNOSTIC). Settled bishops could claim ecclesiastical and doctrinal authority via an unbroken line of APOSTOLIC SUCCESSION. Only bishops could ordain other bishops, priests, and deacons.

In time additional orders arose, including subdeacons, acolytes, exorcists, lectors, or readers of scriptural lessons at the Eucharist, and doorkeepers (Eusebius, *Church History* 6.43.11). In the MIDDLE AGES these came to be called minor orders, but they were abolished at VATICAN COUNCIL II.

At the Council of TRENT Holy Orders (the laying-on of hands) was formally defined as a SACRAMENT, or outward sign of inward grace instituted by CHRIST and conveying the Spirit (session 22). Like BAPTISM, and CONFIRMATION Holy Orders conferred an indelible character on the SOUL, which is never lost even if a priest is defrocked and prohibited from celebrating SACRAMENTS. In case a defrocked person did celebrate a sacrament, that sacrament would be illegal but still valid. Today priests must be 24 and bishops 30 years old, of good character, and not excommunicated in order to receive ordinations. Deacons are exempt from the age requirement.

In the MIDDLE AGES the main function of Holy Orders was to guarantee the legitimacy of the Eucharist offered by priests. Therefore, the priesthood received the most attention. At Vatican II a renewed emphasis was placed on the bishop, who shares preeminently in the priesthood of Christ and is the principal dispenser of the mysteries of God (*Christus Dominus,* Decree of the Bishops' Pastoral Office in the Church). The council also allowed for the ordination of married deacons to relieve the pressures resulting from a shrinking priesthood.

Debate continues over admitting women to Holy Orders. In *Ordinatio Sacerdotalis* (May 22, 1994) Pope JOHN PAUL II, appealing to "the constant and universal Tradition of the Church," stated that it is a "judgment . . . to be definitely held" that the church has no right to confer ordination on women. Then Cardinal Ratzinger, now BENEDICT XVI, argued that this statement was infallible teaching. However, others assert that Paul, who refers to men and women as fellow apostles (Rom. 16:7) and to Phoebe as a deacon (16:1) seems to take a different view. Recent art historians have concluded that many catacomb frescoes clearly depict women celebrating the Eucharist.

Further reading: Paul F. Bradshaw, *Ordination Rites of the Ancient Churches of East and West* (New York: Puebla, 1990); Deborah Halter, *The Papal "No": A Comprehensive Guide to the Vatican's Rejection of Women's Ordination* (New York: Crossroad, 2004); Everett Ferguson, ed., *Church, Ministry and Organization in the Early Church Era* (New York: Garland, 1993).

Holy Roman Empire (Lat.: *sacrum romanum imperium*) (962–1806)

The Holy Roman Empire was a central European collection of states and principalities that emerged out of the lands ruled by CHARLEMAGNE (c. 742–814). It was created with the idealistic goal of protecting the Catholic FAITH at a time when much of Europe was still pagan and when the Byzantine Empire and the Orthodox patriarchy were still considered major threats. Through its long history it served as a bulwark for the Catholic Church until the fracture of the Reformation rendered it irrelevant.

On Christmas Day, 800, Pope Leo III (r. 795–816) named Charlemagne emperor of the Romans. This action was a direct slap at the Byzantine emperors at CONSTANTINOPLE, who still claimed exclusive temporal AUTHORITY over Christendom.

Although Charlemagne himself used the title emperor, the Holy Roman Empire is usually seen as beginning after his death and the division of his realm. The western half continued as the kingdom of the Franks (eventually FRANCE) and the eastern half (including German and Italian lands) was dubbed the Holy Roman Empire, starting with Otto I (912–73). Otto became king of the Germans, but in 962 he reclaimed the imperial title. This date is now generally assumed to be the founding date of the Holy Roman Empire.

Until 1562, all the emperors received their crowns from the pope in Rome. Otto lent great support to the PAPACY and considered BISHOPS to be *domini*, or lords of the realm. Over time, however, a persistent conflict emerged between CHURCH AND STATE, emperor and pope, resulting in wars over control of the PAPAL STATES and in the INVESTITURE CONTROVERSY.

The empire evolved into an elective monarchy (with princes choosing the emperor), a structure set in writing in the constitution of 1338. Later, newly elected emperors had to swear not to attempt to make the office hereditary. However, after 1468 the Habsburgs gained virtual control over the office. The emperors' powers were limited; they had immediate control only over their own inherited territories. France, Denmark, Poland, and Hungary soon opted out. The emperor, called Kaiser in German, was the sole sovereign and monarch of all of GERMANY, but the country was made up of a large number of member states. The major rulers constituted the Imperial Diet, or Reichstag, but the myriad lesser dukes, princes, and lords had autonomous powers within their territories. The emperor was forbidden to intervene in a particular state as long as local rule conformed to the general laws of the empire.

The small group of elector princes who chose the emperor included the bishops of Mainz, Trier, and Cologne, as well as the rulers of Bohemia, the Palatine on the Rhine, Saxony, and Brandenburg. The electors of Saxony became Protestants, and this became a vital factor in the success of the PROTESTANT REFORMATION. After CHARLES V the emperors' influence was progressively diminished.

In the late MIDDLE AGES Holy Roman Emperors like Maximilian I (r. 1493–1519) made a strong attempt to unite the empire, but the effort was brought to naught by the combined forces of the Reformation in the north and the continuing presence of the Turks on the eastern border. Following the Thirty Years' War (1618–48) and the Treaty of Westphalia (1648), the sovereignty of the various German states was spelled out in writing, leaving the empire a mere association of some 360 distinct political entities, widely varying in size and power.

Over the centuries the boundaries of the empire underwent continual change, though its core of Germany, Austria, and Bohemia remained fairly constant. At times it included the northern half of ITALY and parts of the Netherlands. Emperor Francis II (r. 1792–1806) finally and officially disbanded the empire in 1806 at the instigation of Napoléon I, who as emperor fashioned his own CONCORDAT with the PAPACY. The fall of Napoléon (1769–1821) then set the stage for the unification of Germany north of Austria and the establishment of the Austro-Hungarian Empire.

Further reading: Geoffrey Barraclough, *The Origins of Modern Germany* (Oxford: Blackwell 1952); James Bryce, *The Holy Roman Empire* (Oxford: Shrimpton 1864); Friedrich Heer, *The Holy Roman Empire* (New York: Frederick A. Praeger, 1967); Jonathan W. Zophy, ed., *Holy Roman Empire: A Dictionary Handbook* (Westport, Conn.: Greenwood, 1980).

Holy Spirit

In CHRISTIAN and Catholic THEOLOGY the Holy Spirit is the third person of the TRINITY, distinct from but consubstantial, coequal, and coeternal with the Father and the Son as GOD. Throughout Scripture the Spirit is the principle of God's divine activity in CREATION, REDEMPTION, and sanctification.

In Christian interpretation the Spirit moves the waters of creation (Gen. 1:1), is the life-giving energy of God in creation, manifests God's presence to all beings at some level ("The wind listeth where it will," John 3:8), speaks through the prophets (Jer. 31:31–34; Joel 2:28, quoted by PETER in Acts 2:17), inspires the Scriptures, and prepares for the coming of the Messiah. The Spirit overshadowed MARY OF NAZARETH in the INCARNATION (Luke 1:35) and descended on Jesus in the form of a dove at his BAPTISM (3:22) and, as a parallel to Jesus, on the disciples in tongues of fire at the moment of the church's "conception" at Pentecost (Acts 2:1–4). In later theological language the Spirit animates and sanctifies the church (*see* CREED). The Spirit accompanies Jesus throughout his ministry, and Jesus promises a fuller reception of the Spirit to his disciples at the time of his DEATH, RESURRECTION, and glorification (John 14:16–17).

The early church believed that the Spirit was progressively manifest in time. The Spirit is first bestowed on the newly baptized person at baptism and in a special way at CONFIRMATION and at the reception of HOLY ORDERS. The Spirit is often identified with God's love (1 Cor. 13), especially in theologies of the Trinity, and is seen as bearing theological gifts, which are equally beneficial to the whole assembly or church (*see* PAUL THE APOSTLE). The Spirit also bears "fruit," namely, "love, joy, peace patience" (Gal. 5:22–23).

The divinity of the Spirit was the last to be clarified among the three persons of the Holy Trinity. In the fourth century the Pneumatomachoi ("Spirit Opponents") objected to the consubstantiality of the Spirit with the Father and Son. This position was condemned at CONSTANTINOPLE Council I in 381. In recent times there has been a reemphasis on the role of the Spirit in the Pentecostal movement among Protestants and the CHARISMATIC RENEWAL among Catholics. Many consider the theology of the Spirit as a potential spur toward Christian unity.

Further reading: David Coffey: *"Did you receive the Holy Spirit when you believed?": Some Basic Questions for Pneumatology* (Marquette, Mich.: Marquette University Press, 2005); D. Donnelly, A. Denaux, and J. Famerée, *The Holy Spirit, the Church and Christian Unity* (Louvain: Louvain University Press, 2005); Francis MacNutt, *The Nearly Perfect Crime: How the Church Almost Killed the Ministry of Healing* (Grand Rapids, Mich.: Chosen, 2005).

Holy Shroud *See* SHROUD OF TURIN.

Holy Thursday *See* LITURGICAL YEAR.

homily *See* PREACHING.

Hopkins, Gerard Manley (1844–1889)
Victorian poet and Jesuit priest
Born in Stratford, Essex, Hopkins studied at Balliol College, Oxford, where he developed a friendship with poet Robert Bridges (1844–1930) and became a member of the Oxford Movement. Like JOHN HENRY NEWMAN, he became Roman Catholic in 1866 and two years later entered the priesthood. He started teaching in 1882 at Mount St. Mary's College and Stonyhurst College and soon became a professor of Greek at University College Dublin.

Although he published few of his poems during his lifetime, he has become one of Britain's most admired poets. His most famous poems include *The Wreck of the Deutschland, The Windhover,* and *God's Grandeur.* Hopkins broke away from the commonly accepted poetic form of "running rhythm," instead reintroducing "sprung rhythm," based on the older Anglo-Saxon rhythmic structure. He was much influenced by DUNS SCOTUS's idea of *haecceitas* ("thisness"), which he related to his ideas of inscape and instress, which define the uniqueness of all aspects of CREATION.

Further reading: Edward H. Cohen, *Works and Criticism of Gerard Manley Hopkins; A Comprehensive Bibliography* (Washington, D.C.: Catholic University of America Press, 1969); Alan Heuser, *The Shaping Vision of Gerard Manley Hopkins* (Hamden, Conn.: Archon Books, 1968); Anthony John Patrick Kenny, *God and Two Poets: Arthur Hugh Clough and Gerard Manley Hopkins* (London: Sidgwick & Jackson, 1988); Franco Marucci, *The Fine Delight that Fathers Thought: Rhetoric and Medievalism in Gerard Manley Hopkins* (Washington, D.C.: Catholic University of America Press, 1994).

Hsu Chen-Ping, Francis (1920–1973) *Bishop of Hong Kong*
The first Chinese BISHOP of Hong Kong, Francis Hsu was born in Shanghai in 1920 into a Methodist family. He studied at St. John's College, Oxford University, from which he graduated in 1947 with a degree in English language and literature. Upon his return to China, he assumed a post at Nanking Central University. He was in Nanking when he joined the Catholic Church.

Following the Chinese Communist revolution in 1949, Hsu moved to Hong Kong and then in 1955 to Rome, where he continued his studies at Beda College. He was ordained in 1959 and returned to Hong Kong. He became the administrator of the Catholic center and worked with the Catholic press. Hsu was consecrated the auxiliary bishop of Hong Kong in 1967. Two years later he succeeded to leadership of the archdiocese following the retirement of his consecrator, Bishop Lorenzo Bianchi (r. 1951–68). He had only a brief tenure, as he died after only four years in office, but his successor, Cardinal John Baptist Wu Cheng-chung (1925–2002), would become Hong Kong's first cardinal.

Further reading: Sergio Ticozzi, *Historical Documents of the Hong Kong Catholic Church* (Hong Kong: Hong Kong Catholic Diocesan Archives, 1997).

Hughes, John Joseph (1797–1864) *first Catholic archbishop of New York*
Hughes was born in Ireland and came to America with his parents. He attended Mount St. Mary's College in Emmitsburg, Maryland, and was ordained a priest in 1826. He was consecrated BISHOP in 1838 and became ARCHBISHOP in 1850, when Rome elevated the diocese of New York to an archdiocese.

Hughes became famous for his eloquent defense of Catholicism against attacks by Protestant clergy and as a staunch supporter of Irish immigrants. After failing to gain state support for religious schools he founded an independent Catholic school system. He founded St. John's College, now Fordham University, and laid the foundation stone for St. Patrick's Cathedral (*see* CATHEDRAL). During the Civil War he was an ardent defender of the Union and was sent on a diplomatic mission to France by President Abraham Lincoln (1809–65).

Further reading: John R. G. Hassard, *Life of John Hughes, First Archbishop of New York* (New York: Arno, 1969); Lawrence Kehoe, ed., *The Complete Works of the Most Rev. John Hughes, D.D., Archbishop of New York* (New York: American News, 1864); Vincent P. Lannie, *Public Money and Parochial Education; Bishop Hughes, Governor Seward, and the New York School Controversy* (Cleveland: Case Western Reserve University Press, 1968); Richard Shaw, *Dagger John: The Unquiet Life and Times of Archbishop John Hughes of New York* (New York: Paulist, 1977).

Hugh of St. Victor (1096–1141) *philosopher and theologian*

An AUGUSTINIAN canon regular at the Abbey of Saint Victor in Paris, Hugh emerged as one of the most notable medieval theologians of the Catholic Church. Hugh was probably born in Saxony; he was educated at Halberstadt and came to Saint Victor in Paris in 1115 to teach at the abbey school, founded by William of Champeaux (c. 1070–1121). He became the school's master when it was made a college attached to the University of Paris.

As a philosopher Hugh tried to survey the whole of the observed world from a CHRISTIAN perspective. In his *Didascalion* he stated that the pursuit of the highest good begins with a theoretical survey of all branches of knowledge, to which he added practical disciplines necessary to earthly bodies such as commerce. He wrote *The Mysteries of Christian Faith*, one of the first *summae* of THEOLOGY in the MIDDLE AGES. His treatise on grammar and the arts laid the foundation for the curriculum then being developed in the emerging universities of Europe. In his encyclopedic inter-

ests, Hugh can be contrasted with St. BERNARD OF CLAIRVAUX, who fought against the *curiositas* ("curiosity") generated by the new sciences.

As a theologian, Hugh began with FAITH, which he saw as a cooperative activity by the will and the intellect. He defined three stages: acceptance of church teachings without question, reasoning about them, and finally the ascent and mystical encounter of the SOUL with God.

The crowning work of his theological activity was *De Sacramentis Christianae Fidei*. Though ostensibly a treatise on the seven SACRAMENTS, Hugh, like St. AUGUSTINE OF HIPPO, considered all of life a sacrament. He organized biblical and patristic thought into a systematic body of doctrine. Hugh represents a significant step toward THOMAS AQUINAS and the great *summae* of the High Middle Ages. He divided theology into two parts: one treating CREATION and its consequences before the INCARNATION (FALL, law, human knowledge of God, etc.), the second dealing with restoration after the Incarnation (REDEMPTION, church, ethics, and ESCHATOLOGY).

Hugh was one of many celebrated Victorines, including the Breton Adam of St. Victor (d. 1146), a prolific writer of Latin hymns, and the Scotsman Richard of St. Victor (d. 1173), who wrote a major treatise, *On the Trinity*, which treated the TRINITY as the supreme object of contemplation. The Abbey of St. Victor was destroyed in the French Revolution (1789).

Further reading: Abbe Roger Baron, *Hugh of St. Victor* (Notre Dame: University of Notre Dame Press, 1966); Roy J. Deferrari, *Hugh of Saint Victor on the Sacraments of the Christian Faith* (Cambridge, Mass.: Medieval Academy of America. 1951); Hugh of St. Victor, *Didascalicon: De Studio Legendi*, a critical text, ed. C. H. Buttimer (Washington, D.C.: Catholic University of America Press, 1939).

Hus, John (1373–1414) *Czech church reformer*

Hus was a scholar and priest in Bohemia, now part of the Czech Republic. He led a movement to reform Catholicism that in many aspects presaged the PROTESTANT REFORMATION of the next century.

In 1402 Hus became rector and preacher of the Chapel of the Holy Infants of Bethlehem in Prague. He came under the influence of Jerome of Prague (1370–1416), a former student of JOHN WYCLIFFE, a voice for reform in England (*see* GREAT BRITAIN). He began to call for moral reform among priests and also to advocate changes in doctrine and practice. Most notably, he supported distribution of the EUCHARIST to the laity in both kinds of bread and wine, a position later called Utraquism. As a result of his preaching he was condemned by fellow priests and then silenced and excommunicated by his BISHOP.

In 1414 he accepted a summons to appear before the Council of CONSTANCE. Despite a guarantee of physical safety from Holy Roman Emperor Sigismund (r. 1414–37), he was arrested shortly after his arrival in the city and held in prison for a year until finally brought before the council. The council condemned him and ordered him burned at the stake. Hus'a death polarized the church in Bohemia. Following the Reformation several Hussite churches arose, which are still active today.

Further reading: Heiko A. Oberrman, *The Dawn of the Reformation* (Edinburgh: T & T Clark, 1986); Edward Peters, ed., *Heresy and Authority in Medieval Europe* (Philadelphia: University of Pennsylvania Press, 1980); Matthew Spinka, *John Hus at the Council of Constance* (New York: Columbia University Press, 1965).

hymns (Gk.: *hymnos*; Lat.: *carmen*, "song of praise to hero [or God]")

Hymns were originally songs of praise to Greco-Roman gods and heroes. For example, the Greek *Homeric Hymns* were addressed to the Olympian Gods. In CHRISTIAN circles the term came to have an exclusive religious meaning. AUGUSTINE OF HIPPO defined a hymn as "a song with praise of God" (*On Psalms* 148.11). The equivalent genre

in the Old Testament were the "Psalms," which were composed according to Hebraic prosody and often sung in the Temple in Jerusalem. Later Judaic hymns include the *Psalms of Solomon* and the Thanksgiving Hymns, or *Hodayot,* of the QUMRAN community.

Christians adopted the Psalms for their worship services, along with 15 other biblical songs including the Exodus Hymn of Miriam (Exod. 15:1–18) and the Song of Moses (Deut. 32:1–43), to which they added the Magnificat, or Canticle of Mary (Luke 2:46–56).

The celebrated Kenosis Hymn (Phil. 2:6–11) to CHRIST Jesus seems to have come from a pre-Pauline LITURGY, and there are many additional New Testament references to hymns as a key part of Christian worship (1 Cor. 14:15; Heb. 2:12). The matristic and patristic writers mention the frequent use of hymns, some of which are still used, such as the second- to third-century Phos Hilarion, or Joyful Light, in the Eastern Church and the Gloria in the West.

The earliest known postbiblical hymn is CLEMENT OF ALEXANDRIA's Bridle of Colts Untamed (Paidogogos 3:12). The earliest known hymn with musical notation was the early third century Hymn to the Trinity, found among the Oxyrhinchus Papyri (15.1786). The earliest known collection of hymns is the *Odes of Solomon* (before 100). A few early GNOSTIC hymns have survived as well.

Ephraem the Syrian (c. 306–73) composed hymns for every occasion and topic, ranging from the nativity of Jesus to hymns on various heresies. In addition to all these song hymns, the Eastern Church was noted for hymnlike sermons in verse. In the West, the first noted hymn writers were AMBROSE OF MILAN, Hilary of Poiters (c. 315–c. 367), and Venantius Fortunatus (d. c. 600).

In the early church, hymns were used at the EUCHARIST, weddings, and funerals. With the rise of monasticism hymns became a part of the Divine Office, or PRAYER OF THE HOURS, and major feasts. In modern times popular hymns have become associated with major feast days, especially the feasts of MARY OF NAZARETH. Most Catholic hymns, like the Psalms that preceded them, are about the individual's relationship with God or Mary, and very few concern brotherly or sisterly relations or fellowship in the church. Celebrated hymns include the Te Deum Laudamus ("We Praise You, O God"), an early sequence; the Pange Lingua ("Sing! O Tongue"), attributed to THOMAS AQUINAS; the 17th-century "Come, O Come Emmanuel"); and the medieval Salve Regina ("Hail Queen!"), to name only a few. In more recent times Catholics have adopted Lutheran hymns (O Sacred Head Surrounded), hymns by the Congregationist Isaac Watts (d. 1748) and by Methodist founders John (d. 1791) and Charles (d. 1788) Wesley, as well as Negro spirituals. VATICAN COUNCIL II was followed by a spate of new Catholic hymnody, which has increasingly undergone local INCULTURATION, including the adoption of pop music styles. Many new hymn books have been issued over the last 35 years.

Further reading: Wilma A. Bailey, *Music in Christian Worship* (Collegeville, Minn.: Liturgical Press, 2005); John G. Hacker, *Catholic Hymnal* (New York: W.H. Sadler, 1920); John C. Selner, *Catholic Hymns* (Toledo, Ohio: Gregorian Institute of America, 1954); Joseph Szövérffy, *Latin Hymns* (Turnhout: Brepols, 1989); Henry J. Tillyard, *Byzantine Music and Hymnography* (New York: AMS, 1976).

I

icon/iconoclasm (Gk.: *eikon,* "image," "likeness")

Icons are paintings or mosaics of CHRIST, MARY OF NAZARETH—especially as Theotokos, or Mother of GOD—and the saints. They are especially venerated in Eastern Christianity—Orthodox and Catholic—and are sometimes placed on a level that matches the Scriptures. The ethereal and heavenly quality of eastern iconography reflects the influence of Neoplatonism, which placed strong emphasis on the spiritual aspect of earthly events. The biblical stories most depicted included the ANNUNCIATION, the BAPTISM of Jesus in the Jordan, the dormitian (assumption) of Mary, the raising of Lazarus, the Crucifixion (*see* CROSS/CRUCIFIXION), and the Transfiguration.

Iconographers, or icon painters, trace their tradition back to St. Luke the Evangelist, who they believe painted the first image of the Blessed Virgin. Another legend relates how an image of Christ Acheiropoetos (Gk. "not made with hands") appeared on a cloth sent to King Abgar V of Edessa (r. 4 B.C.E.–7 C.E.; 13–50) to heal him. Two noted later iconographers were the MONKs Theophanes the Greek (c. 1330–1405), who brought the Greek iconographic tradition to Russia, and Andrei Rublev (1360–1430), who painted the wonderful icon of the Angels Visiting Abraham at the Oak of Mamre, a prefiguration of the Holy TRINITY, now in the Tretykov Gallery, Moscow.

In EASTERN ORTHODOX churches the screen that divides the sanctuary from the nave is called the iconostasis, and it is covered with icons. Icon painters consider their art to be sacramental and undergo prayer and fasting before painting.

From about 725 to 842 the Eastern Church went through a wrenching Iconoclastic Controversy. *Iconoclast* in Greek means "image-smasher"; the opposite, iconodule, means "image-venerator." Emperor Leo III the Isaurian (r. 714–41) argued that the use of images prevented the conversion of Jews and Muslims and ordered their destruction throughout the Eastern Empire. The policy was reversed in 784 by the empress regent Irene, and then again by the empress Theodora in 843. The occasion is commemorated in the Feast of Orthodoxy, still celebrated in all branches of the Eastern Church.

The Eastern theologian St. John of Damascus (c. 655–c. 750) defended images in several treatises. He argued that "the invisible things of God are made visible through images" and that the INCARNATION of the Son in flesh fully justified icons. The veneration of icons was attacked at the heretical Synod of 754 at CONSTANTINOPLE but legitimated at the Council of Nicaea II in 787 (*see* COUNCILS, ECUMENICAL). Byzantine iconography is undergoing a revival in both East and West.

Further reading: Thousands of icons are available online; John Baggley, *Doors of Perception: Icons and their Spiritual Significance* (Crestwood, N.Y.: St. Valdimir's Seminary Press, 1988); Leonid Ouspensky and Vladimir Lossky, *The Meaning of Icons* (Crestwood, N.Y.: St. Valdimir's Seminary Press, 1982).

Ignatius of Antioch (d. 107) *bishop and martyr*

Almost nothing is known of Ignatius's personal life or career apart from his becoming the second BISHOP of Antioch (Syria) around 69 C.E. He may well have known some of the APOSTLES. He was caught up in the general persecution of the church under the emperor Trajan (r. 98–117), brought to Rome, and fed to the lions in the Coliseum around 107 C.E. His feast day is October 17.

Before his execution, Ignatius wrote seven letters to the churches along his route, one each to Ephesus, Magnesia, Tralles, and Philadelphia, two to the church at Smyrna, and one to Smyrna's bishop, Polycarp. The letters are a rich source about early THEOLOGY, LITURGY, and church organization.

Ignatius's core idea is the divine "economy of salvation": GOD wants to save the fallen world; he prepared the world through Judaism and the prophets and fulfilled his plan in CHRIST (*Magnesians* 9.1–2). Ignatius attacked the DOCETISM of the pre-GNOSTICS by affirming both the humanity and divinity of Christ (*Smyrnians* 1.1; 7) and the fleshly nature of the EUCHARIST (*Philadelphians* 4). He also developed the theology of martyrdom as the perfect imitation of Christ, an idea that permeated much of church life in the first four centuries after Christ.

To Ignatius we owe most of our knowledge of ecclesiastical organization in his day. He is the first to note the role of the single bishop as the head of a diocese. He describes the bishop as the representation of Christ and the authorized teacher and dispenser of BAPTISM and the Eucharist to the community, through which the faithful are united to Christ.

Further reading: G. W. Bowersock, *Martyrdom & Rome* (Cambridge: Cambridge University Press, 1995); Bart D. Ehrman, *After the New Testament: A Reader in Early Christianity* (New York: Oxford University Press, 1998); William R. Schoedel, *Ignatius of Antioch: A Commentary on the Letters* (Philadelphia: Fortress, 1985); Walter H. Wagner, *After the Apostles: Christianity in the Second Century* (Minneapolis: Fortress, 1994).

Ignatius of Loyola, St. (1491–1556) *founder of Jesuit order*

Ignatius of Loyola was born of Basque nobility at the Loyola castle in the Guipuzcoa province of SPAIN. While recuperating from a battle wound he read the lives of the saints (*see* HAGIOGRAPHY) and the *Life of Christ* by Ludolph of Saxony (c. 1300–78) and experienced a religious CONVERSION. Along with several others he founded the JESUITS, or Society of Jesus (SJ), which under his dynamic leadership played a vital role in restoring the fortunes of Roman Catholicism after the PROTESTANT REFORMATION. He was beatified in 1609 by Pope PAUL V and canonized in 1622 by Pope Gregory XV (r. 1621–23). His feast day is July 31.

As a youth Loyola served as a page in the Spanish court of King FERDINAND I OF ARAGON AND ISABELLA OF CASTILE. Trained for the military, he was wounded in battle in 1521, leaving him slightly crippled for life. After regaining his health, he took a vow of chastity, hung up his sword at the altar of the Blessed Virgin at the MONASTERY of Montserrat, and clothed himself in a pilgrim's garb. He then retired to a cave at Manresa—the name today for Jesuit retreats—to devote himself to a year of meditation (1522–23). The spiritual insights he gained were recorded in his *Spiritual Exercises*, a manual for retreats still widely used throughout the world. Ignatius then journeyed to Rome and to the Holy Land, where he tried to convert Muslims.

In 1528 he began a six-year study of THEOLOGY at Barcelona, Alcala, Salamanca, and Paris. In 1534 he drew up plans for a new order with his early compatriots James Lainez, Alonso Salmerón, Nicholas Bobadilla, Simón Rodriguez, Peter Faber, and St. FRANCIS XAVIER. Members of the Society of Jesus took vows of poverty and chastity along with a vow to work in the Holy Land or wherever the pope sent them. As they were preparing to leave, Loyola was ordained a priest in 1537. In 1538 they had an audience with Pope Paul III (r. 1534–49). While waiting to travel to Jerusalem, Pope Paul issued the bull *Regimini Militantis Ecclesiae* (September 27, 1540) that formally constituted the Society of Jesus.

Owing to the Ottoman blockade, the members never did get to go to the Holy Land. Ignatius was elected the Jesuits' first general. He worked on the Society's constitution over the remaining years of his life. Before settling in Rome, where he would die in 1556, he traveled throughout Europe and made a second trip to the Holy Land.

Among Ignatius's accomplishments was the dispatching of Francis Xavier to India in 1542. The Jesuits eventually became a global missionary group and won a reputation for accomplishments in higher education and intellectual endeavor. Though reviled in Protestant countries and by anticlerical writers everywhere (their name was once a pejorative), the Jesuits have founded more than 500 colleges and universities throughout the world.

See also COUNTER-REFORMATION.

Further reading: Candido de Dalmases, *Ignatius of Loyola: Founder of the Jesuits* (St. Louis: Institute of Jesuit Sources, 1985); Harvey D. Egan, *Ignatius Loyola the Mystic* (Wilmington, Del.: Michael Glazer, 1987); Ignatius of Loyola, *Original Testament: The Autobiography of St. Ignatius Loyola* (London: Inigo International Centre, 1985); ———, *Spiritual Exercises and Selected Works,* ed. George Ganss (New York: Paulist, 1991); Andre Ravier, *Ignatius of Loyola and the Founding of the Society of Jesus* (San Francisco: Ignatius, 1987).

imprimatur

Imprimatur is Latin for "let it be printed." The term often appears in conjunction with a second term, *Nihil Obstat,* Latin for "nothing stands in the way," printed on the obverse of a book's title page; it is a sign of approval by Catholic church authorities.

When a Catholic author completes a book, especially if it touches directly on matters of THEOLOGY or church life, he or she will submit the text to the diocese for review. The diocese's censor is generally the first to read it. If the censor finds nothing that contradicts Catholic FAITH or morals, he or she will add the *Nihil Obstat.*

The censor then passes the book to the BISHOP, who also reviews the text. If he finds nothing of which he disapproves, he grants his imprimatur by which he informs the reader that nothing in the volume has been found to be contrary to Catholic faith or morals. The imprimatur suggests that the book has passed through a meaningful review process. Contemporary bishops are quick to note that the imprimatur does not imply their personal approval of the text and/or its content, merely that the text operates within the realm of CHRISTIAN orthodoxy and moral teachings. If the writer is a member of a religious order, he or she might initially submit the text to a superior within the order. If the superior finds it free of error she or he gives the work an *imprimi potest,* meaning, "it can be printed." The superior then forwards it to the bishop for the final imprimatur.

Occasionally, due to the large number of books printed annually, a book makes its way through the process, is granted an imprimatur, but is later discovered to contain errors. If the book has high exposure, the withdrawal of approval may be an occasion of great controversy. Given the wide variety of topics and views openly discussed within the post-Vatican church, many Catholics have argued that the idea of the imprimatur has become outdated. There is a decreasing use of both the imprimature and *nihil obstat*.

Further reading: Elizabeth Bartelme, "Let It Be Printed" *Commonweal* (February 26, 1965) 81:701–703.

Incarnation (Lat.: *in,* "en" + *carnatio,* "fleshment")

The CHRISTIAN doctrine of the Incarnation asserts that the second person of the TRINITY, the Son of GOD, took human flesh when he was miraculously conceived in the Virgin MARY OF NAZARETH, his human mother, by the power of the HOLY SPIRIT (Luke 1:35). In the historical Jesus CHRIST, the divine nature of the eternally begotten Son is united with human nature of Jesus so that he is "fully God and fully man." In the union neither natures are compromised, but rather both are at the same time full and complete. The doctrine is central to the Catholic FAITH, and the Incarnation is celebrated every year at the Feast of the Incarnation, known also as Christmas (*see* LITURGICAL YEAR).

The THEOLOGY of the Incarnation was progressively worked out at the first seven ecumenical councils (*see* COUNCILS, ECUMENICAL), especially at the Council of CHALCEDON and in the theology of ATHANASIUS OF ALEXANDRIA, who set the standard for all future theologies of the Incarnation. The most important addition in the MIDDLE AGES was JOHN DUNS SCOTUS's idea that Christ would have become incarnate even had there been no original SIN, because God created the world with the Christ in mind. Many important modern theologians like KARL RAHNER have accepted and developed this teaching, even though it is not official dogma.

Further reading: James D. G. Dunn, *Christology in the Making: A New Testament Inquiry into the Origins*

Nativity of Jesus Christ (Luke 2:1–20). Woodcut from Marcus Vigerius (1446–1516), *Decachordum christianum* (1507) (*Washington University Library, Special Collections, with permission*).

of the Doctrine of the Incarnation (Philadelphia: Westminster, 1980); H.R. Mackintosh, *The Doctrine of the Person of Jesus Christ* (Edinburgh: T & T Clark, 1912); John Kenneth Mozley, *The Doctrine of the Incarnation* (London: Geoffrey Bles, 1949); Chul Won Suh, *The Creation-Mediatorship of Jesus Christ: A Study in the Relation of the Incarnation and the Creation* (Amsterdam: Rodopi, 1982).

inculturation

Inculturation is the attempt to adapt the CHRISTIAN message of the Good News to any and all cultures so that CHRIST, Scripture, the church, and its doctrines can be understood in the local frame of mind and in light of the experiences of the people receiving and adopting the message. The goal is to make Christianity as accessible and personal as possible so that any culture can accept the FAITH and feel at home in the religion. The hope is to detach the faith from its historic but not intrinsic European and Middle Eastern garb, so that the missionized people can accept Christianity, and not necessarily "Western Christianity."

Although the term "inculturation" has only been in common use for a few decades, the idea behind it has existed in Christian thought and missionary activity since the beginning of the church. Even though it has been called "adaptation," "indigenization," or "reformulation" in the past, the concept of reworking the message of Christ to the local thought patterns, experiences, and understandings of a specific culture has always been an element of evangelization.

MATEO RICCI, a 16th-century JESUIT missionary to China, practiced inculturation when he donned the local dress and allowed converts to continue observing elements of Chinese culture that others considered non-Christian. His book *The True Idea of God* tried to show that Confucian thought was compatible with Christianity. His goal was to make the message of Christ easily understood, relatable, and acceptable within Chinese culture.

Despite efforts by missionaries to inculturate in the past, before VATICAN II the issue of culture per se was never addressed in any church council. Pope PAUL VI began to stress the importance of inculturation. In *Evangelii Nuntiandi* (December 8, 1975) Pope Paul VI stresses the need to adapt the Christian message to a specific people when he says "Evangelization loses much of its force and effectiveness if it does not take into consideration the actual people to whom it is addressed, if it does not use their language, their signs, their symbols, if it does not answer the questions they ask, and if it does not have an impact on their concrete life" (63). Inculturation became so central to evangelization that Pope JOHN PAUL II established a Pontifical Council for Culture in 1982. The new churches of AFRICA are at the forefront of inculturation efforts in today's church.

Further reading: Ernesto Cardinal, *The Gospel in Solentiname*, 2 vols. (New York: Orbis, 1978); Commission on Theological Concerns of the Christian Conference of Asia (CTC-CCA), ed., *Minjung Theology* (New York: Orbis, 1981); Vincent J. Donovan, *Christianity Rediscovered: An Epistle from the Masai* (Notre Dame: Fides/Claretian, 1978); Kosuke Koyama, *Water Buffalo Theology* (New York: Orbis, 1974); J. M. Waliggo, *Inculturation: Its Meaning and Urgency* (Kampala, Uganda: St. Paul, 1986).

indulgences

In Roman Catholicism, an indulgence is a remission of temporal punishment incurred by SIN. After venial sin is forgiven it still requires a punishment, usually carried out in PURGATORY. The punishment can be remitted through the granting of an indulgence, which has the effect of assigning merit to an individual who needs merit. A plenary indulgence remits all of the existing punishment, while a partial indulgence remits only part of the existing punishment. An indulgence is granted by the church for indulgent acts, which include prayer, Scripture readings, and saying the Rosary. Several conditions are necessary for a valid indulgence, including reconciliation, receiving of the EUCHARIST, and complete renunciation of sin.

In 1095 Pope Urban II granted plenary indulgences to anyone who participated in the CRUSADES. Later indulgences got a bad name, because they were frequently abused for personal or financial gain. Notoriously, in 1517 Pope Leo X (r. 1513–21) launched a sale of indulgences to raise money for the building of churches, including ST. PETER'S BASILICA in Rome; Cardinal Johann Tetzel (1465–

Confraternity of the Celestial Rosary. Trinity (Father, Spirit, crucified Son) in the center, with Mary and angels in top panel, patriarchs and apostles, martyrs and confessors, virgins and widows below. Sts. Dominic and Francis are in top left and right corners, and pious intercessors are below, praying the rosary for souls suffering in purgatory (bottom center). Woodcut from Ulrich Pinder (d. 1519), *Speculum Passionis Domini* (1519). *(Washington University Library, Special Collections, with permission).*

1519) is famous for his aggressive salesmanship in that campaign, in which indulgences were granted for money alone, without the necessary indulgent acts. The sale of indulgences was a central critique of the church by Martin Luther (1483–1546) and the PROTESTANT REFORMATION. In 1567, after the Council of TRENT and during the COUNTER-REFORMATION, Pope PIUS V forbade the sale of indulgences, although the granting of indulgences for pilgrimages and other acts of piety continues to this day.

Further reading: Winfrid Herbst, *Indulgences* (Milwaukee: Bruce, 1955); Henry Charles Lea, *A History of Auricular Confession and Indulgences in the Latin Church* (New York: Greenwood, 1968); Dairmaid MacCulloch, *The Reformation* (New York: Viking, 2003); Nikolaus Paulus, *Indulgences as a Social Factor in the Middle Ages,* tr. J. Elliot Ross (New York: Devlin-Adair, 1922).

inerrancy of Scripture

Inerrancy is a common term used to affirm that the BIBLE teaches truth without error. VATICAN COUNCIL II affirmed that "the books of scripture," inspired as they are by the HOLY SPIRIT, "must be acknowledged as teaching firmly, faithfully, and without error that truth which GOD wanted put into the sacred writings for the sake of our salvation" (*Dei Verbum* 11, Dogmatic Constitution on Divine Revelation).

The scientific approach to the biblical text as a human document that came to the fore in the 19th century explains the church's need to redefine the authority of Scripture and the consequent stress on inerrancy. In *Providentissimus Deus* (November 18, 1893) Pope LEO XIII noted that the sacred writers were not being scientific in the modern sense; they "did not seek to penetrate the secrets of nature, but rather described and dealt with things in more or less figurative language, or in terms which were commonly used at the time, and which in many instances are in daily use at this day." This perspective

on biblical authority was reiterated in PIUS XII's *Divino Afflante Spiritu* (September 30, 1943) and freed the church's biblical scholars to explore the various contemporary tools developed for scriptural exegesis.

Contemporaneously with the Catholic Church's development of a new hermeneutic framework to understand the Bible, Protestants were exploring similar language. Because Protestantism placed heavy weight on the authority of the Bible, some strict interpreters, ranging from evangelicals to fundamentalists, came to maintain that the Bible was true in a literal sense, even when speaking on matters of science and history.

See also HERMENEUTICS.

Further reading: James T. Burtchaell, *Catholic Theories of Biblical Inspiration Since 1810* (New York: Cambridge University Press, 1969); Harvie Conn, ed., *Inerrancy and Hermeneutic: A Tradition, A Challenge, A Debate* (Grand Rapids, Mich.: Baker, 1988); James J. Megivern, ed., *Official Catholics Teachings: Bible Interpretation* (Wilmington, Del.: McGrath, 1978); William Most, *Free From All Error: Authorship, Inerrancy, Historicity of Scripture, and Modern Scripture Scholars* (Libertyville, Ill.: Franciscan Marytown Press, 1985).

infallibility

The teaching on infallibility derives from John 16:13, where Jesus assures the APOSTLES that the Spirit of Truth will come and guide them to all truth and from Matthew 28:20, where he assures them "behold I am with you always." Many CHRISTIANS believe the church as a whole is infallible in the sense of guiding its adherents to the truth necessary for salvation. Before VATICAN COUNCIL I, the term was generally understood as applying to the MAGISTERIUM, or teaching office, of the entire church, including BISHOPS and theologians. The idea of infallibility is related to the parallel idea of the indefectibility of the church, the belief that the church will last to the end of time and never depart from the teaching of CHRIST.

The 19th century presented Christianity with a significant challenge. Reason and science were widely held to be the ultimate authorities, by which the teachings of the church could be judged and the authority of the church challenged. Both Protestants and Roman Catholics felt this challenge. Scholars attacked the veracity of the BIBLE and the legitimacy of many traditional beliefs, especially the veneration of the saints and relics.

The response produced a spectrum of efforts, including attempts to clarify the church's accepted standards of authority. Among conservative Protestants, there was an attempt to define the nature of the Bible as the Word of God. One group of theologians identified with Princeton Theological Seminary began to speak of the Bible as infallible and inerrant. To be precise, they suggested that the Bible was infallible on matters of FAITH and morals and inerrant on matters of history and science. The latter affirmation has been revived during the periodic public debates over creationism and intelligent design.

According to Vatican I, infallibility is freedom from error in the core teaching of the church on matters of faith and morals. Vatican I said, "The Roman Pontiff, when he speaks *ex cathedra,* that is, when in discharge of the office of pastor and teacher of all Christians, by virtue of his supreme apostolic authority, he defines a doctrine regarding the faith or morals to be held by the universal church, by the divine assistance promised to him in Blessed Peter, is possessed of that infallibility with which the divine redeemer willed that his Church should be endowed in defining doctrine regarding faith and morals; and therefore such definitions are irreformable of their own nature and not in virtue of the Church's consent."

The council thus asserted that the pope could speak infallibly if a variety of conditions were met. First, the pope himself must speak, as his infallibility cannot be delegated. Second, he must speak as the universal pastor of Christians, not merely as a church theologian or as on matters related to a particular segment of the church. Third, he must speak with the intention of asserting a timeless truth. In fact, since the council's promulgation of the idea, the assertion of a new teaching to be accepted by the faithful has occurred only once, in 1950, when Pope PIUS XII defined the dogma of the bodily assumption of the Virgin Mary into heaven. The declaration of the dogma of the Immaculate Conception in 1854 by Pope PIUS IX, well before Vatican I, is often cited as an additional example of the pope's infallibility, but that declaration preceeded the declaration on infallibility.

While the concept of infallibility does not extend to the documents or encyclicals that periodically are released by the reigning pope or to the pronouncements of any individual bishop or group of bishops, it is assumed that the pope and the bishops speak from the foundation of infallibility and that they generally are to be believed when they speak. The burden of proof for anyone opposing the pope or the episcopacy on matters not directly covered in the church's dogma is on the person who dissents.

In 1971 critics of infallibility point to popes who promoted false teachings, most notoriously Honorius I (r. 625–38). He affirmed monotheletism ("one will") in Jesus Christ and he was condemned by Leo II (r. 682–83) at the Council of CONSTANTINOPLE III in 680–81. German theologian HANS KÜNG set off a debate by arguing that the popes and councils had made many contradictory and erroneous rulings over the centuries. He suggested that Catholics should speak only of a certain "indefectibility" of the church, a church free of faults, a common position in the Western Church for its first millennium and only slowly replaced by the idea of infallibility. Küng was denied his right to teach as a Roman Catholic theologian in 1979. VATICAN COUNCIL II (1962–65) had reaffirmed papal infallibility but had also emphasized that the entire body of bishops in union with the pope teach infallibly when all concur in a single viewpoint on matters of faith and morals in *Lumen Gentium* 25, the Dogmatic

Constitution on the Church. John Henry New-man urged the hierarchy also to consult the laity, noting that during the period of Arianism and Nestorius, vast numbers were heretical, but the laity kept to orthodoxy.

Further reading: Richard F. Costigan, *The Consensus of the Church and Papal Infallibility: A Study in the Background of Vatican I* (Washington, D.C.: Catholic University of America Press, 2005); Hans Küng, *Infallible? An Inquiry* (Garden City, N.Y.: Doubleday, 1971); Brian Tierney, *Origins of Papal Infallibility 1150–1350: A Study on the Concepts of Infallibility, Sovereignty and Tradition in the Middle Ages* (Leiden: E. J. Brill, 1972).

infancy gospels

Ancient writings that focus on the childhood years of Jesus are called infancy gospels. They are among the many documents circulated in the ancient Christian Church whose supposed authorship by one of the Apostles or an associate was ruled to be false. They were deemed not authoritative and not deserving of inclusion in the Canon of Scripture. Most of these books describe the youthful Jesus as a miracle worker.

The Gospel accounts in the New Testament cover a few events surrounding the birth of Jesus, including the visit of the Magi and Wise Men to the manger and the flight of Joseph and Mary into Egypt to escape King Herod's decree. At some point the family returned to Nazareth, where Jesus is said to have grown up, but there is no information from this time to his confrontation in the Temple when he was 12. The infancy gospels attempted to fill this gap with information from those years.

The Infancy Gospel of Thomas opens with Jesus in his fifth year. While playing with his friends, he molds 12 birds out of dirt and claps his hands, and the birds fly off. He is subsequently described as killing someone who bumped into him and blinding people who brought accusations against him.

In the Gospel of Pseudo-Matthew (also known as the Birth of Mary and Infancy of the Sav-

ior), Mary and the infant Jesus go into a pagan temple in Egypt. As they enter the temple, all the deity statues prostrate themselves and break into pieces. Such stories can be found in all the infancy gospels, which include the Arabic Infancy Gospel, The History of Joseph the Carpenter, the Latin Infancy Gospel, the Life of John the Baptist, the Nativity of Mary, and The Protevangelion of James (also known as Gospel of James).

These books, some of which were very popular in the ancient church, generally dropped out of use during the Middle Ages. They were rediscovered in the modern world as a by-product of the study of ancient history. In the 20th century these books have been republished, along with other noncanonical books. Some antichurch groups claim the books were once included in the Bible but removed by church authorities because of their embarrassing content. An early compilation of such apocryphal texts was published in 1927 as *The Lost Books of the Bible and the Forgotten Books of Eden*. The texts of most of these books have now been placed on the Internet.

Further reading: Ron Cameron, ed., *The Other Gospels: Non-Canonical Gospel Texts* (Philadelphia: Westminster 1982); Ronald F. Hock, *The Infancy Gospels of James and Thomas: With Introduction, Notes, and Original Text* (Santa Rosa: Polebridge, 1995); Bruce M. Metzger, *The Canon of the New Testament: Its Origin, Development, and Significance* (Oxford: Clarendon, 1987); Wilhelm Schneemelcher, ed., *New Testament Apocrypha*, 2 vols. (Louisville: Westminster/John Knox, 1989).

Innocent III (c. 1160–1216) *medieval pope*

Innocent III was one of the most powerful popes in history, exercising power both within the church and among the rulers of Europe. He was born Lotario di Segni in Anagni into a powerful Italian family and received a good education in preparation for a career in the church. He rose quickly in the Hierarchy and was 30 years old when his uncle, Pope Celestine III (r. 1191–98), made him a cardinal. In 1198 he succeeded his uncle as pope.

Innocent III assumed the papal chair at a time when the PAPACY was at the peak of its influence and prestige following the reforms carried out by GREGORY VII (r. 1073–85) and the resolution of the INVESTITURE CONTROVERSY by Calixtus II (r. 1119–24). From the beginning of his reign he articulated his perspective that the affairs of the spirit should dominate those of the body. The church represented the spiritual realm and should take precedence over the earthly monarchs who ruled the temporal realm. To him, the pope was the ecclesiastical king of the world, a position he asserted with his use of the title Vicar of Christ. He believed that mere national rulers should abide by his decisions.

His meddling in political affairs, using such tactics as the INTERDICT, was best illustrated in his relations with FREDERICK II (1194–1250). Following negotiations with Frederick's mother, he named him king of Sicily, and upon her death accepted him as his ward. He would later excommunicate Otto IV (r. 1198–1212), Holy Roman Emperor, force him off the throne, and see that Frederick was elected in his stead.

Innocent prevailed in England in a dispute with King John (r. 1199–1216). Problems began when Innocent refused to accept John's candidates for Archbishop of Canterbury and chose his own person. John moved against the church, and in 1209 Innocent placed him under an interdict and excommunicated him. With the nobles supporting the pope, John backed off and agreed to pay an annual tribute to the Holy See. Interestingly, the pope then sided with John when the nobles forced him to sign the Magna Carta. The pope defined John as his vassal who had signed a document without informing his lord. Thus, Innocent declared the Magna Carta a null document.

In 1215 Innocent moved beyond the Gregorian reforms in calling the Lateran Council IV (see COUNCILS, ECUMENICAL), in part to fight against the newer heretical ideas that had emerged, including those of JOACHIM OF FIORE and the CATHARI/Albigensians, and he laid out a program for improving education throughout the church. He also approved the constitutions of the new MENDICANT orders, the Franciscans and Dominicans, and enlisted them to implement the council's reforms.

With hindsight, it appears that some of the council's decisions proved disastrous. It ordered non-Christians in Christian lands (Jews and Muslims) to adopt distinctive clothing and called on the secular authorities to join in the efforts to eradicate HERESY. In 1205 Innocent had already begun efforts to eradicate the Albigensian heresy, and after the council these efforts were strengthened. As the threat grew, the Albigensian Crusade led to the formation of the INQUISITION in 1233 and its placement in the hands of the Dominicans.

Innocent's greatest failure was the Fourth CRUSADE (1202–04). The crusaders, after being blessed by Innocent, were blocked from the Holy Land and turned their energies instead to Zara, a city across the Adriatic from ITALY (in present-day Croatia). For attacking this Christian city, Innocent excommunicated everyone involved. Still, that did not stop the crusaders, who went on to take CONSTANTINOPLE and sack the city. These events would thwart further attempts to heal the SCHISM between East and West well into the 20th century.

Further reading: Charles Edward Smith, *Innocent III, Church Defender* (Baton Rouge: Louisiana State University Press, 1951); James M. Powell, *The Deeds of Pope Innocent III* (Washington, D.C.: Catholic University of America Press, 2004); Damien J. Smith, *Innocent III and the Crown of Aragon: The Limits of Papal Authority* (Aldershot: Ashgate, 2004); Helene Tillman, *Pope Innocent III*, tr. W. Sax (Amsterdam: North-Holland, 1980).

intercommunion   *See* COMMUNION/COMMUNION OF SAINTS; ECUMENISM.

Inquisition (Lat.: *inquisitio,* "judicial inquiry")

In Roman law an *inquisitio* was simply a judicial inquiry. In Christianity it came to mean an inquiry into a person's beliefs to determine whether they are heretical. The term also means the judicial panels that conducted such inquiries in Europe and the Americas for several hundred years.

Originally CHRISTIANS did not use force against heretics and schismatics but rather tried to persuade them and, failing that, sought to excommunicate, exile, or silence them. After AUGUSTINE justified the use of force against DONATISM and developed the theory of a JUST WAR, inquisitional authorities began to use force to extract confessions from heretics and others. The first person known to die after an inquisition was Priscillian of Ávila (d. 385).

In the MIDDLE AGES Pope Lucius III (r. 1181–85) issued the bull *Ad Abolendam* (September 4, 1184), in which he sought the support of the emperor and princes in the repression and elimination of heretics throughout Christendom. St. BERNARD OF CLAIRVAUX, however, sought to preserve the early tradition with his formula *fides suadenda est, non imponenda*—"faith is to be spread by persuasion and not imposed by force." Gregory IX (r. 1227–41) appointed inquisitors to conduct secret examinations of suspected heretics without the benefit of defense witnesses. Many canon lawyers questioned the legitimacy of these inquiries. Most inquisitors were from the DOMINICAN and FRANCISCAN ORDERS, the most famous of which was the Dominican Bernardo of Gui (1261–1331), who wrote a handbook for inquisi-

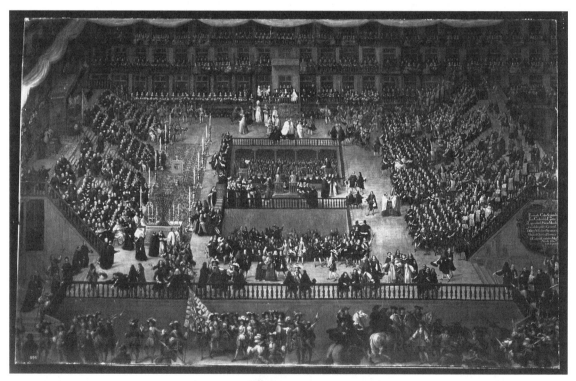

Auto-da-fé in the Plaza Mayor, Madrid, 1680, showing the public trial of *conversos* before a tribunal of the Inquisition *(Art Resource, N.Y.)*

tors. The medieval Inquisition was accompanied by the military extirpation of the CATHARI (Albigensians) and other groups deemed heretical. In 1252 Innocent IV (r. 1243–54) issued the bull *Ad Extirpanda* (May 15, 1252), which justified the use of torture.

The Inquisition was exercised mainly in the heart of the European continent. Often the targets expanded from heretics to political enemies. Philip IV of FRANCE (1268–1314) used the Inquisition to bring down the Knights Templar. Pope JOHN XXII (r. 1316–34) also pursued the Franciscan Spirituals with the Inquisition. The British Isles, Scandinavia, and the kingdom of Castile escaped the Inquisition early on, but in 1477 FERDINAND I OF ARAGON AND ISABELLA OF CASTILE asked Pope Sixtus (r. 1471–84) to set up the Spanish Inquisition to examine which *conversos,* Jews forced to convert to Catholicism, were genuine and which were not (*see* ANTI-SEMITISM). The notorious Tomás de Torquemada (1420–98) was appointed inquisitor general in 1483.

The Spanish Inquisition lasted from 1478 to 1834. It targeted many individuals now celebrated by the Catholic Church, including Sts. IGNATIUS OF LOYOLA and TERESA OF ÁVILA. It instituted the gruesome public ceremony of the auto de fe, or sentence in a matter of FAITH. After a procession, Mass, and sermon, the condemned were dressed in grotesquely embroidered robes and yellow miters and led off to be executed by the secular authorities. The last burning at the stake took place in Seville in 1781.

Pope Paul III (r. 1534–49), who convened the Council of TRENT, established the Roman Inquisition under the Holy Office in 1542 to counteract Protestant heretics. The PAPACY sought to expand the powers of the Inquisition throughout the Netherlands, France and the HOLY ROMAN EMPIRE, but in effect it was successful only in the PAPAL STATES. The most celebrated victim of the Roman Inquisition was the Dominican philosopher Giordano Bruno (1548–1600). After Pope PAUL VI reorganized the Vatican CURIA in 1968, the name

of the holy office was changed to the Congregation of the Doctrine of the Faith. It still conducts inquisitions but without the assistance of secular authorities to punish those found to be in error.

Protestants also conducted their own Inquisitionlike heresy trials, but not on the same scale as the Catholics. The modern papacy has apologized indirectly for the injustices done to GALILEO GALILEI, but it has yet to bring up the question of the Inquisition. Many Catholics try to mitigate the black mark of the Inquisition by pointing to the atrocities of HENRY VIII and others against Catholics.

Further reading: Edward M. Peters, *Inquisition* (Berkeley: University of California Press, 1989); Helen Rawlings, *The Spanish Inquisition* (Malden: Blackwell, 2006); Norman Roth, *Conversos, Inquisition and the Expulsion of the Jews from Spain* (Madison: University of Wisconsin Press, 1995).

interdict

As EXCOMMUNICATION is to an individual, so is interdict to a collective body (country, region, parish). Issued by a pope or other high church official, it denies the SACRAMENTS and ceremonies of the church to the group that receives it. When, for example, a country is placed under an interdict, BAPTISM may occur, but the EUCHARIST may not be served, and priests may not officiate at marriages or burials.

Often interdicts were issued when a monarch had acted against the interests of the church. The hope was that the public would apply pressure to force the monarch to repent. Although he was not the first to use the tactic, Pope INNOCENT III (r. 1198–1216) gave it its name. He freely used it to press the church's concerns with various European rulers. Among the first to feel its brunt were FRANCE, whose ruler Philip II Augustus (r. 1180–1223) tried to put aside his first wife and marry another (1200–01), and England (1200–08), whose king disagreed with Innocent III over the appointment of the next Archbishop of

Canterbury. Interdicts have been less frequent in recent centuries.

Further reading: Sydney R. Packard, *Europe and the Church under Innocent III* (London: G. Bell & Sons, 1930); Richard C. Trexler, ed., *The Spiritual Power: Republican Florence Under Interdict.* Studies in Medieval and Reformation Thought (Leiden: Brill, 1997).

Investiture Controversy

Toward the end of the 11th century, a long-standing struggle over the relative powers of CHURCH AND STATE came to a head in Catholic Europe. The symbolic focus of the struggle between popes and secular lords was the ceremony of investiture, in which BISHOPS were formally vested with the symbols of office.

It had become common practice for kings and lesser feudal lords to interfere in the process of selecting new bishops. They would either appoint the bishop outright or provide a short list of candidates for the approval of the church. When the new bishop was consecrated (by another bishop in the sacrament of HOLY ORDERS), the local ruler would formally invest him with the lands attached to the diocese and accept the bishop's homage as a feudal vassal. The lord would then hand over the symbols of office, the bishop's ring and crosier.

In an attempt to assert the church's autonomy, GREGORY VII HILDEBRAND (r. 1073–85) tried to put an end to these practices. In 1075 he issued a decree forbidding lay investiture. His most intense opposition came from the youthful HENRY IV (1060–1106), the Holy Roman Emperor. In the heat of the controversy, Gregory excommunicated Henry, and Henry called the German bishops together to depose Gregory. Henry finally gave in, and in a famous incident crawled through the snow outside the castle at Canossa in Tuscany to beg the pope's FORGIVENESS. The pope lifted the excommunication in 1077.

The conflict between the two leaders soon revived, however, as rulers and bishops through-

out the empire took sides. Henry's secular enemies elected a new emperor, and in 1080 the pope renewed his excommunication. Henry's clerical supporters declared Gregory deposed and elected an antipope, Clement III (r. 1080, 1084–1100). In 1084 Henry marched on Rome, drove Gregory from the city, and installed Clement in his stead. Over time, Henry's support of Clement turned his own family against him. His son revolted and forced his father from the throne in 1105, but the underlying issues were still unresolved.

Gregory's successors continued to assert his ban on investitures, until finally in 1122, Henry V (1081–1125) worked out a compromise with Pope Calixtuis II (r. 1119–24). Henry abandoned his authority to appoint bishops or invest them with the signs of their office, but he successfully retained the privilege of investing new bishops with their lands and receiving their homage in return.

Further reading: Uta-Renate Blumenthal, *The Investiture Controversy: Church and Monarchy from the Ninth to the Twelfth Century* (Philadelphia: University of Pennsylvania Press, 1988); H. E. J. Cowdrey, *Pope Gregory VII, 1073–1085* (Oxford: Oxford University Press, 1998); Karl F. Morrison, ed., *The Investiture Controversy: Issues, Ideals, and Results* (New York: Holt, Rinehart & Winston, 1971); Gerd Tellenbach, *The Western Church from the Tenth to the Early Twelfth Century* (Cambridge: Cambridge University Press, 1993).

Iona

The tiny island of Iona (3.5 miles by 1.5 miles) lies to the southwest of the Isle of Mull, on Scotland's west coast. It was there, around 563 C.E., that St. COLUMBA (c. 521–97) and 12 companions founded a MONASTERY that became a center for the evangelization of the Picts and Scots. Subsequently, a famous school and large monastic complex were developed on the island. Among the famous residents was Aidan (d. 651), who came to Iona around 635, stayed for five years, and then left to found a school on the island of Lindisfarne.

Vikings attacked Iona for the first time in 802, burning the monastery; they returned in 806 and completed their work by slaughtering the entire community of 68 people. A convent for women of the Benedictine Order was established on the island in 1203, and a Benedictine abbey for males was built about the same time. The Benedictines remained until the PROTESTANT REFORMATION in the 16th century, when they became the target of zealous reformers who dismantled the monastic buildings and tossed them into the sea.

In 1938 Reverend George MacLeod (1895–1991), a minister in the Church of Scotland, began a new ecumenical Iona Community. He suggested that restoring the old abbey might be a means of breaking down the barriers he had seen between working people and church leadership. Restoration of the Benedictine monastery (on the site of Columba's monastery) was completed in 1965.

Further reading: Dauvit Broun and Thomas Owen Clancy, eds., *Spaes Scotorum (Hope of the Scots): Saint Columba, Iona and Scotland* (Edinburgh: T & T Clark, 1999); John Jamieson, *An Historical Account of the Ancient Culdees of Iona, and of their Settlements in Scotland, England, and Ireland* (London: Longman, Hurst, Rees, Orme & Brown, & C. Jameson, 1811); Lucy Menzies, *Saint Columba of Iona: A Study of His Life, Times and His Influence* (New York: E.P Dutton, 1920); Richard Sharpe, ed., *Adomnan of Iona: Life of St. Columba* (New York: Penguin, 1995).

Ireland

Christianity and Catholicism have played an integral role in Irish life for some 1,600 years, ever since Pope Celestine I (r. 422–32) sent the missionary Palladius to the Irish as their first BISHOP as reported in the *Chronicle* of Prosper Tiro of Aquitaine (c. 390–c. 465). In the next century the Briton St. PATRICK converted the unmissionized parts of the island and instituted the Roman type of episcopal structure. Celtic MONASTICISM, however, retained its own structure. Often groups of MONKS, NUNS, and lay people were associated with one MONASTERY that could be governed by a lay *coarb* (Glc. "heir") or *airchendech* (Glc. "chieftain"). Sts. Columkille (d. 597) and COLUMBA were noteworthy monks of this period.

The establishment of Viking towns like Dublin and the arrival of Norse settlers brought Ireland into closer contact with England, which was experiencing the same influx. Archbishops of Canterbury (in England) like Lanfranc (r. 1070–89) and ANSELM sought to reform the Irish church, as did the ARCHBISHOP of Armaugh (in Ireland) St. Malachy (r. 1129–48). The English pope Adrian IV (r. 1154–59) urged English king Henry II (r. 1154–89), married to the formidable Eleanor of Aquitaine (1124–1204), to assert authority over Ireland and to wrest control away from the chieftains, but the outlying territories remained independent.

In subsequent years there was a notable decline in the church, which Observant FRANCISCANS and other orders helped to reverse. When HENRY VIII broke with Rome the Irish Parliament recognized him as head of the Church of Ireland in 1536. With a brief respite under Mary Tudor (r. 1553–58), there ensued a bitter struggle between the British monarch and traditional Catholics in Ireland. Irish chieftain and earl of Tyrone Hugh O'Neill (1550–1616) led a rebellion. After the Irish resisters fled to the Continent in 1607, King James I (r. 1603–25) imported Scottish Presbyterians and English Anglicans to settle in Ireland. The oppression became almost complete when the lord protector Oliver Cromwell (r. 1653–58), victor in Britain's civil war, conquered large parts of Ireland in a bloody campaign in 1649. Priests were expelled and mass was forbidden.

The English Restoration and the accession of James II (r. 1685–88) brought a promise of toleration. However, the Glorious Revolution of 1688 brought William of Orange-Nassau to the throne as King William III of England (r. 1688–1702), and James was crushed at the Battle of the Boyne in Ireland (1690). Irish Catholics went through a period of brutal suppression. Bishops and priests were outlawed. Catholics came under the Penal

Laws and were prohibited from owning land, serving as lawyers or officers, or voting in elections.

These rights, except for holding office, were gradually restored by 1793. Irish nationalist Catholic Daniel O'Connell (1777–1847) used parliamentary methods to gain the remainder of Catholic rights until Catholic Emancipation in Great Britain and Ireland was declared in 1829. However, the Great Hunger of 1845–49, caused by a potato blight and the continued export of Irish grain to England, brought death on a massive scale and drove a large part of the surviving Irish population to the Americas. The population dropped from 7 million to 3.5 million by the census of 1911.

Irish Catholics were long noted for their loyalty to Rome and their traditional devotionalism, in part as an expression of national and class solidarity against British rule. The religion experienced a great revival in the first part of the 19th century. Maynooth College (1795) produced a stream of well-educated CLERGY; new religious orders sprang up, and old ones experienced a renaissance. Catholics supported the Protestant Charles Stewart Parnell (1846–91), champion of Irish home rule, until his affair with Katherine O'Shea (1845–1921) was exposed in the press.

The Easter Rebellion of 1916 was the handwriting on the wall for the British overlords, who agreed to independence in 1921 after many violent skirmishes. The six counties to the north became predominantly Protestant Ulster, still a part of the United Kingdom, and the 26 counties to the south became the Irish Free State, which became the Republic of Ireland in 1948. Struggles continue between Protestants and Catholics in the north, where the two groups are approaching parity in numbers.

The Free State under Eamon de Valera (1882–1975) was heavily influenced by Catholic moral and social teaching, and the church maintained a strong presence in public life. However, since the country entered the European Union in 1973, economic success has been accompanied by social change. In 1985 the government enacted a liberal contraception law over the objections of the bishops, although it passed an antiabortion law in 1983. Church attendance has dropped significantly sine the 1980s. The recent PEDOPHILIA scandals have harmed church credibility.

Further reading: Michael Carroll, *Irish Pilgrimage: Holy Wells and Popular Catholic Devotion* (Baltimore: Johns Hopkins University Press, 1999); Patrick J. Corish, *The Irish Catholic Experience: A Historical Survey* (Wilmington, Del.: Glazier, 1985); Emmet Larkin, *The Consolidation of the Roman Catholic Church in Ireland, 1860–70* (Chapel Hill: University of North Carolina Press, 1985).

Ireland, John (1838–1918) *U.S. archbishop and champion of Americanism*

John Ireland was born in Burnchurch, Ireland, on September 11, 1838. He moved to the United States as a youth of 12 with his family and in 1852 settled in St. Paul. He was an advocate of aligning the Catholic Church with American culture. As a youth with potential, Ireland was sent to FRANCE by Joseph Cretin, then BISHOP of St. Paul, to complete his seminary studies, and he was ordained in 1861. He served as a chaplain during the American Civil War and then returned to St. Paul to become the bishop's secretary.

Ireland was an orator of some skill and won approval from many Protestants when he denounced the local political establishment for high-level corruption. In 1870 he attended VATICAN COUNCIL I as an American representative. He was named bishop coadjutor in 1875, succeeded to the bishop's chair in 1884, and became the first ARCHBISHOP of St. Paul in 1888.

As bishop, Ireland's influence grew, and he was regularly invited to speak before religious and secular organizations. Throughout the first decade of his bishopric, he frequently chose topics that emphasized the Catholic Church's place on the American landscape and called fellow church leaders to take a positive stance toward American culture. He sought to convince non-Catholics of the loyalty American Catholics felt toward the land in which they lived. To these ends, he worked against the continuation of ethnic enclaves within the church and advocated the use of English texts in all the parochial schools.

At the time Ireland was at the peak of his influence, the church in Catholic Europe was facing a number of setbacks due to the secularization of national governments and the resulting loss of the privileged position previously held by the church. While the American Catholic community thrived under the separation of CHURCH AND STATE, in Europe separation had brought major losses. Nevertheless, in 1899, Pope LEO XIII issued an encyclical condemning the ideas that he saw being championed by Ireland and other American leaders under the label *AMERICANISM*.

Ireland and fellow bishops JAMES GIBBONS and John Joseph Keane (1839–1918) of Richmond and Dubuque were quick to respond to the papal document. They noted that the ideas denounced in the encyclical varied considerably from what they had espoused and denied that anyone in the American hierarchy advocated those ideas. The damage had been done, however, and the church withdrew from many areas of participation in American life, such as support for public schools. It did not return until after World War II. Ireland continued to lead the archdiocese of St. Paul until his death on September 25, 1918.

Further reading: John Ireland, *The Church and Modern Society: Lectures and Addresses by John Ireland* (New York: D.H. McBride, 1897); James H. Monnihan, *The Life of Archbishop John Ireland* (New York: Harper, 1953); Marvin R. O'Connell, *John Ireland and the American Catholic Church* (St. Paul: Minnesota Historical Society, 1988).

Irenaeus of Lyons (c. 130–c. 200) *bishop and theologian*

Irenaeus is without doubt the most important orthodox theologian of the second century. Many consider him the first CHRISTIAN theologian who tried to think through the core teachings of the FAITH systematically; he formulated the RULE OF FAITH that became the articles of the CREED. His ideas appear to have been based closely on the BIBLE. His feast day is June 28 in the West and August 23 in the East.

Irenaeus was born in Smyrna, in Asia Minor, where he heard St. Polycarp of Smyrna (c. 69–c. 155) as a child. He studied at Rome and went to Lyons as presbyter and then BISHOP. Though he fought heretics, he sought toleration for the followers of MONTANUS from the bishop of Rome Eleutherius (c. 175–89) and later for the Quartodecimans (who followed the Jewish date of Nisan 14 for EASTER) from Victor I (189–98).

Irenaeus embraced a principle of a single Scripture (with both Old and New Testaments) united by a series of covenants between GOD and humankind (*Against Heresies* 3.11.8). He also retained the early apostolic teaching that the last things that will come at the end of days (the new heaven and new earth) will not be radical departures, as some millenarians like MONTANUS taught, but like the first things. Thus, the end will be a recapitulation and restoration of all things in CHRIST (*Proof of Apostolic Teaching* 6). The kingdom of God will not be some wild utopia but simply the cessation of wars, freedom from bondage, and abundant harvests justly distributed (*Against Heresies* 5.35.1–5), bringing material as well as spiritual benefits. What will pass away is not the world itself but the nefarious schema, or arrangement, beneath which it suffers (5.36.1). Irenaeus framed these two teachings in the three articles of the creed (CREATION, REDEMPTION, and sanctification, or regeneration).

This THEOLOGY must be reconstructed from the tracts Irenaeus wrote condemning the Gnosticism swirling through the Roman Empire at this time, especially the version preached by VALENTINUS. In his struggle with the GNOSTICS Irenaeus stressed the unity of God, who is manifest in the economy of salvation. The 20th-century discoveries of

Gnostic documents at Nag Hammadi show that his accounts of the Gnostics are remarkably accurate.

Further reading: Most of Irenaeus's writings are available online; Robert M. Grant, *Irenaeus of Lyons* (London: Routledge, 1997); Gerd Lüdemann, *Heretics: The Other Side of Early Christianity* (Louisville, Ky.: Westminster John Knox, 1996); Eric Osborn, *Irenaeus of Lyons* (Cambridge: Cambridge University Press, 2001).

Isidore of Kiev (d. 1463) *advocate of union between Eastern and Western Churches*

Isidore of Kiev, who rose to lead the Russian Orthodox Church in the 15th century, became a major advocate of the reunion of the Catholic Church and EASTERN ORTHODOXY. Isidore was born in Thessalonika and educated as a Greek. At some point he moved to CONSTANTINOPLE, where he became a MONK. He eventually became head of the MONASTERY of St. Demetrius there and gained a considerable reputation for his learning.

Isidore rose to prominence as the Byzantine Empire's very existence was under threat from the Ottoman Turks. Church and civil leaders were open to a reunion with the West as a means of staving off defeat. In 1434 Isidore attended the Council of BASEL, which was preoccupied by squabbles over the revival of papal authority, brought to a low point by the western SCHISM (1378–1417). In spite of the problems at Basel, plans were laid for a further gathering at Ferrara, ITALY, at which the topic of reunion with the East was considered.

As preparations for reunion continued, in 1436 Isidore was consecrated metropolitan of Kiev and All Rus, and thus head of the Russian Orthodox Church. He traveled to Moscow in 1437, where he organized a delegation to attend the council about to gather at Ferrara (*see* COUNCILS, ECUMENICAL). Arriving in Italy in 1438, he became one of the Orthodox Church's official spokespersons. He worked steadily for the union both at Ferrara and at Florence, where the council moved in January 1439.

Once a plan of union was reached and the council adjourned, Pope Eugene IV (r. 1431–47) designated Isidore as his legate to Russia and Lithuania. A short time later, while Isidore was on his way back to Russia, Eugene made him a cardinal, one of the very rare occasions in which a person not of the Latin Rite was so acknowledged. He found when he arrived back in Moscow and published the details of the union, however, that none of his fellow bishops were ready to accept it. At the czar's command, the bishops deposed him, and he was imprisoned.

In 1443, Isidore escaped and fled to Rome, where Eugene welcomed him. In spite of Moscow's reluctance to join the Greek Orthodox, efforts at union between Rome and Constantinople continued. In 1452, Eugene's successor, Pope Nicolas V (r. 1447–55) sent Isidore to Constantinople to complete the formal union, which he successfully accomplished. However, a few months later the Turks overran the city; Isidore escaped only by swapping clothes with a dead man and allowing himself to become a slave. As in Moscow, he escaped and made his way back to Rome. He was named bishop of Sabina and later given the now purely honorary titles patriarch of Constantinople and archbishop of Cyprus. He died in Rome.

Further reading: Milton V. Anastos, *Aspects of the Mind of Byzantium: Political Theory, Theology, and Ecclesiastical Relations with the See of Rome.* (Aldershot: Ashgate, 2001); Henry Chadwick, *East and West: The Making of a Rift in the Church: From Apostolic Times Until the Council of Florence* (Oxford: Oxford University Press, 2005); Joseph Gill, *The Council of Florence* (Cambridge: Cambridge University Press, 1961).

Islam (Ar.: *islam,* "submission"; from the same root as *salaam,* "peace")

Islam (literally "submission" to the will of GOD, or Allah) is historically the last of the three Abrahamic FAITHS. It began with the prophet Muhammad (c. 570–629) in the early seventh century. Today the faith claims more than 1.5 billion adherents, called Muslims, and is second in number only to Christianity.

Although Muhammad is considered the founder of Islam, the religion traces its roots back to the prophet Abraham. Whereas Judaism and Christianity contend that God asked Abraham to sacrifice Isaac, Islam claims it was Ishmael (whom both the BIBLE and the *Qur'an* consider the ancestor of the Arabs). Muslims believe that, while Judaism and Christianity received God's genuine revelation, their followers distorted the message over time. They believe that Muhammad, an illiterate merchant from Mecca, was the final prophet in a line that included Noah, Abraham, Moses, and Jesus, who with Muhammad (the "Seal of the Prophets") are the five most important prophets in Islam. Rather than creating Islam, in this view, Muhammad simply restored God's people and called them back into a relationship with him. Unlike Jesus CHRIST, Muhammad is not considered divine, and although he is highly revered by all Muslims, who say "peace be upon him" every time they speak his name, it is blasphemous and punishable to worship him. His life is a model all Muslims try to live by, as captured in the *sunnah,* the sayings and traditions of the Prophet.

In 610 Muhammad began receiving revelations from God, which continued for the course of his lifetime and were compiled shortly after his death in the form of the Qur'an (also written *Koran*), literally 'recitation.' The *Qur'an,* written in Arabic, the "language of God," is the most revered scripture of Islam, as it is considered the literal word of God. It is considered the model of perfection from a literary, grammatical, moral, and divine point of view.

The central doctrine of Islam is the unity and oneness of God. All Muslims agree on five obligatory practices, called the Five Pillars of Islam: the *shahada,* or the profession of faith, which states that "There is no God but Allah, and Muhammad is His messenger"; *salah,* five daily prayer services facing Mecca; *zakat,* an obligatory tithe of a believer's wealth for purposes of redistribution to the poor; *Ramadan,* the month of fasting, worship, and celebration; and the *Hajj,* the pilgrimage to Mecca and Medina that all Muslims must do once in their lifetime if they are physically and economically able.

The two main branches of the faith are Sunni and Shi'a, the former claiming roughly 80 percent of the faithful, the latter around 15 percent, largely living in Iran. The two branches split very early in Muslim history over who would lead the Islamic community after the death of the prophet Muhammad, who did not leave a male heir. Sunni Muslims contend that leadership follows through the companions of the Prophet, whereas Shi'a Muslims argue it follows his bloodline. In Sunni Islam the 'Four Rightly Guided Caliphs,' or leaders, were Abu Bakr, Umar, Uthman, and Ali. Shi'a Islam recognizes only Ali (598–661), the Prophet's nephew, married to his daughter, Fatimeh. Throughout history there has been much conflict and violence between Sunnis and Shi'as, and this continues today. Sufism represents the mystical tradition within Islam.

The expansion of Islam after its inception was astounding. Within 100 years of conquest and conversions, the faith became predominant from Morocco to Central Asia, across three continents, and became important enough in the Byzantine Empire to affect the veneration of ICONs during the Iconoclasm Controversy. The core territories of Islam were ruled by the Umayyad Empire from 705–50, the Abbassids until 935, the Seljuk Turks until the 14th century, and the Ottoman Empire until its collapse in the early 20th century.

The Christian CRUSADES had a powerful impact on the Muslim world. In 1099 the city of Jerusalem, the third-holiest site in Islam after Mecca and Medina, fell to the crusaders. Salah al-Din, or Saladin (1137/38–93), restored Islamic dominance when he defeated the crusaders a century later. He is still revered as a powerful Islamic figure. Another important battle was in 1453, when Mehmed II (1432–81) conquered CONSTANTINOPLE in 1453, ushering in the demise of the Byzantine Empire.

The MIDDLE AGES were a golden age for Islam. Greco-Roman civilization had survived in the East and was carried on and advanced by Muslim scholars and scientists. Such fields as astronomy, mathematics, and medicine thrived under Islam while they languished in the Christian West. The Persian IBN SINA (980–1037), Avicenna in Latin, wrote more than 450 books on philosophy and medicine, and he is considered the "father of modern medicine." IBN RUSHD (1126–98), known as Averroes in the West, is most famous for his summaries and commentaries on ARISTOTLE's works, which eventually made them accessible to Christian thinkers. Al-Andalus, southern SPAIN, was a hotbed of scholarship, with Córdoba as the seat of translation. For hundreds of years Al-Andalus was a place of tolerance and respect, where Jewish, Christian, and Muslim scholars lived and worked side by side.

Interfaith dialogue between Islam and Catholicism has been slow and difficult. The legacies of Arab and Turkish conquest, the Crusades, Western colonialism, and competing claims to the Holy Lands have made it hard even to begin religious dialogue. True dialogue is difficult because Christians and Muslims do not approach the issues from equal planes. The fact that Islam came after Christianity and sees itself as the culmination of God's revelation creates a hierarchy of interpretation. Muslims view the Bible as God's revelation, though distorted and less important than the Qur'an, whereas Christians do not give any weight to the Qur'an. Also, several biblical stories are found in the Qur'an, including the stories of Abraham, Joseph, and Jesus, often with varying details. The strict adherence to monotheism and the oneness of God means that Muslims consider Christianity to be a polytheistic religion due to the doctrine of the TRINITY. Although Muslims revere Jesus as a prophet and recognize his VIRGIN BIRTH, they do not accept that Jesus was crucified, believing it was Judas Iscariot instead.

Further reading: Maria Jaoudi, *Christian and Islamic Spirituality; Sharing a Journey* (Mahwah, N.J.: Paulist, 1993); Imam W. D. Muammad, *Religion on the Line: Al-Islam, Judaism, Catholicism, Protestantism* (Chicago: W. D. Muhammad, 1983); Fazlur Rahman, *Islam* (New York: Holt, Rinehart & Winston, 1966); W. Montgomery Watt, *Muhammad: Prophet and Statesman* (London: Oxford University Press, 1964); A.J. Wensinck, *The Muslim Creed: Its Genesis and Historical Development* (New York: Barnes & Noble, 1965).

Italo-Albanian Catholic Church

The Italo-Albanian Catholic Church is one of the smaller Eastern Rite Catholic bodies. Its members are people of Greek heritage residing in southern ITALY and Sicily. Christianity originally developed in southern Italy and Sicily as a Greek-speaking religion. The process of latinization had only begun when in the eighth century the region was shifted to the jurisdiction of Greek Byzantium, leading to a revival of Greek Christianity. After the Norman French took control of the region in the 11th century, the entrenched Byzantine church was only slowly relatinized.

The gradual disappearance of the Byzantine rite was reversed in the 1400s by the relocation of a group of Albanians into southern Italy. In 1595 a BISHOP was appointed for them, a first step toward full recognition by Vatican authorities. Full recognition finally came in the 19th century.

In 1732 the church established a seminary of its own in Calabria, and a second opened two years later in Palermo. They serve the two dioceses of Lungro, begun in 1919, and Piana degli Albanesi, created in 1937. The MONASTERY of Santa Maria di Grottaferrata (fd. 1004), with its own bishop in residence, is the oldest structure representative of the continuing Greek tradition in Italy. The church has some 60,000 members.

Further reading: Ronald G. Roberson, *The Eastern Christian Churches—A Brief Survey,* 5th ed. (Rome: Pontifical Oriental Institute, 1995).

Italy

No country on earth can rival Italy's importance to Roman Catholicism and its growth in the world. It is the home of VATICAN CITY, an independent state since 1929, and the official residence of the pope, who is patriarch of the West and the Supreme Pontiff and primate of the Catholic Church.

EARLY PERIOD

After its emergence in Jerusalem, Christianity and hence Catholicism found its second primal center in Rome, the capital of the great empire of the ancient world where most CHRISTIANS lived. The Roman Empire at first thwarted the new religion but then facilitated its peaceful spread throughout its vast territories, which reached from Hadrian's Wall in England and the Rhine delta in GERMANY, down to the Straits of Gibraltar, over to Syene in Upper EGYPT, up to the upper Euphrates and Tigris in Mesopotamia, and across to the lands above the Danube. All this territory provided the missionary grounds for the rapidly expanding religion, especially once it became the official religion of the state.

The earliest reference to the presence of Christians in Rome dates from 49 to 50. Roman historian Suetonius says that Emperor Claudius (r. 41–54) expelled the Jews from Rome for the disturbance caused by "Chrestus" (*Claudius* 25.4). PAUL refers to a whole group of fellow workers and APOSTLES there in Romans 16, which is generally dated about 55. The persecution of Christians by Nero in 64 is reported both by Suetonius (*Nero* 16.2) and Tacitus (*Annals* 15.44). At the end of the century St. CLEMENT OF ROME mentions that Sts. PETER and PAUL were both martyred in Rome, a fact that automatically made the city second in importance after Jerusalem (IRENAEUS *Against Heresies* 3.3.2). The earliest community in Rome was Greek-speaking and was composed of hellenized Jews and Gentiles.

Rome became home to many of the early Christian apologists and the funnel for missionary activity from the Middle East to parts West. Irenaeus says that the Roman community became an early defender of orthodoxy and produced the first recorded roster of urban BISHOPS, indicating a belief in APOSTOLIC SUCCESSION (Eusebius, *Church History* 5.6). Church organization in the city grew more elaborate as the number of adherents grew. Bishop of Rome Cornelius (r. 251–53) called a synod of bishops there in 251, showing the city's importance. In the third century there is also evidence for communities in Ravenna, Rimini, and Apulia.

Although there were several cycles of urban and provincial persecutions (under Nero in 64; Domition in 95; Trajan around 110; Hadrian in 124; Marcus Aurelius in 161; Decius in 249; and Diocletian in 297, to name only the largest), the number of martyrs was not nearly as great as popularly believed—perhaps 1,000 in all. Meanwhile, the Christian population swelled, constituting perhaps a third of the empire by the time of CONSTANTINE THE GREAT.

CONSTANTINE TO THE MIDDLE AGES

In 313 Constantine issued the Edict of Milan, which legalized Christianity. The act was less an act of liberality than a political move to win support from the growing Christian population. Constantine and his mother, St. Helena, immediately sought to gratify the wishes of their new clientele. Constantine granted the Roman BASILICA now known as St. John Lateran to the bishop of Rome as his seat and palace. He also began building the first ST. PETER'S BASILICA on Vatican Hill. His mother began a search for the true CROSS and sponsored the building of several churches in the Holy Land, including the Church of the Holy Sepulcher in Jerusalem (*see* ARCHITECTURE). Constantine also convened the first Council of Nicaea in 325 (*see* COUNCILS, ECUMENICAL) to keep the empire unified and to settle the ARIANISM question. The entanglement of the emperor in church affairs would lead to both eastern CAESAROPAPISM and the western INVESTITURE CONTROVERSY.

By 370 the seat of the empire had moved to Milan, leaving the bishop of Rome the most important figure in the city and paving the way for what later would be called the PAPACY. The emperor Gratian (r. 375–83) granted Pope Damasus I (r. 366–84) a rescript, making Rome the court of appeal for all the bishoprics of Italy. In rapid succession Rome had to face the Visigoths, who sacked the city in 410, the Vandals, and the Huns. Theodoric the Great (r. 493–526) set up a permanent Ostrogothic dynasty with Arian sympathies in Ravenna.

The Byzantine emperor JUSTINIAN I (r. 527–65) sought to reunify the empire from his western base in Ravenna. Though he ornamented the churches of Ravenna with wonderful mosaics, his efforts could not prevent the Arian Lombards from invading the Po Valley in 568. The invasion left Rome and the regions around it under the sole protection of the pope, fatefully leading to the later formation of the PAPAL STATES. During these turbulent times, Popes Leo I the Great (r. 440–61) and GREGORY I THE GREAT contributed mightily to the growing power of the papacy and the spread of Christianity to Spain and England. The tendency of eastern bishops to appeal to the Roman bishop for help in solving their many theological disputes added to the pope's prestige. It is from this time that one can speak of an organized papacy in a more formal sense of the term.

Gregory also gave support to St. BENEDICT OF NURSIA, who began his monastic foundations at Subiaco and Monte Cassino. The MONASTERIES of Italy soon became the repository of early biblical manuscripts and patristic writings and helped preserve the learning of the ancient world for future generations. Monasteries also became laboratories for new breeds of animals and technological innovation.

In an attempt to protect themselves from the Lombards and the Byzantine emperors the popes sought help from the Frankish kings, beginning with Pepin III the Short (r. 751–68) and reaching a high point with the coronation of CHARLEMAGNE (r. 771–814) as emperor by Pope Leo III (r. 795–816) on Christmas Day, 800, in St. Peter's

Basilica in Rome. This dangerous liaison led to an unending struggle between the pope and princes over issues of simony, lay investiture, taxation of church property, and so on. Some medieval popes like INNOCENT III and BONIFACE VIII often got the better of their princely opponents, but others were less successful.

Clerical abuse was rife, even at the papal court. DANTE ALIGHIERI both celebrated the glories of Catholicism and excoriated church authorities for the corruption they allowed, which gave rise to many protest movements, including the FRANCISCAN order and GIROLAMO SAVONAROLA in Italy. All seemed to come to a head during the AVIGNON PAPACY and the Western SCHISM, with popes living in luxury in Avignon, France, while antipopes popped up in Italy and elsewhere. Toward the end of the medieval period there was a noted turn toward humanism and the celebration of the powers of humankind.

RENAISSANCE TO ENLIGHTENMENT

The Renaissance church was a very ambiguous creature. On one hand, the Medici popes sponsored the great artists of the time (MICHELANGELO, RAPHAEL) who made the Vatican the jewel of Europe, and on the other hand Borgia popes like ALEXANDER VI corrupted the papacy with illegitimate children, Machiavellian politics, and open warfare. In time the papacy and the Papal States became a lure for the warring monarchs of France, Austria, and Spain. When the PROTESTANT REFORMATION rattled the church to self-consciousness in 1517 to 1520, it still took the papacy 25 years to call the Council of TRENT and bring about lasting reform.

The COUNTER-REFORMATION brought many innovations to Italy: vigorous new religious orders, a new baroque spirituality that spawned luxuriant baroque art forms, and a missionary impulse that reached the ends of the earth. The Enlightenment, however, brought not only criticism of abuse but outright scorn toward many things Catholic, leading to the abolition of clerical privileges, the closing of monasteries, and the confiscation of church property even in Italy itself.

MODERN AGE

Italy in the 19th century was caught between the aspiration for national political unification under the banner of Giuseppe Garibaldi (1807–82) and a papacy struggling to retain its secular states and railing against the incursions of modern scholarship in the field of religion. Through all this, the papacy managed to respond to the social and political challenge of the labor movement and political agitation for social reform. In the middle stood the conflicted PIUS IX, the "Prisoner of the Vatican," who declared the doctrine of the Immaculate Conception (1854), saw nearly every modern enterprise as an invitation to either atheism or error in his *Syllabus of Errors* (December 8, 1864), and called VATICAN COUNCIL I, wherein he declared himself and the papacy to have powers of INFALLIBILITY in matters of faith and doctrine. Meanwhile, he excommunicated Garibaldi for taking away his very secular dominions and refused to recognize the democratic movements of the world.

Despite the reactionary stand of the papacy, the seeds of risorgimento were growing even within the Italian church, with new religious orders, the LITURGICAL MOVEMENT, and the participation of lay Catholics and priests in the movements of modernity. Popes LEO XIII at the turn of the century and Benedict XV (1914–22) began to relent. The Vatican settled its land claims with the state of Italy in the Lateran Treaty of 1929 and succumbed to the blandishments of fascist dictator Benito Mussolini (1883–1945), who had signed the treaty. The church's stance remained conflicted throughout World War II under Popes Pius XI and PIUS XII.

When Pope JOHN XXIII called VATICAN COUNCIL II in 1959, Italy and the rest of the world welcomed the opening up of the Catholic Church to all that was good in modernity. In his encyclicals on social justice, global interdependence, and the scourge of modern warfare, he spoke not only to Catholics but to the world. Since Vatican II the church in Italy has gone through a considerable retrenchment, often almost to the positions and practices of Pius IX. In the meantime the number of priests in Italy and church attendance there plummeted. For the first time in centuries, even the popes were not Italian after 1978.

In 1985 the Vatican renegotiated the Lateran Treaty of 1929. No longer is Catholicism the official religion of Italy. Children no longer receive Catholic instruction in state schools, and the CLERGY no longer receive a salary from the state. While 98 percent of the population is nominally Catholic, some estimates claim that as few as 10 to 19 percent of them attend church with any regularity.

Further reading: K. Baus, *The Imperial Church from Constantine to the Early Middle Ages* (New York: Herder & Herder, 1980); Jean Daniélou & Henri Marrou, *The First Six Hundred Years* (New York: MaGraw-Hill, 1964); Owen Chadwick, *A History of the Popes 1830–1914* (Oxford: Clarendon, 1998); George Holmes, *The Oxford Illustrated History of Italy* (Oxford: Oxford University Press, 2001); John McManners, ed., *The Oxford Illustrated History of Christianity* (Oxford: Oxford University Press, 1993).

J

James II of England (1633–1701) *last Catholic king of England, Scotland, and Ireland*

James II was the second son of Charles I (1600–49) and Henrietta Maria (1609–69) of FRANCE. He was born at St. James's Palace and became the duke of York at the age of 11. He grew up in exile in FRANCE and converted to Catholicism in 1669.

Surprisingly, the Catholic James was accepted as king in 1684 (he was also known as James VII of Scotland). His support waned, however, when he violently suppressed the Monmouth uprising in 1685. He began to institute policies that undermined the Church of England and hinted at his desire to establish a Catholic state, and he frequently appointed Catholics to positions of authority. In 1688 Parliament deposed him in favor of his Protestant daughter, Mary II, and son-in-law, William III of Orange (r. 1689–1702), and he fled to France. James returned to fight and lose the Battle of the Boyne (1690) in Ireland, today celebrated by Orange Order Protestants on July 12, and lamented by Catholics.

James II married twice and had 15 children. He is buried in France. Many of his surviving family members and heirs are buried in ST. PETER'S BASILICA.

Further reading: Peter Earle, *The Life and Times of James II* (London: Weidenfeld & Nicolson, 1972); Lewis Innes, *The Life of James the Second, King of England* (London: Longman, Hurst, Rees, Orme, & Brown, 1816); John Miller, *James II* (New Haven, Conn.: Yale University Press, 2000); David Ogg, *England in the Reigns of James II and William III* (Oxford: Clarendon, 1955).

James the Greater, St. *apostle*

James is the anglicized form of the Biblical Hebrew name Jacob. James was an APOSTLE and the older brother of St. John (Mark 3:17). Jesus bestowed the epithet Boanerges on the two brothers; it can mean either "sons of tumult" or "sons of wrath" (hot-tempered) in Hebrew. His feast day is April 30 in the East and July 25 in the West.

PETER, James, and John form a special group who witnessed the raising of Jairus's daughter (Mark 5:37), the TRANSFIGURATION (Mark 9:2), and the agony of CHRIST in Gethsemane (Mark 14:33). James was later the leader of the Jerusalem church, which closely followed Jewish ritual law and temple worship. Paul calls him "the brother of the Lord" (Gal. 1:19). He was put to death by Herod Agrippa I (r. 42–44) according to Acts 12:2, the only apostle whose martyrdom is mentioned in the New Testament.

A sixth- to seventh-century legend tells that James preached in SPAIN. Though there is no other evidence for this claim, the legend gave rise to the great pilgrimage site of Santiago de Compostela. James's symbol is the sea shell. There is much discussion whether the ossuary that turned up on the antiquities black market in Jerusalem is his. An inscription on the side reads "James, son of Joseph, brother of Jesus"

Further reading: R. R. van Voorst, *The Ascents of James: History and Theology of a Jewish-Christian Community* (Atlanta: Scholars, 1989).

Jansenism

Jansenism was a powerful movement within the Catholic Church, especially in FRANCE, that stressed an AUGUSTINIAN theology that seemed to resemble that of the Protestants in the areas of grace and free will. The movement was eventually suppressed.

Cornelius Otto Jansen (1585–1638) was director of a college at the University of Louvain and then bishop of Ypres. His posthumous book *Augustinus* (1640) influenced such figures as the Abbé de Saint-Cyran (1581–1643), Antoine Arnauld (1612–94), and Antoine's sister Jacqueline Marie Angélique Arnauld (1591–1661), abbess of the famous Cistercian convent of Port-Royal near Paris; they believed Jansen's ideas, derived from AUGUSTINE OF HIPPO, could be used to counteract Protestantism. Antoine Arnauld, author of the noted logical treatise *The Art of Thinking* (1662), developed a stringent approach to the reception of Eucharistic Communion that bordered on scrupulosity, in contrast to the JESUIT teaching on frequent Communion. The philosopher and mathematician Blaise Pascal (1623–62) came under the influence of Port-Royal. French kings and churchmen became deeply involved in the Jansenist controversy up to the French Revolution.

Pope Innocent X (r. 1644–55), in the bull *Cum Occasione* (May 31, 1653), condemned five Jansenist propositions, especially the assertions that without a special grace humans cannot fulfill God's commands, and that grace is irresistible in a state of fallenness (in agreement with Protestantism). Other Jansenist statements were said to deny FREE WILL and to uphold moral pessimism. Arnauld replied that the pope was right to condemn those propositions, but he denied that they were contained in *Augustinus*. Later, Alexander VII (r. 1689–91) revived the attack against the Jansenists, and Arnauld fled to the Netherlands, where he influenced Pasquier Quesnel (1634–1719), who continued the Jansenist tradition.

A resurgence of Janenism early in the next century brought a renewed condemnation by Clement XI (r. 1700–21) in *Unigenitus Dei Filius* (September 8, 1713). A branch of the Jansensist movement, including validly ordained bishops, broke with Rome and became affiliated with the OLD CATHOLICS.

Further reading: James E. Bradley, *Religion and Politics in Enlightenment Europe* (Notre Dame: University of Notre Dame Press, 2001); William Doyle, *Jansenism: Catholic Resistance to Authority from the Reformation to the French Revolution* (Houndmills: Macmillan, 2000); Theophilus Gale, *The True Idea of Jansenisme: Both Historick and Dogmatick* (London: Th. Gilbert, 1669); A. Sedgwick, *Jansenism in Seventeenth-Century France* (Charlottesville: University of Virginia Press, 1977).

Jean-Baptiste de La Salle, St. (1651–1719)
educator, founder of Christian Brothers

Jean Baptist de La Salle, a pioneer in public education, was born in Rheims, FRANCE, of a noble family. He attended the College des Bons Enfants in Reims and the Sorbonne in Paris. He was ordained in 1679. He was canonized in 1900 by LEO XIII. His is feast day is May 15. Pope PIUS XII named him patron of all teachers of youth in 1950.

Full of zeal to serve, and acutely aware of the lack of educational opportunities for the poor, he decided to found free schools open to all children. He faced a variety of obstacles, not the least being his own noble birth—his BISHOP refused to appoint him to one of the poorer neighborhoods, as it would be unsuitable to his social rank. He got around the problem by training tutors and organizing them into the monastic Order of the Brothers of Christian Schools, formed between 1680 and 1684 (*see* CHRISTIAN BROTHERS). LaSalle wrote the order's rules and convoked the first two general chapters. He led the order until his death in 1719. As his work prospered, he ran into new opposition from private tutors who complained that his free schools were taking away clients.

A major innovation in LaSalle's schools was the introduction of French as the language of instruction rather than Latin, which was used in most schools of his day even at the elementary level. He also introduced the classroom, whereby students would be taught as groups, rather than tutored on a one-to-one basis. Students were assigned to classes based on age and reading level. To manage the classes he developed a system of regulations that dictated the daily schedule as well as classroom behavior.

Beginning with free elementary schooling, LaSalle expanded his work to include Sunday schools to teach reading and writing to eager workers whose only leisure was on that day. He developed a teachers' college to train instructors. Given the success of his program, the government began to send him juvenile offenders, and he reorganized juvenile prisons as vocational schools. He also wrote the textbooks used in all these institutions.

LaSalle and the order moved their headquarters to Paris in 1688 and to Rouen in 1705. The order expanded through the 18th century but was nearly destroyed following the French Revolution in 1789. It was able to reorganize beginning in 1802. The order experienced numerous ups and downs as regulations came and went in the gradually secularizing France. The work was all undone in the years after 1904, when teaching by religious in French schools was outlawed. The closing of the French schools, however, was followed by the global dispersion of the Brothers to many countries. From 1904 to 1908, 222 houses were founded overseas, and a number of schools for French students opened in countries bordering France.

LaSalle's original organization continues to the present as the Institute of the Brothers of the Christian Schools, which remains dedicated to educational ministries. While a religious order, its members do not take the traditional monastic vows. Today there are approximately 7,500 La Salle Brothers working in more than 80 countries.

Further reading: William John Battersby, *De La Salle: Saint & Spiritual Writer* (London: Longmans Green, 1950); Jeffrey Gros, *Jean Baptist de La Salle: The Spirituality of Christian Education* (New York: Paulist, 2004).

Jerome, St. (c. 342–420) *translator of Bible to Latin*

St. Jerome is best known for writing the Vulgate, a translation of the BIBLE to Latin from the original Greek, Hebrew, and Aramaic (mostly for the Book of Daniel); his version was used by the Roman Catholic Church until Pope JOHN PAUL II issued the New Vulgate April 25, 1979. He is considered a DOCTOR and FATHER OF THE CHURCH and is patron of theological learning. His feast day is September 30.

Jerome was born Eusebius Sophronius Hieronymus at Stridon, in today's Slovenia. He was baptized in 365 and lived as a hermit in the Syrian deserts. In 379 he was ordained by Bishop Paulinus of Nola (354–431), and soon after he traveled to CONSTANTINOPLE to study Scripture under St. GREGORY OF NAZIANZUS. He later served as secretary to Pope Damasus I (r. 366–83), who commissioned him to produce the Vulgate. In 388 he returned to the Holy Land, where he spent the remainder of his life as a hermit near Bethlehem.

Jerome's Vulgate included the entire Bible except for a few books of the Apocrypha. He also wrote biblical commentaries, polemical treatises, and a dialogue against the Pelagians (*see* PELAGIUS). He was the most learned of the western fathers, especially in Hebrew, and was known for his zealous enthusiasm for monasticism and the ascetic life. He has often been accused of misogyny. His body rests in the Sistine Chapel.

Further reading: Charles Christopher, *Saint Jerome, The Sage of Bethlehem* (Milwaukee: Bruce, 1959); Leonard Hughes, *The Christian Church in the Epistles of St. Jerome* (London: Society for Promoting Christian Knowledge, 1923); J.N.D. Kelly, *Jerome: His Life, Writings, and Controversies* (London: Duckworth, 1975); Charles Martin, *Life of St. Jerome* (London: Kegan, Paul, Trench & Company, 1888); Jean Steinmann, *Saint Jerome and His Times* (Notre Dame: Fides, 1959).

Jesuits

The Jesuits, or the Society of Jesus, is a worldwide educational and missionary order that played a key intellectual and organizational role in combating the PROTESTANT REFORMATION. It was founded in Paris in 1536 by the Spaniard St. IGNATIUS OF LOYOLA and six companions and approved as a religious society by Pope PAUL III in the bull *Regimini Militantis Ecclesiae* (1540). The bull set their goals to be "the progress of souls in Christian life and teaching and the propagation of the faith." The rule and constitution of the society were approved by the membership in 1558.

Ignatius planned to take his followers to the Holy Land, but Ottoman attacks prevented the move. However, the society had taken a special vow to go anywhere the pope sent them in the service of the COUNTER-REFORMATION, and in short order its presence was felt all over the Old and New Worlds, founding humanist institutions of learning, serving as missionaries to the farthest reaches of the world, and fostering the intellectual life of Catholicism at the highest levels. The spirituality of Ignatius, embedded in his *Spiritual Exercises*, informed all the undertakings of the society. The motto of the order is *Ad majorem gloriam Dei* ("For the greater glory of God").

The Jesuits opened their first institution of higher learning at Messina in 1548. It was soon followed by the Gregorianum in Rome. Eventually they founded colleges and universities in all their missionary fields. Under Claudio Aquaviva, general of the society from 1581 to 1615, an elaborate code of Jesuit education was set into place. The order produced noted theologians, including St. ROBERT BELLARMINE (1542–1621), who engaged in reasoned debate with Protestants and was sympathetic to GALILEO GALILEI at his trial, and FRANCISCO SUAREZ (1548–1617), who sought to reconcile the contradictions between THOMAS OF AQUINAS and JOHN DUNS SCOTUS.

In the United States the Jesuits founded the noted universities Georgetown (1789), Fordham (1841), Loyola of Chicago (1870), and many others. Two of the foremost Jesuit theologians of the 20th century, JOHN COURTNEY MURRAY and KARL RAHNER, had enormous influence on VATICAN COUNCIL II. Noted Jesuit paleontologist PIERRE TEILHARD DE CHARDIN wrote *The Phenomenon of Man* (1959) and *The Divine Milieu* (1965), which offered a mystical vision of the evolution of consciousness and its relation to the universe.

Apart from their influence in education, the Jesuits helped shape the modern world through missionary work. St. FRANCIS XAVIER, one of the society's original members, traveled to Goa in India, the Maluccas in Indonesia, and eventually Japan, where he founded the first Christian church in that land. Manuel de Nóbriga went to Brazil. St. Edmund Campion (1540–81) went back to his native England to work with underground recusant Catholics. Michele Ruggieri (1543–1607) and MATTEO RICCI introduced Catholicism with a Chinese flavor to the elite mandarins of Nanjing; ROBERTO DENOBILI sought to convert the

Brahmans of India; Jacques Marquette (1637–75) explored the Great Lakes and the Mississippi with Pierre Jolliet in 1673; and EUSEBIO FRANCISCO KINO, beginning in 1681, established a series of missions in the Sonoran desert, including the famous Mission San Xavier del Bac near Tucson, Arizona. Jesuits have left their missionary footprints throughout the entire world. The movie *The Mission* (1986) featured their missionary work among the Guanari in Brazil.

Another area in which Jesuits seek to fulfill their original charter is conducting retreats for Catholics in various parts of the world, at which the model of the *Spiritual Exercises* is adapted to lay circumstances. Today Protestants and others often attend these retreats. Jesuits also serve in diocesan parishes.

Often in its long history the society has found itself entangled in controversy At the height of the Counter-Reformation Pope PAUL V intervened to try to stifle a bitter argument between the Jesuits, who were accused of FREE-WILL Pelagianism, and their Dominican opponents, who were accused of deterministic Calvinism, to no avail. Later Jansenists attacked Jesuit moral theologians for alleged moral casuistry (*see* JANSENISM). Jesuit INCULTURATION practices in China, including use of native language and dress in the LITURGY and veneration of ancestors, sparked opposition from Dominicans and Franciscans coming from the Philippines in the 17th century, ending with the condemnation of the Chinese rites by Benedict XIV (r. 1740–58) in 1742. Political intrigue motivated Louis XV to expel the Jesuits from FRANCE in 1764. At the urging of the sovereigns of France, SPAIN, and Portugal, Clement XIV suppressed the society in 1773, but members continued to function under the protection of Frederick II of Prussia and Catherine the Great of Russia. Missions also thrived in GREAT BRITAIN and Maryland. Pius VII (r. 1800–23) lifted the ban in the bull *Solicitudo ecclesiarum* in 1814.

Today Jesuits remain the most numerous Catholic religious community in the world, with more than 20,000 members. They publish some of the most prestigious Catholic journals, including *Biblica, Civiltà Cattolica*, and *Theological Studies*.

Further reading: Manfred Bartel, *The Jesuits* (New York: Morrow, 1984); Peter McDonnough, *Men Astutely Trained* (Boston: Free Press, 1992); John W. O'Malley, *The First Jesuits* (Cambridge, Mass.: Harvard University Press, 1992).

Jewish-Catholic relations

The relations between Jews and CHRISTIANS in general and Catholics in particular can be divided between the negative and the positive. Although it is somewhat false to separate the two aspects, the negative relations are covered under the entry ANTI-SEMITISM and the positive are dealt with under this heading.

By way of introduction, it is always important to note that Christianity first emerged from the matrix of first-century Judaism. The first followers of Jesus did not think of themselves but as Jews. The term *Christian* was not used until around 95 and then probably as a pejorative term of abuse (Acts 11:26). The Jesus-followers' BIBLE was the Hebrew Bible; they followed the Torah and its moral prescriptions; they observed the kosher rules; and they saw themselves as the continuation of the original Covenant God made with the Israelites. When Christian became predominantly Gentile in the second century, a differentiation started to set in until the first real marks of division were fixed when CONSTANTINE I THE GREAT started to favor Christianity as Christianity.

Yet under the stress of Gnosticism and Marcionism, second- and third-century Christians were forced to acknowledge their Jewish roots in their retention of the Septuagint version of the Hebrew Scriptures in their CANON OF SCRIPTURE. The Christian theology of CREATION, the FALL, and REDEMPTION in history is almost totally dependent on texts of the first Covenant. Some theologians, like IRENAEUS OF LYONS, incorporated the Jewish

Scriptures into the Christian framework under a rubric of *tota scriptura* ("all scripture"), which recounts God's continuous action throughout all sacred history in a series of increasingly redemptive covenants. Others incorporated the Jewish Scriptures on the model of TYPOLOGY, seeing events in the Old Testament as promises, foreshadowing or images of their fulfillments, types, and realities in the New Testament. (This model, however, had the tendency to subordinate the Old to the New in a kind of supercessionism under which the salvation promised to the Jews was cancelled and transferred to the "true Israel," that is, the Christians, but it sill retained the necessity of incorporating the Jewish Scripture into the Christian framework.)

After Constantine, however, there followed the lamentable history of the marginalization, ghettoization, and persecution of Jews beginning in the MIDDLE AGES and culminating in the Holocaust during World War II. This history was marked by fear, ignorance, contempt, hatred, and violence.

Beginning earlier but culminating in VATICAN COUNCIL II, the Catholic Church solemnly and theologically changed its understanding of its relationship to Judaism as a religion and to Jews as a people. The Vatican II participants, referring to the APOSTLE PAUL's famous lines in Romans 9–11, wrote that the original Covenant and promises given to the Israelites remain valid today in *Lumen Gentium* 16, the Dogmatic Constitution on the Church. In *Nostra Aetate* 4, the Declaration of the Relation of the Church to Non-Christian Religions, the council fathers also acknowledged "the bond that spiritually ties the people of the New Covenant to Abraham's stock." *Nostra Aetate* 4 abides as the innovative key text and reference point for all future developments in Jewish and Catholic relations. The now celebrated paragraph makes no reference to prior patristic, papal, or conciliar statements, but takes the Catholic Church back to the primal biblical text of Paul's Epistle to the Romans 9–11, where he states

unequivocally that Israel, the name God gave to Jacob and his descendants (Gen. 32:28), is still a part of the Covenant and that, mysteriously, "all Israel will be saved" (11:26).

This theological shift had immediate organizational effects. In 1966 Pope PAUL VI established the Vatican Office for Catholic-Jewish Relations under the Secretariat for Promoting Christian Unity. The former was headed by Fr. Cornelius Rijk and the latter by Cardinal Augustin Bea (1881–1968), two pioneers in ECUMENISM and interreligious dialogue. The office was later replaced by the Vatican Commission for Religious Relations with the Jews in 1974, under the presidency of Cardinal Joannes Willebrands (1909–2006). The commission then issued the Guidelines for and Suggestions for Implementing the Conciliar Declaration *Nostra Aetate* 4. Meanwhile, Catholic CLERGY and laypeople became fully engaged participants in interreligious dialogue through such forums as the National Conference of Christians and Jews (1928).

Ten years later the Catholic-Jewish commission published Notes on the Correct Way to Present Jews and Judaism in Preaching and Catechesis (June 24, 1985), which dealt with such topics as Judaism in Catholic religious teaching, the proper relation of the Old and New Testaments, Christianity's roots in Judaism, Jews in the New Testament, and Christian history.

In the United States and other countries the seed planted at Vatican II bore fruit in new agencies such as the United States Bishops Conference Secretariat for Catholic Jewish Relations, established in 1967. The American secretariat fostered Jewish-Catholic dialogue and other exchanges throughout the United States. The United States Catholic Conference also issued its own guidelines, such as Criteria for the Evaluation of Dramatizations of the Passion (1988), which was meant to strip American derivatives of the medieval Passion Play of Oberammergau in GERMANY from its virulently anti-Semitic portrayal of Jews. It also produced many curricular guidelines on the implementation of *Nostra Aetate* 4, including suggested guidelines on dealing with the Holocaust (the Shoah) and more. Many of these projects have been cosponsored by the Anti-Defamation League. Key facilitators of many of these projects were Dr. Eugene J. Fisher, longtime director of the Section for Catholic-Jewish Relations, and Rabbi Leon Klenicki, director of Interfaith for the Anti-Defamation League. The secretariat cooperates closely with the National Association of Diocesan Ecumenical Officers.

On other fronts, many Catholic theologians independently entered into open-hearted dialogue with their Jewish counterparts before, during, and after Vatican II. Not a few have been deeply shaped by the theologies of Martin Buber (1878–1965) and Rabbi Abraham Joshua Heschel (1907–72). Jewish and Catholic biblical scholars have come to work together on the Dead Sea Scrolls of QUMRAN and even the deep background of the texts of the New Testament itself, the authors of which understood themselves to be Jews and not "Christians."

Immediately after his election as pope JOHN PAUL II took giant steps toward closer relations between Catholics and Jews. He was the only modern pope who grew up with close Jewish friends. He met in 1986 with Elio Toaff (1915–   ) the chief rabbi of Rome, whom he addressed as "elder brother" in the faith. Then in 1993 he began diplomatic relations with Israel in the Fundamental Agreement of the Holy See with the State of Israel. The relations were fully normalized in 2004. John Paul constantly referred to *Nostra Aetate* as "an expression of faith" and "an inspiration of the Holy Spirit." Cardinal Walter Kasper (1933–   ), current president of the Commission for Religious Relations with Jews, has stated that *Nostra Aetate* has brought about "an astonishing transformation" in the Catholic Church's self-understanding of its relation to Judaism.

Certain flash points remain between Catholics and Jews, thorniest of which is the question of Catholics targeting Jews for conversion. In 2002 the United States Conference of Catholic Bishops

and the National Council of Synagogues published a joint document, *Reflections on Covenant and Mission* (August 12), in which the Roman Catholics stated that "campaigns that target Jews for conversion to Christianity are no longer theologically acceptable in the Catholic Church." This statement brought immediate relief to Jews and immediate consternation to traditional Catholics. Then Cardinal Avery Dulles stepped into the fray by saying that it is "an open question whether the Old Covenant remains in force today" ("The Covenant with Israel"). In an earlier article, "Covenant and Mission," Dulles cited the many passages in the epistle to the Hebrews in which the author of that non-Pauline work claims that CHRIST is the high priest of a new and better Covenant (8:6) that "abolishes the first in order to establish the second" (10:9). The question then reduces to the decision whether Romans 9–11, the foundation of *Nostra Aetate* 4, is more authoritative than the later text of Hebrews, which manifests the signs of typological supercessionism and, perhaps, of polemical anti-Judaism. Catholics have not yet fully made that decision.

Further reading: All the Vatican and United States Conference of Catholic Bishops statements and guidelines cited above can be found online; Philip A. Cunningham, *Education for Shalom: Religion, Textbooks and the Enhancement of the Catholic and Jewish Relationship* (Collegeville, Minn.: Liturgical Press, 1995); Avery Dulles "Covenant and Mission," *America* (October 14, 2002); ———, "The Covenant with Israel," *First Things* (November 2005) 157:16–21; Eugene J. Fisher and Leon Klenicki, eds., *A New Millennium: From Dialogue to Reconciliation* (New York: Anti-Defamation League, 2000); ———, *Spiritual Pilgrimage: Texts on Jews and Judaism 1979–1995 by John Paul II* (New York: Crossroad, 1995).

Jewish Christianity

The first CHRISTIANS were Jews, and Christianity operated during its first decades as a way within JUDAISM. As the church separated from the Jewish community to become a different religion, the membership became overwhelmingly Gentile. However, a minority of people of Jewish heritage remained in the church, in part due to the Christian evangelists who used the synagogue as an initial preaching base. The vegetarian but Torah-observing Ebionite sect, which held Jesus to be a mere human and not God, survived into the third century in the Transjordan.

Over the centuries, the Jewish community remained a visible presence within the larger Christian community and a source of converts—whether peaceful or forced. Forced conversions were most widespread and had the worst consequences in SPAIN. At the end of the 15th century the INQUISITION pursued so-called secret Jews, who had formally converted (Lat. *conversos*) but were believed to be continuing to practice their Jewish faith in private. ST. TERESA OF ÁVILA, who would eventually emerge as a DOCTOR OF THE CHURCH, was the daughter of a Christian family of Jewish origin that had been persecuted as secret Jews.

In the modern world, individual Jews have converted to Roman Catholicism and subsequently launched efforts to convert their ethnic brothers and sisters. In 1842, Alphonse Ratisbone (1814–84), a Jew whose brother Theodore had converted to Christianity and become a priest, had a vision of the Virgin Mary. As a result, the brothers founded the Congregation of Notre Dame de Sion, which went on to establish convents internationally; its members were devoted to converting Jews (and to a lesser extent, Muslims).

The most prominent Jewish convert to Catholicism in the 20th century was Edith Stein (St. Theresa Benedicta of the Cross) (1891–1942). She was attracted to Christianity as a graduate student under philosopher Edmund Husserl (1859–1938) at the University of Freiburg. In 1922 she formally converted and took immediate steps to join the CARMELITES. She later taught at the college level and became a popular speaker throughout Europe. To protect her from the Nazis, her superiors moved her to Holland in the 1930s, where

the SS caught up with her during the war. She was arrested, sent to Auschwitz, and killed in 1942. Pope JOHN PAUL II canonized her in 1998.

In the years after World War II, support for efforts to evangelize Jews declined markedly. This changing perspective can be seen in the Edith Stein Guild, formed in 1955, which had among its goals providing support for Hebrew Christians, but not the conversion of Jews. The guild also supported the canonization of Stein.

VATICAN COUNCIL II changed the church's perspective relative to the Jewish community and in effect withdrew support for evangelization activities that specifically targeted the Jewish community. While the church welcomes Jewish converts, it has turned its primary attention to dialogue with the Jewish community and attempts to address the harm done to Jews in the past by Christians individually and collectively. The dictates of Vatican II altered the program of the Congregation of Notre Dame de Sion completely and helped reshape the program of newer groups such as the Association of Hebrew Catholics, which works to help Jewish Christians in the Holy Land continue to live as cultural Israelis.

Dissenting from the perspective of Vatican II is the Remnant of Israel, founded in 1977 by Fr. Arthur B. Klyber (1900–99), a Redemptorist who had been active in Jewish evangelism since his conversion in the 1920s. Remnant of Israel is the major organization based in the Catholic Church that primarily seeks the conversion of Jews to Christianity.

See also ANTI-SEMITISM.

Further reading: Clair Huchet Bishop, *How Catholics Look at Jews* (New York: Paulist, 1974); David Goldstein, *Autobiography of a Campaigner for Christ* (Boston: Catholic Campaigners for Christ, n.d.); Waltraud Herbstrith, *Edith Stein: A Biography,* tr. by Bernard Bonowitz. (San Francisco: Ignatius, 1992); Arthur B. Klyber, *Once A Jew* (Chicago: St. Alphonsus Rectory, 1973); Karl Pruter, *Jewish Christians in the United States* (New York: Garland, 1987).

Joachim and Anne, Sts. *parents of Mary, mother of Jesus*

According to later tradition, Anne and Joachim, whose names are not mentioned in the New Testament, were the parents of MARY OF NAZARETH, the mother of Jesus. In the West their joint feast day is, since 1969, July 26, and in the East it is celebrated on September 9.

The legend of the aged parents to whom an angel promises the birth of Mary appears initially in the second-century pseudepigraphal writing the *Protevangelium of James.* The narrative goes on to tell of Mary's presentation in the Temple at age 3, her weaving of the curtain of the Temple, her betrothal to JOSEPH OF NAZARETH, a widower with children, and the Virgin Birth of Jesus in a cave, with a midwife present. The *Protevangelium* served as the source for the devotion to Anne and Joachim in medieval piety and their frequent depiction in art as well as the THEOLOGY of Mary. Their tombs are reputed to be in Jerusalem. Devotion to St. Anne increased proportionately to devotion to the Virgin in the MIDDLE AGES. LEONARDO DA VINCI painted a famous Madonna and Child with St. Anne. Martin Luther (1483–1546) railed against this noncanonical devotion during the PROTESTANT REFORMATION. The shrine of St. Anne-de-Beaupré (fd. 1658) near Quebec City, Quebec, Canada, is the earliest pilgrimage shrine in NORTH AMERICA.

Further reading: E. W. A. Budge, *Legends of Our Lady the Perpetual Virgin and Her Mother Hanna* (London: Medici Society, 1922; rpt.: London: Oxford University Press, 1933); R. F. Hock, *The Infancy Gospels of James and Thomas* (Santa Rosa, Calif.: Polebridge, 1995); G. Schiller, *Iconography of Christian Art* (Greenwich: New York Graphic Society, 1971).

Joachim of Fiore (c. 1135–1202) *abbot and apocalyptic writer*

Joachim of Fiore, one of the most important apocalyptic writers of the medieval era, was born in Calabria in southern ITALY. He is best known for his interpretation of the Book of Revelation, which, he believed, prophesied the events of his own era (*see* APOCALYPSE). He became quite famous as a writer and an adviser of popes and rulers, some of whom he visited, while others came to see him in his isolated monastic home in Calabria.

Raised in relative wealth, as a young man he briefly served as a court official in the Norman kingdom of Sicily. After a religious enlightenment he traveled to the Holy Land. Upon his return he lived as a hermit and then joined the CISTERCIAN Order. He spent much of the following years trying in vain to understand the opaque symbolism of the Book of Revelation. His search was rewarded one Easter morning, he claimed, when he experienced a spiritual illumination on the text. Confident that he now understood Revelation and its relationship to the other biblical books, he began writing his commentary.

His basic insight was of the three stages of history, grounded in a theological understanding of the TRINITY. GOD'S threefold nature was analogous to history's division into three eras—that of the Old Testament (the time of the Father, married priest), the New Testament (the time of the Son, celebate priests), and a coming third era associated with the HOLY SPIRIT (MONKS). From his reading of history, he concluded that the Antichrist was about to appear; the disruption of history he introduces would be followed by the next era of the church's earthly existence, a new golden age of the Holy Spirit. According to Joachim's calculations, the first era consisted of 42 generations, while at most two generations (or 60 years) remained to the era of the Son, which would be followed by the Antichrist and his persecution of the church.

In his apocalyptic view history is dictated by God rather than by the progress of human society. Joachim did not advocate, as did many others after him, opposing the visible forces of EVIL. God would defeat the forces of the Antichrist. Joachim's interpretation of the Book of Revelation and other apocalyptic passages in the Bible differ significantly from the dominant view of the Catholic Church since the fifth century. The church had rejected any attempt to see Revelation as real history and use it as a tool for prophecy.

Joachim published his views in three primary texts, *Liber Concordiae Novi ac Veteris Testamenti*, *Expositio in Apocalipsim*, and *Psalterium Decem Cordarum*, which were produced with stunning illuminations. As his fame grew in the decades after his death, in 1202 the church began to take notice and examine his ideas. In 1215, Lateran Council IV condemned his understanding of the Trinity, a version of what is termed modalism, in which the persons are not seen as eternal and essential to GOD's internal being. However, by the middle of the century a Joachimist faction had emerged among the Franciscans ORDER. Called Spirituals, these Franciscans taught that at the beginning of the 13th century the spirit of life had departed from the BIBLE, to be superseded by Joachim's three books. The Joachimists also predicted that the celibate priesthood would soon cease to exist in favor of monks, filled with the Spirit.

The ideas of these Joachimists were condemned in several steps in the 1250s, but the passing of the year 1260 without the visible changes they had predicted was another blow to the legitimacy of their teachings. Although Joachim's writings and ideas faded away soon after, his apocalyptical approach to history has been periodically rediscovered. Many have claimed that Georg F. W. Hegel's philosophy of history is Joachimite.

Further reading: Bernard McGinn, ed. and tr., *Apocalyptic Spirituality: Treatises and Letters of Lactantius, Adso of Montier-en-Dur, Joachim of Fiore, the Franciscan Spirituals, Savonarola.* (New York: Paulist, 1979); Marjorie Reeves, *Joachim of Fiore and the Prophetic Future* (New York: Harper Torchbooks, 1977); Delno C. West and Sandra Zimdars-Swartz, *Joachim of Fiore: A Study in Spiritual Perception and History* (Bloomington: Indiana University Press, 1983).

Joan, "Pope"

During the MIDDLE AGES a story started circulating throughout Europe that following the death of Pope Leo IV (r. 847–55) on July 17, 855, a woman had been elected pope. In fact, there had been much controversy surrounding the choice of successor, lending credence to the tale. Pope Benedict III (r. 855–58) was at first chosen, but the emperors Lothaire (795–855) and Louis II (822–875) supported an alternate candidate, an excommunicated cardinal named Anastasius. Benedict was formally crowned only in October 855.

Proponents of the Pope Joan story claim that Leo had actually died in 853 and that "Joan" served in his place for two years. She was reputedly a learned woman who disguised herself, went to Rome, and as John Anglicus had a notable career as a cleric. John/Joan was in the right place when Leo died and emerged as the popular candidate. However, during her second year in office, according to the legend, she became pregnant and during a papal procession went into labor and gave birth. She was subsequently sequestered, removed from office, and disappeared from history. The events of her reign were then ascribed to Leo, and the date of his death altered accordingly.

The story circulated into the 17th century, but it has since been largely put to rest by historians who have been unable to find any contemporary records (the first texts of the story are from the 13th century). Today Catholic scholars treat it as a fable. Protestants gave some credence to the story, though it was never a large part of their heated polemics against Catholicism. The story was given new life in the late 20th century by some feminists, who see the story as an argument for female priests and others who see it as simply a means of defaming the Catholic Church.

Further reading: Donna Woolcross Cross, *Pope Joan: A Novel* (New York: Ballantine, 1996); Emmanuel Royidis, *Pope Joan: A Romantic Biography* (London: Verschoyle, 1954); Peter Stanford, *Legend of Pope Joan: In Search of the Truth* (New York: Berkley, 2000).

Joan of Arc, St. (1412–1431) *French visionary and military leader*

Joan of Arc is one of the national heroes of FRANCE and a Catholic saint. Answering a religious call at the age of 17, she commanded the French royal army that helped drive the English out of FRANCE. She was convicted of HERESY and burned at the stake. In 1920 she was canonized. Her feast day is May 30.

Joan was born in Domrémy, Champagne, to a peasant family during the Hundred Years War (1337–1453). At a young age she began receiving supernatural visitations from St. MICHAEL THE ARCHANGEL, St. Catherine, and St. Margaret. They told her to save France from the English and to find the true king of France. In 1429 she convinced Charles VII (1403–61) of her sincerity, and he agreed to let her lead the army at Orléans. After rescuing the city she convinced Charles VII to march on Reims for his coronation. Dressed in armor and carrying a white banner with an image of GOD, two angels on either side, and the words *Jesus* and *Mary*, she led the troops to victory.

After several successful military campaigns, Joan was taken prisoner on May 24, 1430, near Compiègne. She was sold to the English, who tried her for heresy and witchcraft. The court declared her visions demonic, and she was executed on May 30, 1431. In 1456 she was retried and declared innocent and a martyr by Pope Callistus III (r. 1455–58). She is the second patron of France. Irish dramatist George Bernard Shaw (1856–1950) wrote an admiring play about her, *Saint Joan* (1923).

Further reading: Evelyn Everett-Green, *Called of Her Country: The Story of Joan of Arc* (London: S. H. Bousfield, 1891); Deborah A. Fraioli, *Joan of Arc and the Hundred Years War* (Westport, Conn.: Greenwood, 2005); Siobhan Nash-Marshall, *Joan of Arc: A Spiritual Biography* (New York: Crossroad, 1999); Daniel Rankin, trans., *The First Biography of Joan of Arc; With a Chronicle Record of a Contemporary Account* (Pittsburgh: University of Pittsburgh Press, 1964).

John XXIII, Bl. (1881–1963) *pope*

John XXIII was a hugely influential pope who struggled to reform the Roman Catholic Church and give it a more modern face. He summoned VATICAN COUNCIL II and sought to address all issues in the church, including controversial matters such as priestly celibacy, artificial birth control, and Jewish-Christian relations.

Several historic popes and BISHOPS served as exemplars for John XXIII, including GREGORY I (590–604), a pastoral pope who referred to himself as "servant of the servants of God" and sent Augustine of Canterbury to convert England, and CHARLES BORROMEO, scion of the Medici, cardinal archbishop of Milan, and Catholic reformer, who spent his personal wealth caring for the poor of his diocese. More immediately John XXIII found models in LEO XIII, who issued *Rerun Novarum*, the first encyclical to address modern socio-economic problems, Giacomo Maria Radini-Tedeschi (1857–1914), the bishop of Bergamo under whom the future pope first served, and Benedict XV (r. 1914–22), who reined in the antimodernist faction in the Vatican.

Born Angelo Giuseppe Roncalli to a peasant family in Sotto il Monte in Lombardy, he always knew he would be a priest. He never lost touch

Bas-relief of John XXIII and cardinals by Italian sculptor Giacomo Manzù, Door of Death, St. Peter's Basilica (Vatican City) *(Scala/Art Resource, NY)*

with the strong piety and direct simplicity of his ancestors and relatives. Early on he was sent to study in Rome but got drafted into the army instead. The raucous ways of army life shocked him, but he mellowed when he later served as a Walt Whitmanesque orderly in World War I. His war experience led him to become a champion of peacemaking the rest of his life.

The student Angelo was always excited by ideas and not afraid of the modern world and its scientific orientation. In his diaries he criticized St. PIUS X for being afraid of new things. He served as secretary to the bishop of Bergamo and professor of church history before being called to Rome to serve as a minor official in the Congregation for Missions. Against Vatican policy, he supported the Popular Party of Fr. Luigi Sturzo (1871–1959), the only political figure able to stand up to Mussolini. In this struggle he befriended Giovanni Battista Montini, who was to succeed him as Pope as PAUL VI. True patriotism, he preached, was not nationalism but brotherly love.

In 1925 Roncalli's life took a fateful turn. He was appointed apostolic nuncio to Bulgaria with the rank of ARCHBISHOP. As bishop he took the motto *Obedientia et Pax,* in direct challenge to the Fascist motto *Credire, obedire, combattere* ("Believe, obey, fight"). This post removed him from Vatican intrigues and put him into direct, warm contact with Eastern Orthodox Christians and Muslims. From this distance Roncalli could observe dispassionately the Vatican's fateful CONCORDATs with Mussolini and later Hitler. He became a neighbor to the small Bulgarian contingent of Roman and Uniate Catholics, often incurring the displeasure of PIUS XI for reaching beyond his diplomatic brief.

Nine years later Roncalli was appointed apostolic delegate to Greece and Turkey and was stationed in the great city of Istanbul, where he developed a close relationship with the Eastern Orthodox patriarch. While the Vatican was losing its bearings during the war, Angelo, calling in his diplomatic cards, helped to funnel thousands of Jews out of eastern Europe to the Holy Land by issuing certificates of immigration.

As the war ended, Roncalli was appointed nuncio to FRANCE, the most desirable assignment in the Vatican diplomatic portfolio. Quietly he engaged leading French thinkers and theologians—YVES CONGAR, JACQUES MARITAIN, HENRI DE LUBAC, and Cardinal Emmanuel Célestin Suhard (1874–1949)—while the Vatican was reviving its antimodernist propaganda, with French intellectuals as the target.

In 1953 Roncalli was appointed cardinal archbishop of Venice. He came back to Italy expecting to end his life in this post. He visited every parish and set about finding employment for jobless Italians. He worked with everyone, believer and nonbeliever, socialist and communist. He was a reconciler, not a divider. Upon PIUS XII's death in 1958, Roncalli experienced a radical turn of fate when the conclave of cardinals elected him pope as a compromise candidate. He took the name John XXIII. The Vatican cardinals were in for a big surprise. He broke precedents: travelling outside the Vatican, jostling with ordinary people, and removing the hated phrase "perfidious Jews" from Holy Week prayers. His encyclical *Mater et Magistra* (May 15, 1961) addressed the problems of the arms race and economic disparity among the nations.

In 1959 John XXIII issued the call for VATICAN COUNCIL II at St. Paul's Outside the Walls, a church symbolically outside the original precincts of Rome. Over the opposition of the old guard, under Cardinal Ottaviani (1890–1979), the pope allowed the council participants to deliberate on all topics. Before Vatican II was completed, John XXIII died in 1963. His signature encyclical was PACEM IN TERRIS, issued in the year of his death.

Further reading: Jean-Yves Calvez, *The Social Thought of John XXIII: Mater et Magistra* (Chicago: Regnery, 1965); E. E. Y. Hales, *Pope John and His Revolution* (Garden City, N.Y.: Doubleday, 1965); Peter Hebblethwaite, *Pope John XXIII: Shepherd of the Modern World* (Garden

City, N.Y.: Doubleday, 1985); Pope John XXIII, *Journal of a Soul* (New York: McGraw-Hill, 1965); Peter J. Riga, *John XXIII and the City of Man.* (Westminster, Md.: Newman, 1966).

John Chrysostom (c. 347–407) *theologian and doctor of the church*

John was a popular preacher noted for his literal interpretations of Scripture and his stress on asceticism. After he died he was named Chrysostom, Greek for "Golden Mouthed." His feast day is September 13 in the West and November 13 in the East.

Born into a noble family in Antioch, he became an ascetic and lived as a hermit before becoming a deacon in 381 and a priest in 386. He quickly became known for his powerful and practical homilies on various biblical books. He was an opponent of allegorical interpretation. In his homilies *Against Judaizing Christians* he used the phrase *Christ-killers,* which became a club to persecute Jews in the MIDDLE AGES (*see* ANTI-SEMITISM).

In 398 he reluctantly agreed to become BISHOP of CONSTANTINOPLE. He quickly made enemies by attempting to reform the corrupt court and CLERGY and by opposing extravagant wealth. The Patriarch Theophilus of Alexandria (r. 385–412), who sought control over Constantinople, convened the Synod of Oak in 403 and condemned John on 29 charges, including a trumped-up charge of heresy and, more seriously, a charge of insulting the empress. Much to the people's anger and the protests of Pope Innocent I (r. 402–407), John was deposed. He was exiled to Pontus but died before he reached it because of a grueling journey on foot.

Further reading: F. H. Chase, *Chrysostom: A Study in the History of Biblical Interpretation* (London: George Bell, 1887); Dolores Greeley, *The Church as "Body of Christ" According to the Teaching of Saint John Chrysostom* (Notre Dame: Department of Theology, 1977); J. N. D. Kelly, *Golden Mouth: The Story of John Chrysostom, Ascetic, Preacher, Bishop* (Ithaca, N.Y.: Cornell University Press, 1995); W. R. W. Stephens, *Saint John Chrysostom, His Life and Times* (London: J. Murray, 1883).

John Fisher, St. (1460–1535) *bishop and martyr*

Fisher was born in Beverley, Yorkshire, England (*see* GREAT BRITAIN). He studied at Cambridge, becoming ordained in 1491 and receiving a doctorate of divinity in 1501. A major theologian of his time, he became bishop of Rochester (1504) and chancellor of Cambridge (1514). He opposed HENRY VIII's attempt to annul his marriage to Catherine of Aragon (1485–1536). Together with St. THOMAS MORE, Fisher was executed by Henry in 1534. Both were beatified in 1886 by LEO XIII and canonized in 1935 by PIUS XI. They share their feast day, June 22.

Fisher's major theological work was his *Confutatio* (1523), a Latin apologia to help his fellow church leaders refute the growing Lutheran challenge. He also wrote a treatise defending the Catholic understanding of the EUCHARIST against Johann Oecolampadius (1482–1531) of Basel. As chancellor of Cambridge, Fisher was responsible for luring DESIDERIUS ERASMUS to the school. He also became close friends with Sir Thomas More, Henry VIII's lord chancellor, who became high steward of the university in 1525. Like More, he would be caught up in the marital problems of the British king. In 1527 he was called on to rule on the status of Henry's marriage to Catherine of Aragon. He argued that they were, in fact, legally married, and thus Henry could not put her aside and remarry.

In 1534 Henry forced the Act of Succession through Parliament, which declared his marriage to Catherine null and void and legitimized his marriage to Anne Boleyn (c. 1501/1507–36). Fisher and More refused to take the oath accepting the act, an oath that implicitly denied papal authority. On April 17, 1534, Fisher and More were confined in the Tower of London.

While he was in confinement, Pope Paul III (r. 1534–49) named Fisher a cardinal, an act that infuriated Henry. Henry now pressed the recently passed Statute on Treason, which among other provisions made refusal to recognize him as head of the Church of England an act of treason. Neither Fisher nor More could acknowledge Henry's assumed position since to do so would deny papal authority. Condemned at a trial on June 17, 1535, Fisher was executed a week later. His severed head was put on display on London Bridge and subsequently thrown into the Thames. His body and that of More lie buried in the church of St. Peter in the Tower of London.

Further reading: John Coulson, ed., *The Saints: A Concise Biographical Dictionary.* (New York: Hawthorn, 1960); Dowling, Maria, *Fisher of Men: A Life of John Fisher, 1469–1535* (New York: St. Martin's, 1999); Richard Rex, *The Theology of John Fisher* (Cambridge, Cambridge University Press, 1991); Edward Surtz, ed., *The Works and Days of John Fisher: An Introduction to the Position of St. John Fisher (1469–1535), Bishop of Rochester, in the English Renaissance and Reformation* (Cambridge, Mass.: Harvard University Press, 1967).

John of Damascus, St. (c. 675–c. 749)
theologian and doctor of the church

A MONK and a powerful preacher, John became known as a strong defender of ICONS during the Iconoclastic Controversy. His feast day, formerly March 27, is now December 4.

Little is known about his life, and the sources that exist conflict with one another. He was born in Damascus, became the chief financial officer to the Ummayad caliph Abdul Malek (r. 685–705), and served as representative of the CHRISTIANS to the caliph. He apparently lived in harmony with Islam, which he later saw as a Christian HERESY.

At the age of 23 he began to study under the Sicilian monk Cosmas, and he excelled in his studies. During the Iconoclastic Controversy he wrote several treatises in defense of images (*see*

ICON). His writings upset the Byzantine emperor, Leo III the Isaurian (r. 717–41), who managed to turn the caliph against him. He retired to a MONASTERY near Jerusalem and became a monk.

There he continued his theological writings, including his most important work, *Fount of Wisdom*. He also wrote *An Exact Exposition of the Orthodox Faith,* a detailed presentation of the main Christian doctrines. According to his biographer, he died in 749. He is sometimes referred to as the last of the church fathers. In 1890 Pope LEO XIII proclaimed him a DOCTOR OF THE CHURCH.

Further reading: Andrew Louth, *St. John Damascene: Tradition and Originality in Byzantine Theology* (Oxford: Oxford University Press, 2002); Joseph Hirst Lupton, *St. John of Damascus* (London: S.P.C.K., 1882); Valentine Albert Mitchel, *The Mariology of Saint John Damascene* (Turnhout: Henri Proost, 1930); Daniel J. Sahas, *John of Damascus on Islam: The "Heresy of the Ishmaelites"* (Leiden: Brill, 1972); Nomikos Michael Vaporis, ed., *Three Byzantine Sacred Poets: Studies of Saint Romanos Melodos, Saint John of Damascus, Saint Symeon the New Theologian* (Brookline, Mass.: Hellenic College Press, 1979).

John of Monte Corvino (c. 1247–1328)
pioneer Franciscan missionary to China

John of Monte Corvino was a Franciscan missionary to China in the 13th and 14th centuries, serving as BISHOP for the Khanbaliq (Beijing) region in 1313. John was born in southern ITALY. He had already served as a soldier, a magistrate, and a physician when at 26 he decided to join the FRANCISCAN ORDER. In the 1280s he traveled to Armenia and Persia as part of a Franciscan mission. On his return to Rome in 1289 he brought with him an official delegation from King Hethum II of Armenia (r. 1289–1307), which included a bishop of the Nestorian Church who had been born in Khanbaliq (Beijing).

With letters of introduction from the pope, John made his way across India to China, arriving shortly after the DEATH of Kubla Khan in 1294. He was received the following year by Kubla Khan's successor and grandson, Timur (1336–1405, known in the West as Tamerlane) in Khanbaliq. Timur gave him permission to settle in the area and allowed him to preach, and he remained there the rest of his life. John built two churches in Khanbaliq and frequently sent letters back to Rome describing his work. In 1307, based on the letters, the pope named John the ARCHBISHOP of Khanbaliq. He then consecrated several of John's brothers as bishops and sent them to China both to consecrate John (in 1313) and to assist him in growing the church.

John's work did not survive him for long. Most of his converts were from the Mongol ruling class, which was pushed aside by the middle of the 14th century. Christianity, (both Catholic and Nestorian), was destroyed in the process.

Further reading: Samuel H. Moffatt, *A History of Christianity in Asia,* vol. 1 (San Francisco: HarperSanFrancisco, 1992); Arthur Christopher, Moule, *Christians in China Before the Year 1550* (London: S.P.C.K., 1930).

John of the Cross, St. (1542–1591) *mystic and Carmelite reformer*

St. John of the Cross, one of the most important CHRISTIAN mystics and mystical thinkers, was born into a wealthy merchant family in Fontiveros, Spain, as Juan de Yepes y Alvarez. He was canonized by Benedict XIII (r. 1724–30) and declared a DOCTOR OF THE CHURCH in 1926 by Benedict XV. His feast day is December 14.

His encounter with the plague as a hospital worker led him to study with the JESUITS around 1560, but three years later he chose to join the CARMELITES. He later attended the University of Salamanca, where he prepared for his ordination in 1567. As a Carmelite he met St. TERESA OF ÁVILA, another Carmelite and mystic. John joined with Teresa in her attempt to reform the order as part of the COUNTER-REFORMATION in Spain. She called for a return to its austere beginnings as a more intense form of the monastic life. As part of their discipline, following the lead of Teresa, he and the small group of MONKs who gathered around him decided to manifest their commitment to poverty by going barefooted. This practice would become a distinguishing feature of the movement that he and Teresa were leading, and their movement would be referred to as the "Discalced," or "shoeless," Carmelites. He operated somewhat independently until 1572, when Teresa asked him to come to Ávila as the confessor for the Carmelite convent she led. The more moderate Carmelite leadership resisted the growing reform effort, and they had him kidnapped in December 1577.

John's nine months of confinement actually proved a blessing, at least to the larger world, as it was during this time he composed many of his mystical poems, which became among his most widely read writings. After his escape he resumed leadership in the reform and authored a number of other texts describing the mystic life and his experiences. These books joined those of Teresa as some of the classic works of Christocentric mysticism. Their work helped define the nature of the mystical experience and showed clearly how it could be combined with an orthodox THEOLOGY and a life of devotion to CHRIST.

John is particularly remembered for his understanding of the dark night of the SOUL, a common experience of mystics as they seek the experience of complete union with GOD. Along the mystical path, frequently marked by ever-new realizations of divine realities, the mystic often experiences a profound and sometimes lengthy absence of the divine, a feeling of alienation and abandonment by God, made all the more miserable by the contrast with what has been lost.

John kept a low profile until 1582, when the independent status of the Discalced Carmelites was finally achieved, the same year that Teresa died. From then until his death in 1591 he took on various leadership roles within the order. His books were first published in 1619.

Further reading: Gerald Brenan, *St. John of the Cross: His Life and Poetry:* Poetry tr. Lynda Nicholson (Cambridge: Cambridge University Press, 1973); Richard P. Hardy, *John of the Cross: Man and Mystic* (Boston: Pauline, 2004); John of the Cross, *The Collected Works of St. John of the Cross,* tr. Kieran Kavanaugh and Otilio Rodriguez (New York: Doubleday, 1964); ———, *Ascent of Mount Carmel,* tr. E. Allison Peers (Garden City, N.Y.: Image, 1958); ———, *Dark Night of the Soul,* tr. E. Allison Peers. (Garden City, N.Y.: Image, 1959).

John Paul I (1912–1978) *pope*

The lengthy reign of Pope PAUL VI was followed by the very brief reign of Pope John Paul I, who in his choice of name indicated his desire to continue the thrust of VATICAN COUNCIL I and integrate the popular personas of his two immediate predecessors. He was born Albino Luciani on October 17, 1912, at Forno di Canale, ITALY. In 1928, he entered the seminary of Belluno. He completed his studies in 1935 and was ordained a priest. In 1937 he became the vice rector of the Belluno seminary, where he taught moral and dogmatic THEOLOGY, canon law, and art history. He completed his doctorate in theology at the Gregorian Pontifical University in 1947. In 1953 he was named a BISHOP of Vittorio Veneto; Pope Paul VI (r. 1963–78) promoted him to patriarch of Venice in 1969. He received his cardinal's hat in 1973 and on Paul VI's DEATH he was elected pope.

John Paul I served 33 days, one of the shortest terms ever for a pope, and he died on September 28, 1978. Those who knew him cited his humility as his most outstanding characteristic. Following his death, a number of people claimed miraculous cures, and an effort seeking his canonization was begun. His successor took the name JOHN PAUL II. John Paul I's sudden and unexpected death led to a variety of rumors and even conspiracy theories that attributed his death to other than natural causes. To date no evidence has emerged to give the conspiracy theories any credence.

Further reading: A Carmelite Nun, *John Paul I—The Smiling Pope* (Flemington: A Carmelite Nun 1985); Regina Kummer, *Albino Luciani, Papa Giovanni Paolo I: Una vita per la Chiesa* (Padua: Messaggero, 1988); *Nights of Sorrow, Days of Joy; Papal Transition: Paul VI, John Paul I, John Paul II* (Washington, D.C.: National Catholic News Service, 1978).

John Paul II (1920–2005) *pope*

Born Karol Józef Wojtyla in 1920, John Paul II was elected pope in 1978. His reign was remarkably long, allowing him to change the face of the PAPACY at the end of the 20th century.

Karol grew up in a loving but firm household in Wadnowice, Poland, a small town near Krakow. His mother died when he was nine, and his older brother, a doctor, died when he was 12. His father, a retired army officer and tailor, died in 1941 after the Nazi invasion of Poland. Karol himself had two scrapes with DEATH. He was hit by a streetcar as a boy and by a truck as a college student. As pope he would have a much closer encounter when Mehmet Ali Agca (1958–) shot him in St. Peter's Square in 1981. In 1995 members of Al Qaida plotted to assassinate the pope in Manila, but their plot was revealed the day before its execution.

Unlike any previous pope since early Christianity, Karol grew up with Jewish friends. A lifelong friend, Jerzy Kluger, later played a crucial role in such milestone events as John Paul II's diplomatic recognition of Israel, his visit with Elio Toaff (1915–), the chief rabbi of the Great Synagogue of Rome in 1986, and his respectful visit to Auschwitz. Later the pope was to address Jews as "our elder brothers."

He and his father moved to Krakow in 1938 so he could study at Jagiellonian University, where he was both a scholar and an athlete. He skied, which he continued to do as pope, hiked, kayaked, and swam with colleagues. His scholarly passions were religion, theater, and philosophy. Early on he felt called to the priesthood, and he entered an underground seminary during the Nazi occupation. To evade deportation he worked in a stone quarry and later in a chemical plant.

Wojtyla was ordained in 1946 and served as student chaplain while working on a doctorate in philosophy. Studying under the celebrated French Dominican theologian Reginald Garrigou-Lagrange (1877–1964) in Rome, he wrote his thesis on the Carmelite mystic St. JOHN OF THE CROSS. Returning to Poland, he wrote a dissertation at Lublin Catholic University on Catholic ethics and Max Scheler (1874–1928), whose early philosophy centered on value ethics.

Prior to his election as pope, his entire ecclesiastical life was spent under oppression and restriction, first by the Nazis and then by the communists. As a result, Catholicism in Poland remained far more traditional and doctrinally orthodox than in the free world. This bunker mentality provided the church with strength under pressure and provided Wojtyla in his early days with clarity and vision. In his dealings with the communists Wojtyla was later described as "tough but flexible." Asked about his relation to the communist authorities, he is said to have replied, "I am not afraid of them. They are afraid of me." When the Iron Curtain fell, another scenario began to unravel, and the pope wound up chastising even the once unanimous Polish faithful for their liberalization of divorce and abortion laws.

After his return to Poland in 1951, his rise in the Polish HIERARCHY was meteoric. He became professor of ethics and philosophy at the seminary in Krakow and Lublin. In 1958, just 12 years after ordination, Pope PIUS XII named him auxiliary bishop of Kraków. Pope PAUL VI named him ARCHBISHOP in 1964 and cardinal in 1967. Many say that the new archbishop was intelligent, affable, and engaged throughout VATICAN COUNCIL II (1963–65). He apparently made significant contributions to *Gaudium et Spes,* the Constitution on the Church in the Modern World, and on the topic of ethics and religious freedom. After Pope Paul VI removed the topics of birth con-

John Paul II holding a crozier, his cape blowing in the wind *(Foto Rzepa/WpN)*

trol and married clergy from council debate and issued his own encyclical on the former, *Humanae Vitae* (1968), Wojtyla wrote a staunch defense in *L' Osservatore Romano,* the semiofficial Vatican newspaper. Some say he even wrote the encyclical itself. This was a sign that in the aftermath of Vatican II Wojtyla was fully capable of playing the "tough" hand.

Wojtyla was not the first choice in the consistory after the new pope JOHN PAUL I's sudden death in 1978. Elected on the seventh ballot, he broke into tears, tears that often returned in the company of small children. He was the first non-Italian pope since the Dutch Adrian VI in 1523. From the balcony of St. Peter's he proclaimed he accepted out of obedience to CHRIST and the most holy Madonna. MARY OF NAZARETH was to figure heavily in his pontificate.

John Paul II was soon to put his own stamp on the PAPACY. The word that best fits that stamp is solidarity. Under that banner the pope sought to identify with the social and political aspirations of his fellow Poles under the leadership of Lech Wałęsa (1943–) as they struggled against the last oppressive remnants of communism. When he visited Poland shortly after his election in 1978, John Paul II mustered legions who helped bring the regime's hubris to its knees. Literally millions turned out to attend his EUCHARISTS and listen to his words. Soviet premier Mikhail Gorbachev (1931–   ) later acknowledged the pope's influence on the end of communism.

John Paul II made 104 pastoral visits throughout the world and encountered nearly 18 million people at his Wednesday general audiences. The pope sought solidarity with other religions of the world, especially in his call for the universal recognition of the dignity of each individual and of religious freedom. This was in keeping with many doctrinal statements of Vatican II, which hold that the one universal truth is also present in other religions. Thus, John Paul II recognized unity with Jews as "elder brothers" and Muslims as "brothers in faith under one God." He even went so far as to cite the scriptures of Hinduism and Buddhism for their sacred meaning, frightening some traditionalists in and outside the Vatican. Despite these opening ecumenical gestures, the pope never succeeded in truly advancing relations between Rome and the Eastern Orthodox, who remained distrustful of him.

Solidarity also aptly described the pope's beatification and canonization of many holy persons during his pontificate. He wanted to underscore concretely the universal bonding and sanctifying power of the church. He proclaimed 1,338 as blessed and 482 as saints. The blessed and the saints include laity, religious, and clergy. They are from all continents and include martyrs from Korea and the Congo, MAXIMILIAN KOLBE and Edith Stein, who died at Auschwitz, and KATHERINE MARY DREXEL of the United States. In 2003 the pope beatified Mother Theresa of Calcutta. Notably absent, however, was the Salvadoran martyr archbishop Oscar Romero (1917–80), murdered in his cathedral like St. THOMAS À BECKET. Romero had affirmed liberationist themes and championed another kind of solidarity with the Salvadoran peasant poor.

John Paul II was flexible to those outside the church but was capable of inflexibility within the church. For example, he wielded a heavy hand on theologians at the edge. He removed the Vatican II theologian HANS KÜNG from the Catholic faculty at Tübingen. He silenced the Franciscan liberation theologian LEONARDO BOFF, who was later pushed out of the religious life and the active priesthood.

Many theologians, priests, and laity accused the pope and his supporters in the VATICAN CURIA of betraying or seriously thwarting the evangelical reforms of Vatican II. Whereas Vatican II promised a future of collegiality and decentralization, the pope reverted to a traditional monarchical papacy. Crucially, the pope appointed many cardinals and bishops who seemed not in full sympathy with Vatican II and who in their own dioceses emulated the pope's centralized, hierarchical style.

Although the church at large was experiencing severe tests due to a lack of priests, the pope refused to discuss a married priesthood and came close to declaring that ordaining women contradicted the dogmatic teaching of the church (see HOLY ORDERS). When the pedophile scandal wounded the American church, the papacy, apart from a few words, remained aloof and reluctant to remove bishops like Cardinal Bernard Law (931–   ) of Boston, who had effectively tolerated the abuses.

The pope became noted for his crusade against abortion and euthanasia, often accusing the liberal democracies of being "cultures of death." His thinking on this issue was most clearly stated in the encyclical *Evangelium Vitae* (March 25, 1995). He was almost equally adamant against the death penalty except in the most extreme of cases.

Besides his many encyclicals, John Paul II became a prolific author during his papacy. His *Crossing the Threshold of Hope* (1994) became a worldwide best seller. In 2003 he published a book of poems, harking back to his interests as a student in Krakow. Shortly before his death he published *Memory and Identity* (2005), a memoir of his encounters as pope. Characteristically, he referred to same-sex unions as "a new ideology of evil." He also compared abortion to the

Holocaust, much to the consternation of most Jewish leaders.

In 2001 the papal physicians announced that John Paul II was suffering from Parkinson's disease. Although the disease noticeably affected his mobility and speech, the pope fulfilled his public duties until the very end. Many speculated that he might resign, but he always declared that the Lord and the Madonna called him to the papacy, and only they could ask him to give it up. Thousands of devout Catholics and young people thronged St. Peter's plaza to sing hymns and recite the joyful mysteries of the Rosary as John Paul II died on April 2, 2005. He served as pope for 26 years.

There can be little doubt that John Paul II was among the most significant world figures in the last quarter of the 20th century. His theme of solidarity, while illuminating the grand gestures of his papacy, also masked undercurrents of dissatisfaction and discontent that are sure to surface under his successor.

Further reading: Charles E. Curran and Richard A. McCormick, eds., *John Paul II and Moral Theology* (New York: Paulist, 1998); Antoni Gronowicz, *God's Broker: The Life of John Paul II* (New York: Richardson & Snyder, 1984); Robert J. Russell, William R. Stoeger, and George V. Coyne, eds., *John Paul II on Science and Religion: Reflections on the New View from Rome* (Notre Dame: University of Notre Dame Press, 1990); John Saward, *Christ Is the Answer: The Christ-Centered Teaching of Pope John Paul II* (New York: Alba, 1995); James V. Schall, *The Church, the State and Society in the Thought of John Paul II* (Chicago: Franciscan Herald, 1982); David Willey, *God's Politician: Pope John Paul II, the Catholic Church, and the New World Order* (New York: St. Martin's, 1993).

John the Baptist, St. *prophet, baptizer of Jesus*

John the Baptist is revered as a prophet in both Christianity and ISLAM; he is considered to have prepared the way for Jesus. John was the son of Zachariah, a priest of the order of Abijah, and Elizabeth, also of priestly descent (Luke 1:5). According to Luke, an angel foretold Zachariah of John's birth (Luke 1:13–20), but he did not believe and was struck mute for his doubt. He began his ministry at the age of 27, preaching a theme of repentance and the coming kingdom of GOD, and he baptized thousands in the Jordan River. He adopted the style of the Old Testament prophets, dressing in camel hair and eating locusts and wild honey (Matt. 3:4). Jesus came to John from the Galilee and was baptized by him (Matt. 3:15). John's ministry ended a short while later when Herod Agrippa (d. 44) arrested him after he denounced the marriage of Herod's brother, Phillip, to Herodias (Matt. 14:1–12). He was subsequently beheaded.

According to the Gospel of Luke, the Virgin Mary visited Elizabeth when she was pregnant with John, adding to his sanctity. The feast of his nativity is celebrated on June 24, six months prior to Christmas. He is often depicted in sheep's wool with a staff and a lamb.

Further reading: George Horne, *Considerations on the Life and Death of St. John the Baptist* (Oxford: Clarendon, 1777); Carl R. Kazmierski, *John the Baptist: Prophet and Evangelist* (Collegeville, Minn.: Liturgical Press, 1996); Charles H. H. Scobie, *John the Baptist* (London: SCM, 1964); Walter Wink, *John the Baptist in the Gospel Tradition* (London: Cambridge University Press, 1968).

Joseph of Nazareth, St. *spouse of the blessed Virgin Mary and foster-father of Jesus*

According to two of the GOSPELS (Matt. 1–2, Luke 1–2), Joseph was betrothed to Mary at the time of Jesus' birth, although both narratives emphasize her virginity. Joseph died of natural causes in the first century, before the Passion. His feast day is March 19.

Joseph was a pious Jew of Davidic descent (Matt. 1:19). He raised Jesus in his household in Nazareth for at least 12 years (Luke 2:42–51). Although he is mentioned only a few times in the

New Testament, he is often referred to in later traditions. The veneration of Joseph appears to have originated in the East, with the apocryphal "History of Joseph the Carpenter" written between the fourth and seventh centuries. In the West it developed later, and his feast day was not introduced to the Roman calendar until 1479. In 1870 Pius IX declared him Patron of the Universal Church, and in 1889 Leo XIII confirmed his preeminent sanctity next to the Blessed Virgin Mary in his encyclical *Quamquam pluries* (August 15, 1889). He is often depicted holding the child Jesus and a staff.

Further reading: Francis Lad Filas, *Joseph: The Man Closest to Jesus; The Complete Life, Theology and Devotional History of St. Joseph* (Boston: St. Paul Editions, 1962); Gerald J. Kleba, *Joseph Remembered: The Father of Jesus* (Irving, Tex.: Summit, 2000); David P. McAstocker, *The Carpenter* (Milwaukee: Bruce, 1938); Joseph Mueller, *The Fatherhood of St. Joseph* (St. Louis: Herder, 1952).

Jude, St. *one of the Twelve Apostles*

Jude is sometimes referred to as Jude Thaddaeus or Judas of James. He should not be confused with Judas Iscariot, the APOSTLE who betrayed Jesus. He was the brother of St. James the Lesser and a blood relative of Jesus. He preached in Persia and was martyred along with St. Simon. They share the same feast day, June 19 in the East, October 28 in the West. Tradition attributes the Epistle of Jude to him, and he is frequently depicted with a club, the weapon that was used to kill him.

In the late 20th century in the United States, St. Jude gained new prominence when popular actor and comedian Danny Thomas (1914–91) fulfilled a promise he made early in his life to build a shrine to St. Jude. Opening its doors in 1972, the St. Jude Children's Hospital in Memphis, Tennessee, has devoted itself to the study and treatment of catastrophic diseases in children. Jude is the patron saint of lost or improbable

causes, attributable to the fact that early CHRISTIANS were confused between Jude and Judas Iscariot, and therefore devotion to St. Jude was a lost cause.

Further reading: Hazel Fath, *A Dream Come True. The Story of St. Jude Children's Research Hospital and Alsac* (Dallas: Taylor, 1983); Mitch Finley, *Heavenly Helpers: St. Anthony and St. Jude: Amazing True Stories of Answered Prayers* (New York: Crossroad, 1994); Robert A. Orsi, *Thank You, St. Jude, Women's Devotion to the Patron Saint of Hopeless Causes* (New Haven, Conn.: Yale University Press, 1996); Liz Trotta, *Jude: A Pilgrimage to the Saint of Last Resort* (San Francisco: HarperSanFrancisco, 1998).

Julian of Eclanum (c. 386–454) *advocate of Pelagianism*

Julian (or John) of Eclanum was recognized as the most learned of the supporters of PELAGIUS. He was born on the island of Sicily and grew up in southeastern ITALY, where his father was the BISHOP of Apulia. He was initially ordained a deacon in his father's church. Toward the end of his reign Pope Innocent I (r. 401–17) consecrated Julian a bishop and assigned him the see of Eclanum. The following year, when the new pope Zosimus (r. 417–18) issued his anti-Pelagian *Epistola Tractatoria,* John joined 18 other Italian bishops and refused to condemn Pelagius. The Roman emperor subsequently banished Julian along with Pelagius and his followers from Italy in 421.

Julian used his intellectual skills in the service of the new movement and was soon recognized by all as its leading advocate. He systematized Pelagius's ideas, especially his more extreme positions on SIN and FREE WILL, and directed his attention to refuting St. AUGUSTINE OF HIPPO (354–430), Pelegius's strongest and most important critic. Unfortunately, in subsequent centuries texts of his writings were lost, and we know of him only through the many quotations that were cited by Augustine. Augustine's most substantial work against Pelagianism was his *Contra Iulianum* ("Against Julian"), and at the time of his death he was working on a second book against Julian, which he left unfinished.

Soon after leaving Italy, Julian moved to Antioch (Syria) where Theodore of Mopsuestia (c. 350–428) protected him for a while. Theodore, too, however, eventually found his Pelagian faith unacceptable, and Julian moved on to CONSTANTINOPLE. He tried to persuade each new pope to reconsider the condemnation of Pelagianism but was unsuccessful. His refuge in Constantinople ended once Emperor Theodosius II (r. 408–50) had time to understand the issues, and he expelled Julian, who died in 454.

Further reading: Dennis Etumonu Arimoku, *The Polemics of St. Augustine against Pelagius* (Rome: Pontifical Urban University, 1983); Gerald Bonner, *Augustine and Modern Research on Pelagianism* (Villanova: Augustinian Institute, Villanova University, 1972); Eugene TeSelle, *Augustine the Theologian* (New York: Herder, 1970).

Julian of Norwich (1342–1412)

Julian of Norwich was the name given to an anonymous anchoress, a person who lives alone because of a vow to devote her life to prayer and meditation. She lived in a cell adjoining the church of St. Julian in Norwich, in northeast England, which accounts for her name.

Julian was born in 1342. Her writings, which contain very few details of her life, raised her above her anonymity, as her first book was also the first English language book known to have been written by a woman. In her 30th year, in May, 1373, she took ill and believed she was dying. At that point, she experienced a set of 16 visions revealing the love of the Divine. She subsequently recovered and soon thereafter wrote a short book about the experience. A longer text appeared two decades later, the *Sixteen Revelations of Divine Love*. Long lost amid the wealth of Catholic mystical writing, Julian's work has been recovered in the 20th cen-

tury by Catholic and Protestant women seeking a greater role in the life of the church.

Today, Julian is cited for her profound mystical insight and her repeated references to GOD and CHRIST in the feminine gender as "mother." Her work is seen as a precursor of contemporary feminist THEOLOGY. It has also become known for its optimism, in which the central theme is not law or duty but joy and compassion.

Julian seems to have lived a long life, surviving through the period of the Black Death, and dying around 1412. Through the 20th century, numerous editions of her writings were published.

Further reading: Frances Beer, *Women and Mystical Experience in the Middle Ages* (Woodbridge, U.K.: Boydell, 1992); Jennifer P. Heimmel. *"God Is Our Mother": Julian of Norwich and the Medieval Image of Christian Feminine Divinity* (Salzburg: Institut fur Anglistik und Amerikanistik, Salzburg University, 1982); Julian of Norwich, *Revelations of Divine Love* (Baltimore: Penguin, 1984); Brent Pelprey, *Christ Our Mother: Julian of Norwich* (Wilmington, Del.: M. Glazier, 1989).

Julian the Apostate (332–363) *late pagan Roman emperor*

Born in CONSTANTINOPLE, Flavius Claudius Julianus was the nephew of CONSTANTINE THE GREAT and cousin of Constantius II (317–61). He ruled as Roman emperor from 361 to 363. CHRISTIANS refer to him as the Apostate because he converted from Christianity to paganism and is best known for his anti-Christian reforms and support for pagan ideas and practices within the empire.

After surviving the murder of most of his family, he was banished with his half-brother, Gallus, to Macellum, where attempts were made to convert him back to Christianity. When Gallus was made Caesar in 351, Julian was freed. He soon became influenced by Neoplatonic ideas, and he studied at Athens with ST. GREGORY OF NAZIANZUS and ST. BASIL THE GREAT; he also was initiated into the Eleusinian mysteries.

He was presented to the army as Caesar in 355, and as sole emperor he began a program of radical reform. He stopped the persecution of pagans and the destruction of pagan temples, attempted to reestablish pagan worship throughout the empire, forced education in schools to be paganized, wrote and published polemical works against Christianity, and even reinstated exiled heretical bishops to the church in the hope of creating dissension. In 363 he tried to rebuild Solomon's Temple in Jerusalem, but after repeated fires he abandoned his efforts. On June 26, 363, he died when he was struck with an arrow during battle.

Further reading: Robert Browning, *The Emperor Julian* (Berkeley: University of California Press, 1978); Alice Gardner, *Julian, Philosopher and Emperor, and the Last Struggle of Paganism Against Christianity* (New York: G.P. Putnam, 1906); Adrian Murdoch, *The Last Pagan: Julian the Apostate and the Death of the Ancient World* (Stroud: Sutton, 2003); Rowland Smith, *Julian's Gods: Religion and Philosophy in the Thought and Action of Julian the Apostate* (London: Routledge, 1995).

justification (Lat.: *justus*, "just" + *facere*, "to make"; Gk.: *dikaiosyne*, "righteousness")

Justification is the doctrine that a baptized person (*see* BAPTISM) is made or declared to be righteous before GOD through the grace of CHRIST. Catholics and Eastern Orthodox believe that this righteousness reaches the inner person and sanctifies one so that one can cooperate with grace and gain merit through good works. Luther and Calvin taught that righteousness was only imputed from the outside and solely through the merit of Christ, while internally the saved person remains a sinner (*simul justus et peccator* "at once justified and still a sinner"). Luther's teaching of justification by FAITH alone and not by works was rooted in his strong reaction against the sale of INDULGENCES by JOHANN TETZEL, whereby the ignorant were trying to buy their relatives out of PURGATORY with money. Luther equated indulgences with purely human works that in no way could justify the sinner.

All theologies of justification reach back to St. PAUL's epistle to the Romans 4, wherein he says that God counted Abraham righteous by his faith. Early theologians did not focus on this teaching, which was first picked up by AUGUSTINE OF HIPPO and later reemphasized by Luther in the PROTESTANT REFORMATION. The Council of TRENT sought to counteract the Protestant view (session 6) yet contained passages that provided starting points for later dialogue.

A number of modern biblical scholars claim that Paul's thinking on justification has been wrongly interpreted by the modern introspective conscience of the West. In any case, there has been some rapprochement between Lutherans and Catholics on the issue. HANS KÜNG contributed to this dialogue with his book *Justification in the Thought of Karl Barth and the Catholic Church*, first published in 1964 and since revised many times. The Vatican and the Lutheran World Federation issued a *Joint Declaration on the Doctrine of Justification* (1985), which has been posted on the Vatican Web site.

Further reading: Hans Küng, *Justification: The Doctrine of Karl Barth and a Catholic Reflection* (Louisville: Westminster/John Knox, 2004); John Reumann, "Justification by Faith: The Lutheran-Catholic Convergence," *The Christian Century* (October 1977): 942–946; Krister Stendahl, *Final Account: Paul's Letter to the Romans* (Minneapolis: Fortress, 1995).

Justinian I (483–565) *Byzantine emperor*

Justinian I ruled the Byzantine Empire from 527 to 565, restoring its power and reuniting much of the Mediterranean region. His legal and religious reforms had long-term impacts on European civilization.

Justinian became emperor following the death of his uncle Justin I (r. 518–27), whom he had actively assisted in the empire's affairs. Possibly his greatest asset was his wife, Theodora (d. 548), a commoner who had worked her way to power. Justian made her his joint ruler, and this decision proved decisive. When rioting broke out in CONSTANTINOPLE in 532, she was the one who stood firm and saved his throne.

The following year, using the services of two very competent generals, Belisarius (c. 505–65) and Narses (478–573), he began a campaign to recover North Africa, which was under the control of the Vandals. In 535 he began the recovery of ITALY from the Ostrogoths. Both efforts took more than a decade but were eventually successful. They insured the continuing Roman domination of the Mediterranean.

Justinian's most lasting accomplishment was the Corpus Juris Civilis, a new codification of Roman law. It updated and rationalized the existing legal system and greatly influenced subsequent secular and canon (church) law, both East and West. Having articulated his commitment to CAESAROPAPISM, Justinian took an active role in church affairs. The church was still in a process of defining orthodoxy. At the time the great challenge was monophysitism, which taught that Christ had only one divine nature rather than two—divine and human (see COUNCIL OF CHALCEDON; CHRIST; CYPRIAN OF CARTHAGE).

As the Monophysites were a strong presence in the empire, Justinian attempted to mollify them by issuing a decree condemning three theologians who tended toward Nestorianism (the belief that Jesus was two distinct persons), including Theodore of Mopsuetia (d. 428), whom the church had never before condemned. Pope Virgilius (r. 537–55) and other church leaders opposed the edict. Justinian called the Constantinople I Council in 553 to support his position.

Justinian undertook major construction and restoration in Constantinople, culminating in his rebuilding of HAGIA SOPHIA. The earlier building had been a victim of the 532 riots. The end product was an architectural wonder. It is the largest surviving structure from antiquity and is renowned for its expansive dome. Much of our knowledge of Justinian comes from the writings of the historian Procopius (d. 565), especially his *Secret History,* an account of Justinian's court that chronicles much scandalous activity.

Further reading: J. W. Barker, *Justinian and the Later Roman Empire* (Madison: University of Wisconsin Press, 1966); Robert Browning, *Justinian and Theodora* (New York: Praeger, 1971); Asterios Gerostergios, *Justinian the Great* (Belmont, Mass.: Institute for Byzantine and Modern Greek Studies, 1982).

Justin Martyr (c. 100–c. 165) *philosopher, apologist, and martyr*

Justin was a very early CHRISTIAN philosopher and apologist who attempted to defend the FAITH in the context of Greek philosophy. He was born in a Greek pagan home in Flavia Neapolis, now known as Nablus, Israel. He was given a good secular education and began a philosophical quest that led him through various schools. The courage of the martyrs attracted him to Christianity. A personal conversation with an elderly Christian became the catalyst for his actual conversion.

Though now a Christian, Justin wore the common dress of a teacher of philosophy. He argued that pagan philosophy, like Jewish law, was "a schoolmaster to bring us to Christ." (Gal. 3:24) This perspective became a foundation for his discussion with a wide variety of people from various religious and philosophical schools. He founded a school in Ephesus, later transferred to Rome. He used the Stoic idea of the Logos to illuminate the theology of CHRIST as the "incarnate Logos" who is "second to God."

Justin's thought survives in the texts of three books he wrote. The first *Apology* was addressed to Emperor Antonius Pius (c. 86–161) and defended Christians against charges of immorality and atheism. The second was addressed to the Roman Senate. His *Dialogue with Trypho Jew* states that the New Covenant replaced the Old (see TYPOL-

OGY). After many active years, he was arrested for practicing an unauthorized religion and, when he refused to renounce his faith, was beheaded along with six of his students. An account of his trial and death survived as *The Acts of Justin the Martyr.*

Further reading: L. W. Bernard, *Justin Martyr, His Life and Thought* (Cambridge: Cambridge University Press, 1967); Cyril Charlie Martindale, *St. Justin the Martyr* (London: Harding & More 1921); David Rokeah, *Justin Martyr and the Jews* (Leiden: Brill, 2001).

just war

The theory of the just war establishes the limiting conditions and criteria under which a war may be engaged in despite its coercive and destructive nature. It seems fairly certain that Christianity in the first three centuries tended in the direction of PACIFISM. Just war theory relies heavily on the arguments given by St. AUGUSTINE OF HIPPO in various writings.

The Old Testament speaks frequently of the wars of the Israelites and even proposes an image of GOD as a warrior who fights for Israel (Exod. 15). Deuteronomy 20 contains the rules for warfare. But the Hebrew prophets frequently challenged kings and people on their quick reliance on warfare (Hos. 5:11–14; Isa. 31:1–3). Instead, they began to preach on the complete reliance on God.

The New Testament both agrees and disagrees with this tradition. In many PARABLES Jesus promotes complete reliance on God's unstinting providence (Matt. 6:28), and Paul teaches that the principalities and powers of this world have been overcome through the DEATH and RESURRECTION of CHRIST (1 Cor. 2:6–8). In sum, the New Testament came to teach a principle of nonretaliation or nonrevenge (Matt. 26:50–52), a principle that one does not overcome EVIL with more evil but by transforming evil into good (Gen. 50:15–21; Rom. 12:21); and a principle that God's kingdom is spiritual and that the "war" against evil powers

is on the spiritual and heavenly plain (Rev.; John 18:36). CHRISTIANS are called to endure in FAITH (Rev. 1:9).

On the other hand, many New Testament passages show Jesus and the APOSTLES commending soldiers and centurions without requiring them to give up military service (Luke 7:5–17; Acts 10–11). In the second and third centuries the church experienced severe persecution from the imperial state and promoted "beating swords into plowshares" (Isa. 2:4) by refusing military service and doing good even to persecutors (JUSTIN MARTYR, *1 Apology* 39: IRENAEUS, *Against Heresies* 4.34.4; TERTULLIAN, *Against the Jews* 3). A complicating factor was that soldiers were expected to offer sacrifices and libations to the tutelary gods of their battalions, the civil gods, and the emperor. Those few Christians in the army who refused were martyred. Christians did pray for armies to maintain the peace.

However, during these two centuries Christians in increasing numbers enrolled in the army. When CONSTANTINE THE GREAT tolerated Christianity in 313 the situation changed dramatically, later leading Sts. AMBROSE and Augustine to change their attitudes toward war and formulate a just war theory (Augustine, *Against Faustus* 22.69–76). St. THOMAS AQUINAS adopted and adapted Augustine's arguments (*Summa Theologiae* 2a2ae.40). Just war theory has undergone considerable development over time and received an interpretation leaning toward pacifism in *Gaudium et Spes* 77–81, the Pastoral Constitution on the Church in the Modern World, restated in the official *Catechism of the Catholic Church* 2307-17 and the United States Conference of Catholic Bishops *The Challenge of Peace: God's Promise and Our Response* (1983). Pope JOHN PAUL II argued vehemently against war and especially the second Gulf War.

In time moral theologians began to make a distinction between *jus ad bellum* (the right to go to war) and *jus in bello* (right during war) and to lay down conditions, qualifications, and criteria for the pursuit and conduct of warfare. The right-to-war criteria, which are not rigid benchmarks, include war as a last resort, a just cause, the intention to promote good (revenge is absolutely forbidden), proportionality in planning between the good sought and the ill effects of the actual war, a competent authority to declare and justify war, and reasonable expectation of success. The right-in-war criteria include discernment between ethical and unethical means (e.g., torture), and proportional effects, with no uncontrollable injury to the civilian population (a major issue in the age of atomic warfare). Today just war theory is a subject both in moral theology and ethical philosophy.

During the period of the Vietnam War (1965–73) many young drafted Catholics refused to serve on Selective Conscientious Objections grounds that that war failed to meet most criteria of just war teaching. They lost their appeals in the courts.

Further reading: Temaž Mastnak, *Crusading Peace: Christendom, the Muslim World and Western Political Order* (Berkeley: University of California Press, 2002); Eileen Egan, *Peace Be With You: Justified Warfare or the Way of Nonviolence* (Maryknoll, N.Y.: Orbis, 1999); Jean Bethke Elshtain, ed., *Just War Theory* (New York: New York University Press, 2002); Paul Ramsey, *The Just War: Force and Political Responsibility.* (New York: Scribner's, 1968); Michael Walzer, *Just and Unjust Wars: A Moral Argument,* (New York: Basic, 1992).

K

Kells, Book of

The Book of Kells, one of the great artistic creations of the early MIDDLE AGES, is an illustrated manuscript of the four GOSPELs (Matthew, Mark, Luke, and John). The manuscript and illustrations were written on vellum (calfskin), and the whole work was completed around 800.

There is some disagreement over who produced the work. The majority opinion attributes it to Columban MONKS on IONA off the coast of Scotland at a MONASTERY founded by the Irish monk St. COLUMBA. According to this account, the manuscript was brought to the Kells, County Meanth, IRELAND, when the Vikings began raiding Iona, although others believe that the book was produced at the monastery at Kells.

Today the book is kept on public display at the library of Trinity College, Dublin. In the 1660s it was presented to the library by Anglican Henry Jones, the bishop of Meath and former vice chancellor of the university. Most recently, the book has been bound in four volumes. Generally, visitors to the library may see two of the four volumes, one opened to a major decorated page and one showing two pages of the script.

Further reading: *The Book of Kells* (New York: Alfred A. Knopf, 1974); Ruth Megaw and Vincent Megaw, *Celtic Art From Its Beginnings to the Book of Kells* (London:

Front cover of the Book of Kells, c. 800, an ornamented manuscript showing the biblical figures from Revelation 4 who were symbols of the four gospellers; Man (Matthew), Lion (Mark), Ox (Luke), Eagle (John) (Trinity College, Dublin) *(Art Resource, NY)*

Thames & Hudson, 1989); Edward Sullivan, *The Book of Kells* (London: Studio, 1952); *Treasures of Early Irish Art, 1500 B.C. to 1500 A.D.* (New York: Metropolitan Museum of Art, 1978).

Kennedy, John F. (1917–1963) *only Catholic president of the United States*

John F. Kennedy (known politically as JFK) was born in Brookline, Massachusetts, to a wealthy Catholic family active in state politics. He studied at the London School of Economics and at Princeton and Harvard Universities. He served in the U.S. Navy during World War II, receiving a Purple Heart for his actions.

After stints in the U.S. House of Representatives and Senate, JFK ran for the presidency in 1960, defeating Vice President Richard Nixon (1913–94) in a very close race. Although Roman Catholics had long constituted about one quarter of the U.S. population, only one Catholic had ever run for president before—Alfred E. Smith (1873–1974), soundly defeated in 1928 under a pall of ANTI-CATHOLICISM.

Kennedy's FAITH became an important issue in the election campaign, as some voters feared it could impact his decision making as president. In order to allay such fears he addressed a meeting of Baptist ministers in Houston, Texas, on September 12, 1960. In the widely reported speech he said, "I am not the Catholic candidate for President. I am the Democratic Party's candidate for President who happens also to be a Catholic. I do not speak for my church on public matters—and the church does not speak for me."

JFK was assassinated on November 22, 1963, in Dallas, Texas, apparently by Lee Harvey Oswald (1938–63). Many conspiracy theories surround his death. He is buried in Arlington National Cemetery. Although historians rate JFK as an average president, his memory is still revered by millions of ordinary citizens.

Further reading: Thomas J. Carty, *A Catholic in the Whitehouse?: Religion, Politics and John F. Kennedy's Presidential Campaign* (New York: Palgrave MacMillan, 2004); Lawrence H. Fuchs, *John F. Kennedy and the American Catholicism* (New York: Meredith, 1967); John F. Kennedy, *Profiles in Courage* (New York: Harper & Brothers, 1956); ———, *Why England Slept* (New York: Wilfred Funk, 1940); Arthur M. Schlesinger, Jr., *A Thousand Days: John F Kennedy* (Boston: Houghton Mifflin, 1965).

Kim Su-Hwan, Stephen (1922–) *first Korean cardinal*

Stephen Kim Su-Hwan was born on May 8, 1922. He grew up during the turbulent years of Japanese domination, World War II, and the Korean War. He was ordained a priest in 1951 and consecrated a bishop of Masan in 1966. In 1969 he succeeded Paul Maria Kinam Ro (1902–84) as ARCHBISHOP of Seoul and received his cardinal's hat. During almost three decades in office he became a well-known voice for justice and peace in his country. He hosted the 1984 visit of JOHN PAUL II and the 1989 International Eucharistic Congress. He retired in 1998 and was succeeded by Archbishop Cheong Jin-seok (1931–).

Further reading: Sunquist, Scott W., ed., *A Dictionary of Asian Christianity* (Grand Rapids, Mich.: William B. Eerdmans, 2001).

Kingdom of God *See* GOSPEL.

Kino, Eusebio Francisco (1645–1711) *Jesuit missionary and explorer*

Jesuit priest Eusebio Francisco Kino made his mark as a tireless explorer and mapper of the lands of the U.S. Southwest and the Mexican northwest. He founded several important missions among the region's Native American population, most notably the original Mission St. Xavier del Bac near Tucson, Ariz.

Kino was born in Segno, in what is now the Italian Tyrol. He was well educated in the sciences of his day and became a professor of mathematics at the University of Ingolstadt, GERMANY. In 1665 he joined the Society of Jesus and a decade later was assigned to missionary work in the New World. He arrived in Mexico in 1681.

After an unsuccessful attempt to found a mission in Baja California, Kino began work among the Pima people in the area of Arizona and Mexico's Sonora. He opened the first mission at Nuestra Senora de los Dolores in 1687. He became identified with the Pima, helping them in their repeated conflicts with the Apaches to the north and holding off Spanish miners from the south who tried to force them to work in the silver mines in northern Mexico. The Pima mission served as Kino's headquarters for his explorations of the surrounding territory and the founding of additional missions.

Kino made about 40 trips in Arizona, becoming the first European to visit the ruins of Casa Grande, an ancient town built in Arizona by the Hohokam Culture in about 1300. He explored the sources of the Rio Grande, Gila, and Colorado Rivers; his trip along the Colorado in 1701 proved that Baja California was a peninsula and not an island as previously believed. His maps became the standard reference for the next 100 years.

Much of our knowledge of the era derives from Kino's *Favores celestiales* (1708), later translated into English as the *Historical Memoir of Pimería Alta*. Kino died at Mission Magdalena in Sonora in 1711.

Further reading: Herbert E. Bolton, *Padre on Horseback* (Chicago: Loyola University Press, 1963); Eusebio Francisco Kino, *Historical Memoir of the Pimería Alta,* tr. Herbert Bolton, 2 vols. (Cleveland: Arthur Clark, 1919); ———, *Kino's Biography of Francisco Javier Saeta,* tr. Charles W. Polzer (Rome: Jesuit Historical Institute, 1971); Frank C. Lockwood, *With Padre Kino on the Trail* (Tucson: University of Arizona Press, 1934); Charles W. Polzer, *Kino A Legacy: His Life, His Works, His Missions, His Monuments* (Tucson: Jesuit Fathers of Southern Arizona, l998).

Knights of Columbus

In the late 19th century, American Catholic laypeople found themselves at a distinct disadvantage relative to their Protestant colleagues in trades and business. Protestants could avail themselves of a variety of fraternal and service organizations, including secret societies such as FREEMASONRY, to advance their careers. The Freemasons in particular helped their members get better jobs and provided assistance in times of need. The Catholic Church prohibited its members from joining secret societies, especially the Freemasons, which it considered anti-Catholic.

In 1881 these and other problems faced by Catholics in the labor force led a small group of men in New Haven, Connecticut, working with parish priest Fr. Michael J. McGivney (1852–90), to create a Catholic fraternal organization that could provide many of the services available to their Protestant neighbors without violating church strictures against secret societies. They chose the name Knights of Columbus, in honor of CHRISTOPHER COLUMBUS, who was revered by all Americans as a historical figure and by Catholics as the one who brought their religion to the New World.

While designed as a self-help organization, from the start it incorporated elements of concern for the community, both Catholic and otherwise, developing programs to embody the image of knightly defenders of country, family, and FAITH. Among its first actions was the development of an insurance program for widows and orphans of deceased members. It also developed rituals that rivaled those of the Masons and helped draw back any Catholics who had drifted into Masonic lodges. As part of its responsibilities in defending the church, it also emerged as a Catholic anti-defamation league answering charges against the church, especially those challenging the patriotism of American Catholics.

The Knights of Columbus is organized into local councils, regional councils, and a supreme council responsible for the guidance and development of the organization as a whole. By the beginning of World War I the organization had spread throughout the United States and Puerto Rico. As the 21st century began, it had some 1.5 million members and was carrying on an expansive program across the continent and abroad. Today it continues its social and charitable activities and promotes information on the Catholic Church.

Further reading: Maurice Francis Egan and John B. Kennedy, *The Knights of Columbus in Peace and War* (New Haven, Conn.: Knights of Columbus, 1920); Christopher J. Kauffman, *Columbianism & the Knights of Columbus,* (New York: Simon & Schuster, 1992); ————, *Faith and Fraternalism: The History of the Knights of Columbus, 1882–1982* (New York: Harper, 1982).

Knights Templar

The Knights Templar, officially the Poor Knights of CHRIST and of the Temple of Solomon, was a medieval order of monastic knights who made their initial appearance in the aftermath of the First CRUSADE (1095–99). Their primary mission was to protect Christian Jerusalem and secure safe passage for pilgrims to the city. They took the standard monastic vows of poverty, chastity, and obedience.

The immediate cause of the First Crusade was a change in Muslim rulers in Jerusalem, which blocked the way to Christian pilgrims. The crusaders quickly conquered Jerusalem and the Holy Land. Still, the route from Europe, passing through or near other Muslim lands, remained hazardous for any pilgrims. In response, in 1118 a group of nine young men including Hugh de Payen (d. 1136) and André de Montbard (1103–56, the uncle of BERNARD OF CLAIRVAUX) presented to Baldwin II (d. 1131), king of Jerusalem, their plan to create an order of warrior MONKS, the Knights Templar, to protect CHRISTIAN travelers. The order established its Jerusalem headquarters on the Temple Mount at the Al-Aqsa Mosque, which the Templars incorrectly believed to be Solomon's Temple, whence their name.

Hugh de Payens journeyed to the West to attain the church's blessing for the new order. At a council held at Troyes in 1128, the Templars decided to adopt the Rule of St. BENEDICT, as revised by the CISTERCIANS, since several of the original members were Cistercians. They also adopted the Cistercians' white habit, on which they placed a red cross. As the order developed, members assumed one of four primary duties: knight, sergeant, farmer, or chaplain.

The Templars quickly gained a reputation as effective warriors, and recruits flocked to their centers. Wealthy supporters provided them with money and land, upon which they built castles and planted farms. They sought out militarily strategic sites for their fortified centers. Using the octagonal architectural pattern found in the Church of the Holy Sepulchre in Jerusalem (*see* ARCHITECTURE), the Templars also built a number of distinctive round churches, one of the more famous being the Temple Church in London, which served as their British headquarters. The knights also served as de facto bankers for pilgrims going to the Holy Land.

After two centuries of growth, the Knights Templar became powerful enough to be considered a threat by secular rulers. On October 13, 1307, King Philip of France (r. 1285–1314) arrested all its members in his territories on a series of accusations including heresy and sodomy and seized its properties. When the pope did nothing to stop the action, other European rulers acquiesced in the persecution, which culminated when Grand Master Jacques de Molay (c. 1343–14) was burned at the stake.

The Templars' reputation did not die with it, however, and many legends emerged, including their supposed finding of the HOLY GRAIL. It was long rumored the order continued to exist as a secret underground movement that, like the Jesuits, might make a comeback. In the aftermath of the French Revolution (1789–91), a new Templar movement was founded in France in 1805 by two Freemasons, Philippe Ledru (1754–1832) and

Bernard-Raymond Fabré-Palaprat (1775–1838). Though relatively small, it was able to carry on a spectrum of public activities including processions through the streets of Paris. Ledru and Fabré-Palaprat also organized a Gnostic church to compete with Roman Catholicism. The new order and church subsequently spawned several dozen neo-Templar organizations in the 19th and 20th centuries. One such group, founded in post–World War II France, popularly known as the Solar Temple, made headlines in 1994 when nearly 50 of its members, including almost all of its leadership, died in a mass murder-suicide.

The neo-Templar groups, building on the accusations of the order's contemporary enemies, have suggested that the Templars secretly held Gnostic views. Neither the medieval critics nor the modern Templars ever presented much evidence to back their conclusions.

In the 1960s a new Templar legend took shape. Pierre Plantard (1920–2000), a minor figure in France's occult community, developed a theory that the Templars had been founded in order to find and secure documents that would prove the royal claims of the Merovingians, the first royal dynasty of France, who had been usurped. Plantard's ideas were then taken up by other writers as part of an elaborate alternate history of early Christianity. These writers suggested that the Templars had indeed found documents showing that the Merovingians had descended from a union between Jesus and Mary Magdalene, whom Jesus supposedly entrusted to found the Christian church (instead of the usurper, St. PETER) The Templars then hid the evidence at their center in Rennes le Château in France while they served the surviving lineage of Jesus and Mary Magdalene.

This alternate history was elaborated in the 1982 best seller, *Holy Blood, Holy Grail,* from which it was picked up by novelist Dan Brown and integrated into the plot of his international best-selling thriller, *The Da Vinci Code* (2003). Though *Holy Blood, Holy Grail* was published as a nonfiction book, it authors later admitted that the story was a complete fabrication. Brown also picked up on a further expansion of the Templar story concerning a Scottish outpost, the Rosslyn Chapel, which some saw as a possible repository of the Templars' Jerusalem documents.

The Da Vinci Code by no means exhausts the list of Templar conspiracy theories. Canadian writer Laurence Gardner argues that Mary Magdalene was the mother of two sons and a daughter by Jesus, and that Jesus' bloodline was passed through the younger son to the House of Stewart (or Stuart); the present ruling house in England is thus illegitimate, while the late Princess Diana (1961–97), a genuine Stewart descendent, had genuine claims to the throne.

Further reading: Michael Baigent, Richard Leigh, and Henry Lincoln, *Holy Blood, Holy Grail* (London: Jonathan Cape, 1982); Malcolm Barber, *The New Knighthood: A History of the Order of the Temple* (Cambridge: Cambridge University Press, 1994); ———, *Trial of the Templars* (Cambridge: Cambridge University Press, 1978); Dan Brown, *The Da Vinci Code* (New York: Doubleday, 2003); Peter Partner, *The Murdered Magicians: The Templars and Their Myth* (Oxford: Oxford University Press, 1981); Piers Paul Read, *The Templars* (London: Weidenfeld & Nicolson, 1999).

Kolbe, St. Maximilian (1894–1941) *Franciscan martyr at Auschwitz*

Maximilian Kolbe, a FRANCISCAN priest executed by the Nazis at Auschwitz, was born Raymond Kolbe on January 8, 1894, in Poland. He was educated by the Franciscans and in 1910 was received as a novice, at which time he took the name Maximilian. He was sent to Rome to complete his studies and while there was ordained to the priesthood (1918).

Following World War I, he returned to Poland, where he promoted the work of the Militia of the Immaculata, a movement he had founded in 1917 seeking consecration by CHRISTIANS to the Blessed Virgin. In 1927 he opened a center near Warsaw that he called Niepokalanow, or the "City of the Immaculata." By the beginning of World War II in 1939, Niepokalanow had expanded from 18 to 650 resident friars. It was the largest Catholic religious house then in existence.

From Niepokalanow, Kolbe and his associates ran an extensive religious publishing enterprise, including two periodicals, a daily newspaper, and a monthly magazine whose circulation grew to around 1 million. A second City of the Immaculata was opened in Nagasaki, Japan, in 1930. Building on the 1854 declaration of MARY OF NAZARETH's Immaculate Conception as Catholic dogma by Pope PIUS IX, Maximilian moved on to affirm the role of Mary as Mediatrix of the graces of the TRINITY and as Advocate for God's people, themes emphasized by Marian devotees in the last half of the 20th century.

In 1941 Maximilian was arrested, in part for attempting to house displaced Jews, and sent to Auschwitz. A short time later, he offered his life for another prisoner. His captors responded by placing him in an isolated cell to starve to death. Unwilling to wait for him to die, the camp authorities had him killed with a fatal injection on August 14, 1941.

Pope JOHN PAUL II, in pronouncing Maximilian's sainthood in 1982, called him a "martyr of charity." In subsequent years, some have accused Kolbe of acquiescence to general ANTI-SEMITISM that infested the Catholic Church in Poland in the early 20th century.

Further reading: Francis M. Kalvelage, ed., *Kolbe, Saint of the Immaculata* (New Bedford, Mass.: Franciscans of the Immaculate, 2001) Ernesto Piacentini, *Panorama of the Marian Doctrine of Blessed Maximilian Kolbe,* (Kenosha, Wis.: Franciscan Marytown, 1974); Elaine Murray Stone, *Maximilian Kolbe: Saint of Auschwitz* (New York: Paulist, 1997).

Kulturkampf

The Kulturkampf was an intense campaign of anti-Catholic ANTICLERICALISM initiated by German chancellor Otto Von Bismarck (1815–98) as part of his drive to unify GERMANY and build a strong central and secular government. Several developments fed Bismarck's fears. In 1870, a Catholic Center political party was organized in the new German Empire. In 1871, German Catholic BISHOPS supported the declaration of papal INFALLIBILITY at VATICAN COUNCIL I by PIUS IX. At the same time, Bismarck was dealing with various pockets of Catholic discontent in different parts of Germany. Bismarck's concern was shared by a number of German politicians, who opposed any close connection between the Catholic Church and the government.

The Kulturkampf began with the elimination of the Catholic department in the Prussian ministry of culture in July 1871. Bismarck then gave support to JOHANN VON DÖLLINGER, a prominent Catholic intellectual who opposed papal infallibility and led in the founding of the dissenting OLD CATHOLIC Church in Germany. In 1872 he secularized the schools of Prussia and expelled the JESUITS. He faced his harshest opposition when he tried to secularize marriage ceremonies, and many CLERGY refused to obey (for which they were removed from their parishes and on occasion arrested).

Each action by Bismarck increased support for the Catholic Center party as the Catholic community united against a common enemy. Their success in the 1876 elections signaled that Bismarck had overstepped his power, and he began to negotiate with the new pope elected in 1887, LEO XIII. As negotiations continued, many of the regulations Bismarck had initiated were either withdrawn or were not enforced. The Kulturkampf could be said to have ended in 1887, when a practical solution was reached between Bismarck and Leo XIII, in which most of his anti-Catholic laws were nullified. The Kulturkampf spurred hundreds of thousands of German Catholics to emigrate to NORTH AMERICA.

Further reading: Ellen L. Evans, *The German Center Party 1870–1933, A Study in Political Catholi-*

cism (Carbondale: Southern Illinois University Press, 1981); Ronald J. Ross, *The Failure of Bismarck's Kulturkampf: Catholicism and State Power in Imperial Germany, 1871–1887* (Washington, D.C.: Catholic University of America Press, 2000); A. J. Taylor, *Bismarck, the Man and the Statesman* (New York: Vintage, 1967); Lillian Parker Wallace, *The Papacy and European Diplomacy, 1869–1878* (Chapel Hill: University of North Carolina Press, 1948.)

Küng, Hans (1928–) *theologian and social critic*

Hans Küng is the most controversial Catholic theologian in the contemporary world. Küng was born in Sursee, Switzerland, in 1928, studied at the Pontifical Gregorian University in Rome, and was ordained in 1954. He wrote his dissertation at the Sorbonne in Paris on JUSTIFICATION in the THEOLOGY of KARL BARTH (1886–1968). Pope JOHN XXIII appointed him a *peritus,* or expert, at VATICAN COUNCIL II. He taught at the University of Tübingen in Germany until his retirement in 1996, but he remains a strong voice.

Küng's work on justification contributed strongly to the contemporary convergence between Catholics, Lutherans, and others. In *Infallible? An Inquiry* (1971) he forcefully challenged the PAPACY's claims of INFALLIBILITY on historical and doctrinal grounds. He subsequently challenged the church on the issues of birth control and priestly CELIBACY. Pope PAUL VI, who had been close to Küng since Vatican II, did not censure him: However, JOHN PAUL II removed his license to teach Catholic theology as soon as he was elected in 1979 and thereafter refused to meet with him. Perhaps because of Paul VI's protection, he has never been excommunicated and remains a priest. His books *On Being A Christian* (1977) and *Does God Exist? An Answer for Today* (1980) had a worldwide impact across all denominations.

In 1968 then Cardinal Ratzinger, now BENEDICT XVI, was given a position at Tübingen through Küng's influence, but they had a falling out over the student demonstrations and riots

of that year. In September 2005, the new pope invited K|ng to the Vatican for a private consultation that was reported to be friendly.

In his later years Küng has headed the Foundation for a Global Ethic at Tübingen and written prolifically on eternity, reform, politics and economics, women and theology, science and religion, and the spirituality of the world's religions. His influence on educated Catholics has always irritated the conservative bureaucrats in the Vatican.

Further reading: There are many Web sites that carry information on Hans Küng and selections of his many writings; Hermann Häring, *Hans Küng: Breaking Through* (New York: Continuum, 1998); John Kiwiet, *Hans Küng* (Waco, Tex.: Word, 1985); Manuel Rebeiro, *The Church as the Community of Believers: Hans Küng's Concept of the Church as a Proposal for an Ecumenical Ecclesiology* (New Delhi: Intercultural, 2001).

Kung Pinmei, Ignatius (1901–2000) *Chinese cardinal*

Cardinal Ignatius Kung Pinmei was the first native Chinese BISHOP of Shanghai, China, who for more than three decades lived under confinement by the government of the Peoples Republic of China. Kung was born in 1901 into a Catholic family in Shanghai. He was ordained a priest in 1930 and consecrated as the bishop of Souchou in October 1949, shortly after the Chinese Communist Revolution. The following year he was also named bishop of Shanghai and apostolic administrator of Souchou and Nanking. He also headed the Legion of Mary, which became a symbol of defiance against the CHINESE CATHOLIC PATRIOTIC ASSOCIATION, the organization established at the insistence of the government to govern the Catholic Church apart from any authority of the papacy. Expecting to be arrested at any time, he saw to the training of numerous lay catechists to carry on in the absence of episcopal and CLERGY leadership.

Bishop Kung was arrested on September 8, 1955, along with more than 200 priests and lay leaders of the Shanghai diocese. He was brought to trial in 1960 and sentenced to life imprisonment. He remained in isolation for the next 30 years in spite of efforts to visit him and have him freed. In 1985 Kung was released from jail, but he continued to live under house arrest. In 1984 he was allowed to attend a banquet hosted by the Shanghai government on the occasion of a formal visit by Philippine cardinal Jaime Sin (1928–2005). The two were not allowed to speak privately, but Kung was able to indicate his continued loyalty to the pope.

In 1988 the aging Kung was allowed to travel to the United States for medical care. He was subsequently invited to reside in the diocese of Bridgeport, Connecticut, where he remained until December 1997. Through the 1990s he traveled widely, presiding at the EUCHARIST and speaking on behalf of the church in China, where approximately 10 million Catholics remain caught between the rivalry of the bishops loyal to Rome and those loyal to the Patriotic Association.

In 1979, Pope JOHN PAUL II named Kung a cardinal *in pectore* (in the heart of the pope) but withheld any announcement of that fact to anyone, including Cardinal Kung. In 1991 the pope revealed the appointment and presented Kung with his cardinal's hat in ceremonies in Rome on June 29 that year. In 1998, the Chinese government officially exiled Kung by confiscating his passport.

The cardinal died in 2000. He was 98 years of age and before his death the oldest living cardinal.

Further reading: "The Cardinal Kung Foundation," available online. Elisabeth Rosenthal, "Cardinal Ignatius Kung, 98, Long Jailed by China, Dies," *New York Times* (March 14, 2000).

L

LaFarge, John (1835–1910) *stained glass and mural artist*

John LaFarge was a celebrated French-American Catholic artist in stained glass and murals. His son of the same name was a Jesuit priest known for interracial work.

LaFarge originally decided to pursue a career in law, and to that end attended Mount St. Mary's and Fordham University. However, an early ability and interest in art finally came to the fore. Almost from the beginning his work showed a new and innovative use of color as well as the influence of Japanese art, the study of which he pioneered.

In the 1850s he began to experiment with stained glass and developed innovative techniques that allowed his work to be compared to the best of medieval windows. Among the early examples of his work is the "Battle Window" at Harvard. He also illustrated literary works, such as Alfred Lord Tennyson's *Enoch Arden* and Robert Browning's *Men and Women*. He did murals for Trinity Church, Boston (1873), the Church of the Ascension, New York, and St. Paul's Church, New York. A series of wall paintings on Justice still grace the supreme court building in Baltimore, Maryland.

While engaged in painting and other forms of art, Lafarge produced a number of books on related topics. He finished his life as an honored representative of his profession, including the presidency of the Society of Mural Painters.

Further reading: Henry Adams, et al., *John LaFarge* (New York: Abbeville, 1987); John LaFarge, *Considerations on Painting.* (New York: Macmillan, 1895); ———, *The Higher Life in Art* (New York: McClure, 1908).

LaFarge, John (1880–1963) *Jesuit priest and desegregationist*

John LaFarge was a Jesuit priest who engaged in interracial issues in America long before the Civil Rights movement began. He was born to the celebrated artist of the same name and Margaret Mason Perry. After graduating from Harvard in 1901, the younger LaFarge moved to Austria to study THEOLOGY with the JESUITS at the University of Innsbruck. He graduated in 1905 and shortly thereafter entered the order. He spent the next years as a student, teacher, and parish priest, finally landing at the Jesuit rural missions of St. Mary's County, Maryland, the oldest English-speaking Catholic parish in the United States.

In rural Maryland he had his first serious encounter with the problems of racism in America, both in secular society and the church. One of his tasks in Maryland was the establishment of an elementary and secondary school system for the youths, both black and white, of the county.

In August 1926 he joined the staff of *America* (the American Jesuit magazine published in New York City) and served on its editorial staff for many decades. In New York he reflected on his Maryland experience and began to meet leaders from various racial and ethnic backgrounds to bring people together who wanted to work on racial problems. In June 1934, he founded the Catholic Interracial Council of New York, the first of some 40 similar councils in other locations across America. In 1959, the local councils came together to form the National Catholic Conference on Interracial Justice. LaFarge contributed a number of articles to the conference's *Interracial Review.*

In 1937 LaFarge authored the first book offering a Catholic perspective on racial justice, *Interracial Justice.* Pope PIUS XI was so impressed that he asked the author to prepare the draft of a papal encyclical on the race question. *Interracial Justice* was revised and expanded in 1953 as *The Race Question and the Negro* (1953) and followed with *The Catholic Viewpoint on Race Relations* (1956). At the time LaFarge wrote, few were listening, but his work prepared the church for the Civil Rights movement; when it finally broke out in the 1960s the cadre of people he had trained were ready to act. While working toward interracial justice throughout his life he also made time for other diverse duties, including serving as chaplain for the Liturgical Arts Society, in homage to his father.

Further reading: John LaFarge, *The Catholic Viewpoint on Race Relations* (Garden City, N.Y.: Doubleday, 1956); ———, *Interracial Justice.* (New York: America, 1937), rev. ed. as *The Race Question and the Negro* (New York: Longman, 1953).

laity   *See* CLERGY.

Las Casas, Bartolomé de (1474–1566)
bishop and advocate for Native Americans

Las Casas served as a missionary in Cuba and spent much of his life trying to prevent the destruction of the native populations of the Spanish-American colonies. He was born in Seville, SPAIN, in 1474. In 1502 he went to Cuba as a soldier and was rewarded with a land grant. His new land carried with it the right to the labor of any Native people who resided on it. Las Casas slowly moved toward a religious life and in 1513 became the first person residing in the Americas to be ordained a priest. The following year he renounced any claim on the labor of the Natives on his land. He developed a vision of a town in which the Spanish and the Native people would live together as equals and over the next seven years made several trips to his homeland to raise support to found such communities. In 1523 he joined the DOMINICAN Order.

Back in Spain he helped shape a new law passed in 1542 that prohibited enslaving the Native population and attempted to safeguard their rights. In 1544 Las Casas was named BISHOP of Chiapas, and he headed for Guatemala determined to put the new laws into operation. However, he ran into numerous obstacles from countrymen who saw him as blocking their economic goals.

In 1547 he returned to Spain, where he remained for the rest of his life, continuing his efforts to get the Spanish government to give their support to the Native people. He wrote *A Brief Report on the Destruction of the Indians* (or *Tears of the Indians*), an emotional statement on behalf of the Native people that included a dramatic account of Spanish atrocities. The book circulated across Europe. Its English edition did much to create an image of Spain as an overly cruel occupying power, and it was used to justify English action against the Spanish, such as piracy, during Elizabeth I's reign.

In more recent times, Las Casas has been lauded as a human rights pioneer. His critics, however, have seen him as an irresponsible writer who tried to make his case by slandering his opponents.

Further reading: Juan Freide and Benjamin Keen, eds. *Bartolomé de las Casas in History: Toward an Understanding of the Man and his Work* (Rockford: Northern Illinois University Press, 1971); Lewis Hanke, *Bartolomé de las Casas, Historian* (Gainesville: University of Florida Press, 1952); ———. *Bartolomé de las Casas, Bookman, Scholar and Propagandist* (Philadelphia: University of Pennsylvania Press, 1952); Bartolomé de las Casas, *Tears of the Indian: The Life of Las Casas by Sir Arthur Helps* (Williamstown, Mass.: Lilburne, 1970).

Lateran Basilica

The Lateran BASILICA, officially the Patriarchal Basilica of the Most Holy Savior and St. John the Baptist at the Lateran, is the official seat of the pope as the BISHOP of Rome. It is part of a complex of church buildings on Mount Celio. The Lateran is the official CATHEDRAL of Rome, not St. Peter's.

St. John Lateran is a fitting symbol of the transition of Rome from a primarily pagan to a primarily CHRISTIAN city, which gained speed during the fourth century. The emperor CONSTANTINE donated land formerly occupied by a noble family for the construction of what was the first large basilica in the Christian world (*see* ARCHITECTURE). At a major rebuilding in 905, it was dedicated to JOHN THE BAPTIST. Once built, it served as the papal residence until 1309, when the residence was moved to Avignon for a period. The church was largely destroyed by a fire during the AVIGNON PAPACY, providing a rationale for Pope Nicolas V (r. 1447–55) to suggest that an entirely new basilica be built at the Vatican, a church that became ST. PETER'S BASILICA. Pope Clement VIII (r. 1592–1605) finally oversaw the rebuilding of St. John Lateran in time for the Holy Year pilgrimages in 1600.

The church still contains a number of important RELICS. Constantine's mother, St. Helena (c. 250–c. 330), brought a staircase from Jerusalem believed to have been walked on by Jesus during his Passion that wound up at the Lateran. At one point, the stairs connected the church with the papal residence. In the private chapel for use by the popes, the Sancta Sanctorium, rest additional relics including what are believed to be a piece of the True Cross, a lock of hair from the Virgin Mary, a fragment of bread from the Last Supper, and some bones from the two Johns (John the Baptist and John the Evangelist) for whom the church is named.

Further reading: June Hager, *Pilgrimage: A Chronicle of Christianity through the Churches of Rome* (London: Weidenfeld & Nicolson, 1999); Joseph N. Tylenda, *The Pilgrim's Guide to Rome's Principal Churches* (Collegeville, Minn.: Liturgical Press, 1993).

Latin America

Latin America is composed of the lands in Central and South America and the Caribbean that were shaped by Spanish or Portuguese language, culture, and social systems. At one time Latin America extended into much of today's United States, including Florida, Texas, New Mexico, Arizona, and Alta, or Upper, California. There has been a Hispanic revival in the United States due largely to immigration, and Hispanics, at 22 percent, now constitute the largest minority group in the country.

Catholicism arrived in the New World and Latin America with the arrival of CHRISTOPHER COLUMBUS on October 29, 1492. The theme that governed the Spanish quest for a new route to India, which became transformed into a quest to settle New Spain, was *cruz y oro*, "cross and gold." The kings wanted power and wealth, and the church wanted to spread the GOSPEL.

The Treaty of Tordesillas (1494) had the effect of dividing South America between slave-holding Brazil and at least legally free Spanish America. Pope ALEXANDER VI formally granted the kings of SPAIN and Portugal title to the lands of the New World in the bull *Universalis Ecclesiae* (July 28, 1508). In 1569 Philip II of Spain (r. 1556–98) exported the Inquisition to his American lands to preserve the integrity of doctrine and practice there (and to track down any refugees from the Inquisition in Spain).

The papal approbation of the colonies was strengthened by a missionary impulse that arose during the COUNTER-REFORMATION. Missionaries from all the Catholic countries in Europe streamed to the newly opened lands. They came in the wake of the conquistadores, sometimes converting whole tribes and villages at a stroke. The main orders in the work were the JESUITS, FRANCISCANS, and DOMINICANS, but there were a host of others. Missionary activity was dampened in 1530, when Holy Roman Emperor and Spanish king CHARLES V (r. 1516–56) forbade any but the Spanish to missionize his New World dominions. Jesuits sneaked in other Europeans by giving them Spanish names.

In the early 18th century Jesuits set up special compound villages called reductions where Native peoples lived productive and independent communal lives. These missions extended deep into South America and reached into what is now Arizona and California. Outstanding missionaries were Jesuit EUSEBIO FRANCISCO KINO (1645–1711), a Tyrolean who missionized among the Pima of Arizona and Sonora, and the Franciscans ANTONIO MARGIL DE JESÚS (1657–1726), a Spaniard who founded the missions of Texas including the Alamo, and JUNIPERO SERRA (1713–84), a Mallorcan who founded the Amerindian missions of California, including Los Angeles and San Francisco. St. Augustine, Florida, the oldest city in the United States, began as a Spanish outpost in 1565. Conflicts often arose between secular CLERGY and religious orders, especially missionaries like the Dominican BARTOLOMÉ DE LAS CASAS, who championed the rights of indigenous peoples.

Latin American Catholicism has been affected by long-lasting tensions between pure Spanish, mestizos, Indians, and blacks, between colonialism and independence, between Latinization and indigenization, between church and state, and between the status quo and revolution. Today new

conflicts have been added between male dominance (machismo) and feminism and between traditional Catholicism and fundamentalist Protestantism, which is now bringing in significant numbers of converts.

Latin America has also experienced various types of non- or anti-church movements under the names of liberalism (Simón Bolívar, 1783–1830), anarchism, syndicalism, "justicialism" (Juan Domingo Perón, 1895–1974), and MARXISM (in Cuba and Central America). In the early 19th century most Latin American countries gained independence from their colonial overlords, but often the independence movements yielded military dictatorships, sometimes supported by foreign powers such as the United States. The Catholic HIERARCHY's tendency to side with the status quo combined with new ideologies imported from Europe to spark waves of ANTICLERICALISM, most notably in Mexico in the early and middle decades of the 20th century. A notable exception within the church was Fr. Miguel José Guadalupe Hidalgo (1753–1811), who rallied for Mexican independence but was condemned by the Inquisition and executed by the civil authorities.

Throughout history the popular piety of Latin Americans remained steady, vibrant, and often closely allied, if not syncretized, with indigenous religions that preceded the arrival of Christianity or were brought from AFRICA. The Mexican Dia de la Muerte festival combines elements of the Catholic All Souls and All Saints Days with the Aztec ritual of communing with dead children and ancestors in cemeteries. The Quechua of the Andes perform both ancient Incan and Catholic rituals in tandem in a kind of "sacroparallelism." The traditions of African Yoruba religion combine with the Catholic saint system to form the blended religions of Condomblé in Brazil, Voodoo in Haiti, and Santeria in Cuba and now the United States.

The main focus of Latin American piety was a strong devotion to the Blessed Virgin Mary. Our Lady of Guadalupe in Mexico is famous, but each country has its own special image of the Virgin and a marvelous array of *santos,* or saints, to whom devotees resort for help, protection, cures, and hope. Accompanying this devotion are fiestas, pilgrimages to shrines and holy sites, and striking penitential acts like approaching a church on the knees.

By 1950 the state of Catholicism in Latin America was precarious, but Latin America received a revitalizing tonic through VATICAN COUNCIL II, which in turn contributed to the burgeoning LIBERATION THEOLOGY movement throughout Central and South America and in Hispanic sections of the United States. The liturgy became inculturated with mariachi and other instruments. This flame was kept alive by the widely attended Latin American Conferences of Bishops (CELAM) at Medellín, Colombia, in 1968 and Puebla, Mexico, in 1979, under the inspiring leadership of bishops like DOM HELDER CÂMARA, Cardinal Aloíso Lorscheider (1924–), and OSCAR ROMERO. BASE COMMUNITIES began to spring into existence to respond to both the spiritual and material needs of the people.

However, by CELAM IV, held in Santo Domingo in 1992, the situation had become strained within Catholicism. The voices of liberation were still strong but were increasingly met with conservative opposition. Cardinal Ratzinger, prefect of the Congregation for the Doctrine of the Faith in the Vatican (now BENEDICT XVI), condemned liberation theology; Pope JOHN PAUL II, at first open to some liberationist ideas at Puebla, appointed a new set of bishops throughout Latin America who preach reconciliation instead of liberation.

The 1970s and 1980s marked a period of extreme violence in some countries. Tens of thousands died in civil wars in Central America. Archbishop Óscar Romero was assassinated as he celebrated the EUCHARIST on March 24, 1980. Six Jesuits, three nuns, and three lay workers were also killed in the same period. In the 1990s insurgencies in Colombia and Peru also claimed tens of thousands. Today the church in Latin America is in a stalemate between these two tendencies,

although the growth in the number of democracies has been remarkable and there has been economic improvement in some countries.

At the end of his life Pope JOHN PAUL II lamented the growth of fundamentalist Pentecostalism in Latin America. At the same time, perhaps paradoxically, he tried to suppress or deflect the Catholic versions of the phenomenon, CHARISMATIC RENEWAL, and the Latin American base church movements, both of which could be and are responses to the Protestant challenge. About 20 percent of Latin Americans are now Protestants, mostly evangelicals; the Protestant growth rate is at about 8 percent compared to 2 percent for Catholics.

Today there are approximately 425 million Catholics in Latin America and the Caribbean, the largest number on any continent and almost half the number in the entire world. Throughout Latin America 70 percent of the population remains nominally Catholic, but church attendance is far lower. In 2005, many Latin Americans hoped that the widely respected Franciscan archbishop of São Paulo, Brazil, Cardinal Cláudio Hummes (1934–) would be elected the first pope from the Americas. Although their hopes were dashed, their region is bound to play a crucial role in the future of Catholicism.

Further reading: Phillip Berryman, *Stubborn Hope: Religion, Politics and Revolution in Central America* (Maryknoll, N.Y.: Orbis, 1994); Donald E. Chipman, *Spanish Texas, 1519–1821* (Austin: University of Texas Press, 1992); Edward L. Cleary, *Crisis and Change: The Church in Latin America Today* (Maryknoll, N.Y.: Orbis, 1985); Enrique Dussel, ed., *The Church in Latin America 1492–1992* (Maryknoll, N.Y.: Orbis, 1992).

Legion of Mary

The Legion of Mary is a Catholic lay organization founded by Frank Duff (1889–1980), himself a lay Third Order CARMELITE, in Dublin, IRELAND, in 1921. It has two objectives: the spiritual growth of its members through devotion to the Virgin Mary and the building of the church through social service in the members' communities.

The devotional life adopted by Legion members is derived from the writings of St. Louis Marie Grignion de Montfort (1673–1716), author of the classic Marian text *True Devotion to Mary.* Among de Montfort's many accomplishments was the founding of the Company of Mary, a religious order organized for evangelism under the protection of the Blessed Virgin.

Members of the legion engage in a wide variety of activities, from visiting the sick and aged, assisting with religious education programs, and providing outreach beyond the parish. A local spiritual director named by the parish priest directs member activities. Local chapters (praesidia) are associated with other praesidia in a hierarchical organization at the regional (curia), national (senatus), and international levels. The international headquarters remains in Dublin. The life of the organization is described in the organization's *Official Handbook.*

The work spread to the United States in 1931, and the first praesidium was formed at Raton, New Mexico. It has subsequently spread to most parts of the Catholic world and has become the largest lay Catholic organization in the church.

Further reading: Robert Bradshaw, *Frank Duff: Founder of the Legion of Mary* (Bayshore: Montfort, 1985); *Official Handbook of the Legion of Mary* (Dublin: Concilium Legionis Mariae, 1953).

Lent *See* LITURGICAL YEAR.

Leo I the Great, St. (d. 461 C.E.) *early pope and advocate of papal supremacy*

The most important leader of the Western CHRISTIAN community of the fifth century, Leo helped define the role of the pope in the future church. His feast day is November 10. Pope Benedict XIV (r. 1740–58) declared him a DOCTOR OF THE CHURCH in 1754. His *Tome* (449) is known as a standard of CHRISTOLOGY.

Little is known of Leo's early life, including the date and place of his birth. He emerges out of obscurity as a young man and a deacon of the church in Rome during the reign of Pope Celestine I (r. 422–32). He had by this time gained some fame among his contemporaries and had done liaison work between Celestine and the Gauls. Toward the end of the 430s, Leo went to Gaul to negotiate a settlement to their dispute with Emperor Valentinian III (419–55). In 440, while still away, he was elected to succeed Sixtus II (r. 422–40) as pope.

During the early years of his reign, Leo was confronted with a variety of challenges to orthodox Christian belief throughout western Europe and northern AFRICA and was frequently consulted by local leadership as to how they should react. In ITALY both Pelagianism and Manicheanism were manifest. PELAGIUS attacked the concept of original SIN and thereby undercut the importance of GRACE. MANICHAEANISM was a dualistic faith that rejected the omnipotence of God. Leo ordered those found to be Pelagians to publicly renounce the doctrines and affirm the orthodox FAITH. He also ordered the Manichaeans banished from Rome and organized the Italian bishops to drive them from the land.

The controversy with the greatest consequences for Christian doctrine began in 447, when Eutyches (c. 378–454), a prominent priest in CONSTANTINOPLE, was excommunicated by Patriarch Flavian (d. 449), who condemned Eutyches for denying the two natures (human and divine) of CHRIST. Eutyches appealed to Leo, who after investigating the case threw his support to Flavian and the doctrine of the two natures. When in 449 Eutyches called a local church council attended by his supporters, Flavian appealed to Leo to pressure Eastern Roman Emperor Theodosius II (d. 450) to call an ecumenical council (*see* COUNCILS, ECUMENICAL). Leo also lobbied Western emperor Valentinian III (r. 425–455) for his support. The Council of CHALCEDON (451) affirmed Leo's stand; it was a milestone in the development of the orthodox view of Christ. Leo's intervention, especially as it came at the initiative of eastern patriarch Flavian, would later serve to support papal claims of universal jurisdiction.

The settling of the problem with Eutyches was quickly followed by a crisis in Rome. In 452 Attila the Hun (d. 453) invaded northern Italy. Leo met with him and managed to negotiate his departure. However, just three years later Genseric the Vandal (r. 428–77), an Arian Christian from SPAIN, landed his army on the coast of Italy and took Rome without opposition. Though the invaders plundered all the city's treasures before they left, Leo's intervention spared the residents from massacre and the city from burning.

The last years of Leo's life were spent recovering from the Vandal attack. He died November 10, 461, and was buried in ST. PETER'S BASILICA. Following the construction of the present St. Peter's he was reburied with a special altar erected over his body.

Today Leo is especially remembered for his advocacy of the primacy of the See of Rome and the office of the pope. He argued this notion in some of his sermons. Theological appeals from the East, his intervention in the political vacuum, and his force of personality all served to enhance the status of the PAPACY. His correspondence is an important source for history.

Further reading: Nicolas Cheetham, *Keepers of the Keys— A History of the Popes from St. Peter to John Paul II* (New York: Scribner's, 1983); Roy J. Deferrari, ed., *Fathers of the Church, Pope Saint Leo the Great, Letters* (Washington, D.C.: Catholic University of America Press, 1957); Eamon Duffy, *Saints & Sinners: A History of the Popes* (New Haven, Conn.: Yale University Press, 1997).

Leo XIII (1810–1903) *pope and supporter of social reform*

Leo was born March 2, 1810, in Carpineto Romano, ITALY, as Vincenzo Gioacchino Raffaele Luigi Pecci. He served as the ARCHBISHOP of Perugia and in 1853 was appointed cardinal. On February 20, 1878, he was elected pope and served for 25 years until his death. Many call him the first truly modern pope.

Leo's PAPACY was marked by his attempts to reconcile the church to the modern world, often by taking positions on important social and political issues. His encyclicals reestablished the doctrine that science and religion coexist, mandated the study of the rationalist THOMAS AQUINAS, argued the compatibility of Catholicism with democracy, and encouraged modern biblical study and criticism. His bull *Apostolicae Curae* (September 1896) declared ANGLICAN ORDINATION invalid, but he granted recognition of Eastern Orthodox ordinations. His landmark encyclical *Rerum Novarum* set the framework for all future papal social encyclicals.

Further reading: Katherine Burton, *Leo the Thirteenth: The First Modern Pope* (New York: D. McKay, 1962); Edward T. Gargan, *Leo XIII and the Modern World* (New York: Sheed & Ward, 1961); Justin McCarthy, *Pope Leo XIII* (New York: Frederick Warne, 1896); J. Bleecker Miller, *Leo XIII and Modern Civilization* (New York: Eskdale, 1897).

Leonardo da Vinci (1452–1519) *painter, sculptor, architect, engineer, and scholar*

Leonardo was the archetypal Renaissance man. He is most famous for his paintings, such as *Virgin on the Rocks* and *Mona Lisa*. Many of his works were done for the church, such as the *Last Supper* in the Dominican convent of Sta. Maria delle Grazie. His works introduced the style of the High Renaissance.

Born near Florence, Leonardo was raised by his father and recognized as gifted at a young age. From the ages of 14 to 30 he studied with the master Andrea del Verrocchio (1436–88) in Florence. Between 1483 and 1499 he lived in Milan, where he worked under the duke and produced some of his best paintings. When Milan fell to the French, Leonardo began a nomadic life, living in

Mantua, Rome, and Bologna, among other places. During this time he did the majority of his scientific and scholarly work, and he painted the *Mona Lisa,* now in the Louvre. In 1517 he moved to FRANCE, where he died two years later.

Further reading: Kenneth Clark, *Leonardo da Vinci; An Account of His Development as an Artist* (New York: Macmillan, 1939); Michael Gelb, *Da Vinci Decoded: Discovering the Spiritual Secrets of Leonardo's Seven Principles* (New York: Delacorte, 2004); Ivor B. Hart, *The Mechanical Investigations of Leonardo da Vinci* (London: Chapman & Hall, 1925); Richard B. K. McLanathan, *Images of the Universe; Leonardo da Vinci: The Artist as Scientist* (Garden City, N.Y.: Doubleday, 1966).

liberation theology

Liberation theology identifies the church and its GOSPEL message with a social, economic, and political struggle on behalf of poor or oppressed groups and aims to base the church on local spiritual communities. It grew out of the political theology of Johannes Baptist Metz (1928–   ) and was made known to the world with the publication of GUSTAVO GUTIÉRREZ's *Theology of Liberation.*

Modern CHRISTIAN theologies have tended to anchor themselves in one of the three articles of the Christian CREED: CREATION, REDEMPTION, and sanctification. Liberation theology anchors itself primarily in the theology of redemption; the word is interpreted not as restoration, as with IRENAEUS OF LYONS, nor as individual justification, as with Martin Luther, but as liberation of the poor and the oppressed from suffering and bondage. It can be described as an Exodus-type theology, defining redemption as freedom from physical, spiritual, and political bondage. It sees the role of the church to be a prophetic catalyst seeking justice on Earth so that the kingdom of GOD may arrive. Liberation thought was in part a reaction against liberal economic models of "development."

The key biblical texts for liberation theology are Exodus 3:7–8, where God hears the cry of the oppressed people of Israel, and Isaiah 61:1–2, which Jesus cites at the beginning of his preaching about the kingdom: "The spirit of God is upon me . . . to preach the good news to the poor . . to proclaim freedom for prisoners and recovery of sight for the blind, to release the oppressed" (Luke 4:18–19). Liberation theology is interested not just in the conventionally spiritual and in a guarantee of supernatural bliss, but also in bringing about the kingdom of God through political, economic, and social consciousness (Paolo Freire, 1921–97) and action.

Liberationists trace their lineage back to THOMAS AQUINAS's ethic of the common good and the great social encyclicals of the 19th and 20th centuries—LEO XIII's *Rerum Novarum* (1893) and PIUS XI's *Quadragesimo Anno* (1931)—which began to speak about principles of commutative (fairness in exchange) and distributive (the distribution of wealth) justice, democracy, labor unions, and social well-being. This message was furthered in the two conferences sponsored by the CELAM, the Latin American Conference of Bishops, at Medellín, Colombia, in 1968 and Puebla, Mexico, in 1979. Church leaders like DOM HELDER CÂMARA, Cardinal Aloíso Lorscheider (1924–   ) and OSCAR ROMERO prepared the way for the movement with the help of theologians and philosophers like Gustavo Gutiérrez, Jon Sobrino (1923–   ), José Comblin (1923–   ) and Enrique Dussel (1934–   ).

Liberation theology emphasizes several themes of 1) social justice, which it relates to the medieval social philosophy of the common good (Thomas Aquinas, *Summa Theologiae* 1.2.90.2) and to the papal social encyclicals beginning with *Rerum Novarum* and continuing to John XIII's *PACEM IN TERRIS* and PAUL VI's *Populorum Progressio* (March 26, 1967); 2) conscientization, by which the poor and oppressed become conscious of their own real life situations; 3) PRAXIS, or concrete action over mere theoretical analysis; 4) solidarity with the poor as the focus of God's action in time; and 5) base church communities as the social unit from which to bring about liberation.

Liberation theology had a significant impact on political, social, and spiritual movements in LATIN AMERICA throughout the 1960s and 1970s. At first Pope JOHN PAUL II seemed to cautiously embrace these aspirations, as in his speeches to the Puebla conference in 1976, but Cardinal Ratzinger, then head of the Congregation for the Doctrine of Faith and now Pope BENEDICT XVI, issued an official *Instruction on the Theology of Liberation* (1984) that criticized the theory for its similarities to MARXISM and for breaking the ties between clergy and laity. Several liberation theologians were disciplined, notably LEONARDO BOFF and the Indian oblate Tissa Balasuriya (1924–   ).

The movement was weakened by the appointment of more traditional bishops by John Paul II throughout Latin America. Nonetheless, its theories have been influential in feminist theology and in the theology of INCULTURATION. Liberation thought has also had a strong impact on mainstream Protestant theology. Emilio Castro, a Uruguayan Methodist liberation theologian, became the general secretary of the World Council of Churches from 1985 to 1992.

Further reading: Leonardo Boff, *Jesus Christ Liberator: A Critical Christology for Our Time* (Maryknoll, N.Y.: Orbis, 1978); Edward L. Cleary, ed., *Path From Pueblo: Significant Documents of the Latin American Bishops since 1979* (Washington, D.C.: United States Catholic Conference, 1989); Emilio Castro, *Amidst Revolution* (Belfast: Christian Journals, 1975); Gustavo Gutiérrez, *A Theology of Liberation* (Maryknoll, N.Y.: Orbis, 1971); Arthur F. McGovern, *Liberation Theology and Its Critics* (Maryknoll, N.Y.: Orbis, 1989); Juan Luis Segundo, *The Liberation of Theology* (Maryknoll, N.Y.: Orbis, 1976); Paul E. Sigmund, *Liberation Theology at the Crossroads* (New York: Oxford University Press, 1990).

liturgical movement

The liturgical movement for the reform and renewal of CHRISTIAN ritual, especially the EUCHARIST, began in the early 19th century and culmi-

Notre-Dame du Raincy, c. 1911. This is the first architectural expression of the modern liturgical movement in France. (Le Raincy, France) *(Photo by Roger-Viollet Collection/Getty Images)*

nated in *Sacrosanctum Concilium,* the Constitution on the Sacred Liturgy, at VATICAN COUNCIL II in 1963. The movement has had three phases: monastic, pastoral, and universal.

The eras of the Enlightenment and the French Revolution had seen a fierce critique and even persecution of Catholicism, often from the direction of rationalism. In reaction, Romantic age believers looked for sources of renewal within ancient church tradition, especially in the liturgical writings of the early church FATHERS and in the religious sacramentalism of the Gothic period. The search reached across denominations. The German Johann Adam Möhler (1796–1838), a member of the Catholic Tübingen School, viewed the church as a living tradition and organic unity in his *Symbolik* (1832). The OXFORD MOVEMENT within the Church of England fostered similar interests and from the Catholic viewpoint culminated in the profound historical studies of Christian dogma by JOHN HENRY NEWMAN.

The peak of the monastic phase took place under the guidance of the BENEDICTINE Prosper Guéranger (1805–75), who restored the Abbey of SOLESME in FRANCE and published an influential commentary on the feasts of the LITURGICAL YEAR. Dom Joseph Pothier (1835–1932) at Solesme pursued the restoration of medieval plainsong, or Gregorian CHANT, which spread to other monasteries in Europe, most notably Beuron and MARIA LAACH, both of which fostered a new art to accompany the changes in liturgy.

The second, pastoral phase was inaugurated through the liturgical efforts of St. PIUS X. The antimodernist pope promoted the common use of Gregorian chant, active participation in the liturgy, early Communion (around age 7), frequent Communion, and Eucharistic congresses. Pius X issued his now celebrated *Motu Proprio* or Apostolic Letter *Tra le Sollectitudini* (November 22, 1903) on sacred music, in which he gives primacy of place to Gregorian chant and, secondarily, to classical polyphony (as with Giovanni Pierluigida Palestrina 1514/15–94), while striving to remove orchestral and theatrical productions, characteristic of the 19th century, from celebrations of the liturgy. The lasting impetus in the modern liturgical movement came from Lambertin Beauduin (1873–1960), a Benedictine from the Abbey of Mont-César in Belgium, who founded the journal *La vie liturgique* ("Liturgical Life") and brought the liturgical movement into the life of the ordinary parish. This effort was also fostered by Beuron and Maria Laach in Germany and by PIUS PARSCH, author of the influential *The Church's Year of Grace,* in Austria. In France the JESUIT Paul Doncoeur (1880–1961), a leader in the Parochial Action Movement, promoted the liturgy among youth by means of a "Dialogue Mass." At Maria Laach the various streams of the liturgical movement flowed into the lake of liturgical theology under the guidance of Abbot Ildophons Herwegen (1864–1946) and the inspiration of the theologians Odo Casel (1886–1948) and ROMANO GUARDINI, the latter a diocesan priest. Casel and Guardini focused on the Paschal Mystery as central to the life of the church.

Various Benedictine monasteries around the world were instrumental in carrying the liturgical message to a wider audience. Preeminent in this work was Virgil Michel (1888–1938) of St. John's Abbey in Minnesota, who founded the influential magazine *Orate Fratres,* now called *Worship,* and who combined the liturgical movement with the social justice movement. His successor, Godfrey Diekmann (1908–2002), was a key expert in writing *Sacrosanctum Concilium,* the Constitution on the Liturgy, at Vatican II.

The third, renewal phase was preceded by a period of hesitation. The liturgical renewal, especially in Germany, was succeeding well among young Catholics but was resisted by some conservative BISHOPS. Some in the liturgical movement disparaged private devotions, such as the Rosary, ADORATION of the Blessed Sacrament, and devotion to Mary and the SACRED HEART in favor of the public liturgy. Others sought to recreate ancient liturgies without asking whether they would work in a modern setting. PIUS XII both blessed the liturgical movement and sought to stem its excesses in two important encyclicals, *Mystici Corporis* (June 29, 1943) and *Mediator Dei* (November 20, 1947). The general thrust of the movement, however, was to bring people to the liturgy. In the post–World War II period the emphasis shifted to bringing the liturgy to the people: there was a push for the use of local languages, simplification of rituals, reform of Holy Week services, and conducting Mass facing the people. The new directions were shaped in part by advances in biblical studies and by the ecumenical movement (*see* ECUMENISM/ECUMENICAL MOVEMENT).

The liturgical movement came to fruition with the debate over and confirmation of *Sacrosanctum Concilium,* the Constitution on the Sacred Liturgy (1963), the first document to be published at Vatican II. The constitution states that the Divine Liturgy is the extension of "the work of redemption" of Jesus Christ (preface, 2). The liturgy is the foretaste of heaven and the central work of the Mystical Body of Christ. The decree led to a series of liturgical reforms in the 1960s and 1970s pertaining to the Eucharist, other sacraments, the Divine Office, or PRAYER OF THE HOURS, the LITURGICAL YEAR, liturgical books, sacred art, and sacred furnishings. The reforms also opened up the INCULTURATION of the liturgy into non-European contexts.

Some Catholics reacted strongly against these reforms. Archbishop Marcel Lefebvre (1905–91) led a schismatic movement in 1976 that survives today (*see* TRADITIONALISTS). Some Catholics, still in union with Rome, insist on the traditional Tridentine Mass. To a certain extent liturgical reform went beyond Vatican control with the inclusion of lay people into more and more ministerial functions and women as eucharistic ministers and altar servers. Pope JOHN PAUL II sought to contain experimentation and to restrict gender-inclusive language in *Liturgiam Authenticam* (August 10, 2001), issued by the Congregation for Divine Worship and the Discipline of the Sacraments. This has been augmented by Cardinal Joseph Ratzinger's *The Spirit of the Liturgy* (2000), which disparaged "creativity" in liturgy and pled for tradition as he saw it. Yet the liturgical movement has had its day, changing the way Catholics worship and participate in the life of the church around the world.

Further reading: Mark G. Boyer, *The Liturgical Movement* (Collegeville, Minn.: Liturgical Press, 2004); Romano Guardini, *The Spirit of the Liturgy* (London: Sheed & Ward, 1937); Pius Parsch, *The Church's Year of Grace* (Collegeville, Minn.: Liturgical Press, 1953–1959); Joseph Ratzinger, *The Spirit of the Liturgy* (San Francisco: Ignatius, 2000).

liturgical year

The liturgical year is the annual cycle of seasons and feasts that celebrate the birth, EPIPHANY, BAPTISM, death, and RESURRECTION of Jesus CHRIST as well as the lives of saints who partake in the

Paschal Mystery and are models for CHRISTIAN living. The liturgical year comprises both a temporal cycle and a sanctoral cycle. The temporal cycle, also called the Proper of Time, hinges around two subcycles, the Christmas cycle and the EASTER, or Paschal cycle; it is calculated using both the lunar and the solar calendar. Easter and Christmas are the most solemn of the feasts of the liturgical year and have vigil Masses and Vespers and octaves; the LITURGY surrounding EASTER emerged well before that of Christmas. The two major temporal cycles are preceded by periods of preparation and anticipation, called Lent and Advent, respectively, and followed by periods of celebration. Between the two cycles are periods called Ordinary Time. Certain solemnities are considered holy days of obligation, when believers are required to attend the EUCHARIST. All Sundays are solemnities in liturgical rank.

The sanctoral cycle, also called Proper of Saints, follows the fixed dates of the solar calendar and includes solemnities, feasts, and memorials, mostly of the saints, which are fitted into the

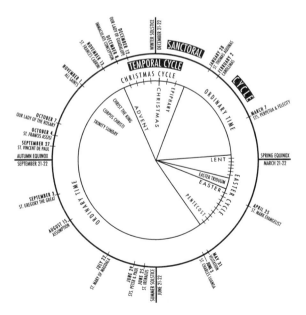

The liturgical seasons *(computer drawing by Aaron Corn)*

temporal cycle. Solemnities are major feast days that include feasts pertaining to MARY OF NAZARETH (Mother of God, January 1; Annunciation, March 25; Assumption, August 15; Immaculate Conception, December 8; Christmas, December 25), St. JOSEPH (March 19), Sts. PETER and PAUL (June 29), the SACRED HEART, and ALL SAINTS (November 1). Feasts include the anniversaries of certain major saints such as St. Mark the Evangelist (April 25). The remaining celebrations in honor of saints (MARTYRS, confessors, doctors, and others) are designated as memorial days. Some feast days are called "movable feasts" and are moved if they come into conflict with a major solemnity.

TEMPORAL CYCLE
Christmas Cycle

Advent The liturgical year begins with Advent (Lat. *adventus* "coming"), which is viewed as a period of waiting for the coming of the Messiah in his INCARNATION as well as for the Second Coming, or Parousia. Advent is a four-week season beginning with the Sunday on or nearest to November 30. The first two Sundays place emphasis on the Second Coming; the last two on the Incarnation. The color of the vestments is purple or violet to signify prayer, penance, abstinence, and fasting (*see* COLORS IN LITURGY). The third Sunday of Advent is called Gaudete, after the opening word of the Introit, or entrance hymn (from Lat. *gaudere* "to rejoice") and the color of the vestments is rose in anticipation of the joy of Christmas.

Christmastide Christmas proper begins with the vigil mass on December 24, popularly called Midnight Mass, plus three solemn masses on Christmas Day. Its octave is the Solemnity of Mary as Mother of God on January 1. The season includes the Feast of the Holy Family (Sunday after Christmas, or December 30 if Christmas and its octave fall on a Sunday) and concludes with the Feast of the EPIPHANY (Sunday between January 2 and 8 in the West; January 6 in the East). In early Christianity Epiphany was the major

solemnity of this season. Vestment color for this period is white, although on Christmas many local traditions allow for gold or other elaborately ornamented vestments of different colors.

Ordinary Time I

The first period of Ordinary Time begins on the Monday after the Sunday following January 6 and lasts until the Tuesday before Ash Wednesday, popularly known as Mardi Gras. The liturgical color is green, which symbolizes growth.

Easter Cycle

Lent The word *lent* comes from Middle English *lenten*, "springtime." In the early church only the few days before Easter were designated for fasting, penance, prayer, and abstinence. This period was gradually extended to three weeks and then to 40 days in commemoration of Jesus' 40-day fast in the desert (Luke 4:1–13), which, in turn, is an echo of the Israelites' 40-year sojourn in the Sinai desert. Lent was originally the time of the preparation of CATECHUMENS for the reception of BAPTISM and the EUCHARIST at the Easter Vigil service. The early Rite of Christian Initiation was restored after VATICAN COUNCIL II (1962–65). The tradition of prayer, penance, fasting, and abstinence also has roots with the MONKS in EGYPT and Syria (*see* MONASTICISM).

The Lenten season begins with Ash Wednesday and lasts until the Easter Vigil. (Mardi Gras, or "Fat Tuesday," is a half-secular, half-religious holiday of revelry that grew up among Mediterranean-based Catholics in anticipation of the austerities that would commence on Ash Wednesday.) Vestments during Lent are violet or purple as a sign of fasting, abstinence, penance, and prayer. The season is made up of five Lenten Sundays. The fourth is known as Laetare Sunday, after the first word of the Introit, or entrance hymn, to the Mass (*laetare* "to rejoice"). This Sunday anticipates the full joy of Easter. Hence, the color of the vestments is muted to rose. Formerly the fifth Sunday was called Passion Sunday, but that name is now reserved to the sixth Sunday. Popularly, Catholics call this Palm Sunday because there is a procession that reenacts Christ's entry into Jerusalem, preceded by worshippers carrying palm branches.

Eastertide/Paschaltide Properly, this second section of the Easter Cycle, also called Holy Week, is called Pascha (Heb. *pesach* "Passover"). It begins with the Easter triduum (Lat. "three days") of Holy Thursday, Good Friday, and Easter Sunday. This part of the Catholic liturgy reaches back to the earliest days of Christian history. It is considered the central and most important part of the liturgical calendar, and all other liturgical celebrations derive from it.

Holy Thursday was called Maundy Thursday in former times, from the word *mandatum* (Lat. "commandment") given by Jesus at the beginning of the washing of the feet (John 13:5, 34). Vestments are white. Holy Thursday liturgy results from a complex development of traditions. It used to include a public reconciliation of Lenten penitents; it still includes a Chrism Mass for the blessing of holy oils by the bishop for use in baptism, HOLY ORDERS, and ANOINTING OF THE SICK and a commemoration of the Last Supper. The Last Supper Eucharist is often held in the evening and includes the ceremony of the washing of the feet. (Today priests renew their commitments to service and CELIBACY at this mass; this emphasis on the priesthood has been criticized as not quite in keeping with the original "whole church" meaning of the Eucharist.). After the mass, the elements of the Eucharist are carried in a procession, during which the *Pange Lingua* hymn is sung, and deposited in a sanctuary. Devout believers frequently keep a vigil at this sanctuary throughout the night. The main altar is then stripped of all vestments.

Good Friday has the simplest liturgy of all the days in the year. It commemorates the death and Passion of Jesus. Vestments are red. There is the liturgy of the Word, the veneration of the CROSS, and the Communion service. The ceremony begins in complete silence, with a large cross covered in purple cloth and laid supine in the middle aisle of the church. Lectors then read passages on the Suffering Servant (Isa. 52:13–53:12), Psalm 31, which contains the words Jesus spoke at his death, and the passages about Jesus as high priest who offers himself in suffering from Hebrews 4:14–16; 5:7–9.

Then the Passion narrative from the Gospel of John (John 18:1–19:42) is read with different persons and the congregation enacting different speaking roles. There are prayers of intercession for the world. One of these prayers, for the "faithless Jews," was removed by JOHN XXIII when he first became pope. Next the cross is unveiled with the priest or deacon singing three times in higher pitches "This is the wood of the cross on which hung the savior of the world," to which the congregation responds "Come let us worship." Congregants approach the sanctuary to kneel and kiss the foot of the crucified Christ. After this the congregation partakes of the Host, consecrated the day before on Holy Thursday. This is not a mass. There is silence once again following the service, and the altar is once again stripped. Good Friday is a day of abstinence for Catholics.

Easter is the celebration of the resurrection of Christ and the fulcrum around which the liturgical year revolves. The most solemn celebration is the Easter Vigil Mass, which is celebrated as close to midnight as possible. This mass begins with the blessing of the new fire outside the church from which the new light of the year is illuminated. From this the Easter candle is lighted for this mass and every Sunday mass throughout the Easter season and thereafter. The water for baptism is blessed, and the neophytes, or catechumens, who have received instruction in the faith during Lent, are baptized. The Easter morning mass contains the famous early sequence hymn *Victimae paschali laudes*. Easter has an octave sequence of feasts, in Rome celebrated at various ancient churches.

Easter is followed by a series of seven Sundays and concludes 50 days later on Pentecost Sunday, the celebration of the descent of the HOLY SPIRIT on the disciples and the foundation of the church as recounted in Acts 2:1–11.

Ordinary Time II

This period includes the remainder of the liturgical year. Vestments are green except for special solemnities. There are three major feasts of the Temporal Cycle that fall during this time. Trinity Sunday, formally established for the whole church in 1334 and held on the Sunday after Pentecost, celebrates the victory of the doctrine of the TRINITY following the first seven ecumenical councils. Corpus Christi is the feast of the sacrament of the body and blood of Jesus, established in 1264, and is celebrated on the Sunday following Trinity Sunday. It echoes the feast of Holy Thursday. The Temporal Cycle concludes with the feast of Christ the King, established in 1925 by Pope PIUS XI to counteract atheism and secularism by proclaiming Christ's sovereignty over families, nations, and the universe. It occurs on the 34th and last Sunday in Ordinary Time. This echoes the Feast of the Ascension.

See also LITURGICAL MOVEMENT; PARSCH, PIUS; VATICAN COUNCIL II.

Further reading: *Didache;* Hipplolytus of Rome, *Apostolic Tradition; Leonine Sacramentary,* Available online; Odo Casel, *The Mystery of Christian Worship* (Westminster, Md.: Newman, 1962); Jean Daniélou, *The Bible and the Liturgy* (Notre Dame: Notre Dame University Press, 1956); Pius Parsch, *The Church's Year of Grace* (Collegeville, Minn.: Liturgical Press, 1953–1959); Vatican Council II, *Sacrosanctum Concilium,* the Constitution on the Sacred Liturgy in *The Documents of Vatican II,* ed. Walter Abbot (New York: America, 1933).

liturgy (Gr.: *leōs,* "people" + *ergōn,* "work" = "work of the people," "public service")

The classical Greek term *liturgy* meant public service in general, including public religious service at the altar. In the Greek Septuagint version of the BIBLE the term was applied especially to the religious services in the Temple in Jerusalem. In CHRISTIAN tradition, the term came to refer to all the public religious offices and ceremonies of the church as opposed to private ones and more especially to the EUCHARIST, the chief religious rite. In a secondary sense the term can refer to specific traditions of liturgical services, such as the Liturgy of the Roman Rite or the Liturgy of St. John Chrysostom. In the Eastern rites *liturgy* almost always refers simply to the Eucharistic celebration. *Sacrosanctum Concilium,* the Constitution on the Sacred Liturgy, at VATICAN COUNCIL II, sought the general reform and renewal of all things liturgical. Liturgy has undergone various forms of INCULTURATION in AFRICA, LATIN AMERICA, and ASIA.

See also LITURGICAL MOVEMENT; LITURGICAL YEAR.

Further reading: Patrick C. Chibuko, *Liturgical Inculturation* (Frankfurt am Main: Interkulturelle Kommunkation, 2002); Charles E. Miller, *Liturgy for the People of God* (New York: Alba, 2001); Dwight W. Vogel, ed., *Primary Sources of Liturgical Theology* (Collegeville, Minn.: Liturgical Press, 2000).

Lombard, Peter (c. 1105–c. 1164) *medieval theologian and bishop*

Little is known of the early years of a poor child named Peter who later became one of the most influential medieval theologians. He was probably born in Novara, Italy, but grew up in Lombardy, which gave him his name.

As a young man he won the patronage of St. BERNARD OF CLAIRVAUX (1090–1153), who facilitated his higher education at Bologna, Rheims, and Paris, where he emerged as a THEOLOGY instructor in the cathedral school of Notre Dame. He subsequently was named CANON of the cathedral (1144), archdeacon of Paris (1156), and BISHOP of Paris (1159).

Lombard completed commentaries on several books of the BIBLE, but he is most remembered for his monumental four-volume theological text called the *Sentences,* completed shortly before his consecration as a bishop. In the *Sentences* he followed a methodology developed much earlier by Isidore of Seville (560–636), ALCUIN, and Paschasius Radbert (c. 790–865), who all compiled biblical verses and quotations from the church fathers to support specific church teachings. Lombard was aware of the new theological directions offered by scholars like PETER ABELARD (1079–1142). Lombard's assemblage of quotations would influence the development of theology well into the 17th century. His work systematically moved through topics relating to GOD, CREATION, INCARNATION, REDEMPTION, the SACRAMENTS, and ESCHATOLOGY.

According to Walter of St. Victor (fl. 1175), a critic of Lombard's, he obtained his bishop's chair by simony. It is more commonly believed, however, that he received it when Philip, the king's younger brother, was chosen and then declined the office in favor of his former teacher.

Lombard apparently died some time in the early 1160s. He is not to be confused with the 16th-century Irish bishop of the same name.

Further reading: Marcia L. Colish, *Peter Lombard* (Leiden: Brill, 1994); Peter of Lombard, *Sententiae in IV libris distinctae,* 3rd. ed., rev. ed. by Ignatius C. Brady, 2 vols. (Grottaferrata: Collegii S. Bonaventurae ad Claras Aquas, 1971, 1981); Philipp W. Rosemann, *Peter Lombard* (Oxford: Oxford University Press, 2004).

Lonergan, Bernard J. F. (1904–1984) *Jesuit philosopher and theologian*

Lonergan was born in Buckingham, Quebec, Canada. After becoming a JESUIT and being ordained in 1936, he did doctoral work on THOMAS AQUINAS and studied broadly in philosophy, theology, economics, and culture. He taught at Toronto, the Gregorian University in Rome, and Harvard University. He was invested a Companion of the Order of Canada in 1970, an honor bestowed on only 150 living people at a time. His reputation as a foundational thinker in the modern world has soared since his death. His *Collected Works* are being published by the University of Toronto.

There are now Lonergan societies on every continent in the world.

Lonergan wrote two seminal works. The first was *Insight: A Study of Human Understanding* (1957, 1992), a work now being compared in stature to John Locke's *Essay Concerning Human Understanding* (1690) and David Hume's *Enquiries Concerning Human Understanding* (1748). It examines the cognitional, epistemological, metaphysical, and methodological implications of what it means to ask, "What do I know and how do I know it?"

The second was *Method in Theology* (1972), in which he examines the processes that theology employs when it reflects on religious experience. Such processes include research, interpretation, history, dialectics, CONVERSION, DOCTRINE, systematics, communication, and their functional interrelationships. A key element in Lonergan's thinking is a shift in focus from the ancient conception of the human as a substance to be acted upon to the liberating idea of the human as a dynamic, autonomous, and interrelating subject, socially, philosophically, and theologically.

Further reading: Frederick E. Crowe, *Developing the Lonergan Legacy* (Toronto: University of Toronto Press, 2004); Mark D. Morelli and Elizabeth A. Morelli, *The Lonergan Reader* (Toronto: University of Toronto Press, 1997); James Marsh, "Self-appropriation: Lonergan's Pearl of Great Price," in Jim Kanaris and Mark Dooley, eds., *In Deference to the Other* (Albany: State University of New York Press, 2004), 53–63.

Louis IX, St. (1214–1270) *crusader king of France*

Louis IX ruled FRANCE for more than four decades and was actively involved in the CRUSADES to extend CHRISTIAN control over the Holy Land. He was canonized in 1297. His feast day is August 25.

Louis was born April 25, 1214, at Poisey. He formally ascended to the throne following the DEATH of Louis VIII in 1226. As he was only 11 years old at the time, his mother, Blanche of Castile (1188–1252), ruled as regent until he came of age. He was educated by DOMINICANS and FRANCISCANS and became a Franciscan lay brother. In 1234 he married.

In 1244 during a serious illness he made a vow to GOD, which he fulfilled by raising an army and leading a Crusade to the Holy Land. In September forces under the sultan of EGYPT captured Jerusalem. As the pope sought to negotiate an alliance with the Mongols under Genghis Khan, Louis raised an army and in 1248 set out for Egypt. His army was routed, and he was captured in April 1250. After finally being freed, he remained in Egypt negotiating for the release of prisoners. He returned on hearing that his mother had died.

Upon his return, Louis IX opened negotiations with Henry III (1207–72), king of England, with the goal of ending hostilities between the two nations. The efforts resulted in the 1259 Treaty of Paris, by which Henry renounced his claims to Normandy and Louis gave Henry certain territories in southern France.

Louis IX proved a patron of both higher learning and Gothic ARCHITECTURE, the two interests coming together in his support of Robert of Sorbonne, who founded the Collège de la Sorbonne in 1253, now the University of Paris, for many years the home of the theological faculty of France for the Catholic Church. Louis's early training appears to have taken root, and he was known for his personal piety and devotion, the latter including the integration of regular prayer, periodic fasting, and penance into his private life.

Louis was dedicated to maintaining peace with his neighbors but also to the return of the Holy Land to Christian control. In the 1260s a new Muslim ruler, Bibars (r. 1260–77), caused considerable trouble for Christians, including the destruction of the church at Nazareth and the capture of Antioch, both of great symbolic value to Christians. Thus, in 1270 Louis again attempted a crusade. His plan was to land at Tunis, convert the local prince to Christianity, and then with a rein-

forced army move on to the Holy Land. However, shortly after landing at Carthage, the plague hit his army and did not spare him. He died in Tunis on August 25, 1270.

The call for his canonization came soon after news of his death reached France. A formal inquiry launched in 1273 resulted in his being named a saint by Pope BONIFACE VIII in 1297.

Further reading: W. C. Jordan, *Louis IX and the Challenge of the Crusade* (Princeton, N.J.: Princeton University Press, 1979); Hans Eberhard Mayer, *The Crusades*, tr. John Gillingham (Oxford: Oxford University Press, 1988); Jean Richard, *Saint Louis: Crusader King of France* (Cambridge: Cambridge University Press, 1992); J. S. C. Riley-Smith, ed. *The Atlas of the Crusades* (New York: Times, 1991).

Lourdes

Lourdes, a small town in southern FRANCE near the Spanish border, became the site of what is possibly the most well-known apparition of the Virgin Mary. Her appearance was accompanied by some extraordinary occurrences and resulted in a lineage of healings among the millions who have made their pilgrimage to the spot where the Virgin is said to have made her presence known.

The extraordinary apparition began when Bernadette Soubirous (1844–79), a young woman who had recently received her first Communion, had her first vision on February 11, 1858. While searching for wood near a natural grotto, she was distracted by a moving rosebush. As she looked a young and beautiful woman appeared above the rosebush. Bernadette dropped to her knees and began to pray, the woman above the rosebush joining in. The woman then disappeared.

Over the next six months, this lady was to appear on 18 occasions. She first spoke to Bernadette during the third apparition. The ninth appearance was crucial; the lady instructed the pliant Bernadette to dig in the ground and drink from and bathe in the water that would emerge.

The lady promised that the water from the spring would have healing powers. Next to the spring, a chapel was to be built.

The naïve Bernadette, considered by many in the village as somewhat slow, presented the local priest with the lady's requests. The priest instructed Bernadette to inquire as to the identity of the lady. In the last apparition the lady identified herself as the Immaculate Conception. Just four years earlier Pope PIUS IX had declared as dogma that the Virgin Mary had been born without original sin in an immaculate conception. That the uninformed Bernadette had articulated such an idea helped convince the parish priest that she had, in fact, seen the Virgin.

In the ensuing years Bernadette asked to enter a religious order but was delayed by a series of illnesses. Eventually the local BISHOP persuaded the Sisters of Nevers to invite her to stay at the Convent of Saint-Gildard. However, her condition deteriorated, and she died on April 16, 1879, at the convent's infirmary. Three days later, the body was placed in a coffin and sealed in the presence of a number of witnesses; 30 years later, in September 1909, her coffin was opened, and her body was discovered to have remained uncorrupted. It can be seen today in the Nevers chapel.

The spring at the grotto became the site of a growing number of cures and continues to flow to the present day. Thousands of cures have been claimed, though only a miniscule number have passed the very strict standards the Vatican-certified medical bureau has established to declare a cure medically unexplainable. The small chapel originally built at the grotto would eventually have a BASILICA erected over it. A nearby church, the Basilica of St. Pius X, was dedicated by Angelo Cardinal Roncalli, later Pope JOHN XXIII, as papal nuncio to France. It can accommodate a crowd of 30,000. Pope PIUS XI canonized Bernadette in 1933.

Bernadette's accounts and the subsequent stories of healing at Lourdes called forth very mixed responses in France from an increasingly secularized public and government. Though Lourdes became world famous as a healing shrine, the French government occasionally imposed restrictions and at one point closed it for several years. Bernadette's story was made into the celebrated movie *The Song of Bernadette* (1943), starring Jennifer Jones (1919–   ) and based on the novel by Franz Werfel (1890–1945).

Further reading: Alexis Carrel, *The Voyage to Lourdes* (New York: Harper, 1950); Ruth Cranston, *The Miracle of Lourdes* (New York: Image, 1988); René Laurentin, *Meaning of Lourdes* (Dublin: Clonmore & Reynolds, 1959); Alan Neame, *The Happening at Lourdes: The Sociology of the Grotto* (New York: Simon & Schuster, 1967; Therese Taylor, *Bernadette of Lourdes: Her Life, Death and Visions* (London: Burns & Oates, 2003).

Lubac, Henri de (1896–1991) *French theologian*
Henri de Lubac, a prominent 20th-century theologian, was born in Cambrai, FRANCE, and while still in his teens (1913) joined the JESUITS. His membership did not keep him from serving in the French army during World War I. After the war he earned a doctorate from the Pontifical Gregorian University in Rome. He was ordained in 1929 and two years later began his teaching career at the Catholic Faculties of Theology of Lyons, where he remained for three decades. Early in his career, he spent much time in the study of the church FATHERS and in 1942, along with his former student JEAN DANIÉLOU, cofounded *Sources chrétiennes,* a series of critical editions of patristic texts with modern translations.

During the Nazi occupation of France, he opposed anti-Semitism and became involved in the resistance. His work against the Nazis finally forced him to leave Lyons and spend the rest of the war in Vals. After the war he resumed his theological career. In the 1950s he became involved in a controversy with some of his more conservative colleagues, whom he accused of misunderstanding scholastic thought by separating Christianity from secular knowledge. This controversy eventually found its way to the Vatican, where objections were raised to his 1946 book, *Surnaturel*, and for a time he was silenced. He turned his attention to other literary pursuits until the theology dispute could be resolved. He became a member of the Academy of Moral and Political Sciences (1957) and joined the faculty at the Catholic Institute of Paris (1959).

By the time VATICAN COUNCIL II opened, Lubac had been found theologically sound. From 1962 to 1965 he served the council as *peritus* (theological expert). In 1983, Pope John Paul II named him a cardinal deacon. De Lubac died in Paris in 1991.

Further reading: Hans Urs von Balthasar, *The Theology of Henri de Lubac* (San Francisco: Ignatius, 1992); Henri de Lubac, *At the Service of the Church: Henri de Lubac Reflects on the Circumstances that Occasioned His Writings* (San Francisco: Ignatius, 1992); ———, *Christian Resistance to Anti-Semitism: Memories from 1940–1944* (San Francisco: Ignatius, 1990); ———, *Theology in History* (San Francisco: Ignatius, 1996); Susan K. Wood, *Spiritual Exegesis and the Church in the Theology of Henri de Lubac* (Grand Rapids, Mich.: William B. Eerdmans, 1998).

Luo Wen Zao (1616–1691) *first native Chinese bishop*

Lua Wen Zao, the first person of Chinese ancestry to become a Catholic BISHOP, was born in 1616 in Fujian Province. In 1631, several friars of the FRANCISCAN ORDER launched a mission in Fujian, and Luo became one of the first converts. He was baptized on September 24, 1633. In 1638 the Franciscans were expelled from the region, and Luo left with them for Macao. He used the next years to learn Latin and master THEOLOGY. He also traveled to Manila, where he studied at the DOMINICANS' St. Thomas College and took a Spanish name, Gregorio de López. In 1650 he was finally accepted into the Dominican Order, and in 1654 he was ordained as the country's first ethnic Chinese Dominican priest. He returned subsequently to Fujian.

In 1664, after a major incident in the Chinese court in Beijing involving the JESUIT scholars who had settled there, all foreign Catholic missionaries were expelled to Canton (Guangzhou), an open port. Being Chinese, Luo was able to remain behind to head the work throughout Fujian and neighboring districts. With the recommendation of his Dominican superiors, he was designated a bishop by Pope Clement X (r. 1670–76). He was consecrated in Guangzhou on April 8, 1685, by Bernardino della Chiesa, a missionary bishop from Italy.

Luo subsequently settled in Nanjing. The foreign priests were allowed to return to their work at the beginning of the 1670s, but Luo continued to exercise his broad episcopal oversight, traveling widely. In 1690, pope Alexander VIII divided Luo's territory into two dioceses centered on Beijing and Nanjing. Luo became the first bishop of Nanjing. Unfortunately, he died the following year. He was succeeded by an Italian. There would not be another Chinese bishop until the 20th century.

Further reading: A. C. Moule, "The Life of Gregorio Lopez," *New China Review* (1919) 1; Scott W. Sunquist, ed., *A Dictionary of Asian Christianity* (Grand Rapids, Mich.: Eerdmans, 2001).

M

magisterium (Lat.: *magister,* "teacher")

The magisterium is the church's legitimate teaching authority, which it received from CHRIST through the APOSTLES (Mark 16:15–16; Matt. 28:18–20; Acts 26:17–18) and which is reinforced by the power of the HOLY SPIRIT (Acts 1:8). Through the magisterium the church is empowered to bring the true message of REDEMPTION and the FORGIVENESS of SIN to all nations.

In the New Testament the magisterium is called a "service" (Gk.: *diakonia*). According to the teaching of VATICAN COUNCIL II, "the teaching office is not above the word of God, but serves it, teaching only what has been handed on, listening to it devoutly, guarding it scrupulously, and explaining it faithfully by divine commission and with the help of the Holy Spirit" (*Dei Verbum* 10, Dogmatic Constitution on Divine Revelation).

Christians, and Catholics among them, have not always agreed about who within the church should exercise this teaching power. The Gospels placed great authority on the "Twelve"—the APOSTLES (Matt. 10:1–4)—with Matthew giving preeminence to PETER (Matt. 16:18). PAUL preached a certain democracy of "gifts" (wisdom, knowledge, healing, etc.) for the common building up of the church (1 Cor. 12), but he did not hesitate to wield his own apostolic authority against other apostles to correct error, which he based on having received his revelation of Jesus Christ (Gal. 1:12). Beginning in the second century the teaching office of the church was gradually removed from wandering teachers, prophets, and apostles and placed in the hands of the sedentary HIERARCHY of BISHOPS, priests, and deacons who could trace the line of their APOSTOLIC SUCCESSION from the "Twelve."

By the time of the Council of Nicaea in 325, Christianity had become a creedal church; its teaching was organized into official CREEDS and other dogma as laid down by provincial and ecumenical councils (*see* COUNCILS, ECUMENICAL), which claimed a monopoly on the ultimate teaching authority and the ultimate truth and anathematized those who did not submit. Individuals could be tested by the hierarchy on the content of their faith and their moral behavior. In the Western Church the teaching office, whether by default or design, became more and more centered in the PAPACY. Although the authority of the councils became generally accepted, in practice, as JOHN HENRY NEWMAN noted, it was the laity and not the episcopacy that remained steadfast throughout the Christological controversies of the third and fourth centuries.

In the MIDDLE AGES the teaching authority of the church was augmented by *magistri theologiae,* "masters of theology," who interpreted both Scripture and tradition to the general church. They accepted the current teaching of the papacy and the HIERARCHY but also revered the authority of the church fathers and their teachings.

The understanding of the role of the magisterium was both altered and narrowed at VATICAN COUNCIL I. Pope PIUS IX wrote the decree on papal INFALLIBILITY and then solicited the agreement of the bishops. At the council 451 voted yes, 88 no, 62 yes with qualifications, and about 91 refused to sign. The decree limited the pope's infallibility to doctrines that are declared EX CATHEDRA ("from the chair" of St. Peter) for the universal church and not simply as a private theologian or even as the bishop of Rome. The doctrine under consideration must be a definition and not simply an explanation. The content is limited to faith and morals and can include something known from natural law. A scientific hypothesis would not be included in this limitation. Finally, the doctrine must be addressed to the universal church and not something that pertains to a part of it, for example the patriarchy of the West as opposed to those in the East. Infallibility is not inspiration (*see* BIBLE), nor is a declared doctrine a new revelation but is believed to come for the "deposit of the faith." By contrast, the President of the Church of Jesus Christ of the Latter-day Saints, popularly known as the Mormon Church, may receive new revelations, even revelations reversing earlier doctrines, as in the cases of polygamy and the admission of African descendants to the priesthood.

Vatican I gave the impression that the magisterium is limited to the papacy alone. Although papal infallibility has been invoked only once since the Vatican I decree—in Pope PIUS XII's declaration of the doctrine of the bodily assumption of MARY OF NAZARETH into heaven in 1950—many theologians and bishops felt that this misperception should be corrected in VATICAN COUNCIL II. *Lumen Gentium* 25, the Dogmatic Constitution on the Church, referred to the texts of Vatican I but also reaffirmed the bishops' role as coteachers of the infallible doctrine of the universal church whose role in the magisterium is derived from their APOSTOLIC SUCCESSION and the bond of communion between all bishops in the world and not compromised by the central and unifying role of the papacy (*Lumen Gentium* 40). Vatican II also stressed the pastoral dimension of the office of the magisterium, namely, the purpose of teaching is not simply the assertion of truth for the sake of truth but for the salvation of the faithful and for the relation between the whole church and the mystery of Christ. John Henry Newman also noted that the role of the laity cannot be excluded from the magisterium either, as it was the laity, not the bishops, who most preserved the orthodox faith during the Christological and Trinitarian controversies (*see* SENSUS FIDELIUM).

Today many make a distinction between the ordinary and extraordinary magisterium. Vatican I pertained to the extraordinary magisterium, that is, solemn decrees of faith or morals pertaining to the faith of the universal church. Solemn decrees have a character of authoritative finality. On the other hand, there is discussion about the infallibility of the statements coming from the ordinary magisterium on such matters as economics, science, SEXUALITY (birth control), and the ORDINATION OF WOMEN. In the last case many claimed that Pope JOHN PAUL II's apostolic letter *Ordinatio Sacerdotalis* (May 22, 1994) was a solemn, definitive statement forever excluding women from the Catholic priesthood. The Congregation for the Doctrine of the Faith, under the presidency of Cardinal Ratzinger, now BENEDICT XVI, issued a clarification, Concerning the Teaching Contained in *Ordinatio Sacerdotalis responsum ad dubium* (October 28, 1995), with the concurrence of John Paul II, that, while requiring "definitive assent," the apostolic letter does not come from the extraordinary but "the universal and ordinary magisterium." In ordinary language, the decision on the ordination of women is practically, but not absolutely, off the table.

Further reading: Charles E. Curran and Richard A. McCormick, *The Magisterium and Morality* (New York: Paulist, 1982); Richard R. Gaillardetz, *By What Authority?: A Primer on Scripture, the Magisterium, and the Sense of the Faithful* (Collegeville, Minn.: Liturgical Press, 2003); ——, *Teaching with Authority: A Theology of the Magisterium in the Church* (Collegeville, Minn.: Liturgical, 1997); Frank Mobbs, *Beyond Its Authority? The Magisterium and Matters of Natural Law* (Alexandria: E. J. Dwyer, 1997); Francis A. Sullivan, *Magisterium: Teaching Authority in the Catholic Church* (Eugene, Ore.: Wipf & Stock, 2002).

Magnificat

Magnificat is the Latin name given to the hymn spoken by Mary of Nazareth in Luke 1:46–55, the name coming from its opening word in the Vulgate translation of the Bible. It has assumed an important place in the Prayer of the Hours, where it forms part of the liturgy said at vespers (evening prayers).

The Magnificat has been compared to a variety of poems in Hebrew literature, most notably the Song of Hannah (1 Samuel 2:1–10). As with Mary, Hannah praises God as a woman to whom special favor has come. Because of its Hebraic form and its Christian content, it has frequently been cited as one of the transitional verses from the Old to the New Testament.

In recent centuries, as Marian devotion has risen in relative importance in the life of the Catholic Church, the fact that the Virgin Mary spoke the prayer has taken on heightened significance. St. Louis de Montfort (1673–1716), whose writings stand as a fountainhead of modern Marian devotion, concluded that Mary not only spoke the Magnificat but also wrote it down; its frequent recitation allows the believer to participate in Mary's spirit and share her sentiments. The Magnificat has come to be a hallmark of the understanding of Mary as the model of the consecrated life.

Further reading: Louis de Monfort, *Jesus Living in Mary: Handbook of the Spirituality of St. Louis de Mont-*fort (Litchfield, Conn.: Montfort, 1994); *Servants of the Magnificat: The Canticle of the Blessed Virgin and the Consecrated Life* (Chicago: Servite Provincialate, 1996).

Manichaeism *ancient dualistic religion and Christian heresy*

Manichaeism was founded in the third century by the Persian ascetic Mani (c. 210–c. 276). It is considered to have been a dualistic religion that posited a cosmic conflict between the realm of God and the realm of Satan, characterized as light and darkness. It was influenced by a late form of Zoroastrianism.

Around 240 Mani emerged to notice as an inspired prophet of a new religion. He was soon forced into exile in India, where he came into contact with Buddhism, but he returned to preach in the Sassanid Persian capital of Ctesiphon after the coronation of his supporter Shapur I (r. 241–72). Shapur I's successor, Bahram I (r. 274–77), attacked Manichaeism, sentenced Mani to death by flaying alive, and banished his followers.

Mani called himself the "Apostle of Jesus Christ" and believed he was the last prophet to come in a long line of men guided by God, including Zoroaster, Hermes, Plato, Buddha, the Hebrew prophets, and Jesus. He considered himself to be the Paraclete that is promised in the New Testament (John 14:16), which Catholicism understands to be the Holy Spirit. The same claim was later made for Muhammad (c. 570–632).

Manichaean theology was a synthesis of the religions of the time, including Zoroastrianism, Christianity, Buddhism, and perhaps Taoism. It shared much with Gnosticism and was based on a belief in the primordial conflict between light (the soul) and darkness (the body). A believer could achieve salvation by identifying with the incorruptible soul, a practice that required strict asceticism. Manichaeans rejected Christian notions of the soul and personal sin. They established a hierarchy of believers based on the level of austerity, distinguishing between the "Elect" and the "Hearers".

The religion spread rapidly in both East and West, establishing itself in EGYPT, Rome, and AFRICA within 100 years. For the 1,000 years it seems to have influenced movements in the West in such places as northern ITALY, FRANCE (*see* CATHARI), SPAIN, and the Balkans, but it flourished primarily in the East, in Babylonia, northern India, western China, and Tibet. In China the movement became identified with Buddhist enlightenment. It appears to have died out in the 13th century. AUGUSTINE OF HIPPO had been a Manichaean for nine years before his conversion to Christianity but became highly critical of the religion, although he did not escape the Manichaean taint entirely in his view of the body and sin.

Further reading: Francis C. Burkitt, *The Religion of the Manichees* (New York: AMS, 1978); A. V. Williams Jackson, *Researches in Manichaeism, With Special Reference to the Turfan Fragments* (New York: Columbia University Press, 1932); Steven Runciman, *The Medieval Manichee: A Study of the Christian Dualist Heresy* (Cambridge: Cambridge University Press, 1947); Serapion of Thmuis, *Against the Manichees* (Cambridge, Mass.: Harvard University Press, 1931); Geo Widegren, *Mani and Manichaeism* (London: Weidenfeld & Nicolson, 1965).

Marcion (c. 70–c. 150) *proto-Gnostic theologian and heretic*

Marcion, a second-century proto-GNOSTIC thinker, was born in Sinope on the Black Sea in today's Turkey. Around 140 C.E. he came to Rome and became a prominent member of its CHRISTIAN church. About four years later he was excommunicated for his teachings. Marcion drew a sharp distinction between the GOD of the Old Testament—angry, severe, just—and the God of Jesus—good, loving, benevolent. According to Marcion, Jesus' mission was not to become the Messiah of Israel; he was instead the Messenger from the higher reaches of the cosmos who came to ransom the human race from the Old Testa-

ment God, "the God of this world" mentioned by PAUL in 2 Corinthians 4:4. He thus rejected the common understanding of the church as the continuation of Israel and of the New Testament writings of the APOSTLES as flowing from those of the Hebrew BIBLE (Old Testament).

Marcion produced the earliest CANON of New Testament books, which he largely restricted to an edited version of Luke's Gospel and ten of Paul's epistles: Galatians, 1 and 2 Corinthians, Romans (minus chapters 15 and 16), 1 and 2 Thessalonians, Ephesians, Colossians, Philemon, and Philippians. He also included part of the Epistle to the Laodiceans, a lost writing attributed to Paul and mentioned in Colossians 4:16.

Following his excommunication he founded a rival church in Rome, which subsequently spread throughout the Roman Empire. The Marcionite Church was a significant competitor to the orthodox church well into the era of CONSTANTINE. Long included in the list of early church heretics, interest in Marcion waned until the 19th century, when scholars studying TERTULLIAN OF CARTHAGE and Ephiphanius of Salamis (c. 310–403), our main source for Marcion, attempted to reconstruct the heretic's writings, especially his text of Luke. More recently, with the growth of a new interest in GNOSTICISM, a new wave of interest in Marcion has appeared.

Further reading: E. C. Blackman, *Marcion and His Influence* (London: S.P.C.K., 1948); John James Clabeaux, *A Lost Edition of the Letter of Paul: A Reassessment of the Text of the Pauline Corpus Attested By Marcion* (Washington, D.C.: Catholic Biblical Association of America, 1989); R. J. Hoffmann, *Marcion: On the Restitution of Christianity* (Chico, Calif.: Scholars, 1984); Robert Smith Wilson, *Marcion* (New York: AMS, 1980).

Margaret Mary Alacoque, St. (1647–1690)

The Visitation NUN Margaret Mary Alacoque founded the devotion to the SACRED HEART, perhaps the most popular Catholic religious devotion in the world. She was canonized by Pius X in 1920. Her feast day is 16 October.

Margaret was born Mary, the daughter of Claude Alacoque and Philiberte Lamyn in L'Hautecord, FRANCE. She was a sickly child who suffered from rheumatic fever. Early on she developed a devotion to the Blessed Sacrament, the consecrated Host placed in a monstrance for adoration, and in 1671 she entered the Visitation Convent at Paray-le-Monial, France. Beginning in December 1673 and for the following year and a half, she had visions of Jesus in the form of a man in long robes pointing to his heart. In a later letter she wrote, "This divine heart is an abyss filled with all blessings, and into it the poor should submerge all their needs. It is an abyss of joy in which all of us can immerse our sorrows. It is an abyss of lowliness to counteract our foolishness, an abyss of mercy for the wretched, an abyss of love to meet our every need." Jesus instructed her to establish a devotion to the Sacred Heart on the first Friday of each month, a holy hour on Thursdays, and a liturgical feast devoted to the Sacred Heart.

Alacoque at first met with rejection, even from her own superior. In 1683 a new superior, Mother Melin, approved the new devotion with the concurrence of the JESUIT Bl. Claude La Colombiere (1641–82). In 1688 a chapel was built to the Sacred Heart at Paray-le-Monial. Soon other chapels were built at other Visitation convents, and the devotion rapidly spread throughout the world. Pope Clement XIII approved the devotion in 1765.

Further reading: St. Margaret Mary Alacoque, *The Autobiography of Saint Margaret Mary,* tr. Vincent Kerns (Westminster, Md.: Newman, 1961); ———. *Letters of St. Margaret Mary Alacoque,* tr. Clarence Herbst (Orlando: Sacred Heart, 1976); Wendy M. Wright, "Inside My Body Is the Body of God: Margaret Mary Alacoque and the Tradition of Embodied Mysticism," in Robert Boenig, ed., *The Mystical Gesture* (Aldershot: Ashgate, 2000), 185–192.

Margil de Jesús, Antonio (1657–1726)
missionary in Spanish America

Antonio Margil de Jesús, a pioneer FRANCISCAN missionary in Central America and Texas, was born in Valencia, SPAIN. He showed an early inclination to the religious life and developed a reputation for humility. In 1673 he entered the Franciscan Order and following four years of education was ordained a priest. Early in the 1680s he was assigned to the New World, and in 1683 he sailed for Mexico.

Soon after his arrival in Veracruz, Mexico, he was assigned to the newly founded College of Santa Cruz in the state of Querétaro. After several years there he set out to establish new missions, eventually founding several in the Yucatán, Costa Rica, and Guatemala. In 1707 he moved to the city of Zacatecas, where he founded the missionary College of Nuestra Señora de Guadalupe de Zacatecas. He headed the college for a decade and then in 1716 joined the new mission in east Texas. In 1717 he led in the founding of Nuestra Señora de los Dolores and San Miguel de los Adaes in Texas and Louisiana. Two years later FRANCE and Spain went to war; as French forces moved westward from New Orleans, the missions were abandoned, and Antonio moved with the rest of the Spanish residents to San Antonio, where he founded a new mission, San José y San Miguel de Aguayo, called by many "the Queen of the Missions."

In 1722 he returned to Mexico, where he worked for the four remaining years of his life. The combination of his self-effacing demeanor and his organizational abilities make Antonio the most famous of the Franciscans to work in 18th-century Texas and Mexico.

Further reading: Carlos E. Castañeda, *Our Catholic Heritage in Texas* 7 vols. (Austin: Von Boeckmann-Jones, 1936–1958; rpt., New York: Arno, 1976). Donald E. Chipman, *Spanish Texas, 1519–1821* (Austin: University of Texas Press, 1992); Eduardo Enrique Ríos, *Life of Fray Antonio Margil, O.F.M.,* (Washington, D.C.: Academy of American Franciscan History, 1959).

Maria Laach

Maria Laach is a former BENEDICTINE abbey located on the bank of Lake Laach, near Andernach in the Rhineland, GERMANY. It dates to 1093, when Palsgrave Henry II of Lorraine began its construction. It was given to the Cluniac Benedictines in the 1120s. It remained in Benedictine hands for the next seven centuries, becoming a center for the monastic life and in certain eras for literature and learning.

In 1873, during Bismarck's KULTURKAMPF, the new resident JESUITS were expelled from the MONASTERY, but in 1892 the Benedictines returned to thrive under a series of outstanding abbots. Early in the 19th century, the brothers became enthusiastic participants in the LITURGICAL MOVEMENT, which aimed to examine and reform the LITURGY to make it more accessible to the faithful. Abbot Dom Ildophons Herwegen, who served from 1913 to 1941, first took the lead; later, Dom Odo Casel (1886–1948) became the movement's leading exponent.

Casel worked on a liturgy-centered vision of Christianity. He centered his work on the idea of mystery, the working out of GOD's plan in history and the culmination of that plan in the Godhead. He saw the great Mystery to be CHRIST in his INCARNATION, death, and RESURRECTION and his visible body, the church. The heart of FAITH is God's revelation to humankind in the series of saving acts and our participation in them. We meet this mystery in ritual action, during which the original redemptive deed is made present in the form of liturgy, through which people participate in the sacred act and receive REDEMPTION. Casel's THEOLOGY would be integral to the liturgical reforms introduced by VATICAN COUNCIL II.

Today, the abbey church stands as a significant example of Romanesque architecture. The complex survives as a hotel and cultural center and is a popular tourist site, while Benedictine MONKS still reside in the monastery proper.

Further reading: Odo Casel, *The Mystery of Christian Worship* (New York: Crossroad, 1999); P. Adalbert Schippers, *Die Stifterdenkmaler Der Abteikirche Maria Laach* (Munster in Westfalen: Achnendorffschen Verlagsbuchhandlung, 1921) ; R. A. Stalley, *Early Medieval Architecture* (Oxford: Oxford University Press, 1999).

Maritain, Jacques (1882–1973) *Thomist philosopher*

Jacques Maritain was a French Catholic philosopher and eminent interpreter of THOMAS AQUINAS. Maritain was born November 18, 1882, into a Protestant family in Paris and grew up in relatively affluent circumstances. He studied at the Lycée Henri IV (1898–99), the Sorbonne 1900–02, and the Collège de France (1903–04), where he studied under Henri Bergson (1859–1941). Following their marriage in 1904, he and his wife, Raissa Oumansoff, a Jew, began a spiritual quest that led them in 1906 to become Catholics.

After a brief time in Hiedelberg, Maritain returned to Paris and began his intense study of Thomas Aquinas. In 1912, he was named professor of philosophy at the Lycée Stanislaus and in 1914 began his long career at the Institut Catholique de Paris. He became a full professor in 1921 and in 1928 was appointed to the chair of logic and cosmology.

Maritain was in the United States in 1940 when German forces overran FRANCE. He remained in America during the war and lectured at both Princeton and Columbia Universities. Following the war, he was named French ambassador to the Vatican (1945–48) but resigned to assume a chair in Thomist studies at Princeton. He retired in 1952 but remained at Princeton until shortly before his wife's death in 1960, when he moved back to France. As a widower, he spent the last years of his life in a MONASTERY at Toulouse. He died there on April 28, 1973.

Through the 1930s, Maritain was the center of a revival of Thomist thought in France and throughout the Catholic world. His attachment to Aquinas brought criticism from the left (his French philosophical colleagues having little use for Catholic thought) and his liberal politics from the right, but his own intellectual accomplishments allowed him to handle both. Along with his many texts that attempted to show the relevance of Aquinas for the understanding of the world, he also actively participated in writing the United Nations Universal Declaration of Human Rights (1948). Among his last books was one that condemned many of the reforms instituted by VATICAN COUNCIL II.

Further reading: Bernard Doering, *Jacques Maritain and the French Catholic Intellectuals* (Notre Dame: University of Notre Dame Press, 1983); Jude P. Dougherty, *Jacques Maritain: An Intellectual Profile* (Washington, D.C.: Catholic University of America Press, 2003); Joseph W. Evans, ed., *Jacques Maritain: The Man and His Achievement* (New York: Sheed & Ward, 1963); William J. Nottingham, *Christian Faith and Secular Action: An Introduction to the Life and Thought of Jacques Maritain* (St. Louis: Bethany, 1968).

Maronite Catholic Church

The history of the Maronite Catholic Church sets it apart from the other Eastern-rite churches (*see* EASTERN CATHOLICISM). It emerged in the fifth century around the charismatic ministry of a man later canonized as St. Maroun (d. 410), who founded a MONASTERY west of Antioch (in present-day Turkey). When Muslims took control of the region, the community fled to the mountainous region of Lebanon, where they survived as a unique, if isolated, community. Their primary BISHOP assumed the title of patriarch of Antioch and the entire East.

When in the 12th century the crusaders set up an autonomous kingdom based in Antioch, Maronite leaders came into contact with Latin Catholic bishops. In 1182 the Maronites decided to affiliate with the Catholic Church. They retained their Syriac LITURGY and made the few necessary doctrinal modifications demanded by Rome (that distinguished it from the Eastern Orthodox Churches). The Maronites viewed themselves as having been in communion with Rome during the centuries prior to the Islamic invasion and then simply having reactivated that communion.

In the 16th century, the region was incorporated into the Turkish-based Ottoman Empire, leading to periodic episodes of persecution of the Maronites. The massacre of thousands of them in 1860 brought the intervention of the French in their defense but also drove many Maronites to emigrate, especially to North and South America and Australia. Continuing unrest in Lebanon after World War II, including periods of civil war, gave further incentives to Maronites to abandon their homeland.

At the start of the 21st century the Maronite Catholic Church, with some 3 million members, was one of the largest of the Eastern Catholic Churches. There are 16 dioceses in the Middle East and diaspora dioceses for Cyprus, Greece, Argentina, Brazil, Mexico, Canada, the United States, and Australia.

The church is headquartered in Bkerke, Lebanon. Its current leader, Mar Nasrallah Boutros Sfeir, was named a cardinal in 1994. The church is active in the Middle East Council of Churches. In 2001 Cardinal Sfeir ordained Robert J. Shaheen (1937–) of St. Louis the first native-born American Maronite bishop.

Further reading: Nikolaus Liesel, *The Eastern Catholic Liturgies: A Study in Words and Pictures.* (Westminster, Md.: Newman, 1960); Ronald G. Roberson, *The Eastern Christian Churches: A Brief Survey,* 5th ed. (Rome: Pontifical Oriental Institute, 1995).

Marriage, sacrament of (Lat.: *matrimonium,* "marriage," "motherhood")

In Catholic teaching marriage is a SACRAMENT of vocation and commitment, that a husband and a wife confer on each other when they take their vows to share their lives together until DEATH. The sacrament is considered incomplete until an intimate union consummates it.

In the Old Testament, marriage was a social institution that GOD ordained from the beginning of CREATION (Gen. 1:27). This is the reason Catholics say that marriage is founded on natural law. The use of the phrase "And Adam knew (*yad'a*) his wife Eve" (Gen. 4.1) implies that the relationship was understood as a covenantal one. Early Israelites allowed polygamy and concubinage, but monogamy came to prevail in postexilic Judaism.

The Torah allowed divorce by the man for "something indecent," but not by the woman (Deut. 24:1). Jewish teachers at the time of Jesus took both strict (Shammai) and more lenient (Hillel) views of divorce. In Greek and Roman law women were allowed to divorce their husbands.

Jesus represented a prophetic and apocalyptic "sharpening" of the Torah (Matt. 5:27–28) and forbade divorce while allowing for the exception in Deuteronomy 24:1: "Whoever divorces his wife except for unchastity and marries another, commits adultery" (Matt. 19:9). Today the Catholic Church does not give heed to that important exception. Although the New Testament allowed for "eunuchs for the kingdom of heaven" (Matt. 19:12), all the early APOSTLES and most deacons, priests, and BISHOPS into the third century were married. It is only after the rise of MONASTICISM that CELIBACY was given a privileged place over married life. Despite this hierarchizing, early theologians like Macarius of EGYPT (d. c. 390) and Maximus the Confessor (d. 662) saw marriage as a type of *theosis,* or elevation of the human spirit into the life of the TRINITY.

PAUL permitted separation and remarriage in cases involving conflict of FAITH (1 Cor. 7:10–15). Today this is known as the Pauline Privilege and has complex rules (*Code of Canon Law* cnn. 1143–49). Another is called the Petrine Privilege "in favor of faith," in which one or both of the marriage partners was not baptized. It is reserved to the Holy See alone. An annulment is a dissolution granted in cases in which the sacrament was not validly conferred in the first place due to various impediments.

In early CHRISTIAN theology the purpose of marriage was seen as threefold: to promote fidelity between the partners, to procreate children, and to effect a sacramental union between the couple (Matt. 19:5, quoting Gen. 1:27 and 2:24). The theme of union was developed in 1 Corinthians 6:17 and Ephesians 5:21–33, where marriage—and not HOLY ORDERS—is seen as the type or metaphor of the relation between CHRIST and the church. This important theological mystery remains undeveloped in Catholicism, perhaps overshadowed by the clericalization of the sacraments. The idea that marriage is a sacrament helped differentiate it from the Roman legal institution and gave it a proper theological framework. The process was not completed until the MIDDLE AGES, when marriage was officially counted among the seven sacraments in the Western Church (THOMAS AQUINAS, *Summa Theologiae* 3, suppl. 49.3).

The procreative aspect of marriage was also clouded by AUGUSTINE OF HIPPO's teaching that original SIN is transmitted through the sexual act, which always contains a taint of SIN. Today this theology is fading in favor of an earlier, more positive view of sexuality as a gift of the self and a reflection of the life of the Trinity (*Catechism of the Catholic Church* 2205). VATICAN COUNCIL II paved the way toward this new THEOLOGY of marriage and family in *Gaudium et Spes* 47–52, Pastoral Constitution on the Church in the Modern World.

In earlier times marriage was preceded with a betrothal ceremony in which promises, gifts, and rings were exchanged. The marriage rite and the exchange of vows was and still is often performed in the context of a nuptial mass that replaced the Roman sacrificial rite of *conferreatio,* whence the tradition of the wedding cake is derived.

Catholicism prohibits the use of "artificial means" in controlling the number of children born to a marriage. The church does permit what it deems the natural "rhythm method," by which couples track the wife's ovulation cycles and restrict intercourse to her infertile periods. When the topic of birth control was broached at VATICAN COUNCIL II, Pope PAUL VI removed it from open discussion and later issued the encyclical letter *Humanae Vitae* (July 25, 1968), which prohibited the use of condoms, birth control pills, or intrauterine devices and reaffirmed the rhythm method.

Many claim that Paul VI relied on the counsel of Archbishop Wojtyla, later JOHN PAUL II, in writing this letter. In any case, the latter later issued the apostolic exhortation *Familiaris Consortio* (November 22, 1981) and the encyclical *Evangelium Vitae* (March 25, 1995), continuing the teaching on birth control. The latest surveys show that the large majority of married Catholic women in the world use some form of artificial birth control according to their own consciences.

Further reading: All the papal documents cited can be found online; Michael G. Lawler, *Marriage and the Catholic Church: Disputed Questions* (Collegeville, Minn.: Liturgical Press, 2002); Philip Lyndon Reynolds, *Marriage in the Western Church: The Christianization of Marriage during the Patristic and Early Medieval Periods* (Leiden: E. J. Brill, 1994); Julie Hanlon Rubio, *A Christian Theology of Marriage and Family* (New York: Paulist, 2003).

Martin de Porres, St. (1579–1639) *first African-American saint*

Martin de Porres, the first person in the Western Hemisphere to be canonized as a saint, was born December 9, 1579, at Lima, Peru, to a Spanish nobleman father and an African former slave, who were not married. He was raised in poverty but early on acquired some knowledge of medicine and skill in caring for the ill from a local surgeon-barber.

As a child of 11, he began working as a servant at a DOMINICAN priory. Combining his little bit of knowledge with a growing compassion for the sick, he began to beg for money to support the nearby poor and sick. Eventually, he was placed in charge of the infirmary. He wanted to become a DOMINICAN brother, but the rules barred black men, which he was considered to be. Martin's own piety in serving the sick eventually led to the Dominicans to change the rule. Martin eventually established an orphanage, a hospital, and an animal shelter in Lima. He became well known for his austere life, his compassion, and his personal devotion to the EUCHARIST.

Martin took ill with a fever in 1639, which claimed his life on November 3. Almost immediately, the Catholic faithful of Lima began to venerate him as the number of healings attributed to him steadily grew. His cause was long in reaching fruition, however. He was beatified in 1873 and canonized only in 1962 by PIUS XII.

Further reading: Giuliana Cavallini, *St. Martin de Porres* (Rockford: Tan Books, 1979); C. Ryan, *Blessed Martin de Porres* (London: Catholic Truth Society, 1953).

martyr   *See* HAGIOGRAPHY.

Marxism

Marxism is the name given to the critical socio-political philosophy developed by Karl Heinrich Marx (1818–83), who founded international communism with Friedrich Engels (1820–95). Marx called his system "dialectical materialism." Claiming to have turned idealist philosopher Georg Friedrich Wilhelm Hegel (1770–1831) "on his head," Marx argued that the institutions of economics, politics, law, and religion reflect not ideas but the material conditions of existence. Against the idealist philosophers of his age, he argued in *Theses Feuerbach* that the real function of philosophy is not simply to understand the world (*theoria*) but to change it (PRAXIS). Together with Engels he wrote the *Communist Manifesto* (1848), urging the workers of the world to unite and overthrow the unjust order. His theory of political economy is contained in *Das Kapital* (1867–84), partly edited by Engels. Religion, he argued, while being the "cry of the oppressed," has been turned into the "opium of the people" by the ruling classes in order to seduce the dispossessed to hope for spiritual rewards in heaven and not to fight for their just due on earth.

In the 19th century the PAPACY was very wary not only of socialism and communism (Marxism) but also of liberalism and democracy itself. Pope PIUS IX spoke against all four in his *Syllabus of Errors* (December 8, 1864). Beginning with LEO XIII's *Rerum Novarum* (May 15, 1891) and extending to JOHN PAUL II's *CENTESIMUS ANNUS* (MAY 15, 1991), intervening popes have not only embraced democracy and certain key elements of political liberalism (popular vote and religious freedom) but also those aspects of socialism that promise to bring a more just distribution of income in society (*see* THEOLOGY). JOHN XXIII's *PACEM IN TERRIS* (April 11, 1963) stands as a watershed in this development. Nonetheless, the popes systematically criticized the materialistic and atheistic aspects of classical Marxism and its communist manifestations.

In the 1960s and 1970s advocates of LIBERATION THEOLOGY embraced aspects of Marxist analysis of the conditions of existence in the Third World in order to free the liberating aspects of the prophetic GOSPEL (Luke 4:16–19) and to better the lives of the poor, both materially and spiritually. They insisted that praxis accompany theory in the doing of theology. Some theologians like Camillo Torres (killed in 1966) embraced violent overthrow of repressive governments, but the vast majority of liberationists adopted peaceful means of social organization and consciencization.

Despite these differences, the liberation movement evoked a stern warning, if not total rebuke, from the Congregation of the Doctrine of the Faith under the presidency of Cardinal Joseph Ratzinger, now BENEDICT XVI, in the *Instruction on Certain Aspects of the "Theology of Liberation"* (August 6, 1984), which charged liberation theologians of reducing FAITH to politics and of a wholesale use of Marx. Liberationists answered

that their agenda is deeply theological and that they use Marx very critically. A second document, *Instruction on Christian Freedom and Liberation* (March 22, 1986), insisted that the goal of liberation theology should be liberating people from SIN and not simply from sinful social structures. With the appointment of more Vatican-oriented bishops in the Third World and the turn of official teaching from the socially informed preferential option for the poor toward spiritual piety, the liberation movement has suffered setbacks but continues.

Further reading: Enrique Dussel, *Ethics and Community* (Maryknoll, N.Y.: Orbis, 1988); Ivan Petrella, *Latin American Liberation Theology: The Next Generation* (Maryknoll, N.Y.: Orbis, 2005); Richard W. Rousseau, ed., *Human Dignity and the Common Good* (Westport, Conn.: Greenwood, 2002; Cyril Smith, *Karl Marx and the Future of the Human* (Lanham, Md.: Lexington, 2005); Willis H. Truitt, *Marxist Ethics* (New York: International, 2005).

Maryknoll

Maryknoll, an American-based foreign missionary society, was founded by Frs. James A. Walsh (1867–1936) and Thomas F. Price (1860–1919). Walsh became interested in foreign MISSIONS and founded a periodical, *The Field Afar,* to promote interest in the work. Price, a North Carolinian ordained as a Catholic priest, began his career in home missions but soon expanded his concern to include foreign missionary activity. The two met in 1910 at a Eucharistic congress held in Montreal and formulated plans for a seminary to train missionaries. They quickly received the approval of the American BISHOPS and in June 1911 traveled to Rome, where Pope PIUS X approved their project as well. The Catholic Foreign Missionary Society of America was a reality before the year ended. The society was headquartered on a hill (knoll) near Ossining, New York, its name chosen because of Walsh and Price's devotion to the Virgin Mary.

At the time Maryknoll was founded, China had received more CHRISTIAN missionaries than any other country. Thus, it was not surprising that China was chosen as the first object of the new society's attention. Price accompanied the first group of three missionaries, Frs. James E. Walsh (not to be confused with the society's cofounder), Francis X. Ford, and Bernard F. Meyer, as the superior for the work, but he died in Hong Kong a year later of a burst appendix. Fr. Walsh stayed at Maryknoll as the society's superior general, a post he retained until his death in 1936. In 1933, Walsh and Maryknoll were acknowledged by his consecration as the titular bishop of Siene.

Among the many people who worked in the background making Maryknoll a reality was Mary Josephine Rogers (1882–1955). She developed an interest in missions while a student at Smith College, where she organized a mission study club. Beginning in 1908, she assisted Walsh and in 1912 was named the head of the women who were working for the society. That group gradually began to think of themselves as pursuing a religious vocation and reorganized in 1920 as the Foreign Mission Sisters of St. Dominic. The Maryknoll Sisters, as they were popularly termed, became a pontifical institute in 1954, at which time their name was changed to Maryknoll Sisters of St. Dominic. In 1925, Rogers, now known as Sister Mary Joseph, became the first mother general, a post she retained until her retirement in 1946. Soon after their founding, the sisters began working alongside the men in the Orient and LATIN AMERICA. A lay affiliate was added in 1975.

Maryknoll missionaries spread out globally to ASIA, AFRICA, and Latin America. They became prominent in South America in the 1960s, where many of the brothers emerged as strong supporters of LIBERATION THEOLOGY. The society has remained on the cutting edge of modern Christian missionary activity as it has made the transition to a decolonialized world and as leadership in global Christianity has passed from the hands of Europeans and North Americans. Its publication affiliate, Orbis Books, is a major publisher of materials on contemporary Christian missions, missionary theory, and global Christianity.

At the beginning of the 21st century, some 1,200 Maryknoll missionaries were at work in more than 50 countries. There are about 720 Maryknoll sisters.

Further reading: Patrick Byrne, *Fr. Price of Maryknoll* (Maryknoll, N.Y.: Catholic Foreign Mission Society of America, 1922); Robert Sheridan *The Founders of Maryknoll* (Maryknoll, N.Y.: Catholic Foreign Mission Society of America, 1980); Daniel Sargen, *All the Day Long* (New York: Longmans, Green, 1941).

Mary of Nazareth (c. 20 B.C.E.–c. 35 C.E.)
mother of Jesus

Mary of Nazareth was the mother of Jesus CHRIST. She has come to have a very important place in the THEOLOGY of Roman Catholicism and EASTERN ORTHODOXY and in the devotions of the Catholic faithful.

HISTORY

In the New Testament Mary appears in three major scenes in the life of Jesus: his birth, his ministry (where she is in the background), and his Passion, DEATH, and RESURRECTION. Mary figures prominently in the GOSPEL birth stories of Matthew 1–2 and Luke 1–2, where she is said to be the betrothed spouse of Joseph when she conceives by the power of the Spirit and gives birth to Jesus while yet a virgin (Matt. 1:20; Luke 1:34). This teaching is called the VIRGIN BIRTH. Somewhat incongruously, Matthew traces Jesus' ancestral line to Abraham and Luke to David through Joseph. Elsewhere the New Testament speaks frequently of Jesus' brothers and sisters, and later tradition goes through hoops in trying to explain these anomalies (Mark 6:3). The two key ideas associated with Mary in the biblical material are her virginity and her maternity.

Mary is much in the background during Jesus' ministry in Galilee. She reappears at the CROSS during the crucifixion scene in the three Synoptic Gospels and is given over to the care of John in the Gospel of John 19:27. Mary is among those who are in the upper room after Jesus' Ascension (Acts 1:14). Any further biographical details did not find their way into written form until second century writings, which are replete with legendary material.

THEOLOGY

The THEOLOGY of Mary is called Mariology. The early theologians mostly viewed Mary typologically as the opposition and inversion of Eve (disobedience/obedience). The medieval tradition picked up on this theme as the Eva/Ave contrast, as in the celebrated ninth-century hymn *Ave Maris Stella* ("Hail, Star of the Sea").

The apocryphal Book of James and the writings of ATHANASIUS OF ALEXANDRIA stressed Mary's "perpetual virginity" (*aieparthenos*), and this necessitated the explanation of Jesus' brothers and sisters as Joseph's children by another wife or as his distant relatives. This theme gave rise to Mary's title as the Blessed Virgin. The Council of EPHESUS (431), in opposition to Nestorianism, upheld Mary's theologically crucial title as Theotokos, or Mother of God. Parallel to the development of the iconography of Mary as Theotokos was the development of Jesus's image as Pantokrator, Ruler (or Judge) of All. The concept of Theotokos shaped the whole course of Byzantine iconography, in which countless ICONS and church mosaics portray Mary as mother of God holding the infant Jesus.

Beginning in the fourth century western theologians began to write of the Assumption of Mary into heaven, body and SOUL. In the Eastern Church this was celebrated as the Dormition, or Falling Asleep of the Blessed Virgin. This teaching was defended by St. Gregory of Tours (538/9–94) in the West and Theoteknos of Livias (fl. 590) in the East. Nevertheless, Mary's Assumption was not declared an infallible teaching of the church

Theotokos, icon of Mary as Mother of God, affirming the teaching of the Council of Ephesus, 431. Image shows Mary holding and pointing to the Christ child, with archangels Michael and Raphael in inner frame and surrounded with David and Solomon, Moses and Aaron, and prophets of the Old Testament. Icon by contemporary icon painter Maria Kukova *(permission of the artist)*

until PIUS XII issued his *Munificentissimus Deus* (November 1, 1950).

The Assumption teaching gave rise to the belief that Mary in heaven intercedes powerfully for the faithful on Earth, a teaching summed up in the title of Mary as Mediatrix of All Graces. Later St. Alphonsus LIGUORI promoted devotion to Mary Mediatrix, and Pope Benedict XV (r. 1914–22) instituted a feast in her honor. Many traditional Catholics in the late 20th century strongly promoted Mary's mediatory role as a dogma.

The next doctrine to be developed was that of the Immaculate Conception, namely, that in view of her role as the coming mother of God, Mary herself was conceived by Sts. JOACHIM AND ANNE without SIN. This doctrine was much debated in the MIDDLE AGES. ANSELM OF CANTERBURY was against it; THOMAS AQUINAS was doubtful, thinking rather that Mary was sanctified in the womb (*Summa Theologiae* 3.27.2). The Franciscan DUNS SCOTUS, followed later by JESUIT theologians, promoted the teaching that Mary was protected from all actual and original sin as part of God's plan of salvation in the INCARNATION. Scotus was careful to note that Mary was in greater need of God's grace mediated through Christ to *prevent* and not simply to *remove* sin (*Reportatio* 16.2.14). Pope PIUS IX proclaimed the doctrine of the Immaculate Conception as an infallible teaching of the church in *Ineffabilis Deus* (December 8, 1854).

During the Middle Ages devotion to the Blessed Virgin grew exponentially. Mary was accorded *hyperdulia* (Gk. *hyper* "more than" + *douleia* "service, veneration"), which is less than the ADORATION due God and more than the veneration due ANGELS and saints. In painting and sculpture angels and saints frequently accompany Mary as her servants. Most of the major CATHEDRALS had Mary as their primary dedication. The formalized image of the Byzantine Theotokos holding the adult-looking Christ child supporting the orb of the world in his hand developed into the images and statues of the tender Madonna holding the baby Jesus whom she knows will be lost to her at his DEATH. The change in imagery paralleled the transition in Christology (*see* CHRIST/CHRISTOLOGY) from divinity to humanity, from Nicaea to Chalcedon.

Devotion to Mary in part reflects another transition in Christian imagery: except in depictions of the CROSS/CRUCIFIXION, Jesus himself took on more and more the august role of the stern ruler and judge of all things at the end of time. This is shown in the Byzantine icon of Christ as the Pantokrator holding his right hand aloft with the index and middle finger signifying his divinity and human-

ity and the other three signifying the TRINITY and his left holding the Book of Life (Rev. 20:15), into which only the names of the saved will be entered. Images derived from this Byzantine prototype were carved in the tympana atop the central portal of Gothic cathedrals all over Europe. When Jesus became the dispenser of stiff justice, the pious faithful retreated to his mother for mercy.

Eastern Orthodoxy has not declared the Assumption a dogma but celebrates the feast. The Orthodox believe that Mary was without

Medieval Madonna and Christ Child. This statue type was very common throughout southern France and Spain. Many show the Madonna and Christ Child with black faces. (Church of St. Philibert, Tournus, France) *(photo by Samuel Leuchli)*

individual, personal sin, but was conceived with original sin to show her solidarity with the rest of humanity. The theologians of the PROTESTANT REFORMATION excoriated the Roman Church for its excessive devotion to saints and the Blessed Virgin, although Luther praised Mary's humility and prayed the Rosary until the end of his life. Later Protestants would accuse Catholics of "Mariolatry." The Church of England's Thirty-Nine Articles prohibited the invocation of the saints and Mary, but Caroline theologians under Charles I of England stressed her holiness and even saw her as a "fountain of grace." High-church Anglicans today hold to teachings similar to the Catholics. The OXFORD MOVEMENT under the leadership of JOHN HENRY NEWMAN accorded the Blessed Virgin Mary a high status.

The theology of Mary underwent a severe feminist critique in Mary Daly's *Beyond God the Father: Toward a Philosophy of Women's Liberation* (1973) as just another aspect of Catholic patriarchalism. Other theologians like ROSEMARY RADFORD RUETHER and the Oblate Fr. Tissa Balasuriya (1924–) have tried to reclaim a new role for Mary in a feminist and liberationist framework, Balasuriya in his 1994 book *Mary and Human Liberation*. (Balasuriya was summarily excommunicated for HERESY by the Congregation for the Doctrine of the Faith in 1997 under prefect Cardinal Joseph Ratzinger, now BENEDICT XVI, but the excommunication was lifted after negotiations.)

At VATICAN COUNCIL II many tradition-minded bishops wanted to add a separate decree on Mary, but the council decided instead to add a chapter to *Lumen Genitum* 52–69, the Dogmatic Constitution on the Church, in which Mary's role is subordinated to the mystery of Christ and God's economy of salvation for the church. Moving opposite to Vatican II, many Catholics today are returning to more traditional Marian theology and devotion.

TITLES

Throughout history Mary has come to receive numerous titles. Besides those noted above—New Eve, Blessed Virgin, Mother of God, Immaculate Conception, Star of the Sea, Mediatrix—various litanies and popular devotions have added many others. A small sampling would include Mother of Divine Grace, Mother Most Pure (very popular in Latin nations as La Purissima), Mother or Our Lady of Good Counsel, Mirror of Justice, Seat of Wisdom, Spiritual Vessel, Mystical Rose (inspiration for the Rosary and for the celebrated painting *Mother of God in the Rose Arbor* by Martin Schongauer, 1445/50–91), Ark of the Covenant, Gate of Heaven, Refuge of Sinners (a strong theme in medieval depictions of Mary), and Queen of Angels. One of the most common titles associated with paintings and statues is Our Lady of Sorrows, which commemorates Mary's affliction at Calvary when Jesus died. This became the source for many paintings and sculptures of the Deposition from the Cross and the pietas, including MICHELANGELO's famous *Pieta* in St. PETER'S BASILICA in Rome.

FEASTS

Formerly, Mary had more feast days commemorating her than did Christ, but liturgical reforms after Vatican II have sought to redress the balance. The first recorded feast, called the Commemoration of Mary, was celebrated the Sunday before Christmas; it developed into the Assumption (August 15), which is a holy day of obligation for Catholics, as is the Feast of the Immaculate Conception (December 8). The Nativity of the Blessed Virgin Mary (September 8) dates from the seventh or eighth century. The Annunciation (March 25) was formerly a feast of Mary but is now counted as the Annunciation of our Lord. The Purification (February 2) is now called the Presentation of Christ. The Visitation of Mary to Elizabeth, formerly celebrated on July 2, is now on May 31. In accord with the liturgical reform of 1969, the Feast of the Circumcision (on January 31, the octave of Christmas) is now celebrated as the Solemnity of Holy Mary, Mother of God, giving due weight to the first formal theological title (Theotokos) given to Mary at the Council of EPHESUS (351). There are also a number of minor feasts of Mary.

DEVOTIONS

A number of Catholic DEVOTIONS have come to be centered on the Blessed Virgin, most of them arising in the Middle Ages. Today they include offices, litanies, prayers such as the Angelus and the MAGNIFICAT, pilgrimages, and novenas (nine-day cycles of devotion), usually associated with major Marian feast days, and the wearing of medals and scapulars. The Rosary holds a special place in Catholic piety to which Pope JOHN PAUL II added new mysteries. Since the 1980s there has been a noticeable return to such traditional Marian devotion.

APPARITIONS

There have been countless apparitions of the Blessed Virgin throughout Christian history, often clothed in colorful folklore and legend. One of the first clearly reported accounts was the appearance of the Theotokos to St. GREGORY OF NYSSA; new apparitions are reported every year.

In modern times stringent criteria must be observed, first by the local bishop and then by the Vatican, before apparitions can be recognized as worthy of devotions and pilgrimages. Some of the more well-known apparitions that have official approval of the church are listed below. With the exceptions of Guadalupe and the Miraculous Medal, all the apparitions were to children or youth. In addition to these, a number of newer apparitions of the Virgin are being investigated or have received local or Vatican recognition as supernatural occurrences. There have also been many reports of as yet unrecognized apparitions, such as in Conyers, Georgia, (1983–98) and the Mojave Desert (1997).

Our Lady of Guadalupe (1531)

The Blessed Virgin appeared four times to the recently converted mestizo (half Aztec, half Spanish) Juan Diego Cuauhtlatoatzin (1474–1548) as "the mother of the true God who gives life." At the fourth apparition she made roses appear in his tilma, or cloak, which he unfolded before the bishop to reveal the image of the Guadalupe now in the BASILICA. Mary is depicted as mestizo, and the image incorporates Aztec elements and colors and a reference to Tonantzin, the Aztec mother goddess. Juan Diego was beatified (2000) and canonized (2002) by JOHN PAUL II on his two visits to the shrine outside Mexico City. Our Lady of Guadalupe is patroness of all the Americas.

Our Lady of the Miraculous Medal (1830)

Mary appeared three times to St. Catherine Laboure (1806–76), a Daughter of Charity of St. VINCENT DE PAUL. At the last appearance Mary asked Catherine to have an image of the Immaculate Conception cast to increase devotion to Mary. The medal soon became known as the Miraculous Medal, which is still worn by millions of Catholics. This appearance influenced the dogma of the Immaculate Conception declared by Pius IX in 1854.

Our Lady of LaSalette (1846)

Mary appeared in the French Alps to Maximin Giraud (age 11) and Melanie Calvat (age 14) in sorrow and tears, calling for penance and conversion.

Our Lady of Lourdes (1858)

This apparition rivals the one at Fatima in popularity and worldwide devotion. Mary showed herself 18 times to 14-year-old Bernadette Soubirous (1844–79) at the Grotto of Massabielle near LOURDES, France, under the title of the Immaculate Conception, calling for penance, prayer, and conversion. Water that flows from a spring at the site of the apparition is considered holy by Catholics and non-Catholics around the world. Bernadette entered the Sisters of Nevers in a convent near the shrine that grew up around Lourdes. When her body was exhumed in 1909, 30 years after her death, it was in a state of preservation. It was reexhumed in 1919 and is now on view in the convent. Bernadette was canonized by PIUS XI in 1933. Thousands of Catholics and non-Catholics make the PILGRIMAGE to Lourdes every year, and thousands have reported cures, which are carefully examined by physicians before being so declared by the church. The latest recognized cure is that of Jean-Pierre Bély (1987), officially noted in 1997. Lourdes was seen by many as a confirmation of the dogma of the Immaculate Conception of Mary. The feast, which used to be universal until 1969, is celebrated on February 11. Jennifer Jones starred in the acclaimed film about Lourdes named *Song of Bernadette* (1943).

Our Lady of Pontmain (1871)

In this little-known apparition, Mary appeared to the farmer children Eugene (age 10) and Joseph (age 12) Barbadette, and students Francoise Richer and Jeanne-Marie Lebosse. Her message was on a banner unfurled at her feet, saying "My son lets himself be moved by compassion."

Our Lady of Fatima (1917)

Mary appeared to shepherdess Lucia de Santos (age 10) and her cousins Francisco (age 9) and Jacinta (age 7) Marto in seven apparitions as Our Lady of the Rosary at Fatima in Portugal. In one of the visions the Sun seemed to approach the Earth. Mary urged saying the Rosary, conversion of sinners, and the consecration of Russia to her Immaculate Heart. She also revealed three secrets that were long kept within the church. Pope JOHN PAUL II, after consulting with the surviving visionary, Sister Maria Lucia de Santos (1907–2005), concluded that the third message referred to the assassination attempt against himself in 1981. Their exchange is published as "The Message of Fatima" by the Congregation for the Doctrine of the Faith on the Vatican Web site. John Paul II beatified Francisco (1908–19) and Jacinta (1910–20) on May 13, 2000. The statue of Our Lady of Fatima has toured the world several times.

Our Lady of Beauring (1932–1933)

Mary appeared 33 times as the Immaculate Virgin and Mother of God, Queen of Heaven, to Andree and Gilberte Degeimbre and Albert, Fernande, and Gilberte Voisin (ages 9–15) on a playground in Beauring, Belgium, calling for conversion of sinners.

Madonna and Christ Child. Ceramic folk sculpture by Rosita and José Sosa, Chulucanas, Peru. *(courtesy Plowsharing Crafts, St. Louis, Mo.; photo by John Huston)*

Our Lady of Banneux (1933)

Mary appeared to Mariette Beco (age 11) eight times as the Virgin of the Poor, promising to intercede for them.

Our Lady of Medjugorje (1981–   )

Beginning in 1981 Mary started to appear to the children Ivanka, Vicka, and Ivan Ivankovic, Mirjana and Ivan Dragicevic, and Milka Pavlovic in the Boznia-Herzegovina village of Medjugorje. Her message is peace, love, faith, prayer, and fasting. The number of pilgrims has reached into the millions, and people of all faiths and no faith report being cured. There has been much conflict between the FRANCISCAN fathers who have sponsored the site and the local bishop. The Congregation for the Doctrine of the Faith has put responsibility for overseeing the authenticity of the visions into the hands of the bishops' conference.

Our Lady of Akita (1969–1978)

Sister Agnes Katsuka Sasagawa, then a postulant in the Order of the Handmaids of the Eucharist in Akita, Japan, began receiving visions of an angelic being, later identified as the Lady of All Peoples and Our Lady of Sorrows. After the apparitions a Katsura (Cerediphyllum japonicum) wooden statue of Mary began to show blood on the right hand and later to shed tears, like many other wooden ICONS and statues throughout the world. The apparitions and occurrences at Akita were deemed supernatural in 1988 by the Congregation for the Doctrine of the Faith.

Our Lady of Rwanda (1981–1983/-   )

In November 1981 Mary appeared to Alphonsine Mumureke (1965–   ), Marie-Claire Mukangang (1961–94), Stephanie Mukamurenzi (1968–   ), Agnes Kamagaju (1960–   ), Emanuel Segatashya (1967–94), and Vestine Salima (1960–   ). She called for prayer and conversion and spoke of the Last Judgment, predicting that if Rwanda did not return to the Lord, there would be "a river of blood." Marie-Claire Mukangang and Emmanuel Segatashya both died during the Hutu-Tutsi genocide. Apparitions ceased for all save Alphonsine in 1983. Archbishop Augustin Misago (1943–   ) of Gikongoro, Rwanda, authenticated the visions in 2001 after consultation with the Vatican.

Our Lady of Betania

Visionary Maria Esperanza (1928–2004) began at an early age to receive apparitions of St. THÉRÈSE OF LISIEUX, the SACRED HEART OF JESUS, and Mary, who appeared to her in Betania, Venezuela, under the title Mary, Virgin and Mother, Reconciler of All People and Nations. At first Maria entered a Franciscan convent, but the Sacred Heart of Jesus appeared to her and told her to sanctify her life as a spouse and mother. On December 8, 1956, in the Chapel of the Immaculate Conception in ST. PETER'S BASILICA, she married Geo Bianchini Giani, with whom she had seven children. Like St. FRANCIS and Padre Pio (1887–1968), she received the STIGMATA, or wounds of Christ, in her hands and side. People claimed she healed, levitated, and bilocated (appeared in two places at the same time). The appearance of blood in a consecrated Eucharistic Host has also been associated with the shrine at Betania. The local church approved the apparitions to Maria Esperanza in 1987.

IMAGES

All the titles and apparitions of Mary discussed above have images and holy pictures associated with them. In addition, a number of special representations of Mary have attained universal veneration. Miracles, visions, healings, and other supernatural phenomena are associated with these noted images of Mary.

One of the most popular is the image of Our Lady of Częstochowa, also called Our lady of Jasna Gora. The icon was brought by Prince Ladislaus Opolszyk to a chapel at Jasna Gora in 1382. Legend says that St. Luke painted the image and that St. Helena found it in Jerusalem and brought it to CONSTANTINOPLE. The image was damaged over the centuries by Tartars and Hussites, and it was repainted virtually anew in 1434. Scholars say the image is a variant of the common Byzantine type called the Virgin Hodegetria (showing Jesus as the Way of Salvation). Our Lady of Częstochowa became patroness of Poland, and her veneration was spread to the world by Polish emigrants.

Another well-known image is the Byzantine icon of Our Lady of Perpetual Help, or Succor, which legend says came from Crete. It was installed in the church of St. Matthew the Apostle in Rome, then transferred by AUGUSTINIANS to Santa Maria in Posterula in Rome, and finally acquired by the Redemptorists and placed in their new church of the Most Holy Redeemer in Rome in 1865. A third popular image of Mary is Our Lady of Mt. Carmel, venerated by CARMELITES and popular throughout the world.

The image of Our Lady of Loreto, near Ancona, Italy, derives its sanctity from a medieval legend that angels transported the house of the Annunciation in Nazareth first to Terstaz in Dalmatia and then to its present site in Italy in 1295. Many churches in the United States are named after Our Lady of Loreto. All scholars today see the house's attribution as unhistorical.

Each local region in the world has its own special image of the Virgin that it venerates. The resurgence of Marian devotion, including its more atavistic manifestations, is due in part to the influence of Pope John Paul II, who brought with him to the pontificate a long-standing devotion to Our Lady of Częstochowa. He dedicated his pontificate to Mary and applied the third secret of Fatima directly to himself.

Further reading: Cornelius X. Friethoff, *A Complete Mariology* (London: Blackfriars, 1958); Mark Garvey, *Searching for Mary: An Exploration of Marian Apparitions across the U.S.* (New York: Plume, 1998); Amy Jill Levine and Maria Mayo Robbins, *A Feminist Companion to Mariology* (Cleveland: Pilgrim, 2005); Elliot Miller and Kenneth R. Samples, *The Cult of the Virgin: Catholic Mariology and the Apparitions of Mary* (Grand Rapids, Mich.: Baker, 1992); Antoine Nachef, *Mary's Pope: John Paul, Mary, and the Church since Vatican II* (Franklin, Wis.: Sheed & Ward, 2000); Ferdinand Nwaigbo, *Mary—Mother of the African Church: A Theological Inculturation of Mariology* (New York: Peter Lang, 2001); Jaroslav Pelikan, David Flusser, and Justin Lang, *Mary: Images of the Mother of Jesus in Jewish and Christian Perspective* (Minneapolis: Fortress, 2005); Wayne Weible, *The Final Harvest: Medjugorje at the End of the Century* (Brewster, Mass.: Paraclete, 1999).

Maximus IV Sayegh (1878–1967) *Melkite Catholic patriarch*

Maximus IV Sayegh, the patriarch of the MELKITE CATHOLIC CHURCH during VATICAN COUNCIL II (1962–65), emerged as a significant force in changing the image and role of the Eastern Catholic patriarchates (*see* EASTERN CATHOLICISM) at a time when the Roman Catholic Church was moving to alter its relationship with EASTERN ORTHODOXY. The Eastern Catholic Churches had emerged over the centuries as various regional church groups left the jurisdiction of the Eastern patriarchs and moved into communion with Rome. The very existence of these churches was a major obstacle to reconciliation between the PAPACY and the ecumenical patriarchate in CONSTANTINOPLE. At the same time, many BISHOPS of the Western, Latin rite were condescending toward the Eastern rite minority within the Roman communion.

At the council, Maximus spoke early and often and in a manner that assumed full equality with the Latin-rite majority of the Catholic Church. For example, he did not speak Latin when he addressed the council. Also, he refused to give precedence to Latin rite bishops over Eastern rite patriarchs. He was a strong voice for the use of the vernacular in the LITURGY of the Mass, which had been the longtime practice in Eastern Rite churches.

In 1965, Pope PAUL VI named Maximus a cardinal. Following his death in 1967, he was succeeded by Maximus V Hakim (r. 1967–2000).

Further reading: Serge Descy, *The Melkite Church: An Historical and Ecclesiological Approach* (Newton: Sophia, 1993).

Medjugorje   *See* MARY OF NAZARETH.

Melkite Catholic Church

The Melkite Catholic Church developed out of a SCHISM within the Syrian Orthodox Church of Antioch in the 18th century. (The word *Melkite* derives from *melek,* the Semitic word for "king.") In 1724, two factions within the church, one headquartered at Aleppo and the other in Damascus, each elected a patriarch. At this point the Ecumenical Patriarch in CONSTANTINOPLE intervened and aligned himself with the Aleppo party. The other patriarch, Cyril VI, was removed from office and forced into exile in Lebanon. Five years later Pope Benedict XIII (1649–1730) inserted himself into the situation. He recognized Cyril as the Antiochean patriarch and joined forces with him to create the Melkite Catholic Church. The new church retained its eastern LITURGY and traditions (including the ordination of married priests) but adjusted its doctrinal stance to accord with Catholic (as opposed to Eastern Orthodox) doctrine.

The Melkite Catholic Church is one of the larger eastern Catholic churches with approximately 1 million members worldwide. Although membership is centered in Syria and Lebanon, it has members in Israel, Palestine, and Egypt; its patriarch carries the additional titles of patriarch of Jerusalem and patriarch of Alexandria (each of which has a parallel Greek patriarch). In 1848 the Ottoman authorities granted the church full recognition, following which headquarters were relocated from Damascus to Sidon, Lebanon. In the late 19th century, Melkite Christians began a global diaspora that saw Melkite communities form in Brazil, Venezuela, Canada, and the United States, all now home to new dioceses. The church is active in the Middle East Council of Churches. In the 20th century, the church moved its headquarters back to Damascus. The present patriarch is Archbishop Georges Bakouney (1962–   ).

Further reading: Serge Descy, *The Melkite Church: An Historical and Ecclesiological Approach* (Newton: Sophia, 1993); Nikolaus Liesel, *The Eastern Catholic Liturgies: A Study in Words and Pictures.* (Westminster, Md.: Newman, 1960); Ronald G. Roberson, *The Eastern Christian Churches: A Brief Survey,* 5th ed. (Rome: Edizioni Orientalia Christiana, Pontificio Istituto Orientale, 1995).

mendicant orders

Taking their name from the Latin word for begging (*mendicare*), the mendicant orders arose in 13th-century Europe and were granted the privilege of wandering and sustaining themselves by labor and charity from the general public (at the time synonymous with the faithful). Unlike other monastic orders, the mendicants at first renounced ownership of corporate property as well as taking the usual individual vows of poverty. The orders appeared in part as a response to Lateran Council IV (1215) (*see* COUNCILS, ECUMENICAL), which had called for renewal of the pastoral mission. The council asked that a cadre of men be chosen to offer free instruction in grammar at every church, assist in preaching in every diocese, and teach THEOLOGY in every metropolitan church. The mendicant friars would meet the need for preaching and teaching. As they eschewed MONASTERIES in favor of a life of wandering, they could go or be sent wherever needs were manifest.

The two most important mendicant orders were the DOMINICANS (Order of Preachers), founded in 1216 by DOMINIC DE GUZMÁN (d. 1221), and the FRANCISCANS, founded in 1223 by St. FRANCIS OF ASSISI (d. 1226). The Carmelites, who emerged over the course of the early 13th century, and the Hermits of St. Augustine (*see* AUGUSTINIANS), formed by uniting several older orders in 1254 and the Mercedarians, would later join them.

The mendicant orders proved an immense success both in recruiting people to their cause and in carrying out the mission to which they had been called across Europe. They were in fact so successful that fellow priests in local churches and the universities, feeling the competition for financial support, began to criticize them. This criticism came to a head in 1274, when the Council of Lyons II included an examination of the mendicants in its agenda. Two prominent mendicant friars, THOMAS AQUINAS and BONAVENTURA (both of whom died that year), came to the orders' defense; their arguments were accepted by the council, which gave the Franciscans and Dominicans its full support and added provisional support for the more recently formed Carmelites and Augustinians (which were given full approval in 1298).

After the first burst of energy, the church HIERARCHY began to regulate the mendicants and use them for various purposes. The mendicants also became embroiled in bitter disputes among themselves and with the PAPACY on whether Jesus' was absolutely poor. In 1300, for example, the papacy ordered friars to seek a license from the BISHOP of any DIOCESE in which they worked. The Council of TRENT gave most of the mendicant orders the privilege of owning corporate property.

The Dominicans would become famous for taking the lead in the INQUISITION and the Franciscans in building the church in the Americas.

Further reading: R. F. Bennett, *The Early Dominicans: Studies in Thirteenth-Century Dominican History* (Cambridge: Cambridge University Press, 1937); Kajetan Esser, *Origins of the Franciscan Order,* tr. Aedan Daly (Chicago: Franciscan Herald, 1970); W. A. Hinnebusch, *A History of the Dominican Order: Origins and Growth to 1550* (New York: Alba House, 1966); C. H. Lawrence, *The Friars: The Impact of the Early Mendicant Movement on Western Society* (New York: Longman, 1994); Henry Charles Lea, *A History of The Inquisition of The Middle Ages,* 3 vols. (New York: Harper & Brothers, 1888).

merit   *See* JUSTIFICATION.

Merton, Thomas (1915–1968) *Cistercian monk, mystic, and prolific author*

Thomas Merton, an American Trappist (CISTERCIAN) MONK and author, was born in Prades, FRANCE. His mother died when he was six and his father when he was 16. He studied at the Oakham School in England; after a year at Cambridge University he moved to the United States and continued his schooling at Columbia University. He wrote his master's thesis on William Blake, a catalyst for his conversion from a lukewarm Anglicanism to Catholicism.

Merton became an instructor at St. Bonaventure's College, now University, in rural New York state and tried to enter the FRANCISCANS. Rebuffed, he encountered the Trappists in 1941 while attending a retreat at their Bardstown, Kentucky, MONASTERY, called Gethsemani. Toward the end of the year he was accepted as a choir novice.

Merton resided at Gethsemani for the rest of his life. In the cloistered atmosphere he had time and was encouraged to write. His most famous book, the best-selling autobiographical *Seven Story Mountain* (1948), revealed a passion-

ate young mystic in the making. Merton would mature over the next two decades. He wrote much on Cistercian spirituality (*see* THEOLOGY). Though remaining at the monastery, he developed an international correspondence with many leading figures of his day, which gave him a worldwide voice. Most notably, he condemned racial violence and the Vietnam War during the 1960s.

In 1968, a new abbot at Gethsemani allowed Merton leave to tour Asia to visit some of his correspondents, during which time he met with the Dalai Lama. He was a leader in ECUMENISM and interreligious dialogue. Unfortunately, he was accidently electrocuted in a Bangkok hotel and died. His body lies buried at Gethsemani.

Merton was a prolific author, turning out almost one new book a year during his 20 years in the monastery. However, a large part of his writings, in accordance with his wish, were not published until 25 years after his death. The most important of the more recently published texts include his dairies.

Further reading: Dennis Q. Mcinerny, *Thomas Merton: The Man and His Work* (Washington, D.C.: Cistercian, 1974); Thomas Merton, *The Ascent to Truth* (New York: Harcourt, Brace, 1951); ———, *Conjectures of a Guilty Bystander* (Garden City, N.Y.: Doubleday, 1966); ———, *Elected Silence—The Autobiography of Thomas Merton* (London: Hollis & Carter, 1949); ———, *The Journals of Thomas Merton,* 7 vols. (New York: Harper, 1995); ———, *The Seven Story Mountain* (New York: Harcourt, Brace, 1948).

Michael I Cerularius (c. 1000–1059) *Eastern Orthodox Ecumenical Patriarch*

Michael I Cerularius was the patriarch of Constantinople in 1054 when relations between Pope Leo IX (r. 1049–54) and the Eastern Church collapsed and the break known as the GREAT SCHISM occurred. Little is known of his early life, though he came from a prominent CONSTANTINOPLE family.

He was groomed for public service, but following the suicide of his brother he entered a MONASTERY. In 1043 he was named patriarch.

Michael became a staunch advocate of the prerogatives of the Eastern Church against the claims of the PAPACY. He also emerged as a vocal critic of what he considered Rome's deviation on a variety of points of belief and practice, and an effective opponent of its temporal power. In the 1050s Pope LEO IX, as monarch of the PAPAL STATES, sought an alliance with the Byzantine emperor to stop the advance of the Normans, then establishing themselves on the island of Sicily. Michael stepped in to block the pope's plans. In 1052, as negotiations between Leo IX and the emperor proceeded, Cerularius ordered several churches in his diocese that used the Latin LITURGY to adopt the Greek liturgy. When they refused he ordered them to be closed.

In 1054, Cerularius insulted Leo's diplomatic legates by refusing to meet with them. Shortly after April 9, word reached Constantinople that Leo had died. On July 16 at Hagia Sophia, Humbert, one of the legates, declared Cerularius and his supporters excommunicated. The act had little support locally; Cerularius convened a Holy Synod and excommunicated all the legates. The emperor tried to step into the quarrel but was unable to quell the rising storm.

As it turned out, the Byzantine throne would soon be vacated; it was held by three different people over the next few years, giving Michael I ample scope to exercise power. But Isaac I Comnenus (r. 1057–59), had Michael charged with treason and exiled. The ship that took him from Constantinople was wrecked, and Michael drowned.

Though Michael did not long outlast the schism he helped cause, his actions had long-standing effects. The break in communion between Eastern and Western Churches has continued for nearly a millennium and has withstood many attempts to heal it.

See also COUNCIL OF FLORENCE; EASTERN ORTHODOXY.

Further reading: Aidan Nichols, *Rome and the Eastern Churches: A Study in Schism* (Collegeville, Minn.: Liturgical Press, 1992); Steven Runciman, *The Eastern Schism: A Study of the Papacy and the Eastern Churches During the XIth and XIIth Centuries* (Oxford: Oxford University Press, 1953).

Michael the Archangel, St. *leader of the faithful angels*

Michael is one of three angels mentioned by name in the BIBLE. He is introduced in chapter 10 of the Book of Daniel to comfort the prophet. Daniel later refers to him as the "great prince" who stands up for Israel during their captivity (Dan. 12). The New Testament epistle of Jude mentions Michael

St. Michael the Archangel slaying the dragon, by Albrecht Dürer (1471–1528) *(Girandon/Art Resource, NY)*

as arguing with the devil over the body of Moses (an incident not mentioned anywhere else in Hebrew literature).

Michael comes into his own in the Apocalypse (Book of Revelation). He is most remembered and acknowledged as the leader of the side of the angels in the heavenly war against the forces of the "dragon" (i.e., Satan). This reference led Western Christian writers to consider Michael the protector of the church, and he was regularly mentioned in the LITURGY of the Mass. He is also seen as the single most prominent angel amid the heavenly hosts, and he is frequently pictured in armor carrying a sword.

In 708, Bishop Aubert of Avranche, FRANCE, in response to a vision of St. Michael, had a church built on the coast of Normandy that now exists on an island (Mont Saint Michel) some two kilometers offshore. The church possesses a red cloth said to have been touched by the angel as well as a slab of marble on which he is reported to have sat. A similar site is located on an island off the coast of Cornwall, where a castle and church were also built in response to a vision of the archangel.

Michael is additionally honored in the liturgical calendar as a saint with special concern for seafarers, the ill, and grocers. His feast day, Michaelmas Day, is September 29 (also the feast day for the archangels Gabriel and Raphael).

Michael's place in western consciousness was heightened by Puritan poet John Milton (1608–74), who vividly described the angel's battle with Satan in his epic poem *Paradise Lost* (1667). In an earlier poem, *Lycidas* (1638), Milton wrote of Michael's legendary role as England's patron-protector against foreign enemies; with civil war approaching, Milton called on England's benefactor to "look homeward, angel," a phrase that became embedded in the country's heritage.

Further reading: Andrew A. Bialas, *The Patronage of Saint Michael the Archangel* (Chicago: Clerics of St. Viator, 1954); Jean Daniélou, *The Angels and Their Mission According to the Church Fathers* (Westminster, Md.: Newman, 1957); David Hugh Farmer, *The Oxford Dictionary of Saints* (Oxford: Clarendon, 1978).

Michelangelo (1475-1564) *Renaissance painter, architect, sculptor, and poet*

Arguably one of the greatest artists of all time, Michelangelo was a prolific artist in many media. Some of his most famous works explored religious themes, including the fresco on the ceiling of the Sistine Chapel in VATICAN CITY, the *Last Judgement* over the altar there, and the sculptures *David*, the *Pietà*, and *Moses*.

Michelangelo Buonarroti was born at Caprese, the son of a noble Florentine. In 1488 he began an apprenticeship with Domenico Ghirlandaio, but after three years he began studying under the patronage of Lorenzo de' Medici (1449–92) and pursued his love of sculpture. In 1496 he went to Rome, where he carved the *Pietà* at the age of 26. He briefly returned to Florence in 1502 and carved *David*, his most famous sculpture, a tribute to the biblical king as a youth before his battle with Goliath. In 1505 he was called back to Rome by Julius II (r. 1503–13) and commissioned to construct the papal tomb. Michelangelo's design was so elaborate that it was never completed, but he finished a sculpture of *Moses* that was to be part of the tomb.

From 1508 to 1512, under pressure from Julius II, he designed and painted the ceiling frescoes in the Sistine Chapel. Those representing Creation are some the most powerful and beautiful paintings ever done. His creation of Adam is reproduced endlessly; it displays the artist's conflict between the humanistic love of the perfect male figure and religious devotion. His interaction with the pope as he painted the ceiling became the focus of the 1965 Charlton Heston film version of Irving Stone's *The Agony and the Ecstasy*. From 1534 to 1541 he painted the *Last Judgment*, also in the Sistine Chapel. Although he is less well known for it, he was also a good poet, dedicating most of his sonnets to his friend the marchessa

Panel from ceiling of Sistine Chapel (Vatican City, Rome) by Michelangelo (1475–1564) showing Eve taking forbidden fruit from the serpent. *(Erich Lessing/ Art Resource, NY)*

Vittoria Colonna (1490/92–1547). Toward the end of his life he was instructed to direct the building of St. Peter's Basilica, of which he designed the dome. He continued in papal employment until his death.

Further reading: Paul Barolsky and Sophie Segur, *Michelangelo and the Finger of God* (Athens: University of Georgia Press, 2003); George Anthony Bull, *Michelangelo: A Biography* (London: Viking, 1995); Ascanio Condivi, *The Life of Michel-Angelo* (State College: Pennsylvania State University Press, 1999); Ross King, *Michelangelo & The Pope's Ceiling* (New York: Walker, 2003).

Middle Ages

In the 15th century, Renaissance intellectuals in Europe began referring to the many centuries between the fall of Rome in 476 and their own day as a single era, which they called the "Middle Ages." In their parochial view, it had been a lost era sunk in superstition, ignorance, and cultural deprivation. Their view was soon reinforced during the Protestant Reformation, whose scholars saw the Middle Ages as a time dominated by the papacy and by a host of practices and theories that

they believed deviated from the original pristine Christianity. The negative judgments began to be challenged only in the Romantic era of the early 19th century. By the late 20th century, the dating of the era itself began to be challenged.

Scholars first called into question both the start and end dates of the era as specialists highlighted its many cultural accomplishments (e.g., the development of the Romance languages, the emergence of new governmental and judicial structures, the modern university, and Gothic architecture) during the 10 centuries traditionally ascribed to it. Reconsideration of the basic outlines of Western history, moving from the earlier parochial perspectives to more globalized viewpoints, are likely to continue, especially as more attention is given to the rise of Islam, the spread of Eastern Orthodoxy through the Slavic world, and pre-Reformation attempts to reform the Catholic Church.

Further reading: David Abulafia et al., *The New Cambridge Medieval History.* (Cambridge: Cambridge University Press, 1995); Norman Cantor: *The Civilization of the Middle Ages* (New York: Harper Collins, 1993); George Holmes, ed., *The Oxford History of Medieval Europe* (New York: Oxford University Press, 1988); David C. Lindberg, *The Beginnings of Western Science: The European Scientific Tradition in Philosophical, Religious, and Institutional Context, 600 B.C. to A.D. 1450* (Chicago: University of Chicago Press, 1992).

millenarianism

Millenarianism is a Christian view of history that foresees the imminent establishment of a thousand-year era of divine order under the reign of Christ, replacing the foibles and suffering of the present age. While various mechanisms for this transition have been proposed, almost all include the Second Coming of Christ and a time of judgment (*see* ESCHATOLOGY.). (This is not the Final Judgment, which will come after the thousand-year period, or millennium.)

Millenarianism usually rests on a literal reading of the biblical books of Daniel and the APOCALYPSE (Revelation), the millennium itself being a direct reference to Revelation 20:1–15. The belief was popular during the first century, but it began to fade by the second in favor of what has become known as amillennialism, which looked for the building of a Christian society on Earth. Revelation 20 was interpreted allegorically, with the millennium referring to the reality of church life from Pentecost to the Second Coming (whose date no one could predict).

Millenarianism in the strictly Christian context, and increasingly in non-Christian contexts in the contemporary world, has emerged sporadically throughout Western history. Prominent proponents include JOACHIM OF FIORE, Thomas Münzer (c. 1488–1525), who led the Protestant Peasant's Revolt (1524–26) and William Miller (1782–1949), who inaugurated the millennialism later known as Seventh Day Adventism. The violence accompanying the brief career of Thomas Münzer as a revolutionary was seized upon to create an image of millennialism as inevitably leading to violence. If anything, however, the truth is quite the reverse. Most millennial groups have been completely free of violence, and many have been programmatically pacifist. In recent times American fundamentalist millenialists have endorsed the use of violence against communist regimes and militant ISLAM. The Vatican has issued many warnings against various aspects of fundamentalism since the 19th century.

Further reading: Norman Cohn, *The Pursuit of the Millennium: Revolutionary Millenarians and Mystical Anarchists of the Middle Ages* (New York: Oxford University Press, 1990); Ted Daniels, *Millennialism: An International Bibliography* (New York: Garland, 1992); Jeffrey Kaplan, *Radical Religion in America: Millenarian Movements from the Far Right to the Children of Noah* (Syracuse, N.Y.: Syracuse University Press, 1997); Richard Landes, *Encyclopedia of Millennialism and Millennial Movements* (New York: Routledge, 2000); Jon R. Stone, *A Guide to the End of the World: Popular Eschatology in America: The Mainstream Evangelical Tradition* (New York: Garland, 1993).

Mindszenty, Joseph Cardinal (1892–1975)
primate of Hungary

Joseph Mindszenty, who in the last half of the 20th century became a symbol of anticommunism, was born in the town of Csehimindszent, in today's Hungary, in 1892. Raised in a pious Catholic environment, he was ordained a priest in 1915. During World War II, he was consecrated BISHOP of Veszprem (1944) but was arrested a few months later by the Nazis. Shortly after the war, in October 1945, Pope PIUS XII named him ARCHBISHOP of Esztergom and primate of Hungary and several months later presented him with his cardinal's hat.

Following World War II, a communist government came to power in Hungary under Soviet control. Mindszenty was arrested in Budapest on December 26, 1948. His FAITH was tested for the next two decades. He was forced to confess under the pressure of mood-altering drugs and sentenced to life imprisonment, although he was released after only a few years. In 1956 he was granted asylum in the American embassy during the failed Hungarian uprising, and he remained there for the next 15 years. He almost immediately began to publicly demand that the Hungarian government accommodate its religious citizens.

Improved relations between Hungary and the noncommunist world presented an opportunity to rescue Mindszenty, and in 1971 Pope PAUL VI arranged for him to resettle in Vienna, Austria, where he died in 1975. His body was later returned to Hungary and buried at the Basilica of Esztergom. Through the 1970s and 1980s, Mindszenty became a symbol of the Catholic religious struggle against the communist governments of eastern Europe. His memory is kept alive by the Cardinal Mindszenty Foundation based in St. Louis, Missouri, which focuses on resistance to what it sees as secular attacks on the Catholic faith.

Further reading: Nicholas Boer, *Cardinal Mindszenty and the Implacable War of Communism against Religion and the Spirit* (London: B.U.E., 1949); *Documents on the Mindszenty Case* (Budapest: Athenaeum, 1949); Stanley G. Evans, *The Trial of Cardinal Mindszenty: An Eye Witness Account* (Birmingham: Religion and the People, 1949); Joseph Mindszenty, *Memoirs, Jozsef Cardinal Mindszenty* (London: Weidenfeld & Nicolson, 1974).

miracles (Lat.: *miraculare,* "to wonder")

In the most traditional sense, a miracle is a divine intervention by GOD for a specific religious purpose, an act that transcends the laws of nature. Modern science has questioned the possibility of miracles because it views the world as a closed system of which the natural laws cannot be violated by a higher power. Earlier scientists did not always agree: Isaac Newton (1642–1727) believed that God was sovereign over creation and could intervene at any time, for example, to correct perturbations in the orbits of the planets. PANTHE-ISM, according to Benedict Spinoza (1632–77), rejected miracles because they are in violation of nature, and since God is nature, they are literally in violation of God. DEISM also rejects miracles based on its belief that God is noninterventionist.

Jewish neo-Aristotelian philosophers, such as Maimonides (1135–1204), argued that miracles are not a current intervention by God but rather events that were preplanned to happen at specific times and places. This is akin to the philosopher Gottfried Wilhelm Leibniz's (1646–1716) idea of preestablished harmony. Many CHRISTIAN theologians have argued that miracles are reasonable and plausible, citing the scriptural miracles in the Old and New Testaments, specifically those performed by Jesus CHRIST.

Catholicism has long accepted the possibility and actuality of miracles. If God is the Prime Mover and First Cause, then it is reasonable to assume God can act in the world because while being responsible for the laws of nature, God is not subject to them. God can perform miracles through divine intervention. Humans, too, can perform miracles if certain conditions are in place. St. FRANCIS OF ASSISI performed hundreds of them during his lifetime and thousands after his death. The Vatican has recorded more than 12,000 events it regards as miracles, such as the well-known healings at LOURDES. A medical commission was set up in 1882 to authenticate miracles at Lourdes. A precondition for CANONIZATION into sainthood was formerly two authenticated miracles each for beatification and CANONIZATION after death. JOHN PAUL II reduced it to one for each.

Further reading: Howard Clark Kee, *Miracle in the Early Christian World: A Study in Sociohistorical Method* (New Haven, Conn.: Yale University Press, 1983); Robert A. Larmer, ed., *Questions of Miracle* (Montreal: McGill-Queen's University Press, 1996); C. S. Lewis, *Miracles, A Preliminary Study* (London: Centenary, 1947); Robert D. Smith, *Comparative Miracles* (St. Louis: B. Herder, 1965); Frederick Robert Tennant, *Miracle and its Philosophical Presuppositions* (Cambridge: Cambridge University Press, 1925).

missions (Lat.: *mittere,* "to send out")

The term *mission* refers to everything the church does to further the kingdom of GOD on Earth. In its plural form, however, it has come to refer more narrowly to the work of evangelization—inviting people into a relationship with God through Jesus CHRIST, usually at some distance from one's home and often in a context foreign to one's social or cultural background. It is seen as a specific response to the great commission, Jesus' words to his APOSTLES to go therefore and make disciples of all nations. (Matt. 28:19).

The APOSTLE PAUL is usually thought of as the first true missionary, though by the time he arrived on the scene, the church was already spreading geographically. Beginning around 38 he made three notable tours of the Mediterranean basin on the coasts of present-day Greece and Turkey, establishing new churches in places where followers of Jesus had been before. He first brought the Gospel to Europe, in response to the "Macedonian call" (Acts 16:9), a dream in which he saw someone asking him to come to Greece and share the message of Jesus.

Simultaneously, the other APOSTLES were said to have gone to different countries. Thomas, for example, is said to have traveled east to Syria and then on to India. Mark, besides traveling with Paul, is claimed as the first missionary in EGYPT (see COPTIC CHURCH), though his exploits there are by no means as well documented as those of Paul. Much of the growth of the church in the first century was accomplished anonymously. Tradition has both Peter and Paul dying in Rome.

As the church grew from its original urban centers, from Jerusalem to Rome, it settled in all parts of the Mediterranean coast. After CONSTANTINE gave Christianity legitimacy within the Roman Empire, it spread beyond its early established territory through the efforts of pioneering MONKS, priests, and BISHOPS. Augustine of Canterbury (d. 604), for example, was sent by Pope GREGORY I to England and, while not the first Christian there, was the first to establish the church on a permanent footing to allow its spread across the country. In like measure, St. BONIFACE established the church in Germany, and Sts. CYRIL AND METHODIUS became the great missionaries among the Slavic peoples.

Beginning in the eighth century, the church's missionary growth in the lands east and south of the Mediterranean was blunted by the emergence of Islam. Once SCANDINAVIA was brought into the fold, the Atlantic blocked further expansion of Latin Christianity. Foreign missionary work came to a virtual standstill for several centuries, though there were a few exceptions, such as the FRANCISCANS' trips into China in the 13th century (see JOHN OF MONTE CORVINO).

The division of the church in 1054 into Roman Catholic and EASTERN ORTHODOX worlds established new possibilities for missions—the Eastern Orthodox lands that seemed less than fully Christian. With the launching of the CRUSADES missionaries followed behind the conquering armies, allowing them to establish Catholic churches in lands generally considered Orthodox territory. This was the origin of EASTERN CATHOLICISM, as Roman Catholic missionaries accepted whole communities of formerly Orthodox into communion with the bishop of Rome.

A new era opened for missionary endeavors in the 16th century. First, the PROTESTANT REFORMATION took a number of countries in western and northern Europe out of the Catholic Church. Countries such as England, Germany, and Holland became targets for future evangelical efforts from Rome. Countries like Poland, which at one point had shown Protestant leanings, were among the territories won back to the Catholic Church during the COUNTER-REFORMATION. Second, the discovery of the Americas and of sea routes to South and East Asia by European explorers opened up huge populations as potential fields for an entirely fresh missionary effort. By this time the church had the assistance of a new set of deployable missionaries, the friars of the mendicant orders, especially the FRANCISCANS, DOMINICANS, and AUGUSTINIANS.

The expansion of the Catholic Church in the 16th century is tied closely to the emergence of the JESUIT order, established in 1540. Its founding principles included a readiness to go anywhere in the world they were sent by the pope or their superiors. By 1552, FRANCIS XAVIER was in India; he was joined within a decade by some 50 colleagues. In the 1580s, MATEO RICCI led the order into China. The first Jesuits in the New World reached Portuguese Brazil in 1549.

Away from Europe, the Jesuits adopted some innovative missionary tactics. In China they led the way in creating a thoroughly indigenized church. Ricci moved quickly to learn Chinese, wear Chinese clothing, and adapt church buildings to local architecture. The Chinese mission also tried to adapt the Chinese custom of veneration of ancestors into Christian worship. Pope Clement XI (r. 1700–21) doomed the Chinese work by the early 18th century in the papal bull *Ex Illa Die* (March 19, 1715).

In South America, the Jesuits created autonomous communities of converts, called "reductions," that allowed native peoples to continue their preconquest ways of life and develop indigenous economies. These towns were eventually seen as obstacles to the expansion of the secular Portuguese colonists, and they were all destroyed by 1750. This devastation was the subject of the American film *The Mission* (1986). Meanwhile, the Jesuits in Europe were making many enemies in the church hierarchy, and by 1773 they were unable to prevent Pope Clement XIV (r. 1769–74) from disbanding the order.

Since the days of CONSTANTINE, CHURCH AND STATE were closely linked in the Christian world, based on an assumption of a religiously uniform society. Such a view left little room for heretics (Christians who differed significantly in their theology from orthodox thought), apostates (those who renounced the Christian faith), and groups that had been resistant to any conversion to Christianity (most notably the Jews). All these groups became fair game for mission work. In the MIDDLE AGES, especially, church leaders, backed by the power of the state, made repeated efforts to force conversion of the Moors and Jews, the most notable success being in the 15th century in SPAIN, which led to the existence of an underground community of Marranos, secret Jews, who outwardly tried to live as Christians.

The emergence of the Albigensians, a heretical community in southern FRANCE, led to the development of the INQUISITION, an organization designed to suppress heretical teachings with the backing of civil authorities and to bring the heretics back to the true faith. After the success of the Albigensian Crusade the Inquisition for a period turned to a less important group, the witches. The activities and often brutal tactics of the Inquisition, which reached for a brief period into the Americas, would for centuries taint the reputation of the church's missionary program.

In 1622, Pope Gregory XV (r. 1621–23) attempted to bring some order to the many missionary endeavors by creating a central Vatican mission office: the Congregation for the Propagation of the Faith, since 1969 known as the Congregation for the Evangelization of Peoples. Its founding was followed by a century of vast missionary expansion of the Catholic Church to take advantage of the global colonial empires being built by Spain, Portugal, and France. Many of the peoples evangelized at that time would come, for good or ill, to associate the arrival of the new faith with their loss of political autonomy. The fact that missionaries were slow to adapt to local cultures and even slower to recruit native converts into the leadership of the church long fed the reputation of the church as a foreign institution, especially in Africa and Asia.

At the end of the 18th century, the church's expansion globally slowed markedly. Historians often blamed the slowdown on the disbanding of the Jesuits and on the French Revolution

Santa Barbara Mission, founded in 1786 by Franciscan friar Fermín Lasuén, successor to Junípero Serra (Santa Barbara, Calif.) *(photo by J. Gordon Melton)*

(1789–91), which removed government support from the church and even imposed restrictions on it. However, it was also at this time that Protestant Britain began to build its global empire, often at the expense of Spain and France, that the Protestant Dutch replaced the Portuguese in several colonial fields, and that various Protestant groups—Moravians, Methodists, and Baptists—began to catch the missionary vision. The movement they launched turned Protestantism from a western and northern European religion into a worldwide movement.

When Africa and China were opened to European expansion in the 19th century, Catholic missionaries had to compete with a host of Protestant missionaries for the allegiance of interested native people (*see* ASIA). More often than not, they were operating as outsiders in lands dominated by governments favoring British Anglicans, German Lutherans, or Dutch Reformed churches. On the other hand, new Catholic missionary orders arose in response to the new fields coming open, such as the Marists (1816), the White Fathers, or Missionaries, to Africa (1868), and the HOLY GHOST FATHERS (reconstituted in 1848 after earlier being disbanded).

The United States would also play a significant role in the Catholic Church's missionary vision, even after the founding of the United States and the establishment of the American HIERARCHY. This predominantly Protestant land remained on the Vatican's list of missionary countries until 1908. Shortly thereafter, two missionary-minded American priests, James A. Walsh (1867–1936) and Thomas F. Price (1860–1919), founded the Catholic Foreign Missionary Society of America, popularly known by the site of its headquarters in New York, MARYKNOLL. Maryknoll would change the image of America in Catholic eyes from that of a missionary-receiving to a missionary-sending country.

The world of missions changed significantly over the course of the 20th century. That change was initiated in Protestant circles with the founding of the ECUMENICAL MOVEMENT, which originated to deal with issues raised on the mission field in Asia, Africa, and Oceania. The movement hoped that the many Protestant churches would stop exporting denominational squabbles into missionary countries, where they were largely irrelevant. The great international conferences held by the movement in the first half of the century provided the platform to discuss problems faced by all in the missionary endeavor and to develop new theoretical models that increasingly recognized the role of the target peoples themselves. The very success of the missions had created a situation that called for de-Westernization.

A new discipline of missiology, pioneered by Protestants in the 19th century, emerged among Catholics early in the 20th. The first chair of missiology was created in 1911 at Münster, Germany, and the first departments were created soon afterward at the Gregorian and Urban Universities in Rome.

The urgency of deconstructing the missionary enterprise and reconstituting it in a swiftly changing world was brought home by a series of political earthquakes: Indian independence (1947), the establishment of the Communist People's Republic of China (1949), the founding of the United Nations (1946), and the rapid collapse of the European colonial empires after World War II (1939–45). The very presence of Western missionaries in non-Western countries where non-Christian religions had always prevailed was called into question. The end of colonialism led to the relatively swift promotion of native lay leaders to priestly roles and outstanding native priests to BISHOPS, ARCHBISHOPS, and cardinals.

From a theological perspective, the mid-20th-century changes in global politics led to challenges of the often unspoken assumptions about the church as a Western institution. The LIBERATION THEOLOGY called for a restructuring of church life and thought away from what it considered to be Western models in favor of South American, Asian, and African models of Christian thinking (*see* INCULTURATION).

VATICAN COUNCIL II served as a watershed event in changing perspectives on the church's missionary life. The various documents from the council emphasized the primacy of God in the church's mission. God sends the Son into the world followed by the activity of the Holy Spirit. The church, as a community of the people in relation to God, participates in God's activity in the world. Mission is the work of the church, that is, all God's people.

This new approach to mission would have the church do mission as the "re-presentation" of Christ to the world. It also calls for a revised understanding of those people who have adhered to another faith either by birth or adult choice. The council saw it important to affirm the existence of other religions and the good that they represent in *Nostra Aetate,* the Declaration on the Relation of the church to Non-Christian Religions. In the future, dialogue with other religions became a part of the church's mission.

Missionary activity also has been recast with some sophistication relative to issues of culture. From the initial attempts by the Jesuits in China to indigenize and the rejection of their approach has come a new idea of inculturation, adaptation to different settings. As articulated in several documents issued through the pontificate of JOHN PAUL II, the process of missionary activity includes bringing the Gospel message to a people (evangelism), allowing the message to be recast in a form familiar to the people (inculturation), and allowing the power of the message to operate toward the liberation of the poor, oppressed, and suffering (*see his Redemptoris Missio,* July 12, 1990).

Further reading: J. C. Dwyer, *Church History, Twenty Centuries of Catholic Christianity* (New York: Paulist, 1985); William Jenkinson and Helene O'Sullivan, eds., *Trends in Missions: Toward the 3rd Millennium* (Maryknoll, N.Y.: Orbis, 1991); Joseph F. McGlinchey, *The Conversion of the Pagan World: A Treatise Upon Catholic Foreign Missions* (Boston: Society for the Propagation of the Faith, 1921); James A. Scherer and Joseph R.

Lang, eds, *New Directions in Mission and Evangelism* (Maryknoll, N.Y.: Orbis, 1992); Scott W. Sunquist, ed., *A Dictionary of Asian Christianity* (Grand Rapids, Mich.: Eerdmans, 2001).

modernism

In Catholic scholarship, modernism was an informal movement of theologians and CLERGY who wanted to update the church with changes in theory and practice. It became a term of opprobrium heaped upon the modernists by more traditional Catholics, especially by St. PIUS X in his encyclicals *Lamentabili* (July 3, 1907) and *Pascendi Domini Grex.* The term also was used in Protestant circles in the early 20th century to denote the liberal wing of Christianity in conflict with fundamentalism over the literal interpretation of the BIBLE and the theory of EVOLUTION.

The Catholic modernists sought to embrace 19th century critical scholarship of the BIBLE, which viewed the biblical authors as products of their historical settings. They tended to emphasize Christianity as a way of life and practice rather than one of intellectualism and scholastic distinction, and they viewed history as the progressive revelation of God. The theologicans most associated with the modernist movement included Alfred Firmin Loisy (1857–1940) and the Oratorian Lucien Laberthonnière (1860–1932). Loisy was a biblical scholar at the Institut Catholique in Paris who applied the historicocritical method to the study of the Bible. Laberthonnière, together with the lay philosopher Maurice Blondel (1861–1941), developed a pragmatic notion of life and faith based on the writings of William James (1842–1910) and Henri Bergson (1859–1941). All three influenced the Englishmen Baron Friederick von Hügel (1852–1925) and Jesuit George Tyrrell (1861–1909), both of whom stressed the cultural context of a living FAITH versus theological abstractions.

Some modernists took heart from LEO XIII's encyclical *Providentissimus Deus* (November 18, 1893) on the use of modern scholarly methods in the study of the Bible, but the tide soon turned against them. Although the laypersons escaped ecclesiastical sanctions, the clerical and religious members of the modernist movement had their books placed on the Index of Forbidden Books and, later on, were excommunicated. Pius X's encyclicals attacked the philosophical and theological foundations of modernism, including the historicocritical method, the stress on the historical Jesus, and the evolution of the institutions of the seven sacraments.

The conflict between modernists and antimodernists raged within the Catholic Church until quelled by Pope Benedict XV (r. 1914–22). In time the Catholic Church embraced the scholarly methodologies of the modernists if not their more extreme theological positions. The modernist tradition had considerable influence on the NOUVELLE THÉOLOGIE movement and, as a result, on VATICAN COUNCIL II. Recently, however, Catholic conservatives and TRADITIONALISTS have been reasserting the old antimodernist positions publically as well as quietly in the Vatican.

Further reading: Scott Appleby, *American Catholic Modernism* (Notre Dame: Notre Dame University Press, 2000); Darrel Jodock, ed., *Catholics Contending With Modernity: Roman Catholic Modernism and Anti-modernism in Historical Context* (Cambridge: Cambridge University Press, 2000); Bernard Reardon, ed., *Roman Catholic Modernism* (Stanford, Calif.: Stanford University Press, 1970).

monastery

A monastery is a dwelling place of MONKS or NUNS living a life in common (*Code of Canon Law* cn. 613). In the history of the CHRISTIAN community certain monasteries, or the communities living there, have given birth to practices, doctrines, and reforms that had far-reaching effects on MONASTICISM in particular and Christianity in general. Among the most important such monasteries are:

St. Anthony, Zafarana, EGYPT. Located 100 miles south of Cairo and just west of the Red Sea, this still functioning COPTIC monastery was founded around 270 and is considered the birthplace of Christian monasticism.

Tabennisi, on the Nile, Egypt. This is the first Christian cenobitic, or communal, monastery in the world; it was founded by Abbot PACHOMIUS around 320. Pachomius directly influenced St. BASIL THE GREAT, who adapted many of his practices for his influential rule, known as the Rule of St. Basil.

St. Catherine, Mt. Sinai. The pilgrim EGERIA visited this monastery around 382. Legend has it that it is the site of the burning bush where Moses spoke with God (Exod. 3:2). This Eastern Orthodox monastery is where Constantin von Tischendorf (1815–74) found the famous *Codex Sinaiticus* in 1854 (*see* CODEX). It is still a place of pilgrimage.

Monte Cassino, near Naples, Italy. This is the site of the communal monastery of St. BENEDICT, considered the father of monasticism in the Western Church. It was founded around 529. Nearly totally destroyed in World War II, it has been completely restored.

Mt. Athos, Greece. Some 20 Eastern Orthodox monasteries are sited on this Macedonian peninsula extending into the Aegean Sea. They were founded by monks of different ethnic origins, starting around 962. Mt. Athos remains a vital spiritual center of EASTERN ORTHODOXY and has produced many bishops for the Eastern Church.

Cîteaux (Lat. *Cistercium*), Burgundy, France. Mother abbey of the CISTERCIAN order, founded in 1098. Cistercians follow a strict, primitive form of the Benedictine rule. BERNARD OF CLAIRVAUX was abbot of Citeaux.

Cluny, France. A reform monastery founded in 909, where choral singing of psalms was highly cultivated. GREGORY VII supported this monastery, which played a large role in the reform of the church.

La Trappe Abbey, near Solvigny, France. Founded in 1122, this reformed Cistercian abbey gave its name to the Trappist order. In 1162 Abbot A. J. Ravé introduced strict observances, which have characterized the order ever since. Gethsemani Abbey, Kentucky, was founded on the model of La Trappe in 1848.

Solesmes, France. A BENEDICTINE monastery founded in 1010 and suppressed during the French Revolution (1789–91), Solesmes was reestablished in 1833 by Dom Prosper Guéranger (1805–75), who fostered the renewal of Gregorian CHANT and became a catalyst in the LITURGICAL MOVEMENT.

Gethsemani Abbey of Our Lady, near Bardstown, Kentucky. Cistercian (Trappist) monastery founded in 1848 by monks from the Breton Abbey of Melleray in France. This was the home abbey of influential Trappist spiritual writer THOMAS MERTON.

St. Meinrad's Abbey, Indiana. Founded in 1854 by two monks from the Swiss Benedictine Abbey of Einsiedeln, this Benedictine monastery is now home to 120 monks. It is the most noted abbey in the United States as a source of liturgical renewal and renewal of the Benedictine way.

See also MONK.

Further reading: Nabia Abbott, *The Monasteries of the Fayy^um* (Chicago: University of Chicago Press, 1937); Christopher Brooke and Lawrence Nugent, *Monasteries of the World* (New York: Crescent, 1982); Marc Cels, *Life in a Medieval Monastery* (New York: Crobtree, 2005); Chris Hellier, *Monasteries of Greece* (London: Tauris Parke, 1996).

monasticism (Gk.: *monos,* "solitary")

Monasticism includes several varieties of CHRISTIAN ascetic religious life, solitary or communal, dedicated to the imitation of CHRIST through vows (religious oaths) of poverty, chastity, and obedience (and in the case of Benedictines, stability). At the point in Christian history when it was no longer dangerous to practice the FAITH, the place formerly held by martyrs as the spiritual heroes of the church was taken up by ascetic and monastic saints. The MONASTERIES that emerged as a result played an outsized role in preserving and developing church traditions.

Monasticism was in part a reaction to the soft life in the church fostered by the Roman imperial authorities after CONSTANTINE THE GREAT officially tolerated Christianity in 313 and later emperors made it the state religion. However, monastic tendencies may have already been present before then. Certain forms of ancient Jewish and early Christian ASCETICISM showed tendencies toward the common life. The Old Testament speaks of Nazirites (Num. 6:1–21) who refused to drink wine or touch dead bodies or unclean foods, as well as bands of prophets who associated themselves with leaders such as Elisha. PHILO OF ALEXANDRIA (*On the Contemplative Life*) refers to the Therapeutae, an ascetic community of Jews who lived near Alexandria in the first century. John the Baptist fits the pattern of a Nazirite prophet; he may have been associated with the Qumran community. The Jewish historian Josephus mentions many similar ascetic personalities and groups in first-century Judea.

Although the New Testament speaks frequently of prayer and fasting, there is little evidence of the ascetic way of life that would later blossom into the full-blown monasticism of the late third and early fourth centuries. Ascetic practices seem to have been stronger among second-century fringe groups later declared heretical, such as the Marcionites (*see* MARCION), the Montanists (*see* MONTANIUS), and the Encratites. Some scholars now suggest that Brahmanic asceticism, Buddhist monasticism, and Neoplatonic philosophical asceticism all contributed elements to Christian monasticism, given the amount of cultural interchange that may have occurred between ancient civilizations in that era.

The first MONKS in the full sense of the term appeared independently in the Syrian and Egyptian deserts in the late third century. St. ANTHONY OF EGYPT set the pattern for all future hermit, or anchorite (Gk.: *anchoresis,* "withdrawal"), monks. ATHANASIUS OF ALEXANDRIA later eulogized his life in the *Life of Anthony*. Anthony began his acetic life at home, then attached himself to a hermit, and finally withdrew to the desert after placing his sister with a group of virgins. These groups of virgins (and widows), in turn, developed into female monasteries. Alone in the desert he experienced assaults by demons and temptations by the devil in the guise of seductresses. Anthony's temptations became a great theme in medieval, Renaissance, and baroque artworks. Anthony served as the prototype of monks who lived mostly alone but assembled for the Lord's Day and other Christian feasts.

Following Anthony, some monks became sedentary while others took up the itinerant path. Itinerant monks survived in Russia until the late 19th century. Some took up odd behaviors: St. Simeon Stylites (c. 390–459) started a fad by spending the last part of his life atop an ancient pillar in Syria, from where he wielded great spiritual influence in the Byzantine Empire.

PACHOMIUS of Egypt (c. 290–347) brought about a major change in the monastic tradition by organizing monasteries for common living throughout Egypt, for both men and women in separate complexes. Anchorite monks had refined the spiritual disciplines of poverty, chastity, fasting, prayer. It was Pachomius's mission to add the disciplines of obedience to a central spiritual authority, self-support through industry, and full communal, or cenobitic (Gk. *koinos* "common"), living.

Pachomius's revolution was further advanced by St. BASIL THE GREAT (330–79) in Cappodocia (Turkey). Basil provided written rules for the ascetic life, coordinated monasteries with the authority of local bishops, and guided monks to provide medical aid and educational services to their surrounding communities. The monasteries in and around Palestine came to be called *lauras*. The rules of St. Basil still guide the monasteries of the East, especially those on Mt. Athos in Greece, which thrive to this day.

During the MIDDLE AGES Eastern monasticism spread throughout the Slavic speaking lands. In 1354 St. Sergius (1314–92) and his brother St. Stepan founded the famous Holy TRINITY monastery at Radonezh near Moscow, which housed the celebrated mural ICON of the Trinity by Andrei Rublev (c. 1370–1430). During the communist era, monasteries in the Balkans and Russia underwent severe persecution and repression, but they are making a comeback today.

The combined influence of Athanasius's *Life of Anthony* and Basil's rules for monks shaped the character of monasticism in the West. John Cassian of Romania (c. 365–433) visited monasteries of the East and laid down the principles of monastic life in *The Institutes*, which had a notable effect in the West.

A pioneer of monasticism in the West was St. Martin of Tours (c. 316–397). He first took up the solitary life in Liguge, France, but he later founded a communal monastery at Marmoutier. As Athanasius did for Anthony, Sulpicius Severus, a disciple of Martin, wrote a HAGIOGRAPHY of him, which inspired many to the monastic life. St. AUGUSTINE OF HIPPO added a new feature after his conversion by AMBROSE OF MILAN. He gathered a group of celibate clergy for regular study and prayer attached to the BASILICA church of the city. This is the origin of the medieval cathedral chapters as well as the seminary system of a bishop surrounded by clergy and candidates for ordination.

It was St. BENEDICT OF NURSIA (c. 468–547) who gave Western monasticism its definitive shape. He began as a hermit in Subiaco, ITALY, but became the leader of several cenobitic monasteries in the region. Then he founded the famous monastery of Monte Casino near Naples. His sister St. SCHOLASTICA founded a parallel abbey for nuns. Besides the monastic threefold requirements of poverty, chastity, and obedience, Benedict added a vow of stability to discourage the sometimes unruly lifestyle of wandering monks. His rule emphasizes hard physical labor and regular hours of prayer (*see* PRAYER OF THE HOURS): "Idleness is the enemy of the soul. Therefore, at fixed times, the brothers should be busy with manual work, and, at other times, with holy reading." *Ora et labora* ("prayer and labor") became the motto of the Benedictine order. The *Rule of St. Benedict* became the model for all future rules of religious orders. Most monasteries are governed by an abbot or abbess who is assisted by a prior and subprior.

Due to the emphasis on study and prayer, monasteries quickly became repositories of the classical literature of Greece and Rome, Scripture, and the theological writings of the early Christian authors. Monks also developed skills as inventors (farm implements, the mill, farming methods) and artists. In the early Middle Ages monasteries became the seedbeds of reform movements, most notably the abbeys of Cluny and Cîteaux. The Calmaldolese and the Carthusians also contributed to monastic reform. The history of women monastics has been much neglected and is only now being written. Irish monasticism developed its own style. Male monks, nuns and lay people lived in separate but conjoined cloisters within abbeys. Irish monks were very evangelical, sending missionaries to Scotland, England, and even Italy.

By the 15th century there were more than 40,000 monasteries throughout Christendom. However, they suffered great losses during the PROTESTANT REFORMATION, including the suppression of the monasteries in England under Tudor rule, during the ANTICLERICALISM of the French Revolution (1784), and during the communist attempt to suppress Christianity itself. Monasticism experienced a revival during the mid-19th century (*see* SOLESMES) and again in the mid-20th century, in the latter case thanks to the writings of THOMAS MERTON. Following the dissolution of the USSR in 1989, Eastern monasticism is undergoing a reinvigoration in Russia. Monasticism has also seen a revival in Prot-

estant, especially Anglican, contexts. Brother Roger Schultz (1937–2005), a Swiss Reformed Protestant, founded the ecumenical Taizé Community in France in 1940. It has drawn countless Christians, non-Christians, and even nonbelievers into a circle of monastic spirituality.

Further reading: St. Benedict, *Rule of St. Benedict,* tr. with intro. by Anthony C. Meisel and M. L. del Mastro (Garden City, N.Y.: Image, 1975); Anselm G. Biggs, *The Benedictine Life* (Belmont: Belmont Abbey, 1974); Peter Brown, *The Body and Society* (New York: Columbia University Press, 1988); C. H. Lawrence, *Medieval Monasticism: Forms of Religious Life in Western Europe in the Middle Ages,* 3rd ed. (New York: Longman, 2000); Thomas Merton, *Seven Story Mountain* (San Diego: Harcourt Brace Jovanovich, 1990); Anselm G. Biggs, *The Benedictine Life* (Belmont: Belmont Abbey, 1974); Miriam Schmitt and Linda Kulzer, eds., *Medieval Women Monastics: Wisdom's Wellsprings,* (Collegeville, Minn.: Liturgical Press, 1996).

monk (Gk.: *monas,* "solitary")

The term *monk* is a popular designation for a member of a male CHRISTIAN community leading an ordered life following vows of poverty, chastity, and obedience. The term was first used to refer to hermits, the essence of whose life was dedication to GOD. Since the time of BENEDICT OF NURSIA (d. c. 547) and his rule, the communal nature of the monastic life has come to the fore, and the term *monk* usually designates one who lives the ordered life under an abbot. A monk may or may not be an ordained priest, though the tendency in the modern world is for monks to assume roles as clergymen.

As religion enters a globalized context, comparisons are inevitably made between Catholic practices and those of other religious traditions. Terms such as *monk* and NUN are frequently used to describe those living an ordered life in, for example, Buddhist and Hindu traditions.

Further reading: William Claassen, *Alone in Community: Journey Into Monastic Life Around the World*

(Leavenworth, Kans.: Forest of Peace, 2000); Hugh Feiss, *Essential Monastic Wisdom: Writings on the Contemplative Life* (San Francisco: HarperSanFrancisco, 1999).

Monk, Maria (c. 1816–1849) *anti-Catholic propagandist*

Maria Monk was the central character in an anti-Catholic hoax in 19th-century NORTH AMERICA that soured Catholic-Protestant relations for many years. In 1836 a lurid anti-Catholic book, *The Awful Disclosures of Maria Monk* (1836), appeared in New York. Monk claimed to have been a NUN in Montreal made pregnant by one of several priests who had raped her. She escaped the convent in order to save her baby's life, it being the common practice, she said, to murder the newborns among the sisters. Although quickly exposed as a hoax, the book went through many reprints, and the story was kept alive for generations.

The real Maria Monk, it transpired, was born in St. Johns, Quebec, and raised in a Protestant family. As a child she suffered from an injury to her brain, to which some attributed her behavior problems as a child and later as an adult. For a short time in her 18th year she was under the care of the Magdalene asylum in Montreal but left after becoming pregnant.

Soon afterward she met William K. Hoyte, leader of the Canadian Benevolent Society, a Protestant organization with strong anti-Catholic proclivities. Hoyte took Monk with him to New York. In concert with other Protestant leaders, including J. J. Slocum and Theodore Dwight, Hoyte put the book together with some background material on Montreal from Monk herself. Monk's book was in the mainstream of three centuries of anti-Catholic writings that date back to the very start of the PROTESTANT REFORMATION. Monk's book would be followed by numerous accounts of Catholic priests and nuns, some alleged, who converted to Protestantism and wrote their stories as exposés of the Catholic Church.

Supporters of the convent in Montreal, the Hotel Dieu hospital, and the Catholic Church published a number of books and articles that discredited Monk's story. Monk responded with a second book, *Further Disclosures by Maria Monk Concerning the Hotel Dieu Nunnery of Montreal* (1836). It contained no information that might refute her accusers. When she bore another child out of wedlock in 1838, her support among even hard-core anti-Catholics dissolved. She died later that year after being arrested for pickpocketing.

The *Awful Disclosures* became part of the standard literature of the anti-Catholic elements within the English-speaking Protestant community, and continues to be periodically reprinted to the present. Today its primary circulation is among small ultrafundamentalist groups.

See also ANTI-CATHOLICISM.

Further reading: Maria Monk, *The Awful Disclosures of Maria Monk Exhibited in a Narrative of Her Sufferings During a Residence of Five Years as a Novice and Two Years as a Black Nun, in the Hotel Dieu Nunnery in Montreal* (New York: Howe & Bates, 1836); ———, *Further Disclosures by Maria Monk Concerning the Hotel Dieu Nunnery of Montreal* (New York: J. J. Slocum, 1836); Gustavus Myers, *History of Bigotry in the United States* (New York: Capricorn, 1960).

Montanus (fl. c. 170) *early Christian sectarian*

Montanism was a CHRISTIAN sectarian movement of the late second century named after its founder, Montanus of Phrygia. The orthodox church quickly suppressed the sect, but remnants of Montanism continued until the eighth century.

After converting to Christianity, Montanus traveled throughout ASIA Minor with two prophetesses, Priscilla and Maximilla, preaching and proclaiming that the New Jerusalem would be established in the village of Pepuza. As an apocalyptic movement it firmly believed in the imminent outpouring of the HOLY SPIRIT, prophesied as the Paraclete in the Gospel of John (14:16). TERTULLIAN, a previous defender of orthodox belief, adhered to Montanism around 206 and became its most widely known proponent. The sect soon developed ascetic tendencies, condemning the existing regulations on fasting as too lax. Along with ascetic traits, followers practiced ecstatic prophecy and speaking in tongues, similar to medieval FRANCISCAN Spirituals, modern-day Pentecostalists, and some Catholics in CHARISMATIC RENEWAL.

Montanism was formally condemned at eastern synods before 200 and by Pope Zephyrinus (r. 198–217) somewhat later. Today, some scholars argue that the Montanists were actually orthodox in their belief if not their practice.

Further reading: John De Sovres, *Montanism and the Primitive Church: A Study in the Ecclesiastical History of the Second Century* (Lexington, Ky.: American Theological Library Association, 1965); Christine Trevett, *Montanism: Gender, Authority, and the New Prophecy* (Cambridge: Cambridge University Press, 1996).

mortal sin   *See also* SIN.

Mundelein, George (1872–1939) U.S. cardinal

George Mundelein spent an outstanding quarter of a century as ARCHBISHOP of Chicago. He was the first American cardinal not of Irish ancestry.

Mundelein was born in New York on July 2, 1872. An outstanding student, he turned down the opportunity to attend the Naval Academy at Annapolis to study for the priesthood. After completing college, he was sent to the Urban College of Propaganda in Rome. He was ordained in 1886.

After his return Mundelein became chancellor of the Brooklyn diocese. In 1906 he was named a domestic prelate in the papal household with the title of monsignor, as a reward for a paper defending Pope PIUS X's anti-modernist position (*see* MODERNISM). He became auxiliary bishop of Brooklyn in 1909.

In 1915 Mundelein was named archbishop of Chicago. His first priority was education, starting with the reorganization of the large parochial school system in the growing archdiocese. He founded a new preparatory seminary and oversaw the opening of Rosary College to expand opportunities in higher education for women. In 1921 he opened a new seminary northwest of Chicago using the charter of the then defunct University of St. Mary of the Lake; he selected the new seminary as the site of the International Eucharistic Congress in 1926.

In 1924 along with former classmate Archbishop Patrick Joseph Hayes (1867–1938) of New York, Mundelein was given his cardinal's hat. Cardinal Mundelein worked to unify the various ethnic groups that were prominent in the archdiocese over stiff resistance, despite their rapid Americanization. He reorganized and expanded Catholic charities, and he established a network of St. VINCENT DE PAUL Societies throughout the archdiocese. Among his last duties was to officiate at the beatification ceremonies for Mother FRANCIS CABRINI in 1938, who in 1946 would become the first American to be canonized.

Further reading: Edward R. Kantowicz, *Corporation Sole: Cardinal Mundelein and Chicago Catholicism* (Notre Dame: University of Notre Dame Press, 1983); James Joseph Walsh, *Our American Cardinals: Life Stories of the Seven American Cardinals: McCloskey, Gibbons, Farley, O'Connell, Dougherty, Mundelein, Hayes* (Freeport, N.Y.: Books for Libraries, 1969).

Murphy, Roland (1917–2002) biblical scholar

Roland Edmund Murphy was born in Chicago on July 19, 1917. He entered the CARMELITE Order as a youth and was admitted to profession in 1935; he was ordained a priest in 1942. He subsequently received degrees in theology and Semitic studies at the Catholic University of America in Washington, D.C., where he began teaching in 1948. He remained there for 22 years.

Murphy's career began propitiously in the wake of the papal encyclical *Divino Afflante Spiritu* (September 3, 1943), which placed new emphasis on biblical studies. He would emerge as one of the leading Catholic Old Testament scholars of the second half of the 20th century, with a specialization in the Hebrew Wisdom books—Job, Psalms, Proverbs, Ecclesiastes, Song of Songs, Wisdom, and Sirach (*see* BIBLE). He also joined the committee that translated both the New American Bible and the New Revised Standard Version. Capping a highly productive career was his work as coeditor with Joseph A. Fitzmyer (1938–) and Raymond E. Brown (1928–98) of the *Jerome Biblical Commentary* (1968) and its revised edition, the *New Jerome Biblical Commentary* (1990). His fellow scholars recognized his accomplishments by electing him for tenures as president of both the Catholic Biblical Association and the Society of Biblical Literature.

Murphy was among the first Catholic scholars to call for "inclusive language"—gender-neutral terms—in the English-language biblical text. In the 1960s, he authored a book on his area of specialty, which he titled *Wisdom, You Are My Sister,* though his publisher persuaded him to retitle it *Seven Books of Wisdom* by the time it was issued.

After many years at Catholic University, in 1971 Murphy became a professor of biblical studies at the Duke University Divinity School (sponsored by the United Methodist Church in North Carolina). He also taught as a visiting professor at Yale, Princeton, and Pittsburgh and was a resident scholar at Washington Theological Union. He spent his retirement, beginning in 1987, at the Carmelite center in Washington, where he died in 2002.

Further reading: Roland E. Murphy, *Introduction to the Wisdom Literature of the Old Testament* (Collegeville, Minn.: Liturgical Press, 1964); ———, *Seven Books of Wisdom* (Milwaukee: Bruce, 1960); Keith J. Egan, Craig E. Morrison, and Marshal J. Wastag, *Master of the Sacred Page: Essays and Articles in Honor of Roland E. Murphy, O. Carm.* (Washington, D.C.: The Carmelite Institute, 1997).

Murray, John Courtney (1904–1967) *U.S.*
Jesuit theologian and Catholic expert on church and state
John Courtney Murray was born September 12, 1904, in New York City. He received his B.A. (1926) and M.A. (1927) at Boston College and his doctorate at the Gregorian University in Rome in 1937. He entered the Society of Jesus in 1920 and was ordained a priest in 1933 (*see* JESUITS). He taught THEOLOGY at Woodstock College, Maryland, from 1937 until his death in 1967. As long-term editor of the Jesuit monthly *America,* he became well known as an interpreter of American life from a Catholic perspective. He also edited the journal *Theological Studies.*

Assuming the role of a public theologian, Murray frequently lectured and wrote about the church's position regarding government and social issues. Following in the footsteps of Archbishops JOHN IRELAND and JAMES GIBBONS, he championed the idea that Roman Catholicism was more than compatible with American constitutionalism. He traced contemporary ideals of freedom to the assertion by Catholic political theory of the church's rights against the state, by implication a limitation on state power. The existence of two parallel structures of order—CHURCH AND STATE—was crucial to the political history of the West: The freedom demanded by the church would lead to other freedoms for both individuals and institutions to operate apart from state control. He saw America developing this basic idea through the instrument of a written document, the Constitution.

Even in the mid-20th century, Murray's public alignment of Catholicism with the conception of a free people under a limited government ran counter to much Catholic thinking in Europe, where the church was still reeling from the loss of power, property, and status as a result of secularization. In the 1950s Murray came under church restrictions in his writing on political and social matters, though in the 1960s he was at least partially vindicated by his participation at VATICAN COUNCIL II, where he made substantial contributions to

Dignitatis Humanae, the Declaration on Religious Freedom. Murray died in New York City in 1967.

Further reading: J. Leon Hooper, *John Courtney Murray and the Growth of Tradition* (New York: Sheed & Ward, 1996); John Courtney Murray, *Bridging the Sacred and the Secular: Selected Writings of John Courtney Murray,* ed. J. Leon Hooper (Washington, D.C.: Georgetown University Press, 1994); ———, *The Problem of God, Yesterday and Today* (New Haven, Conn.: Yale University Press, 1964); ———, *We Hold These Truths: Catholic Reflections on the American Proposition* (New York: Sheed & Ward, 1960); Donald E. Pelotte, *John Courtney Murray: Theologian in Conflict* (New York: Paulist, 1975).

music, liturgical

CHRISTIAN liturgical music had its immediate origins in late Judaic worship, as Christians attended first the Temple in Jerusalem (Act 3.1) and then synagogues as late as the sixth and seventh centuries. Jewish Temple worship included choral singing of psalms and employed many musical instruments, including bells, cymbals, sistras, pipes, horns, trumpets, lyres, lutes, and harps. Trumpets were assigned for special feasts (Num. 10:10), and the *shofar,* or ram's horn, was sounded on Rosh Ha-Shannah and on New Moons.

Philo Judaeus (20 B.C.E.–40 C.E.) wrote that the first-century Therapeutae, a Jewish communal group near Alexandria, practiced unison and antiphonal singing with measured beats and melodies (*Contemplative Life* 80–87). Groups like this could well have set the model for later musical patterns used in the Christian monasteries (*see* MONASTERY) that first arose in EGYPT.

After the destruction of the Temple in 70, synagogue worship abstained from musical instruments as a sign of mourning; early Jewish followers of Jesus seemed to have followed in this tradition. Furthermore, the use of musical instruments in Greco-Roman society was associated with immoral banquet celebrations.

The early Christians worshiped with "psalms, hymns, and spiritual songs" (Eph. 5:19). By the third century Basil of Caesarea (c. 330–79) describes the singing as taking three forms: a precentor, like the Jewish cantor, singing while the people respond with a refrain; antiphonal singing; and unison singing (*Epistle* 107). Antiphons, short response songs, were taken from psalms and received further musical elaboration. Some opposed women singing, in accord with Jewish tradition and because singing women had pagan associations, but others engaged women choruses (Eusebius, *Church History* 7.30.10).

The next liturgical phase was associated with the rise of MONASTICISM and the mode of CHANTS associated with the Divine Office, or PRAYER OF THE HOURS, that evolved in monastic circles. By the MIDDLE AGES the Prayers of the Hours according to Roman reckoning included Matins (middle of the night), Lauds (sunrise), Prime (early morning), Terce (mid-morning), Sext (late-morning), None (whence the word "noon"), Vespers (evening), and Compline (night).

The Eastern and Western Churches developed different liturgical musical styles. All liturgies in the Eastern church are sung—the East knows nothing of what is called Low, or said (spoken), Mass in the West.

Different musical forms emerged within the West as well, along with the different rites, or liturgies, such as Milan, Rome, Toledo, and Metz, but Pepin III (d. 768) and CHARLEMAGNE gave preeminence to the Roman liturgy that GREGORY THE GREAT had reformed two and a half centuries earlier. The associated musical form became known as Gregorian chant. The late Middle Ages developed the beginnings of polyphony in the form of organum, a single line of "ornament" either a fourth or fifth above the original chant line. A form of polyphony also developed in the East, where it was called *kalophonia,* or "beautiful sound."

The PROTESTANT REFORMATION presented a great challenge to Roman Catholicism by introducing new hymns in the vernacular that could be sung by the people and by engaging fine composers to produce great choral works. The Council of Trent did not rise to the challenge and merely affirmed the continuation of Gregorian chant in Latin, allowing some polyphony to enter the LITURGY in the form of motets between sections of the EUCHARIST. Anything that sounded like secular music or that made the text unintelligible was prohibited. Trent wanted uniformity of liturgy and music, with some local variation, throughout the Catholic world. Locally, however, French, German, and Italian dioceses developed vernacular hymnals. In addition, parts of the liturgical Eucharistic prayers were sometimes replaced with hymns of similar meaning.

Despite Trent, musical innovations were already enriching Catholic liturgical music. Clear polyphonic phrasing and linear elegance were introduced by composers like Frenchman Josquin de Pres (c. 1450–75), Venetian Gianmateo Asola (c. 1532–1609), Roman Giovanni Palestrina (1525/6–94), Spaniards Francisco Guerrero (c. 1528–99) and Tomás Luis de Victoria (1548–1611), and Franco-Flemish Orlande de Lassus (1532–94), who was Kapellmeister at the Bavarian court. Guerrero and de Victoria shaped the musical traditions of LATIN AMERICA. Collectively these composers produced masses, motets, psalms, hymns, passions, and litanies on a prolific scale.

Starting in the baroque musical era, instrumental and vocal polyphony flourished or even, as some felt, overwhelmed the text. Vocal compositions approached the theatrical and operatic, as in the masses of Wolfgang Amadeus Mozart (1756–91) and Ludwig van Beethoven (1770–1827) and the monumental *Requiem* of Giuseppe Verdi (1813–1901). A countermovement toward simplicity found supporters such as the late-19th century Society of St. Cecelia, which sought to restore the primacy of Gregorian chant along with the restrained polyphony of Palestrina and his contemporaries. (St. Cecelia, a second-to-third-century martyr, became patroness of music very early in Christian tradition; her feast day is November 22). The society's efforts were reinforced by the growing LITURGICAL MOVEMENT.

In 1903 St. Pius X (r. 1903–14) issued the *motu proprio Tra le Sollecitudini* (November 22), which endorsed Gregorian chant; it encouraged lay participation in liturgical music, while maintaining the Latin Mass. This papal directive governed Catholic music until VATICAN COUNCIL II, which, while embracing the European musical traditions of the church, allowed for the Eucharist in the vernacular and opened the floodgates of musical INCULTURATION. Even secular pop music has made its way into Catholic worship. In reaction, some Catholics, schismatic and not, have returned to the Tridentine Mass, Gregorian chant, and Palestrina motets.

Even within the Catholic mainstream, a tension developed between the pastoral concern to reach the people and the sacred impulse to preserve traditional chant and polyphony or, according to some, "music as art." The Jesuit Joseph Gelineau (1920–   ) sought to mediate this conflict with his new form in psalmody, *The Psalms: A New Translation* (1963). In 1972 the U. S. Catholic Bishops Conference issued the guideline that gave directions for participatory celebrations, *Music in Catholic Worship*. In 1980 the international society Universa Laus published *The Music of Christian Ritual* (1980), which stressed that liturgical music should be subordinate to ritual and text. New musical forms are burgeoning in Latin America, ASIA, and especially AFRICA.

Further reading: Laura Fitzpatrick, "Liturgical Music at the Millennium," in Gerald L. Miller and Wilburn T. Stancil, eds., *Catholicism at the Millennium: The Church of Tradition in Transition* (Kansas City: Rockhurst University Press, 2001); *The Liturgy Documents* (Chicago: Liturgy Training, 2004); Johannes Quasten, *Music and Worship in Pagan and Christian Antiquity* (Washington, D.C.: National Association of Pastoral Musicians, 1964); Eric Werner, *The Sacred Bridge II: The Interdependence of Liturgy and Music in Synagogue and Church during the First Millennium* (New York: KTAV, 1963).

N

Nagasaki Martyrs

Christianity was introduced into Japan in 1549 by the JESUIT St. FRANCIS XAVIER, and it seemed to find a welcoming home. The work thrived for half a century until a series of events brought the mission crashing to the ground. In 1593 a delegation of FRANCISCAN brothers arrived in Japan as the ambassadors of the Spanish governor of the Philippines. They met with the emperor, Toyotomi Hideyoshi (1537–98), who granted permission to establish institutions such as schools and hospitals.

All went well until 1596, when a Spanish ship foundered on the coast and was seized by the Japanese. The angry captain, in a vain attempt to regain custody of his vessel, threatened to use the might of SPAIN, boasting that the Franciscans were even then preparing the country for invasion. Not surprisingly, the emperor moved swiftly to arrest the Franciscans and other Christian leaders. On February 5, 1597, the six Franciscans, three Jesuits, and 17 lay converts were executed—by crucifixion.

Five months later, the emperor ordered all the remaining CHRISTIAN missionaries to leave the country. While the order was not at first enforced, the next several emperors passed anti-Christian legislation and in 1632 made systematic efforts

to eradicate the FAITH. By this time, the Nagasaki Martyrs had been beatified (1627). They were canonized by PIUS IX in 1862 after a new mission in Japan had been started.

Further reading: Joseph Jennes, *A History of the Catholic Church in Japan from the Beginnings to the Early Meiji Era, 1549–1873* (Tokyo: Oriens Institute, 1973); Kazuo Kasahara, ed., *A History of Japanese Religion* (Tokyo: Kosei Publishing, 2001).

Nazism (abbv. Ger.: *Nationalsocializmus,* "National Socialism")

The term *Nazi* arose as a pejorative to contrast it with *Sozis,* or socialists. The word describes the ideological, political, social, and economic system in GERMANY under the Austrian-born demagogue Adolf Hitler (1889–1945). Nazism had twin foundations in the psuedomystical principle of *der Führer* ("the Leader") and the racist principle of a master Aryan race that deserved to rule over the "subhumans" (Slavs, Africans, and especially Jews), which Hitler expounded in *Mein Kampf* (1924–26).

When they came to power, the Nazis exterminated mentally and physically defective people, persecuted homosexuals, imprisoned Jehovah's Witnesses (they refused to honor the state), socialists, and communists, and ultimately pursued a policy of extermination of the Jews, whom they scapegoated for all the ills of Western civilization.

As with Mussolini's FASCISM, the Catholic Church's relation to Nazi Germany is fraught with ambiguity. The church through the Catholic Central Party opposed Nazism during the Weimar Republic (1918–33), but the right wing of the party supported Hitler's coming to power. In the CONCORDAT with Germany in 1933 (called the Reichskonkordat and still in effect in the Federal Republic of Germany), Vatican secretary of state Cardinal Eugenio Pacelli, later PIUS XII, virtually signed away the future of the Christian Democratic Parties, trade unions, and other political organizations in order to preserve the rights of the church to appoint CLERGY, conduct schools, and hold services. The Catholic political leader Konrad Adenauer (1876–1967) was forced into hiding at MARIA LAACH Abbey. Many Catholic Church leaders later showed up at Nazi rallies, most notably Cardinal Michael von Faulhaber (1869–1952) at Munich.

It was only when Hitler turned against the church and started violating the terms of the concordat that PIUS XI issued his encyclical Mit brennender Sorge, "With Burning Anxiety" (March 14, 1937), which condemned Nazi persecution. By then it was too late. Pius XI secretly commissioned American Jesuit JOHN LAFARGE to draft a second encyclical—Humani Generis Unitas, "The Unity of the Human Race,"—which would have condemned Hitler and Nazism outright, but he died before he could issue it. PIUS XII did not follow through. Many Catholics also went to the gas chambers, seemingly abandoned by their church.

Two noble lights of Christian resistance to Nazism did emerge. The first was the Protestant Confessing Church group, inspired by Karl Barth (1886–1966) and led by Pastor Martin Niemöller (1892–1984) and Dietrich Bonhoeffer (1906–45), who formulated the Barmen Declaration (1934) that announced that Christians have only one "Leader," and that is CHRIST. The other was the Catholic movement Weise Rose ("White Rose") in Munich, led by University of Munich students Christoph Probst and brother and sister Hans and Sophie Scholl. They distributed pamphlets condemning Nazism; all three were executed in 1943.

Further reading: James Carroll, Constantine's Sword: The Church and the Jews (Boston: Houghton Mifflin, 2000); John Cornell, Hitler's Pope: The Secret History of Pius XII (New York: Viking, 1999); Daniel Jonah Goldhagen, Hitler's Willing Executioners: Ordinary Germans and the Holocaust (New York: Pantheon, 1965); Beth A. Griech-Polelle, Bishop von Galen: German Catholicism and National Socialism (New Haven, Conn.: Yale University Press, 2002).

Neoplatonism

Plato (427–347 B.C.E.), perhaps the most influential writer-philosopher of the ancient world, had a dramatic impact on Christianity, mostly through the movement he inspired known as Neoplatonism. Plato was a student of the philosopher Socrates, the hero of his dialogues. After his teacher's death in 399 B.C.E., Plato traveled the Mediterranean for a number of years before returning to Athens. He founded the Academy there, the philosophical school whence all subsequent "academies" took their name.

We cannot be certain of Plato's own ideas, as he ascribed different views to the characters in his dialogues, in which Socrates is most often the lead discussant; a few letters also survive. He is often called an "idealist," but it would be more correct to call him an "idea-ist." His early dialogues dealt with questions of virtue and how the SOUL gains knowledge of it (Meno). He became more metaphysical in the later dialogues in which he discussed the Good, the Ideas, or Forms, the immortality of the soul, and the desire for the beautiful. In the Repub-

lic 508–509 he relates how the supreme Good is above being but causes all knowledge, truth, and beauty the way the sun shines on all and generates growth. CHRISTIAN Platonists would relate this idea both to the biblical notion of the creator GOD and to the THEOLOGY of the Light of CHRIST. Plato also held that the *really* real world is a realm of pure being and eternal Ideas (*eidei*), which are far above the shadowy world of becoming and the senses that we inhabit. Christian Platonists would later place great emphasis on the superiority of the spirit, eternity, rest, and the mind and the inferiority of matter, time, motion, and the body. In the *Timaeus* Plato seems to locate the ideas in the mind of God. The Demiurge, who makes the sensible world, looks to these Ideas to fashion the world. The heretic MARCION and many adherents of Gnosticism (*see* GNOSTIC/GNOSTICISM) would identify the Demiurge with the malevolent Creator God of the Old Testament who made the "fallen" world of matter, time, and becoming. In the *Republic* Plato presented the image of the Cave of shadows from which the soul escapes; the Divided Line, which presents a HIERARCHY of knowing ranked in order from opinion, trust, "mathesis" and finally to pure knowledge; and the idea of the soul, with aspects of mind, will, and desire. Humans participate in the life of the highest being to the extent they rise above the world of becoming.

Platonism was mediated to Christian thinkers mostly through the later Neoplatonists Philo Judaeus (c. 20 B.C.E.–50 C.E.), Plotinus (c. 205–70), Iamblichus (c. 245–330), and Porphyry (c. 232–c. 305), who accused Christians of misappropriating Plotinus. Neoplatonic speculation about emanating powers (*dynameis*) shaped much Christian thought about the relation among the persons of the TRINITY, and between the Creator and the creature; it also affected Christian ideas of perfection—the progressive subsumption of the creature into the life of God. AUGUSTINE OF HIPPO employed Porphyry's triadic relations to elucidate the inner life of the soul (memory, understanding, will) as an analogy of the Trinity. Neoplatonism shaped

the ideas of ALLEGORY as practiced in the biblical interpretations of the ALEXANDRINE SCHOOL. DIONYSSIUS the Pseudo-Areopagite transformed the Neoplatonic stages of purification, illumination, and perfection into the mystical theology of the journey of the soul into God.

Platonic and Neoplatonic ideas were the principal shapers of Christian thought until the introduction of ARISTOTLE into the theological framework by Islamic and Jewish philosophers and St. THOMAS AQUINAS and other thinkers of the HIGH MIDDLE AGES. This framework has held sway since then. Marsillo Ficino (1433–99) sparked a Platonic revival in Florence, but it was short lived. The modern thinker SIMONE WEIL has been called a Platonist theologian by many.

Further reading: Paul Firedländer, *Plato* (Princeton, N.J.: Princeton University Press, 1973); Plato, *The Collected Dialogues* (New York: Pantheon, 1966); John M. Rist, *Platonism and its Christian Heritage* (London: Variorum, 1985); A. Hilary Armstrong, *St. Augustine and Christian Platonism* (Villanova, Penn.: Villanova University Press, 1967).

Newman, John Henry (1801–1890) *British theologian and cardinal*

John Henry Newman was perhaps the most prominent British theologian of the 19th century and had a profound effect on both the Church of England and the British Catholic community, which he helped to revive. Newman was born February 21, 1801, in London. At age 15 he had an intense religious experience that led him to study THEOLOGY at Trinity College, Oxford, and at Oriel College, where he won a fellowship and later taught. He was ordained an Anglican priest and in 1828 became vicar at St. Mary's Church, the university parish in Oxford.

An erudite and capable preacher, his sermons drew large crowds, especially as he and a small group of colleagues launched the OXFORD MOVEMENT with the goal of pulling the Church of

England back from its drift into rationalism and liberal theological perspectives. The concerns of the movement found expression in a set of tracts that were widely diffused among British church leaders.

First committed to a conservative Anglicanism, Newman's study of the early church gradually moved him to High Church Anglicanism and then in the early 1840s to Roman Catholicism. Tract number 90 argued that the anti-Catholic paragraphs of the Church of England's Articles of Religion distorted true Catholic belief and practice. This tract led to significant opposition from his Anglican colleagues, and he was forced to leave his pulpit and resign his teaching post at Oriel. Similarly, he later found his motives questioned by the Catholic community.

Over the next three years he considered his position and by 1845 decided he should formally convert to Catholicism. He was received into the church in October 1845, along with several of his followers, and reordained a Catholic priest. In this period, a short 16 years after the Catholic Emancipation Act, the HIERARCHY and diocesan structures had yet to be reestablished after 300 years of severe legal restrictions.

In 1851 Newman moved to IRELAND, founded the Catholic University of Ireland, and spent seven year teaching there. In 1858 he moved to Birmingham and opened an oratory, a house set up for worship and study in the absence of a church facility. He lived a quiet existence until 1863, when he and other Catholic priests came under attack by Anglican priest Charles Kingsley (1819–75), a professor at Cambridge. In response, Newman wrote possibly his most famous work, the *Apologia Pro Vita Sua* (1869), which laid out the course of his own conversion and defended his Catholic stance.

The *Apologia* lifted Newman out of the obscurity into which he had fallen. He began to write prolifically. His 1870 book, *An Essay in Aid of a Grammar of Ascent,* explored the way a searching mind reaches certitude. His work over the next

years led to an appointment as honorary fellow at Trinity College. In 1879, Pope LEO XIII (r. 1878–1903) named Newman a cardinal; it was the first time in several centuries that a nonbishop had been so honored. He wrote forcefully on the SENSUS FIDELIUM and the liberty of CONSCIENCE.

Newman died in 1890. He was declared venerable by Pope JOHN PAUL II (r. 1978–2005) in 1991.

Further reading: Vincent Ferrer Blehl, *The White Stone: The Spiritual Theology of John Henry Newman.* (Petersham: St. Bede's, 1993); Louis Bouyer, *Newman: His Life and Spirituality,* tr. J. Lewis May. (London: Burnes & Oates, 1958); Sheridan Gilley, *Newman and His Age* (London: Darton, Longman & Todd, 1990); Ian Ker, *John Henry Newman* (Oxford: Clarendon, 1988); John Henry Newman, *Newman: Prose and Poetry,* ed. Geoffrey Tillotson. (London: Hart-Davis, 1957).

Nguyen Ba Tong (1868–1949) *Vietnamese bishop*

Nguyen Ba Tong, the first Vietnamese to be consecrated a Roman Catholic bishop, was born in Saigon on August 7, 1868. He served as a parish priest for 18 years before being assigned as the secretary of the DIOCESE of Saigon. In 1932 Pope PIUS XI decided to turn over the work in Vietnam to an indigenous leader and invited Nguyen to Rome, where he consecrated him in 1933 auxiliary bishop of Phat Diem with right of succession. He became the bishop of Phat Diem in 1935.

Nguyen set himself the task of creating a more indigenized church. Among his first steps was to set up a college and seminary to train priests. He strengthened the work of the several orders of NUNS and assigned responsibilities in every parish. His practical accomplishments varied from building a dike to prevent flooding to writing plays, some of which were performed in a theater he built—he believed, with the JESUITS, that the church should contribute to the general culture.

In 1954 Vietnam was divided and a communist government took control of the north. Many priests joined the 700,000 Catholics who fled south. The government confiscated the buildings that housed the church's educational and social welfare programs. Those CLERGY who remained, including Bishop Nguyen, operated under very limited conditions, though they were allowed to lead prayer and celebrate the Mass.

Nguyen died in Phat Diem on August 7, 1968, many years before the government began to loosen its control of a severely weakened church. Because communication with Rome was severely limited through the 1960s, the church did not implement the reforms of VATICAN COUNCIL II. It remains one of the more traditionalist centers of Catholic life and worship.

See also ASIA.

Further reading: Scott W. Sunquist, ed., *A Dictionary of Asian Christianity* (Grand Rapids, Mich.: Eerdmans, 2001).

Nicholas of Cusa (1401–1464) *German Neoplatonic theologian and mathematician*

Nikolaus Kryffs (or Krebs) was born into a well-to-do family in the town of Kues in the Rhineland Palatinate. He would later be known as Nicolas Cusanus, after the Latin name of his birthplace. He was a talented abstract thinker who made contributions in both mathematics and philosophical THEOLOGY. Like the Dominican Giordano Bruno (1548–1600), he broke away from Aristotelian Scholasticism and returned to Plato.

Nicholas chose the church as his career and was successively ordained a priest (1440), named a cardinal (1448), and consecrated as BISHOP of Brixon (1450). He was one of the few people who, like JOHN HENRY NEWMAN centuries later, received a cardinal's hat prior to being named a bishop. He also served as papal legate and papal vicar.

As a mathematician he concentrated on the concept of infinity. From his work he developed the idea of approaching truth but never reaching it completely based on his hypothesis that human comprehension of the universe could at best be incomplete. In his mature years he turned to astronomy, and from his readings and observations of the heavens he made several prescient deductions about the universe. A generation before NICHOLAUS COPERNICUS he argued that the Earth circled the Sun; he further believed that inhabited planets like the Earth circled other stars.

Cusa became famous for his rejection of rationalist theories on the existence or nature of GOD, a perspective offered in his book *On Learned Ignorance*. He reasoned that God as Infinity is largely unknowable and that to know that we do not know is the beginning of wisdom. In God there is a coincidence of all opposites that are found in the finite word. Cusa died in 1464 in Todi.

Further reading: Gerald Christianson and Thomas M. Izbicki, eds., *Nicholas of Cusa on Christ and the Church* (Leiden: E. J. Brill, 1996); Gerald Christianson and Thomas M. Izbicki, *Nicholas of Cusa: In Search of God and Wisdom* (Leiden: E. J. Brill, 1991); Nicholas of Cusa, *Nicholas of Cusa: Selected Spiritual Writings,* tr. Hugh Lawrence Bond. (Mahwah, N.J.: Paulist, 1997); Kazuhiko Yamaki, ed., *Nicholas of Cusa* (London: Routledge/Curzon, 2001).

Nicholas of Lyra (1270–1340) *Franciscan biblical exegete*

Nicholas of Lyra, a FRANCISCAN priest, emerged as one of the great scholars and the foremost Christian BIBLE commentator of the MIDDLE AGES. Little is known of his early life, but he joined the Franciscans as a young man. He showed outstanding intellectual abilities and was allowed to complete his doctorate and join the faculty of the University of Paris (the Sorbonne). He initially became known for his efforts to convert Jews to Christianity, possibly the source of the rumors that he also had a Jewish background.

Nicholas became concerned about the state of biblical studies in his day. His book *Postillae perpetuae in universam Sanctam Scripturam* ("Lasting Analyses of All Holy Scripture") argued for a primacy literal reading of the Bible. He called for improved Latin translations of biblical books, especially those of the Old Testament. Any allegorical or mystical interpretations of the Bible message must be based on an initial literal understanding.

In creating his own commentary on the Bible he drew heavily on Jewish sources, especially Solomon ben Isaac of Rashi (1040–1105), although he always tried to keep his commentary in line with the teachings of the Catholic Church. Church authorities saw his work as a check on the many speculative books on Scripture that had characterized the 13th century. Nicholas's *Postillae* eventually became the first Bible commentary to be printed. Martin Luther (1483–1546) was deeply influenced by Nicholas in his emphasis on the literal and plain meaning of the biblical text.

Further reading: Mark Hazard, *The Literal Sense and the Gospel of John in Late-medieval Commentary and Literature* (New York: Routledge, 2002); Nicholas of Lyra, *Nicholas of Lyra's Apocalypse Commentary,* ed. Philip Krey (Kalamazoo: Medieval Institute, 1997); ———, *The Postilla and Nicholas of Lyra on the Song of Songs,* tr. & ed. James George Kiecker. (Milwaukee: Marquette, 1998).

Nobili, Roberto de'   *See* DE' NOBILI, ROBERTO.

North America

The history of Catholicism in North America cannot be separated from its introduction and development in LATIN AMERICA. The early Latin American mission reached into Florida, Texas, New Mexico, Arizona, and Alta, or Upper, California. Even today, some 22 percent of all American Catholics are of Hispanic origin, and they are exerting growing influence on public and religious life.

CANADA

Basque and Norman Catholic sailors made temporary settlements in Newfoundland in the MIDDLE AGES, but the first French Catholics to reach inland came to Canada as both fur traders and missionaries. In 1535 the explorer and cartographer Jacques Cartier (1491–1557) planted a CROSS at the tip of Gaspé Peninsula, Quebec, where a Mass was also celebrated. Samuel de Champlain (1570–1635), called the "Father of New France," sponsored missionaries to convert the Indian tribes. AUGUSTINIAN Recollects and JESUITS soon arrived in sizable numbers, including the NORTH AMERICAN MARTYRS, who missionized among the Algonquin, Huron, Mohawk, and Wendat. Most French Catholic settlement took place along the St. Lawrence River. The Jesuit Jacques Marquette (1637–75) explored the Mississippi with Louis Jolliet (1645–1700) and established a mission at Kaskaskia, Illinois.

French Canada fell to the British in 1659. Tension between the ruling British Protestants and French Catholics lived on for many generations. Many French "Acadians" fled to Vermont, Massachusetts, France, and Louisiana (the "Cajuns"). Later, facing the threat of a take-over from the nascent United States, the British recognized French Quebec as an autonomous entity within the British Empire, with guarantees for its religion, language, and legal tradition (eventually including the Napoleonic Code, which also still applies in the state of Louisiana).

In the next century Canada saw heavy immigrations of Irish Protestant "Orangemen" and Irish Catholics alike. The Protestants settled mostly in Newfoundland, Nova Scotia, and especially Ontario. Equal numbers later came from Italy, eastern Europe, and the Caribbean, and many of them were Catholic. When Canada became an independent nation in the British Commonwealth in 1857 Quebec won renewed guarantees of religious autonomy, but resentment of Protestant political control in Canada and economic power in Quebec caused periodic nationalist stirrings, which flared up again during the 1970 and 1980s and linger on.

Today there are about 13 million Catholics in Canada, half of them in Quebec Province. Apart from the French, Polish and Ukrainian Catholics have a distinct presence. Canada has a number of outstanding Catholic educational institutions, most notably the University of St. Michael's College in the University of Toronto, where the Pontifical Medieval Institute is housed, and the Université Laval in Quebec City. The noted Jesuit philosopher and theologian BERNARD LONERGAN was a Canadian.

UNITED STATES

The story of Catholicism in the territory now known as the United States of America is complex and varied. It began with Latin American and French missions and settlers, who left permanent footprints in Louisiana, the Southwest, and California.

The English colonies were first settled by Puritans and other Protestant dissenters in New England and Anglicans in the Middle Atlantic and the South. Their legacy left a predominantly Protestant cast and thrust to American religion, which even affected the other religions that later took root. The Protestants experienced cycles of "awakenings" and reform movements, not infrequently tinged with venomous ANTI-CATHOLICISM and ANTICLERICALISM. The one colonial exception was the colony of Maryland, granted in 1637 by James I (r. 1603–25) to Sir George Calvert, known as Lord Baltimore (1606–75), as a refuge for persecuted English Catholics. Catholics also found refuge among the tolerant Quakers in Pennsylvania and in isolated pockets in New York, New Jersey, and Virginia. Toleration of Catholics in Maryland ended when the colony became officially Anglican in 1692. Priests were few in number in the English colonies and were mostly FRANCISCANS and Jesuits.

At the time of the Revolution, which started with the Declaration of Independence in 1776, Catholics numbered only about 25,000, perhaps 1 percent of the population. They were ministered to by just 23 former Jesuits (the order had been suppressed in 1773). JOHN CARROLL, himself a former Jesuit, superior of the mission, and first bishop in America, ardently supported the American Revolution and its democratic principles. The Revolutionary Army direly needed the services of the many young Catholics who joined its ranks. George Washington (1732–99), ever the mediator, suppressed the Anglican celebration of Guy Fawke's Day (November 5), which featured the burning of the pope in effigy, among the troops.

The success of the Revolution and the acceptance of Catholics who supported it instilled a spirit of democracy among churchmen in America. Carroll promoted the use of the vernacular in the LITURGY and a democratic organization in the church, but Rome snuffed out these incipient efforts. Meanwhile, the French Revolution (1789) sent America its exiled priests and NUNS. Native orders began to arise, too, as with the Sisters of Charity, founded by St. ANN SETON to care for the sick and to educate the young. The Louisiana Purchase (1803) more than doubled the size of America (and added a sizable French-speaking Catholic population). Later additions in 1845 (Texas), 1846 (Idaho, Washington, Oregon), and 1848 (California and the Southwest) also increased the Catholic population significantly, many of them Spanish-speaking.

Meanwhile, Catholics in the eastern states were gradually forming dioceses, building hospitals, and establishing school systems. The trusteeship parochial system, in which clergy shared power with the laity, caused problems from the start. Gradually, the American church switched to the corporation model, whereby the local ordinary or bishop is the immediate owner of all church property with the exception of those institutions owned by religious orders.

Between 1820 and 1920 more than 20 million Irish, Italian, German, and east European Catholics immigrated to the United States, where most became laborers in the new urban industries. Often the immigrants formed ethnic churches in ethnic neighborhoods, with the nonliturgical services conducted in the ethnic tongues. As Catholics, especially the urban Irish, began to exert more political clout, they met stiff resistance from Protestants in movements like the Know-Nothing Party (fl. 1850s) and later the Ku Klux Klan. Ironically, anti-Catholic suspicions accomplished some good: the public school movement championed by Horace Mann (1796–1859) owed some of its success to Protestant fears of being overtaken by the success of the earlier Catholic school system.

American bishops followed a very collegial style in the 19th century. This was manifested in the several Baltimore councils and in ecclesiastical structures such as those advocated by JOHN ENGLAND, who held regular councils involving both laity and clergy in his diocese of Charleston, South Carolina. Meanwhile, Pope PIUS IX, reflecting a European context where the church seemed under attack, retreated behind the Vatican walls, responding to intellectual innovation with the *Syllabus of Errors* (December 8, 1864) and the dogma of INFALLIBILITY, which most American bishops opposed. The vigor and creativity of the American church was denounced in Europe and the Vatican as AMERICANISM, which was seen as quasi-heretical. Nevertheless, in 1875 Archbishop John McCloskey of New York (1810–85) was made the first American cardinal; Cardinal JAMES GIBBONS of Baltimore (1834–1921) became the most influential of the early cardinals.

By the early 20th century Catholics had developed a solid parish system, strong parochial secondary schools, and hundreds of institutions of higher learning, including NOTRE DAME UNIVERSITY and Catholic University of America (1889) in Washington, D.C. American Catholics absorbed the energy of their Protestant compatriots and became very activist in promoting their FAITH while upholding the separation of CHURCH AND STATE in their predominantly Protestant country. However, once the papacy condemned Americanism (LEO XIII) and MODERNISM (PIUS X), the Catholic hierarchy of the United States began to retreat. In the 20th century it showed little of the independence toward the Vatican shown by various bishops in Europe and South America.

Catholics suffered one more major bout with prejudice in the 1920s with the rise of the Klu Klux Klan, which targeted Catholic as well as black and Jewish citizens, and with the defeat of Alfred E. Smith (1873–1944) for president of the United States in 1928, largely because of his religious affiliation. This wrong was reversed in 1960 with the election of Catholic JOHN F. KENNEDY (1917–63).

In the second half of the 20th century Catholics thrived as never before. Benefiting from participation in labor unions and from the veterans' benefits in the "G.I. Bill," they rapidly moved up the socioeconomic scale. The Catholic population grew to 42 million by 1960. These Catholics felt invigorated by VATICAN COUNCIL II, which seemed to back their less traditional impulses.

Toward the end of the century, however, dark clouds appeared. As Catholics became suburbanized the formerly vigorous urban parishes became obsolete. Religious vocations dropped markedly. Divisive issues took center stage: the role of women (*see* FEMINISM), the ABORTION question, liberal-conservative feuds in the political arena, and, to add salt to the wounds, the PEDOPHILIA scandal that rocked the highest levels of the clergy. All this shook the confidence of believers and their faith in the church, despite some respected leaders like Cardinal JOSEPH BERNADIN of Chicago.

Despite the difficulties, parishes continue to survive, and Catholics still seek to listen to the GOSPEL of the kingdom of God preached by Jesus CHRIST long ago in Galilee. Of necessity, lay Catholics are taking on more and more important roles in the ministry, administration, and education in America. Today there are about 66 million Catholics in the United States, four times the population of the next-largest denomination, the Southern Baptists.

Further reading: Jay P. Dolan, *In Search of American Catholicism* (Oxford: Oxford University Press, 2003); John Tracy Ellis, *American Catholicism* (Chicago: University of Chicago Press, 1969); David Gibson, *The Coming Catholic Church: How the Faithful are Shaping a*

New American Catholicism (San Francisco: HarperSan-Francisco, 2003); Chester Gillis, *Roman Catholicism in America* (New York: Columbia University Press, 1999); Charles Morris, *American Catholic: The Saints and Sinners Who Built America's Most Powerful Church* (New York: Random House, 1997).

North American Martyrs

The term *North American Martyrs* refers to eight JESUITS (six priests and two lay brothers) who were tortured and killed in the mid-17th century while trying to convert Native Americans of the Huron, Iroquois, and Mohawk peoples. The French had explored the St. Lawrence River Valley as the century began and established a settlement on the site of present-day Quebec in 1608. Over the next half century, they expanded their presence to the southwest toward Lake Ontario.

John de Brebeuf (1593–1649) was the first of the martyrs to arrive, in 1625, and he initiated work among the Huron. Anthony Daniel, Charles Garnier, and Isaac Jogues (1607–46) joined him later. They had some early success despite periodic problems. In 1642, during a war between the Huron and Iroquois, Jogues and lay brother Rene Goupil were captured while on a peace mission to the Iroquois and tortured by them. Though Jogues survived, Goupil became the first of the martyrs to be killed, followed by Jogues and lay brother John de Lalande in 1646, Daniel (1648), John de Brebeuf (1593–1649), Charles Garnier, Noel Chabanel, and Gabriel Lalemant (1649). The Jesuit accounts of their labors now form some of the most important documents on the development of the Catholic Church in America and contain some vivid accounts of the martyrs' last days and hours, marked by unusual courage and faith.

As a group, the Jesuit martyrs were beatified in 1925 and canonized in 1930 by Pope PIUS XI. The death of the martyrs has been commemorated with shrines at Auriesville, New York, and Fort Saint Mary near Midland, Ontario; a number of parish churches have been named for them.

Further reading: Thomas J. Campbell, *Pioneer Priests of North America, 1642–1710* (New York: America, 1913); Edna Kenton and Reuben Gold Thwaites, *Black Gown and Redskins; Adventures and Travels of the Early Jesuit Missionaries in North America, 1610–1791* (London: Longman, 1956); James Comly McCoy, *Jesuit Relations of Canada, 1632–1673: A Bibliography* (Paris: A. Rau, 1937); François Roustang, *An Autobiography of Martyrdom; Spiritual Writings of the Jesuits in New France* (St. Louis: Herder, 1964); R. G. Thwaites, ed., *The Jesuit Relations and Allied Documents* (New York: Pageant, 1959).

Nostra Aetate (October 28, 1965)

Nostra Aetate was VATICAN COUNCIL II's declaration on the church's relationship to the world's other religions; it proposed a dramatic change of direction. The document was originally designed to be a chapter in the statement on ECUMENISM and to focus in particular on Judaism. However, as the council considered the issue, it was elevated into a separate declaration and made universal.

Nostra Aetate encouraged practical cooperation with other religions on matters of common interest, such as social and moral values, as well as dialogue on common themes. For example, it praised ISLAM for its affirmation of monotheism, Buddhism for understanding the limits of materialism, and Hinduism for its emphasis on contemplation and meditation. The beliefs and practices shared with different religions, it was argued, provided an arena in which mutual respect could be acknowledged and conversation pursued.

Reflecting its origins, the document paid particular attention to the church's special relationship to the Jewish community. That relationship is rooted in two facts: Judaism served as the major source of Christianity, yet during their long shared history, the far larger CHRISTIAN community has often persecuted Jews. The document rejected as false a number of common beliefs that underlie ANTI-SEMITISM, especially the idea that the Jews as a people killed CHRIST. It also decried all forms of anti-Semitism. In fact, the declaration summarizes the church's opposition to all forms of discrimination based on race, color, religion, or condition in life.

Nostra Aetate has had a significant practical impact. It became institutionalized through the Pontifical Council for Inter-religious Dialogue, created in 1964, and numerous subsequent dialogical sessions at all levels of the church. During the long pontificate of Pope JOHN PAUL II, his travels around the world featured meetings with leaders of the world's religions. As his pontificate came to a close, he offered public words of apology for the church's sinful actions to people of other faiths, and he often quoted their scriptures in his addresses.

The most dramatic effect was relative to the Jewish community. Following the establishment of the Pontifical Council, in 1971 Pope PAUL VI led in creating a special International Catholic/Jewish Liaison Committee, which was immediately welcomed by Jewish leaders as initiating a new era in Catholic-Jewish relations. The committee has empowered numerous structures for Catholic-Jewish dialogue. Catholic authors explored Catholic support for anti-Semitic acts with renewed candor, including special attention to the role of the church during World War II, when its actions or those of some of its CLERGY directly and indirectly led to the deaths of Jews during the Holocaust.

The insight presented in *Nostra Aetate*, that God did not revoke the Covenant with Israel in making the new Covenant with humanity in Christ has provided a whole new theological agenda for Catholic biblical scholars and a new foundation for the interaction of Jews and Christians. In that light, the church has redirected its activity toward Jews from attempts to convert and control to expressions of repentance for past actions and dialogue aimed at future cooperation.

Further reading: Eugene J. Fisher, *Faith Without Prejudice* (New York: Crossroad, 1993); David Efroymson, Eugene J. Fisher, and Leon Klenicki, *Within Context: Essays on Jews and Judaism in the New Testament* (Collegeville, Minn.: Liturgical Press, 1993); Steven L. Jacobs, ed. *Contemporary Jewish and Christian Religious Responses to the Shoah [Holocaust]* (Lanham, Md.: University Press of America, 1993); Michael Shermis and Arthur Zannoni, *Introduction to Jewish-Christian Relations* (Mahwah, N.J.: Paulist, 1991); Johannes Willebrands, *Church and Jewish People: New Considerations* (Mahwah, N.J.: Paulist, 1992).

Notre Dame, University of

Among the best-known institutions of higher education affiliated with the Catholic Church, the University of Notre Dame was founded on several hundred acres originally purchased by Stephen Badin (1768–1853), the first Catholic priest actually ordained in the United States. Badin left the small plot of land in trust to the BISHOP of Vincennes, Indiana, to be conveyed to anyone who would build a school on the site. In 1842 the land passed to Edward Sorin (1814–93), a priest of the Congregation of Holy Cross, and the university was chartered two years later under the congregation's auspices.

Sorin's goal of building a large school modeled on classic European universities became practical with the immigration of large numbers of European Catholics into the Midwest. Though located in a rural area that seemed inviting to parents, the university was not far from a ring of emerging metropolitan centers, from Cleveland, Ohio, and Detroit, Michigan, to Milwaukee, Wisconsin, and Chicago, Illinois.

At first a small college, Notre Dame grew steadily through the 19th century, adding successively a school of science (1865), a law school (1869), and a college of engineering (1873). Growth slowed only briefly after an 1879 fire that largely destroyed the campus facilities.

In the generation following Sorin's death in 1893, leadership of the school and the Congregation of the Holy Cross were closely related. John A. Zahm (1851–1921), superior of the congregation, followed a variety of strategies for building the academic programs and personnel, and a new generation of scholars made Norte Dame's first contributions to the development of science and technology. Fr. James A. Burns is largely credited with setting Notre Dame on course to become the preeminent Catholic university in North America.

Burns's success cannot be separated from that of a celebrated faculty member, Knute Rockne (1888–1931), the head football coach (1918–31), who inspired his teams to achieve the highest winning percentage of any college football team before or since: 105 victories, 12 losses, and five ties. He brought six national championships to the school and gave it a profile among both Catholics and the wider American community that would have been almost impossible to attain any other way. Growth continued through the 1930s and 1940s under the guidance of Frs. John A. O'Hara (1888–1960) and John J. Cavanaugh (1899–1979).

Notre Dame was well established in 1952 when THEODORE HESBURGH (1917–   ) assumed its leadership. During his 35-year tenure the university became one of the American Catholic Church's leading intellectual institutions. It more than doubled in size and in 1972 made the radical change of admitting female students to the undergraduate school.

In 1967, the Congregation of the Holy Cross relinquished control of the school to an independent board on condition that the president be chosen from among the the Holy Cross Fathers. The school is presently headed by Fr. Edward A. Mallory. His tenure has been marked by an increase in the number of minority students.

Further reading: Arthur J. Hope, *Notre Dame—One Hundred Years* (South Bend, Ind.: University of Notre Dame Press, 1999); George Klawitter, ed., *Adapted to the Lake: Letters By Brother Founders of Notre Dame* (New York: Peter Lang, 1993); Thomas J. Schlereth, *The University of Notre Dame, A Portrait of Its History and Campus* (South Bend, Ind.: University of Notre Dame Press, 1977); Leo R. Ward, *My Fifty Years at Notre Dame* (South Bend: Indiana Province of the Priests of Holy Cross, 2000).

Notre Dame Sisters

Several of the Catholic women's religious orders that emerged in the 19th century are named in honor of Our Lady, the Blessed Virgin MARY OF NAZARETH under one of her titles. Notre Dame means "Our Lady" in French. Julie Billart (1751–1816) and Françoise Blin de Bourdon (1756–1816) started the first Sisters of Notre Dame in 1803 in gratitude for Billart's recovery from a paralytic condition. Founded in Amiens, France, the motherhouse was later moved to Namur, Belgium. The new orders were in part a response to the French Revolution and the poverty it created. Work focused on the education of poor girls. The work spread to England and the United States in the 1840s, to AFRICA in the 1890s, and to ASIA (Japan and China) in the 1920s. By the end of the 20th century, all five continents were involved.

A second congregation devoted to Notre Dame was founded in 1833, sparked originally by the Bavarian government's having closed religious orders in 1809. In the 1820s, Caroline Gerhardinger (1797–1879) decided to start a new order focused on the education of young women. In 1828 the Vatican negotiated a reversal of policy by the Bavarian government. Subsequently, Gerhardinger and a few assistants were able to move into what had previously been a convent and in 1833 started the School Sisters of Notre Dame. Caroline soon became known as Mother Sister Teresa of Jesus. Their rule was approved in 1854. Work spread to the United States in 1847, when Mother Teresa led five sisters to Maryland and Missouri to educate immigrant German-American children. The work spread throughout Europe as well. As the 21st century began, more than 4,300 sisters were at work in 35 countries around the world.

The Notre Dame Sisters, still another group, can be traced to the informal efforts around 1850 of the

Prussian Hilligonde Wolbring, later known as Sister Maria Aloysia (1828–89), to care for children with insufficient parental care. She took her small inheritance and the assistance of a colleague, Elisabeth Kühling (Sister Maria Ignatia), to begin a home for neglected and orphaned children. Her parish priest suggested institutionalizing her work by founding a religious order. The small order thrived for two decades, but the antichurch laws instituted by the Prussian government during the Kulturkampf in the 1870s forced the women to relocate to the Netherlands and the United States. These two locations then became launching pads for the spread of the order internationally. Sisters from the United States opened work in Brazil in 1923, and some from the Netherlands moved to Indonesia in 1934. In 1947, the sisters established an international center in Rome. Since that time expansion has been considerable. Work now is active in more than 15 countries, from Korea to East Africa.

Further reading: Frederick Friess, *Life of Reverend Mother Mary Teresa of Jesus Gerhardinger, Foundress . . . Poor School Sisters of Notre Dame* (Baltimore: St. Mary's Industrial School; 1907); Aimee Julie, *With Dedicated Hearts* (Ipswich: Sisters of Notre Dame de Namur; 1963); Mary Vincentia. *Their Quiet Tread: Growth and Spirit of the Congregation of the Sisters of Notre Dame . . 1850–1950* (Milwaukee: Bruce, 1955); Roseanne Murphy, *Julie Billiart: Woman of Courage* (Mahwah, N.J.: Paulist, 1995); A School Sister of Notre Dame, *Mother Caroline and the SSND's in North America* (St. Louis: Woodward & Tiernan, 1928).

Nouvelle Théologie (Fr.: "New Theology")

Nouvelle Théologie was a theological movement that began in France after World War I and culminated in Vatican Council II. The movement arose in reaction to the general trend in the church in the late 19th century inaugurated by Pius IX when he condemned modernism in his *Syllabus of Errors* (December 8) in 1864. This trend, reinforced by subsequent popes, was coupled with Leo XIII's

elevation of the theology of St. Thomas Aquinas to authoritative status in the seminary curriculum. To many champions of Nouvelle Théologie, the first development blinded the church to inevitable change, and the second narrowed the rich Catholic theological tradition to the thought of single thinker as interpreted by the Neoscholastics. The movement almost came to a halt with Pius XII's *Humani Generis* (August 12, 1950), which aimed to stop the spread of the liturgical movement, ecumenism, existential philosophy, and evolutionary science within Catholic circles.

The key new theologians were the Dominicans Yves Congar (1904–95) and Marie-Dominique Chenu (1895–1990) and the Jesuit Henri de Lubac (1896–1991). Embracing the results of historical research, Congar became the foremost ecclesiologist (theology of the church) of his time. He also engaged in extensive ecumenical activities with Protestants and eastern Christians. Removed from teaching and public preaching, he undertook a study of the church in the New Testament at the École Biblique in Jerusalem.

De Lubac, rejecting the formalism of Neothomism, sought to restore the fathers and mothers of the church to their rightful place by launching with Jean Daniélou the publishing venture *Sources chrétiennes,* which to this day publishes critical editions of patristic and matristic sources. Chenu sought a critical and historical understanding of St. Thomas in the context of his own time. All three influenced the younger theologians Hans Urs von Balthassar and Karl Rahner. Despite earlier condemnations, all three emerged as experts at Vatican Council II (1962–65), where they exerted significant influence on such topics as ecclesiology, sacramental theology, Scripture, and patristic tradition. Their life work seemed in accord with the council's efforts toward both *resourcement* (Fr. "resourcing") and *aggiornamento* (It. "updating") in facing the modern world.

Further reading: Yves Congar, *The Mystery of the Church* (Baltimore: Helicon, 1960); Henri de Lubac,

Catholicism (San Francisco: Ignatius, 1988); Dieter Hoffmann-Axthelm, *Anschauung und Begrift: zur historischen Einardnung von "nouvelle theologie" und "existentialer Theologie"* (Munich: Kaiser, 1973); Marcellino D'Ambrosio, "Resourcement Theology, Aggiornamento, and the Hermeneutics of Tradition," *Communio* (Winter, 1991) 18; available online.

nun (Middle Lat.: *nonna,* "nun")

In popular usage a nun is a female member of a religious order or institute who takes vows of poverty, chastity, and obedience. Some nuns are cloistered, some are not. Technically in canon law the term *nun* applies to religious who live in communal houses to which others are denied access and from which the nuns are generally not allowed to leave (*Code of Canon Law,* cn. 667).

Further reading: Mary Ann Donovan, *Sisterhood as Power: The Past and Passion of Ecclesial Women* (New York: Crossroad, 1989).

Nunes Carneiro Leitao, Melchior (Melchior Miguel Carneiro Leitao)

(1516–1583) *missionary bishop*

The JESUIT priest Jose DeCosta Nunes was the first BISHOP to exercise authority in the Far East after the medieval mission of John of Monte Corvino, (1246–1328) in China. Nunes was born in Coimbra, Portugal. Little is known of his early life, but he joined the Society of Jesus in 1543 and quickly rose in the ranks of the rapidly expanding organization. He was named titular bishop of Nicaea in 1543 and in 1560 became the first bishop of Goa, India, the Portuguese colony chosen by Francis Xavier as the center of Jesuit activity in southern Asia. Seven years later, at Pope PIUS V's direction, he moved farther east to take charge of the work in Japan and China. He settled in Macao (where the Portuguese had established a colony in 1553) and led in the establishment of a number of Catholic institutions, including a hospital and leprosarium.

From his base in Macao Nunes tried to establish a mission in China, but it took almost a decade to see any success. Among his last duties was to welcome MATEO RICCI (1552–1610) to Macao to begin his notable work among the Chinese. He retired in 1581, turning over his duties to the first bishop of Macao Leonardo Fernando de Sa (d. 1587).

Further reading: Sergio Ticozzi, "Carneiro Leitao Melchior Nunes," in Scott W. Sunquist, ed., *A Dictionary of Asian Christianity* (Grand Rapids, Mich.: Eerdmans, 2001); Manuel Texiera, *Macau e sua Diocese,* vol. 2. (Macao: Tipografia da Missão do Padroado, 1940).

O

obedience

Obedience, in which one submits one's own will and desires to that of another, is considered a virtue within Christianity. PAUL THE APOSTLE noted that by Adam's disobedience SIN entered the world and that by CHRIST's obedience many would become righteous. While FAITH is the key to establishing a relationship with GOD, obedience, in imitation of CHRIST, is the virtue that dominates one's daily pilgrimage with God.

Obedience is owed first and foremost to God's expressed will. The content of that obedience is made known in Scripture in Jesus' sayings, for example, the Great Commandment (Matt. 22:37), and through the manifestations of virtues, such as the fruits of the Spirit (Gal. 5:22–23). The church has always taught that obedience or submission to God is absolute.

The church has also taught that obedience to the authorities that God has ordained is also part of the Christian life. Such derived authorities have a claim on obedience that is conditional and takes different forms. Human authorities include, for example, parents, the state, and the church. Human authority always stands judged in so far as it becomes arbitrary, promotes injustice, or directs people away from the will of God.

Obedience is a particularly crucial aspect of the lives of those in religious communities. Upon joining, members take a vow of obedience to those placed in authority over them in a wide range of matters (such as organizing their daily schedule) that would go beyond the bounds of the obedience expected of the average church member. It is understood in religious orders that a special effort is being made by each member to imitate Christ in his obedience to God.

The subject of obedience immediately raises a host of questions concerning the nature of obedience, what mental states and outward acts constitute obedience, who has the authority to enforce obedience and punish disobedience, and what is the relationship between obedience and CONSCIENCE. Such questions are basic to and motivate the discipline of ethics.

Further reading: Quentin de la Bedoyere, *Autonomy and Obedience in the Catholic Church: The Future of Catholic Moral Leadership* (London: T. & T. Clark, 2002); Alois Muller, *Obedience in the Church* (Westminster, Md.: Newman, 1966); Karl Rahner et al., *Obedience and the Church* (Washington, D.C.: Corpus, 1968); H. A. Williams, *Poverty, Chastity, and Obedience: The True Virtues* (London: Mitchell Beazley, 1975).

Oblates of Mary Immaculate

The establishment of the Oblates of Mary Immaculate (OMI) was one of the Catholic responses to the French Revolution (1789).

The Oblates were founded by Eugene de Mazenod (1782–1861), whose family was pushed into exile by the revolution, eventually leading to the divorce of his parents. De Mazenod returned to FRANCE in 1802 and entered a Catholic seminary in Paris in 1808. De Mazenod was beatified in 1975 and canonized in 1995 by Pope JOHN PAUL II. His feast day is May 21.

After his ordination, de Mazenod chose to work among the poor of his home region of Aix. He gathered others to assist in his work of visiting the sick, imprisoned, and alienated of his generation. An informal group emerged assuming the name Missionaries of Provence. When word spread of the missionaries' work and requests for help followed, de Mazenod moved to formalize the company of workers into a religious society, the Oblates of Mary Immaculate, which received papal approval in 1826.

In 1837 de Mazenod was appointed BISHOP of Marseilles, but he continued as head of the Oblates. In 1841, he responded to a request from the bishop of Montreal to extend the Oblate work to the New World. Over the remaining two decades of his life, he recruited more than 450 men to take the Oblates' mission to various parts of the world. The Oblates have become known for their unique vows that include not only poverty, chastity, and obedience but also perseverance until the end—even if the order should dissolve. They have continued to place an emphasis on work among the most neglected members of society—the poor, abandoned, and alienated. They also maintain seminaries for the improvement of CLERGY education and care for several Marian shrines, including the Shrine of the Immaculate Conception in Washington, D.C. The noted Indian Oblate liberation theologian Tissa Balasuriya (1924–   ) was excommunicated by the Congregation for the Doctrine for the Faith under Cardinal Joseph Ratzinger, now BENEDICT XVI, in 1998. The excommunication was lifted the next year.

The Oblates currently have work around the world on every continent from Japan to Brazil to Turkmenistan.

Further reading: Kay Cronin, *Cross in the Wilderness* (Toronto: Missio, 1976); Jean Leflon, *Eugene De Mazenod: Bishop of Marseilles, Founder of the Oblates of Mary Immaculate, 1782–1861,* 4 vols. (New York: Fordham University Press, 1961–70); Donat Levasseur, *A History of the Missionary Oblates of Mary Immaculate: Toward a Synthesis (1815–1985),* 2 vols. (Rome: General House 1989); Josef Metzler, *On All Continents: The Missionary Oblates of Mary Immaculate* (Rome: OMI Information, 1977).

O'Connor, Flannery (1925–1964) *American novelist and short story writer*

Born an only child in Savannah, Georgia, O'Connor attended Georgia State College for Women, where she majored in English and sociology. Although she lived a short life, her two novels (*Wise Blood,* 1952; *The Violent Bear It Away,* 1960) and 32 short stories left an important influence on American literature. She wrote in southern gothic style, focusing on morbid and grotesque characters and situations through whom God's grace could yet work. As a Roman Catholic her writing was influenced by St. THOMAS AQUINAS and by her understanding of the SACRAMENTS. In 1951 she was diagnosed with lupus, the disease that took her father when she was 12. She died on August 3, 1964, and is buried in Milledgeville, Georgia.

Further reading: Jean W. Cash, *Flannery O'Connor: A Life* (Knoxville: University of Tennessee Press, 2002); Richard Giannone, *Flannery O'Connor and the Mystery of Love* (Urbana: University of Illinois Press, 1989); George Kilcourse, *Flannery O'Connor's Religious Imagination: A World with Everything off Balance* (New York: Paulist, 2001); Susan Srigley, *Flannery O'Connor's Sacramental Art* (Notre Dame: University of Notre Dame Press, 2004).

Old Catholics

Across Europe and NORTH AMERICA a number of independent churches use the name *Old Catholic*. Important Old Catholic bodies exist in Switzerland, Austria, the Netherlands, GERMANY, and Poland. In the United States the Polish National Catholic Church and now the Ecumenical Catholic Church (fd. 2001), are the prime examples. All these groups broke with the Roman Catholic Church at some point over the last few hundred years.

The Dutch Old Catholics grew out of an unresolved controversy over the appointment of bishops in the 18th century. The other European Old Catholic groups originated as a protest over the declaration of papal INFALLIBILITY at VATICAN COUNCIL I. The Polish Church originated from a dispute within the Catholic Church in the United States, which in the 19th century was making an attempt to de-emphasize the ethnic and linguistic divisions brought to America from Europe (*see* GEORGE MUNDELEIN).

The Dutch church was able to obtain valid if irregular episcopal orders; through that church the others eventually obtained APOSTOLIC SUCCESSION. In 1889, most of these churches affiliated with one another through the Union of Utrecht and issued a statement of their raison d'être, the Declaration of Utrecht. Traditionally, the Old Catholics and the Anglicans have been in communion, but their relationship has been strained in recent decades over the issue of female priests and BISHOPS (*see* HOLY ORDERS).

In England and the United States (and to a lesser extent elsewhere) apostolic orders from the Netherlands were passed to a former Roman Catholic priest and Old Catholic bishop, Arnold Harris Mathew (1852–1919), who attempted to build an Old Catholic Church in England. Mathew consecrated several bishops there, one of whom brought his episcopal lineage to the United States. The result was the formation in the United Kingdom, Canada, and the United States of a number of small Old Catholic denominations that claim a valid apostolic succession while remaining independent of papal authority. They have through the 20th century followed a variety of paths, although none has been able to form a stable and substantive congregation. Over the years they have made common cause with a number of irregular Eastern Orthodox Churches of a similar nature.

At one point, Mathew discovered that some of the priests associated with him were members of the Theosophical Society, an esoteric organization. When he forced them out of the church, they formed the Liberal Catholic Church, which continued a close relationship to the Theosophical Society and offered an esoteric interpretation of CHRISTIAN teachings. The Liberal Catholic Church now exists in several European countries and North America and has been able to build a larger following than any of the other churches that derived episcopal orders from Bishop Mathew.

In 2001 Catholic priests and laity, reacting against the Vatican's apparent retreat from the spirit of VATICAN COUNCIL II and its stance on sexual issues, formed the Ecumenical Catholic Church. It is currently headed by Archbishop Mark Shirlan and a panel of bishops.

Further reading: Information on the Ecumenical Catholic Church is available online; Peter F. Anson, *Bishops at Large* (London: Faber & Faber, 1964); C. B. Moss, *The Old Catholic Movement* (Eureka Springs, Ark.: Episcopal, 1977); Karl Pruter and J. Gordon Melton, *The Old Catholic Sourcebook* (New York: Garland, 1983); Gary L. Ward, *Independent Bishops: An International Directory* (Detroit: Apogee, 1990).

Opus Dei (Latin for "The Work of God")

Opus Dei is a Roman Catholic institute devoted to encouraging people from all walks of life to fully practice CHRISTIAN principles in daily living. It was founded in 1928 by the Spanish priest St. José Maria Escrivá de Balaguer (1902–75) for lay men; women were admitted in 1930, and eventually it was opened to priests as well. Members do not leave their professions but rather are taught how to incorporate Christian teachings and ethics into their private and public lives. The institute, contrary to its original mission, has become heavily clericalized.

Opus Dei operates educational institutions, conference centers, and residences around the world, with central offices in Rome. It claims more than 85,000 members in 85 countries. In 1982 Pope JOHN PAUL II established it as a Personal Prelature of the Catholic Church. This in effect brought the institute under direct papal supervision. He canonized José Maria Escrivá, the founder, on October 6, 2002.

The organization has long counted many important and influential political and business figures among its membership. Justice Antonin Scalia (1936–) of the U.S. Supreme Court is a member. This has fed groundless popular suspicions that Opus Dei is a secret, power-hungry cult. It has been accused of right-wing political and religious aims and of being tied to the U.S. Central Intelligence Agency. Dan Brown characterized Opus Dei as a sinister organization in his best-selling novel *The DaVinci Code* (2003). Opus Dei members, however, do favor a very traditional understanding of the church and its mission.

Further reading: Vittorio Messori, *Opus Dei: Leadership and Vision in Today's Catholic Church* (Washington, D.C.: Regnery, 1997); Pedro Rodriguez, *Opus Dei in the Church: An Ecclesiological Study of the Life and Apostolate of Opus Dei* (Dublin: Four Courts, 1995); Dominique Le Tourneau, *What is Opus Dei?* (Dublin: Mercer, 1989); Michael J. Walsh, *Opus Dei: An Investigation into the Secret Society Struggling for Power within the Roman Catholic Church* (San Francisco: HarperSanFrancisco, 1992); William J. West, *Opus Dei: Exploding a Myth* (Crows Nest: Little Hills, 1988).

Oratory of Divine Love

The Oratory of Divine Love was a 16th-century reform movement in the Catholic Church. It was formed under the inspiration of Catherine of Genoa (Caterinetta Fieschi, 1447–1510), a FRANCISCAN lay woman who devoted the last three decades of her life to serving the poor and sick.

Over the years Catherine attracted a small group of followers from among the intellectual elite of northern ITALY. An informal group was founded in 1497. Never very large, it nevertheless became a powerful force for reform due to the influence and connections of its members. The Oratory met regularly for prayer and engaged in works of charity among the poor and ill. Over the years, it developed a vision for reforming religious orders and began calling for a general church council to enact needed reforms. Among its first accomplishments was the formation of the Order of the Theatines (sanctioned by the pope in 1524), dedicated to lifting the standards of the CLERGY. The Theatines are today known as the Congregation of Clerks Regular.

The Oratory produced a number of outstanding Catholic leaders including Jacopo Sadoleto (1477–1547), the cardinal who debated with John Calvin; Reginald Pole (1500–58), the cardinal who assisted Mary I of GREAT BRITAIN in her attempt to return the country to the Catholic faith; and Gian Pietro Caraffa (later Pope PAUL IV), who presided over the Council of TRENT.

Further reading: M. R. O'Connell, *The Counter Reformation 1559–1610* (New York: Harper & Row, 1974); J. C. Olin, *Catholic Reform* (New York: Harper & Row, 1990).

Origen of Alexandria (c. 185–c. 254) *one of the first systematic Christian theologians*

Little is known of the early life of Origen, one of the most brilliant and influential CHRISTIAN intellectuals of the third century. He is believed to have been born in EGYPT and seems to have been raised in a Christian home. His father was killed during the persecution of Christians in 200. He had a varied education that included contact with

GNOSTICS of the Valentinian school (*see* VALENTINUS), Neoplatonists, and the writings of PHILO OF ALEXANDRIA.

Origen was only 18 years old when he succeeded CLEMENT OF ALEXANDRIA (c. 150–c. 215) as head of the catechetical school of Alexandria (*see* CATHECHESIS). Soon afterward he began work on his *First Principles,* the first known attempt to produce a comprehensive and systematic presentation of Christian belief. In this work, thoroughly embedded in Greek philosophy, he made a case for the TRINITY, the FALL, human freedom, and the eventual REDEMPTION of all mankind. His Gnostic-like understanding of the Fall as the descent of preexisting souls into material bodies would come back to haunt his reputation.

For almost three decades Origen served as a popular teacher. He introduced his students to the intellectual currents of the time, teaching them to use secular thought to refine Christian teachings and to distinguish the church's affirmations from those of competing philosophical schools and religions. He and his students lived a semimonastic lifestyle and took biblical admonitions seriously. Early in his teaching career, Origen came to understand Matthew 5:29 and 19:12 (eunuchs for the kingdom) to mean that he should castrate himself. His action delayed his ordination for many years.

Origen's fame as a teacher led to invitations to travel and speak. His BISHOP in Alexandria, Patriarch Demetrius (189–232), considered his speaking to be a breach of protocol for a layman and ordered him back to Alexandria, where he remained until 230. During this period, he began his detailed study of the BIBLE, writing a set of extensive commentaries on its different books. For the Old Testament he used both the original Hebrew and the newer Greek text used in most Christian churches, hoping to catch any mistranslations. His *Hexapla,* a critical edition of the Old Testament, and his commentaries on Matthew and John established him as the church's first major biblical scholar. Of all Origen's voluminous work,

only what was translated into Latin has survived. His commentaries did, however, have a significant affect on St. JEROME and later biblical scholars.

In 230 Origen left Alexandria for Palestine, where he was finally ordained by the bishops of Jerusalem and Caesarea. The enraged Demetrius excommunicated, defrocked, and exiled him. Origen settled in Caesarea in 231 and established a new school where he taught for the rest of his life. In 250 a new wave of persecution fell on the church. Origen was taken into custody and tortured. Though he survived and was released, his health was broken, and he died several years later.

Some of Origen's theories, as presented in *First Principles,* came in for criticism in the fourth and fifth centuries. Among the controversial ideas were his affirmation of the preexistence of the soul, his understanding of the Fall as the spiritual soul falling into matter (which seemed to question the goodness of the CREATION and INCARNATION), and the final restoration (Gk.: *apokatastasis*) of all (universal salvation). By the sixth century, these ideas placed Origen in a completely new context, as they came to be associated with a variety of popular heretical notions such as reincarnation, which Origen had specifically condemned.

When his name was connected to a group of Egyptian monks who had developed a somewhat pantheistic understanding of Christianity, a 543 synod in CONSTANTINOPLE issued a condemnation of what it termed Origenism. Later he was explicitly included in a list of heretics promulgated by Constantinople Council II (680). The change in reputation from a popular if controversial Christian thinker to a heretic may account for the loss of so many of his writings. Modern scholarship has helped rehabilitate Origen and reestablish him as an important thinker in the development of the church and an example of the affirmation of FAITH in the face of persecution and torture.

Further reading: Joseph W. Trigg, *Origen* (New York: Routledge, 1998); Henri Crouzel, *Origen* tr. A. S. Worrall (Edinburgh: T & T Clark, 1998); Elizabeth A. Clark,

The Origenist Controversy (Princeton, N.J.: Princeton University Press, 1992); Charles Kannengiesser and William L. Petersen, eds., *Origen of Alexandria: His World and Legacy* (Notre Dame: University of Notre Dame Press, 1988).

Orthodox-Catholic dialogue

As the early church developed in the centuries immediately following the apostolic era, a HIER-ARCHY gradually took shape. All the DIOCESES in a particular region would be tied together under the jurisdiction of a PATRIARCH or chief BISHOP. In the eastern Mediterranean, three major patriarchates emerged, at Jerusalem, Antioch, and Alexandria. In the West, Rome emerged as the central authority. After the capital of the Roman Empire was moved to CONSTANTINOPLE, its patriarch quickly emerged as the most powerful in the East; in 451 the Council of CHALCEDON gave it a status equal to but in second place to Rome, over the protest of Pope LEO I. Given his access to the Byzantine throne, the ARCHBISHOP of Constantinople was soon recognized as the first among the four eastern patriarchs and given the title of Ecumenical Patriarch. To this day, Constantinople has jurisdiction over all Orthodox Christians who live in countries where no canonical, autonomous, or autocephalous Orthodox jurisdiction exists (including much of the Americas).

Pope Leo I's objection can be seen as the start of a slowly growing tension between the Eastern and Western Churches. Some historians trace the split between the churches to the adoption of Latin as the liturgical language in the West instead of Greek. Others note that whereas four patriachates existed in the Eastern Greek-speaking church, only one existed in the West, who exerted disproportionate civil and religious power.

Tension between East and West culminated in the GREAT SCHISM of 1054 when legates sent by Pope Leo IX (r. 1049–54) excommunicated MICHAEL I CERULARIUS (c. 1000–59), the patriarch of Constantinople, and those who supported him.

Archbishop Michael responded by excommunicating Leo. At issue was the claim of papal authority over the other patriarchates, which the Eastern Church considered to be purely honorary. The break was also occasioned by the insertion by the Western Church of the phrase "and the Son" (the FILIOQUE) into the Nicene CREED. The phrase was intended to clarify an obscure theological question about the TRINITY, but the Eastern Church was never reconciled to this unilateral action by the West, which violated an earlier council commitment to maintain a single, unchangeable creed for the whole church. Even after 1054 the Eastern Orthodox and Roman Catholic Churches remained in frequent communication, but they gradually evolved in different directions.

Other divisive issues came into play. During the CRUSADES, a Roman Catholic king, Baldwin I (d. 1118), took the throne in Jerusalem and established Catholic churches and dioceses in the territories of the Eastern patriarchates. Soldiers of the Fourth Crusade in 1204 actually sacked Constantinople.

Early in the 15th century a new effort to heal the schism was initiated as Muslim Turks bore down on Constantinople. In 1438 a council was convened at Ferrara, ITALY (later moved to Florence), with the stated purpose of reuniting the CHRISTIAN world against the spread of ISLAM. The effort had some success, and the Greek delegates signed a lengthy agreement on a variety of divisive issues, such as the use of unleavened bread in the EUCHARIST and the idea of PURGATORY. Before a broad consensus over the agreement could win approval in the East, however, the Turks took Constantinople in 1453, under Sultan Mehmet II (1432–81) and blocked its practical implementation.

Meanwhile, a new irritation for Eastern Church leaders emerged as Catholics began to gather dissenting groups of Orthodox believers into new jurisdictions in communion with Rome. This began in the 12th century; following the establishment of the crusader kingdom of Antioch, the independent Maronites formed the

MARONITE CATHOLIC CHURCH, whose leader was recognized by the West as a patriarch. Over succeeding centuries, wherever Catholic and eastern communities came into geographic or political contact, Eastern Catholic Churches have been formed, the most recent being in the 20th century in India. The process has often led to disputes over church property. In Slavic lands in the 20th century, such property conflicts were exacerbated by the arbitrary actions of antireligious governments that used churches for political ends. With the reemergence of the church in the postcommunist era, these conflicts have become more public in Romania, Russia, and Ukraine.

Fortunately, certain forces worked in the direction of reconciliation in the 20th century, not least the feeling that both churches were under attack by atheistic and secularizing movements, especially in the Soviet Union. Both churches were also influenced by the growing ECUMENISM of the Protestant churches. In 1920 the Ecumenical Patriarch issued an encyclical directed to all Christian Churches calling them to closer relationship with one another. The patriarchate assumed a leadership role in creating the World Council of Churches in 1948.

VATICAN COUNCIL II recast the position of the Catholic Church relative to other Christian bodies. Even before the close of the council, Pope PAUL VI took the lead in initiating a new era in Orthodox-Catholic relations in 1964 by making a trip to Jerusalem for a meeting with Ecumenical Patriarch Athenagoras (d. 1972). The two leaders formally rescinded the 1054 excommunications and in 1965 produced the Catholic-Orthodox Joint Declaration, promulgated simultaneously on December 7 at a public meeting of the Vatican Council and at a special ceremony in Istanbul.

In 1995 Pope JOHN PAUL II followed up on Paul VI's initiative by meeting with Patriarch Bartholomew (1940–), exchanging the kiss of peace with him and issuing a joint statement on Christian unity. Later, amid his statements admitting to and asking for forgiveness for the failures of the Catholic Church, he visited Athens and asked FORGIVENESS for the SIN of the church against Orthodox believers.

However, in the last decades of the 20th century, real gains in overcoming the history of hostility proved elusive. All of the issues—papal primacy, the *filioque* doctrine, the Eastern Catholic churches, and modern property disputes—remained. A number of dialogues have been held by Catholic and Orthodox theologians seeking common ground. Ideas have included mutual affirmation of the nature of one Christian Church that includes both Catholic and Orthodox branches, mutual recognition of sacramental legitimacy, and the collegiality of bishops.

The continued substantive differences between the two communions were visibly manifest in the refusal of the patriarch of Moscow to attend or send a representative to the funeral of John Paul II. John Paul's successor, BENEDICT XVI, has made reconciliation with the Orthodox world a prime goal of his PAPACY.

Further reading: John Borelli and John Erickson, *The Quest for Unity: Orthodox and Catholic in Dialogue* (Crestwood, N.Y.: St. Vladimir Seminary, 1995); Paul McPartlan, ed., *One in 2000? Towards Catholic-Orthodox Unity* (Middlegreen: St. Pauls, 1993); Aidan Nichols, *Rome and the Eastern Churches: A Study in Schism* (Collegeville, Minn.: Liturgical Press, 1992); Ronald G. Roberson, "Catholic-Orthodox Relations in Post-Communist Europe: Ghosts from the Past and Challenges for the Future," *Centro Pro Unione*, (Spring 1993) 43: 17–31.

Ottaviani, Alfredo (1890–1979) *cardinal and Vatican official*

Alfredo Ottaviani was widely viewed as one of the leaders of conservative churchmen during VATICAN COUNCIL II. Ottaviani was born in Rome and raised in a devout Catholic home. He was ordained a priest in 1916 and developed a special expertise in CANON LAW. He also founded the Oasis of St. Rita, an orphanage and school, where he spent a considerable amount of his free time. In 1953 he was named a cardinal and in 1959 appointed the secretary of the Vatican's Holy Office, now the Congregation for the Doctrine of the Faith, with jurisdiction over questions of FAITH and morals.

In 1962, while the Vatican council was in session, he was consecrated the titular BISHOP of Berrhoea. He had already emerged as one of the leading conservative voices at the council and a defender of, for example, papal authority. While opposing a number of the council's initiatives, he retained the respect of all, especially Pope PAUL VI, who in 1966 appointed him pro-prefect of the Congregation for the Doctrine of the Faith. Already in his mid-70s, he would retire two years later.

Ottaviani remained active during his retirement years and is remembered for the "Ottaviani Intervention," a letter he and fellow conservative Cardinal Antonio Bacci (1885–1971) sent to Pope Paul VI in 1969 questioning the adequacy of the new EUCHARIST mandated by the council. It is believed that the letter led to a brief delay in Paul's final approval of the replacement of the Latin Mass with the Novus Ordo Missae. Ottaviani died in 1979.

Further reading: Giuseppe Alberigo and Joseph Komonchak, eds., *History of Vatican II,* 4 vols. (Maryknoll, N.Y.: Orbis, 1995–2004); Robin Anderson and Alfredo Ottaviani, *St. Pius V: A Brief Account of His Life, Times, Virtues & Miracles* (Rockford: Tan, 1989); Alfredo Ottaviani, *The Ottaviani Intervention: Short Critical Study of the New Order of Mass* (Rockford, Ill.: Tan, 1978).

Oxford Movement (1833–45)

In its early stages the Oxford Movement in England was known as Tractarianism, named after a series of publications called *Tracts for the Times,* written by JOHN HENRY NEWMAN, J. Keble, (1792–1866) E. B. Pusey (1800–82), and others (*see*

GREAT BRITAIN). The tracts, taking inspiration from early and medieval Christianity, aimed at restoring the High-Church ideals of the Church of England. They argued for a middle way between "Popery" and what the leaders took to be anthropocentric humanism ("Liberalism").

The series culminated in Newman's tract 90, *Remarks on Certain Passages in the Thirty-Nine Articles* (1841), in which he argued that the articles were generally in consonance with the decrees of the Catholic Council of TRENT. Newman concluded: "The Protestant Confession was drawn up with the purpose of including Catholics; and Catholics now will not be excluded." Tract 90 caused a considerable storm and opposition in the Church of England.

Soon many Oxfordians, including Newman and Henry E. Manning (1808–92), joined the Roman Catholic Church. Both were later elevated to the cardinalate. Within the Church of England, under the leadership of Pusey, the movement led to a greater emphasis on LITURGY and worship, a renewal of monastic orders, and social concern. Newman went on to publish *Essay on the Development of Christian Doctrine* (1845) and other notable treatises. He founded the Oratorians in England. He revived interest in the FATHERS AND MOTHERS OF THE CHURCH among Catholic scholars. Much neglected in his lifetime, many of his ideas on liberty of CONSCIENCE, the MAGISTERIUM, and biblical inspiration came to fruition in VATICAN COUNCIL II.

The Oxford Movement influenced not only THEOLOGY and church but also literature and culture. The poet GERARD MANLEY HOPKINS, for example, embodied its concerns in his poetry.

Further reading: Owen Chadwick, *The Spirit of the Oxford Movement* (Cambridge: Cambridge University Press, 1990); E. R. Fairweather, ed., *The Oxford Movement* (New York: Oxford University Press, 1964).

P

Pacem in Terris (Lat.: "Peace on Earth")
encyclical of Pope John XXIII

Pope John XXIII issued the ENCYCLICAL *Pacem in Terris* (April 11, 1963) just a few months after the Cuban Missile Crisis, which seemed to bring the United States and the Soviet Union to the brink of World War III. At the time the pope was overseeing VATICAN COUNCIL II even as he struggled through the last few months of his life. The encyclical became the signature document of his PAPACY.

John invoked the dignity of all humans, created in the image of GOD (Gen. 1:27), as the foundation for human rights and duties. It was the responsibility of the public authorities to protect and promote those rights and duties by maintaining legitimate social order. He suggested that nations as well as individuals have rights and duties and that "the same law of nature that governs the life and conduct of individuals must also regulate the relations of political communities with one another" (80), thereby providing the conditions necessary for world peace.

The encyclical addressed the arms race and the need for disarmament and called for assistance to underdeveloped nations. It also proposed that an international public authority be established that could act across national boundaries to deal with problems of international dimension. The authority would be created by all nations acting in consensus. John offered his support to both the United Nations (1946) and the Universal Declaration of Human Rights (1948) and expressed the hope that the UN could become an effective safeguard of human rights. He also addressed the issues of racism and minority rights.

While generally applauded in the Catholic world, the encyclical met with mixed reactions around the world. Some thought it utopian or complained of its silence on MARXISM. Others praised it for its clear statement that the church now stood behind human aspirations for peace, justice, and freedom. In any case, the document has stood the test of time. It framed the debate at Vatican II on human rights, religious liberty, and international justice. It still provides Catholic ethicists and believers with principles that help them judge the actions of nations.

Further reading: John C. Bennett and Reinhold Niebuhr, "Pacem in Terris: Two Views" *Christianity and Crisis* 23 (13 May 1963): 81–83; Paul Cremona, *The Concept of Peace in Pope John XXIII* (Malta: Dominican, 1988); Jeremiah Newman, *Principles of Peace: A Commentary* on *John XXIII's Pacem in Terris* (Oxford: Catholic Social Guild, 1964); Edward Reed, ed. *Pacem in Terris: An International Convocation on the Requirements of Peace* (New York: Pocket, 1965).

Pachomius (c. 290–c. 346) *founder of Christian communal monasticism*

Pachomius, an Egyptian convert, became the founder of organized Christian MONASTICISM in the early fourth century. His feast day is May 9. He was born a non-CHRISTIAN in lower EGYPT, but he seems to have been influenced by Christians he met while serving in the army. He was attracted to the ascetic life, and at the age of 20 he moved into the desert, where he learned the particulars of ascetic living from St. Palemon (fl. 340), a disciple of the ascetic St. ANTHONY OF EYGPT (c. 251–356). By the time Pachomius arrived, some of the monks who had chosen the hermit's life had begun to coalesce around a few exemplary individuals whose ways were worthy of imitation. This was the first step in the development of cenobitic, or communal, monasticism.

Pachomius set about to organize these hermits into functioning communities. He moved to Tabennae, an island in the middle of the Nile River, and set up his first community. Those who joined him dropped their individual quests in favor of a common ascetic life under the authority of a spiritual director, with fixed rules and set times for communal prayer (*see* PRAYER OF THE HOURS) and the EUCHARIST. The MONKS were organized into groups (CLOISTERS) and subjected to a schedule for ordering the day and a uniform dress code. Every monk was assigned work and an abbot to oversee his life. Pachomius eventually accepted women into the religious life and organized separate cloisters for them.

The original set of rules developed by Pachomius has been lost, though it is believed that they are reflected in later rules, some of which, like the *Regula Sancti Pachomii,* were named for him. The practices he shaped were the source of the later Rules of St. BASIL THE GREAT and BENEDICT OF NURSIA, which influenced all subsequent monastic life in the eastern and Western Churches, respectively.

Further reading: Athanasius of Alexandria, *The Life of Pachomius,* tr. A. N. Athanassalis (Missoula, Mont.: Scholars, 1975); Dewas J. Chitty, *The Desert a City: An Introduction to the Study of Egyptian and Palestinian Monasticism Under the Christian Empire* (Crestwood, N.Y.: St. Vladimir's Seminary, 1977); Phillip Rousseau, *Pachomius: The Making of a Community in Fourth-century Egypt* (Berkeley: University of California Press, 1985).

pacifism

Pacifism is a belief that people must avoid all violence toward one another and especially refuse to kill one another in war. In the CHRISTIAN world, pacifism has been identified with certain Protestant groups, the so-called peace churches, which include the Church of the Brethren, the various Mennonite groups, and the Society of Friends, or Quakers. Pacifism stands in contrast with JUST-WAR teaching; it has developed a religious rationale for citizens claiming CONSCIENTIOUS OBJECTION to war and refusing to submit to a draft or bear arms.

Just war theory came to prominence as Christianity rose to power in the Roman Empire, and ever since the MIDDLE AGES it has prevailed within the Catholic and most Protestant churches. St. AUGUSTINE OF HIPPO was one of the first theologians to argue in its support. It was intended not as an excuse for war, but rather as a tool to reduce the incidence of war by requiring rulers to justify any belligerence with reference to moral categories and guidelines.

However, there have always been those who found the pacifist ideal the more genuine Christian way and argued for its adoption. The FRANCISCANS have been noted for their advocacy of pacifist ideas, following the model of St. FRANCIS OF ASSISI, who sought to use persuasion rather than force during the CRUSADES.

In the 20th century, the examples of Mahatma Gandhi and Martin Luther King, Jr., have led many to the path of *satyagraha* (Hin. "truth force" and active nonviolence, especially in different arenas of social conflict. Many CATHOLIC ACTION groups have embraced nonviolent pacifism. In the 1930s, DOROTHY DAY began to argue for pacifism and conscientious objection. Day and her Catholic Worker movement nurtured the development of PAX, an American pacifist group. During the Vietnam War, some Catholics who felt that Day's appeal was limited to the far left founded the Catholic Peace Fellowship to bring pacifist ideals to the mainline Catholic Church. The CPF drew inspiration from Pope JOHN XXIII's encyclical *PACEM IN TERRIS*. Philip (1923–2002) and Jesuit Daniel Berrigan (1921–) beginning in the Vietnam era, have led a sustained pacifist movement in the United States, often engaging in symbolic acts of protest.

Meanwhile, in Europe, Pax Christi International was founded in 1945 to encourage postwar reconciliation. In 1972 PAX joined Pax Christi as its American affiliate. VATICAN COUNCIL II had acknowledged the principle of conscientious objection, which was also affirmed by the United States Conference of Catholic Bishops in 1971. A decade later, in its 1983 pastoral, *The Challenge of Peace,* the Bishops Conference further declared pacifism and conscientious objection legitimate expressions of Catholic faith. Pacifists remain a distinct minority within the Catholic Church but have made their presence felt once again during the two Persian Gulf wars.

Further reading: Catholic Institute for International Relations and Pax Cristi, *War and Conscience in South Africa: The Churches and Conscientious Objection* (London: Catholic Institute for International Relations, 1982); Paul Frazier, *Catholic College Students and the Draft* (Nyack, N.Y.: Catholic Peace Fellowship, 1981); Anne Klejment and Nancy L. Roberts, eds., *American Catholic Pacifism: The Influence of Dorothy Day and the Catholic Worker Movement* (Westport, Conn.: Preager, 1996); Ronald G. Musto, *The Catholic Peace Tradition* (Maryknoll, N.Y.: Orbis, 1986).

painting and sculpture

Early CHRISTIANS embraced art for the purposes of instruction and worship. Painting (frescoes), sculpture, and mosaics were the first media they used, followed later by crafts such as ceramic, rock, and metal vessels; intalgio cut stones; textiles: coins; and amulets and medals.

BEFORE CONSTANTINE

The earliest surviving Christian artifacts date to around 200. Some speculate that early Christians followed the Jewish proscription against graven images (Deut. 7:5) and especially images of GOD (Exod. 20:4), but there is little evidence for this. In any case, the prohibition was probably not absolute even for Jews: in Israelite times images of cherubim and other decorations were allowed in the Temple (Exod. 25:1–22; 1 Kings 6:23–29). Archaeologists have found paintings of biblical scenes on the wall of the fourth-century synagogue in Dura Europos on the Euphrates in Syria and mosaics of the zodiac and biblical scenes in the fifth-century synagogue of Sepphoris in Galilee, so even Talmudic Judaism likely allowed for a limited iconographic tradition.

It is almost certain that Christians used ceramic utensils decorated with pagan mythological motifs, although they were apparently allowed only for limited purposes (*see* CLEMENT OF ALEXANDRIA, *Paidogogos* 3.57.1–3.60.1). One must make a distinction between private artifacts (such as silver boxes, or sarcophagi) and communal art (such as paintings in catacombs). Certain pagan images and decorative motifs such as grape vines, peacocks, and urns flowing with water were given a Christian interpretation under the larger schema of the *praeparatio evangelica,* the preparation for the GOSPEL—for example, Orpheus or Apollo as the Good Shepherd. Then, too, Christian clients may simply have commissioned art works from grape clusters signifying the EUCHARIST; sheaves of wheat signifying the Parable of the Tares and the Last Judgment, and others. The symbol of a fish (Gk. *ichthys*) alone or with an anchor (harbor of hope) can refer both to the fish that survived the Flood and the Greek anagram for "Jesus Christ, Son of God, Savior."

Besides the figure of the beardless Good Shepherd, the favorite frescoes portrayed on the walls of the catacombs are not so much illustrations of biblical stories, as in later paintings, but figures and symbols of deliverance from DEATH (Jonah, Isaac, Lazarus, Christ Risen), bondage (Exodus), or peril (Moses Tapping the Rock, Daniel in the Lion's Den, Three Young Men in the Fiery Furnace). Other paintings are of Abraham's Vision of the Three Angels at the Oak of Mamre, and many images of the *orans,* or a standing figure in prayer (the latter form has continued in use in the Eastern Church and in modern times has begun to spread into the West).

Painting of the Good Shepherd in the Catacomb of the Jordani. Note that Jesus is depicted as if he were either Apollo or Orpheus, following earlier Greco-Roman models. (Rome) *(Scala/Art Resource, NY)*

well-known workshops that served non-Christian Romans, GNOSTICS, and members of the other mystery religions such as the cults of Isis, Mithra, Dionysus, or Orpheus.

The first explicitly Christian art was most likely simple crosses; the Chi-Rho (☧, the first two letters in the Greek name *christos*) sometimes accompanied with the letters Alpha and Omega (the first and last letters in the Greek alphabet, used in the Book of Revelation); representations of loaves and fishes referring to Jesus' miracle; doves or ravens from Noah's Ark; peacocks and acanthus foliage symbolizing Paradise; vine and

Corpus, or body, of Christ from Saxony or France; bronze, c. 1150 *(St. Louis Art Museum, with permission)*

North portal of Chartres Cathedral showing Melkizideck, Abraham with Isaac, Moses, Samuel, and David (Chartres, France) *(photo by Frank K. Flinn)*

The Jonah image was the most frequent in early Christian art. He was a symbol of Jesus' death and RESURRECTION and the hope of individual believers (Matt. 12:40; IRENAEUS, *Against Heretics* 55.2; TERTULLIAN, *Resurrection* 58). Jonah is also the subject of several mid-third-century marble statuettes now in the Cleveland Museum of Art. These statues, like the contemporary figures on sarcophagi (stone caskets), are in the late Greco-Roman style; the Jonah iconography is often conflated with Endymion, the mortal shepherd eternally embraced by the moon goddess Selene. There are also frescoes of the Madonna and child that adopt the imagery of Isis and Osiris.

Beginning in the third century, examples of Christian sarcophagi proliferate. The most celebrated is that of Roman prefect Junnius Brassus (d. 359). It shows on the upper register carved reliefs of Christ giving the New Law to Paul and Peter, seated like an emperor over Coelus, the Roman god of heaven, surrounded by the Sacrifice of Isaac and the Arrest of Paul on the left and Christ before Pilate on the right. The lower register shows Christ's Triumphal Entry into Jerusalem, surrounded by Job's Affliction and ADAM AND EVE on the left, and Daniel in the Lions' Den and Paul Led to his Martyrdom on the right. The tradition

of independently standing statues, which flourished in the Latin MIDDLE AGES, ultimately derives from these casket reliefs as well as from carved ivory BIBLE covers that appeared somewhat later. The Eastern Church would never depart from the two-dimensional tradition of the ICON.

CONSTANTINE AND AFTER

As art patrons, CONSTANTINE and his mother, St. Helena, were noted mostly for the many BASILICAS and churches they built to mark Christianity's triumph over the Roman Empire. But the early ecumenical councils (*see* COUNCILS, ECUMENICAL) of the era legitimated other art work as well, such as the great iconic mosaics of Mary as Theotokos and CHRIST as Pantokrator, which were found in many church apses in the first millennium (*see* MARY OF NAZARETH.)

Christian and imperial iconography merged in the mosaic masterpieces of Byzantine art in the East and in the the Byzantine outpost in Ravenna, ITALY; the emperor himself is portrayed as a participant in the liturgical services. The great patron was JUSTINIAN I (482–565). Churches were already being adorned in a scheme of TYPOLOGY, in which Old Testament scenes (shadow) were paired with New Testament ones (type), as at San Vitale in Ravenna.

During the second half of the millennium Christian artistic impulses found expression in the many illuminated Bibles, gospels, and sacramentaries such as the BOOK OF KELLS, the Lindisfarne Gospel, and the ninth century Gospel of Ebbon. These books often had elaborate gold, silver, and ivory carved fronts. The art of reliquaries also developed, especially after Pope GREGORY I approved the long-standing practice of venerating RELICS; this tradition reached a peak in the late MIDDLE AGES.

MIDDLE AGES

The Middle Ages in Europe are noted for the development of the Gothic CATHEDRAL with its New Testament/Old Testament typological schemas, carried out in the stained glass windows and in the sculptural programs around the north, south, and west portals. A new theme for paint-ing and sculpture emerged in the Pietá, Mary holding the body of the crucified Christ in her motherly arms, a form that reached its apex in the Renaissance *Pietá* of MICHELANGELO. The feelings elicited by this image bespeak a new humanism, which was already evident in the painting of Giotto di Bondone (1267–1337). Like other artists, Giotto, who frescoed the life of St. FRANCIS OF ASSISI both in the Basilica of St. Francis in Assisi and in Santa Croce in Florence, benefited from the patronage not only of princes but also of the new mendicant orders, especially the FRANCISCANS and DOMINICANS. Fra ANGELICO

Fresco of St. Francis enduring trial by fire before the sultan of Egypt, by Giotto, 1290–96 (upper church, Basil-ica of St. Francis, Assisi, Italy) *(Scala/Art Resource, NY)*

was himself a Dominican, and his art reflects the religious commitments of his order.

RENAISSANCE AND COUNTER-REFORMATION

Renaissance art rediscovered the forms and beau-ties of Greco-Roman art, which was then being dug up around Rome. Its sponsors were the great princes of Italy like the Medici in Florence, the Sforzas of Milan, the doges of Venice, and the royal courts of Europe. Not the least among these princes were the popes, many of whom were from the lead-ing families. Julius II (r. 1503–13), notorious for corruption, nonetheless commissioned Michelan-gelo to fresco the recently restored Sistine Chapel ceiling with the famous scenes of the creation (*see* MICHELANGELO) and had RAPHAEL (1483–1520) decorate the Vatican Palace, where his *School of Athens* is located.

The favorite sacred images during the Renais-sance were the Madonna and Child and patron saints. Of special note is the Isenheim Altar of Matthias Grünewald (1428–1528), which reveals the depth of the DEVOTIO MODERNA that stands between late Catholicism and the early PROTES-TANT REFORMATION.

During the COUNTER-REFORMATION a new form of intense baroque spirituality (St. TERESA OF ÁVILA, St. IGNATIUS OF LOYOLA) was fostered by the church, along with allegiance to the chair of St. Peter. Giovanni Lorenzo Bernini (1598–1680) gave sculptural and architectural shape to both aspects of this vision in his statue *Ecstacy of St. Teresa of Ávila,* the canopy over the tomb of St. Peter in St. PETER'S BASILICA, and the "motherly arm embrace" of the colonnade and piazza of St. Peter's. The painter Domenicos Theotocopoulos (1541–1614), known as El Greco, and Michel-angelo Caravaggio (1571–1610) made masterly use of chiascuro, or light-and-darkness, reflect-ing the stress at the Council of TRENT on SIN and repentance in the arms of Holy Mother Church. The baroque art of SPAIN was carried by Spanish missionaries to the New World.

The Burial of Count Orgaz, by El Greco, Church of Santo Tomé. This painting is an epitome of Counter-Reformational art. (Toledo, Spain) *(Alinari/Art Resource, NY)*

LATER DEVELOPMENTS

Following the baroque period, much Catholic art became nostalgic, imitative, and given to sentimentality. The invention of lithographic printing fostered the copying of the art of the past rather than fostering the new. Thus, much painting and sculpture became neo-Gothic, neo-Renaissance, and neo-baroque. The rise of the LITURGICAL MOVEMENT in the late 19th and early 20th century gave rise to new art forms in architecture, sacred utensils (*see* UTENSILS, SACRED), VESTMENTS, painting, and sculpture, but even much of that was imitative.

The more interesting religious art of the 20th century was shaped by the Art Nouveau movement of 1900–35. VATICAN COUNCIL II and Pope PAUL VI also contributed to a renovation of liturgical art and an embrace of the modern. JOHN XXIII commissioned Giacomo Manzu (1908–91) to do the Door of Death, the far left doorway in the facade of St. Peter's Basilica. JOHN PAUL II represented a return to traditional piety and traditional art forms and styles. With the INCULTURATION of the Gospel the indigenous arts of the world, especially in LATIN AMERICA and AFRICA, are now being brought into religious and liturgical use; they will no doubt help shape the future of Christian art.

Further reading: Geoffrey Barraclough, *The Christian World* (London: Thames & Hudson, 1981); Pierre du Bourget, *Early Christian Painting* (New York: Viking, 1965); Jannic Durand, *Byzantine Art* (Paris: Terrail, 1999); Antonio Ferrua, *The Unknown Catacomb* (Florence: Nardini, 1990); Emile Mâle, *The Gothic Image: Religious Art in France of the Thirteenth Century* (New York: Harper & Row, 1972); Jeffrey Chipps Smith, *Sensuous Worship: Jesuits and the Art of the Early Catholic Reformation in Germany* (Princeton, N.J.: Princeton University Press, 2002).

Holy Family, anonymous Masai artist. Worldwide peoples are reinterpreting Christian icons through their own cultures. (Kenya) *(courtesy Plowsharing Crafts, St. Louis, Mo.; photo by John Huston)*

Palamas, St. Gregory (c. 1296–1359)
revered Eastern Orthodox mystic and monk

The mystic and MONK Gregory was born around 1296, probably in CONSTANTINOPLE, to a prominent family. As a child he lost his father, and following the example of several family members he decided to become a monk. He joined the community of monks at Mt. Athos, already the center of Eastern Orthodox Monasticism.

Gregory emerged out of obscurity in the 1330s, when he rose to the defense of the prayer discipline called *hesychasm* (Gk.: *hesychia*, "quiet, stillness, peace"), which was widely practiced at Athos. The discipline included the repetition of the Jesus Prayer ("Jesus Christ, Savior, save me, a sinner", leading to an experience of what the monks believed was the light and energy of GOD, sometimes referred to as the light of Tabor, a reference to the tradition that the Transfiguration of Jesus in Luke 28:36 occurred on Mt. Tabor. The discipline had been criticized by humanist Barlaam of Calabria (fl. 1350), who advocated intellectual activity and the pursuit of philosophy as the superior means to know God; the monks, he said, experienced only created effects and not the uncreated GLORY OF GOD.

Gregory developed an apologetic for his fellow monks. He argued that even though God is in his essence unknowable, the divine could be approached through "energies" like the Burning Bush, the Transfiguration, and so on. He drew upon the Cappadocian fathers such as St. BASIL THE GREAT to distinguish between God's essence and the divine economy (God in relation to the CREATION), and he argued that God in relation to the world is still God in the divine fullness.

Gregory's defense won him a decade of controversy. In 1341, a church council at CONSTANTINOPLE discussed and ultimately defended his teachings about God, but his problems were not over. Patriarch John XIV Kalekos (r. 1341–47) favored Barlaam's position and in 1344 found cause to move against Gregory, who was excommunicated and imprisoned. Only with the arrival

of Isidore (r. 1347–49) as the new patriarch in 1347 was Gregory exonerated and freed; in fact, he was named the bishop of Thessalonika (Greece). The practice of *hesychasm* remained a contentious issue in the region, however, and he was able to take up his new post only with the backing of the emperor in Constantinople. In 1351, another church council in Constantinople again discussed Gregory's ideas and again declared them orthodox.

Some of Gregory's writings were later included in the *Philokalia,* the classic compilation of *hesychast* writings first published in 1782. Gregory is considered a saint in the Eastern Church. Though Eastern Orthodox, he has also strongly influenced the mystical tradition of the West.

Further reading: Gregory Palamas. *The Triads* (London: S.P.C.K., 1983); John Meyendorff, *St. Gregory Palamas and Orthodox Spirituality* (Crestwood, N.Y.: St. Vladimir's Seminary, 1997); George C. Papademetriou, *Introduction to St. Gregory Palamas* (Brookline, Mass.: Holy Cross Orthodox, 2004); *The Philokalia: The Complete Text* (London: Faber & Faber, 1995).

pantheism

Pantheism, from the Greek *pan* (all) and *theos* (god), is the belief GOD is everything and hence everything is God. It affirms the absolute imminence of God and the divinity of the world, without much stress on God's transcendence. More a philosophical than a theological position in the West, it is a popular belief permeating many Eastern religions.

In the West, pantheism has generally been opposed by CHRISTIAN thinkers. The most noted pantheist in the West was Benedict Spinoza (1632–77), who identified God and Nature. All beings are modes of the divine. Christianity has generally affirmed the distinction between a transcendent deity and the created world. God is both transcendent (and hence an object of worship) and immanent in the world; although God is the sustainer of CREATION, the divine is never identified with creation itself. Creatures may interact with God as

HOLY SPIRIT and even experience a unity with God, without the differences between God and humanity becoming confused. Christianity has also usually affirmed a "personal" God, while pantheists generally deny the appropriateness of ascribing personal attributes to God.

Pan*en*theism is a modern attempt to resolve the differences between pantheism and Christian theism; it is popularly identified with Alfred North Whitehead (1861–1947) and his student Charles Hartshorne (1897–2000). It was championed in the late 20th century by a movement of "process theology" most often identified with the Methodist John Cobb (1925–   ) and later picked up by Catholic theologians such as RAHNER, KARL, JEAN PIERRE TEILHARD DE CHARDIN, Ewert Cousins, Eulalio R. Baltazar, and Bernard Lee (1932–   ). MATTHEW FOX used it as an element in his creation spirituality.

Panentheism, like pantheism, affirms that the Godhead includes and is present in the cosmos but goes beyond pantheism by also affirming that God transcends the world. From the immanent side, Karl Rahner speaks of "hominization" in which the spiritual destiny of "the Christian is to be a human being, a human being whose depths are divine."

Further reading: Eulalio R. Baltazar, *God Within Process* (Paramus, N.J.: Newman, 1970); Ewert H. Cousins, *Process Theology: Basic Writings by Key Thinkers of a Major Modern Movement* (Westminster, Md.: Newman, 1971); John Hunt, *Pantheism and Christianity* (Port Washington, N.Y.: Kennikat, 1970); Michael P. Levine, *Pantheism: A Non-Theistic Concept of Deity* (New York: Routledge, 1994); Constance F. Plumptre, *General Sketch of the History of Pantheism*, 2 vols. (London: Trubner, 1879).

papacy

The term *papacy* refers to the office and jurisdiction of the pope, the BISHOP of Rome. The powers of the papacy derive from the history and development of the DIOCESE of Rome and its place in the universal church.

The original authority of the pope as the "first among equals" was amplified by two factors. First, Rome was the center of the Roman Empire, where Christianity first spread. Second, Rome was the site of the martyrdom of the apostles PETER and PAUL and thus inherited the mantle of their spiritual and moral authority over the early church and their supreme place in the APOSTOLIC SUCCESSION.

The papacy developed over the first centuries of the church and is documented in the actions of various bishops of Rome. Some of the earliest documents record excommunications by Popes Victor I (r. 189–99) and Stephen I (r. 254–57) of other bishops who refused to accept papal decisions in disputes the popes had been asked to arbitrate. LEO I THE GREAT was a key figure in asserting the dignity of Rome over CONSTANTINOPLE and the city's jurisdiction over the entire Western Church. As the secular power of the Roman Empire shifted from Rome to Constantinople, the church emerged as the most stable and respected international institution in the West at a time when new countries such as FRANCE and GERMANY were just beginning to emerge.

In the eighth century, the pope assumed temporal sovereignty over the former duchy of Rome, the core of what was to become the PAPAL STATES. This act was justified after the fact by a forged document called the DONATION OF CONSTANTINE, purportedly issued by Emperor CONSTANTINE to Pope Sylvester I (314–35). Successive popes would often cite this document as the territory of the PAPAL STATES expanded. Conversely, the 15th-century proof that the Donation was a forgery was later cited as a justification for the incorporation of the Papal States into the modern state of ITALY.

The office of the pope developed as a blend of temporal rulership in the Papal States and moral authority over the church globally. At times the papacy would claim that its spiritual authority took precedence above any temporal authority; this view was initially articulated by Gelasius (r. 492–96), but most powerfully expressed by

BONIFACE VIII (r. 1294–1303). The pope's claim of authority over the Eastern Greek-speaking church would culminate in the SCHISM of 1054 with the mutual excommunications issued by Pope Leo IX (r. 1049–54) and the Patriarch MICHAEL CERULARIUS I (r. 1043–58). This split reached its low point when crusaders sacked Constantinople in 1204; it also led to the establishment of a number of EASTERN CATHOLIC churches as the Roman Catholic Church extended its jurisdiction to those lands dominated by EASTERN ORTHODOXY.

The modern papacy may be said to have begun in 1791, when the Papal States and territories began to be dissolved, first when the territories of Avignon and Venaissin were absorbed into France after the French Revolution (1789). Nearly all the remaining territory was absorbed by Italy in 1870, leaving the present Vatican territory. The loss of the Papal States occurred during the long reign of Pope PIUS IX (r. 1846–78). The refusal to recognize the new state of Italy left the Vatican in limbo until 1929, when the Lateran Treaty formally created the present state of VATICAN CITY.

PIUS IX would set the direction of the church for the next century. A political conservative, he resented the loss of church lands and opposed the democratic political and intellectual modernist changes that were carrying the day in Europe (*see* MODERNISM). At the same time, he encouraged efforts to tighten Rome's control over the church itself, a trend most clearly expressed in the calling of VATICAN COUNCIL I and the issuance of the declaration on papal INFALLIBILITY. He also encouraged the new wave of devotion to the Virgin Mary, with the declaration of the dogma of the Immaculate Conception (1854).

After Vatican I, the papacy emerged as a practical expression of the organizational and teaching leadership placed in the hands of the bishops as a whole but centered on the pope (*see* MAGISTERIUM). Though the pope is described as the "servant of the servants of God," he exerts great influence by his power to name bishops and cardinals. He is most clearly a symbol of the unity of the church.

With the exception of the Coptic pope, the papacy remains distinct among Christian church leaderships, in that the pope is the ruler of a temporal state, albeit a very small one, and the spiritual head of over a billion people. That state, the Vatican, operates as one country among many in the world community. It establishes diplomatic relations with other countries and can make and sign treaties. It is not a member of the United Nations but has established a Permanent Observer Mission. Within the diplomatic world, the church operates as an equal partner but exercises most authority when speaking for Catholics on moral and ecclesiastical issues.

A new era for the papacy began with the reign of Pope JOHN XXIII and the calling of VATICAN COUNCIL II. Since that time, the church has entered into a new, open stance toward the world community, assisted by the tools of modern communication and transportation. The status of the papacy was immensely extended during the lengthy reign of the charismatic Pope JOHN PAUL II, who traveled the world.

Further reading: Frank J. Coppa. *The Modern Papacy since 1789* (London: Longman, 1998); Philippe Levillain, ed., *The Papacy: An Encyclopedia,* 3 vols. (New York: Routledge, 2002); Steven Runciman, *The Eastern Schism: A Study of the Papacy and the Eastern Churches During the XIth and XIIth Centuries* (Oxford: Oxford University Press, 1953); Bruno Steimer and Michael G. Parker, eds., *Dictionary of Popes and the Papacy.* (New York: Crossroad, 2001).

papal bull

In the MIDDLE AGES letters were sealed tight with wax and stamped by *bulla,* or metal seals (often lead or a precious metal), to guarantee their authenticity. By the 13th century, the word *bull* came to mean the letter itself and not just the seal. Somewhat later, any document coming from the papal chancery was called a bull. In more recent centuries, the term has taken on an even more specific designation, being a letter issued from the pope in which he asserts his episcopal authority.

Bulls include decrees for a CANONIZATION, for founding a religious order or society, for nomination of bishops, for some individual dispensations of marriage or religious vows, and for excommunications, apostolic constitutions, and convocations. Many bulls simply document the day-to-day decisions that the pope is asked to rule on, but others have become documents of great historical import. Thus, the papal bull *Summis Desiderantes* (December 5, 1484) issued by Pope Innocent VIII (r. 1484–92) that condemned witchcraft and ordered the punishment of witches set the weight of the church behind the witch hunts then being conducted by the INQUISITION. Another bull, *Inter Gravissimas* (February 27, 1582), issued by Pope Gregory XIII, introduced the GREGORIAN CALENDAR, and in 1570 Pope PIUS V issued a papal bull excommunicating Queen Elizabeth I, marking a significant break between Catholics and British Anglicans (*see* GREAT BRITAIN).

Papal bulls retained the appearance of medieval documents until the 1870s, when Pope LEO XIII simplified the process. He replaced the archaic form of writing previously used by a modern Roman script, and the leaden seal was replaced with a simple stamp. Later changes accommodated modern advances in the composition and reproduction of documents. Documents that contain generally papal teachings are called encyclicals (Lat.: "world circular") although the meaning of *bull* and *encyclical* overlapped before the 20th century.

Further reading: Felician A. Foy, *A Concise Guide to the Catholic Church* (Huntington, Ind.: Our Sunday Visitor, 1984).

papal nuncio

A nuncio is one of the categories of diplomats, legates, or representatives the pope may use in inter-national affairs. A nuncio may be assigned the task of representing the Apostolic See to different governmental bodies, most often a national state. These nuncios may also represent the pope in negotiations with ecclesiastical bodies within that state. A nuncio acts with direct authority from the pope and thus is not subject to the local BISHOPS.

A nuncio enjoys the status of an official ambassador, representing VATICAN CITY as a sovereign state. Because of the stability of the Vatican and its long history as a state entity, a papal nuncio is often recognized by the host country as the ceremonial dean of the corps of diplomats operating there. If that deanship is not recognized, the nuncio is designated a pronuncio by the Vatican. An internuncio is a papal representative who has ecclesiastic but lacks ambassadorial status.

Further reading: Felician A. Foy, *A Concise Guide to the Catholic Church* (Huntington, Ind.: Our Sunday Visitor, 1984); Reginald Poole, *Lectures on the History of the Papal Chancery Down to the Time of Innocent III* (New York: Putnam, 1915).

Papal States

The Papal States formed an independent political entity in central ITALY ruled by the pope as monarch from the eighth century to the unification of Italy in 1871. The country emerged in stages, in part through gifts to the church by secular leaders, even apart from the spurious DONATION OF CONSTANTINE, forged in the ninth century to provide historical justification for the PAPACY's growing temporal power. In 754 Frankish leader Pepin the Short (c. 714–68) gave Pope Stephen II (r. 752–57) the exarchate of Ravenna and other territories, and in return the pope recognized Pepin as the king of the Franks. In 774 his son CHARLEMAGNE confirmed the arrangement, adding the weight of the Carolingian Empire behind the pope.

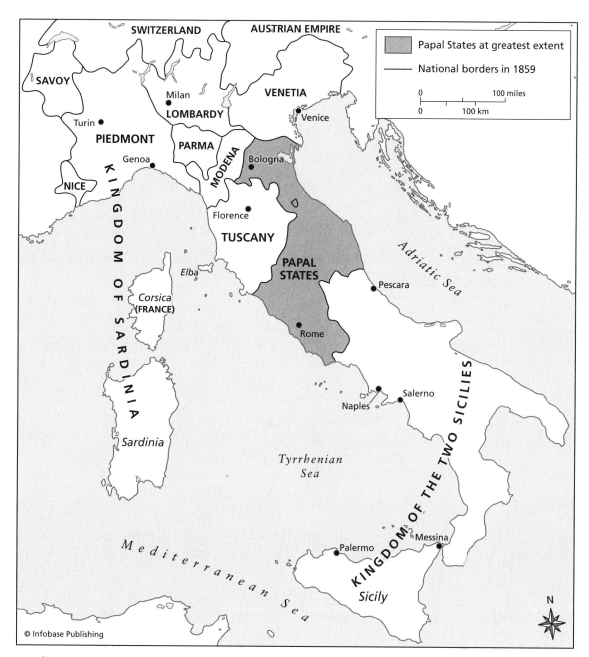

Papal States at their greatest expanse   *(Infobase Publishing)*

popular movement to unite the Italian peninsula into one country, which burst forth in 1848. Austrian and later French forces slowed the inclusion of the Papal States in the new Italy through the 1850s and 1860s. The fall of Napoléon III (r. 1852–70) during the Franco-Prussian War allowed Victor Emmanuel II (r. 1861–78) to seize Rome and complete the unification process, bringing an end to the Papal States.

Initially, Pope PIUS IX, hoping for outside intervention, refused to recognize Victor Emmanuel and designated himself a "prisoner in the Vatican." This stance was also assumed by his successors LEO XIII, ST. PIUS X, and Benedict XV (r. 1914–22) but in muted tones. The stalemate continued until 1929, when Benito Mussolini (1883–1945) negotiated the Lateran CONCORDAT, or Treaty, that created the present VATICAN CITY state with Pope PIUS XI (r. 1922–39).

During the 19th century, the possibility that the United States might establish diplomatic relations with the Papal States (and later Vatican City) became a significant public issue, brought to the fore by repeated waves of ANTI-CATHOLICISM. American Protestant fundamentalists preached that the fall of the Papal States was foretold in Daniel 7. It remained a source of intense debate until late in the 20th century. President Franklin Delano Roosevelt (1882–1945) sent a special envoy to the Vatican during World War II. In the new climate created by VATICAN COUNCIL II and the presidency of JOHN F. KENNEDY, Presidents Gerald Ford (1913–2006), Jimmy Carter (1924–), and Ronald Reagan (1911–2004) were able to appoint special envoys. Then in 1983, William A. Wilson was named the first U.S. ambassador to the Vatican.

Further reading: L. M. Duchesne, *The Beginnings of the Temporal Sovereignty of the Popes, A.D. 754–1073* (London: Kegan Paul, Trench Trubner, 1908); Peter Partner, *The Lands of St. Peter: The Papal State in the Middle Ages and the Early Renaissance* (London: Eyre Methuen, 1972); Allan J. Reinerman, *Austria and the Papacy in the Age of Metternich* (Washington, D.C.: Catholic Univer-

sity of America Press, 1979–1990); Daniel P. Waley, *The Papal State in the Thirteenth Century* (London: Macmillan, 1961).

parable

A parable (or morality tale) is a popular literary form used in the BIBLE. It was once aptly defined as "a metaphor or simile drawn from nature or common life, arresting the hearer by its vividness or strangeness, and leaving the mind in sufficient doubt about its precise application to tease it into active thought" (C. H. Dodd). Metaphor weds one realm of meaning (seed) to another (kingdom) to create an unexpected third (the reign of God). Jesus was known for his use of parables, including several to describe the Kingdom of GOD, which is "already" but not "yet." Parables were among his most well known teachings—the stories of the Good Samaritan (Luke 10:25–37), the Lost Sheep (Matt. 18:10–14), the Sower, and the Prodigal Son (Luke 15:11–32).

In the last half of the 20th century, New Testament scholars have expended considerable energy in exploring the parable form in attempts to tease from it a better understanding of Jesus' message and life in the early church, the decades prior to the written Gospels. They have noted, for example, that parables are typically placed in an introductory setting and that they are followed by statements that attempt to apply or expand on their truths. The parable's metaphor attempts to relate an unknown or lesser-known item with one that is well known and draw a correspondence between them. For example, in Matthew 13, Jesus likens the Kingdom to a mustard seed: both start very small but will suddenly grow very large. The parable challenges everyday consciousness with the expectation of the extraordinary Kingdom (FORGIVENESS, harvest, growth, wedding feast, God's reign).

Further reading: C. H. Dodd, *The Parables of the Kingdom* (London: James Nesbit, 1961); Warren S. Kissinger, *The Parables of Jesus. A History of Interpretation* *and Bibliography* (Metuchen, N.J.: Scarecrow, 1979); Pheme Perkins, *Hearing the Parables of Jesus: Reading the New Testament* (New York: Paulist. 1981); Dan Otto Via, Jr., *The Parables: Their Literary and Existential Dimension.* (Philadelphia: Fortress, 1967).

Parsch, Pius (1884–1954) *theologian of liturgy and devotion*

Pius Parsch, a leader in the early 20th-century revival of liturgical THEOLOGY and devotion, was born into a German family in what is now the Czech Republic and baptized as John Bruno Parsch. Shortly after his 18th birthday in 1904 he became an AUGUSTINIAN friar. Even before his ordination as a priest in 1909 he developed an attraction to and affinity for LITURGY and decided to write a commentary on the breviary. He became a parish priest and studied theology, finally receiving his doctorate at the University of Vienna (1913). He subsequently became a professor of pastoral theology and an instructor of novices. He took a great interest in the liturgy of EASTERN ORTHODOXY.

As an army chaplain during World War I, he became concerned over the soldiers' lack of knowledge of the BIBLE and the lack of any lay participation, above passive attendance, at the Mass. After the war he began to work with the lay people at St. Gertrude's, the parish near his MONASTERY in Klosterneuberg, Austria. He taught them the purpose of the Mass and reshaped it to encourage their participation in its several aspects, including the use of vernacular German. His frequent travels to offer workshops on the new worship format helped lead to the emergence of a lay LITURGICAL MOVEMENT. The movement received the approbation of Pope PIUS X, who had himself previously championed efforts to explain the Mass to the laity in *Acebo Nimis* (April 15, 1905). The participation in the Mass led to more lay participation in the rites of the church year.

Parsch founded two organizations to give focus to the growing movement, the Lay Liturgical Apostolate (which included a publishing house) and the Liturgical Society of St. Gertrude. The church of St. Gertrude became the center where new ideas could be tried out and tested. Parsch's movement came to an end in 1938, when the Nazis moved into the area and took over the monastery property. In 1941 Parsch fled into exile; he returned in 1946 to spend his few remaining years in writing and reviving his work. He was an important source for the changes in liturgy initiated by VATICAN COUNCIL II. His pioneering articles in the journal *Bibel und Liturgie* (1926–   ) were translated as *The Church's Year of Grace* (1953).

Further reading: Norbert Höslunger and Theodor Maas-Eward, *Mit Zähigkeit: Pius Parsch und die biblisch-liturgisch Erneuerung* (Klosterneuburg: Austrian Catholic Biblework, 1979); Parsch, Pius, *The Breviary Explained* (St. Louis: Herder, 1952); ———, *The Church's Year of Grace* (Collegeville, Minn.: Liturgical Press, 1953); ———, *The Liturgy of the Mass* (St. Louis: Herder, 1940).

Passionists

The Passionists are a religious order, the Congregation of Discalced Clerks of the Most Holy Cross and Passion of Our Lord Jesus Christ (abbv. CP) whose stated raison d'être is to revive the memory of the Passion of CHRIST within the Catholic community. The order was founded by Paul Francis Daneo (1694–1775), later to be known as St. Paul of the Cross, who was born and raised in northern ITALY. He was living in Castellazo, Lombardy, where he felt inspired directly by Jesus Christ to found an order and write its rule. Five years later he traveled to Rome and received the pope's blessing for the new community. He was canonized by Pius XI in 1867.

Daneo was ordained a priest by Benedict XIII (r. 1724–30) in 1727. He subsequently formed the first house of the community at Mount Argentaro. Daneo hoped to unite the contemplative and active aspects of piety. That idea proved attractive, and over the next half century 12 congregational houses were established in Italy. In 1741 Benedict XIV (r. 1740–58) approved the Passionists' rule. Clement XIV (r. 1758–59) entrusted the Church of Sts. John and Paul in Rome and an adjacent house to their care. The building continues as the order's motherhouse.

The Passionists were a mendicant order and hence not allowed to possess property except their houses and a few acres of land attached to each. They depended on their own labors and on the voluntary contributions of outside supporters. In predominantly Catholic countries, Passionist brothers have served as assistants to parish priests but commonly serve as parish priests themselves in non-Catholic countries. They have been active in England, the United States, and Australia. They have made the perfection of their own spiritual life and that of those in their care their primary responsibility.

As the 21st century begins, some 2,000 Passionist brothers serve in more than 50 nations. The order is led by a superior general, who is elected to a six-year term. Six consultants from the different geographical regions assist him.

Further reading: Rev. Father Edmund, *Hunter of Souls: A Study of the Life and Spirit of Saint Paul of the Cross* (Westminster, Md.: Newman, 1946); Roger Mercurio, *The Passionists* (Collegeville, Minn.: Liturgical Press, 1992); *Passionists Evangelize the World Today: Passionist Mission on the 3rd Centenary of the Birth of St. Paul of the Cross* (Rome: Editrice Rogate, 1994); St. Paul of the Cross, *The Letters of St. Paul of the Cross* (Hyde Park, N.Y.: New City, 2000).

patriarch

In the BIBLE, the patriarchs in the strict sense are Abraham and his immediate descendants— Isaac, Jacob, and Joseph. More broadly, any of the male ancestors of Israel mentioned in the Book of Genesis can be so designated. During the CHRISTIAN era, the term began to be used to refer to the leading BISHOP in any region that included several dioceses, each of which had its own subordinate bishop. In 451, the emperor JUSTINIAN I (r. 527–63) designated five principle patriarchates—Jerusalem, Antioch, Alexandria, CONSTANTINOPLE, and Rome—and restricted the title of patriarch to the ARCHBISHOPS metropolitan of those five cities. Each of the four Eastern patriarchates came to head an autonomous Eastern Orthodox Church.

In the centuries following the GREAT SCHISM (1054) between Rome and the four Eastern patriarchs, the EASTERN CATHOLIC Churches were founded, characterized by the use of Eastern liturgical rites and communion with Rome. In six of these churches, leadership is placed in the hands of an archbishop with the title of patriarch—the ARMENIAN CATHOLIC CHURCH, the CHALDEAN CATHOLIC CHURCH, the COPTIC CATHOLIC CHURCH, the MARONITE CATHOLIC CHURCH, the MELKITE CATHOLIC CHURCH, and the SYRIAN CATHOLIC CHURCH. These patriarchs recognize and are subordinate to the bishop of Rome. The pope has not recognized the title of patriarch for the head of the UKRAINIAN CATHOLIC CHURCH. Several other eastern Catholics are seeking to reinstitute the rank of patriarch for their rites. Many patriarchs assert that they rank above cardinals.

Further reading: Aziz S. Atiya, *History of Eastern Christianity* (Notre Dame: University of Notre Dame Press, 1968); Edward E. Finn, *A Brief History of the Eastern Rites* (Collegeville, Minn.: Liturgical Press, 1961); Robert F. Taft, *Eastern-Rite Catholicism: Its Heritage and Vocation* (Glen Rock: Paulist, 1963).

Patrick, St. (c. 390–c. 461) *missionary to Ireland*

Born Maewyn Succat in what is now Scotland late in the fourth century, the future St. Patrick was raised in a CHRISTIAN home, his father being a deacon in the local church. As a teenager he was captured by pirates and sold into slavery in northern IRELAND, where he learned Gaelic. After six years working for a herdsman, he escaped and fled to Gaul (modern FRANCE). He spent some time in a MONASTERY school and eventually made his way back to his home in Scotland.

Toward the end of the 420s Patrick had a vision in which he was told to return to Ireland to assist the people. Early in the next decade he arrived there to begin a ministry that would last the rest of his life. He was remembered as a gentle, sincere, affable, and charismatic soul. He won many to Christianity and planted churches throughout the island. He established his headquarters at the monastery he founded at Armaugh (though he was not himself a monk), which also became his seat as the first BISHOP of Ireland. Patrick authored two works, copies of which have survived: an apologetic work in the form of an autobiography, the *Confessio,* and a protest against the slave trade, the *Letter to Coroticus.*

In successive centuries, a variety of pious folk tales grew up around Patrick, who became a legendary figure. He was said, for example, to have used the shamrock as a teaching tool, symbolic of the TRINITY, and he was lauded for expelling all the snakes from the land. Among his first acts was the conversion of a tribal chieftain named Dichu. Dichu was about to kill Patrick but found himself unable to raise his arm.

Patrick died in 461 at Saul, where he had built his first church. March 17, the day of his death, is his feast day but has also become a day of national celebration for the Irish and their friends worldwide. In modern times the saint's day has become known mostly for the amount of alcohol that is consumed by revelers, Catholic and non-Catholic alike.

Further reading: J. B. Bury, *The Life of St. Patrick and His Place in History* (London: Macmillan, 1905); Philip Freeman, *St. Patrick of Ireland: A Biography* (New York: Simon & Schuster, 2004); James Henthorn Todd, *St. Patrick: Apostle of Ireland: A Memoir of His Life and Mission* (London: Wipf & Stock, 2003).

patripassionism

In the centuries when the church was still hammering out the doctrine of the TRINITY, one view that gained considerable support was modalism. It focused on the unity of GOD and understood the three persons of the Trinity to be modes of God's interaction with the world rather than essential expressions of God's reality. One implication of this position was that God the father (Lat. *pater*) had come to earth in the form of CHRIST and had suffered (Lat. *passio*) and died. This opinion was regularly denied by the majority of church leaders and finally excluded from further consideration at the Council of Nicaea II in 787 (*see* COUNCILS, ECUMENICAL)

Patripassionism is most identified with Sabellius (d. 260), a prominent church leader in Rome who was excommunicated both in Rome and later, for good measure, in Alexandria. For Sabellius, God acted in successive modes. While he did not emphasize patripassionism, it was a necessary deduction from his thought.

Further reading: Peter Brown, *The Rise of Western Christendom: Triumph and Diversity* A.D. *200–1000* (Cambridge: Blackwell, 1996); Leo Donald Davis, *The First Seven Ecumenical Councils (325–787): Their History and Theology* (Collegeville, Minn.: Liturgical Press, 1983); Paul L. Gavrilyuk, *The Suffering of the Impassible God: The Dialectics of Patristic Thought* (Oxford: Oxford University Press, 2004); J. N. D. Kelly, *Early Christian Doctrines,* 5th ed. (San Francisco: HarperCollins, 1978).

patron saints

Within the Catholic Church, special recognition is given to saints—those believers who have lived notably holy lives. They are considered to be living now in glory with CHRIST and are hence worthy of being honored and imitated. To them veneration (Gr. *dulia*) is properly offered, although this veneration is distinct from the ADORATION, or worship, that is due only to God. It is proper to seek their assistance by asking God to answer prayers, such as for healing.

Many saints have been seen as having specialized roles as intercessors before God. For example, most saints are first known in the community in which they resided and are expected to help the local residents. Some saints have been especially identified with those who work in a particular vocation or engage in a particular activity. Over time, such saints may be officially designated as patrons for a geographical area, vocation, activity, or need. Such saints are called patrons. Some saints may by their popularity attain official approval for liturgical celebration, given by the VATICAN CURIA office known as the Congregation for the Sacraments and Divine Worship and endorsed by the pope.

Virgin MARY OF NAZARETH, under various names, has often been designated a patron saint. As Our Lady of the Assumption, she is, for example, the patroness of FRANCE, India, Malta, and Paraguay, and as the IMMACULATE CONCEPTION the patroness of Brazil, the United States, and Tanzania. St. George is the patron saint of England (*see* GREAT BRITAIN) and St. ROSE OF LIMA of South America.

Among patrons of occupations are Sts. DOMINIC DE GUZMÁN (astronomers), FRANCIS DE SALES (journalists), and MICHAEL THE ARCHANGEL (police officers, soldiers), ST. JUDE (hospitals, hopeless causes), St. Agnes (young women), FRA ANGELICO (artists), St. Christopher (drivers; he has been removed from the official saints list but is still popular), St. AMBROSE (bee keepers), St. JOSEPH (carpenters), and St. Cecelia (musicians).

Further reading: Michael Freze, *Patron Saints* (Huntington, Ind.: Our Sunday Visitor, 1992); Alice La Plante and Clare La Plante, *Heaven Help Us: The Worrier's Guide to the Patron Saints* (New York: Dell, 1999); Annette Sandoval, *Directory of Saints: A Concise Guide to Patron Saints* (New York: Signet, 1996); Thomas W. Sheehan, *Dictionary of Patron Saints' Names* (Huntington, Ind.: Our Sunday Visitor, 2001).

Paul IV (1476–1559), (r. 1555–1559) *pope*

Giovanni Pietro Caraffa was born at Benevento, ITALY, into a noble Neopolitan family. He emerged as a prominent churchman in the years immediately prior to the PROTESTANT REFORMATION. His quick rise was aided by his uncle Oliviero, the BISHOP of Chiete and a cardinal. He succeeded his uncle as bishop of Chiete (1505) and in 1518 was named the ARCHBISHOP of Brindisi. In 1520, he joined the ORATORY OF DIVINE LOVE, a reformist group inspired by Catherine of Genoa (d. 1510). In 1524 he joined the DOMINICAN reformist Cajetan (1469–1534) in founding the Theatines (also called the Congregation of Clerks Regular), a religious congregation to spread reform through evangelism, parish work, and service to the poor.

During the reign of Paul III (1534–49), Caraffa was placed on the committee charged with reforming the papal court. For his efforts, in 1536 Paul III named him a cardinal and later appointed him archbishop of Naples. His activity in Catholic reform set him against the Protestant agenda, and in 1542 he was placed in charge of the INQUISITION, which he reorganized to better handle Protestant dissent. His often harsh handling of dissidents within the church made him unpopular in many quarters and a surprise choice to succeed to the papal chair in 1555. He was 79 years of age.

Though serving a mere four years, he set an intense agenda. He began by refusing to call the Council of TRENT back into session, suggesting that he could better make reforms himself. From the perspective of history, some of his reforms, such as his demand that bishops actually reside in the territory of their DIOCESE, are seen as positive. Others are seen as stains on his reputation, not the least being his confining the Jews of Rome to a ghetto and making them wear distinctive garb. He also introduced the Index Liborum Prohibitorum (the Index of Prohibited Books) in 1559. Paul IV is also known for opposing Elizabeth I (1533–1603) as she claimed the throne of England on the grounds of her illegitimacy.

Further reading: Donata Chiomenti-Vassallii, *Paolo IV e il Processo Carafa: un caso d'unguista giustizia nel cinque cento* (Milan: Mursia, 1993); Beresford James Kidd, *The*

Counter Reformation, 1550–1600 (London: S.P.C.K., 1963); A. G. Dickens, *The Counter-Reformation* (London: Thames & Hudson, 1968); M. R. O'Connell, *The Counter Reformation 1559–1610* (New York: Harper Brothers, 1974); A. D. Wright, *The Counter-Reformation: Catholic Europe and the Non-Christian World* (New York: St Martin's, 1982).

Paul V (1532–1621), (r. 1605–1621) *pope*

Camillo Borghese, the future Pope Paul V, was born in Rome of a noble family from Siena. Given a good education, he became a priest and slowly moved up in the church's HIERARCHY. He was named a cardinal in 1596 by Pope Clement VIII (r. 1592–1605), and later named cardinal vicar of Rome. He succeeded Leo XI (whose rule lasted less than a month in 1605).

Due to his legal training and conservative views, Paul set a priority of defending the powers claimed and asserted by earlier popes, thus dragging the papacy into a variety of disputes across Europe. His secret agents were in England during the Guy Fawkes Plot (November 5, 1605), when Catholic militants tried to blow up Parliament and kill King James I (1566–1625). The English used their being found out to pin the plot on the PAPACY.

Paul V is most known for being in office when work was completed on St. PETER'S BASILICA, when the works of Copernicus were put on the Index of Prohibited Books, and when GALILEO GALILEI was first censured (1616).

Further reading: John N. D. Kelly, *The Oxford Dictionary of Popes* (Oxford: Oxford University Press, 1986); Thomas Munck, *Seventeenth Century Europe 1598–1700* (New York: Macmillan, 1990).

Paul VI (1920–1978), (r. 1963–1978) *pope*

Pope John Paul VI was born Giovanni Battista Montini on September 26, 1897, at Concesio, Lombardy, ITALY. He was ordained a priest in 1920 and spent most of his early career in the VATICAN CURIA, the papal court. In 1922 he became a pro-secretary to Cardinal Eugenio Pacelli, later Pope PIUS XII. He was named ARCHBISHOP of Milan in 1954 and received his cardinal's hat four years later. He remained in Milan until his election to succeed Pope JOHN XXIII in 1963.

Paul VI ascended to the papal throne in the midst of VATICAN COUNCIL II. He reconvened the council, which continued its reforms, including the replacement of the Latin LITURGY with the vernacular and the reaffirmation of the role of BISHOPS. Following the close of the council, he oversaw the implementation of its many reforms despite the distress they caused to many among the older generation of the faithful around the world. When this generated dissent, he frequently reasserted the primacy of the papal office. Among his statements was his affirmation of Mary as co-redemptrix at the close of Vatican II, whereas the council itself sought to subordinate Mary's FAITH to the work of CHRIST (*Lumen Gentium* 54 Dogmatic Constitution on the Church).

Paul VI was the first pope to leave Italy in more than 150 years. His travels took him around the world. He enlarged the college of cardinals, making room for more cardinals from underrepresented areas, where the church had grown significantly without adequate representation at the highest levels (*see* HIERARCHY).

In the spirit of reconciliation, Paul VI expanded ties with the Protestant world. He addressed the World Council of Churches in 1969 and moved toward doctrinal consensus with Anglicans and Lutherans. He and Ecumenical Patriarch Athenagoras (1886–1972) mutually lifted the reciprocal excommunication of the GREAT SCHISM (1054).

Many thought that the reforms of Vatican II would lead to changes in such issues as divorce, birth control, married priests, and the role of women in the church. The 1970s were a time of widespread discussion on all these social issues. But Paul VI definitively reaffirmed support for priestly CELIBACY in 1967 and prohibited artificial contraception in his encyclical *Humanae Vitae*

(July 25, 1968). While allowing debate through the 1970s on many issues, he did not move to change the traditional stance of the church.

See also ABORTION; HOLY ORDERS; SEXUALITY.

Further reading: William E. Barrett, *A Biography of Pope Paul VI Shepherd of Mankind* (Garden City, N.Y.: Doubleday, 1964); Brian W. Harrison, *The Teaching of Pope Paul VI on Sacred Scripture* (Rome: Pontificium Athenaeum Sanctae Crucis, 1997); National Catholic News Service, *Nights of Sorrow, Days of Joy; Papal Transition: Paul VI, John Paul I, John Paul II* (Washington, D.C.: National Catholic News Service, 1978); *Our Name is Peter: An Anthology of Key Teachings of Pope Paul VI.* (Chicago: Franciscan Herald, 1976).

Paul the Apostle, St. (fl. 55) *greatest missionary of the early church*

Among the early missionaries of the Gospel of Jesus CHRIST, The APOSTLE Paul usually receives the most credit for initially spreading the faith from the Holy Land to much of the Mediterranean basin, including Asia Minor, Greece, Macedonia and Rome. He would have continued on to SPAIN had he not been martyred in Rome (Rom. 15:24, 28). He is also credited for successfully formulating the FAITH and practices of the early church in order to appeal to the Gentiles.

Paul was born into the Hellenistic Jewish community at Tarsus in what is now southern Turkey at the beginning of the Common Era. Paul saw himself as spreading the Gospel of Christ, but he never referred to himself as a *Christian*, a term that was not in use until the end of the first century (Acts 11:26). Paul seems to have been martyred in Rome. In early Christian iconography he is depicted with a book in his hands and later with a sword in reference to the legend of his martyrdom and Ephesians 6:17: "the sword of the Spirit which is the word of God." He shares a feast day with St. PETER, June 29.

Paul as he presents himself in his own epistles (c. 49–62 C.E.) is a very different person from the Paul presented by Luke in the later Book of Acts (c. 95 C.E.) (*see* GOSPEL). In the past biblical scholars tried to reconcile the two portraits, but today they keep the two separate. In any case, Paul has often subsequently been reinterpreted or filtered through the "introspective conscience of the West," as, for example, in AUGUSTINE OF HIPPO and Martin Luther (1483–1546). Paul the missionary has been buried beneath layers of interpretation.

The hardest question is to determine which epistles are by Paul himself, which are from the Pauline tradition, and which are non-Pauline even though Paul's name is attached to them. Most scholars now agree that 1 Thessalonians, 1 Corinthians, 2 Corinthians (which some think is a compilation of separate letters), Philemon (which deals with a runaway slave), Galatians, and Romans are by Paul. The next set of 2 Thessalonians, Ephesians, and Colossians are called deutero-Pauline, that is, they come from a later Pauline school but are not by Paul himself. The epistles in this second group assert the view that we have all died and *have risen* in Christ, whereas the first set assert that we have died but *will rise*. Hebrews is totally unlike Paul; the so-called Pastoral Epistles, 1 and 2 Timothy and Titus, reflect a much later period, being addressed to the "church" in general and not to specific churches.

Paul often stressed certain theological themes (JUSTIFICATION, Law vs. Gospel, predestination), but he was not a systematic theologian as is often claimed (*see* THEOLOGY). For example, he addressed the question of justification by faith in both Galatians and Romans, but he hardly mentioned the terms in the Corinthian letters; there, the issue is ecclesial love and the reciprocity of gifts, for building up the church. Rather than calling him a theologian one can say that Paul, in his own words, experienced a "calling" to serve the Lord in the manner of the Hebrew prophets (Gal. 1:11–17; 1 Sam. 3), although he did not undergo a "CONVERSION" in the classic sense (Acts 9).

Paul is specific rather than universal. He speaks to concrete problems faced by the churches. He places love above "integrity"; he will even forego salvation if it will redeem his fellow Israelites (Rom. 9:3). He talks about justification as a temporal category of God's action in the economy of salvation (Rom. 4), whereas other New Testament writers speak of "forgiveness" as a condition or state of being before God (1 Peter).

Unlike later theologians, often brilliant scholars, Paul looks to the model of Christ, who was utter weakness on the CROSS. Paul favors the stumblers over those who think they have some special wisdom, "inside dope," or secret knowledge leading to salvation (1 Cor. 1:18–2:5). Paul seeks to build up the *ekklesia,* or assembly, of the Lord as a democracy of different gifts, in contrast to the hierarchical *basileia,* or rule, of the Romans under the *Pax Romana,* which was maintained not by love but by the sword.

Paul is also very rhetorical. In Romans he shows he is a master of the Hellenistic literary style of the diatribe. This rhetorical skill can mislead readers. On the question of Jewish circumcision and kosher food laws, tradition taught that Paul was addressing Jews, but recent criticism shows that he is addressing Gentiles who are hankering backward for old Jewish ways. Paul wants them to see that God is always moving forward. The salvation once promised exclusively to the Jews is now being extended to Gentiles "outside the works of the Torah" (Rom. 3:28).

There are certain central themes that Paul does highlight. Against those claiming higher religious status he argues that "in Christ there is neither Jew nor Gentile, slave nor free, male nor female" (Gal. 3:28). This divine impartiality explains why so many women were in high positions in Paul's churches and why he could see Prisca and Aquila as coworkers (apostles) in Christ (Rom. 16:1, 3, 12). The image of the "misogynist" Paul comes not from his genuine letters but from the later deutero-Pauline epistles (Eph. 5:22–6:9; Col. 3:18–4:1), in which women were subordinated to men in line with typical Greco-Roman household codes. The equality theme also shows up in Paul's letter to Philemon, in which he not-so-subtly urges the slaveholder to free his runaway slave Onesimus (v. 16). The theme is extended on an ecclesial level in 1 Corinthians 12, where he rebukes those who claim special charisma from the Spirit, better than their neighbor's. There is only one body, and all members are equally vital for the building up of the church.

The Book of Romans is often parsed as a systematic Pauline theology, but this approach loses Paul's subtlety, as he expounds "the mystery hidden for long ages past but now revealed" (Rom. 16:25–26). Romans is a midrash, a reflection-commentary on the story of Genesis. After the good creation, Adam allowed evil into the world with the single, primal sin. (Paul sees SIN as a time category and not as a status category, as in the concept of original sin.) Sin spread like wildfire and increased in intensity and effect (Gen. 4–6; Rom. 5:20). The result for the Gentiles was that they were given over to their lusts (1:14). Although the Law was meant to redeem, and indeed it does if it is observed (2:26), the history of Israel shows that it has not been observed, and this failure brought the condemnation of God through the mouths of the prophets. God wants not only outward circumcision but circumcision of the heart (1:29; Jer. 31:31–37). Thus, all stand condemned, Gentile and Jew alike. But there is hope. God made a promise (*epangelia*) to Abraham and Sarah, before the Law and circumcision, that they would be the parents of all who have faith, Jew and Gentile alike. Abraham's faith in God's promise justified him in God's sight before the giving of the Law and the Covenant. The birth of Isaac to Abraham and Sarah, who were "dead" in the body, was a foretaste of the resurrection of all to a new life as announced in the Gospel (*evangelion*) of Jesus' death and resurrection. Abraham and Sarah are the true type of Christ. Justification through faith in the Gospel of Christ is resumption in time of the justification in the promise to and the faith of Abraham. The extension of the promise to the nations is something that the prophets, especially 2 Isaiah, proclaimed long ago. Adam was a type "of what was to follow" (5:14) in Genesis 4–6, more sin and more death. With the death and resurrection of Christ, grace gets a toehold in time and will eventually overtake sin and its consequences. Christ is the first fruits (1 Cor. 15:23) in preparation for the full harvest when the Kingdom will arrive, God's glory will be revealed, and creation will be freed from bondage (8:21).

In Romans 9–11 Paul tells his Gentile believers that though his fellow Jews—whom he calls "Israel," the name given directly by God (Gen. 32:26)—said no to the gospel of Christ, they still have the adoption as sons and daughters of God, the divine glory, the Temple worship, the promises, and the ancestry of Christ. Their "no" was providential and to the Gentiles' benefit, and in the end God will be faithful to his original promise. In the final "mystery," known only to God, "all Israel will be saved (11:26)" Paul here is speaking of the real Israel and not talking in terms of supercessionism, the theory that the promises once given to the Jews are cancelled and transferred to Christians.

Further reading: Daniel Boyarin, *A Radical Jew: Paul and the Politics of Identity* (Berkeley: University of California Press, 1994); John G. Gager, *Reinventing Paul* (Oxford: Oxford University Press, 2000); Wayne A. Meeks, ed., *The First Urban Christians: The Social World of the Apostle Paul* (New Haven, Conn.: Yale University Press, 1983); Joseph Plevnik, *What Are They Saying About Paul?* (New York: Paulist, 1986); E. P. Sanders, *Paul.* (New York: Oxford University Press, 1991); Krister Stendahl, *Paul Amongst Jews and Gentiles* (Philadelphia: Fortress, 1976).

pedophilia (Gk.: *pais,* "child" + *philia,* "love")

Pedophilia is the pathological condition in which an adult is attracted to prepubescent and/or underage children and engages in sexual activity with them. The scandals connected with pedophilia provoked the U.S. Conference of Catholic Bishops to commission a study of the problem by the John Jay College of Criminal Justice in New York City in 2002. The study found 10,667 confirmed cases of abuse from 1950 to 2002 by 4,392 priests, or 4 percent of the priest population during that time period. Since 2002 more than 700 priests have been removed from active ministry for pedophilia.

The pedophile scandal in the Roman Catholic Church was a long time brewing until the notorious legal case of Fr. James F. Geoghan (1936–2005) of the archdiocese of Boston, Massachusetts, attracted worldwide attention. Geoghan was convicted of child molestation charges in 2002 and defrocked at the time of his trial. He seems to have molested more than 130 children in various assignments in different parishes and other venues in the Boston DIOCESE. Geoghan was sent to prison, where he was murdered by another inmate.

Geoghan's case uncovered an almost universal pattern among bishops and religious superiors throughout the world of systematically shifting offenders from parish to parish, diocese to diocese, and even country to country in an effort not to "scandalize" the faithful. The news media have reported that BISHOPS and religious superiors often cajoled parents of the victims into silence, made concealed payments to victims, kept the offenses from the knowledge of law enforcement authorities, and very likely engaged in obstruction of justice.

The Geoghan case opened the can of worms in the Boston archdiocese and precipitated the resignation of Cardinal Bernard Law (1931–), who was accused of enabling abuse through failure to act firmly. Pope JOHN PAUL II thereafter appointed Cardinal Law to the VATICAN CURIA and elevated him to cardinal archpriest of Santa Maria Maggiore, one of the four prestige churches of Rome. The appointment was greeted with dismay among Catholics in Boston and elsewhere as sending the wrong signal about church policy.

Boston and other dioceses have negotiated settlements with victims to the tune of several hundred million dollars. There are several organizations that assist survivors of priest pedophilia, most notably SNAP, or the Survivors Network of those Abused by Priests.

Many have accused church authorities of continuing to stonewall on the issue. Former Oklahoma governor Frank Keating (1944–), a prominent Catholic and chairman of the National Review Board to examine the abuse problem, resigned in protest from the board in 2003. The dioceses of Portland, Tucson, and Spokane have gone into bankruptcy, and several more are on the verge. Since the Boston debacle several other scandals have exploded in Los Angeles and Ireland, and the seminary Sankt Pölten in Austria was revealed to be engaged in improper sexual activity and even ran a pornographic pedophile Web site.

Outsiders tend to attribute the pedophile scandal to priests' rule of CELIBACY, but experts discount that. In the general population, most pedophiles are married fathers of children; a married priesthood would not likely solve the problem. Church authorities, including the present pope BENEDICT XVI, have laid some of the blame on the secular culture's acceptance of homosexuality; some traditional Catholics even blame the liberalization brought about by VATICAN COUNCIL II. However, some of the worst cases long predate Vatican II, and in any case the church reforms of the 1960s never involved changes in sexual rules or expectations for Catholics.

The U.S. Conference of Catholic Bishops issued a zero tolerance policy for abuse cases in 1994, but the Vatican asked for changes to protect due process for accused priests. The new policy provides for a confidential inquiry by a bishop upon hearing charges; critics note, however, that ecclesiastical authorities are required by civil law to notify law enforcement immediately upon receiving an allegation in child molestation cases. The issue remains unresolved.

The only certain conclusion is that bishops and religious leaders have failed to heed Jesus' dire warning: "Whoever causes one of these little ones who believe in me to stumble, it would be better for him to have a heavy millstone hung around his neck, and to be drowned in the depth of the sea" (Matt. 18:6). Nothing has damaged the Catholic Church at the turn of the millennium more than the pedophile scandal. Many observers remain perplexed by the Vatican's continuing obtuseness toward the seriousness of the scandal.

Further reading: *Charter for the Protection of Children and Young People* (Washington, D.C.: United States Catholic Bishops Conference, 2002), available online; *The Nature and Scope of the Problem of Sexual Abuse of Minors by Catholic Priests and Deacons in the United States,* A Research Study Conducted by the John Jay College of Criminal Justice (2004), available online at the Web site of the United States Conference of Catholic Bishops; Peter J. Fagan et al., "Pedophilia," *Journal of the American Medical Association* (November 20, 2002) 288: 19, 2458–64; Philip Jenkins, *Pedophiles and Priests: Anatomy of a Contemporary Crisis* (New York: Oxford University Press, 1996); A. W. Richard Sipe, *Celibacy in Crisis: A Secret World Revisited* (New York: Brunner-Routledge, 2003); Charles W. Socarides and Loretta R. Loeb, eds., *The Mind of the Paedophile: Psychoanalytic Perspectives* (London: Karnac, 2004); Peter Steinfels, *A People Adrift: The Crisis in the Roman Catholic Church of America* (New York: Simon & Schuster, 2003).

Pelagius *fifth-century heretic*

Pelagius was a preacher and moral theologian from Roman Britain who argued against the power of original SIN. His views became very popular but were condemned as heretical.

Pelagius was already a respected teacher when he moved to Rome around 400. Shocked at what he believed to be the low level of morality he found in the Roman CLERGY, he began to preach that CHRISTIANS should lead a morally upright life, and that they could. He denied that humans suffered from debilitating original sin. True, Adam had set a bad example, and humans were quick to fall into sin, but once they were justified in CHRIST (*see* JUSTIFICATION) and received BAPTISM, they had the full capacity to keep divine law.

Around 410, Pelagius and his disciple Celestus arrived in Hippo, in North Africa, where St. AUGUSTINE was BISHOP. Pelagius continued on to the eastern Mediterranean, leaving Celestus behind to seek ordination. Celestus, accused of denying the dogma of original sin, was refused, but the incident provoked Augustine to attack Pelagius for teaching that humans could live without sin. Augustine's own dramatic conversion had convinced him that only GOD's grace could overcome sin.

In 415, a synod in Palestine ruled favorably for Pelagius. The next year Augustine responded by organizing two synods in North Africa that came to the opposite conclusion; Pope Innocent I (r. 402–17) supported this stand. In 417, the emperor Honorius (384–423) condemned Pelagius and exiled his followers. In short order another synod in Carthage issued a list of anti-Pelagian statements, affirming the need for child baptism, the necessity of GRACE in leading an upright life, and the impossibility of living a sinless life. The Council of Orange (529) condemned semi-Pelagianism, stating that even the beginning of FAITH comes solely by grace. (Rom. 3)

Pelagius disappeared from history by the end of the decade, but his cause was taken up by JULIAN OF ECLANUM, a bishop from southern ITALY. Julian was exiled but found some support in the East. Pelagianism was finally condemned in 431 by the Council of EPHESUS. Despite this consensus, Pelagianism has continually reemerged in one guise or another. Semi-Pelagians like Luis Molina (1535–1600) claimed that humans have the ability to seek God. It would always lie just below the surface when theologians argued about the human role in conversion, the nature of predestination, and the ability of humans to resist God's grace. The Augustinian views on irresistible grace

sometimes took second place in the MIDDLE AGES to the work of grace in the SACRAMENTS, especially infant baptism, but they reemerged with renewed vigor in the 16th century in the writings of John Calvin (1509–64) and the Reformed Church.

Further reading: Augustine's anti-Pelagian writings are available online; Gerald Bonner, *St. Augustine: His Life and Controversies* (Norwich: Canterbury, 1986); Peter Brown, *Religion and Society in the Age of Saint Augustine* (New York: Harper & Row, 1972); Theodore DeBruyn, tr., *Pelagius' Commentary on St. Paul's Epistle to the Romans* (New York: Oxford University Press, 1993); Robert F. Evans, *Pelagius: Inquiries and Reappraisals* (New York: Seabury, 1968).

penance

A CHRISTIAN understanding of life assumes that each person is a sinner in need of God's FORGIVENESS. In order to receive forgiveness people must confess their SINS, feel sorrow for having committed them, and intend to amend their lives so as to eradicate that sin. In the Catholic Church, the process of receiving forgiveness is seen as highly important and has been given sacramental status as the SACRAMENT OF RECONCILIATION. In the SACRAMENT OF penance, the individual confesses his or her sins to a priest, who listens, assigns the penitent certain acts as reparation for the sin, and pronounces God's forgiveness. On his part, the priest assumes that he has the authority from the church to so act.

Traditionally, the sacrament of penance occurred in a private conversation between the penitent and a priest (a priest confesses his own sin to another priest). In 1973, a new rite of reconciliation was promulgated. It offered three different formats for the performance of the sacrament of penance, the first being the traditional one. The second form was a communal rite of reconciliation, in which two or more penitents go through the steps of a penitential liturgy together, the moment of confession of sin to the priest being the only private part. The third option, usually invoked in an emergency situation when there is a major shortage of priests, includes a general confession of sin followed by a general ablution pronounced by a priest.

Since its introduction in 1973, the communal rite of reconciliation has grown in popularity and is used extensively in the Lenten and EASTER seasons. The service includes an introductory rite (with hymn singing), the reading of Scripture, the litany of reconciliation (with the general prayer of contrition and a litany on forgiveness), a time for individual confession, and the concluding prayers of praise, thanksgiving, and blessing. As a rule, the rite of penance is a prerequisite for participation in the EUCHARIST.

Further reading: Chris Aridas, *Reconciliation: Celebrating God's Healing Forgiveness.* (Garden City, N.Y.: Image, 1987); John Arnold, *The Quality of Mercy: A Fresh Look at the Sacrament of Reconciliation* (Middlegreen: St. Pauls, 1993); Patrick J. Brennan, *Penance and Reconciliation* (Chicago: Thomas More, 1986); James Dallen, *The Reconciling Community: The Rite of Penance* (New York: Pueblo, 1986).

Pentateuch   *See* BIBLE.

perfection

CHRISTIANS generally believe that perfection, a state of being without any moral or spiritual defect or fault, is a characteristic of GOD alone. However, they are also told in Scripture, "Be perfect as your heavenly Father is perfect" (Matt. 5:48).

Christians have tried to resolve this paradox by exploring paths to perfection and debated just what could be achieved; some have suggested that a degree of human participation in God's perfection is possible. British clergyman John Wesley (1703–91), founder of the Methodist movement, called believers to a "perfection in love," suggesting that with God's power they

could reach a point at which their motivation to act conformed to God's will. Wesley's idea drew inspiration directly from the writing of French archbishop FRANÇOIS FÉNELON (1651–1715) but also harked back to St. THOMAS AQUINAS (d. 1274), who taught that perfection in the Christian life derived from acts of charity performed out of love of God and love of neighbor. Even earlier, PETER ABELARD (1075–1142) had spoken of acts of perfect contrition that immediately confer FORGIVENESS of SIN.

Within the Catholic tradition, those in religious orders were considered to be in a "state of perfection" after their vows of poverty, chastity, and obedience. VATICAN COUNCIL II, however, reiterated the point that perfection was the goal of all the faithful, not just the religious, and the term has fallen into disuse.

Today Christians talk about moving toward perfection. A foretaste is available during heartfelt works of goodness, but the fullness remains elusive on one's earthly journey.

Further reading: Réginald Garrigou-Lagrange, *Christian Perfection and Contemplation* (St. Louis: B. Herder, 1937); Asa Mahan, *Scripture Doctrine of Christian Perfection* (Boston: D. King, 1839); Olive Wyon, *Desire for God: A Study of Three Spiritual Classics: François Fénelon, "Christian Perfection"; John Wesley, "Christian Perfection"; Evelyn Underhill, "The Spiritual Life"* (London: Collins, 1966).

Perpetua and Felicity, Sts. (c. 200) *early African martyrs*

Perpetua was a wealthy young married mother in Carthage, today's Tunisia, who converted to Christianity along with her maidservant Felicity around the end of the second century. Both were arrested and sentenced to die during a massive wave of persecution launched by Emperor Septimus Severus (r. 193–211). Perpetua resisted her father's attempts to save her by asking her to reject her FAITH. Felicity, who was then pregnant, also refused to relent. She was allowed to have her child, and a CHRISTIAN woman took it for adoption.

The two women were executed on March 7, 203, by being placed in an arena with a baited cow. They were beheaded after their death. Both were later canonized by popular acclamation. An account of their story, *The Passion of Perpetua and Felicitas,* was later widely circulated. It included paragraphs apparently written by Perpetua herself; it is one of the earliest accounts of the role of women in the ancient church and possibly the first piece of Christian literature written by a woman. It includes details of a variety of visions Perpetua had while in prison. Far from defeating Christianity, martyrdoms like those of Perpetua and Felicity in time drew admiration of Romans who began to compare them to the afflictions laid upon heroes like Hercules.

See also HAGIOGRAPHY.

Further reading: A. Fraschetti, ed., *Roman Women* (Chicago: University of Chicago, 2001.); J. E. Salisbury, *Perpetua's Passion* (London: Routledge, 1997); Rodney Stark, *The Rise of Christianity* (San Francisco: Harper-SanFrancisco, 1997).

personalism

Personalism is a modern philosophical movement, popular among some Catholic thinkers and believers, that puts the idea of personhood at the center of philosophical discourse and personal categories at the center of practice. While basically a philosophical and theological movement, it had practical ramifications for CHRISTIANS as well.

While rooted in ancient philosophy, the personalist movement really emerged only in 19th-century Europe, articulated by theologicans such as the German Protestant Friedrich Schleiermacher (1768–1834) and the British Catholic JOHN HENRY NEWMAN, but most commonly associated with the philosopher-psychologist Rudolph Herman Lotze (1817–81).

One of Lotze's students, Borden Parker Bowne (1847–1910), became the leading exponent of personalism in America. He made it the prevailing philosophy at Methodist–sponsored Boston University, where it was passed on to a variety of Methodist leaders such as Edgar Sheffield Brightman (1884–1954) and Martin Luther King, Jr. (1929–68).

Throughout the 20th century in Europe, the leading personalists were French, including Gabriel Marcel (1889–1973) and JACQUES MARITAIN (1882–1973). The single greatest exponent of the philosophy was Emmanuel Mounier (1905–50), author of *A Personalist Manifesto* (1938). Mounier advanced an idea that resonated well in a Catholic context: that people have a responsibility to take active roles in history, even though they know the ultimate goal of their effort is beyond human history. In their early training, both the current Pope BENEDICT XVI and JOHN PAUL II were notably influenced by personalists.

Peter Maurin (1877–1949) is credited with introducing the personalism of Emmanuel Mounier to DOROTHY DAY and to the Catholic Worker movement. He translated and saw to the publication of Mounier's work, which had already sparked a Catholic revival in FRANCE. In the pages of Day's *Catholic Worker,* the emphasis became the Christian's personal responsibility in history (as opposed to a tendency to withdrawal from the world). Maurin and Day urged their readers to daily acts of mercy toward others.

The Catholic Worker movement brought personalism down to Earth in a program mixing Catholic FAITH, contemplation, and self-examination with social action and work. Members of the movement tried to live out the social doctrine that had been articulated in a series of 19th- and 20th-century papal social ENCYCLICALS, especially LEO XIII's *Rerum Novarum* (May 15, 1891) and PIUS XI's *Quadragesimo Anno* (May 15, 1931). The movement tried to walk a line between bourgeois individualism and industrial capitalism on the one hand and Marxism and fascism on the other, and startled many with its radical assertion that Christian love should be brought from its seeming position of limbo where human affairs are concerned and made to permeate the processes of history.

Further reading: Borden Parker Bowne, *Personalism* (Boston: Houghton Mifflin, 1908); Michael Kelly, *Pioneer of the Catholic Revival: The Ideas and Influence of Emmanuel Mounier* (London: Sheed & Ward, 1979); Jacques Maritan, *The Person and the Common Good* (New York: Charles Scribner's Sons, 1947); Emmanuel Mounier, *Be Not Afraid: Studies in Personalist Sociology* (New York: Harper & Brothers, 1951); ———, *The Personalist Manifesto* (London: Longmans Green, 1938).

Peter the Apostle, St. *leader of the church in Jerusalem, martyr in Rome*

The Apostle Peter emerges in the New Testament as the leader of Jesus' following in his absence. In the years after the formation of the church, he became the leading voice among the Jesus followers in Jerusalem (Acts 1–10). He traveled throughout the region, including Caesarea and Antioch in Syria, and is believed to have moved to Rome, where according to tradition he was martyred. Roman Catholics recognize him as the first BISHOP of Rome and thus the first pope. His feast day, together with St. PAUL, is June 29.

Peter was originally named Simon. In Greek his name is *petros* and Aramaic *cephas*. He is introduced in the first chapter of the GOSPEL of Mark. He and his brother Andrew were the first to be called as APOSTLES, joined immediately by the brothers John and James. Simon, a fisherman by occupation, was told to become an evangelist as a "fisher of men" (Matt. 4:19). Among Jesus' first miracles was the healing of Simon's mother-in-law (Mark 1:30).

Peter's conversation with Jesus recorded in Matthew is crucial to his role. When Jesus asks the apostles "Who do you say I am?" Peter calls him the Anointed One (the CHRIST), the Son of God. Jesus replies, "Blessed art thou, Simon Son of Jonah; for flesh and blood have not revealed it unto you, but my Father who is in heaven. And I say unto you, you are Peter, and upon this rock [Gk. *petros*] I will build my church; and the gates of hell will not prevail against it. And I will give unto you the keys of the kingdom of heaven; and whatsoever you shall bind on earth shall be bound in heaven and whatsoever you shall loose on earth shall be loosed in heaven" (Matt. 16:16–19).

Roman Catholics believe that these words granted Peter the authority he later exercised as pope, or head of the church, and that the authority was passed on to subsequent holders of the papal office. He and his successors wielded the power of designating those who could enter the kingdom. In this viewpoint, being in communion with the pope was a criterion of SALVATION. EASTERN ORTHODOX churches have generally interpreted this passage as applying more broadly to all the apostles; Protestants have generally suggested that it was Peter's confession of faith and his proclamation of the Gospel that was the rock upon which the church would be built.

Peter played a key role in the remaining events of Jesus' life. He emerged as the spokesperson for the apostles and joined James and John as Jesus' most intimate associates at the TRANSFIGURATION (Matt. 17:1–6). His relationship with Jesus was marred by his three-fold denial that he knew Jesus following the latter's arrest, but he regained favor in another famous episode in the Gospel of John. Following his resurrection, Jesus met with Peter and several of the apostles who had returned to fishing. He asked Peter three times, "Do you love me," using the word *agapao* in his question. Peter twice replied that he did love Jesus, but he used the synonym *phileo*. On his third reply he used the word *agapo*, and Jesus accepted his response.

Peter's preeminent role in the early church was manifested on the first Pentecost (Acts 2–3), when he explained to the assembly the different tongues they are hearing. He continued to lead the early Jesus followers at Jerusalem, who were mostly

Jews, but as a result of a vision he advocated that Gentiles did not have to accept Jewish law or be circumcised. (Luke-Acts harmonizes the ministries of Peter and Paul. Paul records bitter conflict in Galatians 2.) At one point, he was arrested and imprisoned. Rescued miraculously, he left Jerusalem. Eventually he arrived in Rome, where he was to be martyred, reportedly by crucifixion. Legend has him asking to be crucified upside down, as he was not worthy to die as Jesus had.

Peter is credited with authorship of the two epistles under his name found in the New Testament, though modern scholarship questions that authorship, especially of 2 Peter. The latter records a variety of traditions about Peter common in the church in the second century; it is evidence of the high status he was accorded but probably reflects a date after his DEATH.

Several writers, including CLEMENT OF ROME, (1 *Clement* 4–6), provide evidence of Peter's work there. According to IGNATIUS OF ANTIOCH, Peter and Paul jointly exercised authority over the CHRISTIAN community in Rome. Writing at the end of the second century, IRENAEUS OF LYONS ascribed the founding of the church in Rome to the pair, who, he wrote, also set in place the episcopal succession. Other evidence, however, strongly suggests that it was not until the middle of the second century that a single, dominant bishop emerged as the clear leader of the body of presbyters and bishops who administered the affairs of the church in Rome. The designation of Peter as the first bishop of Rome first occurs in the third century.

Peter is believed to have been buried on Vatican Hill. Over his grave the emperor CONSTANTINE built a large basilica. This church was demolished in the early 16th century and replaced by the present ST. PETER'S BASILICA. Archaeologists found a marker that some believe was the one placed over Peter's grave prior to Constantine's basilica. The site is directly below Bernini's main altar in the present basilica (*see* ARCHAEOLOGY).

See also PAPACY.

Further reading: Raymond. E. Brown, Karl. P. Donfried, and John Reumann, eds., *Peter in the New Testament: A Collaborative Assessment by Protestant and Roman Catholic Scholars* (New York: Paulist, 1973); Oscar Cullman, *Peter: Disciple, Apostle, Martyr: A Historical and Theological Study* (London: SCM, 1953); W. R. Farmer, *Peter and Paul in the Church of Rome* (New York: Paulist, 1990); D. W. O'Connor, *Peter in Rome: The Literary, Liturgical, and Archaeological Evidence* (New York: Columbia University Press, 1969); Calvin J. Roetzel, *Paul: The Man and the Myth* (Columbia: University of South Carolina Press, 1998).

Philip II (1527–1598) *king of Spain, Catholic champion*

Philip II of SPAIN emerged in the last half of the 16th century as a major defender of Catholic FAITH and interests against the emergent Protestant community in Europe. He was the son of Charles V (1500–58) and Isabella of Portugal (1503–39). As a young man he married Maria of Portugal, but she died in 1545 giving birth. Nine years later he married Mary I (1516–58), who had just become queen of England. Philip backed Mary's efforts to return her country to the Catholic fold. At first Philip was assigned to rule Naples and Sicily within his father's empire, but in 1556 Charles suddenly abdicated and Philip became king of Spain.

Philip's reign began in the midst of a war with England on the continent, which he proceeded to win, driving England from its last continental stronghold at Calais. He was widowed again in 1558. When Elizabeth I (1533–1603) refused his offer of marriage, he subsequently married Elizabeth of Valois (1545–68).

Philip had a love-hate relationship with the PAPACY. He supported its efforts to reestablish Catholicism in England and keep it in the Netherlands, and he and his half-brother John fought the Muslims successfully, but his rulership over southern ITALY was always seen by the pope as threatening his own control in the PAPAL STATES.

Philip's reign brought great wealth to Spain, with colonial conquests such as the Philippine Islands, which are named for him. However, he did little to stave off the empire's eventual eclipse. In the Netherlands, where Protestantism was growing, a revolt against Spanish authority began in 1562 and ended in the Dutch declaring independence in 1581. Meanwhile, England's privateers were undermining Spain's vast American empire. Philip's attempt at a retaliatory invasion of England failed when his massive armada was destroyed in 1588 in one of the most famous naval battles in history.

The defeat of the armada was only partially redeemed by the king's reconquest of Portugal, where his grandfather had once been king. Philip died in 1598 after more than four decades on the throne.

Further reading: Fernand Braudel, *The Mediterranean and the Mediterranean World in the Age of Philip II,* 2 vols. (New York: Harper & Row, 1975); Garrett Mattingly, *The Defeat of the Spanish Armada* (London: Jonathan Cape, 1959); Edward Grierson, *King of Two Worlds: Philip II of Spain* (New York: Putnam, 1974); Peter Pierson, *Philip II of Spain* (London: Thames & Hudson, 1975).

Philo of Alexandria (c. 20 B.C.E.–50 C.E.)
Jewish Neoplatonist theologian and philosopher
Philo of Alexandria, a prominent Jewish scholar and leader of the local Jewish community of the first century, authored a number of biblical commentaries that would become the basis of later Christian ALEXANDRINE SCHOOL of scriptural interpretation. Philo received a good education in both Judaism and Greek literature and philosophy. He developed an understanding of CREATION that relied heavily on Plato. He posited a transcendent deity under whom was the Logos, who contained the divine notions through which he created the cosmos. The individual soul can comprehend the universe. By studying Scripture,

one can come to know the nature of reality and of the divine law. Scripture is to be studied allegorically, and it will divulge an understanding of reality and what one needs to know to lead an ethical and pious life. By following such a life, one attains a likeness to God. God created a good world, and humans can attain that goodness and a sense of unity with GOD.

Philo's works were familiar to CLEMENT OF ALEXANDRIA (c. 150–c. 215), ORIGEN (c. 185–c. 254), CYRIL OF ALEXANDRIA (376–444), and JEROME (345–420). All of them absorbed his allegorical method of interpreting Scripture to one extent or another; it would provide the bridge from the first five books of the Hebrew Bible to the dominant Platonic philosophy of the early century of the Christian era in northern EGYPT.

See also ALLEGORY; BIBLE.

Further reading: English translations of most of Philo's works are now available online; Peder Borgen, *Philo of Alexandria, An Exegete for His Time* (Leiden: Brill, 1997); David R. Runia, *Philo in Early Christian Literature: A Survey* (Minneapolis: Fortress, 1993); ———, "Philo of Alexandria and the Beginning of Christian Thought," *Studia Philonica Annual* 7 (1995): 143–160; Bruce W. Winter, *Philo and Paul Among the Sophists* (New York: Cambridge University Press, 1997).

Pius V, St. (1504–1572), (r. 1566–1572) *pope*
Pope Pius V was born Michele Ghisleri at Bosco, Lombardy, on January 17, 1504. He became involved with the DOMINICAN ORDER early in his life and eventually joined it. He was ordained a priest in 1528 and quickly rose to prominence as a teacher of THEOLOGY and philosophy, a master of novices, and a prior. He matured as the PROTESTANT REFORMATION was taking hold in northern Europe. His feast day is April 30.

In 1556, Pope PAUL IV named Michele bishop of Sutri, and he also served as the inquisitor of the faith for Lombardy (*see* INQUISITION). The following year he received a cardinal's hat and a commission as inquisitor general for all Christendom. Among other accomplishments, he was able to subvert the plan of German emperor Maximillian II (1527–76) to end clerical CELIBACY. In 1566, he succeeded Paul IV as pope.

In an age of COUNTER-REFORMATION, he set an example by his devotion, his personal acts of kindness to the sick, and his refusal to live a luxurious lifestyle. He worked to enforce the decrees of the Council of TRENT concerning priests, BISHOPS, and religious orders.

Paul supported the German Catholics against their Protestant opponents and backed SPAIN against England. He excommunicated Elizabeth I (1533–1603) of England (see GREAT BRITAIN) and supported the claims of her rival, Mary Stuart (1542–87). At the same time, he attempted to unite Europe against the Turks, who had overrun the Balkans and conquered Romania and Hungary. His efforts were rewarded on October 7, 1571, when European naval forces defeated the Ottoman fleet at the Battle of Lepanto, which proved a turning point in the extension of Ottoman Turkish power into Europe.

When he died in 1572, Paul was in the process of forming a new European coalition to oppose Islamic power. A century after his death, he was beatified by Pope Clement X (r. 1670–76), and he was canonized by Pope Clement XI in 1712. In the 20th century, he has been rescued from oblivion and elevated as a hero by post–VATICAN COUNCIL II Catholic TRADITIONALISTS.

Further reading: Robin Anderson, *Pope Pius V* (Rockford, Ill.: Tan, 1989); Lillian Browne-Olf, *The Sword of Saint Michael: Saint Pius V 1504–1572* (Milwaukee: Bruce, 1943); Daughters of St. Paul, *No Place for Defeat: Life of St. Pius V* (St. Paul: Editions, 1987).

Pius IX (1792–1878), (r. 1846–1878) *pope, declarer of the doctrines of the Immaculate Conception and papal infallibility*

As Pius IX, Giovanni Mastai-Ferretti became the longest-reigning pope in history (1846–78); those

32 years witnessed some of the most important events in the life of the modern church. Giovanni studied at the Piarist College in Volterra (1802–09) and later at the Roman Seminary (1814–18) and was ordained a priest in 1819. He held a variety of positions prior to being named ARCHBISHOP of Spoleto in 1827. He became ARCHBISHOP of Omola in 1832 and was given the cardinal's hat in 1840.

Elected to the PAPACY in 1846, Pius IX at first seemed to look with favor on the winds of political change blowing across Europe. However, his outlook changed when revolutionary fervor erupted in ITALY just two years into his reign, and he and the PAPAL STATES he ruled became the targets of nationalists fighting to unite Italy. He had to flee Rome in 1848, and only with the assistance of the French was he able to return in 1850. His position became increasingly untenable, and by 1859 Rome fell to the new Italian state. Pius refused to recognize the new government of Italy, and after the annexation of the Papal States in 1870, he declared himself "prisoner in the Vatican."

Within the church Pius exercised his authority in an increasingly autocratic manner. In 1854, he declared the doctrine of the IMMACULATE CONCEPTION of Mary as dogma. This step brought him the support of many in FRANCE, where a Marian movement had emerged, and was epitomized in the apparition of the Blessed Virgin Mary to St. Bernadette Soubirous (1844–79) at Lourdes in 1858.

Pius asserted his role as vicar of Christ on Earth, using his authority as champion of the new Marian piety. He placed many of the more liberal ideas in society and the church on a *Syllabus of Errors* (July 14, 1864). In 1869, he called VATICAN COUNCIL I, which opened on the Feast of the Immaculate Conception. The council declared as dogma the doctrine of papal INFALLIBILITY, which provoked much dissent in several countries and drove some believers to break away into the OLD CATHOLIC Church.

His struggle against many of the major cultural trends of his times was Pius's legacy to the church. His retarding influence was not overcome until VATICAN COUNCIL II in the 1960s. In 2000, Pope JOHN PAUL II beatified both Pius IX and JOHN XXIII, the popes who called the two Vatican councils. Some say his papal style has returned.

Further reading: Yves Chiron, *Pope Pius IX: The Man and the Myth* (Kansas City: Angelus, 2005); E. E. Y. Hales, *Pio Nono: A Study in European Politics and Religion in the Nineteenth Century* (St. Louis: P. J. Kennedy, 1954); S. William Halperin, *Italy and the Vatican at War: A Study of Their Relations from the Outbreak of the Franco-Prussian War to the Death of Pius IX* (Chicago: University of Chicago Press, 1939).

Pius X, St. (1835–1914) *pope*

Pope Pius X was born Giuseppe Sarto at Riese, Treviso, Venice, which then was under the control of Austria. Son of a poor farmer and seamstress, he felt an early calling to the priesthood. He attended college at Padua and was ordained in 1858. Over the next decades he served as a parish priest and for a time as a spiritual director at the local seminary. Then in 1884 he was named BISHOP of Mantua. He became patriarch of Venice in 1893 and held that office until his election as pope in 1903. He was canonized by PIUS XII in 1954. His feast day is August 21. He is patron of first communicants.

Pius X's pontificate followed the landmark pontificates of PIUS IX (r. 1846–78) and Leo XIII (r. 1878–1903). Pius IX had suffered the dismantling of the PAPAL STATES and the unification of ITALY and withdrew to being "the prisoner of the Vatican." Leo XIII embraced some of the social teachings of the modern world, modern science, and the use of critical methods in the study of the BIBLE, but Pius X continued Pius IX's policies against modernism and the recognition of the Italian republic.

Unlike Leo XIII he had little contact with Anglicans or EASTERN ORTHODOXY. He issued two papal encyclicals, *Lamentabili Sane Exitu* (July 3, 1907) and *Pascendi Dominici Gregis* (August 9, 1907), which specifically attacked modernism and were used to squelch modernist tendencies that had found their way into the church. On September 1, 1910, he promulgated the papal directive that all priests, theological teachers, and confessors take the *Sacrorum Antistitum*, the oath against modernism. He was especially hostile to democracy and hence alienated many American leaders, ecclesiastical and secular. Nonetheless, he made the first overtures with the Italian government that finally led to a normalization of relations with ITALY under PIUS XI in the CONCORDAT called the Lateran Treaty (1929).

Despite his fears of the modern, Pius X undertook a reformation of church music and the restoration of Gregorian CHANT and Renaissance church music in his *Motu Proprio* (November 22, 1903). He strove to replace the 19th-century trend of celebrating the EUCHARIST as a big orchestral and operatic production (*see* MUSIC). He placed great emphasis on the adoration of the Blessed Sacrament and promoted the reception of the Eucharist by children who had attained the "age of discretion" (about seven years) in place of the customary 12 years as well as frequent reception of the SACRAMENT OF RECONCILIATION. He also reformed the VATICAN CURIA and began the modern codification of CANON LAW.

Pius X was remembered for his life of personal devotion. In recent times he has been championed by Catholic conservatives and TRADITIONALISTS who oppose many of the reforms of VATICAN COUNCIL II. The followers of Archbishop Marcel Lefebre (1905–91) call themselves the Society of St. Pius X.

Further reading: Katherine Burton, *The Great Mantle: The Life of Giuseppe Melchiore Sarto, Pope Pius X* (New York: Longmans, Green, 1950); Walther Diethelm, *The Farm Boy Who Became Pope* (San Francisco: Ignatius, 1994); Igino Giordani, *Pius X: A Country Priest* (Milwaukee: Bruce, 1954); Francis Beauchesne Thornton, *Burning Flame: the Life of Pope Pius X* (New York: Benziger Brothers, 1952).

Pius XI (1857–1939), (r. 1922–1939) *pope, signer of Lateran Treaty*

Pope Pius XI, who led the Catholic Church in the years between the two world wars, was known for his conservative THEOLOGY and adherence to traditional Catholic piety. In more recent years, in the wake of the Holocaust, he has been heavily criticized for leading the church into a misguided alliance with fascism and Nazism.

Pius was born Ambrogio Achille Ratti. He was educated at the Gregorian University in Rome and ordained in 1879. He distinguished himself as a staff member of the Ambrosian Library in Milan, becoming chief librarian in 1907. Pope PIUS X appointed him vice prefect of the Vatican Library. In the years after World War I he was called into a diplomatic role as papal legate (1918) and papal nuncio (1919) to Poland. He was named ARCH-BISHOP of Milan in 1921 and succeeded to the papal chair the next year.

Pius XI inherited a critical situation. The church faced a world in turmoil amid political, cultural, and intellectual revolution. The PAPACY itself was in a state of limbo with the government of ITALY, which had stripped away the PAPAL STATES in the preceding century. Pius XI moved first to resolve the diplomatic issues. In 1929 he signed the Lateran CONCORDAT with the Italian government; the pope was recognized as sovereign of the Vatican while he himself accepted a sovereign Italy and its capital, Rome. The Italian government repealed many anti-Catholic laws, and Pius XI did not speak against the invasion of Ethiopia or Italy's role in the Spanish civil war. Pius XI next signed the Reichskoncordat with GERMANY (1933) that included promises of freedom for the church to continue its ministry. This concordat was signed just as Adolf Hitler (1889–1945) was rising to power; he would ignore it as his plans for war fell into place.

In practical terms, the two concordats aligned the papacy with the growing fascist movement in Europe. Pius XI appears to have been motivated by a desire to secure the church's place in the changing world and to find allies in the fight against MARXISM, another rapidly growing force in Europe that he saw as utterly unacceptable. To his credit, he did not ignore the racial philosophy of NAZISM, and openly condemned it in his 1937 *Mit Brennender Sorge,* which was read in churches throughout Germany. At the end of his life he commissioned American Jesuit JOHN LA FARGE to write a draft encyclical addressing racism and ANTI-SEMITISM. It was never promulgated.

Pius XI is recognized for his promotion of higher learning, especially in areas of missiology (the study of missions), the sciences (especially archaeology), and modern communications. He was the first pope to speak on the radio, after having a radio station installed at the Vatican. He also encouraged greater participation of the laity in the life of the church through CATHOLIC ACTION. He died just months before World War II began.

Further reading: Donald Dorr, *Option for the Poor* (Maryknoll, N.Y.: Orbis, 1983); *The Encyclicals of Pius XI,* tr. James H. Ryan (New York: Herder, 1927); Terrence P. McLaughlin, *The Church and the Reconstruction of the Modern World: The Social Encyclicals of Pius XI* (Garden City, N.Y.: Image, 1957); Raymond J. Miller, *Forty Years After: Pius XI and the Social Order: A Commentary* (St. Paul: Radio Replies, 1947).

Pius XII (1876–1958), (r. 1939–1958) *pope*

Pope Pius XII, who led the Catholic church through the difficult years of World War II and its aftermath, would a generation after his death become one of the most controversial figures in the modern church for his actions or inaction relative to NAZISM during the war.

Pius XII was born Maria Giuseppe Giovanni Pacelli into a prominent Italian Catholic family, his grandfather having founded *L' Osservatore Romano,* the Vatican's newspaper, and his father having been one of the Vatican's lawyers. After completing his studies, he was ordained a priest in 1899. He first distinguished himself in the decade prior to World War I by his work on CANON LAW. He was subsequently named apostolic nuncio in Bavaria (1917) and GERMANY (1920). Following the signing of the Lateran CONCORDAT, which normalized the Vatican's relationship with ITALY, Pope Pius XI appointed Pacelli a cardinal in 1929 and named him the Vatican's secretary of state. In this position he negotiated concordats with Bavaria, Prussia, Austria, and ultimately Germany (1933).

A world war was threatening as Pius XII began his papacy in 1939, and he did his best to head it off. He has been criticized, however, for failing to appreciate the scope of Adolf Hitler's plans for empire and the ruthlessness with which he would pursue those plans. Perhaps he was limited by the widespread opinion in the church that FASCISM could be used as a force against MARXISM; he had also become a Germanophile during his years as Vatican secretary of state. Like his predecessor, his primary concern was to protect the freedoms that the concordat had restored to the church in Germany following several generations of anti-Catholic actions by previous German governments.

Much controversy has focused on his attitude toward the Jews during the war. Critics have complained that he turned a deaf ear to the cries of the Jews being massacred in the Holocaust. Supporters have noted that he worked relentlessly to save the Italian Jews and allowed Jews to hide in the church's monasteries and convents. He also allowed Catholics to develop an underground network to protect Jews. After the war, the leader of the Roman Jewish community lauded him and converted to Catholicism. This debate is not likely to be resolved until more historical evidence comes to light.

Pius came out of the war ready to act. He called on the Allies not to hold the German people collectively responsible for the Nazi atrocities, but rather to help them rebound from the war and resume a role in fighting communism. This was a clear statement of the continuity with the policies of his recent predecessors. Also like them, he saw few benefits in the changes wrought by secularization and did not see the need to revisit traditional THEOLOGY in dealing with a rapidly changing world. At times he even condemned those Catholics trying to develop new theological visions.

However, in the little-noticed encyclical *Divino Afflante Spiritu* (September 30, 1940) issued during the war, Pius opened the door to modern biblical criticism. He also issued the important encyclical *Mystici Corporis* (June 29, 1943) that took into account new trends in ECCLESIOLOGY. He also approved new efforts toward a more positive relationship with non-Christian religions, though he later drew back form participating in ecumenical dialogues. He also moved forward in modern communications—he allowed many of his public activities to be filmed for release in newsreels and became the first pope known to mass television audiences.

The Catholic Church experienced significant worldwide growth in the 15 years after World War II. In response, Pius XII oversaw the multiplication of DIOCESEs (from 1,696 to 2,048), greatly increased the number of BISHOPs from non-Western countries, and appointed a number of cardinals from parts of the world never before represented.

Pius XII is remembered for bringing devotion to the Virgin Mary to a new high. As the war ended, he established a Feast to the Immaculate Heart of Mary (Saturday after the Feast of the SACRED HEART OF JESUS) in 1945. In 1950, using the papal authority of doctrinal INFALLIBILITY, he defined the doctrine of the ASSUMPTION of the Virgin into heaven. These acts culminated nearly a century of papal ENCYCLICALS on the Virgin, starting with the definition of the IMMACULATE CONCEPTION by PIUS IX in 1854. Pope Pius XII died in 1958 and was succeeded, surprisingly, by JOHN XXIII.

Further reading: Richard Burke, *The Social Teaching of Pius XII* (Rome: Gregoriana, 1955); Michael Chinigo, ed., *The Pope Speaks: The Teachings of Pope Pius XII* (New York: Pantheon, 1957); John Cornwell, *Hitler's Pope: The Secret History of Pius XII* (New York: Viking;

1999); Margherita Marchione, *Pope Pius XII: Architect for Peace* (Mahwah: Paulist, 2000); ———, *Shepherd of Souls: A Pictorial Life of Pope Pius XII* (Mahwah: Paulist, 2002).

Plato   *See* NEOPLATONISM.

Poland

The Slavic-speaking country of Poland is crucial for understanding the history of Christianity and Catholicism in eastern Europe. Christianity first touched the southern fringes of Poland through the ninth-century missionary efforts of Sts. CYRIL AND METHODIUS to the first Slavic state known as Great Moravia. In 966 Prince Mieczysław I (d. 922) was baptized and married into the CHRISTIAN royal family of Czechoslovakia. Christianity grew but experienced persecution from pagan worshippers for a considerable time.

The central role of the royalty in the life of the church delayed the Polish adopting the 11th-century reforms of Pope GREGORY VII until the 13th century. The waves of invasions by the Tartars strengthened the church and the people's piety. By 1397 Polish missionaries had Christianized Lithuania, which was incorporated into the Polish kingdom. Poland became the ascending power in central Europe under the Jagiellonian dynasty from the 14th to the 16th centuries. During the 14th century many Polish princes supported the cause of JOHN HUS, and the HIERARCHY introduced the INQUISITION to root out heretics. Later many nobles also gave support to the PROTESTANT REFORMATION to secure political and territorial advantages against the powerful king and church.

During the upheavals of these times many religious refugees (Lutherans, Bohemian Brethren, and Socinians) found protection in Poland, which became remarkably tolerant despite the overwhelming Catholic loyalty of the population. In the 16th century Poland remained an island of Catholicism in the middle of Lutheran Prussia to

its west, Hussite Bohemia to its south, and Orthodox Russia to its north and east. At the end of the 16th century the RUTHENIAN CATHOLIC CHURCH and ARMENIAN CATHOLIC CHURCH, formerly in communion with Orthodox Constantinople, formally became Uniate with Rome.

The 17th century saw Catholicism become the national religion of the Polish empire. Piety was centered at the fortress MONASTERY of Jasna Góra ("Bright Mountain") in Częstochowa, which housed the famous Black Madonna. In 1656 King Jan II Casimir (1609–72) dedicated the nation to Mary as patron and queen of the land. Poland developed its own special forms of devotions and hymns, which have survived into the 21st century. This special form of piety aided Polish immigrant communities in Europe and the United States to retain their religious and ethnic identity beyond that of others.

At the end of the 18th century Poland produced one of the most liberal constitutions in Europe but soon suffered partition at the hands of the Prussians and the Russians. The Lithuanian Church reverted to the sway of the czar and the Moscow patriarchy. Though Napoléon Bonaparte (1769–1821) had restored the Duchy of Warsaw, the fate of the nation remained in the hands of its neighbors and enemies (Russia and Austria) throughout the remainder of the 19th century.

Polish independence was reestablished at the Treaty of Versailles in 1919, but both Germany and Russia invaded in 1939 from the west and the east, respectively. At the end of World War II Poland became ethnically unified but suffered under the heavy hand of the Soviets. In the mid-1950s the regime became more liberal, and in the late 1970s the independent trade union Solidarity, under the leadership of Lech Wałęsa (1943–), began a series of strikes in the shipyard city of Gdańsk against the communist government. The election of and triumphal return to Poland by Pope JOHN PAUL II signaled the end of sway of MARXISM over the political and social institutions of the nation. In 1989 Solidarity, the political party that rose out of the strikes, won the national elections. Since then the nation has undergone significant liberalizations on several church-sensitive issues such as divorce, birth control, abortion, and gay rights for which it incurred the censure of the world's first Polish pope, JOHN PAUL II.

Today there are about 35 million Catholics in Poland, about 95 percent of the population. Sunday Mass attendance is very high, 53 percent, in comparison with other European nations. Along with the Republics of IRELAND and SPAIN, Poland remains one of the most homogenously Catholic nations in Europe and the world.

Further reading: *Ksiega tysiaclecia katolicyzmu w Polsce* ("Poland's Millennium of Catholicism") (Lublin, Poland: Catholic University of Lublin, 1969); Jan Kubik, *The Power of Symbols against the Symbols of Power: The Rise of Solidarity and the Fall of State Socialism in Poland* (University Park: Pennsylvania State University Press, 1994); John Radzilowski, *The Eagle and the Cross: A History of the Polish Roman Catholic Union of America* (Boulder, Colo.: East European Monographs, distributed Columbia University Press, 2003); Christopher L. Zugger, *The Forgotten: Catholics of the Soviet Empire from Lenin through Stalin* (Syracuse, N.Y.: Syracuse University Press, 2001).

poverty

In the New Testament, Jesus is noted as telling his APOSTLES, "you shall always have the poor with you" (Matt. 26:11). That observation has proved true. Even amidst the manifest wealth of modern postindustrial societies many families live in a state of deprivation of the material necessities of life—food, clothing, medical care, and shelter. Jesus spoke often of the poor, noting that they would have an honored place in the coming Kingdom of GOD (Luke 6:20). Meanwhile, they were held up as the focus of God's compassion.

PAUL notes that CHRIST became poor so that we could participate in the abundance of his GRACE (2 Cor. 8:9) and admonished CHRISTIANS not to forget the poor in Jerusalem (Gal. 2:10). James noted that God had chosen the poor making them rich in FAITH (James 2:5).

From the many citations concerning the poor, the church was left with certain basic obligations. The involuntary poor must always be objects of concern and charity. Church members are to assist the poor by sharing their relative wealth (*see* THEOLOGY). In more recent years, many Christians have participated in social action in a church context in support of programs to alleviate the suffering of the poor. Identification with the poor has been a decisive element in contemporary LIBERATION THEOLOGY.

Liberation theologians have picked up a theme from several papal social encyclicals and asserted that God and the church have a primary commitment to the poor, a commitment based on the demands of love and justice. In his address to the Puebla Conference of Latin American Bishops (*see* CELAM) and encyclical *Centesimus Annus* (1991), for example, Pope JOHN PAUL II called attention to the world's poor and what he saw as the growth of poverty internationally. Though chastising errors of liberation theologians on some points, on this issue he affirmed his agreement. (Cardinal Ratzinger, now BENEDICT XVI, took a much harder stance against liberation theology.)

The church has also seen in Christ's poverty an ideal and in the adoption of a life that included poverty a most worthy path to spiritual growth. Poverty makes one rely on others and ultimately on God for survival. Voluntary poverty supports one's sense of reliance on God while allowing one to give up the search for wealth and instead use one's life in service to others. Those who join religious orders take a vow of poverty along with their vows of chastity and obedience.

ST. FRANCIS OF ASSISI is known for his special emphasis on poverty. He not only admonished those who joined the order he founded to take vows of individual poverty, but also wanted the order collectively to refuse ownership of property. The Franciscan Spirituals insisted on the absolute poverty of Jesus (Luke 9:58). FRANCISCANS continue to place an emphasis on poverty and the freedom for service it brings.

Further reading: Leonardo Boff, *Cry of the Earth, Cry of the Poor.* (Maryknoll, N.Y.: Orbis, 1997); Gustavo Gutierrez, *A Theology of Liberation* (Maryknoll, N.Y.: Orbis, 1988); Martin Hengel, *Property and Riches in the Early Church* (Philadelphia: Fortress, 1974); Kenneth Baxter Wolf, *The Poverty of Riches: St. Francis of Assisi Reconsidered* (New York: Oxford University Press, 2003).

praxis

The term *praxis* refers to religion expressed in action, in contrast to religion expressed in belief, meditation, prayer, and attendance at religious gatherings. Practicing one's FAITH can take a variety of forms, but in the 20th century the term has usually been used by those who advocate social and political action in an attempt to build a more just society.

Within the Protestant context praxis has been associated with the Social Gospel movement of Walter Rauschenbusch (1861–1918) aimed at building the Kingdom of GOD on Earth. In the Roman Catholic context it has been associated with a variety of movements in which action occurred beyond church walls, such as the worker-priest movement in FRANCE and Belgium and the Catholic Worker movement founded by Dorothy Day (*see* CATHOLIC ACTION). Both Protestants and Catholics joined in the LIBERATION THEOLOGY movement in LATIN AMERICA, which identified with the poor and oppressed as a first order of business and called CHRISTIANS to join in efforts at overthrowing the instruments of secular and sacred oppression.

In contrast to other social movements such as MARXISM and secular socialism, Christian praxis tries to set social action within a worshipful and theological context. THEOLOGY and action interact with each other as the former guides the latter and the latter informs the former. Worship provides a time of empowerment, celebration, and remembrance of the active life, as worshipers connect with God, commemorate often hard-won accomplishments, and pay tribute to those who have given their life in service.

Further reading: Rebecca S. Chopp, *The Praxis of Suffering: An Interpretation of Political and Latin American Liberation Theologies* (Maryknoll, N.Y.: Orbis, 1986); Rosino Gibellini, ed., *Frontiers of Theology in Latin America,* tr. John Drury (Maryknoll, N.Y.: Orbis, 1974); Matthew Lamb, *Solidarity with Victims: Toward a Theology of Social Transformation* (New York: Crossroad, 1982); William R. Stevenson, Jr, ed., *Christian Political Activism at the Crossroads* (Lanham, Md.: University Press of America, 1994).

Prayer of the Hours

The Prayer (or LITURGY) of the Hours, also known as the Divine Office and the Canonical Hours, is a form of public (and private or family) prayer designed to acknowledge the daily cycle of life. It derives from pre-CHRISTIAN patterns of religious culture that celebrated the rising and setting of the sun and the activities of the day and asked protection from the particular dangers of the nighttime world. The APOSTLE PAUL urged his churches to "pray without ceasing" (1 Thess. 5:17). TERTULLIAN, writing in the third century related the practice of constant prayer to eschatological issues—Christians were exhorted to remain alert for Jesus' return (*On Prayer* 4).

The present form of Prayer of the Hours appears to have originated in the practices of MONKS in the Egyptian desert (*see* MONASTICISM). It was anchored in prayer at dawn (Lauds) and dusk (Compline), and often included the basic moments noted in a Roman civil day—the third (Terce), sixth (Sext), and ninth (None) hours (that is, 9 AM, 12:00 noon and 3 PM). Often the pattern might include interrupting one's sleep, rising from bed, and engaging in a brief period of prayer (Matins).

With the development of MONASTICISM, the Litany of the Hours underwent a rich development process. The monastic communities pursued an ideal of praying without cease (I Thess. 5:17). The number and variety of prayers at each gathering of the monks increased. All-night prayer VIGILS were a frequent addition to the weekly and annual schedule. BENEDICTINES included the repetition of the entire Book of Psalms in their average week, and some more extreme orders had members repeating all 150 Psalms daily. This was the context in which varieties of CHANT developed.

In local churches, the Divine Office was anchored by the morning and evening prayer services, which were, compared to the monastic equivalents, relatively short. Most laypeople were unable to attend other gatherings during the day, and these tended to become the preserve of the CLERGY. A standardized schedule of daily prayer for the church was codified around eight daily services known as Vespers (or evening prayer held at twilight), Compline (upon retiring), Matins (in the nighttime), Lauds (at dawn), Prime (beginning of the work day), Terce (9 AM), Sext (noon), and None (3 PM). Church vigils were usually held on the eve of major feast days (such as Christmas or EASTER). The prayers of the Litany of the Hours were built around the texts of the Psalms and other scriptural readings, prayers, antiphons and hymns.

As Christianity became the dominant religion of Europe, attendance at the Prayers of the Hours, even at the start and end of the day, became increasingly neglected by CLERGY as well as laity. A contributing factor was the invention of the breviary, a prayer book that included the litany of the hours. The breviary allowed each individual to have a copy of the text of the Hours; one no longer had to be physically in church to participate in the cycle of prayer. One could pray in one's home at a time that was convenient. The formal, communal recitation of the Hours came to be restricted to major cathedral churches, which hired professionals to say or sing the Divine Office every day. Many noble families commissioned illuminated Books of the Hours. Most notable was the *Tres Riches Houres of the Duc du Barry.*

VATICAN COUNCIL II reformed the Divine Office. The new rules stressed the morning and evening prayers as the hinge of the daily cycle. The cycle was streamlined, and each priest was asked to observe a portion of the Divine Office at his parish. Post–Vatican II breviaries also emphasized that gatherings for daily prayer could be led by laypersons as well as a priest.

Further reading: Stanislaus Campbell, *From Breviary to Liturgy of the Hours: Structural Reform of the Roman Office, 1964–1971* (Collegeville, Minn.: Liturgical Press, 1995); George Guiver, *Company of Voices: Daily Prayer and the People of God* (New York: Pueblo, 1988); Dominic F. Scotto, *The Liturgy of the Hours: Its History and Its Importance in the Communal Prayer of the Church after the Liturgical Reform of Vatican II* (Petersham: St. Bede's, 1987); Robert Taft, *The Liturgy of the Hours in East and West: The Origins of the Divine Office and Its Meaning for Today* (Collegeville, Minn.: Liturgical Press, 1986).

prayers, common (Lat.: *prex,* "prayer," "entreaty")

Prayer is a lifting up of the heart and mind to GOD in supplication, praise, and thanksgiving (Rom. 8:5). Some define prayer as a petition for those things pertaining to salvation. Prayer presents a theological problem. Because God already knows what humanity needs (ORIGEN, *On Prayer* 5), when people pray, they really are only submitting their desires to God's will (THOMAS AQUINAS, *Summa Theologiae* 2.2.83).

Catholics make a distinction between active, oral prayer and contemplative prayer, or meditation. Meditation involves silent reflection and devotion that puts the SOUL into contact with the mystery of God. Oral prayer gathers together the community for petitioning, praising, and supplicating God as the family of CHRIST.

The oldest prayer that came into common use is the Our Father (Lat. Pater Noster), or Lord's

Prayer, which Jesus taught his disciples (Matt. 6:9–13; Luke 11:2–4; *Didache* 8.2.3). It is an eschatological prayer seeking and giving FORGIVE-NESS in anticipation of the coming Kingdom of God, or Heaven. The *DIDACHE* recommends saying the Our Father three times a day at morning, noon, and night. This may have sparked the later PRAYER OF THE HOURS. The Our Father is sung or recited in the Roman EUCHARIST immediately before the reception of Communion. It is also recited in prayer units with other prayers, such as the CREED, the Rosary, the Hail Mary, and the Glory Be to God.

The second-most important but perhaps even more frequently recited prayer, is the Hail Mary (Lat. Ave Maria), based on the angel Gabriel's and Elizabeth's greetings to MARY OF NAZARETH at the ANNUNCIATION (Luke 1:28, 42). It has been set to music many times, including the often-sung version of Franz Schubert (1797–1828). The prayer became common during the CRUSADES when knights and their soldiers prayed for success in recapturing the Holy Land. From 1598 to 1955 it was added to the Prayer of the Hours. Today the Hail Mary is the key prayer in the Rosary.

The most common devotion among Catholics throughout the world, whether in private homes or in public, is the Rosary (Lat.: *rosarium*, "rose garden". The world witnessed the power of the rosary in popular Catholic religiosity when throngs of Catholics recited it in the Piazza San Petro below the Vatican residence of JOHN PAUL II as he died. Surprisingly, the form of the rosary probably was transmitted to Christianity via Islam from Buddhism. Many Buddhists say *om mani padme hum,* "Hail! The Jewel in the Lotus!" when fingering the beads of their rosary. Muslims say a rosary (Ar. *subhah*) composed of 99 or 33 beads, saying in three cycles first "Blessed be Allah!" then "Praised by Allah!" and finally "Allah is Great!" The 99 stands for the 99 names of Allah in the Qur'an. This form of prayer likely passed into Christianity during the period of the Crusades when Christians came into contact with Muslims.

The rosary has always included a concatenation of meditative prayers. The current version was devised by DOMINICANS probably in the 16th century, although legend attributes it to St. DOMINIC DE GUZMÁN of the 12th to 13th century. The Dominican PIUS V did much to spread the devotion after the defeat of the Turks in the Battle of Lepanto in 1571. VATICAN COUNCIL II, while affirming traditional forms of devotion, downplayed types of prayer that did not put Christ at the center. John Paul II fully reinstated the status of the traditional rosary in his encyclical *Rosarium Virginis Mariae* (October 16, 2002). He attempted to thwart objections from ecumenists by saying that the rosary is a form of "contemplating Christ with Mary." He then proceeded to add five new "Luminous Mysteries" that are entirely Christocentric.

Today's rosary is composed of a crucifix, with which one blesses oneself and says the Apostles' CREED. After the Creed, one says an Our Father (on a large bead), three Hail Marys (on small beads), and then a Glory Be to God. There follow five decades of beads (10 Hail Marys each) separated by single beads (Glory Be's). The mysteries are subjects of meditation as one recites the decades of the rosary.

The Joyful Mysteries are 1) the Annunciation of Gabriel to Mary, 2) the Visitation of Elizabeth to Mary, 3) the Birth of Jesus, 4) the Presentation of Jesus in the Temple, and 5) the Finding of Jesus in the Temple. The Joyful Mysteries are said on Mondays, Saturdays, Advent Sundays, and from Epiphany to Lent. The Luminous Mysteries, added by Pope John Paul II, are 1) the Baptism of Jesus in the River Jordan, 2) the Wedding of Cana, Christ Manifested, 3) the Proclamation of the Kingdom of God, 4) the Transfiguration of Jesus, and 5) The Last Supper, the Holy Eucharist. The Luminous Mysteries are for Thursdays, the day of the institution of the Eucharist in Catholic belief. The Sorrowful Mysteries are 1) the Agony of Jesus in the Garden, 2) Jesus Scourged at the Pillar, 3) Jesus Crowned with Thorns, 4) Jesus Carries the Cross, and 5) the Crucifixion. The Sorrowful Mysteries are said on Tuesdays, Fridays, and daily from Ash Wednesday until Easter Sunday. The Glorious Mysteries are 1) the Resurrection of Jesus, 2) the Ascension, 3) the Descent of the Holy Spirit at Pentecost, 4) the Assumption of Mary into Heaven, and 5) the Coronation of Mary as Queen of Heaven and Earth. Pious Catholics often recite the rosary novenas, or nine-day cycles. Devotion to the Rosary has been reinforced by the many modern apparitions of Mary, especially at LOURDES, Fatima, and Medjugorje.

The last of the common prayers is the Glory Be To God, or Doxology (Gk. *doxa* "praise" + *logos* "word of"). The CANON of the Eucharist ends with what is known as the Great Doxology: "Through him [Christ], with him, in him, in the unity of the Holy Spirit, all praise is yours almighty Father, for ever and ever. Amen." The Glory Be, or Lesser Doxology, is "Glory be to the Father, and to the Son, and to the Holy Spirit; as it was in the beginning, is now and ever shall be, world without end. Amen." The Lesser Doxology was added during the early MIDDLE AGES to the PRAYER OF THE HOURS at the conclusion of the recitation of each psalm, and is part of the rosary. Doxologies often conclude hymns.

Another common prayer, still said in some parts of the world, is the Angelus, named for the angel of the Lord who announces the birth of the Messiah (Luke 1:28). The prayer is often said when bells are rung at 6:00 AM, 12:00 noon, and 6:00 PM. Some claim that this prayer was introduced by FRANCISCANS returning from the Holy Land and that it was modeled on the Muslim *salat*, or prayer five times a day.

Further reading: Judith A. Bauer, ed., *The Essential Catholic Prayer Book* (Liguori, Mo.: Liguori, 1999); Lawrence Cunningham, *Catholic Prayer* (New York: Crossroad, 1989).

prelate (Lat.: *prelatus*, "preferred")

A prelate is any CLERGY person with authority (governing power) over a distinct part of the church visible. The most common prelates are the diocesan BISHOPS, who govern particular geographical territories for the church; in common usage the terms *bishop* and *prelate* are interchangeable. However, within the Catholic Church there are a variety of officeholders above the rank of BISHOPS or ARCHBISHOPS, who are also considered prelates, for example, the leaders of some of the large religious orders; many Vatican officials; vicars and prefects apostolic, who act under special mandates from the pope, often in areas where no DIOCESE exists; and vicar generals, who assist territorial bishops. The term *prelate nullius* is used to designate a titular bishop, a bishop whose area of authority is not a geographical territory.

In addition to those mentioned above, who exercise real power and authority, there are also some honorary prelates who have been singled out for their outstanding service and/or accomplishments and who are assigned honorary positions in the "Pontifical Household." Such prelates are addressed as "monsignor," but apart from the privilege of wearing ecclesiastical garb similar to that of a bishop, they exercise no actual authority.

Further reading: Felician A. Foy and Rose M. Avato, *A Concise Guide to the Catholic Church* (Huntington, Ind.: Our Sunday Visitor, 1984).

priest/presbyter (Gk.: "elder," "supervisor")

Presbyter, a Greek word commonly translated as elder, is the most common term used to designate a CLERGY person in the New Testament. The position appears to have derived from Jewish practice whereby elders, as distinct from priests, functioned as leaders of synagogues. As the church spread and APOSTLES became more inaccessible, elders emerged as the primary community leaders. During the first century, the term *presbyter* was interchangeable with *episkopos* (or overseer). Only in the second century did elder and overseer (BISHOP) become two separate offices.

Elders were found in the church at Jerusalem quite early (Acts 11:30), and PAUL is known to have appointed elders in the churches he founded (Acts 14:23). They were assigned to teach and look after the congregations, the teaching function being the most essential. As the church spread from the cities (in which the bishops dwelt), the elders became the chief pastoral officers, whose duties included administering the SACRAMENTS, especially the EUCHARIST. In Latin lands, the term *presbyter* evolved into the modern word priest.

John Calvin (1509–64), founder and leader of the Reformed Church at Geneva, proposed a reorganization of the church that eliminated bishops and placed governance in the hands of groups of elders. Based on his reading of I Timothy 5:17, he concluded that there should be two kinds of elders: ordained teaching elders (clergy) and lay ruling elders. In the average congregation the number of ruling elders usually far outnumbers that of teaching elders. In the English-speaking world, many Calvinist churches are called Presbyterian.

In the discussions and documents of VATICAN COUNCIL II, the term *presbyter* was commonly used in speaking of priests, their office, and their duties. The presbyter is called to identify with CHRIST and seek holiness in his personal life. His vocation is exercised in three roles: shepherd, or pastor, leading a community of the faithful; prophet, preacher of the Word of God; and priest, administering the sacraments.

See also HOLY ORDERS.

Further reading: Donald Goergen, ed., *The Theology of Priesthood* (Collegeville, Minn.: Liturgical Press, 2000); Thomas F. O'Meara, *Theology of Ministry* (Mahwah, N.J.: Paulist, 1999); Kenan Osborne, *Priesthood: A History of the Ordained Ministry in the Roman Catholic Church* (Mahwah, N.J.: Paulist, 1988).

privilege of the faith

In a limited range of circumstances the Catholic Church may allow the ending of a MARRIAGE.

Among the more obscure of these conditions is what is termed the "privilege of the faith," meaning that the church annuls or dissolves the first marriage and a second legal and valid marriage is permitted as a "favor of the faith." Such a privilege is recognized under two circumstances. First, when two people, both non-Catholics, are married and one later converts to the church, the convert may on occasion be allowed to dissolve the first marriage and remarry within the church. Second, in a case in which a church member is married to a nonchurch member, the pope may allow a dissolution of the first marriage in such manner that the member may marry a second time. These two instances are designated the Pauline and Petrine privileges, respectively. The former finds its biblical JUSTIFICATION in the discourse on marriage by Paul in 1 Corinthians 7:12–15. The second derives solely from the power of the pope as Peter's successor.

The privilege of the faith option is relatively rare, but given the size of the church a set of structures have been put in place to handle the petitions. The cases are handled by special tribunals in diocesan CURIA and the VATICAN CURIA.

Further reading: Michael Smith Foster, *Annulment: The Wedding That Was Not* (Mahwah, N.J.: Paulist, 1990); Geoffrey Robinson, *Marriage, Divorce & Nullity: A Guide to the Annulment Process in the Catholic Church* (Ottawa: Novalis, 2000); Eileen Stuart, *Dissolution and Annulment of Marriage by the Catholic Church* (Sydney: Federation, 1994).

probabilism   *See* ALPHONSUS LIGUORI, ST.

procession, liturgical

A liturgical procession is a formal, orderly movement of CLERGY and/or laity from one location to another, symbolizing GOD's action toward the world in loving care and the church as a pilgrim in the world. The most common procession occurs in the EUCHARIST, with the entrance of the PRIEST and those assisting in leading the worship. Processions, often not recognized as such, accompany the reading of the GOSPEL, the offertory, and Communion. More solemn processions occur at high points in the church year (Palm Sunday, the Feast of Corpus Christi).

The Palm Sunday procession reenacts Jesus' entry into Jerusalem before his execution (Luke 19:28–44). In Rome on the Feast of Corpus Christi, the annual Corpus Christi procession moves from St. Peter's Square through the streets of Rome to St. John's Lateran. The procession recreates Jesus' procession from the Upper Room to the Mt. of Olives (Matt. 26:14–35). There are also funeral processions that move from a church to the burial site of a recently deceased church member.

Each nation and village can have its special procession. In many countries an annual festival celebrating the nation's PATRON SAINT will feature a large procession. Typical is the annual veneration of the Virgen de El Viejo on December 8 in Chinandega, Nicaragua; a large procession moves to the church where the statue resides and a special mass is said. St. Willibrord (c. 658–739) is Luxembourg's only saint. On his feast day, November 7, pilgrims journey to Echternach, where he built a church and eventually died. They gather at a bridge over the Sûre River and process a mile to the shrine church. Upon reaching the church, they circle the building and begin a service of prayer. This particular procession is noteworthy as those in the procession make their pilgrimage while dancing. In Santa Fe, New Mexico, devout Catholics process in pilgrimage at Easter from that city to the Santuario de Chimayo, which many call the "Lourdes of America" for its holy, healing dirt.

Further reading: Adolf Adam, *Foundations of Liturgy: An Introduction to Its History and Practice.* (Collegeville, Minn.: Liturgical Press, 1992); Greg Dues, *Catholic Customs and Traditions: A Popular Guide* (Mystic, Conn.: Twenty-third, 1992); Miri Rubin, *Corpus Christi: The Eucharist in Late Medieval Culture* (Cambridge: Cambridge University, 1992).

property

Catholic thought views property through two rather contradictory perspectives. On the one hand, the ownership of property is considered a fundamental aspect of the development of the autonomous human being; on the other hand, voluntary POVERTY, which forgoes the ownership of property, is held out as the ideal in the imitation of CHRIST and is an essential vow for most members of religious orders. MENDICANTS preached the absolute poverty of Christ. GOD gave the world to human beings to hold in stewardship, but the attempt to accumulate and focus on possessions is a primary manifestation of SIN.

Catholic social teaching upholds the right to own property and even considers it an essential right, but it is never absolute. It must be seen in the context of the welfare of the community as a whole (*see* THEOLOGY; THOMAS AQUINAS). Those who own property are obliged to manage their ownership out of concern for others and, for example, with regard to the weakest and poorest in the world. Hoarding property when others are starving is not a right. LIBERATION THEOLOGY, with one of its bases in MARXISM, has challenged both the church's understating of and PRAXIS relative to property ownership.

Voluntary poverty is upheld as a religious ideal in imitation of Christ and his identification with the poor (Luke 9:58; Matt. 25:35). At the same time, not being burdened with the distraction of managing property, one can focus more clearly on one's service to the world.

As the church has grown, it has come to own a significant amount of property. Corporately, it has been, and in places remains, the single largest property owner in the society. Ownership of lands and other vast possessions (*see* PAPAL STATES) has frequently been cited as the cause of corruption not only of church officials but also of entire ecclesiastical structures. The issue typically arises when church holdings are more than sufficient to provide facilities for worship, dispensing charitable goods and services, and supporting ministers. Criticism has been directed particularly at the accumulation of valuable works of art, as in the Vatican Museums, and elaborately adorned buildings.

CANON LAW defines the rules for the church's ownership of property. Much of it is officially owned by particular church office holders such as diocesan BISHOPS, who act as corporations sole, and must be passed to their successors in that office. However, property owned by a DIOCESE is administered collectively; its use, maintenance, and disposal is governed not just by the stated owner but in many cases by trustees, religious orders, financial experts, and other interested parties. Any decisions must be made with due reference to the long-term goals to which the church is dedicated. In the modern world, in which separation of CHURCH AND STATE has become a reality, ownership of church property has been subject to many of the provisions of modern corporate law.

Further reading: Leonardo Boff *Liberation Theology: From Confrontation to Dialogue* (San Francisco: Harper & Row, 1986); William J. Byron, *Toward Stewardship: An Interim Ethic of Poverty, Power and Pollution* (New York: Paulist Press, 1975); Patrick Joseph Dignan, *A History of the Legal Incorporation of Catholic Church Property in the United States, 1784–1932* (New York: P. J. Kennedy & Sons, 1935); Martin Hengel, *Property and Riches in the Early Church: Aspects of a Social History of Early Christianity* (Philadelphia: Fortress, 1974); James V. Schall, *Religion, Wealth and Poverty* (Vancouver: Fraser Institute, 1990).

Protestant Reformation

Of the many traumas endured by the Catholic Church, only the GREAT SCHISM that divided it from EASTERN ORTHODOXY can compare with the Protestant Reformation of the 16th century for its continentwide impact. Most of northern and western Europe (Upper GERMANY, SCANDINAVIA, the Netherlands, GREAT BRITAIN, etc.) were severed from the church, and the great power that

soon arose in NORTH AMERICA was dominated by non-Catholics from the start. All around the world Catholic and Protestant forces have been and often remain in competition for the hearts of the public.

ORIGINS

The Protestant Reformation emerged in an environment of self-criticism on the part of the Catholic Church, in which several reform movements had already appeared, and a variety of changes were under active consideration (*see* COUNTER-REFORMATION). The Protestants, however, demanded changes that were much more extreme; their ultimate success can be explained by their alliance with political leaders pursuing their own temporal interests.

The spark that set off the Reformation was a noisy campaign to sell INDULGENCES in Germany, carried out under the leadership of DOMINICAN preacher JOHANN TETZEL (c. 1465–1519). Tetzel sent the money he raised to Rome to cover bills for the construction of ST. PETER'S BASILICA. Martin Luther (1483–1546), a professor of THEOLOGY at the University of Wittenburg, challenged the practice of selling indulgences and called for a debate on a set of related issues (theses), when he nailed his 95 Theses to the cathedral door at Wittenburg on October 31, 1517. Discussions with theologian JOHANN ECK (1486–1543) and others over the next few years pushed Luther to more extreme positions, such as when he elevated the authority of the BIBLE over that of popes and even church COUNCILS, thus claiming that councils too can err.

Pope Leo X (r. 1513–21) condemned 41 of Luthers *95 Theses* in the bull *Ex surge Domine* (June 15, 1520). But he was protected from the worst consequences by Frederick III, the elector of Saxony (1463–1525), who wanted not only to defend his relatively new university at Wittenburg, but, like several other German princes, also wanted to prevent large sums of money flowing out of his dominions to Rome. In 1521 Luther wrote three famous treatises in which he argued for the priesthood of all believers, developed his understanding that there are only two SACRAMENTS (BAPTISM and the EUCHARIST), and called for the Eucharist to be given to the laity in both kinds (bread and wine). As the writings circulated through the Holy Roman Empire, Luther was summoned to the imperial Diet of Worms (1521), near Frankfurt, where tradition has him proclaiming: "Here I stand. I cannot do otherwise," before Emperor CHARLES V, who presided, and, Johann Eck, the papal legate.

Luther defended his position by appealing to the Bible and reason but in the end was condemned. He was protected by electors and princes in northern Germany, many of whom he won to his cause. The Protestant Reformation was underway.

Luther found immediate support in German-speaking Switzerland when the priest of the cathedral church at Zurich, Ulrich Zwingli (1484–1531), began to sermonize in favor of reform. In 1523 he issued his own set of debating points, the 67 Theses. Following a public debate, the city council supported Zwingli and gave him authority to pursue his reforms, including the abolition of priestly CELIBACY. Zwingli removed all statues from the cathedral and attempted to strip church life of anything not having the direct support of Scripture. From Zurich, the Reformation in a Zwinglian mode spread to Basel and Berne and found some initial support throughout the French-speaking cantons. Luther objected to the smashing of statues and stained glass.

Through the early 1520s, the movement launched by Luther would seem to have been containable. It was largely a German movement, and its two most prominent leaders, Luther and Zwingli, were divided over their approach to reform. However, Catholic authorities were distracted by what seemed to be a more imminent threat. For a generation, Turkish forces had been pushing northward up the Danube. Luther's appearance at Worms was seen as far less important than the fall of Belgrade that same year. In 1526, the Hungarian army was defeated and the

cities of Buda and Pest fell soon afterwards. By 1529, Suleyman the Magnificent (r. 1520–66) was laying siege to Vienna. If the city had fallen the whole of central Europe could have been under attack. While pushed back from Vienna, the Ottoman army would remain a threat for the next century.

With Catholic forces distracted, in 1529 Luther and Zwingli met in an attempt to reconcile their differences and unite the Reformation cause. The so-called Marburg Colloquy found the two men in agreement on most points but unable to agree on the crucial issue of the sacraments. Luther had begun from a basic stance of stripping the church of anything that was opposed by the Bible (as he interpreted it). He retained the idea of the real presence of CHRIST in the sacraments, though he had discarded the idea of transubstantiation (which he saw as magical) and proposed in its stead the idea of consubstantiation. Rather than the substance of the bread and wine of the Eucharist being changed into the substance of the body and blood of Christ, Luther suggested that Christ's substance coexisted with the substances of bread and wine.

Zwingli began his reform from a very different position, arguing that everything should be stripped from the church that was not actually supported by Scripture. He found no scriptural basis for the idea of the real presence. He understood the Eucharist to be merely an ordinance to be followed because it was commanded, its significance being that it was a figurative memorial of Christ's Last Supper with his disciples (1 Cor. 11:24). It had no sacramental meaning. The inability to reach an agreement at Marburg meant that the reforms in Germany and Switzerland would go their separate ways.

The 1530s set the basic shape of the Protestant movement on the European continent. In 1530 Luther and Philip Melancthon (1497–1560) presented Catholic representatives with the Augsburg Confession, in an attempt to work out their differences. It was written so as to emphasize the points in common between the two sides. Even so, the Catholic representatives found the confession unacceptable. It would become the defining statement of Lutheranism that also marked it off from the Reformed Church in Switzerland.

In 1531, Zwingli was killed in Catholic-Protestant fighting in Switzerland. In the vacuum created by his death the center of the Swiss Reformation shifted to Geneva and John Calvin (1509–64). An early reformer, Calvin had to flee Paris in 1533 to Basel, where he would write the first version of the first systematic Protestant theology, the *Institutes of the Christian Religion* (1536). He moved to Geneva later that year and in 1541 became established as the city's ecclesiastical authority.

Calvin had worked out what might have become an acceptable reconciliation between the Lutheran and Zwinglian position on the Eucharist. He suggested that Christ was truly present in the sacraments (thus retaining the sacramental quality of baptism and the Eucharist), but in a spiritual rather than a substantial way. In deference to Zurich he added that Christ was perceivable only to the eye of FAITH. However, by the time he proposed this approach the Swiss and German camps were beyond reconciliation. Calvin's ideas would come to dominate among the western Swiss cantons and among French-speaking Protestants in Strasbourg and throughout France.

With the establishment of Calvin in Geneva, Protestantism was divided into two major camps, the Lutheran and Reformed (Swiss). However, a third group now arose to claim its space within the emerging Protestant realm. As Zwingli carried his reforms forward, there arose in Zurich a group of believers who saw the implications of his sacramental reforms and their challenge to the secular order. They suggested that the church should separate entirely from the state; instead of a church of all citizens, they proposed a church of those who professed faith. They challenged the idea of infant baptism (for which they could find no biblical support) and thought that adults who professed

the new faith should be rebaptized (hence their early name, Anabaptists, or rebaptizers).

The idea of a believers church, united by its profession of faith, sharing the ordinances (baptism and the Lord's Supper), and committed to a disciplined Christian life found little favor within the Catholic, Lutheran, or Reformed Churches. In 1524 Luther authorized the German princes to suppress the "New David," Thomas Münster (1489–1525) in the Peasants' War. Zwingli had driven Anabaptists from Zurich, burning many martyrs in caves. Others adopted MILLENARIANISM and preached the imminent return of Christ. Some of the most radical millenarian Anabaptist zealots took control of Münster, a town in Westphalia, Germany, and turned it into a utopian communal society under the leadership of lay preacher Melchior Hoffman (1495–1543), who believed the city would become the New Jerusalem when Christ returned. After a lengthy siege, the city was captured and the leaders executed.

After the disaster at Münster, the Anabaptists were vilified by association. Their cause was saved by the emergence of new leaders in Menno Simons (1492–1561) and Jakob Amman (c. 1644–c. 1730). A former priest in Holland, Simons articulated his vision of a life in the Schleithein Confession (1527) centered on discipleship and nonresistance to evil. Simons was able to find havens in Germany and Denmark to grow the pacifistic movement. Later Amman would lead a reform of the Anabaptists. Both the Mennonites and Amish would escape persecution in Europe to find refuge and success in North America.

PROTESTANT DISTINCTIVENESS

Luther saw the sale of indulgences as a symptom of what he called works righteousness whereby believers tried to earn salvation by doing trivial good works rather than relying on the grace of God. In the polemics that followed, each side made less-than-accurate accusations about the other. However, there was no escaping that Protestants had replaced much of the basic outline of

Catholic theology and reformed the basic practices of Christian life.

Catholic theology had developed a sacramental vision of the Christian life that carried an individual believer from birth to DEATH. Ideally, a person was baptized into the church as a baby, nurtured in the faith, and confirmed as an adult Christian when he or she moved beyond childhood. As adults, Christians were offered a system to guide them to a Christian life, assisted by communion with Christ in the Eucharist. In their earthly lives, the church offered many opportunities to redress the problem of sin through pilgrimages, the veneration of MARY and the saints, and other forms of spiritual devotion. At the end of this life, a final sacrament prepared one to go to heaven and attain the BEATIFIC VISION.

Protestants felt that many of the features of medieval church life had been corruptions adopted from postbiblical extra-Christian sources. They refocused the attention of the believer on the event of faith in Christ and the justifying and sanctifying power of that event. The great affirmation of the Protestants was that salvation is by faith alone and is not affected by any good works. The faithful should live a life of gratitude for Christ's work.

Protestants found authority for their affirmations in the Bible, the plain message of which, they believed, was accessible to the average Christian, without any allegorical embellishment (see ALLEGORY). No pope or church council was needed to interpret it. However, the fact that so much in the Bible is open to a variety of interpretations would lead later to the splitting of the Protestant movement into many sects.

While Lutherans kept an emphasis on LITURGY and both Lutherans and Anglicans continued to affirm the real presence in the sacraments, as a whole Protestants downplayed the sacraments in favor of the proclamation of the Gospel message. In fact, they all eliminated five of the traditional seven sacraments. Protestants continued to marry and ordain people, they just did not consider marriage or ordination, however solemn, as sacraments.

For John Calvin, the emphasis on the free gift of God in granting salvation to sinners led him to deny any human initiative even in the beginnings of the act of faith. He came to affirm God's absolute sovereignty and predestination as a key element in his theology. At the end of the 16th century, predestination would become a major bone of contention within those churches with Calvinist roots. Dutch Calvinists would turn Calvin's theology into a rigid set of doctrines at the Synod of Dort (1618–19). A form of Reformed faith that affirmed FREE WILL would be articulated by Dutch theologian Jacob Arminius (1560–1609) and transmitted to the free-will Baptists and Methodists, who rejected harsh predestinationism. Another form of Calvinism would be carried to North America by the Puritans.

ENGLAND

As the Reformation moved forward on the Continent, England remained under the rule of a devout Catholic. Soon after Luther appeared on the scene, HENRY VIII (1491–1547) wrote a book attacking him, for which LEO X (r. 1513–21) named him a "Defender of the Faith." Earlier he had married Catherine of Aragon (1485–1536), the daughter of FERDINAND OF ARAGON AND ISABELLA I OF CASTILE, the Catholic rulers of SPAIN, and the widow of his heirless brother Henry VII (1457–1509).

The rise of the Church of England was both similar to and different than the Lutheran and Reformed trajectories. First it arose out of the attempt of Henry VIII to obtain an annulment from Catherine of Aragon on the grounds that she had been the wife of his deceased brother. When that failed he married Anne Boleyn (1507–36), who gave birth to the future Elizabeth I (1533–1603). In the Act of Supremacy (1534) Henry declared himself head of the English church, though he sought to keep the Catholic liturgy intact. Sts. JOHN FISHER and THOMAS MORE refused to sign the act and thereby incurred their executions. Henry then set about the divestment of the MONASTERIES of their holdings and approved the destruction of RELICS, including those of St. THOMAS À BECKET at Canterbury Cathedral.

When Edward VI (1537–53), Henry's legitimate son by Jane Seymour (1509–37), succeeded to the throne, Thomas Cranmer (1489–1556) introduced the English liturgy and took the Church of England in the direction of Calvin's Geneva reform in the first Book of Common Prayer (1549). Cranmer learned much from former Dominican Martin Bucer of Strassburg (1491–1551), who taught at Cambridge University from 1549 to 1551. When Catholic Mary I Tudor (1553–58), daughter of Henry and Catherine, succeeded to the throne, these Protestant advances on the public level were reversed with the assistance of the Oratorian cardinal Reginald Pole (1500–58), one of the champions of the Catholic COUNTER-REFORMATION. Protestant currents remained strong, however.

When she succeeded to the throne, her half-sister, Elizabeth I (1533–1603), sought a middle course between the Reformed Protestantism of Cranmer and the Catholic side of her father. This became known as the Elizabethan Settlement (1559) and became embodied in the Thirty-Nine Articles of 1571. Richard Hooker (c. 1554–1600) was the great champion of the Elizabethan Settlement in his *Law of Ecclesiastical Polity* (1593–1648), which argued against the Puritans for the primacy of natural reason prior to the civil and ecclesiastical polities and to which even scripture and its interpretation is subject. Hooker's theology shaped the future course of the Church of England. Today the Elizabethan compromise can be recognized in the Anglican formula 2 + 5 understanding of the sacraments: 2 = baptism, Eucharist, in deference to the Continental reformers; 5 = penance (RECONCILIATION), CONFIRMATION, MARRIAGE, Extreme Unction (ANOINTING OF THE SICK), and HOLY ORDERS, in unison with the Roman church.

Elizabeth renewed the Act of Supremacy in 1559 and required the Oath of Supremacy recognizing her as spiritual head of the Church of England of all public servants, but many high office holders remained Catholic. Some recusant Catholics went into hiding; others, like the Jesuit martyr St. Edmund Campion (1540–81), who maintained his loyalty to the queen as a Catholic, met their deaths; still others fled to Belgium, where they took refuge at Douai and Louvain and began training priests to sneak back into England. The Archbishop of Canterbury retained the title of primate of England, but today the bishops share power with priests and laity in the General Synod. The Anglican Church's attempt to mediate differences is reflected in the liturgical division between Low Church, which looks like evangelical Protestantism, and High Church, which sometimes can hardly be distinguished from Roman Catholicism.

The basic structures of the present did not take final shape until the organizational consolidation of Archbishop William Laud (1573–1645), who rejected Calvinist predestinationism. In 1622 Laud argued against John Percy (1569–1641, known as "Fisher the Jesuit," that the Church of England and the Roman Catholic Church were parts of the same church.

1700 TO THE PRESENT

All the modern Protestant groups can trace their history to the four churches (Lutheran, Reformed, Anabaptist, and Anglican) established in the 16th century. Particularly important in the diffusion of Protestantism was the maturing Puritan movement in the British Isles in the 17th century. Puritans disagreed over how the church should be organized, giving rise to both Presbyterians and Congregationalists. Baptists emerged arguing for a congregationally based organization, but one separated from any ties to the state. A more radical form of Puritanism appeared as the Society of Friends (the Quakers).

In the 18th century, a revitalization movement appeared in England known as Methodism. It was aligned with the Pietist movement within the

Lutheran church and centered around the small Moravian church in Germany. In the 1730s, the Moravians launched a global missionary movement that was copied by Methodists and Baptists later in the century, and by all of the Protestant churches in the 19th century. Like Roman Catholicism, Protestantism became a worldwide movement. Methodism enjoyed its greatest expansion in North America, where it gave rise to the Holiness Movement (19th century) and Pentecostalism (20th century).

Protestant-Catholic hostility followed the missions to many countries. Catholic anti-Protestantism would be countered by Protestant ANTI-CATHOLICISM. Meaningful attempts to move beyond centuries of hate came only after the World Council of Churches was formed in 1948 and JOHN XXIII was named to the Holy See (*see* ECUMENISM). In his very first encyclical *Aeterni Petri Cathedram* 63 (June 29, 1959), John addressed Protestants as separated brethren, an important step toward recognizing Protestants as legitimate partners in a future dialogue. He then created a Vatican Secretariat of Christian Unity (1960), and Catholics sent official observers to the World Council of Churches in 1968. VATICAN COUNCIL II declared that Protestants were already united with Catholics, sharing one baptism and a common faith in Jesus Christ. Protestant observers were invited to VATICAN COUNCIL II and had input to the proceedings on an indirect basis. Since the 1960s, significant efforts have been made by both Catholics and Protestants to understand each other as brothers and sisters in Christ. More recently the Vatican, however, has retrenched somewhat from the ecumenical openness of Vatican II.

Further reading: Owen Chadwick, *The Reformation* (Harmondsworth: Penguin, 1991); Vergilius Ferm, *Pictorial History of Protestantism* (New York: Philosophical Library, 1957); Harold J. Grimm, *The Reformation Era* (New York: Macmillan, 1954); Hans J. Hillerbrand, ed. *The Oxford Encyclopedia of the Reformation*, 4 vols. (New York: Oxford University Press, 1996); J. Gordon Melton,

Encyclopedia of Protestantism (New York: Facts On File, 2005); Diarmaid MacCulloch, *The Reformation* (New York: Viking, 2003); Wilhelm Pauck, *The Heritage of the Reformation* (Oxford: Oxford University Press, 1961).

psalter (Gk.: *psalmos,* "song" [sung to a harp])

The word *psalter* refers to the biblical Book of Psalms used in the worship of the church. The Eastern Church uses the Greek version of the Septuagint, and the West first used the Old Latin version, then the Vulgate of St. JEROME, and now a new Latin version (1971) that combines fidelity to the Hebrew with some of the felicities of the Vulgate. The breviaries, or prayer books, that contain the PRAYER OF THE HOURS are composed largely of psalms. Beginning in the MIDDLE AGES, MONKS produced psalters and breviaries with elaborate illuminations, as in the *Très Riches Heures of Jean Duc de Berry* (1398–1417).

Further reading: F. O. Büttner, *The Illuminated Psalter* (Turnhout: Brepols, 2004).

pseudepigrapha (Gk.: "written under a false [name]")

In the ancient world, it was common for authors to ascribe their books to famous or ancient persons. Some authors may have been trying to deceive their readers, but others may simply have used the ascription as a grateful acknowledgment to the person who inspired them and whose views they believed to be reflected in their own text. At other times it was a way of simply acknowledging a tradition with which the author identified. Many such pseudepigraphal books circulated among Jews and early Christians, and some even found their way into the BIBLE, such as the epistles to Timothy and Titus in the New Testament, which were most likely not written by PAUL but by an anonymous second-century writer. Modern biblical scholarship has called into question the traditional authorship of a variety of biblical books.

Among the most notable of pseudepigraphal writings are the Book of Enoch, an apocalyptic text recounting Enoch's visionary journeys, the Assumption of Moses, the Apocalypse of Baruch, and the life of ADAM AND EVE. Christian pseudepigrapha of the second and third centuries, written as the CANON OF SCRIPTURE was being set include the very popular *DIDACHE, or Teachings of the Twelve Apostles*, and a number of GOSPELS (lives of Jesus) deemed not apostolic though authorship was assigned to one of the APOSTLES (Gospel of Philip, Gospel of Thomas).

Once excluded from both the Hebrew canon and the Christian New Testament, most pseudepigraphical books were soon forgotten. In the modern world, many of these texts have been rediscovered. They are considered vital documents in understanding the times in which they were written. A variety of modern scholarly collections have been published. Popular editions have also appeared, sometimes presented as secret material allegedly suppressed by the church for various sinister reasons. A number of modern pseudepigraphal books have appeared, such as the *Aquarian Gospel of Jesus Christ* and the *Confessions of Pontius Pilate.*

Further reading: R. H. Charles, *The Apocrypha and Pseudepigrapha of the Old Testament in English* (Oxford: Clarendon, 1913); Edgar Goodspeed, *Famous Biblical Hoaxes or Modern Apocrypha* (Grand Rapids, Mich.: Baker, 1956); Marinus de Jonge, *Pseudepigrapha of the Old Testament as Part of Christian Literature: The Case of the Testaments of the Twelve Patriarchs and the Greek Life of Adam and Eve* (Leiden: Brill, 2003); *The Lost Books of the Bible and the Forgotten Books of Eden* (Nashville: World, 1926); Kurt Niederwimmer and Harold W. Attridge, *The Didache: A Commentary* (Minneapolis: Fortress, 1998).

purgatory (Lat.: *purgare,* "to purge, cleanse")
Purgatory is the state or place where the SOUL after DEATH undergoes further purgation, or cleansing, often imagined as by fire, to rid itself of lesser or venial sins so that it may experience the complete joy of the BEATIFIC VISION OF GOD. It is an intermediate state between HEAVEN AND HELL. Today theologians encompass the teaching on purgatory within the broader framework of the teaching on ESCHATOLOGY.

The idea of purgatory is a late development in western Catholic THEOLOGY, but there were anticipations in late Judaism and early Christianity. The Book of 2 Maccabees 12:40–45 tells that a SIN offering can make atonement for the sins of the dead. (This text is one of the reasons why Protestants later sought to exclude the Apocrypha, among which 2 Maccabees numbers, from the CANON OF SCRIPTURE.) Inscriptions in the walls of CATACOMBS show that prayer for the dead was a common practice by the end of the second century, which is also attested to by TERTULLIAN and St. CYPRIAN OF CARTHAGE. St. AUGUSTINE OF HIPPO confirms the same type of prayers and also speaks of a purifying fire (*City of God* 21.26). St. GREGORY I THE GREAT talks about purgatorial fire removing "light sins" and condones the offering of the EUCHARIST for the deliverance of the soul of one who has passed (*Dialogues* 4.41, 57). St. THOMAS AQUINAS gave the classic theological expression to the doctrine in his *Commentary on the Sentences* (4.21.1) and DANTE ALIGHIERI provided the poetic parallel in the *Purgatorio* of his *Comedia Divina.*

The doctrine of purgatory was also reinforced by the parallel development of the FEAST OF ALL SOULS and masses for the dead. The ecumenical councils (*see* COUNCILS, ECUMENICAL) of Lyons (1274) and FLORENCE (1439) gave the teaching official sanction, but the Eastern Church remained wary of it. The doctrine was denied by the CATHARS and the WALDENSIANS. When it was tied into the preaching of INDULGENCES by the likes of JOHANN TETZEL, purgatory came under broad attack during the PROTESTANT REFORMATION. The Council of TRENT affirmed Lyons and Florence but was very reserved and confined itself to statements about purification after death and prayers for the dead. Purgatory became the subject of voluminous polemics between Catholics and Protestants. Modern Catholic theologians leave many questions about purgatory open. Sts. ROBERT BELLARMINE and ALPHONSUS LIGUORI thought that souls in purgatory could also pray for the living.

Further reading: Catherine of Genoa, *Purgation and Purgatory and The Spiritual Dialogue* (New York: Paulist, 1979); John A. Nageleisen, *Charity for the Suffering Souls: An Explanation of the Catholic Doctrine of Purgatory* (Rockford, Ill.: Tan, 1982); Robert Ombres, *Theology of Purgatory* (Butler: Clergy Book Service, 1978).

Qumran

Qumran is a site above the northwest shore of the Dead Sea, about eight miles south of Jericho, last inhabited in ancient Judean times. There are many caves in the cliffs nearby. In 1948, a young Bedouin discovered several ancient but well-preserved scrolls in one of these caves. In the following years, 11 of the scrolls found their way to Hebrew University and to the American School of Oriental Research, both in Jerusalem. As word spread through the scholarly community, the Dead Sea Scrolls were hailed for what light they might throw on the ancient Jewish world and possibly on the origins of Christianity. Additional scrolls were soon found in other near-by caves, along with numerous artifacts that belonged to the ancient inhabitants of the area.

The rich collection of ancient writings from the caves included texts from the Hebrew BIBLE, Jewish writings known as PSEUDEPIGRAPHA (falsely attributed to various prominent ancient personages), devotional materials, and texts believed to be associated with a Jewish sectarian group that lived at Qumran. Early researchers identified the Qumran community with the Essenes, a Jewish group known from descriptive paragraphs in the writings of Josephus (c. 37–c. 100), a Jewish historian. The Qumranites saw themselves as an eschatological community awaiting the return of the Messiah.

The texts from Qumran have become important items in contemporary religious research. The biblical texts, such as the great scroll of Isaiah, predate the oldest previously known Hebrew texts by more than a millennium. They became vivid demonstrations of the care and accuracy taken in copying and transmitting the Bible, as no significant adjustments to the text had to be made as a result of the Qumran discoveries. The scrolls as a body have yielded numerous new insights into ancient Jewish life, especially the century prior to the rise of Christianity. Early optimistic speculations that the Qumran community might have been a direct predecessor to the Jesus movement and CHRISTIAN church have not materialized, though the documents do expand our knowledge of language and concepts available to the first generation of Christian writers. In the end, the scrolls yield much more information on ancient Judaism than on first-generation Christianity.

Further reading: Robert H. Eisenman, *The Dead Sea Scrolls and the First Christians: Essays and Translations* (Rockport, Mass.: Element, 1996); David Flusser, *The Spiritual History of the Dead Sea Sect* (Tel-Aviv: MOD, 1989); Norman Golb, *Who Wrote the Dead Scrolls? The Search for the Secret of Qumran* (New York: Touchstone, 1995); Geza Vermes, *The Dead Sea Scrolls in English*, 4th ed. (London: Penguin, 1995).

R

Rahner, Karl (1904–1984) *foremost 20th-century Catholic theologian*

Karl Rahner was born in Freiburg, GERMANY. He became a JESUIT and taught at the University of Innsbruck, which was closed by the Nazis in 1936. As the theological expert during VATICAN COUNCIL II he was instrumental in creating the field of FUNDAMENTAL THEOLOGY and played an important role in guiding the Catholic Church into the 21st century.

Rahner's voluminous writings are being gathered in the multivolume *Theological Investigations*. He wrote on the full range of Catholic theological concerns, including the MAGISTERIUM, GRACE, systematic THEOLOGY, and the TRINITY. He focused on theological anthropology, the self-communication of GOD in CREATION and history, and the self and culture. Although God's self-communication to humanity in revelation is an absolutely free offer (grace), it nonetheless reveals humanity's "supernatural existential," or call to and capacity for transcendence.

Grace does not destroy or supplant nature but fulfills it (*Foundations of Christian Faith* 129). Following DUNS SCOTUS, Rahner believed that CHRIST would have become incarnate even if there had been no original SIN because he fulfills the evolutionary development of creation. Rahner invented the term *implicit*, or *anonymous, Christianity*, which describes the act of turning one's heart toward the needs and concerns of the world, regardless of one's religious leanings, such that even an atheist is not excluded from salvation. He reinvigorated the theology of the Trinity as a living part of the religious life, revealing it as God in community.

Toward the end of his life Rahner wrote *Foundations of Christian Faith*, the most systematic of his writings, originally published as independent essays. He wrote in a lucid style, accessible to educated laypeople. Rahner was strongly influenced by St. THOMAS AQUINAS but read him in light of contemporary philosophical discourse, in particular the Enlightenment philosopher Immanuel Kant (1724–1804) and the existential phenomenologist Martin Heidegger (1889–1976). There are many Web sites dedicated to Rahner.

Further reading: John B. Ackley, *The Church of the Word: A Comparative Study of Word, Church, and Office in the Thought of Karl Rahner and Gerhard Ebeling* (New York: P. Lang, 1993); Leo D. Lefebure, *Toward a Contemporary Wisdom Christology: A Study of Karl Rahner and Norman Pittenger* (Lanham, Md.: University Press of America, 1988); Declan Marmion and Mary E. Hines, eds., *The Cambridge Companion to Karl Rahner* (Cambridge: Cambridge University Press, 2005); Bruce Marshall, *Christology in Conflict: The Identity of a Saviour in Rahner and Barth* (Oxford: B. Blackwell, 1987); Louis Roberts, *The Achievement of Karl Rahner* (New York: Herder & Herder, 1967).

Raphael (1483–1520) *Renaissance painter*

Raffaello Sanzi or Santi, better known as Raphael, is among the best-known artists of the Italian High Renaissance, famous for the religious themes that ran through his work. Several of his works were created for the Vatican. His impact on popular Catholic art continues to the present.

Raphael was born in Urbino, ITALY, the son of a painter. As a youth he showed remarkable talent. Around 1495 he was apprenticed in Perugia and gained the immediate attention of the artistic community. In 1501 he received his first notable commission, to paint the *Coronation of the Virgin* for the Church of San Francesco in Perugia. By 1504 he had moved to Florence, already the home of LEONARDO DA VINCI and MICHELANGELO. Here he would become known for his many paintings of the Virgin Mary.

Raphael's career climaxed in Rome. He was called there in 1508 by Pope Julius II (r. 1503–13) and remained there for the rest of his career. The first six years were spent creating a set of frescos in the Stanze, the Vatican papal apartments, around the theme of the historical JUSTIFICATION of the Catholic Church. Among the most heralded of his works are the *Disputà*, a heavenly vision of GOD in assembly with prophets, APOSTLES, and representatives of Christianity through the centuries, and the *School of Athens*, which depicts Christian thinkers in continuity with ancient Platonists. In the background of this latter work is a first representation of ST. PETER'S BASILICA, then also under construction.

Julius's successor, Leo X (r. 1513–21), commissioned a set of 10 tapestries known as the "Acts of the Apostles" for the Sistine Chapel to complement Michelangelo's ceiling. They were hung in 1519. They are still in the Vatican. In 1514, Leo X asked Raphael to help Donato Bramante (1444–1514), one of the architects of St. Peters. Bramante died later that year, and Raphael succeeded him as head of the overall effort.

Raphael just reached his 37th birthday, April 6, 1520, when he died. The funeral of this young man who had accomplished so much in his brief life was held at the Vatican. He was subsequently buried in the Pantheon in Rome.

Further reading: J. J. G. Alexander, *Italian Renaissance Illuminations* (New York: Braziller, 1977); Marcia Hall, ed., *Raphael's "School of Athens"* (Cambridge: Cambridge University Press, 1997); George L. Hersey, *High Renaissance Art in St. Peter's and the Vatican: An Interpretive Guide* (Chicago: University of Chicago Press, 1993); Loren Partridge, *The Art of Renaissance Rome, 1400–1600* (New York: Abrams, 1996).

Raphael, Archangel, St.

Raphael makes his initial appearance in human guise as Azarias in the apocryphal Book of Tobit (*see* BIBLE). He accompanies the younger Tobias to Media and helps the aged Tobit regain his sight. He reveals his true identity as "one of the seven, who stand before the Lord." He, along with Gabriel and MICHAEL, are the only three angels mentioned in Scripture by name.

From this initial appearance Raphael is identified as a healer (as implied by his name, Heb. "God has healed". Some saw him as the angel who moved the waters of the healing pool at Bethesda (John 5). Later church tradition named him the patron of the blind, nurses, and physicians. His feast day is October 24.

Further reading: L. H. Brockington, *A Critical Introduction to the Apocrypha* (London: Duckworth, 1961); Angela Carol, *St. Raphael* (Rockford, Ill.: Tan, 1999).

real presence   *See* EUCHARIST.

recapitulation (Gk.: *apokatastasis*)

Recapitulation, or summing up, is a concept in the early THEOLOGY of REDEMPTION. It holds that salvation was accomplished by the act of GOD through CHRIST, who recapitulated all divine revelation up to the moment of his INCARNATION (Matt. 17:11–12; Acts 3:20–21).

This idea is generally ascribed to IRENAEUS (c. 130–c. 200), the BISHOP of Lyons, FRANCE. Irenaeus developed his idea from a variety of biblical sources, including PAUL's metaphor of Christ as the second Adam (1 Cor. 15:22). For him, Christ's life repeats human history. Christ is all that Adam was, but he does correctly what Adam and his descendents had done wrongly. Thus, Christ became the head of humanity. In Christ all creation is renewed to God. Recapitulation is founded on the principle that the Last Things will be like the First Things restored.

While an important early attempt to understand the nature of redemption, recapitulation was later generally neglected. This theology has been regenerated by the Swedish theologian Gustav Wingren and is now a part of ECOTHEOLOGY.

Further reading: Robert M. Grant, ed., *Irenaeus of Lyons* (New York: Routledge, 1997); J. N. D. Kelly, *Early Christian Doctrines* (London: Adam & Charles Black, 1965); Eric Osborn, *Irenaeus of Lyon* (Cambridge: Cambridge University Press, 2001). Gustav Wingren, *Creation and Gospel* (New York, N.Y.: Edwin Mellen, 1979).

Reconciliation, Sacrament of

The Sacrament of Reconciliation used to be known popularly as confession, and formally as PENANCE, a term still used. It is one of the seven sacraments ritually administered under the leadership of BISHOPS and PRIESTS for reconciling sinners to GOD and to the church. Catholics have appealed to three biblical passages—Matthew 16:16; 18:18,

and John 20:33—as foundation texts for the rite of reconciliation, but biblical scholars of all persuasions no longer find these texts proofs for the institution of the rite.

The New Testament is very clear about the need to confess one's SINS (Luke 5:8); the PARABLE of the Prodigal Son makes confession its central theme (Luke 15:11–32; *see also* James 5:16). However, no formal rite had yet been instituted, as early CHRISTIANS expected the *parousia,* or imminent return of CHRIST (1 Thess. 4:15) and believed that all their sins had been removed through the rite of BAPTISM (which was preceded by a renunciation of sin). There were no clear provisions for those who lapsed or fell away from the narrow path. By the middle of the second century, however, some sort of rite of Reconciliation for a renewed repentance seems to have developed, as attested to in the *Shepherd of Hermas* (*Visions* 2.2.4–5; *Mandates* 4.4.4).

TERTULLIAN refers to a public ritual of Reconciliation at the feet of the presbyters, or priests (*On Repentance* 8). The penitential period for serious sins—apostasy, murder, adultery—often lasted three years or more before one could be reconciled to the communion of believers. A public ceremony later became the common practice in the Roman Rite. Celtic MONASTERIES, by contrast, fostered private and frequent confessions of wrongs and commitments to reform held between MONKS and their abbots and NUNS and their ABBESSES. Irish missionaries to Europe brought this practice with them. In the Eastern Church penance always was bound up with a broader tradition of mysticism and spiritual direction; this remains the case today.

In the MIDDLE AGES the FRANCISCAN Alexander of Hales (1186–1245) popularized what would become the standard THEOLOGY of penance, comprised of contrition, confession, absolution by a priest, and satisfaction, or "doing penance" in the ordinary sense (*Summa Universae Theologiae* Q.19). Canon 25 of Lateran Council IV (1215; *see* COUNCILS, ECUMENICAL) prescribed that all Christians must confess their sins at least once a year.

This led to frequent confession and confessors' handbooks. Franciscans and DOMINICANS became noted as confessors and still are. The leaders of the PROTESTANT REFORMATION denied that penance as a sacrament had been instituted by Christ and saw the penances as so many self-justifying "good works." In response the Council of TRENT affirmed penance as a sacrament yet, in deference to Protestant criticism, also affirmed the complete gratuity of God's grace in Christ.

VATICAN COUNCIL II in *Sacrosanctum Concilium*, the Constitution on the Sacred Liturgy, stated that the new LITURGY for the renamed rite of Reconciliation should explain the sacrament clearly. It must also stress the role of the whole church community with whom a person is to be reconciled, reinstate reconciliation as a public rite as in the early church, and be brief. Texts from the BIBLE were also to be given a prominent place. Today several questions surrounding the sacrament are being discussed: frequency, public absolution in a communal rite, the age for a first confession, and the necessity to confess privately to a priest.

Further reading: James Dallen, *The Reconciling Community: The Rite of Penance* (New York: Pueblo, 1986); R. J. Kennedy, *Reconciliation: The Continuing Agenda* (Collegeville, Minn.: Liturgical Press, 1987); *Rite of Penance* (Collegeville, Minn.: Liturgical Press, 1975).

recusants

Those who remained adherents of the Roman Catholic Church in GREAT BRITAIN in the years after the establishment of the Church of England were called recusants. For a number of years after HENRY VIII broke with the pope, the status of the church remained in debate, and many English people continued to be openly loyal to Rome. However, with the passing of the Act of Uniformity in 1559 early in the long reign of Queen Elizabeth I (r. 1558–1603), the status of Roman Catholics became extremely tenuous. Those who refused to attend Anglican services were subject

to fines. As it became obvious that pockets of Roman Catholic support remained, penalties were increased. Recusants could loose their land or be jailed. They were also denied burial in consecrated land.

The requirements for attending Anglican services remained in effect for more than two centuries but were finally rescinded in 1781. All the laws against Catholics were rescinded in 1829.

See also GREAT BRITAIN.

Further reading: John Bossy, *The English Catholic Community, 1570–1850* (London: Longman & Todd, 1975); Edward Norman, *Roman Catholicism in England* (Oxford: Oxford University Press, 1986); John Richard Roberts, *A Critical Anthology of English Recusant Devotional Prose, 1558–1603* (Pittsburgh: Duquesne University Press, 1966).

redemption (Lat.: *redimere,* "to buy back, ransom")

The term *redemption* overlaps with ATONEMENT, deliverance, and salvation (Lat. *salvere* "to heal"). Most religions of the world teach redemption from SIN, suffering, and DEATH or the cycle of rebirth. In Christianity redemption has two aspects: deliverance from the bondage of sin and restoration to communion with GOD. The implication is that the sinner has been sold into slavery to Satan; Jesus Christ's INCARNATION, death, and RESURRECTION "buys" the sinners back, or redeems them.

In the Song of Miriam (Exod. 15:13) God comes as the redeemer (*go'el*) who delivers Israel from bondage in EGYPT. Like Job (Job 19:25), the psalmist David often calls on God to come as his individual redeemer (Psalm 26:11) to save him from his present affliction. In the New Testament Jesus associates the "ransom of many" with the substitutionary sacrifice of the Suffering Servant in 2 Isaiah (Mark 10:45; Isaiah 53:5–6). Although redemption is associated with the blood of CHRIST only in Ephesians 1:7, this image became central to CHRISTIAN art beginning in the MIDDLE AGES.

Eastern Christian theologians have always seen redemption as a restoration of humanity and its subsumption into the divine life (*theosis*). From the Middle Ages on, Western theologians believed that redemption from original sin enabled the believer to cooperate with grace toward JUSTIFICATION and salvation, but the Protestant reformers denied this element of human cooperation.

Catholics have always upheld the universality of the redemption offered to humankind (1 John 2:2). The followers of John Calvin and Cornelius O. Jansen (*see* JANSENISM) maintained that Christ redeemed only the elect, a position condemned by Pope Innocent X (r. 1644–55) in the papal bull *Cum Occasione* (May 31, 1653).

Further reading: Esther D. Reed, "Redemption," in Gareth Jones, ed., *The Blackwell Companion to Modern Theology* (Oxford: Blackwell, 2004); *Bernard Lonergan, Bernard Lonergan: Three Lectures* (Montreal: Thomas More Institute, 1975).

reincarnation (Sans.: *samsara*; Gk.: *metempsychosis,* "transmigration of the soul to another body")

Reincarnation is the belief, integral to various religious traditions, that the human soul survives DEATH and eventually again incarnates in another human body. In the West, the idea first appeared among ancient Platonic writers. To Plato, the fact that people seemed to know many things before being taught suggested that education was largely a process of assisting the SOUL to remember or recollect what it already knew (Meno 81 c–d; Phaedo 72e).

Reincarnation is widely accepted in Hindu thought, where it is associated with belief in karma (Hindi, "deed with consequences"). Those born in favorable circumstance are the product of favorable karma in previous lives, and those in lowly circumstances may be reaping the consequences of bad karma. Ultimately, Hindus seek to remove the effects of all karma and escape the process of repeated reincarnation. Many Hindus also believe in transmigration, the belief that human souls may reincarnate in lesser animal forms.

A clear statement of reincarnation is found at the beginning of the *Bhagavad Gita,* a popular Hindu sacred text. A slightly different form of reincarnation belief has emerged in Buddhism, as Buddhists deny the existence of an individual substantial soul.

Through Plato, reincarnation entered Western thought, though the belief was later suppressed, as it stands in sharp contradiction to the Jewish and CHRISTIAN mainstreams. In his early writings, ORIGEN (185–c. 254), the first systematic Christian theologian, taught a doctrine of the preexistence of the soul (prior to its birth in a body), a necessary correlate of reincarnation, a belief later condemned by church councils. In his biblical works, Origen explicitly denounced belief in reincarnation. Constantinople II (553) condemned the doctrine of the preexistence of the soul.

Interest in reincarnation revived in the West in the 19th century, in part through the influence of ancient Platonic and Neoplatonic texts, but mostly as a result of encounters with the East. The Theosophical Society, established in 1875, proved an effective means of disseminating Eastern teachings to the West and reviving uniquely Western approaches to the idea. Western advocates of reincarnation tended to see humans on an upward course, in which good karma overcame bad karma.

Theosophists created and spread the modern myth that reincarnation had been widely accepted among Christians before it was suppressed by church fiat at the Council of Constantinople II in 553. There is no historical evidence for the claim, but it has been frequently repeated in books circulating in modern spiritualist and esoteric communities.

Reincarnation stands in stark contrast to CHRIST's affirmations of the goodness of the material world, the importance of one single human existence the unity of the soul, and the ultimate resurrection of the body. The rise of belief in reincarnation has also called attention to the variant definitions of the soul in Christian thought, and a lack of consensus about ESCHATOLOGY, or the Last Things. To counter the preaching of reincarnation by movements such as the New Age, the church has issued various statements opposing the idea, though this has not been a priority concern. The subject has also come to the fore in the various interfaith dialogues with Hindus and Buddhists.

Further reading: Mark Albrecht, *Reincarnation: A Christian Appraisal* (Downers Grove, Ill.: InterVarsity, 1982); Joseph Head, and S. L. Cranston, eds. *Reincarnation: An East-West Anthology* (New York: Julian, 1961); Geddes MacGregor, *Reincarnation in Christianity* (Wheaton, Md.: Quest, 1978); Ian Stevenson, *Twenty Cases Suggestive of Reincarnation* (Charlottesville: University Press of Virginia, 1974).

relics

Strictly speaking, relics are the material remains (usually bones) of deceased saints (those who have been canonized and beatified). In a wider sense, it now also refers to objects closely associated with the saints such as hair, nails, clothing, items they used in daily life, or objects associated with particularly important events in their lives.

Relics became important as the cult of martyr saints grew in the second and third centuries, a time of persecution in the Roman Empire (*see* HAGIOGRAPHY). In fact, it became a requirement that relics (bones) of martyrs be incorporated into church altars where the EUCHARIST was to be celebrated. It is still forbidden to celebrate a mass at an altar devoid of relics, which are sealed in a stone placed in the center of most altars.

The most prized relics in Christendom are those connected directly to Jesus and the events of his life, DEATH, and RESURRECTION. Such relics include the seamless garment he wore, pieces of the True CROSS on which he was crucified, the

crown of thorns he wore, the spear used to pierce his side, the cup from which he drank at the Last Supper (the HOLY GRAIL), and other objects related to the biblical story. Jesus' relics became especially important at the beginning of the fourth century after the church became tolerated under CONSTANTINE. The emperor's mother, Helena (d. 330), who converted to Christianity and toward the end of her life traveled to Palestine, explored Jerusalem and Bethlehem and reportedly found a number of sites and relics of Jesus, among them the True Cross. Helena brought many relics to CONSTANTINOPLE, from where many subsequently found their way to Rome, where they are now housed in the BASILICA of St. John Lateran.

Second only to Jesus' relics are those associated with the Virgin Mary and the 12 APOSTLES. Jesus was resurrected, and the Virgin Mother was translated to heaven, so no bodily remains are extant. However, the bodies of several of the apostles are claimed to have survived. Most notably, the skeletons of PETER and PAUL are believed to be in Rome and that of the apostle James at Santiago de Compostela in northwestern SPAIN.

Beginning at the end of the 11th century, interest in relics grew immensely as crusaders returned with a variety of claimed relics (for example, the blood of Jesus and milk from the Virgin Mary). The new availability of relics coincided with the multiplication of miracle stories about saints, most notably accounts of the unusual preservation of their bodies. The rich and powerful responded by collecting important relics and endowing local churches with them. The building of ST. PETER'S BASILICA occasioned the assembly of possibly the most impressive collection of relics in the world. Among the many treasures claimed to be found there are Veronica's Veil, the Spear of Longinus used at the crucifixion, and a piece of the True Cross.

At the very time these relics were being assembled, DESIDERIUS ERASMUS and Protestants launched a critique of the practice. They challenged both the efficacy of relics and the biblical JUSTIFICATION for their use. Soon they challenged the validity of the relics themselves, as long gaps were found in the historical record of relics supposedly from the time of Jesus and the early church. The Council of TRENT reaffirmed the use of relics but criticized some of the excesses of veneration that had appeared.

In the 20th century, the critique of relics has gained support from scientific research. A number of relics have been proven to have originated at the time when they first "reappeared" on the historical stage, long after their claimed date of origin. Science has not only challenged the historic validity of such relics as the SHROUD OF TURIN and the Crown of Thorns now housed in Paris, it has challenged claims of miracles associated with various artifacts, such as the noncorruptibility of the bodies of various saints.

The Catholic Church does not commonly attempt to either authenticate or debunk relics, but it gives implicit approval by allowing the veneration of some relics and by keeping them in prominent locations. No one, however, is compelled to accept any particular relic, and the church allows its scholars to investigate and critique individual claims.

See also ADORATION.

Further reading: James Bentley, *Restless Bones: The Story of Relics* (London: Constable, 1985); Marie-Madeleine Gauthier, *Highways of the Faith: Relics and Reliquaries from Jerusalem to Compostela,* tr. J. A. Underwood (London: Alpine Fine Arts, 1983); Richard Landes, *Relics, Apocalypse, and the Deceits of History: Ademar of Chabannes, 989–1034* (Cambridge, Mass.: Harvard University Press, 1995); Joe Nickell, *Looking for a Miracle* (Amherst, Mass.: Prometheus, 1998); Russell R. Standish and Colin D. Standish, *Holy Relics or Revelation: Recent Astounding Archaeological Claims Evaluated* (Rapidan: Hartland, 1999).

religious orders

As Christianity became a popular, above-ground movement supported by the leadership of the Roman Empire, it lost some of the intensity that had characterized the apostolic church. It became more inclusive, and inevitably its standards grew lax and its moral rules softened. By the end of the third century many individual CHRISTIANS felt it necessary to withdraw from the mainstream of church life in order to live according to the GOSPEL ideal. ASCETICISM was a common element in their chosen life.

By the middle of the fourth century, some groups of ascetics had coalesced into communities and adopted rules for their common life. The Egyptian PACHOMIUS (c. 290–347) is generally credited with writing the first set of community rules, which St. BASIL THE GREAT codified. The idea of communities of men or women living ordered lives soon spread throughout the Christian world; over the next centuries independent experiments emerged in Gaul (St. Martin of Tours), the British Isles (Sts. COLUMBA and Cuthbert), and Italy (St. Columbanus).

Crucial to the development of the ordered life was the monastic rule, or code, developed by BENEDICT OF NURSIA, the patriarch of Western MONASTICISM. Benedict's rule became the basis for monastic practice for a host of different communities and has remained the most popular rule to the present. The rule provides for a strong ABBESS or abbot (community superior) and stresses the basic communal virtues of obedience, restraint of speech, humility, prayer, and work. It offers guidance for organizing the community and advice on practical matters that are still relevant today. The BENEDICTINE way assumed a stable residential community whose members scheduled their day around the PRAYER OF THE HOURS (the Divine Office). Competing with the Rule of St. Benedict was that of St. Augustine, traditionally traced to AUGUSTINE OF HIPPO (d. 430), which became popular in the ninth century; it was later adapted by the DOMINICANS.

Until the 13th century the various orders were distinguished mostly by their different austerities and devotions. The MENDICANT ORDERS then appeared, offering something quite different. The new orders called for corporate poverty—even the order itself should not own property—and for missionizing the world (as opposed to settling in a resident MONASTERY). This new form of the ordered life was pioneered by Sts. FRANCIS OF ASSISI (1182–1226) and DOMINIC DE GUZMÁN (c. 1170–1221). Members of these orders were called friars, and as they adopted a life of POVERTY, they were enjoined to work but also allowed to beg for their support.

The success of the new mendicant orders aroused opposition from the older orders and from the parish clergy, who felt the competition. But thanks to the aggressive support of leading members of the new orders such as the Dominican THOMAS AQUINAS (d. 1274) and the Franciscan BONAVENTURE (d. 1274), any opposition was laid to rest at the Second Council of Lyons in 1274 (*see* COUNCILS, ECUMENICAL), and the mendicant orders henceforth assumed a prominent role in church life internationally.

The spread of the mendicants had one negative effect—a further restriction on the role of women in the ordered life. They had little opportunity to participate in the service-oriented life of the early Franciscans and Dominicans; the movement of NUNS outside their convents, in imitation of the mendicants, was curtailed (*see* ST. CLARE under FRANCISCAN ORDERS).

A new set of orders was spurred into existence by the PROTESTANT REFORMATION of the 16th century. These new communities, most notably the JESUITS, were oriented toward active ministry in the world—often through teaching and missionary work, as in the case of the Jesuits. The latter in particular were called on to turn back the gains of the Protestants and at the same time spearhead the extension of the FAITH in such faraway locations as India and China, the interior of NORTH AMERICA, and the jungles of South America.

This time women were important participants. The Ursulines are a good example. Founded at Brescia in ITALY, by St. Angela Merici (1474–1540)

in 1535, they are the oldest teaching order of nuns in Roman Catholic history. While many women were successful in creating service-oriented communities, they were continually frustrated by regulations that enforced the bounds of what was considered proper feminine behavior.

In the 19th century, the slow and steady spread of monastic communities that had characterized the previous centuries ran up against a modern world characterized by urbanization, the separation of CHURCH AND STATE, the French Revolution, and the rise of ANTICLERICALISM (*see* CRITIQUE OF RELIGION). Ironically, the post-Enlightenment postrevolutionary world gave birth to literally hundreds of new orders. Many of them were organized for women in response both to new needs in a secularizing society and to changing attitudes toward women that allowed them to pioneer new forms of service in education, nursing, social work, and religious training of youths.

Among the many new 19th-century orders were the Oblate Sisters of Providence, founded in Baltimore, Maryland, in 1829 by St. Mary Lange OSP (c. 1780–1882) and Fr. James J. Jaubert SS. A second is the Sisters of the Holy Family, founded in New Orleans in 1842 by Sr. Henrietta Delille (1813–62). These are the first orders composed of and led by African Americans. These orders provided a new path out of discrimination and even slavery, the lot of most black women in America at the time.

The 20th century was marked by the emergence of many new indigenous orders around the world in what were formerly colonial countries, especially in ASIA and AFRICA. The transition to indigenous control opened space for the formation of many new ordered communities based on local initiatives. Some of these new religious orders are now sending missionaries back to the secularized First World.

Today, the hundreds of religious orders active around the world offer a spectrum of options for those seeking a means to live the ideal Christian life in community with like-minded and like-hearted people. Some live cloistered lives based on contemplative prayer, while others are fully engaged in the world in service to the less fortunate and ill. A few manage premier academic institutions, while others deploy evangelists to the outermost reaches of the world. Common to the orders are vows of obedience, chastity, and poverty.

VATICAN COUNCIL II emphasized the common vocation of every Christian and the possibility of holiness even in nonordered lives in the world. Such affirmations may have narrowed the distinctions between secular priests, the committed laity, and those in orders, at least for some listeners. However, in practice, the demands of the religious life, the constant attention to the Divine Office, the example of fellow members, and the freedom from the encumbrance of mundane concerns continues to set those in religious orders apart as following a distinctive calling within the body of Christ.

Further reading: Peter Brown, *The Body and Society: Men, Women, and Sexual Renunciation in Early Christianity* (New York: Columbia University Press, 1988); Peter Day, *A Dictionary of Religious Orders* (London: Burns & Oates, 2001); Marilyn Dunn, *The Emergence of Monasticism: From the Desert Fathers to the Early Middle Ages* (Oxford: Blackwell, 2000); *Encyclopedia of Monasticism* (London: Fitzroy Dearborn, 1999); Juan Laboa, ed., *The Historical Atlas of Eastern and Western Monasticism* (Collegeville, Minn.: Liturgical Press, 2004); Sandra Schneiders, *New Wineskins: Reimagining Religious Life Today* (New York: Paulist, 1986).

Renaissance (Fr.: "rebirth")

The era of European history from around 1350 to 1550 is known as the Renaissance, when the arts and sciences were "reborn" and flourished, first in ITALY and then throughout Europe, thanks to increased exposure to classical Greco-Roman writing, painting, sculpture, and architecture. The term is also used to characterize other eras, such as the CAROLINGIAN RENAISSANCE and the intellectual renaissance of the 12th century, which was also founded on the rediscovery of certain classical texts. The beginning of the era is most often associated with the Italian author Francesco Petrarch (1305–74), who promoted the study of ancient thought, poetry, and rhetoric.

Renaissance thinkers favored the active life over the contemplative and placed emphasis on a new humanism that celebrated human possibility and achievement. Nicolò Machiavelli (1469–1527) founded his "new science" of politics on his study of Livy (59 B.C.E.–17 C.E.). Leon Battista Alberti (1404–72) rediscovered the principles of perspective and proportion of Vitruvius (c. 90–20 B.C.E.), and architects like Filippo Brunelleschi (1377–1446) put them into effect in churches like San Lorenzo in Florence.

Many historians consider the Renaissance to have been secularist, but it is more true to say that the art of the age was devoted to both sacred and profane themes. Sandro Botticelli (1445–1510) painted both the *Adoration of the Magi* and the *Birth of Venus*. St. THOMAS MORE was both the humanist who wrote *Utopia* and the devout Catholic who underwent beheading for his FAITH. DESIDERIUS ERASMUS wrote the critical, humanist *Praise of Folly* and also edited the first critical edition of the Greek New Testament. On the other hand, the popes who sponsored MICHELANGELO and RAPHAEL often led personally corrupt and irreligious lives. Many see the PROTESTANT REFORMATION as having twin roots in the Jesus-centered piety of the DEVOTIO MODERNA and the humanism of scholars like Erasmus.

Further reading: Joan Gadol, *Leon Battista Alberti: Universal Man of the Renaissance* (Chicago: University of Chicago Press, 1969); Anthony Levi, *Renaissance and Reformation: The Intellectual Genesis* (New Haven, Conn.: Yale University Press, 2002); John W. O'Malley, *Religious Culture in the Sixteenth Century* (Bookfield, Vt.: Variorum, 1993); John T. Paoletti,

Art in Renaissance Italy (Upper Saddle River, N.J.: Prentice Hall, 2006).

Renan, Joseph-Ernest (1823–1892)
orientalist and New Testament critic

Joseph Ernest Renan's biography of Jesus was a landmark in the developing critical study of the New Testament in the 19th century. Renan was born in Brittany and raised in a pious Catholic home by his widowed mother. In 1838 he began his studies at the minor seminary of St. Nicholas de Chardonnet in Paris, followed by work at the major seminary of Issy (1842–44) and at St. Sulpice (1844–45). While studying for the priesthood he became increasingly attracted to modern philosophy and biblical criticism, especially the varieties pursued in Germany (*see* Bible). In 1845 he refused ordination and left the church.

Turning to secular education, Renan completed a university dissertation in 1848 on the study of Greek in the medieval era. In 1869 he finished his first book, *The Future of Science,* but on the advice of friends did not publish it. Instead, he continued his studies in oriental languages and Semitic philology and in 1857 was appointed to a chair at the Collège de France.

In 1863, Renan published the book that was to bring him fame, and, to many, infamy. His *Life of Jesus* appeared in the context of the continuing controversy created a generation earlier by *The Life of Jesus Critically Examined* (1835) by German scholar David Friedrich Strauss (1808–74). However, Renan departed from the skeptical mythological approach of Strauss. He attempted instead to understand Jesus in light of his contemporary geographical, social, cultural, and religious environment. Having traveled to Palestine, Renan could offer much local color, but the book offered little in the way of scholarly historical investigation. Renan's final product was a rather romanticized vision of Jesus, a gentle Galilean in search of a human utopia. Renan also presented a flawed Jesus—ambitious, deceitful, and controlled by sensuality. Renan also denounced Paul as the one who led to Christianity's decadence, popularly summed up in the old saw, "Jesus preached the Kingdom of God; Paul left us the Church."

The *Life of Jesus* would change Renan's life. In 1862, after finally being confirmed in his teaching position at the Collège de France, he was suspended; he was not restored to his position until 1871, when he resumed teaching. In 1884 he assumed an administrative position at the school.

While remembered for his book on Jesus, Renan later wrote in a more genuinely scholarly mode. He completed multivolume *History of the Origins of Christianity* (1866–81), *History of the People of Israel* (1887–93), and the *Corpus Inscriptionum Semiticarum* (1881–?). At the same time, he became more and more skeptical in his personal views, leaving not only the church but altogether renouncing any Christian faith. He had significant influence on the first phase of the quest for the historical Jesus. He died in Paris in 1892.

Further reading: H. G. A. Brauer, *The Philosophy of Ernest Renan* (Madison: University of Wisconsin Press, 1904); M. E. G. Duff, *Ernest Renan: In Memoriam* (New York, 1893); Ernest Renan, *History of the People of Israel,* 5 vols. (Boston: Little, Brown, 1915); ———, *Life of Jesus* (New York: Carleton, 1864); Albert Schweitzer, *The Quest for the Historical Jesus* (New York: Macmillan, 1968).

Resurrection (of Christ) (Lat.: *resurgere,* "to rise again")

Christians believe that Christ rose from the dead to new life after his crucifixion on the cross. However, the earliest creedal formulas do not state that Christ *rose,* but that he *was raised* to life, or resurrected, by God. Specifically, they state that he was resurrected on the third day after the crucifixion, that he appeared to the disciples, and that he was taken into heaven where he is seated at the right hand of the Father, from where he will come again (1 Cor. 15:3–5; Acts 2:32–33).

Resurrection of Jesus Christ, after El Greco (Domenicos Theotocopoulos 1541–1614). Copy of much larger work (1596-1600) in the Prado Museum, Madrid, Spain. *(Mildred Lane Kemper Art Museum, Washington University, St. Louis, with permission)*

Early followers of Jesus shared with various Jewish groups, such as the Pharisees, a belief in the resurrection of the body (Dan. 12:2; Job 19–25–27). Nevertheless, the GOSPEL of Mark in its original form presents no post-Resurrection narrative after Mary of Magdala, Mary the mother of James, and Salome find the empty tomb. The other Gospels do report the resurrection. Interestingly, in those accounts, it is also women, including Jesus' mother, MARY OF NAZARETH, who first discover that the tomb is empty and meet the resurrected Jesus. They in turn take the news to the fearful male disciples. Some biblical scholars have argued that this fact—that women were the first to be entrusted with the Gospel of the death and resurrection of Jesus—can serve as a basis for admitting women to the priesthood.

Paul insists on the centrality of the Resurrection for Christian faith: "If Christ has not been raised, our preaching is useless and so is your faith" (1 Cor. 15:14), and "If Christ has not been raised, your faith is futile, you are still in your sins" (1 Cor. 15:17). The reality of resurrection is key to understanding the rite of BAPTISM. A person is baptized into the DEATH of Christ and emerges with the hope of resurrection (Rom. 6:4). Resurrection of the believer is union with the one body of Christ in what may be called a feed-back metaphor, the believing community forms the literal body of Christ who, in turn, is symbolized by the community.

Christians have often argued over the nature of the resurrected or revivified Jesus. The Gospels of Luke and John insist on the physicality of the raised Jesus (Luke 24:36–43; John 20:26–27). Yet the raised Jesus has extraordinary powers such as passing through locked doors (John 20:19) and being taken up into heaven (Acts 1:9). Paul says that the resurrected body will be transformed so that it is a "spiritual body" (1 Cor. 15:44). In the depiction of the Resurrection on his celebrated Isenheim Altar Matthias Grünewald (1475–1528) painted the risen Jesus as transformed in a luminous aura of resplendent light.

Some advocates of DEMYTHOLOGIZATION claim that the resurrection passages in the BIBLE are mythical. Most Christians, especially Catholics, object to this reading of the text. On the other hand, the New Testament itself at times speaks of resurrection in a nonphysical sense, as in the PARABLE of the Prodigal Son who was once lost and now is found, who once was dead and now is alive (Luke 15:32).

Further reading: Athanasius, *On the Resurrection;* Tertullian, *The Resurrection of the Flesh;* Origen, *On First Principles* 2.10–11—all available online; Carol W. Bynum, *Resurrection of the Body in Western Christianity 200–1336* (New York: Columbia University Press, 1996); Pheme Perkins, *Resurrection: New Testament Witness and Contemporary Reflection* (Garden City, N.Y.: Doubleday, 1984).

revelation (Lat.: *revelatio;* Gk.: *apokalypsis,* "uncovering")

The term *revelation* in its primary sense means the uncovering of something that was formerly hidden. Theologically, revelation has come to mean the self-communication of GOD to people with the truths needed for their salvation. Catholic philosopher-theologians distinguish between truths that reason can determine for itself (e.g., that God exists) and truths that depend totally on God's self-revelation (that God is a TRINITY).

The early CHRISTIAN, but very Jewish, epistle to the Hebrews states: "In times past God spoke to our forefathers through the prophets at many times and in different ways but in these end times God has spoken to us through the Son" (1:1). In the Old Testament God can appear (theophany) in natural forms (burning bush, storm), in visions and dreams (to Joseph), as an angel (Gen. 16:1), or even in human form (Num. 12:8). In prophetic literature God manifests the divine essence and will in the holy words spoken by the prophets (Amos 3:1). God acts in history by making a Covenant with the people, speaking to their forefathers and leaders, and holding them to its terms. In Rabbinic times teachers centered the revelation of God on the Torah, or Pentateuch, the first five books of the BIBLE.

In the New Testament the words and healings of Jesus were seen as the means of God's definitive revelation to humanity. As Simeon says of the infant Jesus, he is "a light for revelation" (Luke 2:23). The Gospels sometimes point to the exclusivity of the revelation through the Son: "No one knows the Son except the Father, and no one knows the Father except the Son and any one to whom the Son chooses to reveal him" (Matt. 11:17). Though God has been revealed in CREATION and CONSCIENCE, PAUL points to the end time saving revelation of the Gospel of Christ in his death and RESURRECTION. The Gospel of John uses the term *phaneroun* ("manifestation" to talk about God's revelation of the divine self in the INCARNATION of the Logos in the flesh (John 1:14–18).

The apologists of the second century were willing to admit that God had been revealed to the ancient Greek philosophers as a preparation for the Gospel but that the definitive and saving revelation depended on the Incarnation of the Logos in the flesh. GNOSTICS wanted to restrict the ultimate revelation to the secret teaching imparted to a select few. The antiheretical writers countered with the argument that the ultimate criterion, or RULE OF FAITH, is the teaching of Christ preserved by the APOSTLES and conveyed to the whole church (IRENAEUS, *Against Heresies* 1.8.1).

At VATICAN COUNCIL II Catholicism widened the definition of revelation. In addition to natural (reason) and special (biblical) revelation, the council's decree *Nostra Aetate* 2, the Declaration on the Relation of the Church to Non-Christian Religions, accepted that the world's great religious traditions shared in the self-communication of God in some sense. Today there is serious debate about how wide and how deep this teaching reaches. KARL RAHNER took an expansive view, while the current Pope BENEDICT XVI takes a narrower view.

Christians who stress the unity and exclusivity of Jesus Christ often rely on John 14:6, where Jesus declares that he is "the way, the truth and the life." However, many Johannine scholars maintain that these words were addressed not to non-Christians, but to Christian groups who did not conform to the Johannine community's understanding of Jesus and his mission.

Further reading: Avery Dulles, *Revelation Theology: A History* (New York: Herder & Herder, 1969); Brian Hebblethwaite, *Philosophical Theology and Christian Doctrine* (Oxford: Blackwell, 2005); Karl Rahner, *Foundations of Christian Faith* (New York: Crossroad, 1984); Joseph Ratzinger, *Dominus Jesus: On the Unity and Salvific Universality of Jesus Christ and the Church,* Congregation for the Doctrine of the Faith (August 6, 2000).

Ricci, Mateo (1552–1610) *pioneering missionary*

Mateo Ricci, the pioneer Catholic missionary to China, was born October 16, 1552, in Macerata, ITALY. He studied law in Rome and then, against his father's wishes, in 1571 joined the Society of Jesus (JESUITS). His subsequent studies at the Roman College emphasized THEOLOGY, science, and ethics. He completed his formal training in 1577 at the University of Coimbra, where he mastered in Portuguese prior to leaving for the Portuguese colony of Goa in southern India. It was in Goa in 1580 that he was finally ordained to the priesthood.

In 1582, Ricci and another Jesuit, Michele Ruggieri (1543–1607), were assigned to launch a China mission. They arrived in Macao in 1583 and initially concentrated on mastering the language. Ricci later moved to Zhaoqing (Chao-ch'ing), not far from Canton. He adopted local dress and set about the task of reaching the learned elite of China, with the ultimate goal of settling in Nanjing (Nanking) and influencing the emperor and court toward Christianity.

To demonstrate his learning to the Chinese, Ricci drew on all of his higher education and linguistic skills. Among his first products was a world map (with China at the center) that was widely circulated and gave the Chinese their first accurate conception of the continents. He later translated several Western mathematics texts, including the first six books of Euclid's *Elements.* By 1588 he had become famous within the Chinese scholarly community.

In 1600 he finally gained an audience with Emperor Zhu Yijun ([Chu Yi-chün] r. 1572–1620) in Beijing and presented him with a clock, a harpsichord, a set of world maps, and a picture of the Madonna, among other items. By this time, he had donned the robes of a Confucian scholar, and he was allowed to move to Beijing (Peking). He and his Jesuit colleagues accommodated themselves to Chinese culture as far as possible. They hoped to demonstrate that there was no theoretical incompatibility between China and the CHRISTIAN faith.

As an evangelist, Ricci wrote a series of tracts on various moral topics and a book, *The True Idea of God,* an apologetic work on Christianity. In the book, he argued that the Confucian thought he encountered in China was a perversion of ancient Confucian thought; the latter, he wrote, had been derived from early Jewish activity in China and included the idea of a transcendent deity. Shorn of its later accretions, Confucian thought could serve as the Gospel for the Chinese. The work, though criticized later for its lack of specifically Christian themes, introduced Chinese readers to a spectrum of basic theological ideas—theism, CREATION, providence, and the existence of HEAVEN AND HELL. He also included an argument for clerical CELIBACY and offered an elemental discussion of Jesus CHRIST.

Ricci made a number of converts, primarily among the Chinese upper classes and intellectuals. His targeting of these people had the added effect of creating a favorable environment for later Christian missionaries. The Jesuits allowed for Chinese veneration of Confucius and family ancestors, used the Chinese words "Tien" (Heaven) and "Shang-ti" (Lord of the Sky) to translate "God" and "Lord," used the Chinese vernacular in religious worship, and allowed offerings to the emperor. These "Chinese Rites" were later condemned by Clement XI (r. 1700–21) and Benedict XIV (r. 1740–58). Under Pius XII, the Sacred Congregation for the Propagation of the Faith (December 8, 1939) issued a directive effectively rescinding Clement XI's decree and allowing for the veneration of ancestors, including Confucius, as "social" in nature and therefore "licit."

Ricci, known as Li Matou (Li Ma-t'ou) to his Chinese contemporaries, died on May 11, 1610, in Beijing. Following his death, the emperor allowed his burial in Beijing. He is remembered kindly even in atheist-oriented contemporary China. In 1983, to commemorate the 400th anniversary of Ricci's arrival in China, an official Chinese magazine published a warm account of Ricci that included a reproduction of a painting of the Madonna and Child originally brought to China by Ricci.

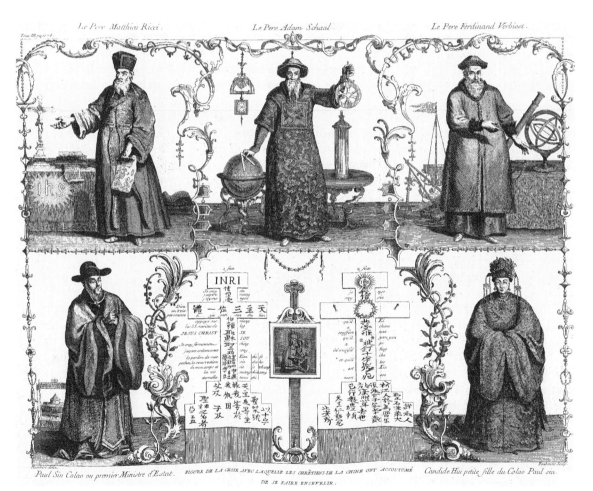

Etching of Jesuit missionaries Mateo Ricci, Adam Schaal, and Ferdinand Verbiest in Mandarin robes with a Mandarin convert and his granddaughter in the lower register (Bodleian Library, Oxford) *(Fordham University Library, Bronx, NY)*

Further reading: Vincent Cronin, *The Wise Man from the West* (London: Ruppert Hart Davis 1955); Mateo Ricci, *China in the Sixteenth Century: The Journals of Matthew Ricci: 1583–1610* (New York: Random House, 1953); Jonathan D. Spence, *The Memory Palace of Mateo Ricci* (New York: Viking, 1984).

rites (Lat.: *ritus,* "a prescribed form of sacred action")

The term *rite* can be used in two senses. It can refer to a particular ritual process, such as BAPTISM, involving separation from secular activity, ritual transformation, and reaggregation with the wider community. Or it can refer to a collection of liturgical, cultural, spiritual, linguistic, and musical forms belonging to a particular subgroup within a broader religious tradition. It is in this sense that one speaks of the Roman, or Latin, Rite, which first developed in the DIOCESE of Rome and spread throughout western Christendom through the efforts of the PAPACY, especially GREGORY I THE GREAT, and of secular rulers like CHARLEMAGNE. The Roman Rite was thoroughly revised at the direction of VATICAN COUNCIL II.

Prior to the hegemony of the Roman Rite, the western CHRISTIAN world supported a variety of regional rites, such as the Ambrosian, Gallican, Celtic, and Mozarabic, with their different liturgical forms and traditions. Remnants of the Ambrosian Rite and CHANT survive in Milan. The same holds for the Mozarabic Rite and chant, which has been reconstructed at the cathedral of Toledo in SPAIN. There are several basic Eastern Catholic rites including the Armenian, Byzantine, Coptic, Melkite, Ethiopian, Maronite, East Syrian, Chaldean, West Syrian, Syro-Malabar, Syro-Antiochene, and Syro-Malankara rites.

Further reading: Edward E. Finn, *These Are My Rites: A Brief History of the Eastern Rites of Christianity* (Collegeville, Minn.: Liturgical Press, 1980); Gordon P. Jeannes, *The Origins of the Roman Rite* (Bramcote: Grove, 1991); Ronald G. Roberson, *The Eastern Christian Churches: A Brief Survey* (Rome: Pontifical Oriental Institute, 1999); Joan L. Roccasalvo, *The Eastern Catholic Churches: An Introduction to their Worship and Spirituality* (Collegeville, Minn.: Liturgical Press, 1992).

Romanian Greek Catholic Church

The Romanian Greek Catholic Church can be traced to the late 17th century. When the Catholic Habsburg rulers of the Austro-Hungarian Empire assumed control over Transylvania from the retreating Ottoman Turks, they encouraged the predominantly EASTERN ORTHODOX population to align themselves with Rome, partly by denying full civil rights to Orthodox believers and partly by supporting JESUIT missionaries. An agreement was reached between Orthodoxy and Catholic leaders in 1698; it was approved at a synod two years later, and the Romanian Greek Catholic Church officially came into existence.

The union worked until 1744, when a revival of Orthodoxy became so strong that the Austrian government gave up its repressive policies. An Orthodox BISHOP was consecrated for Transylvania in 1759, and two communities of about equal strength reemerged. Following World War I, Transylvania was removed from Austria-Hungary and given to Romania, where Orthodoxy prevailed.

In the late 1940s, the new Communist government of Romania forced the Romanian Greek Catholic Church to sever its formal ties to Rome and merge into the Romanian Orthodox Church. To seal the merger, the government had all the Catholic bishops arrested; five died in jail, and a sixth died in 1970 under house arrest. In effect, the Romanian Greek Catholic Church ceased to exist.

In 1990 one of the first actions taken by the post-Ceausescu Romanian government was to repeal the 1948 dissolution decree. Immediately it was discovered that three Catholic bishops had been operating underground, and Pope JOHN PAUL II then appointed bishops to fill all the vacant DIOCESES.

Greek Catholics immediately demanded the return of all their former property. The Orthodox patriarch, eager to reassert his own position in the 1990s, has been slow to return the property on the grounds that in the intermediate years the parishioners have become Orthodox in faith. In spite of the resistance, the Catholic community has been able to recover most of its former property, but efforts continue to secure the remainder of the disputed buildings and land. In 1999 John Paul II visited Romania and met with the Romanian Orthodox patriarch.

The Romanian Greek Catholic Church is led by Metropolitan Lucian Muresan (1931–), the ARCHBISHOP of Fagaras and Alba Julia. The church claims more than 700,000 members.

Further reading: Nicolae I. Branzea and Stefan Ionita, *Religious Life in Romania* (Bucharest: Editura Paideia, 1999); Constantin Cuciuc, *Atlasul Religiilor si al Monumentelor Istorice Religi case din România* (Bucharest: Editura Onosis, 1996).

Roman Missal

The missal is a book containing the materials necessary for participation in the Mass on a week-by-week basis, according to the Latin, or Roman, Rite. The Mass or EUCHARIST, can be divided into two parts, those words spoken at every service, from the opening prayers to the institution of the elements in the Eucharistic ritual, and those words that change weekly, most importantly the readings from Scripture and the prayers appropriate to the day or feast.

The text of the missal changed radically following VATICAN COUNCIL II. Previously, Catholics commonly used the Tridentine Liturgy as affirmed by the Council of TRENT. The missal of Pope PAUL V (1605–21), with the text in Latin, was in general use through the 1960s. It contained in one volume all the elements of the Mass. A new missal, now in the vernacular language of the people celebrating the Mass, was promulgated by Pope PAUL VI (r. 1963–78) after Vatican II and revised under JOHN PAUL II in 2000. It appeared as two books. The first and smaller volume contained the fixed text of the weekly service of the Mass. The second volume, the Lectionary for the Mass, contained all the Scripture readings. These readings, different for each service, are laid out in such a way that over several years a regular participant at the Mass will be taken through the entire Scripture of both the Old and New Testaments with selective readings. The Roman Missal is used by the great majority of Catholic Churches worldwide, though a small number of churches continue to use the Eastern Rite, especially in eastern Europe and the Middle East.

Further reading: F. X. Lasance, *The New Roman Missal* (Palmdale: Christian Book Club of America, 1993); Pierre Loret, *The Story of the Mass* (Liguori, Mo.: Liguori, 1983); Dennis Smolarski, *The General Instruction of the Roman Missal 1969–2002: A Commentary* (Collegeville, Minn.: Liturgical Press, 2003); Paul Turner, *A Guide to the General Instruction of the Roman Missal* (Chicago: Liturgy Training, 2003).

Romero y Galdámez, Óscar Arnulfo
(1917–1980) *archbishop of San Salvador*

Archbishop Óscar Arnulfo Romero y Galdámez, the ARCHBISHOP of San Salvador, became world famous after being assassinated on March 24, 1980, while saying Mass. Romero was born on August 15, 1917, in the town of Ciudad Barrios, in the department of San Miguel, El Salvador. He was educated at the minor seminary in San Miguel conducted by brothers of the Claretian Order and then in 1937 was sent to the major seminary in San Salvador run by the JESUITS. In the midst of his course of study he was invited to study at the Gregorian University in Rome. While there, as World War II was in its initial stages, Romero took note of PIUS IX's opposition to FASCISM and NAZISM.

Romero was ordained in 1942. He began work on a doctorate but was called home by his BISHOP.

"Uncanonized saint" Óscar Romero celebrating mass in San Salvador, El Salvador *(© Christian Poveda/Corbis)*

For a brief period he served as a parish priest in Anamoros but then was assigned to the chancery office as the secretary to the bishop and later the editor of the diocesan newspaper. He was a forceful orator and became well known through the country after assuming duties as a speaker on a radio station.

He emerged as a conservative leader who at first opposed many of the reforms initiated at VATICAN COUNCIL II. He was given the title monsignor and made secretary general of the national bishops' conference. In 1970 he became auxiliary of the archbishop of San Salvador.

In 1974 he was named bishop of Santiago de Maria. His DIOCESE included the town of Tres Calles, where the following year a group of national guardsmen killed five men. Romero complained to the country's dictator. That complaint was the first of a series of critical remarks in sermons and news articles in which he denounced the violence and injustice emanating from the government and called attention to numerous human rights violations throughout the country. In turn, the official newspapers denounced him as an antigovernment fanatic.

Then in 1977, he succeeded the retiring archbishop of San Salvador. Over the years he had opposed both liberal and LIBERATION THEOLOGIES espoused by many of the church leaders in the capital. However, the first months of his bishopric were marked by a series of attacks on priests and poor people. He then became a champion of the poor and the oppressed. In March 1978, reacting to the murder of a priest friend, he cancelled masses throughout the country except for the mass he led at the cathedral in San Salvador, which 100,000 people attended. He had emerged as the major opposition voice in the country.

In 1979, when additional priests were killed and a number of catechists disappeared, Romero continued his vocal opposition to the political and military leadership and received a number of death threats. He appealed to President Jimmy Carter as a fellow Christian to stop arming the Salvadoran regime. Early in 1980 he ordered his close associates to avoid him as he moved about the city lest they be hurt in any violence directed at him. A first assassination attempt missed its mark on March 10, 1980, when a bomb placed near the pulpit in the cathedral failed to explode. However, two weeks later, as he celebrated mass at a small chapel, a single bullet through his heart brought him down.

His death brought worldwide reaction. However, little was done to bring the perpetrators to justice. It was later determined that a former high-ranking army officer named Roberto D'Aubuisson

(1943–92) ordered the assassination. Two years after Romero's death, D'Aubuisson founded a right-wing party in El Salvador. He later ran for president; though defeated, another member of his party was elected in 1999. The site of Romero's assassination has become a place of pilgrimage in El Salvador, and there is an effort for his canonization. Many suspect that his canonization has been delayed lest his admirers make of him the "Saint of Liberation."

Further reading: James R. Brockman, *Romero: A Life* (Maryknoll, N.Y.: Orbis, 1989); ———, *The Violence of Love: The Pastoral Wisdom of Archbishop Oscar Romero.* (San Francisco: Harper & Row, 1988); Plácido Erdozaín, *Archbishop Romero: Martyr of Salvador,* tr. John McFadden and Ruth Warner. (Maryknoll, N.Y.: Orbis, 1981); Jon Sobrino, *Archbishop Romero: Memories and Reflections,* tr. Robert R. Barr. (Maryknoll, N.Y.: Orbis, 1990).

Rose of Lima, St. (1586–1617) *first Western Hemisphere saint*

Rose of Lima, the first person from the Western Hemisphere to be canonized as a saint, was born in Lima, Peru, on April 20, 1586. She was named Isabel Flores y Oliva at birth by her parents, who had migrated from their native SPAIN. She is reported to have shown a tendency to the devotional life even during her childhood years, and through her teen years she was known for her veneration of the Blessed Virgin and the Infant Jesus. She took the name Rose at her confirmation.

During her early years St. CATHERINE OF SIENA became Rose's model, and she began fasting three times weekly and engaging in secret penances. At one point, accused of being vain, she cut her hair and adopted plain clothing. Her increased devotion alienated her from friends and family alike. Family opposition increased when she decided on a celibate life. Her life became focused on a small grotto she had built with the aid of her brother. At the age of 20, she became a DOMINICAN nun.

In the next years, she increased the severity of the penances she practiced. Among other things, she wore a spiked crown that she covered from view with roses. In her mystic encounters with CHRIST, she offered her austerities as penance for personal offenses, for the idolatry she perceived to be practiced in Peru, and for the release of souls from purgatory.

Her life was relatively short; she died at age 31. In the decades after her death, many miracles were attributed to her intercession, leading to her beatification by Pope Clement IX (r. 1667–69), in 1667. She was named a saint just four years later. She was subsequently given the title of Patroness of America (*see* PATRON SAINTS). She has become a very popular saint in NORTH and LATIN AMERICA, often depicted with a crown of roses and holding a CROSS to her breast.

Further reading: Frank Graziano, *Wounds of Love: The Mystical Marriage of Saint Rose of Lima* (Oxford: Oxford University Press, 2004); Mary Fabyan Windeatt, *Angel of the Andes: The Story of Saint Rose of Lima* (Paterson, N.J.: Saint Anthony Guild, 1956).

Rota

The Rota is the second-highest court in the VATICAN CURIA. Its name, which means wheel, is of obscure origin, and may be a reference to the fact that documents used to be wheeled from judge to judge for their consideration. The court declined in responsibility when the PAPAL STATES were lost in the 19th century, but it was given new authority in the reorganization of the CURIA that occurred in 1908.

The Rota is the most active court at the Vatican. It considers cases of marital status, the issue most often sent to Rome for adjudication (*see* MARRIAGE). Most of these cases concern annulments that offer the petitioner the possibility of entering a second marriage.

The Rota consists of 12 members called auditors, about half of whom come from ITALY. Members must be BISHOPS and hold a doctorate in THEOLOGY and CANON LAW. Once appointed, they serve until the age of 70. Each auditor has an assistant, also a doctor of canon law, and the court's work is administered by a large specialized staff.

Further reading: James A. Coriden, *An Introduction to Canon Law* (Mahwah, N.J.: Paulist, 1991); John T. Noonan, Jr., *Power to Dissolve: Lawyers and Marriages in the Courts of the Roman Curia* (Cambridge, Mass.: Belknap, 1970); Ronald T. Smith, *Annulment: A Step-by-Step Guide for Divorced Catholics* (Chicago: ACTA, 1995).

Ruether, Rosemary Radford (1936–)
feminist theologian

Reuther is a Catholic theologian who focuses on issues of gender, social justice (sexism, racism, poverty), ecology, and interfaith concerns as they relate to systematic THEOLOGY. She is the foremost Catholic feminist theologian in United States.

Ruether was born in Minnesota, trained at Scipps College and took her doctorate in patrisitics, the study of the FATHERS AND MOTHERS OF THE CHURCH, at Claremont Graduate School of Theology. She has taught at Howard University, Garrett Theological Seminary, Northwestern University, and the Chicago Graduate Theological Union and currently teaches at the Pacific School of Religion in the Berkeley Graduate Theological Union, where she is Carpenter Professor of Feminist Theology. Reuther was deeply involved in the civil rights, antiwar, feminist, and liberation movements of the 1960s. She is married to Herman Ruether, a political scientist, and has children and grandchildren.

Ruether, a prolific author, established her reputation with *Sexism and God Talk* (1983), a systematic exposition of feminist theology. She critiques traditional Catholic theology, largely patriarchal in orientation, in terms of its language about God and the submissive role of women; she explores Christology (*see* CHRIST/CHRISTOLOGY) and Mariology,

ECOTHEOLOGY, and ESCHATOLOGY. In the opening chapter of *Sexism* she writes: "Theologically speaking, whatever diminishes or denies the full humanity of women must be presumed not to reflect the divine or an authentic relation to the divine, or to reflect the authentic nature of things, or to be the message or work of an authentic redeemer or a community of redemption." She has extended this systematic approach to the recovery of the buried contribution of women's perspectives on issues involving the theologies of ecology (*Gaia and God*, 1992), REDEMPTION (*Gender and Redemption*, 1994), and the crisis of religious nationalism in the Israeli-Palestinian conflict (*The Wrath of Jonah*, 1989). She reaches beyond the received Catholic tradition to include voices of women and non-Catholics. She is currently very engaged in the contribution of women from the Third World to the healing of the planet and in interfaith exchange.

Ruether's theological trajectory can be contrasted with others, such as Mary Daly (1928–), who has remained narrowly centered on women as the primary issue of feminist theology. Ruether contextualizes her theology of women in terms of the broad and interconnected questions of sex, race, class, family, interfaith, and economics. Although called a feminist theologian, what she really proposes is an equi-gender and equi-class theology.

Further reading: Rosemary Radford Ruether, *Sexism and God Talk: Toward a Feminist Theology* (Boston: Beacon, 1983); ———, *Gaia and God* (San Francisco: HarperSanFrancisco, 1992); ——— with Herman Ruether, *The Wrath of Jonah* (San Francisco: Harper & Row, 1989); ———, *Christianity and the Making of the Modern Family* (Boston: Beacon, 2000).

rule of faith (Lat.: *regula fidei;* Gk.: *kanon tes aletheias,* "standard of truth")

The rule of faith was a set of guidelines for CHRISTIAN belief that were developed by the early theologians in their struggle against the many varieties of heterodoxy, including DOCETISM, MARCION, MONTANUS, and the many schools of Gnosticism. The rules took the terms *truth* and *measure* from PAUL's letter to the Galatians (2:14; 6:16); the effort was a step toward the definition of orthodoxy.

For PAUL and others, the Gospel message centered on the DEATH and RESURRECTION of Jesus CHRIST (1 Cor. 15:1–8). The second-century theologians IRENAEUS, TERTULLIAN, and ORIGEN felt the need to frame this central belief between a teaching about CREATION by the Father and another teaching about sanctification or restoration of humanity and creation through the HOLY SPIRIT. The teaching on the goodness of all CREATION, material and spiritual, and its restoration through Christ and the Spirit countered GNOSTIC arguments that matter was either evil or indifferent to salvation. Thus the rule of faith formulation became the kernel from which the formal CREED grew in the third and early fourth centuries.

The classic texts of the rule of faith are found in Irenaeus, *Proof of Apostolic Teaching* 6; Tertullian, *Prescription Against Heretics* 13; and Origen, *On First Principles,* preface. The rule of faith laid the groundwork for all later orthodox theological reflection.

Further reading: C. H. Dodd, *The Apostolic Preaching and Its Development* (New York: Harper, 1944); W. R. Farmer, "Galatians and the Second-Century Development of the Rule of Faith," *The Second Century* (1984) 4:143–70; Gustav Wingren, *Creation and Gospel* (New York: Edwin Mellen, 1979).

Ruthenian Catholic Church

The Ruthenian Catholic Church is an Eastern Rite church that originated in the Carpathian Mountains of southwestern Ukraine, Slovakia, and southeastern Poland. Ruthenians speak a Ukrainian dialect but identify ethnically as Rusyns. Christianity spread into Ruthenia toward the end of the first millennium. When Rome and the Eastern Church severed relations in 1054, Ruthenians adhered to Orthodoxy, but at about the same time Latin Christian Hungary assumed hegemony in the region.

The Hungarian government encouraged the spread of Roman Catholicism into Ruthenia and encouraged the Orthodox faithful to realign with Rome. In 1646, 63 Orthodox priests, most of them Slovakian, entered the Roman Catholic Church through what became known as the Union of Uzhorod. Others joined through two similar mass acts of conversion in 1664 and 1713. By 1720, EASTERN ORTHODOXY had virtually disappeared from Ruthenia. The 18th century saw Latin Rite BISHOPS in the region attempting to replace the Slavic Rite that had continued in use in most parishes. One step in resolving the issue occurred in 1771, when Pope Clement XIV (r. 1769–74), at the request of Holy Roman Empress Maria-Theresa of Austria (1717–80) established a new Ruthenian eparchy (DIOCESE). Seven years later a Ruthenian seminary was opened at Uzhorod. By these steps the Ruthenian Catholic Church (also known as the Byzantine Catholic Church) emerged as a distinctive ethnic church in the region.

After World War I, Ruthenia was incorporated into the new nation of Czechoslovakia. In the 1920s, a group left the Catholic Church and returned to Orthodoxy. Then after World War II, the eastern part of Ruthenia was incorporated into the Soviet Union, and renewed pressure was placed on the church to return to Orthodoxy. Its parishes were placed under the authority of the Russian Orthodox Church and its patriarch in Moscow. Similar efforts against the Ruthenian Church occurred in Poland and Czechoslovakia.

In the late 19th and early 20th century some 500,000 Rusyns migrated to the United States, where the dominant American Latin Rite HIERARCHY opposed their continued use of their Eastern Rite practices. As a result, most of them joined an Eastern Orthodox jurisdiction. A first eparchy in America was finally established in 1924. VATICAN COUNCIL II guaranteed the separate integrity of all

Eastern Rites and put an end to all Latinization in *Orientalium Ecclesiarum* 2, the Decree on the Catholic Churches of the Eastern Rite.

Only with the fall of the Soviet Union did the Ruthenian Catholic Church reemerge. In 1991 Pope JOHN PAUL II reestablished a Ruthenian diocese, the eparchy of Muchaèevo, in the Ukraine. It assumed authority over some 500,000 Rusyn Catholics, but is parallel to both the revived Ukrainian Catholic Church and the Ukrainian Orthodox Church. An American branch of the Ruthenian church now includes four dioceses overseen by a metropolitan residing in Pittsburgh, Pennsylvania. Some 200,000 Ruthenian Catholics remain in the United States. Ruthenian Catholics in Australia and western Europe have largely integrated into the Ukrainian Catholic Church. The American Ruthenian church, sometimes also identified as the Ruthenian-Byzantine-Greek Catholic Church, is headed by Archbishop Basil Schott (1939–   ) and is divided into four dioceses with 243 parishes.

Further reading: Nikolaus Liesel, *The Eastern Catholic Liturgies: A Study in Words and Pictures* (Westminster, Mo.: Newman, 1960); Ronald G. Roberson, *The Eastern Christian Churches: A Brief Survey,* 5th ed. (Rome: Edizioni Orientalia Christiana, Pontificio Istituto Orientale, 1995).

S

sacrament (Lat.: *sacer,* "holy, taboo"; *sacramentum* "oath," "initiation" = Gk.: *mysterion*)

CHRISTIAN sacraments are holy ritual actions believed to have been instituted by Jesus CHRIST as channels of GRACE. Later Catholicism defined a sacrament as an outward and visible sign of an inward and spiritual grace instituted by Christ and entrusted to the church, by which the divine life is communicated to believers. The earliest Christian sacraments were BAPTISM and the EUCHARIST.

BIBLICAL PERIOD

The Latin word *sacramentum* translates the Greek word *mysterion,* which first appears in the late Greek books of the Old Testament Septuagint (Wis. of Sol. 2:22; Dan. 2:28–29, where it meant "hidden counsels" of GOD. In Roman circles *sacramentum* originally meant the solemn oath that a soldier took to the emperor and the gods, binding him to their service. This notion affected the Christian understanding of a sacrament for the first three centuries. The word *mysterion* refers to "hidden things" associated with the rites of initiation common to the mystery religions.

To the APOSTLE PAUL, mysterion meant both God's hidden plan of salvation (Rom. 16:25–26)

to save humankind through the DEATH and RESURRECTION of Jesus, and the rite by which believers enter into Jesus' death with the hope of resurrection (6:3–3–5). There is a political overtone to Paul's daring statement: the followers of Christ are transferring their loyalty from Rome and its emperor to God's appointed Savior, who brings righteousness and salvation.

LATER DEVELOPMENT

The Latin and Greek terms became fully appropriated in Christian language in a struggle to differentiate Christians from GNOSTICS and adherents of the mystery religions in the late second and early third centuries. CLEMENT OF ALEXANDRIA saw Jesus in Christian-Gnostic terms as the "teacher of the mysteries" (*Carpets* 4.25) who leads the soul to immortality. ORIGEN (c. 185–c. 251) thought of baptism as the symbolic mystery of the third day: Jesus' death, descent into hell, and resurrection on the third day (*Homily on Exodus* 5.2). Cyril of Jerusalem (d. 368) taught that in the LITURGY the reality of Christ's DEATH and resurrection is symbolically transferred to the baptized (*Catechetical Lectures* 20). For Ephraem the Syrian (c. 306–373) past and present, heaven and earth, Exodus and Christ's death and resurrection converge in the sacrament through which the HOLY SPIRIT confers grace on the recipient (*Hymns*).

In the fourth century AUGUSTINE OF HIPPO developed the THEOLOGY of the sacrament as a sign that embodies Christ so powerfully that "even if Judas baptizes, it is Christ who baptizes" (*On the Gospel of John* 6.8). This laid the groundwork for the medieval teaching that it is Christ who performs the sacrament (*EX OPERE OPERATO*). In this view a sacrament is a sign, composed of words and elements, that effectively confers the grace of Christ, who is the primary minister. In the MIDDLE AGES it was also believed that certain sacraments (baptism, CONFIRMATION, and HOLY ORDERS) left an indelible mark on the believer, meaning they are permanent and cannot be repeated.

In the 12th century Peter Lombard, in his *Sentences,* was the first to distinguish between sacraments and sacramentals, acts (the Rosary) and objects (holy water) that have a holy character but are not chief means of grace. He counted seven sacraments: baptism, confirmation, the Eucharist, PENANCE (RECONCILIATION), Holy Orders, ANOINTING OF THE SICK, and MARRIAGE. VATICAN COUNCIL II revised the rites of the sacraments, especially baptism, and reinstalled the catechumenate (*see* CATECHESIS/CATECHUMENATE) in *Sacrosanctum Concilium* 64, the Constitution of the Sacred Liturgy. The council took a pastoral attitude toward the sacraments, especially the Eucharist, as the "work of our redemption" (2) in the life of the church. Today penance is called RECONCILIATION and Extreme Unction is called Anointing of the Sick.

The Catholic Church accepts all seven of these sacraments. Anglicans also accept all seven but conceptualize it as 2 + 5, with baptism and the Eucharist considered the greater two. Most other Protestant churches accept only those two as the only sacraments explicitly mentioned in the BIBLE and the only ones in which Jesus partook. The other five are considered to be important rituals, but they are not considered sacraments in a formal sense. Catholics, Eastern Orthodox, and some Protestant bodies have reached substantial agreement on the content and form of baptism and the Eucharist.

Further reading: Cyril of Jerusalem, *Catechetical Lectures* (Philadelphia: Westminster, 1955); Anselm Grün, *The Seven Sacraments* (London: Continuum, 2003); German Martinez, *Signs of Freedom: Theology of the Christian Sacraments* (New York: Paulist, 2003); Joseph Martos, *The Catholic Sacraments* (Wilmington, Del.: M. Glazier, 1983).

Sacred Heart of Jesus

The devotion to the Sacred Heart of Jesus was founded by St. MARGARET MARY ALACOQUE. The feast was established by Clement XIII (r. 1758–69) in 1765 and extended to the whole church by PIUS IX in 1856. It is celebrated on the Friday after Corpus Christi.

The devotion has roots reaching back to biblical times. In the Gospel of John Jesus speaks of living water flowing from his heart (7:38), and when his side is pierced blood and water flow from it (19:33–37). In Byzantine depictions of the Crucifixion (*see* CROSS/CRUCIFIXION) the water and blood symbolize the saving grace from Christ that is shed on the church.

We can speak of a cult of the Wound in the Side of Jesus. This devotion is found in the *Mystica Vine* and *Tree of Life* by St. BONAVENTURE and appears in the visions of St. Mechtild of Hackeborn (d. 1299), St. Gertrude the Great (d. c. 1302) and JULIAN OF NORWICH. In the late MIDDLE AGES the devotion shifted from the pierced side to the pierced heart of Jesus as the font of all GRACE. This form of the devotion was championed by the JESUITS, St. FRANCIS DE SALES, cofounder of the Visitation Sisters, and especially by St. John Eudes (1601–80), who was the first to provide a detailed theological JUSTIFICATION for the Feast of the Sacred Heart. The real catalyst in the devotion came with the visions granted to the Visitation NUN St. Margaret Mary Alacoque, who sought to provide reparations for outrages against divine love, especially the love shown in the Blessed Sacrament. Along with the devotion to the Sacred Heart of Mary, this devotion is the most popular in Catholic piety.

Prints, statues, and holy cards of the Sacred Heart are frequently found in Catholic and other CHRISTIAN homes. The images depict a sweet, almost feminine yet bearded figure of Jesus displaying his wounded heart.

Further reading: Bertrand de Margerie, *Histoire doctrinale du culte au coeur Jésus* (Paris: Mame, 1992); Bernard Haring, *The Heart of Jesus: Symbol of Redeeming Love* (Liguori, Mo.: Liguori, 1983); Raymond Anthony Jonas, *France and the Cult of the Sacred Heart* (Berkeley: University of California Press, 2000); Karl Rahner, "'Behold This Heart!': Preliminaries to a Theology of Devotion to the Sacred Heart," *Theological Investigations 3* (Baltimore: Helicon, 1967).

saints   *See* CANONIZATION; HAGIOGRAPHY.

Santiago de Compostela

Santiago de Compostela, a town in northwestern SPAIN, is reputedly the burial site of the APOSTLE St. JAMES THE GREAT (Span. Santiago). According to legend, James went to this remote corner of the world and then returned to Palestine, where in 42 he was taken prisoner and beheaded. King Herod refused to allow him to be buried. Hence, some of his companions stole the body and put it on a ship. Various accounts suggest the ship was without a crew and manned by angels. After a swift voyage, the ship landed at the mouth of the river Ulla in Galicia. The group who accompanied the body now encountered another obstacle. The local rulers, King Duyo and Queen Lupa, were hostile to Christianity. However, the apostle was eventually buried secretly on an isolated mountainside.

Some eight centuries later, a hermit named Pelayo had an angelic vision while near the burial site. He heard music and saw something shining.

The BISHOP heard music while in the woods near the town and also saw something shining. He called the place where he saw the shining Campus Stellae, Latin for "field of the star," later shortened to Compostela. The occurrence was eventually reported to the bishop in the town of Iria Flavia, the closest community of any size. He began an investigation. As a result the site of the apostle's tomb was reportedly discovered.

The story was then reported to King Alphonse II (765–842), who responded by declaring Saint James the patron of his empire. He ordered the building of a chapel dedicated to Saint James and subsequently two others dedicated to Jesus CHRIST and to Sts. PETER and PAUL. He also had a MONASTERY built there for AUGUSTINIAN monks. From this beginning, the community of Santiago de Compostela emerged.

Word of the discovery and the building of the church spread quickly through the CHRISTIAN West. The news that one of the Twelve Apostles was buried in Spain immediately turned it into a popular pilgrimage site. As pilgrims came to the site, following what became known as the Camino de Santiago (the way of Saint James), the miniscule community grew to become the city of Santiago de Compostela, and the original chapel was replaced with a CATHEDRAL. It came to rival Rome and Jerusalem as a pilgrimage destination. Pope Calixtus II (r. 1119–24) declared a Jubilee grace (i.e., a plenary indulgence) to those who visited the site during those years when July 25 (St. James's feast day) occurred on a Sunday. Alexander III (r. 1159–81) designated Santiago a "holy town."

Beginning in the 14th century, pilgrimages to Santiago slowed markedly, as did pilgrimages in general, one product of the Black Death ravaging Europe. The pilgrimages to Santiago had almost disappeared until in 1878 Pope LEO XIII issued a bull that reiterated the claim that James's remains were in fact at Santiago. Since that time pilgrimages have steadily grown, and today the city is once again a major site for Roman Catholics, Protestants, and even non-Christians to follow the

Camino. The revived interest in St. James led to a wave of place-namings in his honor, especially in Spanish-speaking Latin America; Santiago, Chile, is one example.

Further reading: Horton Davies and Marie-Hélène Davies, *Holy Days and Holidays: The Medieval Pilgrimage to Santiago de Compostela* (London: Associated University, 1982); Maryjane Dunn and Linda Kay Davidson. *The Pilgrimage to Santiago de Compostela: A Comprehensive Annotated Bibliography* (New York: Garland, 1994); David M. Gitlitz and Linda Kay Anderson, *The Pilgrim Road to Santiago: The Complete Cultural Handbook* (New York: St Martin's Griffin, 2000); Michael Jacobs, *The Road to Santiago de Compostela* (London: Viking, 1991).

Savio, Dominic, St. (1842–1857) *youngest nonmartyr saint*

Dominic Savio, the youngest person to be named a saint by the Catholic Church who did not die as a martyr, was born in Riva, Italy. At the age of 12 he encountered St. John Bosco (1815–88), who had begun a ministry to young boys in Turin, ITALY, and he became a student at Bosco's oratory. Savio began to assist Bosco by organizing a protoreligious order among his contemporaries, called the Company of the Immaculate Conception. His feast day is March 9.

Savio became noted for the unusual amount of time he spent in prayer and for the ecstatic state he would enter unpredictably. He professed that he wanted to do everything for the GLORY OF GOD. Never a robust youth, his health began to fail, and by the beginning of 1857 he developed serious lung problems. Treatment (by bleeding) only worsened his condition, and he died in March 1857.

John Bosco was canonized in 1934 (feast day, January 31). At that same time, some believers wanted Savio recognized as well, but his cause was opposed by others who thought he was too young. Pope PIUS XII decided the case in Savio's favor and canonized him in 1954.

Further reading: John Bosco, *The Life of St. Dominic Savio*. Tr. Paul Aronica, 3d ed. (Paramus, N.J.: Salesiana, 1996).

Savonarola, Girolamo (1452–1498)
Dominican fire brand preacher and reformer

Girolamo Savonarola, who attempted to reform the Catholic Church in the generation prior to the PROTESTANT REFORMATION, was born in 1452 into a well-placed family in Ferrara, northern ITALY. He joined the DOMINICAN ORDER at Bologna as a young man in 1474.

Around his 30th year, he emerged from obscurity as a preacher in Florence, but he left the city for a convent in Brescia, where he served as PRIEST. In 1489 he was given a second opportunity at Florence; his fiery oratory caught on, and he became a popular speaker. His major theme was a jeremiad against the SIN and apostasy of his times.

Savonarola's preaching brought him into opposition to the ruling Medici family, especially Lorenzo di Medici (1447–92), who was endowed with wealth, culture, and a spirit of humanism. Lorenzo passed away in 1492 without taking action against the preacher. The following year, with the pope's approbation, Savonarola was named vicar general of the Dominicans in Tuscany, with the task of reforming the order. As he carried out his reforms, he concluded that nothing short of a change of regime in Florence could bring about true reform. He believed that Charles VIII of FRANCE (r. 1483–98) might be the divinely appointed instrument of that change. The French did in fact conquer the city, but their stay was brief. When they left, a republic was constituted, and Savonarola and his followers took control. He moved to turn the city into a theocracy with GOD as sovereign. A variety of puritanical reforms were instituted. Even Sandro Bottecelli (c. 1445–1510), painter of the *Birth of Venus* was cajoled into burning some of his humanist works.

Problems arose in 1495. Savonarola's followers named him a prophet. His critics charged that claiming the gift of prophecy constituted HERESY. He refused to appear and answer charges against him in Rome, and in 1497 the very humanist Pope ALEXANDER VI excommunicated him. Then in 1498, Medici supporters found popular favor in the city's elections. Savonarola was ordered not to preach, and a member of the rival FRANCISCAN order publicly denounced his program. The public turned against him. He was brought to trial on a laundry list of charges and tortured, during which he made a variety of confessions that he later withdrew. He was nonetheless convicted, hanged with two close followers on May 23, 1498, and burned in the piazza of the Palazzo Vecchio. They proclaimed their loyalty to the church and the FAITH to their death.

Further reading: Rachel Erlanger, *The Unarmed Prophet: Savonarola in Florence* (New York: McGraw-Hill, 1988); John C. Olin, *The Catholic Reformation: Savonarola to Ignatius Loyola* (New York: Harper & Row, 1969); Girolamo Savonarola, *The Triumph of the Cross* (London: Sands, 1901); Pasquele Villari, *Life and Times of Girolamo Savonarola* (London: T. Fisher Unwin, 1920).

Scandinavia

Christianity entered Scandinavia in 826, when the German MONK Ansgar (801–865) began a MISSION to what is now Denmark, and later extended to Sweden. The Danish king Harald Bluetooth (d. 986) left a runic inscription dated to 965 that proclaimed the conversion of the Danes. In fact, the conversion took place over many centuries before a majority of the population became CHRISTIAN. The first Danish ARCHBISHOP was named in 1103.

Ansgar moved on to Sweden in 830. The king, Olof Skötkonung (late ninth century), was probably baptized in the year 1000. In 1164, Uppsala was designated as the see of the first archbishop. St. Bridget (Birgitta) of Sweden (1303–73), known for her visions and revelations and the founding of an order, became Scandinavia's first noted saint.

Christianity was introduced into Norway, the land of the Vikings, in the 10th century by missionaries sent from the archbishop of Bremen-Hamburg in GERMANY. The religion spread as the Viking kingdom expanded. The kingdom reached its greatest growth during the reign of Haakon IV (1204–63), at which time it included Iceland, Greenland, the Scottish Islands, Dublin, and the Faeroe Islands. The Black Death hit Norway especially hard and caused the downfall of the kingdom. In 1397 Norway was brought into the united Scandinavia federation under Denmark. Christianity came to Finland in the ninth century but took several centuries to make any substantial headway. In 1216 Finland was incorporated into the Swedish diocese of Uppsala. The first BISHOP of Finland was appointed several decades later, and by the end of the 13th century, Christianity was fully established throughout the country.

When Ólafur Tryggvason (late 12th century), the king of Norway, accepted the Christian FAITH, he saw it as his duty to extend the faith to the then Norwegian territory of Iceland, which still adhered to its old Norse religion. The stage was set for a violent confrontation, but each side chose a spokesperson to argue its merits. The Christian spokesman presented his cause to the pagan leader. Following a period of private contemplation, the pagan leader spoke for conversion to the new faith if the worship of the old gods could continue in the privacy of people's homes. When Norway's power fell, Iceland passed to Danish control in 1380.

The church prospered in Scandinavia through the 15th century but beginning in the 1530s began to align itself with the PROTESTANT REFORMATION. By the end of the century, all of Scandinavia had been brought into the Lutheran camp and remained there exclusively into the 19th century, when a variety of free churches, most with a pietist base, began to arise. Roman Catholicism was outlawed in Denmark in 1569 and in Sweden in 1604, with the other countries following suit. While several attempts were made through diplomacy to reestablish at least a token Catholic presence, they came to little until the 19th century.

Beginning in 1842, Roman Catholicism found an opening in Norway when the first liberalization of the state church's power was enacted. Seven years later Denmark passed a new constitution that included a freedom of religion clause. The laws against Roman Catholicism were relaxed in Sweden in 1873. Through the last decades of the century, the first Roman Catholic parishes appeared across Scandinavia. Throughout the 20th century, growth was slow but steady. In 1953 the Vatican erected the DIOCESES of Oslo, Stockholm, and Copenhagen. The diocese of Helsinki was established two years later. Reykjavik followed in 1968. Norway has some 45,000 members; Sweden, 89,000; Denmark, 35,000; and Finland, 8,000. Many Catholics are immigrants from other parts of Europe and the Mideast.

The Vatican has established diplomatic relations with all of the Scandinavian countries and maintains contact with Denmark, Finland, Norway, and Sweden through a papal nuncio currently residing in Copenhagen. Iceland is in contact through the papal nuncio residing in Dublin, IRELAND. In 2000 Pope JOHN PAUL II canonized St. Maria Elisabeth Hesselblad (1870–1957), who spent many years in the United States as a nurse to Catholics in New York, converted, refounded the order of the Brigittines in Sweden and Europe, and gave refuge to Jews during the fascist era.

Further reading: David B. Barrett, George T. Kurian, and Todd M. Johnson, *World Christian Encyclopedia* (New York: Oxford University Press, 2001); Jón R. Hjálmarsson, *History of Iceland: From the Settlement to the Present Day.* (Reykjavik: Iceland Review, 1993); L. S. Hunter, *Scandinavian Churches: A Picture of the Development and Life of the Churches of Denmark, Finland, Iceland, Norway, and Sweden* (London: Faber & Faber, 1965); Margareta Skog, ed., *Det religiösa Sverige: Gudstjänst-och andaktsliv under ett veckoslut kring millennieskiftet* (Örebro, Sweden: Libris, 2001).

schism (Gk.: *schisma,* "tear," "rip")

A schism occurs when one part of the church formally and willfully withdraws from union with the larger FAITH community, usually over questions of authority. It is contrasted to HERESY.

The most prominent schisms in the history of Christianity were the DONATISM controversy, the GREAT SCHISM between Eastern and Western Christianity, and the Western Schism during the period of the antipopes and the AVIGNON PAPACY. The break with Rome in the PROTESTANT REFORMATION had both schismatic and heretical aspects. The break from the authority of the Vatican by TRADITIONALIST archbishop Michel Lefebre after VATICAN COUNCIL II is the most recent instance of a schism.

Traditionally, the Catholic Church considered that all CHRISTIAN communions not in union with Rome were in a state of material schism and guilty of SIN. This rigid teaching was radically modified at VATICAN COUNCIL II in *Unitatis Redintegratio,* the Decree on Ecumenism, in which Catholicism recognized degrees of COMMUNION, so that those baptized into other Christian denominations share "a certain, albeit imperfect, communion with the Catholic Church" (3). This laid the grounds for serious dialogue on ECUMENISM with other Christian and even interreligious dialogue with non-Christian communities.

Further reading: Yves Congar, *After Nine Hundred Years: The Background of the Schism Between the Eastern and Western Churches* (New York: Fordham, 1959); Stanley L. Greenslade, *Schism in the Early Church* (London: SCM, 1964); Steven Runciman, *The Eastern Schism* (Oxford: Oxford University Press, 1997).

Scholastica, St. (c. 470–543) *early Benedictine monastic leader and twin of St. Benedict of Nursia*

We know little of the early life of Scholastica, the twin sister of BENEDICT OF NURSIA, the founder of the BENEDICTINES. We do know that as a youth she committed her life to GOD.

At some unknown date, Benedict founded his main monastic community at Monte Cassino, ITALY. Shortly thereafter, Scholastica moved to a spot near the town of Plombariola (some five miles from Monte Cassino) where she established a convent that followed her brother's rule. Benedict operated as the spiritual director for Scholastica and her NUNS. Once a year, Scholastica met with Benedict for a time of spiritual consultation. The last such conference occurred just three days before her death in 543. She was buried at the Monte Cassino MONASTERY with her brother. She is considered the patron saint of Benedictine female orders and their convents. Her feast day is February 10.

Further reading: Jane Morrissey, "Saint Scholastica and Saint Benedict: A Paradox, a Paradigm" in Julia Bolton Holloway, Joan Bechtold, and Constance S. Wright, eds., *Equality in God's Image: Women in the Middle Ages* (Pieterlen: Peter Lang, 1991); Kathleen Norris, *The Holy Twins: Benedict and Scholastica* (New York: Penguin Putnam, 2001).

scholasticism   *See* ALBERTUS MAGNUS; BONAVENTURE; DUNS SCOTUS; THOMAS AQUINAS; WILLIAM OF OCKHAM.

Sedevacantism

The term *sede vacante* (Lat. "the chair [of St. Peter] being empty") technically refers to the period between the death of one pope and the election of another. A contemporary movement that believes VATICAN COUNCIL II erred and that the current PAPACY is illegitimate is called Sedevacantism. The movement believes that the Vatican II documents are permeated with HERESY. Hence, beginning with PAUL VI, the holders of the papal office in Rome are deemed heretics. The crux of their argument centers on the abandonment of the Tridentine Latin Mass and the rise of the use of vernacular worship. In addition, the popes are

charged with acting in ways that no true pope would have acted.

The Sedevacantists have created a dilemma for themselves concerning authority within the church. They regard the pope as essential for the church's survival, yet they believe that no pope currently reigns. They also hesitate to name a new valid pope, as that would mean formal SCHISM from the church. They remain a relatively small network of groups waiting for some event that will justify their position and bring, possibly by supernatural means, a valid pope back to Rome.

The largest number of Sedevacantist BISHOPS have orders derived from Archbishop Pierre-Martin Ngo-Dhinh Thuc (1897–1984), the former ARCHBISHOP of Hue, who in the 1970s found himself exiled from his homeland and residing in FRANCE. An archconservative, he consecrated several bishops in SPAIN, for which he was excommunicated in 1976. He repented of his actions. The excommunication was lifted, but in the following years he consecrated additional bishops, and in 1982 publicly stated his view that no pope reigned in Rome. He was excommunicated again in 1983.

The 1975 Spanish consecrations, combined with a set of claimed apparitions of the Blessed Virgin Mary, led to the creation of the Palmarian Catholic Church and the naming of Clemente Domínguez y Gomez (1946–2005), one of the Thuc bishops, as the new pope. He took the name Gregory XVII. He claimed that the Virgin had appeared to him in 1968 near the village of El Palmar de Troya, whence the name of the church. He also claimed that Jesus mystically named him his sub-Vicar with right of succession after PAUL VI's death. The second wave of consecrations, especially those of two bishops in Mexico, made Thuc's episcopal orders available to the TRADITIONALISTS, and in subsequent years more than 100 men were consecrated as traditionalist bishops serving with various branches of Sedevacanists. The episcopal orders through Thuc have been crucially important to the Sedevacantists. While illicit, they are considered valid by Catholic authorities; hence Sedevacantists (though excommunicated) can offer real sacraments to believers (*see* VALIDITY). The Thuc orders also allow the Sedevacantist leadership to avoid seeking Anglican or Old Catholic orders.

The Sedevacantists are now organized in a number of small autonomous communities, among the more important centers being the Union Católico Trento in Sonora, Mexico, and the Congregation of Mary Immaculate Queen in Spokane, Washington. Estimates of support for Sedevacantism range from a few thousand to as many as 10,000 to 20,000 worldwide. The main centers are in NORTH AMERICA and western Europe.

The Sedevacantists are to be distinguished from the much larger segment of traditionalists (such as the Society of Pope Pius X), who, while organized separately, still believe that the current pope is a valid holder of the papal office. Most of them are also distinct from the antipope groups, who have chosen to go through the process of electing an alternative pope to whom they now offer allegiance.

Further reading: Michael Cuneo, *The Smoke of Satan: Conservative and Traditionalist Dissent in Contemporary American Catholicism* (New York: Oxford University Press, 1997).

seminary (Lat.: *semen,* "seed")

Ecclesiastical seminaries are schools, colleges, and universities dedicated to the training and education of the CLERGY. The first seminaries began as cathedral schools attached to the main church of a DIOCESE. St. AUGUSTINE set up one such in Hippo. ALCUIN OF YORK spread the idea of the cathedral school throughout CHARLEMAGNE's empire. Later, the MENDICANT ORDERS founded schools for the education and training of their own members; their schools were attached to the great universities of Europe.

The Council of TRENT mandated that each diocese must either found its own seminary or join with other dioceses in founding joint seminaries. The rules governing seminaries are contained in the Code of Canon Law (cnn. 232–64). With the decline of candidates for the priesthood the minor seminaries (high schools and junior colleges) have almost completely disappeared. Some seminaries have become embroiled in sexual scandals (*see* PEDOPHILIA).

Many religious orders maintain their central seminaries in ROME. They include the Jesuit Gregorianum, the Franciscan Franciscanum, and the Dominican Angelicum. Many American diocesan PRIESTs study at the North American College in Rome, and many BISHOPs have been chosen from among its graduates. The earliest seminary in the United States is St. Mary's Seminary in Baltimore, Maryland, founded in 1791 by Cardinal JAMES GIBBONS and staffed by French Sulpician Fathers.

Further reading: R. Scott Appleby, Patricia Byrne, and William Portiers, ed., *Creative Fidelity: American Catholic Intellectual Traditions* (Maryknoll, N.Y.: Orbis, 2004); J. T. Dillon: *House of Formation: A Catholic Seminary in the 1950s* (Riverside: University of California Press, 2003); J. A. O'Donohue, *Tridentine Seminary Legislation: Its Sources and Its Formation* (Louvain: Bibliotheca Ephemeridum Theologicarum, 1957); Paul Thigpen, *Shaken by Scandals: Catholics Speak Out About Priests' Sexual Abuse* (Ann Arbor, Mich.: Charis, 2002).

sensus fidelium (Lat.: "the sense or understanding of the faithful")

In the Catholic debate about who should perform the teaching function of the church—the MAGISTERIUM—some argue that the pope and the HIERARCHY must share responsibility with all the faithful, CLERGY and lay alike. They believe the *sensus fidelium*—the understanding of the ordinary CHRISTIAN faithful—is fundamentally reliable.

Cardinal JOHN HENRY NEWMAN was the principal champion for consulting the faithful in matters of doctrine. He favored the expression *consensus fidelium*. His key evidence was that during the controversies surrounding ARIANISM in the early church it was the ordinary faithful who kept to an orthodox belief of the INCARNATION of GOD in CHRIST, while a large part of the hierarchy, including popes and BISHOPS in council, often wavered or were confused. Pope Liberius (r. 352–66), for example, at first accepted the decision of the Arian emperor Constantius II (r. 337–61) to condemn St. ATHANASIUS OF ALEXANDRIA for his orthodoxy; he recanted only when the emperor died.

The period of the AVIGNON PAPACY and ANTI-POPES culminating in the Council of CONSTANCE brought into question the nature and extent of papal authority. In the Gallican Declaration of the Clergy of FRANCE (1682), papal primacy was limited by the temporal power of princes, by the authority of a general council and of the bishops, whose consent was necessary to make papal decrees fully infallible, and by the canons and customs of particular churches. In response, VATICAN COUNCIL I declared in the decree on papal INFALLI-BILITY, *Pastor Aeternus* 11, that the declarations of the Roman pontiff are "irreformable of themselves and not from the consent of the Church."

Nonetheless, VATICAN COUNCIL II sought to qualify, if not limit, the splendid isolation of this decree. It upheld the collegial teaching role of all the bishops and also asserted that the laity share in Christ's prophetic office: the "entire body of the faithful, anointed as they are by the Holy One, cannot err in matters of belief" (*Lumen Gentium* 12, Dogmatic Constitution on the Church); the pope and bishops were told to give attention to the *sensus fidelium* (*Lumen Gentium* 35). In practice, this has not been followed. For example, on the question of birth control, surveys show that as many as 70 percent of Catholics worldwide follow their own conscience on this matter. Under Popes JOHN PAUL II and BENEDICT XVI many observers have noticed a return to the spirit, if not the complete letter, of the 19th-century *Pastor Aeternus*.

Further reading: Richard R. Gaillardetz, *By What Authority? A Primer on Scripture, the Magisterium, and the Sense of the Faithful* (Collegeville, Minn.: Liturgical Press, 2003); Maureen Fiedler and Linda Rabben, ed., *Rome Has Spoken: A Guide to Forgotten Papal Statements and How They Have Changed through the Centuries* (New York: Crossroad, 1998); Michael Sharkey "Newman on the Laity," *Gregorianum* (1987) 68/1–2:339–346).

Serra, Junípero, Bl. (1713–1784) *Franciscan missionary to California*

Miguel José Serra i Ferrer was born in Petra, Majorca. Upon joining the FRANCISCANS he took the name Junípero in honor of an early follower of St. Francis. He taught philosophy in Palma and from 1749 at the College of San Fernando in Mexico City. After King Carlos III (1716–88) expelled the JESUITS from Baja, California in 1768, Serra became head of the missions there.

The following year, after founding Misión San Fernando Rey de España de Velicatá in Baja, he led a major expedition up the Pacific coast that established missions at San Diego, Monterey, San Juan, and San Francisco. In 1771 he moved his mission headquarters to Carmel, where he died in 1784 and is interred. Pope JOHN PAUL II beatified him on September 25, 1988. Many Californians support his canonization, but others, including many Native Americans, accuse Serra of enslaving indigenous peoples at his missions.

Further reading: Katherine Ainsworth and Edward M. Ainsworth, *In the Shade of the Juniper Tree; A Life of Fray Junípero Serra* (Garden City, N.Y.: Doubleday, 1970).

Seton, St. Elizabeth Ann Bayley (1774–1821) *first saint born in what became the United States*

Elizabeth Ann Bayley Seton, the first person born in what is now the United States to be canonized by the Catholic Church, was born into a prominent family in the British American colonies. Her family was affiliated with the Church of England, which reorganized as the Episcopal Church after the American Revolution. Her feast day is January 4.

After marrying businessman William Magee Seton in 1794, Elizabeth devoted her free time to organizing a Society for the Relief of Poor Widows with Children. Her husband died in 1803 while they were visiting ITALY. Remaining in that country for a period of time, she was drawn to the Catholic Church. Back in the United States, she formally converted in 1805, an act that isolated her from most of her family. She had become a poor widow with five children of her own to raise.

She eventually moved to Baltimore and opened a school for girls while nurturing the idea of a religious community of women on the model of the Daughters of Charity of St. VINCENT DE PAUL. In 1812 the rule of the Daughters of Charity of Saint Joseph was approved, and the original group of 18 sisters took their vows in 1813. She was elected the first superior of the order and came to be known as Mother Seton. The Sisters of Charity, as the group came to be known, relocated to Emmitsburg, Maryland, where their motherhouse remains today.

In the remaining eight years of her life, Mother Seton composed a set of hymns and gave a number of discourses on the spiritual life. At the same time, she took the lead in expanding the order. While the sisters founded hospitals and orphanages, their primary work was founding schools. Some have credited her with laying the foundation for the parochial school system that became so much a part of Catholic life in the United States.

When Seton died in 1821, 20 houses had already been founded. The prominent American church leader JAMES GIBBONS took up the cause for her canonization. She was finally beatified by Pope JOHN XXIII and canonized in 1975 by Pope PAUL VI. In the years after her death, the Sisters of Charity have undergone a number of changes and now exist as an association of convents and charitable institutions.

Further reading: Joseph I. Dirvin, *Mrs. Seton, Foundress of the American Sisters of Charity* (New York: Farrar, Straus, Cudahy, 1968); Elizabeth Ann Seton, *Elizabeth Ann Seton: A Woman of Prayer: Meditations, Reflections, Prayers, and Poems Taken From Her Writings*, ed. Sister Marie Celeste (New York: Alba House, 1993); ———, *Elizabeth Seton: Selected Writings* (New York: Paulist, 1987); Charles I. White, *Mother Seton, Mother of Many Daughters* (New York: Doubleday, 1949).

sexuality

Sexuality is the general term covering all relations between human beings of a genital or amorous nature and related matters such as gender identity. Christianity emerged from the matrix of Judaism, which heartily approved of marriage and saw offspring as a fulfillment of divine promise (Gen. 15:4–5). Judaism even included the graceful, sensuous, and highly erotic Song of Solomon among its sacred Scripture.

At the time of Jesus the normal expectation was for a man to be married. Members of the Sanhedrin were required to be married and have children. There is no evidence that Jesus was married, but there is also no evidence that he was not. Peter was clearly married (Matt. 8:14–15), as probably were most of the other APOSTLES. In 1 Corinthians 7 PAUL urges everyone not to change their positions in life, given the imminence of the Second Coming. Many have taken this passage to infer that he was not married. But as a Pharisee he would have been expected to be married. In Philippians 4:3 Paul implores his "true yoke-partner" (*gnesie syzyge*) to aid his coworkers. Ancient commentators took this to refer to his wife (CLEMENT OF ALEXANDRIA, *Stromata* 3.53.1).

The late pastoral epistles in the New Testament warn against those who forbid marriage (1 Timothy 4:3). In contrast to the denigration of the body among the followers of Gnosticism and later MANICHAEISM, the orthodox CREED stressed the goodness of the body and material creation.

Some orthodox Christian groups, however, urged sexual abstinence altogether. Furthermore, in the next few centuries church leaders began to take an ascetic view of sexual activity, even in marriage. They forbade premarital and extramarital sex and urged married people to practice sexual moderation and "passionless" sex limited to the purposes of procreation (CLEMENT OF ALEXANDRIA, *Paidogogos* 2.10.91; AUGUSTINE OF HIPPO, *City of God* 14), and contraception was condemned (*Didache* 2.2.).

Beginning as early as the second century, the condemnation of remarriage and the teaching of the perpetual virginity of MARY OF NAZARETH helped create a culture in which the celibate, monastic, and religious life was considered superior to that of laypeople. Augustine located original SIN in the disorder of will, which was manifest in the concupiscence of the flesh. Some, such as Jovinian (d. 405) and JULIAN OF ECLANUM, argued for the goodness of CREATION and for marriage and the equality of a lay life lived in holiness, but their voices were effectively shut out.

In the subsequent tradition Catholicism laid down a rather clinical standard for permissible sexual activity: the insertion of the penis and the ejaculation of semen into the vagina of a spouse solely for the purpose of procreation, preferably without passion. A variety of practices were considered intrinsically EVIL, including contraception by artificial means, coitus interruptus, masturbation, premarital and extramarital sex, and homosexuality.

In time this traditional view of sexuality was modified to allow for a more ample idea of marital love between two people covenanted in MARRIAGE. In modern times this more expansive view owes much to the thinking of FRANZ VON BAADER and the idea of PERSONALISM. Personalism stirred a deeper appreciation of human sexuality as a reflection of the image of God as a community of love. This changed attitude allowed for the use of the rhythm method of birth control (intercourse during the wife's infertile periods) by married couples in PAUL V's *Humanae Vitae* 24 (July 25, 1968). Both Paul VI and JOHN PAUL II affirmed human sexuality and marriage in a way that went far beyond their predecessors, and, most recently,

BENEDICT XVI's first encyclical *Deus Caritas Est* ("God is love," December 25, 2005) affirmed all dimensions of love, including the erotic.

At the turn of the millennium the church was roiled by questions of PEDOPHILIA in the priesthood and homosexuality. For a time Vatican spokespersons tried to blame pedophilia on homosexual orientation, but many psychologists disputed any such connection, although some researchers have argued that a considerable number of PRIESTS today are homosexual in orientation.

In 2005 the Vatican addressed the question of the ordination of celibate homosexuals by issuing the *Instruction Concerning the Criteria for the Discernment of Vocations with regard to Persons with Homosexual Tendencies in View of their Admission to the Seminary and to Holy Orders* (November 29, 2005), written by Cardinal Zenon Grocholewski (1939–) of the Congregation for Catholic Education. The *Instruction* renewed a long-standing ban on sexually active homosexual priests but allowed for the ordination of men who have been celibate for three years, show no deep-seated homosexual "tendencies," and are not "supporters of gay culture." The document has come under severe criticism by many outside Catholicism and some within. The issue of sexuality also plays a key role in the question of the ordination of WOMEN (*see* HOLY ORDERS).

Further reading: Charles E. Curran, *Change in Official Catholic Moral Teaching* (New York: Paulist, 2003); Thomas C. Fox, *Sexuality and Catholicism* (New York: G. Braziller, 1995); John Paul II, *The Theology of the Body: Human Love in the Divine Plan* (Boston: Pauline Books & Media, 1997); Eugene C. Kennedy, *The Unhealed Wound: The Church and Human Sexuality* (New York: St. Martin's, 2001).

Sheen, Fulton J. (1895–1979) *bishop and pioneer in religious broadcasting*

Bishop Fulton J. Sheen's *Life Is Worth Living* was a national popular inspirational television program in the 1950s, appearing weekly in prime time. Sheen later served as ARCHBISHOP of Rochester, New York.

Sheen was born in El Paso, Texas. He attended St. Viator College in Bourbonnais, Illinois, and St. Paul Seminary in Minnesota. Following his ordination as a PRIEST in 1919, he continued his studies at Catholic University of America (CUA) in Washington, D.C., and the Catholic University of Louvain, where he completed his Ph.D. in 1923. He began working as a priest in the diocese of Peoria, but in 1926 he moved to Washington to teach at Catholic University of America, where he remained in various capacities until 1950.

While at CUA, he began his work in religious broadcasting, starting at WLWL Radio in New York in 1928. In 1930 he became the regular speaker on NBC's *The Catholic Hour,* which ran for 22 years. In 1934 he presided at New York's first televised religious service, before the medium was commercialized. In 1951 he launched his weekly television program, *Life Is Worth Living.* The program featured a winsome lecture by Sheen that centered on a set of religious and moral issues common to a wide spectrum of Americans. A majority of his more than 30 million listeners were not Catholics. The show inspired his 1953 best-selling book, *Life Is Worth Living.* Shortly before beginning his television show, Sheen was named director of activities in the United States for the Society for the Propagation of the Faith.

Through his career, the church's HIERARCHY recognized Sheen's accomplishments. In 1930, he was made a papal chamberlain and given the honorary rank of monsignor. In 1966 he was named BISHOP of Rochester and in 1969 titular archbishop of Newport, Wales.

During his years in Rochester, Sheen concentrated his energies on ECUMENISM (following in the spirit of the recent VATICAN COUNCIL II) and POVERTY. However, in contrast to his television persona, his diocesan leadership tended to be autocratic. He resigned in 1969 at the age of 74 during a public controversy over his leadership

style. Before he died, he publicly expressed his disagreement with some of the changes introduced by Vatican II. He died in New York in 1979.

Further reading: D. P. Noonan, *The Passion of Fulton Sheen* (New York: Dodd, Mead, 1972); Thomas C. Reeves, *America's Bishop: The Life and Times of Fulton J. Sheen* (San Francisco: Encounter, 2001); Fulton J. Sheen, *The Electronic Christian: 105 Readings from Fulton J. Sheen* (New York: Macmillan, 1979); ———, *Life Is Worth Living* (New York: McGraw-Hill, 1953); ———, *Peace of Soul* (New York: Whittlesey House, 1949); ———, *Treasure in Clay: The Autobiography of Fulton J. Sheen* (Garden City, N.Y.: Doubleday, 1980).

Shroud of Turin

In the 20th century, the Shroud of Turin, a woven cloth about 14 by 3.5 feet with a human image on it, emerged as one of the most important and controversial RELICS of Christendom. The shroud is believed by many to be the burial cloth of Jesus. It is imprinted with the face and body of a person showing wounds from a crucifixion (*see* CROSS/CRUCIFIXION). Some believe the image appeared at the moment of Christ's RESURRECTION. There are actually two images on the shroud, one of the front of the body and one of the back, as if a person were lain to rest at one end and the other end were wrapped over the top of his head.

The earliest known date for the shroud, now housed in a chapel in Turin, ITALY, is 1355, when its owner, Geoffrey de Charney (c. 1300–56), displayed it at a church in Lirey, FRANCE, claiming that it was CHRIST's shroud. Within two years a pilgrimage medal was struck to commemorate the many believers who had journeyed to see the cloth. It soon came under attack, however, as the local BISHOP questioned the shroud's authenticity and launched an investigation. The controversy continued until one of Geoffrey's descendents passed the cloth to the House of Savoy, later to emerge as the kings of Italy. In 1532, a fire in the chapel where the shroud was housed left burn marks on it as well as water marks from attempts to douse the fire. In 1578, the shroud was relocated to Turin, where it is now housed in the Royal Chapel of the Cathedral of St. John the Baptist. Through the centuries, the shroud resided in a reliquary in the chapel and was taken out for viewing only on special occasions.

The modern story of the shroud began in 1898. Seconda Pia (1855–1941), an amateur photographer, took the first photographs of the cloth and made some newsworthy discoveries. He noticed that the shroud presented a negative image not too different from a photographic negative. Pia's discovery opened a new controversy centered on the shroud's possible scientific credentials, with shroud supporters pointing to its negative image as proof of authenticity and refutation of the charge that it was merely a medieval artifact.

In 1978, a group of scientists, led by American physicist John Jackson, examined the shroud at length. They took new pictures and conducted a series of agreed-upon experiments. Their 1981 report offered a variety of findings that, however hesitant, favored its extraordinary origin, arguing that the image on the cloth was produced during a moment of intense heat emanating from a body that was, at that moment, weightless.

For skeptics, the more definitive experiments were conducted in 1988, when small samples of the shroud cloth were removed and subjected to carbon dating analyses at three different laboratories. All three reported a date of origin between 1260 and 1390, dating that was consistent with the cloth having been produced shortly before Geoffrey de Charney first displayed it.

While debate about the shroud continues, thousands of pilgrims make their way to Turin annually. Meanwhile, a best-selling Spanish novel, *Hermandad de la Sabana Santa* ("The Brotherhood of the Holy Shroud," 2004) by Julia Navarro (1953–), offered the most unique hypothesis. Navarro suggests that the original burial cloth (which may still exist somewhere, hidden by a neo-Templar cult) miraculously generated a clone, the Shroud of Turin. The shroud thus exists as a miraculous relic consistent with the medieval carbon dating.

Further reading: Mark Antonacci, *The Resurrection of the Shroud* (New York: M. Evans, 2000); Vittorio Guerrera, *The Shroud of Turin: A Case for Authenticity* (Rockford, Ill.: Tan, 2000); Mark Guscin, *The Burial Cloths of Christ* (London: Catholic Truth Society, 2000); Joe Nickell, *Inquest On The Shroud Of Turin: Latest Scientific Findings* (Amherst, N.Y.: Prometheus Books, 1998); Ian Wilson, *The Mysterious Shroud* (Garden City, N.Y.: Doubleday, 1986).

Shusaku Endo (1923–1996) *Japanese Catholic novelist*

Shusaku Endo, one of Japan's most highly praised novelists, converted to Catholicism (somewhat reluctantly) at the age of 11 along with his divorced mother. He lived through World War II in Japan and in 1950 traveled to FRANCE to begin three years of study at the University of Lyons.

Much of his writing concerns his struggle with his Catholicism and his efforts to remain both a faithful CHRISTIAN and a good citizen of his homeland. Possibly Endo's best work was *Silence* (1966), which dealt with the martyr's death of a Portuguese missionary to Japan in the 17th century. As a boy he had visited the museum in Nagasaki commemorating the many martyrs of that era, when the Japanese government tried to destroy the church (*see* NAGASAKI MARTYRS).

Other novels include *The Sea and Poison* (1958), *Wonderful Fool* (1959), *The Samurai* (1980), and *Deep River* (1993). Besides his fiction, Endo wrote a number of essays, both religious and secular. He was a very popular radio and television personality. He died in 1996. Three years later a museum dedicated to his life and work was established in Sotome, Japan.

Further reading: Shusaku Endo, *The Final Martyrs* (London: Peter Owen, 1993); ———, *Foreign Studies*

(London: Peter Owen, 1990); ———, *A Life of Jesus* (Mahwah, N.J.: Paulist, 1978); ———, *Silence.* tr. William Johnston (Tokyo: Sophia University, 1970); Mark B. Williams, *Endo Shusaku: A Literature of Reconciliation* (London: Routledge, 1999).

Simeon Stylites, St. (c. 390–459) *hermit saint*

The MONK Simeon (or Simon) Stylites had lived in a MONASTERY for nine years and as a hermit for 10, when around 423 he withdrew to a tiny perch about two cubits (38 inches) in circumference at the top of a Greco-Roman column (in Greek, style), where he lived for seven years, and about 30 years on another taller column. During this time he was dependent on others to bring him food.

Simeon did not lack for attention. As his stay on the pillar lengthened, his fame and his reputation for holiness spread. His feat was viewed as an attempt to lift himself above earthly concerns and resist the downward pull of human nature. He gained a reputation as a miracle worker. Many came to seek his advice and receive his blessing, including no less a personage than the Roman emperor Theodosius II (401–50).

When he died in 459, his body was taken to Antioch (Syria) in a large procession that included a garrison of soldiers. His body was preserved for a time. Evagrius (c. 536–c. 600) left an account of Simeon in his *Ecclesiastical History,* reporting to have seen Simeon's head, considered a most sacred relic, in 580.

Numerous legends grew up around Simeon— that he ate only once a week and not at all during Lent, that he spent the last year of his life standing on one leg, and so on. For several centuries others tried to follow his example. A disciple named Daniel (d. 493) and a later saint who took Simeon's name (often called Simeon the Younger, d. c. 596) were among the more famous ascetics who spent time on pillars.

Further reading: Richard Challoner, *Life of St. Simon the Stylite (389–459)* (Willets, Calif.: Eastern Orthodox, 1977); Robert Doran, *The Lives of Simeon Stylites* (Kalamazoo: Cistercian, 1992); Evagrius Scholasticus, *The Ecclesiastical History of Evagrius Scholasticus,* tr. Michael Whitby (Liverpool: Liverpool University Press, 2000).

sin (Old Eng.: *synn,* "transgression"; Lat.: *peccatum;* Gk.: *harmartia/paraptoma;* Heb.: *hita*)

Fundamentally, the Jewish and CHRISTIAN traditions consider sin to be a turning away from or a rebellion against the command or will of GOD. The paradigm of all subsequent sin is the violation by ADAM AND EVE of God's prohibition against eating of the tree of knowledge of good and EVIL in the midst of the Garden (Gen. 3:6–7), which brought about DEATH and disordered relations between humans and nature itself. The Greek and Hebrew terms also carry a connotation of "missing the mark." Catholics make distinctions between original, venial, and mortal sin.

The Hebrew prophets spoke of individual sinful acts, as when Nathan charged David with the death of Uriah the Hittite (1 Kings 12). However, the main reason they called down divine lawsuits against Israel and its kings was the breach of the social provisions of the Covenant, especially the care of widows, orphans, and the poor. The Psalms place the center of sin in the human heart; they explore the theological and psychological devastation that ensues when sin alienates the believer from the favor of God (Psalm 129: "Out of the depths I cry unto you, O Lord").

In the New Testament there was a deepening of the traditional notion of sin. Sin is rooted not only in the external breach of the divine order but also in the innermost intentions of the sinner (Matt. 5:21–30). Theologians in the second century envisioned sin not so much as a single action but as an orientation that led to the Way of Death instead of the Way of Life (*Didachē* 1.1–6.2). St. AUGUSTINE OF HIPPO later reformulated this duality in his vision of the Two Cities, the City of God and the City of Humans. Early Christians were rigorous about lapses from the Way of Life; the sinner was permitted only a second opportunity after BAPTISM to repent of the serious sins of idolatry, murder, or adultery. When they eventually relaxed this rigor, they needed to develop the SACRAMENT OF RECONCILIATION, or PENANCE.

By the fourth century theologians sought to understand why humans had fallen into sin (see THE FALL. Ultimately they ascribed it to the creatureliness of human nature; CREATION is fallible and liable to change (ATHANASIUS, *On the Incarnation* 3–5). Augustine in *On Marriage and Lust* placed the fault in the perversion of the human will; the vitiation of human nature had been passed from Adam and Eve to all descendants through sexual intercourse, a view that has tainted all Western views of SEXUALITY and from which Christianity and Catholicism are just beginning to emerge. For Augustine sin could be overcome only through the inner workings not of fallen human will but of divine GRACE.

Early theologians did not place total blame on humanity; they saw the trickery of Satan and demons at work in sin (GREGORY OF NYSSA, *Catechetical Orations* 5–6). The overwhelming power of sin led some in the second and third centuries to think that sin and evil were objective, ontological cosmic forces (see GNOSTICS; MANICHAEISM). Most orthodox theologians believed that the mystery of iniquity could not be deciphered directly with rational thought. It had to be approached indirectly through symbols since a fundamental ambiguity remains: humans are destined for the good but inclined to evil. Sin, they believed, must be a more than human force.

In the eighth and ninth centuries, moral theologians developed an elaborate penitential system. They began to make a distinction between venial and mortal sins. The latter are those violations of the moral order serious enough that they destroy the relationship between the sinner and God. A person in the state of mortal sin is prohibited from partaking of the EUCHARIST until the sin is confessed and forgiven in the Sacrament of Reconciliation. Should a person die in that state, he or she is liable to eternal punishment in hell. As JUSTIFICATION for a doctrine of mortal sins these theologians pointed to 1 Corinthians 6:9–10, where PAUL lists sins that would keep a person from inheriting the Kingdom of God: immorality, idolatry, sexual perversion, thievery, greed, drunkenness, revilers, and robbers.

For an act to be a mortal sin, three conditions have to be met: it must be of a grave nature (such as the taking of a human life), it must be committed with knowledge of the seriousness of the act, and there must be the full consent of the will to commit the act. Any act in which one of these conditions is missing or significantly diminished would suggest the act is less than a mortal sin. Those sins that do not qualify as mortal sins are termed venial sins. A person who dies in a state of venial sin is liable to a period of punishment in PURGATORY.

Many contemporary moral theologians, especially BERNARD HÄRING, have argued that the listing and division of sins between mortal and venial leads to a mechanistic, individualistic, and external view of sin and neglects both the deeply interior and the communal aspects of sin. Many Catholics have been led into a confessional trap in which they think that their only grave sins are sexual ones. Häring promoted a return to the pattern of the *Didachē*, which sees grace and sin as life orientations and commitments toward the Way of Life or the Way of Death, and not just a list of sinful acts. The story of the Prodigal Son in Luke 15:1–32 shows that the difference between sin and grace is the difference between death and RESURRECTION.

See also THEOLOGY.

Further reading: J. Patout Burns, *Theological Anthropology* (Philadelphia: Fortress: 1981); Hugh Connolly, *Sin* (London: Continuum, 2002); Paul Levine, *Mortal Sin* (New York: HarperCollins, 1994); Hubert Louis Motry, *The Concept of Mortal Sin in Early Christianity* (Washington, D.C.: Catholic University of America Press, 1920); Paul Ricoeur, *The Symbolism of Evil* (Boston: Beacon, 1969).

Sisters of Mercy

The Sisters of Mercy, an international religious community of women, has become the largest female religious order founded in the English-speaking world. Its founder, Catherine McAuley (1778–1841), grew up in IRELAND when the Anglican establishment imposed by GREAT BRITAIN was still the dominant religious force. Catholic schools had been closed, and while Catholicism survived, it had been severely suppressed. Catherine became the ward of Protestant relatives but quietly retained the Catholic FAITH of her parents. In the early 19th century many of the restrictions on the church began to be lifted. The Catholic Church was fully legalized in 1828. In 1829 established status of the Church of England was withdrawn. The church underwent an immediate and dramatic revival.

McAuley unexpectedly inherited a large sum of money in 1818 from a couple she had helped along the way. She used the funds to start a boarding school for young women with volunteer teachers. Once under way, the community of female teachers looked very much like a convent, though they had not taken vows. At the suggestion of Dublin's ARCHBISHOP, Daniel Murray (1768–1852), the school staff made the transformation to the religious life with a noncloistered rule to allow the women to work among the poor. The Sisters of Mercy was formally organized in 1831.

The women soon became known as the "walking nuns," a local sight and subject of conversation. They soon won over skeptical observers and opened additional convents. Over the remaining decade of her life, McAuley saw to the creation of 12 convents in Ireland and two in England, the first convents to open since the PROTESTANT REFORMATION.

The international spread of the movement began in the 1840s when the first Sisters of Mercy arrived in the United States. They soon fanned out across the country from New York to San Francisco. Once established in a community, they moved as quickly as possible to open a hospital and school. Organization in the Americas pro-

ceeded through several stages. In 1929, 39 of the 60 motherhouses in the United States formed an initial association, the Sisters of Mercy of the Union. At the same time, the movement was spreading to LATIN AMERICA. In 1965, all of the Sisters of Mercy centers in the United States formed a federation, which evolved into the Institute of the Sisters of Mercy of the Americas, formally created in 1991. Their ministry covers a wide spectrum of professions, from pastoral ministry to medicine.

As the 21st century begins, the Sisters of Mercy have work in 25 countries worldwide, including 12 in the Americas. There are over 10,000 sisters worldwide. In the United States, they can be found in most states. McAuley was beatified by Pope JOHN PAUL II in 1990.

Further reading: Mary Carmel Bourke, *A Woman Sings of Mercy* (Harrisburg, Penn.: Morehouse, 1987); Mary C. Sullivan, *Catherine McAuley and the Tradition of Mercy* (Notre Dame: University of Notre Dame Press, 1995).

Smith, Alfred Emanuel (1873–1944) *U.S. Catholic Democratic presidential candidate*

Al Smith, the first Roman Catholic to run for president of the United States on a major party ticket, was born in New York City in 1873. As a youth, he lost his father and put aside his own education to support his family. In 1895, the Democratic Party in New York City (Tammany Hall) secured a job for him in the office of the commissioner of jurors. The job launched a career in politics and public service.

Smith's first elective post was in the state assembly, where he served for 12 years beginning in 1903. His stay culminated in his election as speaker of the assembly in 1913. He moved from the assembly in 1915 to become the sheriff of New York County and then president of the Aldermen of Greater New York City (1917).

An underdog when he entered the race, in 1918 Smith won the New York state governor's office. After a single defeat in 1920, he was reelected for three additional terms. He built a national reputation with his efforts to improve housing, change factory laws, provide better care for the mentally ill, and improve child welfare. Business leaders approved of his efforts to reorganize the state government on a more efficient businesslike basis.

Smith's name initially received serious consideration as a candidate for president in 1924. In 1928 he easily won the Democratic nomination. He ran as an urbanite and lost to Herbert Hoover (1874–1964), who did well in the rural South and West. Smith's chances were damaged by virulent anti-Catholic campaigns in an era when the Ku Klux Klan was active nationally; he was accused of being a stalking horse for the pope (*see* ANTI-CATHOLICISM). Hoover had the bad fortune to be in office when the Great Depression hit and was defeated by Smith's successor as governor of New York, Franklin D. Roosevelt (1882–1945). An embittered Smith gradually fell out with the Democratic Party and its social welfare policies, which he had helped to define. In 1936 and 1940 he supported the Republicans against Roosevelt. He died in New York City on October 4, 1944.

Further reading: William Allen, *Al Smith's Tammany Hall: Champion Political Vampire* (New York: Institute for Public Service, 1928): Paula Eldot, *Governor Alfred E. Smith—The Politician as Reformer* (New York: Garland, 1983); Christopher M. Finan, *Alfred E. Smith—The Happy Warrior* (New York: Hill & Wang, 2002); Franklin D. Roosevelt, *The Happy Warrior, Alfred E. Smith: A Study of A Public Servant* (New York: Houghton Mifflin, 1928); Alfred E. Smith, *Up to Now: An Autobiography by Alfred E. Smith* (New York: Viking, 1929).

Society of St. Vincent de Paul

The Society of St. Vincent de Paul emerged out of the "Conference of Charity," an informal association of Catholic students in Paris, founded in 1833 by Frederic Ozanam (1813–53), Joseph Emmanuel Bailly, Francois Lailier, Augustus Le Tallandier, Paul Lamache, Felix Clave, and J. Devaux. Amid the revolutionary political and social turmoil of the period, the group wanted to explore the role of the church as a benefactor to people. Le Taillandier initiated the idea that a charitable group could help them act out their Christian commitments. Ozanam led in setting up the group, and Bailly, an older man, agreed to take over leadership and direction. The group soon found others who wanted to join their effort.

The work spread throughout the world faster than anyone had imagined. By 1845, when Pope Gregory XVI (r. 1831–46) offered his approbation, the Society was working across FRANCE, in four neighboring countries, and in NORTH AMERICA. By the end of the decade it was in 14 countries. As the work grew the society took St. Vincent de Paul as its patron and assumed its present name.

The society spread throughout the Western world, where members are organized into local conferences. Members devote themselves to personal ministry with those trapped in poverty and to creating institutions to alleviate their suffering—second-hand stores, hospitals, orphanages, and so on. By the end of the 20th century, the society had 875,000 lay and clerical members in 47,000 conferences (teams) in 131 countries. In the United States the society is a major distributor of assistance and surplus food to the poor. Ozanam was beatified in 1997 by JOHN PAUL II.

Further reading: Lucy Archer, *Vincent, Louise, Ozanam.* (Darlington Carmel: Daughters of Charity, 1981); Leonce Celier, *Frederic Ozanam.* (Paris: P. Lethielleux, 1956); *Sketch of the Life of Saint Vincent de Paul and Origin of the Society of the Same Name* (Toronto: Society of Saint Vincent de Paul, 1884).

Soegijapranata, Albert (Albertus Soegijapranata) (1896–1963) *first Indonesian bishop*

Albert Soegijapranata, the first native Indonesian to be named a Catholic BISHOP, was born into a

Muslim family but converted during his college years. He was tutored by a JESUIT priest, Franz van Lith (1863–1926) and subsequently was ordained a Jesuit priest in 1931. He served as both a parish priest and the editor of a periodical, *Swata Tama*. In 1940 he was named vicar apostolic of Semarang, Indonesia, and consecrated the titular bishop of Danada.

In 1942, all of the foreign missionaries in Indonesia were imprisoned, and Soegiapranata and a few native Indonesian priests had to maintain the church through the remainder of the war years. He emerged after the war as a mediating force among the various factions vying for power in the new Republic of Indonesia. He urged his flock to be "A hundred percent Catholic, and a hundred percent Indonesian." He took a leading role in advocating Pancasila, the nationalist ideology that allowed the predominantly Muslim country to adopt a policy of religious freedom. He also served in the Indonesian army as a chaplain.

In 1961, Soegijapranata was elevated to become the first archbishop of Semarang. He subsequently attended the first session of VATICAN COUNCIL II. While in Europe, in 1963, he became ill and went to the Netherlands for treatment, where he died. Indonesian president Sukarno posthumously honored him with the titles of army general and national hero.

Further reading: Scott W. Sunquist, ed., *A Dictionary of Asian Christianity* (Grand Rapids, Mich.: Eerdmans, 2001).

Solesmes

Solesmes, a MONASTERY located in the village of Solesmes in western FRANCE, was founded as a BENEDICTINE priory in 1010. It continued as a monastic center until suppressed in 1791 following the French Revolution (1789).

Solesmes was reopened in 1830 and seven years later was raised to the rank of abbey. Its first modern abbot, Dom Prosper Guéranger (1805–

75), was a devoted student of Gregorian CHANT and made the monastery a center for the revival of the practice. Its work was later caught up in the larger effort of the LITURGICAL MOVEMENT that gained steam at the end of the century. The abbey issued the authoritative LIBER USUALIS (1924), which contains Gregorian chants for feast days and the PRAYER OF THE HOURS.

Today there are two abbeys at Solesmes, located about a block apart: St. Peter for men and St. Cecilia for women, both of which perpetuate the spirituality and performance of Gregorian chant. Both offer a daily schedule of services beginning with the morning high mass. The abbey remains a worldwide center of liturgical renewal.

Further reading: Katherine Bergeron, *Decadent Enchantments: The Revival of Gregorian Chant at Solesmes* (Berkeley: University of California Press, 1998); Cuthbert Johnson, *Prosper Guéranger (1805–75) A Liturgical Theologian: An Introduction to His Writings* (Rome: Pontifico Ateneo S. Anselmo, 1984).

soul (Gmc.: *saiwalo;* Gk.: *psyche;* Heb.: *ruach/nephesh;* Lat.: *anima,* "breath," "wind," "spirit," "animating principle")

Catholics relate the concept of a soul to the theological reality that humans were created "in the image/pattern" of GOD, who breathed into the first human the "breath" (Heb. *nephesh*) of life (Gen. 1:27; 2:7). Both soul and body are in the image of God. The *Catechism of the Catholic Church* 363 sees the soul not only as the principle of life and the human person, but also as the spiritual principle in humanity, the "innermost aspect" of the self.

Plato (427–347 B.C.E.) argued that the soul was simple and immaterial and therefore immortal like God (*Phaedo* 77d–80c). It preexisted the body (*Meno*). Materialists like Democritus (c. 460–c. 370 B.C.E.) and Lucretius (d. c. 50 B.C.E.) seem to have taught that consciousness results from complex physical processes and therefore dissipates when the body disintegrates. GNOSTICS and other ascetics taught that the soul was alien to the body and had its true home away from the material universe.

The classic Catholic THEOLOGY of the soul and body comes from St. THOMAS AQUINAS and his Aristotelian contemporaries, who taught that the soul was the animating form (Gk. *morphe*) and actuality (Gk. *energeia*) of the body (*On the Soul* 2.2). This formulation was given ecclesiastical approval at the ecumenical council of Vienne (1311–12) in the *Constitution on the Catholic Faith*. Like Aristotle, the medievals distinguished between vegetal, animal, and human souls. Though separated from the body at death, the immaterial soul will be reunited with it at the RESURRECTION.

Since the soul is not a result of sexual generation, the medievals taught that the soul is created immediately by God and implanted at some time after a fetus starts developing. Today there is still disagreement about when the soul is united with the embryo, although the Vatican is siding with the moment of conception (*see* ABORTION). The theology of the soul is being developed today by using the resources in the BIBLE in conjunction with the theology of the body. There is much new interest in the "care of the soul" in contemporary spiritual and mystical theology and a growing discussion between theology and neuroscience on the question of the soul.

See also ARISTOTLE; NEOPLATONISM.

Further reading: *Epistle to Diognetus* 6; Tertullian, *On the Soul;* Gregory of Nyssa, *On the Soul and Resurrection;* Augustine, *On the Soul and Immortality*—all available online; Michael Durrant, *Aristotle's De Anima in Focus* (London: Routledge, 1993); Friedrich von Hügel, *Essays and Addresses on the Philosophy of Religion* (London: Dent, 1921/1963); Thomas Moore, *Care of the Soul* (New York: HarperPerennial, 1994); Rhawn Joseph, *NeuroTheology: Brain, Science, Spirituality, Religious Experience* (San Jose: University of California Press, 2002).

Spain *country occupying the Iberian peninsula with Portugal*

Spain has a unique history among the CHRISTIAN countries of Europe. Most of the country was conquered by the Muslims in 711, who together with Jews and Christians created a unique culture, especially in the southern part, which they called al-Andalus. Gradually Christian kings reconquered the Moorish territories until FERDINAND I OF ARAGON AND ISABELLA OF CASTILE united their kingdoms to form the modern state of Spain in 1492.

Spain had been settled by Phoenicians and Greeks on the coasts and by Iberians and Celts inland when it was conquered by the Romans in the second century B.C.E. and renamed Hispania. PAUL talked about going on to Spain in his letter to the Romans 15:24, the implication being that there was already a Jewish settlement there. The emperors Trajan (r. 98–117), Hadrian (r. 117–38), and Marcus Aurelius (r. 161–80) were all born in Spain. Christians gained a footing in the second century C.E. and quickly flourished. CONSTANTINE THE GREAT made Hosius of Cordoba (c. 257–c. 357) his imperial theologian and representative at the Council of Nicaea.

Perhaps as a portent for Spain, the first person known to die under an INQUISITION was the alleged Manichaean bishop Priscillian of Ávila (c. 340–87). In 419 Emperor Honorius (r. 395–423) commissioned his sister Galla Placidia, who was married to the Visigoth king Ataulf (r. 410–15), to secure the peninsula under Roman rule. The ARIANISM of the Visigoth kings was countered by Catholic bishops until Reccared I (r. 586–601), who led his people into the Catholic fold in 589. A number of regional councils were held at Toledo that showed a tendency toward moral rigorism. Spain's most noted scholar in early Christian times was the encyclopedist Isadore of Seville (c. 560–636).

In 711 Muslim Berbers conquered most of the Iberian Peninsula. What ensued were long periods of what many call the *convivencia* (Span. "living together" during which Muslim, Jewish, and Christian culture flourished together. It was during this creative period that the complete corpus of Aristotle was transmitted to the Christians via the Arabic and Jewish philosopher-theologians (*see* ISLAM). Out of this matrix also emerged the Mozarabic Rite and ARCHITECTURE forms (the Alhambra) that were to shape both Spain and its colonies in the centuries to come. Some suspected the Mozarabic rite to have tendencies toward ADOPTIONISM perhaps influenced by the implicit Arianism in Islam's view of Jesus.

Over time Catholic rulers engaged in a piecemeal reconquest of Muslim Spain, often maintaining the culture of the *convivencia*. Of special note is Alfonso X el Sabio ("the Wise", king of Castile and León (r. 1252–84), who fostered learning, art, and music, including the celebrated *Cantigas de Maria* ("Songs of Mary"). Franciscans, Dominicans, and other religious congregations contributed to deepening the already intense spirituality of Spanish Christianity. The founder of the DOMINICAN ORDERS, DOMINIC DE GUZMÁN, was a Spaniard.

Disputes between Muslim rulers gave Ferdinand and Isabella an opening to reconquer al-Andalus, leading to the forced conversion or expulsion of Moors and Jews and their persecution during the Inquisition under the notorious TOMAS DE TORQUEMADA. Ferdinand and Isabella received the titles "Catholic Majesties" from the infamous Pope ALEXANDER VI, himself a Spaniard through his Borgia lineage. A united Spain sponsored the golden age of discovery beginning with CHRISTOPHER COLUMBUS. Spain was ascendant in Europe and the Americas under CHARLES V and Philip II (r. 1556–98). Spain exerted enormous temporal and spiritual influence throughout LATIN AMERICA, the Philippines and its African colonies for centuries; Dominican, Franciscan, Augustinian, and Jesuit missionaries brought about the greatest wave of conversions to Christianity worldwide since the first three centuries after Jesus. The Spanish Empire did not finally collapse until 1898.

During the COUNTER-REFORMATION the contribution of Spaniards was second only to that of Italians in the revival of Catholicism. The founder of the innovative society of JESUITS, St. IGNATIUS OF LOYOLA, was a Spaniard. Along with Ignatius, Carmelites Sts. TERESA OF ÁVILA and JOHN OF THE CROSS opened new paths in spiritual theology, though they were distrusted by their contemporaries.

In the next three centuries Spain experience great upheavals, first in the War of Spanish Succession (1701–14) and then in the conflict between the church and the Bourbon successors to the Spanish throne. Conflict broke out between the traditional HIERARCHY and the educated elites, leading to waves of ANTICLERICALISM both in Spain and the colonies. Kings divested many religious houses throughout Spain. Napoléon I (1769–1821) made his brother Joseph Buonaparte (1768–1844) king of Spain in 1808. Alfonso XII (r. 1875–85) established a pseudoconstitutional monarchy that led to political fracturing.

These tensions carried over into the 20th century, ending in the abdication of Alfonso XIII (1886–1941) in 1931 and the establishment up of a republican government. The disputes between liberals, communists, anarchists, Christian socialists, and regionalists fighting for autonomy precipitated the Spanish civil war (1936–39). Francisco Franco (r. 1939–75) ruled with a "soft" FASCISM as "Caudillo by the grace of God." He sided with the Axis powers (GERMANY, ITALY, and Japan) during World War II but did not declare war against the Allied powers, signed a CONCORDAT with the Catholic hierarchy in 1953 granting the church jurisdictional powers and financial support, and set up Juan Carlos (1938–   ), grandson of Alfonso XIII, as heir to the throne.

Juan Carlos deftly guided Spain into a functioning constitutional monarchy in 1978. Since then Spain has elected both conservative and socialist governments that have progressively disassociated themselves from institutional relations with the Catholic Church. The church's close association with the fascist leadership damaged its appeal to many modern Spaniards who remain nominally Catholic. Today there are more than 40 million Catholics in Spain. There has been a marked decrease in vocations. Not even militant conservative Spanish foundations like OPUS DEI have been able to stem the drift into secularism. Nonetheless, local religious processions continue to be held throughout Spain, and the pilgrimage shrine of SANTIAGO DE COMPOSTELA continues to draw pilgrims from all lands and all faiths.

Further reading: Thomas Glick, Vivian Mann, and Jerrilyn D. Dodds, eds., *Convivencia: Jews, Muslims and Christians in Medieval Spain* (New York: Braziller, 1992); Charles H. Lippy, *Christianity Comes to the Americas, 1492–1776* (New York: Paragon House, 1992); Linda Martz, *A Network of Converso Families in Early Modern Toledo* (Ann Arbor: University of Michigan Press, 2003); Stanley Payne, *Spanish Catholicism: An Historical Overview* (Madison: University of Wisconsin Press, 1984).

Spellman, Francis Joseph (1889–1967)
cardinal and U.S. church leader

Francis Joseph Spellman, the sixth ARCHBISHOP of New York, was born in Whitman, Massachusetts, on May 4, 1889. He attended Fordham University and the North American College at Rome prior to his ordination into the priesthood in 1916. In 1922 he became chancellor of the Boston DIOCESE. In 1925, on a pilgrimage to Rome, he was appointed assistant to the papal secretariat of state, the first American to hold the post. He stayed in Rome for six years, leaving in 1931 on a mission to smuggle a papal document denouncing FASCISM. On his arrival in Paris, he translated the message and released it to the world.

Spellman returned to the United States in 1932 and was soon named auxiliary BISHOP of Boston. He held that post until 1939, when he was named the new archbishop of New York. He was soon appointed to serve in addition as vicar of the U.S. armed forces, placing the care of American Catholic armed forces personnel under his oversight. Spellman used his position to mobilize the Catholic public to back the war effort following the bombing of Pearl Harbor in 1941.

In 1946 Pope Pius XII named Spellman to the College of Cardinals. Credited by the public for assisting the war effort, he used his new position to reopen the issues of Catholic participation in public life. He campaigned to win government funding for parochial schools. Spellman argued that tax money should go to support the education of all American children, even those in religious schools. His position led to an acrimonious debate with former first lady Eleanor Roosevelt, whom he accused of being anti-Catholic. Spellman also argued for the United States to establish formal diplomatic relations with the Vatican. (Relations were established in 1983.)

Spellman served his archdiocese until his death in 1967. His career was defined by the return of the Catholic Church as a force in the American public arena after a generation of silence that followed Pope LEO XIII's 1899 condemnation of AMERICANISM. Spellman thus revived the work of the dynamic 19th-century bishops who helped anchor Catholicism within American life.

Further reading: John Cooney, *The American Pope: The Life and Times of Francis Cardinal Spellman* (New York: Times, 1984); Robert I. Gannon, *The Cardinal Spellman Story* (Garden City, N.Y.: Doubleday, 1962).

spirituality   *See* BONAVENTURE; MEISTER ECKHART; TERESA OF ÁVILA, THEOLOGY.

Stephen, St. (fl. c. 40) *first Christian martyr* (Gk.: *protomartyr*)

St. Stephen, reputedly the first CHRISTIAN martyr, first appears in the biblical Book of Acts 6 (*see* BIBLE) as a "man full of faith and the Holy Spirit" who is chosen to be among the first group of deacons. The deacon's office originated because of a need to free the APOSTLES from such temporal chores as cleaning up after community meals. Stephen is also mentioned as a miracle worker who performed many awe-inspiring acts among the people. It is believed that he was a Greek-speaking Jew.

Stephen's preaching in a Greek-speaking synagogue was his downfall. He was accused of blasphemy and brought before a Jewish council. He defended himself by arguing that the contemporary Jewish community had turned its back on God's purpose for Israel by killing Jesus and failing to keep their own law. His speech reflects how the Gospel message was first preached to the Jewish community.

Angered at Stephen's words, the council led him outside Jerusalem and stoned him to death. As he died, Stephen had a vision of Jesus standing at the right hand of God, and his last words were a prayer that God not hold his executors' actions against them. It has been noted that the Jewish leadership at the time operated under Roman law, which forbade them from carrying out executions without explicit Roman permission. The law was apparently ignored, seemingly out of anger at Stephen's defense. There is no record of any Roman reaction to Stephen's death. The Apostle PAUL appears in the Acts of the Apostles and Luke as a Jew from Tarsus named Saul who persecuted the early church and was present at Stephen's death. Following Stephen's death, those who killed him laid their clothes at Saul's feet.

Early in the fourth century, Paulus Orosius, a confidant of AUGUSTINE OF HIPPO (354–430), went to Palestine to meet with Jerome (c. 342–420). While he was there a body believed by some to be Stephen's was discovered. Orosius brought the relics back with him, and in 424 Augustine had a shrine to Stephen built in the CATHEDRAL at Hippo. The relics were eventually returned to Jerusalem, where in 444 the empress Eudocia (c. 401–60), the wife of Theodosius II (401–50), built a church to house the relics over the spot where Stephen was believed to have been stoned. According to

legend, his relics were later translated to Constantinople and then to Rome.

Further reading: Bruno Chenu et al., eds., *The Book of Christian Martyrs* (Oxford: Clarendon, 1927); W. H. C. Frend, *Martyrdom and Persecution in the Early Church: A Study of a Conflict from the Maccabees to Donatus* (New York: Doubleday, 1967); H. Musurillo, *The Acts of Christian Martyrs* (Oxford: Clarendon, 1972).

stigmata (Gk.: *stigma,* "mark," "brand," "wound")

Stigmata are wounds that appear on a person's body that resemble the wounds suffered by Jesus CHRIST during his Passion. The most common wounds are marks on the hands and feet resembling puncture holes. However, stigmata may also include wounds on the head (from a crown of thorns), back (from whipping), and side (from piecing by a spear).

In recent centuries, St. PAUL's words in Galatians 6:17 that he bore on his body the marks of Jesus have been interpreted to mean that he was the first stigmatist. Previously the passage had been interpreted as referring to another type of affliction, and St. FRANCIS OF ASSISI was credited as the first stigmatist.

Francis's experience was extreme. During the last two years of his life he manifested all five stigmatic wounds. His hands and feet not only showed open wounds but appeared to be pierced through the middle with nails. The nails seemed to be of a bonelike substance and the wounds large enough that a finger could be passed through them. Francis's relatively young demise is attributed in part to the stigmata. Over the next centuries, other renowned stigmatists included Bl. Bienheureuse Luci de Narni (1476–1544) and St. Veronica Giuliani (1660–1727).

The number of reported cases of stigmatism grew in the 19th and 20th centuries, the great majority being women. Among the more well known of the modern stigmatists is Catherine

Emmerich (1774–1824), a German AUGUSTINIAN NUN and visionary. Her stigmata first appeared in 1812. During the ecstasies that accompanied the stigmata, Emmerich described in great detail the last week of Jesus' life. Her accounts would later be collected and published. They remain a popular reading for pious Catholics and were the basis of the Mel Gibson's 2004 film *The Passion*.

The most famous of the 20th-century stigmatists was St. Padre Pio (1887–1968), an Italian Capuchin FRANCISCAN MONK. He received the wounds on his body in September 1918 during a vision of Jesus. As the vision faded, he became aware that his hands, feet, and side were dripping blood. He continued to experience the bleeding throughout his life, though the wounds disappeared shortly before his death in 1968. As word of the stigmata spread pilgrims began to appear at Padre Pio's home monastery in St. Giovanni Rotundo. The experience was interpreted as an answer to Padre Pio's prayer that he be allowed to identify with Christ by a form of participation in his Passion and death.

Rivaling Padre Pio was Thérèse Neumann (1898–1962) of Konnersreuth, Germany. In 1918 she was stricken with a paralysis that left her bedridden and in considerable pain. Several years later, on days connected with the life of St. THÉRÈSE OF LISIEUX, she would experience some degree of healing. Then in 1926, during Lent, she had a vision of Jesus. Afterward a wound opened in her side, and she began to exude tears of blood each Friday. Like Catherine Emmerich, she had a vivid vision of the events of Jesus' crucifixion. The stigmata continued to appear for the rest of her life; it was also claimed that she did not eat any solid food, only a minimum amount of liquid food. The church has taken no positions on Thérèse Neumann but Pope JOHN PAUL II canonized Padre Pio in 2002.

There has been much discussion about psychosomatic aspects of stigmata in terms of self-hypnosis, religious CONVERSION, and spiritual commitment. There are reports of Muslims who experience wounds similar to those of the Prophet Muhammad (c. 570–632) when he first began to preach.

Further reading: Charles M. Carty, *The Two Stigmatists: Padre Pio and Therese Neuman* (Dublin: Veritas, 1956); Jim Gallagher, *Padre Pio: The Pierced Priest* (London: Fount, 1995); Paul Siwek, *The Riddle of Konnersreuth* (Dublin: Browne & Nolan, 1956); Herbert Thurton, *The Physical Phenomena of Mysticism* (Chicago: Henry Regnery, 1952).

St. Peter's Basilica

Officially known in Italian as the Basilica di San Pietro in Vaticano, St. Peter's is the largest church in the CHRISTIAN world (5.7 acres), with a capacity of 60,000. It is the world's most famous Christian church, but technically it ranks second among the five major basilicas of the Catholic Church. Although most papal ceremonies take place here, St. John Lateran is the CATHEDRAL seat of the BISHOP of Rome. Every Christmas Eve the pope celebrates a EUCHARIST in St. Peter's that is televised around the world.

St. Peter's Basilica is named after St. PETER THE APOSTLE, the first bishop of Rome according to Catholic tradition. The church was built over his traditional burial spot, which is believed to be under Bernini's high altar. In 324 Emperor CONSTANTINE I began building a basilica on the site, which had been a cemetery for pagans and Christians. That first St. Peter's, in the architectural style of a Roman BASILICA, consisted of a nave and two aisles.

In the 15th century it was decided that the basilica should be rebuilt, and construction began in 1505 under the supervision of Pope Julius II (r. 1503–13). Donato Bramante (1444–1514) provided the initial design modeled in the form of a Greek CROSS on the basis of earlier plans of LEONARDO DA VINCI. MICHELANGELO redesigned the plan in 1546 and designed the dome, or cupola, in 1558. His plans were faithfully completed by his student, Giacomo della Porta (1541–1604). Michelangelo's famous *Pietà* rests in the basilica.

In 1605 Carlo Maderna (1556–1629) was commissioned to add the nave and the façade. The great baroque master Gian Lorenzo Bernini (1598–1680) designed the famous Cathedra Petri, the Chair of St. Peter, in the apse and the high altar surrounded by fluted twisting columns covered with a baldachino. He also designed and built the two baroque bell towers on the front façade that were later removed when Maderna added the façade. Bernini also designed the colonnade with statues of saints atop surrounding St. Peter's Piazza. The campaign to finance this magnificent edifice included the large-scale sale of INDULGENCES, helping to spark the PROTESTANT REFORMATION.

See also ARCHITECTURE; PAINTING AND SCULPTURE.

Further reading: James Lees-Milne, *Saint Peter's: The Story of Saint Peter's Basilica in Rome* (London: H. Hamilton, 1967); Augustin F. McNally, *St. Peter's on the Vatican* (New York: Stand Press, 1939); Sarah McPhee, *Bernini and the Bell Towers: Architecture and Politics at the Vatican* (London: Yale University Press, 2002); Jocelyn M. C. Toynbee, *The Shrine of St. Peter and the Vatican Excavations* (New York: Pantheon Books, 1957); Roberta Vicchi, *The Major Basilicas of Rome: Saint Peter's, San Giovanni in Laterano, San Paolo fuori le Mura, Santa Maria Maggiore* (Florence: Scala, 1999).

Suárez, Francisco (1548–1617) *Jesuit scholastic philosopher and theologian*

Francisco Suárez was a Spanish JESUIT theologian and political philosopher who emerged as a staunch defender of the power and authority of the Catholic Church. His Scholastic system mediated those of St. THOMAS AQUINAS and Bl. DUNS SCOTUS.

He was trained at the university at Salamanca and matured during the years when the PROTESTANT REFORMATION took much of northern Europe outside the communion of the Catholic Church.

At the same time, nationalism was growing, and rulers were asserting their authority by claiming a divine right of kings; these trends would in the end strip the church of most of its temporal powers.

Suárez became one of the harshest opponents of the divine right of kings, going so far as to deny that any sacred quality adhered to rulers or their offices. In his books *Defensio Fidei Catholicae* (1614) and *De Legibus* (1612), he argued that the power of the state was restricted, in that power is derived from GOD, and all secular law is subordinate to divine law as articulated by God's church.

Suárez authored the first modern treatise on metaphysics, *Disputationes Metaphysicae* (1597). Among the problems he explored was the relationship between predestination and FREE WILL. He used Luis de Molina's (1535–1600) understanding that God's foreknowledge and the action of divine grace preceded the predetermination of human fate. He believed that everyone shared in God's GRACE but that the elect had been granted a special grace so that they inevitably and freely yielded to its influence.

Suárez taught successively at Alcala, Salamanca, and Rome. He died in 1617 in Lisbon, Portugal.

Further reading: Jorge J. Gracia, *Suárez on Individuation* (Milwaukee: Marquette University Press, 1982); Francisco Suárez, *On Beings of Reason* (Milwaukee: Marquette University Press, 1995); ———, *Selections from Three Works of Francisco Suárez* (Oxford: Clarendon, 1944); ———, *Suarez on Individuation: Metaphysical Disputation V, Individual Unity and its Principle,* tr. Jorge J. E. Garcia (Milwaukee: Marquette University Press, 1982).

Suenens, Léon-Joseph (1904–1996) *reformist cardinal at Vatican Council II*

Léon-Joseph Suenens, a cardinal who played a leading role in the reforms enacted at VATICAN COUNCIL II, became world famous in the

1980s as a supporter of the Catholic CHARISMATIC RENEWAL. Suenens was born in Ixelles, Belgium. He completed his studies for the priesthood at the Pontifical Gregorian University in Rome and was ordained in 1927. He taught philosophy at Malines, Belgium, and from 1940 to 1945 at the University of Louvain. In 1945 he became BISHOP of Malines. He was elevated to ARCHBISHOP in 1961 and received his cardinal's hat in 1962.

Suenens was appointed to the commission that planned the agenda for Vatican Council II and emerged during the council as one of the leading voices for reform. In 1972 and 1973 he came into contact with Catholic charismatics and in 1974 published his *Theological and Pastoral Guidelines on the Catholic Charismatic Renewal.* He subsequently invited two American leaders of the movement, Ralph Martin and Stephen Clark, to create an international office in Belgium for the rapidly spreading renewal.

Concerned about some of the independent directions the movement manifested, in 1975 he accepted Pope PAUL VI's request that he become the pope's official adviser on the movement. He subsequently launched efforts to keep the movement within the church both theologically and organizationally, ordering all prayer groups in Belgium to select a priest to lead them. His leadership was important in holding Catholic charismatics in the church while at the same time legitimizing the renewal and calming the fears of brother bishops. He helped find ways around unacceptable theological ideas such as tying the BAPTISM of the HOLY SPIRIT to speaking in tongues and offered clear guidelines for ecumenical activity with non-Catholic charismatics.

Suenens retired as archbishop in 1979 but continued to write and be an active voice in renewal. He retired as papal adviser in 1982 and died in 1996 at his home in Malines.

Further reading: Léon Joseph Suenens, *Christian Life Day by Day* (Westminster, Md.: Newman, 1964); ———, *Ecumenism and Charismatic Renewal: Theo-* *logical and Pastoral Orientations,* (London: Darton Longman Todd, 1978); ———, *A New Pentecost?* (London: Catholic Book Club, 1975); ——— and Dom Helder Câmara, *Charismatic Renewal and Social Action: A Dialogue* (London: Darton Longman Todd, 1980); Vinson Synan, *The Century of the Holy Spirit: 100 Years of Pentecostal and Charismatic Renewal, 1901–2001* (Nashville: Thomas Nelson, 2001).

Suger, Abbé (1081–1151) *abbot of St. Denis and pioneer of Gothic architecture*

The French monastic leader Suger was born into a knightly family. At around nine years old he was dedicated to the abbey of St. Denis, the royal abbey of FRANCE, where its rulers were educated and, in many cases, buried. Some 30 years later, in 1122, he became the MONASTERY's abbot, a position he held until his DEATH.

As the royal abbot, his power rose along with that of the French monarchs, who were consolidating their control of the country. Possibly the height of his power came during the absence of Louis VII (r. 1137–80) on a CRUSADE (1147–49), when Suger virtually ruled the country.

In 1137 Suger began a major renovation of the abbey church of St. Denis. Originally built in 775, the church had been neglected and fallen into disrepair. Beginning on the church's west end, Suger saw to the construction of a new facade that included two towers and three doors. He then moved to the east end, where a new choir was constructed. The completed church became a major event in architectural history, the first Gothic church. Gothic ARCHITECTURE is thus one of the only major architectural styles that can be traced to a single individual. The five French ARCHBISHOPS and thirteen BISHOPS who participated in the dedication ceremony of the new church would take the initiative in developing the Gothic CATHEDRAL throughout the country in the following decades. St. BERNARD OF CLAIRVAUX opposed Suger's lavish expense, arguing for help to the poor instead.

Suger wanted a rich display of light and a har-monically proportioned structure. He appealed to the THEOLOGY of light expounded by DIONYSIUS the Pseudo-Areopagite to justify his expansion of light space for the stained glass windows. The essential structural innovation was the use of ribs, shafts, and buttresses to carry the enormous weight of the stone blocks with which the building was constructed. This innovation allowed ample wall space for the large stained glass windows that give the church unique light effects.

In his mature years, Suger wrote a number of books still of historical importance. They include a biography of Louis VI (1081–1157), fragments of a life of Louis VII (1120–80), an account of the renovation of Saint-Denis, and a volume on his administration of the abbey. He died in 1151.

Suger's church, identified as it was with the French monarchy, became a victim of the Revolu-tion. In 1793–94, it was severely vandalized and its stained-glass windows removed. It was subse-quently turned into a temple of the short-lived cult to reason, then into a warehouse and finally a military hospital. Renovation was started by Napoléon I (1769–1821) and continued through the 19th century, although one of the towers was lost in the process.

Further reading: Jean Bony, *French Gothic Architecture of the 12th and 13th Centuries* (Berkeley: University of California Press, 1983); Otto Von Simson, *The Gothic Cathedral* (Princeton, N.J.: Princeton University Press, 1989); Suger, Abbot of Saint Denis, *Abbot Suger on the Abby Church of St. Denis and its Art Treasures,* tr. Erwin Panosfsky (Princeton, N.J.: Princeton University Press, 1979); ———, *The Deeds of Louis the Fat* (Washington, D.C.: Catholic University of America Press, 1992).

supernatural (Lat.: *super,* "beyond," "above," "exceeding" + *natura,* "nature")

The supernatural pertains to that dimension of reality that is beyond or transcends the realm of the created order. In Catholic belief, the one exception is the GRACE of GOD, which enters into the finite order through the redemptive action of Jesus CHRIST and the HOLY SPIRIT and allows human beings to share in the life of God. The THEOLOGY of nature and grace was given its classic expression in St. THOMAS AQUINAS.

During the Enlightenment Deist followers of Isaac Newton (1643–1727) taught that no super-natural law (miracles) could violate the laws of nature. Deists tended to dispense with the realm of the supernatural. PIUS IX tried to defend super-naturalism against what he took to be the natural-ism in MODERNISM.

Theologians like KARL RAHNER and HENRI DE LUBAC fought the widespread conception that the distinction between the natural and supernatural implies two layers of reality. Rahner introduced the notion of the supernatural existential, which asserts that human existence is fundamentally oriented to life in God, which is granted not via human merit or achievement but comes purely from divine grace. Through God's decree of salvation and grace in Christ, humans are elevated to God in their intrinsic nature. They are rendered capable of receiving the offered grace without distortion or disfigurement of their original created nature.

Further reading: Stephen J. Duffy, *The Grand Horizon: Naure and Grace in Modern Catholic Thought* (Colleg-eville, Minn.: Liturgical Press, 1996); Henri de Lubac, *The Discovery of God* (Grand Rapids, Mich.: Eerdmans, 1996); Karl Rahner, *Nature and Grace* (London: Sheed & Ward, 1963).

Syllabus of Errors

The Syllabus of Errors is a document contain-ing a list of condemned theses or ideas. It was published in 1864 by Pope PIUS IX and attached to his encyclical *Quanta Cura* (December 8, 1864). The list seems to have had several sources, including a list published in 1860 by Bishop Philippe-Olympe Gerbet (1798–1864) of Perpig-nan, FRANCE. In 1849, the provincial council of

Spoleto had requested the pope to issue a list of contemporary errors facing the church.

The syllabus has to be understood in the context of the events of Pius IX's reign. The unification of ITALY has already greatly truncated the PAPAL STATES and was threatening the Vatican's very existence. The pope could easily blame these events on the political, cultural, and intellectual changes of the previous century, which had undermined the traditional role of the church in the life of the people.

The syllabus opens with an attack on philosophies based solely on reason (rationalism) and PANTHEISM (in which God and the world are seen as essentially overlapping rather than separate realities). More specifically, the book pitted the church against the currents of liberalism that had flowed out of the French Enlightenment. Liberalism, as used in the syllabus, refers to a general desire to limit political power and to define and support individual rights. It was thus identified with the French and American Revolutions and the replacement of monarchies with various forms of democracy. The syllabus also condemned a variety of political philosophies (communism, socialism) and groups (secret societies such as FREEMASONRY) that were seen as opposing the church. The pope tried to defend his right to rule the Papal States, though that was now a lost cause.

Narrowly speaking, the syllabus was a reaction to very specific ideas and situations the Catholic Church faced in the mid-19th century. More broadly, it was widely seen as placing the church in opposition to the whole thrust of European and North American political and social history and against modern scientific and political thinking and the use of literary-critical methods in biblical research. The mindset of the syllabus eventually led the PAPACY to condemn the American Catholic leadership when it tried to articulate positive ways of adapting to American democracy, an approach that came to be known as AMERICANISM.

The spirit nurtured by the syllabus of errors reigned supreme until the rise of the NOUVELLE THÉOLOGIE and VATICAN COUNCIL II, where a fresh approach was offered to the church's encounter with the world. The fact that Pope PIUS XI never personally signed the syllabus made it easy to allow it to sink into obsolescence.

Further reading: Frank J. Coppa, *Pope Pius IX: Crusader in a Secular Age* (Boston: Twayne, 1979); E. E. Y. Hales, *Pio Nono: A Study in European Politics and Religion in the Nineteenth Century* (Garden City, N.Y.: Doubleday, 1954); Robert R. Hull, *The Syllabus of Errors of Pope Pius IX: The Scourge of Liberalism* (Huntington, Ind.: Our Sunday Visitor, 1926); *Popes against Modern Errors: 16 Famous Papal Documents* (Rockford, Ill.: Tan Books, 1999).

symbol (Gk.: *syn,* "together" + *ballein,* "to toss")

CHRISTIANS use the word *symbol* in several senses. *Symbolon* was an early term for the CREED or confession of beliefs. More commonly, a symbol is a token representation of a person or reality. For example, keys are a symbol of St. PETER THE APOSTLE. The third meaning, however, is most important: *symbol* as distinguished from *sign*.

Signs are transparent, clear, and univocal in meaning. They point to something outside themselves in an extrinsic way, as in the universal traffic sign of a red circle with a transverse red slash meaning "no." Symbols, by contrast, are opaque and dense and elicit multivocal meanings. Furthermore, they may in some way embody the realities to which they point. The mysteries of faith—the INCARNATION, the SACRAMENTS, the CROSS,—are symbolic in this sense. The very nature of symbols necessitates the task of HERMENEUTICS (interpretation), which strives to disimplicate the symbol, but not entirely because the symbol ultimately is the language of mystery.

In contemporary THEOLOGY symbols occupy a place that rivals the role of ANALOGY and TYPOLOGY in the medieval world. KARL RAHNER sought to give a metaphysics of the symbol: all beings necessarily express themselves through symbols in order to attain their nature. The church is the real symbol of Christ's presence in the world and serves as the primary sacrament through which Christ's GRACE is communicated to the world.

Further reading: Karl Rahner, "Theology of the Symbol," *Theological Investigations* 4: 221–252; Paul Ricoeur, *The Symbolism of Evil* (Boston: Beacon, 1969); George Tracy, *A Theology of Symbol* (Riverton: University Press of Washington, 1979).

synod (Gk.: *syn,* "together" + *hodos,* "way," "coming")

A synod is a gathering where church leaders can debate and resolve questions of DOCTRINE or church life. Within the Catholic Church, synods are held at various levels of the church's structure. In earlier times *synod* was often used synonymously with *council.* There can be both local and universal synods.

Since VATICAN COUNCIL II, a synod of BISHOPS has met periodically at the pope's pleasure. It is composed of selected bishops from around the world, some representing their countries of service, others directly appointed by the pope. This synod serves as an advisory body to the pope on current issues. Generally, the invited bishops engage in conversations with local constituencies on the proposed topics of the upcoming meeting. The synod of bishops has become a major expression of episcopal collegiality in the contemporary church.

However, the term *synod* has often been applied to one-time or limited-time gatherings. For example, as the year 2000 approached, Pope JOHN PAUL II called a meeting in Rome of selected bishops from different continents to discuss the state of the church in light of the approaching new millennium. Synods of bishops from AFRICA, the Americas, Europe, ASIA, and Oceania were held in the closing years of the 20th century.

At the diocesan level, synods have been organized consisting of CLERGY, religious, and laity who meet to offer advice and opinion to the bishop ordinary. Such local synods are not mandated but are allowed. They have often served as an outlet for the articulation of dissent and negative judgments. They can also be instruments for renewal within a DIOCESE by involving large numbers of people in decision making and program development.

At the most recent universal synod in Rome (October 2–23, 2005) the theme was the EUCHARIST but the topics of CELIBACY, PRIEST shortage, and homosexuality dominated the discussions. The Melkite patriarch Gregory III Laham (1933–   ) declared: "Celibacy has no theological foundation."

Further reading: Austin Flannery, ed., *Towards the 1994 Synod of Bishops* (Dublin: Dominican, 1993); *IMBISA Speaks at the African Synod: The Contributions of the Inter-Regional Meeting of Bishops of Southern Africa to the Special Assembly for Africa of the Synod of Bishops 1994* (Harare: Theological Reflection and Exchange Dept. of IMBISA, 1998); Charlton Terry, *Exploring Our Christian Life: In the Light of the African Synod* (Nairobi: Pauline, 1994).

Syrian Catholic Church

In the 18th century, Roman Catholic missionaries spread throughout the Ottoman Empire, especially in what is now Lebanon and Syria. In northwest Syria they encountered members of the Syriac Orthodox Patriarchate of Antioch and All the East, known as the Jacobites. Jacob Baradaeus (d. 578) opposed the teachings of the ecumenical Council of EPHESUS in 431 (and previously affirmed at CONSTANTINOPLE in 381) concerning the nature of CHRIST. These councils affirmed that Christ had both a human and a divine nature, while Jacob, serving as BISHOP of Edessa after 543, held the Monophysite position that Christ had only a divine nature. The controversy caused a SCHISM among the Syrian CHRISTIANS.

The Syriac Orthodox Patriarchate of Antioch and All the East became the dominant Christian group in and around Aleppo. A Catholic mission had unusual success in the Aleppo region through the 1650s, leading in 1662 to the election of Andrew Akhidjan (d. 1677), a Syrian with decidedly Catholic leanings, to head the Syrian Orthodox Church. Problems arose following his death, however, as two factions (one pro-Rome and one independent of Rome) emerged in strength; each elected a patriarch. At this point the Ottoman authorities intervened on behalf of the Orthodox faction. As a result, no bishop was elected to continue the Catholic faction.

The Catholic faction continued to exist but found itself in an increasingly tenuous position, and it was eventually forced underground. Then to the surprise of many, in 1782 the Syrian patriarch suddenly declared his allegiance to Rome, moved to Lebanon, and founded Our Lady of Sharfeh Monastery. He began the first of a new line of Syrian Catholic patriarchs. Finally, in 1828 the Ottoman government granted recognition to the Syrian Catholic Church. In 1850 the headquarters of the church was moved to Mardin, in southwestern Turkey.

Once granted recognition, the Syrian Catholic Church thrived for the next 90 years, but it lost many members during World War I. The PATRIARCH moved to Beirut in the 1920s. The current patriarch is Gregory III Laham (1933–), who was elected in 2000. There are some 1,250,000 Syrian Catholics, most residing in Lebanon, Syria, Turkey, Egypt, and Iraq. Members in North America constitute Our Lady of Deliverance Syriac Catholic Diocese. The church is active in the Middle East Council of Churches. Many Syrian Catholics have been put into grave peril by the Iraqi War II (2002–).

Further reading: Nikolaus Liesel, *The Eastern Catholic Liturgies: A Study in Words and Pictures.* (Westminster, Md.: Newman, 1960); Ronald G. Roberson, *The Eastern Christian Churches: A Brief Survey,* 5th ed. (Rome: Edizioni Orientalia Christiana, Pontificio Istituto Orientale, 1995).

Syro-Malabar Catholic Church

In the 15th century, Portuguese explorers sailed around Africa into the Indian Ocean and eventually landed in India. Here they discovered the Syrian Orthodox Church of Malabar, which traced its origin to the reputed ministry of the Apostle Thomas in the years after the DEATH and RESURRECTION of Jesus. In those areas over which the Portuguese established their hegemony, Catholic missionaries imposed various Roman Catholic liturgical changes and other practices on the church. In 1599, at a SYNOD held at Diamper, these changes were formally accepted by the church's synod, which resulted in the appointment of Portuguese BISHOPS, the adoption of CELIBACY by the CLERGY, and the arrival of the INQUISITION to deal with heretics. Not all agreed with these ways, and in 1653 another synod was held at Diamper, at which time the majority of the church broke with Rome and returned to their pre-Catholic practices and structure.

Upset by events in India, Pope Alexander VII (1599–1655) assigned the CARMELITES the task of dealing with the problem. They were able to persuade some to return to their communion with Rome. As a result of their leadership at this time, Carmelites would continue to hold most of the leading positions in the church until the 1890s. The resultant Syro-Malabar Catholic Church is in full communion with Rome.

Through the middle of the 19th century, a single Roman Catholic structure in India served both Latin rite Catholics and the congregations of the Syro-Malabar rite. Only in 1877 did Pope Leo XIII separate the two groups. In 1896 three vicariates apostolic were designated for the Syro-Malabar Catholic Church, and indigenous BISHOPS were placed in charge. A fourth DIOCESE was created in 1911. Through the 20th century, each of the four dioceses grew to become a province, each headed by an ARCHBISHOP and each including additional dioceses. As the the 21st century begins, there are 24 dioceses in India, half of which are in Kerala. The major ARCHBISHOP cardinal Varkey Vithayathill

(1927–   ) of Ernakulam-Angamly is the current primate of the Syro-Malabar Church.

The Syro-Malabar Catholic Church grew from an estimated 500,000 members in 1930 to some 4,300,000 members by the end of the century. Since the 1960s, members have moved to NORTH AMERICA. There is now a Syro-Malabar eparchy (diocese) for Canada and the United States.

Further reading: Donald Hoke, ed., *The Church in Asia* (Chicago: Moody, 1975); Samuel Hugh Moffett, *A History of Christianity in Asia. Vol. 1: Beginnings to 1500* (San Francisco: HarperSanFrancisco, 1992); S. C. Neill, *A History of Christianity in India,* 2 vols. (Cambridge: Cambridge University Press, 1985).

Syro-Malankara Catholic Church

The Syro-Malankara Catholic Church originated in 1926 out of the somewhat complicated history of south Indian Christianity. It is one of several churches that traces its beginning to the ministry of the Apostle Thomas, who, it is claimed, came to Kerala soon after the RESURRECTION of CHRIST. In the 15th century Indian CHRISTIANS came into contact with the Catholic Church. In 1599 the Indian Christian community accepted the authority of Rome, and in subsequent decades there was an attempt to impose the Latin rite on the church. In 1653, the majority of Indian Christians rejected Roman authority and returned to the Syriac LITURGY that they had previously used. Thus, the Syro-Malabar Catholic Church and the Mar Thomas Syrian Church of Malabar emerged as separate entities.

The Mar Thomas church reestablished its HIERARCHY through the Syriac Orthodox Patriarchate of Antioch and All the East, a church separated from the main body of EASTERN ORTHODOXY over its refusal to accept the formulation of THEOLOGY proposed by the ecumenical councils (*see* COUNCILS, ECUMENICAL) of the fifth century. In the 19th century, the Mar Thomas Church established a relationship with the Church of England, which had recently entered India. Anglican leaders suggested some reforms that led the Mar Thomas Church to split into two branches, the Mar Thomas Syrian Church of Malabar and the Malankara Orthodox Syrian Church. The Mar Thomas Church accepted the reforms suggested by the Anglicans and has established formal communion with the Church of England. The Malankara Church continued with its traditional practices and its communion with the Syriac Orthodox Patriarchate of Antioch and All the East.

In the 1880s, a dispute developed between the Malankara Church and the patriarch of the Syrian Orthodox Church, who began to assert his ownership of the property of the Malankara Church. As that dispute continued into the 1920s, five Malankara BISHOPS opened negotiations with Rome. They asked only that their liturgy be retained and that they remain as bishops of their DIOCESES. On September 30, 1930, two of the five made their profession of the FAITH, and on October 1, two more joined them. The four bishops became head of what is now named the Syro-Malankara Catholic Church. In 1932, one of the four, Mar Ivanios (1882–1953) visited Rome. While there, he was named archbishop of Trivandrum, and his diocese was elevated to become the archeparchy of Tiruvalla.

When the Syro-Malankara Church was established, the Roman Catholic Church had already recognized the Syro-Malabar Catholic Church. Both churches had parishes in the same territory. However, the two churches used very different liturgies (though both eschewed the Latin rite).

Besides the archeparchy (archdiocese), there are three Malankaran exarchies (dioceses) in India. The church has more than 500,000 members. There are scattered congregations across NORTH AMERICA.

Further reading: Ronald G. Roberson, *The Eastern Christian Churches: A Brief Survey,* 5th ed. (Rome: Edizioni Orientalia Christiana, Pontificio Istituto Orientale, 1995).

T

Teilhard de Chardin, Pierre (1881–1955)
paleontologist and theologian of evolution

Pierre Teilhard de Chardin was appointed professor of ontology at the Institut Catholique in Paris in 1911. He participated in several archaeological expeditions in China and AFRICA and was among the original researchers on Peking (Beijing) Man. He trained China's first paleontologists. In 1951 he did research at the Wenner-Gren Foundation, a private anthropological research institute, in New York.

Early in his career Teilhard began to examine a new kind of THEOLOGY that took its inspiration from the scientific milieu; he focused on an ontological understanding of evolution. He saw the biblical stories as metaphors and SYMBOLS of a higher reality. Evolution moves to greater complexity and higher levels of consciousness, as found, successively, in what he called the biosphere, the noosphere (human consciousness), and the agaposphere [cosmic love-based consciousness]. The Risen CHRIST is the nexus of future human society infused with the force of love. The Omega Point is the final state of the universe.

Vatican censors prohibited Teilhard from publishing his theological works during his lifetime. After his death his writings were published by friends outside the ecclesiastical establishment.

Many traditional Catholic theologians claimed that he had an insufficient understanding of SIN and its effects, that he thought the SOUL emerged from materialistic evolution, and that he confused GOD with the evolutionary process. Teilhard did not deny sin or the spirituality of the soul but sought to see them within the evolutionary process. The Omega Point is related to but not the same as God. Many both within and outside the Catholic Church have become devoted to his thought and find in it a way to reconcile science and religion in the modern world.

Further reading: John F. Haught, *Chaos, Complexity and Theology* (Chambersburg: Anima, 1994); Pierre Teilhard de Chardin, *The Divine Milieu* (New York: Harper & Row, 1960); ———, *The Phenomenon of Man* (New York: Harper & Row, 1965).

Tekakwitha, Bl. Kateri (1656–1680) *first beatified Native American*

Kateri Tekakwitha, the first Native American to be considered for sainthood, was born among the Mohawk people of New York in 1656, with the exact place of her birth still a matter of conjecture. Her mother was an Algonquin who had been captured by the Iroquois and saved by her father, an Iroquois. When she was four years old her parents were swept away in a smallpox epidemic, which scarred her own face with pockmarks and impaired her sight. She was subsequently raised by relatives of the Turtle clan. During her teen years, her family attempted, as was the custom, to arrange a marriage for her. Tekakwitha objected.

Though her mother had been a CHRISTIAN, it was not until 1667 that Tekakwitha was introduced to the FAITH by several JESUIT missionaries traveling in Quebec, who stayed briefly with her uncle. She began to think of herself as a Christian, though it was not until some time later, after the clan had moved to a new location along the Mohawk River in what is now Montgomery County, New York, that she was baptized by Fr. Jacques de Lamberville (1641–1710), whose MISSION included her people.

From that time forward Tekakwitha practiced her faith in a most fervent manner. Her determination to remain an unmarried virgin eventually alienated her family, and she was forced to flee. She settled at Caughnawaga (or Kahnawake) near Montreal on the St. Lawrence. Here she found community in the home of Anastasia Tegonhatsihonga, a Christian Indian woman. The group of Catholics among whom she now lived was impressed with her devotion, her prayerfulness, and the chaste lifestyle she had chosen to follow. Her sanctity was respected by both the Native peoples and the French, though the latter refused her request to start an ordered community among Native women.

Tekakwitha died at the St. Francis Xavier Mission at Caughnawaga on April 17, 1680, just 34 years old. Much of what we now know of her was due to her spiritual director, Fr. Pierre Cholenec (1641–1723), who wrote a brief account of her life.

Following her death, devotion to her quickly appeared among the Indians in Caughnawaga and the immediate region. Pilgrimages were made to her grave, and her memory was kept alive. In the 19th century the first petitions for her canonization were made, and in 1884 Fr. Clarence Walworth (1820–1900) oversaw the placing of a monument in her memory. She was declared venerable by Pope PIUS XII in 1943 and beatified by Pope JOHN PAUL II in 1980. Those supportive of her canonization acknowledge her as the "Lily of the Mohawks."

Further reading: *Blessed Kateri Tekakwitha, Mohawk Maiden* (Boston: Daughters of St. Paul, 1980); Margaret R. Bunson, *Kateri Tekakwitha: Mystic of the Wilderness* (Huntington, Ind.: Our Sunday Visitor, 1992); Harold William Sandberg, *Drums of Destiny: Kateri Tekakwitha 1656 to 1680* (St. Meinrad, Ind.: Grail, 1950).

Ten Commandments/Decalogue (Lat.: cum, "with" + mandare, "to order"; Gr.: deka, "ten" + logos, "word," "saying")

The Ten Commandments, also known by their Greek name the Decalogue (symbol "X", are a short list of stipulations imposed by *GOD* on Israel as terms for maintaining his Covenant with them. Three different versions appear in the Pentateuch, in Exodus 34:11–28, Exodus 20:2–17, and Deuteronomy 5:6–11. The commandments are the only words in the BIBLE said to be directly written by God; they were inscribed on two tablet stones of testimony (Exod. 32:16). After Moses smashed them in anger at seeing the golden calf (32:19) they were rechiseled, this time by Moses (34:1).

Most scholars think that the version in Exodus 34, which is very ritualistic in nature, was most likely the earliest. The version in Exodus 20 differs from Deuteronomy 5 in two significant ways. Exodus 20 explains the Sabbath as a commemoration of the Lord's day of rest after creating the world (Gen. 1:28), while Deuteronomy justifies the Sabbath on humanitarian grounds: humans and animals alike need to rest from six days of labor. The last commandment in Exodus 20 forbids a man from coveting his neighbor's wife or possessions;

in Deuteronomy, the commandment forbids coveting his wife or desiring his possessions.

It seems that the last commandment, dealing with desire and coveting, was the first to be violated by human beings. The same Hebrew roots, *hamad* (covet) and *ta'av* (desire), that are used in Deuteronomy's last commandment are used to describe Eve's reaction to the fruit of the forbidden tree (Gen. 3:7).

Tradition later divided the commandments into two tablets, one pertaining directly to God (1–4) and the second pertaining to one's neighbors (5–10). In the 17th century the Puritan dissident Roger Williams (1603–83) would appeal to this tradition in arguing for the separation of the church from the state.

The commandments are short pithy principles grounded in traditional Israelite monotheism. In Matthew Jesus says that he did not come to abrogate the law but to sharpen it, and the prohibition against divorce is an example of that (19:1–8). The commandments in particular were not abrogated in the New Testament, but deepened and given a positive expression; the Law and the Prophets are summed up as the love of God and neighbor (Mark 12:29–31), a summary that is not new but a Midrashic merger of Deuteronomy 6:4–5 ("You shall love the Lord your God," and Leviticus 19:18 ("Love your fellow as yourself"). Jesus' ministry in the Galilee was in great part a renewal of the Covenant between God and the people and gave emphasis to social laws of mutual aid. When the rich man asked Jesus what he must do to gain life everlasting, Jesus cited five commands from the second table and added "do not defraud" (Mark 10:19; Deuteronomy 24:14).

Within the first three centuries CHRISTIANS came to subordinate the interpretation of the Old Testament to its prophetic fulfillment in the New Testament. They also started making distinctions between the legal, moral, and ceremonial law. As Christianity moved out of its Jewish matrix, second-century apologists, especially in their treatises *Against the Jews,* (JUSTIN MARTYR; TERTULLIAN),

claimed that CHRIST either perfected or abrogated all the laws with the exception of the Ten Commandments, which he directly and indirectly affirmed. In Christian eyes, the Sermon on the Mount transformed the moral law, whereas ceremonial law (CIRCUMCISION, kosher rules, purifications, sacrifices) was simply abrogated. Christians took the destruction of the temple in Jerusalem as a sign that God had ended his favor to the Jews and transferred it to themselves and had abrogated the ritual laws, many of which were related to Temple worship.

In a passage many call the New Testament *in nuce,* the prophet Jeremiah promised a new Covenant between God and Israel/Judah with a Torah placed inside and "written on their hearts" (31:31–34). Grounding themselves in the arguments of AUGUSTINE and TERTULLIAN OF CARTHAGE, the great medieval theologians used this text to argue that the Decalogue belonged not to the positive law decreed by God but to natural law (Thomas Aquinas, *Summa Theologiae* 2–2.56.1). Aquinas argued that all the commandments, with the exception of Sabbath worship, could be known by natural reason without the aid of GRACE and revelation.

Following the model of Luther's catechisms, the Council of TRENT included a discussion of the Ten Commandments in the *Roman Catechism* (1563); this component became an essential part of all future CATECHISMS, including the post–VATICAN COUNCIL II *Catechism of the Catholic Church* (1994), where the commandments are discussed in terms of the Christian's life in Christ. There has been a shift from negative prohibition to positive Christian living based on the Sermon on the Mount (Matthew 5:1–7:29) and the Great Commandment to love one another (John 13:34). The Redemptorist moral theologian BERNARD HÄRING contributed to this shift with his groundbreaking *The Law of Christ* (1954).

Further reading: Augustine of Hippo, *On the Spirit and the Letter,* available online; Martin Buber, *On the*

Bible: Eighteen Studies (Syracuse, N.Y.: Syracuse University Press, 2000); *Catechism of the Catholic Church* (Liguori, Mo.: Liguori, 1994); Richard A. Freund, "The Decalogue in Judaism and Early Christianity," in Craig A. Evans and James A. Sanders, eds., *The Function of Scripture in Early Jewish and Christian Tradition* (Sheffield, U.K.: Sheffield Academic, 1998).

Teresa of Ávila (1515–1582) *mystic, saint, and doctor of the church*

The saintliness of Teresa of Ávila was recognized rather quickly after her death; she was beatified in 1614 and canonized a mere eight years later in 1622 by Pope Gregory XV (r. 1621–23). Her writings became classics of mystic literature read alike by Catholics, Protestants, and spiritual seekers of other faiths. However, it was not until 1970, in the wake of VATICAN COUNCIL II and the late 20th-century recognition of the contributions of women to western Catholic history that Pope PAUL VI recognized Teresa's intellectual accomplishments and added her (along with St. CATHERINE OF SIENA) to the list of DOCTORS OF THE CHURCH. Her feast day is July 14.

Teresa was born Teresa de Cepeda y Ahumada near Ávila, SPAIN, into a well-to-do merchant family. One of her grandfathers was a *converso,* or convert from Judaism. When she was 15, her mother died and she was given into the care of some AUGUSTINIAN NUNS. During her stay with them she decided to enter the religious life, and in 1535 she joined the CARMELITE Order. After a number of rather uneventful years, in 1554 she had a dramatic vision of CHRIST that changed her life. It was followed by additional visions each focusing on some aspect of Christ's Passion and suffering.

The visions motivated Teresa to criticize the laxity that had entered into Carmelite life and to launch an effort to call it back to the strict observance that characterized its early years. At that very time the church in Spain was going through the transitions of the COUNTER-REFORMATION, and reform was in the air. Like St. IGNATIUS OF LOYOLA she contributed to baroque mystical THEOLOGY.

Followers of Teresa's reforms could be recognized by their refusal to wear shoes, and the groups became known as the shoeless, or Discalced, Carmelites. Teresa founded a reformed Carmelite convent at Ávila and began to write, starting with an autobiographical essay including an initial survey of mystical prayer. During the mid-1560s, she finished the *Way of Perfection* and the *Meditations on the Canticle.* In 1567, she met John of St. Matthias (later known as JOHN OF THE CROSS), whom she enlisted to extend her reform among the male Carmelites. In 1572 Teresa called him to act as the confessor for her convent at Ávila. Teresa remained as prioress of the Ávila monastery as John tried to spread her reform, except for the nine months he was kidnapped and imprisoned in 1577.

During her last years Teresa wrote her most important book, *Interior Castle.* She began writing it while her *Autobiography* was being examined for HERESY by the INQUISITION. The *Interior Castle* is a detailed description of the steps in the interior life of a mystic. It is all the more important as having been written by a person who was at the same time actively involved in the outward life of the church—traveling, founding convents and MONASTERIES, and advising many people who wrote to her and succeeded in reconciling her mysticism with a life of devotion to Christ.

Further reading: Tessa Bielecki, *Holy Daring: An Outrageous Gift to Modern Spirituality from Saint Teresa, the Grand Wild Woman of Ávila* (Rockport, Mass.: Element, 1994); Cathleen Medwick, *Teresa of Ávila: The Progress of a Soul* (Garden City, N.Y.: Image, 2001); Teresa of Ávila, *The Autobiography of St. Teresa of Ávila* (Garden City, N.Y.: Image, 1960); ———, *Interior Castle* (Garden City, N.Y.: Image Books, 1961); ———, *The Way of Perfection* (Garden City, N.Y.: Image, 1964).

Teresa of Calcutta, Mother (1910–1997) *founder of Missionaries of Charity*

Mother Teresa (or Gonxha) Bojazhiu was born into an Albanian family living in Skopje, Yugoslavia (now Macedonia). When she was 18 she became a NUN with the Sisters of Loreto in Ireland. A year later, having learned some English, she entered the novitiate at Darjeeling, India, and by 1931 was assigned to work in Calcutta.

In 1946 Sister Teresa experienced a calling to serve the poor of Calcutta. With the blessings of her order and church authorities she withdrew from the Sisters of Loreto and moved to one of the poorer sections of the city in 1948. She would soon be joined by a few women who became the nucleus of a new order. The Missionaries of Charity was formally approved as a diocesan congregation in 1950 and as a pontifical institute in 1965. As the order grew it directed its primary focus toward Calcutta's street children and then turned its attention to the dying. Mother Teresa opened several hospices. A natural evolution occurred as the order successively assumed responsibility to serve the homeless and those infected with the most feared and reviled diseases, such as Hansen's disease and AIDS.

Through the 1970s Mother Teresa attracted international attention, and she was given a series of awards, including the Pope JOHN XXIII Peace Prize (1971), the Nehru Prize for her promotion of international peace and understanding (1972), and the Balzan Prize for promoting peace and brotherhood (1979). In 1979 she received the Nobel Peace Prize, an event that made her an international celebrity.

Eventually, the order expanded into other countries and by the mid-1990s included more than 2,300 sisters serving in more than 80 countries. Novitiates were established in Rome, ITALY; Manila, the Philippines; Warsaw, POLAND; Tabora, Tanzania; and San Francisco, California.

In the last years of her life Teresa further endeared herself to her Catholic audience with her defense of the rights of the unborn. In 1994, for example, when she was honored at a National Prayer Breakfast sponsored by the U.S. Congress, she used the opportunity to speak against abortion with her oft-quoted words, "Please don't kill the child. I want the child. Give the child to me."

Mother Teresa died in 1997 and was succeeded by Sister Nurmila as superior general of the Missionaries of Charity, still headquartered in Calcutta. While widely admired in the world, some Indians have expressed muted criticism that her efforts, though noble, failed to address the structures in society leading to the wretched lives of the people she sought to help.

Further reading: Michael Collopy, *Works of Love Are Works of Peace: Mother Teresa of Calcutta and the Missionaries of Charity* (San Francisco: Ignatius, 1996); Sinita Kumar, *Mother Teresa of Calcutta* (London: Weidenfeld & Nicolson, 1998); E. Le Joly, *Mother Teresa of Calcutta: A Biography* (San Francisco: Harper & Row, 1983); R. Serrou, *Teresa of Calcutta: A Pictorial Biography.* New York: McGraw Hill, 1980).

Tertullian of Carthage (c. 160–240) *early theologian/apologist*

Tertullian, a church father important for the development of the doctrine of the TRINITY, was an able opponent of the GNOSTIC heretic MARCION. Later in life he identified with the movement of MONTANUS, thus marring an otherwise outstanding career as an orthodox CHRISTIAN spokesperson.

Tertullian was born in a well-to-do pagan family in Carthage, northern AFRICA. He received a good classical Roman education but later developed strong feelings against philosophy. For reasons not well understood, he converted to Christianity around 195 and put his intellectual training to the service of the church. His *Apology,* written shortly after his conversion, defended church members as law-abiding Romans and denounced their persecution by successive Roman emperors. He pointed out, among other things, that Christianity required its followers to pray for the ruler (one charge often leveled against Christians was that they were committing treason).

Tertullian turned his attentions to Gnosticism, and particularly to Marcion, whose followers seemed the greatest threat in Carthage. His longest single work was *Against Marcion*. In particular, he attacked the Marcionite claim to special revelation and occult knowledge. While still combating the Marcionites, he waded into the debate on the Trinity, which was focused on the effort to reconcile Christ's divinity with monotheism. It was Tertullian who first described God as "one substance consisting in three persons," a major step in the development of a mature Trinitarian position. He also contributed major treatises on BAPTISM, PRAYER, and PENANCE. Against Marcion, he used TYPOLOGY to unite the Testaments. His oft-quoted dictum "I believe because it is absurd" has been misinterpreted for centuries (*see* FAITH AND REASON).

Responding to the 202 edict against Christians (and Jews) issued by Septimus Severus (r. 193–211), Tertullian argued for a pure church that accepted martyrdom if that was its fate. It was this search for purity that led him to the Montanists, a charismatic and puritanical movement that spread through Asia Minor and North Africa. He contrasted the followers of Montanus with the lax and compromising Christians in Rome. Increasingly he stated that martyrdom was the goal of the Christian life. Nevertheless, he lived into his 80s and died a natural death.

Further reading: T. D. Barnes, *Tertullian: A Historical and Literary Study* (London: Oxford University Press, 1971); W. H. C. Frend, *Martyrdom and Persecution in the Early Church* (Oxford: Blackwell, 1964); R. E. Roberts, *The Theology of Tertullian* (London: Longman, 1924); A. D. Sidler, *Ancient Rhetoric and the Art of Tertullian* (London: Oxford University Press, 1971).

Tetzel, Johann (c. 1465–1519) *Dominican friar*

Johann Tetzel, whose selling of INDULGENCES in GERMANY in 1517 provoked Martin Luther to begin the PROTESTANT REFORMATION, was a DOMINICAN preacher at St. Paul's Convent in Liepzig.

Tetzel entered the Dominican Order in 1489. He studied THEOLOGY, taught at the Dominican school in Leipzig, and worked as an inquisitor in Poland. For six years (1504–10) he had also been active as a seller of indulgences. Thus, it was no surprise when at the beginning of 1517 he was appointed the general subcommissary for the sale of indulgences in the church province of Magdeburg. His task took him to Jeuterbock and Zerbst, only 20 miles from Wittenberg, where Luther was a professor of theology. At the time Luther posted his 95 theses calling the sale of indulgences into question, Tetzel was in Berlin pursuing his duties.

Luther's theses received wide publicity when he attached a copy to a letter to Archbishop Albrecht of Mainz (1490–1545) complaining of Tetzel's work and of his sending of money to Rome to build ST. PETER'S BASILICA. Luther also wrote to Pope LEO X. Meanwhile, Tetzel completed a degree of licentiate of theology in the University of Frankfort-on-the-Oder, 1517, and a doctorate of theology the next year, during which time he defended the doctrine of indulgences against Luther's theses in two disputations. Tetzel died in Liepzig in 1519 just as the response to Luther was being organized.

Further reading: Harold J. Grimm, *The Reformation Era, 1500–1650* (New York: Macmillan, 1965); Diarmaid MacCulloch, *The Reformation* (New York: Penguin, 2003); J. J. Vogel, *Leben Des Päbstlichen Gnaden oder predigers Johann Tetzel* (Leipzig: J. Fr. Braun, 1727).

Theodosius I (c. 347–395) *Christian Roman emperor*

Theodosius I, called the Great, is credited with moving the Roman Empire from a general favoritism toward Christianity to a specific support of orthodox CHRISTIAN faith. He was born in SPAIN and rose to power through the army. A lost battle seemed to end his career and force him into retirement, but he was soon rehabilitated and placed in a commanding position. In 379 he became Roman emperor and fostered Eastern CAESAROPAPISM.

Shortly after becoming emperor he became ill. He was baptized as an orthodox Christian by BISHOP Acholius of Thessalonica in the fall of 380, shortly before he arrived in CONSTANTINOPLE. He took his Catholic faith seriously and moved to suppress ARIANISM, which still enjoyed strong support. Among his first acts in CONSTANTINOPLE was to expel the pro-Arian bishop and back the orthodox bishop, GREGORY OF NAZIANZUS. He subsequently called the Council of Constantinople of 381, which backed the orthodox theological position. Theodosius subsequently moved to expel all the Arian bishops from their churches in the eastern half of the Roman Empire in spite of popular opposition in Constantinople, where the majority of the population supported their cause.

In 391, Theodosius banned attendance at pagan worship sites, including the Oracle at Delphi, and barred anyone from decorating images of the pagan gods so as to acknowledge their divinity. While generally protecting pagan sites as part of the empire's artistic heritage, he did order the destruction of the Sarapeum at Alexandria, one of the major pagan temples of the day.

For ordering an indiscriminate massacre in Thessalonika, Theodosius was excommunicated by AMBROSE OF MILAN. He did public penance for several months as part of his effort to have the excommunication lifted. Theodosius was the last great ruler of both East and West of the Roman Empire.

Further reading: Gerard Friell and Stephen Williams, *Theodosius: The Empire at Bay* (New Haven, Conn.: Yale University Press, 1994); Neil B. McLynn, *Ambrose of Milan: Church and Court in a Christian Capital.* (Berkeley: University of California Press, 1994); John Vanderspoel, *Themistius and the Imperial Court: Oratory, Civic Duty, and Paideia from Constantius to Theodosius* (Ann Arbor: University of Michigan Press, 1995).

theology (Lat.: *theos,* "God" + *logos* "word about," "study of")

Theology means simply the word about God or the study of the Godhead. It is the formal attempt to understand and interpret the things of God, both theoretical and practical, revealed in both Scripture and tradition, in a scholarly, methodical, and systematic manner. ANSELM OF CANTERBURY gave a classic formulation to the theological enterprise as *fides quaerens intellectum,* or "faith seeking understanding." Though it can be pursued objectively as an academic subject, theology's true purpose is in understanding and interpreting the truths of God as a service to the community of FAITH.

CHRISTIAN systematic theology began with reflection of the three articles of faith in the theology of IRENAEUS OF LYONS. It includes the doctrines of GOD, Christology, the FALL, redemption through GRACE, ECCLESIOLOGY, the SACRAMENTS, and ESCHATOLOGY. AUGUSTINE OF HIPPO gave an authoritative formulation of the truths of faith for the West in his large corpus of writings.

Creativity and energy continue to inform systematic theology down to the present. A recent development is FUNDAMENTAL THEOLOGY, expounded by KARL RAHNER (1904–84). It finds the ground of theology in God's self-communication to humankind in the story of Israel and Christ as the precondition of human response to God's offer of salvation. Others, like Joseph Ratzinger, now BENEDICT XVI, take a more traditional approach in presenting theology to the lay person.

Moral theology deals with the normative principles of human and Christian action in the world. These include the principles of justice based on God's Covenants with the people. Commutative justice embraces the exchanges between human beings that establish fairness in reciprocal relations and liberation from bondage. Distributive justice seeks the equitable allocation of resources throughout the whole of society and not just the Christian fellowship. Social justice looks to the structural impediments in societies that impede equality in terms of race, class, or gender. The heart of social justice theology is the principle of the common good that St. THOMAS AQUINAS articulated with clarity and force in the *Summa Theologiae* 2.2.90–97, often called "Treatise on Law."

Social justice demands that administrations and governments attend carefully to the conditions of the poorest and most disadvantaged of society, a theme first proclaimed by the prophets of Israel and today most clearly enunciated in LIBERATION THEOLOGY. Without embracing Marxist ideology, liberation theology often employs Marxist analysis to get at structural problems in society. Enrique Dussel, the liberationist theologian, argues in *Ethics and Community* (1988) that the ethic of the GOSPEL challenges the accepted morality of society eschatologically.

The great social themes of moral theology are the subject of several key papal encyclicals (*see* ENCYCLICAL, PAPAL): *Rerum Novarum* (1891) by LEO XIII, *Quadragesimo Anno* (1931) by PIUS IX, *PACEM IN TERRIS* (1963) by JOHN XXIII, *Populorum Progressio* (1967) by PAUL VI, and *Centessimus Annus* (1991) by JOHN PAUL II. While the popes have often critiqued atheistic communism, they have been hardly sparing of the national and international inequities produced by capitalism. Social justice was a central concern of the Latin American Bishops Conferences (CELAM) at Medellín (1968) and Puebla (1979).

Despite the church's century-long focus on the social aspects of moral theology, the media in the West tend to focus attention on those aspects of Catholic moral theology that relate to sexuality: ABORTION, birth control, and homosexuality. Even in these areas, opinion is not unanimous. Many participants in VATICAN COUNCIL II were on the verge of approving the use of the birth control pill. However, Paul VI removed the topic from discussion and issued *Humanae Vitae* (July 25, 1968), written with the help of the future John Paul II, who restated the ban on the pill and on other artificial means in *Evangelium Vitae* (March 25, 1995).

The Catholic Church has always condemned homosexuality; this position was renewed in the doctrinal declaration *Pastoral Care of Homosexual Persons* (October 1, 1986) by Cardinal Joseph Ratzinger, prefect of the Congregation for the Doctrine of the Faith (now BENEDICT XVI). Most recently in 2005 the Vatican proposed to ban even celibate homosexual men from the priesthood, but modified its position after much criticism in the *Instruction on the Priesthood and Those with Homosexual Tendencies* (November 29, 2005).

The condemnation of homosexuality is usually grounded in Leviticus 19, where it is listed along with incest and other sexual irregularities. This chapter is also Jesus' source for the second half of the Great Commandment "Love God with all your heart and all your soul and all your mind and with all your strength [Deut. 6:4–5] and love your neighbor as yourself [Lev. 19:18]" (Mark 12:31). In the Covenant Renewal Discourse, known more commonly as the Sermon on the Plain (Luke 6:17–49), Jesus focuses on the social sins against love of God and neighbor and not the sexual irregularities of Leviticus.

Moral theology also deals with suicide and euthanasia; they were important themes in *Evangelium Vitae*. Most recently the case of Terry Schiavo (1963–2005) drew anguished debate about the treatment of patients who are brain-damaged and comatose for long periods of time. The Vatican bioethicist Bishop Elio Sgreccia (1928–) issued a monitum, or warning, that removing Ms. Schiavo's tube was a step in the direction of euthanasia. Other ethicists pointed to writings of PIUS XII on death and dying that seem to contradict this view. If the Vatican can justify the use of artificial means to extend life beyond its normal course, it may be undermining its argument against artificial means of contraception.

Mystical theology is also called spiritual theology. Mysticism can include ASCETICISM as a discipline in service of the mystical life. In former times theologians often separated the doctrinal from the mystical, or experiential, aspects of theology. Today theologians say this is a false step and that the mysteries contained within the doctrines of faith are also the mysteries that can bring the person into intimate communion with God. Karl Rahner illuminated the theology of the Trinity as a subject both for formal theological reflection and mystical union with God.

In early Christianity mystical theology was deeply affected by Neoplatonism, which valued the spiritual creation far more than the physical and the material, and to a certain extent considered the material world as less good. This tradition held sway from the mystical theology of Pseudo-Dionysius to St. BONAVENTURE.

The mystical theology of the Dominicans MEISTER ECKHARDT and Henry Suso (1295–1366), who innovated a kind of creation mysticism, served as a bridge from the Neoplatonic anti-materialism to the sensual baroque spirituality of TERESA OF ÁVILA and IGNATIUS OF LOYOLA. In recent times Catholic theologians have followed many paths in mystical theology, from a revival of Eckhardt's creation spirituality by MATTHEW FOX, to the incorporation of the Russian mystic tradition and Native American spirituality into the Catholic fold, to a dialogue between Catholic and Hindu spirituality by the Jesuit Anthony de Mello (1937–87). De Mello's mysticism has been criticized by the PAPACY as in part incompatible with Catholic doctrine, but he remains a very popular mystical writer among Catholics and non-Catholics alike.

Further reading: *Catechism of the Catholic Church* (Liguori, Mo.: Liguori, 1994); Charles E. Curran, *The Catholic Moral Tradition Today* (Washington, D.C.: Georgetown University, Press, 1999); Charles E. Curran & Richard A. McCormick, *Dialogue About Catholic Sexual Teaching* (New York: Paulist, 1993); Matthew Fox, *Western Spirituality: Historical Roots, Ecumenical Routes* (Santa Fe: Bear & Co, 1981); Karl Rahner, *Foundations of Christian Faith: An Introduction to the Idea of Christianity* (New York: Crossroad, 1984); Joseph Ratzinger, *Introduction to Christianity* (San Francisco: Ignatius, 2004).

Thérèse of Lisieux, St. (1873–1897) *popular French saint*

Also known as Sister Theresa of the Child Jesus, and as the Little Flower, Thérèse of Lisieux has become one of the most popular saints in the Catholic Church. She was born at Alençon, FRANCE, on January 2, 1873, the daughter of Louis and Zélie Martin. Her parents had both wanted to adhere to the religious life but were prevented by circumstances. However, they were quite supportive of their children who wished to adopt the ordered life. Three of Thérèse's older sisters became CARMELITE NUNS.

Thérèse was only 15 when she initially applied for entrance into the Carmelite convent at Lisieux.

Statue of Thérèse of Lisieux, Kunming, China. She is one of the most popular saints in all of Christianity. (*J. Gordon Melton*)

Refused because of her youth, she took the unusual step of accompanying her father on a pilgrimage to Rome, where they attempted to take advantage of Pope LEO XIII's jubilee to gain his support for her goal. He referred the decision back to the local superior, and her manifest intent helped sway the superior to reconsider her earlier decision. Thus, she was able to join the sisters at the convent in 1888.

Her convent life was notable and noticed by her superior, who ordered her to write an account of what she had experienced and the manner of her reaction to the holy life. Throughout her life she expressed a desire to become a PRIEST. Her autobiography, *Story of a Soul,* was published two years after her death on September 30, 1897. It was translated and published in English in 1901. She called her way of devotion the "Little Way" that centered upon the love of and trust in GOD. It found an immediate response throughout the church. Thérèse was increasingly viewed as a saint who had abandoned herself to the service of God, in contrast to a life of accomplishment in mundane duties.

The canonization process started in 1914 in response to her growing fame and in light of the many miracles attributed to her intercession. She was canonized by Pope PIUS XI in 1925. In 1997, Pope JOHN PAUL II named her a DOCTOR OF THE CHURCH.

Further reading: Michael Hollings, *Therese of Lisieux: An Illustrated Life* (London: W. Collins, 1981); Frances Parkinson Keyes, *Therese, Saint of the Little Way* (New York: Julian Messner, 1950); Thérèse of Lisieux, *The Story of a Soul,* tr. Michael Day, (Wheathampstead: Anthony Clarke, 1973); Hans Urs Von Balthasar, *Therese of Lisieux: The Story of a Mission* (New York: Sheed & Ward, 1954).

Thomas à Kempis (c. 1379–1471) *devotional writer*

Thomas à Kempis, the author of the devotional classic *The Imitation of Christ,* was born in Kempen

in eastern GERMANY. As a young man he moved to Deventer, the Netherlands, and attended the school of the Brothers of the Common Life. The Brothers had been founded by Gerhard Groote (1340–84) and Florent Radewyns, a Deventer priest, as a community of clerics and lay people concerned with the laxity of the CLERGY. The Brethren came together to pursue a life of holiness. They supported their work by selling popular religious texts, including parts of the BIBLE, in the vernacular (rather than Latin). Their vernacular writings later caused them to be seen as precursors of the PROTESTANT REFORMATION.

In 1399 Thomas joined the AUGUSTINIAN Order. He was ordained a PRIEST around 1413. He began work copying texts and writing at Mount St. Agnes MONASTERY near Zwolle, the Netherlands. He wrote several treatises on the monastic life and some devotional essays.

Thomas lived a somewhat mundane monastic life and is remembered only as the purported author of the popular devotional work *The Imitation of Christ.* His authorship is by no means sure, but his name did appear on an early Latin manuscript, and it does reflect the spirituality of the Brothers of the Common Life. Thomas may have copied and edited it using an earlier text produced by Groote. The *Imitation* promotes friendship with and love of Jesus for his own sake. It contains the prayer "Grant me, Lord, to know all I should know, to love what I should love, to esteem most what pleases you, and to reject all that is evil in your sight."

Further reading: J. E. G. De Montmorency, *Thomas à Kempis: His Age and Book* (London: Methuen, 1906); Samuel Kettlewell, *Thomas à Kempis and the Brothers of the Common Life* (New York: G. P. Putnam's Sons, 1882); Thomas à Kempis, *The Imitation of Christ* (Chicago: Moody, 1984).

Thomas Aquinas, St. (c. 1224–1274) *medieval theologian and philosopher*

A DOMINICAN friar who taught at Paris, Naples, and Rome, Aquinas authored the magisterial *Summa*

Theologiae, the foremost theological treatise of the MIDDLE AGES. Blending Christian THEOLOGY with Aristotelian philosophy, his work remained the intellectual standard of Catholic teaching against which all subsequent theology was measured. He was called the Angelic, or Common, DOCTOR OF THE CHURCH and referred to as the "Dumb Ox" due to his girth; he was often painted with a sunburst on his breast, a star, a dove at his ear, a chalice, or an ox. He is the patron saint of universities. Aquinas was buried at the Dominican church in Toulouse. His feast day is January 28.

Thomas, born in the family castle near Naples, was the youngest son of Landulfo d'Aquino, who made his son an oblate at the BENEDICTINE abbey of Monte Cassino. He studied the traditional Platonic liberal arts curriculum at the University of Naples, newly founded by FREDERICK II. At the age of 19 he joined the new mendicant Dominican order. His uncle and brothers objected and had him kidnapped and subjected to the lures of a prostitute to seduce him away. He resisted, earning his later reputation as "Angelic" doctor; he later wrote a treatise against those attempting to "deprogram" young people out of the new MENDICANT ORDERS. After his escape Thomas was sent to the Dominican priory in Paris to study theology at a time when ARISTOTLE's works were entering the university curriculum through the mediation of Islamic and Jewish philosophers and theologians. In 1248 he matriculated at Cologne under ALBERTUS MAGNUS.

Back in Paris, he became a bachelor of Scripture, lecturing on the BIBLE and the *Sentences* of PETER LOMBARD and writing commentaries on Aristotle's principal works. Promoted to master of theology, Thomas wrote the *Summa contra gentiles* ("Summa against the Gentiles", a philosophically informed apology of Christianity intended for missionaries proselytizing among non-Christians, mostly Muslims in SPAIN. He does not deny that there is truth in ISLAM but asserts that it mixes truth with falsehood. He criticizes Islamic philosophers such as Averroes (Ibn Rushd, 1126–98)

St. Thomas debating Averroes (Ibn Rushd) of Cordova, who is lying on the floor. Tempera and gold leaf by Sienese painter Giovanni di Paolo (c. 1399–1482). *(St. Louis Art Museum, with permission)*

who, he believed, put too much reliance on reason over faith. He also wrote treatises criticizing members of the secular faculty, such as William of St. Amour (c. 1210–73) who attacked the mendicants.

From 1259 to 1268 Thomas taught at various Dominican houses in ITALY. For Pope Urban IV he composed the LITURGY for the Feast of Corpus Christi (*see* EUCHARIST) and the *Catena aurea* ("Golden Chain"), a compilation of patristic commentaries on the Bible. While teaching at Sta. Sabina in Rome he began the *Summa Theologiae,* which he worked on until 1273.

Returning to Paris in 1268, Thomas entered into disputations with Siger de Brabant and other radical Aristotelians. He wrote commentaries on Matthew and John, DIONYSIUS the Areopagite's *Divine Names,* Aristotle's *Nicomachian Ethics, Posterior Analytics,* and *Metaphysics,* the CREED, and the Lord's Prayer and Hail Mary (*see* PRAYERS, COMMON). He composed hymns, including *Adoro Te Devote* and *Pange Lingua,* sermons, and prayers throughout his life. While celebrating mass on December 6, 1273, he received a mystical vision after which he said: "Everything I have written seems like straw in comparison with what I have seen and what has been revealed to me." He wrote not another word. He died on the way to the Second Council of Lyons (*see* COUNCILS, ECUMENICAL) in 1274.

The *Summa Theologiae* is composed as a series of questions. Thomas begins by asking whether theology is a science in the Aristotelian sense. He then discusses God (part 1), the movement of all beings toward God as an end (parts 1-2 and 2-2), and the incarnate Christ as the means whereby creatures move toward God (part 3).

Part 1 covers the topics of God's nature, the TRINITY, God the Creator, angels, humans, and divine government. Part 1-2 focuses on humanity: its destiny toward the BEATIFIC VISION of God, its acts, passions, habits, virtues, vices, and sins, and the correction of the last two through law and grace. Part 2-2 treats of life after grace: the theological virtues (faith, hope, and charity), the cardinal virtues (prudence, justice, courage, and temperance), and the charisms, or gifts of the Spirit, relative to the contemplative and active forms of life. Part 3 deals with the Savior (his INCARNATION, ministry, Passion, DEATH, and RESURRECTION), and the SACRAMENTS—the fruits of Christ's redemption of humanity (BAPTISM, CONFIRMATION, the EUCHARIST, and PENANCE). Here the *Summa* abruptly ends. Reginaldo de Piperno (c. 1230–90) Thomas's secretary, sought to supplement the *Summa* by inserting concluding sections from Thomas's commentary on Lombard's *Sentences,* which dated from 30 years before. As Thomas's thinking had evolved considerably between the *Sentences* commentary and the *Summa,* modern editions omit the "Supplement."

Thomas's achievement is best seen as a response to the crisis in medieval Christian theology marked by the divide between Platonic and Aristotelian tendencies. The Platonic strain in the form of NEOPLATONISM prevailed in the first millennium, shaping the thinking of AUGUSTINE and BERNARD OF CLAIRVAUX, and reached a peak in the CAROLINGIAN RENAISSANCE of ALCUIN and the philosophy of the Muslim Avicenna (ibn Sina) (980–1037). As Plato subordinated the shadowy cave of the sensuous and empirical world to the luminous and superior reality of the ideas (*Republic* Book 7), so Christian Platonists subordinated time to eternity, the physical to the spiritual, and the liberal arts, by which we study the world, to theology, by which we know God. In BONAVENTURE, the last of the Neoplatonists, all human effort and insight is devalued and swallowed up in the *unio mystica.*

Thomas represents a paradigm shift that gave philosophical legitimation to the new empirical arts and sciences arising in the MIDDLE AGES—law, medicine, natural science, ARCHITECTURE, and technology. Each art and each science finds its proper place and proper autonomy, not to be submerged in a "higher" viewpoint. Key to this legitimation was the rediscovery of the empirical as the proper, natural object of human knowledge. This explains the turn to Aristotle, who wanted to explain the horse eating hay in the pasture, not the idea of the ideal horse existing in heaven. Thomas made free use of Aristotelian distinctions: cause and effect, substance and accident, form and matter, subject and object, potency and act, being and essence, and so on.

In the early 20th century many self-described Thomists tried to extract a purely philosophical aspect from Thomas's thought, but the doctor, following Augustine and ANSELM, always began from the viewpoint of *fides quaerens intellectum* ("faith seeking understanding"). The underlying categories of interpretation are faith and reason and nature and supernature, or grace. Faith and revelation do not negate reason but correct and complete it. Grace does not negate nature but fulfils it. Thomas stresses the human person as a unity: a soul or spirit incarnate in a body as form infusing matter. This is called hylomorphism, or matter (Gk. *hyle*) informed by soul (Gk. *morphe*).

The senses provide us not "decayed ideas" but beginnings of knowledge: *nihil in intellectu nisi prius in sensu* ("nothing is in the intellect unless it is previously in the senses"). By reason alone the human person can know *that* God is by means of the famous Five Proofs *Summa Theologiae* (1.2.3), but only faith can show *what* God is in all the divine attributes.

Striking a path between equivocity of being (God has "being" totally other than we) on one hand and univocity (God has "being" the same as we) on the other, he asserted that we know God by an analogy of being, "from creatures as their cause, and by way of excellence and negation" (1.13.1 response; *see also* 1.13.5; DUNS SCOTUS). Naturally, the mind seeks to know God in the creatures of creation; supernaturally the soul is destined toward the vision of the divine essence itself, not simply as the Aristotelian *actus purus* ("pure act" and *ipsum esse per se subsistens* ("self-subsisting being") but also as revealed pure love and self-giver of grace. We are aware of this "capacity for God" because we were created in the image and likeness of God (Gen. 1:27). Thus, grace builds on nature. The 20th-century theologian KARL RAHNER would build on this theme of Aquinas.

Thomas' Christology (*see* CHRIST/CHRISTOLOGY) is fully in accord with the formula of Chalcedon: Christ is one person with two natures, fully human, fully divine. Although Scripture seems clear in assigning SIN as the motive for the Incarnation, God is not limited by this and could have become incarnate even if there had been no sin (3.1.3). God descended to the level of humanity so that humanity might be raised to God. The Incarnation is the supreme act of the conferral of the good in CREATION. It is the exaltation of the universe and the divinization of mankind itself through the life of grace it bestows, for grace is the life of God in God's self as the TRINITY.

Thomas presents no formal doctrine of the church in the *Summa*. After treating the Christ he immediately goes into the theology of the sacraments. Implicit in his teaching on the sacraments, however, is the understanding that the church, as the continuation of the Incarnation and redemption in time and space, is the mystical body of Christ (*see* ECCLESIOLOGY) through which the sacraments act both as signs and causes of things that make people holy (3.60.2; 3.64). Earlier Thomas thought that the sacraments were remedies to sin. In the *Summa* they take on an expanded meaning as aids to stages in the spiritual life of individuals and society as a whole. The sacraments are the leavening agents of God in the sanctification of the world.

Thomas was very controversial in his time. In 1277 Robert of Kilwardby (d. 1279), a member of his own Dominican order and archbishop of Canterbury, condemned several of his propositions, and he was seconded by Stephen Tempier, bishop of Paris. These censures were lifted when Thomas was canonized by Pope JOHN XXII in 1323 and declared a doctor of the church by PIUS V in 1567. In the encyclical *Aeterni Patris* (August 4, 1879) LEO XIII enjoined the study of Thomas on all Catholic theological students throughout the world, but not to the exclusion of other theologians. Some critics called this an enshrinement of Thomas that would bind Catholic theology in a 13th-century straightjacket (*see* NOUVELLE THÉOLOGIE). Yet to many, Thomas remains the prime philosophical theologian of Christianity in the West, rivaled only by AUGUSTINE.

Further reading: The *Summa Theologiae* is available online at New Advent and a printed version is the Blackfriar's edition (London, 1964–81); the complete edition of Thomas's works is the Leonine edition (Rome, 1882 ff); Marie-Dominique Chenu, *Toward Understanding St. Thomas* (Chicago: Regnery, 1964); Frederick C. Copleston, *Aquinas* (Harmondsworth: Penguin, 1955); Etienne Gilson, *The Christian Philosophy of St. Thomas* (New York: Random House, 1964); Joseph Pieper, *Guide to Thomas Aquinas* (New York: Pantheon, 1962); James A Weisheipl, *Friar Thomas d'Aquino* (Washington, D.C.: Catholic University of America Press, 1983).

Thomas More, St. (1478–1535) *English statesman and martyr*

A highly successful English lawyer, writer, politician, and public servant, More was executed for opposing the divorce of Henry VIII (r. 1509–47), the event that kicked off the English Reformation. His feast day is June 22, together with St. JOHN FISHER.

More was born in London, the son of Sir John More, and became a page to the Archbishop of Canterbury John Morton (1420–1500) at the age of 13. After attending Oxford University he received his law degree in 1501. He was drawn to the religious life and considered joining a MONASTERY but decided he could not remain celibate and was married in 1505, although he continued strict religious practices and remained a devout Catholic throughout his life.

More coined the word *utopia* in his famous work of the same name, published in 1515; it envisions an ideal nation that abides by natural law and practices religious toleration. After a very successful public career, including being knighted in 1521, serving as Speaker of the House of Commons in 1523, and serving as high steward of Oxford and Cambridge Universities from 1524 to 1525, he succeeded Cardinal Thomas Wolsey (c. 1475–1530) as lord chancellor in 1529.

His political career ended when he opposed Henry VIII's divorce and refused to accept him as head of the English Church. After refusing to take the oath under the Act of Succession, he was imprisoned in the Tower for the next 15 months, where he wrote the *Dialogue of Comfort against Tribulation,* his best devotional book. On July 1, 1535, he was accused of high treason and executed six days later. In 1886 LEO XIII beatified him, and PIUS XI canonized him in 1935. He is the patron saint of lawyers and politicians. More's stand was celebrated in the play and movie *A Man for All Seasons* (1960/1966) by Robert Bolt (1924–95).

Further reading: Benjamin O. Flower, *The Century of Sir Thomas More* (Boston: Arena, 1896); Judith Hillman Paterson, *Thomas More* (Boston: Twayne, 1979); Louis Lohr Martz, *Thomas More: The Search for the Inner Man* (New Haven, Conn.: Yale University Press, 1990); Enid M. G. Routh, *Sir Thomas More and His Friends, 1477–1535* (London: Oxford University Press, 1934).

tiara

The papal tiara is the royal headpiece that was worn by popes for many centuries. Formerly three tiers of the tiara symbolized the pope's roles as BISHOP of Rome, patriarch of the West, and ruler of the PAPAL STATES (later, VATICAN CITY/State). It was used in coronation ceremonies and became a visible symbol of their authority. Its use was discontinued by Pope PAUL VI; JOHN PAUL I was the first modern pope to assume office without being crowned with it. The tiara remains a symbol of the papal office, however, as it still appeared on Pope JOHN PAUL II's coat of arms and the Vatican's flag. Pope BENEDICT XVI removed the tiara from his coat of arms and replaced it with a three-barred bishop's miter. The tiara remains on the Vatican flag and general coat of arms.

Further reading: Felician A. Foy, *A Concise Guide to the Catholic Church* (Huntington, Ind.: Our Sunday Visitor, 1984); Charles Noonan, *The Church Visible: The Ceremonial Life and Protocol of the Roman Catholic Church* (New York: Viking Penguin, 1996); Valerie Pirie, *The Triple Crown: An Account of the Papal Conclaves from the Fifteenth Century to Modern Times* (London: Spring Books, 1965).

tithing

Jewish law required tithing, the setting aside of a 10th of one's income to support a sacred institution or specific sacred causes. The early church financed itself instead through voluntary offerings and from the wages that its ministers earned as they pursued their secular day jobs like PAUL THE APOSTLE.

As the church became the dominant religion in Rome, calls began to be heard for a more institutionalized form of support. As early as the third century, St. CYPRIAN OF CARTHAGE had called for a form of tithing. In the sixth century, many emperors and local rulers began, with church support, to promulgate tithe laws. Over time the laws became more detailed, concerning what was to be tithed (e.g., agricultural crops, livestock, the product of artisans), who would pay the tithe (e.g., landowners, merchants), and who would receive it for the church (e.g., the BISHOP, a parish PRIEST, a religious order, the local prince or magistrate). The practice varied in different countries and regions, and corruption led to periodic revision of the laws.

By the 19th century the emergence of the modern secular state and the gradual acceptance of the separation of CHURCH AND STATE led to a gradual dismantling of the laws supporting the tithe (that is, church tax). In countries like the United States, where Catholics were always in the minority, the church relied on systems of voluntary giving. Such programs have now spread to countries in which Catholicism remains the dominant faith. The current *Code of Canon Law* (cn. 221.1) has a general admission for support of the church and its apostolate.

Many Protestant churches have revived the practice of tithing as an ideal, though only a few denominations make it the norm for members or a requirement for full membership. The Church of Jesus Christ of Latter-day Saints (the Mormon Church) is by far the largest denomination that has strict tithing rules.

Further reading: Catherine E. Boyd, *Tithes and Parishes in Medieval Italy: The Historical Roots of a Modern Problem* (Ithaca, N.Y.: Cornell University Press, 1952); Joseph M. Champlin, *Sharing Treasure, Time, and Talent: A Parish Manual for Sacrificial Giving Or Tithing* (Collegeville, Minn.: Liturgical Press, 1982); Stuart Murray, *Beyond Tithing* (Waynesboro: Paternoster, 2000); Lukas Vischer, *Tithing in the Early Church* (Philadelphia: Fortress, 1966).

titular

The adjective *titular* is applied to DIOCESES and the BISHOPS assigned to them that exist in title only. A titular diocese is usually assigned to a person who holds an administrative position that is deemed equal in honor and authority to what usually adheres to a bishop of a territory, but does not carry the same responsibility for pastoral care. Most Vatican high officials are titular bishops. Titular bishoprics are frequently given to vicars apostolic and papal legates. Auxiliary bishops and missionary bishops are assigned a titular see.

The place names attached to titular sees frequently call attention to parts of the world that once were home to many CHRISTIANS but now are dominated by another FAITH, such as North AFRICA. Those who hold title to such abandoned dioceses are asked to periodically offer prayers for the people in their assigned territory.

Cardinals are assigned titular positions in the diocese of Rome, usually a church. In those cases, the church will often display a picture of the cardinal and his coat of arms, and when in Rome, that cardinal will often say mass at the assigned church.

Further reading: McBrien, Richard P., ed., *The HarperCollins Encyclopedia of Catholicism* (San Francisco: HarperSanFrancisco, 1995).

Torquemada, Tomás de (1420–1498)
Dominican friar and head of Spanish Inquisition
Tomás de Torquemada (or Turrecremata), a DOMINICAN friar, became the head of the Spanish INQUISITION and the major force behind SPAIN's expulsion of the Jews in 1492. Torquemada was himself of Jewish lineage, his grandmother having converted to Christianity. He was born in 1420 in the kingdom of Castile. His uncle, Juan de Torquemada (1388–1468), was a famous Dominican theologian, and Tomás followed his path into the order.

He emerged to prominence as Spain, having largely driven the Muslims out, was struggling to unite into a single Christian kingdom. Castile and the neighboring kingdom of Aragon were united in several steps between 1469, when FERDINAND I OF ARAGON AND ISABELLA OF CASTILE were married, and 1479, when all alternate claimants to their throne were defeated. By the latter year Torquemada had become Isabella's confessor. In 1480, the two monarchs founded the Inquisition in Spain, and in 1483, Torquemada was put in charge.

At this time, Spain had a large community of people derogatorily called Marranos (Span.: "pigs"), secret Jews who outwardly professed Christianity but kept their Jewish faith in the privacy of their homes. Under Torquemada, rooting out Marranos became the primary mission of the Inquisition. He developed a set of guidelines to assist people in identifying the secret Jews, centered on their behavior on Sabbath days and their dietary habits. Anyone discovered to be a Marrano lost his or her property and faced public humiliation—even death at the stake.

In 1490 Torquemada held a show trial of eight Jews accused of crucifying a Christian child. The charge was a variant of the notorious medieval blood libel, which claimed that Jews murdered Christian children to obtain blood for ritual use (*see* ANTI-SEMITISM). No evidence was presented at the trial apart from confessions that had been written under torture. All eight were burned at the stake. After the trial, Torquemada used his access to Isabella and Ferdinand to convince them that the Jews were a threat to the newly unified kingdom and thus should be expelled. The monarchs issued the order on March 31, 1492. They gave the Jews two months to leave. Following the expulsion, Torquemada retired to Ávila and lived quietly in the MONASTERY of St. Thomas. He died there 1498. The historical irony is that the engine of the Inquisition could have easily been turned against Torquemada himself on the basis of his Jewish ancestry.

Further reading: Howard Fast, *Torquemada* (Garden City, N.Y.: Doubleday, 1966); Benito Perez Galdos, *Torquemada* (Irvington: Columbia University Press, 1986); Benzion Netanyahu, *The Origins of the Inquisition in Fifteenth Century Spain* (New York: Random House, 1995).

tradition

Tradition is the body of knowledge, explanation, and practice of Christianity that has been passed down orally through the generations by the church's teachers. It is the accepted and accumulated wisdom of the past up to the present.

Tradition is revealed by GOD and delivered through the prophets, APOSTLES, and subsequent church teachers and leaders. Apostolic tradition differs from ecclesiastical tradition. The former is understood to have been revealed by God to the APOSTLES and the churches they founded; the latter is what is passed on to each subsequent generation of church teachers. Simply put, tradition is the truths, ideas, and customs of the church that are reasonable and agree with divine revelation.

Catholicism has historically placed equal emphasis on Scripture and tradition as dual sources of divine revelation—"the written books and unwritten traditions" in the formulation of the Council of TRENT (session 4, Decree on Scripture and Tradition). During the REFORMATION the issue of tradition was a central point of contention, and Protestants have historically rejected tradition, especially the traditions relating to INDULGENCES, RELICS and PURGATORY. They placed sole authority and all revelation in Scripture (sola scriptura). Anglicans have retained the Catholic practice of accepting tradition as an important element of revelation. One difficulty of the Protestant position is that the canonical books contained in the BIBLE were determined not by the Bible itself but by the theological tradition of orthodoxy that developed over time (*see* CANON OF SCRIPTURE).

Although Trent seemed to speak of Scripture and traditions as two fonts of revelation, VATICAN

COUNCIL II modified this understanding by insisting on the singleness of revelation in *Dei Verbum* 10, the Dogmatic Constitution on Divine Revelation: "Sacred tradition and sacred scripture form one sacred deposit of the word of God, which is committed to the church."

Further reading: Richard P. C. Hanson, *Tradition in the Early Church* (London: SCM Press, 1962); James P. Mackey, *The Modern Theology of Tradition* (New York: Herder & Herder, 1963); George L. Prestige, *Fathers and Heretics: Six Studies in Dogmatic Faith* (London: S.P.C.K., 1963); John E. Thiel, *Senses of Tradition: Continuity and Development in Catholic Faith* (New York: Oxford University Press, 2000).

traditionalists

The sweeping changes in the Roman Catholic Church that followed VATICAN COUNCIL II were not universally welcomed. Some CLERGY and faithful considered them to be radical departures from tradition that threatened the future of the church. Their dismay recalls the reaction of the OLD CATHOLICS of the 1870s to the idea of papal INFALLIBILITY. Just as that group eventually split from the church, the traditionalists, as the 20th-century group has come to be called, have all but severed their ties with the church HIERARCHY.

In the 1970s many leading conservative figures began to speak out against them. In particular they criticized the new vernacular that replaced the Latin Mass that had been standard in Catholic churches around the world since the Council of TRENT. These critics included two ARCHBISHOPS, Pierre Martin Ngo-Dinh-Thuc (1897–1984) of Vietnam and Marcel LeFebvre (1905–91) of Switzerland.

Uncomfortable with the changes, they initially sought a place for conservatives within the church. When their efforts were rebuffed, both began to establish separate communities to preserve pre-Vatican traditions. Eventually, both consecrated bishops to continue the work into the next generations.

Archbishop LeFebvre worked through the 1980s to mobilize a traditionalist following and to train priests to head the new communities. He presented several plans that would allow traditionalists to continue as Catholics in full communion with the Vatican, but they all proved unacceptable to church authorities. His last plan, presented in 1987, asked permission to consecrate three BISHOPS to continue his efforts. Following rejection of his idea, the aging archbishop, with the support of Brazilian bishop de Castro Meyer (1904–91), consecrated four new bishops on his own authority to head the Society of Pius X, the organization he had created for his followers.

In the 1970s traditionalist Vietnamese archbishop Ngo-Dinh-Thuc, then living in exile in ITALY, began working with like-minded conservatives in SPAIN led by Clemente Dominguez Gómez (1946–2005), who was at the time receiving visions of Jesus CHRIST and the Virgin Mary. In 1976, Thuc agreed to consecrate several of the Spanish brothers, for which he was excommunicated. The ban was lifted when he asked FORGIVENESS, but he soon resumed his consecrations. Just before his death in 1984 Thuc publically adhered to SEDEVACANTISM, the claim that the office of the pope was now vacant even though there was a sitting pope. Following Pope PAUL VI's death, the Spanish group, now called the Holy Palmarian Church, declared Gomez to be the new pope.

The bishops in the LeFebvre lineage have remained dedicated to his ideals, and his Society of Pius X is the largest and strongest of the traditionalists groups. In 1983 a breakaway group formed the Society of Pius V in protest against LeFebvre's continued attempts to reconcile with Pope JOHN PAUL II.

The Holy Palmarian Church is the largest of the Thuc groups, but it is largely confined to Spain. There are two small jurisdictions in North America, the Latin Rite Catholic Church headed by Louis Vezelis (1930–   ) and the Congregation of Mary Immaculate Queen, which operates out of Mount St. Michael in Spokane, Washington.

Representatives of the latter group periodically travel around the country promoting devotion to Fatima. Despite their defiance of the post–Vatican II popes, the traditionalists do not reject papal authority in principle, unlike the Old Catholics.

Further reading: Yves Conger, *Challenge to the Church* (Huntington, Ind.: Our Sunday Visitor, 1976); Michael Davies, *Pope Paul's New Mass* (Dickinson, Tex.: Angelus, 1980); Bernard Tissier de Mallerais, *The Biography of Archbishop LeFebvre* (Dickinson, Tex.: Angeklus, 2004); Gary L. Ward, *Independent Bishops: An International Directory* (Detroit: Apogee, 1990).

Transfiguration

The Transfiguration is the Biblical event in which Jesus' appearance dramatically changed in front of three of his APOSTLES—Peter, John, and James. His face shone like the sun, he wore brilliant white clothes, and he appeared with Moses and Elijah. All of them were enveloped in a bright cloud and a voice said "This is my Son, whom I love; with him I am well pleased. Listen to him!"

The event was seen as proof that the law and the prophets recognized the messiahship of CHRIST. It also foreshadowed Christ's future glory in his RESURRECTION (Acts 1:9; 2:33). It is recorded in the three synoptic Gospels (Matt. 17:1–6, Mark 9:1–8, Luke 9:28–36) and alluded to it in 2 Peter 1:16–18 and John 1:14. All three Gospel accounts have the same basic outline and vary only in minor details. According to tradition the Transfiguration took place on Mount Tabor, but scholars disagree, some claiming it was on Mount Hermon or even the Mount of Olives.

The Feast of the Transfiguration is celebrated on August 6. It was first celebrated in the Eastern Church; in the West Pope Callistus III (r. 1455–58) in 1457 instituted the feast to commemorate the victory over the Turks at Belgrade in 1456. In eastern THEOLOGY the Transfiguration was typologically related backward to Moses' transfiguration on Sinai (Exod. 34:30) and forward to humanity's

theosis (Gk. literally, "engoding" and participation in the divine splendor. The Transfiguration became a favored ICON in EASTERN ORTHODOXY.

Further reading: G. H. Boobyer, *St. Mark and the Transfiguration Story* (Edinburgh: T & T Clark, 1942); Dorothy A. Lee, *Transfiguration* (London: Continuum, 2004); John M. Perry, *Exploring the Transfiguration Story* (Kansas City: Sheed & Ward, 1993); Michael Ramsey, *The Glory of God and the Transfiguration of Christ* (London: Darton, Longman & Todd, 1967).

transubstantiation

Transubstantiation is the event that occurs, in the view of many Catholics, at the moment the EUCHARIST is consecrated: the whole substance of the bread and wine turn into the whole substance of the body and blood of CHRIST, although the accidents of the bread and wine—their taste, color, and appearance—remain unchanged. The term was in wide use by the 12th century; belief in transubstantiation was defined as an article of FAITH in 1215 at Lateran Council IV (cn. 1). However, the metaphysical definition of the DOCTRINE was not clarified until after the translation of ARISTOTLE in the 13th century, when ST. THOMAS AQUINAS incorporated the Aristotelian terms of *substance* and *accident* into the definition.

Transubstantiation was a central issue during the PROTESTANT REFORMATION. Martin Luther (1483–1546) preferred to teach the Eucharistic theology of *con*substantiation, whereby the substance of the bread and wine coexist with the substance of the body and blood. Anglicans, and to a lesser extent Lutherans, believe in consubstantiation, thereby agreeing to some extent with Catholics on the real presence of Christ in the Eucharist. Many other Protestant denominations reject both theologies, claiming instead that the Eucharist is a memorial or a symbol. John Calvin's (1509–64) understanding has been called a "functional" presence, whereas Johannes Oecolampadius (1482–1531) in Basel and Huldrich Zwingli

(1484–1531) in Zurich maintained that Christ is only figuratively present through the faith of the believers.

Catholic critics of the doctrine of transubstantiation and its kindred formulations say that it reduces the mystery of the Eucharist to a moment. To them, the rite is a progressive incorporation of the whole believing community—the church as the primal SACRAMENT—into the reality of the new life promised to all in Christ. To parse out the separate parts of the Eucharist, for example the moment of transubstantiation, is to lose sight of the reality of the sacrament as a holistic ritual process. The new liturgy of the church stresses that the GRACE of GOD in Christ arrives equally in the word proclaimed and preached and the sacrament received.

Further reading: Salvatore Bonano, *The Concept of Substance and the Development of Eucharistic Theology to the Thirteenth Century* (Washington, D.C.: Catholic University of America Press, 1960); Michael L. Gaudoin-Parker, ed., *The Real Presence Through the Ages: Jesus Adored in the Sacrament of the Altar* (Staten Island: Alba, 1993); Brian A. Gerrish "Sign and Reality: The Lord's Supper in the Reformed Traditions," in Brian A. Gerrish, ed., *The Old Protestantism and the New: Essays on the Reformation Heritage* (Chicago: University of Chicago Press, 1982) 118–130; Joseph M. Powers, *Eucharistic Theology* (New York: Seabury, 1967).

Trappists

The Order of Reformed Cistercians, popularly referred to as Trappists, arose as a reform movement instigated by the abbot Jean-Armand de Bouthillier de Rancé (1626–1700), who wanted to bring the CISTERCIANS back to their original austere disciplines. The common name derives from the Abbey of La Trappe, in Normandy, FRANCE, where the reform was first implemented. Three MONASTERIES in association with La Trappe were shortly founded in ITALY.

In 1792, at the height of the French Revolution, the government ordered the confiscation of all the property of monasteries. When La Trappe was closed (1792) and its MONKS scattered, Dom Augustine de Lastrange (1854–1927), a retired BISHOP who had joined the order, established a new monastery at Val-Sainte, in the Canton of Fribourg, Switzerland. He instituted a new reform that included a literal observance of the Rule of St. BENEDICT and additional austerities. Monasteries were opened in SPAIN (1793), England, Belgium (1794), and northern Italy. In 1794, Pope Pius VI (r. 1755–99) authorized Val-Sainte as motherhouse of the Trappists, and Dom Augustine was elected abbot. When French forces under Napoleon invaded Switzerland, the Trappists were again displaced; they had no permanent home until Napoleon's defeat allowed their return to France. Dom Augustine was able to purchase the old monastery facilities at La Trappe and rebuild the order.

New monasteries were founded, some following the rules instituted by Abbot de Rancé, and others accepting the more severe rules of Dom Augustine. In 1834 Rome organized all the French houses into the Congregation of the Cistercian Monks of Notre-Dame de la Trappe, eventually recognizing two groupings: the Ancient Reform of Our Lady of La Trappe and the Reform of Our Lady of La Trappe. Both groups flourished and expanded internationally. In 1892, they all joined together with the older Cistercian order into a new Order of Reformed Cistercians, headquartered at the original Cistercian motherhouse at Cîteaux, France.

The order is headed by its general chapter, composed of all the abbots and superiors of member houses, which elects an abbot general who resides in Rome. Each monastery is autonomous and manages its own spiritual and temporal affairs, but all follow a uniform format. Daily life includes prescribed times for LITURGY, the PRAYER OF THE HOURS, or Divine Office, individual prayer and meditation, manual labor, study, meals, and sleep. Monasteries are self-supporting and survive economically from the produce of their labor.

The monks live a cloistered existence. Among the defining characteristics of their daily life is silence; monks refrain from conversation with each other and limit conversation with superiors to a few specified times. New members use their study time to prepare their vows as lay brothers and some for their ordination as PRIESTS.

In the 1840s, the Trappists purchased a farm in Nelson County, Kentucky, and established a monastery called Gethsemani. The original settlement of 44 monks arrived just before Christmas in 1848. After a slow start, the abbey church was completed and dedicated in 1866. The monastery remained a French establishment for several decades but made the transition to English early in the 20th century. Its most famous resident was THOMAS MERTON (1915–68), the celebrated mystical writer. Gethsemani seeded new monasteries that now operate in Georgia, Utah, South Carolina, New York, California, and Chile.

Further reading: Louis Julius Lekai, *The Cistercians: Ideals and Reality* (Kent, Ohio: Kent State University Press, 1977); ———, *The Rise of the Cistercian Strict Observance in Seventeenth Century France* (Washington, D.C.: Catholic University of America Press, 1968).

Treaty of Tordesillas

The Treaty of Tordesillas of 1493 was an agreement mediated by Pope ALEXANDER VI that divided the newly discovered lands along the African coast and in the Americas between SPAIN and Portugal, the two dominant seagoing powers in Europe. Earlier in the century, Portugal had developed a sea route to India and China via the Cape of Good Hope, and an incipient empire had begun to take shape with garrisons and trading posts along the way. The discovery of the Americas by CHRISTOPHER COLUMBUS in 1492 had given Spain access to a potentially vast source of riches.

In 1493 Pope Alexander VI moved preemptively to head off conflict by drawing an imaginary line through the mid-Atlantic west of the Cape Verde Islands (a Portuguese possession). Spain would have possession of any unclaimed territories to the west of the line (which included all of the Western Hemisphere), and Portugal would have possession of any unclaimed territory to the east of the line (including all of AFRICA).

Soon after the initial treaty, as the size of the Americas became better known, Portugal protested and succeeded in negotiating a new line farther to the west. As a result, the portion of the Americas that jutted out farthest to the east, known today as Brazil, was given to Portugal. Delegates of the two countries met at Tordesillas, Spain, to complete the negotiations.

Although not recognized by FRANCE, or GREAT BRITAIN, the other Atlantic powers, the treaty effectively assigned most of the Americas to Spain and the rest to Portugal. Under its protection, in the following decades Roman Catholicism moved unopposed into South and Central America, where it continues to dominate the religious scene.

Further reading: Jerry Brotton, *Trading Territories: Mapping the Early Modern World* (London: Reaktion, 1997); Lyle N. McAlister, *Spain and Portugal in the New World. 1492–1700* (Minneapolis: University of Minnesota Press, 1984).

Trent, Council of (1545-1563)

The Council of Trent was the chief response of Catholicism to the PROTESTANT REFORMATION and the supreme expression of the COUNTER-REFORMATION. For Catholics is was the most important ecumenical council (*see* COUNCILS, ECUMENICAL) after the first seven councils and was determinative of Catholicism until VATICAN COUNCIL II. Trent, whose 25 sessions stretched over many years, can be divided into three main periods. The council was convened by Pope Paul III (r. 1534–49) and concluded under Julius III (1550–55), PAUL IV (1559–65), and Pius IV (1559–64).

In 1518 Martin Luther (1483–1546) called for a "free" general council within the Catholic

Church, of which he was still a member—"free" from the authority of the pope and under the auspices of the Holy Roman Emperor instead. Leo X (r. 1513–21), Hadrian VI (r. 1522–23), and Clement VII (r. 1523–34) were obviously reluctant to agree to these terms. The Vatican was also very conscious that the earlier ecumenical councils of Constance (1414–18) and Florence (1431–42) had very nearly made the council itself supreme over the pontiff. Despite these misgivings, Emperor CHARLES V extracted from Clement VII a promise to hold a reforming council should the Diet of Augsburg (1530) fail to reconcile the disputants.

Attempts to open the council at Mantua and Vicenza came to naught until the border city of Trent was agreed on. In the meantime Paul III directed Cardinals Gasparo Contarini (1483–1542) (made a cardinal while still a layman) and Giovanni Pietro Carafa (later the repressive PAUL IV), to conduct an internal "cleansing of the church" and to reorganize the Vatican offices. Contarini made one last effort to effect a reconciliation at the Colloquy of Regensburg (Ratisbon) in 1541.

During period 1 (1545–47, sessions 1–8) the council decided that participants would vote as individuals and not as national units in order to head off those who supported conciliar supremacy; it was also agreed that doctrinal and disciplinary discussions and decisions would be held and published concurrently. In this period, the council canonized the Nicene-Constantinopolitan CREED (session 3), affirmed both "written books and unwritten traditions" as sources of revelation (session 4), and established the authority of St. JEROME's Latin Vulgate (see BIBLE; TRADITION). In session 5 the council affirmed AUGUSTINE's understanding of original SIN and formulated a doctrine of JUSTIFICATION that allowed for a window into Protestant thought while defending the Catholic doctrine of merit. For the first time all seven SACRAMENTS were determined explicitly as necessary to salvation and as instituted directly by CHRIST (Session 7).

During period 2 (1551–52, sessions 9–14) some Protestant legates from Brandenburg and Wittenburg and the historian Johann Sleidan (1507–56) from Strassbourg attended the initial sessions, but they communicated their views only through the emperor. The council formally defined TRANSUBSTANTIATION in regard to the EUCHARIST and condemned the positions of Luther, Calvin, and Zwingli (session 13). When the Protestant attendees could not get the council to reopen discussion on defined statements, to release the bishops from an oath of fealty to the pope, or to declare the supremacy of the council over the pope, they departed. There were also declarations on penance, or RECONCILIATION, and on Extreme Unction, or the Last Anointing (session 14).

By period 3 (1562–63) all hope of reconciliation with the Protestants was gone, and the newly founded JESUITS made their presence felt. The council decided that COMMUNION in one kind was permissible since Christ is fully present under both species (session 21). Protestants disagreed with this practice, which became normative for Catholic laity until VATICAN COUNCIL II. The remaining sessions dealt with the Mass as a sacrifice, HOLY ORDERS, MARRIAGE, PURGATORY, the veneration of saints, RELICS, and images, or ICONS. The council prohibited the sale of INDULGENCES but allowed FREE-WILL offerings. The council also promoted the writing of a CATECHISM and called for the founding of a SEMINARY in each DIOCESE.

At the conclusion of the council Pius IV published the Profession of Tridentine Faith in 1564. Trent shaped the entire nature of Catholic doctrine and practice until the significant reformulations and reforms of Vatican II. Following the council a revised Vulgate was issued (1592), as was the Roman Catechism for priests (1566), the Breviary (1568), and the Roman Missal (1570). The council served as an effective bulwark against further inroads of Protestantism in Europe. It shaped THEOLOGY, piety, church order, missions, and the fundamental character of Catholicism for the next four centuries.

Further reading: The *Acts of the Council of Trent* are available online; R. Po-chia Hsia, *The World of Catholic Renewal, 1540–1770* (Cambridge: Cambridge University Press, 2005); Michael Mullet, *The Catholic Reformation* (London: Routledge, 1999); Alain Tallon, *Le Concile de Trente* (Paris: Cerf, 2000).

Trinity (Lat.: *tres,* "three" + *unitas,* "unity")

The doctrine of the Trinity is a central CHRISTIAN teaching. It states that GOD is and always has been three distinct persons—Father, Son, and HOLY SPIRIT—who share one divine essence or substance. Catholics believe this doctrine to be both the most profound and the most mysterious of all the church's teachings.

Like the Judaism from which it sprang, early Christianity was strictly monotheistic (Deut. 6:4; 1 Cor. 8:4–6; Acts 17:14–19). Without giving up this strict monotheism, Christians gradually came to believe that Jesus was not simply the Messiah or Anointed One and Son of God but also "Lord" (Rom. 1:4) and that the Holy Spirit was equally, if less explicitly, Lord, too (2 Cor. 3:17). The teaching first came into focus in the precreedal formulas used in BAPTISM (Matt. 28:19; Eph. 4:4–6).

Soon early theologians began to look for prefigurations in the Old Testament, such as the making of humans in "*our* image" (Gen. 1:26, which originally referred to the heavenly council of angels), and the three men who visit Abraham at the oak of Mamre (a scene celebrated in the ICON by Andrei Rublev [c. 1360–1430]). In the second and third centuries theologians tried to formalize the doctrine in ways that retrospectively were deemed heretical. JUSTIN MARTYR employed the Logos (word, reason) doctrine of NEOPLATONISM to explicate the role of the Son, which was often merged with the Wisdom teaching of late Judaism (Prov. 8:22–31). Theophilus of Antioch (fl. 180) introduced the term *trias,* "three," to refer to God, Word, and Wisdom (*Autolycus* 2:15). Some like Justin began to refer to three "divine beings" (*1 Apology* 13.3). Soon they also began speaking

of the outward revelation of the Godhead in the divine "economy" in creation, redemption, and sanctification.

Some conservative Christians became sensitive to criticism that Christians had three gods and embraced what came to be called monarchism (*monos,* "single" + *arche,* "principle"), but this position led to modalism, the Father/Son/Spirit as three aspects of the same God, or ADOPTIONISM, CHRIST as a mere man "adopted" and indwelt by God.

HIPPOLYTUS OF ROME was able to overcome the objections with a refined economic trinitarianism, and TERTULLIAN introduced the all-important terms *trinitas,* "trinity," *substantia,* "substance," and *personae,* "persons." Later Novatian of Rome (fl. c. 350) overcame many objections with his teaching that the Father was "always Father" and therefore eternally had a Son. ORIGEN OF ALEXANDRIA added the formula "eternally begotten Son," which made its way into the CREED. He also asserted that the Father, Son, and Spirit were three distinct *hypostases* in the new sense of "persons." Nonetheless, Origen saw the Son as "a secondary God" (*Celsus* 5.39).

The complicated formulations pertaining to the Trinity were worked out in the first seven ecumenical councils (*see* COUNCILS, ECUMENICAL) and expressed in the creeds. The substantial unity was affirmed against the Arians, the distinction of the persons was affirmed against the Sabellians, and the coeternity and equality of the Son and Spirit with the Father against the Arians and Macedonians. The final formulation was that the Godhead is composed of three distinct persons who share equally one common substance or essence, with the Son proceeding from the Father and the Spirit proceeding from the Father through the Son.

In his profound treatise *On the Trinity,* AUGUSTINE OF HIPPO, using Neoplatonic categories, developed a very subtle "psychological" theory of inner dynamic in the persons of the Trinity, modeled on the relations between memory, understanding, and will in the human mind. Augustine's great insight into the divine *circumcessio,* or "mutual presencing," of the persons of the Trinity is that the distinctness of each lies in their mutual relations in begetting (Father), being begotten (Son), and bonding in love (Spirit). At the same time Augustine championed the FILIOQUE doctrine by which the Spirit is believed to proceed equally from both the Father and the Son. This would later cause great contention between the Latin and Eastern Churches.

BOETHIUS refined the definition of person, and the theologians of the High MIDDLE AGES both reasserted and refined the trinitarian doctrines of ATHANASIUS OF ALEXANDRIA, the Cappadocian Fathers, and Augustine. Lateran Council IV (1215) declared that each of the persons is divine, and the Council of FLORENCE decreed that "everything in God is one except where there is a contrast of relations." This standard medieval formulation was passed on to Protestant Christianity but challenged by the Socinians and Unitarians, who insisted on the singleness of God. In the intervening time the doctrine of the Trinity survived more as a formula than as a living teaching affecting the life of faith.

In recent times the Swiss Reformed theologian Karl Barth (1886–1968) and the Catholic KARL RAHNER have made significant contributions to the theology of the Trinity as a vital part of Christian life. "The Trinity," Rahner said, "is a mystery of salvation" and not something extrinsic to Christian practice and spirituality. Both insist on the identity of the outward manifestation of the Trinity in the economy of salvation and immanent or inward relations of the persons of Trinity among themselves. The triune God who gives of the divine self in revelation is the God of love, which is the essence of divinity itself. God is community, and so are the Christian people.

Further reading: Leonardo Boff, *Holy Trinity, Perfect Community* (Maryknoll, N.Y.: Orbis, 2000); J. N. D. Kelly, *Early Christian Creeds*, 3rd ed. (London: Longman, 1972); Catherine M. LaCugna, *God For Us: The Trinity and Christian Life* (San Francisco: HarperSan-

Francisco, 1991); Jaroslav Pelikan, *The Emergence of the Catholic Tradition, 100–600* (Chicago: University of Chicago Press, 1971); G. L. Prestige, *God in Patristic Thought*, 2nd ed. (London: S.P.C.K., 1952); Karl Rahner, "Remarks on the Dogmatic Treatise 'De Trinitate'" in *Theological Investigations* 9 (1973): 127–144.

Tsung Huai-te, Joseph (1917–1997) *head of official Chinese Catholic Church*

Tsung Huai–te Joseph (or Zong Huaide) was born in China in 1917. He was ordained a PRIEST in 1943 and consecrated a BISHOP in 1958.

After the Communists took power in China, the government expelled all foreign-born religious leaders and demanded that the various religious bodies, including the Roman Catholic Church, drop all ties of financial dependence or organizational subordinance to any foreign bodies—meaning that the Catholic Church could no longer legally submit to the pope in Rome.

In 1940 a Chinese Catholic Cultural Association had been formed to mobilize Roman Catholics in the fight against the Japanese invasion. The Communist government in 1957 replaced this group with a Chinese Catholic Patriotic Association, bringing the church under tight government control and serving to communicate government dictates to the Chinese Catholic community. The association was thwarted during the Cultural Revolution (1966–76), when government agencies banned all public worship and confiscated or destroyed much church property. Bishop Tsung emerged as the public face of the organization in this period.

The Patriotic Association quickly revived in the late 1970s, when the Cultural Revolution was finally suppressed. In the 1980s, Bishop Tsung became chairperson, succeeding Archbishop Pi Sou-Shi. The association claims the right to speak for all Catholics in China, but since it rejects the authority of the pope, a rival HIERARCHY of bishops has arisen in communion with Rome, who also claim to speak for the

Catholic community. These loyalist bishops have had to operate underground in China. The situation has proved confusing to observers, leading some to double their estimates of the size of the Chinese Catholic community.

Tsung served as bishop of Tsi-nan (1958–80) and later of Chow-tsun (Zhou-cun) (1980–97), both in Shan-tung (Shan-dong) Province. He was president of the Chinese Catholic Patriotic Association from 1988 to his death in 1997.

Further reading: Sunquist, Scott W., ed., *A Dictionary of Asian Christianity* (Grand Rapids, Mich.: Eerdmans, 2001).

typology (Gk.: *typos,* "mold," "pattern" + *logos,* "study of")

Types are events, persons, and figures in the Old Testament that are interpreted by CHRISTIANS to be prefigurations and foreshadowings of the Christian dispensation. The type in the first dispensation is contrasted with and compared to the antitype in the second.

Typology is the THEOLOGY of these connections. It is related both to ALLEGORY and ANALOGY but not reducible to these two. The term *typos* (Rom. 5:14) can overlap in meaning with *skia,* "shadow," (Col. 2:17), *hypodeigma,* "copy," (Heb. 8:5), and *parabole,* "figure" (Heb. 11:19).

Perhaps the most celebrated type is in Romans 5:14, where Adam is said to be the "type of the one who is to come," namely CHRIST. However, given the fact that Romans is very much a Midrash on the Book of Genesis, the phrase can also be translated as "what is to come" in the sense of the

increase of SIN and DEATH after the primal sin of Adam. Paul saw the crossing of the Red Sea as a type of BAPTISM (1 Cor. 10:1–6). In the epistle to the Hebrews, the most typological of the books in the BIBLE, the priest-king of (Jeru)salem Melchisedech is seen as a type of Christ (7:13).

Most of the subjects painted on the walls of the CATACOMBS were typological prefigurations. One of the favorites was a figure of Jonah whose three days in the belly of a fish prefigures the RESURRECTION. This sort of typological contrast was continued in the sculpture and windows of the medieval CATHEDRAL. In the ALEXANDRINE SCHOOL of biblical interpretation typology could get merged with a form of allegory in which the Old Testament content was emptied of its meaning and replaced by the New Testament "fulfillment." Some scholars have noted that this leads to theological supercessionism, in which GOD's promise to the Hebrews is voided and transferred to the Christians. Others argue that typology is a way to relate the two testaments and that there is a gentle and benevolent way of relating them by showing that in including the Gentiles God is not excluding the Jews in the plan of salvation.

See also PAINTING AND SCULPTURE.

Further reading: Jean Daniélou, *From Shadows to Reality: Studies in Biblical Typology of the Fathers* (London: Burns & Oates, 1960); Henry N. Klaman, *Jewish Images in Christian Churches* (Macon, Ga.: Mercer University Press, 2000); Emile Mâle, *The Gothic Image: Religious Art in France of the Thirteenth Century* (New York: Harper & Row, 1972); Krister Stendahl, *Paul Among Jews and Gentiles, and Other Essays* (Philadelphia: Fortress, 1976).

U

Ukrainian Catholic Church also called Ukrainian Greek Catholic Church

Christianity spread through the Ukraine from the Byzantine Empire toward the end of the first millennium. At the time of the GREAT SCHISM between the Roman Catholic Church and EASTERN ORTHODOXY in 1054, most Ukrainians remained loyal to CONSTANTINOPLE. However, by the 14th century most of the region came under the control of predominantly Roman Catholic Lithuania. In 1439, Isidore, the Orthodox metropolitan of Kiev, attended the Council of FLORENCE and agreed to a union with Rome. The agreement split Ukrainian CHRISTIANS; many of them rejected the union despite renewed pressure after 1569 from the region's new Polish Catholic rulers.

Toward the end of the 16th century, as Rome was preoccupied in the struggle to suppress Protestantism in eastern Europe, a group of Orthodox leaders began to see union with Rome as a way to head off the complete replacement of Orthodoxy by Latin rite jurisdictions. In 1596, they succeeded in working out a new union in which they kept their Eastern rite, stopped the spread of Latin rite Catholicism, and acknowledged Rome's jurisdiction.

The union worked well for a while, until Orthodox Russia gradually regained control of the Ukraine in the 18th century. Russian authorities promoted Orthodoxy at the expense of Catholicism. They incorporated both the Ukrainian Catholic Church and the surviving Ukrainian Orthodox Church into the Russian Orthodox Church. The Ukrainian Catholic Church survived as a separate entity only in Galicia, western Ukraine, which was part of the Austrian Empire. In 1963 Pope JOHN XXIII made the Ukrainian church a major archepiscopal church.

Galicia was annexed by the Soviet Union after World War II. The Soviet government suppressed the Ukrainian Catholic Church and arrested all of its BISHOPS. The church survived underground during 45 years of Soviet rule. In the meantime, many Ukrainians had migrated worldwide and established Catholic parishes in the United States, Canada, South America, Australia, and Western Europe. These parishes helped keep Ukrainian identity alive during the years of Soviet domination. When the Soviet Union fell apart, a distinctive Ukrainian Catholic Church reemerged, and in 1989 a new bishop of Przemysl was named. Two years later, His Beatitude Lubomyr Cardinal Husar (1933–) moved into his archeparchy residence in Lviv. That same year two seminaries were opened.

Today there are some 5,000,000 members in eleven DIOCESEs in the Ukraine, five dioceses in Canada, and four in the United States. There are also dioceses in Australia, Brazil, and Argentina, with apostolic exarchates appointed for FRANCE, GERMANY, and the United Kingdom.

Further reading: Keith P. Dyrud, *The Quest for the Rusyn Soul: The Politics of Religion and Culture in Eastern Europe and in America, 1890–World War I* (Philadelphia: Balch Institute, 1992); John-Paul Himka, *The Greek Catholic Church and Ukrainian Society in Austrian Galicia* (Cambridge, Mass.: Harvard University Press, 1986); Nikolaus Liesel, *The Eastern Catholic Liturgies: A Study in Words and Pictures* (Westminster, Md.: Newman, 1960).

United States Conference of Catholic Bishops

The United States Conference of Catholic Bishops (USCCB) encompasses all BISHOPs in the United States and the U.S. Virgin Islands and the U.S. territories. It operates based on an original mandate delineated in the VATICAN COUNCIL II document *Christus Dominus,* the Decree Concerning the Pastoral Office of Bishops. Similar national episcopal conferences exist in many countries around the world.

While the USCCB is grounded in the Vatican decree, it exists in organizational continuity with the National Catholic War Council (NCWC), founded in 1917 to help provide chaplaincy and recreational services to Catholics serving in the U.S. armed forces. In the aftermath of the war, in 1919, Pope Benedict XV (r. 1914–22) called on the bishops to join the effort to create a just peace. In response, the American bishops created the National Catholic Welfare Council (soon renamed "Conference," with headquarters in Washington, D.C. Its priority issues included education, immigration, and social action.

Following Vatican II, the Welfare Conference was superseded in 1966 by two organizations: the National Conference of Catholic Bishops (NCCB) and the United States Catholic Conference (USCC). The former attended to the church's affairs in the United States and operated through committees consisting entirely of bishops, though with support staffs as needed. The USCC facilitated collaborative efforts with other Catholics, including laypersons, CLERGY, and religious, to address a wide range of issues of concern. Then in 2001, the two bodies merged into the United States Conference of Catholic Bishops (USCCB).

The USCCB operates through some 50 committees. Among is primary duties has been the issuance of pastoral guidance and policy statements on a wide variety of issues before the church. At the beginning of the new century, the USCCB attained a new level of attention as it was called on to respond to the widespread charges of child abuse that had occurred in different DIOCESEs around the country during the PEDOPHILIA crisis.

Further reading: David M. Byers, *Justice in the Marketplace: Collected Statements of the Vatican and the U.S. Catholic Bishops on Economic Policy, 1891–1984* (Washington, D.C.: United States Catholic Conference, 1985); *Human Sexuality: A Catholic Perspective for Education and Lifelong Learning* (Washington, D.C.: United States Catholic Conference, 1991); *Sharing Catholic Social Teaching: Challenges and Directions.* (Washington, D.C.: United States Catholic Conference, 1998).

utensils, sacred

The general form and style of sacred utensils are governed by the liturgical directives given in VATICAN COUNCIL II's *Sacrosanctum Concilium,* the Constitution on the Sacred Liturgy. The INCULTURATION of the Gospel in indigenous contexts has brought a wide variety of materials and artistic styles into the Catholic tradition, especially in AFRICA, LATIN AMERICA, and ASIA.

The most important SACRAMENT in Catholicism is the EUCHARIST, for which Catholics use the most precious of materials. The principal ritual utensils are the **chalice**, which holds the sacred wine to be consecrated into the blood and the **paten**, which holds the host, or wafer, to be consecrated into the body. The cup also refers to the cup with Jesus' disciples (Mark 10:38). A small **pall** (Lat. *pallium* "cloak") used to be placed over the top of the chalice during the Eucharist.

There are also **ciboria** (Gk. *kiborion* "cup"), covered cups used to transport consecrated hosts to communicants and to store them in a **tabernacle** (Lat. *taberna* "tent"). A tabernacle is a small cabinet, often very ornamented, in which the ciborium with the hosts is placed. It is generally placed on a side altar in a church; a red vigil light shows when the Blessed Sacrament is present inside.

Accompanying the chalice and paten for the Eucharist are the **cruets** (Fr. *cruette* "small jug"), which hold the wine and water that are poured into the chalice during the Eucharist. Today the faithful bring the cruets and unconsecrated hosts to the altar during the Presentation of the Gifts.

Altars are covered with altar clothes during liturgical services. Sometimes pendants are hung in front of altars or elsewhere in the church with the liturgical color according to the season. During the Eucharist **candlesticks** with beeswax candles are kept lit. The **Paschal candle**, consecrated during the EASTER service, is lit on Sundays.

During certain devotions the host is placed in a **monstrance** (Lat. *monstrare*, "to show"), an ornamental vessel to display the Blessed Sacrament for ADORATION. The use of the monstrance became widespread in the 14th century as the frequency of reception of the Eucharist by the faithful decreased. Some pastoral theologians discouraged the adoration of the Blessed Sacrament after Vatican II, but this DEVOTION is undergoing a revival.

During Sunday Eucharists acolytes or altar servers use **censors** or **thuribles** that contain

Chalice with paten. The chalice holds the wine and the paten the host to be consecrated. *(photo by John Huston)*

Monstrance for public display of the Blessed Sacrament during hours of adoration. *(photo by John Huston)*

Censor and thurible *(drawing by Frank K. Flinn)*

live coals and incense, with which the PRIEST or deacon incenses the sacred offerings, the altar, and the congregation as part of the Preparation of the Gifts. The incense is kept in a **boat**, named after its shape, until it is placed in the censor and lit.

During solemn processions either before or apart from Eucharist, the crossbearer carries a **processional cross** at the front of the procession. The cross is often kept in a socket near the altar during the Eucharist.

BISHOPS carry **crosiers**, or shepherd staffs, during solemn ceremonies. It is a symbol of their office as the primary pastors of the flocks within their DIOCESES. Bishops also wear rings, which served as signet seals in former times.

Baptismal font with Easter Vigil candle (All Saints Church, University City, Mo.) *(photo by John Huston)*

Further reading: J. Braun, *Das christliche Altargerät in seinem Sein und in seiner Entwicklung* (Munich: Hueber, 1932); Dennis McNally, *Fearsome Ediface: A History of the Decorated Domus in Catholic Churches* (Lima, Ohio: Wyndham Hall, 2002); Thomas G. Simons and James M. Fitzpatrick, *The Ministry of Liturgical Environment* (Collegeville, Minn.: Liturgical Press, 1984).

V

Valentinus (fl. 100–60) *Gnostic teacher*
Valentinus was a second-century CHRISTIAN teacher who developed a form of GNOSTIC esoteric thought that profoundly affected the church; it also led to the development of an alternative religious tradition in the West that continues to this day. Some have called him "the pope of the Gnostic church."

The little that is known of Valentinus's life is derived from the writings of church fathers such as HIPPOLYTUS OF ROME, TERTULLIAN, and IRENAEUS OF LYONS, who included Valentinus in their list of heretics. Valentinus was born in North Africa, probably in or near Carthage (in what is now Tunisia), around 100. He later moved to Alexandria, where he became a Christian and reportedly received instructions from one of the APOSTLE PAUL's disciples named Theodas (or Theudas). He became a prominent church leader and was probably ordained a priest. Tertullian reported that he was a BISHOP, but there is no other evidence to support that claim. He moved to Rome, where he became very prominent in the Christian community between 135 and 160, from the bishopric of Hyginus (r. c. 138–42) to the beginning of the reign of Anicetus (c. 155–c. 166). According to Tertullian, he was nearly elected bishop of Rome.

Valentinus expounded a peculiar approach to Christianity that denied Jesus's bodily INCARNATION and its correlate, the RESURRECTION of the human body. He was excommunicated around 160 and moved to Cyprus, where he lived for the rest of his life. It was probably during this time that he wrote his most famous work, the *Gospel of Truth*.

For many centuries, the *Gospel of Truth* was known only from the fragments quoted by Irenaeus in the process of refuting it. However, in 1945 a fourth-century copy of the work was found among a group of Gnostic texts uncovered near the town of Nag Hammadi, EGYPT. It was recognized from the quotes that had been cited by Irenaeus. The text was soon translated and published in several European languages, including English. These texts had possibly been hidden by MONKS from a nearby MONASTERY.

Valentinus included in his system all of the elements of what would become Western esotericism—an identification of the secret self with GOD; an understanding of humans as a spark of the divine that had fallen into matter and become trapped; CHRIST, or the Logos, as the revealer who brings the secret knowledge (gnosis) that can lead to escape from the material trap; and a system for operationalizing the gnosis. His basic system would be elaborated upon by a number of disciples in the third century.

Gnosticism manifested tremendous pull on the religious imagination in the years after Valentinus, and in different forms the essential teachings continued to find an audience through the centuries. It would reappear in such movements as the Bogomils and Albigensians. Western esotericism would experience a monumental rebirth in the 17th century with Rosicrucianism, FREEMASONRY, and Theosophy, through which it would be passed to the modern world, where it has experienced a remarkable revival. In the last generation, following the publication of the Nag Hammadi texts, Valentinus has gained a new status as a pioneer of and stimulus to the modern Gnostic movement.

Further reading: Giovanni Filoramo, *A History of Gnosticism* (Oxford: Basil Blackwell, 1990); Bentley Layton, ed., *The Rediscovery of Gnosticism, Vol. 1: The School of Valentinus* (Leiden: E. J. Brill, 1980); Simone Petrement, *A Separate God: The Christian Origins of Gnosticism* (San Francisco: Harper, 1990); J. M. Robinson, ed., *The Nag Hammadi Library in English* (New York: Harper & Row, 1990).

validity

In CANON LAW, the validity of an act, such as a SACRAMENT, often depends on whether certain specific requirements were met before or during the act. Validity is distinct from lawfulness. For example, an excommunicated PRIEST can celebrate a EUCHARIST that is valid (it confers GRACE to the recipient), yet unlawful because the EXCOMMUNICATION prohibits him from offering the sacraments. The rules on validity and lawfulness are contained in the *Code of Canon Law* (cnn. 834–48).

Among the conditions that make a BAPTISM valid are the use of the proper element (water) and the invocation of the Triune God in the baptismal ritual. The performance of the Eucharist requires the words of consecration as the bread

and wine are transformed into the body and blood of CHRIST. Many traditionalists have questioned the validity of the Eucharist performed according to the LITURGIES that flowed from VATICAN COUNCIL II. St. AUGUSTINE OF HIPPO determined the theology of validity in his disputes with the Donatists.

The church has always affirmed that its ministry is in an APOSTOLIC SUCCESSION that can be traced back through a line of BISHOPS to Christ and the APOSTLES. Only a bishop within that lineage can perform a valid ordination of a priest or CONSECRATION of another bishop. According to that minimal condition, the Catholic Church recognizes as valid (though irregular) the orders of the Old Catholic Church but denies validity to ANGLICAN ORDINATION. The Catholic Church also believes that the orders in most Protestant and free churches have lost their validity. Special rules pertain to the ability and condition to contract a valid MARRIAGE in terms of age, consent, and baptismal status. (CODE OF CANON LAW cnn. 1055–1062).

Further reading: Todd Guzie, *The Book of Sacramental Basics* (New York: Paulist, 1981); James A. Coriden, *An Introduction to Canon Law* (New York: Paulist, 1991); Patrick Henry Omlor, *Questioning the Validity of the Masses Using the New All-English Canon* (Reno, Nev.: Athanasius, 1968).

Vandals

The Germanic people who invaded North Africa in the fifth century were generally known as Vandals. They terrorized the Catholic population there and in Italy for a century from their base in Carthage, leaving such a strong memory that their name became synonymous for wanton destroyers.

The Vandals were originally a Germanic tribe that in the fifth century B.C.E. moved from what is now Denmark to the Oder River valley, and in the third century C.E. moved farther south to the Danube River. In 406 the Vandals crossed the Rhine and moved on to the Iberian Peninsula. A generation later they targeted North Africa under their king Gaiseric (c. 400–77), whose military and diplomatic genius kept the Romans and other Germanic tribes at bay for half a century.

In 429, Gaiseric led his people across the Strait of Gibraltar; one by one they attacked the Roman cities along the coast, including Hippo, home of St. AUGUSTINE (354–430), who died in the siege. As the Vandals gained control of the coast they built a fleet of ships and turned to piracy. In 455, they sacked Rome, destroying much of the artistic and architectural heritage of the city.

Among the galling aspects of the Vandal conquest of the largely Christianized cities of North Africa was that while the Vandals were CHRISTIANS themselves, they adhered to ARIANISM. Arian Christians rejected the Trinitarian teaching of the Council of Nicaea (325) and viewed Jesus as the first creation of God, not God himself. The death of so many Catholic Christians at the hands of the Vandals added to the animosity already present among the orthodox majority for the Arian heresy.

Weakened by its own success, the Vandal kingdom was overthrown by an army dispatched from CONSTANTINOPLE in 534. Soon afterward the Vandals ceased to exist as a distinct people. They were absorbed into the Roman community, and their Arian church was suppressed.

Further reading: Poultney Bigelow, *Genseric: King of the Vandals and the First Prussian Kaiser* (New York: G. P. Putnam's Sons, 1918); Thomas Hodgkin, *Huns, Vandals and The Fall of The Roman Empire* (London: Greenhill, 1996); A. H. Merrills, ed. *Vandals, Romans and Berbers: New Perspectives on Late Antique North Africa* (Aldershot: Ashgate, 2004); Malcolm Todd, *Everyday Life of the Barbarians—Goths, Franks and Vandals* (London: B. T. Batsford, 1972).

Vatican City

Vatican City, an independent state located in ITALY and completely surrounded by the city of Rome, is the site of the international headquarters of the Catholic Church, the pope's residence, and the VATICAN CURIA (the church's administrative offices). Vatican City is the smallest country in the world, with a land area of only 1 square kilometer (0.6 sq. miles). The Vatican is the remnant of the former PAPAL STATES, granted to the pope in 754 by the Frankish king Pepin the Short (c. 714–68), and ruled by subsequent popes as monarch until the unification of Italy in 1870.

In the process of creating the modern Italian state, Victor Emanuel II (1820–78) annexed the Papal States. POPE PIUS IX (r. 1848–78) refused to accept the new situation and declared himself a prisoner in the Vatican. His successors, Leo XIII (r. 1878–1903), St. PIUS X (r. 1903–14), and Benedict XV (r. 1914–22) followed suit. Finally, Pope PIUS XI (r. 1922–39) negotiated the Lateran Treaties with Benito Mussolini (1883–1945) that created the independent Vatican City in 1929. The status of the Vatican is fraught with ambiguities, but it allows the tiny nation the ability to establish international relationships with other governments, produce its own currency (the Vatican lira, recently superseded by the Euro), print its own stamps, and issue its own passports. Italy has responsibility for the Vatican's national security.

The 1929 Lateran Treaties privileged Roman Catholicism in Italy. In 1984, however, Italy signed a new concordat with the Holy See that modified various provisions of the prior agreements, including limits on the primacy of Roman Catholicism as the Italian state religion.

The Vatican territory includes ST. PETER'S BASILICA and Square, the apostolic palace, and the Papal gardens. A number of churches—St. John Lateran, Santa Maria Maggiore, St. Paul's Outside the Walls—used by the church but outside the Vatican proper have been assigned extraterritorial status that gives them a variety of privileges as if they were inside Vatican territory. The same holds for the pope's summer residence at Castel Gandolfo.

The name *Vatican* derives from Vatican Hill, which in ancient times was the site of Nero's circus, the place assigned by tradition to PETER's martyrdom. The Emperor CONSTANTINE (c. 288–337) built a basilica there in the fourth century over what was believed to Peter's burial site. This basilica was replaced in the 16th century by the present ST. PETER'S BASILICA (the building of which triggered the PROTESTANT REFORMATION). Contrary to popular understanding, the LATERAN BASILICA, not St. Peter's, is the CATHEDRAL church of the DIOCESE of Rome.

Further reading: Maurizio Calvesi, *Treasures of the Vatican: St. Peter's Basilica, the Vatican Museums and Galleries, the Treasure of St. Peter's, the Vatican Grottoes and Necropolis, the Vatican Palaces* (New York: Portland, 1987); Lilian Gunton, *Rome's Historic Churches* (London: George Allen & Unwin, 1969); James Lees-Milne, *St. Peter's* (Boston: Little, Brown, 1967); Peter J. Toynbee and J. Ward Perkins, *The Shrine of St. Peter and the Vatican Excavations* (New York: Pantheon, 1957).

Vatican Council I (1869–1870)

Vatican I was the 20th ecumenical council (*see* COUNCILS, ECUMENICAL) of the church and the first since the Council of TRENT more than 300 years before. Its main foci were the challenge of MODERNISM and the primacy and INFALLIBILITY of the pope.

Called into session by Pope PIUS IX, the council's decisions reinforced the church's oppositional stance toward the challenge of modern civilization. The groundwork had been laid in 1864 in the pope's *Syllabus of Errors,* which condemned the philosophical and social theories of the time, including rationalism, pantheism, and communism. Vatican I was also a statement of the proper relationship between CHURCH AND STATE just 80 years after the French Revolution had put the two in conflict and only a few years after most of the PAPAL STATES had been annexed by a unified ITALY. The council's decisions were fiercely rejected in many countries, even among elements within the church; the French government banned them from publication.

On June 29, 1868, Pius IX published the bull *Aeterni Patris,* calling for the council. Vatican I officially opened on December 8, 1869, in ST. PETER'S BASILICA in Rome. Although Pius IX invited the Eastern Churches, they rejected his offer on the grounds that the papacy did not pay "due respect to Apostolic equality and brotherhood." He did not invite Anglicans or Jansenists (*see* JANSENISM); on the contrary, he issued a call to Protestants to return to the true church, provoking much negative reaction.

The issue of papal infallibility was not on the council's original agenda, as it would have seemed inappropriate for Pius IX to introduce the topic himself; it was added soon after the council began. Among the many opponents at the council, some argued that the doctrine, if true, did not need to be formalized. JOHN HENRY NEWMAN (1801–90) opposed the issue because he thought it would discourage potential converts.

After much discussion and disagreement, the council declared that the pope was infallible when he spoke formally EX CATHEDRA, that is, as the universal pastor of all Christians on matters of faith and doctrine. The council rejected a proposal by a minority that would have required a concurrence by the church when the pope spoke on dogmatic issues. In protest, 55 council members left Rome the day before the final vote. Amid widespread disagreement and protest over the council, those now known as OLD CATHOLICS separated from communion with Rome.

Two dogmatic decrees were approved at Vatican I. The first was *Dei Filius,* the Dogmatic Constitution of the Catholic Faith, which defined the roles of knowledge, faith, and reason in the interpretation of Scripture. The second was *Pastor Aeternus,* which established papal primacy and papal infallibility.

Due to the modern inventions of the railway and steamship, Vatican I was the most well-attended council in history, with 774 bishops participating out of a total of 1,050. The Franco-Prussian War interrupted the council, and it was not formally closed until the preparations leading up to VATICAN COUNCIL II, which saw itself as the completion of the untreated topics in Vatican I.

Further reading: Richard F. Costigan, *The Consensus of the Church and Papal Infallibility: A Study in the Background of Vatican I* (Washington, D.C.: Catholic University of America Press, 2005); Henry Edward, *The True Story of the Vatican Council* (London: Henry S. King, 1877); James J. Hennesey, *The First Council of the Vatican: The American Experience* (New York: Herder & Herder, 1963); Thomas Mozley, *Letters from Rome on the Occasion of the Ecumenical Council, 1869–1870* (London: Longmans, Green, 1891); Margaret O'Gara, *Triumph in Defeat: Infallibility, Vatican I, and the French Minority Bishops* (Washington, D.C.: Catholic University of America Press, 1988).

Vatican Council II (1962–1965)

Vatican II is probably the most important council for the Catholic Church after Nicaea I and the Council of TRENT, as it ushered in an era of thoroughgoing change in the structures and practices of the church and in its attitudes toward the modern world. The council was announced by Pope JOHN XXIII in 1959. After lengthy preparations, it was convoked in ST. PETER'S BASILICA in Rome with the pope's apostolic constitution *Humanae Salutis,* or Of Human Salvation, on December 25, 1961. There were four separate sessions. John XXIII died in 1963, and Pope PAUL VI oversaw the council to its conclusion.

The council was truly ecumenical, with representatives from around the world, including non-Catholics. Each day began with the celebration of the EUCHARIST in more than 25 different rites from around the world and with the enthronement of the sacred Scriptures on an altar in front of Bernini's main altar. There were more than 3,000 participants, including bishops, theological experts, called *periti,* lay Catholics, members of orders including nuns, and non-Catholic observers. The Eastern Orthodox Church, though invited, did not send observers.

The council immediately became international news. For example, Winston Burdett (1913–) of CBS News announced council events on an almost daily basis. The pseudonymous author Xavier Rynne (who turned out to be the Redemptorist patristic scholar Francis X. Murphy [1914–2002] of the Alphonsianum in Rome) offered chatty updates in the American weekly the *New Yorker.* The operative word on everyone's tongue was the Italian *aggiornomento,* "updating."

In his opening address on December 11, 1961, John XXIII proclaimed two main themes, peace between peoples and social justice, themes that addressed not only Catholicism but the whole world. (Nine days later the Cuban Missile Crisis threatened to engulf the world in nuclear war.) These themes were also central to his signature encyclical, PACEM IN TERRIS.

At the outset of the sessions, the VATICAN CURIA, under the wary scrutiny of Cardinal Alfredo Ottaviani (1890–1979), tried to control the proceedings and write the preliminary drafts, but the BISHOPS in session rejected that approach and put their own theologians to work. Thereafter, progressives had their way on such issues as authorizing the use of local languages in the LITURGY. Cardinals Oscar L. Arnal Liénart (1884–1976) of Lille, Joseph Frings (1887–1978) of Cologne, Leo Josef Suenens (1904–96) of Maline-Brussels, Julius August Döpfner (1913–76) of Munich-Freising, and Bernard Jan Alfrink (1900–87) of Utrecht took informal leadership of the council. Theologians HANS KÜNG, KARL RAHNER, M.-D. CHENU, JOHN COURTNEY MURRAY, and many others played increasingly important roles in framing the ideas and the wording of key documents.

Although the council issued two dogmatic constitutions, one on the church (*Lumen Gentium*) and one on revelation (*Dei Verbum*), the remaining constitutions, decrees, and declarations were pastoral, ecumenical, modernizing, and world-embracing in spirit and manner. There were no anathemas or condemnations, as had been the custom of most previous councils. The council exhibited a confident church looking to reform itself and to offer to the world a vision of the Gospel that Christ transmitted to his disciples.

The Dogmatic Constitution on the Church sees the church as a mystery, communion, and SACRAMENT, not just an institution (*see* ECCLESIOLOGY). The church is the whole people of God, not just the hierarchy. In the Pastoral Constitution on the Church in the Modern World (*Gaudium et Spes*), the church is not only to preach the word of God and celebrate the sacraments but to bring peace and social justice to society at large. In the Decree on Ecumenism *Unitatis Redintegratio* the church is not limited to Catholicism but embraces, in varying degrees, all Christians who seek to follow Christ. The Decree on the Apostolate of the Laity (*Apostolicam Actuositatem*) assigned lay people an equal role in Christian education and the apostolate.

In the all-important Declaration on the Relationship of the Church to Non-Christian Religions (*Nostra Aetate*), the council affirmed that Christ was a Jew, that Christianity was born out of Judaism and has a common spiritual heritage with it, that Jews as a people are not responsible for the death of Christ (4), and that they are not to be persecuted (*see* ANTI-SEMITISM). The council took the daring step of asserting the presence of the "divine mystery" in non-Christian religions; the church, it declared, rejects "nothing which is true and holy" within them (2). God can use all for divine purposes. This decree both legitimated and enhanced the interreligious dialogue that had been embraced by such pioneers as DOM BEDE GRIFFITHS.

Both the Decree on the Bishops' Pastoral Office (*Christus Dominus*) and the Dogmatic Constitution on the Church embraced the principle of episcopal collegiality, thereby modifying the overemphasis on the papacy at VATICAN COUNCIL I. The council also stressed, in the Decree on Priestly Formation (*Optatum Totius*), that priests must be prepared to become true pastors of their flocks.

In a final, daring Declaration on Religious Freedom (*Dignitatis Humanae*) the council, grounding itself on the created dignity of the human person, affirmed the principle of religious liberty for all. This decree shows the direct hand of American Jesuit John Courtney Murray. It placed severe limitations on the old principle that was embodied in the INQUISITION, that "error has no rights."

Historians have discerned two streams that came out of Vatican II. One stream, grounding itself in the Pastoral Constitution on the Church in the Modern World, championed aggionamento, the progressive updating of the church. The other stream, grounding itself in the Dogmatic Constitution on the Church, stressed *ressourcement,* a return to the sources of Catholic tradition as a guide to refurbishing and enriching the church. Both tendencies were present in Vatican II, but some now claim that they have come apart. Hans Küng has charged that Pope JOHN PAUL II and his ally, Cardinal Ratzinger, now BENEDICT XVI, abandoned the aggionamento of Vatican II and retained only the second stream. The new *Catechism of the Catholic Church* (1994), for example, is certainly an admirable re-enrichment out of the tradition, but it shows none of the openness and daring of Vatican II. Critics charge that the Vatican has succeeded in pulling back from collegiality, ecumenical openness, concern for social justice, and dialogue and interchange with other religions. Perhaps the meeting of Benedict XVI and Küng in the fall of 2005 will help bring the two streams back together. However, there is no doubt that the effects of Vatican II will be felt way into the 21st century and beyond.

Further reading: Giuseppe Alberigo, *History of Vatican II* (Maryknoll, N.Y.: Orbis, 1995); Walter Abbott, ed., *The Documents of Vatican II* (New York: America, 1966); Andrew M. Greeley, *The Catholic Revolution: New Wine, Old Wineskins, and the Second Vatican Council* (Berkeley: University of California Press, 2004); Adrian Hastings, ed., *Modern Catholicism: Vatican II and After* (London: S.P.C.K., 1991); Xavier Rynne, *Vatican Council II* (Maryknoll, N.Y.: Orbis, 1999).

Vatican Curia

The Vatican Curia comprises the central offices of the Roman Catholic Church for the entire world.

They surround St. PETER'S BASILICA. Some astute observers have remarked that the Vatican Curia is the first hierarchical corporation formed in the Western world—and its longest lasting.

Throughout the first millennium the papal curia was located in and around St. John Lateran Cathedral, which is still the official CATHEDRAL seat of the pope as BISHOP of Rome. The offices grew in number and scope during the time of GREGORY I THE GREAT and continued to do so into the MIDDLE AGES. There are reports that a second papal residence was built near the Old St. Peter's on Vatican Hill by Pope Symmachus (r. 498–514), which was rebuilt by INNOCENT III. Offices remained at St. John Lateran until the AVIGNON PAPACY. A fire at St. John's in 1309 prevented the pope from taking up residence when the PAPACY returned in 1377. From that time forth St. Peter's became the center of official Catholicism. The various chapels and chambers have undergone significant renovations and alterations through the centuries.

The curia is the means through which the pope exercises supreme, full, and immediate jurisdiction over the universal church. The principle offices include that of the secretariat of state, congregations, tribunals, pontifical councils, the synod of bishops, pontifical commissions, the Swiss Guard, academies, museums, and a post office, bank, and employment office. The most important congregation is the Congregation of the Doctrine of the Faith (formerly called the Holy Office and the Inquisition), which supervises matters of FAITH, the biblical commission, and the commission for the CATECHISM. There are also congregations for oriental churches, worship and the sacraments, canonization procedures, evangelization, the clergy and bishops, those in religious life, and education. There is no congregation for the laity.

The tribunals include the ecclesiastical courts and deal with such matters as INDULGENCES, dispensations, marital annulments, INTERDICTS and EXCOMMUNICATIONS, and HERESY and SCHISM. The ROTA acts as the court of appeal to the Holy See.

The Synod of Bishops acts as a consultative body, a kind of unofficial interim ecumenical council (*see* COUNCILS, ECUMENICAL). Besides the commissions mentioned above, there are also commissions on the BIBLE, cultural heritage, archaeology, and LATIN AMERICA. The special commission Ecclesia Dei was set up by JOHN PAUL II on July 2, 1988, to negotiate reconciliations with TRADITIONALISTS associated with Archbishop Marcel LeFevbre (1905–91). The Swiss Guard has guarded the pope since 1505. In 1527 their commander and 146 others died defending the pope during the sack of Rome by Emperor CHARLES V.

Further reading: There is a Vatican Web site dedicated to a description of all the offices; Bart McDowell, *Inside the Vatican* (Washington, D.C.: National Geographic Society, 1991); John L. Allen, *All the Pope's Men: The Inside Story of How the Vatican Really Works* (New York: Doubleday, 2004); Thomas J. Reese, *Inside the Vatican: The Politics and Organization of the Catholic Church* (Cambridge, Mass.: Harvard University Press, 1996).

Vawter, Bruce (1921–1986) *biblical scholar*

Bruce Vawter was an accomplished biblical scholar who assumed a leading role in the late 20th-century movement for Catholic biblical renewal. Vawter began his religious life in 1942 when he joined the Congregation of Mission (the Vincentians). He was ordained in 1947 and went to Rome for advanced studies. He received degrees in 1952 and 1957 from the Pontifical Biblical Institute. He returned to the United States to teach (1968–86) at Kendrick Seminary (St. Louis), St. Thomas Seminary (Denver), and DePaul University (Chicago). His scholarship was recognized by his colleagues when he was voted president of the Catholic Biblical Association (1961–62).

Vawter achieved prominence largely for his efforts to revive interest in and knowledge of the BIBLE among Catholic laypeople. The biblical renewal movement sought to lead Catholics into a new understanding of the Bible. It encouraged reading and praying with the Scriptures in light of the experience of the mystery of CHRIST combined with knowledge of the teachings of the church. It was also comfortable with a modern awareness of the Bible's historical and cultural dimensions. Vawter's books *A Path through Genesis* (1956) and *The Conscience of Israel* (1961) were aimed primarily at a lay audience.

During his Chicago years, Vawter also became involved in the debates provoked by the reemergence of creationist thought. Creationists are wrong, he said, to assume that belief in CREATION is exclusive of acceptance of the findings of science about the evolution of species.

Further reading: Bruce Vawter, *Amos, Hosea, Micah: With an Introduction to Classical Prophecy* (Wilmington, Del.: Michael Glazier, 1981); ———, *The Conscience of Israel* (New York: Sheed & Ward, 1961); ———, *On Genesis: A New Reading* (Garden City, N.Y.: Doubleday, 1977); ———, *This Man Jesus. An Essay Toward a NT Christology* (New York: Doubleday, 1973).

Vaz, Joseph (1651–1711) *Sri Lanka missionary*

Joseph Vaz, a pioneer missionary to Sri Lanka, was born into the Brahman class in the Portuguese colony at Goa, India, on April 21, 1651. His CHRISTIAN parents saw to his schooling and his mastering of Portuguese and Latin, thus preparing him for entrance into the JESUIT seminary and the Saint Thomas Aquinas Academy. He was ordained a priest in 1676 and subsequently opened a school in his hometown of Sancoale. He later took up a post at Kanara, where his pastoral duties included rescuing Christians from slavery.

Through the 1680s, Vaz developed a desire to minister among the Catholic believers in Sri Lanka. The Buddhist country had once been colonized by the Catholic Portuguese but was then under the control of Dutch Reformed leaders. Vaz affiliated with a new religious order in Goa. Soon after he was elected the order's superior, a position he held until 1686, when he finally found an opportunity

to travel to Sri Lanka. He traveled clandestinely as an itinerant worker, initially settling in the northern city of Jaffna, where he contacted the island's Catholic families and held meetings in the evening. In 1690, Vaz settled in Puttalam, where some 1,000 Catholics resided. He was the first PRIEST in the town for more than 50 years. Two years later he went to Kandy in hopes of obtaining permission from the authorities to operate openly. Instead, he was arrested as a spy. In prison he learned Sinhalese, constructed a prison chapel, and began converting his fellow prisoners.

A turnabout in his situation followed an unusual event in 1696. The kingdom of Kandy was at the time in the midst of a drought. The king turned to the Buddhist monks to pray for rain. None fell. Then Vaz erected an altar, offered prayers, and waited as rain fell everywhere except on him and the altar. As a result, the king granted his permission to freely minister to people throughout his realm.

In 1697, Vaz was named vicar general of Ceylon (the name by which Sri Lanka was then known). In 1699 he settled in Kandy, completing a new church building while working for the king as a translator of Portuguese books to the local language, Sinhala. In spite of continued Dutch control of the island, with the assistance of the king of Kandy he was able to lead in the growth of Catholicism throughout the land.

Vaz died at Kandy on January 16, 1711. Throughout his life he had been a devotee of the Blessed Virgin and had early in his priestly career declared himself a "slave of Mary," an act he documented with a "letter of Enslavement." In 1737, efforts began to have him canonized as a saint. Those efforts did not bear fruit until 1995, when JOHN PAUL II visited Colombo, Sri Lanka, and beatified him.

Further reading: Charles Gasbarri, *A Saint for the New India: Father Joseph Vaz, Apostle of Kanara and Ceylon* (Allahabad: St. Paul, 1961); S. G. Perera, *Life of the Venerable Father Joseph Vaz Apostle of Ceylon*, 2nd ed.,

(Galle: Loyolla, 1953); V. Perniola, *The Catholic Church in Sri Lanka: The Dutch Period*, 3 vols. (Dehiwela: Tisara Prakasakayo, 1983–1985).

veneration of saints   *See* ADORATION.

vestments (Lat.: *vestis*, "garment")

Vestments are the garments worn for liturgical functions. They are not to be confused with religious habits or clerical garments, such as cassocks, worn in the normal course of daily life.

Scenes on catacomb walls and elsewhere indicate that early CHRISTIAN ministers did not wear special garments for BAPTISM or the EUCHARIST. However, such garments were not long in appearing; they have long played an important part of Catholic religious life.

ROMAN RITE

As the Eucharist is the central SACRAMENT of the church, it is fitting to begin with the garments worn for this service. The first is the **alb** (Lat.: *albus*, "white"), a body-length linen garment, which is normally fastened around the waist by a rope called a **cincture** (Lat.: *cinctura*, "girdle," "belt"). Today these inner garments are also often worn by acolytes or altar servers.

BISHOPS, priests, and deacons wear a stole (Lat.: *stola*, "dress worn over tunic"), a narrow band of cloth worn over the shoulders and often ornamented with liturgical motifs like the ChiRho (☧), CROSS, or image of Christ, Mary, or a saint. PRIESTS and deacons wear the stole when officiating at other liturgical functions even when no other liturgical garments are worn. The deacon wears the stole aslant.

Over the alb, cincture, and stole a bishop and priest wear a **chasuble** (Lat.: *casula*, "little house"), an outer liturgical garment often adorned with ornamental motifs. The chasuble was originally the outer cloak of Roman times, retained by the Christian CLERGY after the barbarian invasions in

Priest wearing alb with stole   *(photo by John Huston)*

the fourth century. Later it became a custom for a family to present a chasuble to a newly ordained son. The formal outer garment of a deacon is called a **dalmatic**, after a garment worn in Dalmatia in the second century.

For processions, but not during the Eucharist itself, bishops also wear a **miter** (Gk.: *mitra*, "headband") that has **lappets** hanging from the back and carry a **crozier** (OF: *crosse*, "shepherds crook"). ARCHBISHOPS also wear a **pallium** (Lat.: *pallium*, "cloak"), a band of wool with front and back lappets marked with six dark purple crosses as a sign of their office. The pope may grant the pallium to bishops as a sign of distinction. In processions bishops and priests often wear a **cope** (Lat.: *cappa*, "cape"), which is often highly embroidered with symbols and images.

Clerics have distinct garb for everyday use. A diocesan priest wears a black cassock front-

Priest wearing a chasuble over the alb. The chasuble is worn during the celebration of the Eucharist *(photo by John Huston)*

Eastern Rite priest's vestments with a) *epitrachelion*, b) *zone,* c) *sticharion,* and d) *epigonation.* The priest is standing in front of the iconostasis, which is sacralized by the presence of icons, the Theotokos on the left and Christos Pantokrator on the right. (St. Basil's Orthodox Church, St. Louis, Missouri) *(photo by John Huston)*

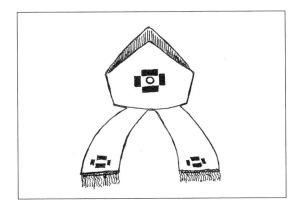

Miter worn by a bishop *(drawing by Frank K. Flinn)*

buttoned robe. In Europe priests often wear a **biretta** (Lat.: *birrus,* "hood"), a four-cornered hat with a tassel on top. Cardinals wear red, and bishops purple, birettas. Formerly a priest and acolytes would wear a **surplice** (ML: *superpellicum,* "over the fur") over a cassock for public devotions. The surplice was often fringed with lace. After the liturgical reforms of VATICAN COUNCIL II, the alb is considered the proper liturgical garment.

Perhaps the most celebrated painting of liturgical vestments and clerical garments is the *Burial of the Count of Orgaz* (see page 496) by Domenicos Theotocopoulos (1541–1614), known as El Greco, located in the church of Santo Tomé in Toledo, SPAIN. It portrays St. Stephen, the deacon and first martyr (Acts 7), in his dalmatic, St. AUGUSTINE OF HIPPO wearing a cope and a miter, another priest in a cope, a priest in a surplice, and a FRANCISCAN and an AUGUSTINIAN friar in their habits.

EASTERN RITES

In the Eastern rites the tunic worn by a deacon is called the *sticharion* and the stole is called the *orarion,* on which crosses and the words "Holy, Holy, Holy" are woven. Higher-ranked deacons wear *epimanika,* or cuffs, under the *sticharion.*

A priest also wears a *sticharion* over which he wears an *epitrachelion* around the neck and reaching to the ankle in front, marked with crosses like the stole in the Western rites. He also wears a *zone,* equivalent to a cincture, cuffs on top of the *sticharion,* and over all a *phelonion,* or cape, equivalent to the chasuble in the West. Hanging from the neck or the belt is an *epigonattion,* a diamond-shaped stiff brocade with a cross on it.

Bishops wear a special chasuble called a *sakkos,* a bishop's stole called the *omophorion,* a pectoral cross and ICON medallions, and a miter that looks like a Persian crown. Bishops also carry two candelabra, one with two candles in the left hand signifying the two natures of CHRIST and one with three candles signifying the TRINITY. A bishop also has everyday clerical garments.

Further reading: Pauline Johnstone, *High Fashion in the Church: The Place of Church Vestments in the History of Art, from the Ninth to the Nineteenth Century* (Leeds: Maney, 2002); David Philipartt, *Clothed in Glory: Vesting the Church* (Chicago: Liturgy Training, 1997); James-Charles Noonan, *The Church Visible: The Ceremonial Life and Protocol of the Roman Catholic Church* (New York: Viking, 1996); Archimandrate Chrysostomos, *Orthodox Liturgical Dress* (Brookline, Mass.: Holy Cross Orthodox, 1981).

Via Dolorosa (Lat.: "Way of Sorrow")

Via Dolorosa ("Via Crucis") is the route taken by Jesus CHRIST following his condemnation by Pontius Pilate, during which he was forced to carry on his back the CROSS on which he would be crucified. The original journey began at the Antonia fortress, built around 35 B.C.E. by Herod the Great and subsequently taken over by the Romans for their garrison, and ended at the hill called Golgotha.

During the early centuries of the CHRISTIAN era, believers initiated the practice of rewalking the route to Golgotha while making note of and meditating on particular events that occurred along the way. Thus, the Via Dolorosa was the basis of the popular practice of praying the Stations of the Cross. The spread of the practice followed the arrival of the FRANCISCANS in the Holy Land in 1342. They encouraged the erection of a set of shrines, both in Jerusalem and back in the Catholic countries, to assist believers in focusing their attention on Christ's Passion. Initially they were placed outdoors; they varied both in number and the specific events commemorated. The Franciscan priest Leonard of Port Maurice (d. 1751) is credited with erecting more than 500 such sets of stations in Europe in the mid-18th century. The current number of stations and their designation was standardized in the 18th century by papal decree. The 14 stations are: 1) Pilate condemns Christ to death; 2) Christ takes the cross; 3) he falls; 4) he meets the Blessed Virgin; 5) Simon of Cyrene is forced to carry the cross; 6) Veronica wipes the sweat from Christ's face; 7) he falls a second time; 8) he meets the women of Jerusalem; 9) he falls a third time; 10) his clothes are removed; 11) he is crucified; 12) he dies; 13) his body is removed from the cross; 14) he is entombed.

Meditation on the Stations of the Cross is an especially popular exercise during Holy Week. The practices have at times been taken to an extreme by some groups focused on penitence, most notably Los Hermanos Penitentes (Span.: "The Penitent Brethren"), the brotherhood of Penitentes who annually reenact the events of Passion Week in as literal a manner as possible, including the crucifixion of a brother that does not lead to death.

Further reading: Paul John Bradley, *My Catholic Devotions* (Gastonia, N.C.: Good Will, 1955); *The Way of the Cross* (Collegeville, Minn.: Liturgical Press, 1978); *Way of the Cross* (Washington, D.C.: Basilica of the National Shrine of the Immaculate Conception, 2001).

Vigil (Lat.: *vigilia,* "a watch")

The term *vigil* originally referred to a variety of worship activities, usually focused on prayer, that occurred in CHRISTIAN settings in the nighttime hours. The primary vigils occurred prior to the annual EASTER celebration, but the term was also used to refer to Matins, which by the sixth century was primarily being observed as the midnight worship in monastic communities.

In the rise of MONASTICISM in EGYPT, belief that the *parousia* would take place at midnight likely influenced the night time hours in the Divine Office or PRAYER OF THE HOURS. Vigils refer back to the women who kept watch at Jesus' tomb (Mark 16:1–2).

Today, vigils primarily refer to times of prayer on the eve of a particularly notable and solemn occasion. The Easter vigil (from dusk to dawn) on Saturday evening before Easter morning remains the most important annual vigil in the LITURGICAL YEAR. It includes the litany of the saints, when worshippers ask saints to pray for those participating in the LITURGY and their loved ones. Vigils may also be held prior to ordination services, funerals, or any Sunday (which are all considered to be like Easter). After the reform of the Roman liturgical calendar in 1969, only Holy Saturday remains as the solemn vigil of Easter.

The primary service that occurs between the death of a church member and the funeral is properly termed the vigil for the deceased, often popularly called the wake. This vigil usually takes place in the deceased's home or a funeral parlor.

The wake service primarily consists of prayers and hymns. Increasingly in the last generation, vigils have become occasions for groups to gather in public and show their support for various causes, from commemorating a tragic event to demanding changes in church life or public policy.

Further reading: Mike Aquilina and Regis J. Flaherty, *How-To Book of Catholic Devotions* (Huntington, Ind.: Our Sunday Visitor, 2000); Bergerm Rupert and Hans Hollerweger, eds. *Celebrating the Easter Vigil.* (New York: Pueblo, 1983).

Vincent de Paul, St. (1581–1660) *missionary to the poor*

St. Vincent de Paul, founder of the Daughters of Charity (with St. Louise de Marillac, 1591–1660) and the Congregation of the Missions (better known as the Lazarists or the Vincentians), spent most of his life in ministry to the poor, the ill, and the enslaved. Vincent was canonized in 1737 and Louise in 1934. His feast day is September 27, and hers is March 15.

Vincent was born in southern FRANCE. As a young man he began his study toward the priesthood with the FRANCISCAN ORDER at Dax. After completing a degree at the Collège de Foix at Toulouse, he was ordained in 1600 and continued his study at the University of Toulouse. A life-shaping event occurred in 1605. While returning home from a trip to Marseille to claim an inheritance, he was captured by Turkish pirates and enslaved for two years. After his escape he spent time in Rome and Paris before becoming a parish priest. In 1619 he was appointed chaplain-general of the galleys, an office that allowed him the opportunity to ameliorate the conditions under which galley slaves lived in French ports.

In 1617, as pastor, he formed the Confraternities of Charity, a group of laywomen who undertook to provide organized material help to the poor. In 1623 Vincent met Louise de Marillac, (1591–1660), who began to work with him in leadership of the Confraternities. Together they founded the Daughters of Charity (1633), which superseded the Confraternities. The Daughters wore high stiff white headdresses and became known affectionately as "God's Geese."

In 1625 all of Vincent's work with the poor came together in his founding of the Congregation of the Mission to evangelize the countryside. The Vincentians would soon develop a far-reaching program that included the education of priests for work in rural areas. The motherhouse was opened in Paris. It suffered during the French Revolution and was eventually confiscated by the new government. A new motherhouse was obtained in 1817.

Apart from the orders he himself founded, Vincent has remained an inspiration to others. In 1833 Frederic Ozanam (1813–53) founded the ST. VINCENT DE PAUL SOCIETY to serve the poor. The society has thousands of chapters in parishes throughout the world and is a principal conduit for distributing food and assistance to the poor in the United States.

Further reading: Louis Abelly, *The Life of the Venerable Servant of God Vincent de Paul, Founder and First Superior General of the Congregation of the Mission,* 3 vols. (New Rochelle, N.Y.: New City, 1993); Emile Bougaud, *History of St. Vincent de Paul, Founder of the Congregation of the Mission and the Sisters of Charity,* 2 vols. (London: Longmans, Green, 1899); Jean Calvet, *Louise de Marillac—A Portrait* (New York: Kennedy, l959); ———, *Saint Vincent de Paul* (New York: David McKay, 1948); J. Dirvin, *Louise de Marillac* (New York: Farrar, Straus & Giroux, l970).

Virgin Birth of Christ

The Virgin Birth doctrine is the belief that Jesus was born of MARY OF NAZARETH by the overshadowing of the Spirit without the agency of a human father. It is sometimes confused with the IMMACULATE CONCEPTION, which actually refers to the conception of Mary by her parents, Sts. JOACHIM AND ANNE, without original SIN.

Scholars generally agree that the Gospels as we now have them first took shape after the death and RESURRECTION of Jesus CHRIST. Thus, the GOSPEL form grew backward from the EASTER event to the ministry of Jesus (Mark), then his birth (Matthew, Luke), and finally before his birth (John).

Early CHRISTIANS were interested primarily in who Jesus was: was he the Messiah, and when did he become manifest as such? The sermon of PETER in Acts 3:20, reflecting a very early Christology, seems to say that Jesus is the Messiah *designatus*, appointed to return in the future; his sermon in Acts 2 seems to say that he became manifest as Messiah at his resurrection. Mark (c. 60–70) sees Jesus' messianic mission beginning with his BAPTISM in the Jordan by John. Matthew and Luke (c. 85–95) see Jesus' messianic role commencing at his birth.

Although the infancy narratives of Matthew and Luke differ on many points, they both agree that Mary became pregnant with the child by the HOLY SPIRIT (Matt. 1:18; Luke 1:35). Matthew refers to Isaiah 7:14, quoting from the Septuagint, the Greek translation of the Hebrew Bible: "Behold a virgin (*parthenos*) shall conceive and bear a son, and his name shall be called Emmanuel." The Hebrew has *almah*, which signifies a woman of marriageable age whether virgin or not.

From early on the DOCTRINE of the Virgin Birth has been given an important place in Christian THEOLOGY, and Mary is given a key role in GOD's plan of salvation. It became a part of the Nicene-Constantinopolitan CREED of 381: "For our sins and for our salvation he came down from heaven and was incarnate of the Virgin Mary." Sts. AMBROSE and AUGUSTINE present the Virgin Birth as part of the mystery of the INCARNATION. "Begotten of the Holy Spirit" in the creed argues against subordination of the Son to the Father, and "born of the Virgin Mary" combats DOCETISM.

Discussions of the Virgin Birth revolve around three aspects: the virginal conception of Jesus in Mary's womb ante partum (before his birth); the virginal birth itself *in partu* (during his birth); and

Mary's continuing virginal status post partum. Catholics are hard put to explain the biblical passages that refer to the "brothers" of Jesus (Matt. 12:46; Mark 3:31; John 2:12, etc.). They take the term to refer to Joseph's children by another wife or to Jesus' "cousins."

Following Ambrose, VATICAN COUNCIL II in the Dogmatic Constitution on the Church (*Lumen Gentium,* 1964) affirms all three aspects of Mary's virginity but clearly subordinates her role to the single mediatorship of Christ, viewing her as the paradigm, or model, of pure FAITH and virtue for members of the church (nos. 52–69). The learned Protestant theologian Karl Barth and Catholic theologian KARL RAHNER have provided subtle discussions of this belief.

Further reading: Walter M. Abbott, *The Documents of Vatican II* (New York: America, 1966); Karl Barth, *Dogmatics in Outline* (London: SCM, 1949); Raymond Brown, *The Birth of the Messiah* (Garden City, N.Y.: Doubleday, 1993); Hilda Graef, *Mary: A History of Doctrine and Devotion,* 2 vols. (New York: Sheed & Ward, 1956); Karl Rahner, *Foundations of Christian Faith* (New York: Seabury, 1978).

virginity

Virginity, the state of having voluntarily refrained form sexual activity, began to attain value during the first century of Christianity (the idea previously having gained some attention in both Jewish and pagan circles). The idea was primarily applied to women, though it could be used at times in reference to sexually chaste males. PAUL calls attention to the manner in which a virgin (a female) can devote herself to GOD apart from the many distractions of a married woman (1 Cor. 7:33–35). However, it was the increased consideration of the Blessed Virgin Mary over the centuries that helped make virginity an ideal for womankind. As the church moved around the Mediterranean basin, CHRISTIAN virginity was contrasted with both the sexual life of pagans and the tainted behavior that surrounded pagan virgins (who were often physically coerced to remain virgins).

During the early centuries of the church, virginity was considered an acceptable option to married life; as ASCETICISM and MONASTICISM spread, rules were promulgated to guide the practice. Beginning in the fourth century, MONASTERIES and CONVENTS became institutions to house those who chose a life of sexual continence. Gradually, chastity became the approved state for Christian PRIESTS. Many of the early church's outstanding thinkers also wrote treatises on virginity, including JOHN CHRYSOSTOM, JEROME, AMBROSE, and AUGUSTINE.

Through the centuries, the extended discussion of virginity (including the problem of virgins who were raped or otherwise violated against their will) drew a distinction between the motivation toward virginity and the physical aspects of remaining a virgin. The Catholic Church teaches that virginity can remain with a woman after she has been violated, a correlate of its teaching that the Blessed Virgin remained a virgin even after giving birth to Jesus. Ideally, virginity is both a state of consciousness and of physical behavior, and in the virginal state there are joys and rewards more than equal to those who participate in physical sexual expressions.

During the early centuries of church life, the act of consecrating virgins became a sacramental rite that included prayers that those so consecrated would remain faithful in their intentions. By the fourth century, those seeking such consecrations became younger and younger, a few being offered for consecration by parents even prior to their birth. This practice led to a law setting age 25 as the youngest one could be consecrated as a virgin.

Without going to extremes in its teachings, the Catholic Church has in the modern world privileged virginity and the life style that accompanies it over the state of marriage. This belief was challenged during the PROTESTANT REFORMATION beginning with Martin Luther (1483–1546), who rejected his monastic vows and married former NUN Katherin von Bora (1499–1552). In partial reaction to Protestant preferences for marriage as the common way of humans in the world, the Council of TRENT pronounced an anathema on teachings that valued marriage equal to or above virginity.

Through the centuries, virginity in the technical sense was required for those entering monastic orders. That requirement was somewhat broken by the Order of the Visitation, a contemplative order founded by St. FRANCIS DE SALES and Jane Frances de Chantal (1572–1641) in the 17th century, which welcomed widows. In more recent times, the requirements of bodily integrity in the case of women is generally no longer required. Women who have been sexually active prior to entrance may offer their repentance in place of their virginity.

Further reading: Thomas Dubay, *A Call to Virginity* (Huntington, Ind.: Our Sunday Visitor, 1977); Raniero Cantalamessa, *Virginity: A Positive Approach to Celibacy for the Sake of the Kingdom of Heaven* (New York: Alba, 1995); Dietrich von Hildebrand, *In Defence of Purity: An Analysis of the Catholic Ideals of Purity and Virginity* (London: Sheed & Ward, 1940).

virtues, cardinal (Lat.: *virtus*, "strength of character")

Virtue is a quality of character and of intellect that enables a person to live an honorable and ethically good life. The medieval philosophers and theologians drew equally on both AUGUSTINE and ARISTOTLE in their theory of virtue. They thought that virtue was not simply a single act of bravery or temperance but an enduring *habitus* (Lat. "habit, customary mode of behavior") or quality of intellect, will, and emotions whereby a person can encounter and deal with individual situations in an ethically appropriate manner. St. THOMAS AQUINAS placed emphasis on the intellectual knowledge of the good, whereas DUNS SCOTUS put it on the will toward the good, but both said both intellect and will had to be in play.

The philosophical cardinal virtues include prudence, temperance, courage, and justice. Prudence allows one to apply knowledge of and will toward the good to concrete situations. Temperance helps a person regulate the sensuous passions to serve the good. Courage balances the tendency toward craven fear with the tendency toward aggressiveness in meeting challenging situations. Finally, justice allows one to maintain fitting relationships with fellow human beings. The overall agency that guides the person to choose the good and avoid evil is called *synderesis* or CONSCIENCE.

While the first four cardinal virtues are sufficient for leading a good life, a person also needs the three cardinal virtues of FAITH, hope, and love (*see* AGAPE) in order to attain the BEATIFIC VISION of God. Faith fundamentally orients a person to God and God's will. Hope sustains and guides a person to attaining union with God, and love is the everlasting virtue that partakes of God's very self and that allows one to love the other selflessly and thereby discover the true self (1 Cor. 13).

The virtues were often depicted in the sculptures and windows of medieval CATHEDRALS. Often they were contrasted with the seven deadly sins of pride, envy, gluttony, lust, anger, greed, and sloth.

Sometime during the 14th century Catholicism fell into a kind of legalistic moralism ("ticking off sins") that lost the underlying thrust of what the original medieval theory of virtue was about: the fundamental orientation of the self toward the good and toward God's gracious self-communication in GRACE. Many theologians during and following VATICAN COUNCIL II have sought to return to this fundamental, biblical understanding of virtue.

Further reading: Aristotle, *Nicomachean Ethics*, available online; Thomas Aquinas, *Disputed Questions on the Virtues*, ed. E. M. Atkins & Thomas Williams (Cambridge: Cambridge University Press, 2005); Josef Pieper, *Faith, Hope, Love* (San Francisco: Ignatius, 1997);

Thomas Shannon, *The Ethical Theory of John Duns Scotus* (Quincy, Ill.: Franciscan, 1995).

VOWS

A vow is a solemn, voluntary promise by someone to perform something for the person to whom the vow is made. In the context of religion, vows are typically made to GOD.

According to Catholic teaching, a valid vow must be freely made by a person with sufficient reasoning capacity, be possible to fulfil, and have a future good in mind. Both priests and religious (MONKS and NUNS) take vows. MONASTICISM developed the three vows of poverty, chastity, and obedience. A monk also took a vow of stability—that he remain in his MONASTERY unless sent by his abbot to found a new monastery. MENDICANTS, especially FRANCISCANS and DOMINICANS, took vows of absolute poverty, which meant that they could use things but not have ownership of them individually or collectively.

Ordinary diocesan PRIESTS take vows of chastity and obedience to their BISHOP or ordinary; they do not take a vow of poverty. In the religious life there is a distinction between temporary vows, usually two to three years, and final or solemn vows, which are for life. Only the PAPACY can dispense a person from solemn vows.

Further reading: Pierre Cotel, *A Catechism of the Vows for the Use of Religious* (Westminster, Md.: Newman, 1953); Charles L. Gay, *The Religious Life and the Vows: A Treatise* (Westminster, Md.: Newman, 1942); Judith A. Merkle, *A Different Touch: A Study of Vows in Religious Life* (Collegeville, Minn.: Liturgical Press, 1998); Eamonn F. O'Doherty, *Consecration and Vows, Psychological Aspects* (Dublin: Gill & MacMillan, 1971); Joyce Ridick, *Treasures in Earthen Vessels, the Vows: A Wholistic Approach* (New York: Alba, 1984).

W

Waldensians

A mainstream Protestant church centered in northern ITALY, the Waldensian Church traces its history back to well before the PROTESTANT REFORMATION. The name derives from a 12th-century Frenchman from Lyons known variously as (Peter) Valdes, Waldo, or Valdo. (The name Peter was added later.) He was a wealthy merchant who after an intense religious awakening decided to live a life of POVERTY in the apostolic example. He soon acquired a following, called the "Poor Men of Lyons," and even sent representatives to the third Lateran Council (1179) to obtain papal approval for his work (*see* COUNCILS, ECUMENICAL). Waldo seems to have had a spiritual commitment to poverty very like that of ST. FRANCIS OF ASSISI. The council rejected them, and in 1182 the ARCHBISHOP of Lyons forbade them to preach. Waldo was subsequently excommunicated along with his followers. Denied the SACRAMENTS, they began to alter their THEOLOGY considerably concerning both the sacraments and the AUTHORITY of the church. They came to see the BIBLE as their authority and began denying other Catholic doctrines such as infant baptism, PURGATORY, and the veneration of saints.

The movement spread to different locations around Europe, but it was strongest in southern FRANCE and northern ITALY—some of the same territory inhabited by the CATHARI. Thus, early in the 13th century, when the church turned against the latter, it was easy to target the followers of Waldo as well. Unlike the Cathari, however, and despite heavy losses to the INQUISITION, the Waldensians survived.

In the 1530s, the surviving Waldensians identified with the PROTESTANT REFORMATION in general and the nearby Reformed Church in Switzerland (under the leadership of John Calvin, 1509–64) in particular. Over the following century they grew to some 100,000 followers, but renewed persecution reduced their numbers drastically in the 17th century. In 1686 they fled to Switzerland but later returned to the mountainous valleys west of Turin, Italy, where they found a haven and survived until granted religious freedom by King Carlo Alberto (r. 1831–49) under the new Italian constitution of 1848.

In the 19th century, the Waldensians took political advantage of the opposition of the Roman Catholic Church to the unification of Italy. They courted the new government and were allowed to evangelize throughout the country. A Waldensian presence was established in most of Italy's major centers, though membership remained relatively small.

Following the changes of 1848, several Protestant churches came to Italy, the first being the Methodists (1859). More than a century later, in 1984, the Italian government removed the Catholic Church as Italy's official religion and entered into concordats with several of the larger groups of religious bodies in Italy, the first with the Waldensian and then the Methodist churches. As such, the two churches were considered to be in partnership with the government and eligible to receive a share of the religious tax. The Waldensians and Methodists now have complete intercommunion and exist in a working union. They are the only Italian-based churches that are full members of the World Council of Churches.

Further reading: R. E. Hedlund, *The Protestant Movement in Italy: Its Progress, Problems, and Prospects* (South Pasadena, Calif.: William Carey Library, 1970); Massimo Introvigne, PierLuigi Zoccatelli, Nelly Ippolito Macrina, and Verónica Roldán, *Enciclopedia delle Religioni in Italia* (Leumann: Elledici, 2001); A. P. Nucciarone, *A Handbook of Church Growth in Italy* (Chestnut Hill: Westminster, 1988); Giorgio Tourn, *The Waldensians: The First 800 Years (1174–1974)* (Torino: Claudiana Editrice, 1980).

weeping icons/statues

Since the early MIDDLE AGES, reports have circulated throughout the CHRISTIAN world of MIRACLES brought about by ICONS (holy pictures) and on occasion even statues. Many have involved healings that come to those who venerate a particular image of Jesus or the Virgin Mary. Others involved instances of seemingly miraculous survival through disasters—war, fires, persecution. One set of stories involves pictures that appear to weep tears or on rare occasions blood, or even a perfumelike substance said to smell like myrrh.

One such icon is Our Lady of Calvary, located at the Kalwaria Zebrzydowska, a site in south central Poland near Krakow. The painting had been given to the Bernardine (FRANCISCAN) Fathers who

maintained the sanctuary. They were the first who noticed the weeping. The icon became a symbol of Polish unity after large parts of the country passed under the control of Austria, Russia, and Prussia in the 18th century. Since the reunion of the country, the icon has been much honored and visited by a regular stream of pilgrims, including Pope JOHN PAUL II in 2002.

A century earlier, a statue of CHRIST located in Rome was observed to weep for several days prior to the invasion and sacking of the city in 1527 by the forces of Charles V (1500–58), the Holy Roman Emperor. Similar stories have been reported to the present, some in a Roman Catholic context and many from Eastern Orthodox churches (where icons have a more central role than in the West). One such weeping picture is the Holy Icon of the Mother of God located in the Nicula Monastery

Weeping icon of the Blessed Virgin Mary, Vietnamese Martyrs Church, Sacramento, California. *(Max Whittaker/ WpN)*

ner Dej, Transylvania, of the Romanian Orthodox Church. The icon was placed in the church in the 1680s, and the first to see it weeping were a group of visiting Austrian soldiers in 1694. They informed the PRIESTs, who also observed the phenomenon. The icon continued to weep for 28 days, and many ill people who touched the tears were healed.

Stories about weeping icons have cropped up occasionally across the centuries, but the number of such reports has increased markedly in the 20th century, partially a factor of improved communications and the sensationalist tendencies of the media. While most of the older reports originated in Europe, the contemporary reports come from around the world, both from countries that are predominantly Christian and others.

Weeping icons and statues have attracted widespread devotion and veneration from people who believe in their miraculous nature, but they have also provoked interest from the scientific community, which has sought to prove or disprove the paranormal element. Tests have been run on the tears to see if they are chemically identical to human tears, and in some cases they have been. Many skeptics seeking mundane explanations for the phenomena have found them, from condensation to dripping ceilings to fraud. Some church authorities, especially in the Eastern Orthodox churches, have objected to any attempt to examine the icons scientifically. Others have been quite willing to allow a broad range of observations and testing.

In the 1990s, the DIOCESE of Civitavecchia, ITALY, ordered a widespread examination of a statue of the Virgin that was weeping blood. The final report, issued at the beginning of 2005, was that the phenomenon remains inexplicable. Opinions about that and other weeping icons and statues appear to shift along a spectrum that coincides with one's belief in the possibility that such phenomena can happen.

Further reading: Joe Nickell, *Looking for a Miracle* (Amherst, N.Y.: Prometheus, 1998); Lisa J. Schwebel,

Apparitions, Healings, and Weeping Madonnas: Christianity and the Paranormal (Mahwah, N.J.: Paulist, 2004); Maria Warner, "Blood and Tears," *New Yorker* 72, 7 (April 8, 1996).

Weil, Simone (1909–1943) *French philosopher and mystical theologian*

Weil was born into a noted Jewish family and graduated with distinction from the École Normal Supérieur, where she studied under the noted philosopher Alain, pseudonym of Emile Auguste Chartier (1868–1951), and embraced MARXISM. Other students called her "the Red Virgin." She served as an anarchist soldier in Spain during the Spanish civil war (1936–39), a militant Marxist labor organizer and inept but sincere factory worker, a stirring teacher, and a CHRISTIAN resistance fighter in France and England, where she escaped during the Nazi occupation of France.

In 1937 Weil had mystical experiences in the chapel of Santa Maria degli Angeli, which St. FRANCIS restored in Assisi, and at Solesmes Abbey, where she fell in love with Gregorian CHANT. She converted but was never baptized. Thereafter, she befriended peasant-philosopher Gustave Thibon (1903–2001) and worked at his vineyard in southern France. She entrusted the majority of her writings to him when she fled to England. She also held long conversations with the Dominican Joseph-Marie Perrin (1905–   ), who helped many Jews escape France during World War II.

On the surface many of Weil's theological assertions border on the unorthodox, but seen from their mystical depth they can take on a profound meaning. Her thoughts were first made known to the world in posthumous collections in French: *The Need for Roots* (1949), *Gravity and Grace* (1947), and *Waiting for God* (1950). She saw in the Greek epics and Plato's philosophy intimations of Christianity. The world plus GOD, she believed, is less than God alone, who delimited the divine fullness to allow for CREATION. Christ on the CROSS reveals both the closest proximity to the Godhead in supernatural obedience and, at the same time, the greatest distance in affliction. Affliction, from which Weil herself suffered deeply, turns the SOUL to seek God. Each religion has its own special truth.

Weil continues to attract serious attention under the auspices of groups like the Simone Weil Society. Some think her a saint for the era of estrangement from God. Many see her as a Christian Platonist. Her mysticism can only be described with one word—fierce.

Further reading: E. Jane Doering and Eric O. Sprinstead, ed., *The Christian Platonism of Simone Weil* (Notre Dame: Notre Dame University Press, 2004); Simone Pétrement, *Simone Weil: A Life* (New York: Pantheon, 1976); Eric O. Springstead, *Christus Mediator: Platonic Mediation in the Thought of Simone Weil* (Chico, Calif.: Scholars, 1983); Miklos Vetö, *The Religious Metaphysics of Simone Weil* (Albany: State University of New York Press, 1994).

Westphalia, Peace of (Treaty of Westphalia)

The Peace of Westphalia is the collective name for a series of agreements reached in the 1640s that finally ended the European wars of religion, the legacy of the split between Roman Catholicism and the PROTESTANT REFORMATION. The initial phase of Catholic-Protestant armed conflict in Europe had been brought to a close in 1555 with the Peace of Augsburg. The agreement gave international legitimacy to Lutheranism and allowed each of the many German territorial rulers to choose whether his dominion would be Catholic or Lutheran. The Calvinists (Reformed Church) were not included in the settlement.

By the beginning of the 17th century, new realities were disturbing the agreement. The COUNTER-REFORMATION was having its effect in reclaiming Protestant lands for Catholicism. The Reformed Church was gaining ascendancy in various lands beyond Switzerland, especially in the Low Countries, various German states, and in eastern Europe. Tension was highest in areas where Protestant and Catholic strength was about equal.

The Thirty Years' War (actually a series of wars with shifting alliances) is generally traced to a revolt by the Protestant majority in Bohemia against Ferdinand II (1576–1637), the Holy Roman Emperor, a Catholic. The conflict spread across Europe wherever tensions were reaching boiling points. As the conflict spread, various states joined in for reasons of national interest, often blurring the religious lines. An initial agreement to end the conflict, the 1636 Peace of Prague, recognized for the first time the Reformed Church.

The last phase of the conflict found the two major Catholic powers on opposite sides, as France allied itself with Lutheran Sweden and the Reformed Netherlands against the Habsburg rulers of Spain and the Holy Roman Empire. After several years of inconclusive fighting, the death of French leader Armand Jean du Plessis (1585–1642), Cardinal Richelieu in 1642 and of Louis XIII (1601–43) the following year presented an opportunity for peace. Louis XIV (1638–1715) ascended the French throne as a child of four, and national leadership passed to his regent, Cardinal Jules Mazarin (1602–61), who set out to bring peace.

A series of agreements were achieved after long negotiations in which Protestant and Catholic diplomats at times refused to meet directly with each other. Some territory changed hands, establishing boundaries that survive to the present. The Peace of Prague was reaffirmed and formal recognition extended to the Reformed Church. The two predominantly Reformed nations, Switzerland and the Netherlands, were recognized as sovereign states. Spain proved to be one of the significant losers, as it gave up claims to the Netherlands and during the conflict lost control of Portugal (which it had seized in 1580). The peace is generally seen as marking the end of religious warfare in Europe.

The framers of the American Constitution often cited the wars of religion as their chief reason for disestablishing religion in the first clause of the First Amendment.

Further reading: Derek Croxton, *The Peace of Westphalia: A Historical Dictionary* (Westport, Conn.: Greenwood, 2001); ———, *Peacemaking in Early Modern Europe: Cardinal Mazarin and the Congress of Westphalia, 1643–1648* (Selinsgrove, N.J.: Susquehanna University Press, 1999); G. M. Lyons and M. Mastanduno, *Beyond Westphalia: State Sovereignty and International Intervention* (Baltimore: Johns Hopkins University Press, 1995).

William of Ockham (William of Occam) (c. 1285-1349) *nominalist philosopher*

Philosopher William of Ockham, an exponent of philosophical nominalism and opponent of the Aristotelian philosophies of THOMAS AQUINAS and DUNS SCOTUS, was born in Ockham, Surrey, England. Little is known of his early life, but as a young man he joined the FRANCISCAN Order. He did his college work at Oxford University and his postgraduate study at the Sorbonne in Paris, where he subsequently taught (1315–20).

In the early 1320s Ockham was drawn into the debates concerning POVERTY among the Franciscans; he supported the views of the more radical wing that Jesus was absolutely poor and that vows of poverty did not allow the order to accumulate wealth either individually or collectively. The members of many wealthy orders, while personally owning nothing, lived somewhat affluent lives. His views were condemned, and in 1324 he was called to Avignon (*see* AVIGNON PAPACY) to be examined by Pope John XXII (r. 1316–34). While there he was placed under house arrest and confined for the next four years.

In 1328, Ockham fled to Munich, where he hoped to find protection with the Holy Roman Emperor Louis IV (1282–1347), who was himself in bad favor with John XXII for resisting papal authority in political matters. He staunchily attacked papal temporal power. Ockham was excommunicated by the pope; the decree was never reversed, and he spent the rest of his life writing in defense of the emperor. He died in Munich in 1347 while trying to negotiate a reconciliation with the church through one of John's successors, Pope Clement VI (r. 1342–52).

Ockham was the foremost logician of the late MIDDLE AGES. He developed a theory of signification and supposition that shapes modal logic today. Although his view on Franciscan poverty caused Ockham the most trouble in his lifetime, his most lasting impact was as a champion of the nominalist philosophical school. The logic of his position led him, among other things, to suggest that the church's major affirmations—the existence of GOD, God's omnipotence, and the immortality of the soul—could not be deduced from philosophical arguments, but were solely the subject of God's revelation.

Ockham's arguments derived from his basic philosophical stance, which asserted that abstract notions like table, triangle, horse, or angel, (called universals at the time) do not have an objective existence, they are simply conventional names (hence the designation nominalists) we gave to different objects. The rigorous application of nominalism led the philosopher to apply the famous principle of "Ockham's Razor": one should not posit any cause to an effect that is not needed to explain it—the shortest satisfactory explanation is the best.

Ockham's Razor was one of the revolutionary ideas that later turned thinkers from ultimate to proximate causes in their attempts to explain phenomena in the world. Hence, it became a major tool for modern scientists seeking to explain the world in ever greater and more precise detail.

Further reading: R. Ariew, *Ockham's Razor: A Historical and Philosophical Analysis of Ockham's Principle of Parsimony* (Champaign-Urbana: University of Illinois Press, 1976); Philotheus Boehner, ed. *William of Ock-*

ham: *Philosophical Writings.* (London: Thomas Nelson, 1957); Arthur Stepen McGrade, *The Political Thought of William of Ockham: Personal and Institutional Principles* (Cambridge: Cambridge University Press, 1974).

women, ordination of

Over the centuries, clerical leadership in the Catholic Church was limited to males. This practice was undergirded by the social structure in which the church emerged and reinforced by certain references to the roles of women in the New Testament and the gender theories of various theologians (*see* SEXUALITY).

The Greeks and Romans believed that only one sex really existed, though it was found in two forms. A woman was considered a watered down version of a man produced by an insufficient amount of vital energy in the fetus (Aristotle, *The Generation of Animals*). Verses from the BIBLE that have been used to support male domination of the church included 1 Corinthians 14: 34 and 1 Timothy 2:11, which admonished women to keep silent in church and to learn silence and subjection.

Drawing on these ideas, among other theologians such as THOMAS AQUINAS saw being female as an impediment to receiving HOLY ORDERS, a purely academic question for him. In various writings, Aquinas considers the role of women and consistently finds women inferior in, for example, intellect. As the female body was inferior to the male's, he wrote, so was her SOUL.

The prohibition of women in the ordained ministry carried into Protestantism, and challenges were not offered until the 19th century. Women first broke the barrier of speaking before audiences that included men, either as lay speakers or evangelists, and then began to assume roles as ordained ministers in some of the newly emerging evangelical sects (Primitive Methodists of England being the first to assign women to formerly male clerical posts).

In the mid-19th century, the first few ordinations of Protestant women occurred, and the first detailed arguments for women ministers began to be heard in the Wesleyan holiness movement. Early advocates of women's ordination included Catherine Booth (1829–90), (cofounder of the Salvation Army) and Methodist Phoebe Palmer (1807–74). Several churches of the Holiness movement would be the first to ordain women on a regular basis; the practice was later passed along to its offshoot, the Pentecostal movement. Advocates argued that female preachers were a sign of the endtime, when "your sons and daughters would prophesy" (Acts 2:17).

However, it was not until the last half of the 20th century that a significant movement to ordain women emerged. It soon won over most representatives of the larger Protestant denominations in America, including Anglicans, Presbyterians, Lutherans, and Methodists. The Baptists have been less receptive to women in clerical roles.

In the Catholic Church, the modern move to ordain women can be traced to the 1930s to a small British organization, Saint Joan's Alliance, which submitted a number of petitions to the Vatican on the subject. Then in the 1970s, an American Catholic laywoman and activist, Mary B. Lynch (1925–79), began to raise the question anew to fellow activists on her Christmas card list. Conversations that grew out of her initial probing led to 1,900 people gathering in Detroit in 1975 to discuss the issue, which in turn led to the founding of a more permanent organization. The incorporation of the Women's Ordination Conference in 1977 and the opening of an office in Washington, D.C., coincided closely with Pope PAUL VI's "Address on the Role of Women in the Plan of Salvation" (January 30, 1977) that reasserted that women were not candidates for ordination.

In spite of Pope Paul VI's statement, a wave of optimism concerning the possibility of change empowered the movement and energized the several conversations between the women's leaders and the National Conference of Catholic Bishops. When JOHN PAUL II came to the United States in 1978, many women took the occasion to ask for change in the church. During his visit, speaking at the Shrine of the Immaculate Conception in Washington, D.C., one of the most prominent women in the church, Mercy Sister Theresa M. Kane, the president of the Leadership Conference of Women Religious, spoke to a room full of nuns calling for the pope to admit women to all levels of service in the church. Catholic nuns have long noted that St. THÉRÈSE OF LISIEUX held a lifelong desire to be a PRIEST and that her canonization in 1934 and declaration as a DOCTOR OF THE CHURCH in 1994 gives implicit approbation to this desire.

John Paul II did not make a definitive response to Kane (though it was generally known that he opposed the idea), and through the 1980s a vigorous discussion on the subject ensued. Hope continually welled up that a change could occur. Adding to that hope was data indicating an acute shortage of priests, a shortage that women might be able to fill.

John Paul II did make a seemingly definitive statement in an encyclical on the ordination of women in the Anglican Church, *Ordinatio Sacerdotalis* (May 22, 1994). He made note of the ongoing discussions and said that through them a misunderstanding had arisen that the question of the ordination of women was merely a matter of church discipline. To clear up that misunderstanding, he stated, "I declare that the Church has no authority whatsoever to confer priestly ordination on women and that this judgment is to be definitively held by all the Church's faithful." (4). That statement effectively ended the debate for the remainder of his pontificate. Some tried to maintain that John Paul II's statement issued from the extraordinary MAGISTERIUM and was therefore infallible. Others, including Cardinal Ratzinger (now BENEDICT XVI), prefect of the Congregation for the Doctrine of the Faith, and KARL RAHNER doubted this interpretation.

While the ordination movement remains active, it has lost much of its steam. Representatives of the Women's Ordination Conference met in 2000 to celebrate their 25th anniversary, but the audience was far smaller than that at the founding meeting. Nevertheless, the meeting led to the founding of Women's Ordination Worldwide, an international network of organizations working for women's ordination. WOW held its first conference in IRELAND in 2001, and 26 countries were represented.

In the summer of 2002, an independently minded BISHOP ordained seven women as Catholic priests as they floated down the Danube River on a boat. The Women's Ordination Conference subsequently announced their support of the Danube Seven, even as the church excommunicated them. More recently, in 2005, one of the women was ordained a bishop and participated in a similar ordination held for North American women on the St. Lawrence River.

Objectors to the ordination of women must overcome the strong biblical fact that the core of the Gospel news—Jesus who was dead but now risen—was entrusted first to women and not men (Mark 16:9; Matt. 28:7; Luke 24:10).

Further reading: Barbara Field, ed., *"Fit for this Office" (Women and Ordination)* (Melbourne: Collins Dove, 1989); Robert J. Heyer, ed., *Women and Orders* (New York: Paulist, 1974); Francis Bernard O'Connor, *"Like Bread, Their Voices Rise!"—Global Women Challenge the Church* (Notre Dame: Ave Maria, 1993); Leonard Swidler and Arlene Leonard, eds., *Women Priests: A Catholic Commentary on the Vatican Declaration* (New York: Paulist, 1977).

Wycliffe, John (c. 1330–1384) *church reformer*
John Wycliffe, a PRIEST and scholar who built a reform movement in 14th-century England, was a graduate of Balliol College at Oxford. He made Oxford his headquarters for the rest of his life. In the 1360s he emerged as a popular preacher and became well known for his criticism of papal and monastic abuse and support of biblical authority. He also challenged the orthodox concepts of

transubstantiation and purgatory. He called the EUCHARIST an "effectual sign."

In 1380 Wycliffe organized followers into a band of poor priests known as the Lollards and sent them around the countryside to spread his ideas. By this time church authorities were trying to move against him. In 1381 councils at Oxford and Blackfriars condemned 24 of his propositions, seconded by Pope Urban VI (r. 1378–89). Nonetheless, he retained massive support in Oxford. While the Lollards spread through the countryside, he worked on the first translation of the Vulgate version of the BIBLE into English (not published until the 19th century).

Wycliffe died quietly in Oxford in 1384. A generation later, the COUNCIL OF CONSTANCE, having condemned Czech reformer JAN HUS, who had similar views, ordered Wycliffe's body exhumed and burned. That order was finally carried out in 1428, his books also being thrown into the fire. Wycliffe is usually seen as an important precursor of the PROTESTANT REFORMATION.

Further reading: A. Kenny, *Wyclif.* (Oxford: Oxford University Press, 1985); ———, ed., *Wyclif in His Times* (Oxford: Clarendon, 1986); Douglas C. Wood, *The Evangelical Doctor* (Welwyn, Eng.: Evangelical, 1984); John Wyclif, *Select English Works of John Wyclif,* 3 vols. ed. T. Arnold, (Oxford: Oxford University Press, 1869–71).

BIBLIOGRAPHY

Abbott, W. M., and J. Gallagher, eds. *The Documents of Vatican II*. New York: American Press, 1966.

Acta Apostolicae Sedis. Vatican City: Vatican, 1909–present.

Adam, Karl. *The Spirit of Catholicism*. Garden City, N.J.: Doubleday, 1929.

Allen, John L. *The Rise of Benedict XVI: The Inside Story of How the Pope Was Elected and Where He Will Take the Church*. New York: Doubleday, 2005.

American Catholic Who's Who. Detroit: Walter Roemig, 1935–1971. Washington, D.C.: National Catholic News Service, 1972–present. Issued biennially.

Annuario Pontificio. Vatican City: Vatican. Issued annually.

Attwater, Daniel. *A Catholic Dictionary,* 2nd ed. New York: Macmillan, 1949.

Barraclough, Geoffrey, ed. *The Christian World: A Social and Cultural History*. New York: Harry N. Abrams, 1981.

Barrett, David. *The Encyclopedia of World Christianity,* 2nd ed. New York: Oxford University Press, 2001.

Beinert, Wolfgang, and Francis Schussler Fiorenza, eds. *Handbook of Catholic Theology*. New York: Crossroad, 1996.

Biedermann, Hans. *The Dictionary of Symbolism*. New York: Facts On File, 1992.

Bissio, Roberto Remo, et al. *Third World Guide 93/94*. Montevideo, Uruguay: Instituto del Tercer Mundo, 1992.

Bokenbotter, Thomas. *A Concise History of the Catholic Church*. New York: Doubleday, 1979.

Bowden, John. *Encyclopedia of Christianity*. London: Oxford University Press, 2005.

Bradley, James E., and R. A. Muller, *Church History: An Introduction to Research, Reference Works and Methods*. Grand Rapids, Mich.: Eerdmans, 1995.

Broderick, Robert, ed. *The Catholic Encyclopedia*. Nashville, Tenn.: Thomas Nelson, 1987.

Buhlman, W. *The Coming of the Third Church*. Maryknoll, N.Y.: Orbis, 1978.

Bunson, Matthew. *Our Sunday Visitor's Encyclopedia of Catholic History*. Huntington, Ind.: Our Sunday Visitor, 1995.

Burghardt, Walter, and William Lynch, ed. *The Idea of Catholicism*. Cleveland: Word, 1964.

Cannon, William R. *History of Christianity in the Middle Ages: From the Fall of Rome to the Fall of Constantinople*. Nashville, Tenn.: Abingdon, 1960.

Carey, Patrick, ed. *American Catholic Religious Thought*. New York: Paulist, 1987.

Catechism of the Catholic Church. San Francisco: Ignatius, 1994.

Catholic Reference Encyclopedia. Charlotte: C. D. Stampley Enterprises, 1968.

Foy, Felician A., and Rose M. Avato, eds. *Catholic Almanac*. Huntington, Ind.: Our Sunday Visitor, 1969–present. Issued annually.

A Catholic Dictionary, rev. ed. New York: Macmillan, 1957.

Chilson, Richard. *Catholic Christianity.* New York: Paulist, 1987.

Clendenin, Daniel B., ed. *Eastern Orthodox Theology: A Contemporary Reader.* Grand Rapids, Mich.: Baker, 2003.

Code, Joseph Bernard. *Dictionary of the American Hierarchy, 1789–1964.* New York: J. F. Wagner, 1964.

Cross, F. L., ed. *Oxford Dictionary of the Christian Church,* 3rd ed. New York: Oxford University Press, 1997.

Curtis, Georgina Pell. *The American Catholic Who's Who.* St. Louis: Herder, 1911.

Cunningham, Lawrence. *Catholic Faith: An Introduction.* New York: Paulist, 1987.

———. *Catholic Faith: A Reader.* New York: Paulist, 1988.

Davis, F., et al., eds. *A Catholic Dictionary of Theology,* 4 vols. New York: Nelson, 1962.

Dehey, Elinor Tong. *Religious Orders of Women in the United States: Catholic. Accounts of Their Origin, Works, and Most Important Institutions, Interwoven with Histories of Many Famous Foundresses,* rev. ed. [Hammond, Ind.: W. B. Conkey, 1930].

Delaney, John J. *Dictionary of American Catholic Biography.* Garden City, N.Y.: Doubleday, 1984.

Delaney, John, and James Edward Tobin. *Dictionary of Catholic Biography.* Garden City, N.Y.: Doubleday, 1961.

de Lubac, Henri. *Catholicism.* New York: New American Library, 1964.

Denziger, Henricus, and Alphonsus Schönmetzer. *Enchiridion Symbolorum Definitionum et Declarationum de Rebus Fidei et Morum,* 34th ed., Rome: Herder, 1967.

Dictionnaire de spiritualité, 16 vols. Ed. M. Villier et al. Paris: Beauchesne, 1935–95.

Dictionnaire de théologie catholique. Ed. Alfred Vacant et al. Paris: Letouzey et Ané, 1951–.

Dolan, Jay P. *The American Catholic Experience: A History from Colonial Times to the Present.* Notre Dame: University of Notre Dame Press, 1992.

Dulles, Avery R. *The Church: A Bibliography.* Wilmington, Del.: Michael Glazier, 1985.

———. *The Theology of the Church: A Bibliography.* Mahwah, N.J.: Paulist, 1999.

Enciclopedia cattolica, 12 vols. Vatican City: l'Enciclopedia cattolica, 1948–54.

Ellis, John Tracy. *A Guide to American Catholic History.* 2d ed., revised and enlarged, by John Tracy Ellis and Robert Trisco. Santa Barbara: ABC Clio, 1982.

Evans, G. R., ed. *The Medieval Theologians.* Oxford: Blackwell, 2001.

Ferguson, Everett, ed. *Encyclopedia of Early Christianity.* New York: Garland, 1997.

Fines, John. *Who's Who in the Middle Ages: From the Collapse of the Roman Empire to the Renaissance.* New York: Barnes & Noble, 1970.

Finney, Paul Corby. *Art, Archaeology, and Architecture of Early Christianity.* New York: Garland, 1993.

Fitzsimons, M. A. *The Catholic Church Today: Western Europe.* Notre Dame: University of Notre Dame Press, 1969.

Foy, Felician, and Rose Avato. *A Concise Guide to the Catholic Church.* Huntington, Ind.: Our Sunday Visitor, 1984.

Freemantle, Anne, ed. *The Social Teachings of the Church.* New York: New American Library of World Literature, 1963.

Gannon, Thomas M. *World Catholicism in Transition.* New York: Macmillan, 1988.

Glazier, Michael, and Monika K. Hellwig, eds. *Modern Catholic Encyclopedia.* Collegeville, Minn.: Liturgical Press, 1994.

Gontard, F. *The Chair of Peter: A History of the Papacy.* New York: Holt, Rhinehart & Winston, 1964.

Hardon, John. *The Catholic Catechism.* Garden City, N.Y.: Doubleday, 1975.

———. *Modern Catholic Dictionary.* Garden City, N.Y.: Doubleday, 1980.

———. *The Question and Answer Catholic Catechism.* Garden City, N.Y.: Doubleday, 1981.

Hennesey, James. *American Catholic Bibliography: 1970–1982.* Working paper series. Charles and Margaret Hall Cushwa Series for the Study of American Catholicism, Series 12, no. 1. Notre Dame: University of Notre Dame, 1982. 41 leaves. Supplement issued as Series 14, no. 1, fall, 1983.

Herberman, C., et al., eds. *The Catholic Encyclopedia,* 15 vols. New York: Gilmary Society, 1913–36.

Hillerbrand, Hans J., ed. *The Oxford Encyclopedia of the Reformation,* 4 vols. New York: Oxford University Press, 1996.

————. *The Reformation: A Narrative History Related by Contemporary Observers and Participants.* Grand Rapids, Mich.: Baker Book House, 1981.

Hillerbrand, Hans J., and Jon Woronoff. *Historical Dictionary of the Reformation and Counter-Reformation.* Walnut Creek, Calif.: Rowman & Littlefield, 2000.

Hughes, Phil. *A Popular History of the Catholic Church* (London: Borns & Oates; New York: Macmillan, 1947, repr., 1961).

Hertling, Ludwig Freiherr von. *A History of the Catholic Church,* tr. Anselm Gordon Biggs. Westminster, Md.: Newman, 1957.

James, Theodore, ed. *The Heart of Catholicism.* Huntington, Ind.: Our Sunday Visitor, 1997.

Jungmann, Josef A. *The Mass of the Roman Rite: Its Origins and Development.* New York: Benziger, 1950.

Keating, Karl. *What Catholics Really Believe: Setting the Record Straight.* San Francisco: Ignatius, 1992.

Komonchak, Joseph, ed. *The New Dictionary of Theology.* Collegeville, Minn.: Liturgical Press, 1993.

Lexikon für Theologie und Kirche, 3rd ed., 11 vols. Freiburg im Breisgau, Germany: Herder, 1993–2001.

Lossky, Nicholas, et al., eds., *Dictionary of the Ecumenical Movement.* Geneva: WCC Publications/Grand Rapids, Mich.: William B. Eerdmans, 1991.

McBrien, Richard P., ed. *HarperCollins Encyclopedia of Catholicism.* San Francisco: HarperSanFrancisco, 1995.

————. *Inside Catholicism: Rituals and Symbols Revealed.* San Francisco: HarperSanFrancisco, 1995.

————. *Lives of the Popes.* San Francisco: HarperSanFrancisco, 2000.

McCabe, James Patrick. *Critical Guide to Catholic Reference Books,* 3rd ed. Littleton, Colo.: Libraries Unlimited, 1989.

McCarthy, Thomas P. *Guide to the Catholic Sisterhoods in the United States,* 5th ed., Washington, D.C.: Catholic University of America Press, 1964.

McKenzie, John L. *The Roman Catholic Church.* London: Weidenfeld & Nicolson, 1969.

McSorley, Joseph. *Outline History of the Church by Centuries: From St. Peter to Pius XII,* 11th ed. St. Louis: Herder, 1961.

Maltby, William S. ed. *Reformation Europe: A Guide to Research II.* St. Louis: Center for Reformation Research, 1992.

Marinelli, Anthony. *The Word Made Flesh: An Overview of the Catholic Faith.* New York: Paulist, 1993.

Melton, J. Gordon. *Encyclopedia of American Religions.* 7th ed. Detroit: Gale, 2002.

————. *The Encyclopedia of American Religions: Religious Creeds,* 2 vols. Detroit: Gale Research, 1988, 1994.

———— and Martin Baumann, eds., *Religions of the World: A Comprehensive Encyclopedia of Beliefs and Practices.* Santa Barbara: ABC-Clio, 2002.

Metford, J. C. J. *Dictionary of Christian Lore and Legend.* London: Thames & Hudson, 1983.

Neill, Stephen. *A History of Christian Missions,* 2nd ed. New York: Penguin Books, 1990.

Nevins, Albert J. *The Maryknoll Catholic Dictionary.* New York: Grosset & Dunlap 1965.

New Catholic Encyclopedia, 18. vols. Washington, D.C.: Catholic University of America Press, 1967–89.

O'Carroll, Michael. *Corpus Christi: A Theological Encyclopedia of the Eucharist.* Wilmington, Del.: Michael Glazier.

————. *Theotokos: A Theological Encyclopedia of the Blessed Virgin Mary.* Wilmington, Del.: Michael Glazier, 1986.

O'Connell, Tim, ed. *Vatican II and its Documents.* Wilmington, Del.: Michael Glazier, 1986.

Official Catholic Directory. New York: P. J. Kenedy, 1913–present. Issued annually.

Orthodoxia. Regensburg, Germany: *Osrkirchliches Institut.* Issued annually.

Ott, Ludwig. *Fundamentals of Catholic Dogma.* St. Louis: Herder, 1954.

The Pope Speaks. Quarterly/Bimonthly. Huntington, Ind.: Our Sunday Visitor, 1954–present.

Pruter, Karl and Gordon Melton, *The Old Catholic Sourcebook.* New York: Garland, 1983.

Quasten, Johannes. *Patrology,* 4 vols. Westminster, Md.: Newman, 1950–60, 1986.

Quin, Mabel, ed. *The Catholic Peoples Encyclopedia.* Chicago: Catholic Press, 1966.

Rahner, Karl, ed. *Sacramentum Mundi,* 6 vols. New York: Herder & Herder, 1968.

Rahner, Karl, and Heinrich Vorgrimler. *Concise Theological Dictionary.* London: Burns & Oates, 1983.

Reese, Thomas. *Inside the Vatican: The Politics and Organization of the Catholic Church.* Cambridge, Mass.: Harvard University Press, 1996.

Reichardt, Mary E., ed. *Encyclopedia of Catholic Literature.* Westport, Conn.: Greenwood Press, 2004.

Roberson, Ronald G. *The Eastern Christian Churches—A Brief Survey,* 5th ed. Rome: Edizioni Orientalia Christiana, Pontificio Istituto Orientale 1995.

Schreck, Alan. *Basics of the Faith: A Catholic Catechism.* Ann Arbor, Mich.: Servant, 1987.

———. *Compact History of the Catholic Church.* Ann Arbor, Mich.: Servant, 1987.

Schroeder, H. J. *Canons and Decrees of the Council of Trent.* St. Louis: Herder, 1941.

Schütz, Bernhard. *Great Cathedrals.* New York: Harry N. Abrams, 2002.

———. *Great Monasteries of Europe.* New York: Abbeville, 2004.

Schwartz, Eduard, and Johannes Straub, eds. *Acta Conciliorum Oecomenicorum.* Berlin: De Gruyter, 1927–71.

Seidler, J., and K. Meyer, *Conflict and Change in the Catholic Church.* New Brunswick, N.J.: Rutgers University Press, 1989.

Shaw, Russell, ed. *Encyclopedia of Catholic Doctrine.* Huntington, Ind.: Our Sunday Visitor, 1997.

Sora, Steven. *Relics from Heaven: Relics from Noah's Ark to the Shroud of Turin.* New York: Wiley, 2005.

Steimer, Bruno, ed., *Dictionary of Popes and the Papacy.* New York: Crossroad, 2001.

Sunquist, Scott W., ed., *A Dictionary of Asian Christianity.* Grand Rapids, Mich.: Eerdmans, 2001.

Thernstrom, Stephan, ed. *Harvard Encyclopedia of American Ethnic Groups.* Cambridge, Mass.: Harvard University Press, 1980.

Thomas, Evangeline, ed. *Women Religious History Sources: A Guide to Repositories in the United States.* New York: Bowker, 1983.

Toynbee, Arnold, ed. *The Crucible of Christianity.* London: Thames & Hudson, 1969.

Tynan, Daniel J., ed. *Biographical Dictionary of Contemporary Catholic American Writing.* Westport, Conn.: Greenwood, 1989.

Vollmar, Edward R. *The Catholic Church in America: An Historical Bibliography,* 2nd ed. New York: Scarecrow, 1963.

Vorgrimler, Heinrich. *Commentary on the Documents of Vatican II,* 5 vols. New York: Herder & Herder, 1967–69.

Walch, Timothy, ed. *The Heritage of American Catholicism,* 28 vols. New York: Garland, 1988.

Water, Mark. *The New Encyclopedia of Christian Martyrs.* Grand Rapids, Mich.: Baker Books, 2001.

Willging, Eugene Paul, and Herta Hatzfeld. *Catholic Serials of the Nineteenth Century in the United States: A Descriptive Bibliography and Union List,* first series, 2 vols. Washington, D.C.: Catholic University of America Press, 1968. Second series, 15 vols. Washington, D.C.: Catholic University of America Press, 1959–68.

INDEX